PENDLETON DISTRICT, S.C. DEEDS

1790-1806

Compiled
by
Betty Willie

Southern Historical Press, Inc.
Greenville, South Carolina

Copyright 1982
By: Southern Historical Press, Inc.

All rights reserved. No part of this publication may be reproduced, stored in a retrieval system, transmitted in any form, posted on to the web in any form or by any means without the prior written permission of the publisher.

Please direct all correspondence and orders to:

www.southernhistoricalpress.com
or
SOUTHERN HISTORICAL PRESS, Inc.
PO BOX 1267
375 West Broad Street
Greenville, SC 29601
southernhistoricalpress@gmail.com

ISBN #0-89308-246-5

Printed in the United States of America

INTRODUCTION

In 1826, Pendleton District was divided into Pickens and Anderson Counties with the name Pendleton disappearing as a contemporary legal entity.

Previous to the year 1768 the only court held in South Carolina was in the City of Charleston. In that year the State was divided into six districts, and Courts of General Sessions and Common Pleas were thereafter established and held in each of the said districts. The judges were authorized to build court houses and other necessary public buildings in some convenient place in each. A court house was established at Ninety-Six, at Cambridge, (See State Statutes, Vol. 7, p. 197.)

At the close of the Revolutionary War all the territory embraced in the present counties of Greenville, Anderson, Oconee and Pickens belonged to the Cherokee Indians, although embraced within the State lines. Many adventurous white people had founded settlements within this territory, and, for their protection from the Indians, the State had built forts in several places, and maintained garrisons therein. All of this territory, except the extreme upper portion of Oconee and Pickens counties was ceded to the State by the Cherokees shortly after the close of the war by a treaty negotiated by Gen. Andrew Pickens near his home on Seneca River. Tradition points out a large oak tree, near the banks of the Seneca River, under which General Pickens met the Cherokee chiefs and made with them the treaty by which the State secured the exclusive possession of this territory.

By Act of 1789, Vol. V., p. 105, the new counties of Pendleton and Greenville were allowed representation in the legislature, each to have one senator and three members in the lower house. At the same session commissioners were appointed to locate a court house for the County of Pendleton. The commissioners were Andrew Pickens, John Miller, John Wilson, Benj. Cleveland, Wm. Halbert, Henry Clark, John Moffett and Robert Anderson. These commissioners purchased from Isaac Lynch a tract of land, about as near the center of the County of Pendleton as practicable, containing eight hundred and eighty-five acres. And the same was conveyed to the said commissioners in trust for the County of Pendleton, as appears by deed dated April 8, 1790, and recorded in book "A", page 1.

Upon this tract of land the Town of Pendleton is located. This tract of land, or a part of it, was laid out into streets and village lots, which were numbered, and the remainder of the tract was divided into what were called "out-lying" lots.

By the Act of 1791, Vol. 7, p. 262, Gen. Andrew Pickens, Col. Robert Anderson, Capt. Robert Maxwell, John Bowen, James Harrison, Maj. John Ford and John Hallum were appointed to purchase land and superintend the building of a court house and jail for the district of Washington. Washington District was composed of the counties of Pendleton and Greenville. The court house was located at Pickensville, near the present Town of Easley.

By the Act of 1798, Vol. VII, p. 283, the name County was changed to District. And at the court house in each of the several districts there shall be held after 1800, Courts of Sessions and Common Pleas, to possess and exercise the same powers and jurisdiction as is held by the district courts. By the same Act, it was enacted that the court for Pendleton District should be held at Pendleton Court House.

PENDLETON COUNTY, SOUTH CAROLINA
CONVEYANCE BOOK A
1790 - 1792

Pages 1-5   8 and 9 Apr. 1790. Isaac Lynch of Pendleton County,
                     Ninety-Six Dist., S. C., Yeoman, to Andrew Pickens,
                     John Miller, John Wilson, Benjamin Cleavelin, Wil-
liam Holbert, Henry Clarke, John Moffet and Robert Anderson, Esquires,
of sd. county, Justices of the Peace of Pendleton Co., for 5 shillings
and for ₺ 25, a tract of land in trust for sd. county, containing 885
acres in sd. county on branches of Eighteen Mile Creek and Three-and-
Twenty Mile Creek, bounding NE and SE on land laid out, SW on Isaac Lynch
all other sides on vacant land, granted to Isaac Lynch 2 July 1787.
Recorded in Bk. VVVV, p. 70.
Wit: Henry Burch, Joseph Box.
Joseph Box made oath 14 Apr. 1790 before Andrew Pickens, J.P.

Pages 6-9   24 and 25 July 1789. Capt. John Goodwyn, of Green-
                     ville County, S. C. to Benjamin Cleaveland, Esq. for
                     ₺ 300 and for five shillings, 300 acres of land in
Pendleton County on Toogaloo River, bounded NE by land laid out to Rob-
ert Looney, SE by Toogaloo River, other sides by vacant land, granted to
sd. John Goodwyn, Esq. 15 Oct. 1784.
Recorded in Bk. BBBB, p. 52.
Wit: Alexander Ramsey, Joseph Jenkins, Jon Boles.
Alexander Ramsey made oath 25 July 1789 before Robert Anderson, J.P.

Pages 10-12   20 Sept. 1787. Field Farrar of State aforesaid con-
                     veys to Thomas Farrar, of Spartanburg Co., S.C. for
                     ₺ 400 sterling, a tract of land containing 640 acres
on Big Beaver Dam Creek, a branch of Toogaloo River, bounded N.W. by the
land laid out to Jacob Milligan, all other sides vacant land at the time
of original survey, granted to Field Farrar 15 Oct. 1784.
Wit: Daniel Symmes, Robt. Looney. Field Farrar and Elizabeth Farrar,
his wife, signed. Daniel Symmes made oath 7 Dec. 1789 before Silv's.
Walker, J.P.
Recorded 10 May 1790.

Pages 13-16   20 Jan. 1790. Jervis Henry Stevens, Professor of
                     music in Charleston, to Major Thomas Farrar, Sheriff
                     of Ninety-Six Dist., for five shillings and ₺ 120
for 640 acres at Cross Roads on the Little Beaver Dam Creek, bounded by
Colonel Stephen Drayton to the NE and at time of survey, all other sides
vacant, granted to Stevens 21 Jan. 1785.
Wit: Joseph Dullis, Samuel Rodgers.
Joseph Dullis made oath before Stephen Drayton, J. P. of Charleston Dist.
on 21 Jan. 1790.

Pages 16-20   25 Aug. 1789. Capt. Louis D. Martin of Pendleton
                     Co., S.C. to Alexander Dromgoole, trader, of Pendle-
                     ton, for five shillings and ₺ 150, two tracts land
in Pendleton County, on Martin's Creek of Keowee River, viz: one tract
of 300 acres, granted to sd. Louis D. Martin 5 Sept. 1785.
Recorded Bk. YYYY, p. 447.
Wit: Alexander Ramsey, Hance Hunter, John Woods.
Signed: Louis D. Martin and Sarah Martin, his wife.
Hance Hunter made oath 28 Aug. 1789 before Robert Anderson, J.P.

Pages 20-23   6 Jan. 1789. Thomas Jones and Betsy Jones, his wife,
                     of Ninety-Six Dist., S.C., planter, to Alexander
                     Drumgoole, merchant, for ₺ 50, 640 acres on First
Creek, branch of Rocky River, granted to Betsy Jones, then Betsy Wilki-
son, 2 May 1785.
Wit: Noah Pittman, John Briner, Louis D. Martin. Signed: Thomas Jones
and Betsy (or Elizabeth) Jones.
John Briner made oath 4 Jun. 1789 before Robert Anderson, J.P.

Pages 23-24   3 May 1790. John Martin of Pendleton Co., S.C. to
                     Phillip Holcom of Union Co., S.C., for ₺ 70, 200 ac.
                     on Mountain Creek, waters of Big Generostee above

1

(Martin-Holcom cont'd): Ancient Boundary Line, bounded by Zachariah Holcom and Tallent's line, originally granted to Thos. Reney in 1784. On 10 Jul. 1788 "a set of printed leases from Thos. Reney to John Martin recorded before Andrew Hamilton."
Wit: John Barnett, John Loyd.
John Barnett made oath 22 Jun. 1790 before And'w Pickens, J.P.

Pages 25-27   14 Nov. 1789. John Smith of Georgia, planter, to Samuel Taylor of Ninety-Six Dist., planter, for ₤ 30 sterling, 200 acres on Tugaloo River. Bounded to the SW by sd. river and all other sides on vacant land.
Wit: Field Farrar, Jon Winn, Jun'r.
Field Farrar made oath before J. Miller, J.P. (no date)

Pages 27-28   5 Apr. 1789. John Huger, Thomas Jones and John Postell, Commissioners of the Loan Office of State of S. C. duly appointed by Act of General Assembly, passed 12 Oct. 1785, to Henry William Desaussure, for 5 shillings and ₤ 273 tract of land in Ninety-Six Dist. on East side of Senekaw River, containing 504 acres granted to Robert Tate in 1784, including Senekaw Old Town and the spot on which Fort Rutledge once stood.
Wit: J. Edwards, Barn'd. Elliott.

Pages 28-30   2 Apr. 1789. John Huger, Thomas Jones and John Postell, Comm. of Loan Office to Henry William Desaussaure---whereas, Robert Tate of Ninety-Six Dist. on 5 May 1785 did borrow on loan of sd. Commissioners, the sum of ₤ 250 -- mortgage to Commissioners, payment due 4 Mar. 1789--land advertised for sale and having exposed to public auction, 5 Apr. 1789, Henry William Desaussure being highest bidder for sum of ₤ 273. Sworn to by John Edwards, Esq., 19 Aug. 1789.
Recorded Bk. C, No. 6, p. 88, Charleston District.

Pages 30-33   Robert Tate, on 27 Jan. 1789, executed certain deed and title to Henry William Desaussure, of Charleston, 540 acres in Ninety-Six District at Seneca on Keowee River, including spot called Fort Rutledge, adjoining Major Taylor, Wm. McCaleb. Signed: Robt. Tate, Susn(Susan?) Tate. Robert Tate confirmed title to Desaussure and Susannah (Tate), his wife, renounces dower.
Wit: E. Ramsey, Wm. Tate.
Recorded 11 May 1790. Ephraim Ramsey made oath 11 May 1790.

Pages 33-35   Ninety-Six Dist., S. C., 9 May 1790. Isaac Lynch, carpenter, to John Lowry, for ₤ 30 sterling, 198 ac. on Eighteen Mile Creek, waters of Keowee River, bounded on SW by Isaac Titworth, SE and NW by James Crowder, NE by David Brag.
Wit: Saml. Lofton, Wm. Lofton. Saml. Lofton made oath 10 May 1790.

Pages 36-38   5 May 1790. Tho. Hallum to John Morrow, for ₤ 60 sterling, for 250 acres, on Eighteen Mile Creek, waters of Keowee River, bounded by Wm. Griffen.
Wit: Saml. Lofton, Wm. Lofton. Samuel Lofton made oath 10 May 1790.

Pages 38-40   25 May 1789. Robert M^{S}Campbell of Orangeburg Dist., S. C., merchant, to Nicholas Darnell, of Greenville Co., S. C., planter, for ₤ 240, for 640 acres in Ninety-Six Dist. above Ancient Boundary Line on Choestoe Creek, bounded by Tugaloo River on S., granted M^{S}Campbell 1 Jan. 1785.
Wit: Gabriel Moffitt, W. H. Lacy, Nathaniel Perry.
Nathaniel Perry made oath 18 Mar. 1789.

Pages 41-44   13 Jan. 1790. John Edwards and William Hort, Esq's., Treasurers of S.C., to Thomas Farrar, Esq., for ₤ 34.13.4.....whereas by Acts of General Assembly, lands which have been granted to persons who have not paid purchase money within time limit are directed to be sold, by Treasurers at Public Auction... Peter Sinkler on 21 Jan. 1785 had grant of 640 acres in Ninety-Six Dist. on Eighteen Mile Creek of Keowee River, bounded by Geo. Kilson , said land sold to Thomas Farrar, highest bidder. (cont'd. next page)

(Pages 41-44 cont'd):
Wit: Richd. H. Homan, Edward Edwards. Edward Edwards made oath 25 Jan. 1790, before John Sandford Dart, J.S.Q.U. at Columbia, S. C.

Pages 44-46   13 Dec. 1787. Edward Goode of Surry Co., N. C. to
                   Thomas Lewis of Greenville Co., S. C., for Ł 100 stg.
                   for 300 ac. on South side of Saluda River, granted
21 Jan., recorded Bk. CCCC, p. 192.
Wit: Ambrose Blackburn, Jno. Lewis, V. Lewis. Vincent Lewis made oath before Isaac Morgan, J.P. in Greenville Co., S. C., 26 Oct. 1789.

Pages 46-47   25 Aug. 1789. John McElroy, late of Laurens Co.,
                   S. C. to Robert Gilleland, of Granville Co., S.C. for
                   Ł 40 sterling, for 300 acres in Abbeville Co., S.C.,
on George's Creek of Saluda River, granted to Patrick Rylie, 1 Jan. 1787. Recorded Bk. PPPP, p. 430. Rylie conveyed to McElroy 1 Apr. 1788.
Wit: David Ross, Henry Machen.
Rec.: 10 May 1790.

Pages 48-50   28 Oct. 1789. Thomas Lewis, of Greenville Co., S.C.
                   to Ambrose Fitzgearld, of same county, for Ł 150 for
                   200 acres in Ninety-Six Dist., bounded by Tugaloo
River, Field Farrar, granted to Peter Finson, 21 Jan. 1785.
Recorded Bk. BBBB, p. 64.
Wit: John Lewis, Vincent Davis, Vincent Lewis. John Lewis made oath before L. A. Alston, J.P., in Greenville Co., 18 Nov. 1789.

Pages 51-52   4 Sep. 1789. Nathan Briant of Greenville Co., S. C.
                   to James Eason, of Pendleton Co. for Ł 50 stg. for
                   125 acres, in Ninety-Six Dist. on waters of Little
Beaver Dam Creek, part of a tract granted John Hunycutt, 6 Nov. 1786, bd. by Eason's Spring Branch and Moses Martin.
Wit: John Briant, Abraham Eason.
Rec: 14 Nov. 1789. Abraham Eason made oath 14 Dec. 1789.

Pages 52-55   11 Feb. 1788. Augustus Merrick of Charleston, S. C.
                   merchant, to Andrew Warnock of Abbeville Co., S. C.,
                   planter, for Ł 3 sterling, 320 acres in Ninety-Six
Dist. on Twenty Three Mile Creek, waters of Savannah River.
Wit: Nichs. Jno. Wightman, Tilly Merrick.
Rec: 7 Feb. 1790. Tilly Merrick made oath 7 Feb. 1790.

Pages 55-57   26 Oct. 1789. Thomas Lewis, of Greenville Co., S. C.
                   to John Gambrill, of Pendleton Co. for Ł 70 sterling,
                   for 328 acres on South side of Saluda River, granted
to Edward Goode, 21 Jan. 1785.
Recorded Bk. CCCC, p. 192, conveyed to Lewis, 13 Dec. 1787.
Wit: Vincent Davis, Vincent Lewis, Wm. Hanby. Vincent Davis made oath before Isaac Morgan, J. P.

Pages 57-59   6 May 1789. Nathan Briant of Greenville Co., S. C.,
                   to George Staton, of Abbeville Co., S. C., for Ł 50
                   sterling, 50 acres in Ninety-Six Dist. on Little
Beaver Dam Creek, waters of Savannah River, being part of a tract granted to John Hunnycutt, 6 Nov. 1786.
Wit: A. Blackburn, James Eason, Job Little. James Eason made oath on 14 Nov. 1789.

Pages 59-60   19 Jun. 1789. William Reed of Pendleton Co., to
                   Isaac Brock, of same, for Ł 10 sterling, 416 acres
                   in Ninety-Six Dist., on South branch of Broadmouth
Creek, waters of Saluda, granted to Reed, 3 Nov. 1788, bounded by John Lowry.
Wit: Hugh Brown, Bn. Starrett. (n.b. Oath recorded on p. 63)

Pages 60-62   10 Apr. 1789. Christopher Casey, of Spartanburg Co.,
                   S. C. to Nathaniel Jackson, of Pendleton Co., for
                   Ł 75, 360 acres in Ninety-Six Dist., on branches of
Big Generostee of Savannah River, bounded by James Jordan, L. Wood, Daniel McCollum. Signed: Christopher Casey and Elizabeth Casey . (cont'd)

3

(Pages 60-62 cont'd):
Wit: Ralph Jackson, Moses Casey, John Couch. (n.b. Oath on p. 64)

Pages 62-63   2 Jan. 1790. William Fowler and Margaret Fowler, his wife, to John Gambrel for ₤ 20, 60 acres on South side of Saluda River, granted 5 Jan. 1789.
Recorded Bk. YYYY, p. 12
Wit: William White, John Smith. William White made oath 2 Feb. 1790.

Pages 63-64   Capt. Hugh Brown made oath to deed p. 59, 13 Mar. 1790.

Page 64   Ralph Jackson made oath to deed p. 60, 15 Apr. 1790.

Pages 64-66   11 Sep. 1789. Joseph Standley and Mary, his wife, to John Maston, for ₤ 30, 177 acres in Ninety-Six Dist. on North side of Bigg Creek of Saluda River, part of a tract originally granted to Elijah Owens, 4 Sep. 1786, conveyed to Standley (no date).
Wit: William Hall, William Roberts, Thomas Standley. William Hall made oath, 8 May 1790.

Pages 66-68   25 Aug. 1789. Jacob Reed and Sarah, his wife, of Abbeville Co., S. C., to John Cobb for ₤ 100 ster'g. 199 acres in Ninety-Six Dist., on Broadmouth Creek, waters of Saluda River, granted Reed, 2 Oct. 1786.
Wit: Aaron Broyles, Isaac Brock. Isaac Brock made oath, 13 Mar. 1790.

Pages 68-69   5 Apr. 1790. Elijah Brown, of Pendleton Co., S. C. to Willey Spiers Brown, of Lincoln Co., N. C., for ₤ 150, 640 acres in Pendleton Co., on Rocky River and Hencoup Creek, granted Samuel Caldwell, 15 Oct. 1784, conveyed to David Hopkins, then to Elijah Brown, recorded Bk. ZZZ, p. 180.
Wit: Joseph Reid, William Drennan, jun'r.
William Drennan, Jr. made oath 5 Apr. 1790.

Pages 69-71   14 Nov. 1789. James Hamilton and Catherine, his wife, to Benjamin Farmer, for ₤ 65 sterling, 100 acres in Ninety-Six Dist., on South side of Saluda River, opposite the mouth of Golden Grove Creek, being a part of a tract granted to James Hamilton's father, dec'd. (no name), 31 May 1784.
Wit: Thomas Gray, Wm. McVey, Elijah Owen. William McVey made oath on 14 Nov. 1789.

Pages 71-76C   MARKS AND BRANDS   RECORDED

                 John Miller (Clk. of County)   31 Jan. 1790
                 John Wilson, Esq.   31 Aug. 1790
                 William Halbert, Esq.   31 Aug. 1790
                 Hugh Brown   31 Aug. 1790
                 John Lewis Davis   (no date)
                 George Nealson   16 Feb. 1791
                 Robert Dowdle   16 Feb. 1791
                 Wm. Read   16 Feb. 1791
                 Alexander Dromgoole   16 Feb. 1791
                 Elijah Stevenson   16 Feb. 1791
                 Daniel Lewis Martin   18 Feb. 1791
                 Robert Evans (on Keowee River)   11 Jun. 1791
                 John Kelly   16 Jun. 1791
                 Joseph Hull   18 Jan. 1793
                 John Miller, junr.   21 Jan. 1793
                 Anslem Roe   21 Aug. 1793
                 Crosby Miller   20 Jan. 1794
                 Thomas Black   10 Feb. 1795
                 David Crawford   30 Dec. 1796
                 Samuel Neel   2 Jan. 1797
                 Julius Gibson   2 Mar. 1797
                 William Smith   2 Mar. 1797
                 Abiel Cobb   2 Mar. 1797

(Marks and Brands cont'd):

Name	Date
Richard Shippe	2 Jun. 1798
Josiah Shippe	2 Jun. 1798
Thomas Jones	8 Oct. 1798
John Callaham	8 Oct. 1798
James Chapman	11 May 1799
Edward Doyle	28 Jul. 1799
James McGuffin	31 Dec. 1799
Kinson Cannon	(no date)
Hartwell Hunnicutt	17 Mar. 1800
William Stanton	14 Oct. 1801
James Doran	6 Jul. 1801
John Rusk	10 Sep. 1802
David Kelton	10 Sep. 1802
Jacob Capehart	15 Mar. 1804
Cornelius Keith	9 Oct. 1804
John McCutchen	27 Apr. 1803
Joseph Taylor	16 Dec. 1805
William Hallums	21 Dec. 1805
Richard Berry	1 Jan. 1806
Nicholas Bishop	22 Jan. 1806
James Rodgers	26 Jan. 1806
Fredrick Johnston	7 Apr. 1806
Holly Vandiver	29 Dec. 1806
Thomas Adams	1 Oct. 1808
George Detworth	23 Oct. 1809
Andrew Davis	1 May 1810
Oliver Woods	25 Jan. 1811
William Woods	25 Jan. 1811
John T. Lewis	12 Oct. 1811
Ratliff Boon	14 Jan. 1812
Elisha Burry(Burriss?)	1 Mar. 1813
James Hobson, Senr.	19 Apr. 1813
William Scott (bricklayer)	5 Jul. 1813
William Johnson	12 Jul. 1813
Isaiah Stephens	6 Oct. 1813
Alexander Brown	19 May 1814
Joseph Grisham	3 Jan. 1815
Elijah Herring	27 Jul. 1816
Jesse Hillion	27 Jul. 1816
James Highsaw	28 Oct. 1816
Wm. Duncan	31 Dec. 1816
Emeriah Felton	6 Jan. 1818
Bailey Barton, Esq.	3 Aug. 1818
John Fields, Senr.	3 Aug. 1818
Richard Lewis	4 Aug. 1819
William Walker	15 Jan. 1820
Benjamin Dickson, Esq.	4 Aug. 1823
John McCallister of Pendleton Village	6 Jul. 1824
Edward Morgan of Pendleton Dist.	19 Nov. 1824
Alexander Moorhead of Anderson Dist.	6 Apr. 1829
Solomon Geer of Anderson Dist.	3 Apr. 1830
Thomas Harrison Lewis	7 Jan. 1832
Thomas J. Newsom	15 Jan. 1834

Pages 77-78   8 Dec. 1789. John Caruthers of Ninety-Six Dist. to Ninginbel (sic) Hamilton, for £ 40, 344 acres in the Ninety-Six Dist. on branches of South Fork of Twelve Mile River, two miles West of Paris's Trading Road. Grant dated: 4 Dec. 1786. Wit: Samuel Jackson, Ephraim Jackson. (n.b. Receipt spells name "Ninian B<u>ll</u> Hamilton") Oath made 17 Mar. 1790, by Samuel Jackson.

Pages 78-80   25 Aug. 1789. Robert Pickens, planter, to John Hamilton, planter, for £ 37, 10 sh., 150 acres in Ninety-Six Dist. on branches of Twenty-Three Mile Creek, waters of Savannah River, bounded by Jacob Gilham.
Wit: Jacob Gilham, Eben Buchanan. Oath made 9 Aug. 1790 by Jacob Gilham.

Pages 80-82   2 Sep. 1789. Peter Finson of Edgefield Co., S. C. to Thomas Lewis, of Greenville Co., S. C., for ₤ 100 sterling, 200 acres on North side of Toogaloo River bounded by Capt. Field Farrar, granted Finson, 25 Jan. 1785. Recorded Bk. BBBB, p. 64.
Wit: James Puckett, Richd. Puckett. James Puckett made oath in Laurens Co., S. C. before Geo. Anderson, J. P., 3 Sep. 1789.

Pages 82-86   25 Apr. 1790. William Jackson and Isabella Jackson, his wife, planter, to Morgan Osborne, planter, for ₤ 30 sterling, 119 acres in Ninety-Six Dist., on the Five Mile Spring Branch, waters of Eighteen Mile Creek, waters of East side of Keowee River, bounded by Samuel Lofton, granted to Henry Chiles, 5 Jun. 1786.
Wit: Tilly Merrick, Thomas Lofton, John Hunnicutt. Tilly Merrick made oath 4 Aug. 1790.

Pages 86-87   11 Jul. 1789. Isaac Gilded, of Abbeville Co., S. C., to John Boren (Boring), of same county, for ₤ 100, 200 acres in Abbeville Dist. of Ninety-Six on branch of South Fork of Twelve Mile River, part of a survey made by Vardry McBee, Deputy Surveyor. Wit: Baley Anderson, William Boren, Isaac Gilder. Capt. Bailey Anderson made oath 8 Sep. 1789.

Pages 88-89   17 Aug. 1787. Baylis Earle, Esq., of Spartanburg Co., S. C., and Baylis Earle, junr., of same co., to Benjamin Selman of Greenville Co., S. C....in consideration for a tract of 287½ acres in Washington Co., Ga., on Derisaw's Creek and 1500 lbs. of tobacco, and one plantation waggon and gear, give receipt for 391 acres in Ninety-Six Dist. on Brandy Creek of Twelve Mile River, granted to Baylis Earle, Jr., 4 Apr. 1785.
Wit: John B. Grigsby, William Martin, Vincent Lewis. (no oath)

Pages 89-91   18 Jun. 1790. Alexander Erwin of Pendleton Co., Cambridge Dist., to Hadbert Tucker of same county, for ₤ 20 sterling, 2-3 acres in Cambridge Dist. on South side of Rocky River.
Wit: George Tucker, Robert Hall, John Hall. Plat included, shows land bounded by Rcbert Hall, James Holmes. Robert Hall made oath 20 Mar. 1790

Pages 91-92   Abbeville Co., S. C. 13 Jul. 1789. John Green, blacksmith of Abbeville Co., to William Skelton, a planter, for ₤ 80, 200 acres on Big Generostee, in Abbeville Co., above the Ancient Boundary Line bounded by Moses Liddle, granted to Green, 23 May 1785. Recorded Bk. IIII, p. 535.
Wit: George Weems, John Barnett. Barnett made oath in Abbeville Co., 9 Feb. 1790, before John Moffet, J. P.

Pages 92-93   17 Jan. 1789. William MacMahen and Mary, his wife, of Pendleton Co., farmer, to Martha Leman, Senr. and Robert Leman, her son, for ₤ 40 sterling, 140 acres -part of a tract of 300 acres granted John Calhoun by patent, 10 Dec. 1784, conveyed to MacMahan, on Twenty-Three Mile Creek of Savannah River.
Wit: William Hallum, Jennet Laman, Saml. H. Dickson. William Hallum made oath 23 Mar. 1790.
Rec: 12 Aug. 1790.

Pages 94-96   19 Nov. 1789. Thomas Cox and Mary, his wife, of the State of Georgia, planter, to Loddy Dobbs of Pendleton Co., "of like occupation", for ₤ 30 sterling, 58 acres granted to Cox by State grant, 3 Dec. 1787, on the Tugaloo River bounded by Capt. Blackburn, Samuel Taylor.
Wit: Barzillai Harrison, Benja. Cleveland. Signed: Thomas and Mary Cocks. Benja. Cleveland made oath 9 Aug. 1790.
Rec: 12 Aug. 1790.

Pages 96-97   19 Oct. 1789. Edward Towry and Betsey, his wife, blacksmith, to John Lewis Davis, joiner, for ₤ 30

(Pages 96-97 cont'd):
sterling, 105 acres granted to Edward Towrey, 3 Nov. 1787, on branch of Chestowee Creek, waters of Tugaloo River, bounded by William McCaleb.
Wit: Nathaniel Perry, Joseph Hand, Benj. Perry. Nathaniel Perry made oath 30 May 1790.

Pages 98-99   20 Oct. 1788. John Gowen and Letty, his wife, of Spartanburg Co., S. C., to Benjamin Barton, of Greenville Co., for Ł 100 str'g, 256 acres in Abbeville Co., south of Saluda River on Twenty-Three Mile River, granted to Letty Gowen by letters patent, 1 May 1786.
Recorded Bk. KKKK, p. 440.
Wit: William Anderson, Allen Gowen, Vinson Anderson. William Anderson and Allen Gowen made oath in Greenville Co., before John Ford, J. P., 13 Dec. 1788.

Pages 99-100   18 Jun. 1790. William McCaleb, planter, for divers causes, grant to James Alexander Douglas, 50 acres on waters of Twelve-Mile River, provided he gives William McCaleb first refusal of purchase, otherwise the intent of this instrument be null and void.
Wit: James Brice, Saml. Taylor. James Brice made oath 9 Aug. 1790.

Pages 100-102   4 Jul. 1788. John Holland of Greenville Co., S. C. Levi Murphree of Abbeville Co., for Ł 100, 200 acres in Abbeville Co., Ninety-Six Dist., on both sides of Buck Creek of Twelve Mile River, granted John Holland, 1 Jan. 1785.
Wit: Baley Anderson, William Anderson, Benjamin Barton. Benjamin Barton made oath 9 Aug. 1790.

Pages 102-103   2 Jan. 1790. George Pierce to Benjamin Starritt for Ł 100 sterling, for 2 different tracts on the south side of the Saluda River, oldest tract of 200 acres granted to George Pierce, 21 Jan. 1785.
Recorded Bk. CCCC, p. 397; "youngest" tract contains 158 acres granted Pierce, 3 Sep. 1787.
Recorded Bk. UUUU, p. 284.
Wit: Wm. Washington, James Moor. Wm. Washington made oath 9 Aug. 1790.

Pages 103-108   2 Sep. 1787. James Jordan, smith, and Margaret, his wife, of Abbeville Co., to Samuel McCollum, weaver, of same, for Ł 5 sterling, 155 acres on North side of Senecha River, plat in Bk. QQQQ, p. 537.
Wit: John Files, Ja. Jos. (sic). John Files made oath 9 Aug. 1790.

Pages 108=111   2 May 1788. Andrew Hamilton of Abbeville Co., farmer, to William Guest, farmer, of same, for Ł 24.11.2 sterling, 200 acres on both sides of Little Beaver Dam Creek, waters of Tugaloo River, bounded by Elijah McCurdy, granted to Hamilton (no date).
Recorded Bk. HHHH, p. 416.
Wit: John Parsons, Charles Bond, Jno. Barton, Solomon King. John Parsons made oath 28 May 1789.

Pages 111-115   26 Feb. 1790. Tilly Merrick, planter, to Alexander Irvin, for Ł 60 sterling, 640 acres in Ninety-Six Dist., on South side of Rocky River, surveyed by David Hopkins for John Turnbull and granted on 16 Jul. 1784.
Wit: James Holmes, George Tucker, Harbert Tucker. Harbert Tucker made oath 9 Aug. 1790.

Pages 115-116   7 Aug. 1790. Alexander Irwine to Robert Hall for Ł 20 sterling, 30 acres beginning at bank of First Creek, granted 15 Oct. 1784.
Wit: Harbert Tucker, Sam'l. Lofton. Harbert Tucker made oath 9 Aug. 1790.

Pages 116-119   14 Oct. 1788, Patrick Forbis, planter, of Abbeville

(Pages 116-119 cont'd):
Co. to James Moore, of same, for Ł 10 sterling, 200 acres in Ninety-Six Dist., above the Ancient Boundary Line on waters of Hencoop, waters of Great Rocky Creek, granted to Forbis for being a soldier in the Continental Line, 5 Mar. 1787.
Wit: Patrick Buchanan, Robert Stevenson, Philmon Waters. Patrick Buchanan made oath 18 Jul. 1789.

Pages 119-122   14 Nov. 1789. John Smith, heir of Ezekiel Smith of Georgia, planter, to William Brooks, of Ninety-Six Dist., for Ł 30 sterling, 200 acres on Tugaloo River, originally granted Ezekiel Smith, 15 Oct. 1784.
Wit: Field Farrar, Jon Winn, Jr. Field Farrar made oath 8 Jan. 1790.

Pages 122-124   96 Dist., 25 Jun. 1790. John Dowdle, planter, to John Calaham, planter, for Ł 70 sterling, 248 acres in 96 Dist., on Beaver Creek, branch of Great Rocky Creek, waters of the Savannah River, part of 600 acres granted to Dowdle, 5 Jun. 1786.
Recorded Bk. LLLL, p. 405.
Wit: Robert Dowdle, Moses Estes, James Dowdle. Plat included, bounded by John Jacks, John Dowdle, Moses Eastridge. Wm. Lesley, deputy surveyor. Robert Dowdle made oath (no date).

Pages 124-125   25 Jun. 1790. John Dowdle, planter, to Moses Estreage, Sr., for Ł 20, 80 acres on Beaver Creek, the branch of Great Rocky Creek, of the Savannah River, bounded by John Callaham, John Dowdle, granted Dowdle 5 Jun. 1786.
Wit: Robert Dowdle, John Callaham, James Dowdle. Robert Dowdle made oath 10 Aug. 1790.

Pages 125-128   4 Jun. 1790. David Read Evans, of Winnsborough, Camden Dist., Gentleman, to Samuel Taylor, Esq., of 96 Dist., fbp Ł 10 sterling, 200 acres on South side of Saluda River, granted to Samuel Croslin, 21 Jan. 1795, conveyed to Evans, 29 May 1788.
Wit: M. Winn, Wm. Roach. Wm. Roach made oath 5 Jun. 1790.

Pages 128-131   29 May 1788. Samuel Croslin, of Fairfield Co., S.C. to David Evans, of same county, Gentl'm., for Ł 5, 200 acres on South side of Saluda River, granted to Croslin 21 Jan. 1785.
Wit: D. Evans, Jno. Winn, Jr. John Winn, Jr. made oath in Laurens Co. S. C., before Jonathan Downs, J. P., 8 Jun. 1790.
Rec: 12 Aug. 1791.

Pages 131-134   7 Jul. 1789. James Moore, planter, to John Todd, planter, for Ł 50 sterling, 200 acres in 96 Dist., above the Ancient Boundary Line, on Hen Coop, waters of Rocky River, granted to Patrick Forbes, for being a soldier in the Continental Line, now belonging to James Moore (n.b. see p. 116).
Wit: Lewis Land, William Todd, John McVey. John McVey made oath on 10 Aug. 1790.

Pages 135-138   13 Apr. 1790. George Weems to William Mackey, for Ł 80 sterling, 246 acres on both sides of Connoross Creek, waters of Keowee Rived bounded by John Lawrence, Robert Waddle, granted to Weems (no date).
Recorded Bk. KKKK, p. 164.
Wit: Alexr. Kilpatrick, Joshua Young, John Clark Kilpatrick. John C. Kilpatrick made oath 30 Jul. 1790.

Pages 138-139   22 Aug. 1788. William McCaleb of Abbeville Co., S.C. to William Young, of same county, for Ł 275, 275 ac. on both sides of Middle Fork of Twelve Mile River, bounded by Mary Kerr, widow, granted to William McCaleb, 16 Jul. 1785.
Wit: James Maxwell, Wm. Maxwell. William Maxwell made oath 22 Aug. 1788.

Pages 140-141   14 Aug. 1787. Ralph Owen and Elizabeth, his wife,

(Pages 140-141 cont'd):
of 96 Dist., Abbeville Co., to James Scott, of same, fow ₤ 40, 300 acres in Abbeville Co., on Washington Creek.
Wit: James Hamilton, Jr., Aaron Boggs. Aaron Boggs made oath in Pendleton Co., 8 Feb. 1790.

Pages 141-143   26 Sep. 1789. Francis Bremar, Esq., of Charleston and James Martin of York Co., S. C., to William Reid of Pendleton Co., S. C. for ₤ 30 sterling, 360 acres in Pendleton Co., on South side of Saluda River on Broadmouth Creek, granted to Bremar and Martin, 3 Apr. 1786. Recorded in the Secretary of State Office (no bk. number).
Wit: Aaron Broyles, B. Starritt, Hugh Brown. Benjamin Starritt made oath 17 Jul. 1790.

Pages 143-145   2 Sep. 1789. Robert Pickens, planter, to Jacob Gilham, planter, for ₤ 37. 10., 150 acres in 96 Dist. on branches of Twenty Three Mile Creek of Savannah River, bounded by John Hamilton.
Wit: Eben Buchanan, John Hamilton. John Hamilton made oath 9 Aug. 1790.

Pages 145-146   22 Jul. 1790. Thomas Coker of Abbeville Co., S. C. to John Green of Greenville Co., S. C., for ₤ 10., 50 acres on Hurricane Creek, South side of Saluda River, part of tract granted to Thomas Coker, whereon he now lives. Recorded Bk. YYYY, p. 408, 22 Jan. 1789, bd. Crawfish Branch, John Johnston.
Wit: Meshack Green, Lewis Green, James Sizemore. Lewis Green made oath 22 Jul. 1790.

Pages 146-150   26 Oct. 1789. John Miles, planter, of Pendleton Co. S. C. to Robert Maxwell, Esq. of Greenville Co., S.C. for ₤ 150, 468 acres on West side of Keowee River, adj. same at mouth of Conneross Creek, granted John Miles, 15 May. 1787. Recorded bk. (SSSS?), p. 197.
Wit: John Caldwell, John Woods. John Woods made oath 23 Sep. 1790.

Pages 150-153   26 Aug. 1790. Tucker Woodson, of Abbeville Co., S. C., planter, to Henry William Dessausure, Esq., of Charleston, for ₤ 45, 200 acres in Pendleton Co. in fork of Tugaloo and Keowee Rivers on both sides of Beaver Dam Creek, waters of Tugaloo, granted Woodson, 3 Apr. 1786.
Recorded Bk. KKKK, p. 312.
Wit: John Woods, Alexander Ramsey. John Woods made oath 23 Sep. 1790.

Pages 154-157   7 Sep. 1790. Col. Robert Anderson, planter, to Charles Rice, planter, for ₤ 80 sterling, 180 acres on West side of Keowee River, granted Anderson on 5 Jun. 1786.
Recorded Bk. LLLL, p. 98.
Wit: Elijah Stinson, John Woods. John Woods made oath 23 Sep. 1790.
Rec: 2 Oct. 1790.

Pages 157-158   29 Obt. 1789. Banister Harper, planter, to William Harper, son of Banister Harper for love and affection and 20 shillings, one Negro woman slave named Cheaney "in what place said Negro shall be found, with increase, except one child named Daniel".
Wit: Robert Anderson, Isaac Linch. ..."This deed of gift by Banister Harper on the express condition that if he should die before 1 Jan. 1791, said Negro woman not be taken from his widow before that time." Robert Anderson made oath 23 Sep. 1790.

Pages 159-160   27 Apr. 1789. Thomas Hallum to Thomas Foster for ₤ 50 sterling, 200 acres on Brushy Creek, branch of Saluda River. Signed by Thomas Hallum and Elizabeth Hallum. Wit: Robert Allison, John Allison, Nimrod Williams.
Robert Allison made oath 15 Jan. 1790.
Rec: 4 Oct. 1790.

Pages 160-161   30 May 1789. Nimrod Williams to Thomas Foster, ₤ 30
                 sterling, for 190 acres on Brushy Creek bounded by
                 Thomas Hallum, William Hobbs, William McWilliams,and
Watson Allison. Signed by Nimrod Williams and Ann Williams.
Wit: William Allison, William McWilliams. William Allison made oath
15 Jan. 1790.
Rec: 4 Oct. 1790.

Pages 162-163   26 Sep. 1787. George Pearce of 96 Dist., to Wm. Wash-
                 ington "for valuable consideration", 130 acres on the
                 South West side of Saluda River, on Tony's Creek to
mouth of Reedy Branch, bd. by William Poor, Rebin Johnson, granted to
Pearce, 1787.
Wit: James Martin, Benj. Starrit, Reuben Johnson. Benjamin Starrit made
oath 9 Aug. 1790. Rec: 4 Oct. 1790.

Pages 163-165   12 Jun. 1790. James Gillison and Jane, his wife, to
                 James Linn, planter, for ₤ 30 sterling, 160 acres on
                 branch of Twenty Six Mile Creek, waters of Seneka
River; grant recorded Bk. EEEE, p. __, 1 Aug. 1785.
Wit: Jonathan Montgomery, James Linn, Jr., James Montgomery. James
Linn, Jr. made oath 9 Aug. 1790.

Pages 166-167   10 Mar. 1788. William Brown and Violet, his wife,
                 of Abbeville Co., to Benjamin Starritt, of same,for
                 ₤ 50 sterling, 306 acres in 96 Dist. on North Fork
of Broadmouth Creek, waters of the Saluda River, granted to Brown on 5
Jun. 1786.
Wit: Joseph Brown, James Brown. James Brown made oath on 9 Aug. 1790.
Rec: 5 Oct. 1790.

Pages 168-171   13 Apr. 1790. John Lawrence of Abbeville Co., to
                 Alexander Kilpatrick, of Pendleton Co., for ₤ 100
                 sterling, 200 acres on both sides of the Conneross
Creek, waters of the Keowee River, bd. by George Weems, Robert Waddle,
William Twitty, granted to Lawrence (no date).
Recorded Bk. EEEE, p. 375.
Wit: Jno. C. Kilpatrick, George Weems, Joshua Young. John Lawrence
made oath 30 Jul. 1790.

Pages 171-175   96 Dist., S. C., 31 Dec. 1788. Thomas Lofton, plan-
                 ter, to William Lofton, planter, for ₤ 50, 630 acres
                 on North Fork of Choestowee Creek in 96 Dist., gran-
ted to Thomas Lofton on 2 Jul. 1788.
Wit: Sam'l Lofton, Sr., Samuel Lofton, William McConnel. Samuel Lofton
made oath 9 Aug. 1790.

Pages 175-176   Mrs. Kitty Burris made oath that her daughter, Jean
                 Burris, now Jean Glenn, was first married to John
                 Evans, who died and left one daughter, Letitia, and
considerable in property, as he was a careful, well managing man.......
daughter then married William Brummett who was not so attentive to his
worldly concerns and spent the full half of what the first husband had
left without adding to the stock, but left issue of two sons....when
said William Brummett was on his death bed, she asked him how he wished
to have his worldly affairs settled...he replied that he wished Letitia
to be made whole, if there was property enough left, signifying that
what was left should be applied to the use of the first husband's child.
John Burt was also present. Date: 21 Jul. 1790. Robert Anderson, J.P.

Pages 176-177   14 Obt. 1788. John Martin of York Co., S. C. to
                 Thomas Woods of York Co., for ₤ 170 sterling, 399
                 acres in 96 Dist., Abbeville Co., on Eighteen Mile
Creek, waters of Savannah River, granted to Martin 6 Mar. 1786.
Wit: Jacob Black, John Black. Jacob Black made oath 16 Sep. 1789.

Page 178   Will of Ralph Wilson, of Abbeville...wife, Jane Wil-
                 son...children: Elizabeth Wilson, George G. Wilson,
                 James W. Wilson, Sarah D. Wilson..."care and educa-
tion under executor until son, James Wharey Wilson, is age 21." Exc:

(Page 178 cont'd):
Thomas Wharey, John Wharey, Stephen Wilson, Jr. Date 9 Oct. 1788. Wit: Jesse Wood, Aaron Derney. (no. rec. date).

Pages 178-179 Will of R. Ralston, of Pendleton Co....wife, Frances ...sons: Lewis and John Raulston, tract of land on tugalooe River, adjoining tract called Village Tract of 150 acres...plantation I live on of 200 acres...(no Exc. named). Date: 17 Ma7 1789. Wit: Jesse Walton, Benj. Harrison.

Pages 179-181 These pages appear to be a record of bond for the executors of Ralph Wilson, deceased. Spaces for names and dates are not filled in.

Pages 181-182 Will of John Johnson, of Pendleton Co., yeoman..... wife (unnamed)...son, Joseph; 200 acres lying on Great Saltketchers in Winton Co., Orangeburgh Dist., S. C....daughter, Elizabeth; 100 acres on Three Mile Creek, waters of Big Saltketchers. Exc: Andrew Jones. Date: 15 Aug. 1790. Wit: Stephen Sullivant, Elizabeth Jones, Joseph Dunklin. Stephen Sullivant made an oath on 8 Nov. 1790.

Page 182 Will of John Linley, yeoman of Pendleton Co...wife, Sarah Linley...unmarried children. Exc.: William Pyle, Jr. and wife, Sarah Linley. DateL 9 Sept.1790. Wit: John Robinson, Joel Halbert, Jacob Visage. John Robinson made oath 11 Nov. 1790.

Pages 183-185 14 Aug. 1790. Joseph Woodall to John Patterson..... grant dated 5 Jun. 1786 to Woodall for 366 acres in 96 Dist., on South fork of Twelve Mile River, now sells 158 acres of original grant, for ₤ 78.10. Wit: John Brown, John Hornidy. John Brown made oath 8 Nov. 1790.

Pages 185-186 9 Nov. 1790. John Robertson to Joseph Woodall for ₤ 29.10, 147 acres in 96 Dist. on Crow Creek, waters of Keowee River, granted to John Robertson, 6 Nov. 1786. Wit: Bailey Anderson, John Langley. Bailey Anderson made oath 9 Nov. 1790.

Page 187 James Shockley to Thomas Shockley, Sr., for ₤ 47.10. sterling, for 5 cows and calves and 2 year old heifer, 2 horses, 18 hogs, 2 beds with furniture. Date: 4 Nov. 1790. Wit: James Jones, only wit. who made oath 8 Nov. 1790.

Pages 188-190 John Moffette, by my hand (to which Frame Woods was jointly bound with me) on 3 Aug. 1784 to George Smith, Josiah Smith, Daniel Desausaure and Edward Darrell (their last name is probably Smith, also. In body of deed they are called "George, Josiah, Daniel and Edward"), for ₤ 1520 sterling, with condition of payment of ₤ 750 on 1 Jan. 1785 "to said Josiah, Daniel and Edward who have survived the sd. George, dec'd,". Wit: J. B. Holmes, William Moore. John Bee Holmes, Esq., Att'y. at Law made oath 10 Dec. 1790.

Pages 190-194 16 Aug. 1785. John Swords, "late a Soldier in the Continental Line of this State", to Lewis Daniel Martin, "late a Captain of the sd. Line", for ₤ 10 sterling for 200 acres in 96 Dist., granted Swords 21 Jan. 1785, on Martin's Creek, waters of Keowee River. Wit: John Bowie, Richard Taliferro ...John Bowie, Esq. made oath before Andrew Hamilton, J. P., Abbeville Co., S. C.

Pages 194-195 9 Nov. 1790. Sturdy Garnier made oath in court that a bond given John Lindley to sd. Garnier for ₤ 300 sterling, to make title to a tract of 280 acres on Big Creek, waters of Saluda River, was returned to John Lindley in May last and Garnier has no demand against Estate of John Lindley.

Pages 195-196   Bill of Sale...Jesse Clements to Culliver Clements,
                     two wagons and six horses...; for ₤ 100 sterling.
                     Date: 20 Aug. 1790. Wit: John Breavert, who made
oath 26 Bct. 1790.

Pages 196-197   10 Nov. 1789. William Love, planter of Abbeville
                     Co., to Barnet Putnam, planter of same county, for
                     ₤ 50, 400 acres on branches of the Generostee, a-
bove Ancient Boundary Line, bd. by John Green, granted to William Love
7 Jan. 1788. Recorded Bk. WWWW, p. 1491.
Wit: Thomas Shockley, Jr., Thomas Shockley, Sr. Thomas Shockley, Sr.
made oath 8 Nov. 1790.

Pages 197-201   27 Jul. 1790. John Smith, late of Wilkes Co., Ga.,
                     planter, to James Madison of Pendleton, S. C., plan-
                     ter, 50 guineas or ₤ 50.7.6 for 200 acres in the 96
Dist., Pendleton Co., on Tugaloo River, granted to John Smith, recorded
Bk. ___, p. ___.
Wit: Alexander Ramsey, John Wood. John Wood made oath 30 Nov. 1790.

Pages 201-202   16 Mar. 1789. William Love, of Abbeville Co., to
                     Thomas Shockley, of same co., for 10 shillings, 150
                     acres granted William Love, 7 Jan. 1788, in Abbe-
ville Co. on a branch of the Savannah River.
Wit: Ja. Jones, Barnet Putman. James Jones made oath 8 Nov. 1790.

Pages 202-203   16 Mar. 1789. William Love of Abbeville Co., to
                     Thos. Shockley, of same, for 10 shillings for 150
                     acres granted to Love, 21 Jan. 1785, on NE side of
Savannah River, being part of 300 acres which 150 acres being the upper
part of sd. granted land, on a branch called Town-house.
Wit: Ja. Jones, Barnard Putman. James Jones made oath 8 Nov. 1790.

Pages 204-206   25 Dec. 1787. George Robuck, of Spartanburg Co., S.
                     C., to Bailey Anderson, of Abbeville Co., ₤ 100 stg.
                     for 440 acres in Abbeville Co., 96 Dist., on both
sides of Middle Fork of 12 Mile River, granted to Roebuck by patent on
7 May 1787....(later amount says ₤ 1000 sterling.)
Wit: William Barnet, Duncin Camron. Abbeville Co., Duncan Cameron made
oath, 29 Sep. 1788.

Pages 206=208   14 Aug. 1790. Joseph Woodall to John Horneday, for
                     ₤ 78.10. for 366 acres in 96 Dist., on South Fork
                     of Twelve Mile River, bd. by Selman; granted 5 Jun.
1786. Wit: John Brown, John Patteson. John Brown made oath 8 Nov. 1790

Pages 208-210   6 Nov. 1789. John Standley to William Halbert, for
                     ₤ 50, 133 acres on Big Creek, in grant called Wash-
                     ington Creek, waters of Saluda River, being part of
tract granted Elijah Owens, 4 Sep. 1786.
Wit: William Hall, William Roberts, William Oaldfield. William Hall
made oath 6 Oct. 1790.

Pages 211-213   6 Nov. 1789. Joseph Standley to William Halbert, for
                     ₤ 50, 50 acres in 96 Dist., on Big Creek, of the
                     Saluda River, part of tract granted to John Nichel-
son, 15 Oct. 1784. Wit: William Hall, William Roberts, William Oaldfield. William Hall made oath 6 Oct. 1790.

Pages 213-215   6 Nov. 1789. Joseph Standley to William Halbert, for
                     ₤ 50, 133 acres on Big Creek, waters of Saluda River,
                     granted to John Nickolson, 6 Oct. 1788.
Wit: William Hall, William Roberts, William Oaldfield. William Hall
made oath 6 Oct. 1790.

Pages 215-217   9 Oct. 1790. Samuel Lofton, Esq., Sheriff of Pendle-
                     ton Co., to John Rolston...whereas, Mark Powell was
                     seized of a tract of 200 acres on Toogaloo River,
known by the name of The Village...Field Farrar in June term last com-

(Pages 215-217 cont'd):

menced Action of Debt for 12.12.4 sterling, also 1.17.3 for costs, by John Bynum, Esq., Clerk of Court at Lexington, 6 Aug. last...on 6 Oct. 1790 at auction, sold land to <u>Lewis</u> Rollston for ₤ 51 sterling (he is called Lewis Rolston in last part of deed several times).
Wit: Thomas Farrar, Wm. Tate. Thomas Farrar made oath 9 Nov. 1790.

Pages 217-219   9 Oct. 1790. Samuel Lofton, Esq., Sheriff of Pendleton Co., to Lewis Rolston...whereas John McGee was seized of a tract of 200 acres on Toogaloo River, bd. by Mark Powell...Field Farrar in June term last began Action of Debt, in Lexington Co., for sum of 12.12.4 sterling, also 1.17.3. sterling for costs...sold to Lewis Rolston at public auction for ₤ 51.
Wit: Thomas Farrar, Wm. Tate. Thomas Farrar made oath 9 Nov. 1790.

Pages 219-222   1 Sep. 1788. Hugh Milling of Camden Dist., S. C., planter, to William Clark of 96 Dist., for ₤ 100, 300 acres on Tugaloo River, known as Milling's Survey, granted 15 Oct. 1784.
Recorded Bk. BBBB, p. 58.
Wit: Jno. Tinkler, David A. Milling. John Tinkler made oath in Fairfield Co., S. C., before John Buchanan, Esq., J. P., 13 Sep. 1788.

Pages 223-224   10 Oct. 1787. John Black, of 96 Dist. to James McAdams, of same, for ₤ 45 sterling, 350 acres, except small piece of 50 acres granted to Craven Moffitt by older grant, in 96 District above the Ancient Boundary Line, on Saluda River granted to John Black, 5 Jun. 1786.
Wit: Gabriel Moffitt, Ebenezer Fain. Ebenezer Fain made oath 20 Jan. 1791. Rec: 5 Feb. 1791.

Pages 225-226   19 Dec. 1789. Joshua Hill of Abbeville Co., to David Durham of Greenville Co., for ₤ 20 received by Phillip Jones in behalf of David Durham for 100 ac. on Rocky Creek, south side of Saluda River, surveyed for James Jones on 6 Jun. 1785 and granted Joshua Hill, 1 Jan. 1787.
Wit: John Cowan, Jr., Ward(?) Hill, William Hammonds. William Hammonds made oath 14 Aug. 1790.
Rec: 7 Feb. 1791

Pages 226-230   19 Aug. 1788. Baylis Earle of Spartanburg Co., to Jesse Goodwin of Greenville Co., for ₤ 50 sterling, for 168 acres on branches of Shoal Creek, waters of Saluda River, granted to Earle by patent 6 Nov. 1786 "in 96 Dist., now called Abbeville Co.".
Recorded Bk. QQQQ, p. 14.
Wit: Baley Anderson, Benjn. Clark. Benjamin Clark made oath 8 Nov.1790.

Pages 230-231   23 Dec. 1788. Watson Allison, of Laurens Co., S. C. to Samuel Torbert, of Abbeville Co., for 20 shillings for 100 acres surveyed for Allison, 20 Aug. 1786, bd. by Samuel Torbert.
Wit: Wm. Edmondson, Andw. Cunningham, Wm. Allison. Andrew Cunningham made oath 9 Mar. 1790.

Pages 231-233   1 Dec. 1787. Dominick Marah, of 96 Dist., to Nathan Page, of Abbeville Co., for 20 shillings for 100 ac. in 96 Dist. on South side of Saluda River, surveyed for Marah 17 Feb. 1786.
Wit: William Osborn, Thomas Osborn, William Reed. William Reed made oath 14 Aug. 1798.

Pages 233-235   96 Dist. 12 Feb. 1791. John Caldwell, planter, to John Callaham, for ₤ 80, 190 acres in 96 Dist. on branches of Great Rocky Creek, called Governor's Creek, granted Caldwell 1 Feb. 1790.
Recorded Bk. B, No. 5, p. 83.
Wit: Adam Files, John McMahen. Adam Files made oath 15 Feb. 1791.

Pages 235-236   30 Dec. 1790. Isaac Lynch and his wife (no name),
                     to Barzellai Harrison, planter, for Ł 25 sterling,
                     100 acres on Tugaloo River, granted Lynch 2 March
1789. Wit: John Miller, Crosby W. Miller. John Miller made oath on
11 Mar. 1791.

Pages 236-238   5 Sep. 1790. John Watson to William Means for Ł 30
                     sterling, 100 acres part of survey of 640 acres on
                     branch of Brushy Creek, branch of the Saluda River,
bd. Wilson.
Wit: Andrew Cunningham, Thomas Caudill, Samuel Means. Samuel Means
made oath 23 Feb. 1791.

Pages 238-240   20 Nov. 1789. John McVey to John Nickelson, for
                     Ł 107 sterling, 200 acres in 96 Dist., on South side
                     of Saluda River, on Washington Creek, granted McVey
3 Apr. 1786.
Recorded Bk. HHHH, p. 445.
Wit: Wm. McVey, Christian Roark. Wm. McVey made oath 8 Feb. 1790.

Pages 240-242   23 Jan. 1786. William Davis and Sarah, his wife, of
                     96 Dist., to Aaron Boages, for Ł 250 sterling, for
                     200 acres on branches of Big Creek, waters of Salu-
da River. Wit: John McVey, William Daves, Robert Richey. John McVey
made oath 8 Feb. 1790.

Pages 242-247   30 Dec. 1789. John Buchanan (also spelled Bowhanan)
                     planter, to Richard Lancaster, planter, for Ł 17, on
                     or before 9 Jan. 1790 and Ł 18 on 9 Jan. 1791, for
200 acres on waters of Hen Coop and Neal's Creek, waters of Great Rocky
Creek.
Wit: James Moore, John Calhoun, John Moore. James Moore made oath on
8 Nov. 1790.

Pages 247-250   19 Nov. 1788. William Forbis, of Abbeville Co., plan-
                     ter, to John Buchanan, planter, of Abbeville Co.,for
                     Ł 30, 200 acres in 96 Dist., above Ancient Boundary
Line on Hencoop, waters of Great Rocky Creek, granted to Forbis for being a soldier in the Continental Line, 5 Mar. 1787., bd. by Patrick Forbis. Wit: James Moore, John Moore, Alexander Moore. James Moore made
oath before Wm. Halbert, J. P. of Abbeville Co. 18 Jul. 1789.

Pages 250-252   11 Mar. 1790. Thomas Roberts and Margaret, his wife,
                     of 96 Dist., to Joseph Bowlin for Ł 6, 55 acres in
                     96 Dist.
Wit: James Scott, John Nickelson, Elijah Owen. James Scott made oath
12 Feb. 1791.

Pages 252-254   2 Feb. 1790. Andrew Lee of Abbeville Co. to Robert
                     Harkness of Pendleton Co. for Ł 100 for two parcels
                     of land in 96 Dist. on Rocky River and Hen Coop Crk.
...one tract of 100 acres granted Lee 15 Oct. 1784; Recorded Bk. AAAA,
p. 212; the other of 121 acres granted Lee 14 Dec. 1786; Recorded Bk.
QQQQ, p. 225. "I, Andrew Lee and Elizabeth Lee my wife, sign."
Wit: Robert Harkness, Jr., James Pettigrew, Thos. Lee. James Pettigrew
made oath in Abbeville Co., 15 Feb. 1791.
Rec: 12 Apr. 1791.

Pages 254-258   19 Aug. 1789. James Shirley,planter of Abbeville Co.
                     to William Anderson, Jr. of Pendleton Co. for Ł 100
                     for 300 acres in 96 Dist. above Ancient Boundary
Line on Beaver Dam Creek, waters of Rocky River, granted James Shirley,
"for Ł 30 sterling paid into Treasury for use of the State". Signed by
James Shirley and Mary Shirley, his wife. (In oath, she is called Mar-
garet).
Wit: James Moore, Thomas Shirley, John Moore. James Moore made oath on
8 Nov. 1790.
Rec: 27 April 1791.

Pages 258-262   24 Dec. 1790. Robert Anderson, and Jane, his wife,

(Pages 258-262 cont'd):
planter, to Levi Pierce, planter, for Ł 25 for 148 acres on Six Mile Creek, bd. on one side by Keowee River, granted to Anderson 2 Feb. 1789. (Signed by Jean Anderson).
Wit: Aaron Terrel, Morgan Osborn. Morgan Osborn made oath 1 Jan. 1791.
Rec: 28 Apr. 1791.

Pages 262-264   4 Sep. 1786. Alexander Eddins of 96 Dist. to James Davis (Lang) (sic), of 96 Dist. for 100 lbs. for 100 acres part of grant of 250 acres to Eddins 21 Jan. 1785 on both sides of Wollono, branch of Saluda River...(in body of deed he is called James Davis (Long).
Wit: Samuel Weaver, Joseph Whitner. Samuel Weaver made oath 14 Feb. 1790. (n.b. mentions another Samuel Weaver).
Rec: 28 Apr. 1791.

Pages 264-268   6 Nov. 1790. John Moore, planter, to Alexander Moore, for Ł 50 sterling, 200 acres in 96 Dist. above Ancient Boundary Line on Great Beaver Dam Crk. of Great Rocky Creek, granted to John Moowe, 1 Mar. 1790, bd. by James Caldwell.
Wit: Joseph Land, James Moore, Richard Lancaster. James Moore made oath 8 Nov. 1790.
Rec: 3 May 1791.

Pages 268-270   28 Mar. 1789. Robert Tate, of Newberry Co., S. C. to Thomas McCants of Abbeville Co., for Ł 20 strg. 240 acres in 96 Dist. on Hen Coop Creek, waters of Savannah River, granted to Robert Tate by patent ____, 1780, containing 640 acres. Signed: Robert Tate, Susn. Tate.
Wit: Bn. Starrit, Margaret Speake. Benjamin Starrit made oath 13 Dec. 1790. Rec: 4 May 1791.

Pages 270-272   28 Mar. 1789. Robert Tate, of Newberry Co. to James Jack of Abbeville Co. for Ł 40 sterling, for 400 ac. in 96 Dist., on Hencoop Creek, waters of Savannah River, granted to Robert Tate by patent (dates blank), 1780, containing 640 acres. Robert Tate and Sun(?) Tate sign.
Wit: Benjamin Starritt, Thomas McCance. Benjamin Starritt made oath on 13 Dec. 1790. Rec: 4 May 1791.

Pages 272-273   13 Feb. 1790. John Wheeler to John Bledsoe, for Ł40 sterling, 103 acres on South side of Saluda River, bd by William Laffoon and John Wheeler, granted to same Wheeler on 3 Oct. 1785.
Wit: Benj. Clark, William Jones. Benj. Clark made oath 14 Feb. 1791.
Rec: 27 May 1791.

Pages 273-275   24 Mar. 1791. John Mauldin, Sr., to Lent Hall, both of Washington Dist., Pendleton Co., S. C., for Ł 25 for 100 acres in Washington Dist. on Governor's Crk. branch of Great Rocky Creek, bd. by William Lesley, Jr., John Mauldin, Blake Mauldin, John Warnock. Wit: Harris Mauldin, Surry (?) Davis, George Tucker. (no oath).
Rec: 27 May 1791.

Page 275   John Mauldin appeared before Elijah Brown, Justice ....declared he sold Nathl. Hall, Sr., 100 acres of land for a certain mare, which he received by hands of John Falconer, who informed the deponent, the above land Mr. Hall purchased and gave to Falkner in consequence of a deed of gift given Nathaniel Hall of his Estate to the amount of(upon) which Falkner told the deponent that he was better pleased than he had been for many years on account of the friendly exchange. Signed: John Mauldin, Sr. Date: 24 Mar. 1791. Rec: 27 May 1791. (no wit.).

Pages 275-278   6 Aug. 1790. Jonathan Clark of 96 Dist., planter, to George Forbes, of same, planter, for Ł 200, 140 acres of land in 96 Dist. on Twenty Six Mile Creek, waters of Savannah River, bd. by David Clark, Bolen Clark, Canady, James

(pages 275-278 cont'd):
Long. Wit: David Clark, John McMah<u>n</u>, Hugh McVey. Plat included. Rec: 30 May 1791. (no oath)

Pages 278-282 18 Mar. 1791. George Shuler and Mary, his wife, planter, to Joseph Chapman, planter, for Ł 200 stg., 305 acres on both sides of South fork of the Saluda River, bd. by Joseph Strabel.
Wit: Bennett Combs, Isaac Miller, John Pendergrass. Benne<u>t</u> Combs made oath 30 Mar. 1781.
Rec: 31 May 1791.

Pages 283-286 21 Oct. 1790. James Simpson, labourer, to Henry Myers, millwright, for Ł 30, 250 acres in 96 Dist. on Big Beaver Dam Creek, surveyed for Robert Blake, 5 Jan. 1785, granted James Simpson "by law", 5 Dec. 1786. Recorded Bk. 0000, p. 417.
Wit: Alexander Ramsay, John Woods. John Woods made oath 24 Nov. 1790.
Rec: 2 Jun. 1791.

Pages 287-288 5 Dec. 1788. David Hopkins, of Chester Co., S. C.to John Henry for Ł 200, 640 acres granted to William Siseland(?), 15 Oct. 1784, conveyed by him to Hopkins land in 96 Dist. on Great Rocky Creek, branch of the Savannah River.
Wit: Jas. Houston, John Young. John Young made oath 9 Apr. 1791.
Rec: 2 Jun. 1791.

Pages 288-290 24 Feb. 1791. Benjamin Alderidge, of Abbeville Co. to John Grisham, of Pendleton Co., for Ł 20 stg., 82½ acres on Little River of Savannah River, part of a tract granted to Ald<u>ridge</u> on 5 Dec. 1785,; Recorded Bk. GGGG, p. 171.
Signed: Benjamin Aldri<u>dge</u>, Rebecca Aldridge.
Wit: John Nast, John Grisham, Sr. (no oath)

Pages 290-292 20 Apr. 1791. Richard Sadler, of Abbeville Co. to Matthew Alexander, for Ł 300 sterling, 180 acres, part of a tract granted to Sadler, 6 Feb. 1786. Recorded Bk. GGGG, p. 405, in 96 Dist. on South Side of Saluda River, on North side of Broadmouth Creek.
Wit: Caleb Conaway, James Mattison. Caleb Conaway made oath 9 May 1791.
Rec: 6 Jun. 1791.

Pages 292-294 17 Jul. 1790. John Dickeson and Ellenor, his mother, to Robert Dickeson for Ł 30 sterling, 100 acres in 96 Dist. on 26 Mile Creek, waters of Savannah River, granted to Michael Dickeson, the husband of Ellenor Dickeson, 5 Jun.1786, bd. by creek and Edward Camp. Signed: John Dickeson, Ellenor Dickeson, Lyddia Dickeson.
Wit: Thomas Case, Moses Jones. Thomas Case made oath 4 Feb. 1791.
Rec: 6 Jun. 1791.

Pages 295-297 30 Apr. 1791. William and Anne Lesley of Abbeville Co., S. C., to John Warnak of Pendleton Co. for Ł 60 for 200 acres on waters of Great Rocky Creek, granted by deed 15 Oct. 1784 "to John War<u>nock</u> from William and Anne Lesley".
Wit: John Miller, Robert Pickens, Ro<u>ber</u>t Dowdle. Robert Dowdle made oath 10 May 1791.

Pages 297-298 10 Feb. 1791. William Millwee, of Laurens Co., S.C. to Lewis Sherrill of Pendleton Co., for Ł 50, 300 acres on Big Beaver Dam Creek, branch of Rocky River, granted Millwee on 15 Oct. 1784.
Recorded Bk. LLL, p. 352.
Wit: Jas. Houston, Samuel Houston. Samuel Houston made oath 12 Feb. 1791. Rec: 8 Jun. 1791.

Pages 299-300 5 Mar. 1790. John Lindley to Enoch Garner, for Ł45 150 acres on North side of Big Creek of Saluda River, being part of 465 acres granted to Elijah Owens on 4 Sep. 1786, conveyed by Owens to Thomas Handley, then by deed to Lindley

16

(pages 299-300 cont'd):
for 150 acres. Wit: Henry Cobb, John Gwin. John Gwin made oath 10 Feb. 1791. Rec: 9 Jun. 1791.

Pages 301-302   1 Oct. 1790. James McAdoo, yeoman, of Cambridge Dist., S. C., to John McCullough, of same, for Ł 30 sterling, 300 acres in Pendleton Co., on waters of Wilson's Creek. Wit: Adam T. (J.?) Files, Richard Cochran. Adam Files made oath 18 Oct. 1790.
Rec: 9 Jun. 1791

Pages 302-304   18 Nov. 1790. William Marchbanks of Pendleton Co., to Baylis Earle, Esq., of Spartanburg Co., S. C. for Ł 50 sterling, 170 acres in 96 Dist. on Young's Crk. of Twelve Mile River, granted to Marchbanks, 1 Jan. 1787, bd. by Young's line. Wit: Bailey Anderson, Abraham Towrey(?). Bailey Anderson made oath 9 May 1791.

Page 305   Sarah Lindley made oath that her husband, John Lindley, was lying on his death bed, (he said) there was one thing he forgot. She asked what it was. He said a colt that was called John (?), he would give to his son, John. He should have the colt above his equal part with the rest of the children. Sworn to 31 Dec. 1790, by Sarah Lindley.
Rec: 9 Jun. 1791.

Pages 305-306   Robert Goodwin, farmer, for love and good will to loving son, Mecager Goodwin...all my goods and chattels now being in my present dwelling house or in my custody. Date: 1 Mar. 1791.
Wit: Nathaniel Ballard, John Langley. John Langley made oath 9 May 1791.
Rec: 9 Jun. 1791.

Pages 306-308   8 Mar. 1791. William Hamilton of York Co., S. C. to Jonas Little, of Pendleton Co., for Ł 16 stg., 100 acres on North Fork of Big Creek, waters of Saluda River, granted Hamilton 14 Jan. 1790.
Wit: Wm. Hamilton, Sterdy Garner. Sterdy Garner made oath 3 May 1791.
Rec: 21 Jun. 1791.

Pages 308-313   21 Mar. 1791. Duncan Camron and Mary, his wife, planter, to James Abbet, planter, for Ł 60, 200 acres in 96 Dist. on Mile Creek, waters of Keowee River, part of 673 acres granted Camron, 1 Oct. 1787, bd. by William Patterson.
Wit: William Patterson, James Hendrex. William Patterson made oath on 9 May 1791.
Rec: 21 Jun. 1791.

Pages 313-317   16 Nov. 1790. William Hallum, planter, to John Patterson, Jr., planter, for Ł 65.10. stg., 200 acres in 96 Dist. on both sides of Golden's Creek of the Twelve Mile River, granted 5 Jun. 1785, except 25 acres contained within lines of a tract granted to Richard Golden, 1784.
Wit: Joseph Chapman, John Patterson, Sr. Joseph Chapman made oath 20 Nov. 1790. Rec: 22 Jun. 1791.

Pages 317-322   20 Apr. 1791. Tilly Merrick, Gentleman, to Francis Millar, planter, for Ł 80 stg., 540 acres part of tract of 640 acres in 96 Dist. on Devil's Fork of Great Generostee Creek, granted Callagan McCarty, 15 Jul. 1784, bd. by Daniel Stringer.
Wit: Daniel Stringer, Thos. Lofton. Danl. Stringer made oath 9 May 1791. Rec: 9 Aug. 1791.

Pages 322-327   9 May 1791. Lewis Daniel Martin, planter, to Alexander Drumgoole, for Ł 200, 2 tracts of 720 acres on Martin's Creek, of Keowee River, one tract of 200 acres granted John Swords, 21 Jan. 1785; Recorded Bk. BBBB, p. 183, conveyed from Swords to Martin 17 Aug. 1785, Pendleton Co., Bk. A, p. 190, the other tract, of 520 acres on waters of Martin's Creek, adj. above

(pages 322-327 cont'd):
tract, granted Martin, 7 Jan. 1790; Recorded Bk. B., No. 5, p. 413. Signed: Louis D. Martin and Sarah, his wife. Wit: Robert Powell, Bartholeme Wollens, Absolum Wollens. Robert Powell made oath 9 May 1791.
Rec: 9 Aug. 1791.

Pages 327-329   96 Dist., 4 Feb. 1791. James Crowther of Abbeville Co., to Moses Jones of Pendleton Co., for Ł 30, 200 acres on Eighteen Mile Creek, waters of Savannah River, bd. by John Miller, Charles Lay, grant bearing date, 2 Jul. 1787.
Wit: Jno. Lovelady, Robt. Hall. John Lovelady made oath 9 May 1791.
Rec: 30 Aug. 1791.

Pages 330-331   30 Jul. 1790. William Rope (Ross?), of 96 Dist. to William Galespy, Sr., planter of same, for Ł 20.8. 354 acres on South side of Saluda River, waters of George's Creek called Pole Bridge Forks, bd. by Galespy, Moses, Thomas Galespy, John Boid, Seneca Road and Henderson.
Wit: Robert Bowen, John Gillespy. Capt. Robert Bowen made oath 23 Jul. 1791. Rec: 30 Aug. 1791.

Pages 332-335   24 Apr. 1791. Francis Miller to Moses Liddle for Ł 20 stg., 127 acres on Devil's Fork of Great Generostee, of Savannah River, part of 640 acres granted to Callgan McCarty on 16 Jul. 1784.
Wit: Joseph Jenkins, Gashem(?) Fulton. Joseph Jenkins made oath 10 May 1791. Rec: 31 Aug. 1791.

Pages 335-339   25 Apr. 1791. Francis Miller to Moses Liddle for Ł 80 stg., 326 acres on Devil's Fork of Big Generostee on East side of Savannah River, part of tract granted Callgan McCarty, 16 Jul. 1784, bd. by Wm. Seawright, Daniel Stringer, Thomas Morrow, William Bennet.
Wit: Joseph Jenkins, Gasham Fulton. Gasham Fulton made oath 11 May 1791.
Rec: 31 Aug. 1791.

Pages 339-343   Nicholas Darnell, planter, to Benjamin Perry, planter for Ł 50 stg., 160 acres on East side of Choestoa Creek, waters of Tugaloo River, part of tract of 640 acres granted to Robert McCampbell, 21 Jan. 1785, bd. by Robert MsCampbell's survey.
Wit: James Darnell, Nathl. Perry, William Elson Davis. William Elson Davis made oath 19 May 1791.
Rec: 10 Sep. 1791.

Pages 343-346   1 Aug. 1787. David McAdoo, of Gillford Co., N. C. to Samuel Jackson of Greenville Co., S. C. for Ł 45 stg., 320 acres in 96 Dist. on branch of Twelve Mile River granted to McAdoo, 4 Sep. 1786.
Wit: Ninian B. Hamilton, Horatio Hamilton. Ninian Bell Hamilton made oath 17 Mar. 1790, Isaac Titsworth signed as witness to receipt of money.
Rec: 14 Sep. 1791.

Pages 346-350   21 Mar. 1791. Duncan Camron and Mary, his wife.... planter, to William Patterson, planter, for Ł 30 stg. for 100 acres in 96 Dist., on Mile Creek, waters of East side of Keowee River, bd. by James Abbet, William Floyd, James Hendrex, Duncan Camron, part of 673 acres granted Camron, 1 Oct. 1787.
Wit: James Hendrex, James Abbet. James Abbet made oath 9 May 1791.
Rec: 16 Sep. 1791.

Pages 351-352   Alice Lowe, for divers causes and valuable considerations, give to my children, William Roberts, Richard Roberts, James Roberts, John Roberts, Thomas Roberts and Alice Roberts, all goods and chattels, household stuff, lands and negros. Date: 9 Sep. 1791. Wit: Elizabeth Miller, Jno. Miller. John Miller made oath 19 Sep. 1791.
Rec: 26 Oct. 1791.

Pages 352-354   4 Aug. 1791. Francis Welchel of Union Co., S. C. to
                   John Davis, of Pendleton Co. for Ł 60 stg. for 200
                   acres in 96 Dist. on both sides of Shoal Creek, a
branch of Saluda River originally granted to Dominic Hollan (Soldier),
recorded Union Co. courthouse Bk. A, no. 1, p. 500, 24 Sep. 1787.......
deed of conveyence -31 Sep. 1785 Francis Hollan and his son, John Hollan
to Francis Welchell.
Wit: Davis Welchel, J. Whitner. Joseph Whitner made oath 19 Sep. 1791.
Rec: 3 Nov. 1791.

Pages 354-355   4 Mar. 1791. William Stevenson to Moses Hopper, of
                   Abbeville Co., planter, for Ł 25 sterling, 140 acres
                   on branch of Big Generostee called Lucas Fork in 96
Dist., bd. by land surveyor Martin sold to Wm. Shelton, John Green, John
and Robert Shelton, above Ancient Boundary Line granted to William Hen-
derson, 7 Feb. 1791. Recorded Bk. C, p. 5.
Wit: John Barnett, Robert Schelton.
Rec: 3 Nov. 1791.

Pages 355-357   1 Oct. 1791. John Miller to Moses Barnes, for Ł 40
                   sterling, 177 acres in Washington Dist. on branch of
                   Conneross Creek, of Keowee River, granted John Twit-
ty, 2 July. 1787. Recorded Bk. VVVV, p. 63.
Wit: Saml. H. Dickson, Crosby W. Miller. Crosby Wilkes Miller made
oath 11 Oct. 1791.
Rec: 16 Nov. 1791.

Pages 357-362   24 May 1791. James Maxwell, late of Mecklenburg Co.,
                   N. C., planter, to John Lewis Davis, of Pendleton
                   Co., cartenter, for Ł 71, 275 acres on Choastoa Crk.
branch of Toogaloo River, granted Maxwell, 3 Nov. 1788. Recorded Bk.
XXXX, p. 544.
Wit: Wm. McCaleb, Jean Anderson. Jean Anderson made oath 26 May 1791.
Rec: 28 Oct. 1791.

Pages 362-366   2 Oct. 1790. Robert MisCampbell of Orangeburgh Dist.
                   S. C., planter, to Lewis Shelton of 96 Dist., for
                   Ł 80, 200 acres on Tugaloo River, bd. by Aaron Smith,
and the River.
Wit: Mordechai Fuller, Ann Box. Mordecai Fuller made oath 15 Jan. 1791.
Rec: 29 Oct. 1791.

Pages 366-367   30 Aug. 1791. James Gillison and Jane, his wife, to
                   Jonathan Montgomery, for Ł 30 stg., 52 acres on the
                   waters of Twenty-Six Mile Creek, bd. by John Pearcy,
James Gillison, Peter Jones.
Wit: James Linn, James Linn, Jr. James Linn made oath 20 Sep. 1791.
Rec: 30 Nov. 1791.

Pages 367-369   24 Jun. 1791. James Gillison to Burgess Reeves, for
                   Ł 54 str'g, 200 acres on North side of Great Rocky
                   Creek of Savannah River, granted Gillison, 17 Oct.
1785. Recorded Bk. QQQQ, p. 114.
Wit: Blake Mauldin, John Harris, Stephen Willet. Blake Mauldin made
oath (no date or rec. date).

Pages 369-371   30 May 1791. Thomas Elliot to Thomas Adams for Ł120
                   sterling, 200 acres in 96 Dist. on Little Beaver Dam
                   Creek, part of a tract granted to John Hunnicutt on
6 Nov. 1785, bd. by James Eason, George Slaton.
Wit: Absolum Bryan, Hardy Bryan, John Beavert. Absolum Brient made
oath 29 Nov. 1791. Rec: 29 Nov. 1791.

Pages 371-372   Israel Pickens, of 96 Dist., give to my children,
                   goods and chattels as follows: daughters Ellinder,
                   Mary, Elizabeth Sturd and Matilday, all household
furnishings to be equally divided...son, John and son, William to have
negros...and son, Israel Pickens, Jr.   Date: __ Jun. 1791.
Wit: Saml. Browne, John Burchfield. Samuel Brown made oath 8 Oct.1791.

19

Pages 372-375   22 May 1789. Moses Shelby, of Green Co., Ga. to
                     Charles Clements of Pendleton Co., for Ł 100 sterling, 133 acres on Broadway Creek, waters of Rocky
River, surveyed for John Woodsides, 13 Jul. 1784, granted to Francis
Miller containing 250 acres. Recorded Bk. HHHH, p. 199.
Wit: Jesse Clements, Wm. Washington, Isai Jones, Culiver Clements.
William Washington made oath 21 Sep. 1791.
Rec: 6 Dec. 1791.

Pages 375-378   2 May 1789. Moses Shelby of Greene Co., Ga. to William Washington of Pendleton Co., for Ł 42, 117 acres
                     on waters of Rocky River, part of a tract surveyed
for John Woodsides, 13 Jul. 1784, granted Francis Miller, containing 250
acres. Recorded Bk. HHHH, p. 199.
Wit: Charles Clements, Jesse Clements, Culiver Clements (her mark).
Charles Clements made oath 24 Sep. 1791.
Rec: 6 Dec. 1791.

Pages 378-379   19 Sep. 1791. James Gillison to John Hutson, for
                     Ł 10 sterling, 100 acres granted Gillison, 15 Oct.
                     1794 on both sides of Six Mile Creek.
Wit: Charles Clements, Robert Anderson. Robert Anderson made oath 20
Sep. 1791. Rec: 7 Dec. 1791.

Pages 379-381   9 Jul. 1791. James Sterritt to William Hall, for
                     Ł 50, 91 acres in Washington Dist. on Fork of Broadmouth Creek, waters of Saluda River, granted William
Brown, 21 Jan. 1785, bd. by Joshua Broyles, William Brown.
Wit: Jer. Burdine, Henry Dobson. Henry Dobson made oath 18 Jul. 1791.
Rec: 8 Dec. 1791.

Pages 381-383   Abbeyville Co., 21 May 1789. Alexander Boyse and
                     Jenat, his wife, planter of Abbeville Co. to William
                     Murray of same, for Ł 160, 320 acres on Pea Creek,
branch of Rocky River.
Wit: John Willson, James Agnew. (no oath)

Pages 383-386   12 Oct. 1790. David Brag, of N. C., planter, to
                     Samuel Neel, planter, of S. C., for Ł 100, 200 acres
                     on Eighteen Mile Creek, bd. by Isaac Titsworth, Col.
Gervais. Signed: David Bragg, by his attorney, Wm. McCaleb.
Wit: Robert Anderson, Wm. Neel McCaleb. Both made oath 15 Feb. 1791.
Rec: 12 Dec. 1791.

Pages 386-387   Seneka, 8 Nov. 1791. Banister Harper and William
                     Harper, appoint John Harper of Halifax Co., Va. our
                     Attorney to act in regard to a tract of land in Halifax Co. to sell, rent or dispose of as he may see fit, etc.....
Wit: Alex.r. Droomgoole, Robt. Looney. Alexander Drumgoole made oath
8 Nov. 1791. Rec: 20 Dec. 1791.

Pages 387-390   12 Aug. 1790. Adam Crain Jones, Jr., of Abbeville
                     Co. to John Robertson of Pendleton Co., for 52.3.9
                     sterling, 200 acres on Twenty-Three Mile Creek, waters of Savannah River, granted Adam Crain Jones, Jr., 15 Oct. 1784.
Recorded Bk. ZZZ, p. 220.
Wit: James Anderson, Thomas Robinson, William Riggs. Thomas Robinson
made oath 6 Nov. 1790.
Rec: 21 Dec. 1791.

Pages 390-394   20 Aug. 1790. Eason Jay and his wife, Abigaile Jay
                     to John Hays, for Ł 30, 100 acres on both sides of
                     Bear Creek, waters of Rocky River, granted to Abigaile Davis, the present wife of Eason Jay, on 5 Nov. 1786. Recorded
Bk. QQQQ, p. 71.
Wit: Daniel Stringer, William Keeton, Thompson Anderson.
Signed: Aeson Jay. William Keaton made oath 21 Jun. 1791.
Rec: 29 Dec. 1791.

Pages 394-398   12 Feb. 1790. Robert Rankin and Leah, his wife, planter, of Pendleton Co., to Andrew Tate (also spelled Teat), of Wilkes Co., N. C., planter, for £ 30 sterling, 154 acres in Pendleton Co. on a branch which is dividing line between said Rankin and said Tate, granted William Herston (also spelled Hairston), 5 Jun. 1786.
Wit: Jesse Wood, John Rankin. Jesse Wood made oath 10 May 1791.
Rec: 31 Dec. 1791.

Pages 398-400   19 Aug. 1791. Alexander Erwin, planter, and Susannah, his wife, spinster, to Robert Tucker, planter, for £ 50, 138 acres on Mulberry Creek, branch of Great Rocky Creek.
Wit: Harbert Tucker, Bartley Tucker, John McMahan. Plat included.... land bd. by Phillip Phagin. Harbert Tucker made oath 20 Aug. 1791.
Rec: 3 Jan. 1792.

Pages 400-402   4 May 1791. Abill Meed to Francis Whelchel for £ 30 sterling, 240 acres granted 4 Jan. 1790, on both sides of Carpenter's Creek, branch of Saluda River.
Signed: Abull Meed. Wit: John Beard, William Whelchel, William Wheller. John Beard made oath 19 Sep. 1791. (name spelled Abrial Mead in oath).
Rec: 4 Jan. 1792.

Pages 402-405   13? Sep. 1791. Robert Waddell of Abbeville Co., to John Clark Kilpatrick of Pendleton Co., for £ 70 for 300 acres on both sides of Snow Creek of Conneross Creek, waters of Keowee River, bd. John Lawrence, George Weems, granted Waddell (no date). Recorded Bk. WWWW, p. 162.
Wit: William Thompson, Andrew Pickens. William Thompson made oath 15 Sep. 1791.
Rec: 11 Jan. 1791.

Pages 405-407   5 May 1791. Thomas Lewis, of Greenville Co., S. C. to Thomas Commander Russell and John Lewis, one of the State of Georgia, and the other of the State of Virginia, for £ 50 sterling, 1300 acres in Pendleton Co. on east side of Brush Creek, granted Thomas Lewis (dates smeared). Recorded Bk. ___, p. ___. Wit: Joseph Mahan, Gesham Kelly, Vincent Davis. Vincent Davis made oath in Greenville Co., S. C. before John Alexander, J. P., 2 Sep. 1791. Rec: 12 Jan. 1792.

Pages 407-410   17 Dec. 1787. Francis Miller to Moses Shelby, for £ 70 sterling, 250 acres in 96 Dist. on Broadway Creek, waters of Savannah River, granted Miller, 21 Jan. 1785. Signed: Francis Miller and Jean Miller.
Wit: James Gillison, L. W. Crawford. James Gillison made oath 20 Sep. 1791. Rec: 17 Jan. 1792.

Pages 410-411   21 May. 1791. Thomas and Mary Burford, his wife, to David Wade, for £ 10 sterling, 335 acres, part of a tract of 600 acres on branch of Broadway, above the Ancient Boundary Line "as will appear by the original granted to David Wade from Thomas and Mary Burford, 14 Dec. 1786."
Wit: Thomas Clement Wade, Shirod Nowland. Thomas Clement Wade made oath 5 Nov. 1791.
Rec: 17 Jan. 1792.

Pages 412-414   9 Jul. 1791. Benjamin Starritt to William Hall for £ 100, 153 acres in Washington Dist., on North Fork of Broadmouth Creek, waters of Saluda River, part of tract granted to William Brown, 5 Jun. 1786, containing 306 acres.
Wit: Henry Dobson, Jas. Brown, Joel Halbert. Henry Dobson made oath 18 Jul. 1791. Rec: 18 Jan. 1792.

Page 414   By his Excellency, Charles Pinckney, Governor and Commander in Chief of South Carolina, to Samuel Lofton, Esquire, by power invested in me, commission Samuel Lofton to be Sheriff of Pendleton Co. Signed in Columbia, 30 Apr. 1790. Peter Freneau, Secretary.

Pages 414-416   20 Jul. 1791. William Read of 96 Dist. to Noblet
                     Johnson, of same, for Ł 100, 303 acres part of 606
                     acres by grant 1 May 1786, on South branch of George's Creek, waters of Saluda River. Recorded in Secretary's Office (no date). Wit: John Johnson, William McKamey, John Armstrong. John Johnson made oath 10 Feb. 1792.
Rec: 13 Feb. 1792.

Pages 416-419   I, William Brooks, taking into consideration that I
                     have a growing family and that I am subject to excess use of spiritous liquors whereby I am liable to be departed of my property by designing men, by which I may be unable to find support for my wife and children...therefore this indenture, between William Brooks, farmer, and Sarah and Margaret Brooks, both daughters of William Brooks, tract of land which I now live, on Tugaloo River, 200 acres...Date: 6 Feb. 1792.
Wit: Wm. McCaleb, Henry Barton. William McCaleb made oath 11 Feb. 1792.
Rec: 13 Feb. 1792.

Pages 419-423   30 Mar. 1792. John Miller, Clerk of Pendleton Co.
                     to William Richardson of the City of London, in England, bookseller, for Ł 300 sterling, 1000 acres on Robert Anderson's Creek, branch of Keowee River, bd. by John Miller, granted Miller, 2 Jul. 1787. Recorded Bk. UUUU, p. 131.
Wit: Crosby Ws. Miller, Mary Ann Miller. Crosby Wilkes Miller made oath 31 Mar. 1792.
Rec: 31 Mar. 1792.

Pages 423-424   John Harris, William McCaleb and William Steele of
                     Pendleton Co. are firmly bound to Andrew Pickens,
                     Robert Anderson and Benjamin Cleveland, Esq.'s.,
Judges of County Court of Pendleton, fow Ł 1500 sterling, we bind ourselves, 28 Jan. 1792...the above John Harris, this day has been duly elected Sheriff of said County to succeed Samuel Lofton, present Sheriff. ...if said John Harris do well and truly discharge the duties of said office, above obligation is null and void.
Rec: 17 Apr. 1792.

Page 424   Pendleton Co. John Ward against Samuel Lofton, Sr.,
                     said Ward made complaint against Lofton of not having delivered three hands of tobacco given to Lofton by Ward's mother (not named). We, appointed arbitrators, do award and declare the charge to be frivolous and that as the accusation was made publicly the reparation should also be that said Ward do publicly acknowledge that he is sorry he made such a complaint against his neighbor, Mr. Lofton. Signed: Andw. Pickens, Saml. Taylor, John Hallum, John Miller. (no date)

Page 424   John Ward of Pendleton Co. having brought a malicious and unjust charge against James Lofton, the
                     youngest son of Samuel Lofton, Esq., Sheriff of the county, a charge of such abhorrent nature as should not even be mentioned amoung men, do confess myself to have been decieved and am most heartily sorry for my conduct, and do promise for the future to conduct myself agreeable to good neighborhood and a good member of Society. And I do hereby acknowledge the forbearance, tenderness and lenity of Mr. Lofton in pardoning my offence. (no date). Signed: John Ward before J. Miller.

Pages 425-427   7 Dec. 1788. James Moore to John Calhoun Anderson,
                     of Abbeville Co. for Ł 50 sterling, 100 acres in Abbeville Co., above Ancient Boundary Line on waters of Great Rocky Creek, bd. by Andrew Ross, granted to James Moore, 15 Oct. 1784. Recorded Bk. ZZZ, p. 244.
Wit: Alexr. Boyse, Charles Willson. Alexander Boyse made oath in Pendleton Co., 12 Dec. 1789. Rec: 14 Jun. 1792.

Pages 427-429   22 Mar. 1791. Benjamin Cornelis, planter, of Pendleton Co. to Bartholomew Weems, planter, of Abbeville
                     Co. for Ł 100 sterling, 407 acres in 96 Dist. on

(pages 427-429 cont'd):
Twenty-Six Mile Creek, waters of Savannah River, a grant to Harry Pearson, 4 Dec. 1786. Wit: George Forbes, Thos. Abbett, George Forbis made oath 30 Mar. 1791. Rec: 15 Jan. 1792.

Page 430   William Robinson reported that Samuel and Joseph Henderson did some years ago (or one of them) did get a child by a Negro woman and on the Wenches telling the same, they said Samuel and Joseph Henderson did beat said Negro woman to death. I do hereby certify that said report is false and groundless, and that I never knew or believe said Samuel and Joseph Henderson to have been guilty of any such thing.
Date: 16 May 1792. Wit: Samuel Torbert, James Loggens. Oath made by Samuel Torbert and James Loggens, 7 May 1792.
Rec: 25 Jun. 1792.

Page 430   Robert Means came personally and made oath that he saw James Cunningham bite a small piece out of the ear of Samuel Henderson of this County. Date: 25 Jun. 1792. Rec: 25 Jun. 1792.

Pages 430-431   Pendleton Co. Thomas Darnell and Nancy Darnell, appeared at the Courthouse, to disclaim any right, title, possession or any other manner of Plea against a certain tract of land, late the property of Solomon King, Jr., containing 114 acres, bd. by South side of Seneca, Solomon King, Sr., John Harris, Thomas Gorman. Date: 14 Jan. 1792.
Wit: Thomas Gorman, Solomon King.
Thomas Gorman made oath 24 Jan. 1792.

#

CONVEYANCE BOOK B
Pendleton Co., S. C.
1701-1795

Page 1   18 Jan. 1791. William Dunlap of Laurens Co., S. C., to Hugh Rogers of Greenville Co., S. C. for Ł 50, 200 acres on North side of 23 Mile Creek, waters of the Savannah River, granted William Dunlap by William Moultrie, Esq., 6 Feb. 1786. Recorded Bk. HHHH, p. 28.
Wit: Lewis Jones, Sarah (R) Riggs. Oath made by Lewis Jones, 26 Jun. 1792 to John Wilson, J. P.
Rec: 26 Nov. 179_.

Pages 2-3   26 Mar. 1791. David Smith, miller, to Thomas Robertson, planter, for Ł 30, 128 acres on 23 Mile Creek, waters of Savannah River in 96 Dist., Pendleton Co., part of 640 acres granted to David Smith, by Thomas Pinckney, Esq., 2 Jun. 1788.
Wit: James Rosemond, Charles Wilson. Plat shows land bounds Thomas Hamilton, David Smith, Surveyor, Robert McCann. Oath made by James Rosemond, 26 Mar. 1791 to John Wilson, J. P.
Rec: 25 Aug. 1791.

Pages 3-5   31 Dec. 1791. Thomas Farrar, Sheriff of Pendleton Co. to Edmund Hollimon (also spelled Hollyman), 640 acres on 26 Mile Creek, bd. on all sides by vacant lands, Hollimon being highest bidder at auction for lands owned by Francis Breen and Luke Breen, debtors to Henry Kennon and Abraham Motte, otherwise Kennon and Motte, plaintiffs in Court of Common Pleas, in 1791, for Ł 35. Plat included. Warrant by Robert Anderson, Esq. laid out to John Hall, Snr., 640 acres on 26 Mile Creek, 15 Jun. 1794. Surveyed by D. Hopkins, D. S. Recorded Bk. A, p. 35. J. N. Brown, Q.V.C certified Thos. Farrar gave title to E. Hollimon.
Rec: 4 Nov. 1792.

Page 5   4 May 1792. Edmund Hollimon, of Edgefield Dist., S. C. to Thomas Farrar, Esq., of Pendleton Co. for Ł 6, for 640 acres on 26 Mile Creek, granted to John Hall, 16 Jun. 1784, by Benjamin Guerrard, Esq.
Wit: (blank) Rec: 4 Nov. 1791.

Pages 6-7   12 Jan. 1792. Benjamin Starritt to William Hall, for Ł 50, 214 acres on Broadmouth Creek, of Saluda River, in Washington Dist., Pendleton Co., granted to William Brown by William Moultrie, Esq., conveyed to Starrett, 5 Jun. 1786, granted 306 acres, held out 214 acres.
Wit: Edward Morgan, Robert Brown, William Hall. Robert Brown made oath 13 Jun. 1792 to William Halbert, J. P.
Rec: 8 Aug. 1792.

Pages 7-8   2 Jan. 1792. Walker Walton, of Franklin Co., Ga. to James Doran of Washington Co., Va. for Ł 90 stg. for 640 acres on Chaughe Creek in Pendleton Co. granted to Jesse Walton, 22 Feb. 1786, by Edward Telfair, Gov. of Georgia. Recorded Bk. III, p. 491, 1 Mar. 1786, again in S. C. Sec. Office in Book marked Georgia Grants, pp. 37-38, 7 Dec. 1787.
Wit: Nathan Perry, Benjamin Perry, Jonathan Dryden. Jonathan Dryden made oath 3 Jan. 1792 to Nath'l. Perry, J. P.
Rec: 11 Jul. 1792.

Pages 8-9   10 Apr. 1792. Samuel Lofton, Esq., Sheriff of Pendleton Co. to William Bennison...whereas Sarah McCollum, Administratrix of George Bennison was seized of 300 acres on E. side of Keowee River at mouth of Deep Creek, 16 Jul. 1784...Thomas Jordan on 20 Dec. 1791 commenced action of debt in County Court at Pendleton against Sarah McCollum, received judgement for 25.13.6Ł, 25 Jan. 1792...land sold to highest bidder at auction, William Bennison, for Ł 40.
Wit: Wm. Lofton, Sam'l Lofton, Jr. Oath recorded on p. 13.
Rec: 16 Aug. 1792.

25

Pages 9-10   24 Oct. 1786. Francis Guthry of Abbeville Co., S.C. planter, to Jehu Pope, of same, planter, for £ 20 for 250 acres in Abbeville Co. on 26 Mile Creek of Savannah River. Signed: Francis Guthry, Sarah (X) Guthry.
Wit: John Norwood, William Cunningham. Oath made by Capt. John Norwood on 25 Jun. 1792 to John Wilson, J.P.
Rec: 8 Aug. 1792.

Pages 10-12   30 Dec. 1792. Francis Miller, farmer, and Jane, his wife, to Richard Walters, Jr. and Thomas Walters, minors, for £ 20, 300 acres on Conneross Creek, a branch of Goodland Creek, bd. by Richard Brooke Roberts, Benjamin Howard on NW, granted Miller by William Moultrie, Esq., 6 Mar. 1786. Recorded Bk. TTTT, p. 38. Signed: Francis Miller, Jane (X) Miller.
Wit: Wm. McCaleb, Robert Anderson. Robert Anderson made oath 24 Jan. 1792 to John Wilson, J.P.
Rec: 1 Mar. 1792.

Page 12   5 Jan. 1792. John Lewis Davis to Eli Davis for £ 40 sterling, 96½ acres on North side of Choestoa Creek, waters of Toogaloo River, adj. NW by John Lewis Davis, 70 acres granted to John Lewis Davis, 5 Dec. 1791, the other 26½ ac. part of tract granted to James Maxwell, 3 Nov. 1788.
Wit: William Hamilton, shoemaker, William Hamilton, Jane Anderson. William Hamilton, shoemaker, made oath to John Wilson, J.P. 12 May 1792.
Rec: 14 May 1792.

Page 13   6 Oct. 1792. Alexander Erwin, planter, and Susannah, his wife, spinster, to John Hall for £ 100, 129 ac. on SW side of Great Rocky Creek. Signed: Alexander Erwin, Susannah (+) Erwin. Wit: George Tucker, Fenton Hall, James Erwin. Plat included, land adj. to Hart(?) Tucker, Robt. Hall, Fergus Cavin, Jas. Thorn(?). George Tucker made oath to Elijah Brown, J.P. 7 Jan. 1791. Rec: 25 Jan. 1792.

Page 13   21 July. 1792. William Lofton made oath to deed of Samuel Lofton, Sheriff of Pendleton Co. (p. 8-9),to John Miller, J. P.

Pages 14-15   13 Nov. 1791. Field Farrar of Camden Dist., S. C., planter, to Humphrey Gibson of 96 Dist., planter,for £ 87, 200 acres on Toogaloo River, granted Norman Martin, 21 Jan. 1785.
Wit: D. R. Evans, Jno. Winn, Jr....Fairfield Co., S. C., John Winn, Esq. made oath to David Reed Evans, J. P., 21 Jan. 1792.
Rec: 25 Jun. 1792.

Pages 15-16   24 Jan. 1792. Stephen Fuller to Michael Whitmer for £ 70, 213 acres granted Fuller, 4 Sep. 1786, in 96 Dist., on South side of Saluda River.
Wit: David Brown, David Hamilton. David Brown made oath to John Wilson, J. P., 24 Jan. 1792.
Rec: 25 Jun. 1792.

Pages 16-18   13 Apr. 1787. Henry Chiles and Sarah, his wife, to William Jackson for £ 25 sterling, 150 acres in 96 Dist. on 5 Mile Creek, branch of 12 Mile Creek, on East side of Keowee River, granted Henry Chiles, 5 Jun. 1786, by William Moultrie, Esq., all sides vacant. Signed: Henry Chiles, Sarah (X)Chiles.
Wit: William Huggins, Thomas Johnson, Robert Huggins. Robert Huggins made oath to John Moore, J. P., 24 Apr. 1792.
Rec: 25 Jun. 1792.

Pages 18-21   13 Apr. 1787. Henry Chiles and Sarah, his wife, to William Jackson for £ 25, 119 acres in 96 Dist. on 5 Mile Spring Branch, waters of 12 Mile Creek, on E. side of Keowee River, bd. NE by Samuel Lofton and vacant land, granted Chiles, 5 Jun. 1786, by Wm. Moultrie, Esq. Signed: Henry Chiles, Sarah (X) Chiles. Wit: William Huggins, Thomas Johnson, Robert Huggins. Robt. Huggins made oath 24 Apr. 1792. Rec: 25 Jun. 1792.

Pages 21-23   9 Dec. 1791. William Jackson and Isabella, his wife, planter, to Anselm Roe, planter, for Ł 65, 150 acres in 96 Dist. on 12 Mile Creek, waters of East side of Keowee River, granted to Henry Chiles, 12 Jun. 1786, by Wm. Moultrie,Esq. Signed: William (O) Jackson, Isabella (d) Jackson.
Wit: John Land, Andrew Roe. Andrew Roe made oath to John Wilson, J.P. 21 Jan. 1792.
Rec: 25 Jan. 1792.

Pages 23-24   19 Oct. 1791. William Prichard of Edgefield Co., SC to James Brown, of Pendleton Co., for Ł 50, 320 ac. in Washington Dist. on 23 Mile Creek, waters of the Savannah River, granted Mary Prichard, 15 Oct. 1794, by Benjamin Guerrard, Esq. Wit: Henry Dobson, Thomas Crow, James Duff. Henry Dobson made oath to Wm. Halbert, J.P., 19 Oct. 1791.
Rec: 10 Sep. 1792.

Pages 24-25   15 Aug. 1792. James Brown to James Hobson for Ł 60 sterling, 300 acres in Washington Dist. on 23 Mile Creek, of Savannah River, granted Mary Prichard, 15 Oct. 1784. Wit: John Miller, Jr., Robert Glenn. John Miller, Jr. made oath to John Miller, J. P., 17 Aug. 1792.
Rec: 10 Sep. 1792.

Pages 25-26   22 Apr. 1791. Francis Miller, planter, to William Bennet, planter, for Ł 70, 180 acres, part of 640 acre tract in 96 Dist., on Devil's Fork, Great Generostee Creek, granted Callagan McCarty, 16 Jul. 1784, adj. William Seawright. Wit: William Seawright, John (X) McCollom. William Seawright made oath to Elijah Brown, 2 Jul. 1791.
Rec: 25 Jun. 1792.

Pages 26-28   31 Dec. 1791. John Smith and Elizabeth, his wife, planter, of 96 Dist. to Zachariah Davis of same for Ł 40, 200 acres on branches of Broadmouth, granted 2 Nov. 1788, by Thomas Pinckney, Esq. Signed: John Smith, Elizabeth (X) Smith. Wit: Henry Farmandis, Mathew Alexander. Mathew Alexander made oath to John Wilson, J.P., 25 Jan. 1792.
Rec: 25 Jun. 1792.

Pages 28-29   19 Jan. 1792. William Honey, planter, and Betty,his wife, to James Matterson, for Ł 100, 100 acres on Broadmouth Creek of Saluda River, part of 200 acres tract granted William Honey, 7 Apr. 1788 by Thomas Pinckney, Esq. Recorded Bk. WWWW, p. 422. Signed: William (H) Honey, Betty (X) Honey. Wit: Mathew Alexander, Francis Clinkscales. Mathew Alexander made an oath before John Wilson, J.P., 25 Jan. 1792.
Rec: 25 Jun. 1792.

Pages 29-30   20 Sep. 1791. William and Elizabeth Honey, planter, of 96 Dist. to James Matterson, planter, for Ł 100 for 80 acres on waters of Broadmouth Creek, part of 200 acre tract granted by Wm. Moultrie, Esq., 6 Feb. 1786. Signed: William (H) Honey, Betty (X) Honey. Wit: Mathew Alexander, William Throop, Francis Clinkscales. Mathew Alexander made oath, 25 Jan. 1792.
No rec. date.

Pages 31-32   2 Nov. 1791. Reverend Robert Smith, Edward Rutledge and John Bee Holmes, Esquires, Assignees in Trust for us of Creditors of Honorable Nicholas Eveliegh, Esq., to Rev. John Simpson for Ł 320, 640 acres above ancient boundary line on Savannah River, 96 Dist., called the Cove, surveyed for Eveliegh on 3 Jul. 1784, by John Purvis. Wit: Henry Rutledge, as to Edward Rutledge, Esq., Thos. Wigglesworth as to Rev. Robt. Smith, H. Bailey as to all three. Henry Bailey made oath to Jas. Nicholson, J. P., 7 Nov.1791.
Rec: 25 Jun. 1792.

Page 32   14 Sep. 1790. Minor Winn of Winnsborough Co., Fairfield Co., S. C., Esq., to Moses Terrell of Pendleton Co., planter, for Ł 50, 200 acres on waters of

(page 32 cont'd):
Toogaloo River, known by the name of Chauga, granted to James Robertson, 21 Jan. 1785, by Benjamin Guerrard, Esq. Recorded Bk. BBBB, p. 78, conveyed to Minor Winn, 11 Dec. 1785.
Wit: Benjn. Cleveland, John Cleveland. Benjamin Cleveland made oath to John Wilson, J. P., 28 Jun. 1792.
Rec: 25 Jun. 1792.

Page 33 2 Sep. 1789. Field Farrar, of Fairfield Co., S. C., Esq., to Aaron Terrell of Pendleton Co., 96 District, planter, for Ł 400, 300 acres in 96 Dist. on Tugaloo River, adj. NE by Henry Stevens, SE on Tugaloo River, vacant lands, granted Farrar, 15 Oct. 1784. Signed: Field Farrar, Elizabeth Farrar.
Wit: D. Evans, Wm. Goode. Receipt wit. by Samuel Taylor, Thomas Farrar. Capt. Field Farrar made oath to Andrew Pickens, J. P. that he signed the above deed, 1 Mar. 1790.
Rec: 25 Jun. 1792.

Pages 33-34 6 Aug. 1791. Aaron Bogs, planter, and Elizabeth, his wife, spinster, to William Young, blacksmith, for Ł 60 sterling, 150 acres on Washington Creek. Signed by Aaron Boggs and Elizabeth (+) Boggs. Wit: William Parsons, John Young, John Nicholson. John Young made oath to Elijah Browne (no date).
Rec: 25 Jun. 1792.

Pages 34-35 27 Oct. 1791. Eleanor Weitzel, executrix to John Weitzel, surgeon, deceased, to Sabra Perkins of Washington Dist., S. C., for Ł 45 stg. for 300 acres of land in 96 Dist. on North fork of Choestoa Creek, waters of Tugaloo River, granted to John Weitzel, surgeon in the Continental Troops of S. C., 16 Jul. 1784.
Wit: Will'm Sloan, John Shannon, John Sitton. John Shannon made oath to John Wilson, 30 Mar. 1792.
Rec: 25 Jun. 1792.

Pages 35-36 4 Jun. 1791. John Warnock and Eleanor, his wife, to Joseph Moss, for Ł 100 sterling, 200 acres on Great Rocky Creek, waters of Savannah River, granted to John Warnock on Bounty, 4 Dec. 1786, by William Moultrie, Esq. Recorded Bk. BBBB, p. 414. Plat included, adj. E. by Blake; NW by Mary Foils and vacant lands. Signed: John Warnock, Ellenor Warnock.
Wit: Andrew Pickens, David Caldwell, Robert Dowdle. Andrew Pickens made oath to Elijah Browne, J. P., 4 Jun. ___.
Rec: 25 Jun. 1792.

Pages 36-38 22 Jan. 1788. Henry Gocher, of Abbeville Co., S. C. 96 Dist., to John Hallum, of same, for Ł 150, 640 acres in 96 Dist. above ancient boundary line on 18 Mile Creek, waters of Savannah River, granted Henry Golcher(sic), 21 Jan. 1784, by Benjamin Guerrard. Signed: Henry (H) Golcher.
Wit: James Lomax, Chas. Wilson. James Lomax made oath to John Wilson, 28 Jun. 1790.
Rec: 25 Jun. 1792.

Pages 38-39 28 Jun. 1768. In the 8th year of His Majesty's reign, Arnold Russell of Long Cane Settlement, Greenville Co., Province of S. C., planter, sold to Samuel Taylor, farmer, of same county, for Ł 150, 150 acres in Greenville Co., on Savannah River, bd. on South where not navigable, all sides vacant, granted 13 Oct. 1759, by his Excellency, William Henry Lyttleyon, Esq., Capt. General and Gov. in Chief of Province of S. C., to Arnold Russell, in Long Cane Settlement. Signed: Arnold (A) Russell, Margaret (+) Russell. Wit: T. Walters, Charles (~) Williams...on 21 Jan. 1768, before Fredrick Winter, Esq. one of his Majesty's Justices for Greenville Co., Thomas Walters and Charles Williams, both of sd. county made oath to above deed. Rec: 25 Jun. 1792. (Pendleton Co.)

Pages 39-40 10 Nov. 1791. Anthony Golding, planter, to Clement Deale, planter, both of Laurens Co., S. C. for Ł200 sterling, for 640 acres in Pendleton Co. on waters

(pages 39-40 cont'd):
of 26 Mile Creek of Savannah River, bd. NE by Golding Tinsley, all other sides vacant, granted to Anthony Golding, 1 Jan. 1785, by Benjamin Guerrard.
Wit: Clement Wells, Alexr. Deale. Clement Wells made oath to John Miller, J. P., 25 Feb. 1792.
Rec: 25 Jun. 1792.

Pages 40-41   5 Oct. 1791. David Waters, of Abbeville Co. to Joseph Whitner of Pendleton Co. by deed dated 17 Jan. 1787. Witnessed by James Lomax, Andrew Porter and Adam Burney, for ₤ 60, 200 acres in 96 Dist. above ancient boundary line on 18 Mile Creek, branch of the Savannah River, granted to Charles Steele on the Bounty. Signed: David (O) Waters.
Wit: Charles Gates, Gedion Clark. Charles Gates made oath to Gabriel Moffett, J. P., 22 Aug. 1792.
Rec: 30 Aug. 1792.

Pages 41-42   24 Oct. 1791. William Love of Abbeville Co. to Charles Bond, of Pendleton Co. for 10 shillings, for 150 acres granted William Love, 21 Jan. 1785, by Benjamin Guerrard, Esq., part of 300 acre tract, the other 150 acres conveyed by William Love to Thomas Shockley, Sr., 16 Mar. 1789, this tract on NE side of the Savannah River, on Townhouse branch.
Wit: James Jones, Daniel Putnam. Daniel Putnam made oath to John Wilson on 8 Mar. 1792.
Rec: 27 Aug. 1792.

Page 42   24 Oct. 1791. William Love of Abbeville Co. to Daniel Putnam of Pendleton Co. for 10 shillings for 255 acres granted to Joseph Love, 7 Apr. 1788, by Thomas Pinckney, Esq., on waters of the Savannah River.
Wit: James Jones, Charles Bond. Charles Bond made oath to Elijah Brown, J. P., 12 May 1792.
Rec: 27 Aug. 1792.

Pages 42-43   25 Jun. 1792. James Long to James Watson for ₤ 100 for 400 acres on both sides of a small creek of the 26 Mile River, waters of the Savannah River, bd. on East by John Owens and Alexander Oliver, granted 15 Oct. 1784, by Benj. Guerrard, Esq.
Wit: George Forbes, James Agnew. James Egnew made oath to Elijah Brown, J. P., 26 Jun. 1792.
Rec: 28 Jun. 1792.

Pages 43-44   27 Aug. 1792. Joab Lawrence to Robert Anderson for ₤ 40, 275 acres on North branch of Cane Creek, called Duito Stamp Creek, granted Joab Lawrence, 2 Jul. 1787, by Thomas Pinckney, Esq.. Recorded Bk. VVVV, p. 130.
Wit: Robt. W. Speed, Wm. McCaleb. Wm. McCaleb made oath to John Miller, J. P., 30 Aug. 1792.
Rec: 31 Aug. 1792.

Pages 44-45   9 Sep. 1790. William Paul of Cheraw Dist., S. C. to John Barton of Pendleton Co. for 50 guineas for 200 acres in 96 Dist. on Chaugee Creek, granted William Paul, 21 Jan. 1785. Signed: Wm. (X) Paul.
Wit: Dd. Hopkins, Robt. Prince. David Hopkins made oath to Charles Simms, Esq., J. P. of Union Co., S. C., 27 Sept. 1791.
Rec: 25 Jun. 1792.

Pages 45-46   26 May 1788. Joseph Brown, Jr., and Jamina, his wife of Abbeville Co. to Joseph Brown, Sr. for ₤ 100 stg. for 170 acres in 96 Dist. on fork of Broadmouth Crk., waters of Saluda River, granted sd. Joseph Brown, 21 Jan. 1785, by Benj. Guerrard, Esq. Signed: Joseph Brown, Jamima Brown.
Wit: Aaron Broyles, Josiah Kennedy. Aaron Broyles made oath to William Halbert, J. P., 30 Aug. 1791.
Rec: 25 Jun. 1792.

Pages 46-47   5 Feb. 1791. John Young of Spartanburg Co., S. C.,
                 to Charles Lay of Pendleton Co. for Ł 50 sterling,
                 100 acres on South branch of Estantowey Creek, waters of Keowee River granted John Young, 4 Sep. 1786. Recorded Bk. MMMM, p. 513.
Wit: Bailey Anderson, Richd. Farrar. Richard Farrar made oath to John Wilson, J. P., 24 Jan. 1792.
Rec: 25 Jun. 1792.

Pages 47-48   2 Apr. 1790. James Cannon and Sarah, his wife, planter, to William Beazley for Ł 30 sterling, 145 acres
                 bd. by Robt. Rankin and Big Reedy Branch, part of a
tract Robert Rankin now lives on, granted to James Cannon, 6 Feb. 1786. Recorded Bk. FFFF, p. 428, conveyed from James Cannon to William Beazley, 6 Feb. 1786. Signed: James Cannon, Sarah (+) Cannon.
Wit: John Beazley, Robert Rankin. Robert Rankin made oath to Elijah Browne, 24 Jan. 1792.
Rec: 25 Jun. 1792.

Pages 48-49   96 Dist., Abbeville Co., ___ day of ___, 1788, Samuel Love, hatter, to Thomas Low, planter, both of
                 Abbeville Co. for Ł 45 stg., 222 acres in Abbeville
Co. on Sadler's Creek, branch of Savannah River, granted Love, 6 Nov. 1786. Recorded Bk. QQQQ, p. 1170.
Wit: John Newman, Gashem Fulton. Gashem Fulton made oath to Jno. Moffett, J. P., 19 Jun. 1789.
Rec: 25 Jun. 1792.

Page 50   Washington Dist., 27 Aug. ___. Thomas Lofton to
                 David Kelton, for Ł 40 stg., 102 acres, part of a
                 tract of 300 acres where Thomas Lofton now lives on
NE fork of 5 Mile Branch, waters of Seneca River, bd. by Thomas Lofton, Samuel Lofton, Sr., Morgan and Wm. Osbourn, granted to Thomas Lofton, 5 Jun. 1786, by Wm. Moultrie, Esq.
Wit: Saml. Lofton, Morgan Osbourn, Saml. Lofton, Jr. Morgan Osbourn made oath to John Wilson, J. P., 28 Aug. 1792.
Rec: 30 Aug. 1792.

Pages 50-51   3 Nov. 1791. William Washington of 96 Dist. to Edwin Smith for Ł 100 stg. for 130 acres on SW side of
                 the Saluda River, bd. by Toney's Creek to mouth of
Reedy branch, William Poor, Reuben Jonston, granted George Pearce in 1787 and conveyed by William Washington to Edwin Smith.
Wit: William Harper, Reuben Johnston. Reuben Johnston made oath to Wm. Halbert, J. P., 26 Jun. 1792.
Rec: 28 Jun. 1792.

Pages 51-52   22 Jun. 1792. Samuel Saxon and Mary, his wife of
                 Laurens Co., S. C. to James McCearly, blacksmith, of
                 Pendleton Co. for Ł 150 stg., 450 acres in Pendleton
Co. on branches of Big Generostee, waters of the Savannah River, adj. to Samuel Durumple, being part of 640 acres granted to Samuel Saxon, 5 Aug. 1786 by Wm. Moultrie, Esq. Signed: S. Saxon, M. Saxon.
Wit: Joshua Downs, James (J) Rains, Thomas Deen. Thomas Deen made oath to John Miller, J. P., 6 Aug. 1792.
Rec: 8 Aug. 1792.

Pages 52-53   2 Feb. 1791. Jesse Saxon of Greenville Co., S. C. to
                 Peter Henly of Abbeville Co. for Ł 24 stg. for 200
                 acres on West side of 23 Mile Creek, waters of Keowee River, granted to Jesse Saxon, citizen, by Thomas Pinckney, Esq. Recorded Bk. VVVV, p. 69.
Wit: John Robinson, Evan Thomas. Evan Thomas made oath to John Wilson, J. P., 24 Jun. 1791.
Rec: 25 Jun. 1792.

Page 54   21 Jan. 1792. James Martin of York Co., S. C. to
                 Moses Liddle of Pendleton Co. for Ł 70, 640 acres on
                 Devil's Fork of Great Generostee Creek, granted to
James Blythe, 18 Jul. 1784, by Benj. Guerrard, Esq. and conveyed to James

(page 54 cont'd):
Martin from William Hort and John Edwards, Esq's., Treasurers of the State of S. C., 8 Apr. 1789.
Wit: Isaac Steel, William Lesly. Isaac Steele made oath to John Wilson, J. P., 24 Jan. 1792.
Rec: 25 Jun. 1792.

Pages 54-55   29 Nov. 1792. Colonel Benjamin Cleveland, Esq., to Little Berry Toney, blacksmith, for Ł 50, 650 acres on both sides of Mill Creek, waters of Chaughe Creek granted to Benjamin Cleveland, 2 Mar. 1789, by Charles Pinckney, Esq., 2 Mar. 1789. Recorded Bk. ZZZZ, p. 82.
Wit: Benjn. Perry, Ambrose ( ) Fitzgerald. Ambrose Fitzgerald made an oath before John Wilson, J. P., 12 Mar. 1792.
Rec: 25 Jun. 1792.

Pages 55-56   Apr. 1792. William Honey, and Betty, his wife, of Washington Dist., Pendleton Co. to Francis Clinkscales, of same, for Ł 40 stg., 100 acres in Washington Dist. on East side of Broadmouth Creek, waters of the Saluda River, being part of 200 acres granted to William Honey, 10 Apr. 1788, by Thomas Pinckney, Esq. bd. by Henry Gocher, Ric'd. Sadler. Recorded Bk. MMMM, p. 9. Wit: Mathew Alexander, James Mattison. Mathew Alexander made oath to Wm. Halbert, J. P., 22 Jun. 1792.
Rec: 25 Jun. 1792.

Pages 56-57   5 Dec. 1791. William Skelton, planter, to William Lesley, planter, for Ł 176, 200 acres on Big Generostee above ancient boundary line, adj. South Moses Liddell, granted John Green, 23 May 1783, by William Moultrie, Esq.. Recorded Bk. IIII, p. 535, granted by John Green to William Skelton, 13 Jul. 1789. Signed: William (W) Skelton.
Wit: Moses Liddell, William Shillito. Moses Liddell made oath to Elijah Browne, J. P., 26 Jan. 1792.
Rec: 25 Jan. 1792.

Pages 57-59   26 Feb. 1792. William Honey and Betty, his wife, to Francis Clinkscales for Ł 60, 377 acres on branches of Broadmouth Creek of the Saluda River, granted to William Honey, 6 Oct. 1788, by Thomas Pinckney, Esq. Recorded Bk. XXXX, p. 475. Signed: William (H) Honey, Elizabeth (X) Honey.
Wit: Mathew Alexander, James Mattison. Mathew Alexander made oath to Wm. Halbert, J. P., 22 Jun. 1792.
Rec: 25 Jun. 1792.

Pages 59-60   29 Sep. 1791. Alexander Erwin, planter, and Susannah, his wife, spinster, to Bartly Tucker for Ł 150 for 120 acres, part of a tract laid out for John Turnbull. Signed: Alexander Erwin, Susannah ( ) Erwin.
Wit: George Tucker, Robt. Tucker, John Holms. George Tucker made oath to Elijah Browne, J. P., 8 Oct. 1791.
Rec: 25 Jun. 1792.

Page 60   9 Sep. 1790. Field Farrar of Fairfield Co., S. C. to Robert Box of Pendleton Co., 96 Dist. for Ł 260 stg., for 200 acres in 96 Dist. on Noyewee Creek and Tugaloo River near Tugaloo Old Town, bd. by Robert MisCampbell, granted to Jesse Grouter (s Soldier), 21 Jan. 1785.
Wit: John Clarke Fitzpatrick, Jno. Barton. John Barton made oath to Nathl. Perry, J. P., 8 Jun. 1792.
Rec: 25 Jun. 1792.

Page 61   12 Aug. 1791. John McCollock, of Spartanburgh Co., S. C. to William Laffoon, of Pendleton Co. for Ł 55 stg. (no acreage given) on South side of Saluda River, adj. Brooses Old Place, surveyed for William Brose, 11 Jun. 1784, granted Andrew Adams, 1 Aug. 1785, by Wm. Moultrie, Esq., transferred by deed to Robert McCoy and from McCoy to John McCollock.
Wit: Benjn. Clark, George Foster, John Wheeler. John Wheeler made oath to John Wilson, J.P., 23 Jan. 1792. Rec: 25 Jun. 1792.

Pages 61-62   21 Jan. 1792. Henry Gotcher to Caleb Conaway for
                   ₤ 100, for 200 acres in 96 Dist. on Broadmouth Crk.,
                   waters of the Saluda River, granted to John Hallum,
15 Oct. 1784 by Benj. Guerrard, Gov.
Wit: John Smith, Henry (H) Gotcher, Jr. Henry Gotcher made oath to Wm.
Halbert, J. P., 15 Feb. 1792.
Rec: 25 Jun. 1792.

Pages 62-63   25 Jun. 1792. James Anderson to John Woodall for
                   ₤ 37 for 188 acres in Washington Dist. on waters of
                   Generostee Creek, waters of Savannah River, granted
Anderson, 3 Oct. 1785, by William Moultrie, Gov. Recorded Bk. FFFF, p.
109. Wit: Jas. Milwee, Joshua Saxon, David Caldwell. David Caldwell
made oath to Wm. Halbert, J. P., 25 Jun. 1792.
Rec: 25 Jun. 1792.

Page 63   5 Feb. 1791. Anderson Thomas, of Fairfield Co.,S.C.
                   to James McKinney of Pendleton Co. for ₤ 256 stg.
                   for 640 acres on Keowee River, granted Thomas on 1
Aug. 1785, by William Moultrie, Gov.
Wit: Bern. Glenn, Ratliff Boon, John (X) Hendricks. Ratliff Boon made
oath to John Wilson, J. P., 28 Nov. 1791.
Rec: 25 Jun. 1792.

Pages 63-64   I, Archibald Gillison, of Abbeville Co., S. C. being
                   low and weak in body, but of sound mind, make this
                   my last will and testament...to beloved wife, Jean
Gillison, my whole estate, both real and personal, during her widowhood
...in case of her remarriage or decease, my four children, Elizabeth
Price, Mary Harris, James Gillison, and Karenhappoch Harris to receive
20 shillings, to be raised from sale of something that can be spared
from the plantation...to daughter, Ann Gillison, at wife's decease or
remarriage, tract of land I now live on, of 125 acres, all household
furniture, cattle, etc....John Gillison, son of my daughter , Ann Gillison, remainder of estate, sufficient for his schooling...I appoint three
friends, James Nash, Stephen Harris, and Larkin Nash, executors.
Date: 3 Jan. 1792.
Wit: George Nash, James Thornhill, Valentine Nash.
Rec: 20 Sep. 1792. (no oath)

Page 64   30 Mar. 1792. James Hamilton to William Honey for
                   ₤ 100, for 200 acres in Washington Dist., Pendleton
                   Co. on North fork of Big Creek, waters of Saluda Riv-
er, granted to James Hamilton, 5 Jun. 1786, by Wm. Moultrie, Esq., Gov.
Recorded Bk. MMMM, p. 9.
Wit: James Hamilton, John Hamilton, Thomas Hamilton. John Hamilton made
oath to John Wilson, J. P., 11 Apr. 1792.
Rec: 25 Jun. 1792.

Page 65   25 Oct. 1791. Robert Craven, planter, to David Brown
                   for ₤ 100 for 404 acres on Crow Creek, branch of the
                   Keowee River (bounded by?) ___ Glenn, Wm. Tate. Sur-
veyed by Robert McCann, deputy surveyor, granted Robert Craven, 11 June
1790, by Charles Pinckney, Esq., Gov.
Wit: David Brown, Jr., Robert (X) Goodwin. David Brown made oath before
John Wilson, J. P., 24 Jan. 1792.
Rec: 25 Jun. 1792.

Pages 65-66   18 Nov. 1791. James Hamilton to Sturdy Garner for
                   ₤ 60 stg. for 186 acres in 96 Dist. on South side of
                   Saluda River, on North fork of Big Creek, granted to
James Hamilton, 6 Oct. 1788, by Thomas Pinckney, Gov.
Wit: Wm. Hamilton, John Craige. William Hamilton made oath to William
Halbert, J. P., 5 Jan. 1792.
Rec: 25 Jun. 1792.

Page 66   13 Oct. 1791. John Pollock and Elizabeth, his wife,
                   to Wimer Siler, for ₤ 30 stg., for 100 acres on 26
                   Mile Creek, bounded NE by Mr. McCollister, N and S
by Mr. Saxon. Signed: John Pollock, Elizabeth Pollock. (cont'd):

(page 66 cont'd):

Wit: Nathaniel Robinson, Benjamin Harris. Benjamin Harris made oath to Wm. Halbert, J. P., 25 Jan. 1792.
Rec: 25 Jun. 1792.

Page 67   8 Jan. 1792. James Gates to John Bourland for Ł 150 for 200 acres, exclusive of 50 acres sold to R. Richardson, in 96 Dist. on South side of Saluda River, above ancient boundary line, bounded NE by Robert Bowen, NW by Richard Richardson, NE by Howell Dowdy and James Goodlett, granted to Gates on 21 Jan. 1785, by Benjamin Guerrard, Esq., Gov.
Wit: Howell Dowdy, Wm. White. Howell Dowdy made oath to John Wilson, J. P., 23 Jul. 1791.
Rec: 25 Jun. 1792.

Pages 67-68   12 Jan. 1792. Rhuben Johnston to William Harper for Ł 150 for 200 acres in Washington Dist., Pendleton Co. on Washington Creek, now called Big Creek, branch of the Saluda River, granted Ruben Johnston, 2 May 1785, by Wm. Moultrie, Esq., Gov. Recorded Bk. DDDD, p. (blank).
Wit: Edwin Smith, Benjn. Bowen, Thomas Bennett. Edwin Smith made oath to Wm. Halbert, J. P., 7 Jan. 1792.
Rec: 25 Jun. 1792.

Pages 68-69   25 Jan. 1792. John Turner and Sophis, his wife, to Ann Jones, for Ł 5, 72 acres on Little Creek of 26 Mile Creek, waters of Savannah River, bd. by Lewis Jones, John Hunnicutt, granted Sophis Turner, 14 Dec. 1786, by William Moultrie, Esq., Gov. Recorded Bk. QQQQ, p. 167. Signed: John Turner, Sophia (X) Turner.
Wit: Jas. Mulwee, Wm. Hall. James Mulwee made oath to John Wilson, J.P. 25 Jan. 1790.
Rec: 25 Jun. 1792.

Pages 69-70   4 May 1792. William Hallum to Robert Bowen, for Ł70 sterling, 300 acres on George's Creek, waters of the Saluda River, granted to William Hallum, 15 Oct. 1784, by Benj. Guerrard, Esq., Gov. Recorded Bk. AAAA, p. 186.
Wit: William Gillespy, Wm. Burney, Samuel Henderson. William Burney made oath to John Wilson, J. P., 13 Jun. 1792.
Rec: 25 Jun. 1792.

Page 70   5 Sep. 1792. Robert Young of Laurens Co., S. C. to Nathan Briant of Pendleton Co., for Ł 40 stg., 200 acres in 96 Dist. on Little Beaver Dam, waters of the Savannah River, granted Robert Young by Benjamin Guerrard, Esq., Gov. 15 Oct. 1784.
Wit: Richard Wallace, Absolum Briant, William Anderson. Absolum Briant made oath to John Wilson, J. P., 29 Oct. 1791.
Rec: 25 Jun. 1792.

Page 71   17 Sep. 1791. Andrew Hamilton to Richard Oldham for Ł 55, "paid in a likely young negro", for 640 acres in 96 Dist., Pendleton Co., on Rocky Creek, branch of Rocky River, granted to Andrew Hamilton, 4 Oct. 1790, by Charles Pinckney, Esq., Gov.
Wit: John Nickleson, John Simpson, James Jordan. John Nickleson made oath to William Halbert, J. P., 21 Jan. 1792.
Rec: 25 Jun. 1792.

Pages 71-72   6 Oct. 1791. Andrew Liddle, and Jean, his wife, a planter, to John Stewart, planter, for Ł 52 stg. for 240 acres on both sides of 12 Mile Creek, in 96 Dist. granted Liddle, 16 Jul. 1784, by Benjamin Guerrard, Esq., Gov. Signed: Andw. Liddell, Jean Liddell.
Wit: Saml. Watt, John Hallum. John Hallum made oath to John Wilson, JP 25 Jan. 1792.
Rec: 25 Jun. 1792.

Page 72   8 Feb. 1792. Kellum Price and Elizabeth, his wife, to John Smith, for Ł 40 stg., 50 acres on Tugaloo River, bd. by Thomas Harris, Sr. and river. Signed: Kellum (P) Price, Elizabeth (X) Price.
Wit: Nathl. Perry, Benjamin Perry. Benjamin Perry made oath to Nathaniel Perry, J. P., 1 Mar. 1792.
Rec: 25 Jun. 1792.

Page 73   10 Dec. 1791. James Jordan, blacksmith, to Daniel Keith, planter, for Ł 50 stg., 200 acres in 96 Dist. on South branch of Big Generostee Creek, branch of the Savannah River, granted to Daniel Keith, citizen, by Thomas Pinckney, Esq., Gov. Recorded Bk. SSSS, p. 370.
Wit: John Simpson, Samuel McCollum. John Simpson made oath to William Nevill, J. P., 10 Dec. 1791.
Rec: 25 Jun. 1792.

Page 73   Henry Willis for Ł 60 sterling sold to Abraham Hunt bed, horses and cattle. Date: 22 Oct. 1792.
Wit: William Nevill, James (X) Garvis.
Rec: 25 Oct. 1792.

Page 74   24 Jan. 1790. Samuel Taylor to Peter Acker, for Ł50 sterling, 200 acres in Washington Dist. on South side of Saluda River, granted Samuel Craslin, 1 Jan. 1785, by Benjamin Guerrard, Esq., Gov.
Wit: James Starritt, Alexander Wiomer. James Starritt made oath before Wm. Halbert, J. P., 25 Jan. 1792.
Rec: 25 Jun. 1792.

Pages 74-75   25 Oct. 1792. Moses Liddle, yeoman to John Simpson, VDM, Minister of the Gospel, for Ł 100, 326 acres on Devil's Fork, branch of Big Generostee Creek, in 96 Dist., now Washington, part of 640 acres granted to Calagan McCartey, 16 Jul. 1784. Recorded Grant Bk. ZZZ, p. 91, bd. by Wm. Seawright, Daniel Stringer, Thomas Morrow, conveyed by Francis Miller to Moses Liddle, 6 Apr. 1791. Recorded Bk. A, p. 335, Pendleton Co., 31 Aug. 1791.
Wit: David Stephenson, Samuel Barr. Samuel Barr made oath to William Halbert, J. P., 8 Oct. 1791.
Rec: 10 Oct. 1792.

Pages 75-77   19 Jul. 1788. James Cannon and Sarah, his wife, of Abbeville Co., S. C., planter, to Samuel Crabtree, of same, planter, for Ł 5 sterling, for 121 acres in Abbeville Co., 96 Dist., on Beaverdam, waters of Savannah River, above ancient boundary line, bd. by Ralph Wilson, granted to James Cannon on 6 Feb. 1786. Recorded Bk. GGGG, p. 396. Signed: James Cannon, Sarah (X) Cannon.
Wit: Ralph Wilson, Jesse Wood. Jesse Wood made oath to John Wilson, JP, 20 Nov. 1792.
Rec: 20 Nov. 1792.

Page 77   27 Oct. 1792. John Harris to Stephen Willis for Ł52 stg., for horses, cattle, household furniture, corn, tools, etc.
Wit: Anthony Laughlin, John Laughlin. Anthony Laughlin made oath before John Miller, J. P., 21 Nov. 1792.
Rec: 3 Dec. 1792.

Page 78   3 Aug. 1792. Mary Kerr, of Abbeville Co., S. C. to William Brown, of Pendleton Co., for Ł 250, 350 ac. in Pendleton Co. on both sides and in fork of the Middle Fork of 12 Mile River, bd. on NE by Mary Creswell, SW by Wm. McCaleb.
Wit: Wm. Young, W. V. Harris. Wm. Young made oath to Robert Anderson, J. P., 8 Nov. 1792.
Rec: 6 Dec. 1792.

Page 79   27 Oct. 1791. John McElveny, of Abbeville Co. to

(page 79 cont'd):
Wm. Young, of Pendleton Co., for Ł 30 sterling, in Pendleton Co., on Earle's Creek of 12 Mile River,adj. to Samuel Earle, granted McElveny in 1786, by Wm. Moultrie, Esq.
Wit: Saml. Lofton, Wm. Lofton, Samuel Lofton, Jr. Samuel Lofton made oath to John Wilson, J. P., 8 Oct. 1792.
Rec: 10 Oct. 1792.

Page 79   25 May 1792. John Hallum to Robert Bowen for Ł 25 stg. for 100 acres on George's Creek, waters of the Saluda River, granted Hallum, 1 Aug. 1785, by William Moultrie, Esq., Gov. Recorded Bk. EEEE, p. 123.
Wit: John Godfrey, Andrew (X) McWilliams, Thos. Grant. Thomas Grant made oath to John Wilson, J. P., 25 May 1792.
Rec: 25 Jun. 1792.

Pages 79-80   14 Sep. 1791. John Butler, of Washington Co., Ga., to John Earle, of Spartanburgh Co., S. C., for Ł 30 stg. for 200 acres in 96 Dist. on the Town fork of 12 Mile River, branch of Keowee River, granted to Robert Butler, a soldier in Capt. Bouris Independent Co., of S. C., John Butler being heir-at-law of Robert Butler.
Wit: Saml. Earle, John Danally. Samuel Earle made oath to George Salmon, J. P. of Greenville Co., S. C., 3 May 1792.
Rec: 25 Jun. 1792.

Pages 80-81   16 Aug. 1791. Benjamin Starritt to John Harper for Ł 45 stg., 272 acres in Pendleton Co., 96 Dist. on NE fork of Little Rocky Creek, waters of Savannah River, granted to Starritt, 4 Jun. 1787, by Charles Pinckney, Esq.,Gov.
Wit: Henry Dobson, Thomas Garner, Sturdy Garner. Henry Dobson made oath to Wm. Halbert, J. P., 19 Oct. 1791.
Rec: 25 Jun. 1792.

Page 81   14 Nov. 1791. John Gowen, of Spartanburg Co., S.C. to Henry Norton, of Pendleton Co., for Ł 60 stg., 294 acres on South side of Saluda River, on East branch of 12 Mile River, granted Gowen, 1 May 1786., bd. by Enoch Hooper on West, Samuel Martin on West.
Wit: William Jameson, William Easley, Enoch Hooper. William Jameson made oath to John Wilson, J. P., 24 Feb. 1792.
Rec: 25 Jun. 1792.

Page 81   27 Sep. 1792. Charles Cotesworth Pinckney, of Charleston, S. C., late Brigadier General of the Armies of the United States of America and Mary, his wife, to General Andrew Pickens, Colonel Robert Anderson, Captain Robert Maxwell, Mr. John Bowen, Major John Ford, Mr. John Hallum, of Washington Dist., S. C., for 60 acres, except 6 acres reserved for said Pinckney for fee, being part of 640 acres in Pendleton Co., Washington Dist., on waters of Brushy Creek, branch of Saluda River, granted to Pinckney, on 15 Oct. 1784.
Wit: Anne Louisa Smith, Will'm. Johnson.

Pages 82-83   28 Sep. 1792. Charles Cotesworth Pinckney, of Charleston, S. C., and Mary, his wife, to General Andrew Pickens, Colonel Robert Anderson, Captain Robert Maxwell, Mr. John Bowen, Major John Ford and Mr. John Hallum, of Washington Dist., S. C....whereas General Assembly by Act of 18 Feb. 1791, appoint Andrew Pickens, Robert Anderson, Robert Maxwell, John Bowen, John Ford, and John Hallum, Commissioners to superintend building of a gaol and a Courthouse, in Washington Dist. and to purchase land for erecting the buildings, most convenient site to be a tract of 640 acres belonging to Charles Cotesworth Pinckney, above the ancient boundary line in Pendleton Co., on waters of Brushy Creek, branch of Saluda River, granted to Pinckney, 15 Oct. 1784, bounding on Thomas Gadsen, Esq., all others on vacant land. Said Commissioners have applied to said Pinckney for 60 acres, part of above tract to build gaol and Courthouse and to form a town by the name of Rockville for sum of 5 shillings, except 6 acres re-

(pages 82-83 cont'd): served by Pinckney as a fee. Wit: Anne Louisa Smith and Will'm Johnson, Jr. Signed: Charles Cotesworth Pinckney, Mary Pinckney. William Johnson, Jr. made oath to Will'm Johnson in Charleston,S.C. 28 Sep. 1792. Thos. Simmons, QV. Plat included....Pursuant to an appointment from Commissioners of Public Buildings for Washington Dist., I have laid out town of Rockville containing 60 acres. Certified 1 Jul. 1792. Signed: Saml. H. Dickson, Deputy Surveyor.
Rec: 14 Nov. 1792.

Pages 83-84   3 Mar. 1782. 96 Dist. Benjamin Ingran, planter, for ₺ 20 stg., paid by Patrick and Alexander McDowell for 640 acres in 96 Dist. on 12 Mile River, waters of Savannah River, granted to James Milwee, 6 Nov. 1786.
Wit: Wiley Glover, Thomas Robertson. Thomas Robertson made oath to Julius Nichols, Jr., J. P. in Abbeville Co., 26 Mar. 1792.
Rec: 18 Dec. 1792.

Pages 84-85   25 May 1792. Jonathan Hicks, of 96 Dist. to Reuben Johnson of same for ₺ 40 stg. for 47 acres on Saluda River, granted to Hicks, 6 Jul. 1787, by Charles Pinckney, Esq. Recorded Bk. A, no. 5, p. 24.
Wit: Edwin Smith, Wm. Smith. Edwin Smith made oath to Wm. Halbert, J.P. 22 Jun. 1792.
Rec: 25 Jun. 1792.

Page 84   8 Jul. 1791. Aeson Jay to Jordan Reeves for ₺ 50 for 125 acres part of 250 acres granted to Aeson Jay in 1788, lying on waters of Big Generostee, waters of Savannah River.
Wit: Jacob Chamlee, Jas. Hillhouse, David Dickey. Joel Chamlee made oath to Elijah Browne, J. P., 18 Nov. 1791.
Rec: 25 Jun. 1792.

Pages 85-86   26 Sep. 1791. Samuel Lofton, Jr. to Duncan Camron, for ₺ 3 for 800 acres on Mile Creek, bd. by Keowee River, granted Lofton, 4 May 1789, by Charles Pinckney, Esq., Gov. Wit: Saml. Lofton, William Patterson, Wm. Lofton. Saml. Lofton, Sr. made oath to John Wilson, J. P., 24 Jun. 1792.
Rec: 25 Jun. 1792.

Pages 86-87   10 Jun. 1789. Mary Smith, of Pendleton Co. to James Buchanan, of Abbeville Co. for ₺ 40 stg. for 130 ac. granted to Mary Smith, 5 Jun. 1786, by Wm. Moultrie, Esq., Gov. on Broadaway Creek, waters of Rocky River, bd. by James Milwee, Daniel McAlester, vacant lands. Signed: Mary ( ) Smith.
Wit: Danl. ( ) McAllister, William McAllister, James Moore. James Moore made oath to John Wilson, J. P., 1 Aug. 1791.
Rec: 25 Jun. 1792.

Page 87   8 Nov. 1792. William Hodges of Abbeville Co. to Jacob Phillips of same, for ₺ 25 stg. for 190 acres in Pendleton Co. on 23 Mile Creek, waters of Savannah River, granted Wm. Hodges, 5 Jun. 1786, by Wm. Moultrie, Esq.,Gov. Recorded Bk. KKKK, p. 630.
Wit: Thos. Foster, Isaac Foster, Wm. Lord, Chs. Wilson, John Henry. Signed: William ( ) Hodges. John Henry made oath to John Wilson, J. P. 28 Nov. 1792.
Rec: 24 Dec. 1792.

Pages 87-88   25 May 1792. Alexander Dromgoole to David Ross for ₺ 60 stg. for 250 acres part of a tract of 791 acres granted Dromgoole, 4 Jul. 1791, by Charles Pinckney, Esq., Gov., recorded Bk. C, no. 5, p. 440.
Wit: Jno. C. Kilpatrick, Wm. McCaleb. Capt. William McCaleb made oath to John Wilson, J. P., 25 Jun. 1792.
Rec: 26 Jun. 1792.

Pages 88-89   14 May 1792. Alexander Dromgoole to Thomas Carri-

(pages 88-89 cont'd): dine, for ₺ 300 stg. for 2 tracts of land containing 720 acres on Martin's Creek, branch of Keowee River, 200 acres originally granted to John Swords, 21 Jan. 1780, released to Lewis Daniel Martin, 7 Aug. 1785, recorded Pendleton Co. Bk. A, p. 190, also conveyed from Lewis Daniel Martin to Dromgoole, recorded Bk. A, p. 322, the other tract of 500 acres on Martin's Creek, granted Lewis Daniel Martin, 1790, recorded Bk. B, no. 5, p. 413, by Charles Pinckney, Esq., Gov.
Wit: Crosby Wilkes Miller, Jeremiah Able. Crosby Wilkes Miller made oath to John Wilson, J. P., 4 May 1792.
Rec: 25 Jun. 1792.

Page 89   14 May 1792. Alexander Dromgoole to Thomas Carradine for ₺ 60 stg. for 536 acres on Martin's Creek, branch of Keowee River, being lower end of tract granted to Dromgoole, containing 791 acres, 4 Jul. 1791, recorded Bk. C. no. 5, p. 440.
Wit: Crosby Wilkes Miller, Jeremiah Able. Crosby Wilkes Miller made oath to John Miller, J. P., 4 May 1792.
Rec: 25 Jun. 1792.

Pages 89-91   9 Jul. 1792. E. Tate McClure to Josiah McClure, planter, for ₺ 40 stg. for 640 acres on South Deep Creek and North side of Seneca River, laid out for James Jordan, surveyed for E. Tate McClure, by William Tate, 24 May 1784 and granted to McClure, 16 Jul. 1784, by Benjamin Guerrard, Gov.
Signed: E. Tate McClure, Josiah McClure.
Wit: Richard Speake, William ( ) Nicholson, Jas. McClure. William Nicholson made oath to Wm. Nevill, J.P., 21 Jul. 1792.
Rec: 10 Dec. 1792.

Pages 91-92   1 May 1791. John Pollock and Elizabeth, his wife, planter, to Alexander Orr, planter, by grant, Jan. 1791 by Charles Pinckney, Esq., Gov., for 175 acres for ₺ 42.10sh. stg.
Wit: Charles Haynie, Robert Rankin, Joseph (JP) Price. Joseph Price made oath to John Wilson, J. P. 27 Aug. 1791.
Rec: 25 Jun. 1792.

Pages 92-93   24 Jan. 1792. David Thornton, of Edgefield Co., S. C., to David Brag, of Pendleton Co., for ₺ 60 stg., for 100 acres on Keowee River, bd. by river, part of 800 acres granted Samuel Lofton, Jr., 4 May 1789, by Charles Pinckney, Esq., Gov., conveyed by Lofton to Dunkin Camron and from Camron to David Thornton.
Wit: Wm. Anderson, Isaac (IL) Lynch, Joseph (X) Brimer. William Anderson made oath to John Wilson, J.P., 4 Jan. 1792.
Rec: 25 Jan. 1792.

Page 93   8 Nov. 1792. Thomas Lofton to Robert Carter for ₺ 120 sterling, 200 acres on NW fork of Choestoe Crk. waters of Tugaloo River, bd. NW by John Skelton, all other sides vacant, granted Lofton, 2 Jun. 1787, by Thomas Pinckney, Esq. Gov. Wit: Saml. Lofton, William Lofton, Margaret Lofton. (oath recorded on p. 102)
Rec: 13 Jan. 1793.

Pages 93-94   23 Mar. 1792. William Murray and Margaret, his wife, of Washington Dist., Pendleton Co. to John Henry, for ₺ 10 stg. for 95½ acres granted Alexander Boyes, 5 Dec. 1785, by Wm. Moultrie, Esq., Gov., part of 320 acres deeded to Wm. Murray, in Washington Dist. above ancient boundary line, on Broadaway Creek, waters of Great Rocky Creek, waters of Savannah River, bd. Mary Atchins. Signed: Wm. Murray, Margaret (X) Murray.
Wit: Jas. Hutson (Houston in oath), James Moore. James Moore made oath to John Miller, J. P., 15 Apr. 1792.
Rec: 25 Jun. 1792.

Page 95   15 Jan. 1793. William McCollock, of North Carolina,
                        to James McCollock (no. county given), for Ł 50 stg.
                        for 200 acres in Pendleton Co. on Griffen's Creek,
waters of Keowee River, bd. SW by Lewis D. Martin, vacant lands on other
granted to William McCollock, 5 Jun. 1786, by Wm. Moultrie, Esq., Gov.
Wit: Saml. Lofton, Thomas Lofton, Margaret Lofton. Saml. Lofton made
oath to John Miller, J. P., 15 Apr. 1793. (1792?)
Rec: 15 Jan. 1793.

Pages 95-96   9 Jan. 1791. Robert Pickens to George Oldham, for
                        Ł 100 stg. for 170 acres granted James Compton, 5
                        Jun. 1786, recorded Bk. LLLL, p. 350, in 96 Dist. on
Broadaway and Pea Creek, branches of Rocky River, bd. S. by John Pepper
and N. by Hezekiah Rice.
Wit: Richard Oldham, John Pepper. John Pepper made oath to John Wilson
J. P., 29 Jan. 1791.
Rec: 25 Jun. 1792.

Pages 96-97   1 Dec. 1789. 96 Dist. John Erwin to William McCa-
                        leb, farmer, for Ł 50 stg. for 250 acres in 96 Dist.
                        on waters of Rocky Creek, granted John Erwin, 6 Nov.
1786. Wit: John Bowie, Saml. Taylor, John Hairston. Samuel Taylor
made oath to William Nevil, Esq., J. P., 25 Jun. 1792.
Rec: 26 Jun. 1792.

Pages 97-98   10 Sep. 1792. William McCaleb to William Drenin,Jr.
                        for Ł 60 stg. for 250 acres where Drenin now lives,
                        granted John Erwin, of 96 Dist., 6 Nov. 1786, on
waters of Rocky Creek, bd. SE by Col. David Hopkins, vacant land.
Wit: Wm. McClaskey, Wm. Thompson. William Thompson made oath to Elijah
Browne, J. P., 8 Oct. 1792.
Rec: 10 Oct. 1792.

Pages 98-99   29 Jan. 1791. Robert Pickens to Richard Oldham for
                        Ł 100 stg. for 150 acres part of a tract granted to
                        James Compton, 5 Jun. 1786, by Wm. Moultrie, Esq.,
Gov., recorded Bk. LLLL, p. 353, in 96 Dist. on Broadaway Creek and Pea
Creek, of Rocky River, bd. by John Pepper.
Wit: John Pepper, Charles Clements. Charles Clements made oath to John
Wilson, J. P., 29 Jan. 1791.
Rec: 25 Jun. 1792.

Pages 99-100   29 Sep. 1792. William Neil, planter, of Lawrence
                        (sic) Co., S. C. to John McClain of Pendleton Co. for
                        Ł 30 stg. for 278 acres in 96 Dist. above the ancient
boundary line, on waters of Rocky River, bd. by John Wilson, granted to
William Neil, 27 Sep. 1784.
Wit: James Moore, Thomas Entrekin. James Moore made oath to John Miller
J. P. 8 Oct. 1792.
Rec: 10 Oct. 1792.

Pages 100-101   15 Dec. 1790. James Martin and Sarah, his wife, of
                        Camden Dist., S. C., doctor, to John Pickens, of 96
                        Dist., planter, for Ł 65 stg., 300 acres in 96 Dist.
on Occony Creek, branch of Keowee River, granted 16 Jul. 1784 to Dr. James
Martin. Recorded Bk. BBBB, p. 21. Bd. by John Loumber on NW and vacant
lands. Signed: James Martin, Sarah Martin.
Wit: John Patterson, Andrew Baskin. John Patterson made oath to Elijah
Browne, J. P., 9 Aug. 1792.
Rec: 10 Oct. 1792.

Page 101   96 Dist..10 Feb. 1790. George Shooler, planter, to
                        Joseph Culton, Sr., for Ł 50 stg., for 200 acres on
                        Rocky Creek, branch of Savannah River, granted George
Shooler, 15 Oct. 1784, by Benjamin Guerrard, Esq., Gov.
Wit: Jas. Douthit, Jno. (X) Pendergrass. Harris Mauldin made oath, he
saw George Shooler acknowledge this deed to Elijah Browne, 26 Jun. 1792.
Rec: 27 Jun. 1792.

Page 102   12 Jan. 1792. Enoch Hooper, of Greenville Co.,S. C.

(page 102 cont'd): to Henry Norton, of Pendleton Co. for Ł 60 stg. for 242 acres on South side of Saluda River, on small branches of 12 Mile River, granted Hooper, 30 May 1782, by Wm. Moultrie, Esq., bd. by John Henderson, Henry Norton.
Wit: Michael Johnson, Gideon (X) Norton, William Edwards.. Michael Johnson made oath to John Wilson, J. P., 24 Feb. 1792.
Rec: 25 Jun. 1792.

Pages 102-103   6 Mar. 1792. Phillip Prator to Alexander Boyse for Ł 50 stg., 238 acres on head branch of 23 Mile Creek, waters of Savannah River, bd. SW by John Prator, SE by Robert McCann, and vacant lands. Granted Phillip Prator, 5 Dec. 1791 by Charles Pinckney, Esq., Gov. Recorded Bk. E, no. 5, p. 139. Signed: Phillip (PP) Prator.
Wit: Robt. McCann, Hartwell Hunnicutt. Robt. McCann made oath to John Wilson, J. P., 10 Apr. 1792.
Rec: 25 Jun. 1792.

Pages 103-104   6 Mar. 1792. John Prator to Alexr. Boyse for Ł 50 stg, 100 acres above ancient boundary line on 23 Mile Creek, waters of Savannah River, part of 400 acres granted to John Prator, 17 Apr. 1788, by Thomas Pinckney, Esq., Gov. Recorded Bk. WWWW, p. 409.
Wit: Robt. McCann, H. Hunnicutt. Plat included. Land bd. on East by William Alexander Boyse, on South by John Prator, on West by Robert Pickens, on North by Phillip Prator. Robt. McCann made oath to John Wilson, J. P., _____ 1792.
Rec: 26 Jun. 1792.

Pages 104-105   3 Feb. 1792. James Thompson to William Hillhouse for Ł 100 for 150 acres granted to Thompson on Beaver Crk branch of Great Rocky Creek, bd. NW by Joseph Culton, vacant lands, being a plantation where John Jackson now lives.
Wit: John Haynie, Wm. McVey. William McVey made oath to Elijah Browne, J. P., 11 Feb. 1792.
Rec: 25 Jun. 1792.

Page 105   23 Jan. 1793. Stephen Strange, Jno. Burton, Dan'l. Ledbetter and James Tate being chosen by Moses Liddel and Wm. Bennet as arbitrators in a certain dispute of land between them, it is our opinion that according to witnesses and Lofton's line and plat being legally proved to us, it is our opinion that the land belongs to Moses Liddel. Witness our hands: James Tate, Stephen Strange, Dan'l Ledbetter, Jno. Burton.
Rec: 25 Jan. 1793.

Page 105   I, Ephraim Mitchell, of St. John's Parish, S. C. am bound to John McClure of Pendleton Co. for Ł 240 stg. payment due, 18 Jan. 1792, and I execute conveyance for 640 acres in Pendleton Co., on George's Creek, branch of Saluda River, known by name of Cunningham's place, granted to Ephraim Mitchell, bd. NW by William Gillaspie, or if granted to James Mitchell, William Read, Mary Read, Elizabeth Read, Sarah Read or Hugh Rose, the obligation shall be equally binding.
Wit: Saml. Bennett, Jr., D. Squier...I do hereby acknowledge and assign my whole right and title to within bond to Charles Bowen, if no right should be made to the land there is no recourse on John McClure, given under my hand, 20 Nov. 1792. Signed: John McClure.
Wit: Charles Stevens, John Bowen.
Rec: 28 Jan. 1793.

Page 106   I, Taply Oldham of Pendleton Co., S. C., for consideration of 9000 weight of good merchantable tobacco paid by Peter Greenlees, of Pendleton Co., deliver to Greenlees, a negro named Charlotte about eleven years old. Signed: Taply (H) Oldham. Wit: Andrew Ruddle, William Herring.
Andrew Ruddle made oath to John Wilson, J. P., 9 Feb. 1790.
Rec: 11 Feb. 1793.

Pages 106-107   96 Dist., Laurens Co., S. C., 30 Nov. 1789. Joseph Gallegly and Sarah, his wife, to Andrew Smith, surgeon of DDD, for ₤ 40 stg. for 500 acres on 23 Mile Creek, waters of Savannah River in 96 Dist., Abbeville Co., excepting 200 acres to be laid off to Robt. Freeman, granted to Joseph Erwin, on 4 Dec. 1786, by Wm. Moultrie, Gov., conveyed to Gallegly, 3 Oct. 1789.
Signed: Joseph Gallegly, Sarah (X) Gallegly.
Wit: Jno. Simpson, Jas. Cummings, Jas. Simpson. Jno. Simpson made oath to John Hunter, of Laurens Co., S. C., 7 Jan. 1793.
Rec: 28 Jan. 1793.

Page 108   Pendleton Dist., S. C. I do hereby acknowledge to have received, as widow of George Bennison, late of said county, from his brother, William Benneson, my full and entire rights of dower as widow of George Benneson.
Date: 22 Dec. 1791. Signed: Sarah (X) McCollum....I, John McCullum, as husband of Sarah McCullum, acknowledge reciept of rights of dower.
Wit: Saml. Lofton. Saml. Lofton, Sr. made oath to John Miller, J. P., 1 Mar. 1793.
Rec: 1 Mar. 1793.

Pages 108-109   5 Jul. 1792. John Lewis Gervais, of Charleston, S.C. to Christopher Strong, of Chester Co., S. C., for ₤ 200 for 640 acres on both sides of 18 Mile Creek, waters of Savannah River, 3 miles below Seneca or Ft. Rutledge, granted to John Lewis Gervais, 16 Jul. 1784.
Wit: Geo. Bampfield, Ralph Almar. George Bampfield made oath to Francis Bremar, J. P. of Charleston, 31 Jul. 1792.
Rec: 31 Jan. 1793.

Page 109   I, Benjamin Land, of Pendleton Co., for divers good causes grant to my son, James Land, all goods, chattels, household stuff, and lands for his use, under direction of Judges of the County. Date: 2 Mar. 1793. Signed: Benjamin (X) Land.
Wit: Wm. Haynie. Wm. Haynie made oath to John Miller, J. P..
Rec: 4 Mar. 1793.

Pages 109-110   10 Nov. 1792. Thomas Farrar, Sheriff of Washington Dist., to Samuel Earle, for ₤ 50 for 500 acres in Washington Dist., being land sold to Earle as highest bidder at auction...William Henderson was seized of during his lifetime of above 500 acres, on Beaver Dam Creek, waters of Tugaloo River, in Nov. term 1788, when Samuel Earle began Action of Debt in Court of Common Pleas, at Cambridge, against John Henderson, Thomas Sumter and ___ Starke, executors of last will and testament of William Henderson, deceased...Samuel Earle obtained judgement, Apr. 1791. Sale held on 1 Oct. 1792.
Wit: Solomon Roe, Wm. Edmondson, William Henderson. Wm. Henderson, Esq. made oath (no date or J. P. named).
Rec: 5 Mar. 1793.

Pages 110-111   Pendleton Co. 6 Nov. 1792. Rowland Cornelius signs over to Rowland Cornelius, my son, a mulatto man named Tap, for value received. Condition of obligation, Rowland Cornelius, Sr. will retain said mulatto until his death, then his son to have full possession. Signed: Rowland ( ) Cornelius, Rowland (+) Cornelius, Jr.
Wit: Henry McWhorter, Wm. Wakefield, William Wakefield made oath to Jno. Wilson, J. P., 4 Feb. 1793.
Rec: 4 Feb. 1793.

Page 111   27 May 1792. Robert Maxwell, Esq., of Greenville Co., S. C., to William Vaughn, planter, of Pendleton Co., S. C., for ₤ 50 for ___ acres on South side of Saluda River, bd. by river and on North by William Vaughn, on South by John Maxwell, where William Vaughn now lives, granted Robert Maxwell, 26 Aug. 1786, by Wm. Moultrie, Esq., Gov. Wit: James (X) ?aughn, Hugh Maxwell. James Vaughn made oath to L. Tarrant in Greenville Co., S.C., 9 Aug. 1792. Rec: 24 Jan. 1793.

Page 112 1 Jun. 1792. John Maxwell to Wm. Vaughn for Ł 50, 165 acres where Vaughn now lives, bd. by Saluda River, surveyed for John Maxwell, 26 Jul. 1784, by Wm. Moultrie, Gov.
Wit: Rt. Maxwell, Hugh Maxwell. Robert Maxwell made oath to L. Tarrant J. P. of Greenville Co., S. C., 22 Jun. 1792.
Rec: 24 Jan. 1793.

Pages 112-113 9 Aug. 1787. Gilbert Mills, of Abbeville Co., S.C., planter, to William McPherson, of same, planter, for Ł 40, 8 shillings, 200 acres in Abbeville Co., granted Gilbert Mills, 5 Jun. 1786. Recorded Bk. KKKK, p. 710, on Generostee Creek, bd. Moses McCarter. Signed: Gilbert Mills, Martha (+) Mills.
Wit: Saml. Green, Andw. Hamilton. John Gilliland, witness to receipt. Andw. Hamilton made oath to John Wilson, J.P., 10 May 1791.
Rec: 24 Jan. 1793.

Pages 113-115 7 Jul. 1792. Thomas Commander Russell and Mary, his wife, of Elbert Co., Ga. to Thomas Edmondson, of Winchester, Va., for Ł 140, for 563 acres in Washington Dist. (late 96 Dist.), on Brushy Creek, bd. NE by Henry Purcell, SE by Theopolis Wyatt, West by Thomas Gadsden, and by vacant lands. Signed: Thomas C. Russell, Mary Russell.
Wit: M. Walker, Wm. Edmondson. Wm. Edmondson made oath to John Wilson, J.P., 25 Jan. 1793.
Rec: 26 Jan. 1793.

Pages 115-117 25 Jan. 1793. Andrew Pickens, Esq., and Rebecca, his wife, to William Richards, trader, for Ł 150, 700 ac. granted to Jesse Spears, 3 Mar. 1788. Recorded Bk. VVVV, p. 464 in 96 Dist. on Oconee Creek, waters of Keowee River, bd. SW by Jesse Spears, Oconee Mountain and vacant lands, conveyed to Andrew Pickens, Esq., 18 Jan. 1789, also a tract of 200 acres granted to John Lumbas, 15 Oct. 1784. Recorded Bk. BBBB, p. 57, conveyed to Pickens, 10 Apr. 1789, in 96 Dist. on Oconee Creek, waters of Keowee River, bd. NE by John Martin, vacant lands. Signed: Andrew Pickens, Rebekah Pickens.
Wit: Wm. McCaleb, Thomas L. Reece. Wm. McCaleb made oath to John Miller 5 Feb. 1793.
Rec: 5 Feb. 1793.

Page 117 27 Jul. 1791. Thomas Wadsworth and William Turpin to John Smith, planter, for Ł 25, 300 acres on Broad Mouth Creek, waters of Saluda, bd. SE by Henry Goucher and William Medling. Signed: Thos. Wadsworth for Wadsworth & Turpin.
Wit: Eugene Brannen, Wm. Young. Eugene Brannen made oath to Thos. Wadsworth, Esq., J.C. of Laurens Co., S. C., 28 Jul. 1791.
Rec: 2 May 1793.

Pages 117-118 25 Oct. 1792. John Smith to Moses Jones for Ł 75 stg for 300 acres on Broadmouth Creek, waters of Saluda, bd. SE by Henry Goucher and William Medling.
Wit: Jno. Lovelady, Dr. Andrew Jones. Jno. Lovelady made oath to John Miller, J.P., 9 Jan. 1793.
Rec: 2 Mar. 1793.

Page 118 1 Mar. 1793. Thomas Moss to John Tippen for Ł 50, for 130 acres, part of a tract granted to Thomas Moss on 5 Mar. 1789, on waters of Big Generostee. Signed: Thomas (X) Moss. Wit: James Long, Thos. Shockley, Daniel Putnam. James Long made oath to John Miller, J.P., 2 Mar. 1793.
Rec: 2 Mar. 1793.

Pages 118-119 21 Jan. 1793. Charles Gates to George Singleton Foster, for Ł 100 stg., 140 acres granted to Gates, 5 Jun. 1786, by Wm. Moultrie, Gov., in 96 Dist. on S. side of Saluda River, bd. N. by Charles Gates, part of 180 acres.
Wit: Wm. (X) James, Mary Ann (X) James, J. Foster. Josiah Fosher made oath to Gabriel Moffett, J.P., 22 Jan. 1793.
Rec: 24 Jan. 1793.

Page 119   Received from Richard Richardson, 1 Mar. 1791, sum
                        of ₺ 10 sterling, in full satisfaction of my right
                        and title to a tract of 700 acres on Dody's Creek,
granted Thomas Lewis, 4 Dec. 1786. Signed: Thomas Lewis.
Wit: J. Whitner. Joseph Whitner made oath to John Wilson, J.P., 24 Jan.
1793.
Rec: 24 Jan. 1793. Plat shows land bounded on North by Richardson, on
E. Doddy land and vacant land, on South fork of Doddy's Creek.

Page 120   10 Aug. 1792. Wm. McBee, of Washington Co., State
                        of Franklin to Wm. Brown of Pendleton Co., S.C. for
                        ₺ 100, 400 acres on both sides of Raven's fork of
12 Mile River, granted Wm. McBee by Wm. Moultrie, Gov., 6 Jun. 1784.
Signed: William (M) McBee. Wit: Uriah Hunt, Jesse (+) Hunt, Thomas
(X) Hunt. Uriah Hunt made oath to Bayley Anderson, J.P., 27 Oct. 1792.
Rec: 24 Jan. 1793.

Pages 120-121   23 Mar. 1792. William Murray and Margaret, his wife,
                        of Washington Dist. to James Parker, of same, for
                        ₺ 50 stg., 150 acres, part of tract granted Alexan-
der Boyes of 320 acres, 5 Dec. 1785, by Wm. Moultrie, Gov., conveyed to
Murray, above ancient boundary line on Broadaway Creek, waters of Great
Rocky Creek, of Savannah River, bd. by Hugh Wartlaw, Esq., William Smith
and Murray's Mill Pond. Signed: Wm. Murray, Margaret (+) Murray.
Wit: James Moore, Wm. Murray. James Moore made oath to William Halbert,
J.P., 28 Jan. 1793.
Rec: 26 Jan. 1793.

Pages 121-122   22 Aug. 1792. Jonas Little to Samuel Brown, for ₺40
                        sterling, 130 acres in Washington Dist., on South
                        side of Saluda River on Dividing ridge of Big Creek
and Saluda River, granted Jonas Little, 10 Oct. 1789, by Charles Pinckney, Gov., bd. by James Hamilton. Signed: Jonas Littell.
Wit: Samuel Barkley, Robert Craig. Samuel Barkley made oath to Wm. Halbert, J.P., 20 Sep. 1792.
Rec: 24 Jan. 1793.

Page 122   16 Sep. 1790. Minor Winn, Esq., of Fairfield Co.,
                        S.C., to Stephen Fuller, planter, of Pendleton Co.
                        for ₺ 40, 200 acres in 96 Dist. on both sides of 18
Mile Creek, waters of Keowee River, bounding North on George Kilson, all
other, vacant lands, granted Winn on ___ 1785.
Wit: Field Farrar, Sam'l. Taylor. Major Sam'l. Taylor made oath to Wm.
Neville, J.P., 26 Jan. 1793.
Rec: 26 Jan. 1793.

Pages 122-123   2 Mar. 1792. John Henry to Thomas Houston for ₺ 100
                        sterling for 320 acres on Great Rocky Creek, branch
                        of Savannah River, where Thomas Houston now lives,
part of 640 acres granted William Sosseland(?), 8 Oct. 1784, by Benjamin
Guerrard, Gov. conveyed to Col. David Hopkins then to John Henry.
Wit: Sam. H. Dickson, William Thompson, Josiah Houston. Samuel H. Dick-
son made oath to Elijah Browne, J.P., 26 Jan. 1793.
Rec: 26 Jan. 1793.

Page 123   26 Jan. 1793. John Norwood to Andrew Riddle for ₺50
                        stg., 173 acres bounded SE by Elias Moore, NE by Rob-
                        ert Stevenson, NW lands unknown, granted Norwood, 3
Dec. 1792. Wit: James Dobbins, Wm. McCaleb. James Dobbins made oath
to Wm. Halbert, J.P., 26 Jan. 1793.
Rec: 26 Jan. 1793.

Pages 123-124   16 Dec. 1792. William Goggins, miller, to Thomas
                        Grant, silversmith, for ₺ 4 stg., for 404 acres on
                        North side of 26 Mile Creek, waters of Keowee River,
bd. NW by Scott, SW by John Morris, vacant lands, granted Goggins by
Charles Pinckney, Gov., 1 Oct. 1792. Signed: William (X) Goggins.
Wit: James Hembree, William Buller. James Hembree made oath to Wm.
Nevill, J.P., 24 Jan. 1793.
Rec: 25 Jan. 1793.

Pages 124-125   25 Jan. 1793. David Jordan, planter, of Pendleton
                     Co. to John Parker, planter, of Abbeville Co., S.C.
                     for Ŀ 100 stg., 200 acres granted Jordan, 2 Oct. ___
on Wilson's Creek, waters of Savannah River, bd. by lands unknown.
Wit: James Moore, Patrick Buchannon. James Moore made oath to Wm. Halbert, J.P., 26 Jan. 1793.
Rec: 26 Jan. 1793.

Pages 125-126   13 Mar. 1788. Saml. Earle of Greenville Co., S. C.
                     to Martin Hulate of Abbeville Co., S. C. for Ŀ 40
                     stg., 112 acres in 96 Dist. on 12 Mile River, granted Earle, 5 Feb. 1787, by Wm. Moultrie, Gov.
Wit: Bailey Anderson, Seth Farrar. Bailey Anderson made oath to Nathl. Perry, J.P., 15 Feb. 1792.
Rec: 24 Jan. 1793.

Page 126   10 Jan. 1792. Richard Pollard to William Norton for
                     Ŀ 60 stg., 300 acres in 96 Dist. on Tomasee River,
                     granted Pollard as his bounty, 21 Jan. 1785. Recorded Bk. BBBB, p. 83.
Wit: John Hallum, Henry Norton. Henry Norton made oath to John Wilson, J.P., 24 Feb. 1792.
Rec: 24 Jan. 1793.

Pages 126-127   Last will and testament of James Wilson...being of
                     sound mind and memory...to my brother, John Wilson,
                     5 shillings...to his oldest son, Robert Wilson, 5
shillings...to my lawful wife, Keziah to have plantation where I now
live, all stock, plantation tools, household furnitures, books, paper
rights and credits...Keziah, my loving wife to be sole executrix.
Date: 16 Apr. 1790. Signed: James (X) Wilson.
Wit: Francis Nunn, William Lowe, Rt. Maxwell.
Rec: 24 Jan. 1793.

Page 127   24 Oct. 1792. Kerby Hubbard, of Lincoln Co., N. C.
                     farmer, to Thomas Hobson of Pendleton Co., farmer...
                     for Ŀ 42 stg., 187 acres on NW side of 23 Mile Creek,
waters of Keowee River, part of 682 acres, bd. by creek and vacant lands,
granted John Portman, citizen, by Wm. Moultrie, Gov. Recorded Bk. OOOO,
p. 418, conveyed to Hubbard, 2 May 1792.
Wit: Peter (P) Henly, Moses Payne. Moses Payne made oath to Wm. Nevill, J.P., 24 Jan. 1793.
Rec: 25 Jan. 1793.

Pages 127-128   8 Dec. 1792. John Darragh to Owen Evans for Ŀ 35 stg
                     for 100 acres on Saluda River, part of 200 acres surveyed for Robert Wilson, adj. John Wilson, granted
18 Nov. 1784. Recorded Bk. IIII, p. 164.
Wit: Samuel Barkley, Thomas Wilson, Andrew (X) Barkley. Samuel Barkley
made oath to Wm. Halbert, J.P., 11 Dec. 1792.
Rec: 26 Jan. 1793.

Pages 128-129   4 Feb. 1792. John Bourdine, of Georgia, to Jacob
                     Kitle, of Pendleton Co. for Ŀ 80 stg. for 139 acres
                     in Washington Dist. on Big Creek, waters of Saluda
River, part of tract granted John Burdine, by Wm. Moultrie, Gov., 5 Jun.
1786, also part of tract conveyed from John Nicholson to John Burdine.
Wit: Jeremiah Burdine, Thos. Garner, William Hatchett. Thomas Garner
made oath to Wm. Halbert, J.P., 23 Jan. 1793.
Rec: 24 Jan. 1793.

Pages 129-130   4 Feb. 1792. John Burdine, of Georgia, to Thomas
                     Garner, of Pendleton Co., for 176 Ŀ stg. for 276 ac.
                     on Big Creek of Saluda River, granted Burdine, 6 Mar.
1786, also part of tract adj. above tract granted Burdine, 5 Jun. 1786.
Recorded Bk. LLLL, p. 333 and Bk. HHHH, p. 466, also part of tract conveyed from John Nicholson to Burdine, in all containing 376 acres.
Wit: Jeremiah Burdine, Jacob (X) Kitle, William Hatchett, Jacob Kitle
made oath to Wm. Halbert, J.P., 23 Jan. 1793.
Rec: 24 Jan. 1793.

Pages 130-131   4 Jan. 1793. William Dorsey of Burk Co., N. C., farmer, to Daniel Ship, of Pendleton Co., miller, for ₤ 80 stg., 300 acres part of survey of 373 acres on 23 Mile Creek, waters of Savannah River, bd. SW by Andrew Roe, all other sides vacant, granted John Davis, then a citizen of S. C., by Charles Pinckney, Gov. Recorded Bk. ZZZZ, p. 84, 2 Mar. 1789, conveyed by Davis to Wm. Dorsey. Signed: William ( ) Dorsey.
Wit: Lewis Cobb, Jacob Rame. Lewis Cobb made oath to Wm. Halbert, J.P. 25 Jan. 1793.
Rec: 25 Jan. 1793.

Page 131   31 Jan. 1793. George Salmon, of Greenville Co.,S.C. to John Fields, of Pendleton Co. for 5 shillings stg. for 290 acres, part of tract granted George Salmon, 4 Jun. 1793, on both sides of Fork of 12 Mile River, bd. by Cameron.
Wit: Lewis Wimberly, Sarah Anderson. Sarah Anderson made oath to Bayley Anderson, J.P., 31 Jan. 1793.
Rec: 5 Feb. 1793.

Pages 131-132   14 Feb. 1793. William Twitty, heir and administrator of the estate of John Twitty, dec'd. of Pendleton Co. to James Ditto, of same, for ₤ 80 stg. for 140 acres on branches of Keowee River, bd. SW by John Twitty, E. by Minor Winn, NW by William McKay, NE by unknown, granted John Twitty, citizen, by Charls. Pinckney, Gov. Recorded Bk. C, no. 5, p. 80.
Wit: George Hayes, John Adly. George Hayes made oath to Wm. Nevill,J.P. 16 Feb. 1793.
Rec: 18 Feb. 1793.

Pages 133-134   2 Feb. 1793. James Ditto to John Adair for 13.3.8 stg., for 140 acres in Washington Dist. on branches of Keowee River, bd. SW by John Twitty, E. by Minor Winn, NE by lands unknown, NW by William McKay.
Wit: John Curry, Benjamin Murry, John Caruthers. (Oath blank-names and dates).
Rec: 20 Mar. 1793.

Page 134   4 Sep. 1792. John Hamilton, planter, of Abbeville Co., 96 Dist., to Samuel Watson, planter, of York Co., S. C., for ₤ 50 stg. for 300 acres on each side of Little Generostee Creek, waters of Savannah River, granted Hamilton, by Benj. Guerrard, Gov.
Wit: Joseph Turnbull, James Turnbull, John Turnbull. James Turnbull made oath to Jno. Harris, J.P., 3 Nov. 1792.
Rec: 24 Jan. 1793.

Pages 134-135   8 Nov. 1792. John Darragh to Samuel Barkley for ₤50 stg., 100 acres on Saluda River, a part of 250 acres surveyed for Darragh, bd. by James Wilburn, granted 7 Nov. 1785. Recorded Bk. FFFF, p. 321.
Wit: John Wilson, Josiah Goodwin, Jas. Hillhouse. John Wilson made oath to Wm. Halbert, J.P., 11 Dec. 1792.
Rec: 24 Jan. 1793.

Pages 135-136   14 May 1792. Isaac Guilder, of 96 Dist. to Mathew Hamilton, of same for ₤ 25 stg. for 65 acres in 96 Dist. on both sides of Little Fork of Eastatoe, a branch of Keowee River. Signed: Isaac (1) Guilder.
Wit: Ninian Bell Hamilton, Abraham Tanzey. Ninian Bell Hamilton made oath to Gabriel Moffett, J.P. (no date).
Rec: 24 Jan. 1793.

Page 136   12 Jul. 1792. Swanson Lunsford to William Wilson for ₤ 100 stg., 640 acres in Washington Dist. on Brushy Creek, waters of Saluda River, bd. NW by Thos Commander Russell, NE by Peter Fayssoux, SE by Gen'l. Moultrie, vacant land. Wit: Jno. Stewart, Charles Huse, Sam'l. Means.
Samuel Means made oath to John Wilson, J.P., 22 Jan. 1793.
Rec: 24 Jan. 1793.

Pages 136-137   12 Nov. 1792. John Landers to Samuel Deane for
                     1.12.8 for 5 acres part of 300 acres granted to John
                     Files, 15 Oct. 1784, on Big Generostee, waters of
Savannah River. Wit: Thomas Leonard, Samuel Bradcutt. Thomas Leonard
made oath to Elijah Browne, J.P., 23 Feb. 1793.
Rec: 25 Feb. 1793.

Pages 137-138   8 Dec. 1790. John Twitty to John Miller, for Ł 40
                     stg., 177 acres in 96 Dist. on branches of Conneross
                     Creek, waters of Keowee River, bd. by vacant lands,
granted to Twitty, 2 Jul. 1787, by Thomas Pinckney. Gov. Recorded Bk.
VVVV, p. 63.
Wit: Robt. Squib, John Miller, Jr. John Miller, Jr. made oath to John
Miller, J.P., 2 Aug. 1792.
Rec: 11 Aug. 1792.

Page 138   16 Jul. 1792. Sarah Dalrumple, Executrix and John
                     Dalrumple, Executor of Estate of Samuel Dalrumple,
                     dec'd. to Edward Wade for Ł 60 stg., 325 acres in
Washington Dist., Pendleton Co. on Mill's Creek, branch of Rocky River,
granted Samuel Dalrumple, 6 Apr. 1789, by Charles Pinckney, Gov. Re-
corded Bk. ZZZZ, p. 279. Signed: Sarah (l) Dalrumple, Jno. Dalrumple.
Wit: John Durley, David (1) Wade, Jas. Milwee. David Wade made oath to
John Miller, J.P., 8 Oct. 1792.
Rec: 6 Oct. 1792.

Page 139   10 Feb. 1792. Thomas Brough, of 96 Dist. and Agnes,
                     his wife, to James Wilson, of Pinckney Dist., S.C.,
                     for Ł 35 stg., 200 acres on North side of Savannah
River, bd. by Pat'k. Calhoun, Jr., William Bozby, Sadler's Creek, grant-
ed to Thomas Brough, 6 Feb. 1786, by Wm. Moultrie, Gov. Signed: Thomas
(X) Brough. Wit: Danl. Garvin, James Brough, Saml. Wilson. James Brough
made oath to Fleming Bates, J.P., in Abbeville Co., S.C., 20 Jan. 1792.
Rec: 8 Oct. 1792.

Pages 139-140   1 Dec. 1792. James Robertson, of Washington Co.,Ga.
                     to James Terrell, of Pendleton Co., for Ł 60 stg.,
                     for ___ acres on Chauge Creek, waters of Tugaloo Riv-
er, granted James Robertson, a soldier by Benjamin Guerrard, 21 Jan.
1785. Recorded Bk. BBBB (no page no.) Signed: James (X) Robertson.
Wit: Saml. Taylor, Blake Mauldin. Blake Mauldin made oath to John Miller, J.P., 1 Dec. 1792.
Rec: 1 Dec. 1792.

Page 140   18 Feb. 1793. Roger Martin to John Mauldin, Jr. for
                     Ł 100 stg., 200 acres in Washington Dist. on both
                     sides of Beaver Creek, waters of Rocky River, bd. on
E. by James Garner, Daniel McCay, Ancil Jarrot.
Wit: Ancil ( ) Jarrot, Ruth Martin. Joab Mauldin made oath to Elijah
Browne, J.P., 2 Mar. 1792.
Rec: 8 Mar. 1793.

Pages 140-141   Mathew Finley made oath he had a note on Joseph Hill
                     for 13.13.4, dated 4 Jan. 1787 on demand with inter-
                     est, which note is lost or misplaced and that he has
received full payment. Sworn: 5 Oct. 1792, to Robert Anderson, J.P.
Rec: 2 Apr. 1793.

Page 141   Washington Dist., Pendleton Co. 13 Feb. 1793. And-
                     rew Smyth, Sr., of Cambridge, 96 Dist., Abbeville Co.
                     S. C., to James Hamilton, of Washington Dist., Pen-
dleton Co., for Ł 30 stg., for 300 acres on 23 Mile Creek, waters of the
Savannah River, part of 500 acres to be laid out to Robert Freneau, as
granted 4 Dec. 1786, by Wm. Moultrie, Gov. to Joseph Irwin and conveyed
by him and Milla, his wife, to Joseph Galligly and from him to Dr. Andrew Smyth. Wit: Archibald Hamilton, Andrew Smyth, Jr., John Chambers.
Archibald Hamilton made oath to John Wilson, J. P., 12 Apr. 1793.
Rec: 13 Apr. 1793.

Pages 141-142   25 Apr. 1792. John Perkins to Joseph Doughty, for

(pages 141-142 cont'd):
£ 60 sterling, 140 acres, part of 340 acres granted Lewis Daniel Martin by Thomas Pinckney, Esq., 2 Jul. 1787. Recorded Bk. TTTT, p. 310, on branch of Conoross Creek, waters of Keowee River, bd. by Solomon Perkins on SE, NE and NW by lands unknown, including the plantation where Joseph Doughty now lives, conveyed by L. D. Martin to John Perkins. Signed: John ( ) Perkins.
Wit: John C. Kilpatrick, Alexr. Kilpatrick. John Clark Kilpatrick made oath to Wm. Nevill, J.P., 19 Jun. 1792.
Rec: 24 Apr. 1793.

Pages 142-143   25 Apr. 1792. Lewis Daniel Martin to John Perkins for £ 40 stg., for 140 acres, part of 340 acres granted Lewis D. Martin by Thomas Pinckney, Gov., 2 Jul. 1787. Recorded Bk. TTTT, p. 310, on Connoross Creek, waters of Keowee River, bd. by Solomon Perkins, vacant lands and land where Joseph Daughty lives.
Wit: Jno. Kilpatrick, James Kilpatrick. Jno. C. Kilpatrick made oath to Wm. Nevill, J.P., 19 Jan. 1792.
Rec: 24 Apr. 1793.

Pages 143-145   14 Mar. 1792. Jacob Gillham to James Compton for £ 55 stg. for 150 acres in 96 Dist. on branch of 23 Mile Creek, waters of Savannah River, part of 640 ac. granted Robert Perkins, then conveyed to Jacob Gillham, 1 Sep. 1789.
Wit: Benjn. Smith, John Perkins, Samuel Norwood. Benjamin Smith made oath to John Wilson, 15 Nov. 1792.
Rec: 24 Apr. 1793.

Page 145   24 Sep. 1791. Robert Pickens, planter, to James Greer, planter, for £ 50 stg. for 200 acres part of tract in 96 Dist. on branches of 23 Mile Creek, waters of Savannah River, bd. by John Prater, the Meeting House, Jacob Gillham, John Hamilton.
Wit: George Forbis, Benjn. Smith, Jacob Gillham. Jacob Gillham made oath to John Wilson, J.P., 24 Sep. 1791.
Rec: 24 Apr. 1793.

Page 146   9 May 1792. Joseph Culton to Robert Stevenson for £ 45 for 200 acres granted George Shulor by Gov. Benjamin Guerrard, Esq., 15 Oct. 1785, on Great Rocky Creek, adj. to John Henry, William Thompson.
Wit: James Dobbins, John Dobbins. James Dobbins made oath to Wm. Halbert, J. P., 8 May 1792.
Rec: 29 May 1793.

Pages 146-147   24 Jan. 1793. Joseph Culton to Robert Stevenson for £ 50, for 250 acres on Rocky River, Beaver Creek, a part of 440 acres granted Joseph Culton, by Benjamin Guerrard, Gov., 21 Jan. 1785, bd. by Eliab Moore, James Dobin, John Brice and Robert Stevenson.
Wit: James Dobbins, John Dobbins, Anne Culton. James Dobbins made oath to John Wilson, J.P., 9 Feb. 1793.
Rec: 29 May 1793.

Pages 147-148   ___, 1793. William Gillispie, planter, and Agnes, his wife, spinster, to Jacob Gillham, (amt. blank) for 100 acres on branches of Canoe Fork of Little Generostee, granted Gillispie, 3 Apr. 1780. Recorded Bk. KKKK, p. 201. Also 57½ acres on SW of above tract granted 21 Jan. 1785. Recorded Bk. CCCC, p. 174. Signed: Wm. Gillaspie, Ann ( ) Gillaspie.
Wit: John Willey, Samuel Wyley. Plat included, land adj. to Wm. Gillespie, Samuel Wyley. John McMahen, D.S. surveyed 21 Jan. 1793. John Willey made oath to John Wilson, J.P., 12 Apr. 1793.
Rec: 16 Apr. 1793.

Page 148   James Gillison for 266 dollars paid by Andrew Pickens, Esq., sold negro man, named Joe, about 25 years old, and negro boy named Boowain(?), about 14 years (cont'd)

(page 148 cont'd):
old. Date: 2 Mar. 1793. Signed: James ( ) Gillison.
Wit: John Miller, William Steele.
Rec: 16 Apr. 1793.

Page 148   John Hunnicutt, of Abbeville Co., S. C., is bound
                  to Wm. Lewis of same, for Ł 100 stg. Date: 4 Sep.
                  1787...condition of obligation for John Hunnicutt to
make deed to 200 acres on branches of 23 Mile Creek, by names of Mulwee's
Creek, in county aforesaid.
Wit: H. Hunnicutt, Eli Hunnicutt. Eli Hunnicutt made oath to John Miller, J. P., 4 May 1793.

Pages 148-149   State of Georgia. 4 Mar. 1793. George Ogg, Esq., of
                  Richmond Co., Ga. to Thomas Peter Carnes, of same co.
                  Attorney at Law, for Ł 200 for 625 acres in Pendleton
Co., S. C. on North branch of Tugaloo, bd. on W. by Thomas Holden, NE by
Robert Thompson, on all others by vacant lands.
Wit: P. J. Carnes, Thomas Farrar. Thomas Farrar made oath to Wm. Edmondson, J.P., in Pendleton Co., 8 Apr. 1793.
Rec: 16 Apr. 1793.

Pages 149-150   10 Jan. 1793. Blake Mauldin, blacksmith, to William
                  Haynie, planter, for Ł 87 stg. for 200 acres on SE
                  side of 18 Mile Creek, of Savannah River, bd. on SE
and SW by John Miller, Esq., on SE by Charles Lay (Say?) and Courthouse
tract, being tract laid out to James Crowther, 2 Apr. 1787. Signed:
Blake Mauldin, Betsey (X) Mauldin.
Wit: Reubin Piles, (blank). Reubin Piles made oath to John Miller, J.P.
10 Jan. 1793.
Rec: 12 Jan. 1793.

Page 150   1 Dec. 1789. Ledford Pain (also spelled Payne) for
                  Ł 10 stg. for 25 acres on fork of Back and Beaver
                  Creek, adj. to John Jackson, Joseph Culton, part of
tract granted to Thomas Morris, conveyed to Payne.
Wit: John Jackson, Alexr. Stevenson, James Stevenson. John Jackson made
oath to John Miller, J.P., 10 Jan. 1793.
Rec: 10 Jan. 1793.

Page 150   8 Jan. 1793. Major Parsons to Blake Mauldin for
                  Ł 150 stg. for 240 acres on fork of Tugaloo and Keo-
                  wee River, part of 2 tracts, one granted Parsons, 5
Jan. 1786, by Wm. Moultrie, Esq., 4 Jun. 1787, the other for 870 acres
granted Parsons, 4 Jun. 1787, by Thomas Pinckney, Esq., bd. by Keowee
River.
Wit: John Jackson, Moses Gaist, Thomas Parsons. John Jackson made oath
to John Wilson, J.P., 9 Jan. 1793.
Rec: 10 Jan. 1793.

Page 151   18 Mar. 1793. Thomas Farrar, Sheriff of Washington
                  Dist., S.C., to Charles Bowen, for Ł 140 stg. for
                  damages and costs expended by Hannah Turpin in her
suit, as administratrix of David Batey, dec'd., in judgement against one
Ephraim Mitchell, for 640 acres in Washington Dist., on both sides of
George's Creek, land being sold to highest bidder, Charles Bowen.
Wit: W. Thompson, Charles Stevens. Waddy Thompson made oath, 18 Sep.
1793 to Wm. Edmondson, J.P.
Rec: 16 Apr. 1793.

Page 152   24 Feb. 1792. Josiah Patterson, of Abbeville Co.,
                  96 Dist., planter, to James Rice, of Pendleton Co.,
                  blacksmith, for Ł 50 stg., for 200 acres in Pendle-
ton Co. on Wolf Creek, branch of 12 Mile River, running on East side of
Glassey Mountain with 20 acres part of adj. 200 acres known as Beaver
Dam, granted to Patterson, 21 Jan. 1785.
Wit: Richard (X) Holden, Archd. Thompson. Richard Holden made oath to
Bayley Anderson, J.P., 22 Sep. 1792.
Rec: 16 Apr. 1793.

Pages 152-153   11 Feb. 1793. William Henderson to Conrad Aderhold
                       for Ł 36 for 243 acres on Rice's Creek of 12 Mile
                       River, part of 450 acres granted to Henderson by Wm.
Moultrie, Gov., 5 Jun. 1786.
Wit: Isaac Miller, John Glenn. Isaac Miller made oath to Elijah Browne,
J.P., 12 Apr. 1793.
Rec: 16 Apr. 1793.

Page 153   28 Dec. 1787. David Loggan, of Abbeville Co., to
                       Elias Roberts, of same, for 20 shillings for 200 ac.
                       in Abbeville Co. on south side of Saluda River, sur-
veyed 24 May 1785 for Loggan.
Wit: Wm. Edmondson, James Miller, James Robinson Miller. Wm. Edmondson
Sr., Esq., made oath to Elijah Browne, J.P. of Pendleton Co., 10 Apr.
1793.
Rec: 16 Apr. 1793.

Page 153   Charles White sold to Bartholomew White by way of
                       debt, mortgage and for a set time the following ar-
                       ticles: 62 acres of land where Charles White now
lives, one horse, now in possession of Charles White, cattle, household
furnishings, none to be removed from possession of Charles White for one
year, then if Charles White should pay Bartholomew White Ł 70 sterling,
then this, mortgage to be in effect. Date: 20 May 1793. Signed: Charles (X) White.
Wit: James Hembree, William Welch.
Rec: 23 May 1793.

Page 154   21 Mar. 1793. William Broose, to William Laffoon,
                       for Ł 40 stg. for 57 acres on South side of Saluda
                       River, granted Broose, 4 Jan. 1790. Signed: Wm.
Bruce. Wit: Isaac Meers, John Keith. John Keith made oath to Gabriel
Moffitt, J.P., 6 Apr. 1793.
Rec: 16 Apr. 1793.

Pages 154-155   12 Feb. 1790. Jesse Baker, planter, to William Mc-
                       Caleb, planter, for Ł 150 stg., for 300 acres on W.
                       side of Keowee River, bd. on S. by Major Sam Taylor,
on all others vacant lands. Signed: Jesse Baker, Grace Baker.
Wit: Robert Howell, Wm. Neal McCaleb. Wm. Neal McCaleb made oath to
John Miller, 22 Apr. 1793.
Rec: 23 Apr. 1793.

Page 155   29 Feb. 1791. Robert Pickens to John Pepper for
                       Ł 100 stg. for 150 acres part of tract granted to
                       James Compton, by Wm. Moultrie, Gov., 5 Jun. 1786.
Recorded Bk. LLLL, p. 350 in 96 Dist. on Broadaway and Pea Creeks, on
branches of Rocky River, adj. on N. by George Oldham, on S. by Richard
Oldham.
Wit: Richard Oldham, Charles Clements. Charles Clements made oath to
John Wilson, J.P., 29 Jan. 1791.
Rec: 16 Apr. 1793.

Page 156   29 Nov. 1790. James Hamilton to John Pepper for
                       Ł 50 stg. for 100 acres granted by Benjamin Guerrard,
                       Esq., Gov., 15 Oct. 1784. Recorded Bk. AAAA, p. 177.
in 96 Dist., South of Saluda River, bd. on NW by Moses Holland, on SE by
William Maples.
Wit: Aaron Boggs, Moses Holland. Moses Holland made oath to Wm. Hal-
bert, J.P., 5 Jan. 1791.
Rec: 16 Apr. 1793.

Pages 156-157   21 Nov. 1790. Thomas Roberts to John Pepper for 100
                       Ł stg. for 150 acres granted by Thomas Pinckney, Gov.
                       5 Jan. 1789. Recorded Bk. YYYY, p. 340, in 96 Dist.
on South side of Saluda bd. on North by river, on NW by James Hamilton,
and Elijah Owens, on South by Elijah Owens and Hamilton. Signed: Thomas
Roberts ( ).
Wit: Mason Bennett, Thomas Bennett. Thomas Bennett made oath to William
Halbert, J.P., 5 Jan. 1791. Rec: 18 Apr. 1793.

Page 157   2 Jul. 1792. William Low to Keziah Wilson for ₤ 7
                    stg. for 123 acres on Hurricane Creek, of Saluda Riv-
                    er, part of a tract William Low now lives on.
Wit: John Wilson, Francis Nunn. John Wilson made oath to Elijah Browne.
(no date).
Rec: 16 Apr. 1793.

Pages 157-158   James Jordan, of Washington Dist., Pendleton Co.,
                    blacksmith, for love and affection I bear my loving
                    son, Adam Jordan, grant to him all my lands, goods
and chattels, and debts. Date: 29 Feb. 1793. Signed: James Jordan.
Wit: Auston (X) Cornelius, John (his mark) Corres, Chs. Travis.....A
true inventory of the property of James Jordan delivered to Adam Jordan
...440 acres on Deep Creek, cattle, blacksmith tools, etc. Date: 27
Feb. 1793, in presence of John QV Corris (could be John Q. Norris),
Austen (X) Cornelius, Chs. Travis.
Rec: 16 Apr. 1793.

Page 158   1 Sep. 1792. John Huggins to Samuel Lofton, Jr., for
                    ₤ 60 stg., 200 acres on both sides of 5 Mile Spring,
                    waters of the Keowee River, bd. on NE by John Lewis
Gervais, on NW by unknown land, vacant land, granted Huggins, 2 Oct.1786,
by Wm. Moultrie.
Wit: John Robinson, Saml. Lofton, Wm. (his mark) Jackson. Saml. Lofton
made oath to John Miller, J.P., 22 Jul. 1793.
Rec: 22 Jul. 1793.

Pages 158-159   7 Mar. 1793. Thomas Lofton to Saml. Lofton for ₤ 15
                    stg., for 64 acres part of plantation where Thomas
                    Lofton now lives, on both sides of 18 Mile Creek, wa-
ters of Keowee River, bd. by John Lewis Gervais, Saml. Lofton, Daniel
Kelton, granted Lofton, 5 Jun. 1786, by Wm. Moultrie.
Wit: Wm. Lofton, John G. Lofton, Samuel Lofton, Jr. William Lofton made
oath to John Miller, J.P., 22 Jun. 1793.
Rec: 22 Jun. 1793.

Pages 159-160   18 Jan. 1790. Adam Crain Jones, Jr., of Abbeville
                    Co., S. C., to Bartholomew White, of Pendleton Co.
                    for ₤ 20 stg., 251 acres in Pendleton Co. on Generos-
tee and Rocky River, waters of Savannah River, granted Jones, 5 Mar.1787,
by Thomas Pinckney. Recorded Bk. RRRR, p. 200.
Wit: Charles (X) White, James Rosamond, James Eddins. (oath names and
dates blank).
Rec: 23 May 1793.

Pages 160-161   I, William Haynie am indebted to Wadsworth, Turpin
                    & Steel for 19.5.5. stg. for security mortgage on a
                    tract of 200 acres on branch of 18 Mile Creek, join-
ing lands with a tract on which Courthouse now stands, lately known as
Capt. Mauldin's plantation, conveyed to me by Mauldin.
Wit: Robt. Norris, Henry Sims. Henry Sims made oath to John Miller,J.P.
20 May 1793.
Rec: 22 May 1793.

Page 161   I, Thomas Buchanan for ₤ 100 stg. have sold to Archi-
                    bald Buchanan all my lands, household goods, horses,
                    cows and other moveables in my possession...120 lbs.
principle and interest to be paid on 1 May 1796. Date: 1 May 1793.
Wit: John Miller, Jr., Crosby W. Miller. John Miller, Jr. made oath to
John Miller, J.P., 24 Jun. 1793.
Rec: 24 Jun. 1793.

Page 161-162   15 May 1793. William Makie to John Portman for ₤ 40
                    stg., 40 acres on North side of Keowee River, grant-
                    ed to William Mackie, 7 Nov. 1791, by Thomas Pinckney
Gov. Signed: William (W) Mackie.
Wit: Jno. C. Kilpatrick, Alxr. Kilpatrick. Alexander Kilpatrick made
oath to Nathl. Perry, J.P., 15 May 1793.
Rec: 24 Jun. 1793.

Pages 162-163   8 Jun. 1793. John Oliver to James Hamilton for Ł 40 stg., 200 acres in Washington Dist. on branch of 23 Mile Creek, waters of Savannah River, granted Samuel Oliver, by Wm. Moultrie, 2 Oct. 1786. Signed: John (his mark) Oliver.
Wit: Wm. Hamilton, James Blair, Josiah Downen. Wm. Hamilton made oath to John Wilson, J.P., 8 Jun. 1793.
Rec: 25 Jun. 1793.

Page 163   18 May 1782. Joel Holcom to John Hornaday for Ł 5 for 80 acres, part of a tract on South side of the Saluda River, branch of North fork of 12 Mile River, granted Joel Holcom by Wm. Moultrie, 1 Jan. 1787. Signed: Joel (his mark) Holcom.
Wit: Wm. Marchbanks, Isaac (E) Gilder, Elijah (his mark) Marchbanks. William Marchbanks made oath to Bayley Anderson, J.P., 1 Feb. 1793.
Rec: 26 Jun. 1793.

Pages 164-165   5 Jun. 1793. John Miller and James Milwee to Farren McKenzie and Duncan McKenzie for Ł 25 stg. for 380 acres in Washington Dist. on Big Beaver Dam Creek, waters of Tugaloo River, granted to John Miller and James Milwee, 2 Jul. 1787 by Thos. Pinckney. Recorded Bk. UUUU, p. 144. Signed: John Miller, Jas. Milwee.
Wit: Jesse (his mark) Coffee, Wm. N. McCaleb. Jesse Coffee made oath to John Miller, J.P., 26 Jun. 1793. Recorded 27 Jun. 1793. John Miller seperately for himself agrees to defend moiety of Duncan McKinzie from all persons.

Pages 165-166   6 May 1793. Harris Mauldin, of Pendleton Co., S.C., to John Johnston, of Abbeville Co., S.C., for Ł 50 stg. for 80 acres in Washington Dist. on Rocky River waters of Savannah River, bd. on SE & SW by William Brown, on SE by John Mauldin, NE by Blake Mauldin and Rocky River. Recorded Bk. B, no. 5, p. 349. Wit: Joab Mauldin, John Mauldin, Sr., Peggy (X) Mauldin. Joab Mauldin made oath to Elijah Browne, J.P., 26 Jun. 1793.
Rec: 27 Jun. 1793.

Pages 166-168   25 May 1788. Lewis Newhouse of Charleston, merchant, to John James Himley of Charleston, merchant, for Ł 500, 10 sh. stg., 640 acres in 96 Dist. on Little Beaver Dam, waters of Savannah, bd. on North by James Bentham, on East by Moses Tomlin, on West by Mr. Aikens, surveyed for Edward Trescott, 26 May 1785, also all tract of 640 acres in 96 Dist. on Little Beaver Dam, be. on South by Moses Tomlin, on East by Col. Peter Horry, on West by Edward Trescott, surveyed for James Bentham, 26 May 1785, also 280 acres in 96 Dist. on South fork of Brushy Creek, waters of Sandy River, surveyed for Daniel Tharin, 8 Jan. 1785, bd. on all sides by vacant land, said three tracts containing 1560 acres.
Wit: Timy Ford, Hen. Will. Desausure...96 Dist., Henry Wm. Desausure made oath to Julius Nichols, Jr., J.P., 2 May 1793.
Rec: 27 Jun. 1793.

Pages 168-169   8 Jul. 1793. George Payne to William Hallum for Ł40 stg., for 158 acres on branch of 18 Mile Creek on North side, bs. on South by Thos. Hallum, on East by Wm. Hallum, surveyed by John Rodgers to Henry Payne, 5 Sep. 1785, granted by Wm. Moultrie, 4 Dec. 1786.
Wit: Robert Baker, John Hallum. John Hallum made oath to John Wilson, J.P., 30 Jul. 1793.
Rec: 2 Aug. 1793.

Pages 169-170   I, Anna Roach, for love and affection I have for my son, William Roach, give him all my goods and chattels now at my dwelling house on Seneca River, and have delivered inventory to William Roach. Date: 5 Aug. 1793. Signed: Anna (X) Roach.
Wit: Joshua (+) Young, Stephen Roach. Joshua Young made oath to John Miller, J.P., 6 Aug. 1793.
Rec: 6 Aug. 1793.

Pages 170-172 30 May 1792. John James Himely of Charleston, merchant, to Samuel Merian of Philadelphia, Pa., for 5 shillings stg. for 640 acres in 96 Dist. on Little Deaver Dam, waters of Savannah River, bd. by James Bentham on the North, on the South by vacant land, on East by Moses Tomlin, on West by Mrs. Aikens, granted to Edward Trescott, 26 May 1785, also, a tract of 640 acres on Little Beaver Dam, waters of Savannah River, bd. on South by Moses Tomlin, on East by Col. Peter Horry, on West by Edward Trescott, surveyed for James Bentham, 26 May 1785, also a tract of 280 acres part of 640 acres in 96 Dist. on South fork of Brushy Creek, waters of Sandy River, surveyed for Daniel Tharin, 8 Jun. 1785, three tracts of 1560 acres. Signed: J. James Himely.
Wit: Henry William Desausure, Wm. Hort...Lewis Newhouse by deed sold these pieces of land to James Himely, 28 May 1788, as agent and friend of Samuel Merian...Abbeville Co., S. C., Henry William Desausure made oath to Julius Nichols, Jr., J.P., 2 May 1793.
Rec: 27 Jun. 1793.

Pages 172-173 26 Jun. 1793. Major Thomas Farrar, Sheriff of Washington Dist., to James Linn and Benjamin Harris for ₺ 100 stg, 640 acres on 26 Mile Creek, waters of the Seneca River, granted John Hall, Sr., 16 Jul. 1784.
Wit: Benjamin Roe, Jonathan Montgomery. Benjamin Roe made oath to John Wilson, J.P., 26 Jun. 1793.
Rec: 27 Jun. 1793.

Pages 173-175 8 Mar. 1793. James Blair to Thomas Smart for ₺ 60 stg., for 231 acres on branch of Conneross Creek, waters of Keowee River, granted John Wardon, 3 Nov. 1788, by Thos. Pinckney, Gov., conveyed from Wardon to Blair, 5 Oct.1792. Recorded Bk. ZZZZ, p. 56.
Wit: Isaac Casey, Thomas Barton. Isaac Casey made oath to Wm. Nevill, J.P., 25 Jun. 1793.
Rec: 27 Jun. 1793.

Page 175 3 Feb. 1792. James Browne to William Brown, by grant dated 2 Oct. 1786, by Wm. Moultrie, Esq., to Jacob Galleyton for 250 acres on Governor's Creek, conveyed to James Browne, 1 May 1790, who now conveys to William Browne for ₺ 40.
Wit: Thomas Hays, Milley Brown. Milley Brown made oath to Elijah Browne J.P., 22 Jun. 1793.
Rec: 27 Jun. 1793.

Pages 175-176 Washington Dist., 24 Jun. 1793. Thomas Lofton, Planter, to Saml. Lofton, Sr., Planter, for ₺ 75 sterling for 100 acres, part of a tract where Thomas Lofton now lives, on NE side of 5 Mile Branch of 18 Mile Creek, waters of Seneca River, bd. on NE by John Lewis Jervais, on NW by Saml. Lofton, on SW by David Kelton, granted 5 Jun. 1786, by Wm. Moultrie.
Wit: Wm. Lofton, Samuel Lofton, Jr., John G. Lofton. Samuel Lofton, Jr. made oath to John Miller, Jr., J.P., 6 Aug. 1793.
Rec: 6 Aug. 1793.

Page 176 13 Jan. 1791. Richard Morrow and his wife to John Parker for ₺ 50 for 327 acres surveyed 14 Jul. 1785, in 96 Dist. on Great Rocky Creek, bd. on SW by Henis, North by Abraham Reid. Signed: Richard Morrow, Margaret Morrow (her mark).
Wit: Thomas (his mark) Gray, John (his mark) Morrow. John Morrow made oath to Wm. Halbert, J.P., 19 Jun. 1793.
Rec: 15 Aug. 1793.

Page 176 9 Jan. 1793. Gabriel Harden of Washington Dist.,S.C. planter, to John Griffen, of same co., planter, for ₺ 50 stg, for 319 acres on branch of 23 Mile Creek, bd. NE and SE by Joseph Jenkins and Andrew Roe, SE by lands of Gabriel Hardin granted, 19 May 1790, by Charles Pinckney. Recorded Bk. B, no.5, p. 342. Signed: Gabriel Hardin, Comfort (+) Harden.
Wit: Wm. Haynie, W. Steele. Wm. Steele made oath to John Miller, Jr., 7 Sep. 1793. Rec: 25 Sep. 1793.

Page 178   18 Feb. 1793. Roger Martin to Ancil Jarrot for ₺ 75
                        stg., 150 acres in Washington Dist. on both sides of
                        Beaver Creek, branch of Rocky River, adj. John Mauldin, Wm. Thompson.
Wit: Joab Mauldin, John Mauldin. John Mauldin made oath to Elijah
Browne, J.P., 1 Jun. 1793.
Rec: 25 Sep. 1793.

Page 178   I, Thomas Betts sold to John Griffen, a negro boy of
                        about 15 years of age, named Billey, for ₺ 50.
Wit: T. Harvey, E. Downing, John Williams, Jr. John Williams, Jr. made
oath to John Hunter, J.P., 14 May 1793.
Rec: 25 Sep. 1793.

Pages 178-180   8 May 1793. Benjamin Clardy and Agnes, his wife, to
                        Thomas Wadsworth and William Turpin, merchants, are
                        bound for the sum of 50.16.5½ sterling, with interest, as security, all tract of 217 acres where Benjamin Clardy now lives,
on NE side of Saluda River, bd. on SE by Capt. Rosmond, on N. by Robert
Maxwell, granted to Wadsworth and Turpin by Wm. Moultrie, 4 Jan. 1787,
conveyed to Clardy, 5 May. 1789. Signed: Benjamin Clardy, Agnes Clardy.
Wit: James Young, Nancy (+) Clardy. 96 Dist. James Young made oath to
John Hunter, J.P., 5 Aug. 1793.
Rec: 25 Sep. 1793.

Page 180   Benjamin Clardy to Thomas Wadsworth and William Turpin, merchants, obligation dated 8 May 1793 for 100.
                        1.12.11. stg., with 50.16.5½ interest to be paid annually before 1 Jan. 1794, security cattle, furniture and tools. Date:
8 May 1793.
Wit: James Young. James Young made oath to John Hunter, J.P., 5 Aug.
1793.
Rec: 25 Sep. 1793.

Pages 180-181   23 Mar. 1793. John Grissam, of Pendleton Co. to
                        Robert Gabie, of Lincoln Co., N. C. for ₺ 5 stg. for
                        1/3 part of Iron Works on Grissam's land on 26 Mile
Creek, with 1/3 part of water said creek affords, except what grist mill
requires, also a piece of ground 25 feet by 50 feet, also free passage
to and from the works.
Wit: Lewis Cobb, James Anderson. Lewis Cobb made oath to John Miller,
J.P., 16 Sep. 1793.
Rec: 25 Sep. 1793.

Pages 181-182   2 Mar. 1793. John Grissam to David Carter for ₺ 5
                        stg. for 1/3 part of Iron Works on John Grissam's
                        land on 26 Mile Creek, with 1/3 part of water said
creek affords, except what grist mill requires, also piece of land 25
feet by 50 feet convenient to works and free passage to and from works.
Wit: Lewis Cobb, James Anderson. Lewis Cobb made oath to John Miller,
J.P., 16 Sep. 1793.
Rec: 25 Sep. 1793.

Pages 182-183   16 Aug. 1793. Hon. William Moultrie, of Charleston,
                        S. C., Esq., to George Ringland, of Charleston, for
                        ₺ 550 stg. for 1100 acres on Cane Creek, on a town
named Cane Creek Town, near the Keowee River, bd. by original grant to
Wm. Moultrie, 16 Jul. 1784, recorded Secretary's Office.
Wit: Jacob Drayton, William Drayton. Jacob Drayton made oath to John
Sandford Dart, I.P.Q.U., in Charleston, 21 Aug. 1793.
Rec: 25 Sep. 1793.

Page 184   17 Mar. 1792. John Logan to Thomas Stone; John Logan, heir at law of Thos. Logan, dec'd., 200 acres
                        in Pendleton Co. 96 Dist., granted to Thos. Logan,
2 Oct. 1786, by Wm. Moultrie for his service or bounty. Recorded Bk.
BBBB, p. 241, on George Creek, waters of Saluda River.
Wit: Joel (+) Cox, Janin (I) Loosk. Sworn to 28 Jul. 1792, to Wm. Edmondson, J.P.
Rec: 25 Sep. 1793.

Pages 184-185   14 Sep. 1790. Thomas Stone, and Mary, his wife, of
                     Pendleton Co. to Thomas Edwards, of Greenville Co.,
                     S. C., for Ł 30 for 100 acres being a grant to John
Loggan, heir at law of Thomas Loggan, dec'd., conveyed by John Loggan
to Stone, on branch of George Creek, waters of Saluda River, bd. by Armstrong, including 1 acre on South side of Creek at a shoal convenient
for a Mill seat. Signed: Thomas Stone, Sary (her mark) Stone.
Wit: Thomas Townes, John Armstrong, John Eaton. Thomas Townes made oath
to Wm. Edmondson, J.P., 16 Sep. 1793.
Rec: 25 Sep. 1793.

Pages 185-186   14 Sep. 1793. Moses Swevillent and Millinder, his
                     wife, of Greenville Co., S.C. to Thomas Edwards, of
                     Greenville Co. for Ł 50 for 150 acres, part of 200
acres in Pendleton Co. on S. side of Saluda River, granted 1 May 1781.
Recorded Bk. IIII, p. 412, bd. by branch above Parris's Waggon Ford, and
Swevillent's line. Signed: Moses Swevillent, Millander Swevillent(+).
Wit: Thos. Townes, Blackmon Ligon, Hewlit Sullivant(n.b. this is also
spelled Swevillent/Swellivent). Thomas Townes made oath to Wm. Edmondson, J.P., 16 Sep. 1793.
Rec: 25 Sep. 1793.

Page 186   14 Sep. 1793. Moses Swillivant and Millinder, his
                     wife, of Greenville Co. to John Eaton, of same, for
                     Ł 20 for 50 acres part of 200 acres granted 5 May
1786, in Pendleton Co., 96 Dist. on S. side of Saluda. Recorded Bk. IIII
p. 412. Signed: Moses Swillivant, Millinder (+) Swillivant.
Wit: Thos. Townes, Blackmon Ligon, Hewlet Sullivent. Thomas Townes made
oath to Wm. Edmondson, J.P., 16 Sep. 1793.
Rec: 25 Sep. 1793.

Pages 186-187   8 Dec. 1788. Sutton Green, of Abbeville Co. to Joseph Dunn, of same, for Ł 85 for 242 acres in 96
                     Dist. on fork of Camp Creek, branch of the Saluda
River, granted to Sutton Green, 7 May 1787, bd. on NE by Wm. Lewis, and
vacant lands.
Wit: Gideon Clark, Nathl. Clark.
   "Be it remembered, that on the day and date mentioned, that livery and siezen(?) was entered into that the sd. Sutton Green
gave the sd. Joseph Dunn a peaceable and quiet possession according to
the due form of law, that is by breaking a twig and pulling up a branch
of turf and delivering it to the sd. Jos. Dunn in presence of us, Gideon
Clark, Nathl. Clark. 8 Dec. 1788."
Gideon Clark made oath to Gabriel Moffett, J.P. 2 Nov. 1793.
Rec: 25 Sep. 1793.

Pages 187-189   6 Feb. 1792. Andrew Pickens, Robert Anderson and
                     Benjamin Cleveland, Judges of the Co. of Pendleton
                     to Thomas Wadsworth, William Turpin and William Steele
the Judges acting as Trustees for county for Ł 7. 15 sh., for 1/2 acre
tract being moiety of Lot #2, one of 6 lots, by Court order, 12 Nov.1790,
were surveyed and staked near spot allotted for public buildings, the
other side of Lot 2, property of John Miller, Clerk of County, and directly opposite the house now occupied by Blake Mauldin, on Lot #1.
Signed: John Miller, Clk. of Co.
Wit: Wm. McGuffin, Henry Sims. Wm. McGuffin made oath to John Miller,
J.P., 19 Jun. 1793.
Rec: 25 Sep. 1793.

Pages 189-191   18 Jun. 1792. Andrew Pickens, Robert Anderson and
                     Benj. Cleveland, Esq., Judges, to William Steele,
                     for 7.15 for lot of 1/2 ac. being moiety of Lot #2
belonging to William Shaw on south, on north by part of Lot #2 belonging
to Wadsworth, Turpin and Steele, directly opposite Lot #1, belonging to
John Grissam. Signed: John Miller, Clerk.
Wit: Wm. McGuffin, Henry Sims.
Wm. McGuffin made oath to John Miller, J.P., 19 Jun. 1793.
Rec: 25 Sep. 1793.

Pages 191-192   10 Nov. 1792. William Jewell, of Washington Dist., Pendleton Co. to John Gilliland, of same, for Ł60 stg. for 200 acres on Brushy Creek, South side of Saluda River, granted Jewell, 5 Jan. 1789.
Wit: William McKamey, John Armstrong, Ann (her mark) Armstrong. Wm. McKamey made oath to Wm. Edmondson, J.P., 1 Feb. 1793.
Rec: 23 Sep. 1793.

Pages 192-193   25 May 1793. James Gillison, of 96 Dist. to Elias Hollingsworth, for Ł 12 stg. for 50 acres on branch of 23 Mile Creek, bd. by Wm. Turpin, land granted to one Martin, Hugh Rogers, Thomas Wadsworth, then granted to Samuel Gillison, son and minor of James Gillison, by Moultrie, 18 Oct. 1785. Recorded Bk. IIII, p. 681. Signed: James (IG) Gillison. Wit: Wm. Steele, Samuel Jones. Wm. Steele made oath to John Miller, J.P., 16 Sep. 1793.
Rec: 23 Sep. 1793.

Pages 193-194   23 Jan. 1793. Isaac Alexander and Margaret, his wife, of Kershaw Co., S. C., to Thomas Garner, of Pendleton Co. for Ł 100 for 250 acres surveyed by Bennet Crafton, D.S., 18 Jul. 1784, on Toney's Creek, waters of Saluda River, adj. to John Burdine. Signed: I. Alexander, Margaret Alexander. Wit: Nat. Alexander, Elias Alexander...Lancaster Co., S.C., Elias Alexander made oath to Hugh White, J.L.C., 6 Feb. 1793.
Rec: 25 Sep. 1793.

Pages 194-195   5 Apr. 1791. Thomas Shirley and Mary, his wife, of Abbeville Co., planter, to Bennet Combs, of Pendleton Co., planter, for Ł 80 stg. for 640 acres in 96 Dist., on 18 Mile Creek, on the old trading road to Keowee, granted to Shirley, 21 Jan. 1785. Signed: Thomas Shirley, Mary (X) Shirley.... Abbeville Co; Richard Shirley made oath to Adam Crain Jones, 23 Jul.1791.
Rec: 25 Sep. 1793.

Pages 195-197   22 Aug. 1793. Bennet Combs and Doratha, his wife, to Thomas Garvin, for Ł 60 stg. for 320 acres on branches of 18 Mile Creek, on old trading road to Keowee, surveyed by Purvis for Thos. Shirley, 3 Jun. 1785. Signed: Bennet Combs and Doratha (her mark) Combs.
Wit: Benjamin Barton, John Holland, Thomas Anderson. Benjamin Barton made oath to Bayley Anderson, J.P., 22 Aug. 1793.
Rec: 25 Sep. 1793.

Page 197   5 Feb. 1793. Joseph Jenkins, of Pendleton Co. to Reuben Pyles of Laurens Co., S. C., for Ł 100 stg. for 160 acres on Keowee River, 23 Mile Creek, adj. to Daniel Ship and land lately owned by Gabriel Hardin, now belonging to John Ward, granted to Jenkins, 4 Dec. 1786.
Wit: Blake Mauldin, J. Whitner. (no oath)
Rec: 25 Sep. 1793.

Pages 198-199   11 May 1793. Solomon King, to Francis King for Ł 15 stg. for 100 acres granted to Solomon King, 5 Jun. 1786. Recorded Bk. LLLL, p. 217, in 96 Dist. on S. side of Seneca River. Signed: Solomon (X) King.
Wit: John King, James Ditto. James Ditto made oath to John Miller, J.P. 16 Sep. 1793.
Rec: 25 Sep. 1793.

Page 199   I, Solomon King sold to Francis King a negro man named James and a negro woman, named Luce, cattle, household furniture for 7 thousand wt. tobacco to be delivered before 25 Nov. 1798. Date: 11 May 1793.
Wit: J. Ditto, Jno. Grindle. James Ditto made oath to John Miller, J.P. 11 Sep. 1793.
Rec: 25 Sep. 1793.

Pages 199-200   11 May 1793. Fields Pewitt to Francis King for Ł20 stg. for 127 acres in 96 Dist. on branch of Connoross, a branch of Keowee River, bd. on SW by John

(pages 199-200 cont'd):
Parsons(?), on SE by Wilson Hollan, on N by James Ingram, granted to Fields(sic), 2 Jul. 1787. Signed: Fields (+) Pe+itt.
Wit: Adam Morris, Jno. McCollum. Adam Morris made oath to John Miller, J.P., 16 Sep. 1793.
Rec: 25 Sep. 1793.

Pages 200-201   I, William Roberts for divers good causes and valuable consideration to my son, John Roberts, give all my goods, chattels, household stuff, lands, negros under direction of Judges of Pendleton Co. Date: 12 Oct. 1793. Signed: William (his mark) Roberts.
Wit: Jane Miller, John Miller, Jr. Jane Miller made oath to John Miller. Jr.. J.P., 12 Oct. 1793.
Rec: 25 Sep. 1793.

Page 201   Camden Dist.. S.C....Whereas, it appears some reports has prevailed in this part of the world respecting Capt. Lewis Martin being married to the subscriber, as her lawful husband, but I do hereby publicly publish and declare that I have neither the right or Claim in any wise to sd. Martin as my husband, nor never had. Date: 16 Jun. 1784. Signed: Rachel (X) Murdock.
Wit: Edward Lacey, Jno. Wallace.
Rec: 25 Sep. 1793.

Pages 202-203   21 Aug. 1793. George Ringland, of Charleston, S.C. to Hon. William Moultrie, of Charleston, a bond of obligation for Ł 1000 stg. with payment of Ł 550 with interest to be paid on or before 21 Aug. 1797...indenture for Ł 550 for 1100 acres on a town known as Cane Creek Town, near Keowee River, granted 16 Jul. 1784.
Wit: Jacob Drayton, William Drayton. Jacob Drayton made oath to John Sandford Dart, J.P.Q.U., 21 Aug. 1793.
Rec: 11 Nov. 1793.

Page 203   6 Apr. 1790. Benjamin Denton, of Greenville Co., N. C. to Joseph Martin of Henry Co., Va. for 40 guineas, for 200 acres on Tugaloo River about 2 miles above Col. Benjamin Cleveland, adj. to Robert Looney and others, same tract Reuben Denton, dec'd. of S. C. granted Reuben Denton as a soldier, Benjamin Denton, his brother, heir at law. Signed: Benjamin (+) Denton.
Wit: Henry Potter, John Craft, William Martin...State of North Carolina, William Martin made oath to Samuel Spencer, J.S.C.L.C., 8 Apr. 1790.
Rec: 13 Nov. 1793.

Pages 203-204   3 Jun. 1793. John Wilson, Esq., Collector of State Tax for Pendleton Co., to John Miller, Jr., Deputy Clerk of the county for Ł1, 4 sh. for term of 7 yrs. expiring 3 Jun. 1800, for 640 acres in Washington Dist., on 18 Mile Crk. for default of a payment of public taxes, granted John Miller, 21 Jan. 1785, by Benjamin Guerrard, Gov. Recorded Bk. CCCC, p. 324.
Wit: Crosby Ws. Miller, Job Smith. Crosby Ws. Miller made oath to John Miller, Jr., J.P., 18 Sep. 1793.
Rec: 13 Nov.1793.

Pages 204-205   7 Aug. 1793. Joseph Irwin, of Lincoln Co., N.C. to Wm. Hamilton, of Pendleton Co. for Ł 30 stg. for 200 acres in Washington Dist. on 23 Mile Creek, waters of Savannah River, part of tract granted Irwin, 4 Dec. 1786, adj. John Ewing Calhoun and creek. Signed: Joseph (I) Irwin.
Wit: Robert Schrimster, William Hamilton, James Hamilton. James Hamilton made oath to John Wilson, J.P., 2 Nov. 1793.
Rec: 13 Nov. 1793.

Page 205   14 Jan. 1793. Elijah Oliver, for divers goods to Robert Looney full power and authority to act in my name and to be my lawful attorney.
Wit: Thomas Farrar, who made oath to John Miller, Jr., C.P.C., 13 Nov. 1793.
Rec: 13 Nov. 1793.

Pages 205-206   7 Aug. 1793. David Bragg to Joshua Dodson, for ₤70 stg. for 100 acres on Keowee River and Mile Creek, part of 800 acres granted Samuel Lofton, Jr., 4 May 1789, conveyed by Lofton to Duncan Camron, from Camron to David Thornton, from Thornton to David Bragg.
Wit: Thomas Creel, Isaac Dodson, Wm. Patterson. Isaac Dodson made oath to John Miller, C.P.C., 21 Dec. 1793.
Rec: 21 Dec. 1793.

Page 206   I, George Tucker, of Pendleton Co. to Elijah Tucker, at present of Halifax Co., Va., sell horses and cattle, also plantation tools, furniture for ₤ 70.
Date: 17 Nov. 1793.
Wit: Albert Robins, Hannah (+) Cobbin. Albert Robbins made oath to J. Miller, 17 Nov. 1793.
Rec: 21 Dec. 1793.

Page 207   24 May 1793. Andrew Warnock, of Pendleton Co., Washington Dist., planter, to John Warnock, of same, for ₤ 10 stg. for 331 acres granted Hugh Warnock, 3 Mar. 1786, on Broadaway, waters of Savannah River, bd. NE by James Daugherty, SE by Hugh Warnock, and vacant lands.
Wit: Joseph Warnock, Michael Warnock, Samuel Warnock. Samuel Warnock made oath to ___, 26 May 1793.
Rec: 21 Dec. 1793.

Pages 207-208   24 May 1793. Andrew Warnock, planter, to Joseph Warnock, for ₤ 10 stg. for 300 acres surveyed for Hugh Warnock on waters of Rocky River, 6 Apr. 1785. Recorded Bk. HHHH, p. 408.
Wit: John Warnock, Michael Warnock, Samuel Warnock. Samuel Warnock made oath to John Wilson, J.P., 8 May 1793.
Rec: 21 Dec. 1793.

Pages 208-209   22 Nov. 1792. Joseph Culton to John Brice for ₤ 100 stg. for 200 acres on Beaver Creek, branch of Rocky River, waters of Savannah, granted Joseph Culton, 21 Jan. 1785.
Wit: Robert Stevenson, Wm. Hillhouse, Joseph Alexander. Plat included. Land bd. by James Thompson, Eliab Moore. Joseph Alexander made oath to Elijah Browne, J.P., 10 Jan. 1793.
Rec: 15 Jan. 1793.

Pages 209-210   29 Apr. 1793. William Reighly, of Abbeville Co., to Ezekiel Pickens, of Charleston, for ₤ 40 for 66 acr's granted 2 Oct. 1786, in Washington Dist. on S. side of Keowee River.
Wit: Samuel Watt, Charles T. Colcock. Samuel Watt made oath to Wm. Nevill, J.P., 16 Nov. 1793.
Rec: 16 Jan. 1794.

Page 210   I, Henry Cobb appoint my son, Jesse Cobb my lawful attorney to make title to 628 acres in Caswell Co. (no state listed), on Stony Fork of Moore's Creek.
Date: 16 Dec. 1793. Signed: Henry (H) Cobb.
Wit: John Oldham, Otheneil Rice, Wm. Grayham...The power was acknowledged before me, Wm. Halbert, J.P., 24 Jan. 1794.

Page 211   14 Feb. 1790. Isaac Titsworth, of Pendleton Co., a planter, to John Lowry, of Abbeville Co., planter, for ₤ 50 stg. for 200 acres in 96 Dist. on 18 Mile Creek, waters of Keowee River, bd. NE by David Bragg, SW by John Miller, granted Titsworth, 21 Jan. 1785. Signed: Isaac (his mark) Titsworth.
Wit: John Willson, Saml. Lofton. (Oath date and name blank).
Rec: 24 Jan. 1794.

Pages 211-212   25 Jan. 1793. Peter Handly to John Lowry for ₤ 60 stg. for 200 acres on W side of 23 Mile Creek, the waters of Keowee River, granted Jesse Lanton, 2 Jul. 1787. Signed: Peter (PH) Handly. (cont'd. next page)

(pages 211-212 cont'd):

Wit: Wm. Lofton, Jas. Ferris, Jas. Brown. Wm. Lofton made oath to Robert Anderson, J.P., 25 Jan. 1793.
Rec: 24 Jan. 1794.

Pages 212-213   17 Nov. 1793. William Huggins of 96 Dist. to Thomas Carey, for Ł 50 stg. for 200 acres on both sides of 18 Mile Creek, waters of Keowee River, bd. SE by John Lewis Gervais, granted 2 Oct. 1786. Signed: Wm. Huggins, Martha Huggins.
Wit: Robert Glen, Thomas Burns. Robert Glen made oath to John Miller, Jr., C.P.C., 7 Dec. 1793.
Rec: 24 Jan. 1794.

Pages 213-215   (dates blank) 1793. Avis Tourtellot, of Pendleton Co., seamstress, to William Thayer and James Thayer, of Charleston, merchants, for 100.13.9., 300 acres on 18 Mile Creek, waters of Savannah River, granted John Hunter, Esq., 15 Oct. 1784, also 170 acres granted Hunter, 5 Feb. 1787.
Wit: Wm. Edmondson, W. Thompson. William Edmondson made oath to John Willson, J.P., 3 Mar. 1794.
Rec: 5 Mar. 1794.

Page 216   24 Jan. 1794. Joseph Whitner to Christopher Wagner for Ł 100 stg. for 427 acres granted Whitner, 17 May 1787, by Thomas Pinckney, Esq., Gov. "for the time being", W. of old boundary line on Camp Creek, waters of Saluda River.
Wit: Samuel Earle, J. B. Earle. Samuel Earle made oath 24 Jan. 1794.
Rec: 24 Jan. 1794.

Pages 216-217   24 Jan. 1794. Caleb Conaway and Mary, his wife, to Thomas Matterson for Ł 50 stg. for 110 acres on the branch of Broadmouth Creek, waters of Saluda River, granted Francis Bremar and James Martin, 9 Mar. 1786. Recorded Bk. JJJJ, p. 384, conveyed from Bremar and Martin to Caleb Conaway. Signed: Caleb Conaway, Mary (+) Conaway.
Wit: James Tate, Jr. Edw. F. McClure, John Tippen. John Tippen made oath to E. Browne, J. P., 24 Jan. 1794.
Rec: 24 Jan. 1794.

Pages 217-218   24 Jan. 1794. Caleb Conaway to Reuben Cox for Ł 50 stg. for 100 acres on branches of Broadmouth Creek, waters of Saluda River, part of 640 acres granted Francis Bremar and James Martin, 9 Mar. 1786. Recorded Bk. JJJJ, p. 384.
Wit: Edward McClure, James Tate, Jr.,John Tippens. John Tippens made oath to E. Browne, J.P., 24 Jan. 1794.
Rec: 24 Jan. 1794.

Pages 218-220   22 Jan. 1794. Caleb Conaway to Robert Kay, Sr., for Ł 100 stg. for 200 acres on Broadmouth Creek of the Saluda River granted John Hallum, 15 Oct. 1784, by Benjamin Guerrard. Recorded Bk. AAAA, p. 185, also a tract of 430 acres part of 640 acres granted Francis Bremar and James Martin, 3 Apr. 1786, by Wm. Moultrie, Gov. Recorded Bk. JJJJ, p. 384. Signed: Caleb Conaway, Mary (+) Conaway.
Wit: Robert Elgin, Reubin (R) Cox, Robert Kay. Robert Kay made oath to E. Browne, J. P., 24 Jan. 1794.
Rec: 24 Jan. 1794.

Page 220   3 Jan. 1792. William Armstrong, of 96 Dist. to John Armstrong, of Abbeville Co. for Ł 40 stg. for 300 acres on Corner Creek, waters of Savannah River in Abbeville Co., granted Wm. Armstrong (no date). Signed: Will'm (X) Armstrong.
Wit: Benjamin Shambly, Mathew (X) Armstrong. Benjamin Shambly made an oath to Wm. Nevill, J. P., 3 Jan. 1794.
Rec: 24 Jan. 1794.

Page 221   21 Feb. 1792. John Hallum of Washington Dist., to
                     John Armstrong of same, for Ł 60 stg., for 140 acres
                     granted Hallum, 5 Jun. 1786, by Wm. Moultrie, in
Washington Dist. on George's Creek, waters of Saluda River. Signed:
John Hallum, Ann Hallum.
Wit: Charles Huse, Andrew Huse. Sworn before Wm. Edmondson, J. P., 19
July 1792.
Rec: 24 Jan. 1794.

Pages 221-222   9 Mar. 1792. Alex'r. Loggan, of Washington Dist. to
                     John Armstrong, for Ł 27 for 200 acres in Washington
                     Dist. on N. branches of George's Creek, waters of
Saluda River, granted Alexander Loggan, 3 Apr. 1786.
Wit: Andrew Huse, Genevary Tomlin(?), David Loggan. Sworn before Wm.
Edmondson, J. P., 19 Jul 1792.
Rec: 24 Jan. 1794.

Pages 222-223   24 Jan. 1793. James Milwee to John Findley for Ł 40
                     for 235 acres part of a tract granted Millwee, by
                     Wm. Moultrie, 17 Nov. 1788, on N side of Saluda Riv-
er. Wit: Peter Acker, Robert Parker, Jessey (X) Gray. Jesse Gray
made oath to Wm. Halbert, J. P., 25 Jan. 1794.
Rec: 24 Jan. 1794.

Page 223   (blank), 1793. Elias Roberts to Andrew Willson for
                     Ł 75 stg. for 100 acres on both sides of George's
                     Creek, S. side of Saluda River, adj. Robert Easley.
Wit: John Blassingame, Thomas Blasingame, Robert Easley. Robert Easley
made oath to Wm. Edmondson, J.P., 3 Jan. 1794.
Rec: 24 Jan. 1794.

Page 224   29 Jan. 1791. Robert Pickens to Kezekiah Rice for
                     Ł 100 stg. for 170 acres, part of tract granted to
                     James Compton, 5 Jun. 1786, by Wm. Moultrie. Record-
ed Bk. LLLL, p. 350, in 96 Dist. on Broadaway Creek and Pea Creek, the
branches of Rocky River, adj. George Oldham.
Wit: John Pepper, Richard Oldham. John Pepper made oath to John Wilson,
J.P., 9 Jan. 1791.
Rec: 24 Jan. 1794.

Pages 224-225   21 Nov. 1793. Robert Waugh to John Adair, merchant,
                     for Ł 100 specie, for 556 acres on Keowee River, bd.
                     by Capt. Littel, Capt. Buchanan, Capt. McCaleb, Sam-
uel Robinson and Elijah Stenson. Signed: Robert Waugh, Sarah Waugh.
Wit: Edw. Adair, John Growly, John Curry. Edward Adair made oath to
John Wilson, J. P., 13 Jan. 1794.
Rec: 24 Jan. 1794.

Pages 225-226   31 Jan. 1793. George Salmon, of Greenville Co.,S.C.
                     to Lewis Wimberly, of Pendleton Co. for Ł 65 stg.,
                     for 300 acres, part of tract granted Salmon, 4 Jun.
1787, on both sides of S. fork of 12 Mile River, bd. by Duncan Camron
and Earle.
Wit: Sarah Anderson, Wiat Anderson. Wiat Anderson made oath to Bayley
Anderson, J. P., 31 Jan. 1793.
Rec: 24 Jan. 1794.

Page 226   27 Mar. 1793. Peter Perkins, of Pittsylvania Co.,
                     Va. to Elisha Dyer. of Pendleton Co., for 30 shill-
                     ings. Va. money, for 206 acres on both sides of Big
Estotoy. Wit: Richd. Farrar, James Walker. James Walker made oath to
Bayley Anderson, J. P., 25 Oct. 1793.
Rec: 24 Jan. 1794.

Page 227   8 Dec. 1792. Zephaniah Roberts of Washington Dist.,
                     S. C. to Timothy Toney, Jr., of Greenville Co., S.C.
                     for Ł 100 for 150 acres granted Roberts, 1 Aug. 1785
by Wm. Moultrie, on S. side of Saluda River, on George's Creek, about 1½
miles from Richd. Parrisses waggon ford. Recorded Bk. EEEE, p. 163.
Wit: Millington (+) Easley made oath to Wm. Edmondson, J. P., 1 Jan.

(p. 227 cont'd):   ...1794. Rec: 24 Jan. 1794.

Pages 227-228 3 Sep. 1792. William Stevenson to Jacob Brazelton for Ł 80 stg. for 200 acres in Washington Dist., on E. side of Keowee River, granted Stevenson, 4 Dec. 1786, by Wm. Moultrie, bd. by Thos. Roach. Signed: William Stenson.
Wit: Jno. Vernor, Jr., James Hamilton. John Vernor made oath to Wm. Nevill, J.P. 24 Jan. 1794.
Rec: 24 Jan. 1793.

Pages 228-229 (blank), 1793. Elias Roberts to Robert Easley, for Ł 75 stg. for 100 acres on S. side of Saluda River, bd. by Robert Easley, Toney, and Andrew Wilson. (n.b. no given name for Toney). Surveyed for David Logan, 24 May 1785.
Wit: John Blasingame, Andrew (A) Wilson, Thomas Blasingame. Andrew Wilson made oath to Wm. Edmondson, J. P., 3 Jan. 1794.
Rec: 24 Jan. 1794.

Pages 229-230 8 Feb. 1793. Thomas Martin, of Charleston, merchant, to Jesse Clements, of Pendleton Co., planter, for Ł 100 for 640 acres on 12 Mile River, bd. NE by Col. Purvis, survey certified by Ephariam Mitchell, 4 Jun. 1784, David Hopkins, D.S.
Wit: Jona. Davis, Charles Clements. Charles Clements made oath to Wm. Halbert, J.P., 13 Jan. 1794.
Rec: 24 Jan. 1794.

Pages 231-232 28 Jul. 1786. Thomas Entrikin, of Lawrence Co., S.C. yeoman, to William Warren, of Newberry Co., S.C. for Ł 40 stg. for 200 acres in Abbeville Co. on branches of Big Beaver Dam on N. side of Savannah River, granted 3 Apr. 1786.
Wit: Josiah East, John Entrikin, Jno. Dalrumple. John Dalrumple made oath to Jno. B. Earle, J.P., of Pendleton Co., 4 Jan. 1794.
Rec: 25 Jan. 1794.

Pages 233-234 26 Aug. 1792. Andrew Pickens, Jr., yeoman, and Margaret, his wife, to William Warren, planter, for Ł50 stg., for 200 acres on both sides of 12 Mile River.
Signed: Andw. Pickens, Margaret (her mark) Pickens.
Wit: William Drennin, John Pickens. (oath blank).
Rec: 25 Jan. 1794.

Pages 234-235 Washington Dist. 24 Nov. 1793. John Fowler and Esther, his wife, to Thomas Millford, for Ł 25 stg. for 174 acres on Wilson's Creek, waters of Rocky River, granted Fowler, 26 Dec. 1792 by Wm. Moultrie, bd. NW by John McCollough, SW by James Pettigrew, SE by John Rutledge. Signed: John Fowler, Esther (+) Fowler.
Wit: Wm. M. Cavindish, William Bladden, Joel Callaham. William Bladden made oath to E. Browne, J.P., 24 Jan. 1794.
Rec: 25 Jan. 1794.

Pages 235-236 18 Jan. 1794. Mary Beard and William Beard, her son, of 96 Dist., to William Bladden of Washington Dist., for Ł 1000 stg. for 100 acres on Wilson's Creek, a branch of Rocky River, granted Mary Beard, 5 Jan. 1786 by Wm. Moultrie.
Signed: Mary (M) Beard, Wm. Beard.
Wit: John Glover, William Pitts. William Pitts made oath to E. Browne, J.P., 24 Jan. 1794.
Rec: 25 Jan. 1794.

Page 236 1 Jun. 1793. James Gillison to William Prichard for Ł 20 stg. for 100 acres, part of a tract granted to Gillison by Thomas Pinckney, 3 Dec. 1787. Recorded Bk. VVVV, p. 215. Bd. by Thomas Hayes on N. and James Garner on N., on NE by Widow Hanks. Signed: James(IC) Gillison.
Wit: Stephen Willis, Luke Hanks. Stephen Willis made oath to Wm. Nevill, J. P., 25 Jan. 1794.
Rec: 25 Jan. 1794.

Pages 236-237   21 Jan. 1794. John Portman to George Portman, for
                      Ł 40 for 145 acres on branches of Connoross Creek,
                      waters of Keowee River, surveyed for John Portman,
where he lives now. Signed: John (P) Portman.
Wit: John C. Kilpatrick, Mordica (X) Fuller. John C. Kilpatrick made
oath to Wm. Nevill, J.P., 25 Jan. 1794.
Rec: 25 Jun. 1794.

Pages 237-238   I, John Portman, for Ł 25 stg. sell to Rowland Burks,
                      cattle, household furniture. Date: 1 Jan. 1794.
                      Signed: John Portman.
Wit: John C. Kilpatrick, Mordica (X) Fuller. John C. Kilpatrick made
oath to Wm. Nevill, J.P., 25 Jan. 1794.
Rec: 25 Jan. 1794.

Page 238   I, Roland Burks, for Ł 20 stg. sell to George Port-
                      man, horses, cattle, household furniture. Date: 1
                      Jan. 1794.
Wit: Jno. C. Kilpatrick, Mordica Fuller. Jno. C. Kilpatrick made oath
to Wm. Nevill, J.P., 25 Jan. 1794.
Rec: 25 Jan. 1794.

Page 238   I, Francis Miller, of Pendleton Co. sell to John Adam
                      Miller, of Greene Co., Ga. (no amount shown), cattle,
                      horses and all the rest of my property that I poss-
ess. Date: 10 Jan. 1793.
Wit: David Dickson, R. C. Royston...Greene Co., Ga., "The foregoing is
a true copy from the records of my office". Date: 13 Jan. 1793. Wm.
Daniel, C.G.C., certify Tho. Houghton is acting J.P. of sd. county.
(no recording date).

Pages 239-240   1 Jan. 1793. Mathew Morgan, yeoman, to Francis Mil-
                      ler, yeoman, for Ł 150 stg. for 130 acres on branch
                      of Big Generostee Creek, waters of Savannah River,
bd. NE by Thomas Moss, granted to Morgan, 7 Nov. 1791, by Charles Pinckney. Recorded Bk. E, no. 5, p. 99.
Wit: Jesse Brown, Alexr. Miller, William (X) Ballard. Jesse Brown made
oath (no. J. P. named; no date).
Rec: 25 Jan. 1794.

Pages 240-241   3 Sep. 1793. Isaac Elledge to Thomas Farrar for Ł60
                      for 350 acres surveyed, 1 Jul. 1789, in Washington
                      Dist. on W. side of Keowee River, bd. SW by John Twit-
ty, N. by John Portman, Sr., granted by Charles Pinckney, 3 Dec. 1792.
Signed: Isaac (X) Elledge.
Wit: Thos. Lofton, Matilda Farrar. Thomas Lofton made oath to Rbt. Max-
well, J.P., 25 Jan. 1794.
Rec: 25 Jan. 1794.

Page 241   18 Jul. 1793. Francis Miller, of Pendleton Co. to
                      John Adam Miller, of Greene Co., Ga. for Ł 200 stg.,
                      for 168 acres on Generostee Creek, part of 336 acres
granted Mathew Morgan, 1791, by Chs. Pinckney. Recorded Bk. E, no. 5,
p. 99. Wit: Jesse Brown, Abner Brown. Jesse Brown made oath to Elijah
Browne, J.P., 28 Jul. ___.
Rec: 25 Jan. 1794.

Page 242   30 Dec. 1793. Francis Miller, of Pendleton Co., to
                      John Adam Miller, "of same place", for 250 lbs. stg.
                      for 160 acres on Generostee, part of 336 acres gran-
ted Mathew Morgan. Wit: Jesse Brown, John Brown, James (X) Moss. Jesse
Brown made oath to John Wilson, J.P., 25 Jan. 1794.
Rec: 25 Jan. 1794.

Pages 242-243   23 Nov. 1793. Isaac Lynch to William McCaleb for
                      118.14.8. for two negro girls, Rose and Minerva.
Signed: Isaac (his mark) Lynch.
Wit: Thos. Creel, Wm. N. McCaleb.
Wm. N. McCaleb made oath to J. Miller, J. P., 26 Nov. 1793.
Rec: 25 Jan. 1794.

Page 243   19 Jan. 1788. Alexander Edens, of 96 Dist., to Geo.
                        Hudson, of the same Dist., for Ł 25, for 147 acres
                        granted 1 Jan. 1787, by Wm. Moultrie, on both sides
of Carrock's Creek, waters of Saluda River. Signed: Alexander (his
mark) Edens, Molley Edens.
Wit: William Blyth, Joseph Harden. Joseph Harden made oath to Gabriel
Moffett, J. P., 24 Aug. 1793.
Rec: 15 Feb. 1793.

Pages 243-244   19 Nov. 1793. William Hamilton to James Hamilton,
                        for Ł 30 stg. for 200 acres in Washington Dist., on
                        23 Mile River, waters of Savannah River, part of a
tract granted to Joseph Ewing, by Wm. Moultrie, 4 Dec. 1786, adj. John
Ewing Calhoun.
Wit: Wm. Vann, John Hamilton. John Hamilton made oath to John Willson,
J. P., 14 Feb. 1794.
Rec: 22 Feb. 1794.

Pages 244-247   11 Apr. 1788. Charles Saxon and Judith, his wife,
                        of Laurens Co., S. C. to Samuel Saxon, their son, of
                        the same county, for Ł 40 stg. for 200 acres on 23
Mile Creek, waters of the Savannah River, in Abbeville Co., granted to
Charles Saxon, 5 Jun. 1786, by Wm. Moultrie. Signed: Charles Saxon, Judith Saxon.
Wit: James Merony, James Yancy. Plat included, bd. N. by Thomas Wadsworth, vacant land on other...Laurens Co., James Yancy made oath to John
Rodgers, J. P., 12 Jun. 1788.
Rec: 6 Mar. 1794.

Page 247   30 Nov. 1793. Samuel Saxon, of Washington Dist., S.
                        C., to Josiah Ship, for Ł 62 stg. for 200 acres in
                        Washington Dist., on 23 Mile River, waters of the
Seneca River, granted to Charles Saxon by States Letter Patent, 5 June
1786, by Wm. Moultrie.
Wit: James Long, David Crawford. James Long made oath to E. Browne, J.
P., 30 Jan. 1794.
Rec: 6 Mar. 1794.

Pages 247-248   10 Sep. 1793. James Houston to Jonah Houston, for
                        Ł 200 stg. for 640 acres on Deep Creek, branch of
                        Seneca River, including fork granted to Houston on
16 Jul. 1785, by Benjamin Guerrard.
Wit: Charles McClure, Thomas Houston. Charles McClure made oath to E.
Browne, J. P., 4 Mar. 1794.
Rec: 7 Mar. 1794.

Pages 248-249   30 Nov. 1792. George Houston, of Abbeville Co., to
                        Jeremiah Starks, of Newberry Co., for Ł 20 stg. for
                        300 acres part of 778 acres in 96 Dist. on branches
of Wilson Creek and Little Generostee, granted Houston, 6 Oct. 1788 by
Thomas Pinckney. Recorded Bk. XXXX, p. 457.
Wit: John McNeel, Phillip Phegans. Phillip Phegans made oath to John
Baylis Earle. J. P., 12 Mar. 1794.
Rec: 12 Mar. 1794.

Page 249   14 Apr. 1792. John Caldwell, of Abbeville Co., to
                        Phillip Phegans, of Pendleton Co., for Ł 20 stg. for
                        300 acres in 96 Dist. on Wilson's Creek, branch of
Great Rocky River, granted to Caldwell, 15 Oct. 1784, by Benj. Guerrard.
Recorded Bk. ZZZZ, p. 191.
Wit: Geo. Tillman. Wm. Bladen. William Bladden made oath to Elijah
Browne, J. P., (no date).
Rec: 12 Mar. 1794.

Page 250   14 Apr. 1792. John Caldwell, and Elizabeth, his wife
                        of Abbeville Co., to Phillip Phegans of Pendleton Co.
                        for Ł 20 stg. for 792 acres in 96 Dist. on Wilson's
Creek, branch of Great Rocky Creek, granted to Caldwell, 24 Apr. 1789,
by Chas. Pinckney. Recorded Bk. ZZZZ, p. 321. Signed: John Caldwell,

(page 250 cont'd): Elizabeth Caldwell. Wit: George Tillman, Wm. Bladon. William Bladen made oath to Elijah Browne, J. P., 17 May 1793.
Rec: 12 Mar. 1794.

Pages 250-251   14 Feb. 1793. Francis Whelchel to James Roberts for ₤ 30 for 244 acres granted to Abuel Meed, 4 Jan. 1790, by Charles Pinckney, on both sides of Carpenter's Creek, branch of the Saluda River. Signed: Francis (F) Whelchel.
Wit: James Culton, Dennis (D) Barnes, William (X) Roberts, James (+) Roberts. James Culton made oath to Gabriel Moffett, J. P., 22 Jan. 1794.
Rec: 14 Mar. 1794.

Pages 251-252   22 Nov. 1792. John Patterson, planter, to Solomon Redman West, for ₤ 50 stg., for 175 acres, part of 200 acrgs on Golden's Creek, waters of Keowee River, granted to William Hallum, 5 Jun. 1786, by Wm. Moultrie. Recorded Bk. LLLL, p. 144, bd. on NW by Richard Golding.
Wit: Abraham Campbell, Little Berry (X) Roch, David (his mark) Ward. Little Berry Roch made oath to J. B. Earle, C.P.C., 24 Mar. 1794.
Rec: 24 Mar. 1794.

Pages 252-253   23 Nov. 1792. John Patterson, planter, to Little Berry Roach, for ₤ 50 stg. for 200 acres, part of 340 acres on Golding's Creek, waters of Keowee River, granted to Patterson, 7 Jul. 1788, by Thos. Pinckney. Recorded Bk. XXXX, p. 209, bd. on NW by Francis Fulcher.
Wit: J. H. Willoughby Pugh, Abraham Campbell, Solomon Redmon (his mark) West. Solomon Redmon West made oath to John Baylis Earle, C. P. C., 24 ___, 1794.
Rec: 24 Mar. 1794.

Page 253   I do hereby acknowledge that I approve of the bargain and sale that John Irwin made with William McCaleb in selling my bounty land of 200 acres on the Cane Creek, and I am fully satisfied and paid by John Irwin for the land. Date: 29 Oct. 1792. Signed: William (+) Farmer.
Wit: John Irwin, Jr. John Irwin, Jr. made oath to Samuel Watt, J. P., 28 Mar. 1793.
Rec: 1 Apr. 1794.

Page 253   4 Nov. 1793. John Pickens to Edward Ware(Were) for ₤ 50 stg. for 100 acres on branch of Great Rocky Crk. bd. on NE by William Thompson, on SW by Samuel Houston, on SE by Garner Green, granted to Pickens by Wm. Moultrie. Recorded Bk. E, no. 5, p. 524.
Wit: Arthur Durley, Andw. Pickens. Arthur Durley made oath to Wm. Neville, J. P., 5 Apr. 1794.
Rec: 9 Apr. 1794.

Page 254   I, Fields Puet, planter, for love and good will to my loving son, Fields Puet, Jr., give all my goods and chattels now being on his land and my dwelling house known as Cane Creek, cattle, 300 acres, in Franklin Co., Georgia, on Garret's River, also furniture in my dwelling house. Date: 1 Apr. 1794. Signed: Fields (X) Puet.
Wit: Alexr. Thomas, William Griffen. William Griffen made oath to Wm. Nevill, J. P., 21 Apr. 1794.
Rec: 21 Apr. 1794.

Pages 254-255   20 Aug. 1793. John Huggins to John Adair for ₤ 100 stg. for 350 acres in Washington Dist., on North & South of 12 Mile River.
Wit: James Walters, Robt. Waugh, John Gurley. Robt. Waugh made oath to Joseph Reed, J. P., 11 Apr. 1794.
Rec: 21 Apr. 1794.

Pages 255-256   2 Feb. 1790. John Johnson to Ebednego Green for ₤50 stg. for 339 acres in 96 Dist., on Hurricane Creek, (cont'd next page)

Pages 255-256 (cont'd):
Saluda River, granted to John Johnson by Wm. Moultrie on 4 Dec. 1786.
Wit: Micaiah Clark, John (B) Brown. John Brown made oath to Wm. Halbert J. P., 26 Mar. 1790.
Rec: 21 Apr. 1796.

Pages 256-257   3 Dec. 1793. Jesse Brown to Alexander McMillen for ₤ 120 stg. for 166 acres, part of 456 acres, granted to John Lauderdale, 3 Dec. 1787, conveyed to Jesse Brown, on Big Generostee.
Wit: Francis Miller, Jean (+) Miller, William (X) Ballard. Francis Miller made oath to E. Browne, J. P., 8 Mar. 1794.
Rec: 21 Apr. 1794.

Page 257   31 Mar. 1791. John Lauderdale to Jesse Brown for ₤ 140 stg. for 200 acres, part of a tract of 456 ac. granted to Lauderdale in 1787, on Big Generostee.
Wit: Vann Walker, Alexr. McMillen, Samuel Walker. Alexr. McMillen made oath to Elijah Browne, J. P., 6 Jul. 1793.
Rec: 21 Apr. 1794.

Pages 258-259   16 Nov. 1793. Dan'l. McCollum, blacksmith, to Dan'l. Ledbetter, planter, for ₤ 150 stg. for 300 acres, a part of a tract of 400 acres on S. side of Big Generostee, branch of Savannah River, granted to McCollum, 4 Jun. 1787.
Wit: Elijah Dyer, William Dyer, Stephen Strange. Stephen Strange made oath to Wm. Nevill, J. P., 23 Apr. 1794.
Rec: 12 May 1794.

Pages 259-260   4 Dec. 1793. John McKinsey, planter, to David Watkins, planter, for ₤ 100 stg., for 320 acres, part of 640 acres granted William Murphey, 16 Jul. 1784, purchased by Peter Conway, 4 Oct. 1788, then conveyed to Edwin Conway, 24 Feb. 1792, from Edwin Conway to John McKinsey, 10 Dec. 1793, on 23 Mile Creek, waters of the Savannah River. Bd. on NE by John Martin, on NW by Andrew Warnock, on SW by John Robinson.
Wit: Michael Warnock, Thomas Black. Thomas Black made oath to John Wilson, J. P., 10 Mar. 1794.
Rec: 17 May 1794.

Page 261   31 Dec. 1793. John McKinsey to Thomas Black, for ₤ 110 stg. for 320 acres, half of a tract of 640 ac. on 23 Mile Creek, waters of Savannah River, Washington Dist., granted to William Murphey by Benj. Guerrard, 15 Jul. 1784.
Wit: Michael Warnock, Peter Black. Peter Black made oath to John Wilson, J. P., 10 Mar. 1794.
Rec: 17 May 1794.

Pages 261-262   13 Mar. 1794. Samuel Jackson to Sarah Sinkler, for ₤ 30 stg. for 100 acres on branches of S. fork of 12 Mile River.
Wit: Joseph Duncan, John Evans. Joseph Duncan made oath to Bayley Anderson, J. P., 13 Mar. 1794.
Rec: 17 May 1794.

Pages 262-263   16 Dec. 1793. John Harris, Esq., Sheriff of Pendleton Co., to William McCaleb...Jun. term 1793. William McCaleb received judgement for 15.19.16 against John Woodside for 400 acres on branches of 18 Mile Creek, waters of Keowee River, bd. by Wm. Swift; Action of Debt in Court of Pendleton against Sam'l. Lofton and Jane Woodside, administrators of the estate of John Woodside, dec'd. Signed: John Harris, S. P. C.
Wit: Joab Lawrence, David McCaleb. David McCaleb made oath to John B. Earle, Esq., 1 May 1794.
Plat of land included...bd. by Wm. Swift.
Rec: 24 May 1794.

Pages 263-266   (dates blank). William McCaleb of Pendleton Co. to (cont'd on next page)

(pages 263-266 cont'd)
Henry William Desausure of Charleston, for ₺ 40 for 400 acres on 18 Mile Creek, of 12 Mile River, waters of the Keowee River, bd. by Wm. Swift, granted to John Woodside.
Wit: Tim Ford, John Kelsell. T. Ford made oath to James Nicholson, J. P., of Charleston Dist., 10 Jan. 1794.
Rec: 10 Jan. 1794.

Page 266   10 Mar. 1794. Jesse Groutcher, of King William Co., Va., to Robert Box, of South Carolina, for ₺ 260 stg. for 200 acres in 96 Dist. on Noyewee Creek and Tugaloo River, near Tugaloo Old Town, bd. on S. by Robert Miscampbell, and vacant lands, granted 21 Jan. 1785. Signed: Jesse Grouter.
Wit: Edward Box, Holley Camp. Edward Box made oath to John Wilson, J. P., 12 Mar. 1794.
Rec: 24 May 1794.

Page 267   28 Feb. 1794. Thomas Lofton, planter, to Hugh Dobbs, for ₺ 70 stg. for 350 acres, part of 2 tracts granted Lofton on NW side of 5 Mile Branch, waters of the Seneca River, bd. by Sam'l. Lofton, David Kelton, William Osborn and by Swift.
Wit: Christopher Strong, Eliz'th. (+) Dunn, John G. Lofton. Christopher Strong made oath to John B. Earle, J. P., 22 May 1794.
Rec: 20 May 1794.

Pages 267-268   Washington Dist., 15 May 1794. Morgan Osborn, planter, to Patrick Finney, for ₺ 20 stg. for 110 acres on 5 Mile Branch of 18 Mile Creek, waters of Seneca River, bd. by Morgan Osborn, Fredrick Glover, Wm. Swift, Hugh Dobbs, a grant of 5 Jun. 1786 by Wm. Moultrie.
Wit: Thos. Lofton, David Kelton, Christopher Strong. Christopher Strong made oath to John B. Earle, 22 May 1794.
Rec: 24 May 1794.

Pages 268-269   21 May 1792. Alexander Irwin and Susannah, his wife, to John Irwin for ₺ 100 for 120 acres on N. side of Rocky River and First Creek, part of a tract granted Alexander Irwin, 15 Oct. 1784. Signed: Alexr. Erwin, Susannah (+) Erwin. Wit: Robert Hall, Nathan Hall, Israel Pickens. Israel Pickens made oath to Elijah Browne, J. P., 23 May 1792.
Rec: 25 May 1794.

Page 269   Washington Dist. 5 Feb. 1794. John Huggins, Sr., to John Huggins, Jr., for ₺ 50 stg. for 50 acres, part of plantation where John Huggins, Sr. now lives on both sides of 12 Mile River, waters of Keowee River, bd. on SE by Huggins and granted John Huggins, Sr., 3 Sep. 1787 by Thomas Pinckney.
Wit: Wm. Lofton, Ezekiel John, Samuel Dalrymple. Wm. Lofton made oath to John B. Earle, Esq., 7 Jun. 1794.
Rec: 7 Jun. 1794.

Pages 269-270   16 Nov. 1793. Benjamin Clardy to Thomas Wadsworth, and William Turpin, merchants, for ₺ 20 stg. for 240 acres on branches of Saluda River, Washington Dist., bd. on SW by Benjamin Clardy, SE and SW by Henry Green, A Eley, Mathias Richardson, NW by Capt. Rosmond, granted to Clardy, 13 Dec. 1791 by Chas. Pinckney.
Wit: Jas. Young, James Boyce. James Boyce made oath to Thos. Wadsworth, J. L. C.
Rec: 7 Jun. 1794.

Pages 270-272   9 Apr. 1793. John Hunter, Esq., and Sarah, his wife, of Laurence Co., S. C., to Avis Tourtellot, of Pendleton Co., S. C., simptress (seamstress?), for ₺200 for 300 acres on 18 Mile Creek, waters of Savannah River, granted Hunter, 15 Oct. 1784, by Benj. Guerrard.
Wit: T. Merrick, Rowland Burgess; Tilly Merrick made oath to John Mitchell, J. P., 29 May 1793.
Rec: 7 Jun. 1794.

Pages 272-273   I, Samuel McAdow, of Gilliford Co., N. C., appoint my friend and brother-in-law, John Caruthers, of Abbeville Co., S. C., my attorney to sign deed of conveyance to David Brown, of Abbeville Co. for 200 acres in 96 Dist. on branches of S. fork of 12 Mile River. Date: 16 Dec. 1788.
Wit: Ninian Bll. (Bell) Hamilton, Samuel Caruthers. Ninian Bell Hamilton made oath to Bayley Anderson, J. P., 1 Jun. 1794.
Rec: 18 Jun. 1794.

Page 273   14 Oct. 1793. Samuel McAdow, of Guilford Co., N.C., to John Conn, of Pendleton Co., S. C., for Ł 20 stg. for 200 acres on S. branch of 12 Mile River, granted, 14 Oct. 1786, by Thomas Pinckney. Signed: Samuel McAdow by:John Caruthers.
Wit: Simeon Conn, Joseph Dunn, Nathaniel (his mark) Reed. Joseph Dunn made oath to Bayley Anderson, J. P., 1 Jun. 1794.
Rec: 18 Jun. 1794.

Pages 274-275   7 Apr. 1789. John Edwards and William Hort, Esq., Treasurers of State to John Martin, Esq., Deputy Surveyor, of 96 Dist...by several acts of the General Assembly, lands which have been granted to persons who have not paid the purchase money for such grants within time limit are directed to be sold by Treasurers at public auction....Alexander Robinson, on 16 Jul. 1784, a grant signed to him was sold at auction when James Martin, Esq. purchased as highest bidder for 17.6.8 for 640 acres in 96 Dist. above the Indian boundary on 23 Mile Creek. Signed: John Edwards, Wm. Hort.
Wit: Adam Gilchrist, Edwards, of Charleston Dist. Edward Edwards made oath to Peter Freneau, 14 Nov. 1794.
Rec: 20 Nov. 1794.

Pages 275-276   4 Mar. 1793. Jesse Clemments to Nathan Nalle, planter, for Ł 100 for 640 acres on 12 Mile River, bd. on NE by Col. Purvis, certified by Ephraim Mitchell, 4 Jun. 1784, surveyed by David Hopkins for Thomas Martin.
Wit: James Clemments, Andrew (C) Crage. James Clemments made oath to Wm. Halbert, J. P., 13 Jan. 1794.
Rec: 24 Jun. 1794.

Pages 276-277   10 Feb. 1794. Andrew Kelly of Washington Dist., to John Reno, of same, for Ł 15 stg. for 267 acres land granted Kelly, 7 Nov. 1791, by Charles Pinckney, in Washington Dist., above old Boundary line on S. side of Saluda River, one mile above Richard Parris's Waggon ford, bd. by Nathan Durham. Signed: Andrew (X) Kelly.
Wit: Aaron (his mark) Crane, Thomas Stone, Jno. Harrison. Aaron Crane made oath to Wm. Edmondson, J. P., 5 Apr. 1794.
Rec: 24 Jun. 1794.

Pages 277-278   22 Feb. 1793. Robert Tucker, planter, to James Stuart, for Ł 50 stg. for 196 acres on branch of Mulberry Creek, branch of Rocky River, waters of Savannah River. Signed: Robert (R) Tucker.
Wit: John McMahen, Thomas Pearman, Aulden (A) Tucker. Plat shows land adj. to John Caldwell, Wm. Bladen, Robt. Tucker, James Holmes, Jno. McMahan, Jas. Young. John McMahan made oath to E. Brown, 21 Jun. 1794.
Rec: 24 Jun. 1794.

Pages 278-279   24 Feb. 1794. Thomas Townes, of Greenville Co., Washington Dist., S. C., to David Wade, of Pendleton Co., Washington Dist., for Ł 15 stg., for 140 acres on S. side of Saluda River above Richard Parris's waggon ford, bd. by Kelly, Swillivant, granted Townes, 4 Feb. 1793, by Wm. Moultrie.
Wit: Jno. (his mark) Reno, John Eaton, Jno. Harrison. John Reno made oath to Wm. Edmondson, 25 Apr. 1794.
Rec: 24 Jun. 1794.

Page 279   10 Nov. 1793. William Todd, of Edgefield Co., S.C., to Robert Easley, of Pendleton Co., for Ł 25 for 100 (cont'd. next page)

(page 279 cont'd) acres, part of 156 acres granted to William Todd, 10 Feb. 1786, by Thomas Pinckney. Recorded Bk. UUUU, p. 452, on S. side of Saluda River.
Wit: Jno. Harrison, Archibald (his mark) Todd, Mary (+) Thompson. John Harrison made oath to Wm. Edmondson, J. P., 23 Jun. 1794.
Rec: 25 Jun. 1794.

Page 280   5 Sep. 1793. We, the Arbitrators chosen on the 1st part of James Jordan, viz: James Long and Moses Liddle, Esq., on the 2nd part of Isham Sharp as Attorney of George Lumpkin, Moses Hayings only appeared, therefore it is deemed by the arbitrators on both sides that the bond be given to George Lumpkin or Isham Sharp, his attorney and shall be forfeited. Signed: James Long and Moses Liddle and Moses Hayaes.
Rec: 25 Jun. 1794.
Wit: Thomas Farrar, John Grissam.

Page 280   9 Oct. 1792. John Smith, Jr., of Pendleton Co., a planter, to Richard Hooper, of Greenville Co., S.C., a planter, for ₤ 100 stg. for 50 acres, bd. on SW by Tugaloo River, granted to Callum Price, by George Matthews, Esq., Gov. of State of Georgia, 27 Sep. 1787, certified in South Carolina in book for Georgia Grants, p. 65, 10 Mar. 1788. Signed: John Smith, Anna Smith.
Wit: Wm. White, Thomas White. William White made oath to Nath'l. Perry, J. P., 7 Oct. 1793.
Rec: 25 Jun. 1794.

Pages 280-281   Jan. 1792. John Simpson, merchant of Laurens Co., S. C., to John Smith, planter, of Pendleton Co., for ₤ 100 for 452 acres in 96 Dist. at confluence of the Brasstown Creek and Tugaloo River, granted to Simpson, 1 Dec. 1788, by Thomas Pinckney.
Wit: David Speers, Thos. (X) Goucher. Thomas Gotcher made oath to John Wilson, J. P., 26 Jun. 1794.
Rec: 26 Jun. 1794.

Pages 283-284   8 Mar. 1788. John Swords, 96 Dist., to John Boyd of same, for ₤ 200 for 640 acres granted to Swords, 3 Apr. 1786 by Wm. Moultrie, in 96 Dist. on both sides of S. fork of George's Creek, waters of Saluda River. Signed: John Swords, Eleanor Swords.
Wit: William Love, James Wallace, David (X) Killough. David Killough made oath to Wm. Neville, J. P., 9 Nov. 1793.
Rec: 25 Jun. 1794.

Pages 284-285   27 Mar. 1793. Benjamin Bowen to William Hall for ₤ 50 stg. for 168½ acres in Pendleton Co., Washington Dist., on Double Branches, waters of Saluda River, granted to Bowen, 5 Jan. 1789 by Thos. Pinckney. Recorded Bk. YYYY, p. 282. Plat shows land adj. to James Reden.
Wit: Joseph Brown, Peter Acker, Robert Sloan. Peter Acker made oath to William Halbert, J. P., 26 Mar. 1794.
Rec: 25 Jun. 1794.

Pages 285-286   23 Jan. 1794. Henry Norton to Thomas Goss, for ₤30 stg. for 336 acres in Washington Dist., on Golden's Creek, waters of 12 Mile River, granted to Norton, 3 Dec. 1792, by Charles Pinckney.
Wit: Mathew (his mark) Mullinix, Jas. Brown. Mathew Mullinex made oath to John Willson, J. P., 10 Mar. 1794.
Rec: 25 Jun. 1794.

Pages 286-288   29 Apr. 1794. Eliab Moore and Rebecca, his wife, to John Pickens, Sr., for 200 guineas, for 340 acres on Rocky Creek, waters of Savannah River. Signed: Eliab Moore, Rebecca (her mark) Moore.
Wit: Robert Dowdle, James Ross, Joseph Pickens. Robert Dowdle made an oath to Joseph Reid, J.P. 25 Jun.1794. Rec: 25 Jun. 1794.

Pages 288-289   6 Jun. 1794. Thomas Farrar, Esq., Sheriff of Washington Dist., to Henry Sims, of same...James Gillison seized of a tract of 179 acres in Washington District, Pendleton Co., on 18 Mile Creek...John Cunningham, of Charleston, S. C., began action of debt against James Gillison, levied sum of Ł 150 stg. On 2 Jun. 1794, Sheriff disposed of sd. land at public auction to highest bidder, Henry Sims for Ł 20 stg.
Wit: W. Thompson, John McGehee. John McGehee made oath to J. B. Earle, 26 Jun. 1794.
Rec: 26 Jun. 1794.

Page 289   I, Elijah Brown, of Pendleton Co., for 86.14.10, pd. by Samuel Brown, of Charleston, for 1 slim negro man named Jacob, about 20 years of age and 1 year old colt. Date: (blank), 1794.
Wit: Jesse Browne, Mason Bennett, Micaiah Clark. Mason Bennett made oath to John Willson, (no date).
Rec: 26 Jun. 1794.

Page 289   I, James Ross, sold to John Ross, Sr., planter, for Ł 30 stg., 2 horses and colt, 3 cows, 2 calves and household furniture. Date: 15 Jun. 1794.
Wit: :James Long, Vann Walker. James Long made oath to J. B. Earle, 7 Jul. 1794.
Rec: 7 Jul. 1794.

Pages 289-290   I, George Ross sold to John Ross, Sr., planter, for Ł 25 horses, cattle, household furniture. Date: 15 Jun. 1794.
Wit: Eliab Moore, James Long. James Long made oath to J. B. Earle, 7 Jul. 1794.
Rec: 7 Jul. 1794.

Page 290   9 Jan. 1794. John Thomas to John Sutherland, for Ł 10 stg. for 50 acres adj. John Sutherland, Archelaus Prater, John Thomas. Granted Ebenezer Fain, 12 Oct. 1787, by Thomas Pinckney. Signed: John (X) Thomas.
Wit: Joseph Geneway, Archelaus Prater. Archelaus Prater made oath to William Nevill, 11 Apr. 1794.
Rec: 10 Jul. 1794.

Pages 290-291   29 Nov. 1792. Thomas Commander Russell, of South Carolina and John Lewis, of Va., to George Humphries, of Pendleton Co., for Ł 60 stg. for 840 acres, part of a tract granted to Thomas Lewis, ___ Dec. 1786, for 1300 acres on Reedy Fork of Brushy Creek. Signed: Tho. C. Russell, John Lewis.
Wit: John Brown, William Welch. John Brown made oath to Wm. Edmondson, J. P., 4 Mar. 1794.
Rec: 10 Jul. 1794.

Page 292   23 Jun. 1794. Lazarus Tilly to Jane Tilly for Ł 100 stg. for 300 acres in Washington Dist., Pendleton Co. on Generostee Creek, waters of Savannah River, granted Richard Morrow, 3 Nov. 1788, by Thomas Pinckney. Recorded Bk. XXXX, p. 525, bd. on E. by Joshua Saxon, on S. by John Dalrymple, on W. by Henry Huston, on N. by James Maroney, released by Morrow to Tilly, 9 Jan. 1793.
Wit: George Warner, John Braselton. George Warner made oath to E.Brown, J. P., 26 Jun. 1794.
Rec: 10 Jul. 1794.

Pages 292-299   7 Nov. 1794. Hugh Middleton and Edward Prince, planters, and Robert Middleton, Esq., of Augusta, Ga. to John Hall, Esq., of Philadelphia, Pa., for 12 shillings stg., for 12,000 acres granted Hugh Middleton and Edward Prince in grants of patents of 1,000 acres each, in Washington Dist., Pendleton Co., on 6 Oct. 1794, between 23 and 26 Mile Creeks, waters of Savannah River. Plats distinguished by letter "A", numbered 1-12...also tract of 22,000 acres in Washington Dist., Pendleton Co., granted Hugh and Robert

(pages 292-299 cont'd):
Middleton, of equal quantity on same date, between Little River and Hencoop Creek, waters of Savannah River. Plats distinguished by letter "B", numbered 1-22...also, 15,000 acres granted Hugh and Robert Middleton between 23 and 26 Mile Creeks, distinguished by letter "C", numbered 1-15...84,000 acres granted Robt. Middleton in 96 Dist., Edgefield Co. Plat distinguished by letter "E", numbered 1-84...94,000 acres granted to Robert Middleton in Washington Dist. on waters of Keowee River, Saluda River, 12 Mile River, 12 and 6 Mile Creeks. Plats no. 218-323. Signed: Hugh Middleton, Edward Prince, Robert Middleton.
Wit: Sam'l. Jack, William H. Jack, Samuel Barnett...Edgefield Co., S.C. Samuel Barnett made oath to Joseph Hightower, J. P., 18 Dec. 1794.
Rec: 26 Dec. 1794.

Page 300   15 Aug. 1793. James Early to John Sutherland for Ł 20 stg. for 40 acres on S. side of Saluda River, granted Ebenezer Fair, 1 Oct. 1787, by Thomas Pinckney. Wit: Lawrence Broadley, John (X) Hayward. Lawrence Bradley made oath to Bayley Anderson, 11 Apr. 1794.
Rec: 10 Jul. 1794.

Pages 300-301   19 Jan. 1793. Richard Morrow of N. C. to Lazarus Tilly of Pendleton Co. for Ł 100 stg. for 300 acres on Generostee Creek, waters of Savannah River, bd. on E. by Joshua Saxon, on S. by John Dalrymple, on W. by Henry Huston, on N. by James Maroney, granted to Morrow, 3 Nov. 1788, by Thos. Pinckney. Recorded Bk. XXXX, p. 521.
Wit: Aaron Boggs, James Maxwell, Robt. Dowdle. Robert Dowdle made oath to E. Browne, J. P., 26 Jun. 1794.
Rec: 10 Jul. 1794.

Page 302   I, Elijah Stevenson for Ł 60 stg. paid to me by John Adair, merchant, one negro woman named Nancy, with her increase. Date: 30 Apr. 1794.
Wit: John Curry, Wm. Thompson.
Rec: 13 Jul. 1794.

Page 302   2 Mar. 1793. John Young, planter, and Mary, his wife, spinster, to William Young, blacksmith, for Ł 40 stg, 51 acres on Little Generostee Creek, Savannah River. Signed: John Young, Mary (+) Young.
Wit: James Young, Alexander Keith. James Young made oath to E. Browne, J. P., 8 Jul. 1794.
Rec: 17 Jul. 1794.

Pages 302-303   14 Jan. 1794. John Young, planter, to James Young, blacksmith, for Ł 50 stg. for all household stuff and implements of household, cattle, horses, Ł 50 to be paid by 25 Dec. 1798.
Wit: William Buchanan, Eben Buchanan. William Buchanan, Jr. made oath to E. Browne, J. P., 12 Jul. 1794.
Rec: 17 Jul. 1794.

Page 303   29 Sep. 1792. William Swift, of Newberry Co., S.C. to James Young, of Pendleton Co., for Ł 7stg. for 55 acres, part of 310 acres on branches of Mulberry Creek, waters of Rocky River, granted William Swift, 5 Feb. 1787.
Wit: Robert Baird, T. R. Rodgers, Aquilla Howard...96 Dist., Abbeville Co., Robert Beard made oath to Wm. Baskin, J. P., 5 Apr. 1794.
Rec: 17 Jul. 1794.

Page 304   20 Sep. 1792. William Lesley, of Abbeville Co., S. C., to William Buchanan, of Pendleton Co., for Ł 70 stg. for 640 acres in Pendleton Co., on Little Generostee Creek, granted to Jacob Drayton, 15 Oct. 1784, conveyed to Lesley, 11 Oct. 1791.
Wit: Mathew Reed, John Pickens, John Buchanan. John Buchanan made oath to John Willson, J. P. 8 Feb. 1793.
Rec: 17 Jul. 1794.

Pages 304-305   8 Feb. 1794. Jean Claton, of Fairfield Co., S. C.,
                   to William Asherst, of Pennington Co., S. C., for
                   Ł 90 for 300 acres granted Francis Wafer, by Thomas
Pinckney, 7 May 1787, conveyed from Francis Fafer to Jean Claton, Nov.
1788, in 96 Dist. on Dody's Creek of Saluda River, bd. on SW by James
Flemin. Signed: Jean (+) Cleaton.
Wit: Isham Cleaton, John (I) Watson, William (his mark) Cleaton...Isham
Clayton made oath to Gabriel Moffett, 11 Feb. 1794.
Rec: 25 Jul. 1794.

Pages 305-306   27 Oct. 1788. William Carpenter of 96 Dist., to Wil-
                   liam Acker (also Asher), of Surry Co., N. C., for
                   Ł 60 for 200 acres in 96 Dist., west of ancient Boun-
dary line, on S. side of Saluda River, granted Carpenter, 4 Apr. 1785 by
Wm. Moultrie. Signed: William (his mark) Carpenter.
Wit: James Jett, William Bourland. William Bourland made oath to Gab-
riel Moffett, J. P., 19 Jun. 1794.
Rec: 25 Jul. 1794.

Pages 306-307   10 Aug. 1794. Morgan Osborn to William Griffen for
                   Ł 40 stg. for 80 acres on N. side of 5 Mile Branch,
                   waters of 18 Mile Creek, part of 2 tracts, one on
194 acres, granted Samuel Lofton, Sr. by Charles Pinckeney, the other
119 acres granted Henry Chiles, by Wm. Moultrie, bd. by David Kelton.
Wit: Joab Mauldin, James (his mark) Gillison, David Kelton. James Gillison made oath to J. B. Earle, 11 Aug. 1794.
Rec: 11 Aug. 1794.

Pages 307-308   5 Aug. 1794. Jno. Campbell of Abbeville Co., plan-
                   ter, to Charles Rice, of Pendleton Co., planter, for
                   Ł 80 stg. for 300 acres on 18 Mile Creek, waters of
Savannah River, on both sides of creek, granted Campbell, 18 Jan. 1785,
by Wm. Moultrie. Recorded Bk. GGGG, p. 95.
Wit: Edward (his mark) Parnel, James Cunningham. Abbeville Co...James
Cunningham made oath to Wm. Baskin, J. P., 6 Aug. 1794.
Rec: 13 Aug. 1794.

Page 309   4 Apr. 1794. John Griffen and Sarah, his wife, to
                   John Ward for Ł 62 for 319 acres conveyed to Griffen
                   on 9 Jan. 1793. Recorded Bk. B, p. 176, Pendleton
Co., bd. by John Junkins, Andrew Roe, on 23 Mile Creek. Signed: John
Griffen, Sarah Griffen.
Wit: James Sims, Isaac Nicholson. Isaac Nicholson made oath to J. B.
Earle, J. P., 14 Aug. 1794.
Rec: 14 Aug. 1794.

Pages 309-310   4 Apr. 1794. William Guest to David Guest for Ł 50
                   stg. for 180 acres on Tugaloo River, part of a tract
                   of 190 acres surveyed for William Guest, 20 Jul.1787
by Thomas Pinckney, conveyed to David Guest, 20 Jul. 1787. Signed: William (M) Guest.
Wit: Moses Guest, Benjamin Guest. Moses Guest made oath to Wm. Nevill,
19 Sep. 1794.
Rec: 12 Dec. 1794.

Pages 310-311   4 May 1793. Robert Carter to Benjamin Perry, for
                   Ł 150 for 200 acres on Middle Fork of Choestoa Creek
                   on waters of Tugaloo River, bd. on NW by John Skel-
ton, granted to Thomas Lofton, 2 Jul. 1787, by Thos. Pinckney.
Wit: Johnson Monroe, Nathaniel Perry. Nathaniel Perry made oath to Jno.
Baylis Earle, J. P. 10 Sep. 1794.
Rec: 12 Sep. 1794.

Page 311   26 Feb. 1789. Robert Lusk, of Union Co., S. C., to
                   John Whitney, of same, for Ł 50 stg., for 240 acres
                   in 96 Dist. on N. fork of 18 Mile Creek, waters of
Savannah River.
Wit: William McCullough, Aaron Lockert, Mary McCullough...Union Co. S.
C. Aaron Lochert made oath to Wm. McCullough, J. P., 20 Feb. 1789.
Rec: 15 Sep. 1794.

Pages 311-313   Abbeville Co., S. C., 16 Jan. 1787. Charles Steele to David Waters, for Ł 53 stg. for 200 acres in 96 Dist. above ancient boundary line on 18 Mile Creek, branch of Savannah or Keowee River, granted 4 July 1785, by Wm. Moultrie. Wit: James Lomax, Adam Porter, Adam Burney...Abbeville Co., Andrew Porter made oath to Hugh Wardlaw, J. P., 29 Aug. 1793...I do hereby sign over my right and title to within release to Joseph Whitner, or his heirs this 5 Oct. 1792. Signed: David (his mark) Waters.
Wit: Charles Gates, Gideon Clark.
Rec: 15 Sep. 1794.

Pages 313-314   28 Nov. 1793. Christopher Williman of Charleston, to Charles Clemments, planter, for Ł 100 for 640 acres in 96 Dist. on Cherokee Creek, Rocky River, of Savannah, on waggon road from Ninty six to Keowee.
Wit: Geo. Metzker, Charles Stewart. Geo. Metzker made oath to Elijah Browne, J. P., 12 Sep. 1794.
Rec: 15 Sep. 1794.

Pages 314-317   20 Nov. 1794. Hugh Middleton, Edward Prince, Robert Middleton and John Blanton, the two former of S. C., the two latter of Ga., to Robert Goodloe Harper, of S. C., for Ł 100 stg. for 30 tracts adjoining each other, containing 1000 acres each, in Washington Dist., Pendleton Co., between Broadaway and Hencoop Creeks, branches of Rocky River, granted Hugh Middleton and Edward Prince, 6 Oct. 1794...also 21 tracts adjoining as appears in Plat A., containing 1000 acres each between 18 and 26 Mile Creeks, waters of Savannah River, granted Hugh and Robert Middleton, 6 Oct. 1794...also, 18 tracts adjoining each other as appears in Plat D., containing 1000 ac. each in 96 Dist., Pendleton Co., on branches of Rocky River, granted to Hugh and Robert Middleton, 6 Oct. 1794. Signed: Hugh Middleton, Edward Prince, Robert Middleton, John Blanton.
Wit: N. H. Bugg, John Swepson. Plats included...Edgefield Co., S. C., Nicholas Hobson Bugg made oath to Joseph Hightower, J. P., 3 Dec. 1794.
Rec: 11 Dec. 1794.

Pages 317-322   1 Dec. 1794. Hugh Middleton and Edward Prince, of S. C., planters, and John Blanton, of Ga., planter, to Hon. Robert G. Harper, Esq., of City of Charleston, S. C., for Ł 5 stg. for 8000 acres on seperate adjoining tracts of 1000 acres each between 18 and 23 Mile Creeks of Savannah River, in Washington Dist., Pendleton Co. Plats marked with letter "B", number 1-8... tract of 72,000 acres of 1000 acres each between Keowee and Saluda Rivers, plats numbered 1-72, marked "D". Signed: Hugh Middleton, Edward Prince, John Blanton, by his attorney, N. H. Bugg.
Wit: Giles Y. Raines, John Whitefield, Joseph Hightower. Plats included...Edgefield Co., S. C. John Whitefield made oath to Joseph Hightower J. P., 3 Dec. 1794.
Rec: 11 Dec. 1794.

Page 322   8 Aug. 1793. Benjamin Cleveland to James Blair for Ł 30 for 200 acres granted Henry Hyrne, 1 Jan. 1785, on Toxaway Creek, branch of Chauga, waters of Tugaloo. Wit: Alexr. Hunter, C. Kennedy...Acknowledged in open court, 15 Sep. 1794, J. B. Earle, J. P.
Rec: 15 Sep. 1794.

Pages 322-323   13 Apr. 1794. Benjamin Cleveland to James Blair for Ł 30 for 200 acres part of 975 acres granted Cleveland, 5 Dec. 1791, by Charles Pinckney, adj. on NW by tract granted Henry Hyrne, 21 Jan.1785, James Blair and Joseph Stepp, on S. side of Toxaway Creek.
Wit: Joseph Stepp, Absolom Cleveland. Acknowledged in open court, 15 Sep. 1794. J. B. Earle, J. P.
Rec: 15 Sep. 1794.

Page 323   13 Jan. 1794. Jno. McVey to Wm. McVey, for Ł 60 stg. for 211 acres granted Nathan Young, 3 Apr. 1785, conveyed from Young to Jno. McVey, 105 acres granted to

(page 323 cont'd):
Jno. McVey, 2 Jan. 1792, by Charles Pinckney.
Wit: Wm. Gillaspie, Jno. McCall. Jno. McCall made oath to E. Browne, 17 Jan. 1794.
Rec: 15 Sep. 1794.

Pages 323-324 10 Feb. 1795. Andrew Kelly to Aaron Crane for Ł 50 for 267 acres in Washington Dist., above old boundary line on S. side of Saluda River, above Richard Parris's waggon ford, granted 7 Nov. 1791, by Charles Pinckney. Signed: Andrew (X) Kelly.
Wit: John (his mark) Reno, David (X) Wade, Jno. Harrison. John Reno made oath to Wm. Edmondson, J. P., 5 Apr. 1794.
Rec: 15 Sep. 1794.

Pages 324-325 30 Oct. 1793. Ralph Owen to Joel Halbert for Ł 50 stg. for 165 acres in Washington Dist., on SE fork of Washington Creek, now called Big Creek, waters of the Saluda River, granted to Ralph Owen, 6 Mar. 1786, by Wm. Moultrie. Recorded Bk. HHHH, p. 363.
Wit: Mason Bennett, John Halbert, John Nicholson. Mason Bennett made oath to Wm. Halbert, J. P., 5 Mar. 1794.
Rec: 15 Sep. 1794.

Pages 325-326 30 Oct. 1793. John Nicholson to Joel Halbert for Ł50 for 80 acres in Washington Dist. on Big Creek, waters of the Saluda, part of a grant to Nicholson, 15 Oct. 1784, by Benjamin Guerrard. Recorded Bk. ZZZ, p. 253.
Wit: Mason Bennett, John Halbert, Ralph (X) Green. Mason Bennett made oath to Wm. Halbert, 5 Mar. 1794.
Rec: 15 Sep. 1794.

Page 326 16 Jan. 1794. Charles Lay to James Walker Wright of Washington Dist., for Ł 150 stg. for 100 acres on the Little Estatoe. Signed: Charles (V) Lay.
Wit: John Cochran, Francis Boren. Francis Boren made oath to Bayley Anderson, 7 Jul. 1794.
Rec: 15 Sep. 1794.

Pages 326-327 22 Mar. 1793. Jervais Henry Stevens, of Charleston, Gentleman, to Benjamin Cleveland, of Pendleton Co., planter, for Ł 30 stg. for 200 acres on Toxaway Creek branch of Chagee, waters of Tugaloo River, granted to Henry Hyrne, Esq., for his faithful services during the War as a Lieutenant in the State Cavalry commanded by Col. Hezekiah Mahan.
Wit: John Davidson, James Blair. (Oath names and dates blank.)
Rec: 15 Sep. 1794.

Pages 327-328 7 Aug. 1794. Jacob Visage and Elizabeth, his wife, to John Miller, for Ł 4 for 150 acres on the SE side of 23 Mile Creek. Signed: Jacob Visage, Elizabeth (X) Visage.
Wit: James Tuffnell, Jonathan Hicks. James Tuffnell made oath to William Nevill, 20 Sep. 1794.
Rec: 20 Sep. 1794.

Pages 328-329 20 Sep. 1794. Jacob Visage and Elizabeth, his wife, to James Tuffnell, for Ł 20 for 200 acres on the SE side of 23 Mile Creek, bd. by John Miller, part of 543 acres granted to Visage. (no date). Signed: Jacob Visage, Elizabeth Visage.
Wit: Jno. Miller, James (+) Doyal. James Doyle made oath to Wm. Nevill, J. P., 20 Sep. 1794.
Rec: 20 Sep. 1794.

Page 329 96 Dist. 3 Nov. 1790. John Jackson, planter, to Hezekiah Davis, Senr., for Ł 20 for 250 acres on Beaver Creek, of Rocky Creek, branch of the Savannah River, bd. on NE by Eless(?) Moore, on NW by John Callaham, on W. by James Cal-

(page 329 cont'd):
houn, on S. by John Armstrong, granted to Jno. Jackson, 26 Dec. 1788, by Benjamin Guerrard. Signed: John Jackson, Ann (X) Jackson.
Wit: John Nelson, Abijah Davis, Hermon (X) Commons. Abijah Davis made oath to E. Browne, J. P., 23 Sep. 1794.
Rec: 1 Oct. 1794.

Pages 329-330   96 Dist. 29 Jan. 1794. Hezekiah Davis, planter, to Abijah Davis, for Ł 35 for 250 acres on Beaver Creek, branch of Great Rocky Creek, of Savannah River, bd. on NE by Eless Moore, on NW by John Callaham, on W. by James Calhoun, on S. by John Armstrong. Granted to John Jackson, 26 Dec. 1788, by Benjamin Guerrard. Signed: Hezekiah Davis, Sarah (X) Davis.
Wit: Jesse Davis, John (his mark) Hunter. Jesse Davis made oath to E. Browne, J. P., 23 Sep. 1794.
Rec: 1 Oct. 1794.

Page 330   4 Jan. 1791. John Jackson, planter, to Jesse Davis, for Ł 20 for 150 acres on Beaver Creek, waters of Rocky River, branch of Savannah, bd. by John Jackson, John Henry, James Johnson, Mark Bird, John Armstrong, granted to Jackson on 30 Nov. 1788, by Benjamin Guerrard. Signed: John Jackson, Anna (X) Jackson.
Wit: James John Orr, Hezekiah Davis, John Nelson. Hezekiah Davis made oath to E. Browne, J. P., 23 Sep. 1794.
Rec: 1 Oct. 1794.

Pages 330-331   7 Aug. 1794. John Butt to William Laffoon for Ł 75 for 365 acres on both sides of Peter's Creek, of the Saluda River, surveyed for Butt, 25 May 1787, where Gideon Clark now lives.
Wit: Benjamin Clark, Charles Gates, Wm. Thompson. Benjamin Clark made oath to Gabriel Moffett, J. P., 13 Sep. 1794.
Rec: 13 Oct. 1794.

Pages 331-332   22 Jul. 1794. Levi Pierce and Elizabeth, his wife, planter, to John Green, planter, for Ł 80 stg., for 148 acres on 6 Mile Creek, bd. one side on Keowee River, granted 2 Feb. 1787, by Charles Pinckney. Signed: Levi (P)Pierce, Elizabeth (her mark) Pierce.
Wit: Elijah Stevenson, Joab Laurence. Elijah Stevenson made oath to Joseph Reid, J. P., of Washington Dist., 2 Jul. 1794.
Rec: 14 Oct. 1794.

Pages 332-334   2 Oct. 1794. Robert Craven, of Pendleton Co., and Abigale, his wife, to J. F. Grimkie, (later called John Faucherraud Grimkie), of Charleston, for Ł 100 stg. for 450 acres on W. side of Keowee River, Pendleton Co., 96 Dist., bd. by land lately belonging to Capt. Wm. Tate and J. F. Grimkie, including a tract of 450 acres granted to Grimkie as military bounty for his services during the War as Lt. Col. in the Army of the United States, and part of 640 acres surveyed for Robert Craven by Samuel J. Dickson, Deputy Surveyor, granted 7 Oct. 1793, by Wm. Moultrie. Signed: Robert Cravens, Abigale (X) Cravens.
Wit: Leonard D. Shaw, John Hinson. Leonard D. Shaw, of Greenville Co., S. C., made oath to J. B. Earle, J. P., 3 Oct. 1794.
Rec: 16 Oct. 1794.

Pages 334-335   To Andrew Pickens, Samuel Taylor and Robert Anderson, Esquires, by lease and release, 2 and 3 day of Oct. 1794 made between Robert Cravens, of Pendleton Co., and Abigale, his wife, to J. F. Grimkie, of Charleston, did convey tract on W. side of Keowee River, Washington Dist., bd. by land lately owned by Capt. Wm. Tate and a tract belonging to sd. Grimkie of 450 acres as a military bounty for his services during the War and by indentures containing 613 acres granted to Craven by Wm. Moultrie, 7 Oct. 1793...said Abigale is not able to travel to make and declare before judges of Common Pleas for her voluntary consent...give full authority for above Andrew Pickens, Samuel Taylor and Robert Anderson, or any two of you to go

(pages 334-335 cont'd):
to said Abigale and take such release as she shall make. Signed: John Rutledge, Chief Justice of the State of Charleston, 30 Jul. 1794.
Wit: Thos. Rhett Smith, Wm. Mason, C.C.P....We, commissioners above named certify on 3 Oct. 1794, that Abigale Cravens was privately examined and she did give her relinquishment of dower. Signed: Andw. Pickens, Sam'l Taylor. Samuel Taylor made oath to J. B. Earle, 3 Oct. 1794.
Rec: 15 Oct. 1794.

Pages 335-336   8 Feb. 1791. John Barton to Robert Box for Ŀ 50 stg. for 146 acres in 96 Dist. on both sides of Barton's Creek, waters of Tugaloo, granted to Barton, 2 Feb. 1786, by Edward Telfair, Governor of Georgia. Recorded in S. C., Georgia Grant Bk., p. 45-46, 24 Jan. 1788.
Wit: Jas. Willborn, Wm. Cleveland. James Wellborn made oath to William Halbert, 26 Jan. 1794.
Rec: 10 Nov. 1794.

Page 336   30 Aug. 1794. Jephs Moss of Washington Dist., to William Gillaspie, Jr., planter, of same, for Ŀ 70 stg. for 150 acres on S. side of the Saluda River on Bowen's Fork, of George's Creek, adj. to Wm. Gillaspie, Jr. and Wm. Gillaspie, Sr., ___ Boyd, and Charles Bowen.
Wit: Charles Bowen, Thomas Henderson, John (his mark) Thomas. Charles Bowen made oath to John Willson, J. P., 10 Nov. 1794.
Rec: 16 Nov. 1794.

Pages 337-338   17 Nov. 1794. Alexander Ramsey and Mary, his wife, of Pendleton Co., to William Dickson, of Newberry Co. for Ŀ 40 stg. for 200 acres on the NW fork of Chaugee Creek, waters of the Tugaloo River, in Washington Dist., bd. on SW by Wm. McCaleb, and by vacant land, granted to Ramsey, 2 Mar. 1789, by Charles Pinckney. Recorded Bk. ZZZZ, p. 92. Signed: Alexr. Ramsey, Mary (X) Ramsey.
Wit: Richard Sloan, Thomas (X) Degaly. Richard Sloan made oath to J.B. Earle, J. P., 18 Nov. 1794.
Rec: 18 Nov. 1794.

Page 338   4 Jul. 1794. Samuel Lofton to William Warren for Ŀ 20 stg. for 200 acres on fork of Chaugee Creek, the waters of Tugaloo River, bd. on SW by Alexander Ramsey, granted 2 Sep. 1793, by Wm. Moultrie. Signed: Samuel Lofton, Jr.
Wit: Jno. Harris, Wm. Lofton, Samuel Jones. William Lofton made oath to Joseph Reid, J. P., 1 Jan. 1795.

Page 339   30 May 1794. Robert Anderson, Esq., to Roland and Richard Burks, for Ŀ 80 stg. for 200 acres on both sides of Connoross Creek, waters of Keowee River, bd. on NW by Capt. Uriah Goodwine, granted to George Brough on Bounty for his service in the late War, 16 Jul. 1794, by Benj. Guerrard. Recorded Bk. BBBB, p. 27 and granted to Robert Anderson, 10 Jul. 1786.
Wit: David Sloan, Job Hinton. Job Hinton made oath to Nath'l. Perry, 20 Jun. 1794.
Rec: 26 Nov. 1794.

Pages 339-340   4 Dec. 1794. Ambrose Fitzgerrald and Sarah, his wife to Richard Brown, of Pittsylvania Co., Va. for Ŀ 80 for 242 acres in Pittsylvania Co., on branches of Shocks Creek, it being their full portion of land devised to them in last will and testament of Richard Brown, deceased, which directed all lands belonging to decedant to be equally divided among his lawful children of which Sarah Fitzgerrald is one, who with Ambrose Fitzgerrald, her husband, has sold to Richard Brown. Signed: Ambrose (his mark) Fitzgerrald, Sarah (her mark) Fitzgerrald.
Wit: Jacob White, Lewis Ralston. Lewis Ralston made oath to Nathaniel Perry, J. P., 4 Dec. 1794.
Rec: 5 Dec. 1794.

Pages 340-341   30 Jul. 1794. John Anderson and Ails, his wife, of
                     Newberry Co., S. C., to James Tate, Jr., of Pendle-
                     ton Co., for Ł 10,000 stg., for 2 tracts in Pendle-
ton Co., adj. Indian Boundary line on N., 1st tract of two hundred thousand acres, granted to Anderson, 7 Oct. 1793, bd. by Tugaloo River on W.
and Tomasee Creek and Little River on E., 2nd tract of one hundred thousand acres, granted 7 Oct. 1793, bd. by Toxaway and Keowee Rivers, on W.
of Indian Boundary Line, 12 Mile River on E. Signed: John Anderson,
Ails Anderson.
Wit: Wm. Irby, James (his mark) Jones, Ann (X) Cobb. Wm. Irby made oath
to Wm. Nevill, J. P., 16 Sep. 1794.
Rec: 31 Dec. 1794.

Pages 341-342   9 Jan. 1794. John Thomas to Archelaus Prater, for
                     Ł 20 stg. for 100 acres on S. side of Saluda River,
                     bd. by James Fleman, John Thomas, John Sutherland,
___ Henderson, part of a tract granted to Ebenezer Fain, 12 Oct. 1787 by
Thomas Pinckney. Signed: John (T) Thomas.
Wit: John Sutherland, Joseph Genaway. John Sutherland made oath to Wm.
Nevill, 11 Apr. 1794.
Rec: 10 Jan. 1795.

Page 342   3 Feb. 1794. William McCaleb to Nathaniel Dennis for
                     Ł 60 stg. for 369 acres in Washington Dist. on Chau-
                     gee Creek, NE fork of Tugaloo River.
Wit: John Griffen, David McCaleb. David McCaleb made oath to J. Baylis
Earle, J. P. 2 Jan. 1794.
Rec: 17 Jan. 1795.

Pages 342-343   4 Jul. 1793. Benjamin Whorton to Thomas Robertson
                     for Ł 70 stg. for 383 acres on Oconee Creek, waters
                     of Little River, branch of Keowee River, granted on
3 Dec. 1792, by Charles Pinckney.
Wit: Wm. McCaleb, James Hendrix. Wm. McCaleb made oat0 to J. Miller,
J. P., 12 Nov. 1793.
Rec: 22 Jan. 1795.

Pages 343-344   2 Nov. 1793. William Lewis of Burke (?) Co., N. C.,
                     to William Hunt, of Pendleton Co., S. C., for Ł 100
                     stg. for 320 acres granted to William Lewis, 5 Jun.
1780, by Wm. Moultrie, W. of Old Boundary Line on Camp Creek of Saluda
River.
Wit: James Gillespie, Mary Gillespie. James Gillespie made oath to Bay-
ley Anderson, 10 Apr. 1792.
Rec: 21 Jan. 1795.

Pages 344-346   28 Sep. 1793. Benjamin Bowen, of Pendleton Co., (for-
                     merly a part of Abbeville Co.) to Robert Sloan of the
                     same, for Ł 85 stg. for 490 acres, on W. side of
Saluda River, Double Creek branch, bd. on W. by Peter Acker, on N. by
Robert Moore, granted to Bowen, 2 Feb. 1789, by Thomas Pinckney.
Wit: George Maxwell, James (X) Reden, Hugh (X) Rynolds. George Maxwell
made oath to Wm. Nevill, 4 Aug. 1794.
Rec: 24 Jan. 1795.

Pages 346-347   20 Apr. 1794. John Glenn to Isaac Bynum for Ł 50 stg.
                     for 600 acres on 12 Mile River, part of 1,000 acres
                     granted to Glenn on 7 May 1793, bd. by David Muphie
and Joel Mody.
Wit: David Murphee, Joel Moody. David Murphree made oath to Bayley Anderson, J. P. 26 Aug. 1794.
Rec: 24 Jan. 1795.

Pages 347-349   2 Jul. 1794. Wm. Hallum and Mary, his wife, of Wash-
                     ington Dist., to Robert Baker, of same, for Ł 70 stg.
                     for 200 acres, part of 2 grants, one by Moultrie, the
other by Thos. Pinckney, 2 Mar. 1787 on W. side of 18 Mile Creek, bd. on
N. by John Anderson, on S. by Thomas Hallum. Signed: William Hallum,
Mary (+) Hallum.Wit: Ambrose Dudley, George Payne. Ambrose Dudley made
oath to John Wilson, J.P., 17 Nov. 1794. Rec: 24 Jan. 1795.

Pages 349-351   19 Jun. 1794. William Poor to James Riding for ₤ 50
                     for 200 acres in Washington Dist., granted to Poor
                     on 1 Dec. 1788 by Thos. Pinckney. Recorded Bk. YYYY,
p. 218. Wit: Meridith Blackburn, Lewis Nelson, Arthur Halbert. Arthur
Halbert made oath to Wm. Halbert, J. P.,.16 Jun. 1794.
Rec: 24 Jan. 1795.

Pages 351-352   15 Feb. 1794. Thomas Garner to William Halbert for
                     ₤ 30 for 90 acres in Washington Dist., on Rutledge's
                     Camp Creek, waters of the Big Creek, part of a tract
conveyed from Isaac Alexander to Thomas Garner, 23 Jan. 1793, granted/
grant recorded Bk. FFFF, p. 117.
Wit: William Harper, Mason Bennett, William Wilson. Mason Bennett made
oath to E. Browne, J. P., 4 Jul. 1794.
Rec: 24 Jan. 1795.

Pages 352-354   17 Sep. 1794. Joseph Williams of Rutherford Co., N.
                     C., to John Earle, "of county aforesaid", for ₤ 60
                     for 200 acres on Middle fork of Connoross Creek, a
branch of Keowee River, granted to John Williams on bounty, 21 Jan. 1785,
by Benjamin Guerrard, certified by Thomas Lewis, deputy surveyor, said
John Williams died intestate, having no issue, Joseph Williams is his
brother and lawful heir.
Wit: William Hannon, Robert Young, George W. Earle. George Washington
Earle made oath to J. B. Earle, J. P., 6 Jan. 1795.
Rec: 26 Jan. 1795.

Pages 354-355   24 Dec. 1794. George Pain to Henry Gasaway for ₤ 25
                     stg. for 150 acres on 18 Mile Creek, waters of the
                     Seneca, bd. on SW by Bennet Combs, on NW by Joseph
Chapman, granted 30 Sep. 1792, by Chas. Pinckney, being part of a tract
of 300 acres. Signed: George Payne.
Wit: Robert Baker, Sarah (X) Baker. Robert Baker made oath to John
Wilson, 4 Jan. 1795.
Rec: 24 Jan. 1795.

Pages 355-356   15 Jan. 1793. George Thompson to William Hunt of 96
                     Dist., for ₤ 40 for 112 acres granted 5 Jun. 1786, by
                     Wm. Moultrie, in 96 Dist. on S. side of Saluda River,
adj. to John Caruthers.
Wit: Moses Hunt, John Mayes. Moses Hunt made oath to Bayley Anderson,
11 Aug. 1794.
Rec: 25 Jun. 1795.

Pages 356-357   2 Feb. 1790. James Compton to Robert Pickens, plan-
                     ter, for ₤ 150 stg., for 640 acres in 96 Dist., on
                     Broadaway and Pea Creeks, branches of Rocky River,
granted 5 Jun. 1796, by Wm. Moultrie. Signed: James (his mark) Compton.
Wit: Robt. McCann, Andrew Huse. Robert McCann made oath to John Wilson,
J. P., 2 Dec. 1790.
Rec: 24 Jan. 1795.

Pages 357-358   12 Mar. 1794. William Thompson to John Moore, for
                     ₤ 50 for 100 acres part of a tract of 545 acres gran-
                     ted to Thompson, 6 Nov. 1786, recorded Bk. 0000, p.
297. Plat shows bd. by ___ Parker, Wm. Thompson. Surveyed by Joshua
Saxon, 10 Mar. 1794.
Wit: John Drennan, Jacob Anderson. Wit: (to receipt)-Abraham Anderson,
Alexander Moore, Jacob Anderson. Alexander Moore made oath to E. Brown,
22 Nov. 1794.
Rec: 24 Jan. 1794.(1795?)

Pages 358-359   1 Feb. 1790. James Compton to Robert Pickens, plan-
                     ter, for 10 shillings, for 640 acres granted Compton
                     on 5 Jun. 1786, by Moultrie, in 96 Dist. on Broada-
way and Pea Creeks. Signed: James (his mark) Compton.
Wit: Robert McCann, Andrew Huse.
Rec: 24 Jan. 1795.
(This was put here by mistake, ought to have been p. 355 before release)
"Quoted from text"......

Pages 359-361   11 Jun. 1793. Clement Owen and John Moore to William
                   Halbert for Ł 50 stg. for 170 acres in Washington Dis.
                   on branch of Big Creek, waters of the Saluda River, a
part of grant to Clement Owen, 4 Sep. 1786, by Wm. Moultrie, bd. by Thomas Wilson. Recorded Bk. MMMM, p. 492. Signed: Clement Owen, John (X) Moore.
Wit: Thomas Gray, Enoch Garner, Ralph Owen. Plat included. Enoch Garner made oath to E. Brown, 4 Jul. 1794.
Rec: 24 Jan. 1795.

Pages 361-363   24 Jan. 1795. John Miller, of Washington Dist., to
                   John Lovelady, for Ł 25 stg. for 150 acres in Washington Dist. on Chaugee Creek, waters of the Tugaloo
River, granted to Miller, 2 Jul. 1787, by Thos. Pinckney. Recorded Bk. SSSS, p. 402.
Wit: Moses Jones, Nathaniel Dennis. Plat included. Moses Jones made oath to John Miller, J. P., 24 Jan. 1795.
Rec: 24 Jan. 1795.

Page 364   I, Waddy Thompson, of Pendleton Co. have sold to
                   Thomas Blassingham, one negro girl named Marie, age
                   about 17 years. Date: 9 Feb. 1794.
Wit: Josiah N. Kennedy, Hugh Morrah. Acknowledged in open court of 1794 by J. B. Earle, J. P., Rec: 25 Jan. 1794. (1795?)

Pages 364-365   26 Jan. 1795. Henry McWhorter, of Abbeville Co. to
                   Thomas Smith, of Pendleton Co., for Ł 25 stg. for
                   162 acres on Broad Mouth Creek, waters of the Saluda
River, granted to William Hone(?), by Gov. Pinckney, 6 Oct. 1788, bd. on W. by Robert Telford. Signed: Henry McWhorter, Jane (X) McWhorter.
Wit: Joseph Brown, Thomas Smith, Benoni Fowler. Joseph Brown made oath to Joshua Saxon, J. P., 27 Jan. 1795.
Rec: 25(?) Jan. 1795.

Page 365   I, John Lauderdale for Ł 50 stg. of my son, James
                   Lauderdale's left him by his grandfather, which I
                   have wasted and run through, do fully grant to said
James Lauderdale one half of a tract of 300 acres that I now live on, bd by Brown and Mills, together with certain cattle, furniture. Date: 2 Jan. 1795.
Wit: Harris Mauldin, Robert Norris, John Mauldin. Harris Mauldin made oath to E. Brown, J. P., 2 Jan. 1795.
Rec: 26 Jan. 1795.

Pages 365-366   I, John Lauderdale for consideration of Ł 50 of my
                   daughter, Sarah Lauderdale, left to her by her grand
                   father, which I have wasted and run through, grant
Sarah Lauderdale one half of a tract of 300 acres, bd. by Thompson and certain cattle, furniture. Date: 2 Jan. 1795.
Wit: Harris Mauldin, Robert Norris, John Mauldin. Harris Mauldin made oath to E. Brown, J. P., 2 Jan. 1795.
Rec: 26 Jan. 1795.

Pages 366-367   6 Dec. 1794. Peter Freneau and Francis Bremar, Esqs.
                   of Charleston Dist., S. C. to Joseph Whitner, of Pendleton Co., for Ł 10 stg. for 640 acres in Washington Dist. on both sides of 18 Mile Creek, waters of the Keowee River, granted to Freneau and Bremar, 1 Mar. 1786, originally surveyed for Henry Hughes.
Wit: Peter Bremar, Thomas Farrar. Thomas Farrar made oath to J. B. Earle, J. P., 24 Jan. 1795.
Rec: 26 Jan. 1795.

Pages 367-368   4 Jun. 1794. Jacob Rami to Joseph Whitner, for Ł50
                   stg. for 400 acres, granted 2 Sep. 1793, by Wm. Moultrie, in Washington Dist. on both sides of 18 Mile Creek, waters of the Keowee River, bd. on SE by Wm. Banister, on NE by Clement Deal, on NW by Golden Tinsley, on NE by Golden Tinsley, on SW and NW by John Campbell, and ___ McGuffin, on E. and SE by Jehu Pope, on SE and SW by Peter Freneau and ___Brimar. (cont'd next page)

(pages 367-368 cont'd):

Wit: Joab Mauldin, W. Steele. Joab Mauldin made oath to J. B. Earle, J. P., 24 Jan. 1795.
Rec: 24 Jan. 1795.

Pages 369-370   13 Aug. 1792. Richard Morrow to Zachariah Walker, for ₤ 50 stg. for 200 acres, part of 480 acres granted to Morrow, 3 Nov. 1788, by ____, on Big Generostee. Wit: Alexr. McMillen, Vann Walker, Jesse Browne. Jesse Browne made oath to E. Browne, J. P., (no date).
Rec: 26 Jan. 1795.

Pages 370-371   20 Jan. 1795. Jesse Coffee to John Henson for ₤ 30 for 130 acres granted to Coffee, 24 Aug. 1787, on Tugaloo River. Signed: Jesse (his mark) Coffee.
Wit: Alex Hunter, Joseph Swilling. Acknowledged in open court by J. B. Earle, 27 Jan. 1795.
Rec: 27 Jan. 1795.

Pages 371-372   4 Mar. 1794. John Kelly, Sr., and Nancy, his wife, of Washington Dist., to Wm. Mitchel, of Washington Dist., farmer, for ₤ 50 for 150 acres on Doddy's Crk. S. side of the Saluda, part of a tract of 331 acres granted John Kelly, Sr., by Wm. Moultrie, 7 Aug. 1786, surveyed by Joseph Whitner, deputy surveyor, bd. by John Kelly, David Smith, Enoch Smith. Signed: John Kelly, Nancy Kelly.
Wit: James Barron, Charles Dodson, Ezekiel Dunnagan. Charles Dodson made oath to John Wilson, 24 Jan. 1795.
Rec: 27 Jan. 1795.

Pages 372-374   18 Nov. 1794. Major Staton, of Greenville Co., S. C. to William Cleveland, of Pendleton Co., for ₤ 100 stg for 200 acres in Washington Dist. on Tugaloo River, Signed: Major (f) Stanton.
Wit: John Hinson, Meridith Blackburn....Greenville Co., S. C. Meridith Blackburn made oath to L. Tarants, Q.P., 17 Nov. 1794.
Rec: 24 Jan. 1795.

Pages 374-375   21 Jan. 1793. William Bell, of Chester Co., S. C., to William Wilson, of Pendleton Co., for ₤ 80 for 100 acres in Washington Dist., granted to Bell, 6 Jun. 1785 by Wm. Moultrie. Recorded Bk. DDDD, (no page no.).
Wit: John Nichelson, James Robinson. John Nichelson made oath to Wm. Halbert, 26 Dec. 1793.
Rec: 27 Jan. 1795.

Pages 375-376   I, Thomas Lesley, for ₤ 30 stg. paid by Andrew Pickens & Co., late merchant of South Carolina, sold one negro man named Sambo about 40 years old, one negro girl named Ciel, about 12 years old, and one bay mare. Date: 11 Apr. 1794. Wit: Moses Liddell, Daniel Stringer. Moses Liddell made oath to J. B. Earle, J. P., 9 Sep. 1794.
Rec: 9 Sep. 1794.

Pages 376-377   27 Oct. 1794. John Mills of N. C., to Wymer Siller, of Pendleton Co., for ₤ 5 for 180 acres on SE side of 26 Mile Creek, part of 640 acres granted Mills, 5 Jun. 1786, by Wm. Moultrie. Recorded Bk. LLLL, p. 215.
Wit: Joshua Saxon, Joseph (X) Huneycut. Plat shows land adj. to Benjamin Harris, John Polock, John E. Calhoun. Joshua Saxon made oath to E. Browne, J. P., 27 Jan. 1794.
Rec: 27 ___, 1795.

Pages 377-379   8 Nov. 1794. Wm. Pyle, Executor of the Estate of John Lindley, deceased, and Sarah Lindley, Executrix .....John Lindley, yeoman, in his lifetime owned sundry tracts of land and other estates. His last will and testament dated 9 Sep. 1790, directed to be sold at public auction, ...auction held 11

(pages 377-379 cont'd):
Dec. 1790, conducted by William Faris...tract of 260 acres to Sarah Lindley as highest bidder, on N. side of Big Creek, waters of the Saluda, part of 400 acres, granted to John C. Martin, 6 Mar. 1786, by Wm. Moultrie. Recorded Bk. HHHH, p. 334, conveyed by Martin to George Pearce, 17 Nov. 1786, conveyed from Pearce to John Lindley, 6 Sep. 1787. Signed: Wm. Pyle.
Wit: Thomas Garner, Lewis Garner, Harper Garner. Lewis Garner made oath to Wm. Halbert, J. P., 8 Nov. 1794.
Rec: 27 Jan. 1795.

Pages 379-382   9 Jun. 1794. Robert Anderson, Esq., to John Shannon, farmer, for Ł 80 for 200 acres, on both sides of the Connoross Creek, waters of the Keowee River, bd. on the N. by James Brough, granted to John Daveys on bounty for the service of Daniel Daveys, deceased, in the late War, deceased 16 Jul. 1784, granted by Benjamin Guerrard. Recorded Bk. BBBB, p. 24, conveyed to Anderson on 10 Jul. 1786. Signed: Robert Anderson, Lydia Anderson.
Wit: Willm. Sloan, Joseph Jenkins. Wm. Sloan made oath to J. B. Earle, J. P., 6 Jan. 1794.
Rec: 25 Jan. 1795.

Page 382   1 May 1790. Jacob Gilleylin to James Brown for Ł50 for 250 acres on Governor's Creek, waters of Rocky River, granted 2 Oct. 1786 by Wm. Moultrie.
Wit: Thomas Turner, John Evans, Thomas Brown. Thomas Brown made oath to E. Browne, J. P., 12 Jul. 1794.
Rec: 28 Jan. 1795.

Page 383   20 Aug. 1794. James Holmes, Sr., to Reuben Degarnet for Ł 500 for 119 acres on Mulberry Creek, branch of Rocky River.
Wit: Fergus Craven, John McMahan, Bartley Tucker. Bartley Tucker made oath to E. Browne, J. P., 30 Jul. 1795.
Rec: 4 Feb. 1795.

Pages 383-386   4 Oct. 1788. Donald Campbell, of 96 Dist., to Lewis Daniel Martin, Esq., for Ł 100 stg. for 296 acres on N. fork of Connoross Creek, waters of Keowee River, granted Campbell, 2 Mar. 1789.
Wit: William Steele, Zephaniah (X) Harrison. William Steele made oath to John Miller, J. P., 1 Feb. 1794.
Rec: 4 Feb. 1795.

Page 386   I, Elias Hollingsworth, sold to Thomas Wadsworth and William Turpin, one road waggon with geers, 4 horses, 2 feather beds and furniture.
Wit: Thomas Garvin, who made oath to J. B. Earle, J. P., 9 Feb. 1794.
Rec: 9 Feb. 1795.

Pages 387-388   I, Blake Mauldin, having failed in making titles to Robert Hammatt for 1 lot of land on ½ acre at Pendleton Courthouse for which I was bound for Ł 60 and whereas, Joab Mauldin has satisfied Hammatt for bond, I am now indebted to Joab Mauldin for 31.16.2, to be paid 14 Jan. 1797, security, one negro woman named Alyce, about 20 years old and one boy named Tom about 17 months old, son of Alyce. Date: 15 Jun. 1795.
Wit: William Steele, Robert Hammatt. Wm. Steele made oath 9 Feb. 1795.
Rec: 9 Feb. 1795.

Pages 388-389   2 Feb. 1795. John Moss to William Lays for Ł10 stg. for 200 acres granted to John Moss on his bounty, 4 Jul. 1791, by Charles Pinckney, bd. on N. by William Lewis, on SE by William Lewis, on Milwee's Creek, waters of 23 Mile Crk., reserving all older granted land within the bounds of sd. lines. Signed: John (O) Moss.
Wit: Sam'l. Neil, William Hobbs. Sam'l. Neil made oath to J. B. Earle, 10 Jan. 1795.
Rec: 10 Feb. 1795.

Pages 389-391   7 Jan. 1791. William Reed, of Pendleton Co., to John
                 Armstrong, of Greenville Co., for ₤ 130 for 606 acres
                 part of 786 acres in 96 Dist., Pendleton Co., on
George's Creek, waters of the Saluda River, granted to Wm. Reed, 1 May
1786, by Wm. Moultrie, where Reed now lives, bd. by Reed and by Noblet
Johnson.
Wit: William Armstrong, John Hamilton. John Hamilton made oath to John
Wilson, 3 Feb. 1795.
Rec: 14 Feb. 1795.

Pages 391-392   11 Dec. 1794. John Armstrong, of Pendleton Co., to
                 William McKemy for ₤ 12 for 30 acres, part of 606 ac.
                 in 96 Dist. on S. branch of George's Creek, waters
of the Saluda, granted to William Reed, 1 May 1786, by Wm. Moultrie.
Wit: Charles Bowen, Charles Stevens. Charles Bowen made oath to John
Wilson, J. P., 2 Feb. 1795.
Rec: 14 Feb. 1795.

Pages 392-393   3 Dec. 1791. William Reed, of 96 Dist., to William
                 McKamy for ₤ 50 for 116 acres part of 606 acres....
                 granted to Reed, 1 May 1786, on branches of George's
Creek, waters of the Saluda, bd. by Noblet Johnson.
Wit: William Jewele, John Armstrong. William Jewele made oath to John
Wilson, J. P., 2 Feb. 1795.
Rec: 14 Feb. 1795.

Pages 393-396   8 Feb. 1792. Noblet Johnson, and Sarah, his wife, of
                 Washington Dist., to William Jewel for ₤ 60 stg., for
                 150 acres, part of 606 acres on S. fork of George's
Creek, waters of the Saluda River, Washington Dist., granted to William
Reed, 1 May 1786, by Wm. Moultrie, bd. by William Reed, Noblet Johnson,
John Armstrong. Signed: Noblet Johnston, Sarah (+) Johnston.
Wit: John Armstrong, William McKamey. William McKamey made oath to Jno.
Wilson, J. P., 2 Feb. 1795.
Rec: 14 Feb. 1795.

Pages 396-397   ____, 1790. William Irby and Henrietta Irby, his
                 wife, of Newberry Co., S. C., to Daniel Symmes for
                 ₤ 100 stg. for 520 acres surveyed for Albert Robins,
in Washington Dist., on waters of Little River of Keowee, bd. on NW by
Ellis Harlin, also 138 acres surveyed for Fields Prewitt, Sr., in Washington Dist. on Cane Creek, waters of the Keowee River. Signed: Wm. Irby, Henrietta (+) Irby.
Wit: James (X) Smith, John Garvin. John Garvin made oath to Robert Gilliam, J. P., 21 Jan. 1795.
Rec: 16 Feb. 1795.

Pages 397-399   13 Mar. 1792. George Nelson to Meshack Green for
                 ₤ 25 stg. for 350 acres in 96 Dist., south of Saluda
                 River, on Little Beaver Dam Creek, waters of Rocky
River, of the Savannah River, part of a tract granted to Nelson, 10 Jun.
1790, bd. by Isaac Horten, George Anderson. Signed: George (his mark)
Nelson.
Wit: Isaac Horton, Jno. Carrell. Isaac Horton made oath to John Wilson,
J. P., 2 Sep. 1792.
Rec: 27 Feb. 1795.

Pages 399-401   23 Apr. 1791. Andrew Liddle, farmer, to John Gris-
                 sam, for ₤ 2 stg. for 100 acres, part of 473 acres
                 on waters of 26 Mile Creek of the Keowee River, bd.
on S. by Francis Gutry, granted to Andrew Liddle by Thos. Pinckney (no
date). Recorded Bk. WWWW, p. 107.
Wit: Jehu Pope, David (D) Carter. David Carter made oath to J. B. Earle
on 5 Sep. 1795.
Rec: 5 Sep. 1795.

Pages 402-403   13 Jun. 1794. George Staton to James Eason for ₤10
                 stg. for 50 acres on both sides of the Little Beaver
                 Dam, part of a tract granted to Staton, 6 Jun. 1791
by Charles Pinckney, bd. by Eason, and Thomas Adams. Signed: George(X)

(pages 402-403 cont'd):
Staton. Wit: Aron Tolinson, William (X) Doss. Aaron Tolinson made oath to Wm. Hall, J. P., 17 Feb. 1795.
Rec: 3 Mar. 1795.

Pages 403-404   4 Oct. 1794. Jesse Miller, Washington Dist., to Wm. Jameson, of the same, for Ł 40 stg. for 180 acres, granted to Joseph Paterson, 21 Jan. 1785, on Woolf Creek, branch of 12 Mile River, on the E. side of Grassy Mountain, line to begin on waggon ford of Cattail branch, adj. to tract of 220 acres granted to Josiah Paterson, conveyed by him to James Rice...condition of this obligation is that Jesse Miller will deliver to Wm. Jamison by 1 Mar. next, one new wagon done after the manner mentioned in the note that Jesse Miller gave to Sam'l. Young, deceased, 4 ___, 1793.
Wit: Thomas Gaw, John McElroy. John McElroy made oath to Robert Bowen, J. P., 21 Feb. 1795.
Rec: 7 Mar. 1795.

Pages 404-405   11 Oct. 1794. William Twitty and Sarah, his wife, & and Ann Twitty, administrators of the estate of John Twitty, deceased, to Sam'l. Gardner for Ł 150 stg. for 200 acres on the Keowee River, granted to John Twitty, 5 Jun. 1786, by Wm. Moultrie, surveyed by Wm. Twitty, by heirship. Signed: William Twitty, Sarah (X) Twitty, Ann (X) Twitty.
Wit: H. Montgomery, John Hays, Wm. Farris. John Hays made oath to J.B. Earle, 16 Mar. 1795.
Rec: 16 Mar. 1795.

Pages 406-407   18 Sep. 1794. Albert Francis Smithson to Benjamin Trammel, both of Greenville Co., S. C., for Ł 40 stg. for 150 acres on branch of Little Estatoe, N. half of 300 acres granted to Smithson, 5 Dec. 1788, recorded Bk. YYYY, p. 22. Signed: Albt. (Albert) Francis Smithson, Sina (+) Smithson.
Wit: Isaac Trammel, William Lax. Isaac Trammel made oath to Gabriel Moffett, 20 Sep. 1794.
Rec: 17 Mar. 1795.

Pages 407-408   2 Oct. 1794. James Tate, Jr., to James Hamilton for Ł 5 stg. for 400 acres, by name of Rich Mountain on Rampey's Creek.
Wit: Edw. T. McClure, William McClure, Jas. Hart. Edward T. McClure made oath to E. Browne, J. P., 18 Mar. 1795.
Rec: 19 Mar. 1795.

Pages 408-409   2 Oct. 1794. James Tate, Jr. to Samuel Tate for Ł5 stg. for 1,100 acres on Estatoe Creek of the Keowee River, head branchs of the Eulonoy Creek of the Saluda River, part of a tract granted to John Anderson and conveyed to James Tate.
Wit: Robt. Tate, Edward McClure, Richard Speake. Edward McClure made oath to E. Browne, J. P., 18 Mar. 1795.
Rec: 19 Mar. 1795.

Pages 409-410   22 Oct. 1794. James Tate, Jr. to Samuel Tate for Ł5 stg. for 200 acres on Connoross Creek, waters of the Chauge Creek, also a tract of 640 acres on Connoross Creek. Wit: Edw. T. McClure, Robt. Tate, Richd. Speake. E. T. McClure made oath to E. Browne, J. P., 18 Mar. 1795.
Rec: 19 Mar. 1795.

Pages 410-411   22 Oct. 1794. James Tate, Jr. to Samuel Tate for Ł5 stg. for 960 acres, part of a tract granted to John Anderson, conveyed to Tate on Little Estatoe Creek of the Keowee River.
Wit: Edward T. McClure, Richd. Speake, Robt. Tate. Edw. Tate McClure made oath to E. Browne, 18 Mar. 1795.
Rec: 19 Mar. 1795.

Pages 411-412   22 Oct. 1794. James Tate, Jr. to Samuel Tate for Ł5 stg. for 640 acres on Cane Creek, branch of the Keo-

(pages 411-412 cont'd):
wee River. Wit: Edw. T. McClure, Richd. Speake, Robert Tate. Edw. T. McClure made oath to E. Browne, J. P., 18 Mar.1795.
Rec: 19 Mar. 1795.

Pages 412-413   22 Oct. 1794. James Tate, Jr. to Samuel Tate for ₤5 stg. for 160 acres on George's Creek, waters of 12 Mile Creek (River), also a tract of 718 acres on the Crow Creek being parcels granted to John Anderson, conveyed to James Tate.
Wit: E. T. McClure, Richd. Speake, Robt. Tate. E. T. McClure made oath to E. Browne, J. P., 18 Mar. 1795.
Rec: 19 Mar. 1795.

Pages 413-414   22 Oct. 1794. James Tate, Jr. to Samuel Tate for ₤5 stg. for 240 acres on Roak Creek, of the Connoross, also 640 acres originally granted to John Anderson, conveyed to Tate.
Wit: Edw. T. McClure, Richd. Speake, Robt. Tate. Edw. T. McClure made oath to E. Browne, 19 Mar. 1795.
Rec: 19 Mar. 1795.

Pages 414-416   3 Feb. 1795. Robert Stevenson and Isabel, his wife, & Blake Mauldin and Elizabeth, his wife, to James Tate, Jr., for 5 shillings stg. for several tracts ....Robert Stevenson and wife, 200 acres, part of 420 acres granted to Robert Stevenson, 1 Dec. 1788, Pendleton Co., formerly 96 Dist...on the Rocky River and Beaver Creek, bd. by land late property of J. Thornton and Norris Smith and Norris Jeulton(?) and Moris and E. Moore on Beaver Creek, including mine of iron ore...Blake Mauldin and his wife, 6 acres including a cascade and seat for water works on Beaver Creek adj. aforesaid parcel of 200 acres...sd. 6 acres part of a tract of 190 acres ... granted to Thomas Morris, 4 Dec. 1786. Signed: Robert Stevenson, Isabel (X) Stevenson. Blake Mauldin, Betsey (O) Mauldin.
Wit: James Brice, Sr., James Brice, Jr., Sam'l. Tate. James Brice, Jr. made oath to E. Browne, J. P., 27 Feb. 1795.
Rec: 19 Mar. 1795.

Pages 416-417   23 Feb. 1795. Robert Stevenson and Isabel, his wife, to James Tate, Jr. for 5 shillings for 10 acres on the E. side of Rocky River, including iron ore mine, part of 490 acres granted to Stevenson, 1 Dec. 1788, in 96 Dist. on the Rocky River and Beaver branch, bd. by late property of Thornton, Norris, Smith and Norris J. Culton, Morris and E. Morris. Signed: Robert Stevenson, Isabel (X) Stevenson.
Wit: James Brice, Sr., James Brice, Jr. James Brice, Sr. made oath to this on 27 Feb. 1795.
Rec: 19 Mar. 1795.

Pages 417-418   27 Oct. 1794. James Tate, Jr. to William Tate for ₤ 5 stg. for one tract of 200,000 acres, bd. by the Tugaloo River and the Indian Boundary line, the other tract of 100,000 acres, bd. by the Toxaway and Keowee River and the Indian Boundary, plat made to John Anderson, 9 Oct. 1793.
Wit: E. Tate McClure, Robt. Tate, Richd. Speake. Edw. Tate McClure made oath to E. Browne, J. P., 18 Mar. 1795.
Rec: 19 Mar. 1795.

Pages 418-419   2 Mar. 1795. David Carter and Mehitable, his wife, to Samuel Tate for ₤ 5 stg. for privileges of 1/3 part of Iron works on 26 Mile Creek, granted by Francis Guthrie to Jehu Pope, by Pope to Jno. Grissan and by Grissan to Carter, viz: middle fire places of iron works with 1/3 part of water which creek affords, except what grist mill requires, also a piece of land 25 feet by 50 to sd. works, also free passage to and from works. Signed: David (D) Carter, Mahatabel (X) Carter.
Wit: Edw. Tate McClure, Benjamin Dickson. Edw. T. McClure made oath to E. Browne, J. P., 18 Mar. 1795.
Rec: 19 Mar. 1795.

Pages 419-421   3 Mar. 1795. John Grissam and Elizabeth, his wife, to James Tate, Jr., for Ł 5 stg. all valuable part of iron works, viz: western fire place on 26 Mile Creek, known by the name of Grissam Iron Works, together with piece of ground of 10 acres on E. side of Iron works, bd. by Guthrie's line, Blake Mauldin and Samuel Little, excepting a plat of ground of 50 square feet previously conveyed by John Grissam to David Carter and Robert Gabby, also coal yard for other two fire places of iron works, lately conveyed to Blake Mauldin and Samuel Tate. Signed: J. W. Griss<u>im</u>, Elizabeth (X) Grissim. (n.b. in previous conveyance #418-419, name is spelled Griss<u>an</u>)
Wit: Edw. T. McClure, David (D) Carter. Edw. T. McClure made oath to E. Browne, J. P., 18 Mar. 1795.
Rec: 19 Mar. 1795.

Pages 421-423   ___, 1795. James Tate, Jr. to Samuel Tate for Ł 5 stg., four tracts of land in all 4,219 acres, part of a tract of 200,000 acres granted to John Anderson, conveyed to James Tate, Jr. as seven different tracts on Toxaway Creek, 1st containing 320 acres, 2nd., 120 acres, 3rd., 360 acres, 4th., 180 acres, 5th., 120 acres, 6th., 160 acres, 7th., 120 acres...also seven different tracts on Chauga, 1st., 225 acres, 2nd., 300 acres, 3rd., 118 acres, 4th., 114 acres, 5th., 140 acres, 6th., 190 acres, 7th., 6 acres ....also 5 tracts on Conoross, 1st., 280 acres, 2nd., 215 acres, 3rd., 100 acres., 4th., 120 acres, 5th., 320 acres.
Wit: Wm. McClure, Edw. T. McClure, Jas. Hart. Edw. Tate McClure made oath to E. Browne, J. P., 18 Mar. 1795.
Rec: 19 Mar. 1795.

Pages 424-425   2 Oct. 1790. James Tate, Jr. to Edward Tate McClure several tracts for 5 shillings stg. on main fork of French Broad River, also tract on Big Estatoe, main fork of Keowee River. Also a tract on Gregories's Creek, branch of 12 Mile River, adj. to Joseph Woodhall. Also, a tract called 6 Mile Spring on the head waters of 12 Mile River. Also, a tract on Toxaway, middle fork of the Keowee River called Horsepasture. Also, a tract at the head of N. fork of Eulony Creek. All tracts granted to John Anderson and conveyed to James Tate, Jr., quantity and boundary appear in plats.
Wit: Richd. Speake, Robt. Tate, Sam'l. Tate. Robt. Tate made oath to E. Browne, J. P., 18 Mar. 1795.
Rec: 19 Mar. 1795.

Pages 425-428   20 Jul. 1789. Evan Thomas, farmer, to William Kerly, for Ł 60 for 191 acres, part of a tract of 383 acres, on the E. side of 23 Mile Creek, of the Keowee River, bd. on N. by John Portman, granted to Evan Thomas, citizen, by Wm. Moultrie. Recorded Bk. LLLL, p. 491. Signed: Evan Thomas, Elizabeth (X) Thomas.
Wit: Lewis Cobb, Elijah Stinson. Lewis Cobb made oath to J. B. Earle, J. P., 23 Mar. 1795.
Rec: 23 Mar. 1795.

Page 428   I, Elias Hollingsworth, farmer, for Ł 30 stg., paid by Thomas Wadsworth and William Turpin, merchants, for horses, a crop of corn, fodder hay.
Wit: James Young, Jas. Boyer. James Young made oath to John Downs, J.P. 15 Feb. 1795.
Rec: 25 May 1795.

Pages 429-430   9 Mar. 1794. John Adair and John Curry to James Adair Waugh for Ł 50 for 556 acres in Washington Dist., bd. on NE by Wm. McCaleb, on NW and NE by John Buckhannon, on NW by George Little, on Keowee River. Signed: Jno. Adair, James Curry.
Wit: Wm. Woodward, Benjamin Murry. Benjamin Murry made oath to J. B. Earle, J. P., 25 Mar. 1795.
Rec: 25 Mar. 1795.

Pages 420-431   9 Mar. 1795. Nathan Austin to Wm. Grant for Ł 100, for 150 acres granted Austin, 7 Mar. 1791, by Charles Pinckney. Recorded Bk. C., no. 5, p. 276, on S. side

(pages 430-431 cont'd.):
of Conoross Creek, of the Keowee River, now in possession of Wm. Grant.
Wit: Wm. Sloan, Jno. C. Kilpatrick, J. P. (no oath).
Rec: 26 Mar. 1795.

Pages 431-433   12 Oct. 1794. Wm. Mackey to Henry Hays for ₺ 60 stg. for 90 acres, part of a tract in 96 Dist., on E. side of the Keowee River, bd. by Wm. Mackey, John Hays, granted to Wm. Mackey, 2 Jul. 1787. Signed: William (W) Mackey, Mary (+) Mackey.
Wit: John C. Kilpatrick, Geo. Hays, John Twitty, John Hays. John Hays made oath to J. B. Earle, J. P., 25 Mar. 1795.
Rec: 26 Mar. 1795.

Pages 433-436   12 Oct. 1794. Wm. Mackie to Henry Hays for ₺ 60 stg. for 150 acres on the E. side of the Keowee River, bd. by Wm. Mackie, James Tate, granted to Mackie, 5 Jun. 1786. Signed: William (W) Mackie, Mary (X) Mackie.
Wit: John Hays, John Twitty, Geo. Hays. Geo. Hays made oath to J. B. Earle, J. P., 20 Mar. 1795.
Rec: 26 Mar. 1795.

Pages 436-438   22 Feb. 1794. James Tate to Henry Hays for ₺ 50 stg. for 48 acres on the E. side of the Seneca River including house and improvements where John Burns now lives. Wit: Geo. Hays, John Hays, John Burns. John Hays made oath to J. B. Earle, J. P., 6 Mar. 1795.
Rec: 26 Mar. 1795.

Page 438   I, Samuel Robinson for love and goodwill I bear my son, Michael Robinson, all goods and chattels, present dwelling house, cattle, beds and furniture. Date: 3 Apr. 1795. Signed: Sam'l. (R) Robinson.
Wit: Geo. W. Earle, Jas. Wood. Certified by J. B. Earle, J. P., 3 Apr. 1795. Rec: 3 Apr. 1795.

Pages 438-441   4 Feb. 1794. Andrew Pickens, Robert Anderson, Robert Maxwell, John Hallum, John Ford and Robert Bowen,Esqs Commissioners chosen by the General Assembly at Town of Pickensville, Pendleton Co. to Michael Smith, carpenter, for ₺ 20, 5 shillings for 1/2 acre lot on Federal Street, corner lot next to Courthouse in Pickensville.
Wit: Wm. Edmondson, Wm. Norton. Wm. Norton made oath to J. B. Earle, J. P., 3 Apr. 1795.
Rec: 3 Apr. 1795.

Pages 441-442   29 Dec. 1794. James McFarron and Isabel, his wife, of Abbeville Co., farmer, to James Eddins, of Abbeville Co., for ₺ 160 stg. for 300 acres on branch of Wilson's Creek, of Great Rocky Creek. Signed: James McFaron, Isabel(her mark) McFaron.
Wit: Robt. Norris, Surry Davis. Surry Davis made oath to E. Browne, J. P., 6 Apr. 1795.
Rec: 8 Apr. 1795.

Pages 442-443   12 Oct. 1794. David Norrington, of Franklin Co.,Ga. to Samuel Taylor, of Pendleton Co., for ₺ 5 for 240 acres in Washington Dist. on Griffen's Creek, branch of Keowee River.
Wit: Sam'l. Taylor, Jr., Thos. Robertson. Sam'l. Taylor, Jr. made oath to J. B. Earle, J. P., 9 Apr. 1795.
Rec: 9 Apr. 1795.

Pages 443-444   12 May 1794. David Norrington, of Franklin Co., Ga. to Samuel Taylor of Pendleton Co., for ₺ 5 stg. for 426 acres in Washington Dist. on the W. side of Keowee River, bd. on SW by Robert Anderson, on SE by Sam'l. Taylor.
Wit: Sam'l. Taylor, Jr., Thos. Robertson. Sam'l. Taylor, Jr. made oath to J. B. Earle, 9 Feb. 1795. Rec: 9 Apr. 1795.

Pages 444-445   Washington Dist. 1 Apr. 1795. Francis Greenwood, schoolmaster, to Charles Rice, planter, for ₤ 50 stg. for 815 acres, surveyed for Greenwood, 12 Aug. 1793, on branchs of the Seneca River, bd. on NW and NE by Jehu Pope, on E. by McGuffin, on SE by General Andrew Pickens and William Crosby, on SW by Col. Robt. Anderson, on SW by John Hays, on SE by Peter Sinkler, granted to Greenwood, 2 Dec. 1793 by Wm. Moultrie.
Wit: Thomas (+) Raper, John Raper. John Raper made oath 9 Apr. 1795 to J. B. Earle, J. P.
Rec: 9 Apr. 1795.

Pages 445-447   3 Feb. 1795. Joel Callahan to Richard Richardson for ₤ 50 stg. for 300 acres granted to Callahan, 1 Jan. 1787 by Wm. Moultrie, in Washington Dist. on branchs of George's Creek and Doddy's Creek of the Saluda River.
Wit: John (+) Callahan, John (F) Fowler. John Callahan made oath to E. Brown, J. P., 4 Feb. 1795.
Rec: 10 Apr. 1795.

Pages 447-448   12 Mar. 1794. James Davis, of Pendleton Co., to William Glenn, of Rockingham Co., N. C. for ₤ 150 stg., (acreage?) on both sides of Olinoy.
Wit: Amos Ladd, John Chastain, Elijah Chastain. Amos Ladd made oath to Baily Anderson, 3 Apr. 1794.
Rec: 10 Apr. 1795.

Pages 448-452   16 Dec. 1794. Edward Camp and Elizabeth, his wife, to Jacob Capehart for ₤ 50 stg. for 120 acres above the Ancient Boundary line, on 26 Mile Creek, of the Savannah River, bd. by Calhoun, Dickerson, and Edward Camp, granted to Camp, 7 Aug. 1786 by Wm. Moultrie for 280 acres in 96 Dist. Signed: Edward Camp, Elizabeth (+) Camp.
Wit: John Hunnicutt, Joseph Jolly. John Hunnicutt made oath to John Wilson, 6 Apr. 1795.
Rec: 16 Apr. 1795. Plat included also.

Pages 452-454   13 Apr. 1795. Andrew Pickens, Robert Anderson, Robert Maxwell, John Ford, John Hallums and Robert Bowen, Esqs., Commissioners by the General Assembly to lay out a town of Pickensville and of the counties of Pendleton and Greenville to Hugh Morrow (also spelled Morrah), carpenter, for ₤ 9 stg. for 1/2 acre lot of land in Pickensville, Lot no. 11, fronting Federal Street.
Wit: J. Brown. John Brown made oath to John Willson, J. P., 4 Apr.1794.
Rec: 16 Apr. 1795.

Page 454   I, Nathan Austin have sold to William Grant...(this is very dim, hard to read), 2 Mar. 1795...do assign my right of within bill of sale to John Hardin(?) & Jeremiah Abil...15 Apr. 1795. Signed: Jacob Womack.
Rec: __ Apr. 1795.

Pages 454-455   19 Sep. 1794. Samuel Lofton to Joshua Reeder for ₤ 60 stg. for 200 acres on both sides of 5 Mile Spg. Branch, waters of Keowee River, bd. on NE by John L. Jervais, granted, 2 Oct. 1786 by Wm. Moultrie.
Wit: Samuel Neil(?), John Warnock, David Alexander. Samuel Neil made oath to J. B. Earle, J. P., 20 Apr. 1795.
Rec: 21 Apr. 1795.

Pages 456-457   1 Feb. 1792. Benjamin Starrett to Samuel Finley(?), for ₤ 100(?) stg. for 160 acres, part of 200 acres granted to George Pearce(?) on the S. side of Seneca River, by Benjamin Guerrard (date?). Recorded Bk. CCCC, p. 39(?).
Wit: John Finley, Samuel Finley. John Finley made oath to Wm. Halbert, J. P., 18 Apr. 1795.
Rec: 20 Apr. 1795. (n.b. this is very dim).

Pages 457-461   9 Jul, 1793. David Jordan to John Tippen for ₤ 250 stg. for 480 acres in Washington Dist. formerly 96 Dist., on Big Jenerostee Creek, branch of Savannah

(pages 457-461 cont'd): River, granted to Jordan, 1 Dec. 1788, by Thomas Pinckney. Recorded Bk. YYYY, p. 233.
Wit: Jesse Brown, James Long, William Tippen. Jesse Brown made oath to Elijah Browne, 15 Jul. 1793.
Rec: 21 Apr. 1795.

Page 461 I, Jeremiah Abels for Ł 60, 11 shillings sold to Mary Roberts, furniture, kitchen ware, sheep, horse. Date: 14 Dec. 1794.
Wit: John (H) Hardin, J. B. Earle. Acknowledged in court, 25 Apr. 1795 by J. B. Earle, J. P.
Rec: 25 Apr. 1795.

Pages 461-464 23 Apr. 1795. Joseph Reed to Charles Stevens for Ł 50 stg. for 201 acres on Little Beaver Dam Creek, bd. on NW by Aquilla Grurand, on SW by the Tugaloo River, on other by vacant land, granted to Reed by William Milwee, Esq. on 2 Dec. 1793.
Wit: Thomas Farrar, David McCaleb. David McCaleb made oath to J. B. Earle, J. P., 24 Apr. 1794.
Rec: 27 Apr. 1795.

Pages 464-467 5 Feb. 1793. Francis Miller and Jean, his wife, to John Adair and James Curry, merchants and co-partners for Ł 50 for 240 acres in Washington Dist. (lately 96 Dist.), on Cain Creek, Little River. Signed: Francis Miller, Jean (+) Miller.
Wit: Joseph Hill, Reece Jones, Wm. McCaleb. Joseph Hill made oath to J. B. Earle, J. P., 27 Apr. 1795.
Rec: 27 Apr. 1795.

END OF BOOK B.

PENDLETON COUNTY, S. C.
CONVEYENCE BOOK C-D
1795-1799

Pages 1-2 14 Feb. 1794. Andrew Pickens, Robert Anderson, Robert Maxwell, John Ford, John Hallum and Robert Bowen, Esqs., Commissioners chosen by the General Assembly to lay out the town of Pickensville and counties of Pendleton and Greenville, to Michael Smith, carpenter of Pendleton Co., for Ł 14 stg. for 1/2 acre lot in Pickensville, known as Town Lot #15. Signed: (by above Commissioners.)
Wit: Robt. Speed, John Couch, W. Steele. Robt. W. Speed made oath to J. B. Earle, J. P., 28 Apr. 1795.
Rec: 28 Apr. 1795.

Pages 2-3 27 Apr. 1793. Nathaniel Williams and Elizabeth, his wife, to Samuel Burton for Ł 21 stg. for 200 acres, on branches of Austin's Creek, waters of Connoross, surveyed for Nathaniel Williams and granted 4 Oct. 1790 by Charles Pinckney, Esq. Signed: Nathaniel (X) Williams, Elizabeth (her mark) Williams.
Wit: Benjamin Ingram, Nathaniel Austin. Benjamin Ingram made oath to Nathl. Perry, J. P., 27 Apr. 1795.
Rec: 29 Apr. 1795.

Pages 3-4 6 Jul. 1792. John Gowen, of Spartanburg Co., S. C. to William Jamison, of Pendleton Co. for Ł 40 stg. for 340 acres granted to Gowen, 1 Jan. 1789 by Thos. Pinckney, in Washington Dist. on both sides of George's Creek, of Saluda River, adj. to land formerly belonging to Edmond Bearden. Signed: John Gowen.
Wit: Jephs Moss, James Earley, Winn (X) Bearden. Jephs Moss made oath to Robert Bowen, J. P., 2 May 1795.
Rec: 4 May 1795.

Page 4   20 Nov. 1791. John Nicholson to William Jamison for
                    ₤ 40 stg. for 225 acres granted to Nicholson, 3 Jul.
                    1786 by Wm. Moultrie, in 96 Dist. on Princes Creek,
of George's Creek of Saluda River.
Wit: Ebenezer Fain, John Black. Ebenezer Fain made oath to Gabriel Moffett, J. P., 17 Sep. 1792.
Rec: 4 May 1795.

Page 5   13 Dec. 1791. Edmond Bearden, of Greenville Co., S.
                    C., to William Jamison, of Pendleton Co., 96 Dist.,
                    for ₤ 40 stg. for 500 acres granted Bearden, 1 May
1786 by Wm. Moultrie, in 96 Dist. on S. side of Saluda above old boundary line on both sides of George's Creek of Saluda River.
Wit: Daniel McCollum, Jesse (X) Langston, Luke (L) Barnet. Luke Barnet made oath to Gabriel Moffitt, J. P., 17 Sep. 1792.
Rec: 4 May 1795.

Pages 5-6   16 Aug. 1792. William Ross (or Rose) to William Jamison for ₤ 12 stg. for 166 acres, part of 809 acres
                    granted Rose(?), 5 Jan. 1789 by Thos. Pinckney, in
Washington Dist., S. of Saluda on Mile Fork of George's Creek, bd. on S. by William Galaspie, Sr., John Gillaspey, and sd. Jamison.
Wit: David Smith, James Hobbs, Luke Barnett. Luke Barnet made oath to Gabriel Moffett, J. P., 17 Sep. ___.
Rec: 4 May 1795.

Pages 6-7   15 Nov. 1790. James Gates to Richard Richardson for
                    200 acres in 96 Dist. on SW side of Saluda River, adj
                    to James Fork of Doddy's Creek, Howell Doddy, granted 21 Jan. 1785 by Benjamin Guerrard.
Wit: John (his mark) Ellege, Isum (X) Bishop. Isham Bishop made oath to Robert Bowen, J. P., 13 Mar. 1795.
Rec: 15 May 1795.

Pages 7-8   12 Dec. 1794. Daniel Bryson, also Brison, of Pendleton Dist. to Thomas Jones of Abbeville Co. for ₤20
                    stg. for 100 acres on Wilson's Creek, granted to Jno.
McKneel by Charles Pinckney, 1789, excepting to Daniel Bryson use of the water of branch.
Wit: George Tillman(?), Phillip Phagans, Lewis (?) Bozeman. Phillip Phagan made oath to E. Browne, J. P., 17 Apr. 1795.
Rec: 2 May 1795.

Pages 8-9   29 Nov. 1792. Samuel Brasher and Feeby, his wife, to
                    Edward Maxwell for ₤ 100 stg. for 402 acres in Washington Dist. on S. side of Saluda bd. on SW by vacant land, on NW by A. W. Mahon, on NE by Perisemon's(?), on SE by John Vanderhorst, Esq., granted Robert S. Brasher. Signed: Robert Samuel Brasher, Feeby (X) Brasher.
Wit: Andrew Huse, Wm. Edmondson. Robt. Samuel Brasher made oath agreeable to law before Wm. Edmondson, J. P., 29 Nov. 1792.
Rec: 30 May 1795.

Pages 9-10   5 Jan. 1795. Moses Barnes, of Rutherford Co., N. C.
                    to George Potts, of Pendleton Co., for ₤ 40 stg. for
                    177 acres in Washington Dist. on branches of Connoross Creek, branch of Keowee River, bd. on all sides by vacant land, and granted to John Twitty by Thos. Pinckney, 2 Jul. 1787. Recorded Bk.VVVV, p. 63, conveyed by Twitty to John Miller, by Miller to Moses Barnes.
Signed: Moses (MB) Barnes.
Wit: Yelverton Neville, William Cummin. William Cummin made oath to J. C. Kilpatrick, J. P., 30 Jan. 1795.
Rec: 3 Jun. 1795.

Pages 10-11   3 Dec. 1794. James Martin, of York Co., S. C. to
                    Alexander Stevenson, of Pendleton Co., S. C. for ₤60
                    stg. for 121 acres part of a tract granted Amos Roberts, 16 Jul. 1784, by Benjamin Garret, Governor, and then conveyed to James Martin, 18 Apr. 1789, on Mountain Creek, branch of Great Generostee Creek. Plat drawn by William Sloan, D.S., 6 May 1791. (cont'd next page)

(pages 10-11 cont'd):

Wit: James Stevenson, Thomas (X) Skelton. Thomas Skelton made oath to E. Browne, J. P., 21 Jan. 1795.
Rec: 6 Jan. 1795.

Pages 11-12   3 Dec. 1794. James Martin, of York Co. to Thos. Skelton, of Pendleton Co., for Ł 100 stg. for 200 acres, part of 640 acres granted to Amos Roberts, 16 Jul. 1784, by Benjamin Garret, and conveyed to James Martin, on Mountain Creek of Great Generostee Creek., bd. by James Stevenson, Alexander Stevenson, Marak's old line.
Wit: James Morrow, James Stevenson. James Stevenson made oath to E. Browne, J. P., 22 Apr. 1795.
Rec: 5 Jun. 1795.

Pages 12-13   8 May 1791. Aeson Jay to Jacob Chamberlain for Ł 35 for 129 acres, part of 254 acres granted Jay, 1788, on Big Generostee, waters of Savannah River, where Jacob Chamberlain now lives.
Wit: Jordan Reaves, Jas. Hillhouse, David Dickey. Jordan Reaves made oath to E. Browne, J. P., 18 Nov. 1791.
Rec: 10 Jun. 1795.

Page 13   19 Feb. 1795. James Ross to Abraham Odam for Ł 10 stg. for 122 acres, granted James Ross on 19 Feb. 1792, by Wm. Moultrie, on W. side of Great Generostee Creek, by by William Drayton, James Martin.
Wit: Brown Ross, Joel Ledbetter. Joel Ledbetter made oath to J. B. Earle, J. P., 3 Jun. 1795.
Rec: 23 Jun. 1795.

Page 14   26 Feb. 1795. Abraham Oldham to Joel Ledbetter for Ł 35 stg. for 122 acres in Washington Dist. on waters of Generostee Creek, of Savannah River, granted James Ross, 4 Mar. 1793, by Wm. Moultrie, bd. on NW by Mathew Thompson, on SW by William Drayton and by vacant land.
Wit: Leon (his mark) Hamilton, John Burford. John Burford made oath to Joshua Saxon, J. P., 21 Mar. 1795.
Rec: 23 Jun. 1795.

Pages 14-16   Washington Dist. 6 Apr. 1795. Thomas Farrar, Esq., Sheriff of Washington Dist. to Patrick McDowell and Alexander McDowell, merchants of the Town of Cambridge, 96 Dist., highest bidders for Ł3, 10 shillings, in judgement against Daniel McCullum, brought by William Young in Court of Common Pleas at Cambridge, for Ł 20, sd. judgement by writ of Fiere Facias attested by Hon. John Rutledge, Esq., Chief Justice, 9 Jun. 1793 who commanded Sheriff to seize all goods and chattels of Daniel McCullum for 640 acres in Pendleton Co. on 26 Mile Creek, bd. on all sides by vacant land. Signed: Thomas Farrar, Sheriff.
Wit: James McCracken, Thos. Anderson...Abbeville Co., I certify I was present and saw Thomas Farrar sign and James McCracken and Thomas Anderson sign as witnesses. Signed: Julius Nichols, J. P., 28 Apr. 1795.
Rec: 24 Jun.1795.

Pages 16-17   11 Apr. 1795. Joseph Brown, Jr. to Peter Hall for Ł 20 stg. for 136 acres surveyed for Brown on 3 Oct. 1785, granted 2 Oct. 1786 by William Moultrie. Recorded Bk. 0000, p. 31 in Washington Dist., on Cherokee Br. of the Savannah River.
Wit: Hugh Brown, Samuel Smith, Anna Brown. Hugh Brown made oath to Wm. Hall, J. P., 16 Jun. 1795.
Rec: 24 Jun. 1795.

Pages 17-18   24 Jan. 1795. John Cox to Hugh Montgomery for Ł 100 for 183 acres in Washington Dist. granted Cox by Chas. Pinckney, 17 Feb. 1790, surveyed by Adam Crane Jones and granted 5 Apr. 1790, on Saluda River. Recorded Bk. N, no. 5, p. 215. Signed: John (X) Cox. (cont'd. next page)..

(pages 17-18 cont'd)

Wit: W. N. Hall, James Vaughn, James Thompson. James Thompson made oath to Wm. Hall, J. P., 25 May 1795.
Rec: 24 Jun. 1795.

Pages 18-19   15 Jan. 1794. James Montgomery and Sarah, his wife, to Joel Ledbetter for £ 5 stg. for 200 acres in Washington Dist. being half of a tract granted to Sarah Montgomery by Chas. Pinckney, 17 Dec. 1789. Signed: James Montgomery, Sarah Montgomery.
Wit: Daniel Ledbetter, William Bennet. Daniel Ledbetter made oath to E. Browne, J. P., 24 Jan. 1794.
Rec: 24 Jun. 1795.

Pages 19-20   15 Sep. 1790. Field Farrar, Esq. of Winnsborough Co., Fairfield Co., S. C., to Equilar Greer (or Green) of Pendleton Co. for 60 Guineas stg. for 200 acres in 96 Dist. on waters of Savannah River called Tugalo, bd. by vacant land, granted John Fleek (or Fluk) by Benjamin Guerrard, 21 Jan. 1785. Recorded Bk. BBBB, p. 116.
Wit: John Robinson, Joel Kilpatrick. John Robinson made oath to John Barton, J. P., 24 Jun. 1795.
Rec: 24 Jun. 1795.

Pages 20-21   1 Jan. 1793. Mathew Alexander to Henry Cobb for £ 200 stg. for 266 acres on Big Creek, of Saluda River, bd. by Isaac Alexander, David Alexander, part of three tracts, 1 of 250 acres granted Mathew Alexander, 21 Jan. 1785, recorded Bk. AAAA, p. 285, 2nd grant of 253 acres, granted 4 Feb. 1788, recorded Bk. WWWW, p. 211.
Wit: Saml. Cobb, Benj. Arnold. Samuel Cobb made oath to Wm. Hall, J.P. 23 Apr. 1795.
Rec: 24 Jun. 1795. (Plat)

Pages 21-23   22 Jan. 1793. Enoch Garner to Henry Cobb for £ 50 stg. for 140 acres on Big Creek and Saluda River, bd. by William Halbert, Enoch Garner, Henry Cobb, part of 465 acres granted Elijah Owens, 4 Sep. 1786. Recorded Bk. MMMM, p. 498, conveyed by Owens to Joseph Handley, by Handley to John Lindley, 5 Sep. 1789 and from Lindley to Enoch Garner.
Wit: Saml. Cobb, Josiah Grimmet. (Plat) Samuel Cobb made oath to Wm. Hall, J. P., 23 Apr. 1795.
Rec: 24 Jun. 1795.

Pages 23-24   24 Jun. 1794. Robert Anderson of Pendleton Co. to Bailey Anderson of Pendleton Co. for £ 50 stg. for 1/2 tract now in possession of Bailey Anderson, lying in Greenville Co., Washington Dist., S. C., on both sides of Checkaroa River of Saluda, by survey made by George Salmon, D. S., 213 acres granted Robert Anderson, 21 Jan. 1785, by Benj. Guerrard, it being half of sd. tract of 106½ acres.
Wit: Joshua Dyer, John Landers Farrar (called Landers Farrar in oath).
Joshua Dyer made oath to W. W. Reed, J. P., 25 May 1795.
Rec: 24 Jun. 1795.

Page 24   I, John Smith of Pendleton Co., planter, for love, good will and affection for my loving wife, Anna Smith, give all my goods, chattels now in my possession, stock and negro boy named Jacob, 300 acres of land with all working tools and shop. Date: 27 Mar. 1795.
Wit: Nathl. Perry, Susanna Perry. Nathl. Perry made oath to Jn. B. Earle, J. P., 24 Jun. 1795.
Rec: 24 Jun. 1795.

Pages 24-25   8 Dec. 1794. Moses Tomlinson to William Honey for £ 100 stg. for 157 acres, in Washington Dist., on E. side of Little Beaver Dam Creek, waters of Rocky River. Signed: Moses (/) Tomlinson.
Wit: John Caldwell, Moses (M) Key, William (/) Key. Moses Caldwell made

(pages 24-25 cont'd):
oath to Wm. Mulwee, J. P., 3 Jun. 1795.
Rec: 24 Jun. 1795.

Page 26   3 Dec. 1794. James Martin, of York Co., S.C. to Henry McDaniel, of Pendleton Co., for Ŀ 5 stg. for 640 acres in Pendleton Co., 96 Dist. on N. side of the Keowee River, granted to Francis Bremar and Peter Freneau, Esqs., 3 Apr. 1785.
Wit: David Sloan, William Gant. David Sloan made oath to J. B. Earle, J. P., 24 Jun. 1795.
Rec: 24 Jun. 1794.

Pages 26-27   25 Apr. 1795. Major Robert Cravens to Henry Burch for Ŀ 20 stg. for 114 acres on Keowee River, surveyed 29 Feb. 1789, bd. by James Gillison and by vacant lands.
Wit: Joshua Dodson, James Hendrix. James Hendrix made oath to J. B. Earle, J. P., 24 Jun. 1795.
Rec: 24 Jun. 1795.

Pages 27-28   25 Apr. 1795. Major Robert Cravens to Henry Burch for Ŀ 20 stg. for 103 acres on Keowee River, surveyed 29 Feb. 1789, bd. by William Tate and by vacant land.
Wit: Joshua Dodson, James Hendrix. James Hendrix made oath to J. B. Earle, J. P., 24 Jun. 1795.
Rec: 24 Jun. 1795.

Pages 28-30   16 Jun. 1793. Eliza Ann Purvis, widow, of Edgefield Co., S. C., to William Murphee, of Pendleton Co., for Ŀ 250 stg. for 640 acres in Pendleton Co. at a place called Seconah, on 12 Mile River, branch of the Savannah River.
Wit: John Bynum, Seth Farrar. John Bynum made oath to W. W. Reed, 17 Jun. 1793.
Rec: 24 Jun. 1795.

Pages 30-31   14 Mar. 1793. John Hennington, of Orangeburgh Dist., S. C., to Richard Holden, of Washington Dist., Pendleton Co. for Ŀ 20 stg. for 100 ac. granted 6 Jun. 1791, by Chas. Pinckney, in Washington Dist. on S. side of Keowee River. Signed: John Hennington, Elizabeth Hennington.
Wit: Ann Sheppard, John Moorhead. John Moorhead made oath to Bailey Anderson, J. P., 1 Apr. 1795.
Rec: 24 Jun. 1795.

Pages 31-32   21 May 1793. Humphrey Gibson, of 96 Dist. to Jacob Gibson for Ŀ 25 for 200 acres granted 21 Jan. 1785, by Benjamin Guerrard to Norman Martin, in 96 Dist. on Tugalo River, bd. on SW by river, on NE by John Smith on NW by Absolom Cleveland. Signed: Humphrey (his mark) Gibson.
Wit: John Smith, Thos. Kelly, Humphrey (his mark) Gibson, Jr. Humphrey Gibson made oath to Benjamin Cleveland, J. P., 7 Aug. 1794.
Rec: 24 Jun. 1795.

Page 32   7 Aug. 1794. Jacob Vance, of Pendleton Co., to Harmon Reed, of Bunckum (sic) Co., N. C. for Ŀ 40 stg. for 140 acres in Pendleton Co., on both sides of S. fork of Doddy's Creek, granted Vance, 5 Jun. 1786 by Wm. Moultrie.
Wit: Nathaniel Clark, Jacob Gardner. Nathl. Clark made oath to Jno. Barton, J. P., 24 Jun. 1795.
Rec: 25 Jun. 1795.

Pages 32-33   5 Mar. 1793. Samuel Martin to John Mullinex for Ŀ 110 stg. for 237 acres in Washington Dis. on Golden Creek, waters of 12 Mile River, granted to Martin, 3 Apr. 1786 by Wm. Moultrie, recorded in the Secretary's

(pages 32-33 cont'd):
                         Office. Signed: Samuel (his mark) Martin.
Wit: Jas. Brown, Thos. Goss(?). James Brown made oath to John Willson, J. P., 5 Mar. 1793.
Rec: 25 Jun. 1795.

Pages 33-34   I, Susannah Crutchfield for Ł 130 stg. paid by Alexander Ramsey, planter, sell 1 negro woman named Nan or Nancy and her two children and her increase forever. Signed: Susanna(h) (her mark) Crutchfield.
Wit: Jno. Green, Jas. Baily, Levi Pierce. Levi Pierce made oath to L. (or S.) Gardner, J. P., 25 Jun. 1795.
Rec: 25 Jun. 1795.

Page 34   23 Dec. 1794. Robert Anderson to Jas. Hendrix for Ł 80 stg. for 160 acres on N. fork of Cane Creek, branch of Keowee River, granted Robert Anderson, 5 Mar. 1787. Recorded Bk. TTTT, p. 111.
Wit: Benjamin Whorton, Anthony Griffen. Benjamin Whorton made oath to Wm. Hall, J. P., 25 Jul. 1795.
Rec: 25 Jun. 1795.

Page 35   I, James Gilliling for Ł 10 stg. paid by Aroph (?) Alexander, sell 1 horse, hogs, 4 acres of corn, standing in the field where I now live, 4 acres of tobacco and 6 acres of wheat standing on sd. plantation, also all goods, furniture, implements of household and all other goods mentioned in schedule. Signed: James Gilliland.
Wit: John Gilliland, Saml. Carnick, James Jones. Samuel Cornick made oath to Joshua Saxon, J. P., 25 Jun. 1795.
Rec: 25 Jun. 1795.

Pages 35-36   3 Dec. 1794. James Martin, of York Co., S. C. to James Stevenson, of Pendleton Co. for Ł 100 stg. for 320 acres, part of 640 acres granted 16 Jul. 1784, by Benj. Guerrard(?), to Francis Albertia(?), by conveyence from Treasurers of the State, 18 Apr. 1789, on Devil's Fork, on a branch of Great Generostee.
Wit: David Dickey, Thomas Morrow. Thomas Morrow made oath to E. Browne, J. P., 22 Apr. 1795.
Rec: 25 Jun. 1795.

Page 36   3 Dec. 1794. James Martin, of York Co., S. C. to James Stevenson, for Ł 80 stg. for 160 ac. part of 640 acres granted Amos Roberts, 16 Jul 1784, by Benj. Guerrard, and conveyed by Treasurers of State to James Martin, 18 Apr. 1789, on Mountain Creek, branch of Generostee Creek, as appears on two plats drawn by William Sloan, D. S., 26 May 1791.
Wit: Thos. Morrow, David Dickey. Thomas Morrow made oath to E. Browne, J. P., 22 Apr. 1795.
Rec: 25 Jun. 1795.

Pages 37-38   ___ Feb. 1794. Nathaniel Bryant, of Pendleton Co. to Robert Maxwell, of Greenville Co., S.C. for Ł 50 stg. for 200 acres on Little Beaver Dam Creek, waters of Savannah River, granted Robert Young, 15 Oct. 1784, by Benj. Guerrard, conveyed to Bryant, 15 Sep. 1791. Recorded Bk. B, p. 70, Pendleton Co. Signed: Nathaniel (+) Bryant.
Wit: John Kellum, Christopher (his mark) Stanton. Christopher Stanton made oath to Joshua Saxon, J. P., 22 Jun. 1795.
Rec: 25 Jun. 1795.

Page 38   30 Dec. 1790. Andrew Pickens, Esq., Justice of the Peace, of Pendleton Co., to William Sloan ...Andrew Pickens in his official capacity, agreeable to law bind unto William Sloan a certain Mullatto mail(male) child named Isaac Williams, now three years old, until age 25. During time of servitude he is to obey the lawful command of his Master, to be diligent and attentive to his Master's interest...William Sloan to provide good and sufficient meat, drink, lodging and apparell fitting for a

(page 38 cont'd):
servant and learn him to spell and read the
Holy Scriptures. Signed: Andw. Pickens, Willm. Sloan...Signed, sealed
and delivered in the presence of Benj. Cleveland.
Rec: 26 Jun. 1795.

Pages 38-39 14 Mar. 1794. John Shannon to Jonathan Cridinton for Ł 15 stg. for 73 acres granted to John Shannon, on Choata (sic) being the plantation where Cridenton now lives.
Wit: William Sloan, Joseph Swilling. Joseph Swilling made oath to John Barton, J. P., 22 Jun. 1795.
Rec: 27 Jun. 1795.

Pages 39-40 We, William Mathews, David Pugh, Enoch Berry, Willoughby Pugh, Henry McWhorter, William Wakefield, Mary Wakefield and Allen Wakefield, do free and let at liberty and never more to be bound a Slave, to enjoy an equal portion of freedom and Liberty as any Free white Citizen, a certain Negro man named Bob, formerly slave of Henry Wakefield, deceased.
Signed: William Mathus, Allen Wakefield, William Wakefield, Enoch Barry, Henry McWhorter, Willoughby Pugh, David (his mark) Pugh, Mary Wakefield. William Mathews made oath that he saw all sign except Henry McWhorter, being all heirs of Henry Wakefield, 10 Jul. 1795, to John Willson, J.P., Henry McWhorter acknowledged he did sign.
Rec: 13 Jul. 1795.

Pages 40-42 17 May 1795. William Twitty, heir of John Twitty, dec'd., to George Hays, for Ł 40 stg. for 200 acres in Washington Dist. on 18 Mile Creek, branch of Keowee River, bd. on E. by land granted to Minor Winn and by vacant land, originally granted to George Kilson, 21 Jan. 1785, conveyed to Minor Winn.
Wit: Thomas Hays, John Hays. Thomas Hays made oath to J. B. Earle, J.P. 17 Jul. 1795.
Rec: 17 Jul. 1795.

Pages 42-44 22 Aug. 1792. John Mulherin(?) of Barbon Co., Ky. blacksmith, to George Smith of Pendleton Co. for Ł 25 stg. for 200 acres on 12 Mile Crk. waters of Savannah River, granted 3 Sep. 1787.
Wit: James Cannon, Joseph Smith, Mary (X) Cannon. James Cannon made oath to J. Miller, J. P., 24 Jun. 1793.
Rec: 21 Jul. 1795.

Pages 44-46 16 Nov. 1795. Samuel Dalrimple and Sarah, his wife, to George Smith for Ł 100 stg. for 160 acres on Big Generostee, waters of the Savannah River, bd. on NW by Richard Morrow, on N. by Joshua Saxon, on E. by David Anderson, on S. by Samuel Saxon, on W. by John Smith, granted 6 Feb. 1786. Signed: Samuel Dalrimple, Sarah (/) Dalrimple.
Wit: James Cannon, Joseph Smith, Rachel Smith. James Cannon made oath to J. Miller, J. P., 24 Jun. 1793.
Rec: 24 Jun. 1794.

Pages 46-48 6 Sep. 1791. William Harper to Moses Perkins for Ł 70 stg. for 300 acres in 96 Dist. on Connoross Crk., waters of Keowee River, granted 16 Jul. 1784, by Benj. Guerrard.
Wit: William Perkins, Willm. Sloan. William Perkins made oath to Nathl. Perry, J. P., 15 Jun. 1794.
Rec: 27 Jul. 1795.

Page 49 I, Robert Kilgore, of Pendleton Co. authorize Daniel Delany, of Pendleton Co., as my lawful attorney in behalf of certain rights and interests I claim to a tract of land in Richmond Co., Ga. on the mouth of Williamson Creek, the undivided right, Daniel Delany is legally empowered to sell. Date: 27 Jul. 1795. Signed: Robert Kilgore.
Wit: Elias Hollingsworth, Eziekeil Buffington, Abm. Buffington. Ezekiel

(page 49 cont'd):
Buffington made oath to Joseph Reid, J. P., 25 Jul. 1795.
Rec: 28 Jul. 1795.

Pages 49-50   I, William Richards, for divers goods, causes and considerations, appoint Mathias Cleveland my lawful attorney to recover and receive all (from all) persons in Pendleton Co. and the Cherokee Nation, money, debts and demands owed to me. Date: 29 Jun. 1795. Signed: W. Richards.
Wit: Matt. Willson, Murwood Timberlake. Murwood Timberlake made oath to Robert Anderson, J. P., 10 Jul. 1795.
Rec: 3 Aug. 1795.

Page 50   I, David Gentry sell to Major Gentry horses, hogs, beds and furniture for 40 dollars. Date: 10 Jul. 1795. Signed: David (his mark) Gentry. Wit: Evin Smith, Jas. McBride. James McBride made oath to Joseph Reid, J. P., 4 Aug. 1795.
Rec: 7 Aug. 1795.

Page 50   I, Field Prewet, donomi conslet(?), appoint Benja. Ingram, my attorney to ask and demand the full sum of Ł 11-10 shillings on a note given Field Pruet, by Adam Wright, 1 Jun. 1794. DateL 17 Apr. 1795. Signed: Field (X) Pruet, John (X) King (he is not mentioned otherwise.)
Wit: Benj. Whorton, James Hendrix, Francis (X) King. Francis King made oath to S. M. Gardner, J. P., 20 Apr. 1795.
Rec: 8 Aug. 1795.

Page 51   We, Field Prewett, Sr. and Field Prewett, Jr., appoint Benjamin Ingram, our attorney to demand and receive full amount of money due us for public service mention in our discharges from Lt. David Mosley. Date: 17 Apr. 1795. Signed: Field (his mark) Prewit, Jr., Field (X) Prewet, Sr., John (X) King.
Wit: Benja. Whorton, James Hendrix, Francis(X) King. Francis King made oath to S. M. Gardner, J. P., 20 Apr. 1795.
Rec: 6 Aug. 1795.

Pages 51-53   20 Nov. 1794. Elias Hollingsworth to Thomas Wadsworth and William Turpin, merchants, for Ł 12 10 shillings for 50 acres on 23 Mile Crk, bd. by creek, Martin, Wm. Turpin, Hugh Rogers, Thomas Hollingsworth. Originally granted to Samuel Gillison, son and minor of James Gillison, by Wm. Moultrie, 18 Oct. 1784. Recorded Bk. IIII, p. 631 and by James Gillison, the father, conveyed to Elias Hollingsworth, 25 ___ 1793.
Wit: James Young, James Boyce. James Young made oath to Jonthn. Downs, J. P., 15 Feb. 1795.
Rec: 8 Aug. 1795.

Pages 53-54   I, John Anderson, of 96 Dist., planter, appoint my true friend, William Tate, of the same, my lawful attorney to convey in my name, two tract of land, one tract of two hundred thousand acres, bd. on W. by Tugalo River, the other tract of one hundred thousand acres, bd. on W. on Toxaway and Keowee River, on N. by old Indian boundary line. Date: 14 Jul.1794.
Wit: Jonas Beard, James Kennedy, John C. Floker...City of Charleston, before Peter Freneau, J. P., James Kennedy made oath, 1 Aug. 1794....... Charleston, Office of Mesne Conveyences, I certify there is no mortgage or record in this office to described 2 tracts, 1 Aug. 1794. Signed: D. Mazyck, Register.
Rec: 17 Aug. 1795.

Pages 54-56   17 May 1794. William Tate, Esq., of 96 Dist. to the Hon. Robert Morris, Esq., of Philadelphia, Pa. and John Nicholson, Esq., of same, for 5 shillings lawful money of Pennsylvania, two tracts granted by the State of S. C., by Wm. Moultrie, Esq., Gov., 7 Oct. 1793. Recorded Bk.1, no. 5, pp. 173 and 174. One tract on the Savannah River, in Washington

(pages 54-56 cont'd):
Dist., bd. on SW by old Indian Boundary Line, on SE by the Toxaway River and Keowee River, on NE by 12 Mile River, containing one hundred thousand acres. The other tract on Savannah River, in Washington Dist., bd. on SW by Indian Boundary, on SE by Tugalo River, on NW by Little River and Tamasee, containing two hundred thousand acres.
Wit: Richard Price, George Honey...18 Nov. 1794, before Isaac Howell, Esq., one of the Judges of Court of Common Pleas for the County of Philadelphia, William Tate acknowledged indenture....Thomas Mifflen, Gov. of the Commonwealth of Penn. certified Isaac Howell, Esq., is a Judge of the Court of Common Pleas, 5 Dec. 1794. Signed: James Trimble, Deputy Sec'y.
Rec: 17 Aug. 1795.

Pages 57-58   6 Jul. 1795. Elias Earle, of Greenville Co., S. C., to Christopher Waggoner, of Pendleton Co., for Ł 9 stg. for 50 acres, part of 576 ac. granted 5 Apr. 1790, by Charles Pinckney, surveyed for Sutton Green, 1 Feb. 1788, in 96 Dist. on both sides of Camp Creek, a branch of Dowdy's Creek, waters of the Saluda, bd. on NW and SW by vacant lands, on SE and W by Joseph Whitner, on NE by James Goodlet.
Wit: John Powell, Thomas Cape. John Powell made oath to W. Reid, J. P., 16 Jul. 1795.
Rec: 19 Aug. 1795.

Pages 58-59   29 May 1794. James Cunningham, of Knox Co., in the Territory of the United States, South of the Ohio, to John Langley, of Pendleton Co., for Ł 40 stg. for 200 acres in Pendleton Co., bd. on SE by Hickory Nut Mountain, on SE by James Gillispie, on NW and NE by John Boyd, surveyed by William Benson, for Samuel Earle, conveyed to Cunningham.
Wit: Nathaniel Bullard, Thos. Chapman. Nathaniel Bullard made oath to W. W. Reid, J. P., 7 Feb. 1795.
Rec: 19 Aug. 1795.

Page 59   I, William Nevill have delivered to Lewis Cobb a negro wench named Phillis for value received.
Date: 29 Mar. 1795. Wit: Abial Cobb, Lophar Tanner. (no oath). Rec: 19 Aug. 1795.

Pages 59-60   6 Jan. 1795. Alexander Powers, of Washington Dist., to Isham Irby, of same, for Ł 100 stg. for 163 acres in Washington Dist. on 23 Mile Creek, part of a tract of 475 acres granted to Powers, 6 May 1793, by Wm. Moultrie.
Wit: John Portman, Charles Irby. Alexander Powers acknowledged deed to J. B. Earle, J. P., 19 Aug. 1795.
Rec: 19 Aug. 1795.

Pages 60-61   2 Apr. 1795. Josiah Paterson, of Abbeville Co. to Howell Miller, of Pendleton Co. for Ł 50 stg. for 200 acres in Pendleton Co. on Woolf Creek, branch of 12 Mile River, on E. side of Glassy Mountain, except 20 acres, part of the sd. 200 acres known as Beaverdam, conveyed to Paterson by James Price, 1 Jan. 1785.
Wit: John Curry, Jesse Wilson. John Curry made oath to Bayley Anderson, J. P., 10 Apr. 1795.
Rec: 24 Aug. 1795.

Pages 61-62   Washington Dist. 26 Aug. 1795. Thomas Farrar, Esq., Sheriff of Washington Dist., to Abraham Elledge...John Cunningham received Judgement against James Gillison for Ł 150...John Rutledge, Esq., Chief Justice of S. C., ordered Sheriff Thomas Farrar to seize all goods, chattels, lands of James Gillison to be sold at auction, highest bidder being Abraham Elledge for Ł 4 stg. for 150 acres on both sides of 26 Mile Creek. Signed: Thomas Farrar, Sheriff.
Wit: Leonard D. Shaw, Thomas L. Reese. Leonard D. Klyne Shaw made oath to J. B. Earle, J.P., 26 Aug. 1795. Rec: 26 Aug. 1795.

Pages 62-64   23 Apr. 1791. Jehu Pope to John Grissam for
                           ₤ 100 stg. for 150 acres on 26 Mile Creek, the
                           waters of Keowee River, part of a survey of 250
acres granted to Francis Gutry, citizen, of Abbeville Co., by Benjamin
Guerrard. Recorded Bk. AAAA, p. 136, made over to Jehu Pope.
Wit: Andr. Liddell, David (B) Carter. David Carter made oath to J. B.
Earle, J. P., 5 Sep. 1795.
Rec: 5 Sep. 1795.

Pages 64-65   22 Feb. 1793. John McCulough to Joel Callahan
                           for ₤ 40 stg. for 138 acres on Beard's Creek.
Wit: John McMahen, James Kile, Andw. Busson(?). Plat shows land bd. on
N. by vacant land, on SE by Jas. McAdo, on W. by McColough. John McMahen
made oath to E. Browne, J. P., 15 Sep. 1795.
Rec: 15 Sep. 1795.

Pages 65-68   3 Dec. 1794. John Cart, of Charleston, S. C.
                           to Charles Clements, of 96 Dist. for ₤ 50 for
                           614 acres (later says 617 acres) on S. fork of
Barker's Creek, in 96 Dist. granted Wm. Wightman, 5 Sep. 1784.
Wit: James Jack, Charles Stuart. Charles Stewart made oath to William
Hall, J. P., 11 Sep. 1795.
Rec: 22 Sep. 1795.

Pages 69-70   Washington Dist. 26 Aug. 1795. Thomas Farrar,
                           Sheriff of Dist., to John Harris...lands of Sam-
                           uel Crofton was siezed for judgement of Andrew
Pickens & Co. for the sum of (blank) and ordered sold at public auction
to the highest bidder, who was John Harris, for ₤ 34 stg. for 302 acres
on both sides of Woolonoy Creek, waters of the Saluda, S. fork. Signed:
Thomas Farrar.
Wit: Leonard Shaw, George W. Earle. Leonard Shaw made oath to J. B.
Earle, J. P., 20 Aug. 1795.
Rec: 2 Sep. 1795.

Pages 70-71   2 Jan. 1792. John Henderson, of Elbert Co.,Ga.
                           to Solomon Roe, of Pendleton Co., 96 Dist., for
                           ₤ 30 stg. for 200 acres, granted Henderson, 4
Sep. 1786, by Wm. Moultrie, on S. side of Saluda, on both sides of 18
Mile Creek, branch of the Savannah River.
Wit: John Boyd, Thomas Green, Thos. Henderson. John Boyd made oath to
John Willson, J. P., 18 Oct. 1794.
Rec: 22 Sep. 1795.

Pages 71-75   20 Apr. 1795. Jacob Capehart to William Steele
                           for ₤ 60 stg. for 120 acres on 26 Mile Creek,
                           bd. by Robt. Dickerson, Calhoun, Edward Kemp,
part of 288 acres granted to Edward Kemp, 7 Aug. 1786, by Wm. Moultrie.
Wit: J. Whitner, Saml. Barr. Joseph Whitner made oath to S. M. Gardner,
J. P., 23 Sep. 1795.
Rec: 1 Oct. 1795.

Pages 75-77   18 Feb. 1793. Stephen Drayton, of Charleston,
                           S. C., to Joshua Lee, of 96 Dist. for ₤ 60 for
                           500 acres on Choestoa Creek, branch of Tugalo,
bd. on SE by lands laid out for John Vanderhorst, granted to Stephen Drayton, 15 Oct. 1784 as Bounty allowed by the State for Army Service, as
Quartermaster General for the Southern Dept. Signed: S. Drayton.
Wit: John McRee, Stephen Ravenell...Charleston, Stephen Ravenell made
oath to John Sanford Dart, J.P.Q.M., 18 Feb. 1793.
Rec: 3 Oct. 1795.

Pages 77-78   20 Jul. 1795. Samuel Lofton, Sr., planter, to
                           James Gassaway for ₤ 50 stg. for 200 acres
                           where Gassaway now lives, part of a tract gran-
ted Lofton by Wm. Moultrie, 4 Feb. 1793, on 18 Mile Creek, branch of the
Seneca of Keowee River, on N. fork of the Savannah River, bd. by Christopher Strong. Wit: J.(?) G. Lofton, Robert Glenn. Robt. Glenn made oath
to J. B. Earle, J. P., 3 Oct. 1795.
Rec: 3 Oct. 1795.

Pages 78-80   4 May 1794. Robert Phillips, of Fairfield Co.,
                       S. C., to Benjamin Armstrong, for Ł 75 for 600
                       acres on the W. side of Keowee River, bd. on
NE by George Liddell, granted John Campbell, 1 Jan. 1785, conveyed to
Robt. Phillips, 20 Apr. 1786.
Wit: Jno. Buckhannon, Robt. Tate, James Brice. James Brice made oath
to E. Browne, J. P., 14 Jun. 1794.
Rec: 13 Oct. 1795.

Page 81   25 Apr. 1791. Marah (later Mary) Files to Adam
                       Files, planter, for Ł 45 for 350 acres above
                       the ancient boundary line on Mountain Creek, of
Big Generostee, branch of the Savannah River, bd. on all sides by patent
land, granted to Marah Files (no date). Recorded Bk. CCCC, p. 177.
Signed: Mary (M) Files.
Wit: John McCollum, John Files. John Files made oath to Wm. Nevill, 21
Feb. 1793.
Rec: 15 Oct. 1795.

Pages 81-82   4 Jul. 1794. John Wheeler and Susannah, his
                       wife, of Pendleton Co., to Samuel Earle, Jr.,
                       of Greenville Co. for Ł 150 stg. for 200 acres
where they now live, on the S. side of S. fork of the Saluda River.
Signed: John Wheeler, Susannah (X) Wheeler.
Wit: William Hawks, Joseph Wheeler, Robt. (R) Bailey. William Hawks
made oath to John B. Grigsby, J. P., 13 Oct. 1795.
Rec: 15 Oct. 1795.

Page 83   27 Mar. 1795. Richard Oldham to George Dil-
                       worth for Ł 60 for 200 acres taken off the S.
                       side of plantation, of 640 acres in Washington
Dist., Pendleton Co. on Broadaway, waters of a creek of Rocky River,
granted to Andrew Hamilton, 4 Oct. 1790, surveyed for Henry Collins Flagg
on 23 Aug. 1784. Recorded Bk. G, no. 5, p. 62, conveyed from Hamilton to
Oldham, bd. by Molly Smith.
Wit: Reuben Clements, Allis Thompson, William Lindley. Allis Thompson
made oath to Wm. Hall, 21 Jun. 1795.
Rec: 19 Oct. 1795.

Page 84   26 Jul. 1795. George Dilworth to Robert Brown
                       for Ł 35 stg. for 200 acres on Broadaway, creek
                       of Rocky River, granted Andrew Hamilton, 4 Oct.
1790, conveyed from Richard Oldham to Dilworth.
Wit: Wm. Gray, Wm. Lindley, George Oldham. William Gray made oath to
Wm. Hall, 5 Oct. 1795.
Rec: 20 Oct. 1795.

Pages 84-86   18 Feb. 1795. Ferrihan McKinsey, planter, to
                       Dunkan McKinsey, for Ł 59 stg. for 380 acres
                       on Big Beaver Dam, waters of Tugalo River,
granted John Miller and James Milwee, 2 Jul. 1787, by Thomas Pinckney(No
book no.), p. 141. Signed: Ferrihan (*) McKinsey.
Wit: William Brooks, Kinneth Findley, Zech. Roberts. Zachariah Roberts
made oath to Nathl. Perry, J. P., 25 Apr. 1795.
Rec: 23 Oct. 1795.

Pages 86-87   7 Jan. 1795. Alexander Kilpatrick to Jonathan
                       Kemp for Ł 150 stg. for 150 acres on SW side
                       of the Keowee River, granted Kilpatrick, 7 Aug.
1785, by Wm. Moultrie.
Wit: Wm. Nevill, John Nevill. William Nevill made oath to Jno. Barton,
J. P., 7 Jan. 1795.
Rec: 24 Oct. 1795.

Page 87   I, Samuel Meirs, of Washington Dist. am firmly
                       bound to Alexander Barron for Ł 100 stg., cov-
enent made to Alexander Barron for 165 acres on which Barron now lives,
agreeable to a plat from John Kilpatrick, 15 Jul. 1791, payment to be
made by Jul. 1, then this obligation is null and void. Date: 10 Feb. 1794
Signed: Saml. Myers. Test: Zech Roberts. Zachariah Roberts made oath to

(page 87 cont'd):
Rec: 3 Nov. 1795.
Nathl. Perry, J. P., 31 Oct. 1795.

Pages 87-88   We, heirs of Elias Dejernit, dec'd. assign to Joab Mauldin our right and title to a negro boy called Tom, about 13 years old, part of Estate of Elias Dejernit, having received full satisfaction. Date: 22 Jun.1795. Signed: Bartley Tucker, Nancy (+) Degernet, Rueben Degernet, Maxd. Kennedy (called Maxfield Kennedy in oath).
Wit: Jeremiah Hall, Sarah Perkins. Sarah Perkins made oath to E. Browne J. P., 29 Sep. 1795.
Rec: 4 Nov. 1795.

Pages 88-90   29 Aug. 1794. Fredrick Glover, of Abbeville Co. to James Harthorn (also spelled Hathorn) for Ł 50 stg. for 214 3/4 acres in 96 Dist. on 5 Mile Branch of 18 Mile Creek, waters of Savannah River, bd. on NE and SE by Thomas Lofton, on NW by William Erwin and by vacant lands, granted to Glover, by patent 1 Mar. 1790, recorded Bk. B., no. 5, p. 164.
Wit: Benj. Glover, John Curry, William Wright....Abbeville Co., William Wright made oath to Hugh Wardlaw, J. P., 2 Sep. 1794.
Rec: 6 Nov. 1795.

Pages 90-91   5 Feb. 1794. Alexander McClusky, planter of Pendleton Co. to Ann Harthorn (Hawthorn), spinster, of Abbeville Co. for Ł 25 stg. for 192 acres in Pendleton Co. on branches of Wilson's Creek and Mountain Creek, part of a tract granted to Andrew Defloor(?), 2 Feb. 1789, by Charles Pinckney.
Wit: William Beck, Andrew Kirkpatrick, Robert Campbell Gordan. Robert Campbell Gordan made oath to Wm. Milwee, J. P., 8 Nov. 1795.
Rec: 7 Mar. 1795.

Page 91   I, Evin Smith, hatter, for Ł 10, 15 shillings, paid by John Adair, sold all household goods, kitchen implements in my possession. Date: 8 Sep. 1795. Wit: William Hamilton, Benja. Merry(?). (No oath).
Rec: 6 Nov. 1795.

Page 92   27 Aug. 1793. Elenor Black, of Pendleton Co., to James Black, of same, for Ł 20 stg. for 152 acres, part of 473 acres granted Elenor Black, 17 Jun. 1785, by Wm. Moultrie.
Wit: Samuel Black, Adam Davis. Samuel Black made oath to J. B. Earle, J. P., 9 Nov. 1795.
Rec: 9 Nov. 1795.

Page 92   1 Oct. 1791. Elinor Black, of Abbeville Co., to Saml. Black, of same, for Ł 20 stg. for 200 acres, part of 423 acres granted Elinor Black, 1785, in Pendleton Co. on branches of Great Generostee Creek.
Wit: John Norwood, William Rupel (Russell), Wm. Black. Wm. Black made oath to J. B. Earle, J. P., 9 Nov. 1795.
Rec: 9 Nov. 1795.

Page 93   I, Robert Glenn, by note dated 20 Apr. 1793 am bound to William Steele for Ł 50 stg. to be paid by 5 Mar. 1795, bargain part of land on which I now live of 198 acres, horses, cattle, furniture. Date: 11 Feb. 1795.
Wit: William (cannot read this), Aaron Steele. Aaron Steele made oath to J. B. Earle, J. P., 19 Nov. 1795.
Rec: 19 Nov. 1795.

Pages 94-97   9 Jan. 1794. Henry William Desaussure, Charleston, to William McCaleb, of Pendleton Co.for Ł 12 for 7 acres part of 504 acres called Fort Rutledge on the Keowee River, adj. to land of Wm. McCaleb, being "a small parcel of low land from the best of the low ground of H. W. Desaussure, (pages 94-97 cont'd):   now occupied and planted by Joel Bradshaw, by a small branch". Wit: Tim Ford, John Kelsall. Timothy Ford made oath to Jas. Nicholson, J. P., Charleston Dist., 10 Jan. 1794...I do hereby agree that I will ...(cannot read) from my wife a proper renunciation of Dower. Signed: Henry W. Desaussure. Date: 10 Jan. 1794.

Page 97   I, James Tate, Jr. sold to Thomas Blair for
                             ₤ 20 stg. a negro boy named Jacob, to be held
                             by Thomas Blair until the said ₤ 20 is return-
ed to Thomas Blair, then the negro to be returned to James Tate. If sd. negro dies within six months, the loss is James Tate's. Date: 29 Jun. 1795.
Wit: Daniel Stringer, Moses Liddle. (no oath).
Rec: 25 Nov. 1795.

Pages 97-98   3 Dec. 1794. James Martin to Thomas Morrow for
                             ₤ 60 stg. for 540 acres, part of a tract grant-
                             ed, 16 Jul. 1785 by Benjamin Guerrard for 640
acres on Great Generostee Creek.
Wit: John Glen, Leonard Morrow. Leonard Morrow made oath to E. Browne, J. P., 22 Apr. 1795.
Rec: 1 Dec. 1795.

Page 98   I, Daniel McCollum sold to Thomas Morrow (later
                             called Sr.) for ₤ 50 stg., cattle, horses, furn-
                             iture, waggon, 8 acres of corn now as it stands
in the field, one set of blacksmith tools. Date: 28 Sep. 1795.
Wit: Jas. Hamilton, Edward Tate McClure. James Hamilton made oath to Joshua Saxon, J. P., 12 Oct. 1795.
Rec: 1 Dec. 1795.

Pages 98-99   18 Nov. 1795. Robert Duncan, of Greenville Co.,
                             S. C., Washington Dist., to James Duff, Sr. of
                             Pendleton Co., Washington Dist., for ₤ 50 stg.
for 267 acres in Washington Dist., Pendleton Co. on branches of N. fork and branches of middle fork of George's Creek, waters of the Saluda Riv- er, granted to Duncan, 7 May 1787, by Thomas Pinckney.
Wit: Robert Henderson, Jr., Hezekiah (H) Collins, Francis Scott. Robert Henderson made oath to William Edmondson, 21 Nov. 1795.
Rec: 1 Dec. 1795.

Pages 99-101   27 Aug. 1793. James Jett to James Duff for
                             ₤ 75 for 530 acres on the prong of George's
                             Creek. bd. by William Jamison and Jett.
Wit: Robt. Henderson, Jr., Saml. Carson Duff, James Henderson. Robert Henderson, Jr. made oath to William Edmondson, J. P., 28 Nov. 1795.
Rec: 1 Dec. 1795.

Pages 101-102   8 Dec. 1792. John Patterson, planter, to Fran-
                             cis Fulcher for ₤ 60 stg. for 148 acres, part
                             of 348 acres on Colding's Creek, waters of the
Keowee and granted to Patterson, 7 Jul. 1788, by Thos. Pinckney. Record- ed Bk. XXXX, p. 209.
Wit: Willoughby Pugh, Enoch Berry. Willoughby Pugh made oath to John Willson, J. P., 11 Apr. 1793.
Rec: 19 Dec. 1795.

Pages 102-103   2 Jul. 1795. Eli Langford to William Tabor for
                             ₤ 48 for 200 acres, part of 446 acres granted
                             Langford, 2 Sep. 1793, by Wm. Moultrie. In 96
Dist. on Crow Creek, waters of Keowee River.
Wit: J. S.(?)(Joseph in Oath) Carleton, John Tubb, Henry Carlton. John Tubb made oath to Joseph Reed, J. P., 19 Dec. 1795.
Rec: 22 Dec. 1795.

Pages 103-104   6 Jan. 1789. David Sloan, of Abbeville Co. to
                             Charles Brannon (Brandon), of same, for ₤ 50
                             stg. for 270 acres in 96 Dist., granted John
Martin, 1 Aug. 1785, by Wm. Moultrie, conveyed to David Sloan, 15 Nov.

(pages 103-104 cont'd):
1788. Wit: John Grindel, Willm. Sloan. John Grindle made oath to J. B. Earle, J. P., 2 Jan. 1796.
Rec: 2 Jan. 1796.

Pages 104-106   21 Jan. 1788. Solomon King, of Abbeville Co., farmer, to John Grindel, farmer, of same, for ₺ 73 stg. for 200 acres on S. side of the Seneca River, bd. by Solomom King and by vacant land, granted to King, 5 Jun 1786, by Wm. Moultrie. Recorded Bk. LLLL, p. 217. Signed: Solomon (X) King. Wit: John C. Kilpatrick, John Twitty, Charles Brandon. Charles Brannon made oath to J. B. Earle, J. P., 2 Jan. 1796.
Rec: 2 Jan. 1796.

Page 106   2 Mar. 1793. Andrew Perkins to John P. Caldwell, for love and good will for John P. Caldwell, also 30 shillings stg., horses, cattle, tools, furniture on condition that Andrew Perkins have use of same as long as he shall live.
Wit: William McElvaney, David Caldwell. David Caldwell made oath to J. B. Earle, J. P., 2 Jan. 1796.
Rec: 2 Jan. 1796.

Page 107   2 Mar. 1793. William Drennan to John Perkins Caldwell for love and good will and 30 shillings stg. for horses, cattle, furniture, tools on condition that William Drennan shall have use of same as long as he shall live.
Wit: David Drennan, David Caldwell. David Caldwell made oath to J. B. Earle, J. P. 2 Jan. 1796.
Rec: 2 Jan. 1796.

Pages 107-108   31 Mar. 1795. John Portman, Sr. to Thomas Hobson for ₺ 5 stg. for 200 acres, part of 800 ac. (no location given). Signed: John (P) Portman. Wit: Lewis Cobb, Christopher (X) Ramsey. Christopher Ramsey made oath to J. B. Earle, J. P., 13 Jan. 1796.
Rec: 13 Jan. 1796.

Pages 108=109   21 Jul. 1795. Thomas Hobson to John Woodall for ₺ 20 stg. for 130 acres, part of 888 acres on waters of 23 Mile Creek, granted John Portman and conveyed to Hobson by deed, "all that he held after he sold 200 ac. to Evan Thomas, 200 ac. to Thomas Hobson, and 200 acres taken by an older right". Signed: Thomas (his mark) Hobson.
Wit: Abiel Cobb, Lewis Cobb. Thomas Hobson acknowledged he signed the above deed to J. B. Earle, J. P., 13 Jan. 1796.
Rec: 13 Jan. 1796.

Pages 109-111   7 Apr. 1789. John Edwards and William Hort, Esq., Treasurers of the State of S. C., to James Martin, Esq., of 96 Dist., by several acts of the General Assembly, lands granted to persons who have not paid purchase money within time limits...James Dutilly on 16 Jul. 1784 was granted land and not having complied with the time, such grant is put up at public auction to the highest bidder, being James Martin for ₺ 19, 6 shillings, 8 pence, on 23 Mile Creek.
Wit: Adam Gilchrist, Edward Edwards...Charleston Dist., Edward Edwards made oath to Stephen Ravanell, J. P., 3 Jun. 1793. Plat surveyed by Dd. Hobson, D. S. Signed: ___? Bremar, Surv. Gen.
Rec: 18 Jun. 1796.

Pages 111-112   I, John Lauderdale, having failed to make payment to Jesse Brown for ₺ 100 stg., by bond to keep him clear of all costs and damages, with the sum of ₺ 20 stg., Jesse Brown signed a judgement to Robert Harkness, on John Harris and John Lauderdale at the January Court in Pendleton, 1795 ....Peter Kays satisfied Robert Harkness on the judgement, I, John Lauderdale stand endebted to Peter Kays for ₺ 20, 6 shillings by 7 Nov. 1796, and now bargain and sell to Peter Kays part of a tract granted William

(pages 111-112 cont'd):
Brown, 4 Dec. 1786 for 294 acres in 96 District on Great Rocky Creek. Recorded Bk. QQQQ, p. 227, bd. by James Thompson, Kays, J. Milsap and by land where John Lauderdale now lives.
Wit: J. Mauldin, Robert Harkness. Robert Harkness made oath to E.Brown, J. P., 21 Nov. 1795.
Rec: 22 Jan. 1796.

Pages 112-113   7 Nov. 1795. John Lauderdale and Milberry, his wife, to Peter Kays, Ł 20 stg. for 160 acres, part of a tract of 294 acres granted William Brown. Signed: John Lauderdale (only).
Wit: J. Mauldin, Robert Harkness. Plat shows land by on E. by James Thompson, on N. by John Lauderdale, on W. by James Bowen, on S. by William Lesley, on branches of Beaver Creek and Reedy River. Robert Harkness made oath to E. Browne, J. P., 21 Nov. 1795.
Rec: 22 Jan. 1796.

Pages 113-114   24 Nov. 1794. William Welch and Jamima, his wife, to Alexander Boyce for Ł 70 stg. for 226 acres on Saluda River, bd. on SW and NW by land surveyed for Robt. Maxwell, on NW by Alexander Boyce, on NW by land surveyed for Michael Killison, on NE by Saluda River, granted Thomas Wadsworth and William Turpin, by Wm. Moultrie, 5 Feb. 1787. Recorded Bk. QQQQ, p. 516, and all that part of a tract lying above Nutonbrough(?) branch which empties into the Saluda River, branch dividing another grant belonging to John Clardy. Signed: William Welch, Jamima (her mark)Welch.
Wit: Henry Guthrie, Stephen Booth. Stephen Booth made oath to John Wilson, J. P., 13 Feb. 1795.
Rec: 22 Jan. 1796.

Pages 114-115   4 Sep. 1794. Joseph and Jane (also spelled Jean) Wornock to John McFall for Ł 75 stg. for 200 acres, part of 300 acres granted Hugh Wornock, 3 Apr. 1786, conveyed to Joseph Wornock by Andrew Wornock, heir of Hugh Wornock. Recorded Bk. WWWW, p. 468, on Neil's Creek, waters of the Rocky River, bd. by Moses Holland, Edward Tate, Stephen Willis, Elisha Bennet, Alexander McLane, plantation where Joseph Wornock now lives. Signed: Joseph Wornock, Jean Wornock.
Wit: Jno. George, Joseph Black. John George made oath to Wm. Mulwee, J. P., 5 Jan. 1796.
Rec: 5 Jan. 1796.

Pages 116-117   29 Apr. 1791. Tilley Merrick, planter, to Jno. Robinson, planter, for Ł 50 for 640 acres in 96 Dist. on 23 Mile Creek, granted James Hartsell, 16 Jul. 1784 by Benjamin Guerrard.
Wit: John (his mark) McKinsey, Adam (X) Wright, Asa Tortellot. Adam Wright made oath to John Willson, J. P., __ Mar. 1793.
Rec: 25 Jan. 1796.

Pages 117-119   6 Jan. 1794. Benja. Cleveland to Charles Kennedy for Ł 50 stg., tract (acreage not given) on Main Chauga Creek, below where Charles Kennedy now lives. Wit: Thos. Jordan, John Davis. Benjamin Cleveland acknowledged deed in open court, 25 Jan. 1796, to J. B. Earle, J. P. Rec: 25 Jan. 1796..."2 acres of above land being shoal where Cleveland built a mill formerly and not far above mouth of small creek, where Cleveland now has a mill...in respect to building a mill above shoal, Kennedy is to have all priviledge, excepting of a grist mill. If Kennedy build a grist mill without Cleveland's consent the above deed to be void."

Page 119   22 Apr. 1794. Benja. Cleveland to Joseph Stepp for Ł 20 for 100 acres on S. side of Toxaway Creek, part of a survey of 975 acres granted Cleveland by Charles Pinckney, bd. by James Blair and sd. Stepp.
Wit: James Blair, Absolom Cleveland. Benja. Cleveland made acknowledgement to J. B. Earle, J. P., 25 Jan. 1795.
Rec: 25 Jan. 1795.

Pages 119-120   22 Dec. 1795. Adam Files to Alexander Stevenson for Ł 45 stg. for 100 acres, part of tract granted Files 15 Oct. 1785, by Benjamin Guerrard, of 350 acres on both sides of Mountain Creek, branch of Generostee Creek, of Savannah River. Recorded Bk. AAAA, p. 220, plat drawn by John Hamilton, 12 Dec. 1795.
Wit: Moses Liddel, Gashim Fulton. Moses Lidd_le_ made oath to E. Browne, J. P., 22 Dec. 1795.
Rec: 25 Jan. 1796. Copy of plat of 100 acres for Jeremiah Files, 1795, certified by Jno. Hamilton.

Page 121   10 Aug. 1795. Edwin Smith, of Washington Dist. to John Clements for valuable consideration for 130 acres on SW side of Saluda River, on Toney's Creek and mouth of Ready Branch, bd. by William Poor, Austin Jo_n_ston and granted George Pearce, 1787, conveyed to Smith.
Wit: Lewis Nelson, Aaron Clements. Lewis Nelson made oath to Wm. Hall, J. P., 23 Jan. 1796.
Rec: 25 Jan. 1796.

Pages 121-122   31 Mar. 1795. Benjamin Starrett, of Washington Dist. to John Clements for valuable consideration for 100 acres on SW side of Saluda River on branch of Toney's Creek, Reedy Branch, bd. by William Poor, George Pearce.
Wit: William Poor, Samuel Cobb. William Poor made oath to Wm. Hall, JP on 23 Jan. 1796.
Rec: 25 Jan. 1796.

Pages 122-123   23 Dec. 1793. John Martin to Asa Cobb for Ł 50 for 177 acres in Washington Dist. on branches of Saluda River, part of a grant to Elijah Owens, 4 Sep. 1786, by Wm. Moultrie, conveyed by Owens to Joseph Standley, from Standley to John Martin. Recorded Bk. MMMM, p. 495.
Wit: William Willson, Mathias Martin. William Willson made oath to Wm. Hall, J. P., 9 Jan. 1796.
Rec: 25 Jan. 1796.

Pages 123-124   19 Jul. 1794. William Willson to Isaac Wilson for Ł 40 stg. for 50 acres in Washington Dist. on S. side of Big Creek, "formerly called Washington Creek", waters of the Saluda River, part of a grant to William Bell by Wm. Moultrie, 6 Jun. 1785, conveyed from Bell to William Willson, recorded Bk. DDDD, p. 295.
Wit: Asa Cobb, Jesse Cobb, John Pepper. Asa Cobb made oath to Wm. Halbert, J. P., 29 Jul. 1794.
Rec: 25 Jan. 1796.

Pages 124-125   26 Oct. 1795. Wm. Stevenson, of Washington District, to William Gillispie, of same, for Ł 100 for 200 acres granted to Wm. Crosby, 15 October 1784, by Benjamin Guerrard, in Washington Dist. on N. side of Seneca River. Wit: John Loggan, David Stevenson. John Loggan made oath to Saml. Porter, J. P., 23 Jan. 1796.
Rec: 25 Jan. 1796.

Pages 125-126   5 Sep. 1792. Robert Dowdle to Thomas Thaxton for Ł 10 stg. for 238 acres surveyed for John Johnston, 28 Dec. 1785, granted Dowdle, 3 Dec. 1787, in 96 Dist. on Broadaway branch of Great Rocky Creek.
Wit: John Wornock, Charles Beni_tt_, James Moon. Charles Ben_n_ett made oath to Wm. Halbert, J. P., 9 Oct. 1792.
Rec: 25 Jan. 1796.

Pages 126-127   11 Feb. 1793. William Vaughn to James Vaughn for Ł 100 stg. for 200 acres on Saluda River part of 2 tracts, one of 165 acres originally granted to John Maxwell, 6 Mar. 1786, recorded Bk. FFFF, p. 57, conveyed to William Vaughn. The youngest grant to Robert Maxwell, 4 Sep. 1786, recorded Bk. NNNN, p. 485 and conveyed to William Vaughn. Signed: William

(pages 126-127 cont'd):
(+) Vaughn. Wit: John (+) Cox, Isaac (+) Cox. John Cox made oath to Wm. Halbert, J. P., 11 Jul. 1793.
Rec: 25 Jan. 1796.

Pages 127-128   7 Jun. 1794. William Murphree to Samuel Ward for ₺ 25 stg. for 200 acres on S. side of the Saluda, on 12 Mile River, and Woolf Creek, a grant to Murphree, 5 Dec. 1791 by Charles Pinckney.
Wit: Ephraim (X) Herring, Joseph Duncan. Ephraim Herring made oath to W. W. Reid, J. P., 21 Apr. 1795.
Rec: 25 Jan. 1796.

Pages 128-129   11 Apr. 1794. William Gillispie, planter, and Ann, his wife, spinster, to Jacob Gilham for ₺ 32, 14 shillings, 4 pence stg. for 100 acres on branches of Conor (sic), fork of Little Generostee, granted Gillispie, 3 Apr. 1786, recorded Bk. KKKK, p. 201, also 50½ acres of SW of tract of 200 acres granted 25 Jan. 1785, recorded Bk. CCCC, p. 174. Signed: William Gillispie, Ann (fancy "A") Gillespie.
Wit: John Willey, Samuel Willie. Samuel Willey made oath to Samuel Porter, J. P., 23 Jan. 1796. (Signed Samuel Wyllie).
Rec: 25 Jan. 1796.

Pages 129-130   6 Aug. 1793. Bevely Cox to John Cox, Jr. for ₺ 55 stg. for 200 acres granted 15 Oct. 1784, by Benjamin Guerrard to heirs of James Alexander, Jr., deceased. On Savannah River, on each side of Big Generostee Creek, Asaph Alexander being lawful heir of James Alexander, Jr., conveyed to Bevely Cox, 6 Aug. 1793. Signed: Bevely (his mark) Cox, Mary (M) Cox.
Wit: James Jones, James Cox. James Jones made oath to Saml. Porter, J.P. 21 Jan. 1796.
Rec: 25 Jan. 1796.

Pages 130-131   29 Dec. 1795. Lott Ivey to Jehu Ivey for ₺ 30 stg. for 106 acres on both sides of Connoross Creek, waters of Keowee River, granted to Lott Ivey, 2 Dec. 1793. Recorded Bk. H, no. 5, p. 105, by Peter Freneau, Esq. Secretary. Wit: Alexd. Kilpatrick, Mary Kilpatrick. Mary Kilpatrick made oath to J. C. Kilpatrick, J. P., 13 Jan. 1796.
Rec: 25 Jan. 1796.

Pages 131-132   2 Jun. 1795. Edwin Wade and Nancy, his wife, to John Wornock, for ₺ 10 stg. for 400 acres, part of tract granted Samuel Dalrimple, surveyed 3 Jul. 1787, on Neal's Creek, of Rocky River. Signed: Edward Wade and Nancy (a fancy mark) Wade.
Wit: Moses Holland, Alexr. McLean, William King. Alexander McLean made oath to E. Browne, J. P., 26 Jan. 1796.
Rec: 26 Jan. 1796.

Pages 132-133   I, William Sloan for ₺ 100 stg. paid by David Sloan, have sold him 2 negro boys, one named Joe, age 13, the other named Sambo, age 12.
Date: 10 Jul. 1794. Signed: Wm. Sloan.
Wit: Samuel Briden. Samuel Briden made oath to J. B. Earle, J. P., 26 Jan. 1796. Rec: 26 Jan. 1796.

Page 133   18 May 1793. Robert Anderson to Benjamin Whorton for ₺ 55 for 275 acres (no further description).
Wit: J. L. Landus, James Hendrix. James Hendrix made oath to J. B. Earle J. P., 26 Jan. 1796.
Rec: 26 Jan. 1796.

Page 134   25 Mar. 1795. Fields Prewit, of Pendleton Co. to Anthony Griffen, of Greenville Co., S. C. for ₺ 30 stg. for 155 acres granted Prewitt, 10 Dec. 1791, by Charles Pinckney. Recorded Bk. D, no. 5, p. 260. On

(page 134 cont'd):   S. fork of Cane Creek, waters of Keowee River.
Signed: Field (X) Prewit. Wit: Benja. Whorton, James Hendrix. James
Hendrix made oath to J. B. Earle, J. P., 26 Jan. 1796.
Rec: 26 Jan. 1796.

Page 134-135   15 Apr. 1795. Fields Prewit (Jr. in body of
                        deed) to Benjamin Whorton for Ł 30 stg. for
                        400 acres on Cane Creek, waters of Keowee River, where Prewit now lives. Signed: Field (f) Prewit.
Wit: James Hendrix, Hannah (X) Hendrix. James Hendrix made oath to J.
B. Earle, J. P., 21 Jan. 1796.
Rec: 26 Jan. 1796.

Pages 135-136   13 Apr. 1795. Field Prewit, Sr. and Field Prewit, Jr. to Robert Duncan for Ł 20 stg. for
                        155 acres agreeable to conditional line made
by Field Prewit and Anthony Griffen. Recorded Bk. D, no 5, p. 260, on
S. fork of Cane Creek, of Keowee River. Signed: Field (X) Prewit, Sr.,
Field Prewit, Jr. (no mark recorded).
Wit: Benjamin Whorton, William (O) Owen, Mary Whorton. Benjamin Whorton
made oath to J. B. Earle, J. P., 26 Jan. 1796.
Rec: 26 Jan. 1796.

Pages 136-137   15 Jul. 1793. Edward Wade, of Washington Dist.
                        to Alexander McLean for Ł 5 stg. for 8 acres,
                        30 poles, on Neal's Creek of Rocky River, part
of a tract laid out for Samuel Dalrimple, 6 Apr. 1789, conveyed by his
executors to Edward Wade, joining plantation where McLean now lives, surveyed by Saml. F. Dickson, D. S.
Wit: Mary Holland, Elisha Bennett, Joseph Wornock. Elisha Bennett made
oath to Wm. Halbert, J. P., 12 Oct. 1793.
Rec: 26 Jan. 1796.

Pages 137-138   6 Apr. 1793. William Buchannon, of Abbeville
                        Co. to Alexander McLean, of Pendleton Co., for
                        Ł 40 stg. for 250 acres granted Buchannon, 6
Nov. 1786, in Washington Dist. above ancient boundary line on Rocky River
bd. on NW by Hugh Wornock and by vacant land. Signed: William (8) Buchanan. Wit: Joseph Wornock, Thomas Buford, Elisha Bennett. Elisha Bennett made oath to W. W. Halbert, J. P., 12 Oct. 1793.
Rec: 6 Jan. 1796.

Pages 138-139   8 Apr. 1793. Alexander McLean to Elisha Bennett for Ł 35 stg. for 125 acres granted Wm.
                        Buchanan on 6 Nov. 1786, conveyed to McLean,
on Neal's Creek of Rocky River, part of 250 acres surveyed for Buchanan,
6 Apr. 1785, bd. on SW by Hugh Wornock, on SE by Stephen Bennett, on NE
by McLean. Wit: Joseph Wornock, Stephen (X) Bennett, Jean Wornock.
Stephen Bennett made oath to W. W. Halbert, J. P., 12 Oct. 1793.
Rec: 26 Jan. 1796.

Pages 139-140   12 Dec. 1792. John Holcom (also spelled Holcombe) to James Linn for Ł 40 stg. for 76 ac.
                        part of 211 acres granted Holcom, 20 Jan. 1788
by Charles Pinckney, on Mountain Creek, of Generostee and Savannah River,
above ancient boundary line, plat by Jonathan Clark. Signed: John (h)
Holcombe. Wit: Robert Linn, Aron Smith. Robert Linn made oath to J.B.
Earle, J. P., 26 Jan. 1796.
Rec: 26 Jan. 1796.

Pages 140-141   22 Jul. 1795. William Norwood to Robert Allison for Ł 50 stg. for 150 acres on 23 Mile Crk.
                        waters of Savannah River, part of tract granted Samuel Norwood by Benjamin Guerrard and at decease of Samuel Norwood,
conveyed to William Norwood, his heir. Wit: William Montgomery, A. C.
Jones, Jr., Joseph (X) Morrison. William Montgomery made oath to W. W.
Hall, J. P., 12 Aug. 1795.
Rec: 26 Jan. 1796.

Page 141　　　　　　　　　10 Sep. 1795. Elizabeth King to Peter Hall
　　　　　　　　　　　　(or Hale) and Robert King for Ł 100 stg. for
　　　　　　　　　　　　1 negro woman, 55 years of age, horses, cows,
all household goods and chattels "for Elizabeth King's children".
Wit: Wm. Beazley, Nathan Nall. Nathan Nall made oath to Wm. Hall, J.P.
5 Jan. 1796. Rec: 26 Jan. 1796.

Pages 141-142　　　　　　　22 Jan. 1796. Francis King to John Ragsdale
　　　　　　　　　　　　for Ł 73 stg. for 100 acres in Dist. of Pick-
　　　　　　　　　　　　ensville, formerly 96 Dist. on S. side of the
Seneca River, plat dated 5 Jun. 1786, granted Sollomon King, Jr., brother of Francis King, citizen, by Wm. Moultrie. Recorded Bk. LLLL,p.217.
Signed: Francis (X) King.
Wit: Thos. Gorman, Judith Gorman. Thomas Gorman made oath to J. C. Kilpatrick, J. P., 26 Jan. 1796.
Rec: 26 Jan. 1796.

Page 143　　　　　　　　　15 Dec. 1795. John King to John Ragsdale for
　　　　　　　　　　　　Ł 100 stg. for 115 acres on S. side of Seneca
　　　　　　　　　　　　River at mouth of Cannoe Landing Branch, part
of a tract granted Solomon King, Jr., 5 Jun. 1786. Signed: John (his
mark) King.
Wit: John Harris, Edwd. Williams. Edward Williams made oath to J. C.
Kilpatrick, J. P., 26 Jan. 1796.
Rec: 26 Jan. 1796.

Pages 143-144　　　　　　　24 Sep. 1795. Robert Box, of Pendleton Co., to
　　　　　　　　　　　　David Humphreys, of Surry Co., N. C., for Ł220
　　　　　　　　　　　　stg. for 200 acres in Pendleton Co., on Noyowee
Creek and Tugalo River, near Tugalo Old Town, bd. on SE by Robt. Miscamp-
bell, originally granted Jesse Geontose(?), Souldier(sic), 26 Jan. 1785.
Signed: Robert (R) Box.
Wit: Harris McKinley Wiley, O. C. Hooper, Jr. Harris Wiley made oath
to Jno. Barton, J. P., 24 Sep. 1795.
Rec: 26 Jan. 1796.

Pages 144-145　　　　　　　I, Charles Travis, of Pendleton Co., for Ł 100
　　　　　　　　　　　　stg. paid by Thomas Stribbling, of Union Co.,
　　　　　　　　　　　　S. C., sold him (no amount named) acres in Pen-
dleton Co., on W. side of Deep Creek, bd. on SE by Robert Green, granted
Samuel Green, 2 Sep. 1793, conveyed to Travis. Date: 20 Jan. 1796.
Wit: Thomas Farrar, J. B. Earle. Thomas Farrar made oath to E. Browne,
J. P., 27 Jan. 1796.
Rec: 27 Jan. 1796.

Page 145　　　　　　　　　I, Charles Travis for Ł 100 stg. paid by Thos.
　　　　　　　　　　　　Stribling, of Union Co., S. C. sold 143 acres
　　　　　　　　　　　　on both sides of 23 Mile Creek, branch of the
Keowee River. Date: 20 Jan. 1796.
Wit: Thomas Farrar, J. B. Earle. Thomas Farrar made oath to E. Browne,
J. P., 27 Jan. 1796.
Rec: 27 Jan. 1796.

Pages 145-146　　　　　　　I, James Jordan for Ł 100 sold to Thomas Strib-
　　　　　　　　　　　　ling 300 acres on W. side of Deep Creek and 26
　　　　　　　　　　　　Mile River, including fork, part of 400 acres
granted James Jorden by Benjamin Guerrard. Recorded Bk. ZZZ, p. 54.
Date: 20 Jan. 1796. Wit: Thomas Farrar, J. B. Earle. Thomas Farrar
made oath to E. Browne, J. P., 27 Jan. 1796.
Rec: 27 Jan. 1796.

Pages 146-147　　　　　　　4 Oct. 1794. Elias Earle, of Greenville Co.,
　　　　　　　　　　　　S. C., to John Butt, of Pendleton Co., for Ł100
　　　　　　　　　　　　stg. for 200 acres granted 4 Mar. 1793 by Wm.
Moultrie, part of 690 acres in 96 Dist. on S. side of Saluda River, on
both sides of Camp Creek, bd. on NW and SW by lands laid out for William
Lewis, Sutton Green and Joseph Whitner, on SE and NE by Charles Gates.
Wit: Jno. McBeath, Benj. Clarke. Benjamin Clark made oath to W. W.Reid
J. P., 20 Jan. 1796.
Rec: 27 Jan. 1796.

Pages 147-149   27 Oct. 1791. John Norwood, of Abbeville Co. planter, to Collen Campbell, of Pendleton Co., planter, for ₤ 100 stg. for 200 acres granted John Norwood, heir at law to Daniel Norwood, soldier, late of the Army, in 96 Dist. on Wallinoy Creek, S. fork of Saluda River, granted to John Norwood, 14 Oct. 1784.
Wit: William (+) Linneard, Honour (fancy "L") Linneard. William Leonard made oath to Elijah Browne, J. P., 18 Nov. 1794.
Rec: 27 Jan. 1796.

Pages 149-150   19 Mar. 1793. William Murphree to Moses Murphree for ₤ 60 stg. for 439 acres in 96 Dist. on S. fork of 12 Mile River, surveyed 9 Aug. 1787. Wit: James Powell, Jonathan (+) Gregory, Aron (+) Murphree. James Powell made oath to Bailey Anderson, J. P., 30 Mar. 1793.
Rec: 27 Jan. 1796.

Pages 150-151   1 Jan. 1795. John Green, planter of Abbeville Co. to Moses Hopper, of Pendleton Co. for ₤ 50 stg. for 150 acres on branches of Big Generostee. Wit: Andw. Hamilton, John Lowry. John Lowry made oath to W. W. Reid, J. P., 28 Jan. 1796.
Rec: 28 Jan. 1796.

Pages 151-152   23 Aug. 1794. James Robertson to Joseph Stepp for ₤ 50 stg. for 200 acres on Chauga Creek, granted Robertson, 1 Jan. 1785, by Benjamin Guerrard. Wit: James Blair, George Simpson. James Blair made oath to Benjamin Cleveland, J. P., 29 Jan. 1796.
Rec: 29 Jan. 1796.

Pages 152-153   ___(blank), 1795. James Hart and Sarah West, his wife, (sic) to Thomas Blair, lately from the Waxhaws, in S. C., now of Pendleton County for 15 guineas for 300 acres on Hamilton's Creek, branch of Savannah River, bd. on SW and SE by Mathew Martin and James Morrow, granted to James Hart, 2 Mar. 1795, by Wm. Moultrie. Signed: Jas., West Hart.
Wit: Jno. Glenn, Moses Liddell, Adam Davis. Moses Liddell made oath to J. B. Earle, J. P., 29 Jan. 1796.
Rec: 29 Jan. 1796.

Pages 153-154   28 Aug. 1795. James Gillespie to John Laughlin for ₤ 35 stg. for 485 acres "excepting what is taken off by Johnston, Dalrymple and Wadsworths older survey" on branch of big Beaver Dam Creek, of Rocky River of Savannah River, bd. on W. by Johnston, on N. by Stephen Anderson, on NE by Dalrymple, on SE by Wadsworth, granted (no date) by Charles Pinckney.
Wit: William Laughlin, Robt. Burby. Wm. Laughlin made oath to William Mulwee, J. P., 5 Jan. 1796.
Rec: 5 Feb. 1796.

Pages 154-155   21 Sep. 1795. Samuel Robertson to John Sutherland for ₤ 40 stg. for 156 acres, excepting a small part held by Robert Anderson, Jr., on S. side of 23 Mile Creek bd. on NE by Richard Speak, granted Samuel Robertson, 7 Jun. 1790 by Charles Pinckney, conveyed to Ickabod Blackledge.
Signed: Samuel Robertson.
Wit: Bennett Aiden, Ichabod Blackledge. Icabod Blackledge made oath to Saml. Gardner, J. P., 16 Dec. 1795.
Rec: 10 Feb. 1796.

Page 155   23 Jul. 1793. Andrew Roe to Isaac West for ₤50 stg. for 200 acres on 23 Mile Creek, waters of the Savannah, part of a tract granted to Roe by Charles Pinckney, 6 Sep. 1790.
Wit: John Robinson, Isaac Nikelson, Jacob (his mark) West. John Robinson made oath to John Wilson, J. P., 25 Jul. 1793. Rec: 9 Feb. 1796.

Page 156   29 Nov. 1794. Thomas Stone to James Bourland for ₤ 110 stg. for 100 acres in Washington Dis.

Page 156 cont'd:	part of a tract granted 2 Oct. 1786, by William Moultrie to John Logan, heir at law of Thomas Logan, deceased, for his "service in the county", of 200 acres on Little George's Creek, waters of the Saluda River, where Stone now lives and conveyed to John Logan, then to Stone.
Wit: John Bourland, Enoch Smith, William Bourland. John Bourland made oath to Robert Bowen, 10 Oct. 1795.
Rec: 9 Feb. 1796.

Page 157	I, Ledford Payne am endebted to James Griffen for ₤ 12...sell him 1 negro man...if note is paid by 1 Jan. 1797, note is null and void.
(hard to read). Date: 10 Feb. 1796. Teste: Jas. Wood.
Rec: 10 Feb. 1796.

Pages 157-158	I, James Martin, of York Co., S. C. am bound to Christopher Casey, of Pendleton Co., for ₤ 40 stg...made title to Casey for 640 acres in Pendleton Co. on branches of Generostee Creek, adj. to Lesley and sd. Casey, granted to David Shaddin. Date: 2 Feb. 1793.
Wit: Jesse Birdsong, John Pucket.....15 Aug. 1795, I assign within note to Reubin Dollar for value received. Signed: Christopher Casey.
Wit: Hugh Atkins, James Shockley...Laurence Co., S. C. John Pucket made oath to Roger Brown, J. P., 10 Dec. 1796.
Rec: 19 Feb. 1796.

Page 158	I, Christopher Casey, of Pendleton Co. am bound to Reuben Dallar, of Spartanburg Co., S. C. for ₤ 100 stg....make title to 640 ac. in Pendleton Co. on the Savannah River, surveyed for David Shadon (?)...If payment is made by 13 Dec. 1795, this debt is null and void. Date: 13 Dec. 1794.
Wit: Ansel Dollar, Thomas Woldrop...Spartanburg Co., Ansel Dollar made oath to Thomas Farrow, J. P., 17 Feb. 1795.
Rec: 19 Feb. 1796.

Pages 158-159	15 May 1794. William Williams, of Washington Dist. to John Duncan, of same, for ₤ 50 stg. for 100 acres, part of a tract granted William Rose, 4 Jun. 1792, by Charles Pinckney for 227 acres in Washington Dist. of S. of Saluda River, bd. on NE and NW by William Jamison, on W. by Joshua Fowler and by vacant lands, where John Duncan now lives. Signed: William (+) Williams.
Wit: William Jamison, John McElroy, William Rose. William Jamison made oath to Bayley Anderson, J. P., 11 Nov. 1794.
Rec: 22 Feb. 1796.

Pages 159-160	12 Apr. 1792. Albert Francis Smithson to Joel Holcom for ₤ 50 stg. for 320 acres on S. side of Saluda River, on branches of 12 Mile Creek "first called Mile Creek now called Rice's Creek", granted to Smithson on 4 May 1789 by Charles Pinckney.
Wit: Joseph Logan, John Tubb. Joseph Logan made oath to Bayley Anderson J. P., 8 Mar. 1794.
Rec: 22 Feb. 1796.

Pages 160-161	10 Jun. 1795. William Beazley to Mary Anderson for ₤ 30 stg. for 50 acres, part of tract granted to James Cannon on 6 Feb. 1786, by William Moultrie, Rec. Bk. FFFF, p. 423, bd. on SE by Big Reedy Branch and Robert Rankin, Wm. Land and Caleb Edmondson. Signed: William (W) Beazley.
Wit: Caleb Edmondson, Isiah Underwood. <u>Josiah</u> Underwood made oath to Wm. Mulwee, J. P., 18 Jun. 1795.
Rec: 5 Feb. 1795.

Page 161	I, John Robinson for ₤ 23 stg., 6 pence, sold to John Turner one negro man named Jefey (or Jesse). Date: 1 Dec. 1795. (cont'd page 106)

Page 161 cont'd:

Wit: Benjamin (B) Turner. Benjamin Turner made oath to J. B. Earle, JP, 29 Feb. 1796.
Rec: 29 Feb. 1796.

Page 161 I, John Turner have sold to my daughter Ann, 1 waggon, horses, horned cattle, hogs for full satisfaction. Date: 25 Mar. 1795. Signed: John (his mark) Turner.
Wit: Thos. Edmondson, Samuel Washburn, Wm. Edmondson. (No oath).
Rec: 29 Feb. 1796.

Page 162 I, Ledford Payne, for £ 55 stg. sold to James C. Griffen, planter, one negro man, named John about 38 years old. Date: 27 Jan. 1796.
Wit: Jesse (+) Ward. Jesse Ward made oath to J. B. Earle, J. P., 1 Mar. 1796.
Rec: 1 Mar. 1796.

Pages 162-163 13 Dec. 1793. Squire Allen to Robert Smith for £ 30 stg. for 272 acres, except part of tract Thomas Farrar takes out of same, adj. to William Guess(?), Thomas Farrar, conveyed by Robert Smith to Allen, 13 May 1786, on Little Beaverdam Creek, of Tugalo River.
Wit: Benjamin Gueat(Guest?), Lee Allen. Lee Allen made oath to J. C. Kilpatrick, J. P., 8 Aug. 1795.
Rec: 1 Mar. 1795.

Pages 163-164 10 Jun. 1795. William Beazley to Caleb Edmondson for £ 75 stg. for 100 acres, part of a tract granted to James Cannon on 6 Feb. 1786, by William Moultrie, Recorded Bk. FFFF, p. 428, bd. on SE by Robert Rankin, on W. by Catherine Miller, Big Reedy Branch, Mary Anderson. Signed: William (W) Beazley.
Wit: Josiah Underwood, James Deviney. Josiah Underwood made oath to Wm. Mulwee, J. P., 28 Dec. 1795.
Rec: 7 Mar. 1796.

Pages 164-165 9 Nov. 1795. Joseph Price to Caleb Edmondson for £ 6 stg. for 30 acres, part of a tract granted to Joseph Price, 3 Dec. 1787 by Thos. Pinckney, Recorded Bk. GGGG, p. 217, bd. on NE by Caleb Edmondson, on N. by (blank), all other sides vacant. Signed: Joseph (JP) Price.
Wit: Josiah Underwood, Polly (her mark) Underwood. Josiah Underwood made oath to Wm. Mulwee, J. P., 28 Dec. 1795.
Rec: 7 Mar. 1796.

Pages 165-166 5 Nov. 1794. Conrad Adderhold to Thomas Goss for £ 30 stg. for 100 acres in Washington Dis. on S. side of Rice's Creek, waters of 12 Mile River, part of a tract granted to William Henderson, 5 Jun. 1786, by Wm. Moultrie. Signed: Jno. Conrad Adderhold.
Wit: Nathaniel Henderson, William Coun(?). (Oath says Brown). Nathaniel Henderson made oath to John Willson, J. P., 19 Sep. 1795.
Rec: 7 Mar. 1796.

Pages 166-167 10 Jul. 1794. Mary Harris and Handy Harris, both of Abbeville Co., and John Harris, of Pendleton Co., to Joseph White, of Pendleton Co.....whereas, John Harris, deceased, late of Abbeville Co., Minister of the Gospel, in his lifetime possessed sundry tracts of land, some of which was directed by his last will and testament to be sold by Mary Harris, executrix, and John Harris and Handy Harris, executors, for £ 45 for 250 acres on E. side of the Keowee River, bd. by River and vacant lands. Granted to Rev. Harris, 15 Oct. 1784, by Benjamin Guerrard, Recorded Bk. AAAA, p. 178. Signed: Mary Harris, Handy Harris, John Harris.
Wit: Saml. H. Dickson, Rebekah Dickson, Jno. Dickson, Sr. Samuel Dickson made oath to Joshua Saxon, J. P., 21 Jan. 1795. Rec: 10 Mar. 1796.

Pages 167-168   13 Mar. 1796. Asaph Alexander to James Turner for ₺ 20 stg. for 200 acres granted on 15 Oct. 1784, by Benj. Guerrard, excepting 40 ac. on W. side of Big Generostee, now in possession of John Simpson.
Wit: William Turner, Aron James. William Turner made oath to E. Browne, J. P., 21 Mar. 1796.
Rec: 2 Mar. 1796.

Page 168   21 Mar. 1795. Joseph Reid, of Pendleton Co., to Joseph Roberts, Jr., of Elbert Co., Ga., for ₺ 5 stg. for 150 acres on branch of Savannah River, in Pendleton Co., part of 200 acres granted to Samuel(?) Love, conveyed from him to John Newman(?), then to Joseph Roberts, Sr., the other 50 acres to James Cox, bd. on NW by John Newman, on SW by Thomas Shockley and James Cox. Signed: Joseph (his mark) Roberts.
Wit: Edward T. McClure, James Tate, Jr., Saml. Tate. Edward Tate McClure made oath to Joshua Saxon, J. P., 28 Mar. 1795.
Rec: 21 Mar. 1796.

Pages 168-169   14 Jan. 1794. Lewis D. Martin to Roland Burks for ₺ 60 stg., for 212 acres, except that part which Martin's line takes off the NE corner, on both sides of Connoross Creek, of Keowee River, granted to Lewis D. Martin, 2 Jul. 1787, by Thos. Pinckney.
Wit: John (P) Portman, Randlof (+) Burks. Randolph Burks made oath to Robert Anderson, J. P., 23 Mar. 1796.
Rec: 24 Mar. 1796.

Pages 169-170   17 Apr. 1791. James Tate, Jr., sadler, of Pendleton Co. to David Moffett, of Lincoln Co. N. C., for ₺ 100 stg. for 320 acres on the E. side of the Savannah River, including mouth of Little Generostee.
Wit: Richd. Speake, Saml. Tate, James Tate. Richard Speak made oath to Wm. Mulwee, J. P., 29 Mar. 1795.
Rec: 25 Mar. 1796.

Pages 170-171   I, Thomas Farrar, planter, for ₺ 50 stg. paid by Samuel Gardner for 240 acres on 18 Mile Ck. bd. by vacant land, granted to Peter Sinkler and held by the Treasurers, purchased by Thomas Farrar as the highest bidder, Recorded Bk. CCCC, p. 387. Date: 3 Mar. 1796. Ack.: by J. Whitner and J. B. Earle, C. C. and J. P.
Rec: 25 Mar. 1796.

Page 171   7 Nov. 1795. James Jordan to William Hamilton for ₺ 10 stg. for 100 acres, part of 400 acres in Pendleton Co., 96 Dist., on 23 and 26 Mile Creeks and Deep Creek, waters of the Keowee River, bd. by James Houston, granted to Jordan, 16 Jul. 1788 by Benj. Guerrard, Recorded Bk. ZZZ, p. 24...."(This deed is continued on p. 179)".

Page 172   1 Jan. 1793. Jones (Jonas) Kile to Solomon Palmour for ₺ 60 stg. for 120 acres on Wolf Creek, waters of 12 Mile River, bd. by James Bremis(?), ___ Bradley, part of 640 acres (granted) to Benjamin Perry, 1 Jan. 1786 by Wm. Moultrie.
Wit: Wm. Marchbanks, Thomas (his mark) Kile. Wm. Marchbanks made oath to Bayley Anderson, J. P., 13 Mar. 1794.
Rec: 28 Mar. 1796.

Pages 172-174   28 Nov. 1794. Christopher Lewis, of Camden Dist., S. C., planter, to Thomas Rustin, of the City of Philadelphia in the Commonwealth of Pennsylvania for "divers other good causes and considerations", tract of 51,000 acres originally surveyed for Wade Hampton and Mark Mitchell, in 96 District to the East of the path to Tugaloo, bd. on E. by Wade Hampton and Mark Mitchell, on other sides by vacant lands...and certain other tract of 40,960 acres originally surveyed for Thomas Sumter, in 96 District, extending across a water course called Shoemaker, bd. by Wade Hampton and Mark Mitchell, granted to Christopher Lewis, by Wm. Moultrie,

Pages 172-174 cont'd:
on 1 Jul. 1793, Recorded Bk. L., no. 5, pages 136 and 192.
Wit: Edw. Shippen, George A. Baker...State of Pennsylvania, Edward Shippen, Esq., one of the Justices of the Supreme Court of the Commonwealth, 18 Dec. 1794. Signed: James Trimble, Sec'y. for Thomas Mifflin, Governor of the State of Pennsylvania.
Rec: 28 Mar. 1796.

Pages 174-176   3 Feb. 1795. Christopher Lewis, of Camden Dist., S. C., to Ezekiel King, of Philadelphia, Pa., for 5 shillings for 27,920 acres on the S. side of the Tenisa(?) River and High Wassa Creek, 96 Dist., S. C., bd. on S. by Wade Hampton and Richard Harrison, on N. by Hampton and on other sides by vacant land, granted by Patent on 1 Jul. 1793 by Wm. Moultrie. Recorded Bk. L, No. 5, p. 125.
Wit: Catherine Baker, George A. Baker...Philadelphia, Penn., Christopher Lewis acknowledged above deed to Isaac Howell, Judge of the Court of Common Pleas, 3 Feb. 1794. Ack. by James Trimble, Dept. Sec'y. for Thomas Mifflin, Governor. (Plat).
Rec: 28 Mar. 1796.

Page 177   6 Apr. 1793. John Breavert to Charles Willson for Ł 9 stg. for 371 acres on Little Beaverdam, waters of the Savannah River, in 96 Dist. granted to Breavert, 6 Feb. 1793, by Chas. Pinckney.
Wit: John (+) McKinsey, Jean Willson, James Simms. Jean Willson made oath to John Willson, J. P., 7 Mar. 1796.
Rec: 29 Mar. 1796.

Pages 177-178   1 Apr. 1791. Thomas Lesley to Isaac Steele, for Ł 60 stg. for 230 acres granted on 22 Jun. 1785, by Wm. Moultrie, on the waters of Great Generostee, joining sd. Steele and Thomas Lesley. Signed: Thomas Lesley, Mary Lesley.
Wit: Aaron James, James Steele. Aaron James made oath to E. Browne, J. P., 29 Mar. 1796. Plat surveyed for Thomas Lesley, 22 Jun. 1785, by Wm. Lesley, D. S.
Rec: 30 Mar. 1796.

Page 178   3 Nov. 1795. Mathew Dickson to Walter Carson Dickson for Ł 55 ..sell him horses, colts, waggon, ploughs, cows, furniture, kitchen utensils, etc. (itemized list).
Wit: Elizabeth Miller, J. Miller. (No oath).
Rec: 31 Mar. 1796.

Page 179   (Continuation of James Jordan deed on p. 171). Wit: Charles Travis, Wm. McClure. Charles Travis made oath to E. Browne, J. P., 29 Mar. 1796. Rec: 5 Apr. 1796.

Pages 179-180   3 May 1794. James Gillispie to Ephraim Harris for Ł 30 stg. for 779 acres granted to Gillispie on 22 Aug. 1791, by Chas. Pinckney, west of old boundary line, on Woolf Creek and Shoal Creek, bd. by Samuel Earle, Samuel Duff, John Gillispie, James Gillispie.
Wit: Samuel Ward, Samuel Duff, Nancy Gillispie. Samuel Ward made oath to W. W. Reid, J. P., 3 Jul. 1794.
Rec: 5 Apr. 1796.

Page 180   16 Jan. 1790. Thomas Lesley to Hugh Simpson for Ł 17 stg. for 72 acres, part of 300 acres granted 15 Oct. 1784 by Benj. Guerrard on the branches of Great Generostee Creek.
Wit: Moses Liddell, Jacob Gilliland. Moses Liddell made oath to E. Browne, J. P., 26 Jan. 1796.
Rec: 5 Apr. 1796.

Pages 180-181   20 Oct. 1795. William Mackie to William(cont'd)

Pages 180-181 cont'd:
Steele for Ł 10 stg. for 170 acres in Washington Dist. on W. side of 23 Mile Creek, Keowee River, part of 332 acres granted to Mackey on 2 Jul. 1787 by Thomas Pinckney, 132 acres sold to Paul Fountain, now occupied by Thomas (?) Payne, that part next to Pendleton Courthouse, bd. by John Portman, Jesse Luiston(?), John Young. Signed: William (M) Mackie.
Wit: Joab Mitchell, Saml. Neel. Joab Mitchell made oath to J. B. Earle, J. P., 8 Apr. 1796.
Rec: 8 Apr. 1796.

Page 181   15 Dec. 1795. James Mulwee to Eli Davis for Ł 50 stg. for 132 acres on Choestoe Creek, on waters of Tugalo River, bd. on all sides by vacant land, granted to Mulwee, 7 Nov. 1791, by Chas. Pinckney.
Wit: W. H. Lacy, Wm. Hudgens. William Hughes Lacy made oath to Nath'l. Perry, J. P., 8 Apr. 1796.
Rec: 12 Apr. 1796.

Page 182   25 Apr. 1794. James Patterson to Absolom Blythe for Ł 80 for 115 acres granted George Salmon, 4 Sep. 1786 by Wm. Moultrie, on S.side of the Saluda River.
Wit: Samuel Vanderpoor, Samuel (+) Burnet(?), George Patterson. Samuel Vanderpool made oath to W. W. Reid, J. P., 10 Feb. 1796.
Rec: 12 Apr. 1796.

Pages 182-183   30 Nov. 1795. James Duff, of Pendleton Co., Washington Dist., to Samuel Burdine, of same, for Ł 90 stg. for 267 acres granted Robert Duncan, 7 May 1787 by Thos. Pinckney, in Washington Dist. on branches of North Fork and branches of Middle Fork of George's Creek, waters of the Saluda River.
Wit: William Eddins, John Yager, John Burdine. John Yager made oath to W. W. Reid, J. P., 30 Nov. 1795.
Rec: 12 Apr. 1796.

Pages 183-184   30 Nov. 1795. James Duff to Samuel Burdine for Ł 90 stg. for 300 acres, part of a tract granted to James Jett, 30 Mar. 1784, by Thos. Pinckney, for 628 acres in Washington Dist. on both sides of a prong of George's Creek, waters of the Saluda River, conveyed by Jett to Duff, 27 Aug. 1793.
Wit: William Eddins, John Yager, John Burdine. John Yager made oath to W. W. Reid, J. P., 30 Nov. 1795.
Rec: 12 Apr. 1796.

Page 185   22 Oct. 1795. John Black, of Lawrence Co.,SC 96 Dist., to John Murphey, of Pendleton Co., for Ł 50 stg. for 212 acres granted to Black on 1 Feb. 1787 by Wm. Moultrie, in Washington Dist. on Town Creek, waters of 12 Mile River.
Wit: William Murphe, Benjamin Barton. William Murphree made oath to W. W. Reed, J. P., 12 Apr. 1795.
Rec: 12 Apr. 1795.

Pages 185-186   16 Feb. 1796. James Sewards or Swords (this name written this way), of Chesterfield Co., Va., to Joseph Williams and Griaff Williams (Jointly), both of Pendleton Co., for Ł 80 stg. for 200 acres in Pendleton Co. on N. side of the Tugalo River, being land whereon the Public Garrison, called Tugalo Station, now stands, land granted to James-Buff (marked out), by the State of S. C., by virtue of Soldiers Bounty Warrant.
Signed: James Sewards, by some called "Swords".
Wit: Wm. Martin, Robert (R) Box, John Smith; William Martin made oath to Joseph Reid, J. P., 11 Apr. 1796.
Rec: 13 Apr. 1796.

Pages 186-187   22 Jul. 1795. Benjamin Clardy and Agnes, his wife, planter, of Pendleton Co., Washington

Pages 186-187 cont'd:
Dist., to Ambrose Hudgens, Sr. for 59.3.9... (amount of acreage not stated), part of tract originally surveyed for William Lowe and granted to Wadsworth & Turpin, 4 Jan. 1787, by Wm. Moultrie, conveyed by Wadsworth & Turpin, 15 Jul. 1789, on Saludy(Saluda) River and Brushy Creek. Signed: Benja. Clardy, Agnes Clardy.
Wit: Jesse Kirby (also spelled Curby), Smith Clardy. Jesse Kirby made oath to R. Maxwell, J. P., 27 Jul. 1795.
Rec: 13 Apr. 1796.

Pages 187-188
1 Oct. 1795. Thomas Wadsworth and William Turpin, Merchants, to Ambrose Hudgins, Sr., planter, for ₤ 10 stg. for 200 acres, part of a tract surveyed for Benj. Clardy and by him conveyed to Wadsworth & Turpin, 16 Nov. 1793, in Washington Dist. on the Saluda River, bd. by Benj. Clardy, Henry Green, Mathias Richardson and Capt. Rosemond. Signed: Thomas Wadsworth for Wadsworth & Turpin, Jane Wadsworth.
Wit: James Young, James Boyce. James Young made oath to John Hunter, J. P., 1 Oct. 1795.
Rec: 13 Apr. 1796.

Page 188
29 Jan. 1796. John Lewis Davis to Basley... (also Basil) Smithson, for ₤ 50 stg. for 66 acres on the S. side of Cheostoe Creek, of the Tugalo River, bd. by Eli Davis, originally granted to James Maxwell, 3 Nov. 1788, by Thos. Pinckney.
Wit: W. H. Lacy, Marsin Smithson. Marsin Smithson made oath to Nath'l. Perry, 9 Apr. 1796.
Rec: 13 Apr. 1796.

Page 189
I, Charles Hughes for ₤ 50 stg. paid by William Owens sold him 150 acres, part of tract of 560 acres granted Charles Hughes by Chas. Pinckney, 25 Feb. 1796, Recorded Bk. C, no. 5, p. 346. Signed: Charles Huse.
Wit: Charles Willson, Robert Swann. Charles Willson made oath to John Willson, J. P., 15 Mar. 1796.
Rec: 14 Apr. 1796.

Pages 189-190
27 Jan. 1796. Captain John Norwood, of Abbeville Co., to James Lindsey, of Pendleton Co. for 20 shillings for 630 acres granted Robert Wallace, 5 Sep. 1785, by Wm. Moultrie, on the S. side of the Saluda River, Washington Dist.
Wit: George Turner, James McCaleb. (No oath).
Rec: 15 Apr. 1796.

Pages 190-191
4 Feb. 1795. James Buchanan, of Abbeville Co. to John George of Pendleton Co. for ₤ 32 5 sh. for 130 acres where George now lives, granted to Mary Smith, of Pendleton Co., 5 Jun. 1786, conveyed to Buchanan, in Washington Dist. on Rocky River, bd. on NW and NE and SE by Dan'l. McAlister, on SW by John Parker, James Milwee; Recorded Bk. NNNN, p. 23.
Wit: John Wornock, Thomas Armstrong, John Moore. John Wornock made oath to Wm. Hall, 8 Nov. 1796.(1795?)
Rec: 16 Apr. 1796.

Page 191
I, Henry Hill sold to Benjamin Barton, one negro woman named Hester. Date: 26 Jan.1796.
Wit: Wm. Marchbanks, Jonas Hill. William Marchbanks made oath to W. W. Reid, J. P., 16 Apr. 1796.
Rec: 18 Apr. 1796.

Pages 191-193
28 Jul. 1789. Gabriel Pickens, of Abbeville Co. to Christopher Long, of Pendleton Dist., for ₤ 100 stg. for 200 acres on N. side of the Savannah River and N. side of the Seneca River at the fork of Saluda and Tugalo Rivers, where Long now lives, granted to William Gabriel Pickens, 5 Jun. 1786. Signed: Wm. Gab. Pickens. (cont'd next page)

Pages 191-193 cont'd:

Wit: George Deavors, Jacob Clearman...Spartanburg Co., S. C., George Deavors made oath to James Jordan, J. P., 27 Apr. 1795.
Rec: 18 Apr. 1796.

Pages 193-194   20 Feb. 1796. John Harris, Sheriff of Pendleton Co., to John James...Mary Devaney being seized of 154 acres in Pendleton Co. on the NW side of a branch dividing line of Robert Rankin and Andrew Tate, Andrew Tate obtained two judgements against Mary and Hugh Devaney, one for 7.12.4, the other for 8.9.3., both with costs. John James for Ł 10 stg. was the highest bidder (by his friend, Andrew Tate). Signed: John Harris. Wit: Thos. Gorman, Saml. Barr. Samuel Barr made oath to John B. Earle, J. P., 18 Apr. 1796.
Rec: 18 Apr. 1796.

Page 194   29 Mar. 1796. James Cunningham, of Knox Co., in the Territory of the United States South of the Ohio, to William Eddins, of Pendleton Co., for Ł 80 stg. for 200 acres on the SE side of Hickorynut Mountain on head branches of Dody's Creek, S. of the Saluda River, surveyed by William Benson for Samuel Earle, who sold to James Cunningham.
Wit: Wm. Crain, John Langley. William Crane made oath to W. W. Reid, J. P., 29 Mar. 1796.
Rec: 18 Apr. 1796.

Pages 194-195   6 Oct. 1795. Christopher Waggoner, of Washington Dist., to Benjamin Eddins, of Abbeville Co., 96 Dist. for Ł 9 stg. for 50 acres, part of 576 acres granted to Elias Earle, 5 Apr. 1790 by Charles Pinckney, surveyed for Sutton Green, 1 Feb. 1788, in 96 Dist. on both sides of Doddy's Creek of the Saluda River, bd. on SE and SW by Joseph Whitner, on SE, NW and NE by vacant lands, on NE by lands surveyed for James Good--tt (torn). Signed: Christopher Wagner, Barbary (X) Waggoner.
Wit: John Yager, Samuel (X) Yager. John Yager made oath to W. W. Reid, J. P., 13 Apr. 1796.
Rec: 18 Apr. 1796.

Pages 195-196   22 Sep. 1795. Christopher Waggoner to Benjamin Eddins, Sr. for Ł 121 stg. for 427 acres granted to Waggoner, 7 May 1787 by Thomas Pinckney, on W. side of old boundary, on Camp Creek, waters of the Saluda River. Signed: Christopher Wagner, Barbary (+) Waggoner.
Wit: John Yager, John Shotwell, Wm. Eddins. John Yager made oath to W. W. Reid, J. P., 13 Apr. 1796.
Rec: 18 Apr. 1796.

Pages 196-199   11 Sep. 1786. Wm. Wrightman, of Charleston, Goldsmith, to James Cart (Cast?), of same, merchant, for Ł 250 stg. for 617 acres on S. fork of Baker's Creek, in 96 Dist., granted to Wm. Wrightman, 5 Sep.1785.
Wit: Jno. Currier, James Nicholson. (Plat). James Nicholson made oath to Daniel Smith, J. P., 9 Mar. 1786 (Charleston?).
Rec: 13 Apr. 1796.

Pages 199-200   22 Nov. 1794. Charles Clements to Nathaniel Reid for Ł 25 stg. for 100 acres in Washington Dist. on Oak Chuskie(?) Creek, waters of Savannah River, part of 640 acres granted Christopher Williman, 15 Oct. 1784 by Benj. Guerrard, conveyed from Williman to Clements, 29 Nov. (___).
Wit: Reuben Clements, Joseph McKam, George (R) Reid. George Reid made oath to Wm. Hall, J. P., 4 Apr. 1795.
Rec: 25 Apr. 1796.

Pages 200-201   21 Sep. 1795. William McKey, farmer, to Moses Payne, farmer, for Ł 20 stg. for 162 acres on W. side of 23 Mile Creek, waters of Keowee River, part of 332 acres bd. on E. by John Portman and vacant land, granted to McKey by Thomas Pinckney (no date). Recorded Bk. SSSS, p. 406...

Pages 200-201 cont'd:
                        Signed: William (his mark) **Mackie**.
Wit: Lewis Cobb, who acknowledged before Samuel Gardner, J. P., (no date
Rec: 25 Apr. 1796.

Page 201   23 Dec. 1795. John Woodall, Sr. to John Wood-
                        all, Jr. for ₤ 30 for 83 acres in Washington
                        Dist., on NW side of Generostee Creek, waters
of the Savannah River, part of 300 acres granted to James Anderson, 3 Oct.
1785, by William Moultrie. Recorded Bk. FFFF, p. 109 and part of 188 ac.
sold from Anderson to John Portman, Sr.
Wit: George Hoge(?), Abraham Howard, Robert (R) Caldwell. "Personally
came **John** Hoge and Robert Caldwell who made oath to Joshua Saxon, J.P."
19 Jan. 1796. Signed: **George** Hoge and Robt. Caldwell.
Rec: 27 Apr. 1796.

Pages 201-202   29 Mar. 1796. John Woodall, Sr., cooper, to
                        John Woodall, Jr., for ₤ 20 stg. for 261 acs.
                        in Washington Dist. on Generostee Creek, the
waters of Savannah River, part of 500 acres granted to John Woodall, Sr.
7 Sep. 1795 by Governor Arnoldus Vanderhorst. Recorded Bk. P., no. 5,
p. 437. Bd. by Drayton.
Wit: George Hoge, Abraham Howard, Robert (R) Caldwell. George Hoge has
made oath to Joshua Saxon, J. P., 2 Apr. 1796.
Rec: 27 Apr. 1796.

Pages 202-203   9 Feb. 1796. Thomas Shockley, Sr., of Pendle-
                        ton Co. to Nathaniel Howard, of Elbert Co.,
                        Ga. for ₤ 20 for 100 acres in Pendleton Co. on
the Savannah River, part of 2 tracts granted to William Love, conveyed
toShockley from Love, on Town House Branch, now called Bond's Branch. Bd.
by Shockley's plantation, "to near the cabbing where James Shockley formerly lived" to the plantation where James Shockley now lives. Signed:
Thomas (T) Shockley.
Wit: Thomas Woodard, Stephen Haynes, Elijah Owens, J. P. Elijah Owens,
Esq., made oath to J. B. Earle, J. P., 3 May 1796.
Rec: 3 May 1796.

Pages 203-204   30 May 1793. 96 Dist., Pendleton Co. John
                        Looney to John Robinson for ₤ 20 stg. for 200
                        acres on E. fork of Baker's Creek, granted to
John Looney.
Wit: Conrad Hukleman, George Hukleman. Conrad Hukleman made oath to E.
Browne, J. P., 30 Nov. 1793.
Rec: 3 May 1796.

Pages 204-205   3 Nov. 1794. Doctor James Martin to John Rob-
                        inson, planter, for ₤ 25 stg. for 320 acres
                        or one half of 640 acres on Barker's Creek,
branch of the NW fork of Long Cane, bd. on the N. by James Miller, and
by vacant lands. Signed: James Martin.
Wit: Sm. Linton, Joseph Calhoun, John Montgomery....Abbeville Co., Sam
Linton (Liuton?), made oath to Fr___es(hand written, difficult to type),
J. P. 25 Mar. 1796.
Rec: 3 May 1796

Page 205   We, Jesse Cooper, Susannah Willis and Margaret
                        Chappell, of Wilks Co., Ga., son and daughters
                        of Enos Cooper, of Pendleton Co., S. C., con-
stitute said Enos Cooper to be our lawful attorney to act in our names to
collect all legacies, debts, etc. due us in Commonwealth of Virginia,Cul-
pepper Co., or any other place. Date: 9 Apr. 1796. Signed: Jesse Cooper, Susannah (X) Willis, Margarett Chappell.
Wit: Peyton Wyatt, Alexander Bohannon....Lincoln Co., Ga., Alexander Bohannon made oath to Gibson Wooldridge, J. P., 29 Apr. 1796.
Rec: May 5, 1796.

Page 206   I, James Martin of York Co., S. C. am firmly
                        bound to James Gordan, of Pendleton Co., for
                        ₤ 300 stg., date 18 Sep. 1786, and will make

112

Page 206 cont'd:
good and sufficient title to 550 acres on the Great Generostee Creek where John Tippen now lives, joining on S. by James Martin, on N. by Luskey, part of a tract granted to John Buck, 16 Jul. 1784, note due on 1 Dec. 1792.
Wit: James Briant, John Tippen; James Briant made oath to John Barton, J. P., 21 Nov. 1795. (James Briant from State of Georgia)...I, James Jordan do assign within contents to John Tippen, in the presence of Chas. Travis, James Long. Date: 1 Jul. 1793. James Long made oath to J. B. Earle, J. P., that he saw James Jordan sign above indorsement to John Tippen, 7 May 1796.
Rec: 7 May 1796.

Pages 206-207
26 Jan. 1796. Samuel Robinson, farmer, to Abiel Cobb, bricklayer, for ₤ 50 stg. for 191 acres being half of tract of 382 acres on the E. side of 23 Mile Creek, waters of the Keowee River, granted to Evan Thomas, then a citizen of South Carolina, 3 Jul. 1786, conveyed to Samuel Robinson, 27 Mar. 1789.
Wit: Lewis Cobb, Topher Tanner. Lewis Cobb made oath to J. B. Earle, J. P., 5 May 1796.
Rec: 7 May 1796.

Page 207
23 Oct. 1795. James Long and Margary, his wife, to Henry Houston for ₤ 80 stg. for 200 acres part of a tract granted Thomas Leonard by Wm. Moultrie, 6 Nov. 1786. Recorded Bk. QQQQ, p. 43. Conveyed to James Long, 10 Oct. 1795, and part granted James Long, 4 Mar. 1793, by Wm. Moultrie. Recorded Bk. E., no. 5, p. 486. On Big Generostee, waters of the Savannah River, bd. by John McCushion(?), Moore, Tilly, Stephen Hinin(?), Ezekiel Boyses(?). Signed: James Long, Margery Long.
Wit: John McCutchen, John Woodall. John McCutcheon (spelled Mc Cushon) made oath to Joshua Saxon, J. P., 31 Oct. 1795.
Rec: 7 May 1795.

Pages 207-208
10 Oct. 1795. Thomas Leonard, planter, to James Long, planter, for ₤ 20 stg. for 160ac. granted to Leonard by Wm. Moultrie, 6 Nov. 1786 on Big Generostee Creek, waters of the Savannah River.
Wit: Samuel Dean, Francis Prine. Francis, Prine, Jr. made oath to Joshua Saxon, J. P., 31 Oct. 1795.
Rec: 7 May 1796.

Page 208
2 Feb. 1792. John McVey to John Sherrard for ₤ 20 for 94 acres, part of 200 acres granted Nathan Young, 22 Oct. 1784, by Wm. Moultrie, on the waters of Little Generostee, conveyed to McVey, 29 Aug. 1789.
Wit: Wm. McVey, Alex. Sherrard. William McVey made oath to E. Browne, J. P., 16 May 1796.
Rec: 7 May 1796.

Page 209
I, Avis Tourtellot, of Pendleton Co., for 195 lbs. stg. paid by William Thayer, of the City of Charleston, merchant, sold him 300 acres on 18 Mile Creek, waters of the Savannah River, granted 15 Oct. 1784, by Benjamin Guerrard to John Hunter, Esq., also a tract of 120 acres bd. on the NE, NW, SE and SW on above tract, granted to John Hunter, Esq., 1787. Date: (blurred) May 1796.
Wit: William Griffen, John Garvin. John Garvin made oath to J. B. Earle J. P., 18 May 1796.
Rec: 12 May 1796.

Page 209
I, Andrew Hamilton, of Abbeville Co., for ₤80 stg. paid by Alexander Sherridan(?), of Pendleton Co., sold him 2 negro wenches, one named Gin about 32 years old, the other name Let(?) about 7 years old. Date: 26 Apr. 1796.
Wit: Wm. Dunlap, W. P. Richard. William Richard made oath to Sm. Linton J. P., 30 Apr. 1796.
Rec: 18 May 1796.

Page 210 1 Jul. 179_. Andrew Hamilton, of Pendleton Co. and Aron Alexander, of Abbeville Co., to William Dickey, of Pendleton Co., for ₺ 70 stg for 250 acres, granted to Aaron Alexander for 100 acres by Benjamin Guerrard, 21 Jan. 1785, on Generostee Creek, and a grant of 150 acres to Andrew Hamilton, 21 Jan. 1785, adj. to above 100 acres. Signed: Andrew Hamilton, Aron Alexander.
Wit: John Willy, John Sherrard (both names dim). John Wyley made oath to Elijah Browne, J. P., 16 Feb. 1792.
Rec: 12 May 1796.

Pages 210-212 10 Oct. 1795. James Abbut and Margaret, his wife, planter, to Anselm Roe, planter, for ₺ 100 for 260 acres in Washington Dist. on Mile Creek, the E. side of Keowee River, part of 806 acres granted to Abbut, bd. on E. by Abner Davis, all other sides vacant. Signed: James (+) Abbutt, Margaret (X) Abbutt.
Wit: Henry Birch, Andrew Roe. Andrew Roe made oath to J. B. Earle, J.P. 23 May 1796.
Rec: 23 May 1796.

Pages 212-213 8 Feb. 1794. Robert Evens to John Gregory for ₺ 15 stg. for 110 acres on Keowee River.
Wit: Robert Beaty, Ezekiel Dunnagan. Robert Beaty made oath to Joseph Reid, J. P., in Washington Dist., 8 Feb. 1794.
Rec: 23 May 1796.

Pages 213-214 12 Oct. 1795. James Abbot, planter, and Margaret, his wife, to Anselm Roe, planter, for ₺ 100 stg. for 249 acres in Washington Dist., on Mile Creek, waters of E. side of Keowee River, part of 673 acres granted to Dunkan Camron, 1 Oct. 1787, by Thomas Pinckney, bd. by land sold to Mr. Collins, conveyed by Wm. Patterson. Signed: James Abbett(+) and Margaret (X) Abbet.
Wit: Henry Burch, Andrew Roe. Andrew Roe made oath to J. B. Earle, J.P.
Rec: 23 May 1796.

Pages 214-215 9 Nov. 1795. Jacob Visage and Elizabeth, his wife, to James Doyal for ₺ 10 stg. for 90 ac. on 23 Mile Creek, part of a tract granted to Visage, 2 Jan. 1793, by Wm. Moultrie. Signed: Jacob Visage, Elizabeth (her mark) Visage.
Wit: James Tuffnell, George Tucker(?). James Tuffnell made oath to Wm. Milwee, J. P., 11 Nov. 1795.
Rec: 1 Jun. 1796.

Pages 215-216 28 Dec. 1790. Samuel Dalrimple to William Harris for ₺ 50 stg. for 320 acres, part of a tract of 640 acres on Generostee Creek, the waters of the Savannah River, granted to Dalrymple.
Wit: Jacob Herring, Isaac Herring, Ephraim (+) Herring. Isaac Herring made oath to Joshua Saxon, 25 Aug. 1795.
Rec: 9 Jun. 1796.

Page 216 23 Jan. 1796. Charles Bowen and Agnes, his wife, of Knox Co., in the Territory of the United States, South of the Ohio to James Duff of Pendleton Co. for ₺ 190 stg. for 640 acres in Washington Dist. on both sides of George's Creek, waters of the Saluda bd. "then by lands now or late" William Reed. Signed: Charles Bowen, Agnes (+) Bowen.
Wit: Saml. Duff, Jas. Cunningham, Thos. Chapman. James Cunningham made oath to R. Bowen, J. P., 29 Mar. 1796.
Rec: 9 Jun. 1796.

Page 217 17 May 1796. John Mauldin, blacksmith, and Sarah, his wife, spinster, to Andrew Middleton Norris for ₺ 60 stg. for 100 acres on Governor's Creek, of the Great Rocky Creek. Signed: John Mauldin, Sarah (+) Mauldin. Wit: Wesley Mauldin, Keziah Mauldin, Thomas Milsap. Plat shows land bd. on N. by Jno. Mauldin, on E. by Harris Mauldin, on S. by

Page 217 cont'd: Surkey(?) Davis, on W. by Nathan Hall. Thomas Milsap made oath to E. Browne, J. P., 13 Jun. 1796. Rec: 20 Jun. 1796.

Pages 217-218   Washington Dist. 14 Mar. 1792. I, William Millwee is justly indebted to James Millwee for Ł 27 1 shilling stg. with interest from 14 Mar. 1792 to 1 Dec. 1794, security for debt, I grant a negro girl, named Mary, 5 years old. Signed: Wm. Millwee.
Wit: John Ridgell, William Cannon...I endorse within mortgage to Jacob Capehart for value received. Date: 27 May 1796. Signed: James Millwee. Wit: Joseph Jolly. Wm. Cannon made oath to Wm. Edmondson, 26 Apr. 1796. Rec: 21 Jun. 1796.

Page 218   I, Elijah Tucker of the State of Virginia have bargained and sold to Harbert Tucker(?) of Pendleton Co., 1 negro man named Jim, a fiddler. Signed: Elijah (X) Tucker. Date: 24 May 1786.
Wit: R. Hall, Richard George, John George. Richard George made oath to E. Browne, J. P., 22 Jun. 1796.
Rec: 24 Jun. 1796. (this deed is very difficult to read).

Pages 218-219   I, Zephaniah Roberts for Ł 7 paid by Eben Light, sold him 250 acres, part of a tract granted to Daniel Bush (or Burk) of 633 acres, 250 acres conveyed to Roberts, 4 Nov. 1794, on fork of Brushy Creek, the waters of Saluda River, dated 23 Jun. 1796. Signed: Zeph. Roberts, W. W. Reid, J. P. I, William Reid, one of the Justices for Pendleton Co., certify that Jane Roberd, wife of Zephaniah Roberds, appeared to relinquish her dower rights. Date: 23 Jun. 1796.
Rec: 24 Jun. 1796.

Page 219   I, John Lewis Davis for Ł 60 stg. sold to Brooks H. Davis, 183 acres on the N. side of Choestoa Creek, waters of the Tugalo River, a part of grant to James Maxwell, 3 Nov. 1788, by Thomas Pinckney. Dated: 2 Feb. 1796.
Wit: James Dernall, Benjamin Perry. James Darnell made oath to Nathn. Perry, J. P., 7 May 1796.
Rec: 24 Jun. 1796.

Pages 219-220   30 Nov. 1793. Joseph Duncan to George Willson for Ł 112 stg. for 242 acres granted Sutton Green, 17 May 1787, by Thomas Pinckney, Green sold to Joseph Dunn. Signed: Joseph Dunn.
Wit: James Gillespie, William (his mark) Cross. James Gillespie made oath to W. W. Reid, J. P., 11 Aug. 1795.
Rec: 24 Jun. 1795.

Pages 220-221   19 Sep. 1795. John Rottin and Mary, his wife, to David Brown for 10 shillings for 340 acres part of 548 acres granted to Thos. Holden on 1 Jan. 1786, by Wm. Moultrie, conveyed to John Rotton, 12 Jun. 1789, on N. side of Tugalo River, on branch called Beaverdam, bd. by William Cox, Joseph Childers, Joseph Reid. Signed: John (R) Rotton, Mary (X) Rotton.
Wit: John Reid, William Brown, James Brown. James Brown made oath to J. B. Earle, J. P., 24 Jun. 1796.
Rec: 24 Jun. 1796.

Page 221   9 Dec. 1794. Duncan Camron, planter, of Green Co., Ga. to William Bowen, of Pendleton Co. for Ł 40 proclamation money for 189 acres on branch of 12 Mile Creek, now in Bowen's possession, granted 17 May 1787, by Thomas Pinckney. Signed: Duncan (his mark) Camron.
Wit: Joseph Logan, Wm. Patterson. William Patterson made oath to W. W. Reid, J. P., 15 Aug. 1795.
Rec: 21 Jun. 1796.

Pages 221-222   1 Feb. 1793. William Benson, of Spartanburgh Co., S. C., to Benjamin Salmon, of Pendleton

Pages 221-222 cont'd:

Co., for Ł 10 for 34 acres, granted to Benson, 3 Dec. 1787 by Thomas Pinckney, in 96 Dist., on the N. fork of Beanay Creek, of 12 Mile River, bd. on the W. by land granted to Baylis Earle, Sr. on other sides by vacant land.
Wit: Joseph Benson, Z. Benson...Greenville Co., S. C., Joseph Benson made oath to Jno. B. Grigsby, J. P., 4 May 1793.
Rec: 24 Jun. 1796.

Pages 222-223

I, John Mauldin, Sr., for 265 dollars paid by Harris Mauldin, sold him 120 acres on Governor's Creek of Rocky River, part of 320 acres granted John Mauldin, bd. on W. by Jacob Gillison, on E. by Robt. Norris where Harris Mauldin now resides. Date: 10 Apr. 1796.
Wit: Nathl. Hall, Patience Crenshaw. Rev. Nathl. Hall made oath to E. Browne, 20 __ 1796.
Rec: 24 Jun. 1796.

Page 223

7 Dec. 1795. Moses Jones and Ann, his wife, to Nevill Mattison for Ł 40 stg. for 100 ac. part of a tract of 300 acres on Broadmouth Creek, waters of Saluda River, bd. by lands sold to William Davis from the same tract, surveyed by William Midlingo(?) for John Smith, 7 Dec. 1784, granted to Thos. Wadsworth and William Turpin, 3 Dec. 1786. Recorded Bk. 0000, p. 560. Signed: Moses Jones, Ann (A) Jones.
Wit: James Moorhead, Thomas Mattison, William Davis. William Davis made oath to Wm. Hall, J. P., 2 Jan. 1796.
Rec: 2 Jun. 1796.

Pages 223-224

Washington Dist. 23 Sep. 1795. James Rose (or Ross), of York Co., S. C. to Sheriff Browster (or Bruster), of Pendleton Co. for Ł 5 for 300 acres in Pendleton Co. on Big Beaverdam Creek of the Savannah River, granted to Rose (or Ross), 5 Jun. 1786, by Wm. Moultrie. Recorded Bk. LLLL, p. 54.
Wit: Jacob Gillispy, Margaret (X) Bru<u>ister</u>. Margaret Bruister made oath to Wm. Mulwee, J. P., 23 Jun. 1796.
Rec: 24 Jun. 1796.

Pages 224-226

15 Aug. 1791. Alexander McDowell, of the Town of Cambridge, merchant, to Sheriff Bruister, of Pendleton Co. for Ł 10 stg. for 59½ acres in 96 Dist., bd. on NE by James Milwee, on NW by Samuel Eakins, on SW by John Gent, on SE by Andrew Ross.
Wit: Julius Nichols, Jr., Eugene Brenan, Nichols Moors. 28 Apr. 1792, Eugene Brenan made oath to Patrick Calhoun, Justice of Abbeville Co., S. C., 28 Apr. 1792.
Rec: 24 Jun. 1796.

Page 226

14 Oct. 1794. William Marchbanks to James Rice, for Ł 15 stg. for 30 acres on the S. side of the Saludy (Saluda) River on Wolf Crk. part of a tract granted to James Henderson, 5 Jun. 1786, granted Marchbanks by Henderson by deed, bd. by James Rice, Marchbanks, on S. side of road.
Wit: Elijah Murphree, Johnston Marchbanks. Elijah Murphree made oath to J. C. Kilpatrick, 12 Apr. 1796.
Rec: 24 Mar. 1796.
(Note: For further information on the Marchbanks Family, contact Mrs. Betty Willie)

Pages 227-228

12 Aug. 1793. James Henderson, of Lawrence Co. S. C., planter, for Ł 100 to George Cimmon(or Cinamore?), planter, of Pendleton Co., for 255 acres part of 800 acres granted Henderson, 5 Jun. 1786, by William Moultrie, bd. on NW by John Boyd Comming, on SW by Solomon Roe and Richard Golden. (also spelled Cinimur, Sinamore).
Wit: Moses Hendricks, Edward Norton, Berryman Roe. Berryman Roe made oath to John Willson, J. P., 10 Mar. 1794.
Rec: 24 Jun. 1794.

Page 228   2 Feb. 1793. Joseph Culton, planter, to Roger Martin for £ 200 stg. for 400 acres on Rockey River of Beaver Creek, adj. to Mary Smith, vacant lands. Recorded Bk. B., no. 5, p. 436. Signed: Joseph Coulton. Wit: John Mauldin, Robert Stevenson, John Lauderdale. John Mauldin made oath to E. Browne, J. P., 3 Jun. 1793.
Rec: 24 Jun. 1796.

Pages 228-229   15 May 1795. William Murphree to James Murphree for £ 90 stg. for 250 acres on N. side of 12 Mile River and Town Creek, part of tract granted to Eliza Ann Purvis, 16 Jul. 1784 and part of a tract granted to William Murphree, 15 Dec. 1791, bd. contracted line by Wm. Murphree and James Murphree marked in presence of Joel Moody and Joseph Duncan.
Wit: Robt. Linn, _____ (blanks)...15 May 1795, I certify I saw following deed signed: W. P. Reed, J. P.
Rec: 24 Jun. 1796.

Pages 229-230   11 Jan. 1794. Alexr. Burns to Moses Murphree for £ 30 stg. for 115 acres in Washington District on branches of N. Fork of 12 Mile River, part of a tract granted to Burns, 1 Apr. 1793 by Wm. Moultrie, bd. William Thompson.
Wit: Benjamin Barton, Moses Hunt. Moses Hunt made oath to Bailey Anderson, J. P., 11 Jan. 1794.
Rec: 24 Jun. 1796.

Pages 230-231   22 Feb. 1794. Samuel Harper, of Washington Dist., to Timothy Stamps, late of County and State aforesaid, for £ 25 for 50 acres in Washington Dist., on S. side of Kiowee River, bd. by river and Henry Burch, Samuel Harper, part of 370 acres granted to James Gillison, 6 Nov. 1786, by Wm. Moultrie, conveyed by Gillison to David Clarke and from Clarke to Harper.
Wit: James Abbet, Craduk(?) (L) Low, Charles Dodson. Charles Dodson made oath to Joseph Reed, J. P., 22 Feb. 1796.
Rec: 24 Jun. 1796.

Pages 231-233   23 Nov. 1790. John Haney and Elizabeth, his wife, to Stephen Willis, for £ 105 stg. for 215 acres granted to Haney by Thomas Pinckney, 3 Nov. 1788. Recorded Bk. XXXX, p. 498; also part of a tract of 200 ac. granted to James Gillison by Benjamin Guerrard, 15 Oct. 1784. Recorded Bk. AAAA, p. 147, on W. side of Hencoop Creek; also 228 acres granted to Joseph Price, 6 Nov. 1786, by Wm. Moultrie. Recorded Bk. QQQQ, p. 4. Signed: John Haynie, Elizabeth (her mark) Hanie.
Wit: James Gillison, George Nash. George Nash made oath to E. Browne, J. P., 20 Sep. 1794.
Rec: 24 Jun. 1796.

Page 234   19 Sep. 1794. Joseph Wornock to Stephen Willis for £ 25 stg. for 102 acres granted Hugh Wornock, 6 Apr. 1786 by Wm. Moultrie. Recorded Bk. HHHH, p. 468, conveyed by Andrew Wornock, heir of Hugh Wornock, deceased, to said Joseph Wornock.
Wit: Patrick Norris, Charles Haynie. Patrick Norris made oath to E. Browne, J. P., 20 Sep. 1794.
Rec: 24 Jun. 1796.

Page 234   I certify I have received from Robert Smith, of York Co., S. C., £ 60 and am endebted to pay Smith £ 30 to be paid in goods in Charleston on order. Date: 21 Jul. 1792. Signed: G. Warley....John Munro of the City of Charleston, watchmaker, made oath he was acquainted with the late cashier George Warley and his handwriting having frequently seen him sign his name and he believes his name was suscribed by his signature. Date: 30 May 1796, before D. Mazyck, J.P.Q.M.
Rec: 24 Jun. 1796.

Pages 234-235   Received from Robert Smith, of York Co., S. C.

Pages 234-235 cont'd:
Ł 180 stg. in part of a bond dated, 9 Jun.1786 given by Smith for a tract on Conoross Creek.
Date: 21 Jul. 1792. Signed: G. Warley....John Munro, of the City of Charleston, watchmaker, made oath to signature, 30 May 1796, before D. Mazyck.

Page 235
I, George Warley, of the City of Charleston, gentleman, am bound to Robert Smith, of York Co., S. C. for Ł 500 stg. in gold or silver at the rate of 4 shillins, 8 pence to the dollar or 1.1.9 to the guinea to be paid to Robert Smith. Date: 9 Jun. 1789....Condition of this obligation...I, George Warley make title to 300 acres on Conoross joining lands formerly belonging to the brother of Wm. (or Mr. Warley), now deceased and upon Robert Smith paying last annual payment of land to said George Warley. Signed: G. Warley.
Wit: Jno. Munro. John Munro made oath to D. Mazyck in Charleston, 30 May 1796.
Rec: 24 Jun. 1796.

Pages 235-236
I, John Booth for 193 dollars paid by Robert McCann sold him one negro girl, named Byna, age 12 years old. Date: 26 May 1796.
Wit: John Boyd, Nicholas Bishop. John Boyd made oath to John Willson, J. P., 24 Jun. 1796.
Rec: 24 Jun. 1796.

Page 236
I, John Booth for 300 dollars sold to Nicholas Bishop, one negro wench, 28 years old, named Cloe and her child, 2 years old, named Cato.
Date: 26 May 1796.
Wit: John Boyd, Robert McCann. John Boyd made oath to John Willson, JP, 24 Jun. 1796.
Rec: 24 Jun. 1796.

Pages 236-237
4 Oct. 1794. Thomas Hood, of Pendleton Co., to Edward Johnston, of Buncum(sic) Co., N. C. for Ł 20 stg. for 100 acres, part of 802 ac. granted to Thomas Hood, 4 Mar. 1793, by Wm. Moultrie, on branch of Dowdy's Creek, of the Saluda River, bd. by Eli Bourland, Thos. Hood, Edward Johnston. Signed: Thomas (H) Hood.
Wit: Henry Jones, John Jones. Henry Jones made oath to Robert Bowen, J. P., 8 Jan. 1796.
Rec: 24 Jun. 1796.

Pages 237-238
6 Aug. 1794. William Ashurst to Edward Johnston, of Bunkum (sic) Co., N. C. for Ł 40 stg. for 100 acres on the SW side of the Saluda River, bd. by Ashurst and Thomas Hood, part of 200 acres granted William Carpenter, 4 Apr. 1785, conveyed to Ashurst.
Wit: William Hunt, George Salmon. William Hunt made oath to Robert Bowen, J. P., 8 Jan. 1796.
Rec: 24 Jun. 1796.

Pages 238-239
I, Peter Roland for Ł 130 sold to Stephen Liddell 100 acres on George's Creek, of the Saluda River, known as Roland's Mill, part of a tract laid out to Patrick Riley, granted 1 Jan. 1787, by Wm. Moultrie, conveyed by Riley to John McElroy, from McElroy to Robert Gilliland and from Gilliland to Peter Roland. Recorded Bk. PPPP, p. 430 for 300 acres bd. by Ambrose Bradley, Roland, Martin Lain, Ebenezer Fain and John Allison. Dated: 25 Feb. 1796. Signed: Peter Rowland.
Wit: Ambrose Bradley, Jesse Liddell. Jesse Liddell made oath to Robert Bowen, J. P., 25 Feb. 1796.
Rec: 24 Jun. 1796.

Pages 239-240
21 Dec. 1795. Henry Clark, of Pendleton Co., to Hannah Shotwell, of Abbeville Co., 96 Dist. for Ł 250 stg. for 270 acres granted to Clark, 3 Oct. 1785, by Wm. Moultrie, in 96 Dist. on S. side of the Saluda River,

Pages 239-240 cont'd:
bd. by that part of tract Henry Clark granted to his son, Isaac Clarke, and now belongs to one Moss and Hannah Shotwell.
Wit: Benj. Clark, Henry Clarke, Jr., Jno. Shotwell. John Shotwell made oath to Robert Bowen, J. P., 28 May 1796.
Rec: 24 Jun. 1796.

Page 240 28 Sep. 1795. John Newman to John Burton for 10 shillings for 25 acres, part of a tract of 324 acres granted to John Dobbs, 15 Apr. 1786, conveyed to Samuel Love, from Love to Newman, for 224 acres, 25 Aug. 1788 on branch of Savannah River, called Sandy Creek, bd. by Vandergriffs, Thos. Gray, Tate.
Wit: James Tate, Jr., James Jones. James Jones made oath to Samuel Porter, J. P., 28 Apr. 1796.
Rec: 24 Jun. 1796.

Pages 241-242 25 Jun. 1792. Charles Rice to Alexander Glenn for £ 65 stg. for 200 acres in 96 Dist., now in possession of Glenn, on both sides of Mile Creek, of 12 Mile River, granted to Rice by patent, 1 Jan. 1789, by Benj. Guerrard.
Wit: James Rice, John Glenn. James Rice made oath to Bayley Anderson, J. P. 15 Jul. 1796.
Rec: 24 Jun. 1796.

Page 242 I, Lewis Edwards deliver to Henry King, by debt of mortgage 75 acres joining William Thopson (sic) and John Moor on a branch of Rocky Creek and 36 acres on another tract joining same tract and Bartholomew White, 2 cows and calves, one set of blacksmith tools, 2 feather beds 2 spinning wheels and household furnishings for £ 10 5 shillings.
Date: 15 Feb. 1796.
Wit: William King, Randsom Thompson. William King made oath to Joshua Saxon, J. P., 11 Jun. 1796.
Rec: 24 Jun. 1796.

Pages 242-243 16 Sep. 1794. Benjamin Aldridge (also spelled Eldridge), of Abbeville Co., S. C. to Hugh Harkins, of Pendleton Co. for £ 70 stg. for 150 acres, a tract...part in Pendleton Co. and part in Abivelle (sic) Co. on Little River, bd. by Barker's Creek, Goudy, Hackleman, Gresham, VanderHorst, Nathaniel Eldridge, part of tract granted to Benjamin Aldridge.
Wit: Wm. Hall, Thomas Crow. Thomas Crow made oath to Wm. Hall, J. P., 19 Mar. 1796.
Rec: 24 Jun. 1796.

Pages 243-244 State of Georgia. 25 Sep. 1795. John Luckie, of Oglethorpe Co., Ga. to Alexander McMillan, of Pendleton Co., S. C., for £ 50 stg. for 259 acres in Pendleton Co., on Big Generostee, branch of Savannah River, part of 585 acres granted John Luckie, 3 Apr. 1786, by Wm. Moultrie. Recorded Bk. KKKK, p. 153.
Wit: Jesse Brown, Amos Ponder, Jesse Willingham...State of South Carolina, Pendleton Co., Jesse Brown made oath to Joshua Saxon, J. P., 21 Feb. 1796.
Rec: 24 Jun. 1796.

Pages 244-245 22 Jun. 1796. Isaiah Vines to John Adam Miller for £ 50 stg. for 148 acres on Mountain Creek, of Big Generostee, granted William Thaker by Thomas Pinckney. Recorded Bk. WWWW, p. 116, conveyed to Joseph Brimer, from Brimer to Vines, except one acres which is (blurred) at an old meeting House for a burying ground.
Wit: Jesse Brown, Benjamin (his mark) Brimer, Robert Miller, Jesse Brown made oath to Joshua Saxon, J. P., (no date).
Rec: 24 Jun. 1796.

Page 245 I, Samuel Gardner, planter, for £ 50 stg. pd.

Page 245 cont'd: by Stephen Roach, sell him 240 acres on West side of 18 Mile Creek, bd. on NW by Bennison, on SW by a Spring Branch, part of 640 acres granted Peter Sinkler, by Benjamin Guerrard. Recorded Bk. CCCC, p. 387. Date: 25 Mar. 1786. Signed: S. M. Gardner.
Wit: William Crosby, Jeremiah (X) Hubbard. Wm. Crosby made oath to J. B. Earle, J. P., 24 Jun. 1796.
Rec: 24 Jun. 1796.

Pages 245-246   23 Apr. 1796. Adam Files to Archabauld Neel for ₤ 80 stg. for 175 acres in Neel's possession, made by indenture, 4 Feb. 1796, one half of tract surveyed 31 May 1784, by Bennet Crafton, D. S., for Adam Files, on W. side of Rocky River.
Wit: Robt. Harkness, John Harkness, John McMahan....Plat shows land bd. on SW by Edward Davis, on N. by Archibald Neel and Alexr. Cavin, on W. by Rocky River. Date: 23 Apr. 1796. Signed: John McMahan, D. S. John McMahan made oath to E. Browne, J. P., 14 May 1796.
Rec: 24 Jun. 1796.

Page 247   I, John Martin, of Laurens Co., S. C., planter for ₤ 15 stg., sold to Wadsworth & Turpin, Merchants, of S. C. 200 acres on both sides of Temossy(?) River, branch of the Keowee River, bd. on NE by William Smith and Richard Pollard and vacant lands. Date: 28 Dec. 1795.
Wit: James Boyce, James Young. James Young made oath to William Hunter, J. P., 16 Feb. 1796.
Rec: 24 Jun. 1796.

Pages 247-248   2 May 1796. Thomas Edmondson to Mary Powel, trustee for Nancy Edmondson, wife of Thomas Edmondson, for love and affection to his wife and to provide for her support, confirm to Mary Powell 200 acres including the plantation where John Powell now lives, part of a tract which Edmondson purchased of Thos. C. Russell, and at the death of Thomas Edmondson to be absolute, estate of Nancy Edmondson to be disposed of as she sees fit. I bind my heirs and executors after my decease to maintain Nancy Edmondson.
Wit: W. Thompson, Wm. Norton. Thomas Edmondson acknowledged above before Wm. Mulwee, J. P., 25 Jun. 1796.
Rec: 25 Jun. 1796.

Page 248   I, Samuel Means for 70 bls. stg. sold to James Edmondson 240 acres part of a survey granted by Charles Pinckney, 4 Jun. 1792, on Middle Fork of Brushy Creek, of Saluda River, bd. by lands laid out for General Pinckney, Russel and Pursley. Date: 25 Mar. 1796.
Wit: Wm. Norton, Robt. Henderson, James Edmondson. William Norton made oath to John Willson, J. P., 1 Jun.1796.
Rec: 24 Jun. 1796.

Pages 248-249   I, Solomon King, planter, for ₤ 80 stg. sold to Thomas Patterson, tract (no acreage) on the E. side of the Seneca River, bd. on N. by John Twitty, on E. by Minor Winn, on W. by river, granted Solomon King (citizen) by Wm. Moultrie. Recorded Bk. LLLL, p. 122. Date: 12 Feb'y 1796. Signed: Solomon (+) King.
Wit: John Ragsdale, James Patterson. James Patterson made oath to S. M. Gardner, J. P., 16 Mar. 1796.
Rec: 25 Jun. 1796.

Pages 249-250   9 Jan. 1796. Alex. Young to George Watts for ₤ 40 stg. for 150 acres granted 5 Sep. 1791, by Chas. Pinckney, on branches of the Savannah River, bd. on NW by James Simpson, and vacant land "(by virtue of the last will and testament of James Tavener, dec'd.)" Signed: Alexr. Young and Agnes (+) Young.
Wit: Wm. Green, Wm. McCurdy. Wm. McCurdy made oath to Saml. Porter, JP, 23 Jun. 1796.
Rec: 25 Jun. 1796.

Page 250   15 Dec. 1793. William and Mary McCune of Ga.,
                                       to Samuel Ross (Rose?), of Pendleton Co., for
                                       Ł 100 for 150 acres on the Savannah River, a
part of 156 acres granted to John McElviny by Wm. Moultrie, bd. by John
Calhoun and Col. John Moffet and river to a small lot of 6 acres divided
by the line of Rose and McCune. Signed: Wm. McCune, Mary McCune.
Wit: Wm. Green, Francis Rose(or Ross). William Green made oath to E.
Browne, J. P., 9 Jan. 1795.
Rec: 25 Jun. 1796.

Pages 250-251   1 Jan. 1795. Richard Oldham to William Lind-
                                       ley for Ł 80 stg. for 92 acres on Rocky Creek,
                                       of the Rocky River, bd. by John Huger, Jas.
Clements, Rubin Clements, part of 640 acres granted Andrew Hamilton, 4
Oct. 1790. Recorded Bk. C, no. 5, p. 62. Conveyed to Oldham.
Wit: Reubin Clements, Benj. Arnald. Reubin Clements made oath to Wm.
Hall, J. P., 7 Nov. 1795.
Rec: 27 Jun. 1796.

Pages 251-252   10 Jun. 1796. James Linn to James Stevenson
                                       for Ł 35 stg. for 76 acres, part of a grant
                                       to John Holcomb, 20 Jan. 1788, by Charles
Pinckney for 211 acres on Mountain Creek, of Generostee, of Savannah Riv-
er, above ancient boundary line, joining Stevenson, plat drawn by Jona-
than Clark.
Wit: Jonathan Gibbs, James Morrow. Jonathan Gibbs made oath to Joshua
Saxon, J. P., 27 Jun. 1796.
Rec: 27 Jun. 1796.

Page 252   I, John King for Ł 80 stg. sold to John Harris
                                       115 acres in Washington Dist., on W. side of
                                       Seneca River, part of 231 acres granted Solo-
mon King, Jr., 5 Jun. 1786, by Wm. Moultrie, on Canoe Branch, bd. by John
Harris. Signed: John (his mark) Harris.
Wit: Thos. Gorman, John Ragsdale. Thos. Gorman made oath to E. Browne,
J. P., 27 Jun. 1796.
Rec: 27 Jun. 1796.

Pages 252-253   I, Thomas Towns, of Greenville Co., S. C. for
                                       Ł 25 stg. sold to Joseph Chapman, of Pendleton
                                       Co., 98 acres on S. fork of the Saluda River,
bd. on SE by Strabler, and vacant lands, granted Towns, 1 Oct. 1792.
Date: 26 Apr. 1796.
Wit: Robert Easley, Jno. Blasingame. John Blasingame made oath to John
Willson, J. P., 13 May 1796.
Rec: 27 Jun. 1796.

Pages 253-254   27 Jan. 1795. Nathaniel Briant to Isum Blan-
                                       kenship for Ł 20 stg. for 80 acres in Washing-
                                       ton Dist. on branch of Big Beaverdam, waters
of Rocky River, bd. by Oliver Charles, Barnabas Farr, Nathan Briant.
Signed: Nathan (B) Briant.
Wit: John Hunter, Absolom Briant. Absolom Briant made oath to John Will-
son, J. P., 15 Jul. 1795.
Rec: 27 Jun. 1796.

Page 254   I, James Gillison for Ł 30 sold to Abraham El-
                                       ledge 90 acres on 26 Mile Creek, part of tract
                                       granted Gillison, 3 Dec. 1788, by Thos. Pinck-
ney, Recorded Bk. VVVV, p. 207, bd. on NW by John E. Calhoun, on NW by
Dickson, on NE by Elledge, on SW vacant, on Cannon's Creek. Signed: James
(his mark) Gillison.
Wit: W. Steele, Joab Mauldin. Joab Mauldin made oath to W. W. Reid, JP,
28 Jun. 1796.
Rec: 28 Jun. 1796.

Pages 254-255   16 Jan. 1796. James Martin of York Co., S.C.
                                       to Harry Terrill of Pendleton Co. for Ł 120
                                       stg. for 320 acres on both sides of Woolenoie
Creek, bd. by Wm. Linch, granted William Powell Lee, 10 Jul. 1784, con-

Pages 254-255 cont'd: veyed by William Hort and John Edwards, Esqs. Treasurers of the State of South Carolina, 17 Apr. 1789 to James Martin.
Wit: William Mitchell, John Martin, William (his mark) Starrett. William Mitchell made oath to W. W. Reid, J. P., 16 Apr. 1796.
Rec: 28 Jun. 1796.

Page 255   15 Jan. 1796. James Martin of York Co. to Harry Terrill for ₤ 300 stg. for 640 acres on both sides of Eastoe Creek, granted Adam Wright, 16 Jul. 1784, conveyed from William Hort and John Edwards, 17 Apr 1789 to Martin.
Wit: William Mitchell, John Martin, William (W) Starrett. William Mitchell made oath to W. W. Reid, J. P., 16 Apr. 1796.
Rec: 28 Jun. 1796.

Pages 255-256   10 Oct. 1793. James Madison of Pendleton Co., to James Yowell of Abeville Co. for ₤ 10 stg. for 167 acres in Washington Dist., granted by Charles Pinckney, adj. 200 acres granted John Smith, on one side, all other sides vacant, on Tugalo River.
Wit: Jas. Davenport, Benja. Cleveland, Samuel Leathers. Benjamin Cleveland made oath to J. B. Earle, J. P., 30 Jun. 1796.
Rec: 30 Jun. 1796.

Pages 256-257   19 Sep. 1795. Jesse Coffee to John Davis for ₤ 30 stg. for 140 acres on Tugalo River, where Thos. Standage now lives. Signed: Jesse (his mark) Coffee. Wit: Benja. Cleveland, Wm. Cleveland. Benjamin Cleveland made oath to J. B. Earle, J. P., 30 Jun. 1796.
Rec: 30 Jun. 1796.

Page 257   27 Oct. 1795. Thomas Crow, of Washington District to John Brown for ₤ 5 stg. for 200 ac's on Brushy Creek of the Saluda River, granted to Crow by States Title Patent, by Wm. Moultrie, 1 Jul. 1793. Signed: Thomas (T) Crow.
Wit: Absolom Brown, Lewis (F)* (his mark*) Green, John Hillen. John Hillen made oath to R. Bowen, J. P., 11 Apr. 1795.
Rec: 2 Jun. 1796.

Pages 257-258   7 Oct. 1795. Samuel Tarbet (also Tarbert) of Washington Dist. to John Brown of same, for ₤ 100 stg. for 200 acres on Brushy Creek, granted Tarbert, 15 Oct. 1785, by Benj. Guerrard, by States Letter Patent, part of 400 acres granted Watson Allison, 20 Aug. 1786, bd. by Samuel Tarbert.
Wit: David Welch, James (his mark) Loggins. James Loggins made oath to W. W. Reid, J. P., 12 Aug. 1796.
Rec: 2 Jul. 1796.

Page 258   I, John Brown for ₤ 200 sold to Robert Sharp Hamilton 200 acres granted Samuel Tarbert by Benj. Guerrard, 15 Oct. 1784 on Brushy Creek of the Saluda River; also 100 acres part of 500 acres surveyed for Watson Allison by James Seaborn, 20 Aug. 1786, bd. on W. by Saml. Tarbert.
Date: 8 Apr. 1796.
Wit: Nathaniel Duncan, James Adams. Jas. Adams made oath to W. W. Reid, 12 Apr. 1796.
Rec: 2 Jul. 1796.

Page 259   I, Charles Hughs, hatter, for ₤ 5 paid by John Willson, planter, for 400 acres, part of 840 acres granted Charles Hughs, on Brushy Creek, waters of the Saluda River, bd. by William McKain, James Willson. Date: 15 Mar. 1796. Signed: Charles Huse.
Wit: William Jewell, Wm. (+) Hunley. Charles Hughs acknowledged in open court, both witnesses signed to Wm. Edmondson, J. P., 15 Mar. 1796.
Rec: 2 Jul. 1796.

Pages 258-260   14 Dec. 1787. Samuel Ridgway, of Greenville
                     Co., S. C., to John Willson, of Abbeville Co.
                     for 20 shillings for 640 acres in Abbeville
Co., on Brushy Creek, branch of S. side of Saluda River, surveyed 20 Apr.
1785 for Ridgway. Signed: Saml. (X) Ridgway.
Wit: Wm. Edmondson, James Cunningham, Alexr. (X) Miller. Wm. Edmondson,
Esq., made oath to John Willson, J. P., 22 Mar. 1796.
Rec: 2 Jul. 1796.

Page 260   10 Jul. 1795. Charity Bristow, of Lawrence
                     Co., S. C. to John Wilson, planter, of Pendle-
                     ton Co. for Ł 100 stg. for 360 acres on Brushy
Creek of Saluda River granted by Letters Patent, 5 Jan. 1786 by William
Moultrie. Recorded Bk. LLLL, p. 36 to Carity Ridgway, bd. by Samuel Ridg-
way. Signed: Charity (her mark) Bristow.
Wit: Hugh Chambless, James Adams. James Adams made oath to W. W. Reid,
J. P., 12 Apr. 1796.
Rec: 2 Jul. 1796.

Pages 260-261   19 Feb. 1793. Morgan Hoord to John McCrosky
                     for Ł 20 stg. for 137 acres granted Morgan
                     Hood, 2 Jan. 1792, by Chas. Pinckney, in Wash-
ington Dist. on George's Creek of the Saluda River, bd. on NE by Leonard
Morgan and John Gowen, vacant land and George Parris Creek. Signed: Morgan Hood.
Wit: William Jamison, George Ross, John (I) Hood. William Jamison made
oath to Robert Bowen, J. P., 23 Sep. 1795.
Rec: 8 Jul. 1796.

Pages 261-262   19 Sep. 1795. James Duff of Washington Dist.
                     to John McCrosky of same, for Ł 12 stg. for
                     200 acres granted 13 Jul. 1792, by Thomas
Pinckney, on N. fork of George's Creek of Saluda River, bd. by Morgan
Hood, Wm. Jamison.
Wit: William Jamison, John McElroy, Thomas Gant. William Jamison made
oath to R. Bowen, J. P., 18 Sept. 1795.
Rec: 8 Jul. 1796.

Page 262   Abbeville Co., S. C. I, John Moore for Ł 20
                     sold to Francis Moore, of same county, 100 ac.
                     in Pendleton Co. on W. fork of Beaver Creek,
branch of Rocky Creek, on both sides of Traiding(?) Path, part of 250 ac.
granted John Moore, 5 Mar. 1787. Date: 18 Jun. 1792.
Wit: Joseph Calhoun, Margaret (her mark) Baly....Abbeville Co., Col.
Joseph Calhoun made oath to F. N. Bates(?), J. P., 18 Jun. 1796.
Rec: 9 Jul. 1796.

Pages 262-263   Abbeville Co. I, John Moore am firmly bound
                     to Francis Moore and John Campbell for Ł 200
                     stg. Date: 18 Jun. 1796....I convey 250 ac.
in Pendleton Co. on Beaver Creek to Moore and Campbell.
Wit: Christopher Conner, Margaret (her mark) Baty(?)....Abbeville Co.,
Christopher Conner made oath to F. N. Bates, J. P., 6 Jun. 1796.
Rec: 9 Jul. 1796.

Page 263   I, William Henderson, yeoman, for divers cause
                     appoint trusty friend, John Martin, my lawful
                     attorney to sell and make titles to a tract of
700 acres being half of a tract of 1400 acres granted Wm. Henderson, the
other half sold to me by Bromfield Nidly and Hally Burton(?), land on Ken-
tukie(?) in Lukia Creek or River. (Note: should this read "in Kentucky
on Lukia Creek?). Date: 10 Dec. 1792.
Wit: William (his mark; looks like "A") Thompson, George Thompson, John
Jones. William Thompson made oath to Bayley Anderson, J. P., 10 Dec.1792.
Rec: 18 Jul. 1796.

Pages 263-264   I, William Henderson am bound to John Martin,
                     "his certain attorney", for Ł 300 stg. Date:
                     10 Dec. 1792....condition, above William Hen-
derson make sufficient title for one half moiety to 700 acres in Kentuc-

Pages 263-264 cont'd: kie. Wit: Peter Thompson, George Thompson.
                                     George Thompson made oath to Geo. W. Earle,
                                     Dpty. C. C., 12 Jul. 1796.
Rec: 12 Jul. 1796.

Page 264   I, James Norton, planter, for love and good
                                     will to my loving son, William Norton, all
                                     goods and chattels now in my possession at my
present dwelling house, 1 mare, 1 featherbed and furniture. Date: 2 Jul.
1796. Wit: James Morris, Henry Foster. Henry Foster made oath to Geo.
W. Earle, Dpty. C. C., 18 Jul. 1796.
Rec.: 18 Jul. 1796.

Pages 264-265   7 Sep. 1794. Stephen Fuller to Peter Reece
                                     for Ł 22 stg. for 87 acres on S. side of the
                                     Saluda, bd. by Charles Gates, John Butt and
river, granted by Wm. Moultrie, 1786.
Wit: Charles Gates, W. M. Shackleford. Charles Gates made oath to J.B.
Earle, J. P., 19 Jul. 1796.
Rec: 19 Jul. 1796.

Page 265   I, Samuel Barkely for love and good will I
                                     bear to my loving son, Andrew Barkley, one
                                     bond on John Arnold for Ł 60 for titles to a
piece of land, dated 26 Nov. 1795; one note on Abraham Barron for Ł 15
dated 18 May 1796, payable 25 Dec. 1798; one note on Abraham Barron for
Ł 15 dated 18 May, payable 25 Dec. 1799; all horses, cows, etc. owned by
Abraham Barron and cattle owned by Hugh Wilson, all household furniture.
Date: 22 Jul. 1796. Wit: J. B. Earle, Geo. W. Earle. Acknowledged 22
Jul. 1796, by J. B. Earle, Clerk of Court.
Rec: 22 Jul. 1796.

Pages 265-266   I, William Hone for divers causes and consid-
                                     erations give to Thomas Hone and Sarah Hone,
                                     of Pendleton Co. all my lands, cattle, house-
hold stuff. Date: 3 Aug. 1796. Signed: William (H) Hone.
Wit: Aaron Wilborn, James Wilborn. Aaron Wilborn made oath to Wm. Hall,
J. P., 3 Aug. 1796.
Rec: 3 Aug. 1796.

Pages 266-267   1 Nov. 1793. Willian Honey, of Greenville Co.
                                     S. C. to Abner Honey, of same, for Ł 20 stg.
                                     400 acres in Pendleton Co. on Big Creek, of
the Saluda River, part of 554 acres granted William Honey by Chas. Pinck-
ney, 1 Oct. 1792. Signed: William (H) Hone.
Wit: Aaron Wilborn, Sturdy Gardner. Sturdy Garnder made oath to Wm.
Hall, 3 Aug. 1796.
Rec: 3 Aug. 1796.

Page 267   15 Sep. 1790. Benj. Harris, of 96 Dist., plan-
                                     ter, to James Cunningham, hatter, of same dis-
                                     trict, for 10 shillings for 400 acres on fork
of Brushy Creek, part of 640 acres surveyed for Robert Anderson's Office
by Benjamin Harris, 200 acres made over by Benjamin Harris to Abraham
Nally and 40 acres to Jacob Earnest, Sr.
Wit: Francis Cunningham, James Linn. Francis Cunningham made oath to William Edmond son, Clerk of Washington Dist., 12 Jul. 1796.
Rec: 4 Aug. 1796.

Pages 267-268   27 Aug. 1793. George Humphries to Jacob Ear-
                                     nest for Ł 10 stg. for 20 acres in Washington
                                     Dist., on S. fork of Brushy Creek, of Saluda
River, part of 1300 acres granted Thomas Lewis by Wm. Moultrie, 6 Dec.
1780, bd. Neil Green.
Wit: John Hillen, Jesse Kirby, Jonathan (a) Moore. Jonathan Moore made
oath to Wm. Edmondson, J. P., 22 Aug. 1793.
Rec: 5 Aug. 1796.

Pages 268-270   5 Aug. 1791. James Cunningham to Jacob Earn-
                                     est, Jr. for Ł 50 stg. for 640 acres on both

Pages 268-270 cont'd: sides of Brushy Creek, of Saluda River, 96
                         Dist., bd. on N. by John Hallum and vacant
land, Abraham Nally, surveyed for Benjamin Harris by Wm. Moultrie, 6 Nov.
1786. Wit: Wm. Farris, Wm. (X) Hodge, Norman Earnest. William Hodge
made oath to John Wilson, J. P., 8 Sep. 1791.
Rec: 5 Aug. 1796.

Pages 270-271   4 Aug. 1794. John Norwood, of 96 Dist., Abbe-
                         ville Co. to Jacob Earnest, Sr., of Washing-
                         ton Dist., Pendleton Co. for ₤ 75 stg. for 275
acres on 23 Mile Creek of Savannah River, in Washington Dist., granted
Norwood by Wm. Moultrie, 5 Dec. 1785.
Wit: Bazzel Hallum, John Pickens. John Pickens made oath to John Will-
son, 23 Apr. 1795.
Rec: 5 Aug. 1796.

Page 272   I, Thomas Farrar, planter, for ₤ 100 stg. sold
                         to Jeremiah Hubbard 400 acres part of 640 ac.
                         on 18 Mile Creek, bd. on NW by George Kilson,
on NE by vacant land, granted Peter Sinkler by Benj. Guerrard. Recorded
Bk. CCCC, p. 387. Date: 23 Mar. 1796....Signed and acknowledged before
B. B. Earle, J. P. and recorded 9 Aug. 1796.

Page 272   I, Peter Burns sold to Lewis D. Martin a still
                         holding 37 gallons for 50 and a half dollars.
                         Date: 25 Jul. 1796.
Wit: D. McCaleb, Leonard D. Shaw. David McCaleb made oath to Geo. W.
Earle, D. C. C., 10 Aug. 1796.
Rec: 10 Aug. 1796.

Pages 272-273   John Pickens and Sarah, his wife, for ₤ 200
                         stg. sold William Richards 300 acres in Wash-
                         ington Dist. on Oconey Creek of Keowee River,
granted 17 Jul. 1784, to Dr. James Martin. Recorded Bk. BBBB, p. 21, bd.
on NW by John Suords(?), conveyed to John Pickens by Dr. James Martin &
Sarah, his wife, 15 Dec. 1790. Signed: John Pickens, Sarah Pickens.
Date: 22 Jan. 1796.
Wit: J. W. Thompson, Saml. McCune. James Thompson made oath to J. C.
Kilpatrick, J. P., 26 Jan. 1796.
Rec: 13 Aug. 1796.

Page 273   24 Mar. 1792. Wm. Young to Nathaniel Newman
                         for ₤ 40 for 200 acres on both sides of Earles
                         Creek, fork of 12 Mile River, bd. on NW by
Samuel Earle, granted John McElvaney by William Moultrie, 4 Nov. 1785.
Wit: Stephen Cantwell, Jno. A. Dunseeth. Stephen Cantwell made oath to
Bayley Anderson, J. P., 23 Jan. 1793.
Rec: 16 Aug. 1796.

Pages 273-274   18 Feb. 1792. Moses Anderson and Mary, his
                         wife, to Johnston Murray for ₤ 40 stg. for 265
                         acres, now in Murray's possession, part of a
tract laid out to Thomas Burfort of 600 acres on branches of Broadaway,
adj. E. land laid out to William Buchanan, W. by Thomas Burfort, granted
Murray by deed from Moses Anderson and Mary, 4 Dec. 1786. Signed: Moses
Anderson, Mary Anderson.
Wit: John Anderson, W. Murry, Jr., William Murry made oath to John Will-
son, J. P., 10 Aug. 1796.
Rec: 17 Aug. 1796.

Pages 274-275   I, Nicholas Darnal for ₤ 150 sold to Martin
                         Hewlet 160 acres on Main fork of Choestoe Crk
                         of the Tugaloo River, part of a tract granted
Robert Miscampbell by Benj. Guerrard, 21 Jan. 1785, bd. by Darnal, Hewlet
and Benj. Perry. Date: 2 Apr. 1796. Signed: Nich. Darnall.
Wit: W. H. Lacy, Wm. McMurtrey, William Darnall. William Hughs Lacy
made oath to Nathl. Perry, J. P., 2 Apr. 1796.
Rec: 17 Aug. 1796.

Page 275: I, John McMahan, planter, for ₺ 30 stg. sold to John Scott, planter, 200 acres in Washington Dist. on NE branches of 23 Mile Creek of the Savannah River, bd. on NE by George Liddel and vacant land, granted to John McMahan, 2 July 1787, by Thomas Pinckney. Recorded Bk. BBBB, p. 458. Wit: Geo. Forbis, William Hamilton, Ann Willson. George Forbis made oath to John Willson, J. P., 22 Feb. 1796.
Rec: 19 Aug. 1796.

Pages 275-276: 9 Mar. 1795, James Jordan to John Portman, Sr. for ₺ 3 stg. for 300 acres, now in his possession, part of 652 acres on Seneca River, bd. by Elisha Maxwell, vacant land, granted to James Jordan, citizen, by Wm. Moultrie. Recorded Bk. G, no. 5, p. 247. Wit: John Portman, Jr., J. Ditto. James Ditto made oath to E. Browne, J. P., 27 Jun. 1796.
Rec: 20 Aug. 1796.

Page 276: 15 Feb. 1796. Jean Miller, of York Co., S.C. to Joseph Kennedy of Pendleton Co., for ₺80 for 289 acres on Big Beaverdam Creek where Kennedy now lives, granted to Jean Miller by patent, 5 Dec. 1785 by Wm. Moultrie. Signed: Jean (her mark) Miller. Wit: James Martin, Francis Miller, Mary Miller. James Martin made oath to Thos. Gillham, J. P. on 15 Feb. 1796.
Rec: 24 Aug. 1796.

Pages 276-277: 12 Feb. 1796. James Martin of York County, S. C. to John Gibson, of Pendleton County for ₺ 70 stg...James Martin by Power of Attorney, vested 19 Oct. 1792, by Charles Miles of Union Co., S. C. to John Gibson, 300 acres in Pendleton Co., on Big Beaverdam Creek, where John Gibson now lives. Signed: James Martin. Wit: Wm. Hanna, Wm. Love, Joseph Kennedy. Joseph Kennedy made oath to Geo. W. Earle, Dept. C.C., 24 Aug. 1796.
Rec: 24 Aug. 1796.

Page 277: 24 Sept. 1790. John Jackson to Edley Linn & William Linn for ₺ 50 for 200 acres on Beaver Creek, bd. by Joseph Culton, James Dobins, John Dowdle. Wit: Wm. Forbes, John Linn. John Linn made oath to E. Browne, J. P., 22 Jun. 1796.
Rec: 26 Aug. 1796.

Page 278: I, Robert Anderson, Esq., for ₺ 75 stg. sold to John Nicholson, planter, for 291 acres on both sides of Weaver's(?) Creek, branch of the Olanoy of the Saluda River, granted Anderson, 8 Oct. 1785, by Wm. Moultrie. Recorded Bk. EEEE, p. 502. Wit: James Blair, Major Lewis. Major Lewis made oath to Geo. W. Earle, Dept. C. C., 2 Sep. 1796.
Rec: 2 Sep. 1796.

Pages 278-279: Washington Dist. 25 Jan. 1796. Jacob Reed & Sarah, his wife, to Wm. Hudgins for ₺ 1 for 359 acres on Mountain Creek, of Generostee, of the Savannah River, granted to Reed, 3 Oct. 1791 by Charles Pinckney, recorded Bk. D, no. 5, p. 134. Signed: Jacob (+) Reed, Sarah (+) Reed. Wit: Jacob Reed, Archebald Reed, Jas. Millwee. James Millwee made oath to Wm. Millwee, J. P., 18 Feb. 1796.
Rec: 6 Sep. 1796.

(Note: page 279 torn off)

Pages 279-280: I, Ephraim Lindsay, of Abbeville Co. for ₺ 80 stg. sold to Benjamin Ragsdale, of Pendleton Co., 200 acres granted Lindsay by Benjamin Guerard, 9 Jan. 1785, on 23 Mile Creek of Savannah River, bd. by John Norwood and vacant land. Date: 31 Mar. 1796. Signed: Ephraim Lindsay, Esther Lindsay. Wit: Thomas Earnest, Wm. McCracken. Thos. Earnest made oath to John Willson, J. P., 21 Jun. 1796.
Rec: 6 Sep. 1796.

Page 280: I, John Moore, of Abbeville County for $40 sold to Jno. Campbell (also spelled Camble), 150 acres on W. fork of Beaver Creek of Rocky River. Date: 29 Mar. 1796. Signed: John Moore, Jean (her mark) Moore. Wit: Joseph Trimble, Wm. Kinley. Andrew Hamilton, Jno. dela Howell witness to receipt....Abbeville Co., Jas. Trimble made oath to Wm. Kinley, J. P., 29 Mar. 1796. Jean Moore relinquished dower. Recorded Bk. no. 3, p. 272, 29 Mar. 1796, examined by John Bowie, C. C.
Rec: 15 Sep. 1796.

Page 281: 15 Jan. 1796. James Martin of York County, S. C. to Nicholas Perkins of Pittsylvania Co., Va., for ₤ 200 stg. for 640 acres in Pendleton Co.; also 640 acres joining the other tract, one granted to Samuel Jones, the other to Patrick Reardon, on small Creek of 12 Mile River, granted 16 Jul. 1784, conveyed from John Edwards and William Hort, Esq., Treasurers of the State of South Carolina, 16 Apr. 1789 to James Martin. Wit: William Mitchell, John Martin, William (his mark) Starritt. William Mitchell made oath to W. W. Reid, J. P., 15 Jan. 1796.
Rec: 15 Sep. 1796.

Pages 281-282: 8 Sep. 1795. Thomas Osbern, Sr. to Daniel Putman for 10 shillings stg. for 505 acres on Big Generostee, granted to Osbern by Thomas Pinckney, 1788, except 150 acres now laid out for Robert Skelton, on fork of Big Branch, bd. on E. by William Lesley, on W. by John Green, on S. by Skelton. Signed: Thos. (T) Orsbern, Sr. Wit: Jacob Skelton, John Rusel. Jacob Skelton made oath to E. Browne, J. P., 13 Aug. 1796.
Rec: 22 Sep. 1796.

Page 282: 20 Oct. 1792. Charles Bond of Elbert Co., Ga. to Daniel Putman of Pendleton Co., for 10 shillings for 75 acres on NE side of Savannah River, part of 300 acres granted to William Love by Benjamin Guerard, 21 Jan. 1785, 150 acres granted by Love to Thos. Shockley, Sr., 16 Mar. 1789, the other 150 acres granted by Love to Charles Bond, 24 Oct. 1791, bd. on SE by Savannah River to a branch called Town House. Wit: Christopher Casey, Isaac Evans. Christopher Casey made oath to E. Browne, J. P., 8 March 1796.
Rec: 22 Sep. 1796.

Pages 282-283: 5 Aug. 1794. Mathew Alexander to James Scott for ₤ 100 stg. for 234 acres in Pickensville Dist. on Big Beaverdam Creek of Rocky River, of Savannah River, bd. by Dr. Olivant, Wm. Moore, Joseph Smith, part of a tract granted to Alexander by Thos. Pinckney, 4 Feb. 1788. Wit: William Smith, Barnabas (+) Fair. Wm. Smith made oath to Wm. Hall, J. P., 8 Jul. 1796.
Rec: 22 Sep. 1796.

(Note: Page number torn off 283 and 284)

Pages 283-284: Washington Dist. 3 Oct. 1795. James Millwee to Robert Moore for ₤ 5, for 93 acres on SW side of the Saluda River, bd. on NW by Peter Accor(?), on SE by Jesse Gray, granted to Millwee by Thos. Pinckney, 7 May 1787. Recorded Bk. RRRR, p. 348. Wit: Peter Acker (see Accor also) John Moore, James Moore. Edwin Smith witness to receipt. Peter Acker & Edwin Smith made oath to Wm. Hall, 15 Sep. 1796.
Rec: 22 Sep. 1796.

Pages 284-285: I, James Hamilton, planter, for ₤ 60 stg. to Alexander Hamilton, planter, for 386 acres, (James Hamilton reserves 40 acres of tract), in Washington Dist. on 18 Mile Creek of the Seneca River, bd. on SE by Jno. Martin, SE & NE vacant land, SE & SW by Mary Leonard, granted Samuel Henry Dickson, 1 Dec. 1788 by Thos. Pinckney. Recorded Bk. ZZZZ, p. 67. Date: 4 Apr. 1796. Wit: John Scott, John Hamilton, Rowley McMahon. John Scott made oath to John Willson, J. P., 12 Apr. 1796.
Rec: 10 Oct. 1796.

Pages 285-286: 31 Mar. 1795. James Millwee, to John Brouster, Jr. for ₺ 40 for 200 acres on 26 Mile Creek, granted to Millwee, 15 Oct. by Benj. Guerrard. Wit: James Linn, Jas. Brouster, James Payne. Jas. Linn made oath to Wm. Millwee, J. P., 21 Mar. 1795.
Rec: 10 Oct. 1795.

Pages 286-287: 8 Sep. 1792. Joseph Dunn to Samuel Clark for ₺ 40 stg. for 200 acres on both sides of Camp Creek of the Saluda River, 2 miles above Old Indian Path, 96 Dist., bd. on NW by Jacob Vanue, vacant land. Wit: Isaac Clark, James Gillispie, Nathl. Clark. Nathaniel Clark made oath to W. W. Reed, J. P., 8 Sep. 1796.
Rec: 21 Oct. 1796.

Pages 287-289: 11 Feb. 1788. Samuel Love, of Abbeville Co., S. C., hatter, to Jacob and Lewis Jones, of same, for ₺ 25 for 100 acres in county and state aforesaid, on the Savannah River at the mouth of Sandy Creek, above old boundary line, bd. by William Tate, William Love, Andrew Sullivan, part of 374 acres granted John Dobbs, 4 Sep. 1786, by Wm. Moultrie. Recorded Bk. MMMM, p. 539, sold to Samuel Love, 11 Jan. 1787. Wit: Jesse Casey, James Jones.....Abbeville Co., - James Jones made oath to Jno. Moffett, J. P., 7 Aug. 1789.
Rec: 21 Oct. 1796.

Pages 289-290: 3 Oct. 1794. Jacob Jones and Lewis Jones, of Pendleton Co., to Thomas Gray, of same, for ₺ 60 for 100 acres, part of a tract granted to John Dobbs, 4 Sep. 1786 by Wm. Moultrie for 324 acres on N. side of the Savannah River, on Sandy Creek, bd. by William Tate, Andrew Sullivan, William Love and river. Wit: John Burton, Chrt. (X) Vandergrift. Chrt. Vandergrift made oath to Saml. Porter, J. P., 9 Jul. 1795.
Rec: 22 Oct. 1796.

Pages 290-291: 10 Sep. 1796. Reuben Reid to Levi Murphree for ₺ 100 stg., for 700 acres on Wolf Creek of 12 Mile River, part of 1,000 acres granted Reed, 2 Jul. 1792 by Charles Pinckney. Wit: Benj. Barton, Moses Murphree. Benjamin Barton made oath to W. W. Reid, J. P., 12 Oct. 1796.
Rec: 22 Oct. 1796.

Page 291: 5 Dec. 1795. Edward T. McClure to David Anderson for ₺ 70 stg. for 500 acres on Main Branch of Middle fork of French Broad River, in Pendleton Co. Wit: James Tate, Saml. Tate, Hezekiah Speak. (Plat). Capt. Samuel Tate made oath to John Baylis Earle, J. P., 10 Oct. 1796.
Rec: 22 Oct. 1796.

Page 292: I, Fredrick Ward, of Abbeville Co., planter, for ₺ 12-10 shillings, sold to Henry Houston, of Abbeville Co., planter, 200 acres in 96 Dist., Pendleton Co., on Rocky River, of the Savannah River, surveyed by J. Martin, D. S., 10 Jan. 1785. Wit: Josiah Chambers, John Sanders. Date: 20 Apr. 1796....Abbeville Co.-Josiah Chambers made oath to Samuel Foster, J. P., 21 Apr. 1796.
Rec: 3 Nov. 1796.

Page 292: I, Samuel Means for $30 paid by Michael Smith sold him 129 acres on Brushy Creek, bd. John Boyd, part of tract granted Means, 9 May 1792. Dated: 12 Feb. 1796. Wit: J. McGehee, Wm. Gunn. John McGehee made oath to Geo. W. Earle, Dept. C. C., 10 Nov. 1796.
Rec: 10 Nov. 1796.

Pages 292-293: I, John Norwood, of Abbeville Co., S. C., planter, for ₺ 130 stg. sold to John Smith of Pendleton Co., 200 acres on Barton's Creek of the Tugalo River, granted Fredrick Ward, 7 Nov. 1785. Date: 11 Nov. 1796. Wit: W. H. Lacy, Blake Mauldin, Nicholas Darnall. Nicholas Darnall made

(Pages 292-293 - Norwood, cont'd): to J. C. Kilpatrick, J. P., 11 Nov. 1796.
Rec: 10 Nov. 1796.

Page 293: 19 May 1796. John Parker to Thos. Chadwick for ₤ 9 stg. for 40 acres and a quarter on Beaverdam, of Rocky River, bd. SW by Widow Dalrymple, S. by Wadsworth, part of tract granted Richard Morrow by Thos. Pinckney. Wit: John Henry, John (X) Horton. John Henry made oath to John Willson, J. P., 10 Nov. 1796.
Rec: 10 Nov. 1796.

Pages 293-294: 23 Apr. 1794. Nicholas Pyle to James Eason for ₤ 100 stg. for 98 acres in Washington District on W. side of Big Creek, of Saluda River, granted Matthew Alexander by Benjamin Guerard, 21 Jan. 1785, conveyed to Pyle, 27 Oct. 1786. Wit: William Bennett, Samuel (+) Pyle. Samuel Pyle made oath to William Hall, 17 Feb. 1795.
Rec: 10 Nov. 1796.

Page 294: Newberry Co., S. C. 24 Jul. 1795. John Cannon of said county, 96 Dist. to William Cannon, of Pendleton Co., Washington Dist., for ₤ 60 stg. for 127 acres, part of tract granted James Daughtry, by Wm. Moultrie, 19 Jan. 1785. Recorded Bk. JJJJ, p. 200, for 270 acres, conveyed to John Cannon, recorded Newberry Co., 28 Nov. 1789, surveyed by James Millwee, D. S. Signed: John Cannon, Elinor (her mark) Cannon. Wit: Jas. Lindsey, Daniel Williams, Cassander Williams. James Lindsey made oath to B. Williams, J. P., 4 Jul. 1795 (in Newberry Co.?).
Rec: 16 Nov. 1796.

Pages 294-295: 27 Apr. 1796. William Cannon, of Pendleton Co., Washington Dist., to Thomas Watson, of same, for ₤ 50 stg. for 127 acres, part of 640 acres granted James Daugherty. Signed: William Cannon, Abigale (+) Cannon. Wit: Lewis Sherrill, Joseph Kennedy, Wm. Millwee. Lewis Sherrill made oath to Wm. Millwee, J. P., 24 Apr. 1796.
Rec: 16 Nov. 1796.

Page 295: Washington Dist. I, Blake Mauldin for ₤ 70 stg. sold to Joab Mauldin 340 acres in fork of the Tugalo and Keowee River, part of 2 tracts, one granted Major Parson, of 64 acres, 5 Jun. 1786, by Wm. Moultrie, the other of 820 acres granted Parsons, 4 Jun. 1787, by Thos. Pinckney, bd. by land deeded by Parsons to Amos Killborn, which crosses little Beaverdam Creek and Abram Casey's land sold to Jacob Holland, Wm. Cox, and John Rotton, also 2 islands in Keowee River. Date: 14 Oct. 1796. Wit: James Jolley, Major Lewis. Major Lewis made oath to Geo. B. Earle, D.C.C., 17 Nov. 1796.
Rec: 17 Jun. 1796.

Pages 295-296: 29 Nov. 1796. John Harris, late Sheriff of Pendleton Co. to Ezekiel Pickens, Attorney at Law, ...Wheras, Thomas Lesley was seized of 300 acres on both sides of a small creek of Great Generostee Creek. Baylis Earle obtained judgement against Lesley and Robert Selfrige for ₤ 68 stg. .....John B. Earle, Clerk of Court at Pendleton Co. directed Sheriff to sell at auction all goods, chattels, lands of Robt. Selfridge and Thomas Lesley, sale held 2 Jan. 1796, for ₤ 15 to Ezekiel Pickens. Signed: John Harris, late Sheriff of Pendleton Co. Wit: James Wood, James Dickson, J. Mauldin. James Wood made oath to Geo. B. Earle, D.C.C., 17 Nov. 1796.
Rec: 17 Nov. 1796.

Pages 296-297: 3 Feb. 1796. John Lewis Davis, planter, to Brooks H. Davis, planter...John Davis is endebted to Brooks H. Davis for ₤ 50, bond to be paid 1 Oct. next...security, one negro man named Jack, all carpenter tools and joiner tools, cattle, sheep, hogs, horses. Wit: Tho. Harrison, Joseph Martin. Thomas Harrison made oath to Nathl. Perry, J. P., 2 Apr. 1796.
Rec: 18 Nov. 1796.

Page 297:   28 Mar. 1795. William Kirby of Washington District to Nathaniel Davis, of same, for ₤ 95 stg. for 190 acres, upper part of 382 acres on 23 Mile Creek of Saluda River, granted Evan Thomas by Wm. Moultrie, 3 Jul. 1786, bd. by Kirby, Abiel Cobb. Wit: Wm. Fariss, John Aden, James Kirby. William Fariss made oath to John Willson, J. P., 15 May 1795.
Rec: 27 Nov. 1796.

Pages 297-298:   29 Mar. 1792. George Nelson to Isaac Horton for ₤ 25 stg. for 100 acres in 96 Dist., S.of Saluda River on Little Beaverdam Creek of Rocky River, part of tract granted Nelson by Charles Pinckney, 17 Jun. 1790. Signed: George (his mark) Nelson. Wit: Jno. Carrell, Wm. Vann. William Vann made oath to John Willson, J. P., 9 Sep. 1795.
Rec: 5 Dec. 1796.

Page 298:   (blank) July 1793. Jacob Saxon to Joseph Land for ₤ 25. Plat shows 100 acres on Generostee Creek, bd. N. unknown, E. unknown, S. by Joseph Saxon, W. by David Anderson. Wit: Wm. Drennan, John Drennan. Joshua Saxon, D.S. William Drennan made oath to E. Browne, J. P., 31 Dec. 1795.
Rec: 13 Dec. 1796.

Page 299:   I, George Nelson sold for ₤ 40 stg. to John Green, 100 acres on Little Beaverdam, bd. by George Anderson, John Green, part of tract granted to Nelson by Charles Pinckney, 7 Jun. 1790. Date: 22 Nov. 1796. Signed: George (his mark) Nelson. Wit: William Nelson, Thomas (T) Green, Nathaniel Eastest. Sworn to Wm. Milwee.
Rec: 13 Dec. 1796.

Page 299:   22 Dec. 1794. James Jett to Joseph Woodall for ₤ 20 stg. for 182 acres on Crow Creek. Wit: William Boren, Nathaniel Bullard. William Boren made oath to Robert Bowen, J. P., 7 Nov. 1796.
Rec: 14 Dec. 1796.

Pages 299-300:   8 Nov. 1796. James Eason, of Pendleton Co., to Josiah N. Kennedy of Greenville Co., S. C. for ₤ 40 stg. for 120 acres in Pendleton Co., formerly 96 Dist., on Little Beaverdam Creek, part of a tract granted to John Hunnicutt, 6 Nov. 1786, by Wm. Moultrie, including Eason Spring Branch. Signed: James (his mark) Eason. Wit: J. McGehee, Ambrose Blackburn. John McGehee made oath to J. B. Earle, J. P., 14 Dec. 1796.
Rec: 14 Dec. 1796.

Pages 300-301:   28 Nov. 1796. James Eason, of Pendleton Co. to Josiah N. Kennedy for ₤ 100 stg. for 50 acres part of tract granted George Staton, 6 June 1794, by Charles Pinckney, on both sides of Little Beaverdam Creek, bd. by Eason and land where Thomas Adams formerly lived. Signed: James (his mark) Eason. Wit: J. McGehee, Amb. Blackburn, John McGehee made oath to J. B. Earle, J. P., 14 Dec. 1796.
Rec: 14 Dec. 1796.

Page 301:   2 Jan. 1797. Henry Capehart, of S. C. to George Capehart, of N. C. for ₤ 20 and interest to be paid 2 Jan. 1799, sold him goods, household furniture (list). Wit: Aaron Hardin, James (his mark) Doil. James Doyle made oath to John Willson, J. P., 16 Jan. 1797.
Rec: 16 Jan. 1797.

Page 302:   On 10 and 11 of Oct. 1796, an election was held for five commissioners to oversee the poor of Pendleton Co., and on the 12th, we the Managers for sd. election met according to law and counted over the votes and found William Steele, William Guest, William Reid, Joseph Brown and John Bryson were legally elected to fill the trust aforesaid.....we recommend that the Clerk of our County Court will put this on record and file it among the papers of the County. Signed: E. Browne, J. Miller,

(P. 302-cont'd) Michael Dickson, Managers(?). Rec: 16 Jan. 1797.

Page 302: I, William Burney for ₤ 22-17-6 paid by William Wallace sold him 700 acres, part of 1000 acres granted Burney by Charles Pinckney, in Washington Dist. on 18 Mile Creek and 23 Mile Creek, of Keowee River, bd. SW and SE by Ephraim Lindsey, NW by Thomas Gadson, SW by Charles Hughes, granted 4 Jun. 1792. Recorded Bk. F, no. 5, p. 39. Wit: Mich. Smith, Wm. Gunn, M. Hamilton.....Elizabeth (her mark) Burney, wife of William Burney released her dower to Andw. Pickens, Judge of Pendleton Co., 16 Nov. 1796. William Hamilton made oath to John Willson, J. P., 15 Nov. 1796. Rec: 16 Jan. 1797.

Pages 302-303: (blank) 1794. Capt. William McCaleb of Abbeville Co., S. C. to William Lindsey of Pendleton Co., for 20 shillings for 175 acres..... granted McCaleb, 5 Sep. 1785 by Wm. Moultrie, on S. side of Saluda River, Washington Dist. Wit: Geo. Tucker, James McCaleb. James McCaleb made oath to William Edmondson, J. P., 27 Jan. 1794. Rec: 16 Jan. 1797.

Page 303: I, Saml. Bryson for ₤ 45 stg. paid by Saml. Barr, sold him one negro fellow named Jack, about 30 years old. Date: 9 Jun. 1796. Wit: Danl. Bryson. Danl. Bryson made oath to E. Browne, J. P., 3 Nov. 1796. Rec: 16 Jan. 1797.

Page 303-304: I, William McKey, of State of Kentucky, planter, for ₤ 60 sold to Isaac Williams of Pendleton Co. all that tract on the branches of the Keowee River, bd. on NW by William McKey, on E. by Peter Sincler, on S. by John Twitty, granted William Mackey by Charles Pinckney, Recorded Bk. C, no. 5, p. 67. Date: 1 Sep. 1796. Signed: William (W) Mackey. Wit: James Patterson, Alexr. Kilpatrick. James Patterson made oath to J. C. Kilpatrick, J. P., 1 Sep. 1796. Rec: 16 Jan. 1797.

Page 304: I, William Mackey, of Kentucky, planter, for ₤ 60 sold to Isaac Williams, of Pendleton Co. tract on E. side of Seneca River, bd. on E. by John Twenty, on NW by vacant land, on SW by river, part of tract bd. by Henry Hays and McKey, granted Mackie by Wm. Moultrie. Recorded Bk. KKKK, p. 632. Date: 1 Sep. 1796. Signed: William (W) Mackey. Wit: James Patterson, Alexr. Kilpatrick. James Patterson made oath to J. C. Kilpatrick, J. P., 1 Sep. 1796. Rec: 6 Jan. 1797.

Page 304: I, Richard Powell for $50 sold to Jane Reese, cattle, crop raised last year and household furniture. Date: 16 Jan. 1797. Wit: Thomas S. Reese. Tho. S. Reese made oath to J. B. Earle, J. P., 24 Jan. 1797. Rec: 24 Jan. 1797.

Page 304: 10 Feb. 1795. William E. Kennedy and Thomas Lofton, of Greenville Co., S. C. to George Selmser(?) for ₤ 20 stg. for 502 acres. Signed: Wm. E. Kennedy, Thos. Lofton. Wit: Josiah Kennedy, B. Starritt. Benjamin Starritt made oath to Joshua Saxon, J. P., 24 Jun. 1795. Rec: 24 Jun. 1797.

Page 304-305: 4 Nov. 1795. Francis King to Jonathan Kemp for ₤ 30 stg. for 127 acres on branches of Connoross, of Keowee River, bd. SW by John Parson, SE by William Wollum, N. by James Ingram, granted Fields Prewit by Thos. Pinckney, 2 Jul. 1787. Signed: Francis (X) King. Wit: Thomas Vick, Sarah (X) King. Thomas Vick made oath to Samuel Gardner, J. P., 14 Mar. 1796. Rec: 24 Jan. 1797.

Page 305: I, Francis Rose voluntarily make my deed of Gift of all my property both real and personal

(P. 305 cont'd) to my beloved wife, Pricilla Rose, 75 acres on Savannah River, bd. by Saml. Rose and Col. John Moffet, Horses, cattle, furniture and plantation tools, excepting one dollar that I leave to my brother, John Rose or his oldest son if any of them is living and I authorize Pricilla Rose to sell or dispose of the property after my decease and I disannull all former deeds of gift, wills whatsoever. Date: 5 Jun. 1796. Signed: Francis (+) Rose. Wit: Thos. McCune, Wm. McCune, J. P., Wm. McCune made oath to Saml. Porter, J. P., 21 Jan. 1797.
Rec: 24 Jan. 1797.

Page 305: 29 Mar. 1794. Samuel Rose and Rhody Rose to Francis (also Frank) Rose for ₤ 50 for 75 ac. on Savannah River, part of 156 acres granted to John McEvanney, 6 Nov. 1786, by Wm. Moultrie, bd. by John Moffitt and river. Signed: Samuel Rose, Rhody(X) Rose. Wit: William Green, Wm. McCune. Wm. Green made oath to Saml. Porter, J. P., 21 Jan. 1786.
(No recording date).

Page 305: I, William Young, of Pendleton Co., appoint Jesse Hunt, of Washington Co., Tenn., my lawful attorney to assign a deed of conveyence from me to Uriah Hunt, of Washington Co., Tenn., lying on Boon's Creek, which land was conveyed to Young by Hunt, adj. Nathl. Davis below and Sharpin Harris above. Date: 17 Sep. 1796. Wit: Wm. Brown, William Hunt. Wm. Brown made oath to E. Brown, J. P., 24 Jan. 1797.
(No recording date).

Pages 305-306: 20 Jan. 1795, Amos Freeman to James Boun for ₤ 80 for 112 acres on branches of 12 Mile River, granted by Thomas Pinckney, 6 Aug. 1787. Signed: Amos (A) Freeman. Wit: Thomas (+) Anderson, William Boun. Wm. Boun, Sr. made oath to Bayley Anderson, J. P., 9 Mar. 1795.
Rec: 24 Jan. 1797.

Page 306: 29 Nov. 1791. Daniel Kelly of Greenville Co., S. C. to Michael Whitmire, Sr. of Pendleton Co. for ₤ 40 for 422 acres granted Kelly on 6 Apr. 1789 by Wm. Moultrie in 96 Dist. on branches of 12 Mile River and Ooliney. Wit: Abraham Powell, Matw. (his mark) Kelly, Henry (+) Whitmire. Henry Whitmire made oath to W. W. Reed, J. P., 14 Oct. 1796.
Rec: 24 Jan. 1797.

Page 306: I, John Mauldin, Sr. for ₤ 60 "at 4/8 pr. dollar" sold to Thomas Millsap 100 acres where Martain now lives on Rocky River, adj. Wm. Hall, Robert Harkness, Elijah Browne, Esq., Robert Norris, granted Samuel McCune and conveyed to Blake Mauldin. Date: 8 Nov. 1796. Wit: Martin Terrell, Wesley Mauldin. Martin Terrell made oath to E. Browne, J. P. (no date).
Rec: 24 Jan. 1797.

Page 306: 29 Dec. 1794. Harris Mauldin to Thomas Millsap for ₤ 30 stg. for 80 acres in Washington Dist. on Rocky Creek, of Savannah River, bd. by John Lindsey, john Mauldin, Rocky River, Robt. Norris, granted John Johnston, recorded Bk. B, no. 5, p. 349. Wit: Wm. Brown, Edward Davis, Joab Mauldin, Edward Davis made oath to E. Browne, J. P., 12 Jun. 1795.
Rec: 24 Jan. 1797.

Pages 306-307: 1 Nov. 1793. Moses Liddell, planter, to John Henderson, for ₤ 40 stg. for 298 acres in Washington Dist. on Great Generostee Creek of Savannah River, half of tract granted John Pironeau(?), 16 Jul. 1784, who conveyed to Ephraim Mitchell, 1 Aug. 1785, from Mitchell to Augustus Merrick, 20 Mar. 1789 (45 acres sold to Richard York out of survey), laid out by John C. Kilpatrick, again surveyed by Tilly Merrick, heir to Augustus Merrick, to Moses Liddell, 1791. Wit: Leonard Morrow, Elijah Nicholson, John Stevenson. Leonard Morrow made oath to E. Browne, J. P., 6 Feb. 1794. Rec: 24 Jan. 1797.

Page 307:	I, James Anderson and Agnes, his wife, for
$50, paid by Abel Honey sold him 150 acres on
Little Beaverdam Creek, part of tract granted
James Anderson by Charles Pinckney, 5 Dec. 1791. Recorded Bk. E, no. 5,
p. 140. Date: 24 Jun. 1796. Signed: James Anderson, Agness Anderson. Wit:
James Wilbun, William (H) Honey...Agnes Anderson released dower to Wm.
Hall, J. P., 23 Jun. 1793.
Rec: 24 Jan. 1797.

Page 307:	11 Jan. 1796. George Oldham to Thomas Crow for
Ł 60 stg. for 170 acres on N. bank of Broada-
way, branch of Rocky River, bd. by Robert
Brown, Hezekiah Rice,...Woodlaw. Wit: George Dilworth, Edmond Lindsey,
Hezekiah Rice. George Dilworth made oath to Wm. Hall, J. P., 11 Jan.1797.
Rec. 24 Jan. 1797.

Page 308:	28 Sep. 1795. James Long, planter, to William
Dickey, planter, for Ł 30 stg. for 150 acres
part of tract granted Henry Pearson by William
Moultrie, 5 Jun. 1785, on Great Generostee Creek, of Savannah River, adj.
Wm. Herring, McDannel, James Long, Joseph Land, Joshua Burns. Wit: Brad-
ock McDonald, Burril Reeves, Timothy Gary(?). Bradock McDonald made oath
to Joshua Saxon, J. P., 31 Oct. 1795.
Rec: 24 Jan. 1797.

Page 308:	I, Joab Laurence for Ł 140 sold to William
Thompson 65 acres part of 885 acres on S. side
of Cain Creek and part of N. side of Cain Crk.
of Keowee River, granted Laurence, 2 Mar. 1789 by Charles Pinckney. Recorded Bk. ZZZZ, p. 133. Date: 3 Jun. 1796. Wit: Michael Speed, Jno.
Green, John (X) Cosby. John Cosby made oath to E. Browne, J. P., 25 Jan.
1797.
Rec: 25 Jan. 1797.

Pages 308-309:	I, Joab Lawance for Ł 30 sold to John Cosby
60 acres, part of 885 acres granted Lawrence
by Charles Pinckney, 2 Mar. 1789 on N. part
of Cane Creek. Date: 3 Jun. 1796. Wit: William Thompson, John Green, Michael Speed. William Thompson made oath to E. Browne, J. P., 25 Jan.1797.
Rec: 25 Jan. 1797.

Page 309:	I, Samuel Taylor for 100 guineas sold to James
Yowell, planter, 200 acres, on Tugalo River,
run for John Smith, Soldier, surveyed by Thom-
as Lewis, D. S., 5 Jul. 1784, adj. land laid out for Reuben Denton, Soldier. Date: 25 Jan. 1797. Wit: Joel Yowell, John Taylor; Joel Yowell
made oath to J. B. Earle, J. P., 25 Jan. 1797.
Rec: 25 Jan. 1797.

Page 309:	19 Oct. 1795, Robt. Looney to Benjamin Cleve-
land, Esq. for Ł 200 stg. for 100 acres on
Tugalo River, bd. Cleveland's, Jesse Coffee,
Robt. Looney. Wit: Robt. Sharp, John Carden...Jan. Court 1797, above deed
was acknowledge and ordered recorded by J. B. Earle, C.C.
Rec: 25 Jan. 1797.

Page 309:	15 Oct. 1795. James Swords, a Soldier to Ab-
salom Cleveland, of Franklin Co., Ga. for Ł50
stg. for 200 acres on NE side of Tugalo River,
in 96 Dist., granted Swords, 21 Jan. 1785 by Benj. Guerard. Wit: James
Blair, David Powers. James Blair made oath to J. B. Earle, C.C., 25 Jan.
1797. Rec: 25 Jan. 1797.

Pages 309-310:	I, Benjamin Cleveland, Esq. for Ł 50 stg. sold
to James Davenport 95 acres on Tugalo River,
part of 200 acres granted Gilbert Grooms,sol-
dier, adj. John Smith, Davenport. Date: 10 Aug. 1796. Wit: James Blair,
John Cleveland. Capt. James Blair made oath to J. B. Earle, J. P., 25 Jan.
1797. Rec: 25 Jan. 1797.

Page 310:   I, Robert Miller, of Union Co., S. C. for
£ 250 stg. sold to Nicholas Welch, of Pendleton Co., 419 acres on 26 Mile Creek, granted to Katharine Miller by Wm. Moultrie, 1785, bd. on E. by Caleb Edmondson, on NE by Jonathan Montgomery. Date: 6 Dec. 1796. Wit: James Hembrie, William Welch. Wm. Welch made oath to Wm. Millwee, J. P. 21 Jan. 1797. Rec: 26 Jan. 1797.

Page 310:   3 Sep. 1796. William Skelton and Patty, his wife, to William Harkness for £ 34 for 100 ac. bd. by John Files, Samuel Henry, Samuel Deen, Jeremiah Files, on Mountain Creek, branch of Big Generostee, part of a. tract granted to David Clark, 5 Feb. 1787 by Wm. Moultrie. Recorded Bk. PPPP, p. 62. Signed: William Skelton, Patty (her mark) Skelton. Wit: Robt. Harkness, William (his mark) Cox. Robert Harkness made oath to E. Browne, J. P., 26 Jan. 1797.
Rec: 26 Jan. 1797.

Pages 310-311:   Washington Dist. 6 Feb. 1793. John Landers & Mary, his wife, to William Harkness for £ 90 for 150 acres, half of a tract on Mountain Creek, of Big Generostee, granted John Files, 15 Oct. 1784 by Benjamin Guerard. Signed: John Landers, Mary (her mark) Landers. Wit: Willm. Cavandish, Adam Files. Adam Files made oath to E. Browne, J. P., 25 Jun. 1795. Rec: 26 Jan. 1797.

Page 311:   22 Apr. 1796. John Perkins to James Standridge for £ 90 stg. for 310 acres on Chauga Creek, granted Perkins by Wm. Moultrie, 24 Nov.1791, now in possession of Standridge. Signed: John (X) Perkins. Wit: William Burton, Joseph Stapp. Joseph Stapp made oath to John Barton, J. P., 28 May 1796. Rec: 26 Jan. 1797.

Page 311:   I, William Millwee for 200 Spanish Mills and dollars sold to Edward Doyle 344 acres on 23 Mile Creek of the Savannah River, surveyed for Millwee, 6 May 1785. Date: 24 Jan. 1797. Wit: Henry Sims, Jas. Brouster, Aaron Guyton(?).....Martha (her mark) Millwee released dower to W.Steele, J. P., 24 Jan. 1797.
Rec: 26 Jan. 1797 (No oath)

Page 311:   I, James Martin, of York Co., S. C.for £ 100 stg. sold to Peter Eakins (or Eaker) and Jonathan Smith, of said county, and state, 640 acres granted to Joseph Hall(?) on 26 Mile Creek, 16 Jul. 1784, by conveyence to Martin. Date: 2 Jun. 1796. Wit: John Smith, John Akins, Daniel Smith....Pinkney Dist., S. C., above deed proven to Wm. McCollock, J. P., 2 Nov. 1796.
(No recording date).

Pages 311-312:   I, James Martin, of York Co., S. C., for £ 40 stg. sold to Harman Cummins 640 acres in Pendleton Co. on Mountain Creek of Great Generostee, bd. on W. by Tho. Leonard, on S. by Walker, including where Cummins now lives. Date: 26 Jan. 1797. Signed: Charles J. Colcock, Attorney for Freneau and Bremar (no explanation for this). Wit: John Hillhouse,Thos. Morrow. Thomas Morrow made oath to Joshua Saxon, J. P., 26 Jan. 1797. Rec: 26 Jan. 1797.

Page 312:   5 May 1795. Edward Ware, of Greenville Co., S. C. to John Martin, of Pendleton Co., for £ 50 stg. for 100 acres now in Martin's possession, on Rocky River, bd. on NE by William Thompson, on SW by Sam'l. Houston, on SE by Gardner Green, granted John Perkins by William Moultrie. Recorded Bk. E, no. 5, p. 524. Signed: Edward (EW) Were. Wit: Arthur Durley, John Drennan. John Drennan made oath to Joshua Saxon, J. P., 29 Feb. 1796.
Rec: 26 Jan. 1797.

Page 312:   3 Apr. 1796. William Low to Francis Nunn (?)

(page 312 cont'd): for Ł 50 stg. for 126 acres on both sides of Hurricane Creek, now in possession of Nunn, part of tract where Low now lives, adj. Smith. Signed: William Low, Margaret (X) Low. Wit: George Oldham, William (W) Stanton....Margaret Low released dower to William Hall, J. P., 23 Apr. 1796. George Oldham made oath to Wm. Hall, 23 Apr. 1796.
Rec: 26 Jan. 1797.

Pages 312-313: I, William Low sold to George Oldham for Ł107 stg. for 261 acres on S. side of Saluda River. Date: 3 Apr. 1796. Signed: William Low, Margaret (X) Low. Wit: Francis Nunn, Hezekiah Rice. Margaret Low released her dower to Wm. Hall, J. L., 23 Apr. 1796.
Rec: 26 Jan. 1797.

Page 313: 5 Jan. 1796. Daniel Brison and Jenny Bryson, his wife, to James Bole for Ł 50 stg. for 200 acres, part of 602 acres granted to John McNeel, 5 Oct. 1789 by Charles Pinckney on Willson's Creek, bd. by Thomas Jones. Signed: Daniel Bryson, Jenny (her mark) Bryson. Wit: Wm. McKay, Wm. McKee, George Stringer. Wm. McKay made oath to E. Browne, J. P., 24 Oct. 1796.
Rec: 26 Jan. 1797.

Pages 313-314: 8 May 1795. James Millwee, of Pendleton Co., to Jesse Gray for Ł 40 stg. for 235 acres on S. side of Saluda River, one half of tract of 470 acres surveyed for John Wagnon and granted to Millwee by Wm. Moultrie, 6 Nov. 1786. Wit: Alx. McDowell, J. McCrackane....96 Dist., James McCracken made oath to Jno. Trotter, Esq., J. P., of Abbeville Co., 21 Jan. 1797.
Rec: 26 Jan. 1797.

Page 314: I, Johnston Murry, planter, for Ł 50 stg. sold to Edward Vandiver, planter, 115 acres of 600 acres granted Thomas Burford on Rocky River, bd. by Ellicksader Meclane (Clerk made note: 'I cant make out them words"...I believe Alexr. McLean."), Thomas Wade, Jno. Wartlaw. Wit: John Wornock. Wit.: John Wornock, Godfry Hartsfield, John Vandiver. Acknowledged to E. Browne, 26 Nov. 1796.
Rec: 26 Jan. 1797.

Page 314: I, David Prewit, of my own free will and accord to to Hezekiah Burrill, my Grandchild, one cow and feather bed, also to Harley Burrell, my grandchild, young cow and colt. Date: 20 Jan. 1797. Signed: David Pruet. Wit: Jesse Brown, Morgan Hood. Jesse Brown made oath to Joshua Saxon, J. P., 20 Jan. 1797.
Rec: 26 Jan. 1797.

Pages 314-315: 21 Jan. 1795. Richard Oldham to Reubin Clements for Ł 60 stg. 294 acres on Rocky Creek of Rocky River, bd. by James Clements, Hezekiah Rice, Wm. Lindley, part of 640 acres granted Andrew Hamilton, 4 Oct. 1790. Recorded Bk. C, no. 5, p. 62, conveyed by Hamilton to Oldham. Wit: William Lindley, Benja. Arnold; William Lindley made oath to Wm. Hall, J. P., 7 Nov. 1795.
Rec: 26 Jan. 1797.

Page 315: I, Peter Gill, of Burk Co., N. C. for Ł 50 sold to William Smith (no county) 100 acres on Mile Creek, S. side of Saluda River, bd. by Wm. Poor, Samuel Martin, Henry Huse. Date: 20 Jan. 1797. Wit: Benja. Price, Lewis Swan. Peter Gill acknowledged deed before George Washington Earle, Dept. Clerk of Pendleton Co., 26 Jan. 1797.
Rec: 26 Jan. 1797.

Page 315: 8 Jan. 1794. James Montgomery, Joner(Joiner?) to William Stevenson, planter, for Ł 40 stg. for 200 acres in Washington Dist. on E. side

(Page 315 cont'd) of the Seneca River, one half of tract granted to Sarah Montgomery, 7 Dec. 1789 by Charles Pinckney, adj. to John Varner, Sr. Signed: James Montgomery, Sarah Montgomery. Wit: William Stevenson, Moses Purvianes. Proved by oath of William Stevenson to E. Browne, J. P., 27 Jan. 1797.
Rec: 27 Jan. 1797.

Pages 315-316: 22 Nov. 1790. James Hamilton, " heir of Pendleton Co." to Asa Cobb for Ł 90 stg. for 100 acres on S. side of Saluda River, granted to James Hamilton's father, deceased, by Benjamin Guerard, 15 May 1784, part of a tract of James Hamilton's father (no name given), bd. by Benja. Farmer. Signed: James Hamilton. Wit: Thomas Bennett, William Maples. Thomas Bennett made oath to Wm. Halbert, J. P., 5 Jan. 1791.
Rec: 27 Jan. 1797.

Page 316: I, Benjamin Green, Jr. of Abbeville Co., for Ł 125 sold to James Alfer of Chatham Co., Ga. 444 acres in 96 Dist. on Little Generostee Creek of the Savannah River in Pendleton Co. Date: 21 Feb. 1797. Wit: Wm. Steele, David McCaleb, J. T. Whittendel. John T. Whittendel made oath to J. B. Earle, J. P., 25 Feb. 1797.
Rec: 21 Feb. 1797.

Page 316: 11 Jan. 1796. James Martin, of Lincoln Co., N. C. to Thomas M. Taggart (could be McTaggart) of Burk Co., N. C. for Ł 65 stg. for 320 acs. half of a tract on E. fork of the Eastatoe Creek, granted James Smith, "who not complying with the laws of the State forefieted his right of Patent and sold at public auction by the Treasurers of the State", 8 Apr. 1789 for 640 acres purchased by James Martin, bd. by Thomas M. Taggart and John McGilliars(?). Wit: Thomas Hogg, John M. Galliart. Thomas Hogg made oath to Thos. Gillham, J. P., 12 Jan. 1796.
Rec: 4 Mar. 1797.

Pages 316-317: 11 Jan. 1796. James Martin of Lincoln Co., N. C. to John M. Gallert, of Burk Co., N. C. for Ł 65 stg. for 320 acres, half of tract granted James Smith and sold at public auction to James Martin, 8 Apr. 1789. Wit: Thomas McTaggart, Thomas Hogg. Thomas Hogg made oath to Tho. Gillham, J. P., 12 Jan. 1796.
Rec: 4 Mar. 1797.

Page 317: I, George Nelson for Ł 10 stg. sold to Meshack Green 700 acres on Little Beaverdam Creek of the Savannah River, bd. on SE and NE by George Anderson and vacant land, granted Nelson, 7 Jan. 1790 by Charles Pinckney. Recorded Bk. P, no. 5, p. 378. Date: 27 Feb. 1797. Signed: George (his mark) Nelson. Wit: Isaac Horton, John Green, Jas. Millwee. Isaac Horton made oath to J. B. Earle, J. P., 11 Mar. 1797...Martha (her mark) Nelson released dower to W. Steele, J. P., 12 Mar. 1797.
Rec: 12 Mar. 1797.

Pages 317-318: 22 Mar. 1792. Thomas Findley of Abbeville Co. to William Stevenson of Pendleton Co. for Ł100 stg. for 260 acres in Washington Dist. on E. side of the Keowee River, granted Findley, 5 Dec. 1785 for 465 acres, the other part sold to Wm. Moral, bd. on S. by Ambrose Hudgens. Wit: William Morril, Moses (X) Purvines. William Morril made oath to Wm. Nevill, J.P. 31 Dec. 1792.
Rec: __ Mar. 1797.

Page 318: 14 Oct. 1792. William Brown of Wilks Co., Ga. to John Lauderdale of Pendleton Co. for Ł 100 stg. for 294 acres on Great Rocky Creek, granted Brown, 4 Dec. 1786, at the mouth of Beaver Creek, adj. Rachel Thompson, Widow Woman's land, Jacob Gillilan, John Mauldin. Recorded Bk. QQQQ, p. 227. Wit: Samuel Croft, James Linn. James Linn made oath to E. Browne, J. P., 18 Jan. 1797.
Rec: 16 Mar. 1797.

Page 318: We, Robert Rankin and Margaret Wood, Executors of Jesse Wood, both of Pendleton Co. for Ł 20 stg. sold to Peter Kays (no amount shown), in Washington Dist. on Big Generostee Creek of the Savannah River, adj. to Joshua Saxon, Widow Smith and Kay's land, surveyed for George Smith. Date: 14 Dec. 1796. Signed: Margaret (X) Wood, Robert Rankin. Wit: Nolly Marsley (or Masters), Rachel (X) Rankin. Nolly Masters(?) made oath to Joshua Saxon, J. P., 17 Sep. 1796. Rec: 18 Mar. 1797.

Pages 318-319: We, John Lauderdale and Milberry, my wife for Ł 50 stg. sold to Peter Kays & Co., 134 acres in Washington Dist. on Great Rocky Creek of the Savannah River, beginning at the mouth of Beaver Creek, bd. by James Thompson, Kays, Widow Mauldin, Thos. Milsap. Date: 7 Nov. 1796. Signed: John Lauderdale, Milberry (X) Lauderdale. Wit: Lazarus Tilly, Danl. Rutherford, John Tuggle. Lazarus Tilly made oath to Joshua Saxon, J.P., 14 Mar. 1797. Rec: 18 Mar. 1797.

Page 319: I, William M. Cavindish sold to Peter Kays & Co., for Ł 20, 200 acres in 96 Dist. on the branches of Wilson's Creek of the Savannah River, bd. on SE by John McColough, on NE by James Kell. Date: 6 Feb. 1796. Wit: Rachel Smith, William G. Smith, Mary Smith. Rachel Smith made oath to Joshua Saxon, 30 Aug. 1796. Rec: 18 Mar. 1797.

Page 319: I, William Lesly, of Abbeville Co., for $100 sold to Peter Kays, of Pendleton Co., 200 ac. on branch of Beaver Creek, granted William Lesley, Jr., 7 Nov. 1791. Date: 10 Mar. 1797. Signed: William Lesley. Wit: Jean (X) Evans, Arthur Durley, plat shows land adj. SW by Jas. Thompson and Wm. Brown, S. by Jacob Gilliland, vacant land. Arthur Durley made oath to Joshua Saxon, J. P., 16 Mar. 1797. Rec: 18 Mar. 1797.

Pages 319-320: 5 Nov. 1792. Jonas Little to Isaac Roberts for Ł 50 for 186 acres in Washington Dist. on Big Creek of the Saluda River, granted to William Hamilton, by Charles Pinckney, 1 Feb. 1790. Recorded Bk. B, no. 5, p.113. Signed: Jonas Littell. Wit: James Wilbern, Sturdy Garner. James Wilbern made oath to Wm. Hall, J. P., 3 Aug. 1796. Rec: 25 Aug. 1797.

Page 320: 17 Sep. 1796. Isaac Roberts and Mary, his wife to Sturdy Garner for Ł 47 for 186 acres in Washington Dist. on Big Creek of Saluda River, granted William Hamilton, 1 Feb. 1790 by Charles Pinckney. Recorded Bk. B, no. 5, p. 113. Signed: Isaac Roberts, Mary (X) Roberts. Wit: Charles Bennett, James Scott, Abner Hone. Charles Bennett made oath to Wm. Hall, J. P., 18 Mar. 1797. Rec: 25 Mar. 1797.

Pages 320-321: 11 Jul. 1795. David Clarke to William Bodenhammer for Ł 80 for 200 acres on Hurricane Creek, granted Clarke, 21 Jan. 1785, bd. on W. by John Johnson and vacant land; also, 127 acres adj. tract granted Johnathan Clarke, 4 Dec. 1786...Signed and sealed and delivered to James Wilbern, lawful Attorney for William Bodenhammer. Wit: James Anderson, James Wilbern, Thomas Coker. James Anderson made oath to John Willson, J. P., 11 July 1795. (No recording date)

Page 321: Mar. 1793. Jacob Kille(?) to Enoch Garner for Ł 50 stg. for 131 acres in Washington Dst. on N. side of Big Creek, of Saluda, part of tract granted John Burdine by Wm. Moultrie, 5 Jun. 1786. Signed: Jacob (X) Kille. Wit: Thomas Garner, William Halchell(?). Thomas Garner made oath to Wm. Hall, JP, 18 Mar. 1797. Rec: 25 Mar. 1797.

Page 321: 5 Jan. 1794. Wm. Black of Abbeville Co. to John Hodge, of Pendleton Co. for ₤ 10 for 200 acres on N. fork of Big Creek, granted Wm. Coulter, 4 Jul. 1785, by Wm. Moultrie, left by will to said Wm. Black. Wit: James Hodge, John Alexander. Jas. Hodge made oath to Wm. Hall, JP, 24 Feb. 1797. Rec: 25 Jan. 1797.

Page 322: 24 Feb. 1797. John Hodge to Thomas Hona (also Honae) for ₤ 30 for 200 acres on N. fork of Big Creek, of Saluda River, granted William Coller, 4 Jul. 1785 by Wm. Moultrie. Recorded Bk. BBBB, p. 309. Wit: James Hodge, William Hona. John Hodge made oath to Wm. Hall, J.P., 24 Feb. 1797. Rec: 25 Mar. 1797.

Page 322: I, William Burney, planter, for ₤ 25 stg.... sold to Thomas Pilgrim for 100 acres, part of 1000 acres granted Burney by Charles Pinckney, in 96 Dist. on 18 and 23 Mile Creeks of the Keowee River, bd. on SE by Ephraim Linsey, SW by Ephraim Linsey, NW by Thomas Gadson, SW by Charles Hughes. Recorded Bk. F, no. 5, p. 39. Date: 11 Nov. 1790. Wit: John Hallum, John Edmondson, Jacob Earnest. John Hallum made oath to John Willson, J. P., 16 Nov. 1796...Washington Dist., Elizabeth (her mark) Burney, wife of William Burney released dower to Andw. Pickens, Judge, 16 Nov. 1796. Rec: 30 Mar. 1797.

Page 323: I, Jacob Rame for 5 shillings sold to Thomas Rapier 100 acres where Rapier now lives, bd. by Joseph Whitner, Daniel Kelley, Deale and Tinsley, being part of 404 acres granted Rame, 2 Sep. 1793. Date: ___ Aug. 1796. Wit: John Griffen, Abner A. Steele. Abner Alexr. Steele made oath to G. W. Earle, D.C.C., 30 Mar. 1797. Rec: 30 Mar. 1797.

Page 323: I, Jacob Rame for ₤ 54 stg. sold to Daniel Kelly, 100 acres part of 404 acres granted to Rame, 2 Sep. 1793, adj. Wm. Banister, Peter Freneau and Francis Bremar, Esq., Joseph Whitner and lands claimed by Clement Deale, deceased, on E. branches of 18 Mile Creek, including the plantation where Rame now lives. Date: 26 Apr. 1796. Wit: W. Steele, William Hunter. William Hunter made oath to G. W. Earle, D.C.C., 30 Mar. 1797. Rec: 30 Mar. 1797.

Pages 323-324: 17 Jul. 1796. John Calhoun of Abbeville Co., planter, to John Norwood, of same, planter, for ₤ 100 for 200 acres on Tugalo River in Dist. of Cambridge, in lands set apart for Continental Soldiers of this State, 12 Jan. 1785, granted to Peter McGrew and conveyed by McGrew to Calhoun, 5 Dec. 1786. Wit: Wm. McMahan, A. C. Martin, John Porter. William McMahan made oath to John Willson, J. P., 7 Dec. 1796. Rec: 31 Mar. 1797.

Page 324: 4 Jan. 1793. John Varner, Jr. to John Varner, Sr., for ₤ 100 stg. for 357 acres in Washington Dist. on E. side of Seneca River, granted John Varner, Jr., 5 Jun. 1786 by Wm. Moultrie, bd. on W. by Seneca River, on N. by Ambrose Hudgins, on E. by Sarah Varner, on S. by George Varner. Wit: E. T. McClure, George Vernor. George Vernor made oath to E. Browne, J. P., 4 Jan. 1793. Rec: 3 Apr. 1797.

Pages 324-325: I, J. C. Kilpatrick for ₤ 60 stg. sold to Edward Box, 260 acres on both sides of Noyewee Creek, of Tugalo River, granted John C. Kilpatrick, 4 Oct. 1790, by Charles Pinckney. Date: 2 Nov. 1796. Wit:Thos. Gibson, George Blair. Thomas Gibson made oath to Jno. Barton, J. P., 7 Mar. 1797. Rec: 8 Apr. 1797.

Page 325:					10 Nov. 1796. John Harris, late Sheriff of
						Pendleton Co. to Moses Jones...whereas, James
					Millwee was seized of 150 acres on both sides
of Town Creek, of Tugalo River, granted by Charles Pinckney, 7 Nov.1791
...Edward Mannan got judgement against Millwee for Ł 12-18 shillings stg.
John B. Earle, C.C.P., directed Sheriff to sell goods, chattels, houses,
lands of Millwee at public auction, 4 Jun. 1796...Moses Jones, highest
bidder for Ł 30 stg. by his friend, Joab Mauldin. Signed: John Harris,
late Sheriff of Pendleton Co. Wit: James Dickson, William Griffen,
James Wood. James Wood made oath to Geo. W. Earle, D.C.C., 17 Nov.1796.
Rec: 14 Apr. 1797.

Pages 325-326:				23 Apr. 1796. Adam Files to Edward Davis for
					Ł 80 stg. for 125 acres now in Davis' posses-
					sion, one half of tract surveyed 31 May ___
by Bennet Crafton. Wit: Robert Harkness, John Harkness, John McMahan.
Plat shows land bd. on E. by Rocky River, SE by Fergus Cavin, SW and N.
by Archib. Neil. Surveyed 23 Apr. 1796 by John McMahan, D.S. who made
oath to E. Browne, J. P.
Rec: 14 Apr. 1797.

Page 326:					12 Apr. 1797. John Langley to William Eddens
						for Ł 70 stg. for 150 acres on S. side of
						Hickorynut Mountain on one of the branches of
Wolf Creek, of 12 Mile River, bd. by 200 acres first granted Samuel Earle
now belonging to Wm. Eddens, sold to him by Langley, part of 779 acres
granted James Gillispie, 5 Sep. 1791 by Charles Pinckney, conveyed to
Langley. Wit: Samuel (his mark) Yeager, Moses Cantrell(M), William (H)
Heath. Samuel Yager made oath to J. B. Earle, J. P., 14 Apr. 1797.
Rec: 14 Apr. 1797.

Pages 326-327:				23 Apr. 1796. Thomas Edmondson of Pendleton
					Co. to John Edmondson of Charles City Co., Va.
					for Ł 500 stg. for plantation where I now live
adj. to tract belonging to Genl. Pinckney on which the Town of Pickensville is laid out, which tract I purchased from Thomas C. Russell with
the following slaves: Nancy, Terris, Punch, Toney and Samuel, otherwise
called Jeff, also household furniture and stock of all kinds...reversing
to myself the disposal of a lifes estate...and uncontrolled power of disposing of 200 acres out of part of my plantation...the true intention
being, I am now in actual possession of tract and negros, etc....I con-
sider it my duty as a parent to provide for his children, so to my son,
John Edmondson to be divided as he may think proper after my death between my sons George and Benjamin Edmondson, Mary Boulwar, daughter of
Phillip P. Boulwar and Thomas Edmondson, son of my son, William Edmondson and I give John Edmondson full power to take possession of my property immediately after my decease. Signed: Thos. Edmondson. Wit: Jas.
Edmondson, W. Thompson. Waddy Thompson made oath to G. W. Earle, J. P.,
17 Apr. 1797.
Rec: 17 Apr. 1797.

Page 327:					22 Feb. 1797. Peter Chambless of Orangeburgh
					Dist., S. C. to John McClain of Pendleton Co.
					for Ł 25 stg. for 200 acres on branches of S.
Broadway Creek, bd. on NE by John McClain, on SE by Grayham, vacant land,
granted 20 Feb. 1797 by Charles Pinckney. Wit: Josiah Houston, Wiley Bishop. Wiley Bishop made oath to Joshua Saxon, J. P., 31 Mar. 1797.
Rec: 17 Apr. 1797.

Page 327:					3 Jun. 1795. Mathew Willson of Abbeville Co.
						to John McClain of Pendleton Co. for Ł 25 for
						285½ acres on branches of Broadway of Great
Rocky Creek, bd. on N. by Hugh Wardlaw, on NW by William Smith, on SW by
John Miller, on SE by William Neil, part of tract granted Willson, 7 Aug.
1786. Wit: William Wardlaw, Mary (m) Wordlaw. William Wordlaw made oath
to E. Browne, J. P., 14 Oct. 1795.
Rec: 17 Apr. 1797.

Pages 327-328:				I, John Adam Miller, of Pendleton Co. for Ł100
					stg. sold to James Hannah of Elbert Co., Ga.

(Pages 327-328 cont'd): 150 acres on Big Generostee Creek, part of a tract granted Matthew Morgan, recorded Bk. E., no. 5, p. 99, conveyed to Francis Miller, then to John A. Miller, including all that land where Francis Miller now lives, bd. by Thomas Moss. Date: 2 Dec. 1796. Wit: Jesse Brown, George Grizel, Alexr. McMillin. Jesse Brown made oath to Joshua Saxon, J. P., 8 Apr. 1797. Rec: 17 Apr. 1797.

Page 328: 4 Jan. 1793. George Vernor to John Vernor, Jr. for Ł 40 stg. for 218 acres in Washington District on E. side of Seneca River, granted to George Vernor, 4 Dec. 1786, by Wm. Moultrie, bd. on N. by John Vernor, Jr., on E. by Sarah Vernor. Wit: James Hamilton, Mary (+) Vernor. James Hamilton made oath to E. Browne, J. P., 23 Jan. 1793. Rec: 17 Apr. 1797.

Pages 328-330: 1 Dec. 1796. John Harris, of Washington Dist. planter, to Lewis Tresevant, of the City of Charleston, Attorney at Law, for Ł 25 for 236 acres in Pendleton Co. (formerly called 96 Dist., but now in Washington Dist.) on 26 Mile Creek, granted, 4 Nov. 1791 to James Millwee, bd. on NE by David Anderson, on SE by James Mackelwee, on SW and SE vacant land, NW and NE by James Saxon. Signed: John Harris, Mary Harris. Wit: George Shuler, Alexr. Barron. George Shular made oath to Joshua Saxon, J. P., 17 Apr. 1797. Rec: 17 Apr. 1797.

Page 330: I, Moses Jones for Ł 100 stg. sold to Charles England 120 acres on Toxaway Creek, fork of Chauga, waters of Tugalo River, granted Jones on 1 Apr. 1793, surveyed by William Sloan, bd. on NE and SE by Thomas Piney, Esq. and vacant land. Date: 5 Apr. 1796. Wit: James Blair, Robert Powell...Washington Dist., Capt. James Blair made oath to G. W. Earle, D.C.C., 20 Apr. 1797. Rec: 20 Apr. 1797.

Page 330: 4 Feb. 1797. Benjamin Whorton to James Caddell (?) for Ł 40 stg. for 200 acres on S. side of Cain Creek, bd. by Calopsane's(?) South line. Wit: John Beazley, Obern Buffington. Obern Buffington made oath to Joseph Reed, J. P., 22 Apr. 1797. Rec: 23 Apr. 1797.

Page 330: 15 Aug. 1791.(?) Burrill Bobo, of Spartanburgh Co., S. C. to Joseph Logan(?) for Ł 60 stg. for 165 acres surveyed by Andrew Thompson, 1 Apr. 1785 for Bobo, on branch of Keowee River called Crow Creek, granted 5 Jan. 1785. Signed: Burrell, Elizabeth (+) Bobo. (Note: Burrell Bobo and Elizabeth Bobo). Wit: James Rice, William Murphree, John Tubb (?). James Rice made oath to Bailey Anderson, J. P., 20 Apr. 1793. Rec: 1 May 1797.(very dim).

Pages 330-331: I, Josiah N. Kennedy of Greenville Co., S. C. for Ł 405 stg. sold to William Stephens, merchant, of Charleston, 8 parcels of land in Pendleton Co. containing in all 4,186 acres; one of 120 acres on Little Beaverdam Creek, part of tract granted John Hunnicutt by Wm. Moultrie, 6 Nov. 1786, bd. by James Eason's Spring Branch, Moses Martin; one of 50 acres on both sides of Little Beaverdam Creek, adj. above tract granted George Slaton by Charles Pinckney, 6 __ 1791; one of 637 acres on Beaver Creek, branch of Rocky River, granted Josiah N. Kennedy by Chas. Pinckney, 7 Nov. 1791, bd. on SW by James Martin, on SE by Wm. E. Kennedy, vacant land; one of 1000 acres; another of 318 acres on Beaver Crk. Rocky River, both granted Josiah N. Kennedy, 7 Nov. 1791, bd. on NE by James Martin, on SE by Jos. Calhoun, Wm. E. Kennedy, on NW by John Jackson; another of 714 acres, part of tract granted Joseph Kennedy, 7 Sep. 1789 by Chas. Pinckney, recorded Bk. ZZZZ, p. 471, conveyed by J. N. Kennedy, Exr. of Joseph Kennedy, deceased; another of 648 acres part of a tract granted James Milwee, 6 Apr. 1789 by Chas. Pinckney, recorded Bk. ZZZZ, p. 226; another of 654 acres, part of a tract granted Ebenezer

(Pages 330-331 cont'd):   Kennedy, 7 Sep. 1789 by Charles Pinckney, recorded Bk. ZZZZ, p. 502. Date: 8 Apr. 1797.
Wit: Wm. Bowen, Jno. McGehee. John McGehee made oath to Wm. Hall, J.P., 28 Apr. 1797.
Rec: 5 May 1797...Sarah Kennedy, wife of Josiah N. Kennedy released dower to Wm. Hall, J.P., 4 May 1797. Signed: Salley Kennedy.

(Note: Copier does not cross "T's", difficult to distinguish between L and T).

Page 331:   I, Samuel Watt of Abbeville Co., Esq., for ₤ 200 stg. sold to Peter Perkins of Pittsylvania Co., Va., planter, 250 acres in "96 Dist. at time of grant, but now in Washington Dist.", on both sides of Woolenoy Creek, S. fork of the Saluda River, bd. by James Davis, granted to Watt, 16 Jul. 1785 by Benjamin Guerrard. Date: 10 Apr. 1797. Wit: Bannister Stone, James Kellay, Wm. Lynch. Bannister Stone made oath to Wm. Edmondson (no date).
Rec: 16 May 1797.

Pages 331-332:   3 Jan. 1796. Robert Duncan of Greenville Co., S. C. to Ezekiel Potts for ₤ 80 stg. for 155 acres, bd. by Field Prewet, Anthony Griffen, Wm. Sloan. Recorded Bk. D, no. 5, p. 260, on S. fork of Cain Creek, of Keowee River. Wit: Benj. Whorton, Jesse Neville. Jesse Neville made oath to J. C. Kilpatrick, 7 Nov. 1796.
Rec: 16 May 1797.

Page 332:   I, Lewis D. Martin for ₤ 15 stg. sold to John Harris 236 acres in Washington Dist. on 26 Mile Creek, granted James Millwee by Charles Pinckney, 4 Nov. 1791 and sold at Sheriffs Sale. Date: 11 Apr. 1796.
Wit: Saml. Barton, Benj. Ingram...Washington Dist., Benjamin Ingram made oath to J. B. Earle, J. P., 29 May 1797.
Rec: 29 May 1797.

Page 332:   I, Benjamin Ragsdale, planter, for ₤ 20 stg. sold to Thomas Caudell, planter, 25 acres a part of 200 acres granted Ephraim Lindsey in Washington Dist., formerly 96 Dist. on 23 Mile Creek, of Savannah River, bd. on E. by John Norwood, on S. by Wm. Burney, granted Ephraim Lindsey by Benj. Guerrard. Recorded Bk. CCCC, p. 296. Date: 3 Feb. 1797. Wit: Thomas Pilgrim, Jacob (his mark) Earnest, Michael (his mark) Pilgram. Thomas Pilgrim made oath to John Willson, J. P., 21 Mar. 1797.
Rec: 3 Jun. 1797.

Page 332:   I, Jacob Earnest, planter, for ₤ 20 sold to Thomas Caudell, planter, 50 acres, part of 275 acres granted John Norwood by Wm. Moultrie, bd. on E. by Samuel Norwood, on N. by Gadson, on W. by Ephraim Lindsey. Recorded Bk. TTTT, p. 355.(255?) Date: 10 Apr. 1797. Signed: Jacob (X) Earnest. Wit: James Jett, Chas. Willson, Alexander Glenn. Alexander Glenn made oath to John Willson, J. P., 10 Apr. 1797.
Rec: 3 Jun. 1797.

Pages 332-333:   I, Norman Martin of Salem Co., S. C., planter, for 87 ac.(87 pounds?) sold to Humphrey Gibson of Pendleton Co., 200 acres on Tugalo River, granted to Martin. Signed: Norman (X) Martin. Wit: Benjamin Deason, William Nelms, Robert (X) Singleton....Salem Co., S. C., Robert Singleton made oath to Joseph Douglas, J. P., 15 Mar. 1796....Pendleton Co., Benjamin Deason made oath to John Barton, J. P., 3 Oct. 1796.
Rec: 3 Jun. 1797.

Page 333:   I, Joel Webb, planter, for $40 sold to John Portman, Elder, planter, 652 acres on Keowee River, below the mouth of 18 Mile Creek, granted to James Jordan, 6 May 1793, by Wm. Moultrie, sold by Sheriff to Webb. Date: 8 Jun. 1797. Wit: Archer (his mark) McDaniels. W. Earle,......
(cont'd next page)

(Page 333 cont'd): Washington Dist., George W. Earle made oath to J. B. Earle, J. P., 8 Jun. 1797.
Rec: 8 Jun. 1797.

Page 333: I, John Robinson, planter, for 130 acres sold to Zachariah Taliaferro, Attorney at Law, 230 acres on E. branch of 23 Mile Creek. Date: 8 Mar. 1797. Wit: W. Steele, Robert Pickens, Geo. Forbis...Sarah Robeson wife of John Robeson released dower to William Steele, J. P., 9 March 1797. Robert Pickens made oath to John Willson, J. P., 11 Apr. 1797.
Rec: 8 Jun. 1797.

Pages 333-334: State of Georgia. 2 Jun. 1797. James Luckie, of Oglethorp Co., Ga. to Alexander McMullen, of Pendleton Co., S. C., for $300 for 259 ac. in Pendleton Co. on Big Generostee, part of 585 acres granted to John Luckie, 2 Nov. 1793, by Wm. Moultrie, conveyed by John Luckie to James Luckie, 2 Nov. 1793. Wit: John Ponder, Wm. L. Luckie, Stephen Bullard. Stephen Bullard made oath to Joshua Saxon, J. P., 13 Jun. 1797.
Rec: 14 Jun. 1797.

Page 334: I, Robert Looney for $100 sold to David Barton, 3 mares, 6 cattle, pigs, sheep, furniture, blacksmith tools, etc. Date: 1 Feb. 1797. Wit: Thomas Farrar, Cyprian Farrar. Maj. Thos. Farrar made oath to J. B. Earle, J. P., 17 Jun. 1797.
Rec: 17 Jun. 1797.

Page 334: I, Robert Looney for $500 sold to David Barton 200 acres on Cane Creek, of Tugalo River, adj. John Humphrey, granted 21 Jan. 1785 by Benj. Guerrard. Date: 1 Jan. 1797. Wit: Thomas Farrar, Cyprian Farrar.... Maj. Thomas Farrar made oath to J. B. Earle, J. P., 17 Jun. 1797.
Rec: 17 Jun. 1797.

Page 334: I, Robert Looney for $1,000 sold to David Barton, 200 acres adj. Jesse Coffee near mouth of Chauga Creek, granted 15 Oct. 1784 by Benj. Guerrard, Esq. Date: 1 Jan. 1797. Wit: Thomas Farrar, Cyprian Farrar. Maj. Thos. Farrar made oath to J. B. Earle, J. P., 17 Jun. 1797.
Rec: 17 Jun. 1797.

Page 334: I, Richd. York, for $170 sold to Stephen Whitmire 74 acres. Date: 16 Nov. 1796. Signed: Richard (his mark) York. Wit: James Morrow, William Anderson...above land laid out for James Brock on both sides of Generostee Creek, part of 200 acres surveyed 4 Oct. 1796. William Anderson made oath to Joshua Saxon, J. P., 15 Apr. 1797.
Rec: 24 Jun. 1797.

Pages 334-335: I, John Ferguson for $43 sold to William Anderson 80 acres. Date: 13 Apr. 1797. Signed: John Ferguson. Wit: James Stevenson, Stephen Whitmire...Plat shows land bd. on E. by John Ferguson, SW by Richd. York, S. by Big Generostee Creek, part of 640 acres granted John Perenieu(?), surveyed 7 Oct. 1796...John McMahen, D.S. James Stevenson made oath to Joshua Saxon, J. P., 15 Apr. 1797.
Rec: 24 Jun. 1797.

Page 335: I, Stephen Whitmire for $170 sold to William Anderson, 74 acres. Date: 13 Apr. 1797. Wit: James Stevenson, Alexander Stevenson. Above tract is part of 200 acres laid out for James Brown, on both sides of Big Generostee, surveyed 4 Oct. 1796. James Stevenson made oath to Joshua Saxon, J. P., 15 Apr. 1797.
Rec: 24 Jun. 1797.

Page 335: I, Stephen Whitmire for $100 to William Anderson for 114 acres granted Whitmire, 1793, by Wm. Moultrie. Date: 13 Apr. 1797. Wit: James

(Page 335 cont'd): Stevenson, Alexander Stevenson. James Stevenson made oath to Joshua Saxon, J. P., 15 Apr. 1797. Rec: 24 Jun. 1797.

Page 335: I, William Means for ₤ 150 sold to Amos Adkison 350 acres; one of 100 acres part of 640 acres granted Samuel Ridgway by Wm. Moultrie, 5 Jun. 1786, conveyed to John Willson, then to Means, on Brushy Creek, N. fork of the Saluda River; the other 250 acres part of a tract granted Samuel Bush by Moultrie, adj. above tract, on both sides of Brushy Creek, bd. by Wm. Willson, and Roberts. Date: 11 Oct. 1796. Signed: William Means, Jane Means. Wit: John Wilson, John Hamilton. John Hamilton made oath to Robert Bowen, J. P., 1 Apr. 1797. Rec: 24 Jun. 1797.

Page 335: (Here the page number is repeated - 335, and should be 336)

Pages 335-(336): I, William Satterfield, for ₤ 50 sold to Abraham Elrod for 204 acres on Saluda River (corner torn) on Ferrls and John Trip, Dyche, (smeared), part of tract granted Augusteen Blackbourn by Thos. Pinckney, 2 Apr. 1786, conveyed to Saterfield, 19 Jan. 1795. Date: 20 Dec. 1796. Signed: William (W) Saterfield, Rachel (X) Saterfield. Wit: Thomas Payn (?), Christopher Stanton. Christopher Stanton made oath to R. Bowen, J. P., 1 Apr. 1797. Rec: 24 Jun. 1797.

Page 335 (336): 14 Jan. 1797. James Duff to Joshua Fowler for ₤ 50 stg. for 668½ acres on head branches of George's Creek of the Saluda River. Wit: B. Mauldin, Jesse Miller, William Jameson. Blake Mauldin made oath to Robt. Bowen, J. P., 20 Jan. 1797. Rec: 24 Jun. 1797.

Page 335 (336): We, Thomas Edwards and Mary Ann, my wife, of Greenville Co., S. C., for ₤ 100 sold to George Harrison of Pendleton Co., 150 acres in Pendleton Co. on the Saluda River "at noted place of Parrisses", granted by Wm. Moultrie, 1 May 179_. Recorded Bk. JJJJ, p. 412. Conveyed by Sullivant to Edwards. Date: 11 Mar. 1797. Signed: Tho. Edwards, Mary Ann Edwards. Wit: James Jewell, (?) Williams, James Jewell (repeat). James Jewell made oath to and William Edwards signed with him, Robert Bowen, 24 Jun. 1797. Rec: 24 Jun. 1797.

Page 335 (336): I, Reuben Pyles for ₤ 26 sold to Joseph Ship 160 acres where Ship now lives, granted Joseph Jenkins, adj. Daniel Ship, John Ward, transferred from Jenkins to R. Pyles. Date: 22 Jun. 1797. Wit: J. Mauldin, Aaron Steele. Joab Mauldin made oath to J. B. Earle, J. P., 24 Jun. 1797. Rec: 24 Jun. 1797.

Page 335 (336)-337: 27 Oct. 1796. Christopher Long, taylor, to David Brown for ₤ 50 stg. for 86 acres on N. side of the Savannah River and N. side of the Seneca River, at the fork of Seneca and Tugalo Rivers, where David Brown now lives, granted Gabriel Pickens, 5 Jun. 1785, conveyed to Long. Signed: Christopher (X) Long. Wit: Saml. Tate, John Brown, Joseph Brown. Samuel Tate made oath to E. Browne, J. P., 26 Jun. 1797. Rec: 26 Jun. 1797.

Page 337: I, James Ditto for ₤ 50 stg. sold to Jas. Patterson 145 acres on branches of Keowee River, bd. on SW by John Twitty, deceased, on SE by Minor Winn, on NW by Wm. Mackey, granted John Twitty, dec'd. and by William Twitty, his heir, conveyed to Ditto, granted by Charles Pinckney. Recorded Bk. C, no. 5, p. 80. Date: 1 Sep. 1796. Wit: Isaac (X) Williams, William Dennis. Isaac Williams made oath to J. C. Kilpatrick, J. P., 1 Sep. 1796. Rec: 26 Jun. 1797.

Page 337: I, Moses Guest for Ł 15 stg. sold to David Humphreys 37 acres on N. side of Tugalo River, part of a larger tract granted Guest by Geo. Matthews, Governor of Georgia. Plat shows land bd. on S. by Humphreys, on E. by the river, on N. by Saml. Guest, on W. vacant. Wit: Rich'd. Hooper, Morgan Guest. Richard Hooper made oath to Nathl. Perry, 20 Nov. 1796. Rec: 26 Jun. 1797.

Page 337: I, James Blair for $200 sold to William Martin 200 acres granted Reuben Denton who served as a Soldier in the State of South Carolina, now in possession of Martin, on Tugalo River. Date: 9 May 1797. Wit: Joel Yowell, Taliferro Shelton. Joel Yowell made oath to J. B. Earle, J. P., 26 Jun. 1797. Rec: 26 Jun. 1797.

Page 337: I, William Lowe, for Ł 85 stg. sold to Hezekiah Rice 185 acres on S. side of Saluda River, on Hurricane Creek. Date: 23 Apr. 1796. Signed: William Lowe, Margaret Lowe. Wit: George Oldham, Francis Nunn. Margaret (X) Lowe, wife of William Lowe, released dower to William Hall, J. P., 23 Apr. 1796. George Oldham made oath to W. Hall, 23 Apr. 1796. Rec: 26 Jun. 1797.

Pages 337-338: 9 Feb. 1795. William Hamilton to William Killen for Ł 60 stg. for 120 acres on N. branch of 12 Mile River. Wit: Mirah Miller, Robert Killen. Mirah Miller made oath to John Willson, J. P., 12 Nov. 1796. Rec: 26 Jun. 1797.

Page 338: I, John Hallum for Ł 30 sold to Blake Mauldin 100 acres on George's Creek of the Saluda River, granted Thomas Hallum by Benj. Guerard, 15 Oct. 1784, recorded Bk. AAAA, p. 181. Date: 28 Oct. 1796. Wit: Thomas Lamar, J. Mauldin. J. Mauldin made oath to Wm. Edmondson, J. P., 28 Oct. 1796. Rec: 26 Jun. 1797.

Page 338: 23 Mar. 1797. George Thompson to William Wiatt for Ł 75 for 200 acres on N. fork of 12 Mile River, part of a tract bought of James Martin, 10 Jul. 1784 in Washington Dist., W. of Old Indian Boundary Line, bd. by Thompson, Moorhead, Wiatt, Combs, Rose Reese. Wit: William King, James (X) Barnett. James Barnett made oath to W. W. Reed, J. P., 22 Apr. 1797. Rec: 26 Jun. 1797.

Page 338: Washington Dist. I, William McGuffin, planter, for $50 sold to John Hays 69 acres on NE side of Keowee River, bd. on NE by Henry Hays, on SE by John Hays, on NW by Robert Maxwell, vacant land. Date: 4 Jan. 1797. Wit: Andw. Liddell, Aaron Hill, Daniel Kelly. Daniel Kelly made oath to G. W. Earle, D.C.C., 27 Jun. 1797. Rec: 27 Jun. 1797.

Page 338: I, John Hays, planter, for $50 sold to Joshua Ham 69 acres on NE side of Keowee River, bd. W. and S. by Henry Hays, NW by Robert Maxwell, vacant land. Date: 8 Mar. 1797. Wit: E. Williams, William Crosby, Alexander Patterson. William Crosby made oath to G. W. Earle, D.C.C., 27 Jun. 1797. Rec: 27 Jun. 1797.

Pages 338-339: I, Thomas Gorman for Ł 15 stg. sold to John Harris, 20 acres in Washington Dist. on W. side of Seneca River, part of tract of 173 ac. granted by Wm. Moultrie to William Hollum, 2 Oct. 1786. Date: 10 Feb. 1796. Wit: John Ragsdale, George Bond. George Bond made oath to John Willson, J. P., 27 Jun. 1797. Rec: 27 Jun. 1797.

Page 339: 24 Oct. 1795. James McCarley of Greenville Co., S. C., blacksmith, to Joshua Burris of Pendle-

(Page 339 cont'd:) ton Co., planter, for £ 150 stg. 450 acres, part of tract granted Samuel Saxon by William Moultrie, 7 Aug. 1786 on Great Generostee Creek of Savannah River, where Burris now lives. Wit: Robert King, Thomas Houston, William King. Robert King made oath to Joshua Saxon, J. P., 11 Jun. 1796. Rec: 28 Jun. 1797.

Page 339: I, James Millwee for £ 20 sold to Joseph Martin 190 acres granted Millwee by Chas. Pinckney, 2 Mar. 1789. Date: 5 Jul. 1797. Wit.: Meridath (his mark) Hunnicutt, Margaret Brouster. Mordray Hunnicutt made oath to Wm. Millwee, J. P., 5 Jul. 1797. Rec: 5 Jul. 1797.

Pages 339-340: 1 Nov. 1796. Edward Tate McClure and Josiah McClure, of Pendleton Co., to Henry McWhorter, Jr. of Pickensville Dist., planter, for £ 100 for 233 acres in 96 Dist. Signed: Edward T. McClure, Joshia McClure, Margaret (+) McClure. Wit: Jas. Hamilton, Jno. McWhorter, William McClure. James Hamilton made oath to Joshua Saxon, J. P., 31 Mar. 1797. Rec: 5 Jul. 1797.

Page 340: 14 Jan. 1792. William Riggs to Samuel Elrod for £ 60 for 150 acres in 96 Dist. on 26 Mile Creek on Beaverdam Creek of Savannah River, bd. by John Hunnicutt, Saml. Elrod, Col. Robt. Anderson, William Riggs, part of tract granted Riggs by Wm. Moultrie. Wit: James Anderson, Saml. Riggs. James Anderson made oath to J. B. Earle, J. P., 4 May 1797. Rec: 5 Jul. 1797.

Page 340: I, Peter Bremar, of Town of Columbia, S. C., for £ 50 sold to Daniel McCoy, 600 acres in 96 Dist. on Rocky River, bd. on SW by Norris and Mary Smith, on SE by Joseph Culton, on N. by Norris, surveyed, 6 Feb. 1786. Wit: James Sanders Guignard, John (his mark) McCoy. John McCoy made oath to Joshua Saxon, J. P., 28 Jun. 1797. Rec: 5 Jul. 1797.

Page 340: 20 May 1797. Thomas Robinson to Thomas Kenady for £ 40 stg. for 150 acres part of tract granted Benjamin Whorton for 383 acres. Recorded Bk. F, no. 5, p. 389, on Oconey Creek, branch of Little River, fork of Keowee River. Wit: Isaac (his mark) Harnage, Samuel Gibson. Thomas Robertson made oath to J. B. Earle, J. P., 20 Jun. 1797. Rec: 5 Jul. 1797.

Page 340: 10 Apr. 1791. William Adams of Abbeville Co. to William Dickey of Pendleton Co. for £ 40 stg. for 250 acres granted Adams by Wm. Moultrie, 5 Jun. 1786 on Little Generostee. Wit: Nathaniel Weed, James McCarter, David Clark. Nathaniel Weed, Sr. made oath to F. M. Bates, J.P., (of Abbeville Co.?), 10 Jun. 1791. Rec: 20 Jul. 1797.

Page 341: I, William Dickie and Ann, my wife for $200 sold to Alexander Sherard 250 acres; 150 ac. granted Andrew Hamilton, 21 Jan. 1785. Recorded Bk. CCCC, p. 234; 100 acres granted Aaron Alexander, 21 Jan. 1785, Recorded Bk. AAAA, p. 541, adj. each other. Date: 12 Jul. 1797. Signed: William Dickey, Ann (her mark) Dickey. Wit: Elizabeth (her mark) Boyd, W. Richard. William Richard made oath to Jno. Barton, J. P., 13 Jul.1797. Rec: 20 Jul. 1797.

Page 341: 1 Jul. 1790. Alexander McCrery and Margaret, his wife, to Alexander Sherard for £ 40 for 200 acres, granted James Hammanger by Benj. Guerard, 21 Jan. 1785, conveyed to McCrery, 19 Sep. 1787, on Generostee. Signed: Alexr. McCrery, Margaret (M) McCrery. Wit: John Willey, John Sherard. John Wiley made oath to Elijah Browne, J.P., 16 Feb. 1797. Rec: 20 Jul. 1797.

Page 341:   21 Apr. 1791. William Simpson to Alexander
                                 Sherrard for ₤ 40 stg. for 178 acres granted
                                 Simpson, 4 Oct. 1790 by Charles Pinckney on
Little Generostee. Wit: William Dickey, John Simpson. William Dickey
made oath to Elijah Browne, J. P., 16 Feb. 1792.
Rec: 20 Jul. 1797.

Page 341:   I, John Sherrard, Sr. for $500 sold to John
                                 Sherrard, Jr., 640 acres granted 2 May 1785.
                                 Recorded Bk. DDDD, p. 265. Date: 20 December
1796. Wit: John Watt, Andrew Hood. John Watt made oath to E. Browne, JP,
28 Dec. 1796.
Rec: 20 Jul. 1797.

Pages 341-342:   12 Aug. 1794. John Pickens, Sr., planter, and
                                 Sarah, his wife, to Isaac Harnage for ₤ 30
                                 for 109 acres granted John Pickens by William
Moultrie, 7 Jan. 1793 on Oconney Creek of Little River of Keowee of Savan-
nah in 96 Dist., bd. on NW by Doctr. Martin, vacant lands. Signed: John
Pickens, Sarah Pickens. Wit: John McCollum, Eliab Moore. Col. Eliab
Moore made oath to Joshua Reed, J. P., 27 Jun. 1797.
Rec: 20 Jul. 1797.

Page 342:   24 Aug. 1793. John Young of Spartanburgh Co.
                                 S. C. to Hardy Owens of Pendleton Co. for
                                 ₤ 47 stg. for 350 acres on both sides of 18
Mile Creek, granted by Wm. Moultrie, 1786. Wit: H. M. Wood, George Salmon. Greenville Co., S. C., Henry Machen Wood made oath to George Salmon, J. P., 7 Jun. 1794.
Rec: 20 Jul. 1797.

Page 342:   10 Feb. 1797. Anthony Golding, of Lawrence
                                 Co., S. C. to James Hobson of Pendleton Co.,
                                 for $80 for 150 acres on W. side of 23 Mile
Creek of the Keowee River, part of 640 acres granted Mary Prichard, 5 Oct.
1784, conveyed to Golding, bd. on E. by James Hobson, on W. by Jane Deale,
on SW by John Portman. Wit: Thomas (his mark) Hobson, John Woodall. John
Woodall made oath to J. B. Earle, J. P., 17 Jul. 1797.
Rec: 20 Jul. 1797.

Pages 342-343:   5 Dec. 1795. Robert Kirkwood, Hugh Kirkwood
                                 and Nathan Kirkwood to John Bowie, Esq. of
                                 Abbeville Co. for ₤ 50 for 200 acres in Wash-
ington Dist. on Connoross Creek of Keowee River, bd. on NW by John Bowie,
vacant land, granted John Bowie as Executor of Estate of Hugh Kirkwood,
deceased, for his children which by last will now on record in the Office
of the Clerk of Common Pleas, in 96 Dist., was ordered to be equally divided among his children, Robert Kirkwood, Hugh Kirkwood, and Nathan Kirkwood. Signed: Robert Kirkwood, Nathan Kirkwood (only). Wit: Thomas Jeffres, Sally Reed, George Bowie. Miss Sally Reed made oath to Hugh Wardlaw, J. P. of Abbeville Co., 26 Jul. 1797.
Rec: 27 Jul. 1797.

Page 343:   I, John Hunnicutt for ₤ 25 sold to David Smith
                                 102 acres on the NW branch of 23 Mile Creek,
                                 of the Savannah River, bd. on SE by Thomas
Hamilton, on N. by David Smith, vacant land, granted Hunnicutt, 2 July
1787 by Thomas Pinckney. Recorded Bk. VVVV, p. 73. Date: 12 Aug. 1797.
Wit: Job Smith, James Cansler, Wm. Rankin. Wm. Rankin made oath to John
Willson, J. P., 15 Aug. 1797.
Rec: 18 Aug. 1797.

Page 343:   South Carolina. I, William Payne of Georgia,
                                 for ₤ 20 stg. sold to Orman Morgan of "State
                                 aforesaid", 200 acres on N. side of Tugalo
River, bd. by James Alexander, Jacob Buchannon. Date: 22 Feb. 1797. Wit:
Thomas Harbin, Francis Calloway. Francis Calloway made oath to Nathl.
Perry, 10 Aug. 1797.
Rec: 18 Aug. 1797.

Pages 343-344:   I, Orman Morgan of Pendleton Co. for Ł 20 sold to Caleb Barton 200 acres bd. on SW on Tugalo River and vacant land, granted William Payne, 4 Feb. 1786 by Edward Telfair, Governor of Georgia and recorded in the Secretary's Office of South Carolina, 24 Jan. 1788. Date: 29 April 1797. Wit: Henry C. Barton, Lewis Rolston. Henry C. Barton made oath to Nathl. Perry, J. P., 29 Apr. 1797.
Rec: 18 Aug. 1797.

Page 344:   13 Jul. 1797. Robert Scott of Lawrence Co., S. C. to Elizabeth Polock of Pendleton Co. for Ł 100 stg. for 200 acres on S. Broadaway of the Savannah River, granted James Scott, now deceased, upon the Bounty granted Soldiers of this State, now possessed by Robert Scott, being the whole and sole heir to James Scott, granted 2 May 1785 by Wm. Moultrie. Recorded Bk. BBBB, p. 275. Wit: Patrick Scott, Jos. Galligly, James Pollock....Lawrence Co., S. C., Patrick Scott made oath to Joseph Dillard, J. P., 13 Jul. 1797.
Rec: 25 Aug. 1797.

Page 344:   I, Thomas Farrar for Ł 20 stg. sold to Mary Thompson 220 acres on Generostee Creek, part of tract granted Gilbert Neyle, bd. by land surveyed for Drayton, David Pruit, John Ross (or Rose). Date: 1 October 1796. Wit: James Ross, William B. Ross. James Ross made oath to Joshua Saxon, J. P., 17 Aug. 1797.
Rec: 22 Aug. 1797.

Page 344:   I, Mary Thompson, widow, for Ł 8 stg. sold to Peter Keys & Co., 14½ acres, part of tract granted Gilbert Neyle, 3rd Monday in Apr. 1786 by Wm. Moultrie, on Big Rocky fork of Generostee, of Savannah River, bd. by Peter Keys, Mary Thompson, David Pruit. Wit: James Long, David Ross. Plat. James Long made oath to Joshua Saxon, J. P., 10 Aug. 1797.
Rec: 22 Aug. 1797.

Page 344:   Whereas, Peter Bayley, late of the City of Charleston, S. C., Attorney at Law by his last will and testament dated 13 Jun. 1785, among other bequests, gave Thomas Drayton, 2nd. son of William Drayton, Esq., Banister (Barrister?) at Law, tract of 640 acres in 96 District, lately granted to him....Thomas Drayton has since departed life, intestate, and said tract became right of Jacob Drayton, Hannah Drayton, Mary Charlotte Wilson, Sarah Motte Drayton and William Drayton, his surviving brothers and sisters, who have agreed to sell for Ł 55 stg. to Peter Keys of Pendleton Co. 640 acres in 96 Dist. on branch of Big Generostee Creek, of the Savannah River above the ancient Boundary line, granted 15 Oct. 1784 to Peter Bayley. Date: 6 Jul. 1797. Signed: Jacob Drayton, H. Drayton, S. M. Drayton, M. C. Wilson, W. Drayton. Wit: James Long, W. Young. James Long made oath to Joshua Saxon, J. P., 10 Aug. 1797.
Rec: 22 Aug. 1797.

Pages 344-345:   I, William Turpin, Merchant, for consideration of same value in land conveyed to me by Thomas Wadsworth sold him my right to the following tracts of land, they being tracts jointly held by Thomas Wadsworth and William Turpin (viz) - in Washington Dist.: one tract of 640 ac. on Big Beaverdam Creek, waters of Savannah surveyed by John Martin, and granted to Timothy Knap, 4 Jul. 1785; one tract of 250 ac. surveyed by Joshua Saxon for William Turpin, granted 6 Feb. 1786, on branches of the Generostee; one tract of 640 ac. on 23 Mile Creek, surveyed by John Hunter, granted Stephen Wadsworth, 7 Nov. 1785; one tract of 267 ac. surveyed by John Hunter, granted Susannah Wadsworth, 7 Nov. 1785, on 12 Mile Creek; one of 375 ac. on 23 Mile Creek, surveyed by Joshua Saxon, granted Thomas Wadsworth, 7 Nov. 1785; one of 300 ac. on branches of Generostee Creek of Savannah River, surveyed by Joshua Saxon, granted to Thomas Wadsworth, 28 May 1785; one of 300 ac. on branches of Generostee, surveyed by Saxon, granted Thomas Wadsworth, 3 Oct. 1785; one of 483 acs. on Beaverdam and 23 Mile Creeks, surveyed by Saxon, granted Thomas Wadsworth,

(Pages 344-345 cont'd): 7 Nov. 1785. Date: 2 May 1797. Signed: Willm. Turpin. Wit: James Boyce, William Turpin, Jr. ....I, Peter Brounetheau, one of the Justices of the Quorum of the State of South Carolina certify that Mary Turpin, wife of William Turpin, released her dower, 8 May 1797....Lawrence Co., S. C., James Boyce made the oath to William Neil, J. P., 21 Aug. 1797.
Rec: 27 Sep. 1797.

Page 344: I, James Millwee for Ł 70 stg. sold to Josiah N. Kennedy, in Greenville Co., S. C., 648 ac. in Pendleton Co. on 26 Mile Creek, granted to Millwee, 6 Apr. 1789 by Charles Pinckney. Recorded Bk. ZZZZ, p. 226. Date: 8 Apr. 1797. Wit: Joshua Kennedy, Joseph Kennedy. Joseph Kennedy made oath to Wm. Hall, J. P., 1 Aug. 1797.
Rec: 24 Aug. 1797.

Page 344: I, William E. Kennedy of Washington Co., Ga. for Ł 50 stg. sold to Josiah N. Kennedy, Merchant of Greenville Co., S. C., 644 acs. in Pendleton Co., part of tract granted William E. Kennedy, 7 Sep. 1789 by Charles Pinckney. Recorded Bk. ZZZZ, p. 502. Date: 11 Apr. 1797. Wit: Andw. Kennedy, John Birdsong. Andrew Kennedy made oath to Wm. Hall, JP, 1 Aug. 1797.
Rec: 24 Aug. 1797.

Pages 344-345: 10 Jun. 1792. John Hunnicutt to George Nelson for Ł 60 for 208 acres in 96 Dist. on 26 Mile Creek of the Savannah River, bd. on NW by David Clarke and John Hunnicutt and vacant land, granted Hunnicutt by Thos. Pinckney, 7 Apr. 1788. Wit: H. Hunnicutt, Rolin Hunnicutt. Rolin Hunnicutt made oath to John Willson, J. P., 22 Feb. 1794.
Rec: 24 Aug. 1797.

Page 346: 5 Jul. 1794. George Nelson to Patrick McCoy for Ł 80 for 281 acres in Washington (Co.?) on 26 Mile Creek of the Savannah River, bd. NW by David Clarke, John Hunnicutt, granted Hunnicutt. Signed: Geo. (his mark) Nelson. Wit: Geo. Forbes, Fredrick (X) Keel. George Forbes made oath to John Willson, J. P., 8 Nov. 1794.
Rec: 24 Aug. 1797.

Page 346: I, John Hunnicutt for Ł 60 sold to Patrick McCoy 208 acres on 26 Mile Creek of Savannah River, bd. on NW by David Clarke, all other sides by John Hunnicutt, surveyed by Jonathan Clarke, granted Hunnicutt by Thomas Pinckney, 7 Apr. 1788. Date: 10 Aug. 1797. Wit: John Morrow, John Jones. John Morrow made oath to J. B. Earle, J. P., 24 Aug. 1797.
Rec: 24 Aug. 1797.

Pages 346-347: 10 Feb. 1796. James Martin of York Co., S. C. to James Rogers of Pendleton Co. for Ł 40 for 372 acres on 23 Mile Creek, granted Martin, 6 Mar. 1780, by Wm. Moultrie, with all rights "which remains out of the lines of land claimed by Wadsworth and Turpin and Pritchard and a survey where Samuel Robertson lives"..."said James Martin and (blank) Martin, his wife" grant to James Rogers. Wit: Adam Rogers, Richard Robinson. Adam Rogers made oath to J. B. Earle, J. P., 29 Aug. 1797.
Rec: 29 Aug. 1797.

Page 347: I, Andrew Boddin of Camden, S. C. for Ł 28 sold to James Blair of Pendleton Co., 200 ac. in 96 Dist. on N. branches of Toxaway Creek, surveyed for James Madison, 2 Apr. 1793. Granted John Calvert by Arnoldus Vanderhorst on Monday, 6 Jul. 1795. Date: 9 Aug. 1797. Wit: Jas. Wyly (Wily in oath), Thos. Crews. Thomas Crews made oath to Jno. Barton, JP, 29 Aug. 1797.
Rec: 30 Aug. 1797.

Page 347: Lawrence Co., S. C. I, Thomas Entrekin for Ł 50 stg. sold Wm. Millwee of Pendleton Co.,

(Page 347 cont'd): 200 ac. on 26 Mile Creek of Savannah River. Date: 11 Mar. 1796. Wit: William Neill, Samuel Neill....Mary (+) Entrekin released dower to John Hunter, J. P. of Lawrence Co., 11 Mar. 1796. William Neill, Esq. made oath to John Hunter, J. P., 11 Mar. 1796.
Rec: 1 Sep. 1797.

Pages 347-348: I, William Millwee and Martha, my wife, for Ł 50 stg. sold to Randol Hunnicutt 200 acres on S. side of 26 Mile Creek of Savannah River granted Thomas Entrekin, 21 Jan. 1785 by Benj. Guerrard. Date: 18 Jan. 1797. Signed: Wm. Millwee, Martha (her mark) Millwee. (her mark appears to be "O") Wit: Henry Sims, Aaron Guyton...Martha (M) Millwee (mark is different here) released dower to W. Steele, J. P., 24 Jan. 1797. Aaron Guton made oath to John Willson, J. P., 24 Jan. 1797.
Rec: 2 Sep. 1797.

Page 348: 28 Jan. 1792. William White to Patrick Early for 10 shillings for 100 acres part of 200 ac. granted John Love, 7 Apr. 1788 by Thos. Pinckney on Savannah River. Signed: William (X) White, Mary (X) White. Wit: James Shields, Hugh Atkins, Daniel Putman. James Shields made oath to John Willson, J. P., 8 Mar. 1792.
Rec: 4 Sep. 1797.

Page 348: 23 Apr. 1795. Collin Campbell to Cornelius Keeth for Ł 20 stg. for 100 acres where Joseph Dunn now lives, part of 200 acres granted John Norwood, heir at law of Daniel Norwood, Soldier, 15 Oct. 1784, on Ooleney Creek, of Saluda. Wit: William Keith, John Keeth. William Keith made oath to W. W. Reed, J. P., 23 Apr. 1795.
Rec: 4 Sep. 1797.

Pages 348-349: 96 Dist., S. C. 22 Jul. 1789, William Brown and Margaret, his wife, to William Lesley, joiner, (later, Ju'r.) for 640 acres on Broadaway Creek of Great Rocky Creek, granted Margaret Lesley (now wife of William Brown), 5 Jun. 1786 by Wm. Moultrie. Recorded Bk. KKKK, p. 693. Signed: Wm. Brown, Margaret Brown. Wit: Thomas Lesley, Wm. McKee...,.96 Dist. Abbeville Co., William McKee made oath to Samuel Watts, J. P., 1 Jul. 1794.
Rec: 11 Sep. 1797.

Page 349: 12 Nov. 1793. John Norwood of Abbeville Co., to Benjamin Clarke, of Pendleton Co. for Ł 40 stg. for 100 acres, part of tract granted to Norwood, 16 Jul. 1784 on S. side of Saluda River, adj. John Wheeler, Col. Henry Clark. Wit: jon. Clarke, John Wheeler, Absolom Blythe. John Clarke made oath to W. W. Reed, J. P., 7 Mar. 1796.
Rec: 12 Sep. 1797.

Page 349: 16 May 1795. Bailey Anderson, Esq. to Bennett Combs for Ł 200 stg. for 345 acres, part of tract granted George Reobuck, 7 May 1786 in Washington Dist., bd. by John Robertson, Bailey Anderson. Signed: Bayley Anderson, Mary Anderson. Wit: Jesse Murphree, Leonard (X) Farer. Jesse Murphree made oath to Wm. Reid, J. P., 7 Oct. 1797.
Rec: 7 Oct. 1797.

Page 350: I, Martin Hewlet for Ł 60 stg. sold to Bennett Combs 112 acres on 12 Mile River, granted to Samuel Earle by Wm. Moultrie, 5 Feb. 1787. Date: 7 Oct. 1797. Wit: Daniel Ship, John Easley, Abram Duff. Abraham Duff made oath to W. W. Reid, J. P., 7 Oct. 1797.
Rec: 7 Oct. 1797.

Page 350: I, Jehu Pope of Pendleton Co. for Ł 50 stg. sold to George Reese 333 acres on branch of 18 Mile Creek of Keowee River, adj. on SW to

(Page 350 cont'd): George Benison, part of 494 acres granted to Pope by Wm. Moultrie, 4 Mar. 1793. Wit: Thomas (X) Alexander, J. Whitner. Joseph Whitner made oath to G. W. Earle, D.C.C., 18 Sep. 1797. Rec: 18 Sep. 1797.

Page 350: I, Jehu Pope, late of State and County for Ł 175 sold to George Reese 200 acres on W. side of 18 Mile Creek, granted George Bennison, bd. by Peter Singlar, conveyed to Pope, 2 Feb. 1789. Recorded in Abbeville, Bk. 2, p. 147 and 148. Date: 18 Feb. 1797. Wit: Joseph Whitner, Thomas L. Reese. Joseph Whitner made oath to G. W. Earle, D.C.C., 18 Sep. 1797. Rec: 18 Sep. 1797.

Pages 3501-351: 3 Apr. 1797. William Chapman and Darkey, his wife, to Robert Baker for Ł 40 stg. 96 acres part of two grants, "one by Moultrie, the other by Thos. Pinckney, 5 Mar. 1787" on 18 Mile Creek, bd. by Robert Baker, and Ambrose Dudley. Signed: William (+) Chapman and Darky (+) Chapman. Wit: Geo. Payne, Ambrose Dudley. Ambrose Dudley made oath to John Willson, J.P., 6 Jul. 1797. Rec: 18 Sep. 1797.

Page 351: 25 Jun. 1796. Edward Camp to Benjamin Turner for Ł 60 stg for 173 acres on SE side of Milwee's Creek. Wit: John Turner, Simon Doyle. John Turner made oath to John Willson, J.P., 18 Sep. 1797. Rec: 18 Sep. 1797.

Pages 351-352: 1 Mar. 1795. James Polock and Elizabeth Polock, Administrators of the Estate of John Pollock, deceased, to Nathaniel Robison for Ł 40 for 225 acres on 26 Mile Creek, part of 1000 acres granted John Pollock, dec'd. by Thomas Pinckney, 2 Jun. 1788. Recorded Bk. KKKK, p. 92. Signed: Elizabeth Pogue, James Pogue. Wit: James Linn, Jas. Brouster, James Millwee....Plat shows land adj. Randol Hunnicutt on N., on W. by Jas. Pollock, on E. by Calhoun, on SE by Wimer Lober, on S. by James Brouster. Receipt signed by Elizabeth Pogue, James Pogue. Jas. Linn made oath to Wm. Millwee, J.P., 25 Mar. 1795. Rec: 18 Sep. 1797.

Page 352: 2 Oct. 1792. Thomas Moss to Jonathan Watson for Ł 30 stg. for 50 acres, part of 170 ac. granted Samuel Moss, 1787, on Big Generostee, of Savannah River, bd. by Richland Creek, John Tippen, Matthew Morgan. Signed: Thomas (X) Moss. Wit: John Sutherland, Price Williams, Jesse Brown. Jesse Brown made oath to John Varner, J.P., 11 Dec. 1797. Rec: 12 Dec. 1797.

Page 352: 31 Aug. 1792. Phillip Phagens to Stephen Leverette for Ł 20 stg. for 200 acres in 96 Dist. on Ready Fork of Willson's Creek, branch of Rocky River, part of 792 acres granted John Caldwell by Charles Pinckney, Recorded Bk. ZZZZ, p. 321. Signed: Phillip (P) Phagan. Wit: George Tillmon, William Bladen, William Bladen made oath to E. Browne, J.P., 20 Sep. 1797. Rec: 20 Sep. 1797.

Pages 352-353: 22 Jul. 1795. William Bladen to Henry Millford for Ł 30 stg. for 300 acres adj. old Boundary Line, part of 504 acres granted to Bladen, 5 Nov. 1792. Recorded Bk. E, no. 5, p. 379. On branch of Great Rocky Creek, and Willson's Creek. Wit: Stephen Leverette, John Harkness. Plat shows land adj. on E. by Wm. Bladon, on SE by James Martin, on W. by Phagan. Stephen Leverette made oath to E. Browne, J.P., 20 Sep. 1797. Rec: 20 Sep. 1797.

Page 353: 5 Nov. 1795. John Patterson to Elijah Mayfield for Ł 90 stg. for 158 acres conveyed to Patterson by Joseph Woodall, 14 Aug. 1790, on S. fork of 12 Mile River. Wit: John Cochran, Joshua Dyer, Josiah Dyer. John

(Page 353 cont'd): Cockran made oath to W. W. Reid, J.P., 25 Sept. 1797. Rec: 27 Sep. 1797.

Pages 353-354: 27 Sep. 1797. Elijah Mayfield and Elizabeth, his wife, to George Miller for Ł 90 stg. for 159 acres on S. fork of 12 Mile River, conveyed by John Patterson, 5 Nov. 1795. Signed: Elijah (X) Mayfield, Elizabeth (X) Mayfield. Wit: J. Mauldin, James Wood...Washington Dist., Elizabeth Mayfield released dower to Wm. Steele, J.P., 27 Sep. 1797. Joab Mauldin made oath to Wm. Steele, J.P., 27 Sep. 1797.
Rec: 27 Sep. 1797.

Page 354: Washington Dist. I, George Miller, planter, for Ł 100 stg. sold to Thomas Hinesly, 425 acres in two surveys joining each other, one granted Miller, 5 Feb. 1787, by Wm. Moultrie, the other granted 22 Oct. 1792, by Chas. Pinckney, on Golding's Creek of 12 Mile River. Date: 27 Sep. 1797. Wit: J. Mauldin, Saml. Neel...Washington Dist., Mary (M) Miller, wife of George Miller, released dower to Wm. Steele, J.P., 27 Sep. 1797. Joab Mauldin made oath, 27 Sep. 1797.
Rec: 27 Sep. 1797.

Page 354: I, John Buchannan, of Fairfield Co., S. C., Administrator of the Estate of Robert Buchannan, for $200 sold to Jesse Coffee, of Pendleton Co., planter, 200 acres on Middle Fork of Connoross Creek of Keowee River, granted Robert Buchannon, Soldier, dec'd, by Benj. Guerard on 21 Feb. 1785. Date: 7 Oct. 1797. Wit: John Pratt, Jno. Robb, Wm. McMorries...Fairfield Co., John Pratt made oath to Wm. Robertson, J.P., 7 Oct. 1797. Rec: 14 Oct. 1797.

Pages 354-355: 5 Apr. 1797. George Ross of York Co., S. C. to William Jolly, Sr. of Pendleton Co., for Ł 50 stg. 257 acres on 26 Mile Creek, granted Ross on 1 May 1786 by Wm. Moultrie. Recorded Bk. JJJJ, p. 466. Wit: John Bird, James Clark, Wilson Jolly. Wilson Jolly made oath to William Millwee, J.P., 24 Oct. 1797.
Rec: 24 Oct. 1797.

Page 355: I, William Steele, Merchant, for $120 sold to Samuel Neel, planter, 138 acres on NE branch of 18 Mile Creek of Savannah River, bd. on NW by Isaac Lynch, on NE by David Brag, John Lewis Gervais, on SE by Samuel Lofton, granted Robert Glenn, 16 Feb. 1786, by Charles Pinckney. Date: 15 Feb. 1797. Wit: James Wood, Joab Mauldin. Joab Mauldin made oath to John Varner, J.P., 25 Oct. 1797.
Rec: 25 Oct. 1797.

Page 355: 29 May 1797: Joseph Webb to William Mulican, Jr. for Ł 40 stg. for 300 acres, part of the tract granted James Jordan "on land belonging to Jas. Chandler and land belonging to Isham Irby", on the Seneca River. Wit: Sion (+) Holly, James Chandler...Washington Dist., Sion Holly made oath he saw Joseph Webb "otherwise called Joel Webb" sign above deed to G. W. Earle, D.C.C., 1 Nov. 1797.
Rec: 1 Nov. 1797.

Page 355: I, Jacob Capehart for $350 sold to Joab Mauldin 120 acres on 26 Mile Creek, bd. on E. by Calhoun, on N. by Robert Dickerson, on S. by John Turner, part of 288 acres granted Edward Camp by Wm. Moultrie, 7 Aug. 1796, conveyed to Capehart. Date: 9 Aug. 1797. Wit: D. McCaleb, John Griffen...Plat. Washington Dist., Margaret (X) Capehart, wife of Jacob Capehart, released dower to Wm. Steele, J.P., 12 Aug. 1797. David McCaleb made oath to G. W. Earle, D.C.C., 18 Aug. 1797.
Rec: 4 Nov. 1797.

Page 356: I, Martha Henderson, Widow of the late William Henderson, and Nathaniel Henderson, her son for $28 and 50¢ sold to John Counrod Ader-

(Page 356 cont'd): holt, taylor (tailor), 100 acres on 12 Mile River (now known as Rice's Creek), granted to William Henderson by Wm. Moultrie, 5 Jun. 1786,for 450 acres. Recorded Bk. MMMM p. 37. Date: 10 Jun. 1797. Signed: Martha (+) Henderson, Nathaniel Henderson. Wit: Abraham Duk, Margaret (+) Henderson, Jane(O) Henderson. Abraham Duk made oath to John Willson, J. P., 10 Aug. 1797. (No recording date).

Page 356: I, Thomas S. Reese, Sheriff of Pendleton Co. sold to Joel Webb 640 acres on Saluda River below the mouth of 18 Mile Creek, "sold as property of Jas. Jordan at the instance of Waddy Thompson". Date: 6 May 1797. Wit: W. Thompson, William (X) Mullican....Washington District: William Mullican made oath to G. W. Earle, D.C.C., 1 Nov. 1797. Rec: 4 Nov. 1797.

Page 356: I, James Lindsey for ℔ 200 stg., sold to Thomas Blasingame, 377 acres on the branches of the Saluda River, bd. by Zebulon Gervison, Robert Easley. Date: 16 Aug. 1796. Wit: Robert Easley, John Blasingame.....Washington Dist.: Elizabeth (e) Lindsey, wife of James Lindsey, released dower to Andw. Pickens, Judge of Pendleton Co., 15 Nov. 1796. John Blasingame made oath to R. Bowen, J.P., 13 Nov. 1797. Rec: 14 Nov. 1797.

Pages 356-357: I, James Lindsey, of Jackson Co., Ga., for $300 sold to Thomas Blasingame, of Pendleton Co., 175 acres on Saluda River. Date: 9 Nov. 1797. Wit: John Blasingame, Francis (X) Blalock....Washington Dist.:... Elizabeth (e) Lindsey released dower to Benja. Cleveland, Judge of Pendleton County. John Blasingame made oath to R. Bowen, J.P., 13 Nov. 1797. Rec: 14 Nov. 1797.

Page 357: 2 Dec. 1796. Hamilton Reid to Moses Murphree for ℔ 50 stg. for 859 acres on S. fork of 12 Mile River, granted to Reid by Charles Pinckney, 12 Jun. 1792. Wit: Daniel Stuart, Izan (+) Murphree. Daniel Stuart made oath to W. W. Reid, J.P., 13 Feb. 1797. Rec: 14 Nov. 1797.

Page 357: We, Isabellah McChesney, William Asher and wife and William Young and wife, for valuable consideration and one dollar sold to Walter McChesney 100 acres in Rockbridge Co., Virginia, on Walker's Creek being plantation of Walter McChesney, deceased, joining Henry Camponel and William Wardlaw. Date: 10 Nov. 1797. Signed: Isabel McChesney, William Ashurst, Mary Ashurst, William Young, Jean Young. Wit: Robt. Akin, Thomas (H) Hood. Robert Akins made oath to R. Bowe, J.P., 13 Nov. 1797. Rec: 20 Nov. 1797.

Pages 357-358: I, James Hobson, planter, for 40 Federal dollars sold to Christopher Ramey 100 acres on W. side of 23 Mile Creek of Keowee River, a part of 640 acres granted to Mary Preachard by Benjamin Guerard, bd. on NW by Jane Deale, on SW by John Woodall. Date: 1 Dec. 1797. Signed: James (his mark) Hobson. Wit: Lewis Cobb, Nathaniel (his mark-fancy "N") Davis. Lewis Cobb made oath to Geo. W. Earle, D.C.C., 2 Dec. 1797. (No recording date)

Page 358: I, Josiah Ship, for $5.00 sold to Isaac Alewatters, 258 acres on 23 Mile Creek, bd. on W. by Josiah Ship, on NW by Isaac Alewatters, surveyed 9 Nov. 1797 by Jonathan Clark, D. S. Date: 6 Dec. 1797. Wit: J. W. Grissam Mary (X) Grissam, Susannah (+) Grissam. John W. Grissam made oath to G. W. Earle, D.C.C., 6 Dec. 1797. Rec: 6 Dec. 1797.

Page 358: 2 Nov. 1797. William Gillispey, Sr. of Pendleton County to Thomas and James Gillispey of the State of Virginia, for ℔ 20 stg. for

(Page 358 cont'd): 354 acres on George's Creek of the Saluda River, bd. by Gillespy, Moss, Thomas Gillespy, John Boyd, John Gillespey to Seneca Road. Signed: William (X) Gillespey. Wit: Wm. Payne, Thomas Boyd. William Payne made oath to John Willson, J. P., 11 Nov. 1797. Rec: 6 Dec. 1797.

Page 358: I, William Gillispie, Sr. sold to William Gillispie, Jr., a negro boy named Jack for $300 ...Dated: 4 Nov. 1797. Signed: William (/) Gillispie. Wit: Wm. Payne, James Cooper. James Cooper made oath to John Willson, J. P., 13 November 1797. Rec.: 6 Dec. 1797.

Pages 358-359: 10 Aug. 1793. John Hunnicutt, planter, to John Morrow for Ł 100 stg. for 227 acres, surveyed by Jonathan Clark, granted 7 Sep. 1789 by Charles Pinckney. Recorded Bk. ZZZZ, (no page number), on 26 Mile Creek of Savannah River, bd. on E. by David Clark and lands unknown. Wit: Andrew Wornock, David Smith. Andrew Wornock made oath to J. B. Earle, JP. 24 Aug. 1797. Rec: 24 Aug. 1797. ("Neglected to be recorded at time given, although it bears the same date").

Page 359: I, John Hunnicutt, planter, for Ł 100 stg. for 227 acres surveyed by John Clark, on 26 Mile Creek of the Savannah River, bd. on E. by David Clark and unknown, granted by Charles Pinckney, 12 Nov. 1789.Recorded Bk. ZZZZ, p. 503. Date: 10 Aug. 1797. Wit: Patrick McCoy, John Jones. Patrick McCoy made oath to J. B. Earle, J.P., 24 Aug. 1797. Rec: 24 Aug. 1797.

Page 359: I, David Hamilton, of Washington Dist. for $250 sold to Alexander Glenn, 148 acres on both sides of Rice's Creek, of 12 Mile River, bd. by Charles Rice. (No date). Wit: Enoch Berry, Jon Stuart. Enoch Berry made oath to R. Bowen, J.P., 7 Oct. 1797. Rec: 11 Dec. 1797.

Pages 359-360: I, Robert McCrary of Lawrence Co., S. C. for Ł 60 sold to Samuel Dean of Pendleton Co. 440 acres part of 640 acres granted McCrary by Wm. Moultrie, 7 Aug. 1786, on Mountain Creek of Savannah River, recorded Bk. MMMM, p. 28, bd. by Samuel Dean, Harmon Cummins, Saml. Houston, Jonathan Watson, Brymer, Files. Date: 29 Mar. 1797. Wit: John Bollan, John McCrary, John (P) Portman....Lawrence Co., S. C., John Bourland made the oath to George Whitmire, J. P., 29 Mar. 1797. Rec: 18 Dec. 1797.

Page 360: 17 Jun. 1794. Jacob Herring to Samuel Dean for Ł 20 stg. for 125 acres, part of a tract granted to Capt. Rainey (date blank), on Big Generostee of Savannah River, bd. by land where Richard Beauduet(?) now lives. Wit: Thos. Linard, Griffith James. Thomas Leonard made oath to E. Browne, J.P., 26 Oct. 1797. Rec: 18 Dec. 1797.

Page 360: 15 Aug. 1794. William McCaleb to Daniel Delaney for Ł 15 stg. for 100 acres on branch of Choestoe Creek, part of a tract granted to McCaleb, 2 Jul. 1787 by Thos. Pinckney, now in possession of Delaney. Wit: W. H. Lacy, Benja. Perry. Wm. Hughs Lacy made oath to Nathl. Perry, 2 Mar. 1796. Rec: 18 Dec. 1797.

Page 361: 4 Dec. 1795. Jacob Holland, Jr. of Abbeville Co., S. C. to Daniel Delaney for Ł 60 stg. for 200 acres, on small creek of Connoross of Savannah River, granted Holland, 4 Jul. 1795 by Wm. Moultrie. Wit: Jacob Holland, Thomas Holland. Jacob Holland made oath to Nathl. Perry, 1 Jan. 1796. Rec: 18 Dec. 1797.

Page 361: 10 Oct. 1795. Joshua Lee to Daniel Delaney

(Lee-Delaney cont'd): for ₤ 60 stg. for 354 acres on NW branch of Choestoe Creek of Tugalo River, granted to Lee by Thos. Pinckney, 2 Jul. 1787, bd. on SW by Wm. McCaleb, and vacant lands. Signed: Joshua (X) Lee. Wit: W. H. Lacy, David Sims. W. H. Lacy made oath to Nathl. Perry, J.P., 2 Apr. 1796.
Rec: 18 Dec. 1797.

Pages 361-362: 19 Nov. 1792. Charles Rolland of Pendleton Co. to Isaac Jones of Elbert Co., Ga. for ₤ 80 for 162 acres part of a tract granted John Shannon by Chas. Pinckney. Signed: Charles (X) Rolland. Wit: Reuben Simpson, John Smith, Henry (+) Highsaw. Reuben Simpson made oath to Nath. Perry, J.P., 12 Aug. 1794.
Rec: 18 Dec. 1797.

Page 362: 8 Jan. 1795. Benjamin Howard and Lucy, his wife, of Abbeville Co., to Edmond Mannon, of Pendleton Co. for ₤ 40 stg. for 300 acres in Washington Dist., Pendleton Co., on branch of Connoross, called Goodland Creek, granted Benjamin Howard, by Wm. Moultrie, 3 Apr. 1786. Bd. on SW by Robert Coram. Recorded Bk. KKKK, p. 161. Signed: Benja. Howard, Lucy Howard. Wit: Martin Howard, Elijah (X) Walker, Jno. Mannon. Elijah Walker made oath to J. C. Kilpatrick, J. P., 9 Dec. 1797. (no rec. date).

Page 362: I, Moses Perkins for ₤ 80 stg. sold to Henry Gotcher 240 acres on both sides of Connoross Creek of Keowee River, granted Perkins by Wm. Moultrie, 1 Jan. 1793, bd. by Moses Perkins, Saml. Henson. Date: 3 Oct. 1796. Wit: Wm. Barton, John Barton, Jr. William Barton made oath to John Barton, J. P. (no date).
Rec: 18 Dec. 1797.

Page 362: I, Edmund Mannon for ₤ 30 sold to Elijah Walker 60 acres, part of 300 acres where Mannon now lives, on S. side of Goodland Creek, of Connoross Creek. Signed: Edmond (X) Mannon. Wit: Gideon Hogg, William Kilpatrick. Gideon Hogg made oath to J. C. Kilpatrick, J. P., 18 Dec. 1797.
Rec: 18 Dec. 1797.

Pages 362-363: 5 Apr. 1797. Joshua Burris to James Burris for ₤ 50 for 100 acres part of 640 acres granted Samuel Saxon by Wm. Moultrie, 7 Aug.1796 on Big Generostee Creek, of Savannah River, including plantation where James Burris now lives, by deed from Samuel Saxon to James McCarely then to Joshua Burris. Wit: Elijah Herring, Jesse Davis, Noah Nelson. Oath says Elijah Walker made oath to John Varner, 18 Dec. 1797.
Rec: 20 Dec. 1797.

Page 363: I, Bennett Combs of Washington Dist. for ₤3 sold to Williby Brotton 107 acres on NW side of 15 Mile Branch of Savannah River, part of tract granted Thomas Shirely by Benj. Guerard, 25 Jan. 1785. Date: 20 Dec. 1797. Wit: Wm. Hunter, Fredrick (F) Johnston. Doctor Wm. Hunter made oath to George W. Earle, D.C.C., 20 Dec. 1797.
Rec: 20 Dec. 1797.

Page 363: Washington Dist., I, Bennett Combs for ₤ 70 sold to Fredrick Johnston 213 acres on 15 Mile Branch of Savannah River, part of tract granted Thos. Shirely by Benj. Guerard, 25 Jan. 1788, bd. by Willoby Brotton. Date: 20 Dec. 1797. Wit: Wm. Hunter, Willoby (+) Brotton. Dr. William Hunter made oath to G. W. Earle, D.C.C., 20 Dec. 1797.
Rec: 20 Dec. 1797.

Page 363: Washington Dist., I, Henry Gasaway for ₤ 10 sold to Elias Hollingsworth (no amount given) on NW branch of 15 Mile Branch of Savannah River, granted by Charles Pinckney, 15 Sep. 1792 to Geo. Payne. Date: 27 Dec. 1797. Wit: Saml. Cherry, Adam Rogers; Saml. Cherry made oath to Geo. W. Earle, DCC, 27 Dec. 1797. Rec: 27 Dec. 1797.

Pages 363-364: 27 Dec. 1797. James Millwee, farmer, and his wife, Margaret, to Ezekiel Buffington, farmer, for Ł 50 stg. for 740 acres on S. side of the Keowee River on both sides of Little River, granted 15 Mar. 1787. Signed: Jas. Milwee, Margaret (m) Millwee. Wit: W. Steele, John Garvin. William Steele made oath to G. W. Earle, D.C.C., 28 Dec. 1797. Rec: 28 Dec. 1797.

Pages 364-365: 15 Mar. 1794. Isaac Harlston, planter, to Caleb Starr for Ł 75 for 400 acres on both sides of Cane Creek, of Keowee River. Wit: Tho. Corbett, William Harleston....Charleston Dist., S. C., Thomas Corbett made oath to James Downs, J.P., 17 Apr. 1794. Rec: 28 Dec. 1797.

Page 365: I, Thomas Morrow for $20 sold to Leonard Morrow half the priviledge of a mill and still seat with necessary bounds and timber. Date: 30 Sep. 1797. Wit: Elisha Cook, Samuel Glen. Samuel Glen made oath to John Verner, J.P., 7 Oct. 1797. Rec: 28 Dec. 1797.

Page 365: 8 Sep. 1796. Thomas Morrow, Sr. to Leonard Morrow for Ł 50 stg. for 138 acres on Devil's fork and Great Generostee Creek, bd. Thomas Morrow, Sr. Wit: Jas. Hart, Thomas Morrow. Thomas Morrow made oath to John Verner, J.P., 7 Oct. 1797. Rec: 28 Dec. 1797.

Page 365: I, Thomas Morrow for $80 sold to James Morrow 120 acres on Great Generostee Creek, part of Thomas Morrow's tract, bd. by Jno. Ferguson, Stevenson, Leonard Morrow, Thos. Morrow, Jr. Date: 30 Sep. 1797.

Page 365: 6 Sep. 1796. Thomas Morrow, Sr. to Thomas Morrow, Jr. for Ł 40 for 111 acres on Generostee Creek. Wit: Jas. Hart, Leod. Morrow. Leonard Morrow made oath to John Vernor, J.P., 7 Oct. 1797. Rec: 28 Dec. 1797.

Page 365: I, Boling Clarke for $300 sold to Joseph Clarke a negro fellow named Sambo. Date: 27 Dec. 1797. Wit: Richard Golden, Wm. Golden, Elizabeth Golden. Richard Golden made oath to G. W. Earle, D.C.C., 28 Dec. 1797. Rec: 28 Dec. 1797.

Pages 365-366: I, Boling Clarke for Ł 60 stg. sold to Joseph Clarke the lower part of 2 tracts, granted to Boling Clarke, 21 Jan. 1785 by Benj. Guerard. Recorded Bk. AAAA, p. 433 and 426, on branches of E. side of 23 Mile Crk. bd. by Jonathan Clarke, Joseph Clarke, 400 acres. Date: 5 Jan. 1796. Wit: Josiah Johnson, Jeptha Johnson, Boling Clarke, Jr. Josiah Johnson made oath to John Willson, J.P., 16 Jul. 1796. Rec: 28 Dec. 1797.

Page 366: 25 Aug. 1794. Thomas Kelly, of Franklin Co., Ga. to John McIroy of Pendleton Co. for Ł 50 stg. for 181 acres granted Thomas Kelly on 5 Feb. 1787 by Wm. Moultrie in Pendleton Co., on both sides of McAdams Crk. branch of the Saluda River and a small branch of George's Crk. Wit: Wm. (W) Taylor, Jesse Legrand. William Taylor made oath to Benja. Cleveland, J. P., 26 Aug. 1794. Rec: 28 Dec. 1797.

Page 366: 12 Oct. 1792. John McEarley (also McCarley), sadler, to Richard Prince, planter, for Ł 40 for 173 acres above the ancient boundary line on branches of Mountain Creek, of Big Generostee, branch of Savannah River, granted by Gov. Pinckney to Samuel Henry. Wit: John (X) Howard, (cont'd next page)

(Page 366 cont'd):   John (h) Holcomb. John Holcomb made oath to John Vernor, J. P., 27 May 1797.
Rec: 28 Dec. 1797.

Page 367: 18 Feb. 1793. John Holcomb, planter, to Richard Prince for Ł 20 for 100 acres above the ancient boundary line on Mountain Creek of Big Generostee, branch of the Savannah River, bd. where John Holcomb formerly lived, granted by Charles Pinckney. Signed: John (h) Holcomb. Wit: Josiah Prince, Thomas (X) Skelton. Josiah Prince made oath to John Verner, J. P., 27 Mar. 1797.
Rec: 28 Dec. 1797.

Page 367: 10 Sep. 1796. James Martin of Lincoln Co., N. C. to John Hay of Pendleton Co. for Ł 20 stg. for 320 acres on Mountain Creek of Big Generostee, where John Hay now lives, it being one half of a tract granted to Dorrel Cross, 16 Jul. 1784, for 640 acres, then by Treasurers of the State of same to James Martin, the other one half of tract conveyed to Zachariah Holcomb. Wit: Zachariah (his mark) Holcomb, John Rudifill, Peter (X) Hay. Peter Hay made oath to E. Browne, J. P., 27 Oct. 1797.
Rec: 28 Dec. 1797.

Page 367: I, Richard Prince for $100 sold to Thomas Hay for 100 acres on Mountain Creek of Big Generostee, bd. by Wm. Skelton, part of a tract granted John Holcomb by Charles Pinckney. Date: 1 Sep. 1797. Signed by Richard (R) Prince, Edea (E) Prince. Wit: William Skelton, Josiah Prince. William Skelton made oath to E. Browne, J. P., 28 Dec. 1797.
Rec: 28 Dec. 1797.

Pages 367-368: 19 Mar. 1796. Phillip Holcomb, of Union Co., S. C. to John Tippen of Pendleton Co. for Ł70 stg. for 200 acres surveyed by David Hopkins, granted to Thomas Henry 1784, conveyed to James Martin, then to Phillip Holcomb, on Mountain Creek, of Big Generostee of the Savannah River, bd. by James Stevenson, Stephen Whitmire, Mark Castleberry, William Castleberry. Wit: Jonathan Gibbs, Rachel (X) Holcomb. Jonathan Gibbs made oath to Joshua Saxon, J. P., 10 Nov. 1797.
Rec: 28 Dec. 1797.

Page 368: I, Jonathan Whatson for Ł 30 sold to John Tippen 50 acres, part of 179 acres surveyed for Thomas Moss on a branch of Big Generostee Crk. 18 Aug. 1781 by John Cowen, Jr., including the plantation where Edward McColister now lives. Date: 19 Dec. 1797. Signed: Jonathan Watson. Wit: John Brown, George Tippen, Stephen Ballard. John Brown made oath to John Vernor, J. P., 10 Dec. 1797.
Rec: 28 Dec. 1797.

Page 368: I, James Milwee for $10 sold to Benj. Brimar (no amount) on Mountain Creek, part of grant to Jacob Reid by Charles Pinckney, 3 October 1791. Date: 17 Jan. 1797. Wit: Samuel Henry, Mary (X) Henry. Saml. Henry made oath to E. Browne, J.P., 27 Oct. 1797.
Rec: 28 Dec. 1797.

Pages 368-369: 10 Nov. 1790. Henry Childs (also Chiles), a planter, of Abbeville Co. to John Land, planter, of Pendleton Co., for 5 shillings stg. for 150 acres in 96 District above the ancient boundary line, on 12 Mile River of the Keowee River, granted to Childs by Wm. Moultrie, 4 Dec.1786. Signed: Henry Chiles, Sarah (X) Chiles. Wit: Joseph (/) Land, Tom (O) Forson, (called Ferguson in oath), Sam (X) White. Joseph Land made oath to John Willson, J.P., 25 Jun. 1792.
Rec: 29 Dec. 1797.

Page 369: 5 Feb. 1795. William French to John Hutson for Ł 67 for 200 acres on the S. fork of 12 (cont'd on next page)

(Page 369 cont'd): Mile River, bd. by Baylis Earle's old line, now called Selmans. Wit: Isaiah Lewis, Lewis Wimberly, Isaac Wimberly. Lewis Wimberly made oath to W. Reid, J. P., 13 Feb. 1796.
Rec: 29 Dec. 1797.

Pages 369-370: 17 Feb. 1794. Nathaniel Perry to John Young for Ł 27 for 168 acres on the NW branches of Ravin's Creek of 12 Mile River, bd. by Robert Willson and vacant land, granted to Perry, 4 Sep. 1786. Wit: Wm. Young, Benja. Perry. William Young made oath to Bayley Anderson, 13 Mar. 1794.
Rec: 29 Dec. 1797.

Page 370: 3 Nov. 1795. James Jett to William Brown for (blank) lbs. stg. for 297 acres granted Jett on 2 Sep. 1793, W. of old Indian boundary on both sides of Raven fork of 12 Mile River, bd. on SW by William Brown, NW by John Young, vacant land. Wit: Bennett Combs, John Robinson. Bennett Combs made oath to G. W. Earle, D.C.C., 29 Dec. 1797.
Rec: 29 Dec. 1797.

Page 370: 22 Sep. 1795. Peter Kinza to Isaac Bynum for Ł 80 stg. for 202 acres on N. side of 12 Mile River. Signed: Peter (+) Kinza. Wit: David Murphree, Peter Burrell. David Murphree made oath to W. W. Reid, J. P., 22 Oct. 1797.
Rec: 29 Dec. 1797.

Page 370: I, Zachariah Holcomb for Ł 60 stg. sold to Joseph McCarley, 160 acres on Big Generostee Date: 27 May 1797. Signed: Zachariah (Ø) Holcomb. Wit: J. McMahan, James McCarley, James Brown. Plat shows land bd. on E. by Wid(ow) Loyd, on SE by Jas. McCarley, on SW by Thos. Hays, on NW by vacant land, on N. by part of above tract, surveyed by John McMahan, D.S., 23 May 1797. James Brown made oath to John Vernor, J. P., 28 Dec. 1797.
Rec: 29 Dec. 1797.

Pages 370-371: I, James Scott for Ł 30 sold to Charles Ellitt, 100 acres on branches of Big Creek of the Saluda River, part of 443 acres granted to Ralph Owne by Wm. Moultrie, 6 Mar. 1780. Recorded Bk. HHHH, p. 207. Date: 5 Mar. 1797. Wit: William Young, William Bell. (Plat). William Bell made oath to Wm. Hall, J. P., 20 Oct. 1797.....Nancy (E) Scott, wife of James Scott released dower to Benj. Cleveland, Judge, 11 Nov. 1797.

Page 371: I, Henry Burdine for Ł 20 sold to Charles Ellitt for 50 acres on Big Creek of the Saluda River, part of 200 acres granted to William Davis by Benjamin Guerard, 21 Jan. 1785; also part of 132 acres granted Matthew Alexander, 2 Mar. 1789. Date: 25 Mar. 1797. Wit: William Young, William Bell. William Bell made oath to Wm. Hall, J. P., 28 Oct. 1797. Nancy Burdine, wife of Henry Burdine, released dower to Benj. Cleveland, 11 Nov. 1797.
Rec: 29 Dec. 1797.

Page 371: 23 Mar. 1797. George Thompson to James Gipson for Ł 45 for 100 acres on N. fork of 12 Mile River, part of tract bought of Martin in Washington Dist., W. of old Indian boundary line, bd. by Gipson and Thompson. Wit: William King, James (X) Barnett. James Barnett made oath to W. W. Reid, J. P., 25 Apr. 1795.
Rec: 29 Dec. 1797.

Page 372: 14 Nov. 1796. Peter Kays and Lettice, his wife & Co., to John Tuggle for Ł 50 stg. for 60 ac. bd. by Widow Smith, Jane Tilly. Signed: Peter Kays & Co., Lettice Kay. Wit: John McMahan, John Hillhouse. Wit. to receipt: William Smith, Rachel Smith. John McMahan made oath to Joshua Saxon, J. P., 31 May 1797.
Rec: 30 Dec. 1797.

Page 372: 18 Nov. 1796. Peter Kays and Lettice, his wife, & Co. to John Tuggle for Ł 5, "all that land the George Smith plat represents, said plat in hands of John Rankin and Margarite Wood, Exr. of Jesse Wood", on Generostee Creek, bd. by Joshua Saxon, Widdow Tilly, creek dividing Wood and Tuggle, Widow Smith. Signed: Peter Kays & Co., Lettice Kay. Wit: Rachel Smith, John Smith. **William** Smith made oath to Joshua Saxon, J. P., 20 May 1797. Rec: 30 Dec. 1797.

Pages 372-373: 12 Dec. 1789. William Farmer to William McCaleb, farmer, for Ł 15 stg. for 200 acres in 96 Dist. on both sides of Cane Creek, a branch of the Keowee River, granted to Farmer on 4 Dec. 1786 by William Moultrie. Signed: John Taylor, his Attorney. Wit: Dd. Cunningham, Saml. Taylor. Samuel Taylor made oath to J. B. Earle, J. P., 1 Jan. 1798. Rec: 1 Jan. 1798.

Page 373: I, Bennett Combs for $341 sold to John Gipson 250 acres on both sides of 15 Mile Branch of the Savannah River, granted by Charles Pinckney, 5 Mar. 1792, bd. by Mary Gibson. Date: 29 Dec. 1797. Wit: Moses Hunt, Saml. Cherry. Moses Hunt made oath to G. W. Earle, D.C.C., 29 Dec. 1797. Rec: 1 Jan. 1798.

Pages 373-374: 4 Jan. 1798. Samuel Taylor and Elenor, his wife, to Ezekiel Buffington for Ł 125 stg. for 200 acres on Little River of Keowee River bd. on NW by Eleazer Turner, granted Matthew Hair by Benjamin Guerard, on 21 Jan. 1785. Signed: Saml. Taylor, Elenor Taylor. Wit: W. Steele, J. Mauldin. Joab Mauldin made oath to J. B. Earle, J.P., 5 Jan. 1798. Rec: 5 Jan. 1798.

Page 374: 29 Dec. 1797. William Griffen and Margaret, his wife, to David Kelton for Ł 40 stg. for 80 acres on N. side of 5 Mile Branch of 18 Mile Creek, part of 2 tracts; one granted Samuel Lofton by Charles Pinckney, for 394 acres, bd. on NE by David Kelton, Childs (now sold). Signed: William Griffen, Margret(+) Griffen. Wit: Hugh Dobbs, Jon McDole, John Glenn. Hugh Dobbs made oath to J. B. Earle, J.P., 6 Jan. 1798. Rec: 6 Jan. 1798.

Page 374: 5 Mar. 1796. Albert Robins of Greenville Co., S. C. to George Stamps of Pendleton Co. for Ł 40 stg. for 144 acres on Little River of Keowee River of Savannah River, bd. on NW, NE. and SE. by Fields Pruet, Sr., on NW by Saml. Taylor, granted Albert Robins by Arnoldus Vandrhorst, 7 Dec. 1795. Wit: John Vickrey, Christopher Vickrey. John Vickrey made oath to Joseph Reid, J.P., 11 Mar. 1796. Rec: 10 Jan. 1798.

Pages 374-375: I, Samuel Taylor, planter, for $80 sold to George Stamps 70 acres on S. side of Little River (except 1 acre laid off to Samuel Taylor nearest Shoal), part of 640 acres granted Taylor. Date: 10 January 1798. Wit: W. Steele, Geo. W. Earle. George Washington Earle made oath to J. B. Earle, J.P., 10 Jan. 1798. Rec: 10 Jan. 1798.

Page 375: I, John Cannon of 96 Dist., Newberry Co., for Ł 50 stg. sold to Mary Rigdale, widow, of Pendleton Co., Washington Dist., 127 acres, part of 640 acres granted James Daugherty, 3 Apr. 1786, recorded Bk.JJJJ, p. 200, by Wm. Moultrie, conveyed to Cannon 270 acres, 8 Sep. 1789, recorded Newberry Co. Date: 19 Sep. 1796. Wit: William Lofton, Sr., Abigale (her mark) Loftin, Jas. Lindsey, Sr.....Newberry Co., James Lindsey, Sr. made oath to John Speake, Esq., J. P., 20 Sep. 1796. Rec: 10 Jan. 1798.

Page 375: I, Daniel McCoy for $200 sold to John McCoy

(McCoy cont'd): 273 acres, part of tract granted Peter Bremar, 6 Feb. 1786. Date: 23 Jun. 1797. Signed: Daniel (X) McCoy. Wit: James (+) Gerld, Ecor (Eaker in oath) (X) Thaker, John McMahen. Plat shows land bd. on E. by Ansel Garrod, on SE by Jas. Thompson, on S. by John Norris, on W. by Rocky River, on N. by said tract surveyed on 23 Feb. 1797 by J. McMahen. James Jarret made oath to E. Browne, J. P., 10 Jan. 1798.

Page 375-376: 13 Oct. 1792. Elijah Mayfield to James Brown for Ł 100 stg. for 240 acres in Washington Dist. on Golden's Creek of 12 Mile River, granted 5 Feb. 1787 by Wm. Moultrie. Signed: Elijah (X) Mayfield. Wit: John Yager, Samuel Yager. John Yager made oath to Wm. Reece, J.P., 23 Jun. 1797. Rec: 20 Jan. 1798.

Page 376: 15 Jan. 1794. Isaac Mayfield to James Brown for Ł 60 stg. for 428 acres in Washington District on Golden's Creek of 12 Mile River, granted 5 Feb. 1787 by Wm. Moultrie. Signed: Elijah (X) Mayfield. Wit: John Yager, Samuel Yager. John Yager made oath to Wm. Reece, J.P., 23 Jun. 1797. Rec: 20 Jan. 1798.

Page 376: 15 Jan. 1794. Isaac Mayfield to James Brown for Ł 60 stg. for 428 acres in Washington Dist. on Golden's Creek of 12 Mile River, granted 2 Jan. 1792 by Charles Pinckney. Signed: Isaac (his "R" mark) Mayfield. Wit: James Duff, Jr., Henry Burdine. James Duff made oath to W. Reid, J.P., 26 Jun. 1797. Rec: 20 Jan. 1798.

Page 376: 25 Apr. 1795. Limon French to George Karr for Ł 70 stg. for 183 acres granted Co.(Col.?) Robert Anderson, 20 Apr. 1785 on both sides of a branch of Oolenoy Creek of the Saluda River, bd. on NW and NE by John Vanderhorst, and vacant land. Wit: Stephen Adams, who made oath to Wm. Reid, J.P., 25 Apr. 1795. Rec: 20 Jan. 1798.

Pages 376-377: 11 Apr. 1793. Ebenezer Fain to William Reid for Ł 50 stg. for 150 acres on S. branch of Oolenoy Creek, granted Robert Willson, by Thomas Pinckney, 5 Dec. 1787. Recorded Bk. TTTT, p. 604...."on 8 May 1791 in presence of John Adams, Sr. and Henry Adams, Robert Anderson sold to Ebenezer Fain". Wit: William (X) Farmer, John Roberts. John Roberts made oath to R. Bowen, J.P., 20 Jan. 1798. Rec: 20 Jan. 1798.

Page 377: 9 Sep. 1790. Alexander McClosky of Abbeville Co. to Samuel Wiley of Pendleton Co. for Ł40 for 200 acres, granted 4 Jun. 1787 by Thomas Pinckney, on Little Generostee. Wit: Alexd. Sherard, John Sherard. Alexander Sherard made oath to E. Browne, J.P., 16 Feb. 1792. Rec: 24 Jan. 1798.

Pages 377-378: 20 Jan. 1797. Isaac Harnage, planter, to William Richard, merchant, for Ł 40 stg. for 109 acres in 96 Dist. on Oconney Creek of Keowee River, adj. to Dr. James Martin, granted 7 Jan. 1793 by Wm. Moultrie. Wit: James Files, Mathew Cleveland. James Files made oath to J. B. Earle, J.P. 24 Jan. 1798. Rec: 24 Jan. 1798.

Pages 378-379: 16 Nov. 1791. Samuel Dalrymple, yeoman, and Sarah, his wife, to John Smith, planter, for Ł 100 stg. for 128½ acres on Big Generostee of the Savannah River, bd. on E. by George Smith, on S. by William Herring, on N. by Joseph Smith, granted 6 Feb. 1786. Signed: Samuel Dalrymple, Sarah (/) Dalrymple. Wit: Rachel Smith, James Cannon, George Smith. Rachel Smith made oath to Joshua Saxon, J.P. 22 Jan. 1798. Rec: 22 Jan.1798.

Page 379:   19 Apr. 1793. Benjamin Perry to Jonas Bishop for ₤ 20 for 590 acres on the branches of Mill and Woolf Creeks, of 12 Mile River, bd. on NW and SW by Benjamin Perry, granted Perry, 6 Aug. 1787. Wit: Nathl. Perry, Susannah Perry. Susannah Perry made oath to Nathl. Perry, J.P., 19 Apr. 1793. Rec: 24 Jan. 1798.

Pages 379: 4 Mar. 1794. Jonas Bishop to Christopher Harmon of Elbert Co., Ga. for ₤ 100 for 360 ac. on branches of Mill Creek and Woolf Creek of 12 Mile River, granted Benj. Perry, 6 Aug. 1787. Signed: Janes Bishop. Wit: Jno. Conrod Adderhold, Thomas Goss, Abraham Duk. Abraham Duk made oath to Wm. Edmondson, J.P., 30 Jul. 1794. Rec: 24 Jan. 1798.

Pages 379-380: 19 May 1794. Jones Bishop of Pendleton Co. to Christopher Harmon of Elbert Co., Ga. for ₤30 stg. for 148 acres on Mill Creek and Woolf Creek of 12 Mile River, bd. SE, SW, N & NE by Perry, granted Jones Bishop on 3 Feb. 1794. Signed: Jones Bishop. Wit: Abraham Duk, Jonas Hill. Abraham Duk made oath to Wm. Edmondson, J.P., 30 Jul. 1794. Rec: 24 Jan. 1798.

Page 380: I, Christopher Harmon of Pendleton Co. for ₤ 100 sold to Abraham Duk 200 acres. Date: 30 Dec. 1797. Signed: Christopher (C) Harmon. Wit: John Conrod Adderhold, James Jett. John Conrod Aderhold made oath to E. Browne, J.P., 24 Jan. 1798. Rec: 24 Jan. 1798.

Page 380: 6 Jul. 1797. William Moore to John Fields for $200 and ₤ 50 for 205 acres granted John Young and Joseph French on both sides of 12 Mile River, bd. on SE by Moses Murphree, on NE by Fields, on W. by Saml. Jackson. Signed: William (X) Moore. Wit: Lewis Wimberly, Noah Wimberly. Lewis Wimberly made oath to W. Reid, J.P., 17 Oct. 1797. Rec: 24 Jan. 1798.

Page 380: We, Peter Keys and Lettice Keys and Co. for ₤ 125 sold to James Thompson 494 acres at the mouth of Beaver Creek on S. side of Rockey River, adj. Thompson, Wm. Brown, dec'd, Harris Mauldin, Thomas Milsap and Great Rocky Creek. Date: 4 Nov. 1797. Signed: Peter Kays & Co., Lettice Keys. Wit: Robert King, Lent Hall. Lent Hall made oath to E. Browne, J.P. on 22 Jan. 1798. Rec: 24 Jan. 1798.

Pages 380-381: I, Richard Sadler of Pendleton Co. for ₤ 25 stg. sold to Robert Swain of Abbeville Co., 312 acres on branches of Barker's Creek of Savannah River, bd. on SW by David Greer, on E. by William Reid, on N & W by Jas. Allen, granted to Sadler by Chas. Pinckney, 2 Jan. 1787. Recorded Bk. 2N5, p. 159. Date: 1 Sep. 1797. Wit: Thomas Donalson, James Thornhill....Abbeville Co., Thomas Donaldson made oath to Reuben Nash, J.P., 21 Sep. 1797. Rec: 24 Jan. 1798.

Page 381: I, Thomas Hamilton for ₤ 40 stg. sold to William Scott 200 acres in 96 Dist. on W. branches of 23 Mile Creek of the Savannah River, granted Hamilton by Wm. Moultrie, 5 Jun. 1786. Date: 27 Dec. 1797. Wit: John Powell, Benj. Smith, David Smith. John Powell made oath to John Willson, J.P., 27 Dec. 1797. Rec: 24 Jan. 1798.

Page 381: Washington Dist. I, David Smith for ₤ 30 .. sold to William Scott 100 acres part of 640 acres granted Smith by Tho. Pinckney, 7 Jun. 1788 in 96 Dist. on 23 Mile Creek, bd. on NE by Job Smith, SW by Jonathan Clarke, John Robinson. Recorded Bk. XXXX, p. 94. Date: 27 Dec. 1797. Wit: Thos. Hamilton, John Powell, Martin (X) Eubanks. Plat shows land bd. on

(Smith-Scott cont'd): N. by Robinson, on E. by Rankin, on S. by Rankin, on W. by Grimes. Thomas Hamilton made oath to John Willson, J.P., 27 Dec. 1797. Rec: 24 Jan. 1798.

Page 381: I, John Buchannon of Fairfield Co., S. C. for Ł 10 stg. sold to William Hinson of Pendleton Co., 200 acres on the Keowee River, granted to John McCree by Benj. Guerard, 1785. Date: 7 Oct. 1797. Wit: John Pratt, John Robb, Jesse Coffee. Jesse Coffee made oath to John Barton, J.P., 13 Jan. 1798. Rec: 24 Jan. 1798.

Pages 381-382: I, Samuel Little for Ł 30 stg. sold to John Portman 20 acres on 26 Mile Creek and Pearces Creek, part of 2 tracts; one granted to David Jordan for 204 acres, 17 Feb. 1791 bd. by Gutrie; the other 10 acres part of 150 acres granted Gutrie, 15 Oct. 1784, bd. by 26 Mile Creek, Pearces Creek, John Morris, Smith. Date: 3 Nov. 1797. Wit: James Hembree, Mark (+) Pitts. James Hembree made oath to Wm. Millwee, J.P., 24 Jan. 1798. Rec: 24 Jan. 1798.

Page 382: 23 Mar. 1795. Roger Martin to James Garner for Ł 30 stg. for 100 acres on branches of Beaver Creek, part of 400 acres laid out for Joseph Culton. Recorded Bk. ___, no. 5, p. 436. Wit: John Mauldin, James (his mark) Stroud. John Mauldin made oath to E. Browne, J. P., 29 Dec. 1797. Rec: 24 Jan. 1798.

Page 382: I, John Moore, Merchant of Charleston for Ł 70 stg. sold to John McCutchen 500 acres on Big Generostee Creek, bd. by Widow Tilly, Henry Houston, John McCutchen, John Ross. Date: 7 Apr. 1797. Wit: James Crawford, Peter Keys. Peter Keys made oath to Joshua Saxon, J.P., 15 Nov. 1797. Rec: 24 Jan. 1798.

Page 382: I, John Ross, planter, for Ł 50 stg. sold to John McCutchin 200 acres on Big Generostee Creek, bd. by Henry Houston, John McCutchin, Ross, James Long. Date: 15 Nov. 1797. Signed: John (/) Ross. Wit: Petr. Keys, James Ross. Peter Keys made oath to Joshua Saxon, J.P., 15 November 1797. Rec: 24 Jan. 1798.

Page 382: I, William Steele for Ł 100 stg. sold John McCutchin a negro woman named Molly and her two children, Hannah and Isaac. Date: 27 Jul. 1796. Wit: J. Mauldin, James Wood. Joab Mauldin made oath to Joshua Saxon, J. P., 25 Jan. 1798. Rec: 25 Jan. 1798.

Pages 382-383: 13 Mar. 1797. John Todd to Adam Todd for Ł30 stg. for 100 acres, part of 200 acres granted Patrick Forbush, 15 Mar. 1787 on Hencoop Creek, of Great Rocky River, part of a tract where Adam Todd now lives. Wit: Elisha Bennett, Jenny Todd, Sarah Bennett. Elisha Bennett made oath to Wm. Hall, J.P., 25 Jul. 1797. Rec: 25 Jan. 1798.

Page 383: 25 Aug. 1796. Johnston Murray of Elbert Co., Ga. to Elisha Bennett of Pendleton Co. for Ł 15 for 150 acres, part of 600 acres upon Broadaway Creek of Rocky River, bd. by Alexander McLean, Edward Vandiver, Tho. Burford, granted to Tho. Burford, 4 Dec. 1786 by Wm. Moultrie. Wit: William Murray, John Murray, Anna Murray. John Murray made oath to E. Browne, J.P., 3 Sep. 1796. Rec: 25 Jan. 1798.

Page 383: 21 Nov. 1795. William Hunt to Edward Wilson for Ł 80 stg. for 150 acres on Camp Creek of the Saluda River. Wit: Richd. Thompson, Jehu Lawler. Jehu Lawler made oath to R. Bowen, J. P., 18 Jan. 1798.(cont'd):

(Hunt-Wilson cont'd): Rec: 25 Jan. 1798.

Page 383: We, George Harrison and Elizabeth, my wife, for Ł 100 sold to William McClure 150 acres where Harrison now lives, on the Saluda River at Parris' ford, conveyed from Swelivant to Edwards, then to Harrison. Date: 17 Oct. 1797. Signed: George Harrison, Elizabeth (her mark) Harrison. Wit: James Allard, Simon (his mark) Lovelady, Robt. Harrison. Simon Lovelady made oath to R. Bowen, J.P., 25 Nov. 1797. Rec: 25 Jan. 1798.

Page 384: I, John Willson and Elizabeth, my wife, for Ł 50 stg. sold to John Darrah 100 acres on S. side of the Saluda River, part of a tract granted to Willson, 21 Jan. 1785 by Benj. Guerard. Date: 12 Sep. 1797. Signed: John Wilson, Elizabeth (her mark) Wilson. Wit: John Wilson, Jr., John T. Hamilton. John Hamilton made oath to E. Browne, J.P., 12 Nov. 1797. Rec: 25 Jan. 1798.

Page 384: I, George Wilson for Ł 112 stg. sold to John Loller (also Lawler) 242 acres on Shoal Crk. of the Saluda River, granted to Sutton Green, 17 May 1787. Date: 17 Feb. 1797. Signed: George (O) Wilson. Wit: John Bourland, James (Q)(his mark?) Garrison; John Bourland made oath to R. Bowen, J.P., 18 Jan. 1798. Rec: 25 Jan. 1798.

Page 384: I, Samuel Watt, Esq., of Abbeville Co. for Ł 25 sold to John Gipson, carpenter of Pendleton Co. 723 acres in 96 Dist. (now in Pendleton Co.) on Big Beaverdam of Tugalo River, granted Watt by Charles Pinckney, 7 Jan. 1788. Date: 15 Mar. 1797. Wit: William Welch, Lewis Sherrill. Lewis Sherrill made oath to G. W. Earle, D.C.C., 25 Jan. 1798. Rec: 25 Jan. 1798.

Page 384: 12 Dec. 1797. Major Papon (or Passon) to Amos Kilburn for Ł 30 stg. sold 200 acres, part of 870 acres surveyed for Papon(?) by Jon. C. Kilpatrick, D.S., granted by Thos. Pinckney, 4 Jun. 1787 in Washington Dist. on forks of the Tugalo and Keowee Rivers, beginning at Camp branch on the Keowee. Wit: Farley Thompson, William Bates. William Bates made oath to John Vernor, J.P., 23 Jan. 1798. Rec: 25 Jan. 1798.

Pages 384-385: I, Edward Wade for Ł 28 sold to John Taylor 70 acres on both sides of Neal's Creek part of a tract granted Samuel Dalrymple, conveyed to Wade. Recorded Bk. ZZZZ, p. 279. Date: (blank) 1797. Wit: Peter Greenlee, Stephen Willis. Stephen Willis made oath to E. Browne, J.P., 2 Oct. 1797. Rec: 25 Jan. 1798.

Page 385: 25 Jan. 1796. Joseph Brown and Aaron Broyles to Edwin Smith for Ł 150 for 400 acres in Washington Dist. on Broadmouth Creek of the Saluda River, part of 929 acres granted to Brown and Broyles, 10 April 1791. Recorded Bk. D, no. 5, p. 504. Surveyed by James Millwee, D.S., bd. by Joseph Brown, William Fowler, Richard Bullock, Little Creek and Reedy fork of the Saluda River. Signed: Joseph Brown, Jr., Aaron Broyles. Wit: Jacob Reed, Thomas Smith. Jacob Reed made oath to Wm. Hall, J.P., 15 Jan 1798. Rec: 25 Jan. 1798.

Page 385: 26 Jan. 1796. Joseph Brown to Edward Smith for Ł 150 stg. for 150 acres in 96 Dist. on Broadmouth Creek of the Saluda River, part of a tract granted Nathaniel Aldridge, 5 Mar. 1789. Surveyed by Thomas Lofton, D.S. Recorded Bk. TTTT, p. 110; also 2 other tracts granted to Giles Gantt, bd. by Nathaniel Aldridge, Wm. Reed, Joseph Brown, on NW side of Broadmouth Creek, including Saw Mill and Grist Mill. Signed: Joseph Brown, Jr. Wit: Jacob Reed, Thomas Smith. Jacob Reece made oath to Wm. Hall, JP, 13 Jan. 1798. Rec: 25 Jan. 1798.

Pages 385-386: 26 Mar. 1795. Richard Oldham to James Clements for Ł 32 stg. for 100 acres on branch of Rocky Creek of Rocky River, bd. by Charles Clements, Charles Stuart, William Lindley, part of 640 acres granted Andrew Hamilton, 4 Oct. 1790. Recorded Bk. C, no. 5, p. 62. Conveyed from Hamilton to Oldham. Wit: Reuben Clements, William Lindley, William Wordlaw. William Lindley made oath to Wm. Hall, J.P., 7 Nov. 1795. Rec: 25 Jan. 1798.

Page 386: I, Bennett Aden for $50 sold to John Ritchey (Richey) 100 acres on W. side of 23 Mile Crk. of Keowee River, part of 500 acres granted by Arnoldus Vanderhorst, bd. on E. by Jesse Laxton, on N. by Wm. Mackey, on W. by Stephen Fuller. Date: 4 Jul. 1797. Wit: Jacob Gillispie, John Brouster. Jacob Gillispie made oath to Joseph Reed, 4 Jul. 1797. Rec: 26 Jan. 1798.

Page 386: 9 Jun. 1796. John Haynie and Stephen Haynie to Joseph Wornock, for Ł 32 stg. for 200 ac. where Joseph Wornock now lives, part of 3 tracts; one of 200 ac. granted James Gillison, 15 Oct. 1784, recorded Bk. AAAA, p. 14, conveyed to John Haney; one of 200 ac. granted to John Haney, 16 Oct. 1789, recorded Bk. ZZZZ, p. 226; one of 479 ac. granted Stephen Haney, 2 Mar. 1795, recorded Bk. P, No. 5, p. 139. Signed: John Haynie, Stephen Haynie. Wit: Thos. Hanks, Stephen Willis. Capt. Stephen Willis made oath to E. Browne, J.P., 3 Sep. 1796. Rec: 26 Jan. 1798.

Pages 386-387: We, John Laughlin, Moses Whitlow and Sarah Dalrymple for Ł 96 stg. sold to Joseph Thompson 670 acres, granted Samuel Dalrymple by Charles Pinckney, 7 Jun. 1790, on Coldwater Creek of Rocky River of Savannah River, bd. on E. by John Hilhouse, on SE by John Dowdle, on W. by Joshua Saxon, on NE. by Henry King, on N. by vacant land. Date: 1 Jan. 1798. Signed: John Laughlin, Moses Whitley, Sarah (+) Dalrymple. Wit: William King, Henry King, Robt. Thompson. William King made oath to E. Browne, J. P., 23 Jan. 1798. Rec: 26 Jan. 1798.

Page 387: 6 Apr. 1797. Stephen Barton to Joseph Reed for Ł 20 for 119 acres on Keowee River, bd. NW and SW by Felix Warley, where Joseph Reed now lives, granted Bartin, 3 Oct. 1796 by Arnoldus Vanderhorst. Signed: Stephen Berten. Wit.: Joseph Hill, William Hays, Noah (X) Langley. Joseph Hill made oath to J. B. Earle, J.P., 26 Jan. 1798. Rec: 26 Jan. 1798.

Page 387: 28 Dec. 1796. William Floyd, Jr. to Reuben Login for Ł 40 for 100 acres on Keowee River bd. by Mile Creek, Dunkin Camron's old line, granted Dunkin Camron by Thos. Pinckney. Signed: William (X) Floyd. Wit: Alexr. Floyd, George Tubb. George Tubb made oath to W. Reid, J.P., 25 Jan. 1798. Rec: 26 Jan. 1798.

Page 387: I, William Mullican of Washington Dist. for Ł 50 sold to John Russel 240 acres on N. side of Keowee River, part of 652 acres granted to James Jordan by Wm. Moultrie. Date: 9 Jan. 1798. Signed: William (X) Mullican. Wit: Thos. Stribling, Nancy Stribling. Thomas Stribling made oath to J. B. Earle, J.P., 26 Jan. 1798. Rec: 26 Jan. 1798.

Pages 387-388: I, John Verner, Sr. for $20 sold to John Verner, Jr. 21 acres, my part of Fishery that lies below Upper fish traps, on Seneca River on W. bank, including fish trap put into said river by James Cox, including four islands. Date: 5 Aug. 1797. Wit: William Wakefield, George Verner. William Wakefield made oath to Wm. Millwee, J.P., 29 Jan. 1798. Rec: 29 Jan. 1798.

Page 388: I, Peter Jones for Ł 80 stg. sold to John Cinnemur 133 acres, part of 233 acres granted to Jones, 6 Feb. 1792 by Charles Pinckney, in 96 Dist. on Doddy's Creek, of the Saluda River, bd. on SW by Thos. Lewis and Peter Jones, NE and NW by Geo. Thompson, NE by Howell Doddy. Date: 19 Apr. 1796. Signed: Peter Jones, Elizabeth (her mark) Jones. Wit: William Bourland, Noah Cinnemur. Noah Cinnemur made oath to Wm. Reed, J.P., 8 Dec. 1797. Rec: 29 Jan. 1798.

Page 388: I, Peter Jones for Ł 80 sold to John Cinnemur 158 acres granted Jones by Wm. Moultrie, 6 Feb. 1792 in 96 Dist. on Buck Creek of Saluda River above ancient boundary line. Date: 19 Apr. 1792. Signed: Peter Jones, Elizabeth (/) Jones. Wit: William Bourland, Noah Cinnemur. Noah Cinnemur made oath to Wm. Reed, J.P., 19 Apr. 1796. Rec: 29 Jan. 1798.

Page 388: 18 Oct. 1797. Andrew Ruddle to Eliab Moore for $300 for 173 acres, bd. SE by Eliab Moore, NE and NW by Robert Stevenson, granted John Norwood, 3 Dec. 1792. Wit: Robert Dowdle, Petr. Keys. Peter Keys made oath to Joshua Saxon, J.P., 25 Jan. 1798. Rec: 29 Jan. 1798.

(Page number torn off).
Page 388: I, James Hart sold to William Copeland all my property, land, notes in my possession, 20 Apr. 1795. Signed: James (X) Hart. Wit: Samuel Torbert, who made oath to Bill of Sale to Wm. Edmondson, 9 Oct. 1795. Rec: 29 Jan. 1798.

Pages 388-389: 9 Apr. 1793. William Allen (later Allison) of Washington Dist. to William Copeland for Ł 100 stg. for 60 acres on Brushy Creek, part of 400 acres granted Watson Allison by States Letter Patent by Wm. Moultrie, 4 Dec. 1786. Signed: William Allison. Wit: Stephen (X) Low, James Cunningham. Stephen Low made oath to R. Bowen, J.P., 19 Dec. 1795. Rec: 29 Jan. 1798.

Page 389: 24 Mar. 1795. Samuel Talbot of Washington District to William Copeland of the same, for Ł 50 stg. for 70 acres on N. side of Brushy Creek, of Saluda River, part of 200 acres granted William Edmondson by States Letter Patent by Benjamin Guerard, 15 Oct. 1784, bd. by Wm. Copeland, Thomas Foster. Signed: Samuel Torbert. Wit: David (+) Kirby, Thomas Doggett, Fredrick Bowen. David Kirby made oath to John Willson, J.P., 11 Apr. 1795. Rec: 29 Jan. 1798.

Page 389: Abbeville Co., I, John Robinson for Ł 50 sold to Thomas Sidney Reese of Pendleton Co; 100 acres on branch of 26 Mile Creek of Savannah River, bd. NW by John Jones, SE by Eli Hunnicutt, SW by John E. Calhoun, granted Michael Dickson, 1785. Date: 13 Sep. 1797. Signed: John (R) Robinson. Wit: Alexr. Boyse, Moses Liddell. Alexr. Boyse made oath to J. B. Earle, J.P., 30 Jan. 1798. Rec: 30 Jan. 1798....Abbeville Co., Jean (her mark) Robinson, wife of John Robinson released dower to Adam Crane Jones, 1 Dec. 1797.

Page 390: Washington Dist. 29 Jan. 1798, Thomas Farrar, Sheriff of Washington Dist. to Joseph Eaton, whereas, the land of James Beaty has been seized, 334 acres on 6 Mile Creek...Clayton Rogers, Executor of Hope's Estate obtained Judgement against James Beaty for Ł 50 stg....John Rutledge, Esq., Chief Justice of State levied Ł 53 stg. and ordered land to be sold at auction to highest bidder, being Joseph Eaton for Ł 5 stg. Signed: Thomas Farrar, Late Sheriff of Washington Dist. Wit: Wm. Edmondson, D. McCaleb. David McCaleb made oath to G. W. Earle, D.C.C., 5 Feb. 1798. Rec: 5 Feb. 1798.

Page 390: 4 Apr. 1793. Levi Murphree and Mary, his wife

(Page 390 cont'd): to Thomas Edwards for Ł 35 stg. for 135 ac. on Cowpen Creek of Ooloney. Signed: Levi (his mark) Murphree. Wit: Joseph Roberts, William (X) Roberts, William Robins made oath to Bayley Anderson, 11 May 1795. Signed: William Robins. Rec: 13 Feb. 1798.

Page 390: I, Joseph Martin for $700 sold to Joseph Oliver 214 acres in Washington Dist. on 26 Mile Creek of Keowee River, bd. NW by Joseph Martin, SE by Widow Caswell, granted by Wm. Moultrie, 22 Jan. 1793. Recorded Bk. F, no. 5, p. 526. Date: 13 May 1797. Wit: A. Boyse, Robert Clarke. Alexander Boyse made oath to John Willson, J.P., 7 Jul. 1797. Rec: 28 Jan. 1798.

Page 391: Whereas, Alexander Ervin was seized of 140 ac on E. side of Rocky Creek, bd. by Joseph and John Erwin, Fenton Hall, Robert Hall...and whereas, Asa _____ made judgement against Alexander Erwin for Ł 35-1-4, I, John Harris, Sheriff on 7 Jan. 1794 sold tract, as directed by law to John Erwin, by his friend, William Steele, being highest bidder for Ł13 stg. Date: 13 Oct. 1797. Signed: John Harris. Wit: Hardy Owen, William Shackleford. (Plat). William Shackleford made oath to W. Steele, J.P., 5 Nov. 1797....At request of Mr. Israel Pickens, I have laid out tract where Alexr. Erwin now lives, surveyed 13 Nov. 1796. Signed: John McMahan D.S. Rec: 1 Mar. 1798.

Page 391: I, John Harris for $300 sold to John Scott 640 acres on Willson's Creek, of Savannah River, bd. W. by Thomas Clarke, S. by John Bryson. At time of survey bd. S. by John Caldwell, and vacant land. Date: 13 Oct. 1797. Wit: W. Steele, M. Pickens...Mary Harris, wife of John Harris released dower to Wm. Steele, 13 Oct. 1793. William Steele made oath to J. B. Earle, J.P., 3 Mar. 1798. Rec: 3 Mar. 1798.

Page 391: Washington Dist. I, Henry Branyon of Abbeville Co. for Ł 5 stg. sold to Thomas and John Branyon of Abbeville Co., jointly 300 acres in Washington Dist., Pendleton Co., on Crooked Creek, of Little Generostee, granted by Wm. Moultrie, 1 May 1786. Recorded Bk. KKKK, p.376; Thomas Branyon to have 150 acres, John Branyon to have 150 acres. Date: 1 Mar. 1798. Wit: James Wood, J. Mauldin. Joab Mauldin made oath to J.B. Earle, J.P., 3 Mar. 1798. Rec: 3 Mar. 1798.

Page 392: 9 Jun. 1793. Lewis Daniel Martin, planter, & Sarah, his wife, to Joseph Hall, planter, for Ł 130 stg. for 200 acres on Martain's Creek, S. side of Keowee River, granted Benjamin Newsom, on Bounty for his services as Lieutenant in the American Army, 21 Jan. 1785, by Benj. Guerard. Recorded Bk. BBBB, p. 151. Conveyed to Martin, 27 Nov. 1790; also 227 ac. in Washington Dist. (alias 96 Dist.) on Griffen's Creek, of Keowee River, granted Martin, 2 Jul. 1787, by Thomas Pinckney. Recorded Bk. UUUU, p. 148. Signed: Lewis D. Martin, Sarah Martin. Wit: John Knox, Thomas Kennedy. John Knox made oath to G. W. Earle, D.C.C., 5 Mar. 1798. Rec: 5 Mar. 1798.

Pages 392-393: 1 Mar. 1798. Andrew Roe to Jacob Capehart for Ł 100 for 90 acres on 23 Mile Creek of Savannah River, part of 338 acres granted Roe by Charles Pinckney, 6 Sep. 1790. Recorded Bk. C, no. 5, (no page number). Wit: Jonathan Hicks, Jr., Anselm Roe. Jonathan Hicks, Jr. made oath to G. W. Earle, DCC, 5 Mar. 1798. Rec: 5 Mar. 1798.

Page 393: 3 Jul. 1795. Timothy Reeves to Richard Haney for Ł 60 stg. for 182 acres, part of tract granted David Clarke, 5 Feb. 1787, on Big Generostee of Keowee River, in Washington Dist. conveyed to Benjamin Haney by Clarke, from Haney to Reeves, bd. N. by James Long, E. by Henry Person, S. by remaining tract. Wit: James Long, George Reeves. James Long made (page 393 cont'd): oath to Joshua Saxon, J. P., 31 Oct. 1795. Rec: 12 Mar. 1798.

Page 393: 13 Feb. 1797. Job Barnard of Buncomb Co., N. C. to Joseph Woodall of Pendleton Co. for Ł 40 stg. for 291 acres on both sides of Georges Creek of 12 Mile River, granted Barnard, 27 Nov. 1793. Wit: James Tubb, Wm. (+) Tubb, George (O) Tubb. William Tubb made oath to John Willson, J. P., 11 Apr. 1797.
Rec: 16 Mar. 1798.

Pages 393-394: 17 May 1795. Samuel Crabtree of Iredale Co., N. C. to Margaret McElvaney of Pendleton Co. for Ł 50 stg. for 121 acres on Rocky River, bd. on E. by Robert Maxwell, on S. by Houston, on N. by Ralph Wilson.... granted James Cannon by Wm. Moultrie. Recorded Bk. GGGG, p. 396. Conveyed from Cannon to Crabtree. Wit: Thomas Cole, Joseph (I) Irwin. Joseph Erwin made oath, that he carried deed to be signed to Crabtree, oath made to Wm. Millwee, J. P., 3 Jul. 1797.
William McElvaney swore that this is deed he, the deponent drew and gave to Joseph Irwin for purpose of getting signed by Samuel Crabtree.
Rec: 25 Mar. 1798.

Page 394: I, Margaret McElvaney, Jr. of Abbeville Co. for Ł 40 sold to Joseph Gray of Pendleton Co. 121 acres granted James Cannon by Wm. Moultrie, sold by Cannon to Samuel Crabtree, from Crabtree to Margaret McElvaney, 7 May 1795, on Beaverdam Creek of the Savannah River, bd. on E. by Robert Maxwell, Esq., on S. by Houston, on N. by Elijah Williamson. Recorded Bk. GGGG, p. 396. Signed: Margaret McElvaney, Sr., Margaret McElvaney, Jr. Wit: Anthony Wm. Elton, William McElvaney, Elenor Elton. William McElvaney made oath to Wm. Millwee, J. P., 21 Feb. 1797.
Rec: 25 Mar. 1798.

Page 394: I, Mary Thompson, Widow, for divers causes give to my beloved daughter, Hannah Bowman, wife of Jesse Bowman, one negro girl named Rigne, about 3 years old, not to be sold or traded but to remain the property of Hannah Bowman. Date: 20 Nov. 1797....If Hannah Bowman should die without heir, the above negro shall revert back to the nearest heir of the Thompson family. Wit: James Long, William Gambriel. James Long made oath to Joshua Saxon, J. P., 15 Mar. 1798.
Rec: 26 Mar. 1798.

Page 394: 21 Mar. 1798. Josiah East of Laurence Co., S. C. to Jesse Davis of Pendleton Co. for $120 sold him 270 acres on Generostee Creek, surveyed by John Hunter. Wit: Lewis Bennett, Jethro Walker, John Walker ....Laurence Co., Jethro Walker made oath to Joseph Downs, J. P., 22 Mar. 1798. Rec: 30 Mar. 1798.

Pages 394-395: 13 Nov. 1797. James Martin of Lincoln Co., N. C. to Peter Perkins of Stokes Co., N. C. for Ł 100 for 320 acres in Pendleton Co. on both sides of Ooloney Creek of the Saluda River, part of 640 acres granted to William Powell Lee, 16 Jul. 1784 by deed from William Hort and John Edwards, Esqs., Treasurers of the State of S. C., 7 Apr. 1789, to Martin. Wit: Abraham Perkins, Moses Starrett, William (W) Starrett. Abraham Perkins made oath to G. W. Earle, D.C.C., 9 Apr. 1798.
Rec: 9 Apr. 1798.

Page 395: We, Thomas Wadsworth and William Turpin, Merchants, for Ł 60 stg. sold to William Steele, Merchant, one half acres lot being moiety of Lot #2 in Village of Pendleton Courthouse, which was conveyed to Wadsworth & Turpin & Steele by Andrew Pickens, Robt. Anderson and Benjamin Cleveland, Esqs., Commissioners of Pendleton Co. Date: 27 Mar. 1798.Wit: James Boyce, Lewis D. Martin, Jas. Young. Lewis D. Martin made oath to G. W. Earle, DCC, 10 Apr. 1798. Rec: 10 Apr. 1798.

Page 395: I, Charles Hughs for ₤ 30 sold to Robert Swan 100 acres, part of 560 acres granted Hughs by Charles Pinckney, bd. by William Owens. Date: 25 Feb. 1796. Wit: Chas. Willson, William Owens. William Owens made oath to Wm. Edmondson, J. P., 3 Feb. 1797. Rec: 10 Apr. 1798.

Page 395: I, John Wilson, Judge of Pendleton Co, certify Mary Harris, wife of John Harris, released dower in deed to Lewis Tresevant, 17 April 1798. (See deed p. 328).

Page 395: I, John Wilson, Judge of Pendleton Co. certify that Sarah (her mark) Martin, wife of Lewis D. Martin, released dower in John Harris deed, 26 Jun. 1798. (See p. 332).
(Note by Clerk - "the two above relinquishments were taken after deeds were recorded.")

Pages 395-397: 12 Feb. 1798. James Kilgore to Arnoldus Vanderhorst and Thomas Waring, as Executors of Major John VanderHorst, dec'd., for ₤ 206 stg. 15-10, for 150 acres in 96 Dist. on branches of Ready Creek, called Ready fork, surveyed for Samuel Saxon, 24 Nov. 1784, granted to Richard Richardson, 5 Sep. 1785; also 400 acres on Enoree River, surveyed 5 Jan. 1775, on Warrant dated 8 Sep. 1774, granted Daniel Hugar, 15 Oct. 1784; also, 640 acres on Saluda River, above Old Indian Boundary, bd. on NE by William Righly, granted John VanderHorst, 16 Jul. 1784. Wit: A. VanderHorst, Jr., Wm. Bowen, Horatio Grifen, Lewis Tresevant. Lewis Tresevant made oath to J. B. Earle, J. P., 11 Apr. 1798. Rec: 12 Apr. 1798.

Page 397: I, Lewis Daniel Martin of Washington Dist., planter, for ₤ 50 stg. sold to Richard Stevnes, Master of the Ship "Hope", 640 acres in Washington Dist., formerly 96 Dist., on Connoross Creek of the Keowee River, bd. NE by Major Bowie, SW by Thomas Stevenson. Date: 21 Mar. 1798. Wit: James S. Neilson, Lewis Tresevant. Sarah Martin, wife of Lewis D. Martin released dower to John Harris, J. P., 7 Apr. 1798. Lewis Tresevant made oath to J. B. Earle, J. P., 14 Apr. 1798. Rec: 15 Apr. 1798.

Pages 397-398: 5 Jul. 1794. Phillip Phagans to George Tillman for ₤ 20 stg. for 240 acres on S. side of Willson's Creek of Rockey River, bd. by Isaac Mitchell, part of two tracts and one whole third; two granted John Caldwell by Benj. Guerard and Charles Pinckney; one granted Phillip Phagans by Charles Pinckney. Wit: Isaac Mitchell, Jr., Phillip (his mark) Phagans, Jr. Phillip Phagans made oath to J. B. Earle, J. P., 16 Apr. 1798. Rec: 10 Apr. 1798.

Page 398: 2 Feb. 1798. William Pritchard of Edgefield Co. to James Sims of Pendleton Co. for $111 for 230 acres on 23 Mile Creek, part of tract granted Pritchard, 15 Oct. 1784. Wit: Michael Dickson, John Dickson, Sr., Saml. H. Dickson. Michael Dickson made oath to J. B. Earle, J. P., 16 April 1798. Rec: 16 Apr. 1798.

Page 398: I, James Martin of Lincoln Co., N. C. for ₤ 100 stg. sold to Richard Robinson of Pendleton Co., 640 acres on 23 Mile Creek, where Robinson now lives, granted Andrew Robinson, 16 Jul. 1784, conveyed from Wm. Hort and John Edwards, Treasurers of S. C., 8 Apr. 1789. Date: 14 April 1798. Wit: John Robinson, Jacob (his mark) West, William Parmore. John Robinson made oath to J. B. Earle, J. P., 16 Apr. 1798. Rec: 16 Apr. 1798.

Pages 398-399: 21 Mar. 1797. Jacob Wisage to Zachariah Morgan for ₤ 30 for 90 acres, part of tract gran-

(Pages 398-399 cont'd): ted Visage by William Moultrie on 23 Mile Crk. Wit: John Robinson, Elisha Robinson, Jacob (his mark) West. John Robinson made oath to G. W. Earle, DCC, 16 Apr.1798. Rec: 16 Apr. 1798.

Page 399: 25 Dec. 1797. John Grissom, Sr. of Pendleton Co. to John Shurley of Abbeville Co. for $1,366 for 692 acres on Little River of the Savannah River; 589 acres, part of tract of 640 acres granted by Benja. Guerard, 21 Jan. 1785, bd. SE by Widow Stevenson; also 88 acres bd. SW on above tract, granted Margaret Stevenson by Wm. Moultrie, 6 Nov. 1786; also 15 acres on NE side, part of tract granted Benj. Aldridge by Moultrie, 1785; Recorded Bk. GGGG, p. 471, including mill and mill pond, bd. Phillip Saler, John Grissom. Signed: John (JG) Grissom, Sr., John Grissom,Jr. Wit: John Robinson, Joshua Shirley, Phillip (S) Sa<u>lor</u>. John Robinson made oath to G. W. Earle, DCC, 16 Apr. 1798. Rec: 16 Apr. 1798.

Page 399: 26 Nov. 1789. Henry Pearson of 96 Dist. to Benjamin Craig of Pendleton Co. for Ł 10 for 457 acres in 96 Dist. on 26 Mile Creek of Savannah River, granted 4 Dec. 1786. Recorded Bk. PPPP, p. 258. Wit: Jonathen Clark, Anthony Golding, Mary (X) Pearson. Jonathan Clark made oath to John Willson, J. P., 19 Dec. 1789. Rec: 16 Apr. 1798.

Pages 399-400: 14 Dec. 1789. Benjamin Craig to Randolph Hunnicutt for Ł 100 for 457 acres in 96 Dist. on 26 Mile Creek of Savannah River, granted on 4 Dec. 1786. Recorded Bk. PPPP, p. 258. Signed: Benja. (C) Craig. Wit: Jothn. Clarke, David Clarke, Charity (c) Clarke. Jonathan Clarke made an oath to John Willson, J. P., 19 Dec. 1789. Rec: 17 Apr. 1798.

Page 400: I, Samuel Lofton, planter, for Ł 20 sold to James Gasaway, planter, 105 acres granted to Lofton by Wm. Moultrie, 4 Feb. 1793. Date: ___ Dec. 1797. Wit: William Griffen, Thomas (his mark) Carey, David Kelton. Thomas Cary made oath to J. B. Earle, J.P., 16 Apr. 1798. Rec: 17 Apr. 1798.

Page 400: 3 Oct. 1795. Edward Wade to Andrew McAlester for Ł 60 stg. for 150 acres surveyed by James Millwee, 3 Jul. 1787, where William Wilson now lives, on Neil's Creek of Rocky River, bd. NE by Hugh Wornock, SE by Thomas Burford and Robert Dowdle. Signed: Edward Wade, Nancy (+) Wade. Wit: Nathaniel McAlester, Wm. Wilson, Alexander McAlester. Alexander McAlester made oath to J. B. Earle, J.P., 16 Apr. 1798....Plat represents 150 acres laid off from Edward Wade to James Oldham. James Millwee, DS.

Pages 400-401: I, William Hall for $100 sold to Joseph Brown 168 acres in Washington Dist. on Double branches of the Saluda River, part of tract granted Benj. Bowen by Thos. Pinckney, 5 Jan. 1789, bd. by William Hall, Jamimah (X) Hall. Wit: David Brown, Joseph Brown, Arthur Halbert. Joseph Brown made oath to Wm. Hall, J.P., 16 Sep. 1796....Jamimah Hall released dower to Andrew Pickens, J.P., 19 Sep. 1796. Rec: 17 Apr. 1798.

Page 401: I, Nicholas Darnal for Ł 200 sold to Jacob Shelor 220 acres on both sides of Choestoe Creek of the Tugaloo River, bd. by Nicholas Dernal, Benjamin Perry, Martin Hewlett, Robert Harrison. Date: 2 April 1798. Wit: Wm. White, Robert Harrison. William White made oath to Nathl. Perry, J. P., 3 Apr. 1798. Rec: 17 Apr. 1798.

Page 401: I, Barzilla Harrison of Pendleton Co. for Ł 70 stg. sold to Richard Echols of Franklin

(Harrison cont'd): Co., Georgia, 100 acres on SE of Tugalo River granted Isaac Lynch by Charles Pinckney on 2 Mar. 1789. Date: 13 Nov. 1797. Wit: Lewis Rolston, John Rolston. Lewis Rolston made oath to Nathl. Perry, J.P., 30 Nov. 1797. Rec: 18 Apr. 1798.

Pages 401-402: 3 Jul. 1795. Francis Fulcher of Washington Dist. to Joshua Reider (Reader) of same, for ₤ 100 stg. for 148 acres, part of 348 acres on Golden's Creek of 12 Mile River, granted John Patterson, 17 Jul. 1788 by Thos. Pinckney. Recorded Bk. XXXX, p. 209. Bd. on NW by John Patterson. Signed: Francis (his mark appears to be "T") Fulcher. Wit: William Jones, Thomas Finley. Thomas Finley made oath to G. W. Earle, DCC, 24 Apr. 1798. Rec: 24 Apr. 1798.

Page 402: I, Isaac Alewaters for $50 sold to Josiah Ship 25 Acres on 23 Mile Creek where Josiah Ship now lives, conveyed by Ship to Alewaters. Date: 2 May 1798. Wit: Sin. (Simon in oath) Doyle, Daniel Sargent. Daniel Sargent made oath to G. W. Earle, DCC, 2 May 1798. Rec: 3 May 1798.

Page 402: 3 Jan. 1796. Andrew Pickens, Robert Anderson, John Miller and John Willson, Esqs., Commissioners appointed by Act of General Assembly for laying off Town of Pendleton and erecting a Courthouse, to Walter Scott Adair for ₤ 20, a lot of land in Town of Pendleton, known in Plan of Town as Lot no. 1. Signed: Robert Anderson, John Willson, Jno. Miller (only). Wit: E. Adair, Louis D. Martin. Edward Adair made oath to G. W. Earle, DCC, 28 Apr. 1798. Rec: 3 May 1798.

Page 402: I, John Leonard of Newberry Co. for $300 sold to Alexander Hamilton of Pendleton Co., 200 acres in Washington Dist. on 18 Mile Creek of Savannah River, granted Locklin Leonard by Thos. Pinckney, 5 Mar. 1787, bd. by Mary Leonard. Date: 9 Jan. 1798. Wit: John Hamilton, Joseph Clarke, James Hamilton. James Hamilton made oath to John Willson, J.P., 9 March 1798. Rec: 17 May 1798.

Pages 402-403: I, Sarah Love for $87 sold to Henry McWhorter Sr., 1 mare, 1 woman's saddle and bridle, 2 cows, calves, featherbed, chest and other movable property. Date: 22 May 1798. Wit: William McClure. Jas. Hamilton. William McClure made oath to John Verner, J.P., 22 May 1798. Rec: 22 May 1798.

Page 403: 5 Nov. 1796. David Clark to John Grissom for ₤ 65 for 262 acres on Keowee River, granted Clark, 2 Jan. 1792 by Chas. Pinckney. Wit: Rattliff Boon, Balaam Mauldin. Ratliff Boon made oath to W. W. Reid, JP, 15 May 1798. Rec: 22 May 1798.

Page 403: I, Benjamin Smith for $60 sold to James Chapman 137 acres in 96 Dist. now Washington District on 23 Mile Creek of Savannah River bd. SW & SE by Ezekiel Pilgrim, granted by Chas. Pinckney, 2 Mar. 1789. Recorded Bk. ZZZZ, p. 104. Date: 13 Dec. 1797. Wit: James Rosamond, Jr., Jno. McMurry, Chas. Willson. James Rosamond made oath to John Willson, J. P., 20 Dec. 1797...Ruth (X) Smith, wife of Benj. Smith released dower to John Willson, J.P., 20 May 1798. Rec: 26 May 1798.

Page 403-404: I, Joseph Duncan for ₤ 50 sold to Rice Duncan 185 acres on 12 Mile River. Date: 30 April 1798. Wit: John Byrd, Charles (X) Durham. John Byrd made oath to James Jett, J. P., 25 May 1798. Rec: 2 June 1798.

Page 404:   2 Apr. 1798. William Stevenson, planter, and
                             Jenny, his wife, spinster, to John Hamilton
                             (also Hambleton) for $50 and 50¢ for 200 ac.
except 57 ac. that William Galaspie sold to Jacob Gilham, granted William
Gilaspie, 21 Jan. 1785, for 572 ac. on both sides of Canoe fork of Little
Generostee of Savannah River. Recorded Bk. CCCC, p. 174. Signed: Wm. Stevenson, Jenny (her mark) Stevenson. Wit: James Stevenson, John Hamilton.
James Stevenson made oath to John Willson, J.P., 1 Jun. 1798...Jenny Stevenson, wife of William Stevenson released dower to John Willson 1 June
1798. Rec: 2 Jun. 1798.

Pages 404-405:   I, William Burney, planter, for 30 lbs. stg.
                             sold to Joseph Angling, planter, 100 acres
                             part of tract in Washington Dist., on the NE
branches of 23 Mile Creek of Savannah River, bd. SE by James Lindsey.
Date: 25 Apr. 1798. Wit: Benjamin Ragsdale, Jesse Ragsdale, Asa (+) Ragsdale....Plat shows land bd. on N. by Wallis, on E. by Wallis, on S. by
Ragsdale, on W. by Wallis. Jesse Ragsdale made oath to John Willson, J.P.
12 May 1798....Elizabeth (+) Burney, wife of William Burney released dower to John Willson, 12 May 1798. Rec: 11 Jun. 1798.

Page 405:   I, James Chandler, planter, for ₺ 80 stg.sold
                             to William Brister, planter, 220 acres on the
                             Keowee River, surveyed for Elisha Maxwell on
4 Jan. 1787 by Arnoldus Vanderhorst. Date: 15 Jan. 1798. Wit: Thomas Vick,
Samuel (+) Brister. Samuel Brister made oath to John Verner, J.P., 16 Jun.
1798. Rec: 21 Jun. 1798.

Page 405:   23 Dec. 1797. Benjamin and John Arnold of
                             Greenville, and Lurance Co.'s, S. C. to Andrew Barkley of Pendleton Co. for ₺ 60 stg.
for 400 acres in Pendleton Co. on Rocky Creek of Savannah River, part of
1,000 acres granted Benjamin Arnold, 5 Sep. 1791. Signed: Benjn. Arnold,
John Arnold. Wit: Samuel Barley, David Ridgway. Samuel Barkley made oath
to Wm. Millwee, J.P., 22 Jun. 1798.
Rec: 23 Jun. 1798.

Page 405:   12 Mar. 1795. Zachariah Walker of Pendleton
                             Co. to William Anderson of Spartanburgh Co.
                             S. C. for ₺ 82 stg. for 150 acres part of
486 acres granted Richard Morrow 3 Nov. 1788. Recorded Bk. XXXX, p. 546.
Also, part of 200 acres conveyed to Walker; Also part of 200 acres where
Walker now lives, to exclude 50 acres where Saml. Walker now lives on Big
Generostee Creek. Wit: Jesse Brown, Leonard Morrow, Thomas Glen. Leonard
Morrow made oath to John Verner, J.P., 22 Jun. 1798.
Rec: 25 Jun. 1798.

Pages 405-406:   19 Nov. 1796. David Brown and Jane, his wife,
                             to Saml. Brown for ₺ 30 stg. for 111 acres on
                             N. side of Toogalo River, bd. by Thomas Armstrong, part of 558 acres granted Thomas Holden, 1 Jan. 1787, conveyed
part to John Rotten, 12 Jun. 1789, from Rotten to Brown, 1794. Signed:
David Brown, Jean (X) Brown. Wit: John Brown, Joseph Brown. Joseph Brown
made oath to W. Hall, J.P., 22 Jun. 1798.
Rec: 25 Jun. 1798.

Page 406:   Washington Dist. I, Joshua Broyles for $150
                             sold to Samuel Brown 100 acres on both sides
                             of Hencoop Creek, branch of Rocky River, part
of tract granted John Grayson by Benj. Guerard, 25 Jan. 1785, conveyed
from Martin to Broyles, bd. by Harkins and John Hall. Date: 12 Aug. 1797.
Wit: Aaron Broyles, David Brown. Aaron Broyles made oath to Wm. Hall, JP,
12 Aug. 1797....Elizabeth (X) Broyles, wife of Joshua Broyles released
dower to John Willson, J.P., 17 Feb. 1798.
Rec: 25 Jun. 1798.

Pages 406-407:   I, Meshack Stevens of Knox Co., Tenn. for ₺60
                             stg. sold to Joshua Dyer of Pendleton Co. 483
                             acres in 96 Dist. on both sides of Estatoe
Creek, of the Keowee River, bd. by John Thomas, granted to Stevens by Wm.

(Stevens cont'd): Moultrie, 1790. Date: 30 May 1798. Signed: Meshack (his mark) Stephens. Wit: James Anderson, Josiah Dyer. Josiah Dyer made oath to W. Reid, J. P., 25 Jun. 1798. Rec: 26 Jun. 1798.

Page 407: 13 Dec. 1796. James Martin of York Co., S.C. to William Thompson for Ł 30 stg. for 160 ac. on both sides of Town Creek, of 12 Mile River bd. by William Thompson, Francis Jones, part of 320 acres granted Samuel Thompson 16 Jul. 1784 by Benj. Guerard, conveyed to Martin. Wit: Thomas Lofton, Jesse Murphree. Jesse Murphree made oath to W. Reid, J. P., 20 Dec. 1797. Rec: 26 Jun. 1798.

Page 407: 28 Mar. 1797. George Thompson to Wm. Thompson for Ł 25 for 180 acres on fork of 12 Mile River, surveyed by David Hopkins, D.S. for William Thomas, part of tract granted by William Thomas to George Thompson. Wit: James Jett, Thomas Wafer. James Jett made oath to G. W. Earle, DCC, 25 Jun. 1798. Rec: 26 Jun. 1798.

Page 407: 28 Mar. 1797. George Thompson to Richard Thompson for Ł 25 stg. for 200 acres on the N. fork of 12 Mile River, bd. by Richard Thompson, James Gibson, Bennett Combs, part of tract conveyed from Wm. Thomas to George Thompson. Wit: James Jett, Reuben Reid. James Jett made oath to G. W. Earle, DCC, 25 Jun. 1798. Rec: 26 Jun. 1798.

Pages 407-408: I, Jonathan Gregory for Ł 50 sold to James Jett 314 acres. Date: 25 Sep. 1797. Signed: Jonathan (+) Gregory. Wit: Nathan Nall, Wm. (+) Bush. Nathan Nall made oath to G. W. Earle, J.P., 25 Jun. 1798. Rec: 26 Jun. 1798.

Page 408: 16 Nov. 1796. John McCrosky to James Hagood for Ł 25 stg. for 137 acres on George's Creek of the Saluda River, bd. NW by Leonard Morgan, John Garvin, other sides by George Parris Creek, granted Morgan Hood on 2 Jan. 1792, conveyed from Hood to McCrosky. Signed: John McCrosky, Margaret (X) McCrosky. Wit: Sterling Hightower, Mary Bullion. Sterling Hightower made oath to W. Reid, J.P., 21 Jun. 1798. Rec: 26 Jun. 1798.

Page 408: 16 Nov. 1796. John McCrosky to James Hagood for Ł 30 stg. for 200 acres, part of tract granted James Duff, 13 Jul. 1792, on George's Creek of Saluda River, bd. by Morgan Hood, Wm. Jameson. Signed: John McCrosky, Margaret (X) McCrosky. Wit: Sterling Hightower, Mary Bullion.... Sterling Hightower made oath to W. Reid, J.P., 21 Jun. 1798. Rec: 26 Jun. 1798.

Page 408: I, Benjamin Clarke and Patience, my wife, for Ł 35 stg. sold to James Hagood 100 acres, part of tract granted John Norwood on 16 Jul. 1784 on S. side of Saluda River, bd. by Col. Henry Crake's old place, John Wheeler, deed to Clarke by Norwood. Date: 24 Jan. 1797. Signed: Benjamin Clarke, Patience (P) Clarke. Wit: Wm. Laffoon, George S. Foster, Solomon (X) Banks. Wm. Laffoon made oath to Wm. Reid, J. P., 25 Jun. 1798. Rec: 26 Jun. 1798.

Pages 408-409: I, William Martin of Pendleton Co. for $800 sold to Lodwick Dobbs of Franklin Co., Ga., 400 acres in three surveys: one of 100 acres granted William Martin; one of 200 acres granted to Reuben Denton on the Tugalo River; one of 100 acres granted Edward Rice, bd. by each other. Date: 30 Jan. 1797. Wit: Wm. Cleveland, Daniel Hammack...Frances Martin, wife of Wm. Martin released dower to Benj. Cleveland, 16 May 1798. Daniel Hammack made oath to Jno. Barton, 18 Jun. 1798. Rec: 26 Jun. 1798.

Page 409: 2 Mar. 1796. John Martin of York Co., S.C., to John Clemens of Pendleton Co. for Ł 125 for 11 acres, part of tract in Washington District on N. side of Saluda River, including mill where Clements now lives and granted George Pearce and conveyed to Martin. Wit: Drury (M) Morris, James (his mark) Riden. James Riden made oath to Wm. Hall, J.P., 5 Mar. ____. Rec: 26 Jun. 1798.

Page 409: 24 May 1798. Eliab Moore and Rebecca, his wife, to Peter Greenlees for Ł 150 stg. for 300 acres on both sides of Broadaway Creek, granted Eliab Moore by Benj. Guerard, 16 Jul. 1784. Recorded Bk. ZZZ, p. 87. Signed: Eliab Moore, Rebecca (her mark) Moore. Wit: Patrick Norris, J. Pickens, Joseph Pickens made oath to E. Browne, J.P., 17 Jun. 1798. Rec: 26 Jun. 1798.

Pages 409-410: I, Wm. McKain of Abbeville Co. for Ł 87 stg. sold to John Jones of Abbeville Co. 326 ac. granted by Wm. Moultrie, 25 Nov. 1794. Recorded Bk. K, no. 5, p. 538, on 23 Mile Creek of Savannah River. Date: 29 Sep. 1797. Wit: Robert McCann, Hannah McCann. Hannah McCann made oath to Robt. McCann, J.P., in Pendleton Co., 25 Jun. 1798. Rec: 26 Jun. 1798.

Page 410: 4 Jun. 1796. Robert Willson of York Co., S.C. to Hugh Wilson, Jr. of Pendleton Co. for Ł 30 stg. for 50 acres, part of 200 acres granted Robert Wilson by Chas. Pinckney, 18 Nov. 1784, on S. side of the Saluda River, bd. on W. by Owen Evans, to Wilson's ford on Saluda to Cambridge. Signed: Robert Wilson, Elizabeth Wilson. Wit: James Jamison, Joseph Jamison, John Hope....York Co., James Jamison made oath to Tho. Gilham, JP, 4 Jun. 1796. Rec: 26 Jun. 1798.

Page 410: 6 Aug. 1793. Asaph Alexander to Bevely Cox for Ł 100 stg. for 200 acres granted 15 Oct. 1784 by Benj. Guerard to James Alexander, Jr., deceased, on the Savannah River, on both sides of the mouth of Big Generostee Creek Asaph Alexander being the lawful heir of James Alexander, Jr., dec'd. Wit: James Jones, John Cox. James Jones made oath to Saml. Porter, 26 Jan. 1796. Rec: 26 Jun. 1796.

Pages 410-411: I, Joseph Clark for Ł 60 sold to Thomas Coker 200 acres where Coker now lives, part of the tract granted Bowlen Clark by Benj. Guerard, 21 Jan. 1785. Recorded Bk. AAAA, p. 433. Wit: Jacob (X) Harvick, Nicholas Harvick, Geo. Forbes. Nicholas Harwick made oath to John Wilson, J.P., on 16 Jun. 1798....Mary (X) Clark, wife of Joseph Clark made oath to John Wilson, 16 Jun. 1798. Rec: 26 Jun. 1798.

Page 411: I, Sheriff Brouster for Ł 50 sold to Aaron Guyton 300 acres on Big Beaverdam Creek granted James Ross by Wm. Moultrie, 15 Jun. 1786. Recorded Bk. LLLL, p. 54, conveyed from Ross to Brouster. Date: 29 Apr. 1796. Signed: Sheriff (his mark) Brouster.* (Note: this appears to be his given name not a title). Wit: Joseph Jolly, William Jolly, William (his mark) Adkins. Joseph Jolly made oath to Wm. Millwee, J.P., 9 Nov. 1796... Elenor (her mark) Brouster, wife of Sheriff Brouster released dower to Robert Anderson, J.P., 24 Jun. 1796. Rec: 26 Jun. 1798.

Page 411: I, Sheriff Brouster for Ł 50 stg. sold to Aaron Guyton 40 acres bd. by James Milwee, Beaverdam Creek, Brouster, part of 100 acres granted Alexander McDowell by Wm. Moultrie, 5 Feb. 1787, conveyed from McDowell to Brouster. Date: 9 Apr. 1796. Signed: Sheriff (his mark) Brouster. Wit: Joseph Jolly, William Jolly, William (his mark) Adkins. Joseph Jolly made oath to Wm. Millwee, J.P., 9 Nov. 1796...Elinor (B) Brouster released dower to Robert Anderson, 24 Jun. 1796. Rec: 26 Jun. 1798.

Page 412: I, John McKeady of Abbeville Co. for ₤ 15 stg. sold to Alexander Sherrard 199½ acres on Little Generostee of Savannah River, granted McKeady, 4 Nov. 1793 by Wm. Moultrie. Recorded Bk. J., no. 5, p. 403. Signed: John McKeady. Wit: Henry Loosk, John Sherrard. John Sherrard made oath to Nathan Lusk, J. P., 22 May 1798. Rec: 26 Jun. 1798.

Page 412: Greenville Co., S. C. I, Elias Earle for 5 shillings sold to Isham Clayton 435 acres on Eastetoe, branch of Keowee River, surveyed for Isham Clayton, 6 Aug. 1789, granted Elias Earle, 4 Dec. 1797 by Chas. Pinckney. Date: 1 Jan. 1798. Wit: Jno. Gowin, James Reynolds. John Gowen made oath to David Goodlett, J.P., (in Pendleton Co.) 9 Feb. 1798. Rec: 26 Jan. 1798.

Page 412: 24 Mar. 1797. Isaac Linch to Isaac Titsworth for ₤ 40 for 301 acres in 96 Dist. on branch of Keowee of Savannah River, bd. S. by Robt. Craven, E. by Wm. Tate, N. by Richd. Brook Roberts, granted by William Moultrie, 2 Sep. 1793. Signed: Isaac (ǂL) Lynch. Wit: Zephaniah (X) Harris, Joshua (X) Holden, Abraham Hargiss. Abraham Hargiss made oath to Joseph Reid, J.P., 1 Apr. 1798. Rec: 20 Jun. 1798.

Pages 412-413: I, George Goodwin for $100 sold to William Parsons 206 acres on Big Creek of Saluda River, part of 291 acres granted Clement Owin by Wm. Moultrie, 6 Mar. 1786. Recorded Bk. HHHH, (no. page number). Date: 2 Feb. 1797. Signed: George (g) Goodwin, Mary (+) Goodwin. Wit: Edmund Parsons, Charles Bennett, John Goodwin. Charles Bennett made oath to Wm. Hall, J.P., 4 Feb. 1797....Mary (X) Goodwin released dower to John Wilson, J.P., 17 Feb. 1798. Rec: 26 Jun. 1798.

Page 413: 28 Dec. 1797. John Martin of Lincoln Co., N.C. to Hugh Moore of Pendleton Co. for ₤ 80 stg. for 640 acres granted John Hathorn, 16 Jul. 1784, conveyed from John Edwards and Wm. Hort, Treasurers of the State, 8 Apr. 1789 to Martin, on Oolenoy Creek of the Saluda River. Wit: Amos Ladd, Samuel Lewis. Samuel Lewis made oath to Wm. Reid, J.P., 12 April 1798. Rec: 26 Jun. 1798.

Page 413: Washington Dist. I, William Shaw of Abbeville Co. for $171 sold to Joseph Brown 200 acres in Washington Dist. on Hencoop Creek of the Savannah River, granted James McConnell by Wm. Moultrie, 7 Nov. 1785. Recorded Bk. GGGG, p. 42. Date: 28 Feb. 1798. Wit: Joseph Brown, Charles Sims. Joseph Brown made oath to Wm. Hall, J.P., 23 Jun. 1798. Rec: 26 Jun. 1798.

Page 413: I, Bennett Combs for $300 sold to Mary Gibson 390 acres on 15 Mile Branch of Savannah River, granted by Chas. Pinckney, 5 Mar.1792, bd. by John Gibson. Date: 29 Dec. 1797. Wit: Moses Hunt, Saml. Cherry. Moses Hunt made oath to G. W. Earle, DCC, 29 Dec. 1797. Rec: 26 Jun. 1798.

Pages 413-414: 4 Dec. 1795. Charles Hunt to Charles Hunt, Jr. for ₤ 50 stg. for 150 acres on Connoross Crk. part of tract surveyed by Chas. Hunt, 22 Jul. 1790. Wit. Daniel Willis, Washington (X) Hunt. Daniel Willis made oath to John Harris, J.P., 20 Jun. 1798. Rec: 26 Jun. 1798.

Page 414: 10 Mar. 1798. Samuel Lofton, Sr. to Benjamin Jackson for ₤ 25 stg for 30 acres, part of 2 tracts: one granted Saml. Lofton, Sr. by Wm. Moultrie, 1793; the other granted Thos. Lofton by Moultrie, 1786, on E. side of 18 Mile Creek, bd. by Thos. Carey, Chris. Strong. Wit: William

(Lofton-Jackson cont'd):   Griffen, John G. Lofton. John G. Lofton made
                           oath to Wm. Reid, J. P., 26 Jun. 1798.
Rec: 26 Jun. 1798.

Page 414:   I, Obern Buffington for Ł 20 sold to William
                           Beazley 25 acres on N. side of Cain Creek of
                           Keowee River, part of 567 acres granted Ezekiel Buffington and Allis Harling, 5 Mar. 1792 by Chas. Pinckney. Recorded Bk. D, no. 5, p. 416. Date: 28 Dec. 1797. Wit: John Beazley, William Trapp. John Beazley made oath to Joseph Reid, J.P., 29 Dec. 1797.
Rec: 26 Jun. 1798.

Pages 414-415:   10 Jan. 1791. John Simpson to Aaron James for
                           Ł 60 stg. for 210 acres granted Simpson on 5
                           Jan. 1789, on Big Generostee. Wit: Jacob Gilleylen, Thomas Turner. Thomas Turner made oath to E. Browne, J.P., 12 Feb. 1796. Rec: 26 Jun. 1798.

Page 415:   I, Thomas Lesley for Ł 27 stg. sold to Aaron
                           James 87 acres on Great Generostee Creek of
                           Savannah River, where Asaph Alexander now lives, part of tract granted Henry Long by Wm. Moultrie, 10 Aug. 1793. Date: 1 Aug. 1796. Wit: James Turner, Chris. Winder. James Turner made oath to John Verner, J.P., 26 Jun. 1798.
Rec: 26 Jun. 1798.

Page 415:   Whereas, Robert Selfridge was in possession
                           of 640 acres on Wilson's Creek of Savannah
                           River, bd. S. by Jno. Caldwell, W. by Thos. Clark, S. by John Bryson....whereas, Baylis Earle made judgement against Selfridge for 64-11-1....now, I, Thomas Sidney Reese, Sheriff of Pendleton Co. sold tract to John Harris, Esq., highest bidder, for $150. Date: 28 Jul. 1797. Signed: Thomas S. Reece, Sheriff. Wit: Saml. Barr, R. Bowen. Samuel Barr made oath to J. B. Earle, J.P., 26 Jun. 1798.
Rec: 26 Jun. 1798.

Page 415:   I, Lewis Dinkins, of Town of Columbia, S.C.,
                           for Ł 50, sold to Michael Barrett of said
                           town and State, 500 acres in Pendleton Co. on George's Creek, bd. NE by John Carew, NW by Robert Easley, SW by Wade and Fleming, E. by Siddle, granted Dinkins by Chas. Pinckney, 2 Jul. 1798. Date: 14 Jul. 1798. Wit: H. M. Gowen, Richd. Homan....Camden Dist., Richland Co., S. C., Richard Homan made oath to Harris Turner, J.P., 14 Jul. 1798. Rec: 23 Jul. 1798.

Pages 415-416:   I, John Carewe, of Town of Columbia, S. C.,
                           for Ł 50 sold to Michael Barrett, of Columbia, 500 acres in Washington Dist., Pendleton Co., on George's Creek, bd. NE by Lewis Dinkins, SE by Wilson and Easley, SW by Jenny Marie Alkin, granted John Carew by Charles Pinckney, 2 Jul. 1798. Date: 13 Jul. 1798. Signed: John Carewe. Wit: Wm. Howell, John Dickey, Richd. H. Homan....Camden Dist., Richland Co., Richard H. Homan made oath to Harris Turner, J.P., 14 Jul. 1798.
Rec: 23 Jul. 1798.

Page 416:   I, Jenny Maria Alkin of Columbia for Ł 50
                           sold to Michael Barrett of Columbia 500 ac.
                           in Washington Dist., on George's Creek, bd. NW by Toney and Wilson, NE by Michael Boulyer, SE by David Hughs, SW by John Carew, granted Jenny Marie Alkin by Chas. Pinckney, 2 Jul. 1798. Date: 14 Jul. 1798. Wit: Martyn Alin, Lydia Rutland....Camden Dist., Richland Co., Martyn Alkins made oath to Harris Turner, J. P., 14 Jul. 1798.
Rec: 23 Jul. 1798.

Page 416:   I, Michael Boulgar of Columbia for Ł 50 sold
                           to Michael Barrett 500 acres in Washington
                           Dist. on George's Creek, bd. NE by Phillip Brasher, SE by Tho. Blasingame, SW by Jenny M. Alkins, NW by Widow Hill, granted Boulger by Charles Pinckney, 2 Jul. 1798. Date: 14 Jul. 1798. (cont'd next page).

(Boulger cont'd): Signed: Michael (M) Boulger. Wit: Martyn Alkin, Richd. Homan....Camden Dist., Richland Co., S. C., Martyn Alkin made oath to Harris Turner, J. P., 14 Jul. 1798. Rec: 23 Jul. 1798.

Page 416: Columbia, S. C. 18 May 1798, I agree to allow Richard H. Homan 960 acres part of 1,920 acres on Big and Little George's Creek, in Pendleton Co., Richard Homan to discharge all expenses attending running same...I agree to place no obstruction to the sale of above land in consequence of a sale by Tho. Farrar, late Sheriff of Washington Dist., ... wherein I became purchaser. Signed: Michael Barrett. Wit: Martyn Alkin ....Camden Dist., Richland Co., S. C., Martyn Alkin made oath to Harris Turner, J. P., 14 Jul. 1798. Rec: 23 Jul. 1798.

Page 416: I, Michael Barrett have appointed Richard Hatfield Homan my Attorney for special purpose to dispose of all lands as are my property on Big and Little George's Creek, in Pendleton Co., and which were bought for me by Waddy Thompson at a sale made of same by Thomas Farrar, Esq., Sheriff of Washington Dist. in 1793, and which are described: No. 1, 2, 3. (Note: no other description). Date: 14 Jul. 1798. Wit: Martyn Alkin... Camden Dist., Richland Co., S. C., Martyn Alkin made oath to Harris Turner, J. P., 14 Jul. 1798. Rec: 23 Jul. 1798.

Pages 416-417: We, Zachariah Holcomb and John Hays sold to Elizabeth Thrisher 100 acres bd. by Martin, John Loyd. Date: 3 Feb. 1798. Signed: Zachariah (∅) Holcomb, John (X) Hays. Wit: John Tippen, William Skelton, John McMahon. Capt. John Tippen made oath to Joshua Saxon, J. P., 9 Apr.1798. Rec: 23 Jul. 1798.

Page 417: Whereas, John McCambridge, dec'd, formerly possessed of 1,000 acres on Little Beaverdam Creek of Toogalo River...James McClure, in June last, get a judgement against John Henry, administrator of the goods ..chattels...lands of John McCambridge, and were ordered sold by Sheriff to the highest bidder (amount blank) to James McClure. Date: 6 Jan.1798. Signed: Thomas S. Reese, Sheriff. Wit: John Gage, James Anderson. Both made oath to Robert McCann, J. P., 26 Jan. 1798. Rec: 28 Jun. 1798.

Page 417: I, John Martin of Union Co., S. C. for Ł 50 sold to Thomas Farrar of Pendleton Co., 200 acres on Little Beaverdam Creek of Toogalo River, granted Martin 7 Aug. 1786 by Wm. Moultrie. Date: 2 Apr. 1798. Wit: Jos. C. Gist, W. Thompson. Waddy Thompson, Esq. made oath to J. B. Earle at Pickensville, 10 Apr. 1798. Rec: 23 Jul. 1798.

Page 417: I, John Martin of Union Co. for Ł 50 sold to Benjamin Hickman of Pendleton Co. 200 acres on Little Beaverdam Creek of Toogalo River, including Hurricane, bd. NE by Dortos Fredrick Sunn, SE by Capt. James Wilson, granted Martin 7 Aug. 1786 by Wm. Moultrie. Date: 2 Apr. 1798. Wit: Jos. C. Gist, W. Thompson. Waddy Thompson, Esq., made oath to J.B. Earle, J. P., 10 Apr. 1798. Rec: 23 Jul. 1798.

Pages 418-419: 14 Apr. 1795. George Naylor of Augusta, Richmond Co., Ga., Esq., to Abraham Morhouse of Philadelphia, Commonwealth of Pennsylvania, Merchant, for 5 shillings, lawful money of Penn. for 100,000 acres in Washington Dist. on Keowee and Little River (lengthy description) granted by Wm. Moultrie, 6 Oct. 1794, registered in Office of Secretary of State in Bk. N, no. 5, #34-133. Wit: David Allison, Jos. Boggs...15 Apr. 1794, before Matthew Clarkson, Esq., Mayor of the City of Philadelphia appeared

(Naylor-Morhouse cont'd): George Naylor, Esq. and acknowledged above indenture. Rec: 6 Aug. 1798.

Page 419: 9 Apr. 1798. Thomas Farrar of Pendleton Co. to Samuel Earle of Greenville Co., S. C. for ₤ 80 stg. for 640 acres on Big Beaverdam Crk. of Toogalo River, granted Capt. Field Farrar by Benj. Guerard, 15 Oct. 1784, bd. by Jacob Milligan. Wit: J. B. Earle, Wm. McCaleb; J. B. Earle made oath to John C. Kilpatrick, 1 Aug. 1798. Rec: 6 Aug. 1798.

Pages 419-420: 5 Dec. 1795. David Lewis Anderson and Rachel, his wife, of Laurens Co., S. C. to Joseph Jolly and James Moorhead, of Pendleton Co. for ₤ 100 stg. for 200 acres on branch of Town Creek, granted Anderson by Benj. Guerard, 15 Oct. 1784. Recorded Bk. ZZZ, p. 123. Signed: David Ls. Anderson, Rachel Anderson. Wit: John Hughs, James Laughlin. James Laughlin made oath to Wm. Millwee, J. P., 8 Jul. 1797. Rec: 6 Aug. 1798.

Page 420: Washington Dist. I, Thomas Carey for ₤ 80 stg. sold to William Griffen 200 acres in Washington Dist. on 18 Mile Creek E. side of Keowee River, bd. by John Lewis Gervais, granted William Huggins by Wm. Moultrie, 2 Oct. 1786. Recorded Bk. BBBB, p. 399. Date: 5 Jan. 1798. Signed: Thomas (O) Carey. Wit: John G. Lofton, Robert Glenn, Samuel Lofton, Jr. Robert Glenn made oath to J. B. Earle, J. P., 1 Jan. 1798. Rec: 6 Aug. 1798.

Page 420: 11 Mar. 1797. John Hamilton to Owen Evans for ₤ 40 stg. for 81 acres on S. side of Saluda River, granted Hamilton 5 Dec. 1791. Signed: John (his mark) Hamilton, Mary (M) Hamilton. Wit: John Wilson, Sr., Hugh Wilson, John Wilson, Jr. Hugh Wilson made oath to Wm. Hall, J.P., 17 Feb. 1798. Rec: 6 Aug. 1798.

Pages 420-421: 11 Jan. 1796. Asa Cobb to Reubin Johnston (also Johnson) for ₤ 50 stg. for 60 acres in Washington Dist. on S. side of Saluda River, part of 200 acres granted James Hamilton by Benj. Guerard, 15 Oct. 1784, bd. by Benjamin Farmer. Wit: John Pepper, Peter Greenlees, Saml. Pepper. John Pepper made oath to Wm. Hall, J. P., 18 Mar. 1797. Rec: 6 Aug. 1798.

Page 421: I, Abraham Barren of Greenville Co., S. C., for ₤ 60 sold to James M. Wilbourn of Pendleton Co., Washington Dist., 185 acres on the Saluda River. Date: 23 Jan. 1798. Wit: William Hone, Hugh Wilson, Thomas Hone. William Honey made oath to Wm. Hall, J. P., 25 Jun. 1798. Rec: 6 Aug. 1798.

Page 421: I, George Goodwin of Greenville Co., S. C. for ₤ 7, 10 shillings stg. sold to Charles Bennett 68 acres on Saluda River, part of 291 acres granted Clement Owen by Wm. Moultrie, 6 Mar. 1786. Recorded Bk.HHHH (no page number). Date: 4 Feb. 1797. Signed: George (g) Goodwin, Mary (X) Goodwin. Wit: Thomas Bennett, Crafford Goodwin. Thomas Bennett made oath to Wm. Hall, J.P., 4 Feb. 1797...Mary Goodwin, wife of George Goodwin released dower to John Wilson, J. P., 17 Feb. 1798. Rec: 6 Aug. 1798.

Page 422: I, Joseph Bowlin and Valentine, my wife, for ₤ 50 stg. sold to Dickerson Garrett 65 acres on Saluda River. Signed: Joseph (X) Bowlin, Valentine (her mark-arrow pointed up) Bowlin. Wit: William Bell, John Hall. William Bell made oath to Wm. Hall, J. P., 18 Jun. 1796...Valentine Bowlin released dower to Wm. Hall, J. P., 18 Jun. 1796. Rec: 6 Aug. 1798.

Page 422: I, Dickerson Garrett for ₤ 40 stg. sold to

(Dickerson Garrett cont'd): Thomas Bennett 65 acres on S. side of Saluda River. Date: 17 Feb. 1798. Wit: John Harper, Walter Bell. John Harper made oath to Wm. Hall, J. P., 17 Feb. 1798...Lidia (+) Garrett released dower to John Wilson, J. P., 17 Feb. 1798. Rec: 6 Aug. 1798.

Pages 422-423: I, Nancy Jones of Washington Dist., planter, for Ł 37-10 shillings, sold to Adam Lukey, planter, 72 acres in 96 Dist. on Little Creek of 26 Mile River of Savannah River, bd. E. by Lewis Jones, W. by John Hunnicutt, granted Sophia Case by Wm. Moultrie, 4 Sep. 1786. Recorded Bk. C., p. 598. Date: 23 Jan. 1797. Signed: Nancy (her mark) Jones. Wit: John Jones, Saml. Burney, Wm. Burney. Samuel Burney made oath to Wm. Reid, JP, 28 Jun. 1798. Rec: 6 Aug. 1798.

Page 423: I, William Rigs of Washington Dist., planter, for Ł 30 stg. sold to Andrew Oliver 50 acres part of tract on Little Creek of 26 Mile Crk. of Savannah River, bd. W. by Adam Lukey, E. by Robt. Hunnicutt, Wm. Rigs, and Andrew Oliver, Wardlaw, granted William Rigs by Wm. Moultrie, 5 Jun. 1786. Recorded Bk. N, p. 174. Date: 27 Jan. 1797. Signed: William Riggs, Sarah (X) Riggs. Wit: Saml. Burney, Adnr. Porter. Samuel Burney made oath to Wm. Reid, J. P., 28 Jun. 1798. (No recording date).

Page 423: We, William Anderson and Eliza Ann, my wife, and James Prichard, joint heirs of the late Eleanor Prichard, of Edgefield Co., S. C., for Ł 50 stg. sold to William Pritchard, of same place, 640 acres granted Eleanor Prichard 15 Oct. 1784 on 23 Mile Creek, Pendleton Co. Date: 18 Jan. 1798. Signed: W. Anderson, Eliza Ann Anderson, James Prichard. Wit: Hugh Dickson, Thos. Anderson, Caleb Holloway. Hugh Dickson made oath to Robt. McCann, J. P., 27 Jun. 1798. Rec: 6 Aug. 1798.

Pages 423-424: I, William Prichard of Edgefield Co. for $350 sold to John Dickson of Pendleton Co. 359 ac. on 23 Mile Creek, bd. E. by lands granted to Wm. Prichard, SE by Ephraim and Richard Robinson, NW & SW by Dutilley, NE by James Prichard. Date: 19 Jun. 1798. Wit: Hugh Dickson, W. Anderson, Thomas Anderson. (Plat). Hugh Dickson made oath to Robt. McCann, J. P., 21 Jun. 1798. Rec: 6 Aug. 1798.

Page 424: 27 Nov. 1788. John Hunter, Esq. of 96 Dist. to Elazon Smith, of same, for Ł 45 stg. for 155 acres now in his possession, on 23 Mile Creek of Savannah River, bd. by Hugh McBee, Thomas Abbott, Bowling Clark, granted Hunter by Wm. Moultrie, 1 May 1786 (now says 255 acres). Wit: Jonathn. Clark, Jean Hunter, Margaret Hunter. Jonathan Clark made oath to John Wilson, J. P., 21 Mar. 1795. Rec: 6 Aug. 1798.

Page 424: I, John McCutchin and Ann, my wife, for Ł 78 stg. sold to Peter Keys 200 acres in Washington Dist. on Big Generostee of Savannah River, bd. by Mr. Moore, McCutchin, Wm. Hurtin, Widow Tilly. Date: 1 March 1798. Signed: John McCutchin, Ann (A) McCutchin. Wit: Joshua Saxon, Jesse Bowman. Joshua Saxon, J. P. certified he saw deed signed 20 Mar. 1798. Rec: 6 Aug. 1798.

Page 424: I, Samuel Lovingood for $30 sold to Samuel Taylor 112 acres bd. on SE by John Shannon, granted Lovingood 6 Oct. 1794. Date: 3 May 1798. Wit: John Taylor, J. B. Earle. J. B. Earle made oath to G. W. Earle DCC 10 Jul. 1798. Red: 6 Aug. 1798.

Pages 424-425: I, Jacob Capehart, planter, for Ł 20 sold to

(Capehart cont'd): Amos Nation, planter, 30 acres on 23 Mile Creek, bd. by Hobson, part of tract granted Capehart by Wm. Moultrie. Date: 15 Mar. 1798. Wit: Lewis Cobb, Moses Payne. Lewis Cobb made oath to G. W. Earle, DCC, 21 Jul. 1798. Rec: 6 Aug. 1798.

Page 425: 3 Jul. 1798. Eli Hunnicutt and Martha, his wife, to John Jones for £ 10 stg. for 50 ac. on Jones' Creek of 26 Mile Creek, bd. on N. by Lewis Jones, on SE by Jones' Creek, part of 482 acres granted Hunnicutt by Wm. Moultrie, 4 Oct. 1786. Recorded Bk. 4, P, p. 240; also tract of 20 acres on Jones' Creek bd. by above tract, part of 300 acres granted Michael Dickson by Wm. Moultrie, 5 Jun. 1786. Recorded Bk. 4 J, p.419. Signed: Eli Hunnicutt, Martha (X) Hunnicutt. Wit: James Jolly, Jesse Jolly. James Jolly made oath to Wm. Millwee, J. P., 3 Jul. 1798. Rec: 6 Aug. 1798.

Page 425: I, John Moore of Iredale Co., N. C. for $500 sold to Alexander Cavin 200 acres granted to John Wornock, 4 Dec. 1786 on W. side of Rocky River. Recorded Bk. BBBB, p. 414. Conveyed to Joseph More. Signed: Joseph (his mark) More. Wit: John McMahen, William Cook. William Cook made oath to E. Browne, J. P., 11 Aug. 1798. Rec: 17 Aug. 1798.

Pages 425-426: Washington Dist. 7 May 1794. Thomas Grant to John Cox for £ 91 stg. for 304 acres granted William Goggings by Chas. Pinckney, 1 Oct. 1792, then to Thomas Grant, on 26 Mile Creek bd. by John Morris, Scoots. Wit: Benj. Dickson, Charles (his mark) White. Benjamin Dickson made oath to Wm. Millwee, 7 Aug. 1797. Rec: 17 Aug. 1798.

Page 426: 21 Aug. 1797. William Hutton of 96 Dist. of Abbeville Co. to Aaron Moore of 96 Dist. of Pendleton Co. for £ 60 for 453 acres granted 7 Jan. 1793 by Wm. Moultrie in Washington Dist. on Shoal Creek of Keowee River of Savannah River. Wit: John (X) Queal, Elizabeth McKinley, Samuel Dickson and Wm. McKinley witnessed receipt, 21 Aug. 1797. John Quel made oath to Wm. McKinley, J. P., 21 Aug. 1797. Rec: 18 Aug. 1798.

Page 426: Washington Dist. I, Richard Robinson for £25 stg. sold to John Morgan 184 acres on both sides of 23 Mile Creek, part of tract granted Alexander Robinson 16 Jul. 1784, sold by John Edwards and Wm. Hort, Esq.s, Treasurers of State to James Martin, 7 Apr. 1789. Date: 20 Aug. 1798. Wit: Jacob (X) West, William Black, William Pasmore. William Pasmore made oath to J. B. Earle, J. P., 21 Aug. 1798. Rec: 21 Aug. 1798.

Pages 426-427: I, Richard Robinson for £ 25 stg. sold William Pasmore 184 acres, part of tract granted Alexander Robinson 20 Jul. 1784, sold by the Treasurers to James Martin 7 Apr. 1789, on W. side of 23 Mile Creek, bd. by Pasmore, Jonathan West. Date: 24 Apr. 1798. Wit: James Tuffnell, Jacob (his mark) West, Michael (his mark) West. Jacob West made oath to J. B. Earle, J. P., 21 Aug. 1798. Rec: 21 Aug. 1798.

Page 427: I, Simeon Theus, Treasurer of the State of South Carolina for £ 50 stg. sold to Jacob Lynch the following tracts of land: 300 acres on N. branch of the Keowee River, bd. by Brook Roberts, on E. by river, on S. by John F. Grimkie; tract of 640 acres on E. side of Keowee River, "comprehending the spot of ground whereon Fort Prince George was formerly built"; said tracts mortgaged by William Tate to insure his bond to Commissioners of the Loan Office for paper medium, mortgage no. 233, in the Treasury Office. Date: 4 Apr. 1798, at Charleston, S. C. Wit: John McCall, Lyon Levy. Rec: 21 Aug. 1798.

Page 427: I, Samuel Burton for $170 sold to Samuel Barr one negro boy named Joe, about 8 years old. Date: 6 Jan. 1798. Wit: W. Steele. William Steele made oath to G. W. Earle, DCC, 23 Aug. 1798. Rec: 23 Aug. 1798.

Page 427: I, Joseph Duncan for $210 sold to Jesse Tatum 120 acres on Wolf Creek. Date: 21 Apr. 1798. Wit: John Bird, Sr., Sarah Bird. John Bird, Sr. made oath to James Jett, J.P., 23 Aug. 1798. Rec: 27 Aug. 1798.

Pages 427-428: 2 May 1798. Joseph Duncan to Edward Tatum for $260 for 130 acres, part of tract granted to Duncan 6 Feb. 1786. Wit: Jesse Tatum, Wm. Marchbanks. Jesse Tatum made oath to James Jett, 25 Apr. 1798. Rec: 27 Aug. 1798.

Page 428: I, John Jenkins for $150 sold to Jeremiah Thompson 143 acres on Crow Creek. Date: 11 Aug. 1798. Signed: John (X) Jenkins, Susanna (X) Jenkins. Wit: Adam Heath Thompson, Rice Duncan. Adam Heath Thompson made oath to James Jett, J. P., 24 Aug. 1798. Rec: 27 Aug. 1798.

Page 428: 16 Apr. 1796. George Slaton to Isham Blankinship for Ł 50 stg. for 100 acres in Washington Dist. on Little Beaverdam of Rocky River part of tract George Slaton now lives on, bd. by Thomas Adams. Signed: George (his mark) Slaton. Wit: Jeremiah (B) Ellrod, Oliver Charles. Oliver Charles made oath to Wm. Hall, J. P., 28 Jun. 1796. Rec: 8 Sep. 1798.

Page 428: 14 Jan. 1795. Thomas Wade to George Vandiver for Ł 10 stg. for 100 acres, part of 486 ac. surveyed for Wade, 16 Sep. 1791,on Neel's Crk of Rocky River, bd. by Stephen Bennett, David Wade. Signed: Thomas Clements Wade. Wit: Elisha Bennett, Edward (X) Wade, David (X) Wade. Elisha Bennett made oath to Joshua Saxon, J. P., 20 May 1797. Rec: 13 Sep. 1798.

Page 429: I, Benjamin Turner for 150 Spanish Mill dollars sold to Arthur Mitchel 100 acres where Mitchel now lives, on 23 Mile Creek of the Savannah River. Date: 15 Sep. 1798. Signed: Benjamin (B) Turner. Wit: Simon Doyle, Elias Turner. Simon Doyle made oath to John Verner, 17 Sep. 1798. Rec: 17 Sep. 1798.

Page 429: I, Benjamin Turner for Ł 40 sold to Simon Doyle 73 acres where Doyle now lives, bd. by Arthur Mitchel, on 23 Mile Creek of Savannah River. Date: 15 Sep. 1798. Signed: Benjamin (B) Turner. Wit: Elias Turner, Arthur Mitchel. Arthur Mitchel made oath to John Verner, J. P., 17 Sep. 1798. Rec: 17 Sep. 1798.

Page 429: I, John Turner for $150 sold to James Simmons 200 acres where Simmons now lives, bd. by Simon Doyle, on 23 Mile Creek of Savannah River. Date: 17 Sep. 1798. Wit: Isaac Alewaters, Simon Doyle. Simon Doyle made oath to John Verner, J. P., 17 Sep. 1798. Rec: 17 Sep. 1798.

Page 429: I, Joel Ledbetter and Kitty, my wife, for Ł40 stg. sold to Ezekiel Stanley 122 acres in Washington Dist. on Big Generostee Creek of Savannah River, granted James Ross by Wm. Moultrie, 4 Mar. 1793, bd. by Guilbert Neyle, Patr(?) Bayley. Signed: Joel Ledbetter, <u>Katy</u> (X) Ledbetter. Wit: Daniel Ledbetter, Prudence Hix. Daniel Ledbetter made oath to Joshua Saxon, J. P., 5 Aug. 1798. Rec: 8 Aug. 1798.

Page 430:   I, Ezekiel Stanley and Rhoda, my wife, for
                         $200 stg. sold to Peter Keys 122 acres grant-
                         ed James Ross by Wm. Moultrie, 4 Mar. 1793,
conveyed to Ezekiel Standley in Washington Dist. on Big Generostee Creek
of Savannah River, bd. by Gilber Neyle, Peter Bayley. Date: 29 Sep. 1798.
Signed: Ezekiel Stanley, Rhoda (X) Stanley. Wit: William B. Ross, David
Ross. David Ross made oath to Wm. Millwee, J. P., 8 Oct. 1798.
Rec: 8 Oct. 1798.

Page 430:   Spartang.(Spartanburgh?) Co., S. C. 5 April
                         1797, Burrell Bobo to Wm. Stuart, both of
                         Sparten. for $400 for 194 acres on both sides
of Little River of Keowee River in Pendleton Co., part of 550 acres granted Bobo by Wm. Moultrie, 5 Feb. 1787. Signed: Burrill Bobo, Elizabeth(X)
Bobo. Wit: Chaney Bobo, Elizabeth (X) Summer, George Suler. George Shuler made oath to Joseph Reed, 10 Nov. 1797.
Rec: 8 Oct. 1798.

Page 430:   10 Oct. 1796. George Shuler to William Stuart
                         for 37 shillings, for 100 acres bd. by Bobo.
                         Wit: Edward Hase(?), Jacob Reece. Edward
Hase made oath to Joseph Reed, J. P., 15 Mar. 1798.
Rec: 8 Oct. 1798.

Pages 430-431:   10 Oct. 1795. George Shuler to William Stuart
                         for ₤ 20 for 50 acres on both sides of Crav-
                         en's Creek of Little River, bd. by Rt. Craven
and Bobo. Wit: Edward Hases(?), Jacob Reece. Edward Hases made oath to
Joseph Reed, J. P., 15 Mar. 1798.
Rec: 8 Mar. (Oct.?) 1798.

Page 431:   15 Apr. 1797. Burrell Bobo of Spartang. Co.,
                         S. C. to George Shuler of Pendleton Co. for
                         $400 for 330 acres, part of 530 acres grant-
ed to Bobo by Wm. Moultrie, 5 Feb. 1787, on Little River of Keowee River.
Signed: Burrell Bobo, Elizabeth (X) Bobo. Wit: William (X) Stuart, Eliza-
beth (X) Summer, Chaney Bobo. William Stuart made oath to Joseph Reece,
J. P., 10 Nov. 1797.
Rec: 8 Oct. 1798.
(Note: the name Joseph Reece looks like Reed in some places.)

(Page numbers are torn off pages 431-436).

Page 431:   I, Edward Johnson of Bunkum (sic) Co., N. C.
                         for $400 sold to John Byass Blackwell of
                         Greenville Co., S. C., 100 acres in Pendle-
ton Co. on SW side of Saluda River, bd. by Wm. Ashurst, part of 200 ac.
granted Wm. Carpenter, 4 Apr. 1785, conveyed to Wm. Ashurst, from Ashurst
to Edward Johnson, bd. on SE & SW by Thomas Hood, NW by Ashurst. Date: 27
Jul. 1797. Wit: Thos. Harrison, Charles Barron, George Bradley. George
Bradley made oath to E. Browne, J. P., 16 Apr. 1798.
Rec: 8 Oct. 1798.

Page 431:   We, Ebenezer Bourland of Pendleton Co., Ed-
                         ward Johnson of Buncum Co., N. C. for $100
                         sold to John Byass Blackwell of Greenville
Co., S. C. 100 acres: by Bourland 15 acres and by Johnson 85 acres in
Pendleton Co., on SW side of Saluda River, part of 802 acres granted to
Thomas Hood, 1793, bd. by Wm. Ashurst, Wm. Hunt, John Lollar. Date: 28
Jul. 1797. Signed: Edward Borland, Edward Johnson. Wit: William Thurston,
George Bradley, Benjamin Borland. George Bradley made oath to E. Browne,
J. P., 16 Apr. 1798.
Rec: 8 Oct. 1798.

Pages 431-432:   2 Nov. 1793. John Buchannon of Abbeville Co.
                         to David Alexander of Pendleton Co. for ₤ 20
                         stg. for 107 acres, one fourth part of plan-
tation on Cherokee Creek of Hencoop Creek, NW branch of Savannah River,
granted Buchannon by Thos. Pinckney, 7 Jul. 1788. Recorded Bk. XXXX,p.223
and bd. by David Alexander. Wit: Stephen Willis, James Alexander, David

(Buchannon-Alexander cont'd): Alexander. Stephen Willis made oath to Wm. Hall, J. P. (no date). Rec: 8 Oct. 1798.

Page 432: I, Joseph Duncan for $600 sold to Solomon Murphree 374 acres. Date: 7 Dec. 1797. Wit: James Jett, David Murphree, Wm. Murphree. Moses Murphree made oath to W. Reed, J. P., 8 Oct. 1798. (Signed by David Murphree.). Rec: 8 Oct. 1798.

Page 432: We, Auldin Tucker and Clary, my wife, for $200 sold to John McCollister 100 acres bd. by Robert Tucker, Blair, Jeremiah Hall, Henry Milford, James Stuart, Bartley Tucker and John McCollister. Date: 1 Aug. 1798. Signed: Auldin (X) Tucker, Clary (X) Tucker. Wit: J. McMahen, Robert Tucker, Samuel Emison. Samuel Emison made oath to E. Browne, JP, 6 Oct. 1798. Rec: 8 Oct. 1798.

Pages 432-433: We, Harbert Tucker and Fannie, my wife, for $200 sold to John McCollister 100 acres where Robert Tucker now lives, bd. by Mulberry Crk., Bartley Tucker, James Martin. Date: 1 Aug. 1798. Signed: Harbert Tucker, Fanney Tucker. Wit: John McMahen, Samuel Emison, Robert (R) Tucker. Samuel Emison made oath to E. Browne, J. P., 6 Oct. 1798. Rec: 8 Oct. 1798.

Page 433: 27 Jul. 1795. Fergus Caven to Samuel Emison for Ł 60 stg. for 135 acres granted Cavin on 1 Dec. 1791 by Chas. Pinckney, bd. by Cavin on the N., on S. by James Corls, on SE by Alex. Erwin, on NW by Matthew Corls, on E. by Rocky Creek of Savannah River, above the ancient boundary line. Signed: Fergus Cavin, Hannah (her mark-arrow pointed down) Cavin. Wit: Nathan McAlister, George Stringer. Nathan McCollister made oath to E. Browne, J. P., 3 May 1797. Rec: 8 Oct. 1798.

Page 433: 18 Aug. 1798. William Gillispie, Sr. to William Gillispie, Jr. for Ł 60 stg. for 193 ac. on S. side of Saluda, on George's Creek, Middle Fork. Signed: William (/) Gillispie. Wit: Saml. C. Duff, James Cunningham, James Duff. James Cunningham made oath to Robt. McCann, J. P., 20 Aug. 1798. Rec: 8 Oct. 1798.

Page 433-434: I, William Gillispie, Sr. for $100 sold to William Gillispie, Jr., one waggon, geers, all my plantation tools, all furniture, one horse, 1 cow and calf. Date: 20 Aug. 1798. Signed: Wm. (/) Gillispie. Wit: Saml. C. Duff, James Duff, James Cunningham. James Duff made oath to G. W. Earle, DCC, 18 Sep. 1798. Rec: 8 Oct. 1798.

Page 434: 11 Aug. 1798. Robert Harkness to John Harkness for Ł 100 stg. for 2 tracts in Washington Dist. on Rocky Creek and Hencoop; one tract of 100 acres granted Andrew Lee by Benj. Guerard. Recorded Bk. AAAA and p. 212, 15 Oct. 1784; the other of 121 acres granted by Wm. Moultrie to Andrew Lee, 4 Dec. 1786. Recorded Bk. QQQQ, p. 225. Wit: Jas. Thompson, John Glasgow. James Thompson made oath to E. Browne, J. P., 11 Aug. 1798. Rec: 8 Oct. 1798.

Page 434: I, Robert Harkness for $500 sold to James Harkness all goods and chattels mentioned, cattle, hogs, sheep, 1 eighty gallon still and vessels, horse, waggon, household implements, etc. (itemized list). Date: 11 Aug. 1798. Wit: Jas. Thompson, John Glasgow. James Thompson made oath to E. Browne, J. P., 11 Aug. 1798. Rec: 8 Oct. 1798.

Pages 434-435: I, Robert Harkness for $100 sold to Margaret Harkness all goods and chattels mentioned: 1 mare, 2 cows, featherbed and bed clothes, (itemized list). Date: 11 Aug. 1798. Wit: Jas. Thompson, John Glasgow. James Thompson made oath to E. Browne, J. P., 11 Aug. 1798. Rec: 8 Oct. 1798.

Page 435: 3 Jul. 1789. John Prater, planter, to Robert Pickens, planter, for Ł 80 stg. for 200 ac. part of tract in 96 Dist. on 23 Mile Creek of Savannah River. Wit: Robt. McCann, Alexr. Boyse. Robert McCann made oath to John Willson, J. P., 2 Dec. 1790. Rec: 8 Oct. 1798.

Page 435: 28 Aug. 1792. Robert McCann, planter, to Robert Pickens, planter, for Ł 6 stg. for 280 acres now in Pickens possession, on 23 Mile Creek of the Savannah River, part of 688 acres granted McCann by Charles Pinckney 3 May 1790. Wit: Jonathan Hicks, Levi Wimpy....Plat shows bd. NE by Alexr. Boyse, NW by Jno. Prater, W. by Robt. Pickens, SW by Alexr. Boyse, SE by R. McCann, E. by R. McCann. Levi Wimpy made oath to John Willson, J. P., 13 Oct. 1792. Rec: 8 Oct. 1798.

Page 436: I, Alexr. Boyse for $400 sold to John Pickens 200 acres on 23 Mile Creek of Savannah River, bd. NW by Robt. Pickens, NE by David Wimpy, SW by Robt. McCann, granted John Hodges by Benj. Guerard. Date: 7 July 1788. Wit: Bazzel (+) Smith, Hannah McCann. Bazzle Smith made oath to Robt. McCann, J. P., 7 Jul. 1798....Jane Boyse (X), wife of Alexander Boyse released dower to John Willson, J. P., 30 Aug. 1798. Rec: 8 Oct. 1798.

Page 436: I, James Prichard of Edgefield Co., S. C., planter, for Ł 50 stg. sold to William Prichard, of same place, Surveyor, for 640 acres in Pendleton Co. on 23 Mile Creek of Savannah River, granted 15 Oct.1784. Wit: Solomon Cox, Thos. Anderson. (Plat)....Edgefield Co., Solomon Cox made oath to Arthur Simkins, JEC, 19 May 1798. Elizabeth (X) Prichard released dower to Arthur Simkins, 19 May 1798. Rec: 20 Oct. 1798.

Pages 436-437: I, William Prichard of Edgefield Co., S. C., Surveyor, for $200 sold to Jane Reese of Pendleton Co. 200 acres in Pendleton Co. on 23 Mile Creek of Keowee River, bd. SW by Wm. Prichard, part of 640 acres... granted James Prichard, 15 Oct. 1784, by Benj. Guerard, by Letters Patent and conveyed to Wm. Prichard 14 Apr. 1798. Date: 6 Apr. 1798. Wit: Edwin Reese, Leah Reese. Edwin Reese made oath to Robt. McCann, J. P., 6 June 1798....Plat shows land bd. on N. by John Dickson, on W. by Prichard. Rec: 20 Oct. 1798.

Page 437: I, William Burton of Abbeville Co. for Ł 30 stg. sold to Crafford Goodwin of Greenville Co., S. C., 220 acres on NW branch of Keowee River, tract surveyed for Wiley Glover, 21 Oct. 1789, granted by Charles Pinckney to Burton, 9 Feb. 1791. Date: 30 Oct. 1797. ..."except my wife's dower forever"...Wit: John Goodwin, John Burton, Thomas Beaty. John Goodwin made oath to W. Reed, J. P., 10 Feb. 1798. Rec: 20 Oct. 1798. (No signature of or by wife.)

Pages 437-438: 1 Mar. 1796. Col. Benjamin Cleveland to Henry Dodson for Ł 20 stg. for 116 acres in Washington Dist. on Toxaway Creek, part of 950 ac. granted Cleveland by Chas. Pinckney. Wit: Absolom Cleveland. Absolom Cleveland made oath to Jno. Barton, J. P., 21 Nov. 1796. Rec: 20 Oct. 1796.

Page 438: 1 Feb. 1794. Wm. Lofton to Matthew Russel for Ł 100 stg. for 430 acres where Russel now

(Lofton-Russel cont'd): lives, on N. fork of Choestoe Creek of Tugalo River, part of tract granted Tho. Lofton by Thomas Pinckney, 2 Jul. 1787, and sold to Wm. Lofton. Wit: Saml. Lofton, John G. Lofton. Samuel Lofton made oath to G. W. Earle, DCC, 27 Oct. 1798. Rec: 27 Oct. 1798.

Page 438: I, Francis Bremar of Charleston, S. C. for Ł 50 sold to John McKenzie of Big Beaverdam Creek, 450 acres in 96 Dist. on Big Beaverdam Creek of Tugalo River, granted Jacob Milligan, conveyed to Bremar. Date: 19 May 1798. Wit: Ann Elliott, Geo. Ioor. Ann Elliott made oath to Isaac Motte Dart, Notary Public (Charleston?), 19 Mar. 1798. Rec: 28 Oct. 1798.

Pages 438-439: 4 Jun. 1794. Thomas Farrar, Sheriff of Washington Dist. to John Wilson, Esq....whereas, John Miller was seized of 640 acres on Big and Little Beaverdam Creek of Tugalo River, Jane Chapley obtained judgement against Miller for Ł 60 stg....William Edmondson, Clerk of Court of Common Pleas, Washington Dist., directed all lands, goods, chattels of John Miller to be sold at public auction to the highest bidder, being John Wilson, Esq. for Ł 9-10 shillings stg. Wit: Benj. Smith, Jacob Capehart. Benj. Smith made oath to Wm. Edmondson, J. P., 24 Jun. 1794. Rec: 31 Oct. 1796.

Page 439: 16 Dec. 1797. James Henderson to Wm. Marchbanks for Ł 35 stg. for 131 acres on S. side of the Saluda River on Wolf Creek of 12 Mile River. Wit: John Henderson, Matthew (his mark) Henderson. John Henderson made oath to Rt. Bowen (no date). Rec: 12 Nov. 1798.

Pages 439-440: 1 Jun. 1789. Francis Breen of Charleston, merchant, to Andrew Bay, of same place, Attorney at-law for Ł 100 stg. for 640 acres in 96 Dist. on 26 Mile Creek, surveyed 12 Jan. 1784 for Peter Bremar, granted by Wm. Moultrie to Breen, 2 Jan. 1786. Wit: Wm. Robertson, Wm. Cleland. William Robertson made oath to James Nicholson, J. P. of Charleston Dist. 4 Sep. 1790....Plat surveyed 12 Jan. 1785 by D. Hopkins, Dept. Surv..... Signed: F. Bremar, Sur. Genl. Rec: 12 Nov. 1798.

Page 440: I, Jane Deale sold to Abner A. Steele one negro boy named Tour for $216 and 14¢. Date: 14 Nov. 1798. Signed: Jane (X) Deale. Wit: James Wood who made oath to G. W. Earle, DCC, 15 Nov. 1798. Rec: 15 Nov. 1798.

Clerk had note: "This page carried over (441)", refers to pg. 441 and 442 being misnumbered as 441 and 442 again.

Page 441: I, Benjamin Starrett for $40 sold to Joshua Reeder 100 acres bd. by Reeder, part of tract granted by Wm. Moultrie. Recorded Bk. T., no. 5, p. 2. Date: 26 Jun. 1798. Wit: Simon Reeder, Jonathan Reeder. Simon Reeder made oath to James Jett, 26 Jun. 1798. Rec: 15 Nov. 1798.

Page 441: I, Alexander Boyse for $200 sold to William Otwell 150 acres on Brushy Creek of Saluda River, bd. on SW by John Clardy, on SW by Wm. Faris and Tho. Earnest, NW by Michael Kiltison, NE by Wm. Otwell. Date: 7 Sep. 1798. Wit: David Grimes, William Otwell. William Otwell, Jr. made oath to Robt. McCann, J. P., 19 Oct. 1798. Rec: 15 Nov. 1798.

Page 441: I, Alexander Boyse for $400 sold to William Otwell 100 acres bd. NE by Saluda River, SW by John Clardy, NW by Alexander Boyse, Michael Kiltison. Date: 6 Sept. 1798. Wit: David Grimes, William Otwell.....

(Boyse-Otwell cont'd): William Otwell, Jr. made oath to Robt. McCann on 19 Oct. 1798. Rec: 15 Nov. 1798.

Page 441: I, James Hamilton, planter, for Ł 25 stg. sold to James Stevenson, planter, 150 acres in Washington Dist. on SE branches of 23 Mile Creek of Savannah River, part of a tract granted Joseph Erwin, 4 December 1786 by Wm. Moultrie, bd. on SE by James Blair. Wit: Archibald Hamilton, W. W. Burney, R. Wallace. William Burney made oath to Robt. McCann, J.P. on 26 Jun. 1798. Rec: 15 Nov. 1798.

Pages 441-442: 25 Jun. 1798. Josiah McClure, planter, to William McClure, planter, for Ł 40, 112 acres, part of 640 acres granted Edward McClure and conveyed to Josiah McClure on Deep Creek of Seneca River. Wit: Jas. Hamilton, Austin (+) Cornelius. James Hamilton made oath to J. C. Kilpatrick, J. P., 27 Jun. 1798. (Plat). Rec: 15 Nov. 1798.

Page 442: I, Charles Stevens of Pendleton Co., carpenter, for $100 sold to William Crow of Edgefield Co., S. C., 252 acres on Little Beaverdam Creek of Toogaloo River, granted Stevens by Arnoldus Vanderhorst on 7 Dec. 1793, surveyed for Joseph Reed 9 Mar. 1789. Date: 31 Oct. 1798. Wit: Squire Allen, James Bradberry. Squire Allen made oath to Geo. W. Earle, DCC, 31 Oct. 1798. Rec: 15 Nov. 1798.

Page 442: Peter Wagnon to Daniel Willis for Ł 30 for 125 acres on Big Beaverdam Creek of Toogaloo River, part of 348 acres granted Benjamin Hickman, 31 May 1791 by Wm. Moultrie, running from Camp's ford to Kee's ferry, bd. by Richd. Medlin, Lewis Medlin, John Bradberry. Date: 11 Jun. 1797. Signed: Peter (his "fancy L" mark) Wagnon. Wit: Lucy (X) Moore, Charles Hunt. Charles Hunt made oath to John Harris, J. P., 20 Jun. 1798. Rec: 15 Nov. 1798.

Page 441 (again) 10 Nov. 1795. George Forbes, of Washington Dist. to Thomas Black for Ł 12 stg. for 100 acres on 23 Mile Creek of Keowee River, part of 394 acres granted Forbes by States Letter Patent by Wm. Moultrie, 3 Jun. 1793. Wit: Wm. Faris, Wm. Blair. William Faris made oath to John Wilson, J. P., 17 Feb. 1796. Rec: 17 Nov. 1798.

Page 441: 16 Aug. 1794. Benjamin Cleveland to Daniel McMillin for Ł 50 stg. for 200 acres, part of 975 acres granted Cleveland by Chas. Pinckney, 5 Dec. 1791, bd. on NW by James Blair on Toxaway Creek, a fork of Toogalo River, N. by Benj. Cleveland, Joseph Stepp. Wit: Alexr. Hunter, John Cleveland. John Cleveland made oath to John Barton, J. P., 10 Apr. 1795. Rec: 19 Nov. 1798.

Page 441: 18 Sep. 1789. David Clarke of Pendleton Co. to Samuel Harper of Spg. Co., S. C. for Ł200 stg. for 270 acres on Keowee River, surveyed for James Gillison by Wm. Lesley, D.S., bd. N. by river, vacant land. Wit: William Jamison, James Abbet, Hance Harper. William Jamison made oath to Robt. McCann, J. P., 16 Nov. 1798. Rec: 20 Nov. 1798.

Pages 441-442 (again): I, Joel Webb, planter, for $80 sold to Thomas Vick 50 acres on Keowee River, below the mouth of 18 Mile Creek, part of 642 acres granted 6 May 1793 by Wm. Moultrie to James Jordan and sold by Sheriff of Pendleton Co. to Joel Webb, bd. by Wm. Mullican. Date: 17 Mar. 1798. Wit: William (X) Brister, Nancy (X) Vick. William Brister made oath to John Verner, 31 Oct. 1798. Rec: 20 Nov. 1798.

Page 442:   20 Jun. 1798. Meshack Stephens of Knox Co.,
                                    Tenn. to Joel Terrell of Pendleton Co. for
                                    £ 50 stg. for 488 acres on Big Eastotoe of
Keo. River. at fork of Mile Creek and Charlotte's Creek, bd. John Thomas,
granted by Chas. Pinckney, 6 Dec. 1798. Signed: Mesheck (his mark) Stephens. Wit: John Terrell, Rowland Chiles, Amilew(?) Childs. John Terrell made oath to W. W. Reid, J. P., 24 Nov. 1798.
Rec: 27 Nov. 1798.

Page 442:   20 Jun. 1798. Milley Stephens of Knox Co.,
                                    Tenn. to Joel Terrell of Pendleton Co. for
                                    £ 140 stg. for 488 acres on Big Eastatoe of
Keowee River, bd. by John Thomas, granted by Chas. Pinckney, 6 Dec. 1790.
Signed: Milley (+) Stephens. Wit: John Terrell, Roland Chiles, Amilew
(X) Chiles. John Terrell made oath to W. W. Reid, a Magistrate, that he
saw Milley Stephens, wife of Meshack Stephens sign within deed and he
saw Rowland (spelled Bowland) Chiles and Amilew Chiles sign, 24 November
1798. Rec: 27 Nov. 1798.

Pages 442-443:   10 May 1795. Jonathan Clark to Micajah Clark
                                    for £ 50 stg. for 158 acres on S. branch of
                                    Hericane of Saluda River, where Micajah Clark
now lives, part of 212 acres granted Jonathan Clark by Wm. Moultrie, 4
Dec. 1786. Recorded Bk. PPPP, p. 197. Wit: James Clark, John Johnson, Josiah Johnson. John Johnson made oath to Robt. McCann, 19 May 1798.......
Jenny Clark, wife of Jonathan Clark, released dower to John Wilson, J.P.,
27 Nov. 1798.
Rec: 27 Nov. 1798.

Page 443:   24 Jun. 1797. William Rose to Samuel Harper
                                    for £ 14 stg. for 200 acres granted to Henry
                                    Burch, 2 Jan. 1793, bd. by Harper, Gillison,
Robt. Craven. Wit: John McElroy, Elizabeth (X) Harper. Elizabeth Harper
made oath to Joseph Reed, J. P., 11 Dec. 1798.
Rec: 12 Dec. 1798.

Pages 443-444:   18 Feb. 1793. John Wilson to Robert Gray for
                                    £ 20 stg. for 147 acres bd. on S. by land
                                    laid out to Thomas Entrican, now belonging to
Andrew Pickens, NE by Robt. Gray, part of 295 acres granted John Wilson,
3 Dec. 1792, on Rocky Creek. Wit: James Rankin, Robert Rankin, Joseph
(JP) Price. Robert Rankin made oath to Wm. Millwee, J. P., 13 Aug.1798.
Rec: 12 Dec. 1798.

Page 444:   4 Sep. 1797. Edward T. McClure of Pendleton
                                    Co. to Farley Thompson of Elbert Co., Ga. for
                                    £ 50 stg. for 200 acres on W. side of Seneca
River, granted Robert Tate, 1784, conveyed to Edw. T. McClure, 1790, bd.
NW by David Sloan, E. by the Seneca River. Wit: James Tate, Saml. Tate.
James Tate made oath to John Verner, 25 Jan. 1798.
Rec: 12 Dec. 1798.

Page 444:   28 Jun. 1798. Isaac Lynch to Isaac Titsworth
                                    for £ 52 stg. for 150 acres on W. side of the
                                    Keowee River, bd. by Grimkie, Isaac Titsworth
and Field Pruet, part of a bounty granted Wm. Tate. Signed: Isaac (IL)
Lynch. Wit: Nathl. Harbin, Samuel Harbin, Jesse Harbin. Nathaniel Harbin
made oath to James Jett, 10 Aug. 1798.
Rec: 12 Dec. 1798.

Pages 444-445:   8 Jun. 1798. Isaac Lynch to Zephaniah Harrison for £ 50 for 160 acres on Main Crow Crk.
                                    part of tract known as Fort Prince George,bd.
by Isaac Lynch, Henry Burch, near Cabbin Jacob Reece formerly lived in.
Signed: Isaac (IL) Lynch. Wit: Nathl. Harbin, Saml. Harbin, Jesse Harbin.
Nathaniel Harbin made oath to James Jett, J. P., 10 Aug. 1798.
Rec: 12 Dec. 1798.

Page 445:   9 Mar. 1794. James Wafford, D. Surveyor of
                                    Spartanburg Co., S. C. to Alexander Boyse of

(Wafford-Boyse cont'd): Pendleton Co. for Ł 20 for 150 acres, part of 650 acres granted Wafford, 7 Apr. 1788, on Brushy Creek of Saluda River, bd. by Jewell, Allison, Earnest, Humphries land, now Alex. Boyse land. Wit: William Humphries, Margaret (+) Wafford. William Humphries made oath to Robt. McCann, J. P., 29 Jul. 1798.
Rec: 12 Dec. 1798.

Page 445: I, John Wilson, Esq. for $300 sold to James Bradberry 640 acres on Big and Little Beaverdam Creek of Tugalo River, granted John Miller and sold at Sheriff's sale by Thomas Farrar, late Sheriff of Washington Dist. purchased by John Wilson to Exclude 40 acres on William Shilleto's line, which was taken off by an older survey of Squire Allen. Date: 31 Oct. 1798. Wit: Charles Stevens, Squire Allen. Squire Allen made oath to G. W. Earle, DCC, 31 Oct. 1798.
Rec: 12 Dec. 1798.

Pages 445-446: I, James Martin of Lincoln Co., N. C. for Ł 120 sold to Executors of Thomas Reese, deceased, of Pendleton Co. for Henry Dobson Reese, infant son of Thomas Reese, dec'd, 640 acres on both sides of 23 Mile Creek. Date: 27 Jun. 1798. Wit: Edwin Reese, Hugh Dickson. Edwin Reese made oath to G. W. Earle, DCC, 28 Nov. 1798....York Co., S. C.,... Lilly Martin, wife of James Martin, released dower to John McClannihan, J. P., 1 Oct. 1798.
Rec: 12 Dec. 1798.

Page 446: Laurence Co., S. C. I, Richard Griffen of said county for $320 sold to John Griffen of Pendleton Co., 320 acres in Pendleton County near the Courthouse, where John Griffen now lives, part of 640 acres granted Goldin Tinsley, conveyed to me, 11 Sep. 1788. Wit: J. R. Brown, Martha Hallum, David Crow. Martha Hallum made oath to G. W. Earle, DCC, 10 Dec. 1798. Plat shows bd. on N. by Henry Sims, on W. by Steele and Public Lands, on E. by Walker and Gillispie, on SE by James Griffen....96 Dist., Elinor Griffen, wife of Richard Griffen released dower to J. R. Brown, J. P., of Newberry Dist., S. C., 24 Aug. 1798.
Rec: 12 Dec. 1798.

Pages 446-447: I, William McCaleb for $600 sold to John Baylis Earle 300 acres on W. side of Keowee River, bd. on S. by land laid out to Maj. Saml. Taylor, being bounty tract granted Captn. Jesse Baker. Date: 20 Jun. 1798. Wit: D. McCaleb, Joel Foster. David McCaleb made oath to G. W. Earle, DCC, 5 Dec. 1798.
Rec: 12 Dec. 1798.

Page 447: I, William McCaleb, planter, for $100 sold to John Baylis Earle, 359 acres on W. side of Keowee River, bd. NE & NW by bounty survey, NW & SW by Saml. Taylor, SW by Jesse Baker, NE & SE & SW by Banister Harper, surveyed by Thos. Lofton, 24 Aug. 1791, granted McCaleb by Arnoldus Vanderhorst, 4 Apr. 1796. Date: 20 Jun. 1798. Wit: D. McCaleb, Joel Foster. David McCaleb made oath to G. W. Earle, DCC, 5 Dec. 1798.
Rec: 12 Dec. 1798.

Page 447: I, Thomas Boyd, for (no amount) sold to Blake Mauldin 147 acres on George's Creek, bd. NW & NE by Hallum, SW & NW by Rowland and Bowen, SW by Gillispie. Date: 22 Dec. 1797. Wit: Geter Lynch, Michl. Smith. Michael Smith made oath to Wm. Edmondson, J. P., 22 Dec. 1797.
Rec: 12 Dec. 1798.

Page 447: Washington Dist. 13 Aug. 1798. Patrick Fenny a planter of Pinckney Dist., S. C. to John G. Lofton of Washington Dist. for $130 for 110 acres on 5 Mile Branch of 18 Mile Creek of the Seneca River, bd. by Morgan Osborn, Fredk. Glover, Wm. Swift, Hugh Dodd, granted by Wm. Moultrie on 5 Jun. 1786. Wit: Solomon Lofton, Sr., Samuel Lofton, Jr., Christopher

(Fenny-Lofton cont'd): Strong. Samuel Lofton, Sr. made oath to G. W. Earle, J. P., 15 Dec. 1798. Rec: 15 Dec. 1798. (Deed was signed: Patrick Phinney).

Page 448: Washington Dist. I, John Hudson for ₤ 10 sold to Arthur McAdoo 136 acres on Connoross Creek of Seneca River, granted by Wm. Moultrie to Hudson, 2 Sep. 1793. Date: 7 Apr. 1798. Wit: John G. Lofton, Samuel Lofton, Jr., Wm. Shelby. John G. Lofton made oath to G. W. Earle, J. P., 15 Dec. 1798. Rec: 15 Dec. 1798.

Page 448: I, James Curry of Abbeville Co. for ₤ 100 sold to Samuel Houston of Abbeville Co., a planter, "his part of half of 4 tracts" surveyed by Thomas Lofton, D.S. for John Adair and James Curry as tenants in Common; 1st tract of 452 acres; 2nd tract of 697 acres; 3rd tract of 339 acres and 4th tract of 278 acres, in 96 Dist. on the Keowee River. Date: 10 Jul. 1796. Wit: Robert Brackenridge, Joseph (his mark) Spence, with Robert Brackenridge making oath to Samuel Watt, J. P., 17 Dec. 1798. Rec: 19 Dec. 1798.

Page 448: 29 May 1797. William Millwee to Wm. Laughlin for $114 for 76½ acres on Town Creek of 26 Mile Creek, part of tract granted Millwee on (in) 1784 by Benj. Guerard, bd. by James Pogue. Signed: Wm. Millwee, Martha (M) Millwee. Wit: John Laughlin, James Pollock. James Pogue made oath he was present and saw deed signed to Wm. Millwee, J. P., 29 Dec. 1798. Rec: 2 Jan. 1799.

Pages 448-449: I, John Mills of Wake Co., N. C. for $300 sold to Joseph Green 200 acres in Pendleton Co. on 26 Mile Creek of Savannah River, part of the tract granted Mills. Date: 13 Oct. 1796. Wit: Nancy (/) Saxon, Hugh Mills. I certify above deed was signed before me, 13 Oct. 1796. Signed: Joshua Saxon, J. P. Rec: 3 Jan. 1799.

Page 449: I, John Whisenhunt of the Cherokee Nation for $300 sold to John Taylor, a negro fellow of the name Tom, formerly the property of John Craig of Pendleton Co., the said Tom not being present to deliver.....I authorize Taylor to take him into possession as his property, wherever he may be found, and in case Taylor shall not receive the negro, I oblige myself to refund $300. Date: 2 Jan. 1799. Signed: John (X) Whisenhunt. Wit: Thomas McCreight, Robt. Waugh. Thomas McCraight made oath to J. B. Earle, J. P., 8 Jan. 1799. Rec: 8 Jan. 1799.

Page 449: 31 Oct. 1795. James Jett to Elisha Dyer, Sr. for ₤ 10 stg. for 514 acres bd. by tract granted Athantious Thomas "known by name of Qualhache", on both sides. Wit: William Boren, Nathan (+) Nations. William Boren made oath to Wm. Reid, J. P., 31 Oct. 1795. Rec: 12 Jan. 1799.

Page 449: 2 Apr. 1796. Athanatius Thomas of Chester Co. in S. C. to Elisha Dyer of Pendleton Co. for ₤ 50 for 335 acres on Eastatoe Creek, granted by Wm. Moultrie. Recorded Bk. EEEE, p. 240. Wit: Caleb Dyer, Anderson Thomas, John Thomas. Caleb Dyer made oath to Wm. Reed, J. P., 2 April 1796. Rec: 12 Jan. 1799.

Page 450: I, James Kilgore of Greenville Co., S. C. for ₤ 15 stg. sold to Moses Hendrix of Pendleton Co. 230 acres, part of 330 acres granted by patent, 15 Dec. 1796, conveyed to Absalom Powell, 100 acres, on S. side of Saluda River, on Carpenter's Creek, bd. by Joseph Whitner, William Bruce, Cunningham, survey for Moses Hendrix and Absalom Martin. Date: 11 Apr. 1798. Wit: Colin Campbell, Thomas Linard. Colin Campbell made oath to W. Reid, 29 May 1798. Rec: 14 Jan. 1799.

Page 450: 20 Aug. 1794. Jacob Vance, planter, to Moses Hendrix, planter, for Ł 1 for 100 acres, part of 200 acres granted Vance, 6 Mar. 1786, in 96 Dist. on both sides of Camp Creek, of Saluda River. Wit: Samuel (S) Martin, Absalom Martin. Absalom Martin made oath to W. Reid, J. P., 22 Aug. 1794. Rec: 14 Jan. 1799.

Pages 450-451: 22 Aug. 1794. Jacob Vance, planter, to Samuel Martin, blacksmith, for Ł 1 for 100 acres, part of 200 acres on Saluda River, granted to Vance, 6 Mar. 1786 by Wm. Moultrie, on both sides of Camp Creek. Wit: Moses Hendrix, Absalom Martin. Moses Hendrix made oath to Wm. Reid, JP, 22 Aug. 1794. Rec: 14 Jan. 1799.

Page 451: I, Nathaniel Perry for Ł 50 sold to Levi Murphree 608 acres on Buck Creek of 12 Mile River, granted Perry by Wm. Moultrie, 4 Sep.1786. Date: 8 Jan. 1798. Wit: Benjamin Perry, William Darnell. Benjamin Perry made oath to Nathl. Perry, J. P., 23 Jan. 1799. Rec: 23 Jan. 1799.

Pages 451-452: 13 Aug. 1792. Robert Pickens, planter, sold to David Wimpy, planter for Ł 22, 208 acres on 23 Mile Creek of Savannah River, Washington Dist., part of 280 acres conveyed from Robert McCann, 28 Aug. 1792. Wit: Jonathan Hicks, Levi Wimpy....Plat shows land bd. on N. by Alexr. Boyse, on E. by Robt. Pickens, on S. & W. by Robt. McCann. Levi Wimpy made oath to John Willson, J. P., 13 Oct. 1792. Rec: 23 Jan. 1799.

Page 452: I, William Chapman for love, good will and affection I bear my Father, Joseph Chapman, do give him all and sundry goods, chattels in my possession: horse, colt, hogs head of tobacco and household furniture, (itemized list). Date: 22 Jan. 1799. Signed: William (X) Chapman. Wit: Job Smith, John Smith. Job Smith made oath to G. W. Earle, DCC, 24 Jan. 1799. Rec: 24 Jan. 1799.

Page 452: Francis Bremar and Peter Freneau of Charleston, on __ day ___, did appoint James Martin, Esq. then of Pendleton Co., our lawful Attorney to sell and dispose of a parcel of land in which we were interested with the sd. Martin, which belonged to us jointly....now for several causes, we have thought it fit to revoke sd. Power of Attorney and now constitute our friend, Charles Jones Colcock, Esq. to be our Attorney. Signed: 10 Jun. 1797 in Charleston. Wit: Seth Paine, Jacob Edney. Jacob Edney made oath to E. Darrell, Jr., J. P., in Charleston, 13 Jul. 1797. Rec: 24 Jan. 1799.

Pages 452-453: I, Henry McDaniel, Sr. for Ł 30 stg. sold to John Portman 100 acres on N. side of Keowee River, part of where I now live, bd. by McDaniel, Southern. Date: 24 Jan. 1799. Signed: Henry (+) McDaniel. Wit: George Verner, Alexr. Young. Alexr. Young made oath to John Verner, JP, 24 Jan. 1799. Rec: 24 Jan. 1799.

Page 453: I, John Portman for Ł 30 stg. sold to Henry McDaniel, Sr. 20 acres on 26 Mile Creek and Pearces Creek, part of 2 tracts: one of 10 acres, part of 204 acres granted David Jordan, 17 Feb. 1791, bd. Guthrie; the other 10 acres, part of 150 acres granted Guthrie, 15 Oct. 1784, on 26 Mile Creek and Pearce's Creek, bd. John Morris. Signed: John (his mark) Portman. Date: 23 Jan. 1799. Wit: George Verner, Alexr. Young. Alexander Young made oath to John Verner, J. P., 24 Jan. 1799. Rec: 24 Jan. 1799.

Pages 453-454: Abbeville Co., 96 Dist. 28 May 1791. John Irwin, planter, to John McWhirter, blacksmith, both of 96 Dist., for eight Thousand weight

(Irwin-McWhirter cont'd): good tobacco for 250 acres above the old boundary line on Rocky River, "in county aforesaid", bd. on SE by William Lesley, on SW & NW by David Hopkins. Wit: John Irwin, James Buchannon. Thomas Buchannon made oath to John Willson, J. P., 20 Sep. 1791. Rec: 24 Jan. 1799.

Page 454: 23 Nov. 1792. Spilsby Glenn, of Union Co., S. C. to Thomas Shockley, of Pendleton Co., for Ł 5 stg. for 54 acres in 96 Dist. on the Savannah River, granted Glenn by Chas. Pinckney, 6 Dec. 1790, recorded Bk. C, no. 5, p. 120. Wit: John P. Sartor, Sarah Sartor, Joseph Hollingsworth....Union Co., S. C., John P. Sartor made oath to Thos. Blasingame, J. P., 1 Jun. 1793. Rec: 24 Jan. 1799.

Pages 454-455: 16 Jul. 1796. Thomas Shockley, Sr. to Thomas Shockley, Jr. for $100 for 100 acres, part of tract granted Wm. Love by Benj. Guerard, 21 Jan. 1785, on Savannah River. Signed: Thomas (T) Shockley. Wit: John Newman, Fergus Cavin. John Newman made oath to John Verner, J. P., 8 Sep. 1798.

Page 455: I, James Allison for $160 sold to Francis Clinkscales 140 acres on Saluda River, bd. by John Gambrell, Reuben Cox, James Allison, William Vaughn, granted Allison. Date: 8 Jan. 1799. Signed: James (his mark) Allison, Elizabeth (+) Allison. Wit: Thomas Mattison, William Clinkscales and Reuben (R) Cox. Thomas Mattison made oath he saw James Allinson, Sr. and Elizabeth, his wife, sign to Wm. Reid, J. P., 24 Jan. 1799. Rec: 24 Jan. 1799.

Page 455: I, James Allison for Ł 20 stg. sold to William Williamson 85 acres on S. fork of Saluda River on Little Creek. Date: 29 Dec. 1798. Signed: James (+) Allison, Sarah (+) Allison. Wit: Thos. Jordin, Arris Cox. Thomas Jordan made oath to Wm. Hall, J. P., 5 Jan. 1799. Rec: 24 Jan. 1799.

Page 455-456: 26 Jul. 1793. James Porter of Abbeville Co. to Usley Doss of Pendleton Co. for Ł 40 stg. for 187 acres, where Usley Doss now lives, run by Thomas Lofton for Porter, granted by Chas. Pinckney, 1 Feb. 1790. Wit: Absolom (A) Bryant, William (his mark) Doss. Absolom Doss made oath to John Willson, J. P., 20 Aug. 1793. Rec: 24 Jan. 1799.

Page 456: Washington Dist. I, William Vaughn for $150 sold to William Cox 100 acres on Saluda River, bd. by James Vaughn, part of 165 acres granted John Maxwell, 6 Mar. 1786, conveyed to Vaughn, recorded Bk. FFFF, p. 574. Date: 24 Dec. 1798. Wit: Thos. Jordan, Isaac (X) Cox. Thomas Jordan made oath to Wm. Hall, J. P., 5 Jan. 1799. Rec: 24 Jan. 1799.

Page 456: I, James Jett for Ł 5 stg. sold to William Lynch 350 acres in 96 Dist., granted to Jett by Wm. Moultrie, 2 Sep. 1793, on both sides of Eastatoe of Keowee River, bd. by Wm. Lynch, Elisha Dyer, Sr. and the tract granted Athanalius Thomas, by Benj. Guerard. Date: 1 Dec. 1797.Wit: John Terrell, Amos Ladd, Edward Murdine. Edward Murdine made oath to W. Reed, J. P., 3 Jan. 1799. Rec: 24 Jan. 1799.

Pages 456-457: 15 Jan. 1798. Peter Perkins of Stokes Co., N. C. to William Lynch of Pendleton Co. for 160 lbs. currant money of Va. for 320 acres on S. side of Woolonoy Creek, of Saluda River, part of 640 acres granted William Powell Lee, 16 Jul. 1784, conveyed by Wm. Hort and John Edwards, Esq. the Treas. of State, 7 Apr. 1789. Wit: Abraham Perkins, William (X) Quillen, Charles Newman. Abraham Perkins made oath to G. W. Earle, DCC, 9 Apr. 1798. Rec: 24 Jan. 1799.

Page 457: 15 Jan. 1798. Peter Perkins of Stokes Co., N. C. to William Lynch of Pendleton Co. for Ł 200 stg. for 250 acres, bd. by James David, granted Samuel Watt by Benj. Guerard, 17 Jul. 1785, on both sides of the Woolonoy Creek on Saluda River. Wit: Abraham Perkins, Charles Newman, William (X) Quillen. Abraham Perkins made oath to G. W. Earle, DCC, 9 Apr. 1798. Rec: 24 Jan. 1799.

Page 457: 26 Oct. 1797. Elisha Dyer to William Lynch for Ł 50 stg. for 167 acres on Eastatoe Crk., part of tract granted Athenatius Thomas by William Moultrie, 1 Aug. 1785. Wit: Joshua Dyer, B. Stone. Joshua Dyer made oath to W. Reid, J. P., 27 Oct. 1797. Rec: 24 Jan. 1799.

Pages 457-458: (No. torn off). I, Matthew Alexander for $857 sold to Isaac Clements 270 acres on Broadmouth Creek of the Saluda River, bd. by James Mattison, Francis Clinkscales, Robert Kay, Nevil Mattison, Matthew Alexander, part of two tracts: one granted Richard Saddler, 6 Feb. 1786; the other granted Matthew Alexander, 7 May 1792. Wit: Hugh Clements, Henry Trussell, Walter Manning. Hugh Clements made oath to W. Reed, J. P., 24 Jan. 1799. Rec: 24 Jan. 1799.

Page 458: 3 May 1797. George Thompson to Archabald Boyd for Ł 40 "in good trade" for 100 acres on 12 Mile River, part of tract bought of William Thompson, 1784, in Washington Dist., W. of Old Indian Boundary Line, bd. by Boyd, Mayfield. Wit: William King, Robt. Linn. William King made oath to James Jett, J. P., 4 Dec. 1798. Rec: 24 Jan. 1799.

Pagr 458: 1 Jan. 1799. William Boyd to Micajer Smithson for $600 for 350 acres, granted 3 Jul. 1787 by Thos. Pinckney to Boyd, on both sides of Coffe's Creek of Tugalo River. Wit: Wm. White, John Hooper, Matthew B. Hooper. Mathew Hooper made oath to Nathl. Perry, J. P., 10 Jan. 1799. Rec: 24 Jan. 1799.

Pages 458-459: 21 Jan. 1799. William Lynch of Pendleton Co. to William Sutherland of Rockingham Co., NC for 700 silver dollars for 320 acres on both sides of Woolenoy Creek of Saluda River, part of 640 acres granted William Powell Lee, 16 (smeared) 1784 by conveyence from William Hort and Jno. Edwards, Esqs., Treas. of State, 7 Apr. 1789. Wit: Amos Ladd, Joseph Ladd, John Ladd. Amos Ladd, Sr. made oath to Wm. Reed, J. P., 24 Jan. 1799. Rec: 24 Jan. 1799.

Page 459: 31 Jan. 1795. William Hall to Thomas Davis for Ł 45 stg. for 100 acres on Little Creek of Saluda River, granted John Blair by Thos. Pinckney, 5 Jan. 1789. Wit: Walter Manning, James Mattison, Lewis Davis. Walter Manning made oath to Wm. Hall, J. P., 28 Jan. 1797. Rec: 24 Jan. 1799.

Page 459: 16 Aug. 1798. Meshack Green to Christopher Creder for Ł 40 for 100 acres, part of tract granted George Nelson by Chas. Pinckney, on Rocky River, Little Beaverdam. Signed: Mesheck (his mark) Green. Wit: Geo. Anderson, John Green, Thomas Green....Creasey (+) Green, wife of Mesheck Green, released dower to John Wilson, J. P., 24 Jan. 1799. George Anderson, Esq., made oath to Robt. McCann, J. P., 24 Jan. 1799. Rec: 24 Jan. 1799.

Page 459: I, John Verner, Sr. for Ł 40 sold to David Verner 224 acres on Sandy Creek of Savannah River. Date: 6 Aug. 1797. Wit: Wm. Wakefield, William Stevenson. William Stevenson made oath to John Verner, J. P., 26 Aug. 1797. Rec: 24 Jan. 1799.

Page 460:   26 Dec. 1797. David Gillispie to Robert Hix for Ł 100 stg. for 150 acres, part of tract granted Gillispie, 1786, on Keowee River, bd. John Verner, Christopher Hargraves, Joel Ledbetter. Wit: John Whitworth, Josiah Underwood. Josiah Underwood made oath to John Verner, J. P., 29 Dec. 1797. Rec: 24 Jan. 1799.

Page 460:   I, Samuel Houston of Abbeville Co., planter, for $500 sold to George Stevenson, 532 acres part of two tracts: 200 acres surveyed by David Hopkins, 28 Jun. 1784; 332 acres surveyed by William Lesley, 5 Oct. 1785, joining each other on Mountain Creek of Generostee. Date: 8 June 1797. Wit: Wm. Lesley, Elinor (+) Chalmers...Abbeville Co., William Lesley made oath to Samuel Watts, J. P., 9 Jun. 1799...Grizzel (her mark) Houston, wife of Samuel Houston, released dower to Andrew Hamilton, J.P., in Abbeville Co., 24 Jan. 1799. Rec: 24 Jan. 1799.

Pages 460-461:   I, Thomas Hone for $150 sold to William Elliot 195 acres in Washington Dist. on Big Creek of Saluda River. Date: 26 Oct. 1798. Wit: Aaron Wilborn, James Wilborn. Aaron Wilborn made oath to Wm. Hall, J. P., 24 Dec. 1798. Rec: 24 Jan. 1799.

Page 461:   14 Feb. 1795. Isaac Willson to William Harper for Ł 80 for 60 acres on Big Creek of Saluda River, part of 400 acres granted John Martin by Wm. Moultrie, 6 Mar. 1786, conveyed to George Pearce, then to Jonathan Hix, from Hix to Willson. Signed: Isaac (X) Willson. Wit: Wm. Poor, Harper Garner, Henry Townley. Henry Townley made oath to Wm. Hall, J. P., 10 Mar. 1798. Rec: 24 Jan. 1799.

Page 461:   I, Samuel Snoddy of Sumner Co., Tenn. for $300 sold to Walter Bell of Pendleton Co., 621 acres on Little River Creek of Rocky River, granted David Ramsey, Esq. in trust for heirs of Fergus Snoddy, dec'd by Wm. Moultrie, 3 Oct. 1785, recorded Bk. FFFF, p. 186. Date: 1 December 1797. Wit: George Dilworth, Samuel Thompson, William Bennett. William Bennett made oath to Wm. Hall, J. P., 2 Dec. 1797. Rec: 24 Jan. 1799.

Page 462:   I, George Humphries for Ł 30 stg. sold to James Foster, Jr., 100 acres, part of 1300 acres granted Thomas Lewis on S. fork of the Brushy Creek, bd. by Abednego Green. Date: 31 Dec. 1798. Signed: George (his mark) Humphries. Wit: Joseph (E) Erwin, Henry (HG) Green. Joseph Erwin made oath to Robt. McCann, J. P., 22 Jan. 1799. Rec: 24 Jan. 1799.

Page 462:   I, Joshua Lee of Green Co., Ky. appoint John Shannon of Pendleton Co., my Attorney with free power to deliver titles to 500 acres in Pendleton Co. on Choestoa Creek, granted Stephen Drayton. Date: 1 May 1798. Signed: Joshua (X) Lee. Wit: W. Womack, Moses Perkins. Moses Perkins made oath to G. W. Earle, DCC, 25 Jan. 1799. Rec: 25 Jan. 1799.

Page 462:   I, Patrick McDowell of the Town of Cambridge, Abbeville Co., S. C. for Ł 25 stg. sold to John Rusk of Pendleton Co., 207 acres in Washington Dist. on Crow Creek of Keowee River, bd. on NW by Col. Hopkins and vacant land. Date: 16 Jan. 1799. Wit: Thomas Farrar, Wm. McCaleb. Major Thomas Farrar made oath to G. W. Earle, DCC, 25 Jan. 1799. Rec: 24 Jan. 1799.

Pages 462-463:   I, William Asherst for $250 sold to William Hunt 100 acres on SW side of Saluda River, bd by Asherst, part of 200 acres granted William Carpenter, 4 Apr. 1785, conveyed to William Asherst, bd. by Wm. Hunt and

(Asherst-Hunt cont'd): Asherst. Date: 10 Jan. 1799. Wit: James Bowland, James (X) Garoson. Oath blank.
Rec: 24 Jan. 1799.

Page 463: 16 Apr. 1795. James Gillispie to Mark Ward for ₤ 40 stg. for (no amount shown), part of 779 acres granted Gillispie, 22 Aug. 1791 by Chas. Pinckney, W. of Old Boundary on Woolf Creek of 12 Mile River, bd. by John Gillispie, Saml. Duff, Samuel Earle, Ward, Abel Fike. Wit: Samuel Ward, Ephraim (X) Herring. Abel (X) Fike made oath to W. Reid, J. P., on 16 Apr. 1795.
Rec: 25 Jan. 1799.

Page 463: Washington Dist. 19 Jul. 1794. Francis Greenwood, Schoolmaster, of Pendleton Co. to James Pratt of Chester Co., S. C. for ₤ 10 stg. for 100 acres, being N. part of 815 acres granted Greenwood by Wm. Moultrie, 2 Dec. 1793, bd. by Gen'l. Robert Anderson's ferry road, Francis Greenwood, William McGuffin, on Seneca River. Wit: Joseph Jenkins, Robert Anderson, Jr. Joseph Jenkins made oath to J. C. Kilpatrick, J. P., 3 Sep. 1798. Rec: 25 Jan. 1799.

Pages 463-464: 7 Apr. 1789. John Edwards and William Hort, Esq., Treasurers of the State of South Carolina to Charles Crowley....whereas, by several Acts of the General Assembly of the State, lands which have been granted to persons who have not paid the purchase money within time limit and are directed sold at Public Auction...a grant to Samuel Caldwell on 15 Oct. 1784, and not having complied with the terms, land sold at auction to Charles Crowley as the highest bidder for ₤ 16 for 640 acres on Rocky River, Hencoop Creek. Wit: Edward Edwards, Thos. Nicholls....Charleston, Thos. Nicholls made oath to John Jordan, J. P.....received from Elijah Brown, Esq., of Pendleton Co., ₤ 150. In consideration, I hereby assign over above lease and my right and title of the whole premises to Elijah Brown. Date: 24 Oct. 1791. Wit: Patrick Spieren, Samuel Browne. Samuel Browne made oath to Wm. Nevill, J. P., 25 Jun. 1794.
Rec: 25 Jan. 1799.

Pages 464-465: 12 Dec. 1797. John Gregory to Gregory Watts for ₤ 45 stg. for 110 acres on E. side of the Keowee River, bd. by Wm. Harris and vacant land, and river, granted Robert Evins. Wit: Joseph Hill, Hugh Wardlaw, Isabella Reed. Joseph Hill made oath to Joseph Reid, J. P., 25 Jun. 1799.
Rec: 25 Jan. 1799.

Page 465: I, Loddy Dobbs and Sarah, my wife, sold to Larkin Cleveland 50 acres for $300, on Toogalo River, bd. on E. by Wm. Cleveland, on W. by Wm. Brooks, on S. by river, granted Thomas Cox. Date: 28 Dec. 1798. Signed: Loddy (his mark) Dobbs. Sarah (her mark) Dobbs. Wit: Benj. Cleveland, N. Cleveland. Neely Cleveland made oath to J. B. Earle, J. P., 25 Jan. 1799. Rec: 25 Jan. 1799.

Page 465: I, William Baker and Elizabeth, my wife, for $150 sold to Thomas Barton 126 acres on Cain Creek, of Toogalo River, bd. by Baker and John Kees, granted Michael Wilkinson. Date: 10 Oct. 1798. Wit: John Robison, John Kees. John Robison made oath to J. C. Kilpatrick, J. P., 25 Jan. 1798. Rec: 25 Jan. 1799. (Note: Elizabeth did not sign).

Page 465: I, Jehu Pope for ₤ 15 sold to Levi Moore 132 acres on 18 Mile Creek of Keowee River, bd. by Whitner, Geo. Reese, part of 494 acres granted Pope, 4 Dec. 1793. Date: 10 Apr. 1796. Wit: George Reese, Anna Reese. George Reese made oath to Michael Dickson, J. P., 29 Jan. 1799. (Note: Anna Reese is called "wife of George Reese" in oath).
Rec: 29 Jan. 1799.

Page 466: 25 Jun. 1798. David Brown and Elizabeth, his wife, to David Nolin for $257.12 for 404 ac.

(Brown-Nolin cont'd): on Crow Creek of the Keowee River, granted Robert Craven by Chas. Pinckney, 9 May 1790, bd. by Barne Elenn, Wm. Tate. Signed: David Brown, Elizabeth (her mark) Brown. Wit: Sihon(?) Busby, Berryman Roe. Sinn(?) Busby made oath to James McKinney, J. P., 25 Jun. 1798. Rec: 29 Jan. 1799.

Page 466: Washington Dist. 1 Mar. 1796. Robert Cravens, planter, to John Kelly, planter, for ₤ 20 stg for 160 acres on Keowee River. Wit: Thos. Lofton, John Carruthers, James Kell. James Kell made oath to Joseph Reed, JP on 30 Mar. 1797. Rec: 4 Feb. 1799.

Page 466: I, William Sturges, lawfully constituted Attorney for Francis Lee, of the City of Charleston, for ₤ 30 sold to John Turner, 200 acres part of 547 acres granted Francis Lee on 26 Mile Creek of the Savannah River. Date: 29 Sep. 1798. Signed: Wm. Sturges. Wit: Joseph Jolly, Wilson Jolly. Joseph Jolly made oath to Jonathan Montgomery, J. P., 18 February 1799. Rec: 18 Feb. 1799.

Pages 466-467: I, Edward Camp for ₤ 50 stg. sold to John Turner 168 acres where Turner now lives on 26 Mile Creek of the Savannah River, bd. by Sexton, surveyed for Camp, 1785. Date: 8 Feb. 1799. Wit: William (+) Case, Elias Turner. William Case made oath to Jonathan Montgomery, J. P., 18 Feb. 1799. Rec: 18 Feb. 1799.

Page 467: I, Squire Allen for ₤ 40 sold to William Gist (Guest) 50 acres on Little Beaverdam Creek of Toogalo River, part of tract granted Robert Smith, 1 Jan. 1787 by Wm. Moultrie, conveyed from Smith to Allen, 30 Dec. 1793, bd. by Thomas Farrar, William Guest. Date: 4 Jan. 1798. Wit: Thomas Farrar, Matt. Michie. Thomas Farrar made oath to John B. Earle, J. P., 18 Feb. 1799. Rec: 18 Feb. 1799.

Page 467: I, Thomas Shanklin of Abbeville Co. for $200 sold to Daniel Delaney of Pendleton Co. 200 acres on Connoross Creek, granted by William Moultrie, 5 Sep. 1785, recorded Bk. FFFF, p. 27. Date: 4 Feb. 1799. Wit: Alexander White, Alexander (A) White, Sr. Alexander White made oath to Nathan Lusk, J. P., 4 Feb. 1799...Hannah Shanklin released dower to Nathan Lusk, 4 Feb. 1799. Rec: 19 Feb. 1799.

Page 467: I, Levi Moore sold to Charles Rice for ₤ 15, 132 acres on 18 Mile Creek of Keowee River, bd. by McGuffin, Whitner, Geo. Reese, part of 494 acres granted Jehu Pope, 4 Mar. 1793, conveyed by Pope to Moore, 10 Apr. 1796. Date: 10 Jan. 1799. Signed: Levi (+) Moore. Wit: Joseph Whitner, Edward Williams, Edward Williams made oath to G. W. Earle, DCC, 25 Feb. 1799. Rec: 25 Feb. 1799.

Pages 467-468: I, William McCaleb, planter, sold to William Steele, merchant, one negro man named Samson, for $600. Date: 13 Feb. 1799. Wit: James Wood, Crosby W. Miller. James Wood made oath to G. W. Earle, DCC, 4 Mar. 1799. Rec: 4 Mar. 1799.

Page 468: I, John Morgan for ₤ 25 stg. sold to Jonathan West 92 acres, part of tract granted Alexander Robinson, 16 Jul. 1784, sold by John Edwards and William Hort, Treas. of State, 7 Apr. 1789 to James Martin, Esq. on W. side of 23 Mile Creek. Date: 19 Nov. 1798. Signed: John (X) Morgan. Wit: Hugh Rogers, William Passmore. William Passmore made oath to G. W. Earle, DCC, 4 Mar. 1799. Rec: 4 Mar. 1799.

Page 468: I, Thomas Raper, planter, for $100 sold to John Aden, planter, 218 acres on E. side of 23 Mile Creek, bd. on W. by Evin Thomas, on S. vacant, on W. by Jno. Grissom, bought of Robert Linn, on N. by creek, granted Blake Mauldin by Arnoldus Vanderhorst. Date: 28 Jun. 1797. Signed: Thomas (+) Raper. Wit: Lewis Cobb, Andrw. Liddell. Andrew Liddell made oath to G. W. Earle, DCC, 4 Mar. 1799. Rec: 4 Mar. 1799.

Page 468: I, Thomas Blair for Ł 20 sold to Moses Liddell, Sr., 300 acres on Hamilton Creek of the Savannah River, granted by Arnoldus Vanderhorst to James Hart, 2 Mar. 1795. Recorded Bk. R., no. 5, p. 142. Date: 26. Jan. 1798. Wit: John Henderson, John Simpson, Andw. Liddell. Andw. Liddell made oath to G. W. Earle, DCC, 4 Mar. 1799. Rec: 4 Mar. 1799.

Page 468: For consideration of $280 paid to me by John Craig, I have sold him 1 negro, Tom. Date: 25 Dec. 1798. Signed: John Ruske. Wit: John Wilson, Robert Waugh. Robert Waugh made oath to Bill of Sale to J. B. Earle, J. P., 9 Jan. 1799. Rec: 7 Mar. 1799.

Pages 468-469: 27 Sep. 1791. Dunkin Camron of Franklin Co., Ga. to William Floyd of Pendleton Co. for 900 acres, now occupied by Floyd; 200 acres part of 673 acres granted Camron, 1 Oct. 1787 by Thos. Pinckney; 70 acres, part of 800 acres granted Samuel Lofton, Jr. by Chas. Pinckney, bd. SW by the Keowee River and vacant land: likewise a certain Fishery or half of the Fishery, conveyed from David Thompson to Camron. Signed: Duncan (his mark) Camron. Wit: James Jendrix, Alex. Floyd. Alexander Floyd made oath to Henry Burch, J. P., 9 Feb. 1799. Rec: 7 Mar. 1799.

Page 469: I, David Grimes for $43 sold to Alexander Boyse 40 acres on Beaverdam and Hurricane Creeks, part of 160 acres granted 7 May 1787 to Charles Ridgway. Date: 7 Sep. 1798. Wit: Josiah (+) Smith, Wm. Otwell. Josiah Smith made oath to Joseph Reid, J. P., 12 Nov. 1798. Rec: 7 Mar. 1799.

Page 469: I, David Grimes for $75 sold to Alexander Boyse 20 acres on Hurricane Creek of the Saluda River. Date: 7 Sep. 1798. Wit: Josiah (+) Smith, Wm. Otwell. Joshua Smith made oath to Joseph Reid, J. P., 12 Nov. 1798. Rec: 7 Mar. 1799.

Page 469: I, William Otwell for $600 sold to Alexander Boyse 860 acres on Hurricane Creek of Saluda River, bd. SW by John Booth, NW & NE by Micajah Clark, vacant land. Date: 7 Sep. 1798. Wit: David Grimes, Josiah Smith made oath to Joseph Reed, J. P., 12 Nov. 1798. Rec: 7 Mar. 1799. ..."the Justice has wrote Joshua instead of Josiah in some parts of the probates above".

Page 470: 2 Feb. 1799. William Bennison of Abbeville Co. to John Grissom, Jr. for $428 for 248 ac. on Keowee River and Deep Creek, part of tract granted Benjamin Guerard, 10 Jul. 1784 to George Bennison, bd. Edward McClure. Wit: John Shirley, John (IG) Grissom, Sr., John Grissom, Sr. made oath to John Vernor, J. P., 22 Feb. 1799. Rec: 8 Mar. 1799.

Page 470: I, David Wimpee for Ł 40 sold to Levi Wimpee 296 acres on Brushy Creek of Saluda River, granted by Chas. Pinckney, 2 Apr. 1792. Rec. Bk. D., no. 5, p. 552. Signed: David (D) Wimpey. Wit: Robert Orr, Gabriel Foster. Robert Orr made oath to Robert McCann, 10 Jan. 1799.

Page 470: I, Alexander Boyse for Ł 75 stg. sold Robert Orr 100 acres including place where Orr now lives, on 23 Mile Creek of Savannah River,... "part of a four acres tract" granted John Prater by Thos. Pinckney "7 or 17th" Apr. 1788. Recorded Bk. WWWW, p. 409, conveyed to Boyse, 16 March 1792. Date: 5 Oct. 1798. Wit: David Grimes, Wm. Otwell. William Otwell made oath to Robt. McCann, J. P., 6 Oct. 1798...Jane Boyse, wife of Alexander Boyse, released dower to Robt. McCann, J. P., 1 Mar. 1799. Signed: Jean (X) Boyse. Rec: 8 Mar. 1799.

Pages 470-471: I, Alexander Boyse for Ł 35 stg. sold Robert Orr 130 acres, part of 238 acres granted to Phillip Prater, 5 Dec. 1791, conveyed Boyse, 6 Mar. 1792. Recorded Bk. B., p. 102 (Pendleton Deeds?), on 23 Mile Crk. and 26 Mile Creek of Savannah River. Date: 5 Oct. 1798. Wit: David Grimes, Wm. Otwell. Wm. Otwell made oath to Robt. McCann, J. P., 6 Oct. 1798...Jane Boyse, wife of Alexander Boyse released dower to Robert McCann, 1 Mar. 1799. Signed: Jean (+) Boyse. Rec: 8 Mar. 1799.

Page 471: 31 Oct. 1795. William Mackey to John Williams for Ł 75 stg. for 193 acres, part of 246 ac. granted 3 Apr. 1786 by Wm. Moultrie to Geo. Weems; in 96 Dist. S. of Saluda River, on Connoross Creek of Keowee River. Signed: William (W) Mackey, Mary (X) Mackey. Wit: Richard Woolbanks, William Eddins. Richard (R) Woolbanks made oath to Robert Bowen, J. P., 6 Nov. 1795. Rec: 8 Mar. 1799.

Page 471: 31 Oct. 1795. William Mackey (also spelled McKey) to John Williams for Ł 22 stg., 77½ acres granted 4 Oct. 1790 by Chas. Pinckney, in 96 Dist. on both sides of Connoross Creek of the Keowee River, bd. on NE by Geo. Weems and vacant land. Signed: William (W) Mackey, Mary (X) Mackey. Wit: Richard Woolbanks, William Edens. Richard (R) Woolbanks made oath to Robert Bowen, J. P., 6 Nov. 1795. Rec: 8 Mar. 1799.

Pages 471-472: I, J. C. Kilpatrick for Ł 30 sold to John Williams 75 acres on SW side of Connoross Creek of Keowee River, bd. John Williams and granted Kilpatrick by Chas. Pinckney, 6 Feb. 1792, now in possession of Williams. Date: 21 Mar. 1799. Wit: Gideon Hogg, James Kilpatrick. James Kilpatrick made oath to John Barton, J. P., 24 Jan. 1798. Rec: 8 Mar. 1799.

Page 472: I, Betty Haire of Sullivan Co., Tenn. have land in South Carolina coming to me by virtue of the Service of my Husband, Matthew Haire, dec'd, in the late American War, and property that he took into that State...I constitute John Tally of Sullivan Co., Tenn. my Attorney to recover land and property. Date: 18 Feb. 1799. Signed: Betty (+) Hare..... State of Tennessee, Sullivan Co., Feb. session, 1799, Betty Haire acknowledged above Power of Attorney to Matthew Rhea, C.S.C., 18 Feb. 1799. Rec: 11 Mar. 1799.

Page 472: I, John Talley of Sullivan Co., Tenn. for $185 sold to Samuel Taylor and John Baylis Earle of Pendleton Co., S. C., 200 acres in Pendleton Co. on Little River, branch of Keowee, bd. Eleazer Turner, and vacant land, granted Matthew Hare (Soldier) by Benj. Guerard, 21 January 1785, and I bind myself against the Heirs of Matthew Haire, dec'd. Date: 11 Mar. 1799. Signed: John Tally, Attorney for Betty Hare. Wit: Sam'l. Cherry, G. W. Earle. Samuel Cherry made oath to G. W. Earle, DCC, 11 Feb. 1799. Rec: 11 Mar. 1799.

Page 472: I, Matthew Har, being of sound mind but considering a long and dangerous journey leave this as my last will and testament. I give my older brother 5 shillings and every one of my brothers equal with my

(Will of Matthew Har(e) cont'd): old brother...likewise, I give my older sister 5 shillings and my second oldest sister 5 shillings...likewise orphant child that is bound to me I allow her sufficient learning at my expense...also all the rest of my goods & chattels, land I give to my wife, Elizabeth and make her my sole Executrix. Date: 26 Sep. 1776. Signed: Matthew (his mark) Hare. Wit: David Looney, John Adair...State of North Carolina, Sullivan Co., November Session, Elizabeth Hare exhibited in open Court last will and testament of Matthew Hare, dec'd. Probate according to Law...Ordered letters of Execution issued to Elizabeth Hare...from Minutes of Court. Teste: Matthew Rhea, C.S.C....State of Tenn., Sullivan Co., the above is a copy of the will of Matthew Hare filed and recorded in this Office. Date: 18 Feb. 1799. Matthew Rhea, C.S.C., Rec: 11 Mar. 1799.

Page 472: 28 Dec. 1795. John Reid to Robert Hynes (also Hines) for Ł 35 stg. for 200 acres on N. side of Little River, part of 476 acres granted to John Reid by Chas. Pinckney, 3 Dec. 1792, bd. Major Taylor. Wit: George Tubb, Alex. Floyd, Susanna (her mark) Reese. George Tubb made oath to Jos. Reid, J. P., 11 May 1798. Rec: 11 Mar. 1799.

Page 473: I, John Sharrar, Sr. for Ł 85 stg. sold John Sharrar, Jr., 320 acres in two surveys: one of 94 acres, part of 200 acres conveyed by John McVey to John Sharrar, Sr.; the other being whole of 226 acres surveyed for Matthew Young, 21 Jul. 1787, granted John Sharrar, Sr. on Generostee Creek. Date: 20 Feb. 1799. Wit: Petr. Keys, W. Richard. William Richard made oath to G. W. Earle, DCC, 16 Mar. 1799. Rec: 16 Mar. 1799.

Page 473: I, William McClesky for Ł 40 sold Andrew Hood 150 acres on Crooked Creek of Savannah River, granted McClesky by Wm. Moultrie, 1 May 1786. Date: 24 Jul. 1798. Wit: J. Mauldin, W. Steele. Joab Mauldin made oath to G. W. Earle, DCC, 16 Mar. 1799...Isabalah (I) McClesky, wife of William McClesky made dower release to John Harris, J.P., 13 Aug. 1798. Rec: 16 Mar. 1799.

Page 473: I, Peter Keys & Co. for $100 sold William Richards 640 acres in Washington Co (Dist.) on Rocky fork of Generostee of Savannah River, granted Peter Beaty. Date: 17 Aug. 1798. Wit: Mary Moore, Jno. L. (or S.) Rushton. John (L.?) Rushton made oath to Sm. Finton, J. P., 23 Feb. 1799. Rec: 16 Mar. 1799.

Page 473: I, Daniel D'oyley of Charleston, for $200 sold to Fredrick Lanier of Pendleton Co. 200 acres in 96 Dist. on Beaverdam Creek of Tugaloo River, granted as Bounty Land to D'oyley as a Lieutenant in the 1st Continental Regiment of South Carolina. Date: 7 Mar. 1799. Wit: Geo. Caborne, F. Brimer. Francis Brimer made oath to Danl. Jas. Ravinel, J. P., 9 Mar. 1799. (in Charleston?). Rec: 23 Mar. 1799.

Pages 473-474: I, Charles Willson for Ł 14 stg. sold Hezekiah Posey 171 acres on Little Beaverdam Creek of Rocky River, bd. NE by Thomas Ellet, James Eason, granted John Brevert by Chas. Pinckney, 4 Feb. 1792. Recorded Bk. B., No. 5, p. 131. Date: 9 Mar. 1799..."NB - I do not warrant above lands from no person but myself and heirs and John Bevert and his heirs or Cleamaindor Bevart"(sic). Signed: Charles Willson. Wit: Robert McCann, Samuel Owens. Samuel Owens made oath to Robert McCann, J. P., 9 Mar. 1799. Rec: 23 Mar. 1799.

Page 474: I, Jacob Capehart for Ł 60 sold Hezekiah Posey 262 acres on 26 Mile Creek, granted Capehart by Wm. Mutrie, 6 Jan. 1794. Recorded Bk. K, no. 5, p. 59. Date: 23 Mar. 1799. Wit: William Steele, James Wood.

(Capehart cont'd): James Wood made oath to G. W. Earle, D.C.C., 23 Mar. 1799. Rec: 23 Mar. 1799.

Page 474: I, Jacob Visage of Abbeville Co. for $5.00 sold to Benjamin Nicholson 60 acres on 23 Mile Creek in Pendleton Co., part of 543 ac. granted Visage by Wm. Moultrie, 7 Jan. 1793. Recorded Bk. F., no. 5, p. 501, bd. John Miller, James Tuffnell, James Doyle, Martin. Date: 25 Mar. 1799. Wit: Hezekiah Posey, Thomas Visage. Thomas Visage made oath to G. W. Earle, D.C.C., 1 Apr. 1799. Rec: 1 Apr. 1799.

Page 474: I, Benjamin Jackson, planter, sold to William Griffen 300 acres, part of 2 tracts: one was granted Samuel Lofton, Sr. in 1793; the other granted Thomas Lofton in 1786, both by Wm. Moultrie, on E. side of 18 Mile Creek, bd. Thomas Casey, Christ. Strong. Date: 1 Apr. 1799. Wit: Jas. Dickson, G. W. Earle. George W. Earle made oath to J. B. Earle, J. P., 1 Apr. 1799. Rec: 1 Apr. 1799.

Pages 474-475: I, James Linn, Sr., planter, for $350 sold to Lewis Cobb, planter, 246 acres on S. side of 23 Mile Creek, granted Linn by Wm. Moultrie. Date: 7 Jan. 1799. Wit: William Steele, Jacob Capehart. William Steele made oath to G. W. Earle, DCC, 1 Apr. 1799...Sarah (X) Linn, wife of James Linn, released dower to John Willson, J. P., 8 Jan. 1799. Rec: 1 Apr. 1799.

Page 475: I, Joseph Whitner for 5 shillings sold to Charles Rice 30 acres in Washington Dist. on W. side of 18 Mile Creek of Keowee River, part of 190 acres transferred from Jacob Rame to Whitner, recorded Pendleton Records, 26 Jan. 1796, Bk. B, p. 367. Date: 11 Feb. 1799. Wit: Moses Payne, John Young. Moses Payne made oath to G. W. Earle, DCC, 2 Apr. 1799. Rec: 2 Apr. 1799.

Page 475: I, John Henry Stevelie of Burk Co., N. C., merchant, appoint my loving son, Fredrick Stevelie of State and County aforesaid, merchant, my lawful Attorney to collect all sums of money, debts, rents, goods, etc. belonging to me. Date: 1 Jun. 1793(?). Wit: J. McDowell, JP, Peter Moll, JP. ..Burk Co., N. C., I certify John McDowell and Peter Moll are acting Justices for this county. J. Erwin, C.C., 14 Jun. 1793. Rec: 2 Apr. 1799.

Page 475: I, James Millwee for £10 sold to Wm. Chisom 70 acres on 26 Mile Creek, granted Michael Dickson by Wm. Moultrie, 5 Jun. 1786. Date: 27 Feb. 1798. Wit: Marady (mark) Hunnicutt, William Hunnicutt, Jno. (his mark) Hunnicutt. Meridy Hunnicutt made oath to Jonathan Montgomery, J.P., 1 Apr. 1799. Rec: 5 Apr. 1799.

Page 475: I, Zebulon Garrison of Pendleton Co. sold to Pleasant Easley of Greenville Co., S. C. 137 acres on Saluda River. Date: 8 Oct. 1797. Wit: John Blasingame, Jas. Blasingame. John Blasingame made oath to D. Goodlett, J.P., 8 Feb. 1799. Rec: 6 Apr. 1799.

Page 475: I, David Clark for £30 sold to Henry Hill 130 acres, part of tract on E. side of Keowee River, including mouth of Suder Creek. Date: 25 Mar. 1799. Wit: James McKinney (called James McMahon in oath), Jonas Hill. Jonas Hill made oath to Henry Burch, J.P., 8 Apr. 1799. Rec: 8 Apr. 1799.

Page 476: 2 Nov. 1795. John Boyd to William Cox for £20 for 163 acres on Carpenter's Creek. Wit: W. M. Bruce, Jacob Vance. William Bruce made

(Cox-Boyd cont'd): oath to Wm. Reed, J. P., 19 Jul. 1798. Rec: 8 Apr. 1799.

Page 476: I, Thomas Edmondson for ₤ 30 sold to Philip Boulware 100 acres, part of tract (no further description). Wit: W. Hamilton, Wm. Vann. William Hamilton made oath to William Edmondson, Clerk of Court of Common Pleas, 19 Jul. 1797. Rec: 10 Apr. 1799.

Page 476: Sumner Co., Tenn. I, William Young of said County and State, am bound to William Griffen of Pendleton Co., S. C. for 2,000 dollars on 14 Jan. 1799 and give William Griffen the following tracts on Middle fork of 12 Mile River: 1st, of 160 acres known as Wm. Hunt's improvement; 2nd of 130 acres known as Dowthit's Place; 3rd of 200 acres known as the Long Survey; 4th of 100 acres known as Camron's Tract; 5th of 200 acres joining Camrons' and Robertson's lines; 6th of 100 acres next to Camron's, known by Wm. Brown. Date: 14 Jan. 1799. Signed: Wm. Young. Wit: William Brown, Sargent Griffen, A. Wilkinson. William Brown made oath to G. W. Earle, DCC, 11 Apr. 1799. Rec: 11 Apr. 1799.

Page 476: William Williamson of York Co., S. C. to Lawrence Bradley of Pendleton Co. for ₤ 50 stg. for 300 acres on S. side of Saluda River.... where Bradley now lives. Date: 26 Nov. 1791. Signed: Wm. Wmson. Wit: W. Lancaster, John James...Spartanburg Co., William Lancaster made oath to Isham Harrison, J.P., 20 Apr. 1792. Rec: 11 Apr. 1799.

Pages 476-477: Ebenezer Fain of Buncumb Co., N. C. to Lawrence Bradley of Pendleton Co. for $50.00 for 48 acres bd. by Cornelius Ford, on Saluda River, part of tract granted Fain, 1 Oct. 1787 by Thos. Pinckney. Date: 23 Nov. 1798. Wit: James Fleming, Ambros Bradley. Ambros Bradley made oath to Rt. Bowen, J.P., 15 Feb. 1799. Rec: 11 Apr. 1799.

Page 477: I, William Henson for ₤ 27 sold to Joshua Gotcher 200 acres on Keowee River, granted to John McCree by Benj. Guerard, 1785. Date: 9 Feb. 1798. Signed: Wm. (X) Henson. Wit: Samuel (S) Henson, Joseph Hyde. Samuel Hinson made oath to John Barton, 13 Jan. 1798. Rec: 15 Apr. 1799.

Page 477: 3 Apr. 1799. William Jamison and Margaret, his wife, to Samuel Burdine for $340 for 150 acres on George's Creek, of Saluda River,... granted John Gowen, 1789, then by deed to Jamison, 1792, bd. McCrosky, Daniel McCollum. Signed: William Jamison (only). Wit: John McCrosky,Luke Barnett, Abraham Burdine. Luke Barnett made oath to Robt. McCann, J.P., 10 Apr. 1799....Margaret (O) Jamison, wife of William Jamison released dower to Robert McCann, J.P., 11 Apr. 1799. Rec: 15 Apr. 1799.

Page 477: I, John Hallum for ₤ 150 sold to Isaac Elrod 127 acres on Brushy Creek; also, 200 acres on Brushy Creek, adjoining above tract, both tracts granted John Hallum. Date: 15 Dec. 1798. Wit: Willm. Faris, Thomas Earnest, Stephen Booth. Stephen Booth made oath to Robt. McCann, J. P., 11 Apr. 1799. Rec: 15 Apr. 1799.

Pages 477-478: I, Thomas Foster of Bunkum (sic) Co., N. C. for $100 sold to Isaac Elrod of Pendleton Co. for 30 acres (torn) on Brushy Creek; also 30 acres granted William Hobbs, bd. by Talbot. Date: 5 Dec. 1798. Wit: Wm. Faris, Stephen Booth, Thomas Earnest. Stephen Booth made oath to Robt. McCann, J. P., 11 Apr. 1799. Rec: 15 Apr. 1799.

Page 478:   I, James Martin of Lincoln Co., N. C. for
             Ł 100 sold to Matthew Dickson, Jr., 640 ac.
             on 26 Mile Creek of Seneca River, granted to
James Patterson and by John Edwards and William Hort, Esq.s., Treasurers
of the State to Martin. Date: 16 Feb. 1799. Wit: D. McCaleb, John Griffen.
Witness to receipt - James Given. James Given and John Griffen made oath
to John Willson, J. P., 13 Apr. 1799.
Rec: 15 Apr. 1799.

Page 478:   I, John Aden for $250 sold to Ambrose Barnett
             118 acres, granted Blake Mauldin by Arnoldus
             Vanderhorst, 1 Aug. 1796, on E. side of 23
Mile Creek. Date: 30 Mar. 1799. Wit: Jacob Capehart, Nathaniel (N) Davis.
Nathaniel Davis made oath to John Willson, J. P., 15 Apr. 1799...Anne(X)
Eden, wife of John Aden released dower to John Willson, 15 Apr. 1799.
Rec: 15 Apr. 1799.

Page 478:   5 Feb. 1797. Robert Boyse of Abbeville Co.,
             to Micajer Smithson for Ł 15 stg. for 112½
             acres surveyed for Isaac Thrasher, on Cuffee
Creek, branch of Choestoa of Tugalo River, bd. on SE & SW by Wm. Boyd.
Wit: William White, Bartley Smithson, Marson Smithson. Marson Smithson
made oath to G. W. Earle, DCC, 27 Apr. 1799.
Rec: 27 Apr. 1799.

Pages 478-479:   I, Hugh Alexander Nixon of Orangeburgh Dist.,
                 S. C., planter, for Ł 20 stg. sold to John
                 Smith, of same, planter, 200 acres in Wash-
ington Dist. on N. branches of Connoross Creek of Keowee River, granted
Nixon. Date: 20 Apr. 1798. Wit: Lemuel Phillips, Elizabeth (X) Nixon....
Orangeburgh Dist., Samuel Phillips made oath to Thos. Fairchild, J. P.,
30 Jun. 1798. ...I, Hugh Alexander Nixon, one of the Justices of Quorum
certify Elizabeth (X) Nixon, wife of Hugh Alexander Nixon released dower,
20 Apr. 1798.
Rec: 29 Apr. 1799.

Page 479:   I, William Richard of Abbeville Co. for $100
             sold to Peter Keys of Pendleton Co., 640 ac.
             in Washington Dist. on Rocky fork of Jener-
ostee of Savannah River, granted Peter Beaty. Date: 4 Feb. 1799. Wit: Robert Love, P. Richard. Robert Love made oath to Joshua Saxon, J. P., 6
Apr. 1799. Rec: 29 Apr. 1799.

Page 479:   I, John Smith of Orangeburgh Dist., S. C.,
             planter, for Ł 20 stg. sold to Peter Keys of
             Pendleton Co. 200 acres in Washington Dist.
on N. branch of Connoross Creek of Keowee River, bounty land, granted to
Hugh Alexander Nixon, by Benj. Guerard, 21 Jan. 1785, conveyed to Smith.
Date: 28 Apr. 1798. Wit: James Long, William Ross, Robert Elliot. James
Long made oath to Joshua Saxon, J. P., 5 Mar. 1799.
Rec: 29 Apr. 1799.

Page 479:   I, Thomas Black for $100 sold to Elisha Rob-
             inson 394 acres granted George Forbes on 23
             Mile Creek. Date: 29 Apr. 1797. Wit: Willm.
Farris, William Black. William Black made oath to George W. Earle, DCC,
27 Apr. 1799. (No recording date).

Page 479:   I, John Robinson, planter, for $200 sold to
             William Robinson and Elisha Robinson (no ac.)
             part of tract of 640 acres on 23 Mile Creek
granted Jas. Hacket by Benj. Guerard, except part sold by me to Jacob
West. Date: 1 Apr. 1799. Wit: G. W. Earle, D. McCaleb. David McCaleb made
oath to G. W. Earle, DCC, 29 Apr. 1799.
Rec: 29 Apr. 1799.

Page 479:   I, John Robinson, planter, for $50 sold to
             Amos Robinson (called Amos Garrett Robinson)
             (no amount of acreage), part of tract I live

(Robinson cont'd): on, on 23 Mile Creek, of 640 acres granted Jas. (ink blot) by Benj. Guerard, includes all that part on E. side of 23 Mile Creek, except which is sold to Jacob (torn off). Date: 6 Apr. 1799. Wit: G. W. Earle, DCC, D. McCaleb. David McCaleb made oath to G. W. Earle, 29 Apr. 1799. Rec: 29 Apr. 1799.

Pages 479-480: I, John Robinson for ₤ 30 stg. sold to Jacob West 150 acres, part of 640 acres granted to James Hackett by Benj. Guerard (part of this deed is torn). Date: 1 Apr. 1799. Wit: G. W. Earle, D. McCaleb. David McCaleb made oath to G. W. Earle, DCC, 29 Apr. 1799. Rec: 29 Apr. 1799.

Page 480: I, James Martin of Lincoln Co., N. C. for ₤ 96 stg. sold to John Dickson of Pendleton Co. 640 acres on Keowee River. Date: 2 Apr. 1799. Wit: Saml. Feemster, Stewart Brown, Wm. Bratton, Jr. Samuel Feemster made oath to Jos. (?) Palmer, J. P., 2 Apr. 1799. Rec: 30 Apr. 1799.

Page 480: State of South Carolina. John Martin empowered David Ross to make title to Leban Oakley for 400 acres where Oakley now lives...I, David Ross for ₤ 50 stg. sold to Leban Okley 400 acres granted to John Martin by Wm. Moultrie, 3 Apr. 1786, on Middle fork of Connoross of the Savannah River. Date: 15 Oct. 1798. Signed: David Ross for John Martin. Wit: Robert Powell, Daniel Daughty, James Ross. Daniel Doty made oath to Joseph Reed, J. P., 17 Apr. 1799. Rec: 30 Apr. 1799.

Page 480: I, Alexander Boyse for ₤ 20 stg. sold David Wimple, 100 acres, part of tract granted to Philip Prater by Chas. Pinckney, 5 Dec. 1791, conveyed to Boyse, 6 Mar. 1792, recorded in Clerk's Office, Pendleton Co. in Bk. B, p. 102, on 26 Mile Creek of Savannah River, on Hurricane Creek of Saluda River and head waters of 23 Mile Creek, called Half Moon, bd. by Robert Orr, David Wimpee. Date: 1 Mar. 1799. Wit: Robert Orr, Adin Wimpee. Eden Wimpee made oath to Robt. McCann, J. P., 1 May 1799. Rec: 3 May 1799.

Page 480: I, John Portman, Sr. for ₤ 86 stg. sold Samuel Taylor: 40 acres, granted Wm. Mackey on 7 May 1791, conveyed to Portman, on Keowee River; also tract adjoining above, granted James Jordan, sold at Sheriff's Sale to Joel Webb, conveyed to Portman, bd. by Portman and Bennett Aden; also 100 acres on Keowee River, bd. by other tracts, conveyed to Portman by Henry McDaniel, bd. by McDaniel, Samuel Southern, on Keowee River, below mouth of 18 Mile Creek, in whole 300 acres. Date: 4 May 1799. Signed: John (his mark) Portman, Sr. Wit: Lewis Cobb, John Taylor. John Taylor, Esq., made oath to G. W. Earle, J. P., 4 May 1799. Rec: 4 May 1799.

Pages 480-481: I, John Portman, Sr., appoint John Portman, Jr., my grandson, of Lincoln Co., Ky. my lawful attorney to collect all sums of money, debts due to me. Date: 4 May 1799. Signed: John (his mark) Portman, Sr. (Wit: names torn off). Lewis Cobb made oath he saw Power of Attorney signed with George Washington Earle, 4 May 1799. Rec: 4 May 1799.

Page 481: I, James Millwee for ₤ 100 sold to Hugh Brown, 300 acres on Toogalo River, granted Millwee by Chas. Pinckney, 5 Sep. 1791, recorded Bk. C., no. 5, p. 533. Date: 10 Jul. 1797. Wit: Aaron Broyles, Jacob (HR)Reed. Aaron Broyles made oath to Wm. Hall, J. P., 10 Jul. 1797....Margaret (+) Millwee, wife of James Millwee released dower to John Willson, 20 August 1798. Rec: 7 May 1799.

Page 481:   I, Michael Cain, of Abbeville Co. sold to Joseph Dernall 200 ac. on Conoross Creek, granted Denis Obrien, who conveyed to Cain (no amount) Date: 28 May 1799. Signed: Michael (c) Cain. Wit: Joseph Black, Jesse Kennedy. Jesse Kennedy made oath to Wm. Baskin, J. P., 8 May 1799......
Mary (m) Cain, wife of Michael Cain, released dower to Wm. Baskin, J.Q.U. in Abbeville Co., 8 May 1799.
Rec: 9 May 1799.

Page 481:   5 Feb. 1799, John Thomas, of Richland Co., SC to David Lewis, of Pendleton Co. for Ł 500 for 140 ac. on N. side of Keowee River. Wit: Wm. Hopkins, Mary (+) Hopkins, Thos. Wafer. Thomas Wafer made oath to Henry Burch, J. P., 12 Apr. 1799.
Rec: 11 May 1799.

Page 481:   I, Stephen Strange and Elizabeth, my wife, for 40 dollars sold to Daniel Ledbetter (no amount ac.) granted Strange, 4 Mar. 1798. Recorded Bk. R, no. 5, p. 418. Date: 8 Mar. 1799. Signed: Stephen Strange, Elizabeth (X) Strange. Wit: Ezekiel Stanley, Richard Holley. Ezekiel Stanley made oath to John Verner, J. P., 5 Mar. 1799.
Rec: 21 May 1799.

Pages 481-482:   I, Leban Okely for 130 dollars sold to Ezekiel Stanley, 200 acres, part of tract granted John Martin by William Moultrie, 3 Apr. 1786. Recorded Bk. KKKK, p. 324, sold to David Ross, from Ross to Okely, on North fork of Conner (sic) Creek. Date: 7 May 1799. Signed: Leban (his mark) Okely. Wit: Daniel Doughty, Daniel Ledbetter. Daniel Ledbetter made oath to G. W. Earle, J. P., 21 May 1799.
Rec: 21 May 1799.

Page 482:   28 Feb. 1788. James Kennedy, Esq., Sheriff of Charleston Dist., S. C. to Peter Keys........
Whereas, Daniel Jinkens, in Court of Common Pleas, Charleston, obtained Judgement against Robert Dillon, Administrator of William Marshall, deceased, who died intestate, for debt of Ł3000 stg. and costs.....Honorable John Fishereaud(?) Grimkie, Esq., Justice of Court, on 12 Nov. 1787, ordered all goods and chattels and Real Estates of William Marshall, dec'd. to be levied for the debt.....and also against William Marshall, Jr., heir at law of dec'd......James Kennedy, Sheriff, took possession of 640 ac. in 96 Dist. on S. side of 26 Mile Creek, granted to Agnes McGlaulin, 15 Oct. 1784, by Benj. Guerard, and was advertised in the State Gazette.....James Kennedy for Ł 16 (? torn) stg. sold to Peter Keys. Wit: James Courtney, D. O. Conner. James Courtney made oath to W. Marshall, J. P., Charleston (?).
Rec: 22 May 1799.

Page 482:   We, James Moore and Mary, my wife, of City of Charleston, S. C., for Ł 20 stg. sold to Peter Keys, of Pendleton Co., 300 acres in Washington Dist., on Big Generostee, of Savannah River, granted James Mulroney and conveyed from Mulroney to Catherine Guarantee, conveyed from Catherine Guarantee to Jno. Smyth, from Smyth to John Moore, bd. by Widow Tilly, Squire Saxon, Saml. Saxon, John Durley, Johnston Lance, John McCutchin. Date: 26 Nov. (?-ink blot). Signed: John Moore, Mary (X) Moore. Wit: Isaac (X) Steele, Thomas Divine.....Charleston Dist., S. C., Thomas Divine made oath to W. Pennington, Q. U., 4 May 1799.
Rec: 22 May 1799.

Page 482:   Washington Dist., I, John Hays, planter, for 50 dollars sold to Thomas Hays, 190 acres on N.E. side of Keowee River, part of 382 acres granted John Hays by Arnoldus Vanderhorst, 5 Dec. 1796. Date: 17 Dec. 1798. Signed: John Hays, Mary (X) Hays. Wit: Edw. Williams, Henry Hays, Jr. Henry Hays, Jr. made oath to G. W. Earle, D.C.C., 25 May 1799.
Rec: 25 May 1799.

Pages 482-483:   Washington Dist. I, Thomas Hays, planter, for

(Pages 482-483 cont'd): 50 dollars sold to Henry Hays, Jr., 100 ac. on N.E. side of Keowee River, part of tract granted John Hays by Arnoldus Vanderhorst, 5 Dec. 1796, conveyed to Thomas Hays. Date: 16 Dec. 1798. Signed: Thomas Hays, Margret (X) Hays. Wit: Edw. Williams, Henry Hays, Sr., John Hays. Henry Hays, Sr. made oath to G. W. Earle, D.C.C., 25 May 1799. Rec: 25 May 1799.

Page 483: I, William Stuart for ₺ 80 stg. sold to William Bruce 160 acres, part of 320 acres "formerly to Robert McDowell". Date: 8 Mar. 1796. Signed: William Stewart. Wit: Charles Gates, John Bruce. Charles Gates made oath to George Foster, J. P., 1 Jun. 1799. Rec: 13 Jun. 1799.

Page 483: 15 Mar. 1790. Robert McDowell, of Spartanburg Co., S. C. to William Bruce, of Pendleton Co. for ₺ 75 for 160 acres, part of 320 acres, granted McDowell, 21 Jan. 1785, by Benjamin Guerard, in 96 Dist. on both sides of Warrior's Creek, commonly known as Carpenter's Creek, of Saluda River, W. of Old Indian Boundary Line. Wit: Elias Earle, Wm. Stuart. Elias Earle made oath to G. W. Earle, D.C.C., 11 Apr. 1799. Rec: 13 Jun. 1799.

Page 483: 4 Nov. 1793. Francis Whelchel to Dennis Barnes for ₺ 60 stg. for 140 acres, part of 240 acres granted by Charles Pinckney, 4 Jan. 179_, on (torn off) da (Saluda(?) River, bd. by Wm. Bruce. Wit: Francis Whelchel, Jr., John Whelchel, Joel (X) Owenby. Joel Owenby made oath to (torn off, as was rec. date).

Page 484: I, Michael Dickson for 50 dollars sold to Thomas Richard, 224 acres on branches of 18 Mile Creek, of Savannah River, bd. on N.W. by Michael Dickson, Esq. Date: 25 Jan. 1799. Wit: Wm. McGuffin......I certify I saw Michael Dickson sign above deed and that Wm. McGuffin was a witness. W. Reed, J. P. Rec: 13 Jun. 1799.

Page 484: 9 Dec. 1788. Andrew Wornock, of 23 Mile Crk. 96 Dist., planter, to Margaret Blare (Blair) of 23 Mile Creek, for ₺ 60 for 320 acres, now in her possession, in 96 Dist. on N. side of 23 Mile Creek, of Savannah River, bd. on W. by John Calhoun, on E. by John Robinson. Wit: John Willson, Benjn. Smith. Benjamin Smith made oath to John Willson, J. P., 10 Apr. 1799.....Mary (X) Wornock, wife of Andrew Wornock, released dower to John Willson, 9 Apr. 1799. Rec: 13 Jun. 1799.

Page 484: I, Robert Smyth, of Abbeville Co. for $100 sold to James Lafoy, of Pendleton Co., 200 ac. granted Nathaniel Bradwell of Charleston Dist. of S. C. as his Soldier's Bounty, 3 Sep. 1784, in 96 Dist. on N. fork of Choestoa Creek, of Toogalo River. Date: 24 Dec. 1798. Wit: Turner Harris, John (his mark) Lively.....Abbeville Co., John Lively made oath to Saml. Foster, J.P., 7 Jun. 1799. Rec: 22 Jun. 1799.

Page 484: I, Charles Stevens for ₺ 100 stg. sold Joseph Reed 201 acres on N.E. side of Toogalo River and Little Beaverdam Creek, bd. on N.W. by Aquilla Greer, granted Joseph Reed by Wm. Moultrie, 2 Dec. 1793. Date: 1 Jan. 1799. Wit: David Sloan, George Reed. Capt. David Sloan made oath, 24 Jan. 1799. (Rest torn off).

Page 485: I, John Hallum for $600 sold to John Gibson, planter, 429 acres granted Hallum, recorded Bk. WWWW, p. 123, 7 Jan. 1788 by Thomas Pinckney, on Big Beaverdam Creek of Toogalo River, where John Gibson now lives. Date: 15 Nov. 1798. Wit: Robert Anderson, Wm. Womack. Robert Ander-

(Pages 482-483 cont'd): 50 dollars sold to Henry Hays, Jr., 100 ac. on N.E. side of Keowee River, part of tract granted John Hays by Arnoldus Vanderhorst, 5 Dec. 1796, conveyed to Thomas Hays. Date: 16 Dec. 1798. Signed: Thomas Hays, Margret (X) Hays. Wit: Edw. Williams, Henry Hays, Sr., John Hays. Henry Hays, Sr. made oath to G. W. Earle, D.C.C., 25 May 1799. Rec: 25 May 1799.

Page 483: I, William Stuart for Ŀ 80 stg. sold to William Bruce 160 acres, part of 320 acres "formerly to Robert McDowell". Date: 8 Mar. 1796. Signed: William Stewart. Wit: Charles Gates, John Bruce. Charles Gates made oath to George Foster, J. P., 1 Jun. 1799. Rec: 13 Jun. 1799.

Page 483: 15 Mar. 1790. Robert McDowell, of Spartanburg Co., S. C. to William Bruce, of Pendleton Co. for Ŀ 75 for 160 acres, part of 320 acres, granted McDowell, 21 Jan. 1785, by Benjamin Guerard, in 96 Dist. on both sides of Warrior's Creek, commonly known as Carpenter's Creek, of Saluda River, W. of Old Indian Boundary Line. Wit: Elias Earle, Wm. Stuart. Elias Earle made oath to G. W. Earle, D.C.C., 11 Apr. 1799. Rec: 13 Jun. 1799.

Page 483: 4 Nov. 1793. Francis Whelchel to Dennis Barnes for Ŀ 60 stg. for 140 acres, part of 240 acres granted by Charles Pinckney, 4 Jan. 179_, on (torn off) da (Saluda(?) River, bd. by Wm. Bruce. Wit: Francis Whelchel, Jr., John Whelchel, Joel (X) Owenby. Joel Owenby made oath to (torn off, as was rec. date).

Page 484: I, Michael Dickson for 50 dollars sold to Thomas Richard, 224 acres on branches of 18 Mile Creek, of Savannah River, bd. on N.W. by Michael Dickson, Esq. Date: 25 Jan. 1799. Wit: Wm. McGuffin......I certify I saw Michael Dickson sign above deed and that Wm. McGuffin was a witness. W. Reed, J. P. Rec: 13 Jun. 1799.

Page 484: 9 Dec. 1788. Andrew Wornock, of 23 Mile Crk. 96 Dist., planter, to Margaret Blare (Blair) of 23 Mile Creek, for Ŀ 60 for 320 acres, now in her possession, in 96 Dist. on N. side of 23 Mile Creek, of Savannah River, bd. on W. by John Calhoun, on E. by John Robinson. Wit: John Willson, Benjn. Smith. Benjamin Smith made oath to John Willson, J. P., 10 Apr. 1799.....Mary (X) Wornock, wife of Andrew Wornock, released dower to John Willson, 9 Apr. 1799. Rec: 13 Jun. 1799.

Page 484: I, Robert Smyth, of Abbeville Co. for $100 sold to James Lafoy, of Pendleton Co., 200 ac. granted Nathaniel Bradwell of Charleston Dist. of S. C. as his Soldier's Bounty, 3 Sep. 1784, in 96 Dist. on N. fork of Choestoa Creek, of Toogalo River. Date: 24 Dec. 1798. Wit: Turner Harris, John (his mark) Lively.....Abbeville Co., John Lively made oath to Saml. Foster, J.P., 7 Jun. 1799. Rec: 22 Jun. 1799.

Page 484: I, Charles Stevens for Ŀ 100 stg. sold Joseph Reed 201 acres on N.E. side of Toogalo River and Little Beaverdam Creek, bd. on N.W. by Aquilla Greer, granted Joseph Reed by Wm. Moultrie, 2 Dec. 1793. Date: 1 Jan. 1799. Wit: David Sloan, George Reed. Capt. David Sloan made oath, 24 Jan. 1799. (Rest torn off).

Page 485: I, John Hallum for $600 sold to John Gibson, planter, 429 acres granted Hallum, recorded Bk. WWWW, p. 123, 7 Jan. 1788 by Thomas Pinckney, on Big Beaverdam Creek of Toogalo River, where John Gibson now lives. Date: 15 Nov. 1798. Wit: Robert Anderson, Wm. Womack. Robert Ander-

Page 488: (Blank) Jan. 1796. Thomas Stribling and Elizabeth, his wife, to Josiah McClure for Ł 40 stg. for 100 acres on 26 and 23 Mile Creeks at confluence of sd. Creeks, bd. by James Houston. Signed: Thos. Stribling, Betsey (+) Stribling. Wit: Edward T. McClure, Shadrack (+) Elkins. Edward McClure made oath to Patrick Norris, J.P., 24 Jun. 1799. Rec: 24 Jun. 1799.

Page 488: I, John McKinsey for Ł 60 sold to John Tappley, 200 acres on Big Beaverdam Creek, bd. Henry Myres, R. Miller. Date: 19 Jan. 1798. Wit: Alexr. Kilpatrick, William Kilpatrick. William Kilpatrick made oath to (torn), 24 May 1799. Rec: (torn)

Page 489: We, Thomas C. Russell and Mary, my wife, of Lincoln Co., Ga., for Ł 65 sold to Hosea Tapley of Pendleton Co., 200 acres on both sides of Connoross Creek, granted Russell, 16 Jul. 1784. Date: 4 Feb. 1799. Signed: Tho. C. Russel, Mary Russel. Wit: Harriet Russel, John Tapley. John Tapley made oath to J. B. Earle, J.P., 24 May 1799. Rec: 24 Jun. 1799.

Page 489: I, Joseph Martin for $400 sold to Aaron Terrill 190 acres granted to sd. Millwee (sic) by Charles Pinckney, 2 Mar. 1789. Date: 10 Mar. 1799. Wit: Merit Martin, Archd. Terrill. Archabald Terrill made oath to Wm. Cleveland, J.P., 19 Jun. 1799. Rec: 24 Jun. 1799.

Page 489: I, William Steele for 260 Milled Dollars sold to Robert Seego, 320 acres on Cane Creek of Keowee River, surveyed for Steele, 29 Sept. 1786. Date: (blank) 1799. Wit: Michael Smith, Benjn. Laurence. Benjamin Laurence made oath to Henry Burch, J.P., 24 Jun. 1799. Rec: 24 Jun. 1799.

Page 489: I, Isham Clayton, of Greenville Co., S. C. for 200 dollars sold to Peter Thompson of Pendleton co., 435 acres on S. fork of Eastatoe Creek of Keowee River. Signed: Isham (I) Clayton. Wit: John McBeath, John Hunt. (Most of oath torn).

Page 490: I, Joel Terrill for 420 dollars sold to John Cochran all my right and title to all that tract on 12 Mile River, where Cochran now lives, land left to me by my Father's last will and testament....I empower Executors and Administrators of sd. Harry Terrill, dec'd. to make lawful titles in lieu of my self. Date: 25 Feb. 1799. Wit: Sanders Light, Stephen Reed. Sanders Light made oath to W. Reed, J.P., 25 Feb. 1799. Rec: 24 Jun. 1799

Page 490: 31 Jul. 1790. John Caldwell, Jr., planter, to John Bryson, late of N. C., for Ł 50 stg. for 150 acres granted Caldwell by William Moultrie, 1786, on Willson's Creek. Wit: Hugh Baskin, Danl. Bryson. Danl. Bryson made oath to E. Browne, J. P., 5 May 1798. Rec: 24 Jun. 1799.

Page 490: Abbeville Co., 31 Jul. 1790. John McNeel to John Bryson of N. C. for Ł 50 stg. for 300 ac part of tract granted McNeel by Charles Pinckney, 5 Oct. 1789, surveyed by Wm. Lesley, D.S. Wit: Henry Long, Danl. Bryson. Danl. Bryson made oath to E. Browne, J.P., 5 May 1798. Rec: 24 Jun. 1799.

Page 490: I, Richard Walter, planter, am bound to Elijah Stevenson for Ł 100 stg., 12 Aug. 1789....consideration to make sufficient title to 150 ac on Seneca River, bd. on N.W. by Benjn. Laurence, on S.E. by Col.Anderson,

(Page 490 cont'd): then above obligation is null and void. Wit: Robert Anderson, Wm. McCaleb....14 Dec. 1790, I assign over my right and title to within bond to Samuel Robinson for value rec'd. Signed: Elijah Stinson. Teste: Tho. Lofton, Capt. William McCaleb made oath to G. W. Earle, D.C.C., 22 May 1799. Rec: 24 Jun. 1799.

End of Book C-D

. . . .

DEED BOOK E

Pendleton Co., S. C.
1799
Pendleton District, S. C.
1800

Page 1: We, Auldin Tucker and Clery, his wife, for $300 dollars sold to William Blair (Blare) on Rocky River at old boundary line. (very dim). Date: 2 Aug. 1798. Signed: Auldin (X) Tucker, Clery (X) Tucker. Wit: John McAlister, Nathaniel McAlister, James McAlister. Nathan McAlister made oath to John Wilson, J.P., 8 Jun. 1799. Rec: 24 Jun. 1799.

Pages 1-2: Daniel McAlister and Agness McAlister for Ł 34 stg. sold to Alexander McAlister 200 ac. on Broadaway, branch of Rocky River, of the Savannah River, surveyed by David Hopkins, 10 Jan. 1785, granted by Wm. Moultrie, 1 May 1786. Date: 8 Jan. 1789. Signed: Daniel (his mark) McAlister, Agness (A) McAlister. Wit: Nathan McAlister, William Blair, John George. John George made oath to John Willson, J.P., 8 Jun. 1799. Rec: 24 Jun. 1799.

Page 3: Abbeville Co. Elizabeth Swift of Newberry Co. for Ł 28 sold to Matthew Alexander, of Pendleton Co., 216 ac. on Broadmouth Creek of the Saluda, beginning at line of Pendleton Co. and Abbeville Co., granted Wm. Swift. Date: 20 Nov. 1798. Signed: Elizabeth Swift. Wit: Patk. McDowell, Wm. Linvill. Patrick McDowell made oath to Charles Devanport, J. P. of Abbeville Co., 2 Mar. 1799. Rec: 24 Jun. 1799.

Pages 3-4: I, George Head for $80 sold to Amos Atkinson 25½ acres, part of 640 acres granted Samuel Ridgway, 5 Jun. 1786, on Brushy Creek. Date: Dec. 1797. Signed: Geo. (X) Head. Wit: Wm. Farris, Richard Head. Richard Head made oath to Robert Bowen, J.P., 15 Jun. 1799. Rec: 24 Jun. 1799.

Pages 4-5: I, Thomas Wafer for $992 sold to James Barren 382 acres on Keowee River. Date: 18 Feb. 1799. Wit: Richard Holden, David (B) Brown. David Brown made oath to Henry Burch, 12 Apr. 1799. Rec: 24 Jun. 1799.

Pages 5-6: 5 Nov. 1795. John Boyd to Thomas Boyd for Ł 100 for 631 acres on branches of Georg's Creek. Wit: Henry Norton, John Boyd, Jr. John Boyd made oath to William Edmondson, J.P., 31 Dec. 1797. Rec: 24 Jun. 1799.

Pages 6-7: I, Robert McCann, Esq. for Ł 55 stg. sold to Thomas Boyd ___ on Little River granted McCan, 4 Jun. 1792 by Charles Pinckney. (dim)

205

(Page 6-7 cont'd): Date: 23 Aug. 1798. Wit: John Pickens, William Rose. William Rose made oath to Robert McCann, J. P., 23 Aug. 1798.
Rec: 24 Jun. 1799.

Pages 7-8: We, Felix Warley and Ann Warley, of City of Charleston, S. C. for ₤250 stg. sold to John Clark Kilpatrick of Pendleton Co., 400 acres on Connoross, branch of Keowee River, bd. on W. by land laid out to Capt. George Warley. Recorded Book of State Bounty Grants, p. 62, 15 Oct. 1784 made to Major Joseph Warley, who died intestate, Felix Warley being heir at law. (Date too dim to read). Wit: W. Richard, James Lynch. W. Richard made oath to J. B. Earle, J.P., (date ___).
Rec: 24 Jun. 1799.

Pages 9-10: Washington Dist. Joseph Chapman of Pendleton Co., planter, for $650 sold to Joseph Smith, planter, 300 (?) acres on S. side of 12 Mile River, and S. side of Goldings(?) Creek, granted Michael(?) Golding, 24 Jun. 1784 by Benjamin Guerard. Date: 25 Aug. 1798. Signed: Joseph (+) Chapman. Wit: William Killen, John Hallum. Mary (X) Chapman, wife of Joseph Chapman, released dower to John Willson, J.P., 12 Nov. 1798. John Hallum made oath to John Willson, 26 Sep. 1798.
Rec: 24 Jun. 1799. (very dim).

Pages 10-11: 3 Sep. 1789. Benjamin Clark and Patience, his wife, to John Nicholson for ₤ 50 stg. for 176 acres on Weaver's Creek of Oolenoy of the Saluda River, granted to Clark, 4 Jun. 1787. Signed: Benj. Clark, Patience (her mark) Clark. Wit: Issac Davis, Joseph Carleton. Joseph Carleton made oath to W. Reid, J.P., 23 Jul. 1798.
Rec: 24 Jun. 1799.

Pages 11-12: I, Nathan Young for $250 sold to John Buchannon 160 acres on branches of Little Generostee Creek, being S. end of tract granted to Nathan Young, 2 Sep. 1793, and divided by Jno. McMahon, 7 Feb. 1799. Date: 8 Feb. 1799. Signed: Nathan (Y) Young. Wit: Francis Beaty, David Beaty. Francis Beaty made oath to Nathan Lusk, J. P., 9 Feb. 1799. Jane (I) Young released dower to Nathan Lusk, J.P., 9 Feb. 1799.
Rec: 24 Jun. 1799.

Page 13: I, Nathan Young for $250 sold to John Buchannon 145 acres on branches of Little Generostee Creek, being N. end of survey granted to Young, 2 Sep. 1793. Date: 8 Feb. 1799. Signed: Nathan (Y)Young. Wit: Francis Beaty, David Beaty. Francis Beaty made oath to Nathan Lusk, JP, 9 Feb. 1799. Jane (I) Young released dower to Nathan Lusk, 9 Feb. 1799.
Rec: 24 Jun. 1799.

Page 14: I, Thomas Davis and Keziah, his wife, for 420 dollars sold to Nimrod Smith (also spelled Smyth), 200 acres, part of survey granted to Davis for 1000 acres, on both sides of Little Creek, adj. to lands laid out for Francis Clinkscales, granted by Charles Pinckney; also, 100 ac. granted to Reuben Cox, 10 Aug. 1785, by Wm. Moultrie, conveyed by Cox to Davis, 13 Mar. 1787, being tract of 200 ac. whereon Thomas Davis now lives. Date: 19 Aug. 1797. Signed: Thomas (+) Davis, Keziah (Her mark) Davis. Wit: Reubin Nash, William Waddle. Reubin Nash made oath to E. Browne, J.P., 19 Aug. 1799.
Rec: 24 Jun 1799.

Pages 14-15: I, Bennett Combs of Greenville Co., S. C. for $600 sold to Jacob Light of Pendleton Co. 170 ac. on 12 Mile River, bd. by William Murphree, Caleb Boyd, Geo. Thompson, Samuel Earle. Date: 24 Jun. 1799. Wit: James Jett, Abin (X) Light. Dolley (+) Combs, wife of Bennett Combs released dower to John Willson, J.P., 31 Mar. 1799- (marked through) 1800. Abin Light made oath to Henry Burch, J.P., 24 Jun. 1799.
Rec: 24 Jun. 1799.

Page 16:   I, Samuel Henderson for $440 sold to Peter
                               Keys a negro woman, named Nancy, about age 17,
                               and her child, named Esther, about 8 months
old. Date: 1 Aug. 1798. Wit: Joshua Saxon, Lazarus Tilley. Lazarus
Tilley made oath to J. B. Earle, J.P., 25 Jun. 1799.
Rec: 25 Jun. 1799.

Pages 16-17:   We, Peter Keys and Lettice, my wife, for ₤200
                               stg. sold to Joseph Betterton, 200 acres in
                               Washington District, on Big Generostee of the
Savannah River, bd. by Samuel Saxon, John Durley, Peter Keys. Date: 6
Apr. 1799. Signed: Peter Keys, Lettice Keys. Wit: Josiah Elliott,
David Pruitt, Michael Pruitt. David Pruitt made oath to Joshua Saxon,
J. P., 1 May 1799.
Rec: 25 Jun. 1799.

Page 17:   I, Leban Okely for ₤ 30 stg. sold to George
                               Lowry (Loury), tract whereon Lowry now lives,
                               part of tract granted to John Martin by Wm.
Moultrie, 3 Apr. 1786. Recorded Bk. KKKK, p. 324. Date: 20 Oct. 1798.
Signed: Leban (his mark) Okely. Wit: John Burks, Isaac Loury, Bn.
Starritt. Benjamin Starritt made oath to John Hallum, 11 Apr. 1799.
Rec: 25 Jun. 1799.

Pages 17-19:   I, John Boyd, Sr. for $500 sold to John Boyd,
                               Jr., 600 acres (rest of description too dim
                               to read). Date: 12 Sep.(?), 1798. Wit:
Thomas Boyd, William Pugh(?), Stephen Merrill. Thomas Boyd made oath to
James Jett, J. P., 12 Sep. 1798.
Rec: 25 Jun. 1799.
(Note: description is clearer in release).

Pages 19-20:   I, John Ross for ₤ 30 stg. sold to Jehu Cook
                               213 acres on Jenerostee(?) Creek, bd. on N.W.
                               by George Hays and Gilbert Nail and vacant
land, granted Ross by Charles Pinckney, 5 Jun. 1797. Recorded Bk. Q, no.
5, p. 394. Date: 22 Dec. 1798. Signed: John (/) Ross, Barbarra (B)
Ross. Wit: _____ (smeared) Ross, David Prewitt, Charles Hamilton. David Pruitt made oath to Joshua Saxon, J.P., 21 Dec. 1798.
Rec: 28 Jun. 1799.

Page 20:   We, James Martin and Francis Bremar for ₤ 60
                               sold to David Pruitt (no acreage stated) in
                               96 District on Great Generostee, branch of the
Savannah River, surveyed for Joseph Walker, 26 Jun. 1784. Date: 13 Apr.
1799. Wit: Matthew Dickson, Eliza B. Thompson. Matthew Dickson made
oath to John Willson, J. P., 13 Apr. 1799.
Rec: 25 Jun. 1799.

Pages 20-21:   I, David McCleskey of Abbeville Co. for $214
                               sold to Archabald Buchannon of Pendleton Co.
                               150 acres, part of tract granted McCleskey by
Thomas Pinckney, on bank of the Savannah River, bd. by James Tate. Date:
7 Mar. 1799. Wit: John Middleton, Caleb Baker. John Middleton made
oath to Nathan Lusk, J. P., 21 Jun. 1799.
Rec: 25 Jun. 1799.

Pages 21-22:   Washington Dist., Pendleton Co. I, Thomas
                               Livingston, of Abbeville Co. for $370 sold to
                               Robert Tellford of Pendleton Co., 400 acres
on S. fork of Broadmouth Creek of Saluda River, bd. by Oliphant, Joseph
Brown, part of tract granted Andrew Williamson for 400 acres. Date: 10
Dec. 1798. Wit: Bn. Starritt, Isaac (X) Rice. Benjn. Starrett made oath
to W. Reid, J. P., 25 Jun. 1799.
Rec: 25 Jun. 1799.

Page 22:   I, Thomas Vick, planter, for ₤ 20 stg. sold
                               to Henry Lard, planter, 120 acres on Keowee
                               River, part of 220 acres granted 20 November
1794 by Wm. Moultrie to Vick, adjoining Jonathan Kemp, surveyed for John

(Page 22 cont'd):   Portman. Date: 27 Nov. 1798. Wit: Jonathan Kemp, Elizabeth Kemp. Jonathan Kemp made oath to John Harris, J. P., 25 Jun. 1799. Rec: 25 Jun. 1799.

Pages 22-23:   We, Elijah Mayfield and Elizabeth his wife, for $600 sold to Bennett Combs 270 acres on 12 Mile River, bd. by William Murphree, Archd. Boyd, George Thompson, Nathl. Newman. Date: 12 Apr. 1799. Signed: Elijah (M) Mayfield, Elizabeth (X) Mayfield. Wit: Stephen Mayfield, Isham Mayfield. Isam Mayfield made oath to Henry Burch, J. P., 24 Jun. 1799. Rec: 25 Jun. 1799.

Pages 23-24:   I, James Martin of Lincoln Co., N. C. for 50 lbs. stg. sold to Job Smith of Pendleton Co. 270 acres, except that part that intersects with Pilgrim's land, bd. on NW by Hamilton, granted David Sisson(?) for 296 acres. Date: 16 Apr. 1799. Wit: William Hamilton, Rowley McMillan, Jr. William Hamilton made oath to John Hallum, J. P., 16 Apr. 1799. Rec: 25 Jun. 1799.

Pages 24-25:   24 Jan. 1793. John Henderson and Martha, his wife, to Richard Burdine for Ł 40 stg. for 266 acres, part of tract granted Henderson 1 Jan. 1787 by Wm. Moultrie. Recorded Bk. PPPP, p. 434. On Long Branch of N. fork of George's Creek and Saluda River, known as Henderson's Bluff (Ruff?). Signed: John Henderson (only). Wit: Thomas Blair, James Carrick. James Carrick made oath to John Vernor, J. P., 24 Feb. 1799. Martha (X) Henderson released dower to Robert McCann, J. P., 25 Jun.1799. Rec: 25 Jun. 1799.

Pages 25-26:   We, William Jewell and Elizabeth, my wife,for $300 sold to John Armstrong 150½ acres on S. fork of George's Creek on Saluda River, part of tract granted William Reed by Wm. Moultrie, 1 May 1786, bd. by William Reed, Noblett Johnson, John Armstrong. Date: 3 Mar. 1798. Signed: William Jewell, Elibeth (X) Jewell. Wit: George Archer, John Hamilton. George Archer made oath to William Edmondson, J. P., 3 Mar. 1798. Rec: 25 Jun. 1799.

Pages 26-28:   I, James Anderson, planter, for $370 sold to William Lewis, Jr., planter, 320 acres on 26 Mile Creek, granted Joseph Web(?) by William Moultrie. Date: 2 May 1799. Wit: Hugh Saxon, Benjamin Lewis. Agnes Anderson, wife of James Anderson, released dower to Robert McCann . Benjamin Lewis made oath to Geo. W. Earle, D.C.C., 7 Oct. 1799. Rec: 7 Oct. 1799.

Pages 28-30:   15 Oct. 1795. Hennery Burch (later called Henry Burk), farmer, of Pendleton Co., Washington Dist. to William Rose for Ł 137 stg. for 1070 acres; 114 acres granted, 5 Mar. 1792 by Charles Pinckney to Robert Cravens, on Keowee River of the Savannah River; also part of 956 acres granted by Wm. Moultrie to Hennery Burch on branches of Shoal Crk. and Cornhouse Creek of Keowee River. Signed: Henry Burch. Wit: Jones Hill, Charles Bradley, Charles (X) Williams. Charles Williams made oath to William Reid, J. P., 12 Nov. 1795. Rec: 25 Jun. 1799.

Pages 30-32:   1 Sep. 1792. James Gillispie to Robert Boid, by lease made over from David Henderson to James Gillispie for 156 acres adj. Hickory Nut Mountain on Shoal Creek of Saluda River and 12 Mile River, granted David Henderson by Wm. Moultrie 5 Jun. 1785, sold to Robert Boyd by Henderson for Ł 30 stg., bd. by Robert Boyd, Samuel Duff; also part of the tract granted Gillispie by Charles Pinckney, 5 Sep. 1791, adj. above tract, George Russell, Shoal Creek and 12 Mile River. Wit: Daniel Tripplett, Saml. Gillispie, Steven Cantrell. Steven Cantrell made oath to Wm. Reid, J. P., 22 Aug. 1792. Rec: 25 Jun. 1799.

Pages 32-34: 1 Sep. 1792. James Gillispie to Robert Boid for Ł 6 stg. for 25 acres part of tract granted 5 Sep. 1791 from Charles Pinckney, W. of old boundary line for 779 acres on Shoal Creek of Saluda River and Woolf Creek of 12 Mile River, bd. by George Russell, Sara Russell. Wit: Stephen Cantrell, Daniel Tripplett, Samuel Gillispie. Steven Cantrell made oath to W. W. Reid, J. P., 22 Aug. 1792.
Rec: 25 Jun. 1799.

Pages 34-35: 6 Jun. 1795. John Tinnison to Robert Boid for Ł 70 for 93 acres, granted 2 Mar. 1789 by Charles Pinckney, west of old boundary line, on SE branch of 12 Mile River. Wit: William Crain, Joel Veaugn. Joel Veaugn made oath to W. W. Reid, J. P., 7 Aug. 1795.
Rec: 25 Jun. 1799.

Pages 36-37: 11 Mar. 1797. Owen Evans to Thomas Wilson for Ł 40 stg. for 100 acres on S. side of Saluda River, granted Evans, 18 Nov. 1784. Signed: Owen Evans, Agnes (X) Evans. Wit: Hugh Wilson, John Wilson, Jr. John Wilson made oath to Wm. Hall, J. P., 10 Jun. 1797.
Rec: 4 Jul. 1799.

Pages 37-38: I, William Turpin of Charleston, merchant, for $200 sold to John Griffen of Pendleton Co., 360 acres on branches of 23 Mile Creek of the Savannah River, surveyed by John Saxon, 10 Jan. 1799. Wit: Joseph Ship, John Wilson. Joseph Ship made oath to G. W. Earle, D.C.C., 5 Jul. 1799.
Rec: 5 Jul. 1799.

Pages 38-42: 10 Dec. 1790, John Davis to William Dosey (Dasey?) for Ł 80 stg. for 300 acres on 23 Mile Creek of Keowee River, bd. SW by Andrew Row, granted John Davis by Charles Pinckney. Recorded Bk. ZZZZ, p. 84. Signed: John (I) Davis. Wit: Lewis Cobb, Evan Thomas. Lewis Cobb made oath to G. W. Earle, D.C.C., 5 Jul. 1799.
Rec: 5 Jul. 1799.

Pages 42-44: 21 Feb. 1793. James Hendrix to Elexander (also Alexander) Floid (Floyd) for Ł 60 stg. for 100 acres on Mile Creek of Keowee River, part of 673 acres granted Dunkin Camron, 1 Oct. 1787 by Thomas Pinckney and conveyed by Camron to Hendrix. Wit: William Floid, Thomas Hargis, Elisha Floid. Elisha Floid made oath to Hennery Burch, J. P., 9 Feb. 1799. Rec: 21 Jul. 1799.

Pages 44-45: I, William Chism for Ł 10 sold to Robert Dickerson 70 acres on 26 Mile Creek, granted to mical Dickerson by Wm. Moultrie, 5 Jun. 1786, bd. by James Jolly. Date: 3 Apr. 1799. Wit: James Jolly, Joseph Johnson. James Jolly made oath to G. W. Earle, D.C.C., 2 Aug. 1799.
Rec: 2 Aug. 1799.

Pages 46-50: 31 Jan. 1794, Samuel H. Dickson, yeoman, to Joseph Smith, planter, for Ł 3 stg. for 331 acres on 12 Mile River of Keowee River of the Savannah River, bd. SW by 12 Mile River, NE by Macbrid. Wit: Hugh Dickson, Samuel Clowney, James Dickson. Hugh Dickson made oath to Mical Dickson, J. P., 7 Aug. 1799.
Rec: 7 Aug. 1799.

Pages 50-51: I, Mary Creswell of Laurence Co., S. C. for $200 sold to John Keeth of Pendleton Co. 200 acres in Pendleton Co. on Wallenor Creek bd. SE by Samuel Watt, NW by John Norwood, granted Mary Creswell, 25 Jan. 1785. Date: 20 Jul. 1799. Signed: Mary (c) Creswell. Wit: Robert Creswell, Robert Mayson. Robert Creswell made oath to W. W. Reid, J.P., 19 Aug. 1799.
Rec: 13 Jul. 1799.

Pages 51-53:   Abbeville Co., 24 Aug. 1799, John Williams of Abbeville Co. to John MacMillin of Pendleton Co. for $15 for 200 acres in Pendleton Co. on W. branches of Generostee Creek of Savannah River, bd. SW by David Jordin, granted John Williams (bounty land) by Thomas Pinckney, 7 Jul.1788. Signed: John (his mark) Williams. Wit: Samuel Weems, William Marbrough ....Abbeville Co., 26 Aug. 1799. Samuel Weems made oath to Samuel Foster, J. P.
Rec: 11 Sep. 1799.

Pages 53-54:   26 Aug. 1799, William Floid (Floyd) to John Grisham for $700 for 350 acres on NE side of Keowee River and Mile Creek part of tract granted by Charles Pinckney, 2 May 1789 to Samuel Lofton, Jr. Recorded Bk. B., no. 5, p. 148. Wit: Balam Mauldin, Alexr. Floyd. Balam Mauldin made oath to Hennery Burch, J. P., 28 Aug. 1799.
Rec: 3 Sep. 1799.

Pages 54-56:   20 May 1799. John Shannen to William Jenkins for $185 for 200 acres on Choestoe Creek of Tugaloo River, part of tract where Shannen now lives, on a conditional line made by Francis Jenkins and Isaac James. Wit: Isaack Jones, Thomas Jinkins. Francis Jinkins witness to receipt. Francis Jinkins made oath to Mikall Dickson, J. P., 22 Jul. 1799.
Rec: 3 Sep. 1799.

Pages 57-58:   27 Jan. 1795, John Portman to John Bruster for Ł 50 for 240 acres, part of 682 acres on W. side of 23 Mile Creek, bd. S. by Joseph Lankson (?), Martin, granted William Martiall(?), Esq., Governor of State of S. C. Recorded Bk. OOOO, p. 510. Signed: John (P) Portman. Wit: William Millwee, Samuel Bruster. Samuel Bruster made oath to William Millwee, J. P., 25 Jan. 1799.
Rec: 3 Sep. 1799.

Pages 58-59:   I, Thomas Millsap of Abbeville Co. for $600 sold to John Tinsley of Abbeville Co., 100 ac on Rocky River in Pendleton Co., bd. by Wm. Hall, Robert Harkness, Elisha Brown, Esq. and Robert Norris, granted to Samuel McCane, conveyed to Blake Mauldin, then to the conveyer. Wit: William Fletcher, Thomas Tinsaley. Thomas Tinsley made oath to Samuel Watt, J. P., 14 Mar. 1799.
Rec: 13 Sep. 1799.

Pages 60-61:   Washington Dist., Pendleton Co., I, Joab Mauldin for $600 sold to Samuel Earle of Greenville Co., S. C. 340 acres in fork of Tugalo River, part of 2 tracts: one, granted Major Passon(?), for 64 acres, 8 Jun. 1786 by Wm. Moultrie; the other for 820 acres granted Lewis Passon (?), 11 Jun. 1787 by Thomas Pinckney on Keowee River and Little Beaverdam Creek, bd. by Graham(?) Carey line, (since sold to Jacob Holland),Wm. Cox, John Rotton. Date: 10 May 1799 (cannot read witnesses names.) Blake Mauldin signed oath. Jean (X) Mauldin, wife of Joab Mauldin released dower to John Wilson, J. P., 17 Sep. 1799.
Rec: 17 Sep. 1799.

(Note: Here the pages get very faded, most unreadable. I have tried to read as much as I can, but may be mistakes in reading the names...BW)

Pages 61-62:   I, William Lesley of Abbeville Co. for $5 sold to Pricilla Turin(?) of Pendleton Co., 50 ac. on branches of Savannah River, west corner of tract surveyed for John Caldwell, 6 Nov. 1792, bd. by Thomas Turner(?), James Carlile, Thomas Turin. Date: 26 Apr. 1799. Wit: James Turner, Asaph Alexander, John McMahan, D.S. states he ran line 2 Aug. 1799. (No oath). Rec: 17 Sep. 1799.

Pages 62-63:   I, John Prater, planter, for $646.50 sold to Zachariah Taliferro, Esq. 300 acres on the E. branch of 23 Mile Creek of Keowee River, bd.

(Pages 62-63 cont'd): Taliferro's line. Date: 21 Aug. 1799. Wit: Richard Head, John Pickens. Elianor (O) Prater released dower to Robert McCann, J. P.C. 6 Sep. 1799. Richard Head and John Pickens made oath to Robt. McCann, J. P., 21 Aug. 1799. Rec: 17 Sep. 1799.

Pages 64-66: 18 Nov. 1796. William Wallace, merchant, to William Burney, planter....William Burney is endebted for several (to Burney) sums of money, amounting to $593.99, due on three seperate bonds payable 1 January 1799. For security, Wallace deeds 700 acres, part of 1000 acres granted Wallace (marked through) Burney by Charles Pinckney, 4 Jun. 1792, on 18 and 23 Mile Creeks of Keowee River, where Wallace now lives. Signed: William Wallace. Wit: W. C. Hamilton, Jacob (his mark) Earnest. Jacob Earnest made oath to John Wilson, J. P., 26 Sep. 1798. Rec: 14 Sep. 1799.

Page 66: I, Robert Childress (Childers) sold to Robert Bowen a negro girl named Cate for $300. Date: 2 Dec. 1798. Wit: John Bowen, Thomas Gillispie. John Bowen made oath to John Hallum, J.P., 14 Sep. 1799. Rec: 14 Sep. 1799.

Pages 66-68: Laurens Co., S. C. I, Robert Spence for Ł 20 stg. sold to Lewis Sherrill of Pendleton Co. 110 acres in Washington Dist. on Beaverdam Creek of Savannah River. Date: 2 Jan. 1799. Signed: Robert (R) Spence. Wit: William Millwee, Joseph Kennedy.....Laurence Co., Joseph Kennedy made oath to William Nall, J. P., 2 Jan. 1799. Nancy (X) Spence, wife of Robert Spence released dower to Jonathan Downs, J.L.C., 13 May 1799. Rec: 21 Sep. 1799.

Pages 68-69: I, Joseph Green for $300 sold to Isham Green 200 acres on 26 Mile Creek of Savannah River, part of 640 acres granted John Mills. Date: 1 May 1798. Wit: James (not clear), Hugh Mills. Hugh Mills made oath to ___, 9 May 1798. Rec: 2 Sep. 1799. (this not clear).

Page 69: I, Isham Green for $80 sold to James Brister (rest not clear)..........
Rec: 25 Sep. 1799.

Page 69-70: (____ not clear).......sold to Alexander Boise for $100 for 180 acres on NE branches of Beaverdam Creek of Savannah River _____ (rest not clear).

Pages 70-71: Shadrich Noling to Spence(?) Mitchell Date: ___ Apr. 1799. Signed: Shadrack (N) Noling. Wit: Doyle Land, Simon Doyle, William Doyle. (Rest not clear).

Page 71: Robert Maxwell(?) of Greenville Co. to James Tate for Ł 160 for 200 acres where Joshua Hamm (?) ....(unreadable).........

Pages 71-73: Francis Greenwood _____ (not clear) _____ granted 2 Dec. 1793. Recorded Bk. H.(?), no. 5, p. 19, by Wm. Moultrie, in Washington Dist. on Keowee River, bd. by Col. Anderson and others ....Jane Anderson signed oath as witness. Elizabeth (X) Greenwood, wife of Francis Greenwood released dower to John Wilson, J. P. (date not clear). Rec: 8 Oct. 1799.

Pages 73-75: 2 Aug. 1793, Richard Oldham, of Pendleton Co. to Christopher Willimon (Williams?) of City of Charleston for Ł 100 for 640 acres in Washington Dist. (also called 96 Dist.) on both sides of 12 Mile River of Keowee River, granted Owens 6 Feb. 1786 by Wm. Moultrie. Recorded Bk.

(Pages 73-75 cont'd:) HHHH, p. 6___, Mentions Robert Anderson and Christopher Willimon(?) tenants in common. Wit: John Hallum, Archeble Owings; John Hallum made oath to John Wilson, J. P., 24 Jan. 1794. Rec: 5 Oct. 1799.

Page 75: Personally came Mr. James Turner before George W. Earle, J. P., and made oath to William Leslie conveyence and that Asaph Alexander signed with him. Date: 17 Sep. 1799. (See pp. 61-62).

Page 76: 96 Dist., We, John Slaitor, Sr., Jno. Slaitor, James George Slaitor and Levi Slaitor (name could also be Stanton, Staitor) are bound to Robert Anderson, Esq. for ŧ 500 stg. and give titles to "land to be surveyed by direction of Robert Anderson on bounty warrants of 200 acres each", total of 600 acres. Signed: John (his mark) Slaitor, Sr., Geo. (v) Slaitor, John Slaitor, Levi (his mark) Slaitor. Wit: Moses Liddle, John Risll. Moses Liddle made oath to George W. Earle, J. P., 6 October 1799.....(land was bestowed as bounty for service in Independant(?), commanded by Capn. John More during the War (this not clear reading).

Pages 76-78: I, Robert Anderson, Esq., for ŧ 75 stg. sold to Alexander Ramsey, planter, 200 acres..... granted John Slaitor(?) on the bounty. Recorded Bk. BBBB, p. 177, on Seneca Creek, W. side of Keowee River; also 100 acres granted Robert Anderson, Citizen, recorded Bk. CCC, p. 490(?) (rest unreadable)....Lydia Anderson, wife of Robert Anderson released dower to John Wilson, J. P., 16 Apr. 1799. On 20 Sep. 1798, Thomas Martin made oath to J. C. Kilpatrick, J. P. Rec: 9 Oct. 1799.

Pages 78-79: Daniel Stringer to John Carrick(?) for ŧ 60 stg. for 470 acres on Generostee Creek with Mill, being part of tract granted James Martin(?) _____, Jacob Chamberland and part originally granted to Stringer. Date: 27 Apr. 1799. Wit: James Morrow, Alexander Stephenson. James Morrow made oath to _____, J. P. Mary (Y) Stringer, wife of Daniel Stringer released dower to John Wilson, J. P., 4 May 1799. Rec: 21 Oct. 1799.

Pages 79-80: 10 Dec. 1792(?), William Gunter to Jacob(?) Holland (...body of deed unreadable). Signed: William Guntor, Ann Guntor. Wit: Hennery Loury, Thomas Holland. Thomas Holland made oath to William Cleveland, J. P. Date: _____. Rec: 22 Oct. 1799.

Pages 80-81: 7 Aug. 1797, Hennery Lowery to Jacob Holland for 100 lbs. stg. for 233 acres granted Lowery 2 Dec. ___. ....Wit: Hugh Patrick, James Lowery. Hugh Patrick made oath to William Cleveland, JP. Date: ___. Rec: 22 Oct. 1799.

Pages 81-82: 3 Sep. 1792, James Keith to James Holland and Andrew Holland for ŧ 15 stg. for 170(?) acres in 96 Dist. on both sides of S. fork of Big Beaverdam Creek. Wit: John (X) Loury, David Keith. John Loury made the oath to John Harris, J. P., 20 Oct. 1799. Rec: _ Oct. 1799.

Pages 82-83: 17 Feb. 1796, James Holland and Andrew Holland to Jacob Holland _____(rest unreadable)....

Page 83: Samuel Gardner to William Steele(?) _____ Date: 14(?) Oct. 1799. Wit: George W. Earle, Joseph Taylor. George W. Earle certified he was a witness, 28 Oct. 1799. Rec: 28 Oct. 1799.

Page 84: Washington Dist., David McCaleb for 140 dollars sold to James McGuffin ___ acres surveyed for Charles Lay(?) on 18 Mile Creek, bd. William Steele. Date: ___. Signed: D. C. McCaleb. Wit: George W. Earle, Francis Greenwood. Francis Greenwood made oath to Geo. W. Earle, DCCJP, 25 Oct. 1799. Rec: 28 Oct. 1799.

Pages 84-85: Washington Dist., I, Samuel Dickson for $50 sold to Francis Greenwood 135 acres on branch of Keowee River of Savannah River, bd. NW by Genl. Robert Anderson, SW by Lieutenant Robert Anderson and vacant lands. Date: 5 Jan. 1797. Wit: James McGuffin(?), Richard Shipp, John Young. Wm. (?) McGuffin made oath to Geo. W. Earle, DC, 20 Oct. 1799. Rec: 28 Oct. 1799.

Pages 85-86: I, Charles Rice, planter, for Ł 32 sold Francis Greenwood, planter, 40 acres part of 180 (?) acres granted Robert Anderson, recorded Bk. QQQQ (or LLLL), p. 98, 7 Sep. 1790 (description not clear).......... Date: 2 Sep. 1798. Wit: Robert Anderson, Lydia Anderson.....Mary Rice, wife of Charles Rice released dower to John Wilson, J. P., _ Jan. 1799. Nov. 1798, Robert Anderson made oath to J. C. Kilpatrick, J. P. Rec: 28 Oct. 1799.

Pages 86-87: 8 Oct. 1798, Peter Perkins of Stokes Co., NC to William Glenn of Pendleton Co. for Ł 100 stg. for 116 acres (later says 117 acres) on Wollonoy Creek. Signed: Peter Perkins, Agnes Perkins. Wit: Thos.(?) Perkins, Bennet Combs, N. Perkins. Bennet Combs made oath to W. Reid. Rec: ___(faded).

Pages 87-88: I, William Millican, Jr. of Pendleton Co. for Ł 60 stg. sold to William Millican, Sr. of Greenville Co., S. C., my stock of cows and hogs. Date: 4 Nov. 1799. Wit: Hugh Crumbley, James Sims. James Sims made oath to Jonathan Montgomery, J. P., 5 Nov. 1799. Rec: 4 Nov. 1799.

Page 88: I, Daniel Ross on _____(date blank) appoint Leonard D. Hall(?), Esq. then of Pendleton Co. my lawful attorney to sell tract of land in Pendleton Co. on Martin's Creek of Seneca River, which I purchased from Alexander Dromgoole. Date: 8 Nov. 1799. Wit: D. C. McCaleb, Jos. Taylor. Jos. Taylor made oath to Geo. W. Earle, DCC, 5 Nov. 1799. Rec: 8 Nov. 1799.

Pages 88-89: I, Michael Barrett of Charleston, Att'y. at Law for Ł 100 stg. sold to Patrick Duncan of Charleston, 200 acres in Pendleton Co., on Little George's Creek. Date: 27 Apr. 1799. Wit: John Nicholson, Thomas Duncan(?). John Nicholson made oath to Wm. Edmondson, J. P. _ Nov. 1799. Rec: _ Nov. 1799.

Pages 89-90: I, Charles Goodwin, Attorney at Law of Winton Co., S. C., for Ł 10 sold to Thomas Benson of Greenville Co., planter, 100 acres on Uloney Creek, branch of S. fork of Saluda River, granted Goodwin by Thomas Pinckney. Recorded Bk. SSSS, p. 307. Date: 13 Apr. 1798. Wit: Benjamin Hankins (only) who made oath to Wm. Edmondson, J. P., 14 Dec. 1799. Rec: _____

Pages 90-92: 2 Dec. 1793. William Gilham, and Jane, his wife, to George Smith for Ł 30 for 54-3/4 acres on 12 Mile River of Savannah River, a part of tract granted Arthur McAdoo and transferred to Gilham. Granted 21 Jan. 1785. Signed: William Gilham, Jane (/) Gilham. Wit: Sarah Gilham, Moses May, James Cannon. Moses May made oath to Joseph Reed, JP, 7 Aug. 1799. Rec: 14 Nov. 1799.

Pages 92-93:   I, George Smith for Ł 40 stg. sold to John
                 Simpson 52-3/4 acres on 12 Mile River. Date:
                 19 Oct. 1799. Wit: John E. Calhoun, Howard
Calhoun. John E. Calhoun made oath to J. B. Earle, J. P., 12 Nov. 1799.
.....Plat shows land bd. on SE by William Warren and 12 Mile River.
Signed: Samuel H. Dickson, D.S.
Rec: 11 Nov. 1799.

Pages 93-94:   I, Robert Smith and Elizabeth, my wife, for
                 Ł 80 sold to Abner Honey, 140 acres, part of
                 771 acres on Branch Dam Creek, bd. by Widow
Gibson and James Swan, granted Smith, 6 Jun. 179_. Date: 23 Aug. 1798.
Signed: Robert Smith, Elizabeth (her mark) Smith. Wit: Charles Hunt,
John Tapley. Charles Hunt made oath to John Harris, J. P., 10 Oct. 1799.
Rec: 11 Nov. 1799.

Pages 94-95:   I, Robert Smith and Elizabeth, my wife, for
                 Ł 30 stg. sold to Abner Honey 159 acres, part
                 of 170 acres off lower end of tract granted
Smith, 6 Jun. 1794. Date: 7 Sep. 1799. Signed: Robert Smith and Elizabeth (her mark) Smith. Wit: Charles Hunt, John Tapley. Charles Hunt
made oath to John Harris, J. P., 18 Oct. 1799.
Rec: 14 Nov. 1799.

Pages 95-96:   I, Patrick More for Ł 75 sold to Hugh Moor
                 102 acres on both sides of Woloney Creek. Date:
                 4 Feb. 1799. Wit: L. Juleen(?), A. B. Matlock,
Bennit Moor. Absolom Matlock made oath to William Reid, J. P., 3 July
1799. Rec: 19 Nov. 1799.

Pages 96-98:   20 Jun. 1795, William McCaleb to William Hughs
                 Lacy for Ł 100 stg. for 400 acres on Choestoe
                 Creek, waters of Toogaloo River; 200 acres be-
ing a bounty granted James McIlwee, 2 May 1785 by Wm. Moultrie; the other
200 acres being part of 446 acres granted Wm. McCaleb, 2 Jul. 1787 by
Thomas Pinckney, 100 acres surveyed for Solomon White, 100 acres for Daniel Dulaney. Wit: Daniel Sims, Brooks Davis. Brooks Davis made oath to
Nathl. Perry, J. P., 9 Apr. 1796.
Rec: 22 Nov. 1799.

Pages 98-99:   22 Jan. 1798, William Rose to Charles Dodson
                 for Ł 50 stg. for 114 acres on S. side of the
                 Keowee River, granted Robert Cravens by Chas.
Pinckney, 5 Mar. 1792 and from Cravens, granted to Hennery Burch, then
conveyed to William Roose. Signed: William Ross. Wit: Abraham Hagis,
John Umphries, Delinham(?) Dodson. Abraham Hargis made oath to James
McKinney, J. P., 12 Jan. ___.
Rec: 27 Nov. 1799.

Pages 99-101:   26 Jan. 1798, Hennery Burch to Charles Dodson
                 for Ł 50 stg. for 103 acres on N. side of the
                 Keowee River, granted Robert Cravens by Chas.
Pinckney, 5 Mar. 1792, conveyed to Burch. Wit: Abraham Hagis, John Humphries, Isaac Umphries. Abraham Hargis made oath to James McKinney, JP,
12 Dec. ___.
Rec: 27 Nov. 1799.

Pages 101-102:   7 Oct. 1795, James Gillispie to John Yager for
                 Ł 30 stg. for (no amount), part of tract gran-
                 ted Gillispie, 22 Aug. 1791 by Chas. Pinckney,
W. of old Boundary Line, on Wolf Creek, bd. by John Langley, John Yager,
John Gillispie, Boyd, James Gillispie, Ephraim Gurrin(?). Wit: William
Crain, Joseph Duff. William Crain made oath to George Foster, J. P., 14
Sep. 1799.
Rec: 13 Dec. 1799.

Pages 102-103:   7 Oct. 1795, James Gillispie to John Yager for
                 Ł 50 stg. (no amount acreage), granted 5 Jul.
                 1785 to David Henderson by Wm. Moultrie for
156 acres on Camp and Shoal Creek of Saluda River, conveyed from Hender-

(Pages 102-103 cont'd.):   son to Gillispie, bd. by Yager, Robert Boyd.
                           Wit: William Crain, Joseph Duff. William
Crain made oath to George Foster, J. P., 14 Sep. 1799.
Rec: 13 Dec. 1799.

Page 104:   2 Mar. 1798, John McCollough to John Callaham
                           for Ł 50 stg. for 200 acres on head branches
                           of Mulberry Creek of Savannah River, bd. NW
and NE by Martha Coyles, other sides by land granted McCullough by Chas.
Pinckney, 7 Feb. 179_. Recorded Bk. C, no. 5, p. 224. Wit: Thomas Milford, John Milford. Thomas Milford made oath to Patrick Norris, J. P.,
13 Sep. 1799.
Rec: 13 Dec. 1799.

Pages 105-107:   7 Sep. 1787, Nathan Young of Aberville, 96
                           Dist., planter, to John Beaty of same, planter, for Ł 35 stg. for 128 acres on Little
Generostee, bd. on SW by Robert Loosk, SE by Nathan Young, part of 370
acres granted Nathan Young by Wm. Moultrie, 21 Jun. 1787. Signed: Nathan
(his mark) Young, Jane (her mark) Young. Wit: William Beaty, Robert
Loosk. William Beaty made oath to Nathan Lusk, J. P., of Pendleton Co.,
23 Aug. 1798.
Rec: 13 Dec. 1799.

Pages 107-109:   21 Apr. 1796, James Cannon, planter, to John
                           Cannon, planter, for natural love and affection, for 55 acres in 96 Dist., Pendleton Co.
on 12 Mile River, E. side of Keowee River, granted James Cannon, 3 Oct.
1791. Wit: Jesse(?) Hillen, Joseph Smith, Isaac Herring. Jesse (or
Joseph- this was written over) Hillen made oath to John B. Earle, J. P.,
13 Dec. 1799.
Rec: 13 Dec. 1799.

Pages 109-110:   I, James Cannon for $125 sold to John Cannon
                           82 acres on Cain Creek of Keowee River, part
                           of a tract laid out for Humphrey Coob(?), conveyed to William Reid(?), then to James Cannon, then to Elijah Herring
and from Herring to James Cannon. Date: 27 Jul. 1799. Wit: Wiley Ledbetter, Joseph Hillin. Jesse Hillin made oath to J. B. Earle, J. P., 13
Dec. 1799.
Rec: 13 Dec. 1799.

Pages 110-112:   15 Oct. 1798, Elenor Pickens to Elijah Herrin,
                           planter, for natural love and affection, 300
                           acres on Conoross Creek in 96 Dist. bd. Thomas
Shanklin, part of tract granted Elenor Pickens, 6 Feb. 1786. Recorded Bk.
GGGG, p. 464. Signed: Elenor (E) Pickens. Wit: Josiah Elliott, Isaac
Herring. ...Received from Elijah Herrin $300, 15 Oct. 1798. Isaac Herring made oath to Joseph Reid, J. P., 8 Jun. 1799.
Rec: 13 Dec. 1799.

Pages 112-113:   8 Oct. 1795, Humphrey Coob (later Cobb) ..of
                           Greenville Co., S. C., to William Reed of Pendleton Co. for Ł 20 for 264 acres in Pendleton Co., on Cain Creek, granted Cobb by Chas. Pinckney, 1 Oct. 1792. Wit:
Jesse Brown, Nathan Reed, Nathaniel Reed. Joseph Brown made oath to
Joseph Reid, J. P., 28 May 1796.
Rec: 13 Dec. 1799.

Pages 113-115:   19 Sep. 1797, William Reid, planter, to James
                           Cannon, planter, for natural love and affection, for 82 acres in 96 Dist. on Cain Creek
of Keowee River, granted 1 Oct. 1792 to Humphrey Cobb. Signed: William
(X) Red. Wit: Benjamin (X) Land, Jesse Hillin....Received from James
Cannon $115. Date: 19 Sep. 1797. Benjamin Land made oath to Jonathan
Saxon, J. P., 20 Feb. 1798.
Rec: 13 Dec. 1799.

Pages 115-117:   10 Feb. 1798, James Cannon, planter, to Elijah
                           Herrin, planter, for natural love and affec-

(Pages 115-117 cont'd.): tion for 82 acres on Cain Creek of Keowee River, part of tract granted 1 Oct. 1795 to Humphree Cobb. Wit: Elisha Herring, Erasmus (X) Tolesson, Benjamin (X) Land. Benjamin Land made oath to Joshua Saxon, J. P., 10 Feb. 1799. Rec: 13 Dec. 1799.

Pages 117-119: 28 Sep. 1798, Elijah Herrin, planter, to James Cannon, planter, for natural love and affection for 82 acres in 96 Dist. on Cain Creek of Keowee River, part of tract granted 1 Oct. 1792 to Humphre Cobb, conveyed from him to William Reed, from Reed to James Cannon, then to Elijah Herrin, and from Herrin to James Cannon. Wit: Jesse Hillin, Mary (+) Hillin.....receipt from Cannon for $125. Date: 28(?) Sep. 1798. Jesse Hillin made oath to Joseph Reid, J. P., 17 Apr. 1799. Rec: 13 Dec. 1799.

Pages 119-126: I, William Read, of City of Charleston, Doctor of Phisick, for $640 sold to Francis Bremar, of Charleston, A. T. L., these several tracts of land, viz: 640 acres in 96 Dist. on N. fork of George's Creek, of Saluda River bd. S. by Rebeckah Reed, W. by John Hallum, E & N by land surveyed 1 Jul. 1784 by Bennet Crafton, D.S. for William Reed; 640 acres in 96 Dist. on both sides of George's Creek, of Saluda River, bd. N. by William Read, surveyed 1 Jul. 1784 for Mrs. Rebecca Reed; 640 acres on S. branches of George's Creek, bd. NW by Hugh Rose, NE by Zaphaniah Roberts, surveyed 20 Jul. 1784 for Elizabeth Read; 640 acres on George's Creek, bd. NW by Ephram Mitchell, NE by Zephaniah Roberts, surveyed 19 Jul. 1784 for Hugh Rose, which several tracts granted William Read, 15 Oct. 1784. Date: 19 Oct. 1799. Wit: Artemas B. Darby, William Gillison. Artemas Bernham Darby made oath to Stephen Ravenell, J. P., 21 Oct. 1799.....Pendleton Co., Washington Dist., Artemus Burnham Derby made oath to William Edmondson, J. P., 10 Dec. 1799. (the other witness is called William Pellison in oath).....pp. 121-124, plats of land, pp.124-125, descriptions of grants made by Artemus B. Darby, D. S.

Pages 126-127: I, John Head for $100 paid by Charles Waters and sold to Charles Waters' daughter, Fanny Waters, 76 acres laid out to Alexander Mahan, conveyed from Mahan to Charles Waters and from Waters to John Head, part of tract laid out to Robert Samuel Brashars and conveyed to Col. Maxwell and from Maxwell to John Head, granted by Thos. Pinckney in 1789 "the sd. Waters to have peaceful possession during his and his wife, Mary Waters, lifetime". Date: 5 May 1799. Wit: James Head, Peter (X) Head. Peter Head made oath to William Edmondson, J. P., 7 Aug. 1799. Rec: 21 Dec. 1799.

Pages 127-128: I, Mary Leboon(?) for $100, paid by Charles Waters, sold to Fanny Waters, daughter of sd. Charles Waters, 2 horses, 11 head of cattle, 16 hogs, featherbed and furniture. Date: 4 May 1799. Wit: James Head, Peter (+) Head. Peter Head made oath to William Edmondson, J. P., ___ Aug. 1799. Rec: 21 Dec. 1799.

Pages 128-129: 5 Oct. 1799, John Winn to David Sloan for $100 for 200 acres where John Win now lives, surveyed 27 Jan. 1792, granted Hanah Mason by Chas. Pinckney; also 1 horse, 2 cows and calves. Signed: John (O)Winn. Wit: Richard Speak, William Sloan. William Sloan made oath to J. B. Earle, J. P., 21 Dec. 1799. Rec: 21 Dec. 1799.

Pages 130-131: I, Brittan Willis, planter, for Ł 50 stg.sold to David Sloan, 140 acres in Washington Dist. on Generostee Creek, bd. W. by Shadrack Ingran(?), surveyed for Willis 11 Sep. 1786, granted by Thos. Pinckney. Date: 24 Aug. 1799. Signed: Britten (M) Willis. Wit: Thomas Stribling, William Sloan. William Sloan made oath to J. B. Earle, J. P., 21 Dec. 1799. Rec: 21 Dec. 1799.

Pages 131-132: 21 Dec. 1799, John Moorhead to James Barnett of Charleston (?) Co., S. C. for Ł 65 stg. for 150 acres on both sides of N. fork of 12 Mile River, bd. by Pendleton Waggon Road, a conditional line between Bennet Combs and Abner Robertson(?), _____ Hicks. Signed: John Morehead, Sarah (her mark) Morehead. Wit: James Sesson(?), Sarah Montgomery. James Sesson(?) made oath to Jonathan Montgomery, 23 Dec. 1799. Rec: 23 Dec. 1799.

Pages 132-133: I, Nicals Perkins of Stokes(?) Co., N. C. for $600 sold to John Easley of Pendleton Co., 600 acres on Rice's Creek of 12 Mile River, surveyed by David Hopkins, D.S., 11 Jun. 1784 for Patrick Bardon(Rardon) Date: 8 Oct. 1799. Signed: N. Perkins. Wit: James Trehern(?), Harmon Hawkins, H. D. L. J. Stone....."Be it remembered that one Kirks(?) has a claim of a tract of 40 acres in one corner of within deed and I, John Easley, do hereby relinquish all claim to the sd. Keeks(?)". Date: 13 Oct. 1799. Wit: Harmon Hawkins, Randolph Riddle. Harmon Hawkins made oath to Robert Bowen, J. P., 12 Nov. 1799. Rec: 1 Jan. 1800.

Pages 133-134: 28 Dec. 1792, Benjamin Perry to Jonas Hill for Ł 30 for 300 acres on Woolf Creek of 12 Mile River, bd. SE by Francis Bradley, NW by James Bruce, part of 640 acres granted Perry, 5 Jun. 1786 by Wm. Moultrie. Wit: Nathaniel Perry, Robert Carter. Robt. Carter made oath to Nathaniel Perry, J. P., 1 Jan. 1800. Rec: 1 Jan. 1800.

Pages 134-135: I, William Rose(?), planter, for $300 sold to Solomon Palmer, planter, 300 acres in Washington Dist. on both sides of Cornhouse Creek of Little River, bd. N. side of Norton's old path. Date: 6 Oct. 1799. Wit: Wm. Rose, Jr., Hudson Rose(?), Jonathan (+) Palmer. Jonathan Palmer made oath to Hennery Burch, J. P., 8 Oct. 1799. (very dim).

Pages 135-136: I, Thomas Blair, planter, for $150 sold to Moses Liddle one long posted walnut bedstead, with feather bead (bed?), 2 cotton sheats, 2 blankets, 2 covered bolsters and pillows, 1 short posted cherry beadstead with feather bed, 2 cotten sheats, 2 blankets, 2 covered bolsters and pillows, 1 round walnut dining table, 1 corner cupboard with a quantity of bouls, plates, dishes, teacups, sausers, coffee and tea pots and sundry other cooking ware, four chests, 1 gun case, bottles, etc., cattle, horses, corn and cotten that is now planted or shall be raised of the plantation which I now dwell on. Date: 15 Apr. 1799. Wit: William McCleskey, Christopher Wonder. (No oath). Rec: 4 Jan. 1800.

Pages 136-137: We, Thomas Blair and Jane, my wife, planter, for $500 sold to Moses Liddle a negro wench named Sarah and her child named Charlott. Date: 24 Dec. 1798. Signed: Thomas Blair, Jane Blair. Wit: William McClesky, Elizabeth Liddle. (No oath) Rec: 4 Jan. 1800.

Pages 137-138: 20 Feb. 1798, Samuel Burton to William Grant for Ł 40 stg. for 200 acres granted Burton by Chas. Pinckney, 4(?) Oct. 1790(?), recorded bk. C, no. 5, p. 270, in 96 Dist. on Cornhouse Creek, of Austin(?) Crk. of Keowee River, according to plat given by Nathaniel Williams. Wit: Abraham Able, William Bannister. Abraham Able made oath to J. C. Kilpatrick, J. P., 7 Jul. 1798. Rec: 4 Jan. 1800.

Pages 139-140: 9 Mar. 1793(?), John Hollan to John Davis for Ł 60 for 200 acres on Shoal Creek of Saluda River in Washington Dist., granted Domico(?) Holland. Wit: Bennet Combs, William Whelchel. Bennet Combs made oath to Baly Anderson, J.P., 12 Mar. 1798. Rec: 5 Jan. 1800.

Pages 140-141: I, Joseph Reed (called Sr. in the oath) for $150 sold to George Walker Reed (also Read) 50 acres on N. side of Tugalo River, part of a tract granted Joseph Reed by Wm. Moultrie, 2 Dec. 1793. Wit: David Sloan, Obediah Trimmer. Joseph Reed, Jr. (not listed as witness) made oath to John Vernor, 9 Nov. 1799. Rec: 5 Jan. 1800.

Pages 142-143: I, Thomas Hindsley, am bound to William Parsons for $460 in Silver or Gold, and give title to 212 acres on Golden's Creek where Thomas Hinsley now lives. (no date). Wit: Thomas Brown, Aaron Boggs, Edmond Parsons. Aaron Boggs and Edmond Parsons made oath to John Wilson, J. P., 6 Jan. 1800. Rec: 7 Jan. 1800.

Pages 143-144: We, Hennery Husten and Kiza, his wife, for $550 sterling money sold to Peter Keys 200 ac. in Washington Dist. on Big Generostee Creek, of Savannah River, bd. John McCutchin, James Long, Steven Herrin, Widow Tilley and Peter Kees; 160 acres of sd. 200 acres was granted Thomas Leonard by Wm. Moultrie, 16 Nov. 1786; remaining part granted James Long 4 Mar. 1793. Date: 28 Oct. 1799. Signed: Hennery Huston, Kiza (X) Huston. Wit: James Long, James Roose (Ross in oath). James Long made oath to Joshua Saxon, J. P., 4 Nov. 1799. Rec: 9 Jan. 1800.

Pages 144-146: I, William Otwell of Pendleton Co. for $350 sold to Elliott Clardy of Laurens Co., 250 ac part of 2 grants conveyed to Otwell by Alexander Boyse, on Brushy Creek of Saluda River, bd. by John Clardy, land called (cannot read this)...and Marchant land, Thomas Earnest(?) and Robert Kellison. Date: 7 Aug. 1799. Wit: Alexander Boyse, John McEwen...... Deborah (X) Otwell, wife of William Otwell released dower to Robert McCann, J. P. 18 Sep. 1799. (no oath). Rec: 10 Jan. 1800.

Pages 146-147: 19 Nov. 1799, James Jett to Neriah(?) Lewis for ₤ 50 for 225½ acres on S. side of Keowee River, bd. SW by Kelly, NE by Kennedy. Wit: Edward Burrows, Savannah (mark) Burch, David Lewis. David Lewis made oath to Joseph Reed, J. P., 27 Nov. 1799. Rec: 13 Jan. 1800.

Pages 147-148: Peter Fenn for $100 sold to Thomas Fields 700 acres on Little River of Keowee River, bd. by Ellis Harbin, ____ Bobo, Fields land. Granted 10 Mar. 1793. Date: 4 Jan. 1800. Signed: Peter (P) Finn. Wit: John Huggins, Jacob Reece. Jacob Reece made oath to Hennery Burch, J. P., 4 Jan. 1800. Rec: 13 Jan. 1800.

Page 148: I, Matthias Turner for (no amount) sold Stephen Roberts 50 acs. on Hurricane Creek of 26 Mile Creek, bd. by Craig, part of a tract granted Martha Vann by Arnoldus Vanderhorst. Date: 27 Nov. 1799. Wit: Simon Doyle, Spence Mitchell. Simon Doyle made oath to Jonathan Montgomery, J. P., 7 Jan. 1800. Rec: 16 Jan. 1800.

Pages 149-150: I, John McClure sold to Isom Mathews for $100 a sertain still, no. Eighty Gallons and nine still tubs, feather bed and furniture, woman's saddle, large pot, etc., my crop of corn, spinning wheel. Date: 9 Oct. 1799. Wit: John Boyd, Jr., George Boyd. John Boyd made oath to Robert Bowen, J. P., 20 Jan. 1800. Rec: 21 Jan. 1800.

Pages 150-155: 6 Jan. 1799, ____(this is blank) Tathum, of the Town of Lexington in Fayette Co., Commonwealth of Kentucky, Esq. Attorney for Abraham

(Pages 150-155 cont'd): Morehouse, of the county of Montgomery, New York, Esq., to P. H. N. Tot Bastrop of Town of Lexington, Esq.,....by deed of conveyence, 14 Apr. 1795, made between George Naylor of Augusta, Georgia, Esq., to Abraham Morehouse of Philadelphia, Commonwealth of Pennsylvania, Merchant, for 100,000 acres in Washington Dist., Pendleton Co., on Little River of Keowee River, granted by the State of S. C. by 100 grants of 1,000 acres each by Governor William Moultrie, 6 Oct. 1794, registered Bk. N, no. 5, numbered 34-133 ....said P. H. N. Tot Bastrop and Abraham Morehead agreed to purchase by Charles Tatham, Attorney for Morehouse, for $100,000. Signed: Abraham Morehouse, by his Atty. in fact, Charles Tathum (Lathum?), in the presence of James Bliss.....State of Kentucky, Lexington Dist........I, Thomas Bodley, Clerk of the Court, certify this indenture was acknowledged before me by Charles Tathum, Attorney for Abraham Morehouse, 6 Jun. 1799.....I, Buckner Thurston (Huiston?), Judge of Court for Lexington Dist. certify Thomas Bodley is Clerk of Court. Recorded: Liber Tet N. A. Folio 146, signed, Zachariah Allen, Not'y. Pub. of Balt(?) City(?) Rec: 16 Jan. 1800.

Pages 155-161: 7 Oct. 1799, P. H. N. Tot Bastrop of Lexington, Fayette Co., Commonwealth of Ky., Esq. to Francois de Block, of the City of Baltimore, Maryland, his attorney in fact, to James P. Boyd, Esq. of Baltimore,.Md. Indenture dated 14 Apr. 1795, between George Naylor of Augusta, Richmond Co., Esq. to Abraham Morehouse, then of Philadelphia, Pa., Merchant, for 100,000 acres in Pendleton Co. (same description in above deed), the sold to P. H. N. Tot Bastrop, who now sells to James P. Boyd for $100,000 (rest unreadable).....State of Maryland, Baltimore Co..... (unreadable).
Rec: 16 Jan. 1800.

Pages 161-164: I, James Nash, Sr. for $357 sold to Jehu Orrs tract of (no amount) on Hen Coop Creek, granted Thomas Jenkins 5 Jun. 1786 by Wm. Moultrie, bd. by Jehu Orr, William Aldrus(?), Stephen Harris. Date: 3 Aug. 1799. Wit: Geo. Manning, James Nash, Jr., Valentine Nash...Ann Nash,wife of James Nash, released dower to John Wilson, J. P., 21 Jan. 1800. Geo. Manning made oath to Patrick Norris, J. P., 23 Jan. 1800.
Rec: 25 Jan. 1800.

Pages 164-166: I, Joel Terrel for $400 sold to Micaiah(?) Clark 488 acres on both sides of Big Estatoe Creek of Keowee River, including plantation where Clark now lives, part of tract granted Meshack Stephens by Chas. Pinckney, sold to Terrel, bd. by Thomases Old Line, Meshack Stephens old line. Date: 8 Sep. 1799. Wit: Robert Dowdy, Bolin Clark. Bolin Clark made oath to Hennery Burch, J. P., 14 Sep. 1799.
Rec: 27 Jan. 1800.

Page 166: I, Saml. Terrill sold to James Moreman a sett of surveying instruments for $33. Date: 17 Jan. 1800. Wit: J.(?) Jervis. (No oath).
Rec: 28 Jan. 1800.

Pages 166-168: Washington Dist., I, Bennett Combs for $200 sold to John Hunt 80(?) acres on N. side of 12 Mile River, on W. side of the Mile Creek, bd. lines to Turner's old house. Date: 4 Aug. 1798. Wit: Abner Robertson, James Wardlaw. Thomas Wardlaw made oath to Hennery Burch, J. P., 21 Dec. 1799.
Rec: 29 Jan. 1800.

Page 168: Washington Dist., I, Aaron Terrel, planter, for $887.50 sold to Christopher Strong, planter, a negro man named Tomm and his wife, named Milley, and their two children named tom and hennery. Date: 12 Oct. 1799. Signed: Aaron Terrill. Wit: Saml. D. Terrell, Sarah Strong (no oath.
Rec: 1 Feb. 1800....."(see probate p. 181 by mistake)".

Pages 169-170: I, Daniel Dulaney for $150 sold to Jonathan Critington 100 acres. Date: 18 Sep. 1799. Signed: Daniel (X) Delaney. Wit: W. Womack(?), Kinson Cannon. William Womack(?) made oath to Joseph Reed, J. P. 14 Dec. 1799. Rec: 13 Feb. 1800.

Pages 170-172: 8 Jan. 1800, James Baty to James Cannon for $150 for 100 acres on Connoross, part of the tract granted to John _____, 9 Nov. 1791 by Wm. Moultrie. Signed: James (B) Baty. Wit: Kinson Cannon, Geo. Baty. Kinson Cannon made oath to J. B. Earle, J. P., 13 Feb. 1800. Rec: 13 Feb. 1800.

Pages 172-174: May 1796, Cullem Price to Kinson Cannon for £ 80 stg. for 172 acres granted by Wm. Moultrie, 19 Nov. 1791, now in possession of William Warmach. Signed: Callem (P) Price. Wit: W. Womack, John Smith. William Warmack made oath to J. C. Kilpatrick, J. P. ....(not readable)...

Pages 174-176: 7 Feb. 1800, John Hardin, planter, to Robert Yearwood, planter, for £ 40 stg. for 148(?) acres, part of tract on Little Beaverdam Crk. of Tugalo River, granted Hardin .....(rest very dim).....J. B. Earle,JP, ...John (H) Hardin, Ann (A) Hardin signed receipt. Samuel Carlile, witness.
Rec: 14 Feb. 1800.

Pages 177-178: 20 Aug. 1796, John Glenn to James Carrick for £ 25 stg. for 135 acres granted Chrisr. Kirsey by Chas. Pinckney, 2 Feb. 1789, bd. by Dan'l. Keith(?), Wm. Seright, John Jolly(?). Wit: Daniel Keith, Jonathan Gibbs, J. Underwood. Daniel Keith made oath to Joshua Saxon, J. P., 25 August 1796.
Rec: 21 Feb. 1800.

Pages 178-179: 4 Jul. 1797, Mordica Fuller to Benonia Fowler for £ 50 stg. for 82 acres in 96 Dist. on the Noyewee River of Tugalo River. Wit: John Smith, John Roberts. John Roberts made oath to John Barton, J. P., 22 Feb. 1800 (cannot read recording date).

Pages 179-180: I, William Young, am firmly bound to Bennet Combs for $1500. Date: 23 Sep. 1796, and make title to 275 acres on N. fork of 12 Mile River, plantation I now live on. Date: 1 Mar. 1798. Signed: W. Young. Wit: John Morehead(?), Nathan (X) Turner. Nathan Turner made oath to Danl Murphree, J. P., 26 Feb. 1800.
Rec: 27 Feb. 1800.

Pages 180-181: I, John Thomas, of Richland Co., S. C. for £ 35 stg. sold to Henry Hill, of Pendleton Co., 50(?) acres on N. side of Keowee River, part of 250(?) acres granted John Thomas, 1 Aug. 1785. Date: 26 Nov.1799. Wit: Jno. McLemore, (cannot read), Robert McAfee. Robert McAfee made oath to H. Burch, J. P., 15 Jan. 1800.
Rec: 24 Feb. 1800.

Page 181: Personally appeared before John Harris, J. P. and made oath to bill of sale (hard to read).. seems to be oath to Aaron Terril deed on p. 168. Date: 1 Feb. 1800. Signed: Saml. D. Terrell.

Pages 181-183: 10 Aug. 1796, John Harris, Sheriff of Pendleton Co. to Lewis Daniel Martin....James Millwee was seized of 236 acres on 26 Mile Creek of Keowee River, John and Sarah Dalrymple having obtained judgement against James Millwee for £ 18. 19 shillings stg., therefore all goods, chattels, lands of Millwee ordered sold at public auction, 4 Jun. 1796 to Lewis Daniel Martin for £ 11 stg. Signed: John Harris, S. of P.C. Wit: Saml. Barton, John Clayton. Saml. Barton made oath to Joshua Saxon,

(Pages 181-183 cont'd): J. P., 10 Mar. 1800. Rec: 10 Mar. 1800.

Pages 183-184: I, John Dickson for $800 sold to Thomas Robertson 640 acres on Keowee River. Date: 13 Mar. 1800. Wit: D. Mozley, James Wood. James Wood made oath to Geo. W. Earle, DCC, 13 Mar. 1800. Rec: 13 Mar. 1800.

Pages 183-184: I, William Jackson for $400 sold to James Martin 100 acres on SW branch of Rocky River,.. part of tract granted Danl. McCoy, 5 Nov. 1792. Date: 30 Sep. 1799. Signed: William (O) Jackson. Wit: Roger Martin, James Garner. James Garner made oath to Patrick Norris, J. P., 2 Dec. 1799. Rec: 13 Mar. 1800.

Pages 185-186: I, John Thomas of Richland Co., S. C. for Ł70 stg. sold to James McAfee of Greenville Co. 200 acres on Keowee River, part of 250 acres granted John Thomas, 1 Aug. 1782(?). Date: 24 Nov. 1799. Wit: Jno. H. Lomax, David Myres, Robert McAfee.....Washington Dist., Robert McAfee made oath to Henry Burch, J. P., 15 Jan. 1800. Rec: 13 Mar. 1800.

Pages 186-187: I, Matthew Alexander of Franklin Co., Georgia for $400 sold to Elijah Wyatt of Pendleton Co. 200 acres on Broadmouth Creek of Saluda River. Date: 29 Jan. 1800. Wit: James Mattison, Nimrod Smith...James Mattison made oath to Reuben Nash, Justice of Abbeville Co....Martha (M) Alexander, wife of Matthew Alexander released dower to John Williams, J.Q. of P. C., 11 Mar. 1800. Rec: 13 Mar. 1800.

Pages 187-189: I, James Maxwell of Macklinburgh Co., N. C., planter, for $200 sold to Robert Hacket(?) of Pendleton Co., 293 acres surveyed for Jas. Madison, 23 Aug. 1787 and granted to James Maxwell, 23 Aug. 1788 by Thos. Pinckney, in Washington Dist. on Tucksoa(?) Creek of Toogaloo River. Date: 12 Dec. 1799. Wit: David Sloan, James McCollum. David Sloan made oath to J. B. Earle, J. P., 15 Mar. 1800. Rec: 15 Mar. 1800.

Pages 189-190: I, William Richard of Abbeville Co., for Ł10 stg. sold to Thomas Richard of Pendleton Co. 109 acres on 18 Mile Creek of Savannah River, bd. on NW by Wm. McGuffin and Genl. Andrew Pickens. Date: 1 Jul. 1797. Wit: William Gray, Wm. (X) Ottery(?). William Gray made oath to Geo. W. Earle, J. P., 13 Nov. 1800. Rec: 13 Mar. 1800.

Pages 190-191: I, James Martin of Lincoln Co., N. C. for $300 sold to Joab Lewis of Pendleton Co. 560 acres on 12 Mile Creek, where Lewis now lives, ... granted John Ducass(?), 16 Jul. 1784. Date: 25 Apr. 1799. Wit: William ( ) Thompson, Isaiah Lewis. William Thompson made oath to Hy. Burch, JP, 1 Dec. 1799. Rec: 13 Mar. 1800.

Pages 191-192: 15 Sep. 1799, Lewis Eaton to John Boren for Ł 5 stg. for 152½ acres on 12 Mile River, bd. on SE by Samuel Jackson. Signed: Lewis (X) Eaton. Wit: Isaiah Lewis, W. Boren. William Boren made oath to Wm. Reed, J. P., 11 Mar. 1800. Rec: 13 Mar. 1800.

Pages 192-193: I, Samuel Jackson for $650 sold to Isaiah Lewis 240 acres on branch of S. fork of 12 Mile River, part of survey granted David (Daniel?) McAdoo for 320 acres. (100 acres on S. side was conveyed to Sarah Sinckler, widow). Date: 7 Sep. 1799. Wit: Jacob Lewis, Joab Lewis. Jacob Lewis made oath to W. Reid, JP, 15 Feb. 1800. Rec: 13 Mar. 1800.

Pages 193-194: 15 Sep. 1799, Lewis Eaton to Isaiah Lewis for £5 stg. for 50 acres on S. fork of 12 Mile River, part of survey granted to Eaton by Chas. Pinckney, 2 Apr. 1798. Signed: Lewis (X) Eton. Wit: John Borin, W. Borin. William Borin made oath to W. Reid, J. P., 24 Feb. 1800. Rec: 13 Mar. 1800.

Pages 195-196: I, Robert Sharp Hamilton of Stokes Co., N. C. for $650 sold to George Dillard of Pendleton Co. 200 acres granted Samuel Talbert by Benj. Guerard, 15 Oct. 1784, in 96 Dist. on Brushy Creek of Saluda River; also 110 acres granted William (Wilson?) Allison by Wm. Moultrie, 4 Dec. 1786. Date: 15 Nov. 1799. Signed: Rt. S. Hamilton. Wit: John Wilson, W. Copland, Wm. Pegg. John Wilson made oath to Robert Bowen, J.P., 7 Mar.1800. Rec: 13 Mar. 1800.

Pages 196-197: I, John Brown sold to George Dollars (also Dillard) for $50 for 70 acres, part of 337 ac. granted John Brown, 3 Dec. 1793 by Charles Pinckney, on N. side of Brushy Creek. Date: 20 Jan. 1800. Signed: John Brown, Anna (X) Brown. Wit: John Wilson, James (+) Merritt. John Wilson made oath to Robert Bowen, J. P., 7 Mar. 1800. Rec: 13 Mar. 1800.

Pages 196-197: 1 Nov. 1797(?), William Jackson to Daniel McCoy (amount ?)...for 46 acres on Great Rocky Creek of Savannah River, bd. on NW by Andrew Norris(?). Signed: Daniel (+) McCoy. Wit: Josh. Alexdr., Richard (R)Dodd. Richard Dodd made oath to Patrick Norris, J. P., 8 Mar. 1800. Rec: 13 Mar. 1800.

NOW CALLED PENDLETON DISTRICT

Pages 198-199: Pendleton Dist., 7 Mar. 1800, I, Jonathan and Mariam Ruth (no amount) sold to William Jackson 1 mare and 11 head of cattle. Signed: Jonathan Ruth, Maryam (M) Ruth. Wit: James Garner, John (X) Jones(?), Benj. Hall. James Garner made oath to Patrick Norris, J. P., 11 Mar. 1800. Rec: 13 Mar. 1800.

Pages 199-200: 17 Feb. 1797, Peter Finn and Thomas Fields to William Stuart for £3 stg. for 300 acres on branches of Little River, bd. by Eli Harlin and Boles. Signed: Peter (his mark) Finn, Thomas Fields. Wit: Henry Burch, Jehu Brown. Henry Burch made oath to W. Reid, J. P., 11 Mar. 1800. Rec: 13 Mar. 1800.

Pages 200-201: I, George Martin and Charity Martin of Greenville Co., S. C. for $150 sold to Danl. Sargent of Pendleton Co., 320 acres on branches of 23 Mile Creek, tract laid out to James Lewis Yancy and granted Tempy Martin, 6 Dec. 1786, by Wm. Moultrie. Recorded Bk. QQQQ, p. 232. Date: 14 Jan. 1800. Signed: George Martin, Charity Martin. Wit: Duncan Camron, L. Camp. L. Camp made oath to Wm. Cleveland, J. P., 12 Mar. 1800. Rec: 13 Mar. 1800.

Pages 201-203: 18 Jan. 1795, Robert George to Alexander Young for £15 for 144 acres granted 4 Aug. 1794 by Wm. Moultrie to Robert George, on Generostee Creek of Savannah River. Signed: Robert (+) George. Wit: Andw. Young, James Young. Andw. Young made oath to Nathan Lusk, J. P., 18 Jan. 1800. Rec: 13 Mar. 1800.

Page 203: 3 Mar. 1800, I certify I sold Capt. Aaron Broyles 3 negroes, 2 fellows and 1 negro woman, one named Peter, one named Joe(?), and the wench, Lucy. Signed: Joseph Brown. Wit: Hugh Brown, Anne Brown. Hugh Brown made oath to Robt. McCann, J. P., 14 Mar. 1800. Rec: 14 Mar. 1800.

Page 204:   I, Edwin Reese for $400 sold to Waddy Thompson a negro boy named Jack about 19 years old. Date: 15 Mar. 1800. Wit: Robt. McCann, David Sloan. David Sloan made oath to Geo. W. Earle, D.C.C., 10 Mar. 1800. Rec: 15 Mar. 1800.

Pages 204-206:   12 Feb. 1799, Moses Liddle to Daniel Keith,Sr. for Ł 50 stg. for 35 acres, part of tract granted Callegan McCarty and transferred to Moses Liddle by Francis Miller, on W. side of Devil's Fork of Great Generostee Creek, plat made by Edw. McClure, 7 Feb. 1799. Wit: Edwd. T. McClure, James Morrow. Edw. T. McClure made oath to John Vernor, J. P., 13 Feb. 1799. Rec: Mar. 1800.

Pages 206-207:   I, William McGregor for $200 sold to Daniel Keith, Jr., 185 acres on Great Generostee Crk. and Devil's Fork, part of 1,000 acres granted Nemar Holden (Holson?) by Wm. Moultrie, 1 Jan. 1787, conveyed to Wm. McGregor, 6 Jul. 1799, plat made by Edw. T. McClure, 29 Jun. 1799, bd. on S and SW by John Dickson, Jr., on N and NE by Dl.(?) Ledbetter. Date: 8 Nov. 1799. Wit: Edw. T. McClure, John Tippen. Edw. Tate McClure made oath to Joshua Saxon, J. P., 8 Nov. 1799. Rec: 15 Mar. 1800.

Pages 207-208:   I, John Baylis Earle of Pendleton Co. for Ł40 stg. sold to Asa Meeks 200 acres on fork of Cain Creek, granted John Williams, a bounty grant, 21 Jan. 1785 by Benj. Guerrard, surveyed by Thomas Lewis, D.S. Date: 17 Mar. 1800. Wit: James Wood, Gilbert Hancock. James Wood made oath to Geo. W. Earle, D.C.P.D., 17 Mar. 1800. Rec: 15 Mar. 1800.

Pages 208-209:   Whereas, Jno. Hunnicutt was seized of 208 ac. bd. on NW by Wm. David Clark and Jno. Hunnicutt.....whereas, Alexander Boyse, in June of 1792, received a judgement against Hunnicutt and lands were ordered sold at public auction......Patr. McCoy, highest bidder for $60. Date: 19 Mar. 1799. Signed: E. Reese, Sheriff of Pendleton Co. Wit: Jno. Hunter, G. W. Earle. George Washington Earle made oath to J. B. Earle, J. P., 24 Jun. 1799. Rec: 17 Mar. 1800.

Pages 209-211:   Washington Dist., 1 Apr. 1795, Benjamin Green, Jr. of Abbeville Co. to William Nicholson of Pendleton Co. for Ł 25 - 18 shillings (Ł 10 already paid, the remainder to be paid by 1 Jan. 1796) for 250 acres on Little Generostee Creek of Savannah River, bd. on SW by Henry Lusk, granted Benjamin Green, 2 Sep. 1793 by Wm. Moultrie. Wit: Geo. Crawford, Samuel McGill. Samuel McGill made oath to John Vernor, J. P., 19 March 1800. Rec: 20 Mar. 1800.

Pages 211-212:   I, Henry McDaniel, Sr. for Ł 5 stg. sold to John Simpson one acre on 26 Mile Creek and Pierce's Creek, part of 150 acres granted to Francis Guttery, 15 __ 1784. Date: 12 Oct. 1799. Signed: Henry (+) McDaniel. Wit: Wm. Cunningham, James Chandler. William Cunningham made oath to John Harris, J. P., 4 Apr. 1800. Rec: 4 Apr. 1800.

Pages 212-214:   I, John Ewing Colhoun for 5 shillings sold to John Simpson 50 acres on W. side of 12 Mile River, the NE end of plantation where John E. Colhoun now resides, bd. on N. by land formerly owned by William Gilham, now land of John Simpson, all other sides bounding John Ewing Colhoun. Date: 12 Nov. 1799. Wit: Jno. Green, J. C. Kerr. Jno. Green made oath to Nathan Lusk, J. P., 11 Mar. 1800. (Plat by Joseph Whitner, D.S., 18 Sep. 1799). Rec: 4 Apr. 1800.

Page 214:   I, Henry Kyle(?) of Union Dist., S. C. for
                            $300 sold to William Hunter of Pendleton Dist.
                            a negro woman named Isobel, age 22. Date: 14
Mar. 1800. Wit: James White, John Hunter. John Hunter made oath to Geo.
W. Earle, D.C.P.D., 9 Apr. 1800.
Rec: 9 Apr. 1800.

Pages 215-216:   Whereas, John Jackson was seized of 1,000 ac.
                            on Beaver Creek of Rocky River, granted Jack-
                            son, bd. on NW by James Dobbing, on NW by Jos.
Colton, on SW, NW and NE by James Thompson.....John McMahon received a
judgement against John Jackson for L6-10 shillings.....lands, goods and
chattels of Jno. Jackson and Saml.(?) Leathers to be sold at public auc-
tion, William Hunter, highest bidder for $170. Signed: E. Reese, S.P.C.
Wit: William Griffen, Charles Bond. Charles Bond made oath to Geo. W.
Earle, D.C.P.C., 9 Apr. 1800.
Rec: 9 Apr. 1800.

Pages 216-217:   18 Feb. 1797, George Shuler of Washington Dis-
                            trict to Edward Hayse (Hays) for 150 acres on
                            Little River of Keowee bd. by William Stuart,
Geo. Smith(?), Shuler; granted George Shuler by patent by Wm. Moultrie,
21 Jan. 1792. Wit: William Stuart, Jacob Reed. William Stuart made oath
to Joseph Reed, J. P., 10 Apr. 1800.
Rec: 10 Apr. 1800.

Pages 218-219:   24 Apr. 1798, Edward Hase to William Parsons
                            (?) for L 48 stg. for 150 acres bd. by Wm.
                            Stuart on Smelcer(?) Creek, Shuler, on Little
River, granted George Shuler, 21 Jan. 1792 by Wm. Moultrie. Wit: Alexr.
Floyd, William Floyd. Alexander Floyd made oath to Joseph Reed, J. P., 8
Apr. 1800. Rec: 10 Apr. 1800.

Pages 219-220:   13 Sep. 1799, Reubin Logan to Elias Turner for
                            $240 for 100 acres on Mile Creek of Keowee Riv-
                            er, bd. by Dunkin Camron, granted by Thomas
Pinckney, being part of old survey to Dunkin Camron. Wit: Jacob Capehart,
Zephiniah (+) Harris. Zephiniah Harris made oath to Henry Burch, J. P.,
15 Feb. 1800.
Rec: 12 Apr. 1800.

Pages 220-221:   I, Martha Vann for $200 sold to Matthias Tur-
                            ner ____ acres on Hurricane Creek of 26 Mile
                            Creek, granted Martha Vann by Arnoldus Vander-
horst. Date: 25 Jul. 1799. Signed: Martha (V) Vann. Wit: Henry Linse(?),
Samuel Morris. Henry Linse(?) made oath to Jothn. Montgomery, J.P., 22
Mar. 1800. Rec: 12 Apr. 1800.

Pages 221-222:   I, Benjamin Nicholson for $10 sold to William
                            Pasmore 543 acres, granted Jacob Visage, bd.
                            by James Doyle, James Tuffnell, John Miller,
Richard Robinson. Date: 27 Nov. 1799. Signed: Benjamin (X) Nicholson.Wit:
Wm. Sims, Hugh Rogers, Jonathan (O) West. William Sims made oath to Geo.
W. Earle, D.C.P.C., 16 Apr. 1800.
Rec: 16 Apr. 1800.

Page 222:   Personally came Robert Honey, being duly sworn
                            saying that to the best of his knowledge and
                            information that his son, Abel Honey is about
twenty one years old. Date: 21 Dec. 1798. Sworn to Wm. Millwee, J.P.
Signed: Robt. Honee.
Rec: 17 Apr. 1800.

Pages 222-223:   I, Abel Honey for $300 sold to James Green
                            150 acres on Little Beaverdam Creek of Rocky
                            River, granted James Anderson, 5 Dec. 1791 by
Chas. Pinckney. Recorded Bk. E, no. 5, p. 140. Date: 25 Dec. 1799.Signed:
Abel (X) Honey. Wit: James Anderson, Isaac Humphries. James Anderson made
oath to Robt. McCann, J. P., 22 Jan. 1800.
Rec: 17 Apr. 1800.

Pages 223-224:   I, David McCaleb for $100 sold to George Capehart 130 acres surveyed 13 Feb. 1795(?) on 18 Mile Creek of Keowee River, bd. on SE by Chas. Rice, on NE by Goldin, on NW by John Guffin(Griffen?), on SW by Lee. Date: ___ Apr. 1800. Signed: D. McCaleb, Martha McCaleb. Wit: Samuel Cherry, John Hunter. John Hunter made oath to Geo. W. Earle, D.C.P.C., 17 April 1800. Rec: 17 Apr. 1800.

Pages 224-225:   I, Abner Honea for divers good causes and considerations give and grant to William Honea all my land and household stuff ...(very dim) Date: 20 Jan. 1800. Wit: Abner Honea, Sr., John Reynolds, Bart. Reynolds, Milburton(?) Reynolds. Abner Honea, Sr. made oath to J. B. Earle, ___ Feb. 1800. (Rec:...(dim).

Pages 225-226:   John Davis, Sr.(?) to George Kile(?) ..(can not read), 200 acres in Washington Dist. granted Danl. Holland by patent, 1 Jan. 1785(?). Wit: ...(cannot read). Abel Kile (or Hill) made oath to Wm. Reed, J. P., 10 Jan. 1798.
Rec: ___ Apr. 1800.

Pages 226-227:   13 May 1793, Tilly Merick of City of Charleston, Merchant, to William Guest of Pendleton Co., planter, for $80 for 200 acres on East side of Beaverdam Creek of Toogalo River, bd. by Alexr. Kilpatrick,.... granted Augustus Merrick, 1 Feb. 1787. Signed: Tilly Merrick, Ex'tor to Augustus Merrick...Wit: Willm. Turpin, Samuel Maverick.......Charleston, Samuel Maverick made oath to William Turpin, J. Q., 7 Feb. 1800.
Rec: 10 Feb. 1800.

Pages 229-231:   15 May 1794, Saml. H. Dickson and Rebecca, his wife, to Saml. Houston for ⅃ 30 stg. for 364 acres on Little Beaverdam Creek of Rocky River of Savannah River, bd. on N. by Goodwin, granted Dickson, 2 Feb. 1789. Signed: Samuel H. Dickson, Rebeccah Dickson. Wit: Nathan Loosk, Charles McClure. Charles McClure made oath to E. Browne, 25 Jun. 1794(?).
Rec: ___ Mar. 1800.

Pages 231-233:   I, Thomas Burford for ⅃ 60 stg. sold to James Gilliland 200 acres on W. side of Broadaway Creek of Rocky River, part of 2 tracts; one granted Thos. Burford by Wm. Moultrie, 5 Jun. 1786, recorded Bk. NNNN, p. 207; the other granted Thomas Burford by Benj. Guerrard, 21 Jan. 1785, recorded Bk. DDDD, p. 44. Wit: John McWhorter, James Dowdle. John McWhorter made oath to Robt. McCann, J. P., 27 Jul. 1799....Mary Burford, wife of Thomas Burford released dower to Robert McCann, 27 Jul. 1799.
Rec: 12 Mar. 1800.

Pages 233-234:   3 Mar. 1800, William Tabour to Phillip Cox for $569 for 200 acres granted 2 Sep. 1793 by Wm. Moultrie to Ely Langford for 400 acres in 96 Dist. on Crow Creek of Keowee River, conveyed from Langford. Signed: William Tabor. Wit: ___ Tubb(?), John Beazley. John Beazley made oath to Joseph Reed, J. P., 3 Mar. 1800.
Rec: 14 Mar. 1800.

Pages 234-235:   I, Patrick McDowell for $50 sold to Thomas Hargis 252 acres on Mile Creek granted Alexander McDowell, 22 Jul.(?) 1788. Date: 10 Dec. 1799. Wit: J. McCracken, Wm. McCourty.....96 Dist., William McCourty made oath to Wm. Nibbs, J. Q, 26 Dec. 1799.
Rec: 15 Mar. 1800.

Pages 236-237:   16 Jul. 1795, John Hardin to Littleton Meeks for ⅃ 20 for 120 acres, part of 415 acres, including plantation where Meeks now lives on Little Beaverdam and branches of Conneross, granted Hardin, 1 Apr. 1793, recorded Bk. G, no. 5, p. 157, by Peter Bremar pro(?) Secretary. Wit; Robert Anderson, Lot Price(?). Robert Anderson made oath to John Barton,

(Pages 236-237 cont'd.):   J. P., 10 Mar. 1800. Rec: 15 Mar. 1800.

Pages 237-239: 19 Nov. 1796, David Browne and Jane, his wife, to Thomas Armstrong for Ł 30 stg. for 111 ac. on N. side of Toogalo River, bd. by James ___ and Saml. Brown, part of 558 acres granted Thomas Holden, 1 Jan. 1787, conveyed part to John Rotten, 12 Jun. 1789, from Rotten to David Brown 1794(?). Signed: David Brown, Jane (X) Brown. Wit: Samuel Brown, Joseph Brown. Samuel Brown made oath to William Hall, J. P., 21 Jan,1797? Rec: ___ Mar. 1800.

Pages 239-240: 8 Apr. 1799, Joseph Logan to Joseph Woodall for $500 for 160 acres on both sides of Bobon(?) Creek, branch of Keowee, granted Burrell Bobo, 5 Jan. 1786. Signed: Joseph Logan, Sr.. Wit: James Jett, Joseph Logan, Jr. James Jett made oath to Henry Burch, J. P., 10 Mar. 1800. Rec: 15 Mar. 1800.

Pages 240-241: We, Josiah Burton and Mary Burton & Co.(?), of Abbeville Co. for $120 sold to Charles Duncan of Pendleton Co. 200 acres in 96 Dist. on Chagua Creek of Toogaloo River, bd. on N. by Indian Boundary Line, surveyed by Thomas Lofton, D.S., 5 May 1790, granted by Chas. Pinckney, 5 Sep. 1791(?). Date: 27 Feb. 1800. Signed: Josiah Burton, Mary (X) Burton. Wit: Samuel Hinson, Archibald Shew(?).....Abbeville Dist., Samuel (S) Hinson made oath to Ebenezer Miller, J. P., 27 Feb. 1800. Rec: 10 Apr. 1800.

Pages 241-242: I, Charles Tucker for $170 sold to Jesse Coffee 300 acres on fork of Conneross, known as White's Ford, joining Jesse Coffee's land and Thomas Rapers, Moses Perkins, where Charles Tucker now lives. Date: 31 Dec. 1798. Signed: Charles (CT) Tucker. Wit: Larkin (X) Brown, Hayes Blare. Hayes Blair made oath to Geo. W. Earle, D.C.P.C., 5 ___ 1800. Rec: 5 May 1800.

Pages 242-243: I, Samuel Hinson for Ł 50 sold to Jesse Coffee 150 acres on both sides of Connoross Crk. of Keowee River, being upper part of survey granted Moses Perkins, where Jesse Coffee now lives, bd. by Hinson, Coffee. Date: 13 Jan. 1798. Signed: Saml. (S) Hinson. Wit: Joshua Gotcher, James Davenport, Charles (CT) Tucker. Joshua Gotcher made oath to John Burton, J. P., 13 Jan. 1800. Rec: 5 May 1800.

Pages 243-244: I, John Hogg sold to Margarett Atkins the following articles: (lists cows, mares, oxen,cart, household furnishings, etc.) Date: 1 April 1800. Signed: John Hoge. Wit: Hugh Crumbless, Wm. Mullican; Wm. Mullican made oath to Joshua Saxon, J. P., 2 May 1800. Rec: 5 May 1800.

Pages 244-245: 29 Jun. 1798, Isaac Lynch to Nathaniel Harbin for Ł 80 for 150 acres on W. side of Keowee River, about 3/4 of a mile below Fort Prince George, bd. by Fields Pruitt, Isaac Tittsworth, part of 300 acres granted William Tate, 16 Jul. 1784. Signed: Isaac (IL) Lynch. Wit: Isaac Titsworth, Saml. Harbin, Jesse Harbin, - Isaac Tittsworth made oath to James Jett, J. P., 10 Aug. 1798. Rec: 14 May 1800.

Page 246: I, Thomas George of Franklin Co., Ga. sold to Kenneth Findley of Pendleton Co. a negro wench known by name of Agga about 25 years of age for $400. Signed: Thomas (X) George. Wit: Benjamin (O) Duncan, ooni(?) Duncan. Benjamin Dunkin made oath to Wm. Cleveland, J. P., 25 Apr. 1800. Rec: _____ 1800.

Pages 246-247: I, Henry Rice of Granger, Tennessee appoint my son, Charles Rice of Pendleton Dist., my

(Pages 246-247 cont'd.): lawful attorney to sell a tract of land of 460 acres granted to me on Rice Creek and Wolf Creek of 12 Mile River. Date: 29 May 1800. Wit: W. Steele, James Wood. Wm. Steele made oath to Michael Dickson(?), J. Q. Date: (cannot read). Rec: __ Jun. 1800.

Pages 247-248: I, Peter Horry(?) for Ł 160 sold to Obediah Trimmier(?) __ hundred acres in 96 Dist. on __ Creek, granted 1 Jan. 1785. Date: 13 Dec. 1799. Wit: Paul Lapier (or Trapier?), Francis Baxter. Paul Trapier(?) made oath......Mary Margaret Horry released dower to Francis C. Deliessiline(?), J. Q....(dates, etc. all very dim).

Pages 248-249: 20 Jun. 1797(?), John Callaham, planter, to Robert Gray(?), planter, for Ł 80 stg. for 225(?) acres on Beaver Creek of Rocky Creek of Savannah River, part of tract granted by Wm. Moultrie, 5 Jun. 1786(?), recorded Bk. LLLL, p. 405(?) to John Dowdle, certified by William Lasley(?), conveyed by Dowdle to John Callahan, 20 Jun. 1790, bd. on NE by John Dowdle, on SE by Elander Pickens, on SW by John Jackson, on NW by W. E. Cannady. Wit: (appears to be)..Wm. McClosky, Abijah Davis........ (oath, deed very dim in center).

Pages 249-250: Samuel Taylor and John Baylis Earle sold to Ezekiel Buffington for __ for 200 acres on Little River, branch of Keowee, bd. on NE by Eliazer(?) Turner, granted Mathew Hare (Soldier) by Benj. Guerrard, 21 Jan. 1785. (rest was unable to read).

Pages 250-251: _____ to John Armstrong 194 acres on Beaver Creek _____
Date: 30 Jan. 1800. _____

Pages 251-252: _____, Wm. Hunter to Jesse Davis _____ Date: 13 Jan. 1800. Wit: William Hillhouse, John (X) Armstrong. John Armstrong made oath he saw Doctor Wm. Hunter sign _____ (rest unreadable).

Pages 252-253: 96 Dist., 10 Sep. 17__, John Gabriel, planter, to Hezekiah Davis(?) for Ł 27 for 180(?) ac. on Big Generostee, granted by Gov. Pinckney to John Gabriel. Wit: Abijah Davis, Joseph (X) Brimer. Abijah Davis made oath to Elijah Brown, J. P., 13 Feb. 1796.
Rec: __ Jun. 1800.

Pages 253-254: _____, Robert Gray, planter, to Van Davis (_____) 150 acres part of tract granted by Wm. Moultrie 1786(?), recorded bk. LLLL, p. ___. Signed: Robert Gray, Elizabeth Gray. Wit: Jesse Davis, Joseph Hall.

Pages 254-255: _____, Hezekiah Davis, blacksmith, to Van Davis for $90(?) for ___ acres part of 180 ac. granted John Gabriel by Thos. Pinckney 1788. Signed: Hezekiah Davis, Sarah(?) Davis. Wit: Jesse Davis, Van Davis, Archibald Shelton, Joseph Hall. Van Davis made oath to Joshua Saxon, JP,

Pages 255-256: I, Golding Tinsley of Newberry Dist. for $220 (?) sold to James Wood (or Hood) 242 acres on 18 Mile Creek of Savannah River, granted John Hunter, Esq., 5 Feb. 17__. Recorded Bk. QQQQ, p. 590. Date: 21 Feb. 1800. Wit: John Griffen, Jno. Hunter. John Hunter made oath to D. McCaleb, D.C.P.C. for John B. Earle.....Newberry Dist., Mary Tinsley released dower to Jacob R. Brown, J.Q.N., 5 Jun. 1800.
Rec: 9 Jun. 1800.

Pages 257-258: 16 Nov. 1798, James Cannon, planter, to John Nugent, hatter, for natural love and affection, 80 acres in 96 Dist., on 12 Mile Creek,

(Pages 257-258 cont'd.): E. side of Keowee River, granted 1 Oct. 1791 part of tract now in possession of Isaac Herrin. Wit: John Cannon, John Hillian, Fany (X) Cannon. John Cannon made oath to Joseph Reed, J. P., 7 Mar. 1800. Rec: 9 Jun. 1800.

Page 259 (torn): 21 Jan 1797, Nicholas Welch to Caleb Edmondson for Ł 40 stg. for 100 acres part of tract granted Catherine Miller by Wm. Moultrie, 1 Aug. 1785. Recorded Bk. EEEE, p. 248. Signed: Nicholas (X) Welch. Wit: Arthur Durley, Wm. Millwee. Arthur Durley made oath to Wm. Millwee, JP, 21 Jan. 1797. Rec: 16 Jun. 1800.

Pages 260-261(torn): 11 Nov. 1799, Mary Harris and Handy Harris of Abbeville Co. and John Harris of Pendleton Co. to William Tabour of Pendleton Co., hatter... .....whereas, John Harris, deceased, late of Abbeville Co., Minister of the Gospel, in his lifetime possessed tracts of land which by his last will and testament did direct to be sold.....Mary Harris, Executrix and Handy Harris, John Harris, Executors, being named and appointed by last will and testament, make this indenture for Ł 50 to William Tabor for 153 acres on W. side of Keowee River bd. by River, John Derson's land he sold to Thomas Robertson, granted Reavriend(sic) Harris 3 Sep. 1787 by Thos. Pinckney. Recorded Bk. UUUU, p. 268. Signed: John Harris, Handy Harris, Mary Harris. Wit: Wm. Davis, Rt. Davis, Andw. Harris. Andw. Harris made oath to John Harris, J. P., 4 Mar. 1800. Rec: 16 Jun. 1800.

END OF BOOK E

(Note: There was no index for this book...bw)

PENDLETON DISTRICT CONVEYENCES

BOOK F

1800 - 1802

"Pendleton records have been inherited by Anderson. In 1828, Pendleton District was divided into Anderson and Pickens Districts. Pendleton County and District records were transferred to the custody of Anderson District, which explains the presence of Pendleton documents among the records of Anderson County."
"Pages 305 and 308 were missing from the volume at the time of lamination" - County Records Division, South Carolina Dept. of Archives and History.
"On page 52, is an indenture, recorded in 1797, which does not fall within the regular dates of the records, 1800-1802" - County Rec. Div.

Note: Nearly all of this book is very faded. Some of the edges are in condition to read, so I will do the best I can to abstract them....BW

Pages 1-3 (torn): I, William Thayer of City of Charleston, Merchant, for love and goodwill I bear my cousins, Lydia Tourtellot, Betsy Tourtellot and Nancy Tourtellot, daughters of Asa Tourtellot, and Avis Symms, formerly Avis Tourtellot, of Pendleton Co., grant to them, reserving unto the said Avis Symms, their mother, the use and improvement of the following, during her natural life, 300 acres on 18 Mile Creek of Savannah River, granted by Benj. Guerrard, 15 Oct. 1784 to John Hunter; also, 170 acres, bd. above tract, granted John Hunter, 5 Feb. 1787, conveyed to William Thayer, 15 Mar. 1796. Date: 16 Feb. 1796. Wit: Dan Symms, T. Merrick...Charleston Dist., Sarah Thayer released dower to John Mitchell, J. Q., 16 Apr. 1796

(Pages 1-3 cont'd):   .....Wm. Thayer of Charleston acknowledged he
                              signed above deed, 16 Apr. 1796.
Rec: 16 Jun. 1800.

Pages 4-5 (torn):   I, John Miller, of Abbeville Co. for £ 50 stg.
                              sold to Samuel D. Terrell of Pendleton Co.,
                              250 acres surveyed for Adam Right. Date:
Dec. 1798. Wit: Peter Irons, J. D. Terrell....Abbeville Co., Rachael Miller, wife of John Miller, released dower, __ Dec. 1798. John D. Terrell
made oath to Wm. Cleveland, J. P., in Pendleton Co.
Rec: 16 Jun. 1800.

Pages 5-6:   I, John Thomas, of Richland Co., S. C. for
                              £ 100 stg. sold to Jeremiah Fields of Pendleton Co., 250 acres in Washington Dist., formerly 96 Dist., on Eastatoa Creek of Keowee River, granted Thomas on 1
Aug. 1785 by Wm. Moultrie. Recorded Bk. EEEE, p. 162. Date: 23 May 1799.
Wit: William R. Tucker, Wm. Hopkins, Anderson Thomas...Richland Co., William R. Tucker made oath to John Herons, J. P., 23 Aug. 1799.
Rec: 16 Jun. 1800.

Pages 6-7:   (faded...) _____ was seized of 130(?) ac.
                              on 18 Mile Creek _____ Seneca River bd. SE
                              by David McCaleb(?), SW by William Gray(?)
___, by James ____ and public land which Court house stands on _____
Lewis D. Martin obtained judgement ____ £ 11-5 shillings against Charles
Lay(?).......public auction on 4 Sep. 1797 did sell above tract to David
McCaleb for £ 60 by his friend, Major Thos. Farrar, being highest bidder
_____ where sd. Robert Maxwell hath lately deceased and hath not executed titles for sd. land unto David McCaleb ___ therefore I, Henry Micham,
now Sheriff of Washington Dist. and successor in _____ of the sd. Robert
Maxwell _____ of £ 60 ____ do grant to sd. David McCaleb 640 acres(?)
described. Date: 12 Oct. 1799. Wit: H. M. Wood, Joseph Whitner. Joseph
Whitner made oath to D. McCaleb, for J. B. Earle, 10 Jun.(?) 1800.
Rec: 14 Jun. 1800.

Pages 7-9:   Whereas, Charles Lay was seized of two tracts
                              of land, to wit: one tract ____ on Chonoross
                              Creek, of Keowee River, granted Lay 2 July
1787 by Thos. Pinckney; other tract of 925 acres on Connoross Creek ...
......(rest not readable)...William Steel, his heirs and assigns forever.
Date: 4 Oct. 179_. Signed: H__ Wood. Wit: John Miller, D_____. John
Miller made oath to D. McCaleb for J. B. Earle.
Rec: 19 Jun. 1800.

Pages 9-10:   _____ for $100 sold to William __
                              200(?) acres, part of tract granted by his
                              Excellency ____, Esq. and conveyed to the sd.
David McCaleb by Henry William(?) Wood(?), 12 Oct. 1799, bd. by James
Armstrong, John Miller and Great Road leading from Pendleton Court House
to Capt. Wm. McCaleb, near mouth of 12 Mile River ____ (rest unreadable).
....mentions William Steele. Date: 24 _____. Plat almost unreadable,
date 8 Jun.(?) 1800. Signed: _____ Farrar, J. B. Earle, J. P.,
Rec: 19 Jun. 1800.

Pages 11-12:   I, James Steuart(?) for $400 sold to Robert
                              McCreight 196 acres on __ Creek of Rocky River, part of two tracts; one granted John ____;
the other to Wm. Mattocks, 2 Mar. 1792, recorded Bk. D, no. 5(?), p.___.
Date: 23 Nov. 1799. Wit: John McCallister, Thomas Jenkins(?), J. P. Bole
(?), John Maloney(?)....Plat: 196 acres bd. on W. by __ Addins(?), E. by
Jas. Holman, SW by Robt. Tucker, SE by road to Baskins...Margaret Steuart
released dower to Wm. Baskin, J.Q., _____ 1799. Signed: Mary A. (M)Steuart
.....Abbeville Co., James Bole made oath to Wm. Baskin, __ Dec. 1799.
Rec: 21 Jun. 1800.

Pages 12-13:   5 Oct. 1797, Jesse Gray to Peter Aker for $200
                              (hard money) for 185 acres near mouth of Bee
                              Branch, bd. by J.(?) Bagwell and sd. Gray.
Signed: Jesse (+) Gray, Huldah (X) Gray. Wit: Peter Aker, Jr., Joseph

(Pages 12-13 cont'd): Aker. Joseph Aker made oath to Wm. Hall, JP, 19 Jun. 1800. Rec: 20 Jun. 1800.

Pages 13-14: I, Robert Moore of Sivear(sic) Co., Tensee. (sic) for $143 sold to Jesse Gray 190 acres on S. side of the Saluda. Date: 26 Sep. 1798. Wit: Wm. Halbert, John Lindley(?), Jas. Halbert. Wm. Halbert made oath to John Hallum, J. P., 26 Jul. 1799.
Rec: 26 Jun. 1800.

Page 15: I, John Young for $400 sold to Francis Beaty 300 acres on Little Generostee Creek, granted Mathew Young, 17 Jun. 1785. Recorded Bk. B., no. 5, p. 203. Signed: John Young, Rachel Young. Wit: John Buchannon, Nathan Beaty.....Rachel Young, wife of John Young, released dower to Joshua Saxon, J. P., 7 Jun. 1800. John Buchannon made oath to _____, 13 Jul. 1799.
Rec: 26 Jun. 1800.

Pages 16-17: 29 Sep. 1795, Charles Waters to Peter Leboon, Sr., for £ 24 for 200 acres granted 5 Jan'y. 1789 by Thos. Pinckney to Alex(?) Mahen, in Washington Dist. on branch of Saluda River, bd. by Robert Samuel Brasher (?). Recorded Bk. YYYY, p. 333. Signed: Charles (W) Waters. Wit: Jas. Head, John Head, Jas. (W) Satterfield. James Head made oath to Robert McCann, J. P., 25 Jun. 1800.
Rec: 25 Jun. 1800.

Pages 17-18: (very dim)....Seems to be a Power of Attorney from ......Michael Trip(?) to Alexr. _____ Date: 5 Mar. 1795. Signed: Robert William, C.C. _____ Stokes Co., N. C. ...I, Mathew Brooks (or Brock) presiding Justice for the time being certify that Robert Williams is subscribing Clerk _____

Page 18: (deed unreadable).....appears to be signed by Geo. Foster(?). Oath unreadable except date ...22 Feb. 1800. Signed: James Neel, Michael Dickson, J. P.

Page 19: (Unreadable)

Page 20: (Mostly unreadable).....Date: 23 __ 1800. Wit: James Pinnell, Claiborn Cullon(?).....Personally came before me, John Johnson, Esq. (faded) and made oath he saw _____ (Commissioner of Ft. Johnson?)...sign and that he with Claiborn Clifton(?)_____, date: 23 Feb. 1800. Signed: John Johnson, J. P.,_____.
Rec: 23 Jun. 1800.

Pages 21 through 26: (Unreadable)

Page 27: (Unreadable)...signed: Benjamin Lawrence, Rachel (X) Lawrence. Wit: John MacCrary, William Thompson.

Pages 28 through 29: (Unreadable)

Pages 30-31: 10 Mar. 1800, Levi Robins to James Gray for $150 for ____ hundred ac. ____ granted 2 Sept. 1793 by (Wm.?) Moultrie....(unreadable). Wit: John Burton, Samuel Boydston. Samuel Boydston made oath to Joseph Reed (date.......unreadable).
Rec: 4 Aug. 1800.

Page 32: (Unreadable)....mentions Joab Mauldin. Signed: David Hughs(?). Wit: John Mauldin, Wylie(?) Mauldin _____. Rec: 11 Aug. 1800.

Pages 33-34: _____ 250 ac. Signed: James Cunningham, Excr. Wit: Richard Nally, ___ (X) Sexton,

(Pages 33-34 cont'd):   Aaron Nally _____. Receipt signed by Abraham
                         Nally _____ (rest not clear).

Pages 34-36:   _____, between Benjamin Harris and Cary,
                         his wife _____ and Abraham Nally _____ 600 ac.
                         on Brushy Creek, bd. on N. by lands laid out
for Thomas Hallum _____. Signed: Benjamin Harris, Karenhapuck (O)
Harris. Wit: Jonathan (?) Moore, Thomas Foster (?) ____ 27 Jan. _____
Jonathan (?) Moore made oath _____.
Rec: 5 Aug. 1800.

Pages 36-37:   _____ on fork of Brushy
                         Creek, Saluda River, granted said Benjamin
                         Harris by Wm. Moultrie, 6 Nov. 1786 _____
sd. tract joining Hallum's survey _____(rest not clear).

Pages 37-38:   (Deed unreadable). _____ personally came
                         James McCaleb and made oath he saw Wm. McCal-
                         eb sign....(rest not clear).

Page 38:   (Unreadable)

Pages 39-40:   _____John Reynold made oath
                         he saw Thomas Gorman sign deed _____
                         (Rest is unreadable).

Pages 40-41:   (Deed unreadable).........Wit: Isaac Payne,
                         James Baker(?). Date: 1 Oct. 1800(?). Saml.
                         Baker made oath he saw Lewis Atkins sign deed.
(More, but cannot read).

Page 41:   20 Mar. 1800, this is to certify that we, the
                         underwritten subscribers doth hereby relin-
                         quish all claim to the Estate of Hugh Rogers
(?) deceast(sic) towards his _____ consent that Hugh Rogers, Jr.
may enjoy forever and his heirs as witness our hands. Signed: Paul Capehart, Moses Payne, Jas.(?) (X) Rogers, Adam Rogers, Sarah (X) Rogers....
.......(witnesses not clear). Thomas Davis made oath (no. J. P.), 16
Sep. 1800.
Rec: 16 Sep. 1800.

Pages 41-42:   _____ Motte, of City of Charleston, for 25
                         s. sold to Andrew Boddan, of Columbia(?), S.C.
                         200 acres in Washington Dist. on Little Beav-
erdam Creek, granted Charles Motte as a Bounty for his services as a Major in the State War of American Revolution, he the sd. ____ Motte being lawful son and heir of Major Charles Motte. Date: 21 Feb. 1799.
Signed: Jacob Motte. Wit: William Hives(?) Grine, Peter Chirrouth(?).
(cannot read......) made oath to Peter Freneau, J. P., 16 Dec. 1799.
Rec: 2 Nov. 1800.

Pages 42-43:   (most of this not readable.........) 30 shil-
                         lings paid by Andrew Boddan _____ containing
                         856 acres; 356 acres surveyed for Joseph ____
21 Nov. 1800, situated in 96 Dist., Abbeville Co., on both sides of the
branches of N. fork of Estertoway(?) including two small branches of the
S. fork of Eastertowy, waters of Keowee; one other tract of 300 acres
surveyed for Benjamin Gowan(?), 21 Jun. 1785(?), in 96 Dist. above the
ancient boundary line on 23 Mile Creek; one other tract in 96 Dist. of
200 acres surveyed for Henry Young, 15 Jun. 1795, on both sides of Seneca River, bd. on SE by John Passon; three said tracts granted by William
Moultrie to sd. Daniel Faust, 4 Feb. 1793. Date: 20 Sep. 1796. Signed:
D. Faust. Wit: R. Hendrick, Saml. Green. Samuel Green made oath ....
(not clear)....10 Jan. 1800.
Rec: 7 Nov. 1800.

(Note: Not only is the writing very dim, the penmanship is bad...BW)

Pages 43-44:   I, Samuel Buchanan (or Buckman), Lieutenant
                         in the late Army of the United States, for

(Pages 43-44 cont'd): Ł 1 sold to Andrew Bodden, of Richland Co., S. C., 200 acres in 96 Dist., Pendleton Co., laid out as bounty land, 25 Aug. 1784, by John Martin, D.S. granted 21 Jan. 1785 by Benj. Guerrard; also, 640 acres on 26 Mile Creek of Savannah River, bd. by land laid out to Joseph Irwin(?), originally surveyed for Samuel Buckman, 15 Jul. 1784 by B. Crofton, D.S. and granted Buckman 15 Oct. 1784 by Benj. Guerrard. Date: 23 Sep. 1799. Signed: S. Bockman. Wit: Richard Wood Craft(?), William Rives, Jr. William Rives, Jr. made oath to Peter Freneau, J.P.Q.U., 16 Dec. 1799. Rec: 20 Nov. 1800.

Page 45: I, Bennett Combs am firmly bound to Joseph Chapman for "thirty hundred dollars". Date: 6 Aug. 1798 and make title to tract of 275 ac. plantation I now live on, bd. on N. by 12 Mile River. Wit: John Gibson, John Chapman. John Chapman made oath to Paul Hallum(?), J. P., 20 Sep. 1799. Rec: 22 Oct. 1800.

Pages 45-46: We, Commissioners for laying off and disposing of the Public lands adjoining Pendleton Courthouse for $35 sold to John Harris one lot of land containing 1 acre. Date: 12 Jun. 1800. (rest unreadable).

Page 46: (Unreadable)

Page 47: (Deed unreadable). Wit: Wm. Hunter, John Taylor.......(appears deed is signed by Andrew Pickens, Robert Anderson, John Wilson, who were the Commissioners for laying off the land. Appears to be several deeds by Commissioners on these pages.)

Page 48: (Top of this page signed by the Commissioners ...probably ending a preceeding deed.)

Pages 48-49: We, Andrew Pickens, Robert Anderson, John Wilson, Commissioners for __ hundred dollars sold to John Bayles Earle, lot of land of 1 acre. Date: 20 Jun. 1800. Wit: Wm. Hunter, D. McCaleb. Signed: Andrew Pickens, Robert Anderson, John Wilson. Rec: 15 Aug. 1800.

Page 49: Personally came and swore on his oath that he saw the Commissioners.....(?)...of the lots of land adjoining Pendleton Courthouse in favor of John Adair, George Capehart, William Shackelfort(?), John Taylor and John B. Earle deeds and that John Hunter was a witness with him and that David McCaleb was a witness to John B. Earle deed. Date: 14 Aug. 1800. Signed: Wm. Hunter to J. B. Earle, J. P.

Pages 49-50: I, George Umphries for $420 sold to Cornelius Green 100 acres, part of 1,300 acres granted Thomas Lewis(?), 4 Dec. 1786, on Little Beaver Creek, bd. by Wm. McCuron(?) and Lewis. Date: 27 Aug. 1800. Signed: Geo. (his mark) Umphries. Wit: Phillip P. Boulware, John Phillips. Phillip P. Boulware made oath to Robert McCann, J. P., 29 Aug. 1800. Rec: 27 Aug. 1800.

Pages 50-52: Last day of Nov. 1794, William Buckann to Ebenezer Buckhannon for 5 shillings for 150 ac. on Generostee Creek, measured out for Jacob Duton, 15 Oct. 1791. Signed: William Buckhannon. Wit: John Buckhannon, Jas. Denham, Margarett Denham....Personally appeared Robert (blank) and made oath he saw above witnesses sign, 9 Aug. 1797, to John Verner, J.P. Rec: 9 Aug. 1797.

Pages 52-53: I, William Lafoon sold to John Bledsow(?) a parcel of land on S. side of the Saluda River granted William Bruse "a part thereof Andrew Addams(sic)", bd. by William Thompson, William Lafoon, across corner of tract granted John Welch. Date: 23 Aug. 1800. Wit: Samuel Earle, John

(Pages 52-53 cont'd): Hankins. Samuel Earle made oath 2 Sep. 1800. (no J. P.). Rec: 2 Sep. 1800.

Pages 53-54: I, Baylis Earle of Spartanburg Co., S. C. for L 30 stg. sold to John Cockran of Pendleton Co., 170 acres on Young's Creek, of 12 Mile River, bd. by John Young, William (?) Young. Date: 31 May 1800. Wit: Samuel Hopkins, William Lyntch, Susannah Colley. Wm. Lyntch made oath to Wm. Hall, J. P., 4 Aug. 1800. Rec: 21 Aug. 1800.

Pages 54-55: Samuel Eakins of State of Georgia for $100(?) sold to Hugh Bruster(?) ___ ac. on Big Beaverdam of Savannah River, bd. by Thomas ___, James Williams (cannot read rest of deed)....Date: 10 Jan. 1800. Signed: Samuel Eakins, Jane (X) Eakins. Wit: Wm. ___, Jas. Bruster(?). James Bruster(?) made oath to ___ Montgomery, J. P......Georgia, Jackson Co. 22 Aug. 1800, Jane Eakins released dower to John Pittman, J. P. Rec: 21 Jul. 1800.

Pages 55-56: I, Henry Lince(?) for $100 sold to Stephen Roberts 125 acres on Hurricane Creek of 26 Mile Creek, bd. on E. by Clark, on W. by Keath Martin(?), on N. by ___. Date: 29 Mar. 1800. Wit: Arron(?) Doyle, Thos. Simmons(?). ....(Cannot read oath). Rec: 2 Aug. 1800.

Pages 56-57: I, William McCaleb for L 50 stg. sold to John Doss(?) ___ (cannot read this) by Thomas Lofton, D.S., granted by Thos. Pinckney, __ Jul. 1787, on Coffee's Creek. Date: 19 Sep. 1800. Wit: Edward Adair (?), Robt. Waugh. _ Sep. 1800, Robert Waugh made oath to J. Bayles Earle, J. P. Rec: __ Sep. 1800.

Pages 57-59: 14 Dec. 1794, Aron Neel to Thomas Neel for L 54(?) ....(cannot read). Wit: John Lofton, Thomas Lofton...(oath not clear).....

Pages 59-60: 7 Jul. 1795, Robert Smith ___ on W. side of Little Beaverdam Creek of Tugaloo River, part of tract originally surveyed for Robert Smith and granted to William Griffen, 6 Jun. 1791 by Charles Pinckney. Recorded Bk. C(?), no. 5, p. 399, containing 771 acres; the other 200 acres ___ May 1792 and again conveyed to Robert Smith by John Dison(?) 1794. Wit: Alexander Kilpatrick, James Kilpatrick. (Receipt of money appears to be from James Swan.) (No oath). Rec: 1 Oct. 1800.

Pages 60-62: 27 Sep. 1796, Aaron Neel and Thomas Neel, both planters, to James Neel, planter, for L 70 stg. for 200 acres on Cuffee Creek of 23 Mile Creek of Seneca River, bd. on NE, SE and SW by Lewis Daniel Martin line, George Ferbush, on NW by John Martin, granted Aaron Neel by Wm. Moultrie, 2 Jan. 1795. Signed: Thomas Neel (only). Wit: Wm. Shelby, Sarah Shelby. William Shelby made oath 29 Sep. ___. Rec: 1 Oct. 1800.

Pages 62-64: ___ 1796, Henry Green and Caroline, his wife to Benjamin Clarridy(?) for L1 - 5 s., 200 ac. on Hurricane Creek of Saluda River, part of a tract of 670 acres granted Henry Green by Chas. Pinckney, 17 Nov. 1791. Recorded Bk. ___, no. 5, p. 186. Signed: Henry (HG) Green, Caroline (X) Green. Wit: Smith Clarridy(?), Ambrose Hudgins. Smith Clarridy(?) made oath to William Hill, J. P., 3 Jul. ___. (Plat shown but cannot read Rec. date.)

Pages 64-65: Henry Cox for Love and natural affection I bear for my wife Polley Cox and for her support, deliver unto Alexander Wall(?) as the Trustee for my wife, the following property, viz: one horse, 1 cow with

(Pages 64-65 cont'd): yearling, feather beds and furniture, one cotton wheel (other items - unreadable). Date: 21 Apr. 1800. Wit: J. B. Earle, Joseph Taylor. J. B. Earle made oath to ....(no. J. P.), 24 Aug. 1800. Rec: 26 Aug. 1800.

Pages 65-66: We, Commissioners for laying off Publick lots and lands adjoining Pendleton Courthouse for $110 sold to John Hunter 2 lots of land adjoining Town of Pendleton, No. 11 on which the goal(?) at present stands (probably the jail)..and No. 5(?) containing 11 acres, bd. by Major John Griffen. Date: 20 Jun. 1800. Signed: Andrew Pickens, Robert Anderson, John Wilson. Wit: Wm. Hunter, J. B. Earle. J. B. Earle certified deed. Rec: 14 Aug. 1800.

Page 67: James McCaleb for divers good causes and considerations appoint David McCaleb my lawful Attorney to make titles to 650 acres on Cain Creek of Keowee River....(not clear to read)...John Barton(?) and Baylis Ninon's(?) _____ to John Barton and Baylis _____ (very dim, appears to be bond of debt). Date: 1 Sep. ___. Wit: Thos. Hunter, John Hunter. John Hunter made oath to J. B. Earle, C.P.D., 19 Sep. 1800. (No recording date).

Pages 67-69: I, John Cannon(?) for $80 sold to _____ Date: 7 Dec. 1799. Signed: John Cannon. Wit: James Waters, John Gilliam. John Gilliam made oath to John Baylis Earle, C.P.D. Date:_____
Rec: 7 Nov. 1800.

Pages 69-70: I, William McCaleb for _____ sold to David McCaleb 1,211 acres on N. side of Seneca River. Date: 25 Aug. 1800. Wit: James Wood, Thomas Farrar. James Wood made oath to J. B. Earle, C.P.D., __ Aug. 1800. Rec: 3 Sep. 1800.

Pages 70-71: I, George Humphries for $150 sold to Abednego Green 100 acres on Little Brush Creek, part of 1,000 acres; 30 acres granted to Thomas Sears, 6 Dec.(?) 1786. Date: 5 May 1800. Signed: George (His mark) Humphries. Wit: Alexander Boyse, Jas.(?) McDowell. Alexander Boyse made oath to John Wilson, J. P., 31 Oct. 1800. Rec: 2 Nov. 1800.

Pages 71-73: I, John Harris for $200 sold to William Reed 300 acres on both sides of Uoloney Creek, S. fork of Saluda River, granted Samuel Crofton, conveyed by Thomas Farrar, Sheriff of Washington Dist. to John Harris. Date: 26 Jan. 1800. Wit: J. C. Kilpatrick, Jas. Dickson.....Mary Harris released dower to Robt. McCann, J. P., 20 Jun. 1799. J. C. Kilpatrick made oath to _____ Hallums, J. P., __ Oct. 1800. Rec: 29 Oct. 1800.

(Note: The recording dates are mixed; no explanation...BW)

Pages 73-74: 9 Dec. 1793(?), Lewis D. Martin for £ 60 stg. sold to Aaron Neil 400 acres on both sides of Cuffee Creek, of 23 Mile Creek of Seneca River, bd. on NE by land surveyed for William Dunlap, granted 5 Apr. 1786(?) by Wm. Moultrie. Wit: Samuel Lofton, Agnes (X) Lofton. Lewis D. Martin acknowledged deed to J. B. Earle, J. P., 10 Oct. 1800. Rec: 24 Oct. 1800.

Pages 74-75: I, Ambrose Barnet for $50 sold to Nathaniel Davis 35 acres, part of tract granted Blake Mauldin by Arnoldus Vanderhorst, 5 Aug. 1796 on E. side of 23 Mile Creek. Date: 9 Jan. 1800. Signed: Ambrose (X) Barnett. Wit: John Sutherland, John Martin. Ambrose Barnett acknowledged deed (no J. P.), 24 Nov. 1800. Rec: 13 Nov. 1800.

234

Pages 75-76: I, Isaac Herring for $60 sold to Joseph Smith 60 acres on Connoross and small creek by the name of Fuller's Creek, part of land laid out to Ellander Dickens, conveyed to Elijah Herring, from him to Isaac Herring. Granted 7 Feb. 1786. Date: 9 Apr. 1800. Wit: James Conner, Elijah Herring. James Conner made oath to John B. Earle, C.P.D., 27 Oct. 1800. Rec: 27 Oct. 1800.

Pages 76-77: I, Daniel Delinny for $100 sold to Joseph Smith 50 acres on small creek of Connoross Creek by name of Fuller's Creek, part of the tract laid out to Thomas Hamilton, conveyed to Daniel Delinny, granted 5 Sep. 1785. Date: 16 Sep. 1799. Signed: Daniel (X) Delenny. Wit: James Conner, Isaac Herring. James Conner made oath to John Barton, J. P., 26 Mar. 1800. Rec: 27 Oct. 1800.

Pages 77-78: I, Ezekiel Able for $140 sold to William Thompson(?) 140 acres on Little Beaverdam of Tugalo River. Date: 20 Jan. 1800. Wit: Barth. Reynolds, Jeremiah Reynolds. Barthm. Reynolds made oath to J. B. Earle, C.P.D., 15 Oct. 1800. Rec: 16 Oct. 1800.

Page 79: I, James Martin am firmly bound to David Dickey for Ł 150 stg. Date: 16 Mar. 1791, condition of obligation - to make title to 320 acres on Great Generostee Creek, part of 640 acres. Wit: Adam Meek, John Martin. Adam Meek made oath to Thomas Gilham, 22 Aug. _____. Rec: 15 Oct. _____.

Pages 80-81: 9 Oct. 1796, John Tallant to John Holcom for Ł 20 for 80 acres, bd. by Jonathan Gibbe's land on Mountain Creek of Big Generostee of the Seneca River, granted to John Tallant, 10 Dec. 1789 by Chas. Pinckney. Recorded Bk. B, no. 5, p. 3. Signed: John (X) Tallant. Wit: Ezekiel Putman, Adam Castlebetty. Ezekiel Putman made oath to Joshua Saxon, J. P., 31 Mar. 1797. Rec: 6 Oct. 1800.

Pages 81-83: I, Mark Castleberry for Ł sold to John Holcom 130 acres including whole improvement where I now live, part of 2 tracts joining together: one surveyed by Thomas Finley for Robert Bog 1785, granted Robert Maxwell 1788 for 42 acres; the other, 88 acres, part of tract surveyed by John C. Kilpatrick for Richard York, 3 Feb. 1787, granted John Tallant, 21 Nov. 1789. Date: 2 Dec. 1797. Wit: Jonathan Gibbs, Adam Davis, Jonathan Gibbs made oath to John Varner, J. P., 25 Dec. 1797. Rec: 24 Oct. 1800.

Pages 83-84: I, Joshua Broils and Elizabeth, his wife, for Ł 30 stg. paid by Samuel Harkins and sold to Ketron Harkins and Joseph Harkins 263 acres on Hencoop Creek of Rocky River, part of tract granted Jno. Grason 1785; recorded Bk. CCCC, p. 174(?). Date: 2 May 1796. Signed: Joshua Broyles and Elizabeth (/) Broils. Wit: Hugh Harkins, Thomas McCant...Elizabeth Broils released dower to William Hall, J. P., 7 May 1796. Rec: 13 Oct. 1800.

Pages 84-85: 16 Apr. 1791, William Boyd of Abeville Co., S. C. to David Stephenson of Pendleton Co. for Ł 100 stg. for 174 acres granted 7 Jan'y 1788 by Thos. Pinckney, in 96 Dist., waters of Savannah River, now in possession of Stephenson. Wit: Samuel McCleskey, William Lee.....Abbeville Co., Saml. McCleskey made oath to William Baskin, J. P., 16 April 1791. Rec: 18 Oct. 1800.

Pages 85-86: 21 Aug. 1797, Nicholas Perkins of Pittsylvania Co., Va. to Jesse Byneham of Pendleton Co. for Ł 200 stg. for 640 acres on Rice's Creek

(Pages 85-86 cont'd): Wit: Abraham Perkins, Peter Perkins, Bennet Combs. Capt. Bennet Combs made oath to Wm. Reed, 21 Aug. 1797. Rec: 4 Oct. 1800.

Pages 86-87: I, John Boyd, Sr. for $800 sold to George Boyd 800 acres on George and Goldin Creeks of 12 Mile River and Seneca River, part of sundry tracts bd. by Thos. Boyd, Jno. Boyd, Sr., Jno. Boyd, Jr., W. Jimeson. Date: 8 Oct. 1800. Wit: Robert Boyd, Jno. Boyd, Jr. Robert Boyd made oath to Wm. Reed, J. P., 9 Oct. 1800. Rec: 7 Oct. 1800.

Pages 87-88: I, Walter Bell for $500 sold to Kannon (also Kenon) Brazeal 201½ acres on Rocky Creek of Rocky River, part of 640 acres granted David Ramsey, Esq., intrusted for the heirs of Fergus Snoddy, deceased, granted 3 Oct. 1785. Date: 2 Mar. 1799. Wit: James Clements, Benj. Clements. Benjamin Clements made oath to Robert McCann, J. P., 11 Apr. 1799 .....Kiziar (XX) Bell, wife of Walter Bell, released dower to Robert McCann, 11 Apr. 1799. Rec: 14 Oct. 1800.

Page 88: I, Aaron James for L 10 stg. sold to Bavester Barton ...(no amount)...bd. by Thos. Turner, John Simpson, Wm. Lesley and sd. Barton. Date: 27 Jun. 1798. Wit: James Turner, Mary Barton. James Turner made oath to John Varner, J. P., 1 Mar.1800. Rec: 4 Oct. 1800.

Pages 88-89: I, John Ross for L 20 stg. sold to William McGreger (Megreger) 50 acres on Jenerestee Creek, part of tract where John Ross now lives bd. by Alexander (M.G.?) William and James Long and Generostee Creek. Date: 21 Oct. 1797. Signed: John (e) Ross. Wit: James Ross, Samuel Dean. James Ross made oath to John Varner, J. P., 11 Mar. 1800. Rec: 14 Oct. 1800.

Pages 89-90: 6 Jul. 1799, Thomas Holden of Laurence Co., S. C. and Margaret, his wife, to William Megregory of Pendleton Co. for L 30 stg. for 185 acres in Washington Dist. on branch of Generostee called Devil's fork, of Savannah River, part of 1,000 acres granted Holden by Wm. Moultrie, 1 Jan. 1787, bd. by Holden, Keith, Ledbetter(?). Signed: Thos. Holden, Margaret Holden. Wit: Joel (O) Pierson, Peramon Tate...Laurence Co., S. C., Joel Pierson made oath to Danl. Wright, J. P.,...(Oath signed - Joel Pereman). Rec: 14 Oct. 1800.

Pages 90-91: 26 Jan. 1800, Saml. Rose and Rhoda, his wife to David Stevenson for $200 for 100 acres bd by Savannah River, John Calhoun, conditional line made by Samuel Rose and Francis Rose, deceased, Wm. Millwee(?), granted 6 Nov. 1786 to Jno. McKourney(?). Signed: Samuel Rose, Rhoda(X) Rose. Wit: James Brown, Daniel Wall. James Brown made oath to Nathan Lusk, J. P., 12 Feb. 1800. Rec: 18 Oct. 1800.

Page 92: I, George Humphries for L 30 stg. sold Jeremiah Foster 52 acres in Washington Dist. on lower S. fork of Brushy Creek of Saluda River part of tract of 1,300 acres granted Thos. Lewis by Wm. Moultrie, 6 Dec. 1786, bd. by Jacob Earnest, T. Brown. Date: 6 May 1796. Signed: George (his mark) Humphreys. Wit: Stephen Boothe, David Grimes. David Grimes made oath to Jno. Wilson, J. P., 10 Apr. 1797. Rec: 3 Nov. 1800.

Pages 92-93: I, Joseph Smith for L 40 stg. sold Peter Keys 60 acres on Big Jenerostee Creek of Savannah River, part of survey granted Saml. Dalrumple by W. Moultrie, 6 Feb. 1786, bd. by Widow Tillys(?), Stephen and Chas.

(Pages 92-93 cont'd): Harris, Widow Smyth and land laid out to George Smythe, which bounds Joshua Saxon. Date: 8 Aug. 1800. Signed: Joseph (X) Smith. Wit: R. Thompson, Elijah Herring. Robert Tomson made oath to J. B. Earle, J.P., 2 Oct. 1800. Rec: 2 Oct. 1800.

Pages 93-94: _ Sep. 17_8, ...(very dim)...Martha Crouder of Pendleton Co., Washington Dist., to Isaac Jennings(?), for $120 for 100 acres on Saluda River, bd. by James Fleming, Jno. Thomas, John Sutherland, Henderson, part of tract granted Ebenezer Fain, 12 Oct. 1787 by Thos. Pinckney. Signed: Martha (X) Crouder. Wit: Laurence Bradley, William (O) Owl(?) William Owl(?) made oath to Robert Bowen, J.P., 12 Aug. 1800. Rec: 14 Oct. 1800.

Page 94: Daniel Stringer of Jackson Co., Ga. personally appeared before John Varner, J.P. of Pendleton Co., S. C. after being duly sworn states he has reason to believe that a certain note which he had on Mr. John Carrick of this Dist. for $300 was Fallonously (sic) taken from his possession in the State of Georgia. The note was due in April past. Date: 20 Jun. 1800. Rec: 17 Oct. 1800.

Pages 95-96: I, John Buckhannon of Town of Winsborough in Fairfield Dist., S. C., tavernkeeper, for ₤30 sold to Robert Glen of Pendleton Dist., planter, 200 acres on Middle Fork of Connoross Creek of Keowee River, granted to Harrison (sic), bd. on S. by Robert Buckhannon. Date: 11 December 1800. Wit: Thomas (O) Carey, Phillip Carolan....Sarah Buckhannon, wife of John Buckhannon, released dower ...(no J. P. named) (no date). Thos. Carey made oath to J. B. Earle, J.P., 15 Dec. 1800. Rec: 15 Dec. 1800.

Pages 96-97: I, Jonathan Kemp for $150 sold to Jno. Harris 127 acres on Conoross of Keowee River bd. SW by John Passon, SE by Wm. Holland, N. by James Ingram, conveyed from Fields Prewitt and Francis King, granted to Fields Prewitt by Thos. Pinckney, 2 Jul. 1787. Date: 14 Aug. 1799. Wit: David Gorman, Demcy (+) Kemp. David Gorham made oath to John Harris, J.P., 13 Aug. 1799. Rec: 18 Oct. 1800.

Page 97: I, Hugh Rose, late of Charleston but now of Kingdom of Great Britain, Gentleman, for ₤ 5 stg. sold to William Read of Charleston, Doctor of Physick, 640 acres in 96 Dist. on George's Creek of Saluda River, bd. on E. by land laid out to Ephraim Mitchell, Esq., on SE by land laid out to Zephaniah Roberts, granted Hugh Rose, 15 Oct. 1784, by Benjamin Guerrard. Date: 5 Mar. 1799. Wit: Neel MacNeal, George H. Inglis(?). Neal McNeal made oath to G. Reed, J.P.Q.U., 3 Nov. 1800. Rec: 16 Dec. 1800.

Page 98: 4 Jan. 1785, Elizabeth Reed of Charleston. SC of Hudson(?) Fort, to William Read of the City and State aforesaid, Doctor of Physick, for ₤ 5 for 640 acres in 96 Dist. on S. branch of George's Creek of Saluda River, bd. on N. by land laid out to Hugh Rose, Zephaniah Roberts, and granted Elizabeth Read by Benjamin Guerrard, 15 Oct. 1784. Wit: Brian Cape, Thomas Simon. Thomas Simon, Esq. made oath to Jacob Drayton, J.Q. (in Charleston?), 16 Sep. 1800. Rec: 16 Dec. 1800.

Pages 98-99: 5 Jul. 1793, Jones Bishop to Henry Willbanks for ₤ __ for 100 acres on both sides of Wolf Creek, part of 539 acres granted Benjamin Perry, 8 Aug. 1787, conveyed to Bishop, 9 Apr. 1793. Wit: William Marchbanks, Charles Loyd. William Marchbanks made oath to Bailey Anderson on 4 Aug. 1794. Rec: 29 Dec. 1800

Pages 99-100: I, Joseph Eaton(?) for Ł 20 sold to Robert Beaty 160 acres on 26 Mile Creek of Keowee River, bd. on NW by land surveyed for James Gillison, on SE by land surveyed for Robert Anderson, part of the tract granted James Beaty by Chas. Pinckney, 16 Feb. 1789. Date: 6 Nov. 1799. Signed: Joseph (X) Eaton. Wit: John Hudson, Wm. Scott. J. Hudson made oath to John L. Reed, J.P., 15 Aug. 1800.
Rec: 29 Dec. 1800.

Page 101: I, Joab Mauldin for $450 sold to James Shirly 120 acres on 26 Mile Creek, bd. by Calhaon? (Calhoun?), Robert Dickeson, John Turner, part of 288 acres granted Edward Kemp by Wm. Moultrie, 7 Aug. 1786, conveyed by Kemp to Jacob Capehart. Wit: James Waters, James Wood. James Wood made oath to (no J.P.), 23 Dec. 1800.
Rec: 20 Dec. 1800.

Pages 101-1-2: I, Isaac Steele for $600 sold to Henry Wilbanks two tracts: one granted Steele by Benj. Guerrard, 15 Oct. 1784; the other granted to Alexander Black, conveyed to Steele for 120 acres, all above land except 20 acres formerly conveyed to Joseph Roberts. Date: 10 Mar. 1800. Wit: Mosses Liddle, Elizabeth Liddle....Martha (a) Steele released dower to Joshua Saxon, 27 Mar. 1800. Elizabeth Liddle made oath to John Varner, J. P., 15 Apr. 1800.
Rec: 29 Dec. 1800.

Pages 102-104: 22 Mar. 1796, William Fowler for Ł 10 stg. sold to Benoni Fowler 100 acres on Broadmouth Creek of Saluda River, bd. by Joseph Brown & William Fowler. Signed: William (W) Fowler. Wit: Richard Bullock and Jeremiah Fowler. Richard Bullock made oath to Wm. Hall, J.P., 26 March 1796. (1799?)
Rec: 16 Oct. 1800.

Pages 104-105: 11 Feb. 1799, Jacob Bouthman to John Deering for $400 for 200 acres in Washington Dist. on Pain Creek of Toogaloo River, part of 400 ac. granted Godpherry(?) (Godfrey?) Isbell. Wit: John Deering, Jr., Richard Daniel. John Deering made oath to William Cleveland, J.P., 4 Mar. 1799.
Rec: 17 Oct. 1800.

Pages 105-106: I, Alexander McMillian for $150 sold to William Megrogor 62½ acres on Generostee Creek, part of tract granted John Lucky(?). Date: 28 Feb. 1800. Wit: E. T. Meclure, James Long. James Long made oath to John Varner, J.P., 11 Mar. 1800.
Rec: 14 Oct. 1800.

Pages 106-107: 15 Sep. 1794, James Cunningham of Washington Dist., planter, to William Copeland, planter, for 10 shillings for 30 acres on Brushy Creek granted John (?) Lofton for 200 acres, 23 Apr. 1789, by Thomas Lofton, D. S., now bd. by Samuel Talbut, Tho. Albert(?), William Copeland. Wit: John (X) Cunningham, Andrew Cunningham. Andrew Cunningham made oath to William Edmondson, J.P., 21 Feb. 1799.
Rec: 3 Dec. 1800.

Pages 107-108: Whereas, by bond of obligation, I am firmly bound to Francis Bremar for $1,000 to be paid by 16 Dec. 1801 _____ that I, William Edmondson bargain and sell the following property, viz: (lists sows, cattle, house and kitchen furniture, plantation tools). Date: 19 Dec. 1800. Signed: William Edmondson. Wit: Joab Mauldin. Joab Mauldin made oath to Robert Bowen, J.P., 3 Jan. 1801.
Rec: 5 Jan. 1801.

Pages 108-109: I, William Edmondson of Pendleton Dist. am firmly bound to Francis Brimar of City of Charleston for $1,000. Date: 19 Dec. 1800.

(Pages 108-109 cont'd): Wit: Joab Mauldin. Rec: 5 Jan. 1801. (No oath).

Pages 109-110: Washington Dist., We, Thomas Findley and William Findley for $300 sold to Henry Garner - 251 acres where Thomas Findley now lives on S. side of Golden's Creek, granted by Wm. Moultrie, 6 Jan. 1792 to Thomas Findley. Date: 24 ___ 1799. Signed: Thomas Findley, William Findley. Wit: Simon Reaves, John Hallum. John Hallum made oath to Basil Hallum, J. P., 8 Oct. 1800.
Rec: 1 Jan. 1801.

Page 110: I, Henry Mills for love and good will I bear my son, James Mills, give him all my household and kitchen furniture, hogs, colt and my crop of corn. Date: 13 Oct. 1780. Signed: Henry (H) Mills. Wit: Tunstall Chandler. (No oath).
Rec: 15 Oct. 1800.

Pages 110-111: I, James Matteson and Frances, my wife, of Pendleton Co. for Ł 20 sold to Benjamin Matteson of Abeville Co. ___ acres on Broadmouth(?) Creek. Date: 23 May 1798. Signed: James Matteson, Frances (X) Matteson. Wit: Lewis Davis, Nimrod Smith. Lewis Davis made oath to Wm. Hall, J. P., 25 May 1798.
Rec: 19 Jan. 1801.

Page 111: Abbeville Co., S. C., I, John George sold to Richard George of Pendleton Co., one negro woman named Jean(?), sd. George bought from John Right; also, colt, hogs, loom, one pooling(?) rack, and dropping (?) bars, all my crop of grain together with every article I possess excepting the "Orphan's Estate" for $160. Date: 1 Oct. 1800. Wit: Robert Harkness, Benj. George. Benjamin George made oath to J.(?) Harris, J.P. (no date).
Rec: 24 Oct. 1800.

Page 112: Personally came before John B. Earle, Clerk of Pendleton Dist., Jesse Ward and Robert Hammet and made oath they were present and did see Isaac Williams of Pendleton Dist., and John Lynch of the State of Georgia, engage in a fight at Pendleton Courthouse in which the above named Williams did bite off the right ear of sd. Lynch, also the sd. Isaac Williams came for the record in person with Jesse Ward and Robert Hammet and acknowledged himself to be guilty of the fact. Sworn, 16 Jan. 1800. Signed by Jesse Ward, Rt. Hammet, Isaac Williams.
Rec: 16 Feb. 1801.

Pages 112-113: I, John Alexander of Pendleton Dist. for $250 sold to Samuel Black of Aberville Dist., 200 acres on E. side of Barker's Creek, granted Thomas(?) Harges(?), conveyed to James Allen, then conveyed to John Alexander, bd. by Wm. Whiteman. Date: 4 Apr. 1800. Wit: Paul Davis, Samuel Brown. Paul Davis made oath to Wm. Hall. J.P., 19 Apr. 1800...Elinor (E) Alexander, wife of John Alexander released dower to John Wilson, J. P., 19 Apr. 1800.
Rec: 11 Apr. 1800(?) (1801?)

Pages 113-114: William Millwee for $100 sold to Andrew Oliver (?) 200(?) acres granted Millwee by Wm. Moultrie, 6 Feb. 1786 .....(body of deed unreadable) .....Date: 18 May(?) 1800. Wit: George Nash, James Moore. James Moore made oath to Robert (___ faded), 18 Oct. 1800. (Rec. date not clear).

Pages 114-115: ___(faded) James McCaleb to...(David McCaleb in oath) ___ 650 acres; one tract of 200 acres on both sides of Cain Creek of Keowee River; one tract of 300 acres surveyed for Wm. McCaleb(?) on W. fork of Cain Creek, ___ (rest not clear reading). Date: 21 Sep. 1800. Signed: James McCaleb. Wit: William Hunter, Thomas Hunter. Doctor William Hunter made

239

(Pages 114-115 cont'd): oath to John B. Earle, C.P.D., 20 Nov. 1800. Rec: 21 Nov. 1800.

Page 115: I, Henry McWhorter sold to Sarah Love one negro woman named Lib, also one negro girl named Sharlot, also one mulatto girl named Rachel. Date: 26 Jan. 1800. Signed: Henry McWhorter, Jane McWhorter. Teste: Henry A. McWhorter. Henry A. McWhorter made oath to John Varner, J.P., 16 Jul. 1800. (No rec. date).

Page 116: We, Alexander Powers and Florence, his wife, for Ł 70 stg. sold to Shadrack Chandler 100 acres, bd. by John Morris, Thomas Ford(?), Edward T. McClure, part of tract granted Powers by Wm. Moultrie, 3 April 1793. Date: 7 Jan. 1800. Signed: Alexander Powers, Florence Powers. Wit: Edward T. McClure, John Hall. Edward T. McClure made oath to Michael Dickson, J.P., 2 May 1800. Rec: 15 Jan. 1801.

Page 117: I, David McCaleb and Matilda, my wife, for $10 sold to George Capehart 14 acres (faded) (in) Pendleton Town (cannot read rest)....... Date: 20 Jan. 1801. Signed: D. McCaleb, Matilda McCaleb. Wit: Jacob Capehart, John Jones. Jacob Capehart made oath to John B. Earle, C.P.D., 21 Jan. 1801. Rec: 24 Jan. 1801.

Pages 117-118: I, Samuel Harper...(to Samuel Harbin?..faded) for ___ hundred twenty five dollars ___ part of tract conveyed (for?) James Gillison by William Lesley of 300 acres on S. side of Keowee River, ___, a part conveyed (for?) Henry Birch ___ between sd. Samuel Harbin and Nathan ___. Date: 2 Oct. 1799. Signed: Saml. Harper, Rith (X) Harper. Wit: James Smith, Sihon(?) (S) Busby, Nathan (X) Boon. N. Boon made the oath to Henry Burch, J.P. 4 Feb. 1799. Rec: 13 Dec. 1800. (very dim).

Pages 118-120: 25 Sep. 1800, Thomas Farrar, Sheriff of Pendleton Dist. to William Lofton(?).......... whereas, Ephraim Mitchell in his lifetime was seized of 300 acres, granted to him as Administrator of the Estate of John Gelblanks(?), dec'd. ..(in trust?) for heirs of sd. deceased, on N. fork of Choesta(?) Creek, of Toogaloo River,....whereas, Henry(?) Stephens obtained judgement against Joseph Johnston, Administrator of Ephraim Mitchell (deceased?) for Ł 17,000.....(therefore?) all goods, chattels, houses, lands and Real Estate of Joseph Johnston to be sold at publick auction, date 7 Jul. 1800.....William Sullivan for $120, being highest bidder. Wit: David McCaleb, George Capehart. David McCaleb made oath to John B. Earle, C.P.C., 26 Sep. 1800. Rec: 20 Nov. 1800.

Pages 120-121: I, John Powel, planter, for $100 sold to Ephraim Merrit, planter, 293 acres surveyed on 4 Aug. 1797, in Washington Dist. on Little River granted John Powel by Charles Pinckney, 2 Jul. 1789. Date: 9 Aug. 1799. Wit: Stephen Merret, William Ross. Stephen Merret made oath to Henry Burch, J.P., 26 Jan. 1801. Rec: 27 Jan. 1801.

Pages 121-122: I, James McCaleb for $500 sold to David McCaleb two tracts; one of 500(acres?), the other of 130 acres on Richland Creek above Shoal near where waggon road crosses the Creek, surveyed for James McCaleb by Thos. Lofton, D.S. Date: ___ Sep. 1800. Wit: William Hunter, Thomas Hunter. Doctor William Hunter made oath to John B. Earle, C.P.D., 25 Nov. 1800. Rec: 21 Nov. 1800.

Pages 122-123: I, David Smith for $200(?) sold to Thomas Hammet(?) (or Hamilton) ___ acres on 23 Mile Crk _____. Date: 5 May 1800. Wit: Wm. Orr,

(Pages 122-123 cont'd):   Wm. Rankin.....Rebecca (X) Smith, wife of Da-
                          vid Smith released dower to John Wilson, J.P.
                          (date not clear). Wm. Rankin made oath to
John Wilson, J.P., 16 Aug. 1800.
Rec: 5 Dec. 1800.

Page 127:   (This page has been inserted here).

Page 122:   (Repeated)

Pages 123-124:   20(?)____ 1794, _____ for ⱡ 40 paid by
                          sd. Rose(?) _____ 109 acres, tract of
                          land granted _____ Young (mentions John Jenk-
ins....believe he made deed)_____. Wit: _____ Moorehead, _____
Moorehead.
Rec: 20 Jan. 1801.

Pages 125-126:   I, George Humphrey for $150 sold to (left out)
                          McClardy, 150 acres part of tract granted to
                          Mss(?) Wadsworth and Turpin on Saluda River on
Brushy Creek. Wit: Phillip Bowles , Benj.(?) Clardy....Charlotte (X) Humphrey, wife of George Humphrey, released dower to Robert McCann, 28 Oct.
1800. Benjamin Clardy made oath to Robt. McCann, J.P., 28 Oct. 1800.
Rec: 20 Jan. 1801.

Pages 126-127:   I, Mathew Kitchens for $100 sold to Simon
                          Doyle ____ ac., half of tract of 677 acres
                          granted Mathew Kitchens on Hurricane Creek by
Thos. Lofton, surveyed 22 Feb. 1786, recorded 8 Jan. 1787 (rest not able
to read).

Pages 127-128:   I, William Rose for _____ sold to John Pow-
                          ell 150 acres on Conoross Creek, granted
                          _____ 20 May 1793. Date: 23 Oct. 1799(?). Wit:
Stephen Merrit, Hutson Rose. (rest unreadable.)

Page 128:   (Deed too dim to read). Signed: Bennett Combs.
                          Wit: J. M. Boran, Samuel Jackson, John Hunt.
                          Oath was signed Wm. Boran, 25 Apr. 1800......
(oath says deed to Nathaniel _____). David Murphree, J. P.
Rec: 14 Oct. 1800.

Pages 128-129:   I, Mathew Kitchens for $80 sold to Simon Doyle
                          _____ (rest unable to read).

Pages 129-130:   (Top of deed not clear)...John B. Earle, Clk.
                          of sd. County and directed Thomas S. Reese,
                          Sheriff of sd. county to levy and sell to Jon-
athan Akey(?) tract of 102 acres, being highest bidder....whereas, Judges
of County Court order the succeeding Sheriff to make titles to land ____
_____ (rest unreadable). Date: 1 Dec. ____.
Rec: 10 Nov. 1800.

Page 130:   (unreadable).........signed: Andrew Pickens,
                          John Wilson, Robert Anderson. Wit: John E.
                          Calhoun, William Steele.

Page 131:   (unreadable).....signed and witnessed as the
                          above deed. Oath looks as if Doctor William
                          Hunter was the grantee. John B. Earle, C.P.D.
(Recording date blank).

Page 132:   (Cannot be read).

Page 133:   (Unreadable)......release to Roger Murphrey
                          one certain parcel of land in Pendleton Co.

Pages 133-134:   (Unreadable)......bargain and sell to Polly
                          and Rebecca Young of sd. State and County one

(Pages 133-134 cont'd):   cow.....(rest unreadable).

Pages 134-135:   (Unreadable).........ninety eight acres on 26(?) Mile Creek _____ granted to Randolph Hunnicutt, 5 Nov. 1792, by Charles Pinckney...........(rest unreadable).

Pages 135-137:   ___ Apr. 1793(?), Henry Green of Washington Dist. to Isaac Davenport of Newberry Co. for Ł 55 stg. for 666(?) acres now in his actual possession _____ on Saluda River.......(rest unreadable).

Pages 137-138:   _____said William Mullican.... _____ tract of land except what is taken by Abraham Howard unto sd. Wm. Mullican _____ _____the daid(deed?) Joseph Prince do warrant_____

Pages 138-140:   _____Henry Green to Joseph Davenport of Newberry(?) Co., S. C. for 1 shilling for 676 acres on Hurricane Creek of Saluda River, Washington Dist., granted Henry Green by State Patent by Charles Pinckney, 4 Nov. 1791....................Signed: Henry (HG) Green. Wit: William _____, John Keely. ...Greenville Co., _____ saw Henry Green and his wife, Ann _____.

Pages 140-141:   _____between George Naylor of Augusta, Richmond Co., Ga., Esq. to Abraham Moorehouse of Philadelphia, Pennsylvania for 100,000 acres on Keowee and Little River, Washington Dist., granted by the State of South Carolina, 100 grantes of 1,000 acres each, 6 Oct.1794. (rest unreadable).

Pages 141-142: (page # repeated) _____confirm unto sd. James P. Boyd, also party hereto _____ body of land containing 100,000 acres .....Now this indenture, the sd. James Boyd for $100 to Francois do Blok (also Block) _____.

Pages 142-143:   _____, Hugh Montgomery, of Pendleton Co. to David Folkner of Greenville Co. for Ł 40 stg. _____(body of deed not readable).....receipt witnessed by Benjamin Arnold, Elijah Bennet.

Pages 144-145:   (Unreadable).........deed signed by Reuben(?) Johnson. Wit: John Halbert, John Lyle.

Page 145:   (Unreadable)

Page 146:   (Unreadable).........Oath signed by John G. Lofton to J. B. Earle, J.P. Rec: 10 Apr. 1801.

Pages 147-148:   (Unreadable).

Page 149:   _____ deed signed by Benjamin Clardy. Wit: William (W) Stanton, William Fary.

Pages 150-151:   (Unreadable).

Page 152:   (Unreadable) ....Wit: Benjamin Bowen, William Bennett.

Pages 153-154:   (Unreadable).

Page 155:   (Unreadable).....deed signed by Andrew Boddan. Wit: R. Witherspoon, Rd. Homan.

Page 156:   (Unreadable).....mentions "the sd. James Sanders Guignard, his heirs and assignes _____

Page 157:	(Unreadable).
Page 158:	(Unreadable).....Wit: J. G. Guignard(?), Rich. Homan.
Page 159:	(Unreadable).
Page 160:	(Unreadable).....mentions "sd. Matthew Richardson's land on Saludy River."
Page 161:	(Unreadable)....mentions Matthew Richardson.
Pages 162-164:	(Unreadable).
Page 165:	(Unreadable)....mentions Matthew Richardson _____ by sd. William Hallum _____.
Pages 166-167:	(Unreadable).
Page 168:	(Unreadable).....mentions John Oldham.
Pages 169-170:	(Unreadable).
Page 171:	(Unreadable).....oath signed: Isaac (X) Williams. Michael Dickson, J.P. Rec: 12 Mar.1801.
Page 172:	(Unreadable).
Page 173:	(Unreadable) _____ deed witnessed by John Hunter, _____ Merritt(?). Plat shows land of 400 acres bd. on all sides by vacant land, laid out to Capt. James Mitchell (bounty?).
Pages 174-175:	(Unreadable) ....Thomas Clemen(?) on Broadaway Creek, of Keowee River, part of a tract granted Thomas Burford, 4 Dec. 1786. _____. Wit: Adam Todd, Alexr. McLean.
Page 176:	(Unreadable).....mentions James Powell....... on banks of 12 Mile River containing 100 ac.
Page 177:	(Unreadable).
Page 178:	(Unreadable)....receipt whereof is hereby acknowledged that the sd. William Boren _____
Pages 179-182:	(Unreadable).
Page 183:	(Unreadable)......oath signed: James Jones. John Varner, J.P. Rec: 13 Apr. 1801.
Page 184:	(Unreadable).
Page 185:	(Unreadable)....deed signed by William Butler. Wit: William (+) Prince, Hugh Chambless.
Pages 186-187:	(Unreadable).
Page 188:	(Unreadable).....unto sd. Peter Edwards against him _____.
Page 189:	(Unreadable).
Page 190:	(Unreadable).....deed signed: Thomas Patterson. Wit: Arron Steel, Peter Ragsdale.
Page 191:	(Unreadable) ......Wm. Sloan appeared before me to make oath to deed and that Danl. Mason was also a Witness.

Page 192:   (Unreadable).

Page 193:   (Unreadable)....Wit: Kenon Breazele, Benjamin
                            Clements. Oath signed: 24 Feb. 1801 by Benjn.
                            Clements, Wm. Hall, J.P. Rec: 10 Mar. 1801.

Page 194:   (Unreadable).....mentions "John Ragsdale
                            signed receipt. Signed: Luke Smith to Wm. Reed,
                            J.P." Rec: 9 Mar. 1801.

Page 195:   (Unreadable)......mentions "Solomon King by
                            Wm. Moultrie, Esq. Recorded Bk. LLLL, p. 217"

Page 196:   (Unreadable).....mentions "said Henry Dobson,
                            his heirs and assigns forever_____"

Page 197:   (Unreadable).....mentions "Peter Ragsdale his
                            heirs and assigns forever. The sd. tract con-
                            tains 135 acres _____"

Page 198:   (Unreadable) ......deed signed by John W. Gri-
                            sham, _____ mentions John McCutchin.

Pages 198-199:   _____ for $150 sold to Peter La-
                            boon 150 acres on Brushy Creek. Wit: Samuel
                            Barr, _____. Signed: William (?) Hambray,
Selah Hambray(?) (Note: Hambray may be Hembree), released dower _____

Pages 199-200:   I, George Cox for $300 sold to James Merritt
                            90 acres on Brushy Creek of Saluda River, part
                            of tract granted Watson Allison, 4 Dec. 1786
bd. by Samuel Talbert, William Allison, Stephen _____. Date: 5 May 1801.
Signed: George (GC) Cox. Wit: John Booth, Obadiah Merrit. Obadiah Merrit made oath to John Wilson, J.P., 12 May 1801.
(No recording date).

Page 201:   I, John Cox, Sr. for good will to my loving
                            son, Beaverly(?) Cox, the whole plantation
                            where I now live to include 150 acres. Date:
30 Mar. 1789. Signed: John (/) Cox. Wit: James Hembree, George Brown.
George Brown made oath to John B. Earle, C.P.D., 16 Apr. 1801.
Rec: 16 Apr. 1801.

Pages 202-203:   We, John Brown and Anna Brown for $500 sold
                            to James Merrit 20(?) acres granted James
                            Jones, part of 200 acres and part of a tract
granted Thomas _____, 1 Jul. 1793, on a conditional line between Jere-
miah Fuller and Merrit, bd. by David Welihistine(?). Date: (blank) 1801.
Signed: John Brown, Anna (X) Brown. Wit: Peter Laboon, Samuel Barr......
Anna Brown, wife of John Brown released dower to John Willson, J.Q., 12
May 1801. Peter Laboon made oath to John Willson, 25 May 1801.

Pages 203-204:   I, Jeremiah Able and Elizabeth, my wife, for
                            $30 sold to Hosea Tapley 114 acres, part of
                            500 acres granted Able, on Connoross Creek,
bd. by Hosea Tapley, Burrel Green, Samuel Thacker, Richard Nall. Date:
3 Oct. 1799. Signed: Jeremiah Able, Elizabeth Able. Wit: John Tapley,
Burnwell Green. Burnwell Green made oath to John Harris, J.P., 7 Feb.
1801. Rec: 1 Jun.(?), 1801.

Pages 204-205:   _____do grant to Levi More all that
                            tract _____ Creek, Keowee River, bd. ___
Harley's land, E. by Connoross Creek, granted by Charles Pinckney, 9 Feb.
1789. Date: 26 Sep. 1796. Signed: John (C) Peek. Wit: Charles Clayton,
Major Loggins, John Clayton. Major Loggins made oath _____

Pages 205-206:   John Patterson and wife, Ann, for $82 sold to
                            Henry Garner 84 acres, part of 586 acres...
                            granted 4 Apr. 1796 to Joshua Reader by Arnol-

(Pages 205-206 cont'd.): dus Vanderhorst, on Golden's Creek of 12 Mile River, bd. by Willomon and Patterson. Date: 26 Nov. 1800. Signed: Ann Patterson, John Patterson. Wit: John Stewart, Simon Reeder. Simon Reeder made oath to Basil Hallum, J.P., 6 Mar.1801. Rec: 9 Mar. 1801.

Pages 206-207: I, Solomon West and Jane, his wife, for $264 sold to Henry Garner 54 acres, part of 200 ac. granted 5 Jun. 1786 to William Killiam (or Hallum?) by Wm. Moultrie, on Golden's Creek. Date: 5 Feb. 1801. Signed: Solomon West, Jane West. Wit: John (J) Patterson, Henry (+) Phinny (or Phinry?). John Patterson made oath to Basil Hallum, J.P., 6 Mar. 1801. Rec: 9 Mar. 1801.

Pages 207-208: We, John Patterson and Ann, his wife, for $150 sold to Henry Garner 63 acres on both sides of 12 Mile River. Date: 5 Feb. 1801. Signed: John Patterson (his mark), Ann (her mark) Patterson. Wit: John Moore, Henry (X) Phinry. Henry Phinery made oath to Basil Hallum, J.P., _____ Mar. 1801. Rec: 9 Mar. 1801.

Pages 208-209: 18 Dec. 1794, Little Bury Roch for £ 50 stg. sold to John Patterson 200 acres on both sides of Golden's Creek bd. by line run for Richard _____. Signed: Little B. Roach, Jane (X) Roach. Wit: John Chapman, Henry (X) Penry. Henry Penry made oath to Basel Hallum, J.P., 6 March 1801. Rec: 9 Mar. 1801.

Pages 209-210: I, Joshua Reeder for $82 sold to John Patterson 84 acres, part of 286 acres granted 4 Apr. 1796 to Reeder by Arnoldus Vanderhorst, on Golden's Creek of 12 Mile River. (rest unreadable).

Pages 211-212: (Unreadable).....with interest at date herein limited _____ sum of $20 for damages of the sd. Edward Penman (or Periman?) which he sustained as well as by reason of the sd. debt _____ (rest unreadable).

Page 213: (Unreadable).....mentions Samiel Robinson, his heirs and assigns _____ that the sd. Thomas Lehre(?), Sheriff of aforesaid sold and conveyed _____ (rest unreadable).

Page 214: (Unreadable).

Page 215: (Unreadable).....mentions goods and chattels houses, lands of sd. David Ramsey _____

Page 216: (Unreadable).....mentions sd. David Ramsey hath or had in which he the sd. John Heart, Sheriff aforesaid can legally grant and convey _____.

Page 217: (Unreadable).....mentions the premises unto Saml. Robinson ....

Page 218: (Unreadable).....deed signed by David Ramsey. Wit: John Mc cluck(?), James Henmar.

Page 219: (Unreadable).

Page 220: (Unreadable).....mentions Ellis Harlin, "the receipt whereof the sd. _____ granted, bargained and sold _____.

Page 221: (Unreadable).....Wit: Caleb Hair, Oburn (X) Buffington. Receipt says above named Ezekiel Buffington and Ellis Harlin _____ £ 100 current money _____. Signed: Field (X) Prewit.

Page 222:   (Unreadable).

Page 223:   (Unreadable) ___ mentions Field Prewit, planter.

Page 224:   (Unreadable) ___ mentions Ellis Harlin, his heirs and assigns a tract of 180 acres ___

Page 225:   (Unreadable) ___ Clement Wade and Mary Wade, my wife, for $190 paid by Elisha Bennett ___

Page 226:   (Unreadable) ___ deed signed by Agnes (+) Wade, Thomas C Cts. Wade, Mary (+) Wade. Wit: Adam Todd, Alexr. McLean.

Pages 227-229:   (Unreadable).

Pages 230-231:   I, Thomas Woods(?) of York Dist. for ₤ 100stg. sold to John Prator Odell(?) of Pendleton District ___. Date: __ Mar. 1801. Wit: William Hamilton, Wm. Woods....York Dist., Loraina Woods released dower to Wm. Smith, ___.

Pages 232-236:   (Unreadable).

Page 237:   (Unreadable).....Wit: Robert Powell, Griffen (+) Hardin. Oath says Adam Burchfield was a witness, also. John Hardin, J.Q.

Page 238:   (Unreadable) ....oath mentions John Griffen and James Wallace and "he did see Jonathan Johnson sign receipt."

Page 239:   (Unreadable) .....Thomas Wafer signed oath to Henry Burch, J.P., 8 Oct. 1800. Rec: 9 Mar. 1801.

Page 240:   (Unreadable) ...."the sd. William Rose and his heirs and assigns."

Pages 241-242:   (Unreadable)...mentions, in description of land, William Rose, Henry ___, John Wakefield (?) on George's Creek of Saludy River ___ John Singleton doth warrant to Isaac James. Date: ___ 1796. Signed by John Singleton, Rutha (?) Singleton. Wit: Stephen James, Lewis Singleton .....Greenville Dist., Stephen James made oath to ___, 3 May ___. Rec: 11 Mar. 1801.

Page 242:   I, Robert Biggs (or Riggs) sold to John Young ___ (unreadable).

Pages 242-243:   I, John ___ of Buford Dist., S. C. for $290 sold to William ___ King 240 acres surveyed for Jacob John, 10 Jan. 1785, in 96 Dist. on Bear Creek ___.

Pages 243-244:   (Unreadable).....mentions 392 acres granted by ___ Pinckney, ___ Sep. 1791, by Richard Hood conveyed to James ___ on George's Crk. of Saludy River ___...sd. tract of 205 acres ___ and all Estate rights, title, interest of him the sd. James Hughs ___. Signed: James Hughs. (Oath___) signed by William Eddins.

Page 244:   (Unreadable) ___ mentions Richard Nall(Nate) ___ - on Connoross Creek of Keowee River, bd. on S. by Capt. Warley, granted ___ 2 Feb. 1789. Signed: Levy (+) More. Wit: Burwell Green, Matilda Powell ___.

Page 245:   (Unreadable)...mentions James Slatern(?)....

(Page 245 cont'd):   (later appears to be Slater).....Wit: William
                             Norton, Thomas Robertson. William Norton made
oath he saw Thomas Field sign within deed to James Slater. Henry Burch,
J. P., 9 Feb. 1801.
Rec: 9 Mar. 1801.

Pages 246-246(?):   (Unreadable)......Wit: Jas. H. Ramsey, _____
                             Receipt for $450. Oath says "Personally appeared before Ephraim Ramsey - one of the Justices _____ Mary Ramsey, wife of within named Joseph Hall Ramsey .....
(rest is unreadable.).

Page 247:   (Unreadable).

Page 248:   (Unreadable)....deed signed Thomas Field. Wit:
                             James McKinney, George Shuler.

Page 249:   (Appears to be a Bill of Sale)......Frankey,
                             age _____. _____ I hereby warrant to W.
                             Thompson. Date: __ Mar. 1801. (Signature not
                             readable). Teste: Alexander Boyse.

Page 249:   Orangeburgh Dist. _____, of Winton _____ and
                             Samuel Taylor have entered into a contract __
                             (cannot read)___ ac. in Pendleton Dist. for
$80 to be paid by 1 Nov. 1799. Signed: James Furce(?). Wit: Hugh Patterson, Phillip Millin.....State of Georgia, Laurens Co., the within bond
from James Furce to Samuel Taylor _____.
Rec: 12 Mar. 1801.

Page 250:   I, Jesse Hillion(?) for $200 sold to Peter
                             Rice _____ on Keowee River, part of a tract
                             conveyed to William Reed _____. Levi Reese
signed oath to Henry Burch, J.P., 9 May 1801.
Rec: 19 Jun. 1801.

Pages 250-252:   Whereas, Robert Maxwell of Greenville Co.,
                             deceased, in his life time possessed 300 ac.
                             on Saludy River, granted Maxwell, 4 Dec. 1796
-Recorded Bk. NNNN, p. 579 _____ mentions William Ferrell, his
heirs and assigns. Date: 11 Mar. 1800. Signed: Mary Maxwell, Robert Anderson. Wit: Wm. Morrison, Major Lewis. (Oath _____)

Pages 252-255:   I, William Turpin of Charleston, S. C. surviving co-partner of Turpin & Wadsworth and
                             whereas, Thomas Wadsworth, in his lifetime
took up grant of 640 acres in 96 Dist. on N. branches of 23 Mile Creek,
of Savannah River, bd. by Wm. Turpin, Felix McKeeswick(?), granted 15
Oct. 1784, recorded Bk. ZZZ, p. 346, and though in name of Thomas Wadsworth did in fact, belong to co-partnership of Wadsworth & Turpin. On
3 Feb. 179___ sd. Wadsworth made out in name of Wadsworth & Turpin, it appears that after an allowance of £ 2-10 s. the deficiency of
the land sold, the purchase money has been paid with interest to said
Thomas Wadsworth, balance of £ 5. 3s. 9 p. still due is unpaid and the
sd. Michael Dickson and sd. Thomas Wadsworth in his lifetime put in possession _____ (unreadable). Date: 5 Feb. 1801. Wit: Jacob Ford, Thomas
Johnston.....We, Subscribing Trustees named in the last will of Thomas
Wadsworth for receiving and applying his property to the purpose in his
will _____. Signed: John E. Calhoun, Henry Wm. DeSaussure _____
make to sd. Dixon titles _____. Thomas Johnson signed oath to
John Willson, J.Q.
Rec: 4 Jul. 1801.

Pages 256-257:   I, Richard Speak for $215 sold to Isaac Williams(?) _____. Wit: David Sloan (only)
                             who made oath to Michael Dickson, J.P., 4 Jul.
1801. Rec: 4 Jul. 1801.

Pages 257-259:   I, Eliab Moor to Jacob Holland for $300 for
                             860 acres, formerly run for Thomas Harrison,

(Pages 257-259 cont'd): on Togalo River, granted by Thos. Pinckney to Moore, 31 Dec. 1787. Date: 25 Jul. 1800. Wit: William Ross(?), William Jones. William Jones made oath to William Cleveland, J. P., 23 Jul. 1800.
Rec: 24 Jul. 1801.

Pages 259-260: I, David Sloan for $300(?) sold to Charles Brandon 100 acres on Smith(?) Creek of Keowee River granted John Martin by Wm. Moultrie, 1 Aug. 1786, bd. by Charles Brandon on the W. Date: 23 Feb. 1797. Wit: Robert Hashel, William Sloan. Robert Hashel made oath to J. B. Earle, C.P.D., 4 Jul. 1801.
(Recording date cannot be read).

Pages 260-263: Whereas, James ____ was seized of 2 tracts: one of 47 acres on N. E. branch of 23 Mile River, of Keowee River, bd. on NE land surveyed for Christopher Curtis, on SW land surveyed for John (?) Oliver; the other tract of 150 acres, part of 640 acres granted Robert Pickens, released to Jacob Gilham, 2 Sep. 1789....Basil(?) Allum (Hallum?) in 1790 recovered judgement vs. sd. James Compton, goods, chattels, lands sold to highest bidder, Saml. Barr for $23 by E.(?) Reese, late Sheriff of Pendleton Co. Date: 27 Jan. 1799. Signed: E. Reese, S.P.C. Wit: A. Boyse, Robert Pickens. Alexander Boyse made oath to John Willson, J. P., "he saw Edward Reese sign deed", 21 Apr. 1800.
Rec: __ Jul. 1801.

Pages 263-264: I, William H. Lacy for $600 sold to William H. Cockerham 300 acres on Choestoy Creek of the Toogaloo River, part of tract granted to James McIlwee by Wm. Moultrie, 2 May 1785; and part of tract granted William McCaleb 2 Jul. 1787 by Thos. Pinckney. Date: 3 Dec. 1800. Signed: W.H. Lacy, Martha (X) Lacy. Wit: William White, Richard Hooper. William White made oath to John Barton, J.P., 29 Apr. 1801.
Rec: (cannot read date).

Pages 264-265: I, William Stuart for $250 sold to Amos Richardson 157 acres, part of tracts granted to Burrel Bobo, 5 Feb. 1787 and George Shuler,3 Jan. 1793 on Little River of Keowee River, on lines of sd. Richardson, William Nicholson and Bobo. Date: 22 Oct. 1800. Signed: William (X) Stuart. Wit: Wm. (W) Mitchell, W. Nicholson, John Mitchell. William Mitchell made oath to Hennery Burch, J.P., 25 Apr. 1801.
Rec: 12 Jul. 1801.

Pages 265-267: I, William Stuart for $250 sold to William Nicholson 197 acres, part of tract granted to Burrel Bobo, 5 Feb. 1787, bd. by Shular, Nicholson and Amos Richardson, on both sides of Little River of Keowee River (cannot read date). Wit: William (X) Mitchell, John Mitchell, Amos Richardson. William Mitchell made oath to Henery Burch, J.P., 25 Apr. 1801.
Rec: 21 Jul. 1801.

Pages 267-269: I, William Stuart for $50 sold to Wm. Nicholson and Amos Richardson 300 acres granted to Peter Finn on Little River of Keowee River. Date: 22 Oct. 1800. Signed: William (X) Stuart. Wit: Wm. Mitchel(X),John Mitchel. William Mitchel made oath to Henery Burch, J.P., 25 Apr. 180_
Rec: 12 Jul. 1801.

Page 269: Edgefield Co., S. C., I, Barkley Martin, Sheriff of sd. County, sold a negro fellow by the name of Tom, the property of John Glass(?),by attachment proved by John Young from Aquilla Miles, J.P., and sold to highest bidder, which was James Young for Ł 53. Date: 9 Aug. 1790. Signed: West Cook (witness?), Barkley Martin, S.E.D.
Rec: 21 Jul. 1801.

Pages 269-272: 29 Oct. 1800, John Roberts, Thomas Roberts, Elsa Growgan, Wm. Lourance, Legatees of the

(Pages 269-272 cont'd):   Widdow Elsa Love, deceased, to Jacob Capehart,
                               for $222 for 222 acres on Sadler's Creek of
                               the Savannah River, granted Samuel Love by Wm.
Moultrie, 6 Nov. 1786, conveyed from Samuel Love to Thomas Love and at
the death of Thomas Love, Elsa Love, his wife, conveyed to the sd. legatees. Signed: John (his mark) Roberts, Thomas (R) Roberts, Elsa (X) Growgan. Wit: Moses Liddle, Saml. Tate, Joseph Roberts. (William Lourance
signed receipt with others.) Saml. Tate made oath to J. B. Earle, C.P.D.
15 Mar. 1801.
Rec: 15 Mar. 1801.

Pages 272-273:   I, William Golaspy and Susander, his wife, for
                               $110(?), sold to John Brown (called Col. John
                               Brown in oath) 302 acres on Middle Fork of
George's Creek, bd. by Robt. Bowen, Esq., granted William Golaspy, Sr.
and William Golaspy, Jr.; one dated 1 Aug. 1785, the other 7 Apr. 1788,
where William Gollaspy now lives. Date: 20 Oct. 1800. Signed: William
Gillispy. Susandar Gillispy. Wit: Saml. Duff, Wm. Brown. Wm. Brown
made oath to Robert Bowen, J.P., 11 Dec. 1800.
Rec: 10 Mar. ____.

Pages 273-275:   I, Christopher Strong for $1,700.28 sold to
                               William Hunter, 640 acres on both sides of 18
                               Mile Creek of Savannah River, granted to John
Lewis by Governor Guerard. Date: 5 May 1801. Wit: John Taylor, John Hunter. Elizabeth (X) Strong made oath to J. B. Earle, J.P., 20 Jun. 1801.
(No recording date).

Pages 276-277:   I, John Bohannan of Fairfield Dist., S. C....
                               (Buchannon in oath)...planter, for $500 sold
                               to Elsy (also Elsi) Hunt, planter, of Greenville Dist., S. C., 300 acres on Chauga Creek of Tugalo River. Date: 12
Mar. 1801. Wit: J. B. Blackwell, Robert Welch. J. B. Blackwell made oath
to George Foster, J.P., (in Pendleton Co.) 13 May 1801.
Rec: 20 Jun. ____.

Pages 277-278:   I, Benjamin Hickman for $300 sold to Luke
                               Smith 200 acres on Little Beaverdam Creek of
                               Tugalo River, bd. NE by Dr. Fredrick Sunn(?),
SE by land laid out to Capt. James Wilson, granted John Martin, 7 Aug.
1786 by Wm. Moultrie. Date: 14 Mar. 1801. Wit: John Mitchell, Solomon
Smith. John Mitchell made oath to John Harris, J. P., 26 May 1801.
Rec: 4 Jul. ____.

Pages 279-280:   I, Francis Lecy, Shopkeeper, of Charleston for
                               Ł 50 sold to Joseph Jolly of Pendleton County
                               100 acres on NW side of 26 Mile Creek of Savannah River, part of 547 acres, bd. by Robert Dickinson and land claimed
by Wm. Turpin. Date: 1 Jan. 1801. Signed: Francis Ley. Wit: John Turner,
Joseph Green. Joseph Green made oath to J. B. Earle, C.C.P.D., 4 Jul.
1801. Rec: 4 Jul. ____.

Pages 280-281:   I, John Wickley of Beauford Dist., S. C. for
                               $200 sold to William J. King 200 acres surveyed for Jacob John 22 Mar. 1785 in 96 District
on 23 Mile Creek. Date: 23 Feb. 1801. Wit: John Fellow, Wm. L. Murdock..
....Beauford Dist., John Fellows made oath to John Peeples, J.P., 23 Feb.
1801. Rec: 5 Aug. ____.

Pages 281-284:   15 Jan. 1801, Wm. Shelby and Sarah, his wife,
                               to Mathew (also Marthew) Armstrong for $60 for
                               100 acres bd. by land laid out to William Turpin, Edw. Kemp, part of tract granted Lewis D. Martin by Wm. Moultrie, 3
Apr. 1801, on 23 Mile Creek. Signed: Willm. Shelby, Sarah Shelby. Wit:
Edward Cemp, James Armstrong. James Armstrong made oath to J. B. Earle,
C.P.D., 18 Jul. 1801.
Rec: (cannot read date).

Pages 284-285:   I, John Simpson for $100 sold to Samuel Anderson 39 acres on 26 Mile Creek of Senekaw(sic)

(Pages 284-285 cont'd): River. Date: 20 Jul. 1801. Wit: Wm. Cunningham, Wm. McGuffin. Wm. McGuffin made oath to John Harris, J. P., 20 Jul. 1801. Rec: 4 Aug. 1801.

Pages 286-288: 96 Dist., 11 Aug. 1791, Thomas Wadsworth to John Harris for £ 20 for 295 acres on 12 Mile River, bd. NW by land laid out to Mitchael Dickeson. Signed: Thomas Wadsworth for Wadsworth & Turpin. Wit: Stephen Cantrell, John Trotter. Stephen Cantrell made oath to Thomas Wadsworth, Esq., J.C., 17 Aug. 1791. (No recording date).

Pages 288-290: I, William Hunter for $37 sold to John Timmons, 100 acres on Beaver Creek, bd. SW by Jesse Davis, SE by John Brice, NW by William Hilhouse. Date: 17 Aug. 1801. Wit: John Hunter, Jonah Elliott. Jonah Elliott made oath to J. B. Earle, 14 Aug. 1801....Plat, "At request of William Brice I have surveyed tract of 100 acres." Signed: Robert Harkness, 13 Aug. 1801. Rec: 14 Aug. 1801.

Pages 290-291: 10 Mar. 1801, Robert Easley of Pendleton Dist. and Caty Benson of Greenville Dist., S. C., have entered into a marriage contract and I, Robert Easley agree that if he should die previous to Caty Benson to give her one good horse, one good feather bed and furniture, one woman's saddle and Caty Benson acknowledges his (her) self fully satisfied with same and I, Caty Benson, in case the marriage should take place between me and Robert Easley and if he should die previous to me, I hereby relinquish all claim, rights and dower as wife of Robert Easley. Signed: Robert Easley, Caty (X) Benson. Wit: John Young, John Blasingame........ Greenville Dist. John Blasingame made oath to D. Goodlett, J.Q., 18 Jul. 1801. Rec: 22 Jul. ____.

Pages 292-293: I, Joseph Smith for $150 sold to William Stow (?) (or How) 300 acres on 12 Mile River, bd. James McBride, John Huggins. Date: 5 August 1799. Signed: Joseph Smith, Ruth (+) Smith. Wit: John Huggins, Mary (X) Huggins. John Huggins made oath to Joseph Reid, J.P., 9 Nov. 1799. Rec: 21 Aug. 1801.

Pages 293-295: I, William Stow (or How) for $150 sold to John Huggins 300 acres on 12 Mile River, bd. James McBride, John Huggins, granted 30 Mar. 1793 (date or signature not readable). Wit: John Donnalson(?), William Evett (?). Henry Burch, J.P., 4 Jul. 1801. Rec: 24 Jul. 1801.

Pages 295-297: I, William Lesly of Abbeville Co. for $65 sold to Joseph Pickens of Pendleton Co._____. _____. Wit: John W. McKinley, John Pickens. (Oath unreadable).

Pages 297-298: I, William T. King of Beauford Dist., S. C. for $50 sold to Thomas Stribling 200 acres surveyed for Jacob Tonn(?) 22 Mar. 1785, and granted John Weekley, 4 Sep. 1786 and from Weekley to King, 23 Feb.1801, in 96 Dist. on 23 Mile Creek. Date: 8 Jun. 1801. Wit: William Cunningham, J. Stribling. William Cunningham made oath to John B. Earle, C.P.D...... Jesse Stribling was also a witness, 24 Aug. 1801. Rec: 24 Aug. 1801.

Pages 298-301: 25 Jan. 1801, Moses Jones for £ 11 sold Jeremiah Fowler 54 acres on Brasstown(?) Creek of Tugalo River, bd. by Moses Jones. Wit: William Jones, Moses Jones. William Jones made oath to John Barton, J.P., 25 Aug. 1801. Rec: 26 Aug. 1801.

Pages 301-302: _____ £ 100 stg. paid by

(Pages 301-302 cont'd): William Murphree for 640 acres on N. side of 12 Mile River. Date: 9(?) Feb. 1797. Signed: John Robertson. Wit: John Bynum, John Chandler. John Bynum made oath to David Murphy, J.P., 27 Jun. 1801.
Rec: 28 Aug. 1801.

Pages 303-305: I, Harbert Tucker for $300 sold to Benjamin Farmer 150 acres, "land which I did live on now he lives on", on Mulberry Creek, Rocky River, bd. by land claimed by Bartlett and Auldin Tucker, John McAlister, Wm. Blair, granted Tilly Merrick as part of a larger survey made by James Millwee, D.S., 20 Mar. 1790. Date: 23 May 1801. Wit: John (X) Griffen, James Garner....Fanny Tucker, wife of Harbert Tucker, released dower to E. Browne, J.Q., 23 May 1801. James Garner made oath to E. Browne, J.P., 23 May 1801.
Rec: 8 Aug. 1801.

Pages 305-308: _____ for $200 sold to John Farrow 226 acres granted William Grayham surveyed by James Milwee, 18 Dec. 1792, recorded Bk. C, p. 153 (Pendleton Deeds?), 23 Mar. 1793, on Rocky River, bd. S. by Thomas Wade. Date: 7 Apr. 1801. Signed: James (his mark) Parkadur(?).Wit: James Cooper, Henson (X) Day. Henson Day made oath to Wm. Hall, J.P., __ _____.

Pages 308-310: _____ to Briton Farrar for 320(?) acres granted Wm. Cunningham, 22 Mar. 1793 _____, bd. by Thomas Mayfield. Date: 6 Aug. 1801. Signed: John (X) Farrar. Wit: Charles Clements, Benjamin Clements. Charles Clements made oath to Wm. Hall, J.P., 26 Aug. 1801. Rec: __ Aug. 1801.

Pages 310-311: I, Thomas Harrison, Sr. for $600 sold to Wm. Cleveland 575 acres on Beaverdam Creek of the Tugaloo River, granted sd. Harrison, 2 Feb. 1786(?). Date: 18 May 1801. Wit: N. Cleaveland, Thomas Holland. Thomas Holland made oath to Michael Dickson, J.P., 5 Jul. 1801.
Rec: 15 Aug. 1801.

Pages 312-314: Washington Dist., 15 Sep. 1798, John G. Lofton to William MCadoo (McAdoo) _____ 110 acres bd. by Morgan Osborn, Fredrick Glover, William Swift, Hugh Dodd, granted by Wm. Moultrie, 5 Jun. 1786. Wit: Wm. Gilham, Samuel Lofton, Jr., Arthur McAdow. William Gilham made oath to J. B. Earle, C.C.P.D., 17 Aug. 1801.....receipt was for Ł 20 stg.
Rec: 19 Aug. 1801.

Pages 314-316: 25 Mar. 1801, Perin Faro (also Farro) to James Parkadur for $140, one negro wench named Charlot about 16 years of age and one negro fellow named Abraham, 9 years of age, one negro wench named Hannah, 5 years of age. (There are three signatures, all last names Farrow, appear to be Perrin, John and Sarah Farrow). Wit: James Asher, Robert Duncan, Austin Mayfield ....(Oath unreadable).
Rec: _____ 1801.

Pages 316-318: We, Matthew and Martha Dickson for $228 sold to Matthew Dickson, Sr. 440 acres on 26 Mile Creek of Seneca River, part of 640 acres..... granted James Patterson and by John Edwaters and William Hort, Esqs., Treasurers of the State to Capt. James Martin of North Carolina and by Capt. Martin to Matthew Dickson, Sr. Signed: Matthew Dickson, Martha Dickson. Wit: _____ Dickson, Walter C. Dickson. Walter Dickson made oath (unreadable).
Rec: 16 Aug. 1801.

Pages 318-324: 21 Apr. 1785(?), John Kerr, hatter, to David Ramsey, physician, Ł 50 for 640 acres in 96 Dist. on Wilson's Creek, bd. by Alexander Noble, Wm. Halbert(?), surveyed by Patrick Calhoun to John Kerr, recorded

(Pages 318-324 cont'd): Bk. CCCC, p. 297. Wit: W. T. Harrison, Charles Snowden, William Mallack(?), Jacob Morris. William T. Harrison made oath to Charles Few, Esq., J.P., of Charleston Dist., 21 May 1801. (No recording date).

Pages 325-332: 22 Apr. 1785, William Mallack, watchmaker, to David Ramsey for 5 shillings for 640(?) acres in 96 Dist. above the ancient Indian Boundary line, near head of Wilson's Creek, branch of Rocky River, bd. part on land surveyed for John Kerr and part _____. Wit: George Warley, George Munro. John Kerr made oath to Charles Few, J.Q., 21 Mar. 1801, that he saw deed signed. (No recording date).

Pages 332-333: I, David McCaleb for $400 sold to Jacob Chamles(?) 200 acres on both sides of Cane Creek of Keowee River, granted Wm. Farmer as bounty, 4 Dec. 1786 by Wm. Moultrie, surveyed by John C. Kilpatrick, D.S. Date: 27 Mar. 1801. Wit: Field Farrar, Wm. (X) Casselbury. Field Farrar made oath to John B. Earle, C.P.D., 10 Sep. 1801. Rec: 28 Mar. 1801.

Page 334: I, Thomas Ware, planter, for 200 acres conveyed by Nicholas Madgett of Town of Columbus, S. C., merchant, sold him a negroe woman by name Patty and her future issue. Date: 14 Oct. 1801. Wit: James Jett, James Anderson. James Jett made oath to John Willson, J.P., 14 Oct. 1801. Rec: 14 Oct. 1801.

Pages 335-337: We, Arnoldus VanderHorst and Thomas Waring,Sr. qualified Executors of the last will of John VanderHorst, late of Charleston, deceased, for Ł 226. 13 s. 4 p., sold to Andrew Boddin and Robert Lithgow of Camden Dist., S. C., 640 acres in 96 Dist., S. of Saluda River on Connoross .... above the ancient boundary, granted George Adirs(?), 1 Aug. 1785; also, 640 acres in 96 Dist. on Cherokee Creek, bd. SE by land laid out to Wm. Barnett, granted Joshua Toomer, Esq., 15 Oct. 1784. Date: 10 Feb. 1798. Wit: J. F.(?) Chion, Hiram Wells, for A. VanderHorst and George Mathews, Daniel Smith for Waring, Sr......Personally appeared Oliver Cromwell who swore he saw deed signed and that John F. Chion signed before Stephen Ravenell, J.Q., 11 Jun. 1798. Danl. Smith, Esq. made oath to Stephen Ravenell, 11 Jun. 1796. Rec: 14 Oct. 1801.

Pages 337-338: I have sold at publick sale three likely young negroes of first quality to Wm. Coker, 2 women and one fellow: Sary, Jeany and Jacob, which I warrant the 2 women to be good cooks, good washers and ironers, and the fellow to be a good field worker, for $900. Date: 26 Oct. 1801. Signed: Thos. Coker. Teste: Jonathan Clark, Henry Clark. Jonathan Clark made oath to John Willson, J.Q., 2 Nov. 1801. Rec: 2 Nov. 1801.

Pages 338-339: I, William Marchbanks of Smith Co., Tn., Administrator of the Estate of William Young, deceased, within Dist. of Pendleton, S. C. do appoint Benjamin Barton of Pendleton Dist., my Attorney to recover and receive money, goods and effects payable or belonging to me. Date: 18 Mar. 1801(?). Wit: James Jett, Joshua Barton, Saml. Smith. James Jett made oath to David Murphree, J.P., 10 Sep. 1801. Rec: 13 Sep. 1801.

Pages 339-340: 20 Feb. 1801, William Ranfrow and Agnes, his wife, to Elisha Dyer, both of Franklin Co.,Ga. for Ł 10 for 150 acres on E. of Savannah River bd. by John Simpson, Gabriel Perkins. Signed: William (O) Ranfrow, Agnes (A) Ranfrow. Wit: John Reid, Nimrod House. John Reid made oath to John Verner, J.P., 10 Oct. 1801. Rec: 13 Oct. 1801.

Pages 340-342: State of Georgia, 26 Jul. 1799, Moses Chiles of Washington Co., Ga. to William Young, formerly of Pendleton Co., S. C. for $200 for 100 acres in Pendleton Co., granted Wm. Moultrie (by?) 1 Jan. 1787. Signed: Moses (X) Chiles. Wit: Duncan Carman (Duncan Camron), Nim. Robuck(Nimrod Burk), J.P., John Glenn, J.P. Duncan Camron made oath and swore Nimrod Burk and John Glenn both signed to John Verner, J.P., 13 Mar. 1801. Rec: 13 Sep. 1801.

Pages 342-344: I, Robert Hamon borrowed $160 from Robert Anderson, Esq. and have given bond for $324, condition for payment of $162 payable in 12 months, with interest and now mortgage one negro boy named Sam, near 12 years old. If debt paid in 12 months sd. Sam reverts back to Robert Hamon during which time sd. negro boy is to remain in possession of Hamon. Date: 2 Jul. 1799. Wit: Jas. C. Oneilly(?). Rec: 16 Oct. 1801.

Pages 344-346: 28 Dec. 179_, Jacob Holland to Alexander angilly(?) ____ lbs. stg. 1_ acres conveyed by James Holland on Big Beaverdam ____ granted 16 ___ 1787 ____ Moses Guest made oath to William Cleveland,JP, 18 Dec. 1797. Isaac Chaney and Richard Maynard signed as witnesses. Rec: 28 Nov. 1801.

Pages 346-347: 30 Nov. 1801, William Thompson to Drury Thompson for Ł 100 stg. for 300 acres bd. on E. by Joseph Culton, on N. by Thomas Drennan, on W. by John Drennan and Lewis Edwards, on S. by John Moore and King, part of 2 tracts granted William Thompson; 1 of 300 acres granted by Benj. Guerard, 15 Oct. 1784, recorded Bk. ZZZ, p. 330; the other of 543 acres by Wm. Moultrie, 10 Nov. 1786, recorded Bk. OOOO, p. 297, where William Thompson formerly lived. Signed: Wm. Thompson, Mary Thompson. Wit: D. McCaleb, John Thompson. David McCaleb made oath to John B. Earle, C.P.D. 11 Dec. 1801. (No recording date).

Pages 348-349: 9 Dec. 1799, James Maxwell of Macklinburg Co., N. C. to John Elkins of Franklin Co., Ga. for $150 for 130 acres in Pendleton Dist. _____ James McCullum made oath to John Verner, J.P., and swore Richd. Allen was a witness. Date: 16 May 1801. Rec: 4 Jan. 1802.

Pages 349-351: 27 ___ 1801, Moses Harris to John Gibson for $150 for 300 acres on Cane Creek of Tugalo, bd. by sd. Gibson, N. by Dunkin McKinsey, NW by Alis Woods, W. land laid out to James Clarke, now in possession of sd. Harris, also Featherbeds, cows, calves, hogs,pots and kettles, quantity of corn and tobacco. Wit: James Jenkins, William Dickson. James Jenkins made oath to John Taylor, Q.U., 30 Dec. 1801. Rec: 30 Dec. 1801.

Pages 351-352: I, John Griffen for $1,600 sold to John Taylor 320 acres, part of 640 acres granted Goldin Findley and sold by him to Richard Griffen and by Griffen to me, 24 Aug. 1798. Date: 4 Jan. 1802. Wit: James Wood, James Williams, Alexander Kilpatrick. Alexander Kilpatrick made oath to John B. Earle, C.P.D., 6 Jan. 1802. Plat shows land bd. on NE by John Hunter, Wm. Shackleford, on NE by Thos. ____(faded), on S. by James Griffen.

Pages 354-355: I, David Grimes of Pendleton Dist. to James White of Pickensville, Pendleton Dist. sorrel horse, branded on rear shoulder "R: and on rear buttock "H". Date: 15 Sep. 1801. Wit: Michael Smith (no oath nor recording date).

Page 355: I have agreed to let David Grimes have above described sorrell horse until Christmas next for use of 2 s. 4 p. stg. ____ , 15 Sep.1801. (cannot read witnesses). Rec: 13 Oct. 1801.

253

Pages 355-359: 1 Mar. 1793, Arthur McAdoo, yeoman, to William Gilham, planter, for ₺ 70 stg. for 200 acres on both sides of 12 Mile River, granted 25 Jan. 1785, recorded Bk. CCCC, p. 40. Wit: James Cannon, Jesse Hillen and John Upton. James Cannon made oath to J. Miller, J.P., 29 Apr. 1793. Rec: 13 Jul. 1802.

Pages 354-356: (Repeated).

Pages 359-361: 12 Nov. 1793, Ebonezer Fain to John Sutton(or Sitton) for ₺ 20 stg. for 100 acres, part of 918 acres granted 1 Oct. 1797 by Thos. Pinckney, in Washington Dist. on N. fork of Blyth's Branch, bd. on NE and NW by Williamson and Moffitt, on SW and SE by John Kelly. Wit: Alex Hunter, Jno. McAdams. John McAdams made oath to Robert Bowen, J.P., 28 Feb.1795. (Cannot read recording date).

Pages 361-362: 13 Sep. 1793, Lawrence Brandley (also Bradley) to John Sutton for ₺ 10 stg. for 100 acres granted 21 Jan. 1785 by Benj. Guerard to William Williamson for 300 acres in Washington Dist. on Saluda River, on N. fork of Blyth's branch, bd. by Williamson. Wit: Ambros Bradley, John Thomas. Ambros Bradley made oath to Robert Bowen, J. P., 19 Mar. 1796. (No recording date).

Pages 363-365: I, Alexander Hamilton for $100 sold to George Cannimore 100 acres in Washington Dist. on 18 Mile Creek of the Savannah River, part of a tract granted Larkin(?) Leonard by Thos. Pinckney, conveyed to Hamilton by John Leonard, bd. corner "commonly known as Samuel Dickson's corner", Mary Leonard, crossing Parrises Old Road. Date: 24 Mar. 1798. Wit: Wm. Hamilton, Edmond Parsons. Jean (X) Hamilton, wife of Alexander Hamilton released dower to John Wilson, J. P., 12 Apr. 1798. William Hamilton made oath to John Wilson, J. P., 12 Apr. 1798. (Cannot read recording date).

Pages 365-366: I, James Turner for ___ lbs. sold to Thomas Buchannan _____ granted by Benjamin Guerard, 15 Oct. 1784(?) on Great Generostee of Savannah River. Date: 9 Apr. 1796. Wit: Isaac Steele, John Bowhannon. (Cannot read oath). Rec: 17 Dec. 1801.

Pages 366-367: 3 Aug. 17__, Alexander Keith and his wife to Samuel Bowen (or Rowen) both of Pickensville, Pendleton Co. for ₺ 40 stg. for 150 acres on Middle Fork of Beaverdam of Tugaloo River in Pickensville Dist., bd. NW by land laid out for Daniel Keith, on SW by William Liddle, granted Alexander Keith by Wm. Moultrie. Signed: Alexander Keith, Agnes (X) Keith. Wit: George Sheilds, William Barron. William Barron made oath to William Nevil, J. P., 25 Jan. 1794. (No recording date).

Pages 367-368: I, James Swan of Logan Co., Ky., empowered John Gibson to be my lawful Attorney to collect debts owed to me. (rest unreadable).Oath dated 10 Feb. 1801 to Wm. Cleveland, J. P. Rec: 12 Feb. 1802.

Pages 369-370: I, Isaac Steel for $200 sold to Joseph _____ _____ acres _____ granted Steel 10 Oct. 1784; also ___ acres granted Widow Black _____ _____ Martha Steel, wife of Isaac Steel released dower to Joshua Saxon, 27 Mar. 1800. (No oath).

Pages 370-371: _____ Date: __ Aug. 1801. Signed: ____ Tucker, Mary (X) Tucker. Wit: ____ _____, Collum Price. Cullum (X) Price made oath he saw Charles Tucker and Mary Tucker sign deed and that Clayton Pashel(?) and Thomas Lay also signed as witnesses. Date: 14 Aug. 1801. John Barton,

(Pages 370-371 cont'd):   J. P., Rec: 5 Feb. 1802.

Pages 371-372:   I, William Hunter for $35 sold to James Steveson _____ acres on Beaver(?) Creek, bd. Bruce(?), Ellinor Pickens, James Dobbins and _____. Date: 10 Oct. 1801. (Cannot read witnesses). _ Oct. 1801, Samuel Cherry(?) made oath, Leonard Anderson(?) was a witness. J. B. Earle, J. P. (cannot read dates).

Pages 372-373:   I, John McKenzie(?) for Ł 50 stg. sold to James Carwine(?) 100 acres part of 400 acres granted Jacob Miligan(?) on Big Beaverdam Crk of Tugalo, bd. by John Tapley, Thos. Farrar. Date: 7 Feb. 1799. Wit: John Pinkerton _____. John Pinkerton made oath and Samuel Rowan was also witness. (Cannot read J. P. or dates).

Pages 373-374:   _____ unto Robert Portwood 247 acres on S. side of Conoross Creek of Keowee River, bd. by land laid out to James Ingran, granted Ingran 1 Jan. 1787 by Wm. Moultrie. Date: _ Oct. 1801. Signed: Benjamin Ingram. Wit: John Harris, Andrew Harris, James Ingram. James Ingram made oath to John Harris, J. P., _ Oct. 1801. Rec: 4 Feb. 1802.

Pages 374-377:   13 Feb. 1802, Craven Moffett of Washington Co. Ga. to Phillip Sutton of Buncombe Co., N. C. for Ł 30 stg. for 200 acres granted 1 Aug. 1785 by Wm. Moultrie to Moffett, on Crooked Creek, Pendleton Co. _____. Wit: Joseph Maxwell, Nancy Moffett. Joseph Maxwell made oath to John Taylor, J. P., 16 Oct. 1802. (1801?). Rec: 15 Feb. 1802.

Pages 377-378:   _____ Robert Dickason mentioned. _____ David Moore made oath he saw James Mitture(?) sign deed with Joseph Jolly and Matthew Dickason as witnesses. Date: 26 Dec. 1801. John Taylor, JP, Rec: 26 Dec. 1801.

Page 379:   _____. Wit: Robert Portwood, John Mitchell, George Vandever. Robert Portwood made oath to John Harris, J.P., 13 Jan. 1802. Rec: 4 Feb. 1802.

Page 380:   _____. Wit: Marthy Aden, Bennet Aden. Bennet Aden made oath he saw Joshua Young sign conveyence to Israel Blag(?), 3 Oct. 1801. Michael Dickson, J. P. Rec: 13 Oct. 1801.

Page 381:   _____ Robert White signed deed. James Carrick made oath _____. Peter Keys, J. P. Rec: 24 Oct. 1801.

Page 382:   Alexander Ramsey for $200 _____

Pages 382-383:   Bill of Sale _____ to James White _____ brands R and H. Date: 15 Sep. 1801. Signed: David Grimes. Wit: Michael Smith. (Note: see p. 354 as this appears to be the same).

Pages 383-384:   _____ mentions Alexander Hamilton. Dower signed by Jean (X) Hamilton, 10 Feb. 1802. John Wilson, J. P. Rec: 13 Feb. 1802.

Page 385:   (Unreadable).......Oath _____ see George Forbes suscribe his name. Signed: Michael Warnock. Rec: 17 Feb. 1802.

Page 386:   (Unreadable).....Oath mentions Thomas Cooker(?). Signed: Jonathan Clark. Rec: 17 Feb. 1802.

Page 387:   (Unreadable).....signed: John Taylor (Seal).

Page 388:   (This number was skipped).

Page 389:   (Unreadable).

Pages 389-390:   I, Israel Blag(?) for Ł 40 stg. sold to Lewis
                             D. Martin .....(rest is unreadable).

Pages 390-392:   I, John Boyd for $100 sold to George Canamur
                             (rest of deed is unreadable)...Signed: John
                             Boyd. Wit: _____ Hamilton, George Boyd.....
Mary Boyd, wife of John Boyd released dower to John Wilson, J.Q., Jan.
1802. William Hamilton made oath to John Wilson, J.Q., 5 Jan. 1802.
Rec: 11 Jan. 1802.

Pages 392-393:   5 Jun. 1801, John Green to Elizabeth Smith for
                             Ł 30 stg. for 75 acres on Rocky Creek of Sa-
                             vannah River, bd. George Anderson, John Green,
Keowee Road _____. Wit: Daniel (X) Pitman(?), Andrew Berkley. Dan-
iel Pitman made oath to Robert McCann, J.P., 19 Nov. 180_.
Rec: 5 Jan. 1802.

Pages 393-394:   I, James Black for divers causes appoint Dav-
                             id Watters(?) my lawful Attorney to collect
                             sums of Money due me (rest unreadable)......
Date: 4 Jan. 1802. (No witnesses recorded). Thos. Black made oath to
John Taylor, J.P., 11 Jan. 1802.
Rec: 11 Jan. 1802.

Pages 395-396:   (Cannot read this.......mentions John Robert-
                             son, _____ Calhoun,.....probably land des-
                             cription) _____ sd. John Ewing Calhoun, his
heirs and assigns. Date: 2 Nov. 1801. (Cannot read signature). Wit: B.
Green, William Anderson. Benjamin Green made oath to J. B. Earle, J. P.,
and that he saw James Millwee sign deed. Plat: (unreadable) certified
28 Dec. 1788 by James Millwee, D.S.
Rec: 2 Nov. 1801.

Pages 396-397:   I, Benjamin Ingram for $100 sold to Lewis D.
                             Martin (no acreage) tract in Pendleton Dist.,
                             formerly 96 Dist. on Conoross Creek of Keowee
River, bd. N. by Lewis D. Martin, NW by Austin, SW by Charles Hunt, S.
by Lewis D. Martin, E. by James Ingram. (Cannot read date). Wit: David
Hammon(?), William Dennis(?). (No oath).
Rec: 10 Feb. 1802.

Pages 397-398:   I, Robert Smith for $100 sold to Asa Kemp 300
                             (?) acres on both sides of Conoross Creek of
                             Keowee River, bd. E. by Major Boyse(?),grant-
ed George Warley _____ a record of a bond given to Calt. George
Warley for titles to above land to Robert Smith, recorded Pendleton Co.,
Bk. D, p. 234, 24 Jun. 1796 _____: Dower released by Elizabeth Smith,
11 Dec. 1801. John Taylor, J.Q. Receipt to J. B. Earle.
Rec: 12 Dec. 1801.

Pages 398-399:   _____ unto James McAdams, his
                             heirs and assigns. Date: 26 Jan. 1802. Signed
                             by James L.(?) Guignand. Wit: Andw. Boddan,
R. H. Waring.....Richland Dist., Andrew Boddan made oath to __ Taylor,
J. P., 6 Jan. 1802. (Cannot read recording date).

Pages 399-400:   _____ (unreadable) __ dollars sold to H. Hun-
                             nicutt 150 acres in Pendleton, on 26 Mile Crk.
                             of Savannah River, granted Eli Hunnicutt, bd.
_____ Calhoun to Hickory Branch, Robert Parker, to a big survey belong-
ing to General Anderson, part of tract granted Ely Hunnicutt by William
Moultrie, 4 Dec. 1786. Date: 14 Jan. 1802. Signed: Eli Hunnicutt. Wit:
James Mulwee, Anthony (+) Dickason. Anthony Dickason made oath to J. B.
Earle, CPD, 15 Dec. 1802. (Cannot read recording date).

Page 400: (Cannot read).......on Coffy Creek, 206 acres granted William Shelby, 20 Oct. 1797, sold by Shelby to John Swords. Wit: John Swancy, Elizabeth Swancy. John Swancy made oath to John B. Earle, CPD, 25 Aug.1801. Rec: 24 Jan. 1802.

Page 401: 17 Dec. 1800, Samuel Lofton, Jr. to Charles Williams for Ł 15 for 200 acres granted Lofton 2 Apr. 1798, on branches of 12 Mile River ...Wit: John G. Lofton, Samuel Carlile. Samuel Carlile made oath to J. B. Earle, CPD, 13 Nov. 1801. Rec: 13 Nov. 1801.

Page 402: 9 Sep. 1801, William Thompson to Benjamin Barton for $50 for 300 acres, bd. by Robert Torrens. Signed: Wm. (+) Thompson. Wit: _____ Wardlaw, Adam H. Thompson. James Wardlaw made oath to David Murphree, J. P., 1 Dec. 1801. Rec: 30 Dec. 1801.

Page 403: I, Jane _____ give and deliver the following property to James Hallums (list of household items too dim to read) ___ and money due him from the Estate of William Hallums. _ Feb. 1801. (Appears to be Jane Payne who signed.) Wit: B. Starrat, Robert Walker. Robert Walker made oath to J. B. Earle, CPD, 21 Feb. 1801. Rec: 21 Feb. 1801.

Pages 403-404: I, Abner Honie for $300 sold to William Honie 400 acres on Big Creek, granted William Honie, Sr. by Charles Pinckney, 1 Oct. 1792. (Cannot read date). Wit: Thomas Honie, Wm. (+) Honie. Thomas Honie made oath to William Hall, J.P., 3 Oct. ____. Rec: 24 Oct. 18__.

Pages 404-405: I, Amos Kilburn(?) of Pendleton Dist. to Samuel Earle, Esq. of Greenville Dist. for Ł 15 stg. for 50 acres on W. branch of Keowee River, part of tract granted Major Parsons, bd. by sd. Earle _____ (rest unreadable).

Pages 405-406: _____ Sutherland for $200(?) _____ for 150 acres on 23 Mile Creek, "except small part supposed to be held in an old right of Robert Anderson, Jr." being a grant to Samuel(?) Robison by Chas. Pinckney _____. Wit: John Sutherland, Hollinsworth Vandiver. John Sutherland made oath to John Harris, J. P., 15 Oct. 1800. Rec: 3 Feb. 1802. Hollinsworth Vandiver also made oath.

Pages 406-407: William Stevenson(?) of Pendleton Dist. for $375 sold to William Richardson of Abbeville Dist. a negro boy named Bob about 14 years of age, 4 feet, 5 inches high _____. Oath signed by Alex Sherard. Nathan Lusk, J. P.

Pages 407-408: I, Bennet Combs for $550 sold to James Wardlaw 240 acres _____(unreadable).

Pages 408-409: I, James _____ Right name Daniel Puttman my attorney to demand from William Childers note granted me in my name 12 Apr. 1796, due 1 Sep. 1797 and a bond granted me from Joel Calliham due 28 Apr. 1796(?) ...... Oath dated 21 Nov. 1801. Rec: 17 Dec. 1801.

Page 409 (numbered 409 again): _____(unreadable) a negro man, one other negro girl named Hannah to sd. Benjamin _____ (Harrison in oath) after my decease and that of my wife, Caty Harrison, during his life then sd. negros to (descend?) to William Langford, son of Hetty Langford, also the house property and

(Page 409 cont'd): and stock that I, Thomas Harrison have given to sd. Benjamin _____. Signed: Thomas Harrison. Wit: _____, Richard Shipp. Richard Shipp made oath to William Cleveland, J. P., 14 Jan. 1801.
Rec: 24 Feb. 1802.

Pages (409)-411: 3 Nov. 1785, Francis Bonneau, of Charleston, house carpenter and Hannah Bonnear, his wife, to John Ewing Calhoun for £ 120 stg. _____
..........Signed: Francis Bonneau, Hannah Bonneau. Wit: Benj. Waller, Benj. Elfe(?) (Ellis?) _____

Page 411: (Unreadable).........(deed).....Personally appeared _____ Shipp before William Cleveland, a Justice, being sworn said he saw Thomas Harrison sign within deed to Jacob _____, 14 Jan. 1802.
Rec: 24 Feb. 1802.

Pages 411-412: For consideration of good will and affection to my son, Benjamin Harrison, grant to him 200 acres on Tugalo River ......(unreadable).
Signed: Thomas (X) Harrison. (rest unreadable).

Pages 412-414: (Unreadable).........bargain and sell to Asa Kemp 200 acres on Keowee River on both sides of Little Beaverdam Creek of Tugaloo River, granted Tucker Woodson(?), 3 Apr. 1786 by Wm. Moultrie. Signed: Henry Wm. Desaussure. (Cannot read witnesses).........Eliza Desaussure, wife of Henry W. Desaussure, released dower to _____, 1 May 1800. Receipt was for £ 135 stg. Wit: Major Parsons. Major Parsons made oath to John Harris, J. P._____ (dates unreadable).

Pages 414-415: (Unreadable).........John A. Miller _____ Capt. John Tippen(?) form myself and my heirs. Signed: James Sloan. Wit: James Long, James Hannah, John A. Miller.......Margaret Hannah (sic) released dower to Elijah Browne, J. P. (rest unreadable).

Pages 415-416: _____(unreadable)_____ for 58 acres _____ sd. Benjamin Cleveland and his heirs we the heirs of Larkin Cleveland, Deceased,................Date: 25 Nov. 1801. Wit: Rezen Sprigg, William Brooks. Heirs: William Cleveland, John Cleveland, Nell (or Neil) Cleveland, John McDaniel, Jeremiah Cleveland, Benjamin Harrieson, Mary Cleveland .....(rest is unreadable)....

Pages 416-417: (Unreadable)......sold to John Bynum, 24 Jan. 1799. Signed: Patrick McDowall. Wit: Noah Cennemur, Jas. McCracken. Plat is for 640 ac. on 12 Mile Creek, bd. on all sides by vacant land. Receipt is for £45 stg. Noah Cannimur made oath to R. Bowen, J. P., _____.
Rec: 13 Oct. 1801.

Pages 417-418: I, Thomas Milsap for $200 sold to Stephen Holoway, 80 acres on S. side of Rocky River, bd. by James Thompson, John Tinsley, granted John Johnston, recorded Bk. B, no. 5, p. 349. Date: 18 Feb. 1801. Wit: Winston Hall, Lent Hall, John Hall. Lent Hall made oath to E. Browne, J.Q., 3 Aug. 180_. Kezia Milsap, wife of Thomas Milsap released dower to E. Browne, 8 Aug. 1801.
Rec: 3 Oct. _____.

Pages 418-419: Washington Dist., I, William Jackson and Sarah, my wife, for $350 sold to John McFall 200 acres in 96 Dist. on Rocky River, granted to Mary Smith by Wm. Moultrie, 5 Jun. 1786, transferred to William Jackson 7 Feb. 1799, part of 207 acres surveyed by John McMahen, D.S. Date: 7 May 1800. Signed: Wm. Jackson, Sarah Jackson. Wit: John Reeves, Jr., John Reeves, Sr. John Reeves, Jr. made oath to Patrick Norris, J.P., 21 May 1800.
Rec: 2 Sep. 1802.

Pages 419-420:   I, James Dinson, planter, for $200 sold John Rush that part of property be it in negros or whatever kind belonging to me and my wife... (not named), part of the Estate of Mrs. Margaret Sinkler, deceased, in Prince William County, Virginia. Date: 11 Aug. 1801. Signed: James Dinson. (only). Wit: John Adair, Joseph Hunnicutt. John Adair made oath to Joseph Reed, J. P., 29 Aug. 1801.
Rec: 30 Aug. 1801.

Pages 420-421:   I, John Buckanon for ___ lbs. sold to Edward Cox 200 acres on Tugaloo River, granted Ezekiel Adams, 15 Sep. 1785. Date: 26 Mar. 1801. Wit: Joseph Evans, Robert Looney. Robert Looney made oath to William Cleveland, J. P., 6 Apr. 1801.
Rec: 12 Oct. 1801.

Page 421:   I, Jehu Reed for $20 sold to William Fortune 75 acres on Cain Creek of Tugalo River, bd. by Pendleton Isbell and Callaway, part of grant to Joshua Eckels, 1794. Date: 7 Jul. 1801. Wit: Thomas Harbin, Francis Callaway. Francis Callaway made oath to William Cleveland, J.P., 17 Dec. 1800. Rec: 12 Oct. 1801.

Page 422:   I, Daniel Ross of the Cherokee Nation for $130 sold to Thomas Caridine of Pendleton Co. 250 acres on Martin's Creek of Seneca River, part of 791 acres granted Alexander Dromgoole, 4 Jul. 1791 by Chas. Pinckney. Recorded Bk. C, no. 5, p. 140(?). ...the sd. 250 acres conveyed from Dromgoole to Daniel Ross. Date: 30 Nov. 1799. Wit: Sarah Earle, John Glenn. Sarah Earle made oath to John B. Earle, CPD, 4 Oct. 1801.
Rec: 4 Oct. 1801.

Pages 422-423:   10 Mar. 1800, Thomas Field to Isaac Hill for $80 for 250 acres ......(unreadable).......... Amos Richards made oath to Henry Burch, _____.
Rec: __ Aug. 1801.

Pages 423-424:   I, James Johns(?) of Marion(?) Co., S. C. for $50 sold to Thomas Hamilton of Greenville Dis. 206 acres on George's Creek of Saluda River.. .....(rest unreadable).

Pages 424-425:   _____Warnock(?) _____(unreadable).....on 23 Mile Creek, part of tract granted Hugh Wornock, 1 May 1786.....(rest unreadable)......

Pages 425-426:   I, Jonathan Moore for $100 sold to Charles __ _____ 100 acres part of tract granted Benjamin Clardy, bd. by Green, Mathias Richardson, _____(unreadable)_____.

Page 426:   (Unreadable)......Hugh Rogers ___Oct. 1801... Margaret Rogers, wife of Hugh Rogers, Hugh Rogers, Jr., his assigns to maintain his mother _____. Signed: Jacob Capehart, William Shackleford, Moses Payne, Adam Rogers. Wit: _____ Robinson, William Pasmore. Ephraim Robinson made oath to John B. Earle, CPD, 2 Nov. 1801.
Rec: 2 Nov. 1801.

Page 427:   (Unreadable).........Wit: Samuel Cherry, James Stephenson. James Stephenson made oath to J. B. Earle, __ Oct. 1801.

Pages 427-428:   I, William Hart (or Hort), of City of Charleston for $500 sold to Aaron Broyles(?) of Pendleton Co., 640 acres on NE side of Broadmouth Creek of Saluda River, bd. SW by Joseph Brown, granted William Hart, 15 Oct. 1784; also, 628 acres in 96 Dist. on Broadmouth Creek, bd. by Hugh Brown, Dr. Osiphant...(rest unreadable). Wit: _____, Dr. James Ravenell. Dr. James Ravenell made oath to Quartermas B. Darby (in Charles-

(Pages 427-428 cont'd):   ton?), 18 Jan. 180_. Rec: 15 Oct. 1801.

Pages 428-429:   I, Little James Hamilton of Pendleton Dist. for $250 sold to Abel Anderson of Bunkum(sic) Co., N. C., 200 acres on 23 Mile Creek of the Savannah River, granted Samuel Oliver, 2 Oct. 1786. Wit: William Hamilton, James Anglin, A. C. J. Anderson. Archibald Cook Johnston Anderson made oath to John Wilson, J.Q., 1 Oct. 1801. Rec: 15 Oct. 1801.

Pages 429-430:   I, James Denson, planter, for divers causes appoint my trusty friend, John Rusk, stonemason, my attorney to recover from Margaret Sinkler, her heirs, executors of Prince William Co., Va., all part of estate belonging to James Denson and wife, in negros or whatever property _____. Date: 11 Aug. 1801. Wit: John Adair, Joseph Hunnicutt. John Adair made oath to Joseph Reid, J. P., 26 Aug. 1801. Rec: 30 Aug. 1801.

Pages 430-431:   I, Hezekiah Rice for $464 sold to Wm. Stanton 125(?) acres bd. by Saluda River _____ Date: 12 Feb. 1800. Wit: Ezekiel Watkins, Thomas Crow. Ezekiel Watkins made oath to William Hall, J. P., 12 Jul. 1801. Rec: 12 Jul. 1801.

Pages 431-433:   I, James Scott for $800 sold to Abner McMillian 200 acres on Saluda River, granted 6 Mar. _____. Date: 7 May 1800. Wit: Robt. McCann, John Robinson, Charles Wilson. Nancy Scott released dower to John Wilson, J. Q., _____ 1800. Robt. McCann made oath to John Wilson. (No dates).

END OF BOOK F

Note: The first index to Book F is badly written and faded. It has been marked out and some thoughtful clerk with a clear handwriting has recopied it. He and I don't agree on the spelling of some names. I am including this grantor index because much of this book is unreadable. Pages of the index were not microfilmed in order, there are some page numbers that I couldn't make out as they were in the fold and couldn't be verified as the pages themselves were unreadable.....BW

Askew, Samuel to Hugh Bruster	54	(Numbers are same as in the
Abel, Ezekiel to Wm. Thompson	77	original book)
Alexander, Jno. to Saml. Black	112	
Adams, Thos. to Roger Murphy	132	
Beckman, Saml. to Andrew Bodden	44	
Buckhannon, Wm. to Ebnz. Buckhannon	51	
Barnett, Ambrose to Nathl. Davis	74	
Broyles, Josh to Hutson & Harkin	83	
Boyd, Wm. to David Stephenson	84	
Boyd, Jno. to Geo. Boyd	86	
Bell, Walter to Cannon Brazeal	87	
Buckhannon, Jno. to Robt. Glenn	95	
Bishop, Jones to Henry Wilbanks	98	
Baulham, Jacob to Jno. Dearing	104	
Boyd, Jas. P. to Francis DeBlock	140	
Boggs, Rob. to John Young	142	
Bell, Walter to G. Dilworth	151	
Boren, Wm. to Jno. Fields, Sr.	178	
Brooks, Geo. to Jas. Shockley	182	
Butler, Wm. to David Hembree	185	
Brown, Jno. to Jas. Merritt	202	
Boggs to Young	242	
Buckhannon, Chas. to Rich. Gray	353	
Bradley, Laurence to Jno. Sutton	361	
Blagg, Israel to L. D. Martin	389	
Boyd, Jno. to Geo. Cennemore	390	
Black, Jas. to David Watkins	393	

(Original Index cont'd):

Bonneau, Hannah to J. E. Calhoun	409
Buckhannon, Jno. to Edw. Cox	420
Blair, Margaret to Michl. Warnock	424
Cunningham, Jas. to Abm. Nally	33
Capehart, Jacob et al to Hugh Rogers	41
Combs, Bennet to Jno. Chapman	45
Commissioners to Jno. Adair	45
Commissioners to Geo. Capehart	46
Commissioners to Wm. Shackleford	46
Commissioners to Jno. Taylor	47
Commissioners to Jno. B. Earle	48
Cox, Henry to Polly Cox	64
Commissioners to Jno. Hunter	65
Cannon, Jno. to Peter Finn	67
Castleberry, Mark to Jno. Holcum	81
Crowder, Martha to I. January	93
Cunningham, Jas. to Wm. Copeland	100
Combs, Bennet to Nathl. Newman	128
Commissioners to Thos. Hunter	130
Commissioners to Wm. Hunter	131
Commissioners to D. McCaleb	132
Clardy, Benj. to M. Richardson	147
Commissioners to S. Cherry	176
Clements, Jas. to Jno. Griffen	193
Cox, Geo. to Jas. Merritt	199
Cox, Jno. to Beverly Cox	201
Coker, Thos. to Wm. Coker	337
Chiles, Moses to Wm. Young	340
Combs, Bennet to Jas. Wardlaw	407
Cleveland, Wm. & others to Ben. Cleveland	415
Delaney, Danl. to Jas. Smith	76
Drennan, Jas. to R. & P. Young	133
Desaussure, H. W. to Wm. Guest	147
Duncan, Jos. to Jas. Powell	176
Duncan Rice (surname Rice) to Jas. Powell	177
Deering, Jno. to Jacob Bokman	195
Dickson, Math., Jr. to Mathew Dickson, Sr.	316
Doran, Jas. to Henry Kyle	389
Desausure, H. W. to Asa Kemp	412
Denson, Jas. to John Rusk	419
Denson, Jas. to John Rusk	429
Earle, Baylis to Jno. Cochran	54
Eaton, Joseph to Rob. Beaty	100
Edmondson, Wm. to Frs. Bremar	107
Edmondson, Wm. to Frs. Bremar	108
Easley, Rob. to Caty Benson	290
Forbes, Geo. to David Watkins	18
Faust, Danl. to Andw. Bodden	42
Fowler, Wm. to Benoni Fowler	103
Finley, Thos. & Wm. to Henry Garner	109
Farrar, Thos. to Wm. Sullivant	118
Farmer, Benj. to S. Cobb	169
Farrar, Thos. to Patr. Duncan	172
Fley, Saml. to Aug. H. Hyndman	210
Farrar, Thos. to David Sloan	233
Fields, Thos. to James Slater	245
Fields, Thos. to James Slater	24
Furse, Jas. to Saml. Taylor	249
Farrow, Jno. to Briton Farrow	308
Farrow, Perrin to Jas. Parkhadur	314
Fain, Ebenezer to John Sutton	359

(Above is listed Pain in index, but is clearly Fain in text).

Forbis, Geo. to U. & E. Forbes	386
Fowler, Jerh. to Moses Jones	398

(Original Index cont'd):

Gray, Jesse to Peter Aker	12
Grisham, Jno. to Simon Doyle	30
Gorman, Thos. to Robt. Portwood	39
Green, Henry to Benj. Clardy	62
George, Jno. to Richard George	111
Green, Henry to Isaac Davenport	138
Garrett, Dickeson to Culliver Clements	116
Guess, Henry to Wm. Eddins	186
Grisham, Jno. to Jno. McCutchin	198
Gillaspy, Wm. to John Brown	272
Griffen, Jno. to Jno. Taylor	351
Grimes, David to Jno. White	354
Green, Jno. to Elizabeth Smith	392
Guignard, Jas. to Jas. McAdams	398
Hallum, Jno. to Elias Hollingsworth	21
Hawks, Fras. to Saml. Earle	26
High, David to Joab Mauldin	32
Harris, Ben. to A. Nally	34
Harris, Ben. to A. Nally	36
Humphries, Geo. to Col. Green (also listed Umphries)	50
Humphries, Geo. to Aledness Green	70
Harris, Jno. to Wm. Reid	71
Herring, Isaac to Jos. Smith	75
Holden, Thos. to Wm. McGregory	89
Humphries, Geo. to Jerh. Foster	92
Harper, Saml. to Saml. Harbin	117
Humphries, Geo. to John Clardy	125
Huggins, Ambrose to Saml. Moore	153
Hallum, Wm. to Math. Richardson	162
Hembree, Wm. to Peter Laboon	198
Hart, Jno. to Saml. Robinson	215
Hughs, Jas. to Henry Guess	243
Hillion, Jesse to Peter Reese	250
Hickman, Ben. to Luke Smith	277
Harrison, Thos. to Wm. Cleveland	310
Hamon, Robt. to Robt. Anderson	342
Holland, Jacob to Alexr. Alagilly (or Angilly)	344
Harris, Moses to John Gibson	349
Hamilton, Alexr. to Geo. Cannimore	363
Hunter, Wm. to Jas. Stevenson	371
Hamilton, Alex. to Andw. Hamilton	383
Harvick, Jacob to Nicholas Harvick	385
Hunnicutt, Eli to H. Hunnicutt	399
Honie, Abner to Wm. Honie	403
Harrison, Thos. to Ben. Harrison	409
Harrison, Thos. to Jacob Holland	411
Harrison, Thos. to Ben. Harrison	411
Hunnicutt, Jas. to Jno. Tippen	414
Hill, Isaac to Thos. Fields	422
Hart, Wm. to Aaron Broyles	427
Hunter, Wm. to Wm. Anderson	427
Hamilton, Jas. to Abel Anderson	428
James, Wm. to Adam Rogers	29
James, Aaron to Beniston Barton	88
Jenkins, Jno. to Rose Reese	124
Jenson, Reubin to Wm. Harper	144
Johnson, Jonth. to Rob. Powell	138
Ingram, Jas. to Rob. Portwood	373
Ingram, Jas. to L. D. Martin	396
Jackson, Wm. to Jno. McFall	418
Jones, James to Tho. Hamilton	423
Kelton, Nichl. to Larkin Tarrant	20
Kemp, Jonth. to Jno. Harris	96
Kitchens, Nathl. to Simon Doyle	126
Kitchens, Nathl. to Simon Doyle	128

(Original Index cont'd):

Kerr, Jno. to Saml. Robinson	217
Keys, Jno. to Rob. Looney	247
King, T. Wm. to Thos. Stribling	297
Keith, Agneth to Saml. Bowen	366
Kilbourne, Amos to Saml. Earle	404
Laurence, Ben. to John Knox	24
Laurence, Ben. to John Knox	26
Laffoon, Wm. to Jno. Blerdin	52
(appears to be Bledso to me)	
Lince, Henry to Stephen Roberts	55
Lofton, John Guy deposition	146
Low, Wm. to Maths. Richardson	160
Lindley, Sarah to Wm. Harper	160
Lehere, Thos. to Saml. Robinson	211
Lacy, H. Wm. to Wm. Cockerham	262
Ley, Francis to Jos. Jolly	279
Lesley, Wm. to Jos. Pickens	295
Lofton, G. Jno. to Wm. McDow	312
Lofton, Saml. to Chas. Williams	401
Miller, Jno. to Saml. D. Terrell	4
McCaleb, David to Wm. Steele	9
Moore, Rob. to Jesse Gray	13
McCaleb, Wm. to Israel Gillison	37
McCollister, Math. to Frs. McCollister	38
Moore, Jacob to Andw. Bodden	41
McCaleb, Wm. to John Doss	56
McCaleb, Jas. to Davd. McCaleb	67
McCaleb, Wm. to Davd. McCaleb	69
Martin, Jno. to Davd. Dickey	79
Mauldin, Joab to Jas. Shirley	101
McMillion, Alex. to Wm. McGregory	105
Mills, Henry to Jas. Mills	110
Mattison, Jas. to Ben. Mattison	110
McCaleb, Jas. to Dav. McCaleb	114
McWhorter, Henry to Saml. Love	115
McCaleb, Davd. to Geo. Capehart	117
McCaleb, Jas. to Dd. McCaleb	120
Montgomery, Hugh to Folkner	142
Mayfield, Elijah to Edwin Rain	150
McCollister, Jesse to Selah McCollister	187
McMahan, Peter to Dd. Welch	189
Miller, Jane to Henry Dodson	190
McCollister, Danl. to Robt. McCollister	225
McCann, Rob. to Field Peutt	
Moore, Levi to Richd. Nall	244
Maxwell, Mary & Rob Anderson to John Terrell	250
Moore, Eliab to Jacob Holland	258
McCaleb, Davd. to Jacob Chamble	332
Martin, Barkley to Jas. Young	269
Maxwell, Rob. to Jno. Elkins	348
McDow, Arthur to Wm. Gilham	355
McKinsee, Jno. to Jas. Carodine	372
Moffet, Craven to Phil. Sutton	374
Moffet, Craven to Phil. Sutton	376
Millwee, Jas. to Rob. Dickson	378
McDowell, Patk. to Jno. Bynum	416
Milsap, Thos. to Stephen Holaway	417
Moore, Johnth. to Obediah Green	425
Milwee, Jas. to John U. Calhoun	395
Nicholson, Wm. to Alex. Sharrar	2
Neele, Aaron to Thos. Neele	57
Neele, Aaron to Thos. & Jas. Neele	60
Neele, Aaron to L. D. Martin	73
Neele, Thos. to Edw. Kemp	160
Norwood, Jos. to Wm. Gambrell	181

(Original Index cont'd:)

Orr, Alex. to Larkin Camp	2
Oldham, Jno. to Culiver Clements	
Otwell, Wm. to Curtis Lord	18
Putman, Danl. to Mosses Liddell	19
Perkins, Nichl. to Jesse Bynum	85
Powers, Alex. to Shadr. Chandler	116
Powel, Jno. to Stephen Merritt	120
Powel, Jno. to Solomon Palmer	129
Prince, Jas. to Wm. Mullican	137
Powel, Rob. to J. C. Kilpatrick	170
Patterson, Thos. to Wm. Mitchel	190
Portman, Jno. to Dd. Sloan	192
Patterson, Thos. to Petr. Ragsdale	197
Peek, Jno. to Levi Moore	204
Patterson, Jno. to Henry Garner	205
Patterson, Jno. to Henry Garner	207
Prewit, Field to Ezl. Buffington	220
Prewit, Field to Ezl. Buffington	222
Prewit, Field to Ezl. Buffington	223
Prewit, Field to Ezl. Buffington	224
Powell, Jno. to J. C. Kilpatrick	237
Parkaden, Jas. to Jno. Farrow	306
Pain, Ebenz. to Jno. Sutton	359
(checked this - it is Fain)	
Payne, Jane to Jno. Hallum	403
Reggs, Wm. to Jas. Anderson	22
Robins, Levi to James Gray	30
Rogers, Adam to H. Rogers	41
Ross, Jno. to Wm. McGregory	88
Ross, Saml. to Danl Stephenson	90
Rose, Hugh to Wm. Reid	97
Read, Elizabeth to Wm. Reid	98
Rose, Wm. to Jno. Powel	127
Reese, Edwin to Jonth. Lindley	129
Robinson, Jno. to D. Williams	184
Rise, Chas. to Peter Edwards	188
Ragsdale, Jno. to Jno. Mitchel	194
Ragsdale, Jno. to Wm. Mitchel	195
Roach, L. Benj. to Jno. Patterson	209
Reeder, Joshua to Jno. Patterson	209
Ransay, Davd. to Saml. Robinson	218
Rose, Wm. to Jno. Singleton	240
Ramsay, H. Jos. to Wm. McPherson	246
Reese, Thos. to Saml. Barr	260
Roberts, Jno. to Jacob Capehart	269
Robertson, Jno. to Wm. Murphree	301
Renfro, Wm. to Elisha Dyar	339
Ramsey, Alex. to Wm. Shackleford	382
Reid, Jehu to Wm. Fortune	421
Ross, Danl. to Hugh Carodine	422
Rogers, Hugh to Adam Rogers	426
Rice, Hezekiah to Wm. Stanton	430
Stewart, Jas. to Jas. McCreight	11
Smith, Rob. to James Swan	60
Smith, Jos. to Peter Keys	93
Steele, Isc. to Henry Willbanks	101
Smith, Dd. to Thos. Hamilton	122
Satterfield, Jas. to Jon. Synard	145
Singleton, Jno. to Isaac James	241
Speaks, Richd. to Isc. Williams	250
Sloan, Dd. to Chas. Brandon	259
Stuart, Wm. to Amos Richardson	264
Stuart, Wm. to Wm. Nicholson	265
Stuart, Wm. to Wm. Nicholson	267
Strong, Chrs. to Wm. Hunter	273
Shirley, Wm. to Mathw. Armstrong	281
Simpson, Jno. to Sal. Anderson	284
Smith, Jos. to Wm. Stone	292

(Original Index cont'd):

Stow, Wm. to Wm. Huggins	293
Swan, Jas. to Jno. Gibson	368
Steele, Isc. to Jos. Roberts	369
Smith, Rob. to Asa Kemp	397
Shelby, Wm. to Jno. Swords	400
Sotherland, Jno. to Geo. Vandiver	405
Stevenson, Wm. to Wm. Richardson	406
Shields, Jas. to Danl. Putman	408
Scott, James to Aber McCillion	431
Thayer, Wm. to Lydia Tourtelott, Betsy and Nancy Tourtelott	1
Thomas, Jno. to Jeremiah Fields	5
Tallant, Jno. to Jno. Hallum	80
Timms, Wm. to Jno. Smith	134
Tucker, Harbert to Ben. Farmer	303
Thomas, Wm. to Drury Thompson	346
Turner, Jas. to Thos. Beauhannon	365
Tucker, Chas. to Nathl. Perry	370
Taylor, Jno. to L. D. Martin	387
Thompson, Wm. to Ben. Barton	402
Umphries, Geo. to Cornl. Green	50
VanderHorst, to Andw. Bodden	335
Vandiver, Geo. to Saml. Martin	377
Wood, M. H. to Davd. McCaleb	6
Wood, M. H. to Wm. Steele	7
Watters, Chas. to Peter Laboon	16
Whitmire, Henry to Isc. Gillison	25
Williams, Isc. to Jno. Lynch	112
Wade, David to Thos. C. Wade	176
Winn, Jno. to David Sloan	191
West, Solomon to Henry Garner	206
Wade, David to Thos. C. Wade	225
Wade, Thos. C. to David Wade, Jr.	227
Woods, Thos. to John P. Odle	230
Weekley, Jno. to Wm. King	242
Whitner, Jos. to W. Thompson	249
Wadsworth & Turpin to Michael Dickson	252
Wickley, Jno. to Wm. I. King	286
Wadsworth & Turpin to John Harris	286
Ware, Ths. to Nichs. Madgett	334
White, Robt. to Dl. Ledbetter	381
Young, Joshua to Israel Blagg	380

End of Original Index

PENDLETON DIST., S. C. CONVEYENCES

BOOK G 1801-1804

Page 1: Bill of Sale, printed by Freneau and Parne, Samuel Taylor, of Abbeville Dist. for $807 sold to Peter Keys 5 negroes to wit.......
Caesar and his wife Cela and their three children, Ceasor, Betty and Bob.
Date: 4 May 1801. Wit: D. McCaleb, John Taylor.
Rec: 4 May 1802. (No oath).

Pages 2-3: Andrew Bay for $250 sold to Elihu Hall Bay of the City of Charleston, 640 acres...... granted 16 Jul. 1784 to James Dutilly, who conveyed to me in 96 Dist. on 23 Mile Creek. Date: 15 Jul. 1801. Wit: James Scurlock, Rebeca Scurlock.......Mississippi Territory, Town of Natchez, ...James Scurlock made oath to John Henderson, Notary Public, 15 Jul. 1801.
(No recording date).

Page 4:   William Parmer to George Smelser, part of a tract granted George Shuler, bd. by William Stuart, the line of Parmer and sarah Ragland and line of Shuler and Edward Hare (Hase?) for 135 acres for $200 on Smelser Creek of Little River of the Keowee River. Date: 2 Dec. 1801. Wit: W. Nicholson, W. Brevart. William Nicholson made oath to John Barton, J. P., 9 Mar. 1802.
Rec: 9 Mar. 1802.

Pages 4-5:   Ambrose Foster for $100 sold to William King 194 acres on Conoross Creek of Keowee River, bd. by Miller. Date: 11 Jan. 1802. Wit: B. Green, James Kilpatrick. (No oath).
Rec: 9 Mar. 1802.

Pages 5-6:   William Thompson for $600 sold to Jacob Light, Sr., 270 acres on 12 Mile River, bd. by William Murphies, Archibald Boys, George Thompson, Samuel Earle. Date: 14 Dec. 1801. Wit: James Jett, E. Murphree. James Jett made oath to David Murphree, J. P., 26 Jan. 1802.
Rec: 10 Mar. 1802.

Pages 6-8:   4 Feb. 1802, Charles Lay to James and A. Beach Stephens for $400 silver (later says James Stephens and A. Beach) for 100 acres on Estertoe Creek of the Keowee River. Signed: Charles Lay, Anna Lay. Wit: J. Terrill, William H. Terrill. Joel Terrill made oath to John Cochran, J. P.
Rec: __ Mar. 1802.

Pages 8-9:   4 Feb. 1802, Charles Lay to James Stephens and A. Beach for $200 for 65 acres on Little Eastotoe, granted 31 Aug. 1791 by Charles Pinckney. Signed: Charles Lay, Anna Lay. Wit: J. Terrill, William H. Terrill. J. Terrill made oath to John Cochran, J. P., 6 Feb. 1802.
Rec: 10 Mar. 1802.

Page 9:   I, Thomas Harrison for love and good will I bear to my son-in-law, William Cleveland, one negro woman called Hannah and her increase, and one negro man called Cooper, after the death of myself and wife, Caty Harrison, with all household property and stock that I have formerly given to him. Date: 14 Jan. 1802. Signed: Thomas Harrison, Sr. Wit: J. D. Terrell, Richard Shipp. Richard Shipp made oath to John Barton, J. P., 9 Mar. 1802.
Rec: 10 Mar. 1801.

Page 10:   John Hawks for £ 5 stg. sold to Peter Weaver 100 acres on Oolonoye Creek of the Saluda River, part of 390 acres granted John Hawks by Charles Pinckney, 22 Nov. 1797. Date: 3 Jan. 1798. Wit: Nathaniel Reed, Colin Campbell. Nathaniel Reed made oath to William Reed, JP, 3 Feb. 1798.
Rec: 8 Mar. 1802.

Pages 10-11:   6 Mar. 1801, James Kilgore of Greenville Dist. to Thomas Lineard of Pendleton Dist. for $1000 for 640 acres on both sides of Wollenoy Creek, surveyed by John Vanderhorst, Esq., granted by Benjamin Gignard (sic). Wit: Colin Campbell, James Coffey. Kiziah Kilgore released dower to Elijah Browne, J.Q., 18 Mar. 1801. Colin Campbell made oath to William Reed, J.P., 22 Feb. 1802.
Rec: 8 Mar. 1802.

Pages 11-12:   Aaron James for $150 sold to Michael Steele 87 acres on Great Generostee Creek of Savannah River, part of tract granted Henry Long by Wm. Moultrie, 16 Aug. 1793, purchased by Thomas Lesley, 1 Aug. 1796. Date: 1 Oct. 1801. Wit: Nimrod Kelly, John Patterson. Nimrod Kelly made oath to E. Browne, J.Q., 9 Mar. 1802. Rec: 9 Mar. 1802.

Page 12:	James Martin of York Co., S. C. am firmly
bound to James Hilhouse of Pendleton Co. for
₤150 stg., date 16 Mar. 1794. Condition -
to make titles to 320 acres on Great Generostee Creek of the Savannah
River, part of tract adjoining John Tippen. Wit: David Dickey, John Martin. David Dickey made oath to Peter Keys, J.P., 8 Mar. 1802.
Rec: 9 Mar. 1802.

Page 13:	John H. Blackburn of Jackson Co., Ga. for
$25 sold to William Copeland of Pendleton
Dist., 100 acres bd. by my line, Wm. Durham.
Date: 2 Dec. 1801. Wit: William Welch, William Durham. William Durham
made oath to William Edmondson, J.Q., 6 Mar. 1802.
Rec: 8 Mar. 1802.

Pages 13-14:	Abel Anderson, planter, for $150 sold John
Wilson 200 acres on 23 Mile Creek, granted
Samuel Oliver by Wm. Moultrie, 2 Oct. 1786
by. on E. by Samuel Barr, on N. by John Blair, on W. by James Stephenson, on S. by John E. Calhoun, Esq. Date: 25 Jan. 1802. Wit: Saml.Barr,
A. Boyse. Rosanah, wife of Abel Anderson, released dower to John Wilson, J.Q., 25 Jan. 1802. Capt. Samuel Barr made oath to John Wilson,JP,
25 Jan. 1802.
Rec: 8 Mar. 1802.

Pages 14-15:	John A. Blackburn of Jackson Co., Ga. for
$50 sold to William Durham 140 acres, bd.
by Durham and "my line leading from Alr.
Copeland to George's Creek Iron Works, to take in Meeting house tract,
along McAdam's line to Widow Curry (Iron car only excepted)". Date: 2
Dec. 1801. Wit: William Copeland, William Welch. William Copeland made
oath to William Edmonson, J.Q., 6 Mar. 1802.
Rec: 8 Mar. 1802.

Page 15:	Aaron Kilbun of Pendleton Dist. for ₤15stg.
sold to Samuel Earle, Esq. of Greenville
Dist., 50 acres on W. of Keowee River, part
of tract granted Major Parsons (this deed was not finished - had note:
Recorded in other book.)

Page 15:	William Reed had granted to him 319 acres
on Wolonoy Creek, bd. by land laid out to
John Adams and Robert Wilson of which Peter
Weaver was to have 100 acres on NE corner, bounds agreed on by both parties, who was joint tenants, which I warrant and defend. Date: 14 Feb.
1797. Signed: William Reed. Wit: David Reed, Nathaniel Weaver. Oath
says David Weaver appeared and made oath and that Nathaniel Reed was a
witness, 6 Mar. 1802 to Colin Campbell, J. P.
(No recording date).

Page 16:	4 Mar. 1801, Ellis Sutliffe of Charleston,
Innkeeper, to John A. Miller of Pendleton
Dist., for $600 for 640 acres on Big Generostee Creek, granted John Sutliffe by Benjamin Guerard, 15 Oct. 1784.
Wit: Jesse Brown, John Griffen, William Welch. Jesse Brown made oath to
Peter Keys, J.P., 14 Mar. 1801.
Rec: 8 Mar. 1802.

Pages 16-17:	18 Aug. 1795, Timothy Reeves to Jesse Brown
100 acres on Generostee Creek, part of 282
acres granted David Clark, conveyed to Benjamin Reney, from Reney to Reeves, bd. on W. by James Long, on S. by Alexander McMillian, on E. by Elisha Garlant and James Long, to include
improvement that Elisha Garlant formerly lived at. Wit: James Clayton,
Burrell Reeves, Richard Haney. Richard Haney made oath to Peter Keys,
J.P., 15 Jan. 1802.
Rec: 8 Mar. 1802.

Page 17:	8 Oct. 1789, Benjamin Rainey of Wilkes Co.,
Ga. to Timothy Reeves of Pendleton Co.,SC.,

(Page 17 cont'd.): for Ł 100 stg. for 282 acres on Generostee Creek, 96 Dist., granted David Clark, 5 Feb. 1787, recorded Estate Book 16 Sep. 1778, p. 648 (no number). Wit: Alexander McMillian, Richard Bradcut. Richard Bradcut made oath to John Wilson, J.P., 21 Dec. 1789. Rec: 8 Mar. 1802.

Page 18: 20 Dec. 1799, Ferdinand Hopkins of Chester Co., S. C. to William Bynum of Pendleton Co. for $75 for 740 acres, part of 2,782 acres granted Hopkins 2 Jan. 1792, on Wolf Creek and Reed Creek. Wit: James Jett, Jesse Murphree. James Jett made oath to David Murphree, J.P., 12 Mar. 1802. Rec: 19 Mar. 1802.

Page 18: William J. King of Beauford Dist., S.C. for $250 sold to John Reeves 240 acres surveyed for Jacob John, 10 Jan. 1785, in 96 Dist. on Bear Creek. Date: 18 Nov. 1801. Wit: Geo. Manning, Jehu Orr. George Manning made oath to E. Browne, J.Q., __ Jan. 1802. Rec: 8 Mar. 1802.

Page 19: 17 Oct. 1789, David Clark of Pendleton Co. to Benjamin Rainey of Wilkes Co., Ga. for Ł 40 stg. for 282 acres on Generostee Crk. of the Savannah River, granted Clark, 5 Feb. 1787, recorded Bk. (blank). Wit: Alexander McMillian, Richard Bradcut. Richard Bradcut made oath to John Wilson, J.P., 21 Dec. 1799. Rec: 8 Mar. 1802.

Pages 19-20: 10 Sep. 1795, James Shields to John Watson for Ł 25 stg. for 100 acres, part of 290 ac. granted Shields 10 Nov. 1790 by Charles Pinckney, in 96 Dist., above Indian boundary on Savannah River, bd. NE by James Miscanders(?), NE and NW by William Lesley, bd. Aston line run for James Alexander. Wit: James Jones, Robert Scelton. Robert Skelton made oath to William Hall, J.P., 26 Jan. 1796. Rec: 8 Mar. 1802.

Pages 20-21: James Nash, Sr., planter, for $100 sold to Larkin Nash, planter, 230 acres on W. side of Hencoop Creek, part of 640 acres granted Thomas Jenkins, 6 Jun. 1786, recorded Bk. LLLL, p. 134 (except what belongs to Auguston Harris). Date: 27 Jan. 1802. Wit: Geo. Manning, John Reeves. (No oath). Rec: 8 Mar. 1802.

Pages 21-22: James Loggins and Susanah, his wife, for $150 sold to Andrew Cauharn(?), 56 acres on the Saluda River, bd. by James Cauhorn and Craven's Creek, part of tract granted Samuel Salbert, Jr. Date: 26 Sep. 1801. Signed: James Loggin, Susannah Loggin. Wit: Joel Morton, Jr., David W. Mitchell. Joel Morton made oath to Robt. McCann, J.P., 30 Oct. 1801. Rec: 20 Mar. 1802.

Pages 22-23: Joshua Lee of Green Co., Ky. for $1,000... sold to Willoby Pugh of Pendleton Dist., a planter, 500 acres on Chestoe Creek of the Tugalo River, granted Stephen Drayton, Esq., 15 Oct. 1784 by Benjamin Guerard. Date: 22 Oct. 1800. Wit: J. (Josiah in oath) Foster, John Shannon, Edmond Manning. John Shannon made oath to John Burton, J.P., 19 Feb. 1802. Rec: 8 Mar. 1802.

Pages 23-24: Washington Dist., George Shular, planter, for Ł 125 stg. sold to Willoughby Pugh, planter, 41 acres part of two surveys: the first granted Shular 2 Feb. 1789 by Chas. Pinckney; the other granted on 4 Jan. 1790, on Golden's Creek of 12 Mile River. Date: 18 Jun. 1790. Signed: George Shuler, Mary Shuler. Wit: Wm. Matthews, John Stuart ..... Washington Dist., Mary Shular, wife of George Shular, released dower to

(Pages 23-24 cont'd.): William Steele, J.P.C., 6 Jun. 1797. Capt.
William Matthews made oath to Robt. McCann,
J. P., 9 Jan. 1798.
Rec: 8 Mar. 1802.

Page 24:	25 Nov. 1801, Elisha Dyar and his wife, Levina, of Franklin Co., Ga. to John Brown of Pendleton Co., S. C. for ⅃ 5 stg. for 150 acres on E. side of the Savannah River, bd. on S. by John Simpson, on N. by William Gabriel Perkins. Signed: Elisha Dyar, Levina Dyar. Wit: John Reid, William Reid. John Reid made oath to John Verner, J.P., 5 Mar.1802.
Rec: 8 Mar. 1802.

Page 25:	John Byas Blackwell of Greenville Co., S. C. for $100 sold to William Hunt of Pendleton Co., 100 acres on SW of the Saluda River, part of 802 acres granted Thomas Hood, 1793, bd. by Asher, Wm. Hunt,and James Allen. Date: 30 Nov. 1802. Wit: Reuben Maiston, Shadrack Gibbs. Shadrack Gibbs made oath to George Foster, J.P., 17 Feb. 1802.
Rec: 8 Mar. 1802.

Pages 25-26:	John Byas Blackwell of Greenville Co. for $550 sold to William Hunt, 100 acres on SW side of the Saluda River, part of 200 acres granted William Carpenter, 5 Apr. 1784, conveyed to William Asher, then to Edward Johnston, from him to Blackwell, bd. on SE and SW by Thomas Hood. Date: 20 Jan. 1802. Wit: George Garison, Frances Esther. Frances Esther made oath to George Foster, J. P., 17 Feb. 1802.
Rec: 8 Mar. 1802.

Pages 26-27:	12 Jan. 1798, John Newman, to Jehu Reed for 10 shillings for 50 acres part of 200 acres on Craven's branch of the Savannah River, granted Samuel Love by Thomas Pinckney, 17 Jan. 1788, conveyed to Newman 11 Feb. 1788. Wit: Thomas Shockley, Jr., James Jones. Thomas Shockley made oath to John Barton, J.P., 8 Mar. 1802.
Rec: 8 Mar. 1802.

Pages 27-28:	John Burton and Ann, his wife, planter, for $150 sold to James Shockley 175 acres by name of Bond's old place, bd. by Barnet Putman and Hail's line, formerly Casey's line, Shockley. Date: 23 October 1801. Signed: John Burton, Ann Burton. Wit: Saml. Tate, James Tate...... James Tate made oath to John Burton, J.P., 8 Mar. 1802.
Rec: 8 Mar. 1802.

Pages 28-29:	Jehu Reid for $95 sold to James Shockley 40 acres surveyed by John McMahan, D.S., part of 200 acres granted Samuel Love 7 Jan.1788 and conveyed to John Newman 11 Feb. 1788, bd. by William Love, James Shockley, Daniel Earp and Jehu Reid. Date: (blank) 1801; Wit: Edward Watts, Aquilly Shockley. Aquilla Shockley made oath to John Verner,JP., 2 Mar. 1802.
Rec: 8 Mar. 1802.

Pages 29-30:	John Tinsley for $600 sold to Thomas King, 100 acres on Rocky River, bd. by Lent Hall, Robert Harkness, Elijah Brown, Esq. and by Robert Norris, granted Samuel H. Lance, conveyed to Blake Mauldin, then to Thomas Milsap and by him to Tinsley. Date: 9 Jan. 1802. Wit: Winston Hall, Lent Hall. Lent Hall made oath to E. Browne, JQ, 26 Feb. 1802. Adah Tinsley, wife of John Tinsley, released dower to E. Browne, J.Q. (No date)
Rec: 9 Mar. 1802.

Pages 30-31:	Hugh Rogers and James Rogers for $400 sold to John Dickson, Jr., 200 acres where Hugh Rogers now lives, granted William Dunlap 6 Feb. 1786, on 23 Mile Creek of the Keowee of the Savannah River. Date: 16 Mar. 1802. Signed: James Rogers, Hugh Rogers. Wit: Hugh Dickson, James Houston. Margaret Rogers, wife of the late Hugh Rogers, deceased, and

(Pages 30-31 cont'd.): Nancy Rogers, wife of James Rogers and Jeany Rogers, wife of Hugh Rogers, released dowers to John Wilson, J.Q., 19 Mar. 1802. Signed: Margaret Rogers,Nancy Rogers, Jenny Rogers. James Houston made oath to John Wilson, J.Q., 19 Mar. 1802.
Rec: 22 Mar. 1802.

Pages 31-32: Culliver Clemments for $175 sold to Reuben Clements 150 acres on Big Rocky Creek of Rocky River of Savannah River, part of 214 acres granted Culliver Clements 1 Jan. 1798 by Charles Pinckney. Date: 7 Oct. 1799. Wit: George Dilworth, James Clement. George Dilworth made oath to Wm. Hall, J.P., 2 Mar. 1802.
Rec: 8 Mar. 1802.

Pages 32-33: William Vaughn for $200 sold to Isaac Cox 100 acres on the S. of the Saluda by James Vaughn, William Cox. Date: 11 Aug. 1800. Signed: William (X) Vaughn. Wit: James Vaughn, Abraham Childers. James Vaughn made oath to William Hall, J.P., 11 Aug. 1800.
Rec: 8 Mar. 1802.

Pages 33-34: James Blair of Franklin Co., Ga. for $100 sold to Jeremiah Hollingsworth of Laurens Dist., S. C., 415 acres, on both sides of Chauga Creek of Tugalo River, granted James Blair, 1 Dec. 1800, recorded Bk. UUU, (no page number). Date: 8 Mar. 1802. Wit: J. C. Kilpatrick, John Barton, J.P. (No oath).

Pages 34-35: 28 Aug. 1795, Aaron Boggs to Henry Burdine for Ł 125 stg. for 200 acres in Washington Dist. of Bigg Creek of the Saluda River, granted William Davis by Benj. Guerard, 21 Jan. 1785, recorded Bk. BBBB, p. 178. Wit: William Bell, William Young. William Bell made oath to Wm. Hall, J.P., 22 Dec. 1797.
Rec: 27 Mar. 1802.

Pages 35-36: 28 Mar. 1796, Berry Medlock to William Bowling for Ł 30 stg. for 50 acres, part of a tract made over to sd. Littleberry Matlock (sic) from David Smith, conveyed to Smith from John Kelly, granted Kelly by Wm. Moultrie, 1786, on Dowdy's Creek of the Saluda, bd. by Smith and Matlock. Signed: Littleberry (his mark) Matlock. Wit: Benoyni Bourland, Coren (X) Mitchel. Benani Bourland made oath to David Murphree, J.P., 27 Mar. 1802.
Rec: 29 Mar. 1802.

Page 37: George Shular sold to William Mitchel....a certain part of tract granted Burrel Bobo 5 Feb. 1787, on old indian path, bd. line of Mitchel and Nicholson, Shular, Edward Hays. Date: 22 Oct. 1800. Wit: William Norton, ____ Richardson, W. Nicholson. Amos Richardson made the oath to Henry Burch, J.P., 25 Apr. 1801.
Rec: 29 Mar. 1802.

Pages 37-38: 25 Apr. 1796, William Bourland to William Mitchell for Ł 15 stg. for 50 acres, part of tract deeded from John Kelly to David Smith, from Smith to Littleberry Medlock, from Medlock to Bourland..... granted Kelly 1796, on Dowdy's Creek of Saluda River, bd. by Bourland, Joseph Leeper. Wit: John McCleery(?), Benoni Bourland, John Bourland. Benjamin Bourland made oath to David Murphree, J.P., 27 Mar. 1702.
Rec: 29 Mar. 1802. (Signed: Benoni Bourland).

Pages 38-39: John Dover sold to William Mitchell (no amt given) 50 acres bd. by John Kelly, Thomas Hood. Date: 24 Mar. 1800. Wit: W. W. Bruce, Robert Akins. Robert Akins made oath to George Foster, J.P., 29 December 1800. Rec: 29 Mar. 1802.

Pages 39-40: Clabourn Harris for $200 sold to David Harris 140 acres on E. side of Hencoop Creek, part of tract granted Joseph Price by Wm. Moultrie, 6 Nov. 1786, conveyed from Price to John Haynie and from Haynie to Clabourn Harris, bd. on N. by John Harris, on W. by M. Willia, on E. by John Philpott, on S. by Philpott and John Haynie. Date: 5 Nov. 1801. Wit: Stephen Willis, John (X) Philpott. John Philpott made oath to E. Browne, J.Q. (no date).
Rec: 8 Mar. 1802.

Pages 40-41: 1 Sep. 1796, James Duff to Elijah Hammond for £ 30 stg. for 100 acres on N. side of N. fork of George's Creek, bb. by John Gillaspie, and Henderson, part of tract James Duff sold to Samuel Burdine. Wit: Samuel Duff, William Hammonds. Samuel C. Duff made oath to Robert Bowen, J.P., 7 Sep. 1796.
Rec: 22 Mar. 1802.

Pages 41-42: John and Violet Hood for $100 sold to John Waters, Jr., 50 acres on both sides of Buck Creek of the Saluda River, part of 2 tracts ....one of 300 acres granted Peter Thompson Feb. 1790 and the other one granted Amos Freeman, bd. by Freeman. Date: 28 Aug. 1801. Signed: John (X) Hood, Violet (X) Hood. Wit: John Waters, Thomas Hood, Isaac James. John Waters made oath to Robert Bowen, J.P., 29 Nov. 1801.
Rec: 22 Mar. 1801. (1802?)

(At this point, many of the marks in the signatures were left blank ... labeled "his or her mark".)

Page 42: 7 Nov. 1801, John Hood for $300 sold to John Waters 138 acres granted Amos Freeman 20 Oct. 1786, on Jones fork of Dowdy's Creek of the Saluda River. Signed: John Hood, Violet Hood. Wit: Ransom Banks, John Watters. John Watters, *Jr.* made oath to Robt. Bowen, J.P., 22 Mar. 1802.
Rec: 22 Mar. 1802.

Page 43: I, John Reno for $200 sold to John Watters 100 acres, part of 276 acres granted Andrew Kelly 7 Nov. 1791 by Chas. Pinckney, on S. side of the Saluda River, one mile above Parris's ford, bd. by Nathan Durham, sd. Kelly. Date: 22 Nov. 1799. Signed: John (X) Reno. Wit: Joab Mauldin, Robert Sutterfield, John Waters. John Waters made oath to Robt. Bowen, J.P., 23 Feb. 1800.
Rec: 22 Mar. 1802.

Pages 43-44: (date blank) 1802, Clabourn Harris to John Harris for $30 for 60 acres bd. by John Laughlin on NE, by Stephen Willis on NW, by John Harris and Clabourn Harris on SW, part of tract granted Joseph Price by Wm. Moultrie 6 Nov. 1786, conveyed to John Haynie then to Clabourn Harris, on Hencoop Creek, to where Public road leads to Shirley's Mill. Wit: Rhatio Durley, David Harris. David Harris made oath to E. Browne, J.P., 6 Mar. 1802.
Rec: 8 Mar. 1802.

Pages 44-46: 96 Dist., William Hunter, Deputy Surveyor, with Mary, his wife, of Laurence Co., S. C. to John Gent, planter, of "state and county aforesaid" for £ 65 stg. for 300 acres on Big Beaverdam of Savannah River, recorded Bk. 4 F, p. 89 in Secretary's Office by Wm. Moultrie 3 Oct. 1785. Date: 10 Oct. 1786. Signed: William Hunter, Mary Hunter. Wit: John Dalrymple, Charles Morgan, Sarah Entrican. Charles Morgan made oath to Robert C. Nash, J.P., of Abbeville Co., 28 Feb. 1800.
Rec: 12 Nov. 1801.

Pages 46-47: William Laffoon for $50 sold to Drury Thompson 100 acres part of tract on Saluda River bd. by Laffoon and John Bledso. Date: 8 Oct. 1801. Wit: Richard Thompson, Rutherford Laffoon. Richard Thompson made

(Pages 46-47 cont'd.): oath to George Singleton Foster, J.P., 10 Oct. 1801. Rec: 8 Mar. 1802.

Page 47: Humphrey Cobb and Nathan Reid, both of greenville Co., S. C. for $50 sold to John Rusk of Pendleton Co., 706 acres on Cain Creek of Keowee River, granted Cobb by Chas. Pinckney, 1 Oct. 1792, bd. by William McCaleb. Date: 19 Dec. 1799. Wit: William Hunter, Samuel Cherry. Levise Cobb, wife of Humprhey Cobb and Jean Reid, wife of Nathan Reid, released dower to Hudson Berry, J.Q., 27 Dec. 1799. Signed: Levise (X) Cobb, Jenny (X) Cobb. (No oath). Rec: 8 Mar. 1802.

Pages 47-48: 19 Nov. 1792, Hugh Brown of Pendleton Co., to David Speers of Laurence Co., S. C. for Ł 100 for 936 acres in 96 Dist. on 26 Mile Creek of the Keowee River. Wit: Robert Blake, James Mulwee. James Milwee made oath to John Wilson, J.Q., 9 Mar. 1802. Rec: 8 Mar. 1802.

Pages 48-49: John Tapley for $380 sold to David Sloan 200 acres, part of 450 acres granted Jawl Meligan, conveyed to Francis Bremar, then to John McKenzie, from McKenzie to Tapley, on Big Beaverdam Creek of the Tugaloo River, bd. by John McKenzie and Tapley. Date: _ Feb. 1802. Wit: Robert Hacket, David Sloan. Robert Hacket made oath to E. Browne, J.Q. (No date). Rec: 10 Mar. 1802.

Page 49: John Verner for $200 sold to Jowl Ledbetter 495 acres bd. by Verner, Ledbetter, Robert Hix and James Morrow, granted Verner by Wm. Moultrie 29 Nov. 1794. Date: 6 Mar. 1802. Wit: John McMillian, James Jones. Rec: 10 Mar. 1802. (No oath).

Page 50: John Taylor for $600 sold to Lewis Daniel Martin the following lots of land in the Village of Pendleton, sold as No. 18, 19 & 20, each containing 1 acre, fronting lots on S. owned by Samuel Taylor and General Andrew Pickens, on W. by David McCaleb and on NE by lots owned by William Hunter. Date: 29 Dec. 1801. Wit: Samuel Cherry, Thomas Gazaway. Samuel Cherry made oath to J. B. Earle, C.C., 10 Feb. 1802. Rec: 10 Feb. 1802.

Pages 50-51: Ely Hunnicutt for $700 sold to H. Hunnicutt 150 acres on 26 Mile Creek of Savannah River granted Ely Hunnicutt by Wm. Moultrie 4 Dec. 1786, bd. by Evin Calhoun, Robert Parker, General Anderson. Date: 14 Jan. 1802. Signed: Eli Hunnicutt. Wit: James Mulwee, Anthony Dickason. Anthony Dickason made oath to J. B. Earle, C.P.D, 15 Feb. 1802. Rec: 15 Feb. 1802.

Pages 51-52: 2 Jan. 1793, David Whitchel(?) to William Jullin for 170 acres for Ł 50, granted 17 May 1787 by Thos. Pinckney to Joseph Whitner, for 304 acres in 96 Dist. above old boundary line on both sides of Carpenter's Creek of the Saluda River, bd. on SE and NE by John Davis, William Davis. Signed: Davis Whilell(?). Wit: Joseph Culton, Samuel Mars. Samuel Morse made oath to W. Reid, J.P., 10 Oct. 1797. Rec: 8 Mar. 1802.

Pages 52-53: William Murphree, Sr. for $800 sold to James Jett 235 acres on Town Creek of 12 Mile River. Date: 25 Sep. 1801. Signed: William Murphree. Wit: John Stuart, John Chandler. John Chandler made oath to David Murphree, J.P., 25 Sep. 1801. Rec: 8 Mar. 1802.

Pages 53-54: Henry Lard, planter, for $100 sold to David Sloan, 225 acres on W. side of Keowee River.

(Pages 53-54 cont'd.):   ...granted Thomas Vick, 20 Nov. 1794 by Wm.
                           Moultrie, bd. by John Portman, Jonathan
Kemp. Date: 30 Mar. 1801. Wit: William Sloan, John Looney. William Sloan
made oath to E. Browne, J.Q., 9 Mar. 1802.
Rec: 10 Mar. 1802.

Page 54:   30 Jan. 1795, Benjamin Clark to Peter Julien
                           and John Julien for Ł 70 stg. for 158 acres
                           on Peter's Creek of Saluda River, granted
Clark, 1 Feb. 1790. Wit: John Powell, William Julien. John Powell made
oath to William Reid, J.P., 30 Jan. ___.
Rec: 8 Mar. 1802.

Page 54:   I, Jacob R. Brown, Justice of Quoram, cer-
                           tify Sarah Griffen, wife of John Griffen,
                           appeared to release dower to John Taylor.
Date: 3 Feb. 18__(torn). Signed: Sary Griffen.

Page 55:   Mark Thompson of Greenville Co., S. C. for
                           $300 sold to Drury Thompson of Pendleton
                           Dist., 247 acres on Peters Creek of Saluda
River, granted by Chas. Pinckney, 4 Dec. 1797. Date: __ Jul. 1801. Wit:
Wm. Hawks, Jonathan Davis. William Hawks made oath to George Foster, JP
13 Oct. 1801.
Rec: 10 Mar. 1802.

Pages 55-56:   John Lowery of Abeville Dist. for $200 sold
                           to William Gilham of Pendleton Dist. 200 ac
                           on 18 Mile Creek of Keowee River, granted
Isaac Titsworth, also part of tract granted Isaac Lynch of 198 acres bd.
above tract. Date: 25 Mar. 1801. Wit: William Baskin, John Gillham. Sarah Lowry, wife of John Lowery, released dower to William Baskin, J.Q.,
25 Mar. 1802. John Gilham made oath to John Taylor, J.Q., 5 Apr. 1802.
Rec: 9 Apr. 1802.

Pages 56-57:   1 Apr. 1801, John Duncan of Washington Co.,
                           Va. to Nathaniel Duncan of Pendleton Dist.
                           for $100 for 100 acres on George's Creek of
Saluda River, conveyed from William Rose (Ross?) to William Williams, ..
then to Duncan, 15 May 1794. Wit: David Duncan, Daniel Duncan. Daniel
Duncan made oath to Robt. Bowen, J.P., 20 Jul. 1801.
Rec: 13 Oct. 1801.

Pages 57-58:   Whereas, my notes bearing dates, viz: 1 Oct.
                           1800 for sum of $77; 24 Sep. 1801 for $269;
                           10 Feb. 1801 for $40; 2 Oct. 1801 for $45;
2 Oct. 1801 for $31.27, I am firmly bound to James White for $1,000 on
condition of payment of $460.52 before 25 Dec. 1801, secure to James
White. I, John Wilson for 5 shillings sold James White the following
property: one negro boy, Joseph, age 6 years; one negro boy, Ned, age 14;
one tract of 102½ acres about two miles below Dickensville on the main
road leading to Charleston on the Saluda River; household furniture and
cattle, the corn in one field, about 10 acres, hogs and tools. Date: 2
Oct. 1801. Wit: Michael Smith, James Wilson. Both made oath to John Wilson, J. P., 2 Oct. 1801.
Rec: 10 Mar. 1801.

Pages 59-60:   David Graham of Pendleton Dist. for $350
                           sold to Buckner Smith of Spartanburgh Dist.
                           for 150 acres on Hurricane Creek of Saluda
River, bd. by Eby Stephens Booth, on SE by William Arratts(?), SW and NW
by Alexander Boyse. Date: 16 Mar. 1801. Signed: David Grimes. Wit: A.
Boyse, Joseph Martin. Alexander Boyse made oath to John Wilson, J.P., 30
May 1801. Nancy Grimes, wife of David Grimes, released dower to John Wil-
son, J.Q, 30 May 1801.
Rec: 25 Sep. 1801.

Pages 60-61:   22 Dec. 1800, Jacob Capehart to Jonathan
                           Hicks, Sr. for $5 for 50 acres, part of a
                           tract on S. side of 23 Mile Creek of Savan-

(Pages 60-61 cont'd.): nah River, granted Andrew Ross(?) by Chas. Pinckney, 6 Sep. 1790, recorded Bk. C., no. 5, (no. page) for 338 acres, then sold to Hicks. Wit: William Shackleford, Thomas Hopson. William Shackleford made oath to J. B. Earle, C.C. (No date).
Rec: 5 Sep. 1801.

Pages 61-62: John Vance for ₤ 50 sold to Moses Hendricks 440 acres, part of 640 acres granted Vance by Wm. Moultrie, 1 Jan. 1786, on both sides of Camp Creek of the Saluda River, 96 Dist., bd by Joseph Davis and Cunningham. Date: 16 Sep. 1801. Wit: David Hendricks, George Hill. George Hill made oath to Robt. McCann, J.P., 12 Oct. 1801.
Rec: 12 Oct. 1801.

Pages 62-63: 3 Feb. 1801, John Wardlaw, son of Hugh Wardlaw, Esq., to John Warnock for $250 for 121 acres, part of 311 acres granted John Wardlaw, 4 Jul. 1785, recorded Bk. EEEE, p. 42, on Broadaway Creek of Savannah River, bd. by William Lesley. Signed: J. N. Wardlaw. Wit: James Caldwell, David Cochran, James E. Vandiver. Mary Anne (X) Wardlaw, wife of John Wardlaw, released dower to Andrew Hamilton, J.Q., 3 Feb. 1801. Edward Vandiver made oath to E. Browne, J.Q,, 1 Oct. 1801.
Rec: 13 Oct. 1801.

Pages 63-64: Alexander McCollister and Sarah, his wife, for $300 sold to Dudley Hammond 200 acres on Broadaway Creek of Rocky River of Savannah River, granted David Hopkins, 1 May 1786 by Wm. Moultrie. Signed: Alexander McCollister, Sarah McCollister. Wit: J. Pickens, Britain Griffen, Wm. McCollister. Joseph Pickens made oath to P. Norris, J. P., 2 Jan. 1802.
Rec: 10 Mar. 1802.

Pages 64-65: John Haynie for $40 sold to Timothy Orr, 50 acres, part of 108 acres surveyed for Haynie 24 Apr. 1788, recorded Bk. N, no. 5, p. 219 ...in 96 Dist., on Bear Creek of Rocky Creek, bd. by Stephen Harris. Date ____ 1801. Wit: Stephen Willis, Charles Haynie. Elizabeth Haynie released dower to E. Browne, J.Q., 22 Sep. 1801. Charles Haynie made oath to E. Browne, J.Q., 29 Sep. 1801.
Rec: 10 Mar. 1802.

Pages 65-66: William Allen for $80 sold to Robert Orr (no amount) on Little River bd. by Elisha Brown. Date: (blank) 1801. Wit: Timothy Orr, John Shirly. Mary Allen, wife of Wm. Allen, released dower to Elijah Brown, J.Q., 29 Dec. 1801. Timothy Orr made oath to E. Browne, J.Q. ____ (blank) 1801.
Rec: 10 Mar. 1802.

Pages 66-67: John Grisham, Jr., for ₤ 20 stg. sold to Timothy Orr, 364 acres, "except what is taken off by Jeremiah Morgan, about 4 or 5 acres" on Bear Creek of Rocky River, granted Grisham, 2 Sep. 1793 by Wm. Moultrie. Date: 30 Oct. 1801. Wit: Benjamin Bowen, David Brown, Britain Griffen. Patsey Grisham, wife of John Grisham, released dower to E. Browne, J.Q., 30 Oct. 1801. Signed: Martha Grisham. David Browne made oath to E. Browne, J.Q., 30 Oct. 1801.
Rec: 10 Mar. 1802.

Pages 67-68: Charles Clements, of Pendleton Co., for $214 sold to Roger Murphey, Sr. of Laurence Co., S. C., 335 acres on Cherokee Creek of Savannah River, bd. by Perron Farrow, Nathan Nall, part of 641 acres granted 5 Nov. 1792 by Chas. Pinckney. Date: 17 Mar. 1800. Wit: James Clements, Roger Murphey, George Dilworth. Agnes Clement, wife of Charles Clement, released dower to Joshua Saxon, J.Q, 18 Nov. 1800. George Dilworth made oath to William Hall, J.P., 11 Apr. 1801.
Rec: 19 Apr. 1802.

Pages 68-69: Matthew Ledbetter for Ł 25 sold to Joseph Waldron 123 acres on Village Fork of Cain Creek of Keowee River, granted Charles Plunket by Wm. Moultrie 2 Dec. 1793. Date: 27 Aug. 1801. Signed: Matthew Ledbetter, Rebeckah Ledbetter. Wit: Jesse Nevill, James Conner. James Conner made oath to Henry Burch, J.P., 12 Oct. 1801.
Rec: 12 Oct. 1801.

Pages 69-70: Samuel Burton for $400 sold to Asa Kemp 330 acres on Littlebeaverdam Creek of Tugaloo River, granted by Chas. Pinckney, recorded Bk. R, p. 393, now in possession of Kemp. Date: 16 Sep. 1799. Wit: John Tapley, James Kilpatrick. Elizabeth Burton, wife of Samuel Burton, released dower to John Taylor, J.Q, 13 Oct. 1801.
Rec: 13 Oct. 1801. (No oath).

Pages 70-71: William Lowe for Ł 50 stg. sold to William Stanton 88 acres on S. side of Saluda River bd. by Mathias Richardson. Date: 23 April 1796. Signed: William Lowe, Margaret Lowe. Wit: George Oldham, Francis Nunn. Margaret Lowe released dower to William Hall, J.Q., 3 Apr. 1796. George Oldham made oath to Wm. Hall, J.P., 23 Apr. 1796.
Rec: 12 Oct. 1801.

Pages 71-72: Major James Hamilton for Ł 5 stg. sold to Capt. Samuel Tate, 646 acres on branch of 26 Mile Creek, granted Hamilton by John Drayton, 4 Aug. 1800, bd. by Ross, Daniel McCollum, Mart Martin. Date: 19 Sep. 1801. Wit: Robert Tate, David Carton, William Singleton. William Singleton made oath to John Verner, J.P., 13 Oct. 1801.
Rec: 13 Oct. 1801.

Pages 72-73: Daniel Simms of Pendleton Dist. for $200 sold to Tadira(?) Foster of Laurence Dist., S. C., 200 acres on Little River of Keowee, granted Daniel Symmes by Chas. Pinckney. Date: 1 May 1801. Wit: David McCaleb, John Griffen. Avis Simms, wife of within named, released dower to John Taylor, J.Q, 2 Sep. 1801. David McCaleb made oath to J. B. Earle, J.Q, 10 Oct. 1801.
Rec: 10 Oct. 1801.

Pages 73-74: 6 Oct. 1801, Eli Langford, Sr. of Greenville Dist., S. C. to Matthew Langford of Pendleton Dist., for ___ hundred dollars for 376 acres on Sugar(?) Creek of Keowee River, bd. by William Tabor, Eli Langford, Sr., Eli Langford, Jr., part of tract granted Langford, Sr., 1793. Signed: Eli Langford, Sarah Langford. Wit: John Stewart, Eli Langford. John Stewart made oath to David Murphree, J.P., 8 Apr. 1802.
Rec: 9 Apr. 1802.

Pages 74-75: John Ross for $672 sold to Johnathan Hemphill, 336 acres on Great Generostee, granted John Mullin, 16 Jul. 1784, including all land on W. side of creek, bd. by John Sison. Date: 5 Sep. 1801. Signed: John (X) Ross. Wit: Wm. Brown Ross, Edward T. McClure. Barbara Ross, the wife of within named, released dower to Elijah Browne, J.Q., 14 Feb. 1802. Edward Tate McClure made oath to E. Browne, J.Q., 19 Feb. 1802.
Rec: 10 Mar. 1802.

Pages 75-76: 1 Apr. 1800, John Lowry of Abbeville Co., SC to John Richy of Pendleton Co., for $900 (no amount of acreage) on W. side of 23 Mile Creek, granted Jesse Saxon(?) by Thos. Pinckney, 2 Jul. 1787. Wit: William Baskin, James Richey. Sarah Lowry, wife of John Lowry, released dower to William Baskin, J.Q., 3 Sep. 1801. James Richey made oath to J. B. Earle, J.Q. (no date).
Rec: 4 Oct. 1801.

Pages 76-77: 13 Apr. 1795, William Thomas of the State of Georgia, to George Thompson of Pendleton

(Pages 76-77 cont'd): Co. for Ł 120 stg. for 640 acres on 12 Mile River, granted 7 Jul. 1784, in Washington Dist., W. of old boundary line, on both sides of river. Wit: John Clarkson, William Thompson. William Thompson made oath to William Reed, J.P., 30 Jul. 1795.
Rec: 14 Oct. 1801.

Pages 77-78: 24 Mar. 1798, Isaac James of Washington District to David Duncan of the same, for $100 for 100 acres granted John Nicholson, 3 Jul. 1786, conveyed from Nicholson to Wm. Jamison, 20 Nov. 1791, then from Jamison to William Rose, from Rose to John Singleton, from Singleton to James; the other part was granted to John Wakefield, conveyed to Wm. Rose, then to Singleton, then to James, 27 Oct. 1796, on head waters of George's Creek main fork of the Saluda River. Wit: William Jamison, Daniel Duncan, Robert Hammond. Robert Hammond made oath to William Reed, JP 27 Sep. 1798.
Rec: 13 Oct. 1801.

Pages 78-79: 14 Dec. 1795, Aaron Neel, planter, to William Shelby, planter, for Ł 50 stg. for 300 acres on Cuffee Creek of 23 Mile River.... granted by Wm. Moultrie, 3 Apr. 1786 to Lewis D. Martin. Wit: Thomas Lofton, John G. Lofton. (No oath).
Rec: 10 Mar. 1802.

Pages 79-80: 5 Apr. 1796, Jonas Hill to Samuel Bradcut for Ł 70 stg. for 200 acres on Wolf Creek of 12 Mile River, near Parrises Old Road, bd. Hill and John Cantrell, Solomon Palmer, Howell Miller, Henry Walbanks part of 640 acres granted by Wm. Moultrie to Benjamin Perry, 1786. Wit: William Marchbanks, William Miller. William Miller made oath to David Murphree, J.P., 15 Dec. 1800.
Rec: 14 Oct. 1801.

Pages 80-81: John Portman of the State of Kentuckie(sic) planter, for $110 sold to Bennet Aden of Pendleton Co., planter, 100 acres, part of tract on N. side of Keowee River, granted James Jordan by Wm. Moultrie. Date: 26 Mar. 1800. Wit: A. Cobb, James Wood. James Wood made oath to J. B. Earle, J.Q., 10 Mar. 1802.
Rec: 12 Mar. 1802.

Page 81: Griffen Brown, planter, for $100 sold to Christopher Vickery(?), 198 acres granted by William Moultrie, 2 Dec. 1793 on Little River. Date: 7 Mar. 1800. Wit: B. Green, Jr., William Hayes. William Hayes made oath to Joseph Reid, J.P., 7 Mar. 1800.
Rec: 16 Apr. 1802.

Page 82: Joseph Taylor for $140 sold to Charles Bond one lot in the Village of Pendleton of 1 ac bd. on W. on Public Square, S. by lot owned by Thomas Hunter, E. by lot owned by William Shackelford. Date: 18 Sep. 1801. Wit: William Hunter, Samuel Cherry. William Hunter made oath to J. B. Earle, C.P.C. (no date).
Rec: 10 Mar. 1802.

Pages 82-83: John Craig for $150 sold to Stephen Roberts 333 acres on 26 Mile Creek, bd. by Mitchell. Date: 16 Sep. 1801. Wit: Simon Doyle, Arthur Mitchel. Simon Doyle made oath to John Montgomery, J.P., 13 Oct. 1802.
Rec: 13 Oct. 1802.

Pages 83-84: Joseph Reed and George Miller(?) Read sold to Robert Hackett(?) 151 acres on branch of N. side of Tugalo River, part of 200 acres granted Joseph Read by Wm. Moultrie, 2 Dec. 1799.(?) Date: 13 Nov. 1801. Wit: Obediah Trimmer, Jesse Stribling, John McMillion. Jesse Stribling made oath to John Harris, JP, 6 Apr. 1802. Rec: 10 Mar. 1802.

Page 84:   John McKinsey(?) for ___ hundred dollars sold to Henry McCoy, 100 acres on Big Beaverdam, part of tract granted Jacob Milligan (?) conveyed to Francis _____, then to John McKinsey(?). Date: 15 Mar. 1802. Wit: Obediah Trimmer, James McClure(?). Obediah Trimmer made oath to John Harris, J.P. (no date).
Rec: __ Apr. 1802. (Very dim).

Page 85:   10 Aug. 1800, Thomas Martin and his wife, Ruth, to John Taylor, Jr., for $200 for 200 acres granted John Moorhead, Sr. Signed: Thomas Martin, Ruth Martin. Wit: Langston Drew(?), John Taylor. Ruth Martin released dower to Joshua Saxon, J.Q., ___ 1800. Langston Drew(?) made oath to Joshua Saxon, 16 Oct. 1801. (Very dim).

Page 86:   John Kasey(?) and Luvisy(?) his wife, for ___ hundred dollars sold to John Guthrie(?) (cannot read the amount).....granted John Palmer by Wm. Moultrie, ____ Apr. 1793(?). Date: 24 Sep.(?) _____ (rest unreadable).

Pages 86-87:   William Gilham to William Warren......... (amount?)...granted Arthur McDow, 21 Jan. 1785(?). Wit: J. A. Kilpatrick, John Simpson(?). Alexander Kilpatrick made oath to John Wilson, J.Q., 19 April 180_. Jane Gilham, wife of William Gilham, released dower to John Wilson J.Q. 19 Apr. 1802.
Rec: 19 Apr. 1802.

Pages 87-88:   Nicholas Welch of Pendleton Dist. for $1000 to William Gray of Laurence Dist., S. C., 255 acres granted Catherine Miller ___ June 1783, recorded Bk. EEEE, p. 248, by Wm. Moultrie, _____. Date: __ Apr. 1802. Wit: _____. There is a dower release, appears to be signed by Margaret _____. Rec: 19 Apr. 1802.

Pages 88-89:   William Gilham for ___ dollars sold to John Simpson _____. Wit: J. B. Earle, James __ Jane (X) Gilham released dower to John Wilson, J.Q., 19 Apr. 1802. John Baylis Earle made oath to John Wilson, 19 Apr. 1802.
Rec: 19 Apr. 1802.

Pages 89-90:   I do hereby swear that (I) will not molest in anywise my wife Rebecah and I will not take her child from her nor cause it to be by any person by my consent or knowledge unless it is judged by any of her neighbors that she misused it or let it suffer _____(not readable) by actual agreement between her and myself provided the child is not to be taken out of the county _____. Date: 11 Jun. 1801. Signed: Berry Moore. John Harris, J.P.
Rec: 24 Apr. 1802.

Page 90:   William Wakefield for $180 sold to John Braselton(?) 194 acres granted George Vance (?) by Arnoldus Vanderhorst, 7 Nov. 1795, and made to me _____. Date: 24 Mar. 1801. Wit: Jarel Megahe, Relick Verner(?). Oath _____(unreadable). John Verner, J. P. 24 Mar. 1801.
Rec: 13 Oct. 1801.

Page 91:   On 8 Jan. 1800, peaceable and quite possession of the plantation on George's Creek, S. side of the Saluda known as Hugh(?) Roses tract of 640 acres joining Ephraim Mitchell and Zephaniah Roberts, tract was delivered by Andrew Wilson, person in possession, to Francis Bremar, Esq., by payment of 2 barrels of corn. Signed: Andrew Wilson. Wit: Hezekiah Johnston, Jesse _____. Hezekiah Johnston made oath (date and name of J.P. blank).
Rec: 10 Oct. 1801.

Pages 91-92:   William Gilham for $100 sold to James Waters 222 acres, part of 2 tracts;one granted Wil-

(Pages 91-92 cont'd): liam Gilham, the other granted Arthur McDow. Date: 10 Apr. 1802. Wit: James Wood, A. Kilpatrick. Jane (X) Gilham released dower to John Wilson, J.Q., 19 April 1802. Alexander Kilpatrick made oath to John Wilson, _____ 1802. Rec: __ Apr. 1802.

Pages 92-93: 25 Aug. 1796, James Martin of York County, S. C. to John Ross of Pendleton Dist. for Ł 100 stg. for 640 acres on Great Generostee where John Ross now lives. Wit: _____ Martin.

Pages 93-94: (Most of this unreadable).........mentions Francis Bremar, Esq. of Charleston .... that the said George Corley .... Signed: George Corley. Wit: Stephen Huff (only) who made oath to Wm. Edmondson, J.Q., 8 Feb. 1802. Rec: 10 Mar. 1802.

Pages 94-95: James Milwee, planter, for $67 sold to John Ewing Calhoun 50 acres on 26 Mile Creek bd. on N. by Michael Dickson, on E. by John Robinson, on S. by John Ewing Calhoun, on W. by Edward Kemp. Date: 2 Nov. 1801. Wit: B. Green, William Anderson. Plat surveyed by James Millwee, D.S., 25 Dec. 1788. Benjamin Green made oath to J. B. Earle, J.P., 22 Nov. 1801. Rec: 2 Nov. 1801.

Page 95: (Unreadable).......Date: 2 Feb. 1799. Oath says Mary Smith to William Jackson. Wit: Eliab Moore, John Smith. Eliab Moore made oath to Patrick Norris, J.P., 14 May 1800. Rec: 4 Sep. 1801.

Page 96: 7 Oct. 1796, Johnston Marchbanks to Abel Hodges for Ł 60 stg. for 220 acres on both sides of Rice's Creek of 12 Mile River, part of tract granted 4 May 1789 by Thos. Pinckney, recorded Bk. ZZZZ, p. 322 to Albert Smithson. Wit: Jesse Miller, Samuel Bradcut, John Birchfield. Samuel Bradcut made oath to John Barton, J.P., 13 Oct. 1801. Rec: 14 Oct. 1801.

Page 97: 26 Apr. 1802, Notice is given to all persons by no means to trade or deal with Charity Harris my wife on my account as she has left my bed without just cause whatever. I am resolved to pay no debts by her contract given. Signed: Benjamin Harris. (No witness).

Pages 97-98: John Field, Sr. and John Field, Jr. for $440 sold to Isaiah Lewis a negro man named Ceasor, about 20 years old, about 5 feet, 7 in. high. Date: 5 Apr. 1802. Wit: Robert Sinkler, John Boren. John Boren made oath to John Cochran, J.P., 1 May 1802. Rec: 1 May 1802.

Page 98: Israel Pickens for $150 sold to Fenton Hall 150 acres on First Creek of Rocky River, bd by John Evins, Alexander Cavin, Fenton Hall and Israel Pickens. Date: 8 Dec. 1801. Wit: Harbert Tucker, John Hall, William Hall. William Hall made oath to E. Browne, J.Q., 10 Feb. 1802. Rec: 20 May 1802.

Pages 98-99: I, Field Farrar am bound to John Robinson, 10 Sep. 1787, condition that I make titles to him to 200 acres on Tugaloe River. Wit: Thomas Farrar, Godfrey Isbel. (No oath).

Pages 99-100: 15 Sep. 1790, Field Farrar of Winnsborough of Fairfield Co., S. C. to John Robison of Pendleton Co. for 200 acres in Robison's possession in 96 Dist. on Tugalow River, granted by Benjamin Guerard on

(Pages 99-100 cont'd):   20 Jan. 1785, recorded Bk. BBBB, p. 16.Wit:
M. Winn, John C. Kilpatrick. Receipt of
L 40 stg. paid by John Robison. J. C. Kilpatrick made oath to Joseph Reed
J.P. 8 Oct. 1798.
Rec: 8 May 1802.

Pages 100-101:   James Millwee for $100 sold to John Vick-
rey 500 acres on Crooked Creek of Little
River, bd. by Robins, Brogden, part of
1000 acres granted James Millwee by Wm. Moultrie, 6 Nov. 1786. Date: 15
May 1801. Wit: Robert Anderson, Levi Robins. Levi Robins made oath to Joseph Reed, J.P., 16 May 1801.
Rec: 16 Apr. 1802.

Page 101:   David Pruitt for $100 sold to Joseph Wood-
all 100 acres surveyed 26 Jun. 1784 for Joseph Walker. Date: 7 Sep. 1799. Wit: Mich-
ael Pruett, Stephen Chastain. Stephen Chastain made oath to Joshua Saxon
J.P. 3 May 1800.
Rec: 26 May 1802.

Pages 101-102:   2 Aug. 1799, David Pruitt to Benjamin Cham-
ble for $800 for 200 acres on Big Generos-
tee Creek at mouth of Rocky fork. Wit:John
Tippen, (Capt. John Tippen in oath), Josiah Elliott, Morgan Hood. Josiah
Elliott made oath to Joshua Saxon, J.P., 6 Nov. 1799.
Rec: 26 May 1802.

Pages 102-103:   Samuel Lofton, Jr. for $60 sold to Caleb
Williams 200 acres on NE branches of 12
Mile River, part of 500 acres granted to
Lofton 2 Apr. 1789 bd. NW by William McCaleb. Date: 6 Mar. 1801. Wit:
Samuel Cherry, John C. Lofton. Samuel Cherry made oath to J. B. Earle,
27 May 1801.
Rec: 27 May 1801.

Page 103:   Willis Jones for $44 sold to Lewis Jones,
Sr. a sorrell horse, cows. Date: 3 Dec.
1801. Wit: John Smith, Lewis Jones, Jr.
John Smith made oath to Saml. H. Dickson, J.P., 11 Mar. 1802.
Rec: 26 Mar. 1802.

Page 104:   Daniel Putman for $10 sold to Thomas Put-
man 80 acres on Big Generostee Creek of the
Savannah River, part of 505 acres granted
Thomas Asburn, Sr., 7 Jan. 1788 by Thos. Pinckney. Date: 28 Jan. 1802.
Wit: Jacob Skelton, John Roberts. Jacob Skelton made oath to John Verner,
J.P., 6 Jan. 1802.
Rec: 27 May 1802.

Pages 104-105:   John Barnett for $10 sold to Thomas Putman
70 acres on Baker's fork of Big Generostee
Creek of Savannah River, part of 360 acres
surveyed for William Stevenson, 21 Aug. 1786 by Thomas Finley, granted
Stevenson, 14 Jan. 1791 by Chas. Pinckney. Date: 6 Jun. 1801. Wit: James
Barnett, Jacob Skelton. Jacob Skelton made oath to John Verner, J.P., 6
Jan. 1802. Rec: 27 May 1802.

Pages 105-106:   Drury Thomas and Martha Thomas sold to John
Hillhouse, Sr., 100 acres on fork of Nel-
son's Creek, including houses and buildings
settled by John Thompson and John Raden. (No price). Date: 23 Feb. 1802.
Signed: Drury Thompson, Martha Thompson. Wit: James Garner, William
Welch, William Thompson. William Thompson made oath to Patrick Norris,
J.P., 9 Mar. 1802.
Rec: 2 Jun. 1802.

Pages 106-107:   Harmon Cumings for $500 sold to Robert Will-
son 160 acres on branches of Willson's crk.
part of 640 acres surveyed for John Baker

(Pages 106-107 cont'd): Ruston by David Hopkins, D.S., 28 Jun.1784. Date: 1 Jan. 1801. Signed: Harmon (X) Cummins. Wit: Samuel Dean, Joseph Dean. Plat laid off 1 Mar. 1800 by Jno. McMahen. Joseph Dean made oath to E. Browne, J.Q., 27 Feb. 1802. Rec: 2 Jun. 1802.

Page 107: Daniel Pitchford for $300 sold to Luke Hamilton 205 acres on Generostee Creek, part of tract granted William Lesley, 6 March 1786, bd. by John Sules(?), Joseph George, William Brown(?) and John Callahan. Date: 2 Mar. 1802. Signed: Daniel Pitchford, Rebecah Pitchford. Wit: Isaac Mitchel, Eli Pitchford. Isaac Mitchel made oath to E. Browne, J.Q., 1 May 1802. Rec: 2 Jun. 1802.

Pages 108-109: Jonas Hill for $80 sold to John Powell part of tract _____ (rest unreadable).

Pages 109-110: Benjamin Cleveland, Esq. of Pendleton Co. sold to Absolem Cleveland of Franklin Co., Ga., planter, for $300 for 300 acres ..... granted 15 Oct. 1785 by Benj. Guerard to John Godwin(?) .... (rest unreadable).

Pages 110-111: 31 Dec. 1801, John _____ of City of Charleston to _____ for $200 for 640 acres. Signed: John _____, Sr. (Unreadable).

Pages 111,112: Thomas Harrison, Sr. for love and good will give to my son, Robert Harrison one negro woman named Lucy and her children, David, Sollomon, Jenny and Jude. Date: 14 Jan. 1802. Signed: Thomas (X) Harrison, Sr. Wit: John D. Terrell, Richard Shipp. Richard Shipp made oath to William Cleveland, J.P., 14 Jan. 1802. Rec: 5 Jan. 1802.

Pages 112-113: 27 Mar. 1802, John Huggins to William Evitte for $400 for 331 acres on 12 Mile River on E. side of a branch of Keowee River of Savannah River, bd. on SW by 12 Mile River, NE by McBride. (Plat)...... granted by William Moultrie to Samuel H. Dickson, 30 Mar. 1793. Signed: John Huggins, Mary (X) Huggins. Wit: Richard Blackstock, John Todd. Richard Blackstock made oath to Samuel H. Dickson, J.P., 5 Jul. 1802. Rec: 5 Jul. 1802.

Pages 113-114: Abraham Nally for $129 sold to Aaron Nally 100 acres, part of 640 acres on S. fork of Brushy Creek of the Saluda River where Aaron Nally now lives, bd. by Jacob Earnest. Date: 24 May 1802. Signed: Abraham (X) Nally. Wit: Wm. Faris, Jno. Faris. William Faris made oath to Robt. McCann, J.P., 28 Jun. 1802. Rec: 7 Jul. 1802.

Page 114: William Hobbs for $45 sold to James White a mare about 6 years old. Date: 30 Jan'y. 1802. Wit: John Powell (only) who made the oath to Wm. Edmondson, J.Q., 19 Jun. 1802. Rec: 25 Jun. 1802.

Page 115: Thomas Farrar for $400 sold to Field Farrar 200 acres on Little Beaverdam of Toogaloo River, granted John Martin. Date: 4 June 1802, condition that Hugh McClannan not be interrupted until Field Farrar being of age. Wit: Cyprian Farrar, Thomas Hunter. Thomas Hunter made oath to J. B. Earle, clerk, 2 Jul. 1802. Rec: 3 Jul. 1802.

Pages 115-116: Hannah Shotwell and Reuben Shotwell for $530 sold to James Hagood (no amount), part

(Pages 115-116 cont'd): of 2 tracts, one granted by Wm. Moultrie to Henry Clark, 3 Oct. 1785, the other by Arnoldus Vanderhorst to Reuben Shotwell, 5 Dec. 1781, on S. fork of the Saluda near Hunt's ford, bd. by line of James Hagood and Hannah Shotwell and by Norwood. Date: 24 Nov. 1801. Signed: Hannah Shotwell, Reuben Shotwell. Wit: Samuel Earle, George Shotwell, Jephs Moss(?). Jephs Moss(?) made oath to George Foster, J.P., 8 Dec. 1801.
Rec: 8 Mar. 1802.

Pages 116-117: John Verner for $200 sold to Joel Ledbetter 495 acres bd. by Ledbetter, Robert Hix and Verner's land which was formerly James Morrow's, granted John Verner by Wm. Moultrie, 29 Nov. 1791. Date: 6 Mar. 1802. Wit: John McMillian, James Jones. John McMillian made oath to J.B. Earle, 16 Mar. 1802.
Rec: 16 Mar. 1802.

Pages 117-118: Robert Telford for Ł 60 stg. sold Thomas Smith 200 acres on Broadmouth Creek of the Saluda River, part of 406 acres granted to Telford by Chas. Pinckney, 4 Jan. 1792, recorded Bk. F, no. 5, p. 26. Date: 17 Jan. 1799. Wit: Robert McCrery, Frasiers(?) Farmer. Isabela (X) Telford released dower to John Wilson, J.Q., 19 Apr. 1800. Robert McGregory made oath to William Hall, J.P., 19 Jan. 1799. Signed: Robert McCrery.
Rec: 10 Jun. 1802.

Page 118: David Clark for $150 sold to James McAfee (no amount given) acres on W. side of the Keowee River, granted Clark, 8 Nov. 1791. Date: 8 Mar. 1802. Wit: William (X) Staggs, Daniel Boon. Daniel Boon made oath to Henry Burch, J.P., __ Mar. 1802.
Rec: 12 Mar. 1802.

Page 119: Thomas Davis of Linkoln(?) Co., Ga. for Ł 5 stg. sold to Lewis David of Pendleton Co. 100 acres on S. side of Little Creek of the Saluda River. Date: 1 Apr. 1799. Wit: William (X) Cox, Isaac (X) Cox, James Martin, J.P. William Cox made oath to ____(blank) Date: (also blank). Rec: 3 Jul 1802.

Pages 119-120: John Ward for $30 paid by Daniel Shipp for Jas. C. Griffen, sold to Jas. C. Griffen 50 acres, part of survey for 319 acres.... granted Gabriel Hardin, Apr. 1789 by Chas. Pinckney, bd. by Griffen and crossing road from the Pendleton Court House, Daniel Shipp, on 23 Mile Creek. Date: 3 Oct. 1801. Wit: John Griffen, Major Lewis. Major Lewis made oath to J. B. Earle, J.Q., 27 Apr. 1802.
Rec: 27 Apr. 1802.

Page 120: Capt. Benjamin Brown for $47 sold to John McMahen 300 acres on Richland Creek of the Conoross Creek of the Keowee River, given Capt. Brown for his service during the last war. Date: 18 Jan. 1802. Wit: W. Black, William Brown, Hezekiah Morris. Hezekiah Morris made oath to Joseph Black, J.P., 17 Jul. 1802.
Rec: 18 Jul. 1802.

Page 121: David Smith for $210 sold to William Orr, Merct., all one half (of) both grist mill and saw mill as they both now stand, and are occupied by David Smith and William Rankin, on 23 Mile Creek, in an equal co-partnership from hence with William Rankin. Date: 19 Feb. 1802. Wit: William Forbus, Robert Pickens, Wm. McMahen. Robert Pickens made oath to John Wilson, J.Q., 19 Feb. 1802. Rebecah (X) Smith, wife of David Smith released dower to John Wilson, J.Q., 18 Mar. 1801.
Rec: 20 Jul. 1802.

(Note: The clerk in many cases has left out key words, in many places. I have inserted them to keep continuity...BW).

Page 122:   Turner Harwood in special confidence in my
                                   trusty friend, William Murphree, appoint
                                   him my attorney to recover my debts, lands
and premises I have in the State of Tenesee (sic). Date: 13 Jan. 1802.
Signed: Turner (X) Harwood. Wit: John Murlew, James Caldwell. James Marlow made oath to David Murphree, J.P., 13 Jul. 1802.
Rec: 13 Jul. 1802.

Pages 122-123:   James Powell, Sr., for confidence in my
                                   trusty friend, William Powell, appoint him
                                   my attorney to recover all debts and demands (due) me in Chatham or Wake Co., N. C. Date: 21 Jul. 1802. Signed:
James Powell. Wit: Samuel (X) Stephens, William Murphree, James (X) Powell. Samuel Stephens made oath to David Murphree, J.P., 21 Jul. 1802.
Rec: 22 Jul. 1802.

Pages 123-124:   William McMahen, planter, for $200 sold to
                                   William Orr, Merchant, 150 acres, part of
                                   300 acres granted John Calhoun by William
Moultrie 10 Dec. 1788 on N. side of 23 Mile Creek of the Savannah River,
bd. on NW by Andrew Wornock, where William McMahen now lives. Date: 18
Mar. 1802. Wit: John McMahen, John Wilson. John McMahan made oath to John
Wilson, J.Q., 18 Mar. 1802.
Rec: 20 Jul. 1802.

Page 124:   Thomas (no name but is Payne) of Franklin
                                   Co., Ga. am firmly bound to Thomas Harrison of Pendleton Dist. and release to Thomas Harrison 101 acres, plat by Kilpatrick, part of tract granted Thomas
Payne on Choestoe Creek bd. on NW by Shilor(?), on SE by Rolston, on NE
by Harrison. Date: 18 Feb. 1800. Signed: Thomas (X) Payne. Wit: Thomas
Keys, Thos. Bibb. Thomas Keys made oath to William Cleveland, J.P., 13
Mar. 1802.
Rec: 16 Jul. 1802.

Pages 124-125:   18 Dec. 1799, peaceable and quiet possession of a tract on George's Creek bd. by
                                   Rebeccah Reed, John Hallum and David Hughs
(is) delivered by Stephen Huff in Washington Dist. to Francis Brimer of
Charleston, Esq., by payment of three barrels of corn, next fall. Signed
by Stephen (X) Huff. Wit: Thomas Edmondson (only) who made oath to William Edmondson, J.Q., 11 Feb. 1802.
Rec: 5 Jul. 1802.

Pages 125-126:   Joseph Clark for $25 sold to Jean (Jain)
                                   Copling 40 acres on W. side of 23 Mile Crk
                                   and S. side of Blare's Branch, part of a
tract granted Bolin Clark by Benj. Guerard, 21 Jan. 1785, recorded Bk.
AAAA, p. 428. Date: 30 Jan. 1798. Wit: Wm. Rankin, Thomas Coker. Mary
(X) Clark, wife of Joseph Clark, released dower to John Wilson, J.Q., 4
Feb. 1799. William Rankin made oath to Robert McCann, 25 Jul. 1798.
Rec: 21 Jul. 1802.

Pages 126-127:(page number torn off) 11 Feb. 1802, Thomas Shockley, of
                                   Abbeville Dist. to Robert Harrison of said
                                   State and Dist. for $400 for 200 acres on
Choestoe Creek, granted Shanklin 9 Jun. 1784 by Wm. Moultrie, recorded
Bk. DDDD, p. 376. Wit: Obadiah Trimmer, Robert Anderson. Abbeville Co.,
Hannah Shanklin, wife of Thomas Shanklin (not Shockley), released dower
to William Baskin, J.Q., 8 Feb. 1802. (No oath).

Page 127 (torn off):   William Banister for $100 sold to Lewis D.
                                   Martin 280 acres on 18 Mile Creek bd. on
                                   SE by John Portman and Henry Young, "except what may be taken by survey on what McDole now lives and the tract
granted to John Portman". Date: 10 Nov. 1801. Signed: William (X) Banister. Wit: Joseph Whitner, W. Steele. Joseph Whitner made oath to J. B.
Earle, J.P., 6 Nov. 1801.
Rec: 6 Nov. 1801.

Pages 127-128: John Cannon for $100 sold to James Cannon, Jr., 50 acres on N. side of Cain Creek of the Keowee River, part of tract laid out to Humphrey Cobb, conveyed to William Reed, from Reed to James Cannon,Sr. and from him to Elijah Hering, from Hering to James Cannon, Sr. and from him to John Cannon, original plat made 1 Oct. 1792. Date: 2 Jan. 1802. Wit: Peter Reece, Samuel Martin. Peter Rees made oath to Josiah Foster, J.P., 4 Feb. 1802.
Rec: 5 Jun. 1802.

Pages 128-129: John G. Lofton for $100 sold to Thomas Hunter following lands, viz: 200 acres granted myself 1 Sep. 1800 on Cidar Creek, fork of Chauga Creek of Toogaloo River; tract of 190 acres granted me 1 Sep.1800 on Cidar Creek fork of Big Chauga, bd. "two above mentioned tracts".....
(Only two listed, must have left out one description...BW) Date: 15 Feb. 1802. Wit: Samuel Cherry, George Capehart. Samuel Cherry made oath to John Taylor, J.Q., 29 Jul. 1802. Agnes Lofton, wife of within named, released dower to John Taylor, J.Q., 26 Apr. 1802.
Rec: 29 Jul. 1802.

Pages 129-130: Henry and William Simms for $425 sold to Thomas Hunter 206 acres on 23 Mile Creek of the Seneca River, bd. on SE by John Taylor, Esq., on NE and NW by John Ward and J. B. Earle, Esq., on SW by Daniel Shipp. Date: 31 Dec. 1801 Signed: Henry Simms, William Simms. Wit: John Taylor, Samuel Cherry. Samuel Cherry made oath to John Taylor, J.Q., 29 Jul. 2801. Jane Simms, wife of Henry Simms, and Fanny Simms, wife of William Simms, released dower to John Taylor, J.Q., 31 Dec. 1801.
Rec: 29 Jul. 1802.

Pages 130-131: Peter Reece for Ł 50 sold to Moses Cannemur 263 acres surveyed 29 Jun. 1797 in Washington Dist. on both sides of 18 Mile Creek, bd. on NE by Wallace, on N. by Gadson, on SW and SE by Solomon Roe. Date: 25 Dec. 1797. Wit: Moses Hendrix, Matthew (X) Mullinnix.Moses Hendrix made oath to James Jett, J.P., 11 Apr. 1798.
Rec: 2 Aug. 1802.

Page 131: John Willson for $101.26 sold to Samuel Taylor a negro boy named Ned, age 15 years ...condition that John Willson pay Samuel Taylor $101.26 by Dec. 5, obligation is void. Date: 6 Oct. 1801. Wit: Jacob Capehart, Chas. Maxwell. Jacob Capehart made oath to John Barton, J.P. (no date).
Rec: 10 Mar. 1802.

Pages 131-132: William Hunter for $10 sold to Lewis D. Martin one lot of land in the Village of Pendleton, of 1 acre, bd. on S. and E. by lots now owned by Lewis D. Martin. Date: 10 Jul. 1802. Wit: Saml. Cherry, David McCaleb. Ann Hunter, wife of within named, released dower to John Taylor, J.Q., 19 Jul. 1801. Samuel Cherry made oath to J.B. Earle, 28 Jul. 1802.
Rec: 28 Jul. 1802.

Pages 132-133: Andrew Pickens, John Wilson, Robert Anderson, Commissioners for disposing of Public Lands at and adjoining Pendleton Courthouse sell to William Steele for $203 the following lots: Lot #19 of 30 acres; #18 of 18 acres; #10 of 11 acres; #29, #30, #32 and #45 of 1 acre each, according to plat of the Village of Pendleton made by Robert McCann, Esq. Date: 14 Oct. 1801. Wit: John E. Calhoun, Thomas Hunter. Thomas Hunter made oath to J. B. Earle, C.C.C., 29 Jul. ___.
Rec: 29 Jul. 1802.

Pages 133-134: 21 Apr. 1785, John Kerr, hatter, to David Ramsey, Physician, for 5 shillings for 640 acres in 96 Dist. (above) the ancient boundary line, on Wilson's Creek, bd. on S. by land surveyed for Alexander

(Pages 133-134 cont'd): Wabbe(?), on E. by land surveyed for William Mallock, was surveyed for Kerr by Patrick Calhoun, Esq., recorded Bk. CCCC, p. 259. Wit: William Matlock, Jacob Morris.
Rec: 10 Aug. 1802. (No oath).

Pages 134-135: 21 Apr. 1785, William Matlock, watchmaker, to David Ramsey, Physician, for 5 shillings for 640 acres in 96 Dist. above ancient boundary line at head waters of Wilson's Creek of the Rocky River, bd. S. by John Kerr, surveyed for Mallock by Patrick Calhoun, Esq., recorded Bk. CCCC, p. 290. Wit: George Warley, George Munro. (No oath).
Rec: 10 Aug. 1802.

Pages 135-137: 22 Aug. 1785, John Kerr, hatter, to David Ramsey, Physician, for £ 50 for 640 acres bd. on S. by Alexander Noble, on E. by William Mattock, recorded Bk. CCCC, p. 299. Wit: William Mallock, Jacob Morris. Wit: to seal of John Kerr was W. P. Harrison, Charles Snowden. William P. Harrison made oath to Charles Tell, Esq., J.P. of Charleston Dist., 21 May 1801.
Rec: 10 Aug. 1802.

Pages 138-140: 22 Apr. 1785, William Mallock, watchmaker, to David Ramsey, Physician, for £ 50 for 640 acres on Wilson's Creek, 96 Dist., bd. by John Kerr, recorded Bk. CCCC, p. 290. Wit: George Warley, George Morris. Wit: to receipt, John Kerr. John Kerr made oath to Charles Tell. JP 21 May 1801.
Rec: 10 Aug. 1802.

Pages 140-141: Shadrack Nolen for $549 sold to Henry Hill 404 acres on Crow Creek, granted to Robert Craven, 1790. Date: 2 Jun. 1802. Wit: William _____, John Grisham, Jr., Abraham Harges. William McFarland made oath to Henry Burch, J.P., 2 Jun. 1802.
Rec: 3 Jul. 1802.

Pages 141-142: I am endebted to Samuel Taylor for $22 and secure to him land where I now live of 100 acres on 26 Mile Creek, conveyed from Abm. Ellage to sd. Hembree, obligation to be paid by 25 Dec. next. Date: 18 Jul. 1802. Signed: William Hembree. Wit: Gladdah Calloway, James Armstrong, M. Hammond. Michael Hammond made oath to John Taylor, J.Q., 10 Aug. 1802.
Rec: 18 Aug. 1802.

Page 142: Alexander Floyd for $130 sold to John Grisham, Jr. 100 acres on Mile Creek, occupied by Joel Muda(?), part of tract granted to Duncan Camron, 1787 by Chas. Pinckney. Date: 26 Sep. 1801. Signed by Alexander Floyd and Nancy Floyd. Wit: James Kell, Thomas Harges. Thomas Harges made oath to John Barton, J.P., 12 Oct. 1801.
Rec: 2 Aug. 1802.

Page 143: 1 Mar. 1798, Jacob Boghman to James Alexander, planter, for £ 3 stg. for 500 acres on Cane Creek of Tugaloo River, bd. SW by James Alexander, granted Boghman by Chas. Pinckney, 21 Feb. 1795. Signed: Jacob Baufman, Elizabeth Baughman. Wit: Robert Saxton(?), Gaddah Calloway. Gaddeth Calloway made oath to Wm. Cleveland, J.P., 5 Apr. 1799.
Rec: 28 Jul. 1802. (Name was spelled Bauthman in oath).

Pages 143-144: 11 Feb. 1802, Thomas Shanklin of Abbeville Dist. to Robert Harrison of sd. district and State, for $400 for 200 acres on Choestoe Creek, granted Shanklin, 9 Jun. 1785, by Wm. Moultrie, recorded Bk. DDDD, p. 376. Wit: Obediah Trimmer, Robert Anderson. Abbeville Dist. ... Hannah Shanklin, wife of Thomas Shanklin, released dower to Wm. Baskin, J.P., 8 Feb. 1802. Obediah Trimmer made oath to J.B. Earle, 8 Feb. 1803.

Pages 144-145: 22 Aug. 1801, Thomas Collin, William Killigan (Holligan?), Esq., planter, to James Alexander for $120 for 60 acres on N. fork of Cain Creek of Toogalew River, bd. on NE by Woods and Holligan(?), on SW by Robert Saxon and Hilligan, part of tract granted to Godfrey Isbell by Thomas Pinckney. Signed: Thomas Collins, Wm. Hilligan(?). Wit: Rezin Spriggs, Joseph E. Veneable. Joseph Veneable made oath to William Cleveland, J.P., 2 May 1802. Rec: 18 Jul. 1802.

Pages 145-146: 10 Feb. 1794, Godfrey Isbell of Franklin Co., Ga., planter, to James Alexander of Pendleton Co., planter, for Ł 75 stg. for 100 acres on Cain Creek of Toogalow River, part of 200 acres granted to John Atterson, soldier, by Benj. Guerard, 21 Jan. 1784, conveyed to Minor Winn, Esq., then to Isbell, 14 Feb. 1790. Signed: Godfrey Isbell, Hannah Isbell. Wit: James Clark (John (X) Alexander. John Alexander made oath to Nathl. Perry, J.P., 14 Feb. 1794. Rec: 28 Jul. 1802.

Pages 146-147: 9 Jul. 1796, John Grisham to Samuel Little for Ł 20 stg. for 40 acres, part of 204 ac. granted to David Jordan, 22 May 1802, recorded Bk. C., no. 5, p. 5, in Washington Dist. on 26 Mile Creek of the Keowee River, bd. by Andrew Liddle. Signed: J. W. Grisham. Wit: Daniel Duncan, Rachel (X) Conger. Oath 11 Sep. 1802 (left out name) J. B. Earle, Clk. (No date).

Pages 147-148: Henry Garner for love and good will to my son, John Garner, all lands I bought of John Patterson, on both sides of Golden's Creek of 12 Mile River, part granted William Hallum, and part granted to Joshua Reeder, both of 200 acres (after decease of my wife and muself), independent of all former gifts, grants and wills. Date: 17 Sep. 1802. Wit: Samuel Taylor, M. Hammond. Michael Hammond made oath to John Taylor J.Q., 17 Sep. 1802. Rec: 17 Sep. 1802.

Pages 148-149: Jas. Smith for $200 sold to Robert Fullerton 150 acres on Fuller's Creek of Conoross Creek, bd. by Elijah Hering and Isaac Hering, part of tract laid out to Ellender Pickens, conveyed from him to Elijah Hering, from him to Isaac Hering and from Isaac Hering to James Smith; also part laid out to Thomas Shanklin, from him to Daniel Delany, then to James Smith. Date: 6 Mar. 1802. Signed: Joseph Smith. Wit: Jas. Fuller, John Gregory, Charnel Darden. John Gregory made oath to Josiah Foster, J.P., 2 Apr. 1802. Rec: 25 Sep. 1802 (called Joseph Smith in oath).

Pages 149-150: William Thompson for $600 sold to Jesse Hall 151 acres on Cain Creek of Keowee River, part of 2 tracts: one granted to Jacob Lawrence by Chas. Pinckney 2 Mar. 1789, the other surveyed by Samuel H. Dickson. Date: 16 Sep. 1801. Wit: Thos. Lofton, Jean Lofton. Thomas Lofton made oath to Joseph Reed, J.P., 2 Jun. 1802. Rec: 23 Sep. 1802.

Pages 150-151: Robert Scott of Laurens Dist., S. C. for $620 sold to Major Lewis of Pendleton Dist. 320 acres, part of 640 acres granted Scott by Wm. Moultrie, 5 Jun. 1786, recorded Bk. NNNN, p. 124, on 26 Mile Crk. of the Savannah River. Date: 26 Feb. 1802. Wit: J. A. Elmore, John Lewis. Isabella (X) Scott, wife of Robert Scott, released dower to John Elmore, J.P., Laurens Co., 10 Jul. 1802. (Oath blank). Plat.

Pages 151-152: William Gilham for $1000 sold to Elam Sharpe 200 acres on 18 Mile Creek of Savannah River, granted Isaac Titsworth. Also, part of tract granted Isaac Lynch adjoining above tract of 198 acres. Date: 9 Ap. 1802. Wit: J. B. Earle, M. Hammond. John B. Earle made oath to John Tay-

(Pages 151-152 cont'd): lor, J.Q. 9 Apr. 1802. Jane Gilham, wife of William Gilham, released dower to John Taylor, 10 Apr. 1802.

Pages 152-153: James Canseller for $50 sold to John Swansey 100 acres, part of 200 acres granted Elizabeth Adair (or Oliver) by Wm. Moultrie 4 Sep. 1786, on 23 Mile Creek of Keowee River. Date: 7 Oct. 1801. Wit: John Kensler, Margaret (X) Wilson. Elizabeth Canselor released dower to John Wilson, J.Q., 7 Oct. 1801. John Cansellar made oath to John Wilson, 7 Oct. 1801. Signed: John Kenselar. Rec: 24 Oct. 1802.

Pages 153-154: 8 Jan. 1802, Thomas Shockley, Sr. of State of Georgia, to Thomas Shockley, Jr. of S.C. for $500 sold 100 acres on Savannah River where Thomas Shockley formerly lived "according to plat until lands conveyed by sd. Thomas Shockley, Sr. to Quil_ Shockley and all below the Townhouse and Bond branch", granted William Love by Guereard. Signed by Thomas (X) Shockley. Wit: William Salter, Robert Black. Robert Black made oath to E. Browne, J.P., 12 May 1802. Rec: 29 Sep. 1802.

Pages 154-155: 4 Mar. 1802, Thomas Shockley to William Salter for $200 for 100 acres on Savannah River on Newman's branch, bd. by Thomas Shockley, Sr. and Thomas Shockley, Jr., part of 2 tracts granted Spilsby Glenn and William Love. Wit: Ro. Black, Polley (X) Salter. Robert Black made oath to E. Browne, J.P., 12 May 1802. Rec: 29 Sep. 1802.

Page 155: 26 Mar. 1799, David Noland to Shadrack Noland for Ł 60 for 404 acres, granted 14 Dec. 1789 by Chas. Pinckney to Robert Cravins in 96 Dist. on Crow Creek of Keowee River. Signed: David Nolind, Nancy Nolind. Wit: Lewis Edwards, Benjamin (X) Turner. Benjamin Turner made oath to Henry Burch, J.P., 29 Jun. ___. Rec: 3 Jul. 1802.

Page 156: Aron Broyles for $400 sold to James Mattison 640 acres on Broadmouth Creek of Saluda granted William Hirt(?) 15 Oct. 1784, bd. by William Poore. Date: 12 Mar. 1801. Wit: Elijah Wyatt, Francis Clinkscales. Francis Clinkscales made oath to E. Browne, J.Q., 19 Jun. 1802. Phanny Broyles released dower to E. Browne, J.Q. 19 Jun. 1802. Rec: 3 Jul. 1802. Dower release was signed: Francis Clinkscales.)

Page 157: Samuel Taylor borrowed of William Richards $1000 and gave bond of $2000, condition of payment before 1 Jan. 1803 and mortgage for 5 negroes, viz: one negro man named Nero, about 30 years old, one negro woman, named Dine about 30 years old and her three children, Ransome(?), Frank and Jim. Date: 9 Mar. 1801. Wit: Obediah Trimmier, G. W. Earle.....Greenville Dist., George W. Earle made oath to J. B. Earle, 9 Mar. 1802. Rec: 11 Oct. 1802.

Page 158: Jonathan Smith for $12 sold to Aron Smith, 12 acres laid out by James Millwee, D.S., part of tract granted Joseph Hall, on 26 Mile Creek, conveyed by James Martin to sd. Smith and Peter Akins (Akers) Date: 6 May 1802. Wit: James Linn, Sarah (X) Linn. James Linn made oath to John Montgomery, J.P., 10 May 1802. Rec: 12 Oct. 1802.

Pages 158-159: 31 Jan. 1801, William Asher to George Keith for $450 for 300 acres on Doddy's Creek of the Saluda River, bd. by Samuel Looper, Enock Smith and William Crane, granted 19 Aug. '86 (sic) to Francis Wafer. Signed: William Asherst. Wit: J. Mackey, Samuel Looper, Wm. Crain. Samuel Looper made oath to Colin Campbell, J. P., 11 Oct. 1802. R- (same)

Pages 159-160:   4 Mar. 1802, Hugh Simpson to John Roberts (no amount) for 172 acres including 150 ac. granted Simpson by Thos. Pinckney, 4 Aug. 1788, and 22 acres granted Thomas Lesley, 15 Oct. 1784, by Benj. Guerard and conveyed to Simpson. Wit: Daniel Putman, Michael Steele. Daniel Putman made oath to John Wilson, J.Q, 11 Oct. 1802.
Rec: 12 Oct. 1802.

Pages 160-161:   Benjamin Whorton for $100 sold to Zachariah Holcomb 200 acres on Cane Creek bd. Caleb Harris (or Starr), Prewett's old line, the sd. Holcomb and Jas. Hughey. Date: 14 Dec. 1801. Signed: Benja. Whorton, Mary Whorton. Wit: William Smith, Thomas Williams. William Smith made oath to Henry Burch, J.P., 19 Dec. 1801.
Rec: 15 Oct. 1802.

Page 161:   James Blair for $250 sold to Joseph Stapp 100 acres, part of tract conveyed to Blair by Col. Benjamin Cleveland, bd. by James Stewart and Blair, Daniel McMillion, on Toxaway Creek. Date: 5 Nov. 1798. Wit: James Airwick, George Blair. James Airwick made oath to Nathaniel Perry, J.P., 5 Nov. 1798.
Rec: 15 Oct. 1802.

Pages 161-162:   Ambrose Foster for $400 sold to Burwell Green one black stud horse. Date: 12 Dec. 1801. Wit: Peter Wagnon, Griffen Brown. Griffen Brown made oath to John Harris, J.P., 6 Nov. 1802.
Rec: 7 Nov. 1802.

Pages 162-163:   George Vandiver, Sr., for Ł 30 sold George Vandiver, Jr. 100 acres on Neals Creek, bd by Bennet (rest is too dim to read).......
Date: 17 Nov. 1800. Wit: William Lewis, Edward Vandiver. Edward Vandiver made oath to E. Browne, J.Q., 11 Oct. 1801.
Rec: 12 Nov. 1802.

Page 163:   George Walls for $400 sold to John Hamilton one negro wench named Charlot about 15 yrs of age. Date: 15 Sep. 1802. Wit: Min. Sherrard, Samuel Stevenson. Miranda Sherrard made oath to Nathan Lusk, J.P. 4 Oct. 1802.
Rec: 9 Nov. 1802.

Pages 163-164:   George Hoge for $250 sold to Daniel William 223-1/4 acres (no description). Date: 8 Oct. 1802. Wit: Hugh Crumbless, John Woodall. John Woodall made oath to P. Keys, J.P., 11 Oct. 1802.
Rec: 12 Oct. 1802.

Pages 164-165:   I, George Pots (also Potts) give to my two grand-daughters, Matilda Smith and Malinda Smith, daughters of William Smith and Nancy, his wife, all the articles mentioned: to Matilda Smith, one feather bed and furniture, two cows and calves, now in Smith's care; to Malinda Smith, one hunting saddle, lent to her mother, two cows and calves, to dispose of at their will when they come to the years of maturity. Date: 2 Oct. 1802. On 11 Oct. 1802, George Potts acknowledged to J. B. Earle, Clk. - signed: George (X) Potts.
Rec: 11 Oct. 1802.

Page 165:   24 Jul. 1802, Robert Harrison and Nancy, his wife, to James Burgess for $400 for 125 acres on Tugaloo River, part of a tract granted to Robert Miscampble by Benj. Guerard, 21 Jan. 1785, bd. by Harrison, ___ Darnell, Martin Hewlett. Signed: Robert Harrison, Nancy Harrison. Wit: John Carn Opea(?) (X) Burgess. Opea Burgess made oath to William Cleveland, J.P., 30 Sep. ___.
Rec: 19 Nov. 1802.

Page 166:   William Shelby for $10 sold to John Swords 150 acres, part of tract granted Shelby on 23 Mile Creek bd. by Swords, David Watkins. Date: 23 Mar. 1802. Signed: Wm. Shelby, Sally Shelby. Wit: Benjamin Lewis, William Swords. <u>Sarah</u> Shelby, wife of William Shelby, released dower to John Wilson, J.Q., 2 Oct. 1802. William Swords made oath to John Wilson, 2 Oct. 1802.
Rec: 17 Nov. 1802.

Page 167:   James Nash for $300 sold to George Nash one negro boy named Harry, and one negro girl named Rose(?). Date: 19 Oct. 1801. Wit: John Reeves, W. Solomon Prewit(?). John Reeves made oath to P. Norris, J. P., 19 Oct. 1801.
Rec: 24 Nov. 1802.

Pages 167-168:   Britain George of Spacklingburg (sic) Co., S. C. for $200 sold to Henry Bouyer of Stokes Co., N. C. 120 acres on 23 Mile Crk granted to George, 2 Jan. 1797, also 42 acres on S. side, adjoining the creek, granted Hugh Warnock and purchased from William Blair by John Wilkinson, who sold to George. Date: 19 Nov. 1798. Signed: Br<u>itton</u> (X) George. Wit: Joseph Erwin, Joseph (X) Bouyer. Joseph Bow<u>yer</u> made oath to John Willson, J.P., 16 Feb. 1799.
Rec: 24 Nov. 1802.

Pages 168-169:   7 Jan. 1799, James and Thomas Gillispy of Russell Co., Va. to Thomas Boyd of Pendleton Co., S. C. for $300 for 245 acres on Brown Creek of George's Creek of the Saluda River. Signed: James Gillispy, Thos. Gillispy. Wit: John Gillispie, Ebel Hodge. John Gillispy made oath to Robert Bowen, J. P., 28 Dec. 1799.
Rec: 13 Oct. 1802.

Pages 169-170:   William Bennit for $200(?) sold to Laban Smith 100 acres on fork of Little Creek bd. by John Harper, granted David Ravenor, Esq. in trust for heirs of Fargus Snoddy, deceased, by Wm. Moultrie, 3 Oct. 1785, recorded Bk. FFFF, p. 186. Date: _ Sep. 1801. Wit: Benjamin Clemments, Spenser Griffen. Benjamin Clemments made oath to William Hall, JP, 8 Han. 1801.
Rec: 12 Oct. 1801.

Page 170:   Hugh McVay for Ł 40 stg. sold to Thomas Risener 85 acres on 26 Mile Creek of the Savannah River, bd. by Jonathan Clark, James Long and Boling Clark. Recorded Bk. C, p. 539 (Pendleton Co.?), 5 Jul. 1791. Date: 17 May 1796. Wit: Joseph Clark, Mary (X) Clark, Fanny (X) McVay. Joseph Clark made oath to Robt. McCann, J.P., 4 Dec. 1802.
Rec: 7 Dec. 1802.

Page 171:   14 Aug. 1792, David Clark to Hugh McVay for Ł 25 (amount of acreage blank) on 26 Mile Creek of the Savannah River, bd. James ____, James Long, Jonathan Clark, Boling Clark, recorded Bk. C, p. 539 on 5 Jul. 1791. Wit: Matthew Parker, Joseph Clark, Thos. Abbett. Hugh McVay assigned over within tract to Thomas Risener in the presence of William Golding. Joseph Clark made oath to Rt. McCann, J.P., 4 Dec. 1802.
Rec: 7 Dec. 1802.

Page 172:   Daniel Weaver for Ł 20 sold to David Weaver 110 acres granted to Daniel Weaver, 1796 on Wolleynoy Creek, bd. on E. by Creswell, on SE by Cares(?), on NW by Mallock, on S. by John Swerling. Date: 29 Dec. 1797. Wit: John Hawks, Zephaniah Roberts. Certified by Wm. Reed, JP, (no date).
Rec: 12 Oct. 1802.

Pages 172-174:   Plat of Joshua Broyles' land, bd. on E. by Jas. Allen, on N. by Joshua Broyles, on S.

(Pages 172-174 cont'd): by Wm. White.....Washington Dist., Joshua Broyles for $100 sold to John Hall 120 ac. on Hencoop Creek of Rocky River, part of tract granted to John Grason(?) by Benj. Guerard, 23 Jan. 1785, conveyed from James Martin to Broyles. Date: 12 Aug. 1797. Wit: Francis Farmer, William (X) Wight. Francis Farmer made oath to Wm. Hall, J.P., 31 Aug. 1797. Elizabeth (X) Broyles, the wife of Joshua Broyles, released dower to John Wilson, J.C.P., 17 Feb. 1798. Rec: 11 Oct. 1802.

Pages 174-175: Benjamin Brown and Susanah, his wife, of Abbeville (Co.) for $50 sold to Jonathan Gillison of Pendleton (Co.) 50 acres part of tract granted Capt. Benjamin Brown on the Bounty for 200 acres on N. fork of Connoross Creek of Keowee River. Date: 5 Nov. 1801. Signed: Benjamin Brown. (only). Wit: James (X) Gillison, Saml. H. Dickson, Rebecah Dickson. James Gillison made oath to Samuel H. Dickson, J.P., 29 Sep't. 1802. Rec: 9 Oct. 1802.

Page 175: James Ross for Ł 2 stg. sold to George Brandon 254 acres on Generostee Creek bd. by Morgan Hood and Draton. Date: 17 Jan. 1797. Wit: William B. Ross, Francis (X) Ross. William Ross made oath to Peter Keys, J.P., 6 Mar. 1802. Rec: 3 Dec. 1802.

Pages 175-176: Personally appeared before me Eligah Isaac and on oath that on 6 April past an affray took place between deponant and Micajah Bond in which the deponant bit off a piece of sd. Bond's left ear...... (believes). Date: 20 Dec. 1802. Signed: Elijah Isaac before Saml. H. Dickson, J.P. Lewis Skelton appeared and said he witnessed the fight or scuffle. Date: 20 Dec. 1802. Rec: 20 Dec. 1802.

Page 176: Samuel Ross for Ł 2 stg sold to George Brandon 254 acres on Generostee Creek bd. by Morgan Hood and Drayten. Date: 17 Jan. 1797. Wit: Wm. B. Ross, Francis Ross. William Ross made oath to Peter Keys, J.P., 6 Mar. 1802. Rec: 3 Dec. 1802.

Pages 176-177: Alexander Kilpatrick for $300 sold to David Guest 295 acres on both sides of Big Beaverdam Creek of the Toogaloo River, granted by Wm. Moultrie, 5 Jun. 1786, taken off NW corner of old survey of Jacob Holland. Date: 9 Jun. 1797. Wit: John Hunt, John Peterson. John Hunt made oath to J. C. Kilpatrick, J.P., 29 Dec. 1797. Rec: 20 ___ (blank).

Pages 177-178: Nicholas Madgett of Columbia, S. C., merchant, for one negro wench named Patty, sold to Thomas Ware of Pendleton Co., 200 acres on head waters of Beaverdam Creek in fork of Toogalow and Seneca. Date: 14 Aug. 1801. Signed: N. Madgett & Co. Wit: James Jett, James Anderson. James Jett made oath to John Wilson, J.Q, 14 Oct. 1801. Rec: 13 Oct. 1802.

Pages 178-179: 7 Jan. 1800, Joseph Hall to Benjamin Goss (also Gawzey) for 200 acres on both sides of Little River of Keowee River, bd. John Caruthers, Elias Wileman, Belfield Wood and Samuel Ross, granted by Chas. Pinckney, 3 Dec. 1792. Wit: Thomas Boyd, Thomas Cureton. Thomas Cureton made oath to Henry Burch, J.P., 29 Jul. 1801. Rec: 12 Oct. 1802.

Pages 179-180: William Moore for $60 sold to Joshua Smith 100 acres on N. fork of Hericane Creek, part of 2 tracts granted to William Otwell at mouth of branch below William Moore's house, crossing Coker's old line ...Date: 23 Mar. 1798. Signed: William (X) Moore. Wit: William Faris,

(Pages 179-180 cont'd): William Copeland. (William Faris) made oath to Robt. McCann, J.P., 19 Oct. 1802. Rec: 20 Oct. 1802.

Pages 180-181: David Dunlap sold to William Richards for $187.87 and give bond for $375.87, to be paid by 1 Apr. 1802, and mortgage 1 mare 5 years old, 1 colt 3 years old, one sorrel gelding 8 years old and other. Date: 20 Sep. 1802 (note says carried over to page 183).

Pages 182-183: Jacob Boshman(?) of Clabourn Co., Tenesy (sic) appoint Rezin Sprigg my Attorney to recover one note against John Deuring(?) for $200, $116 with interest, also judgement against Joseph Venable that he had on Thomas Mills, also receipt from Moses Harry giving by note(?) ...(unclear). Date: 13 Dec. 1802. Signed: Jacob Bowsman(?). Wit: John Rogers, John Rogers, Sr. Claibourn Co., Tn., John Rogers, Jr. made oath to William Rogers, J.P., 23 Dec. 1802. Walter Evans, Clerk of the Court of Pleas and Quarter Sessions of Claibourn Co. certify William Rogers is acting Justice of Peace. Rec: 1 Jan. 1803.

Page 183: Signed: David Dunlap in presence of Robt. Waugh, James Gilkison. Robert Waugh made oath to Robert McCann, J.P., 12 Oct. 1802. Rec: 13 Oct. 1802. (Continued from page 181- David Dunlap to William Richards).

Pages 183-184: Joshua Smith for $60 sold to Cyrus Yancy 100 acres on N. fork of Hericane Creek part of 2 tracts granted William Otwell, bd. by William Moore, Coker's old line, Otwell's old line. Date: 18 Oct. 1802. Signed: Joshua (X) Smith. Wit: Stephen Booth, Backster (X) Risenison(?). Stephen Booth and Baxter Simpson made oath to Robt. McCann, J.P., 18 Oct. 1802. Rec: 20 Oct. 1802.

Pages 184-185: 22 Feb. 1794, John Bukhannon, planter, to Britain Griffen for Ł 35 stg. for 212 ac. on Cherokee Creek of Hencoop of Savannah River, part of tract granted Buckhannon for 428 acres, 26 Jun. 1787. Wit: Alexr. Moore, Andrew Bradley, Peter Griffen. Peter Griffen made oath to E. Browne, J.P., 7 Aug. 1794. Rec: 11 Nov. 1802.

Pages 185-186: James Linn for $100 sold to Aron Smith 29 acres laid out by James Millwee, D.S. part of two tracts: one granted James Gillison 1 Aug. 1785, by Wm. Moultrie, the other granted James Linn 6 Oct. 1794 by Wm. Moultrie. Date: 6 May 1802. Wit: Jonathan Smith, Eliazer (X) Smith. (Note - Elizabeth in oath). Jonathan Smith made oath to John Montgomery, J.P., 16 May 1802. Rec: 12 Oct. 1802.

Pages 186-187: Drewry Thompson for $195 sold to John Linn 96 acres on Rocky River, of Savannah River, bd. by John Stell. Date: 15 Feb. 1802. Wit: John Ramsey, Nicholas Welch. John Ramsey made oath to P. Keys, J.P., 16 Feb. 1802. Rec: 10 Jan. 1803.

Pages 187-189: William Shelby and Sarah Shelby for $100 sold to John Sords (Swords?) 100 acres on 23 Mile Creek, bd. by Armstrong, Wadkins, Lewis D. Martin's old survey. Date: 10 Jul. 1802. Signed: Wm. Shelby, Sally Shelby. Wit: John Swancy, William Swords. Sarah Shelby, wife of William Shelby, made release of dower to John Wilson, J.Q., 2 Oct. 1802. William Swords made oath to John Wilson, 2 Oct. 1802. Rec: 17 Nov. 1803.

Pages 189-190: Edward Hughey for $20 sold to Zachariah Holcomb 15 acres on Cain Creek of Little

(Pages 189-190 cont'd): River, of Keowee River, part of that tract formerly belonging to Henry Barran, bd. by Henry Barran, Fiedl Pewit, Sr. Date: 1 Mar. 1802. Wit: James Smith, James (X) Hughey. James Hughey made oath to Josiah Foster, J.P., 21 Aug. 1802. Rec: 15 Oct. 1802.

Pages 190-191: Henry Burdine for $350 sold to William Halbert 120 acres, pa bert 120 acres, part of tract granted to William Davis, Soldier, by Benj. Guerard, 21 Jan. 1785, conveyed from Davis to Aaron Boggs and from Boggs to Burdine, on S. fork of Big Creek of the Saluda River, bd. by Burdine, Charles Elliott, and Rhoden. Date: 7 Nov. 1801. Wit: Jacob Buzbie, Thomas Hall. Jacob Buzbie made oath to Wm. Hall, J.P., 9 Nov. 1801. Nancy (X) Burdine, wife of Henry Burdine, released dower to John Wilson, J.Q., 26 Dec. 1801. Rec: 11 Oct. 1802.

Pages 191-192: John Edmondson for $50 sold to James Watson 100 acres on Rice's Creek, part taken from Thomas Edmondson's tract. Date: 8 Jul. 1802. Signed: John Edmondson, George Edmondson, Benjamin Edmondson, Mary (X) Edmondson. Wit: James White, John Wilson, A. Boyce, Thomas Edmondson. Alexander Boyse made oath to John Wilson, J.Q., 8 Jul. 1802. Rec: 11 Jan. 1803.

Pages 192-193: Robert Scott of Lawrence Dist., S. C. for $640 sold to Major Lewis of Pendleton Dist. 640 acres, 2 tracts of 320 acres granted Scott, 5 Jun. 1786, recorded Bk. NNNN, p. 124 and 141, on 23 Mile Creek, of the Savannah River. Date: 26 Feb. 1802. Wit: J. A. Elmore, John Lewis .....Lawrens Dist., Isabella, wife of Robert Scott, released dower to John A. Elmore, J.Q., 24 Feb. 1802. John Lewis made oath (Pendleton Dist.) to N. Hammond, D.C., 20 Nov. 1802. Rec: 27 Aug. 1802.

Pages 194-195: James McDonald of Pendleton Dist. for Ł 60 stg. sold to James Sutton of Franklin Co., Ga., 100 (acres) on N. side of Choestoe Creek of Toogalow River, part of tract granted to James Millwee, 2 May 1785, by Wm. Moultrie, bd. by William Baker, Joshua Lee. Date: 7 October 1797. Signed: J. McDannelly, Martha McDannelly. Wit: James (X) Asholok?, Moses Payne, William Hawkins McDanell. James Ashlock made oath to Nathaniel Perry, J.P., 7 Nov. 1797. Rec: 17 Jan. 1803.

Pages 195-196: John Gibson for $255 sold to Francis Jenkins 167½ acres, where Jenkins now lives on S. fork of Beaverdam of Toogaloe River part of tract granted to Samuel Watt by Chas. Pinckney, recorded Bk. YYYY, p. 493. Date: 5 Sep. 1801. Wit: Thomas Rusel, Matthew Pinkerton. Thomas Rusel made oath to John Harris, J.P., 12 Jun. 1802. Rec: 11 Dec. 1802.

Pages 196-198: Benjamin Whorton for $200 sold to Phillip Cox 150 acres, part of tract on N. fork of Cain Creek, bd. by Benjn. Whorton and Phillip Cox, granted Job Laurence, 2 Jul. 1787 by Thos. Pinckney, recorded Bk. VVVV, p. 130. Date: 7 Feb. 1801. Wit: Elijah Floyd, John Beazley. John Beazley made oath to Joseph Reid, J.P., 30 Oct. 1802. Rec: 23 Nov. 1802.

Pages 198-199: Phillip P. Boulware for $130 sold to John Edmondson 100 acres on Middle fork of Brush Creek, part taken off from Thomas Edmondson's tract. Date: 10 Sep. 1800. Wit: James McDowell, Benjamin Edmondson. Benjamin Edmondson made oath to John Wilson, J.Q., 8 Jul. 1802. Rec: 11 Jan. 1802.

Pages 199-200: 13 Feb. 1795, William Sloan to Field Prewit for 5 shillings for 300 acres granted by Chas. Pinckney, 10 Dec. 1791, recorded Bk.

(Pages 199-200 cont'd): D., no. 5, p. 260, on S. side of Cane Crk. of Keowee River. Wit: George Tarwater, Field Prewit, Jr. George Tarwater made oath to John Taylor, J.Q., 29 Jan.1803. (No recording date).

Pages 200-202: Moses James for $600 sold to William Clark 151 acres, surveyed for James Millwee, 15 Jan. 1788, in 96 Dist., on Brasstown Creek of Tugaloo River. Date: 6 Jul. 1801. Signed: Moses Jones. Wit: David Humphreys, William Fowler, Thos. N. Gibson. William Fowler made oath to John Barton, J.P., 15 May 1803(?). Nancy Jones, wife of Moses Jones, released dower to John Taylor, J.Q., 13 Jan. 1802. Signed: Anna (X) Jones. Rec: 25 Oct. 1802.

Page 202: Jacob Chamlee for $50 sold to William Chamlee 66½ acres, part of tract granted to Wm. Farmer, 4 Dec. 1786 by Wm. Moultrie, recorded Bk. BBBB, p. 417. Date: 24 Feb. 1802. Wit: Oden (X) Castleberry, Jas. Starrett. Edwin Castleberry made oath to Josiah Foster, J.P., 24 Dec. 1802.
Rec: 10 Feb. 1803.

Pages 202-203: Josiah McClure for $120 sold to Capt. David Sloan 200 acres on Deep Creek of Savannah River, where Widow Mogot McClure now lives, part of a tract granted to Edwd. T. McClure, 16 Jul. 1784 by Benjamin Guerard, conveyed to Josiah McClure, 9 Jul. 1792, bd. on N. and NW by Stribling, on SW by William McClure. Date: 14 Apr. 1802. Wit: William Morril, David Sloan, Jr. (Oath blank).

Pages 203-204: Willis Benson of Greenville Dist. for $100 sold to Russell Cannon of Pendleton Dist. (no amount) on both sides of Wolf Creek. Date: 18 Oct. 1802. Wit: Elijah Murphree, Joseph Dosett, Elijah Murphree made oath to David Murphree, J.P., 25 Dec. 1802.
Rec: 31 Jan. 1802. (1803?)

Pages 204-205: Andrew Barkley for $100 sold to John Wilson (Jr. in oath) 100 acres on Saluda River, part of tract granted John Darragh, 7 Nov. 1784, recorded Bk. FFFF, p. 321. Date: 22 Sep. 1802. Signed: Samuel Barkley, Andrew Barkley. Wit: John Craig, Joseph (X) Brown. John Craig made oath to E. Browne, J.P., 12 Oct. 1802.
Rec: 12 Oct. 1802.

Pages 205-206: David Anderson for $200 sold to Benjamin Dickson 128 acres on 26 Mile Creek, granted by Chas. Pinckney to Walter C. Dickson. Date: 27 Dec. 1802. Wit: John Love, Walter (X) Pool. John Love made oath to John Montgomery, J.P., 6 Jan. 1803.
Rec: 10 Jan. 1803.

Pages 206-207: Thomas Fields for $70 sold to Asa Hill 200 acres on Long Branch of Little River, bd. by land where William Williams now lives, Isaac Hill, Thomas Fields, William Stewart. Date: 30 Mar. 1801. Wit: James Smith, Wilson Beavart. James Smith made oath to Henry Burch, J.P., 11 Sep. 1801.
Rec: 12 Oct. 1802.

Pages 207: Moses Pheagans of Abbeville Dist. for $25 sold to Hugh Milligan & Co. of Dist. and State aforesaid, 262 acres on Beard's Crk. Pendleton Dist., granted William Moore Cavendish, 1792, then conveyed to Pheagans. Date: 8 Oct. 1802. Wit: Joseph Houston, Wm. Calhoun, Jr...... Abbeville Dist., Wm. Calhoun, Jr. made oath to Wm. Tatum, J.P., 19 Jan. 1803. Rec: 5 Feb. 1803.

Page 208: (Plat). Basil Hallum and Susanah Hallum for $1000 sold to James Chapman 299 acres

(Page 208 cont'd): on 18 Mile Creek of the Savannah River, part of 2 tracts granted Basil Hallum and Henry Goucher, bd. on NE by John Hallum, on SW by William Hubbard and William Hallum. Date: 7 Sep. 1802. Signed: Basil Hallum, Susanah Hallum. Wit: John Hallum, Sam. Baker. John Hallum made oath to John Willson, J.Q., 17 Jan. 1803. Rec: 19 Jan. 1803.

Page 209: By John Taylor, J.Q., certify Ann Long, formerly wife of William Twitty, did this day appear and relinquish to George Hays all claim of dower, 19 Feb. 1803. Signed: Ann (X) Long. Rec: 19 February 1803. (I did not find this deed in the index...BW)

Pages 209-210: Samuel Cherry, Elizabeth Weir, of Chester Dist., Samuel Talbert, of York Dist., James Loggins of Pendleton Dist., Wm. Hall of Union Dist., being only persons having right to tract of land surveyed for our father, Saml. Talbert, Sr., 2 Jun. 1784, sell to George Dilworth of Pendleton Dist. for $250 for 200 acres on N. fork of Brushy Creek, S. side of the Saluda River, bd. on SE by land surveyed for Samuel Tarbert. Date: 24 Jan. 1803. Signed: Saml. Cherry, Elizabeth Weir, Saml. Tarbert, James (X) Loggins, William Hall. Wit: Thomas Cherry, Richard Addis. Richard Addis made oath to Wm. Edmondson, J.P., 12 Feb. 1803. Rec: 22 Feb. 1803.

Pages 210-211: Charles White to Benjamin Dickson for Ł 30 stg. for 60 acres, part of tract granted to William Stone by Chas. Pinckney, 6 Apr.1789 and conveyed to William Cannon, then to White, on 26 Mile Creek, bd. by Dickson. Date: 22 Sep. 1794. Wit: Abraham (X) Eledge, Matthew Dickson. Abraham Eledge made oath to John Montgomery, J.P., 6 Jan. 1803. Rec: 10 Jan. 1803. For renunciation of dower, see Book I, p. 191.

Pages 211-212: Isaac Nicholson for $70 sold to Anthony Griffen 33½ acres, part of a tract granted Jesse Nevill, 6 Mar. 1797, on both sides of Conoross Creek. Date: 25 Jan. 1803. Wit: John Pounds, B. Starritt. B. Starritt made oath to James Starritt, J.P., 25 Jan. 1803. Rec: 29 Jan. 1803.

Pages 212-213: Isaac Sanders and Sarah, his wife, for $200 sold to Richard Standridge 150 acres on S. branch of George's Creek, Saluda River. Date: 17 Aug. 1801. Signed: Isaac (X) Sanders, Sally (X) Sanders. Wit: Alexander Patterson, John Armstrong. John Armstrong made oath to Robert Bowen, J. P., 10 Apr. 1802. Rec: 23 Feb. 1803.

Pages 213-214: Washington Dist., Crosby W. Miller for $40 sold to Anthony Griffen (no amount) granted Miller, 15 Aug. 1787 by Chas. Pinckney. Date: 29 Mar. 1800. Wit: Thomas Lofton, Mary (X) Whorton. Mary Whorton made oath to James Starritt, Esq. (No date). Rec: 29 Feb. 1803.

Page 214: Arthur Macadow (sic) for $20 sold to Anthony Griffen 25½ acres, part of tract granted Naace(?) Meeks, 7 Oct. 1799 by Edward Rutledge, Esq. on Conoross Creek. Date: 25 Jan. 1803. Signed: Arthur McAdoo. Wit: John Pounds, B. Starritt. Benjamin Starritt made oath to James Starritt, J.P., 25 Jan. 1803. Rec: 29 Jan. 1803.

Page 215: Isaiah Lewis for $700 sold to John Field, Jr. (no amount) on 12 Mile River, part of tract granted David Macled(?) and part of granted to Lewis Eaton. Date: 5 Apr. 1802. Wit: John Borin, John Feld. John Borin made oath to John Cochran, J.P., 9 Oct. 1802. Rec: 12 Oct. 1802.

Page 216:   Thomas Milsap, planter, for $400 sold to
                               Andrew McAlister, Yeoman, 200 acres on Wil-
                               son's Creek, granted Martha Coil, 15 Mar.
1787, recorded Bk. TTTT, p. 98. Date: 24 Aug. 1802. Wit: Charles Terrell,
Samuel Emison, Alexander McAlister. Kezia (X) Milsap, wife of Thomas Milsap, released dower to Elijah Browne, J.Q., 2 Sep. 1802. Andrew McAlister
made oath he saw Samuel Emberson, Charles Merrell and Alexander McAlister
sign as witnesses. E. Browne, Q.U., 24 Sep. 1802.
Rec: 11 Oct. 1802.

Page 217:   William Killen for $61.78½ sold to James
                               White feather beds, furniture, one bay mare
and cows and calves. Date: 8 Oct. 1802. Wit: James Wilson (only), who
made oath to Wm. Edmondson, J.Q., 8 Oct. 1802.
Rec: 14 Oct. 1802.

Pages 217-218:   Bartemius Reynolds for $400 sold to John
                               Rusk a negro boy about 18 years old called
                               Daniel. Date: 11 Feb. 1801. Wit: James Wood,
John Griffen. James Wood made oath to J. B. Earle, 24 Feb. 1803.
Rec: 2 Jul. 1802.

Pages 218-219:   William Warren for $400 sold to John Rusell
                               100 acres, part of tract granted to Andrew
                               Pickens, Jr., on 12 Mile River, 100 acres
of sd. tract conveyed from Warren to Thomas Kemp, bd. by Kemp and Rusell.
Date: 17 Nov. 1802. Signed: Wm. (X) Warren. Wit: Moses Liddell, M. Hammond. Michael Hammond made oath to John Taylor, J.Q., 8 Jan. 1803. Rebecca Warren, wife of the within named, released dower to John Taylor, 8
Jan. 1803.
Rec: 2 Mar. 1802.

Page 219:   James Anderson, Sr., planter, for love and
                               goodwill to my son, James Anderson, Jr.,all
                               my goods and chattels in my dwelling house,
also four negroes, to wit: (Smeared, appears to be...) Henry, ___oll,
Alice, and Sam, horses and cattle. Date: 26 Feb. 1803. Wit: John Swancy,
John Willson. John Shwansey made oath to John Willson, J.Q., 6 Feb.1803.
Rec: 1 Mar. 1803.

Pages 220-221:   23 Feb. 1799, Major Parsons is endebted to
                               Robert Anderson, Esq., for $186.50 upon
                               bond of penalty of $373 payable by 1 Jan.
next, mortgage 460 acres on both sides of Connoross Creek, bd. by Robert
Anderson, granted to Parsons, 3 Sep. 1798, recorded Bk. S., no. 5, p.203,
examined by Stephen Ravenell, Esq., Secretary ...(fades out here......)

Pages 221-222:   John Murphree for $420 sold to Aron Mur-
                               phree 212 acres on Town Creek of 12 Mile
                               River. Date: 23 Dec. 1798. Wit: David Mur-
phree, William Murphree. William Murphree made oath to David Murphree,JP
4 Feb. 1803.
Rec: 11 Feb. 1803.

Pages 222-223:   31 Jan. 1801, Charles Clements for $60 sold
                               to James Todd 200 acres on Broadmouth Creek
                               of the Saluda River, bd. by Richard Major,
part of tract granted to Clements (too dim to read....) mentions Bk. N.,
no. 5, p. 229...(witnesses not clear enough to read)...Agnes Clements released dower to Elijah Browne, J.Q., 20 Mar. 1801. Jacob Barbee made oath
he signed with John Murphree to Wm. Hall, J.P., 28 Mar. 1801.
Rec: 9 Feb. 1803.

Pages 223-225:   9 April 1795, Alexander Mahan of Washington
                               Dist. to David Welch for ₤ 70 stg. for 129
                               (?) acres on Brushy Creek of Saluda River,
granted by Thos. Pinckney, 5 Jan. 178_. Signed: Alexander Mahan, Margaret Mahan. Wit: Elizabeth (X) Laboon, Cate Laboon. Elizabeth Light, formerly Elizabeth Laboon, made oath, replied she cannot write her name, but
for them to put it down and that her sister also signed. William Welch

(Pages 223-225 cont'd): made oath he was also present. Robert McCann, J.P., 15 Nov. 1800(?).
Rec: 24 Jan. 1803.

Pages 225-226: 7 Jan. 1803, William Warren, planter, to Ebenezer Smith, planter, for $300 for 116 acres, part of 200 acres granted by Chas. Pinckney, bd. by John Land, William Warren and 12 Mile River. Signed: William (X) Warren. Wit: John Rusel, M. Hammond. Rebecca Warren, wife of William Warren, released dower to John Taylor, J.Q., 8 Jan. 1803. Michael Hammond made oath to John Taylor, Q.U., 8 Jan. 1803.

Pages 226-227: Joseph Woodall for $100 sold to Benjamin Chamble 100 acres, surveyed 26 Jun. 1784 for Joseph Walker. Date: 14 May 1802. Wit: Alex. McMillion, Abraham Moore. Abraham Moore made oath to Peter Keys, J.P., 11 Oct. 1802.
Rec: 8 Jan. 1803.

Pages 227-228: William Welch for $160 sold to Isaac Elrod 220 acres on N. side of Brushy Creek, bd. by William Welch and Isaac Elrod (except what Killison and Blackburn have taken). Date: 29 Jan. 1803. Wit: Wm. Faris, John Faris. William Faris made oath to Robt. McCann, J.P., 31 Jan. 1803. Rec: 21 Feb. 1803.

Pages 228-229: Boling Clark for £ 50 stg. sold to Jonathan Clark 320 acres (later says 200 acres) on 23 Mile Creek, where Jonathan Clark now lives, granted to Boling Clark, 21 Jun. 1785 by Benj. Guerard, recorded Bk. AAAA, (no page number), on Line to branch that runs between two plantations where Jonathan Clark and Joseph Clark now live. Date: 8 May 1796. Wit: Josiah Johnston, Jepthae Johnston. Boling Clark witnessed receipt. Josiah Johnston made oath to John Willson, J.P., 16 Jun. 1796.
Rec: 8 Feb. 1803.

Pages 229-230: Benjamin Starritt for $700 sold to James Doran 200 acres, granted John Daveys(Davis) (?), 16 Jul. 1784, by Benj. Guerard, on both sides of Conoross Creek of the Keowee River, bd. by James Brough. Date: 5 Mar. 1802. Wit: John Nichols, James Fuller.
Rec: 21 Feb. 1803. (Oath blank).

Page 230: William Welch for $190 sold to Obediah Merritt 120 acres on Brushy Creek. Date: 29 Jan. 1803. Wit: John Booth, Elijah Moor. Elijah Moore made oath to Robert McCann, J.P., 5 Feb. 1803.
Rec: 21 Feb. 1803.

Page 231: Samuel Taylor for $320 sold to Shadrack Chandler 640 acres on N. side of Keowee River, granted to Jonathan Clark, 22 March 1785. Date: 12 Mar. 1803. Wit: Samuel Cherry, Moses Liddell. (No oath).
Rec: 18 Mar. 1803.

Pages 231-232: David Clark for $500 sold to Jonathan Clark 395 acres on Harricane Creek of 26 Mile Crk of Seneca River, bd. on NW unknown, on W. by Osburn, granted David Clark by Chas. Pinckney, 2 Oct. 1797. Date: 7 Jun. 1800. Wit: John Cochran, Bolin Clark, Micach(?) Clark. Michach Clark made oath to Robt. McCann, J.P., 3 Aug. 1801.
Rec: 8 Feb. 1803.

Pages 232-233: Thomas Foster for $200 sold to William Welch 300 acres on Brushy Creek, bd. on line between Foster and Copeland and Isaac Elwel. Date: 29 Jan. 1803. Signed: Thomas Foster, Elizabeth (X) Foster. Wit: William Faris, John Johnson. William Faris made oath to Rt. McCann, J.P., 31 Jan. 1803.
Rec: 21 Feb. 1803.

Pages 233-234: Ferdinand Hopkins of Chester Dist., S. C., for $125 sold to John Ubanks, Jr. of Pendleton Dist., 251 acres, part of 2,225 ac. granted Hopkins by Chas. Pinckney, 2 Jan. 1792, on Gililin's Creek of 12 Mile River, bd. by John Eubanks, Jr. I acknowledge my signature in the presence of Mr. William Hubbard. Signed: Ferdn. Hopkins. William Hubbart made oath to John Willson, J.P., 30 Dec. 1802. Rec: 7 Mar. 1803.

Pages 234-235: James Martin of Lincoln Co., N. C. for $300 sold to John Hallum of Pendleton Dist. for 640 acres on 18 Mile Creek and 12 Mile River, granted Thomas Roberts. Date: 17 Aug. 1802. Wit: John Hallum, Ann(X) Hallum. John Hallum made oath he saw Mary Hallum sign as witness, 23 Feb. 1803 to Josiah Foster, J.P., 23 Feb. 1803.

Pages 235-236: David Watkins and Tempy Watkins, his wife, for $5 sold to William Shelby 100 acres,bd. by James Neil, part of 374 acres granted to George Forbes by Wm. Moultrie, 3 Jun. 1793, on Cuffey Creek of 23 Mile River. Date: 27 Jan. 1801. Signed: David Watkins, Tempy Watkins. Wit: John Swancy, Thomas Black. John Swancy made oath to John Wilson, J.Q., 22 Nov. 1802. Rec: 22 Dec. 1802.

Pages 236-237: George Hogge and Mary Hogge for $100 sold to John Woodall 100 acres on Great Generostee Creek of the Savannah River, granted Hogge, 29 Mar. 1799 by Edward Rutledge, Governor of S. C. Date: 5 Nov. 1802. Signed: George Hoge, Mary Hoge. Wit: John Woodall, Jr., Jonth. Hemphill, Robert Colwell. Robert (X) Kolwell made oath to P. Keys, J.P. 13 Nov. 1802. Rec: 12 Mar. 1803.

Page 238: 10 Sep. 1795, Jordan Reeves of Pendleton Dist. to Thomas McGregger of Laurence Co., S. C. for Ł 70 stg. for 125 acres on Big Generostee Creek, part of 254 acres granted Aeson Jay by Thos. Pinckney, recorded Bk. WWWW, p. 103, sd. 125 acres conveyed to Reeves, bd. on NE by James Hillhouse, on S. by Alex. McClusky, on W. and NW. by Jacob Chamble and Daniel Stringer, where Jordan Reeves now lives. Wit: Jesse Brown, George Grizsel, Simon Walker. Jesse Brown made oath to Joshua Saxon, J.P., 16 Nov. 1797. Rec: 26 Nov. 1802.

Page 239: Jonathan Thompson for $80 sold to Rose Reese 100 acres on 12 Mile River, bd. William Thompson, at mouth of S. fork of Mile River. Date: 6 Jan. 1803. Wit: Isaac January, David Murphree. Isaac January made oath to David Murphree, J.P., 6 Jan. 1802. Rec: 20 Jan. 1803.

Pages 239-240: John Powell for $12.50½ sold to William Nicholson 150 acres granted Jonas Hill, 2 Dec. 1799, on Cornhouse Creek of Little River of Keowee River, bd. by Jonas Hill, Fredrick Williams. Date: 12 Apr. 1802. Wit: Isaac Hill, Joshua Robins. Isaac Hill made oath to Henry Burch, J.P., 7 Jan. 1803. Rec: 24 Jan. 1803.

Pages 240-241: I, Elizabeth Manning am endebted to Elijah Walker, planter, for $30 and interest for 12 months, and for $60 mortgage one feather bed and furniture, 200 weight of merchantable pork, six pewter plates and one small pot, other items. Date: 28 Dec. ___. Signed: Elizabeth Mannin. (No witnesses or oath). Rec: 4 Mar. 1803.

Pages 241-242: William Shackleford for $120 sold to James Wood one lot in the Village of Pendleton,

(Pages 241-242 cont'd): of 1 acre. Date: 8 Mar. 1803. Wit: A. Kilpatrick, Aaron Steele. Alexander Kilpatrick made oath to Samuel H. Dickson, J.P., 30 Mar. 1803. Rec: 31 Mar. 1803.

Page 242: Charles Bond for $200 sold to Capt. James Wood 1 acre and No. 25 (in the Village of Pendleton?) bd. on W. on Public Square, S. by Thomas Hunter, E. by William Shackleford. Date: 15 Feb. 1803. Signed: A. Kilpatrick, Aaron Steele. Aaron Steele made oath to J. B. Earle, JP, 19 Mar. 1803. Rec: 3 Apr. 1803.

Pages 242-243: Benjamin Brimer for $100 sold to Samuel Henry 110 acres bd. by Brimer's old line, Andrew Tate and Files, granted Jacob Reed by Chas. Pinckney, 2 Oct. 1791, conveyed to James Millwee and from him to Brimer. Date: 27 Jan. 1802. Wit: David Dickey, William Henry. David Dickey made oath (no J. P.), 15 Jan.1803. Rec: 20 Mar. 1803.

Pages 243-244: Benjamin Brimer for $150 sold to Samuel Henry 390 acres, part of tract where Brimer now lives. Date: 27 Jan. 1802. Wit: David Dickey, William Henry. William Henry made oath to Hezekiah David, J. P., 11 Mar. 1803. Rec: 20 Mar. 1803.

Pages 244-245: Samuel Lofton, Sr. for $500 sold to William Hunter 170 acres, bd. by Hunter, 18 Mile Creek, David Kelton. Date: 27 Mar. 1802. Wit: Samuel Cherry, L. Payne. (Oath blank). Rec: 26 Mar. 1803.

Pages 245-246: Blake Mauldin for $1,500 sold to James Jett 47 acres on Big George's Creek of Saluda River. Date: 15 Nov. 1802. Wit: Solomon(X) Rozett, George Russel. Solomon Rosell made oath to Wm. Edmondson, J.P., 30 Mar. 1803. Rec: 4 Apr. 1803.

Pages 246-247: Sarah Williams for $62 sold to Major Lewis one feather bed and furniture, one chaff?, (chest?), bed and kitchen utinsels, 25 yrs. of six hundred warp chaine(?), one cradle, 1 pair cotton cards, 12 lbs. weight picked cotton, cow and calf, etc. Date: 17 Apr. 1803. Wit: John Holland, Nancy (X) Holland. (No oath). Rec: 24 Mar. 1803.

Pages 247-248: George Forbes for ₤ 65 stg. sold to John Oliver 140 acres where Forbes now lives on 26 Mile Creek of the Savannah River, bd. S. by James Martin, W. by Joseph Clark and Jonathan Clark. Date: 16 Nov.1802. Wit: Alexr. Oliver, John Hunnicutt. Alexander Oliver made oath to Robt. McCann, J.P., 16 Nov. 1802. Elizabeth (X) Forbes released dower to John Wilson, J.Q., 16 Nov. 1802. Rec: 2 Mar. 1803.

Page 248: Samuel Tate for ₤ 30-17 s.-6 p. sold Lewis D. Martin one negro girl named Hannah. Date: 13 Mar. 1803. If bond paid by 14 Mar. 1804 then sale will be void. Wit: Obediah Trimier, David Sloan. Rec: 23 Mar. 1803. (No oath).

Page 249: Isaac Williams for $150 sold to John Reed 133 acres on E. side of Keowee River, part of a tract granted to William McKey by Chs. Pinckney, recorded Bk. KKKK, p. 632, bd. by sd. McKay. Date: 18 Mar.1803. Signed: Isaac (X) Williams. Wit: Henry Hays, Joshua (X) Ham. Joshua Ham made oath to J.B. Earle, J.P., 19 Mar. 1803. Rec: 20 Mar. 1803.

Pages 250-251: Nathl. Hall for $300 sold to Maldin Tucker (could be Aleden) 93 acres, the W. part of Robert Hall's land, now dest.(sic) on First Creek and Rockey River, (except where Robert Hall's, dest., Spring is), bd. by Bartley Tucker and Benjamin Farmer. Date: 13 May 1802. Wit: James Erwin, John (X) Prewit, Patience (X) Prewit. Dorcys Hall, wife of Nathaniel Hall, released dower to Elijah Browne, J.Q., 13 May 1802. James Erwin made oath to E. Browne, J.Q., 13 May 1802. Rec: 17 Mar. 1803.

Pages 251-252: 15 Feb. 1802, Robert Henderson of Jackson Co., Ga. to Patty McDaniel and Henry McDaniel as Administrators of Henry McDaniel, Jr., dec'd., for $126 for 150 acres on N. side of the Keowee River, bd. by Glen, granted to Henderson by Wm. Moultrie. Wit: Nimrod (X) Kelfin Blag, Tim Warhurst, John McDaniel. (No oath). Rec: 14 Mar. 1803.

Page 252: Thomas Robertson for Ł 60 stg. sold Henry Whitmire 150 acres, part of 383 acres..... granted Benjamin Whorton, recorded Bk. F, no. 5, p. 389, on Oconee Creek of Little River of Keowee River, bd. by Thomas Kenedy. Date: (blank). Wit: James Files, Christopher (X) Whitmire. James Files made oath to Henry Burch, J.P., 23 Oct. 1802. Rec: 17 Mar. 1803.

Page 253: John Sison for $180 sold to Peter Keys 130 acres on Big Generostee of the Savannah River, "supposed to be granted to Mullin" bd. by line of Keys and John Mauldin(?). Date: 30 Nov. 1802. Wit: Lazs. Tilly, James Sison. Lazarus Tilly made oath to J. George, J.P., 4 Jan.1803. Rec: 17 Mar. 1803.

Pages 253-254: Isaac Williams for $150 sold to Joshua Ham 150 acres on E. side of Keowee River, part of tract granted William McKey by William Moultrie, recorded Bk. KKKK, p. 623, bd. by Wm. McKey and Henry Hoge. Date: 18 Mar. 1803. Wit: Henry Hays, John Reid. John Reid made oath to J. B. Earle, Clk. 19 Mar. 1803. Rec: 26 Mar. 1803.

Pages 254-255: 3 Apr. 1795, Henry, Sr. (sic) (Loury) to Henry Loury, Jr. for Ł 10 for 100 acres on Beaverdam Creek of the Toogaloo River, bd. on SW by Jacob Holland, on W. by land surveyed for General Huger, granted Henry Loury, Sr. by Wm. Moultrie, 2 Dec. 1793. Wit: Thomas Farrar, Peggy Farrar. (No oath). Rec: 15 Mar. 1803.

Pages 255-256: James Graham for $160 sold to Nathaniel Estes 185 acres on Generostee Creek of Savannah River, laid out for Robert Peacock, bd. on SW by Joseph Land, on NW by Bartholomew White. Date: 16 Feb. 1803.Wit: John Linn, James Parker. John Linn made oath to Hezekiah Davis, J.P., 16 Mar. 1803. Rec: 15 Mar. 1803.

Pages 256-257: John Ervin and Alexander Ervin for $1,000 sold to Harbert Tucker 250½ acres on the N side of Rocky River, granted Alexander Ervin, 15 Oct. 1784, part of 3 tracts. One of 68½ acres where John Ervin now lives, 140 acres where Alexander Ervin lives, which was sold as his property by John Harris, Sheriff, also 42 acres adjoining Hall's Mill Dam on First Creek, referred to by plat made by John McMahan, D.S. Date: 2 Nov. 1802. Wit: John Farmer, Benjamin Browne. John Farmer made oath to E. Browne, J.Q., 2 Nov. 1802. Unity (X) Ervin released dower to E.Browne J.Q., 2 Nov. 1802. (wife of John Ervin, the only one to release...BW). Rec: 15 Mar. 1803.

Pages 257-258: John Young is bound to Alexander Sherrard for $180 and as security, 200 ac. in 96

(Pages 257-258 cont'd): Dist., on Little Generostee Creek granted Matthew Young and by right of inheritance became property of John Young, also, 140 acres granted Matthew Young, a part of 440 acres, 2 Sep. 1793, conveyed to John Young, 15 Feb. 1800. Date: 25 Feb. 1803. Wit: Wm. Richards, James Young. William Richards made oath to Nathan Lusk, J.P., 25 Feb. 1803. Rec: 15 Mar. 1803.

Pages 258-260: Charles Clemments for $40 sold to Reuben Brock 130 acres on W. fork of Barker's Crk of the Savannah River, bd. by Brock, David Green, Thomas Brown and Isaac Brown, part of 617 acres granted William Wightman, 5 Sep. 1785 by Wm. Moultrie. Date: 9 Sep. 1797. Wit: Samuel Brown, William Brown, James Willson. James Willson made oath to William Hall, J.P., 30 Dec. 1797. Rec: 14 Mar. 1803.

Pages 260-261: 8 Aug. 1795, Joel Vaughan of Washington Dist., to Absolom Fares, of same, for Ł 50 stg. for (no amount), part of tract granted 27 Aug. 1791 by Chas. Pinckney to James Galaspey, conveyed to Vaughan 27 Jul. 1793, W. of old boundary line on Wolf Creek, of 12 Mile River and Daughdew(?) Creek of the Saluda River, for 779 acres, bd. by John Langley, William Edings, Daughty, Jacob Vance's land, now Samuel Martin's and John Tenison's land now Stephen Cantrel's. Wit: Robert Boud, John Hood. John Hood made oath to Robert Bowen, J.P., 11 Apr. 1797. Rec: 16 Mar. 1803.

Pages 261-262: 19 Feb. 1802, John Harris to Thomas Cureton for $200, 140 acres granted to William Young 3 Dec. 1792 on Town Creek of 12 Mile River, bd. by Abraham Powell, Edward Harris and Wm. Robertson (excepting small corner taken by Natheal Newman's land). Wit: Isaac Meirs, Archibald Harris, Henry Griffen. Isaac Meirs made oath to George Foster, J.P., 9 Oct. 1802. Rec: 11 Mar. 1802.

Page 262: Lewis Rolston is bound to Thomas Harrison for Ł 30 stg., 2 Feb. 1791, and makes title to 12 acres on Tugalowe River, joining the lands formerly the property of Mr. Payne, to be paid on or before 1 May next. Wit: Godfrey Isbell, Hannah (X) Isbell. (No oath). Rec: 15 Mar. 1803.

Pages 262-263: 14 Feb. 1799, Nathaniel Newman to William Griffen for $400 for 350 acres, granted to Newman, 7 Dec. 1794, on Town Creek of 12 Mile River, bd. by Newman and Powell. Wit: Eli Langford, Green Collier, Stephen Cantrell. Stephen Cantrell made oath to George Foster, J.P., 14 Nov. 1799. Rec: 14 Mar. 1803.

Page 263: Received of John Hamilton $480 for a negro fellow named Jaible, about 19 years of age. Date: 27 Jan. 1803. Signed: Samuel Duff. Wit: Reese Bowen, James Hamilton. (No oath). Rec: 14 Mar. 1803.

Pages 263-264: Stephen Roach for $600 sold to Mary Story 240 acres on W. side of 18 Mile Creek, bd. on NW by George Reese, part of 640 acres granted Peter Sinker. Date: 5 Jul. 1802. Wit: James Starret, B. Starret. Rebeccah Roach wife of Stephen Roach released dower to John Willson, J.Q. 15 Mar. 1803. (No oath). Rec: 25 Apr. 1803.

Pages 264-265: Nimrod Smith for $250 sold to James Mattison 106 acres on Little Creek of Saluda River, granted Thomas Davis, then to Nimrod Smith. Date: 8 Feb. 1803. Wit: A. Boyse, William Williamson. Lettice (X) Smith, wife of Nimrod Smith, released dower to Elijah Browne, Q. U., 28

(Pages 264-265 cont'd): Feb. 1803. William Williamson made oath to E. Brown, 28 Feb. 1803.

Pages 265-266: 20 Oct. 1792, Daniel Putman to Isaac Evans for 10 shillings stg. for 115½ acres on the Savannah River, part of a tract granted to Joseph Lowe, by Thos. Pinckney, 17 Apr. 1788, and William Love being the lawful attorney of sd. Joseph Love, conveyed tract of 250 acres to Daniel Putman, 24 Oct. 1791, bd. by land granted to William Love. Wit: Christopher Casey, Charles Bond. Christopher (Casey) made oath to E. Browne, JQ, 8 Mar. 1794.
Rec: 13 Mar. 1803.

Pages 266-267: 1 Jun. ___, Charles Herd of Abbeville Co. to William Forbes of Pendleton Co. for ₤5 stg. for 70 acres now in the possession of Forbes, surveyed for Herd, 3 Oct. 1786, bd. on NE by John Wornick on the Rocky River. Wit: Eliab Moore, Isaac Logans. (No oath).
Rec: 7 Apr. 1803.

Pages 267-268: 21 Mar. 1801, Henry Woolbanks to Abraham Duck(Duke?) for $350 for 125 acres on Wolf Creek of 12 Mile River, bd. by John Tatum, Howell Miller and Samuel Bradcut, part of tract granted Benjamin Perry and part granted Josiah Patterson. Signed: Henry Wilbanks. Wit: John Wilbanks, James Brown. John Wilbanks made oath to John Verner, J.P., 11 Apr. 1801. Phebe Woolbanks, wife of Henry Woolbanks, released dower to E. Browne, J.Q., 20 May 1801.
Rec: 14 Mar. 1803.

Pages 268-269: 4 Dec. 1802, Isaac Elwaters to George Hogwood (later spelled Hagood) for $200 for 200 acres on Wolf Creek, bd. by Earle, to conditional line by Isaac Atwater and Patterson Chiloke(?),(later Childers), witnessed by Jesse Suggs, Robert Boyd, Gillaspy and Duff. Signed: Isaac Alewaters. Wit: Chil. Merony, Isaac (X) Janeway. Isaac January made oath to David Murphree, J.P., 4 Jan. 1803.
Rec: 11 Mar. 1803.

Pages 269-270: ___ Dec. 1790(?), Telly Merrik (also Tilly Merrick) of the City of Charleston, Merchant, to William Forbes of 96 Dist., planter, for ₤9 stg. for 200 acres in Forbes possession, part of tract surveyed for John Wornock, 18 Aug. 1785 and certified for Augustus Merick, 13 Jan. 1787, bd. on E. by David Hopkins, on Rocky River in 96 Dist. Wit: John Oldham, John Warnock. (No oath).
Rec: 7 Apr. 1803.

Pages 270-271: Samuel Bradcut for $100 sold to Abraham Duck 100 acres on Wolf Creek, part of tract granted to Benjamin Perry by Wm. Moultrie, 5 Jun. 1786, bd. by Howell Miller. Date: 20 Oct. 1801. Wit: Jesse Miller, Wm. Millen, John Highsmith. William Miller made oath to David Murphree, J.P., 24 Oct. 1801. Susanah Bradcut, wife of Samuel Bradcut, released dower to John Willson, J.Q., 27 Oct. 1801.
Rec: 14 Mar. 1803.

Pages 271-272: Mark Ward for $200 sold to Isaac Alewaters 100 acres on Wolf Creek, bd. by Earle, line between Ward and Abel Fike, line between John Gillaspy and Samuel Duff. Date: 8 Mar. 1802. Signed: Mark (X) Ward. Wit: James Jett, Hudson Ross. James Jett made oath to John Cohran, J. P. 14 Mar. 1803.
Rec: 4 Mar. 1803.

Page 272: Richard Thompson and Elizabeth Boyd for $250 sold to Lewis Easten (later Eaten), 100 acres on S. fork of 12 Mile Creek bd. by Archable Boyd and Elijah Mayfield. Date: 13 Nov. 1802. Signed: Richard (X) Thompson, Elizabeth (X) Boyd. Wit: James Thompson, William Mur-

(Page 272 cont'd): phree. James Thompson made oath to David Murphree, J. P., 13 Nov. 1802. Rec: 15 Mar. 1803.

Page 273: William Shelby for $150 sold to John Cary 120 acres, part of 2 tracts, one granted George Forbus, the other granted Aaron Neal bd. by William Sims, on Cuffey Creek of 23 Mile Creek. Date: 19 Jul.1802. Wit: Thos. Laymar, Robert Masey. (No oath). Rec: 26 Apr. 1803.

Pages 273-274: John Maxwell for $20 sold to George Tucker 403 acres surveyed for John Waddell, 6 Jan. 1800, on Rocky Branch of 18 Mile Creek of Seneca River, bd. on NE by John Woodside, on SE by Andrew Pickens, on SW by William Gilham, on S. by John Miller. ____1803. Wit: M. Hammond, B. W. Finley. (Oath blank).

Page 274: Wm. Thompson for $200 sold to Lewis Eaten 100 acres on S. fork of 12 Mile (Creek) bd. by Archable Boyd and Elijah Mayfield. Date: 30 Nov. 1802. Wit: Wm. Murphree, James Thompson. William Murphree made oath to David Murphree, J.P., 16 Dec. 1802. Rec: 15 Mar. 1803.

Pages 275-276: Nathaniel Nall for $220 sold to Samuel Stephens 220 acres on 12 Mile River, part of 640 acres bd. by Nall and John McEntire. Date: 4 Nov. 1802. Signed: Nathan Nall. Wit: John McEntire, John Edwards. John Edwards made oath to John Wilson, J.Q., 4 Nov. 1802. Mary (X) Nall, wife of Nathan Nall released dower to John Wilson, 4 Nov. 1802. Rec: 15 Mar. 1803.

Page 276: Nathan Nall for $400 sold to John McEntire (no amount) part of 640 acres on 12 Mile River. Date: 4 Nov. 1802. Wit: Samuel Stevens, John Edwards. John Edwards made oath to John Willson, J.Q., 4 __ 1802. Mary Nall released dower to John Willson, 4 Nov. 1802. Rec: 15 Mar. 1803.

Page 277: John Reeves for $20 sold to John Heaten 104 acres on Mountain Creek of Savannah River, part of 428 acres surveyed 18 Mar. 1800 for Reeves by John McMahan. Date: 21 Oct. 1801. Wit: Hezekiah Davis, Jonathan Watson. (Plat). Hezekiah Davis made oath to E. Browne, Q.U., (no date). Rec: 15 Mar. 1803.

Pages 277-279: 30 Sep. 1795, Jesse Goodwin of Washington Dist. for Ł 200 stg. to John Langley for 328 acres, part of two surveys adjoining each other on Shoal Creek of the Saluda River; the first of 168 acres granted to Balis Earle by Wm. Moultrie, 6 Nov. 1786, recorded "Grant Bk. the second NQQQQ, p. 14". The second adjoining the above tract granted to James Gillispie by Chas. Pinckney, 5 Sep. 1791, recorded Bk. D., no. 5, p. 52, bd. by Jep Goodwin. Wit: John Yager, George Rusille. John Yager made oath to William Reed, J.P., 30 Sep. 1795, but was signed by George Yager. Rec: 15 Mar. 1803.

Page 279: William Butler, formerly planter, for $100 sold to David Hembry one horse. Date: 6 Mar. 1803. Wit: James (X) Butler, who made oath to Colin Campbell, J.P., 14 Mar. 1803. Rec: 14 Mar. 1803.

Pages 279-280: William Forbes and Margaret Forbes for $256 sold to John Heury (Fleury?) 270 acres on both sides of Rocky River, 200 acres granted Augustus Merrick, 5 Feb. 1787, the other 70 acres granted Charles Hea-

301

(Pages 279-280 cont'd): rel, 2 Jun. 1788. Signed: Wm. Forbes, Margaret Forbes. Wit: Andrew Warnock, Michl. Warnock. Michael Warnock made oath to John Willson, J.Q., 28 May 1801. Margaret Forbes released dower to John Willson, J.Q., 28 May 1801. Rec: 7 Apr. 1801.

Pages 280-281: Capt. Field Farrar was entitled for certain services, to Military bounty lands from the Government of the United States and Capt. Field Farrar died intestate.....I, Thomas Farrar, being his heir at law appoint Thomas T. Tucker, Treasurer of the United States, my attorney to convey and dispose of my rights and titles to Warrants of Bounty Lands. Date: 14 May 1803. Wit: Joseph Taylor, Samuel Cherry. Samuel Cherry made oath to John Taylor, Q.U., 14 May 1803. Rec: 14 May 1803.

Pages 281-282 (torn off): I, James Love appoint Thomas Butler of Logan Co., Ky. my lawful attorney to demand and give receipt for all monies, goods and chattels due me by David Stone, Executor of the Estate of Henry McDaniel, dec'd., late of Pendleton Co., S. C., by legacy bequeathed to me or my wife, Sarah Love, lately McDaniel. Date: 15 Mar. 1803. Wit: Thomas (X) McDaniel, Caleb Lindsey....State of Tennessee, Knox Co., Thomas McDaniel made oath to James Cozby, J.P., 17 Mar. 1803.....I, Archibald Roane, Gov. of the State of Tn., certify James Fazby is acting Justice of Peace for Knox Co. Great Seal of Tn. affixed at Knoxville, 17 Mar. 1803. William Maclin, Secretary. Rec: 2 May 1803.

Pages 282-283 (torn off): William Rose, Sr., for $300 sold to David Lewis (no amount) on N. fork of Little River of the Keowee River, bd. on N. by James Slaton (or Slator), on S. by Jolley, part of three tracts. Date: 10 Jan. 1803. Wit: William McFarland, Samuel Harbin. William McFarland made oath to Henry Burch, J.P., 10 Jan.1803. Rec: 5 Jun. 1803.

Pages 283-284: William Bourland and James McClure for $600 sold to Titus Fox 200 acres on S. fork of Dawdy's Creek of the Saluda River, bd. by Howell Dawdy, Talton Hasley, Joseph Looper, John Davis, William Bourland, and Harmon Read's old line. Wit: John Bourland, Wm. Davis. Wm. Davis made oath to George Foster, J.P., 26 Oct. 1802. Rec: 14 Mar. 1803.

Pages 284-285: 20 Sep. 1800, Thomas Robinson to John Kelly for $130 for 88 acres, part of tract Robinson lives on, on the Keowee River, bd. by John Kelly. Wit: James Kell, Robert Kell. James Kell made oath to Joseph Reed, J.P., 11 Oct. 1800. Rec: 5 Apr. 1803.

Pages 285-286: 22 Jun. 1792, William Guffin, weaver, to John Knox for Ł 20 stg. (no amount acreage) on both sides of Little Beaverdam Creek of the Toogalow River, surveyed for Robert Smith, 6 Aug. 1790, granted Guffin, 6 Jun. 1791 by Chas. Pinckney, recorded Bk. C., no. 5, p. 298...... Signed: William McGuffin. Wit: Reece Jones, Jane Anderson.....I assigne my right and title to Robert Smith for value received, 14 Sep. 1793..... Signed: John Knox. Wit: Mary (X) Ramsey. Jane Anderson made oath to J.B. Earle, Clk., 10 Jan. 1803. Rec: 6 Jun. 1803.

Pages 286-287: Love (Lane?) Mullins for $32 sold to George Capehart 100 acres on N. side of Toogalow River, part of 330 acres William Guest made Lease and Release to Gershim Allen, granted William Guest for 69 acres, 3 Mar. 1788. Condition, if Lane Mullins pays Capehart $32, above is null and void. Date: 16 Mar. 1803. Signed: Love(?) Mullins. Wit: Aaron Steele, Benjamin Ragsdale. Steele made oath to J. Taylor,1 Jun.1803. Rec:4 Ju.1803

Pages 287-288:   Joseph Chapman of Pendleton Dist. sold to
                                   Blake Mauldin of Greenville Dist., 403 ac.
                                   by two surveys, (part) in Greenville and
(Part) in Pendleton Dist. on both sides of the Saluda River, opposite
Table Mountain, 305 acres granted Joseph Strobel, 16 Jul. 1784 by Benj.
Guerard, recorded Bk. AAAA, p. 35, and 98 acres granted Thomas Towns on
1 Oct. 1792 by Chas. Pinckney, on S. side of Saluda, adjoining the above
tract, recorded Bk. F., no. 5, p. 208. Date: 30 Dec. 1800. Wit: Joseph
Gillison, John Mauldin. John Mauldin made oath to George Foster, J. P.,
15 Apr. 1803.
Rec: 6 Jun. 1803.

Page 288:   John Reede for $8 sold to George Capehart
                                   a negro boy named Abrom, about 21 years of
                                   age.....condition if John Reide pay Cape-
hart $8 by 1 Oct. next, obligation is void. Date: 1 Sep. 1802. Signed:
John Reed. Wit: M. Hammond, John (X) Richards. Michael Hammond made oath
to J. B. Earle, Clk., 8 Jun. 1803.
Rec: 4 Jun. 1803.

Pages 288-289:   Peter Gray of Spartanburg Dist., S. C. for
                                   ₤ 100 stg. sold to Baylis Earle of Spartan-
                                   burg Dist., 640 acres on Connoross Creek,
in fork of Toogalow and Keowee Rivers, granted Peter Gray, 15 Jan. 1785
by Wm. Moultrie. Date: 31 Dec. 1802. Wit: Eaton Walker, Gabl. Benson.....
Spartanburg Dist., Gabriel Benson made oath to James Jordan, J.P., May 18
of 1803. Rec: 20 May 1803.

Pages 289-290:   Willoughby Pugh, planter, for $700 sold to
                                   John Verner, planter, 250 acres, where I
                                   now live, on Choestoe Creek of Toogalow Ri-
ver, bd. by David Pugh, Vanderhorst, granted Stephen Drayton by Benjamin
Guerard. Date: 25 Dec. 1801. Wit: Wm. Wakefield, Jean (X) Varner. Will-
iam Wakefield made oath to John Barton, J.P., 15 May 1802. Elizabeth (X)
Pugh, wife of Willoughby Pugh, released dower to John Willson, J.Q., 9
May 1802. Rec: 1 Jun. 1803.

Pages 291-292:   8 Sep. 1795, Anselm Roe, planter, to James
                                   Watson, planter, for natural love and af-
                                   fection I bear James Watters, 150 acres in
96 Dist. on 12 Mile River, E. side of Keowee River, recorded Pendleton
Co., Bk. B., p. 21, 25 Jun. 1792, by John Miller, now in possession of
James Waters. Wit: William Gilham, John Huggins, Samuel Waters. Samuel
Watters made oath to John Taylor, J.Q., 21 Apr. 1803.
Rec: 27 Apr. 1803.

Pages 292-293:   11 Jun. 1795, Joseph Stepp, Sr. and Joseph
                                   Stepp, Jr., for ₤ 50 for 100 acres on S.
                                   side of Toxaway Creek, part of 975 acres
granted Col. Benjamin Cleveland, bd. by Cleveland and James Blair, where
Joseph Stepp, Sr. now lives. Wit: William Martin, Martin Williams. William Martin made oath to John Barton, J.P., 22 Nov. 1796.
Rec: 14 Mar. 1803.

Pages 293-294:   David McCaleb for $2,275 sold to William
                                   Steele, Esq., the following tracts of land,
                                   to wit: one lot of 16 acres, no. 13 in the
Village of Pendleton Courthouse, reference plat made by Robt. McCann, Esq;
300 acres, part of tract granted Charles Lay on both sides of 18 Mile Crk
adj. above 16 acres, SW to 18 Mile Creek at bridge going to the Stone
Meeting House, except 14 acres conveyed by McCaleb to George Capehart on
SE corner, adj. Town lots. Date: 9 May 1803. Wit: James Wood, J. B. Earle
...James Wood made oath to John Taylor, Q.U., 10 May 1803.
Rec: 10 May 1803.

Pages 294-295:   4 Apr. 1803, David McCaleb, Sheriff of Pen-
                                   dleton Dist., whereas, Dolly Combs and oth-
                                   ers were seized of 150 acres on 12 Mile Ri-
ver, Samuel Earle obtained Judgement against Dolly Combs and others for
$580, whereas, all goods, chattels, houses and lands were sold at public

(Pages 294-295 cont'd): auction 7 Mar. 1803 for $51 to Dolly Combs she being highest bidder. Wit: M. Hammond, George Edmondson. Michael Hammond made oath to J. B. Earle, Clk. 7 Jun. 1803. Rec: 18 Jun. 1803.

Pages 295-296: John Hunter of Pendleton Dist. for $400 sold to Samuel Hunter, Jr. of Augusta Co., Va., two lots in the Town of Pendleton, no. 11, on which the Gaol of the County used to stand, no. 1, of 11-3/4 ac. bd. by Major John Taylor on one side and by lots laid out in the Town of Pendleton and the Commons for sd. Town. Date: 24 Oct. 1802. Wit: J. B. Earle, M. Hammond, John Mills. Michael Hammond made oath to J. B. Earle, Clk., 3 Mar. 1803. Rec: 7 Mar. 1803.

Page 296: Hollingsworth Vandiver for $110 sold John Coxx 170 acres on E. side of 23 Mile Creek of the Savannah River, part of tract granted 2 Mar. 1801 by John Drayton, Governor. Date: 23 Dec. 1802. Signed: Hollingsworth (X) Vandiver. Wit: John Taylor, Moses Liddell. Moses Liddell made oath to J. B. Earle, Clk., 8 Jun. 1803. Rec: 8 Jun. 1803.

Pages 297-298: 20 Oct. 1792, Charles Bond of Elbert Co., Ga. to Isaac Evans of Pendleton Co., for 10 shillings stg. for 75 acres, part of 300 acres granted William Love by Benj. Guerard, 1 Jan. 1785, on N. E. side of the Savannah, 150 acres of same tract conveyed by William Love to Thomas Shockley, Sr., 17 Mar. 1789, the other 150 acres conveyed by Love to Charles Bond, 24 Oct. 1791, bd. by Savannah River and Isaac Mother's ;amd/ Wit: Christopher Casey, Daniel Putman. Daniel Putman made oath to E. Browne, J.P., 8 Mar. 1794. Rec: 13 Mar. 1803.

Page 298: William Gillispy, planter, for $11 sold to James Willson, planter, 2½ acres, being within Willson's fence, part of the tract where Gillispy now lives, surveyed for William Cosby. Date: 5 Feb. 1803. Wit: William Willson, Hugh Willson. Hugh Willson made oath to Samuel H. Dickson, J.P., 11 Mar. 1803. Rec: 15 Mar. 1803.

Pages 298-299: 28 Dec. 1802, Jacob Capehart to William Willison for $300 for 222 acres on Saddlers Creek of the Savannah River, granted Samuel Love by Wm. Moultrie, 3 Oct. 1786, recorded Bk. QQQQ, p. 117. Wit: Moses Payne, Mary (X) Payne. Moses Payne made oath to Samuel H. Dickson, J. P., 15 Mar. 1803. Rec: 15 Mar. 1803.

Pages 299-300: George Smith for $230 sold to James Evett 200 acres, above where Smith lives, granted Charles Mulhering by Thos. Pinckney, 3 Sep. 1789, on 12 Mile River. Date: 12 Aug. 1802. Signed: George Smith, Charity (X) Smith. Wit: James Watters, Richard Blackstock. Richard Blackstock made oath to Samuel H. Dickson, J.P., 13 Mar. 1803. Rec: 13 Mar. 1803.

Pages 300-301: William Claton (later Slaton) of Greenville Co., S. C. for $50 sold to William Honey of Pendleton Dist., 100 acres on N. fork of Big Creek of Saluda River, part of tract granted James Hamilton by William Moultrie, 30 Mar. 1792, given to Sarah Slaton, wife of William Slaton by deed of Gift, 3 Aug. 1796. Date: 30 Apr. 1802. Signed: William Slaton. Wit: W. C. Hamilton, Thomas Hone. Sarah (X) Slaton released dower to John Willson, J.Q., 29 Oct. 1802. William Hamilton made oath to John Wilson, J.Q., 29 Oct. 1802. Rec: 15 Mar. 1803.

Pages 301-302: Mary Jones, John McWhirter and Robert Mc-

(Pages 301-302 cont'd): Whirter for $250 sold to Samuel Brown 250 acres (no location). Date: 9 Mar. 1802.
Signed: Mary (X) Jones, John McWherter, Robert McWherter. Wit: Thomas Brown, John McWherter. Thomas Brown made oath to Robt. McCann, J.P., 9 Oct. 1802. Rec: 15 Mar. 1803.

Pages 302-303: James Martin of Lincoln Co., N. C. for $1,200 sold to Jonathan Hemphill of Pendleton Dist., 640 acres granted John Parker, 16 Jul. 1784 and by John Edwards and William Hort, Esqs., Treasurers of the State to John Martin, 9 Apr. 1789, on Generostee Creek of Savannah River, bd. by John Tippen. Date: 10 Nov. 1802. Wit: Samuel Hillhouse, Moses Faris, William J. Walker. William Walker made oath to Hezekiah Davis, J. P., 15 Mar. 1803.
Rec: 15 Mar. 1803.

Pages 303-304: John Prater Odell for $500 sold to Jonathan Reeder a negro woman, named Lusa, with a girl child named Leah. Date: 7 Jul. 1802.
Signed: John (X) Prater Odell. Wit: Joshua Reeder, who made oath to J.B. Earle, 16 Mar. 1803.
Rec: 25 Aug. 1802.

Page 304: Christopher Hargraves for ₤ 50 stg. sold James Johnson 140 acres on the Seneca River where Johnson now lives. Date: 21 Aug. 1799.
Wit: William Bennett, Cooper Bennett. William Bennett made oath to John Verner, J. P., 14 Sep. 1799.
Rec: 14 Mar. 1803.

Page 305: Jesse Hall for good will I bear toward my (son?) Zachariah Hall, freely give all my Estate, real and personal consisting of 150 acres of land, cattle, feather beds and furniture, etc. Date: 7 Jan.1803.
Signed: Jesse (X) Hall. Wit: Thos. Lofton, John Adair. (No oath).
Rec: 10 Jan. 1803.

Pages 305-306: Samuel Lofton for $150 sold to James Watters 150 acres part of 500 acres granted to Samuel Lofton by Chas. Pinckney, 2 April 1798, on 12 Mile River. Date: 31 Mar. 1801. Wit: B. Starrett, James Lofton. Benjamin Starrett made oath to John Taylor, J.Q., 29 Jun. 1803.
Rec: 26 Apr. 1803.

Pages 306-307: John Blithe of Greenville Dist. for $500 sold to Dyer Tally of the same, 221 acres on S. side of Saludy River, known as my old place, part of two tracts granted by Benj. Guerard to Joseph Copeland and sold to John Blythe. Date: 1 Aug. 1801. Signed: John (X) Blythe. Wit: P. Bradford, William Hunt. Phil Bradford made oath to Colin Campbell,JP 14 Mar. 1803.
Rec: 14 Mar. 1803.

Pages 307-308: John Hallum, planter, for $200 sold to Charles Clements 302 acres on Pea Creek of the Savannah River, granted 1 Feb. 1790 by Chas. Pinckney. Date: 14 Oct. 1801. Wit: Joel (X) Braseal, Daniel Owen. Joel Braseal made oath to D. Murphree, J.P., 11 Mar. 1803.
Rec: 14 Mar. 1803.

Pages 308-310: 19 Apr. 1796, James Hodges of Abbeville Co. to Reuben Brock of Pendleton Co. for ₤ 30 stg. for 500 acres in Washington Dist,part of 1,000 acres granted Hodges, 2 Jan. 1792, by Chas. Pinckney, recorded Bk. D, no. 5, p. (blank), on Barker's Creek of Little River of Savannah River. Wit: Benjamin Aldridge, Samuel Evans, Loyd Brock. Loyd Brock made oath to Wm. Hall, J.Q., 13 Jan. 1795.
Rec: 14 Mar. 1803.

Pages 310-311: Henry Bower for $155 sold to Andrew Oliver

(Pages 310-311 cont'd): 168 acres, being one tract of 120 acres granted Britain George, 5 Jan. 1797, branch of 23 Mile Creek of the Savannah River, the other of 48 acres, part of tract granted Hugh Warnock, bd. on SW by above tract, granted by Warnock to Margaret Blair, then to William Blair, then to John Wilkinson and from him to Britain George, from George to Bower. Date: 13 Dec. 1802. Signed: Henry (X) Bower. Wit: Job Smith, Samuel Oliver. Job Smith made oath to John Willson, J.Q., 13 Dec. 1802. Margery (X) Bower, wife of Henry Bower released dower to John Willson, 13 Dec. 1802.
Rec: 10 Jun. 1803.

Pages 311-312: Jacob Earnest for $500 sold to William Brown 240 acres on 23 Mile Creek, on line of Thomas Coddle, Jacob Earnest. Date: 7 Feb. 1803. Signed: Jacob (X) Earnest. Wit: William Faris, James Foster. James Foster made oath to Wm. Edmondson, J.Q., 15 Apr. 1803.
Rec: 15 Apr. 1803.

Pages 312-313: William Turpin of Charleston, Merchant, for Ł 266-13.4.sold to Nicholas Bishop of Pendleton Co., planter, 640 acres on N.branches of 23 Mile Creek of the Savannah River, bd. on SE by lands sold by Thomas Wadsworth to Michael Dickson, on NW by Henry Hunter, on SW by land granted Lydia Maveck, on SE by Camp and Cary land, granted Turpin by Ben. Guerard, 21 Jan. 1785. Date: 2 Mar. 1803. Wit: Samuel H. Dickson, Andrew Pickens, Jr. Mary Turpin, wife of William Turpin, released dower to Paul Hamilton, Q.U. (Charleston?), 4 Mar. 1803. Samuel Dickson, Esq., made oath to J. B. Earle, Clk., 23 Jul. 1803.
Rec: 12 Jul. 1803.

Pages 313-314: Robert Allison and Rebeccah Allison for $400 sold to William Hamby 150 acres on 23 Mile Creek, which by decease of Samuel Norwood was conveyed to his heirs, William Norwood (no further explanation ...BW). Date: 25 Feb. 1803. Signed: William Allison, Rebeca (X) Allison. Wit: William Montgomery, Michael Ragsdale. William Montgomery made oath to Wm. Edmondson, Q.U., 25 ___ 1803.
Rec: 15 Jul. 1803.

Pages 314-316: 7 Oct. 1795, James Gillispy to Ezrel (also Ezekiel) Atkins for Ł 12 stg. (no amount of acreage), part of 644 acres granted 22 Aug. 1791 by Chas. Pinckney, on 12 Mile River, on line marked in presence of Robert Goodwin and Jesse Goodwin. Wit: Stephen Cantrell, William (X) Gibson. Stephen Cantrell made oath to Colin Campbell, J.P., 24 Aug. 1802.
Rec: 26 Jul. 1803.

Page 316: Francis Greenwood for $100 sold William Steele and James Wood one bay mare, about nine years old and 10 head of cattle. Date: 5 Apr. 1803. Wit: D. McCaleb, A. Kilpatrick. Alexander Kilpatrick made oath to John Taylor, Q.U., 26 Jul. 1803.
Rec: 26 Jul. 1803.

Pages 317-318: James Kilbourne, of Pendleton Dist. to Samuel Earle of Greenville Dist. for $250 for 200 acres on W. side of Keowee River, part of a tract granted Major Parsons, including island's fish traps and fisheries. Date: 23 Jan. 1803. Wit: Giddeon Hester, John Crow Foster, James Cox. Elizabeth (X) Kilbourne, wife of Amos Kilbourne, released dower to Obadiah Trimier, J.Q., 1 Feb. 1803. John Crow Foster made oath to Obadiah Trimier, 21 Apr. 1803.
Rec: 15 Jun. 1803.

Pages 318-319: Bernd. Glenn of Union Dist., S. C. for $1,000 sold to Samuel Harper of Pendleton Dist., 420 acres, part of 640 acres granted Glenn, 16 Jun. 1794, on Crow Creek, being remainder not taken by intersections of Mr. Tate's lines. Date: 9 Jul. 1803. Wit: Benjamin Herndon, Simon (X) Jenkins, Jonathan (X) Whitten. Jonathan Whitten made

(Pages 318-319 cont'd): oath to Levi Casey, J. Q., 29 Jul. ____.
Rec: 3 Aug. 1803.

Pages 319-320: Joseph Land for Ł 60 stg. sold to Charles Willson (no amount of acreage), part of a tract where Willson now lives, bd. James Willson, David Caldwell, Wm. Drennan and William Lesley. Date: 14 March 1803. Signed: Joseph (X) Land, Sarah (X) Land. Wit: David Drennan, James Willson. David Drennan made oath to John Willson, J.Q., 15 Mar. 1803.
Rec: 5 Apr. 1803.

Pages 320-321: Robert Smith for $115.62½ sold to William Steele and James Wood two geldings, waggon and geers. Date: 11 Jul. 1803. Wit: Jane Star (X) Ditto, Alexander Smith. Alexander Smith made oath to J.B.Earle Clk. 10 Aug. 1803.
Rec: 10 Aug. 1803.

Pages 321-322: Richard Minton, heir of Richard Minton, Sr. for $60 sold to Andrew Johnston Liddell,Jr. 40 acres on NW side of 26 Mile Creek, bd. SW by land originally granted to Andrew Liddell, Sr., NW by William Felton. Date: 4 Jul. 1803. Wit: Samuel Cherry, Moses Liddell. Samuel Cherry made oath to John Taylor, J.Q., 12 Aug. 1803.
(No recording date).

Page 322: Joel Terrell made oath that a tract of land lying on Little Eatatoe (sic) containing 157 acres, granted to William Young, transferred to Richard Farrar, from him to John Cochran, from Cochran to Joel Terrell and that the deed of conveyence from Cochran is now lost. Date: 2 Sep. 1803. David Murphree, J.P., Rec: 3 Sep. 1803.

Pages 322-323: Richard Minton, Heir of Richard Minton, Sr. for $60 sold to Andrew Liddell, Jr. 40 ac. on NW side of 26 Mile Creek, bd. by William Felton on NW. Date: 4 Jul. 1803. Wit: Samuel Cherry, Moses Liddell. Samuel Cherry made oath to John Taylor, J.Q., 12 Aug. 1803. (Jul.?)
Rec: 12 Jul. 1803.

Pages 323-324: 22 Mar. 1802, John Barnet to James Barnet for $200 for 100 acres on N. fork of 12 Mile River, on both sides of River, bd. by Wardlaw, Witt, Combs, old line between Robertson and Barnet. Signed by James (X) Barnet. Wit: Abner (X) Robertson, James Wardlaw. Abner Robertson made oath to David Murphree, J.P., 20 Mar. 1802.
Rec: 12 Oct. 1803.

Page 324: William Lesley of Abbeville Dist. for $60 sold to John McWherter of Pendleton Dist., blacksmith, 30 acres on Broadaway Creek, part of tract granted Margaret Lesley. Date: 16 Sep. 1803. Wit: Charles Willison, Robert Woods. Charles Willison made oath to William Lesley, JP 16 Sep. 1803. Rec: 11 Oct. 1803.....Plat - shows land bd. by John McWherter on N., on E. by Wm. Drenan, on S. by Wm. Lesley.

Page 325: 17 Jul. 1801, John Mors to Philimon Crane for $120 for 100 acres part of tract granted James Abbet by Wm. Moultrie, bd. Abbets old line, Aaron Crane, Phillimon Craine and Alexander Murphree. Signed: John (X) Morse. Wit: Aaron (X) Crane, William (X) Crane. William C.Crain made oath to David Murphree, J.P., 29 Jun. 1803.
Rec: 29 Jun. 1803.

Page 326: Andrew Oliver for $100 sold to John Jones 215 Acres on 26 Mile Creek, granted William Mulwee, bd. by Wardlaw. Date: 20 Oct.1803. Wit: James Dickson, William Jolly. James Dickson made oath to Saml. Houston, J.P., 26 Oct. 1803.
Rec: 28 Oct. 1803.

Pages 326-327: James Paterson for $100 sold to James Lambert 120 acres on Keowee River, part of 140 acres granted John Twilly (Twitty), 27 Sep. 1790, recorded Bk. B., no. 5, p. 80. Date: 19 Mar. 1803. Wit: Peter Ragsdale, Arron Steel. Peter Ragsdale made oath to John Taylor, Q.U., 18 Mar. 1803. Rec: 26 Aug. 1803.

Pages 327=328: 12 Sep. 1796, Robert Craven to Belfield Wood for ₤ 50(?) for 330(?) acres on both sides of Little River of Keowee River, granted by Chas. Pinckney, 3 Dec. 1792. Signed: Robert Cra<u>ving.</u> Wit: Norsale(?)(Nenah in oath) Lewis, James Barren. James Bar<u>ren m</u>ade oath to James McKinsey, J.P., 19 Nov. 1798(?). Rec: 10 Oct. 1803.

Pages 328-329: Lewis Wimberly for $120 sold to Charles Lay 200 acres on S. side of 12 Mile River, bd. Salmon. Date: 30 Oct. 1802. Signed: Lewis Wimberly, Polly (X) Wimberly. Wit: A. Ladd (<u>Amos</u> in oath), John Field. John Field made oath to John Cochran, J.P., 3 Mar. 1803. Rec: 12 Oct. 1803.

Page 329: I, Fredrick Lanier hereby assign my right and possession to 450 acres on Big Beaverdam Creek, on fork known as Hughe's tract, I am now in possession of since Fall of 1797, to William Cleveland, Esq., for value rd. Date: 1 Sep. 1802. Signed: Fredrick La<u>y</u>nier. Wit: William Harrison, Thos. Holland. Thomas Holland made oath to J. B. Earle, 11 Aug. 1803. Rec: 11 Aug. 1803.

Pages 329-330: Franklin Co., Ga., on 22 Jun. 1801, I, Larkin Cleveland, of the State and County aforsaid, relinquish to Rev. John Cleveland of Pendleton Dist., S. C., 50 acres on N. side of the Toogaloe River, part of 450 acres granted me and being same where I now live. Wit: N. Cleveland, David Cleveland.....Pendleton Dist. - N. Cleveland made oath to Wm. Cleveland, J.P., 25 Jun. 1803. Rec: 11 Aug. 1803.

Pages 330-331: David Dunlap, planter, for $142 sold Benjamin Armstrong a negro wench, named Nancy, about 9 years of age, middle sized, pitted with the small pox, $142 to be paid by 15 May 1804, with interest, then this deed and a certain note given by me to William McCrone (is) transferred to Benjamin Armstrong. Date: 20 Aug. 1803. Wit: Edwd. Adair, Robert Waugh. Edward Adair made oath to J. B. Earle, 23 Aug. 1803. Rec: 23 Aug. 1803.

Pages 331-332: Francis Brimer and James Martin for $100 sold to John Elston 640 acres on Toogaloo River, near Tooloo (sic) Old Town, surveyed by Thomas Lewis, granted Brimer and Martin. Date: 15 Mar. 1803. Wit: Thomas Farrar, Peter Brimer. Thomas Farrar made oath to Obadiah Trimier, J. Q., (no date). Rec: 12 Oct. 1803.

Page 332: William Davis of Abbeville Co. for $650 sold to James Thompson of Pendleton Dist. 200 acres on E. side of Great Rocky Creek, granted David by Benj. Guerard, 1 Jan. 1785, recorded Bk. AAAA, p. 298. Date: 2 Mar. 1802. Wit: D. Gillispie, Stephen Willis. Stephen Willis made oath to E. Browne, 1 Sep. 1803. Rec: 10 Mar. 1803.

Page 333: Samuel Robinson for $150 sold to William Hamilton 97 acres, part of 498 acres granted Robinson 5 Feb. 1798, on Seneca Creek, W. side of Seneca River. Date: 3 Jun. 1802. Wit: John Knox, Robert Waugh. John Knox made oath to Jno. Adair, JP, 20 Jul. 1803. Rec: 28 Oct. 1803.

Pages 333-334: Moses Hopper for $10 sold to Ezekiel Putman 150 acres on Big Generostee Creek of Savannah River, surveyed for John Calhoun, 27 May 1785, granted John Green, 7 Nov. 1791. Date: 15 Oct. 1801. Signed: Moses (X) Hopper. Wit: Thomas Putman, Jacob Skelton. Jacob Skelton made oath to John Verner, J. P., 6 Jan. 1803. Rec: 15 Oct. 1803.

Pages 334-335: Robert Anderson and Mary Caruth, Executors of the Estate of Robert Maxwell, dec'd. for $275 sold to William Townsend 539 acres on Coxes Creek of Rocky River of Savannah River, granted Mary Caruth, then by name of Mary Anderson, by Wm. Moultrie, 3 Oct. 1785, recorded Bk. EEEE p. 491. Date: 29 Oct. 1802. Wit: Joseph Black, James Dalrymple. James Dalrymple made oath to John George, J. P., 10 Sep. 1803. Rec: 13 Sep. 1803.

Pages 335-336: Andrew Pickens, John Willson, Robert Anderson, Commissioners for disposing of Public Land adjoining Pendleton Courthouse for $70 sold to Samuel Taylor one lot of land in Pendleton Village of 1 acre bd. on W. by Lot #15, on N. by Lot #16, on E. by Public lot where public buildings stand and on S. by the street. Date: 7 May 1803. Wit: J.B. Earle, D. C. McCaleb. (No oath). Rec: 24 Oct. 1803.

Pages 336-337: Lewis Wimberly for $900 sold to Charles Lay 300 acres on S. fork of 12 Mile River, bd. by Porter, Cannon and Earle. Date: 30 Oct. 1802. Signed: Lewis Wimberly, Polly (X) Wimberly. Wit: A. Ladd, John Field ....John Field made oath to John Cochran, J. P., 3 Mar. 1803. Rec: 12 Oct. 1803.

Pages 337-338: William Resoner, planter, for $100 sold to Howard Ducksworth, planter, 121 acres,.... where Resoner now lives, part of tract granted John Hunter, on Big Beaverdam Creek of Rocky River, bd. by Thomas Martin, James King. Date: 30 May 1803. Wit: Benjm. (X) Ducksworth, Thomas (X) Martin. Benjamin Ducksworth made oath to R. McCann, J.P., 15 Nov. 1803. Rec: 18 Nov. 1803.

Pages 338-339: Thomas Hood for $150 sold to Samuel Copeland 100 acres on Dowdy's Creek of Saluda River, part of tract granted Hood 11 Mar. 1793, bd. by William Asher. Date: 22 Mar. 1803. Signed: Thomas (X) Hood. Wit: John Stewart, Joseph Looper. Joseph Looper made oath to John Campbell, J. P., 11 Oct. 1803. Rec: 11 Oct. 1803.

Pages 339-340: Alexander McClean for $205 sold to Solomon Geer 200 acres on Neel's Creek, part of 3 tracts: the first granted William Buckhannon, the second to Thomas Burford, the third to Samuel Dalrymple. Date: 17 Sep. 1803. Wit: James Gilleland, James Gwen Dowdle (says Samuel G. Dowdle in oath). James Gilliland made oath to John George, J. P., 10 Oct. 1803. Ann (X) McClain released dower to E. Browne, Q. U., 7 October 1803. Rec: 10 Oct. 1803.

Pages 340-341: David Lewis for $350 sold to George Goodwin 382 acres on N. fork of Little River of the Keowee River, bd. on N. by James Slator, on N.E. by Thos. Boyd and Belfield Woods and bd. on Joshua Robins land, part of 4 tracts. Date: 25 Aug. 1803. Wit: Joshua Robins, Crafford Goodwin. Crafford Goodwin made oath to John Cochran, J. P., 7 Oct. 1803. Rec: 11 Oct. 1803.

Pages 341-342: Moses Mays for $250 sold to William Honie, Sr. 298 acres on 6 Mile Creek of Keowee River, granted Mays 3 Nov. 1794, recorded Bk. C., no. 5, p. 116. Date: 16 Aug. 1800. Wit: John Willson, Jr., Hugh

(Pages 341-342 cont'd): Willson.....I certify I saw deed signed & Witnessed by Hugh and John Willson..James Wilborn, J. Q., 16 Aug. 1803. Rec: 10 Oct. 1803.

Pages 342-343: By my bond or obligation, I am firmly bound to John Bowland, Jr., for $1,000, payment of $500 on or before 21 Oct. 1804 and that I, Daniel Boin for 5 shillings sell him 3 mares, one bay, one yearling, cows and calves, all household and kitchen furniture, plantation tools, 37 gallon still, stock of grain. Date: 24 Nov. 1800. Wit: James Bouland, Wm. McClain. James Bolding made oath to Wm. Edmondson, Q. U., 24 Nov. 1803. Rec: 26 Nov. 1803.

Pages 343-344: 20 Jan. 1795, Joshua Gotcher(?) to Robert Kay for £ 10 stg. for 137 acres in Washington Dist. on Broadmouth Creek of Saluda River, bd. on NE by Joseph Brown and Benoni Fowler, on SW by Mr. Gotcher, on W. by Joseph Reed. Wit: Charles Kay, Benoni Fowler, Wm. (X) Donolson. Benoni Fowler made oath to Wm. Hall. J. P., 28 Jan. 1795. Rec: 10 Oct. 1803.

Pages 344-345: 17 Sep. 1797, Thomas Farrar, late Sheriff of Pendleton Dist., Washington Dist., to Thomas Stribling....Whereas, James Houston was seized of 300 acres on 23 and 26 Mile Creek, and whereas, James Jordan obtained a judgement against James Houston for £ 40 stg., John Rutledge, Esq., Chief Justice of the State, directed Sheriff to sell all the Real Estate, Chattels, etc. at public auction and on 1st Monday and Tuesday of March 1794, did sell property to Thomas Stribling for 50 shillings as the highest bidder. Wit: Joab Mauldin, G. W. Earle. Geo. W. Earle, made oath to W. Thompson, Q. U., 10 Oct. 1803.

Pages 345-346: Hartwell Hunnicutt for $330 sold to James Moore 150 acres on 26 Mile Creek of Savannah River, granted Eli Hunnicutt by Wil'm. Moultrie, 4 Dec. 1786, bd. by Ewin Calhoun, Robert Parker, Big Survey belonging to General Anderson, part of a tract of 150 acres deed from Eli Hunnicutt to H. Hunnicutt. Date: 15 Jun. 1802. Wit: Randp. Hunnicutt, Joseph Jolly. Randol Hunnicutt made oath to Samuel Houston, J. P. 11 ___ 1803. Rec: 16 Aug. 1803.

Pages 346-348: William Turpin of Charleston, Merchant, for £ 63. 6. sold to Elizabeth Dickson... (also Dixon) of Pendleton Dist., 200 acres being Eastern part of tract granted Lydia Mavrick by Gov. Guerard, 13 Oct. 1784, on 23 Mile Creek, bd. by Michael Dickson, Samuel Henry Dickson. Date: 2 Mar. 1803. Wit: Saml. Dickson, Andrew Pickens, Jr. Mary Turpin, wife of William Turpin, released dower to Paul Hamilton, J. Q. (Charleston?), 18 Aug. 1803. Rec: 18 Aug. 1803.

Page 348: 7 Mar. 1800, Shadrack Ingram to William Bedellon(?) for £ 10 stg. for 200 acres on Savannah River. Wit: John Cooper, William Skelton. (Note: Cooper was marked out and changed to Cook). John Cook made oath to John Verner, J. P., 17 Mar. 1800. Rec: 12 Oct. 1803.

Page 349: Joseph Land for $77 sold to Charles Wesley Willson 50 acres on Great Rocky Creek, bd. by Charles Willson. Date: 14 Mar. 1800. Signed: Joseph Land, Sarah (X) Land. Wit: David Drinnan, Charles Willson. Charles Willson made oath to John Willson, J. P., 15 Mar. 1803. Rec: 13 Oct. 1803.

Pages 349-351: 5 Apr. 1803, Thomas Farrar, late Sheriff of Pendleton Dist., to John George........ whereas, Henry W. Desausare, et al, heirs of Daniel Desausare, was seized of 640 acres on Beaverdam Creek, head-

(Pages 349-351 cont'd): waters of Rocky River, judgement obtained by Mary Desausare against Henry W. Desausare, et al, (amount blank). John F. Grimke, Sr., Assoc. Justice directed Sheriff to sell all goods, chattels and lands at Public auction, 2 Feb. 1800, John George was highest bidder at $60. Wit: D. C. McCaleb, Jesse Stribling. David McCaleb made oath to John Taylor, Q. U., 8 Sep. 1803.
Rec: 11 Apr. 1803. (Sep.?)

Pages 351-352: Jean Wylie, relic and Adminstratrix for Estate of Samuel Wylie, late of Pendleton Dist., dec'd., for $115 sold to Jean Wilie relic and Administratrix of Estate of John Wilie, 180 acres surveyed for David Harris 10 Mar. 1790, bd. NE by Willis Brazel, S. by John Barty, granted 13 Jul. 1792. Date: 4 Sep. 1803. Signed: Jean Wilie. Wit: Jacob Gillhan, Elexr. Bohannon. Jacob Gillham made oath to James Tate, Q. U., 24 Sep. 1803.
Rec: 11 Oct. 1803.

Pages 352-353: James Sutton for $300 sold to Trion(?) Fuller 100 acres on N. side of Chestoe Creek of Toogaloo River, granted James McKeen(?) 2 May 1785 by Wm. Moultrie, bd. William Baker, Joshua Lee. Date: 22 Jan. 1803. Rec: 10 Oct. 1803.

Pages 353-354: James McGuffin for $200 sold to William McGuffin 100 acres, part of survey of Lays (?) on SW side of 18 Mile Creek. Date: 29 Jul. 1803. Wit: Hugh McGuffin, John Ford. John Ford made oath to John Taylor, J.Q., 13 Aug. 1803.
Rec: 12 Aug. 1803.

Pages 354-355: John Justice to William Stuart for $200 for 100 acres on both sides of Weaver's Creek of Woolnoy Creek of Saluda River, part of tract granted Benjamin Oliver by Chas. Pinckney, 2 Mar. 1789 and sold by John Oliver to Justice. Date: 1 Aug. 1801. Wit: Matthew Keith, James Brown. Matthew Keith made oath to Colin Campbell, J. P., 4 Feb'y. 1802. Rec: 12 Oct. 1803.

Pages 355-356: William Stevenson for $340 sold to John Ledbetter 175 acres, part of 400 acres granted Sarah Verner by Thos. Pinckney, 7 Dec. 1789, 200 acres conveyed from James Montgomery and his wife, Sarah, (formerly Sarah Verner), to Stevenson, 28 Jan. 1794, recorded Pendleton Bk. D., Folio 315, on Savannah River, bd. John Verner, Sr., William Stevenson, Joel Ledbetter. Date: 8 Feb. 1803. Wit: Hardeman Bennet, James Jones. James Jones made oath to H. Ledbetter, J.P., 11 Oct. 1803.
Rec: 12 Oct. 1803.

Pages 356-357: 27 Dec. 1800, John Yager of Laurence Co., S. C. to John Smith of Pendleton Co., for $60 for 50 acres on Wolf Creek of 12 Mile River, part of 779 acres granted by Chas. Pinckney, 5 Sep. 1791, bd. by James Gillispie's old line, NW by Elisha Herrin and John Yager, Robert Boyd, and John Smith. Wit: Robert Boyd, John Crain. Robert Boyd made oath to Geo. Foster, J.P., 4 Apr. 180_.
Rec: 12 Oct. 1803.

Page 357: 28 Nov. 1803, sold to Isaac Alewaters by James Oneal one sow, the same sow I got from Isaac January and 12 shoalts. Signed: James Oneal. Wit: Solomon (X) Banks. (No oath).
Rec: 2 Dec. 1803(?).

Pages 357-358: Robert Anderson for $100 sold to William Steele and James Wood 200 acres including improvement where Francis Greenwood now lives, bd. road leading to Gen. Anderson's Ferry, part of 815 acres..... granted Francis Greenwood, conveyed to Robert Anderson, 27 Feb. 1799....

(Pages 357-358 cont'd): Date: _____ 1803. Wit: Wm. Hunter, A. Kilpatrick. Alexander Kilpatrick made oath to J. B. Earle, 19 Apr. 1803. Rec: 7 Dec. 1803.

Pages 358-359: John Waddell for $20 sold to George Tucker 403 acres surveyed for Waddell, 6 Jan.1800 on Rocky branch of 18 Mile Creek of Savannah River, bd. NE by John Woodside, SE by Andrew Pickens, SW by William Gilham, S. by John Miller. Date: _____ 1803. Wit: M. Hammond, B.W. Finley. B. W. Finley made oath to Samuel Dickson, J.P., 6 Dec. 1803. Rec: 20 Apr. 1803.

Pages 359-360: William (marked out) James Wood for $240 sold to William Shackleford 242 acres on 18 Mile Creek of the Savannah River, granted John Hunter, Esq., 5 Feb. 1787, recorded Bk. QQQQ, p. 590. Date: 2 Oct. 1800. Wit: Robert Hammett, Andrew Liddell. Robert Hammett made oath to Samuel H. Dickson, J. P., 30 Apr. 1803. Rec: 30 Apr. 1803.

Pages 360-361: 10 Jun. 1803, Edmond Reese to John White for $300 for 100 acres on S. side of 26 Mile Creek, granted Michael Dickson by Ben. Guerard, 1 Jan. 1785, recorded Bk. CCCC, p. 115, bd. SW by John E. Calhoun, E. by Eli Hunnicutt, SE by John Jones, NE by Robert Dickeson. Wit: Samuel Cherry, Moses Liddell. Moses Liddell made oath to Saml. H. Dickson, 6 Dec. 1803. Rec: 8 Dec. 1803.

Pages 361-362: 15 Feb. 1798, John Hunter to William Risoner for Ł 25 for 121 acres in Washington Dist. on Big Beaverdam of Rocky River,part of tract granted Hunter, where he now lives, bd. by Mr. Wadsworth, Joseph Smith, John Hunter and William Risoner. Wit: John Null, Phillip Null. Phillip Null made oath to Robt. McCann, J. P., __ Nov. 1803. Rec: 18 Nov. 1803.

Pages 362-363: Henry Purdy of Abbeville Co., planter,for $125 sold to Benjamin Ducksworth of Pendleton Co., planter, 200 acres on Big Beaverdam Creek of Rocky River, surveyed for Purdy 17 Jun. 1784, granted by Benj. Guerard, recorded Bk. AAAA, p. 471. Date: 23 Mar. 1795. Wit: Thomas (X) Martin, Barnabus (X) Fair, and David Greer. Barnabus Fair made oath to Robert McCann, 13 Nov. 1799. Rec: 7 Dec. 1803.

Pages 363-364: William Griffen for $650 sold to Jonathan Reeder 200 acres on 18 Mile Creek of Keowee River, bd. by John Lewis Gervice(?).. "that part granted by Wm. Moultrie to William Huggins, 2 Dec. 1786 and recorded Bk. BBBB, p. 399, being excluded, it being sold off"; 30 acres, part of 2 tracts, one granted Samuel Lofton, Sr., in 1793, the other to Thomas Lofton, 1786 by Wm. Moultrie, on E. side of 18 Mile Creek, bd. by grant to Wm. Huggins and Christopher Strong (discription not clear).Date 9 Jan. 1802. Wit: John Hunter, William McDow. William McDow made oath to Saml. H. Dickson, J. P., 6 Dec. 1803. Rec: 25 Aug. 1802.

Pages 365-366: 6 Dec. 1803, David McCaleb, Sheriff of Pendleton Dist., to Ezekiel Noble of Charleston Dist.....whereas, William Wallace, now dec'd. was seized of 416 acres on 26 Mile Creek of the Savannah River, bd. NE by Warnock, NW by Thomas Hamilton.....Ezekiel Noble obtained Judgement for $1,943. Honorable John T. Grimke directed all goods, chattels, Real Estate of William Wallace, dec'd. to be sold at public auction on 6 Jun. 1803 to highest bidder, Ezekiel Noble for $60. Wit: M. Hammond, Geo. Edmondson. Michael Hammond made oath to Saml. H. Dickson, J.P., 6 Dec. 1803. Rec: 13 Dec. 1803.

Pages 366-368: 6 Dec. 1803, David McCaleb, Sheriff of Pen-

(Pages 366-368 cont'd):   dleton Dist. to Ezekiel Noble, of Charleston Dist....whereas, William Wallace, dc'd. was seized of 700 acres on 18 Mile Creek, Keowee River, bd. SW and SE by Ephraim Lendies(?), NW by Thomas Gadsden, Ezekiel Noble obtained Judgement against Wallace for $1,943, all goods, chattels, Real Estate of sd. William Wallace, dec'd., sold at public auction 7 Sep. 1803 to highest bidder, Ezekiel Noble for $380. Wit: A. Boyse, Wm. Hamilton. Alexander Boyse made oath to Saml. Dickson, J. P., 6 Dec. 1803.
Rec: 12 Dec. 1803.

Page 368:   21 Nov. 1803, Sir, we have received the Public Goal (Gaol) of Pendleton Dist. and the undertaker, Mr. John Rush (Rusk) has a right to received the obligation. Will you please order it to be given up to him or his order and oblige your humble servants, Robert Anderson, Andrew Pickens, Joseph Whitner and Wm. Steele, Comm. of the Public Buildings in Pendleton Dist. Signed: Paul Hamilton, Esq., Comptroller of the firearms and Revenues of the State.
Rec: 16 Dec. 1803.

Page 368:   I sold and delivered to John Adams for $60 one bed and furniture, 2 cows and yearlings also 12 head of shoalts and one sow, one wheel and cards, one red chest. Date: 21 Nov. 1803. Signed: James O'Neal. Wit: Jodah (X) Adams. Judith Adams made oath to Colin Campbell, J. P., 13 Dec. 1803.
Rec: 15 Dec. 1803.

Pages 368-369:   Jesse Posey for $300 sold to Samuel Taylor 300 acres on NW side of 18 Mile Creek, the Seneca River, bd. NE by Tilly Merrick, W. by Simon Guest, S. by David Kelton and Dr. Hunter, part of 2 tracts granted Samuel Lofton; one for 229 acres by Wm. Moultry, 4 Feb. 1793, the other by Chas. Pinckney, 1 Aug. 1791. Signed: Jesse H. Posey. Wit: Saml. Cherry, Moses Liddell. Moses Liddell made oath to Saml. H. Dickson, 5 Dec. 1803. Rec: 20 Dec. 1803.

Pages 369-370:   Micaiah Clark and Lurany, his wife, for $100 sold to John Wortman 400 acres, part of 1000 acres granted Clark 1792, bd. land sold by Clark to Daniel Wallis, Meshack Green, on Hurricane and Big Crks. Date: 22 Nov. 1803. Signed: Micaiah Clark, Lurany Clark. Wit: G. W. Terrell, William H. Terrell. George Washington Terrell made oath to James Starrett, J. P., 9 Dec. 1803.
Rec: 20 Dec. 1803.

Pages 370-371:   Jeremiah Files for $40 sold to Thomas Boyd 100 acres on Little River of Keowee River, part of 945 acres granted John Caruthers, bd. by McCann. Date: 4 Feb. 1802. Wit: Gideon Norton, James Smith. Gideon Norton made oath to James Starrett, J. P., 22 Nov. 1803.
Rec: 3 Dec. 1803.

Pages 371-372:   1 Nov. 1803, Littleberry Matlock and Christian, his wife, of Granger (sic) Co., Tenn. to William Boling of the State of Kentucky, formerly of Pendleton Co., S. C. for ₺ 30 for 50 acres in Pendleton Co., on Dowdy's Creek, bd. by David Smith and Matlock. Signed: Little Berry (X) Matlock, Christian (X) Matlock. Wit: Catharine (X) Michel, Major Lee. Catharine Mitchel made oath to Thomas Hargis, J. P., 27 Dec. 1803.
Rec: 30 Dec. 1803.

Pages 372-374:   5 Apr. 1796, William Bourland of Pendleton Co. to William Mitchel of Pendleton Co. for ₺ 15 stg. for 50 acres, part of tract made over from John Kelly to David Smith, from Smith to Little Berry Matlock, and from Matlock to Bourland, granted Kelly 1786 by Wm. Moultrie, on Dowdy's Creek of the Saluda, bd. by Bourland, Joseph Luper. Wit: John McClury, Benjamin Bourland, John Bourland.....Henderson Co., Ky., I, Abose Barbour, Clerk of this county, certify that Thomas Prater and Richard Davis, who received acknowledgement of Martha Bourland, the wife of sd.

(Pages 372-374 cont'd):   William Bourland, to deed of conveyence, are acting Justices of this county. Date: 16 Nov. 1803. Signed: Am. Barbour.....Henderson Co., Ky., I, Aeneas Mccollister, Presiding Justice of the County Court, certify that Ambrose Barbour is Clerk of Court, duly elected and sworn. 16 Nov. 1803. Rec: 30 Dec. 1803.

Pages 374-375:   21 Oct. 1803, Alexander Sterrett and Mary, his wife, of Buncomb Co., N. C. to John Davis (later John Dorin; also Dover) for 50 acres on Dowdy's Creek of the Saluda River (no amount of money?) part of 150 acres granted Starrett by Wm. Moultrie, Feb. 1794, bd. by Kelly. Signed: Alexander Sterrett, Mary Sterrett. Wit: William Mitchel, Catharine (X) Mitchel. William Mitchel made oath to Thomas Hargis, J. P., 29 Dec. 1803. Rec: 30 Dec. 1803.

Page 375-376:   James Ferguson and Martha Ferguson for $800 sold to Richard Berry 331 acres, part of 3 tracts, to wit: one granted William Gray for 300 acres, conveyed to Ferguson, NE part conveyed to John Gregory & SW part conveyed to William Duky, bd. by Gray and Gregory. Also, 60 acres part of tract granted John Tarvetor(?) and conveyed to Martha Ledbetter and from Ledbetter to William Wamock, from Womack to Ferguson, bd. Gray, also, one tract of 120 acres granted Wm. Womack, conveyed to Ferguson on Conneross Creek. Date: 3 Oct. 1803. Signed: James Ferguson, Martha Ferguson. (No witness.) I hereby certify James Fergeson and Martha, his wife signed deed of conveyence, 3 Oct. 1803, Obadiah Trimmier, Q. U. Martha Fergeson released dower to Obadiah Trimmier, 3 Oct. 1803. Rec: 10 Oct. 1803.

Pages 376-377:   Charles Martin of Charleston, bricklayer, for $100 sold to William Norton, of Pendleton Dist., 200 acres, formerly 96 District, on both sides of Temasee River of Keowee River, bd. SE by Richard Pollard and William Smith, at time of survey, granted John Martin. Date: 8 Apr. 1803. Wit: Wm. Leech, James (X) Gillison. James Gillison made oath to Samuel H. Dickson, J. P., 16 Nov. 1803. Rec: 17 Nov. 1803.

Pages 377-378:   William Murphree for $120 sold to William Gamletion (later Gamblin) 230 acres on 12 Mile River and Town Creek, bd. by Norton and Luke Barnard. Date: 7 Jun. 1803. Wit: Jesse Murphree, William Curl. William Curl made oath to David Murphree, J. P., 7 Jun. 1803. Rec: 10 Oct. 1803.

Pages 378-379:   Jesse H. Posey for $248 sold to Samuel Taylor 223 acres on N. branch of Cane Creek, of Keowee River, surveyed by John C. Kilpatrick, granted Elenor Brooks 2 Jul. 1787. Date: 7 Sep. 1803. Wit: George Edmondson, Moses Liddell, Michl. Warnock. Moses Liddell made oath to John Taylor, Q. U., 6 Jan. 1804. Rec: 7 Jan. 1804.

Pages 379-380:   Plat of 290 acres bd. N. by Tilly Merrick, W. by Simon Guest, S. by David Kelton and Dr. Hunter, E. by 18 Mile Creek, resurvey for Samuel Lofton 10 Apr. 1802 by John G. Lofton, D. S.....I, Samuel Lofton for 300(?) sold to Jesse H. Posey 290 acres, part of 2 tracts granted Samuel Lofton; one for 575 acres by Wm. Moultrie, 4 Feb. 1793, the other by Chas. Pinckney, 1 Aug. 1792. Date: 13 Oct. 1802. Wit: Joseph Taylor, John Jones. John Jones made oath to Saml. H. Dickson, J. P., 5 Dec. 1803. Rec: 27 Sep. 1803.

Pages 380-382:   Stephen Strange and Elizabeth, his wife, for L 30 stg. sold to John Woodall, Jr. (no amount acreage), the N. end of tract granted Stephen Strange 4 Mar. 1798, recorded Bk. R., no. 5, p. 418. Date ____ 1803. Signed: Stephen Strange, Elizabeth Strange. Wit: Daniel Williams, William Gambrel. Daniel Williams made oath to John McMillian, J.P.

(Pages 380-382 cont'd): 7 Jan. 1804. Rec: 10 Jan. 1804.

Pages 382-383: Elisha Robinson for certain reasons and causes give my beloved son, Thomas Carter Robinson all that tract where I now live, composed of parts of tracts granted James Hacket and George Forbes, conveyed to me by my father, John Robinson and my father-in-law, Thomas Black, on N. side of 23 Mile Creek. Date: 10 Dec. 1803. Wit: Saml. H. Dickson, Rebeckah Dickson. Samuel H. Dickson, Esq., made oath to John Taylor, Q. U., 26 Dec. 1803. Rec: 26 Dec. 1803.

Pages 383-384: Thomas Stribling and Elizabeth, his wife, for $50 sold to Caleb Baldwin (no amount) on 23 Mile Creek at mouth of first spring branch below the mill of Caleb Baldwin, bd. grant of Charles Travis.... granted John Weekly by Wm. Moultrie. Date: 3 Jul. 1803. Signed: Thomas Stribling, Elizabeth Stribling. Wit: J. Haile, Edw. T. McClure, H. McCray, Saml. Tate. Cap'n. Saml. Tate made oath to Obadiah Trimmier, QU, 27 Dec. 1803. Elizabeth Stribling released dower to Obadiah Trimmier on 28 Dec. 1803. Rec: 4 Jan. 1804.

Pages 384-385: 1 Jun. 1803, John Mors to William C. Crane for $50 for 25 acres on both sides of Mile Creek, bd. by Wm. Crane, Jesse Crane, Archibald Bourland, part of 806 acres laid out for James Abbet by Samuel Dickson, D. S., granted Abbet by Wm. Moultrie, 4 Mar. 1793. Signed: John (X) Mors. Wit: Philemon Crane, Aaron (X) Crane. Phillimon Crane made the oath to David Murphree, J. P., 29 Jun. 1803. Rec: 29 Jun. 1803.

Pages 385-387: Elias Phillips for $250 sold to Andrew Wilson 150 acres, part of two tracts, one of 200 acres, part of 500 acres granted Joseph Erwin by Wm. Moultrie, 4 Dec. 1786, on 23 Mile Creek of Savannah River, bd. by John Willson and Calhoun. The other of 60 acres, part of the tract granted John Willson, 5 May 1790 by Chas. Pinckney, on 23 Mile Crk. of Savannah River, being that part sold and whereon Ezekiel Wills now lives, bd. by Saml. Norwood and John Willson. Date: 15 Dec. 1802. Wit: William Willson, Samuel Oliver. Samuel Oliver made oath to John Willson, Q. U., 21 Dec. 1802. Rec: 4 Jan. 1804.

Pages 387-388: John Ivie for $100 sold to Burrel (Burwell) Green 106 acres granted Lott Ivie by the Governor of the State, 2 Dec. 1798, on both sides of Connoross Creek, now in possession of Green, conveyed by Lott Ivie to John Ivie, 20 Dec. 1795, recorded Clerk's Office of the County, 25 Jan. 1796. Date: 17 Apr. 1798. Signed: John (X) Ivie. Wit: Alex. Kilpatrick, J. C. Kilpatrick. John C. Kilpatrick made oath to John Harris, J. P., 13 Jul. 1800. Rec: 5 Jan. 1804.

Pages 388-389: Joshua Burrouse for Ł51 stg. sold to John Burrouse 100 acres on Big Generostee of Savannah River, bd. by Thomas Burrouse. Date: 26 Dec. 1803. Signed: Joshua Burris. Wit: Thomas Burris, Elisha Herring, James Burris. Thomas Burris made oath to Jfh(?) Davis, J. P., 14 Jan. 1804. Rec: 10 Jan. 1804.

Pages 389-390: Jeremiah Able and Elizabeth, his wife, for $50 sold to Burrill Green 241 acres on Conneross Creek, bd. by Green, Mary Morris, H. Tapley. Date: 26 Oct. 1799. Wit: Wm. Grant, Ezekiel Able. Ezekiel Able made oath to John Harris, J. P., 13 Oct. 1801. Rec: 6 Jan. 1804.

Pages 390-391: Benjamin Oliver of Pendleton Dist. for Ł 40 sold to John Justice of Bunikon (sic) Co.,

(Pages 390-391 cont'd): N. C., for 100 acres granted Oliver in 1789 on Beaver Creek of Woolonoy of Saluda River. Date: (blank). Wit: David James, John Pendergrass. David James made oath to W. Reid, J. P., 8 Oct. 1796. Rec: 10 Oct. 1803.

Pages 391-392: John Parker for $275 sold to James Todd... 110 acres where David Gray now lives, bd. by Robert Spearson, Mary Smith. Date: 27 Nov. 1803. Wit: David Drinnan, Daniel J. Gray. (No oath). Rec: 2 Jan. 1804.

Pages 392-393: Ann Smith for $350 sold to Thomas Millsap 490 acres on Connoross Creek and Choestoey part of 650 acres granted John Smith by Wm. Moultrie, 2 Sep. 1793, recorded Bk. __, no. 5, p. 246, bd. by Caleb Price and Matthew Rusel. Date: 26 Jan. 1803. Signed: Ann (X) Smith. Wit: William Price, Jesse Nevill. Wm. Price made oath to Jas. Starritt, J. P., 26 Jan. 1803. Rec: 2 Jan. 1804.

Pages 393-394: Saml. Braidon (Breadon) for Ł 38. 3. 9. sold to Alexander Sherrard one black horse 5 years old, one sorrell colt, 3 cows set of carpenter tools, household furniture, 17 gallons of whickey, now in hands of Patrick Calhoun. Date: 2 Jun. 1803. Signed: Saml. Bridon. Wit: William Bunney(?), John Robinson. William Buney made oath to Nathan Lusk J. Q., 2 Jun. 1803. Rec: 13 Jun. 1803.

Pages 394-396: 10 Feb. 1797, William Gallespie to Gershim Fulton for 10 shillings for 56 acres on Sandy Creek of the Savannah River - part of 455 acres granted Gillaspy by Wm. Moultrie, 30 Nov. 1795, recorded in Bk. P., no. 5, p. 536. Signed: William Gillispie. Wit: Alexander Young, William Willson. William Willson made oath to John McMillion, J.P., 13 Jan. 1804. Rec: 14 Jan. 1804.

Page 396: Sidney Redden sold to Nancy Redden one sorrel mare, fornerly property of George Verner, sold by Verner to me, and one sorrel colt for $150. Date: 17 Jan. 1804. Signed: Sidney (X) Redden. Wit: John George, John Whittworth, John George made oath to James Starrett, J.P. 17 Jan. 1804. Rec: 20 Jan. 1804.

Pages 397-398: Daniel Putman of Pendleton Co., lawful attorney of James Shields of Green Co., Tenn. in Consideration of $100 paid by John Cox, of Pendleton Co. for 142 acres on Savannah River, granted James Shields 10 Nov. 1790, bd. by John Cox, William Lesley, James Shield, Robert Scelton, John Evens, John Watson. Date: 3 Oct. 1802. Wit: Edward Cox, John Franer. Signed:Daniel Putman, Attorney for James Shield. Edward Cox made oath to James Tate, Q. U., 23 Jul. 1803. Rec: 5 Nov. 1803.

Pages 398-399: 3 Jul. 1795, John Morris of Pendleton Co. to Robert Gibbie of Lincoln Co., N. C. for Ł 50 stg. for 258 acres, part of a tract granted John Morris by Wm. Moultrie, on 26 Mile Creek, bd. by Daniel McCollum, David Carter. Wit: Richd. Speake, B. Mauldin, David (X) Carter. David Carter made oath to E. Browne, Q. U. 11 Oct. 1803. Rec: 12 Oct. 1804.

Pages 399-400: William Marshall of Charleston, Attorney at Law-for Ł 100 sold to John Hallum of Pendleton Co., 640 acres on 18 Mile Creek of Savannah River, granted Daniel Milner. Date: 13 Feb. 1798. Wit: Jas. Horne, William Hallum. William Hallum made oath to Wm. Reed, J.P., 13 Nov. 1799. Rec: 10 Jun. 1803.

Pages 400-401: Stephen Barton for $250 sold to Thomas Mil-

(Pages 400-401 cont'd): sap, 172½ acres, being one half of tract granted John Tarwater by Wm. Moultrie on 19 Nov. 1791 on Connoross of Keowee River. Date: 10 Aug. 1803. Wit: Josiah Foster, Daniel (X) Delany. I certify I witnessed above deed, Josiah Foster. J. P., 11 Aug. 1803.
Rec: 2 Jan. 1804.

Pages 402-403: James Martin of York Co., S. C. for $400 sold to Isaac Hudson and Charles Morgan, both of Pendleton Co., 640 acres, including part which lies out of Charles Morgan's claim where he now lives, also part (lower) claimed by A. D. Montgomery, originally granted Alexander McConnel, 16 Jul. 1784 and by William Hort and John Edwards, the Treasurers of the State to James Martin, 8 Apr. 1789, on 12 Mile River, above Anderson's old mill. Date: 11 Jan. 1800. Wit: James Wardlaw, John Hunt. James Wardlaw made oath to David Murphree, J. P., 20 Mar. 1802.
Rec: 21 Jan. 1804.

Pages 403-404: 2 Feb. 1796, James Long, planter, to Stephen Herrin (also Herring), sadler, for Ł 30 stg. for 73 acres where Bradock McDonale now lives, part of tract granted Henry Person by Wm. Moultrie, 5 Jun. 1785, on Great Generostee Creek of the Savannah River, bd. SE by William Dicky, NW by James Long, N. by James Dicky, NE by Stephen Herrin. Wit: Bradock McDonald, Ezekiel (X) Boggs. Bradock McDonald made oath to Joshua Saxon, J. P., 21 Nov. 1796.
Rec: 21 Jan. 1804.

Pages 404-405: Thomas Stribling for Ł 30 sold to Ann Gibson and Willey Roberds, her son, 200 ac., including whereon Gibson and Roberds now live, granted James Houston and by judgement against Houston by James Jordan, John Rutledge, Chief Justice of the State, directed Thomas Farrar, the Sheriff of Washington Dist. to sell to Stribling, being highest bidder. Date: 22 Jul. 1803. Wit: Arthur Johns, Saml. Haile. Arthur Johns made oath to Obdh. Trimmier, Q. U., 26 Dec. 1803.
Rec: 21 Jan. 1804.

Pages 405-406: John B. Earle for and in consideration of Major Samuel Taylor, dec'd., having willed me a tract on W. side of Keowee River, on condition that I should make William Taylor, his son, a title to the tract of 640 acres on E. side of sd. River, granted Sarah Taylor, now sell to William Taylor tract adjoining Samuel Taylor, where he lived and died. Date: 5 Sep. 1803. Wit: A. Boyse, Jas. Starrett, Alexander Boyse made oath to John Taylor, Q.U., 5 Sep. 1803.
Rec: 24 Jan. 1804.

Pages 406-407: Received 18 Nov. 1803, of Taylor and Cherry $290 in full for a negro woman named Sarah about 30 years of age. Signed: Matthew Hooper. Wit: Moses Liddell. (No oath or recording date).

Pages 407-408: Three years after present date, we or either of us, promise to pay John McFall the sum of $120 for value received. Date: 11 Feb. 1803. Signed: Perrin (X) Farrow, John (X) Farrow, Sarah (X) Farrow. Wit: James Cooper, Adam Todd, Michael (?) Bennett.....This indenture of 11 Feb. 1803, Perrin Farrow, John Farrow and Sarah Farrow to John McFall for $120 to sell one negro boy about 13 years of age, named Abraham, until payment is made on or before 11 Feb. 1806. Wit: James Cooper, Adam Todd, Michael Bennet. (No oath).
Rec: 21 Jan. 1804.

Pages 408-410: 5 Mar. 1794, William Thompson for Ł 40 stg. sold to Thomas Drinnan 150 acres granted Thompson, 1784, on Rocky River of Savannah River, bd. land sold to Edward Ware by Thompson, James Caldwell, William Drinnan, land that Thomas Drinnan now occupies. Signed: William Thompson and Mary Thompson. Wit: William Drinnan, Saml. Robertson.....William

(Pages 408-410 cont'd): Drinnan made oath to John George, J. P.,19 Jan. 1804. Rec: 21 Jan. 1804.

Page 410-411: Orman Morgan and Polly, his wife, for $150 sold to John Lawrence 303½ acres on Cain Creek of Toogalow River, where Morgan now lives. Date: 5 Dec. 1801. Signed: Ormane Morgan (only). Wit: Robert Looney, Willoughby Pugh. Robert Looney made oath to Wm. Cleveland, J. P.,15 Dec. 1801. Rec: 13 Oct. 1803.

Pages 411-413: Baveaster Barton for L 10 stg. sold John Cox 40 acres, bd. by Thomas Turner, John Simpson and the sd. Barton, granted William Lesley. Date: 21 Mar. 1803. Wit: Edward Cox, John Hall. Edward Cox made oath to James Tate, Q. U., 23 Jul. 1803. Rec: 5 Nov. 1803.

Pages 413-414: James Dilson for love and good will I bear my loving sons, James Harris Dilson and Charles Desley Willson...(Note: the names are clearly spelled this way...BW)...grant unto sd. James Harris Willson and Charles Wesly Willson 10 head of cattle, 2 shots (sic), 18 hogs and 1 gray mare together with all my goods and chattels. Date: 11 Mar. 1803. Signed: James Willson. Wit: David Drinnan, John McWhorter. David Drinnan made oath to Nathan Lusk, J. P., 15 Mar. 1803. Rec: 5 Apr. 1803.

Pages 414-415: 22 Aug. 1795, James Abbet to John Mors for L 33 for (no amount) on both sides of Mile Creek, bd. by Abbet and Mors, Abner Davis, part of tract of 806½ acres laid out by Samuel Dickson, D. S., granted by Wm. Moultrie, 4 Mar. 1793. Wit: Samuel Mors, Abner Robins. Samuel Mors made oath to Jos. Reed, J. P., 8 Jul. 1798. Rec: 29 Jun. 1803.

Pages 415-416: John Holcom mortgages and make bill of sale for 200 acres to William Turner on Big Generostee Creek, bd. by Thomas Buckhannon, Joseph Robits, John Beard, Michael Steele, tract where Nimrod Cilla now lives, for $80 and interest on or before 4 Dec. 1803. Date: 4 Jul. 1803. Signed: John Holcomb. Wit: Alex. Turner, Pricilla Turner, Robert Turner. Robert Turner made oath to James Tate, Q. U., 9 Oct. 1803. Rec: 8 Oct. 1803.

Pages 417-418: Solomon West for $400 sold to John Chapman 140 acres granted by Wm. Moultrie, 6 Jun. 1786, on Golden's Creek of 12 Mile River, bd. by Joseph Chapman. Date: 21 Jan. 1803. Signed: Solomon (X) West. Wit: John Eubanks, William Hubbard. Jean (X) West, wife of Solomon West, released dower to John Willson, Q.U., 1 Mar. 1803. Wm. Hubbard made oath to John Willson, 1 Mar. 1803. Rec: 27 Jan. 1804.

Pages 419-420: Thomas Risoner for L 40 stg. sold Benjamin Ducksworth 85 acres on 26 Mile Creek of the Savannah River, bd. by John Clark, James Clark (marked out), James Long and Bolin Clark, recorded Bk. C., p. 539, 15 Aug. 1800. Date: 15 Aug. 1800. Signed: Thomas (X) Risoner. Wit:George Forbes, Thomas Coker. Geo. Forbes made oath to Robt. McCann, J. P., 5 Mar. 1803. Rec: 15 Mar. 1803.

Pages 420-421: John Young for $280 sold John Chapman 50 acres where James Gibson and Mills now live part of 168 acres granted Nathaniel Perry in 1786 on SW branch of Raven's Creek of 12 Mile River. Date: 29 Jun. 1800. Wit: Joseph (X) Chapman, John Hudson. Joseph Chapman made oath to W. Reid, J. P., 24 Jun. 1800. Rec: 27 Jan. 1804.

Pages 421-422: Burwell Green for $100 sold Hosea Tapley 50 acres on Conneross Creek, part of the tract granted Lott Joie (probably Ivie), 2 Dec. 1793, bd. by Tapley and the Creek. Date: 17 Sep. 1803. Wit: J.C. Kilpatrick, John Merrill. John Merrill made oath to Obadiah Trimmier, Q. U., 10 Oct. 1803.
Rec: 10 Oct. 1803.

Pages 422-423: 6 Jan. 1803, Elizabeth Thresher for $200 sold to James Kennedy (no amount) bd. by Martin's old line and John Loyd. Date: 6 Jan. 1803. Signed: Elizabeth (X) Thresher. Wit: William Skelton, Joseph Dean. William Skelton made oath to Hezekiah Davis, Es., 15 Jan. 1803.
Rec: 22 Sep. 1803.

Page 423: (Plat) - I have caused to be admeasured and laid out to Richard B. Robert 300 ac. in 96 Dist. on W. side of Keowee River. Date: 9 May 1794. Signed: Ephraim Mitchell, S. G., Surveyor General Office, Charleston, (S. C.), 3 Sep. 1803, Vol. XIII, p. 257. The above plat is a true copy taken from the records and examined by Artimas B. Douby, D. S. G.

Pages 424-426: 7 Nov. 1803, David McCaleb, Sheriff of Pendleton Dist. to Henry Burch, Esq...... Richard Brook Roberts, now dec'd., was seized of tract granted Roberts as a Military Bounty of 300 acres on W. side of the Keowee River, whereas, Morton Brailsford and Sebastion Keely, otherwise Brailsford & Keely, Merchants, obtained judgement against Roberts in his lifetime, for Ł 35 from 31 Jul. 1790, the sd. Brailsford survived Sebastion Keely and obtained judgement against James Kennedy as Administrator for Richard B. Roberts....Hon. John T. Grimke, Clerk of the Court at Charleston, directed the Sheriff to sell all goods, chattles, houses and lands of R. B. Roberts at public auction 7 Nov. 1803 to Henry Burch for $309 as the highest bidder. Wit: Thos. Stribling, Wm. Hamilton. William Hamilton made oath to John Taylor, Q.U., 28 Jan. 1804.
Rec: 28 Jan. 1804.

Pages 426-427: 26 Dec. 1797, Jacob Holland to William Cox for Ł 12 stg. for 100 acres, part of the tract granted Thomas Holden by the Gov. of the State 1 Jan. 1787, and was made over to Peter Lane by deed 12 Dec. 1788, on N. side of the Togalow River, bd. by David Brown, John Rotten, William Cox, where Joseph Childress did live, and Jacob Holland. Signed by Jacob Holland and Mary Holland. Wit: William Bates, William Guest. Wm. Guest made oath to Obadiah Trimmier, Q. U. 22 Nov. 1803.
Rec: 12 Dec. 1803.

Pages 427-428: William Steele for $200 sold Joseph Barton 227 acres, granted William Steele, Esq. by Chas. Pinckney, on Cain Creek of the Keowee River, bd. by William McCaleb, William Steele. Date: 28 Jan. 1804. Wit: William Hamilton, John Head. William Hamilton made oath to John Taylor, Q. U., 28 Jan. 1804.
Rec: 28 Jan. 1804.

Pages 428-429: I, Robert Anderson of Edgefield Co., S. C. am firmly bound to Aaron Broyles of Pendleton Co. for Ł 400 stg. on 23 Oct. 1790 and I make titles to 200 acres on E. side of Broadmouth Creek of the Saluda River on both sides of the Big Branch, bd. SE by Jacob Reed, SW by John Cobb, laid out for Robert Anderson 16 Jul. 1784, obligation to be paid 20 Oct. next, then above is null and void. Date: 23 Oct. 1790. Wit: Benjamin Bowen, William Gotcher. (No oath).
Rec: 12 Oct. 1803.

Pages 429-430: James Cochran for $500 sold to William Montgomery 150 acres at mouth of Cochrans spring branch of S. side of Saluda River, bd. by William Saterfield, David Durham, Craven's Creek, William Tripp

(Pages 429-430 cont'd): and Samuel Tarbert. Date: 5 Apr. 1803. Signed: James (X) Cochran. Wit: James Cochran, Benjamin Ragsdale. James Cochran made oath to Wm. Edmondson, J.P. 5 Apr. 1803.
Rec: 11 Oct. 1803.

Pages 430-431: 3 Dec. 1802, Thomas Hopson to William Prince of Union Dist., S. C. for $50 for 200 acres on 23 Mile Creek of the Savannah River, where Hopson now lives, bd. by Old Mr. Hobson, Capehart and James Barnett. Signed: Thomas (X) Hobson, Anne (X) Hopson. Wit: Jacob Capehart, Isham Prince and Ezekiel Barnet. Isham Prince made oath to David _____ (in fold of book), 6 Jul. 1803.
Rec: 7 Oct. 1803.

Pages 432-433: 13 Jun. 1789, Peter Lance to William Cox for Ł 10 stg. for 100 acres where Cox now lives, on both sides of Little Beaverdam Creek of the Toogalow River, part of a tract granted Thomas Holden and made over to Peter Lance, 25 Dec. 1788. Signed: Peter (X) Lance, Flora (X) Lance. Wit: John (X) Rotten, John (X) Lance, John (X) Pason. John Rotten made oath to Andw. Pickens, J. P., 25 Feb. 1790.
Rec: 12 Dec. 1803.

Pages 434-436: Thomas Morrow, Jr. of Pendleton Dist. for $300 sold to Robert Gilmore of Abbeville Co., 111 acres where Morrow now lives, on Great Generostee Creek, made out to him by Thomas Morrow, Sr. Date: 4 Nov. 1802. Wit: John Carrick, Jas. Houston. Elizabeth Morrow, wife of Thomas Morrow, released dower to James Tate, J. Q., 11 Mar. 1803. James Houston made oath to A. Boyse, J. P., 7 Feb. 1804.
Rec: 8 Feb. 1804.

Pages 436-438: John McCarly and Sarah, his wife, sold to John Stuart for $325 for 200 acres granted Mary Beard, 5 Jun. 1786 by Wm. Moultrie, conveyed by Mary Beard, 5 Jun. 1786, on Big Generostee Creek of Savannah River. Date: 2 Nov. 1803. Wit: Abe Sharrard, Thomas Milford. Sarah McCarly, wife of John McCarly, released dower to James Tate, Q. U., 7 Dec. 1803. Alexander Sherrard made oath to Nathan Lusk, J. P., 23 Jan. 1804.
Rec: 5 Feb. 1804.

Pages 438-440: 13 Oct. 1794, William Bruce to Michael Whitmire for Ł 10. 11 shillings for 147 acres part of a tract granted to Bruce on 4 Jan. 1790, by Chas. Pinckney, for 882 acres W. of Old Boundary, bd. by John Butts, Stephen Fuller and Charles Gates. Wit: John Powell, Earle Lewis. John Powel made oath to W. Reid, J. P., 30 Jan. 1795.
Rec: 13 Sep. 1803.

Pages 440-441: Lewis Cobb, planter, for $360 sold Thomas Holland, planter, 256 acres on E. side of 23 Mile River, granted James Linn, Sr. on 5 Feb. 1786 by Wm. Moultrie, recorded Bk. RRRR, (no page number). Date: 11 May 1802. Wit: Lewis D. Martin, W. Steele. Sally (X) Cobb, wife of Lewis Cobb, released dower to Obadiah Trimier, Q. U., 13 Nov. 1803.
Rec: 13 Oct. 1803.

Pages 441-443: Thomas W. Waters of Newberry Dist., S. C. for $1,000 sold to George Head of Pendleton Dist., 800 acres on both sides of the Brushy Creek of which 100 acres now belong to Andrew Hughes, the balance intended to be conveyed to Head, granted by Wm. Moultrie for 640 acres, bd. by Andrew Hughes, Saml. Peg, Wm. Peg, Nat Adams, James Head, Adkerson and John Wilson. Date: 26 Mar. 1796. Wit: David, Waters, John Head .....Newberry Dist., Fanny Waters, wife of Thomas Willoughby Waters, released dower to Benjamin Long, J. Q., 7 Apr. 1803. David Waters made the oath to Benj. Long, 7 Apr. 1803.....Pendleton Dist., John Head made oath to Wm. Edmondson, Q. U., 9 Aug. 1803.
Rec: 10 Aug. 1803.

Pages 443-444: Able Fike for $150 sold to Alston Alewaters 100 acres on 12 Mile River on Wolf Creek, bd. by Fike, Mark Ward, John Langley and John Gillespie. Date: 28 Jan. 1804. Wit: Isaac Alewaters, John Woodall. Isaac Alewaters made oath to John McMillion, J. P., 31 Jan. 1804. Rec: 1 Feb. 1804.

Pages 444-445: 17 Nov. 1803, before John Willson, Justice of Quoram, came James Hamilton who swore he saw Samuel Duff sign written bill of sale to John Hamilton and Reece Bowen was also witness. (Refers to deed on p. 263...BW).

Pages 445-446: William Murphree for $100 sold Christopher Kirksey, Sr. 640 acres on N. side of 12 Mile River. Date: 17 Jun. 1802. Wit: William Kirksey, Lewis Eaton (X), William Kirksey made oath to David Murphree, J. P. 16 Sep. 1802. Hannah (X) Murphree, wife of William Murphree released dower to John Willson, J. Q., 24 Nov. 1803. Rec: 14 Jan. 1804.

Pages 446-447: Nathaniel Reed for $150 sold to William Watson 267 acres on Cany Creek, branch of Little River of Keowee River. Date: 11 Feb. 1800. Signed: Nathaniel (X) Reed. Wit: Anselm Roe, William Humphries. Anselm Roe made oath to Thos. Harges, J. P., 3 Jun. 1803. Rec: 9 Jul. 1803.

Pages 447-448: Pendleton Dist., I take this method to inform the public that Samuel McGill, having spoken disrespectfully of my father's family respecting a voyage they went on to Charleston together there they sold their cotton and Samuel McGill rec'd. all the money and that night they came out of town. McGill said he would put the money in one of the salt bags that night they came as soon as father knew that McGill had taken of Enoch's money he ordered Mother to go after it my two sisters went with her Enoch Young being there McGill brought out the money his wife and son and my Mother Brother Enoch and my two sisters being present counted one hundred dollars of Enoch's money and took it home and a little after McGill knowing that father was abroad went to a Justice of the Peace charged upon oath my Mother Brother and two sisters with taking a quantity of dollars from him obtained a warrant against them made prisoners of two the whole then was throwd into an arbitration and following award made that is the undernamed Arbitrators being chosen by the family of John Young and Samuel McGill to arbitrate and settle controversies untill this date do award that each party pay their own costs & from Samuel McGill paying Enoch Young eleven dollars and thirty nine cents in the term of one month then all controveries to cease. Signed: 11 Mar. 1803. Arbitrators: James Brown, Thomas Heany, Francis McCalaster, William Ross, Daniel Brison.....NB: Samuel McGill reported when he came home that he had left part of his money in Charleston but when he was called to declare the truth upon oath then he sayeth when he looked over his papers and recollected he had brought all home and left none of it now this award planely discovers that instead of Enoch Young taking money from Samuel McGill, sd. McGill was still his debtor. 1803. Signed: James Young.
Rec: 11 Oct. 1803. (Note: this is copied as written, i. e. - punctuation, etc....BW)

Pages 448-450: 15 Apr. 1803, Joseph Price and Elizabeth, his wife, to John Filanagan (also Felanigam and Flanagan), for $500 for 145 acres on N. fork of Town Creek, granted Price by Thos. Pinckney, 1787, recorded Bk. VVVV, p. 217, and laid off by Price for John Watson. Signed: Joseph Price, Elizabeth (X) Price. Wit: M. Hammond, Moses Liddell. Moses Liddell made oath to John Taylor, Q. U., 16 Apr. 1803. Elizabeth Price released dower to John Taylor, 16 Apr. 1803.
Rec: 16 Apr. 1803.

Pages 450-451: 16 Mar. 1795, Peter Graham and Nancy, his

(Pages 450-451 cont'd): wife, to Samuel McCully for Ł 5 stg. for 270 acres granted Graham, 5 Mar. 1792 on Rocky Creek, bd. NE by Stephen Bennet, where Peter and Nancy now live, also 40 or 50 acres, part of tract granted Prichard Stone, 3 Sep. 1792, conveyed to Graham and reaches as far as the Road leading from John Tood to Stephen Bennet's. Signed: Peter Graham, Nancy (X) Graham. Wit: Joseph Warnock, Joseph Black, Daniel Gray. Joseph Warnock made oath to P. Norris, J. P., 18 Dec. 1802. Rec: 11 Oct. 1803.

Pages 451-452: John Tippen for $100 sold to William Tippen 130 acres on Big Generostee Creek of the Savannah River, part of tract surveyed for Thomas Moss, 18 Aug. 1786 by John Bowan, Jr. and granted to Moss on 5 Mar. 1787 by Thos. Pinckney. Date: 14 Jun. 1803. Wit: Jonathan Gibbs and Levy (X) Prince. Jonathan Gibbs made oath to E. Browne, Q. U., 30 Jan. 1804. Rec: 9 Feb. 1804.

Pages 452-454: Richard Heney (or Henry) to Matthew Long (no amount) for 170 acres on Big Generostee of Savannah River, where I now live, bd. by James Long, Lindsay Payne, Jesse Browne, Garland, John Hamilton, Hezekiah Davis, Esq. and land granted Henry Parsons, part of tract granted Davis Clack (or Clark) by Wm. Moultrie, 16 Sep. 1786, conveyed from Clark to Benjamin Rainey and from Rainey to Timothy Reeves, from Reeves to Henry on 3 Jul. 1795. Date: 20 Oct. 1803. Signed: Richard (X) Henry. Wit: James Long, William Tippen. William Tippen made oath to H. Davis, J. P., 20 Oct. 1803. Sidney (X) Hayney, wife of Richard Hayney, released dower to E. Browne, Q. U., 4 Nov. 1803. Rec: 9 Feb. 1804.

Pages 454-455: Richard Walter of Polusky (sic) Co., Ky. for $160 sold to Joseph Griffen of Pendleton Dist., 1/2 of tract granted to Francis Miller, 6 Mar. 1786 by Wm. Moultrie on Conneross and Goodland Creeks, bd NW by land laid out for Richard Brooks Roberts and land laid out for Benj. Howard. Date: 18 May 1801. Wit: Josiah Foster, Alexander Ramsey, James Ferguson. Josiah Foster made oath to John Barton, J. P., 12 Oct. 1802. Rec: 16 Mar. 1803.

Pages 455-456: 13 Oct. 1792, William Buchannon to Joseph Buchannon for Ł 70 for 300 acres bd. by Andrew Young, Isaac Watts, part of tract granted Jacob Drayton, 15 Oct. 1801, conveyed to Wm. Lesley, 11 October 1791. Wit: John Buchannon, Benjamin Buchannon. Benjamin Buchannon made oath to John Verner, J. P., 9 Aug. 1797. Rec: 11 Oct. 1803.

Page 457: John Hunter for consideration of Jacob Gillaspy having become my security for the payment of $116 to Fuller, for a bay gelding, now in order to identy Gillaspy, I sell him sd. horse, three halters, kettles, plantation waggon and 20 muskrat skins, if note is not paid off then due. Date: 6 Jul. 1803. Wit: J. B. Earle, John Wilson. (No oath is shown). Rec: 22 Dec. 1803.

Pages 457-459: David Greer for $50 sold to Reuben Brock, 100 acres on Barker's Creek of the Savannah River, bd. by James Allen, Reuben Brock, John Robinson, part of 74 acres granted David Greer, 1 Sep. 1794 by Wm. Moultrie. Date: 22 Jun. 1797. Wit: David Brock, David Spradling, Loyed Brock. James Brock made oath he saw David Spradling and Loid Brock witness deed to Aaron Broyles, J. Q., 7 Oct. 1803. Rec: 10 Oct. 1803.

Pages 459-460: Mary Dearing, widow, for divers good cause appoint James Alexander my lawful attorney to recover from Rizin Sprigg, Administrator of the Estate of John Dearing, dec'd., all of the Estate to which I

(Pages 459-460 cont'd): am lawfully entitled to by my dower. Date: 16 Feb. 1801. Wit: Hillery Mills, John Will<u>men</u>. John Wi<u>lmon</u> made oath to Wm. Cleveland, J. P., 18 Oct. 1803. Rec: <u>12</u> Oct. 1803.

Pages 460-461: James Caldwell of Abbeville Dist. for $100 sold to James Gilliland of Pendleton Dist. 177 acres on both sides of Rocky River, bd by David Caldwell, John Still, Thomas and Joseph Drinnan, Charles Wilson ...part of tract granted (Caldwell?). Date: 13 Dec. 1803. Wit: James Caldwell, Jr., David Caldwell. David Caldwell made oath to John George, J. P., 4 Jan. 1804. Rec: 20 Feb. 1804.

Pages 461-462: John Tapley for $100 sold to Jeane Monk, 344 acres bd. NE by Isaac Huger and McCambridge, SE by James Swann, SW by Absalom Legate, NW by Henry Lowry, granted Tapley, 5 Mar. 1798. Date: 17 Dec. 1800. Wit: William Hickman, David Stone. William Hickman made oath to Obadiah Trimmier, Q. U., 8 Jul. 1803. Rec: 15 Aug. 1803.

Pages 463-464: Duncan McKinzie for $375 sold to Benjamin Hickman 150 acres on S. fork of Big Beaverdam Creek of Toogalow River, granted to John Miller, 2 Jul. 1787. Date: 19 Mar. 1803. Wit: Fra. Jenkins, Daniel Keith. Pronus(?) Jenkins made oath to Wm. Cleveland, J. P., 19 Mar. 1803. Rec: 3 Sep. ____.

Pages 464-465: Ann Gibson and Wiley Roberts, her son, for Ł 15 stg. sold to John's (sic) 100 acres, inclīding where "the sd. Arthur now lives" ...part of tract granted James Houston by James Jordan, being land Thomas Farrar, Sheriff of Washington Dist., sold to Thomas Stribling, conveyed from Stribling to Ann and Wiley, beginning at head of branch where Ann and Wiley live. (The grantee's full name is not recorded...BW). Date: 22 Jul. 1803. Signed: Ann (X) Gibson, Wiley (X) Roberds. Wit: Thomas Stribling, John Haile. Thomas Stribling made oath to Obadiah Trimmier, Q. U., 26 Dec. 1803. Rec: 21 Jan. 1804.

Page 465: David McCaleb is bound to Samuel Taylor for $3,200. Date: 4 Jun. 1801, McCaleb made title to house and lot which he resides with the exception of the part on the public ground for which McCaleb is to obtain from the Commissioners a lease to sd. Taylor for as long as term as house shall remain of any use, the obligation is void. Wit: J. B. Earle, Wm. Sloan. (No oath). Rec:28 Jan. 1804.

Pages 465-466: Hugh Moore for $100 sold to Tire(?) Light 150 acres on both sides of Wolenoy Creek of Saluda River, part of tract Moore now lives on. Date: 1 Feb. 1803. Wit: Wm. Linch Bery(?), Robert B. Mallock (called Absolom in oath). Oath is signed by Wm. Lynch, 12 Mar. 1803. to John Cochran, J. P., Rec: 11 Oct.1803.

Pages 466-468: 13 Sep. 1802, Benjamin Laurence and Rachel his wife, to John Adair for $120 (later says $270) for 71 acres on N. side of Cane Creek of the Keowee River, bd. on SW by land laid out for Jacob Laurence ...part of tract granted Benjamin Laurence by Wm. Moultrie, 21 Feb.1893, 21 acres shall be taken off E. end. Wit: Samuel Dinis, Joseph Hill. Samuel Dinis made oath to Jos. Reid, J. P., 15 Sep. 1801. Rec: 10 Feb. 1804.

Pages 468-469: William Thompson for $300 sold James Jett 160(?) acres on both sides of Town Creek, of 12 Mile River, bd. Adam Gilchrist,line

(Pages 468-469 cont'd): run by Joseph Whitner for Wm. Murphree and granted sd. Murphree, 5 Dec. 1791 and Luke Barnard. Date: 1 Nov. 1803. Wit: Elijah Murphree, Alexander Burns. Elijah Murphree made oath to David Murphree, J. P., 1 Nov. 1803. (No recording date).

Pages 469-471: 14 Feb. 1795, William Thompson to John Drinan for Ł 30 stg. for 109 acres, now in possession of Drinan on Rocky River, granted Wm. Thompson by Wm. Moultrie, recorded Bk. 0000, p. 297. Signed: Wm. Thompson, Mary Thompson. Wit: Wm. Drinnan, Robert Smith. Wm. Drinnan made oath to John George, J. P., 8 Feb. 1804. Rec: 27 Feb. 1804.

Pages 471-473: James Rice of Clabourne Co., Tn. for $600 sold to John Tatum of Pendleton Dist. 300 acres on both sides of Wolf Creek of 12 Mile River, part of several tracts granted James Rice, Josiah Patterson and James Henderson, bd. by Patterson's line where it crosses old Keowee Road, Tatum, Abraham Duke, James Rice, Reuben Read and William Marchbanks ....Date: 29 Oct. 1803. Wit: James Jett, Nathaniel Tatum. Nathaniel Tatum made oath to John Cochran, J. P., 28 Dec. 1803. Rec: 27 Feb. 1804.

Pages 473-474: 4 Apr. 1803, David McCaleb, Sheriff of the Pendleton Dist., to Dolly Combs......Dolly Combs, and others, were seized of 572 ac. on 12 Mile Creek and Crow Creek. Samuel Earle obtained judgement against Dolly Combs and others for $586. John Baylis Earle, Clerk of Dist., ordered Sheriff to sell all goods, chattels and lands at public auction on 7 Mar. 1803. Dolly Combs was highest bidder for $50. Wit: Wm. Hamilton, Moses Hendrix. Wm. Hamilton made oath to David Murphree, J. P., 11 Oct. 1803. Rec: 5 Dec. 1803.

Pages 474-476: 16 Aug. 1803, Baley (Bailey) Anderson of Warren Co., Ky. to William Robinson (also Robertson) of Pendleton Dist. for Ł 60 stg for 84 acres, part of tract granted George Roabuck, 7 May 1787, on both sides of Middle Fork of 12 Mile River. Wit: Joshua Barton, Richard Collins. Joshua Barton made oath to David Murphree, J. P., 19 Sep. 1803. Rec: 6 Feb. 1804.

Pages 476-477: James Sanders Guignard of the Town of Columbia, S. C., planter, for $30 sold Edward Adair, Jr. 488 acres on S. side of Cane Creek, bd, NE by Adair and Curry, NE by William Moultrie's land, surveyed for Edward Adair, 11 May 1798, granted Jacob Faust by Edward Rutledge 5 Aug. 1799, conveyed by Faust 16 Feb. 1801, recorded Pendleton Bk. F., pp. 157-158. Date: 21 Sep. 1801. Wit: R. H. Waring, Andw. Bodden....... Richland Dist., S. C., Robert Waring made oath to Marlyn Alkin, J. P., 11 Apr. 1803. Rec: 10 Feb. 1804.

Pages 477-478: David Greer for $80 sold William Townsend 110 acres on Coxes Creek, Rocky River, of Savannah River, granted Greer by Charles Pinckney, recorded Bk. D., no. 5, p. 638. Date: 7 Feb. 1804. Signed by David Greer, Hannah (X) Greer. Wit: James Dalrymple, Thomas Lolloer. James Dalrymple made oath to Jno. George, J. P., 18 Feb. 1804. Rec: 3 Mar. 1804.

Pages 478-480: John Robinson, Sr. of Abbeville Dist. for $100 sold to Jonathan Clark of Pendleton Dist., 150 acres on W. side of 23 Mile Crk granted Robinson by Benj. Guerard, 15 Oct. 1784, where Benjamin Mulligan now lives. Date: 8 Sep. 1803. Signed: John Robertson. Wit: John Robinson, Jr., Peggy (X) Robinson, Benjamin (X) Mullican. Benjamin Mullican made oath to John Willson, Q. U., 29 Sep. 1803. Rec: 27 Oct. 1803.

Page 480: Personally appeared John Burris who made

(Page 480 cont'd): oath that he gave and delivered to Robert Glen his right to a red cow. Date: 20 Aug. 1803. Signed: John (X) Burris to Thomas Hargis, J. P. Rec: 14 Mar. 1804.

Pages 480-481: John Adair and Samuel Houston for $100 sold to Jesse Frost 100 acres surveyed for John Adair and James Curry, 7 Feb. 1793, on both sides of Little River, bd. by Daniel Tredaway. Date: 19 Jan. 1803. Wit: Wm. (X) Tredaway, Henry Houston, Burton (X) Daniel. William Tredaway made oath to John Adair, J. P., 30 Jan. 1804. Rec: 7 Mar. 1804.

Pages 481-482: John Reeves for $231 sold Benjamin Fuller 169 acres part of tract granted Peter Brimar, 6 Feb. 1786, bd. on S. by James Thompson, on E. by Jean Norris, on N. by John Reeves, on NW by Daniel McCoy, on SW by Ansel Jeuett. Date: 14 Jan. 1804. Wit: John Mauldin and Jonathan Ruth. Jonathan Ruth made oath (no date). Sarah (X) Reeves, wife of John Reeves, released dower to Elijah Browne, Q. U., 14 January 1804. Rec: 3 Feb. 1804.

Page 483: 21 Mar. 1804, John Bledsoe to William Bledsoe for $100 for part of tract John Bledsoe now lives on, bd. by Wherter (sic), bank of Saluda River, lines of John and Wm. Bledsoe. Signed: John (X) Bledsoe. Wit: Thos. Calloway, William Bledsoe, Mark Thompson. Thomas Calloway made oath to John Cochran, J. P., 21 Mar. 1804. Rec: 26 Mar. 1804.

Page 484: James Jett for $120 sold to William Steele and James Wood, 47 acres on both sides of George's Creek of the Saluda River on N. side to bridge and across bridge to S. bank to an island near the forge. Date: 5 Mar. 1804. Wit: James Starret, John Rusk. James Starret made the oath to Alex. Boyse, J. P., 5 Mar. 1804. Rec: 21 Mar. 1804.

Pages 485-486: 21 Jun. 1798, John Martin to Samuel Gibson for $100 sold 85 acres, now in Gibson's possession on Rocky Creek, bd. John Drinnan and granted John Perkins by Wm. Moultrie, recorded Bk. E., no. 5, p.524. Wit: Arthur Durley, Wm. Laughlin. William Laughlin made oath to P.Keys, J. P., 18 ___ 1802. Rec: 19 Mar. 1804.

Pages 486-487: John Colcom for $300 sold James McCarley 200 acres on Mountain Creek of Big Generostee of the Savannah River, part of two tracts, one surveyed for Richard York, 3 Feb. 1787 by John Kilpatrick and granted John Tallant, 1789 by Chas. Pinckney, the other surveyed for Robert Boyd, 23 Aug. 1785 by Thomas Finley and granted Robert Maxwell on 3 Mar. 1788 by Thos. Pinckney, bd. by Jonathan Gibbs. Date: 8 Jan.1801. (?). Signed: John (X) Holcom. Wit: Jonathan Gibbs, Jonathan Watson. Jonathan Watson made oath to John Verner, J. P., 14 Apr. 1801. Tabitha(X) Holcomb, wife of John Holcom, released dower to James Tate, Q. U., 6 of Dec. 1803. Rec: 3 Apr. 1804.

Pages 488-489: John Holcom for $50 sold John McCarley 50 acres on Mountain Creek of Big Generostee bd. by Big Survey, John McCarley. Date: 28 Jan. 1803. Signed: John (X) Holcom. Wit: Jonathan Gibbs, Mary (X) Gibbs. Jonathan Gibbs made oath to Hezekiah Davis, J. P., 6 Apr. 1803. Rec: 3 Apr. 1804.

Pages 489-490: John McMahan for $79.15 sold William Steele and James Wood 300 acres on both sides of Richaland Creek of Connoross of Keowee River, granted Cap'n. Benjamin Brown for his services in the late Revolutionary War, conveyed from Brown to John McMahan, 11 Jan. 1802. Date:

(Pages 489-490 cont'd): 15 Mar. 1804. Wit: Wm. Hunter, J. C. Kilpatrick. William Hunter made oath to A. Boyse, J. P. 3 Apr. 1804. Rec: 21 Mar. 1804.

Pages 490-491: George Tucker for $400 sold Thomas Hunter all property I now possess, horses, cattle and hogs, 200 bushels of corn, household furniture, farm utensils.....condition of this bill of sale, if George Tucker have use of sd. property, at end of one year to return, with their increase. Date: 10 Feb. 1804. Wit: Wm. Hunter, B. W. Finley. William Hunter made oath to A. Boyse, J. P., 3 Apr. 1804. Rec: 26 Mar. 1804.

Pages 491-493: Joshua Reeder, of Pendleton Dist., for $750 sold to Phillip May of Anson Co., N. C., 450 acres on both sides of Golden's Creek of 12 Mile River, 140 acres granted John Patterson, 7 Jul. 1788 by Thos. Pinckney, recorded Bk. KKKK, p. 209, bd. NW by John Patterson. Also, a part of the survey of 100 acres granted Benjamin Starret, 6 Jan. 1794 by Wm. Moultrie, recorded Bk. Z(?), no. 5, p. 402. Date: 14 Mar. 1804. Signed: Joshua Reader. Wit: William Pace, Joshua Sturart(?). William Pace made oath to Jno. Willson, Q. U., 16 Nov. 1804. Elizabeth Reider, wife of Joshua Reider, released dower to Jno. Wilson, 19 Mar. 1804. Rec: 30 Mar. 1804.

Pages 493-494: Cornilious Green for $420 sold Abednigo Green (called Sr. in oath) 100 acres part of 1,300 acres granted Thomas Lewis, 4 Dec. 1786 on Little Brushy Creek, bd. William McCrown, Lewis, Riggs, Jeremiah Foster. Date: 29 Mar. 1804. Wit: Abednigo Green, Wm. N. Boyse. Abednigo Green made oath to A. Boyse, J. P., 29 Mar. 1804. Rec: 3 Arp. 1804.

Pages 495-496: William Gillaspie, planter, for $700 sold to Thomas Lindsay, Sr., of Newberry Dist., S. C., planter, 200 acres except 2½ acres conveyed to James Willson, granted William Crausby, where Gillaspie now lives, also a tract adjoining above tract, containing 300 acres, granted Wm. Gillaspie. Date: 8 Dec. 1803. Wit: Geo. Wells, Daniel Thweat, and John Speake. George Wells made oath to H. Speake, J. P., 31 Mar. 1804. Rec: 4 Apr. 1804.

Page 496: Nathaniel Davis gives to my son, Thomas Davis, 100 acres on 23 Mile Creek bd Cob, Barnet, Nathaniel Davis, Thomas Hix...... part of tract granted Evan Thomas by Wm. Moultrie, 1786. Date: 18 Oct. 1800. Signed: Nathl. (X) Davis. Wit: Jacob Capehart, Margaret (X) Capehart. Jacob Capehart made oath to John McMillin, J. P., 15 Mar. 1804. Rec: 11 Apr. 1804.

Pages 497-498: 19 Apr. 1800, James Smith to George Russell for $100 for 200 acres part of survey of 877(?) acres bd. sd. Russell, Richard Woolbanks and Samuel Crane. Wit: William Clayton, James Coffey. William Claton made oath to Colin Campbell, J. P., 13 Mar. 1804. Rec: 14 Mar. 1804.

Pages 498-499: James Hallums for $250 sold to James Parsons, part of 640 acres granted Thomas Roberts on Golden's Creek of 12 Mile River, 200 acres sold to Hallums on W. side of Cider Rocks. Date: 9 Nov. 1803. Wit: Edmond Parsons, William Parsons. William Parsons made oath to John Willson, Q. U., 3 Apr. 1804. Nancy (X) Hallum released dower to John Wilson, 3 May 1804. Rec: 5 May 1804.

Pages 499-500: Henry Gasaway for $400 sold to Thomas Gasaway 476 acres on 26 Mile Creek of Keowee River, bd. S. by John Green and John Hud-

(Pages 499-500 cont'd):   son, 1/2 of tract of 952 acres granted to Henry Gasaway by John Drayton, 7 Sep.1801.
Date: 17 Nov. 1803. Wit: John Griffen, Benjamin Gasaway. Benjamin Gasaway made oath to A. Boyse, J. P., 2 Apr. 1804.
Rec: 2 Apr. 1804.

Pages 500-502:   Mathew Langford for $1,000 sold Jared Nelson 376 acres on Sugar Creek of Keowee River, bd. by Eli Langford, Sr., Eli Langford, Jr., William Tabor, part of tract granted Eli Langford, Sr. by Governor Moultrie, 1786; also, part of tract granted Eli Langford, Sr., by Gov. Moultrie, 1793. Date: 9 Apr. 1792. Wit: Joshua Reeder, Isaiah Kirksey. Josiah Kirksey made oath to John Willson, Q. U., 17 Feb. 1804. (Signed: Isaiah Kirksey).
Rec: 25 May 1804.

Pages 502-503:   Henry Gasaway for $300 sold Thomas Gasaway 100 acres on Six Mile Creek of Keowee River, being NE part of 770 acres granted to Gasaway by Jno. Drayton, 7 Sep. 1802, also, to include 100 acres bd. by Susanah Brown on SE and on NE by Moses Mays, NW by Robert Evans. Date: 17 Nov. 1803. Wit: John Griffis, Benjamin Gasaway. Benjamin Gasaway made oath to A. Boyse, J. P., 2 Apr. 1804.
Rec: 2 Apr. 1804.

Pages 503-504:   Elizabeth Liddell, Widow and lawful Executrix of Moses Liddell, dec'd., for $300 sold to Elijah Nicholson 201(?) acres on Devil's fork of Great Generostee Creek of the Savannah River, bd. Martin and part of 640 acres granted James Blithe, 17 Jul. 1784, conveyed by John Edwards and William Hort, Treas. of the State, to James Martin of York Co., S. C., 8 Apr. 1786, conveyed by Martin to Moses Liddell, dec'd. by deed dated 21 Jan. 1792, recorded Pendleton Bk. B, p. 54. Date: ___ Mar. 1804. Wit: John Rusell, Adam Davis. Adam Davis made oath to Nathan Lusk, J. P., 10 Mar. 1804.
Rec: 13 Mar. 1804.

Page 504:   Elisha Robinson for $50 sold Thomas Black one horse, 9 head of cattle, all my household furniture. Date: 12 Jan. 1804. Wit: John Taylor, H. Dobson Reese. Major John Taylor made oath to M. Hammond, D. C., 29 May 1804.
(No recording date).

Page 505:   Nancy Stover for myself and my husband, Obadiah Stover, for $30 sold to William Richards one cow and calf, dishes, one bed and covers, all my wearing apparel and household furniture. Date: 17 May 1804. Signed: Nancy (X) Stover. Wit: Ezekiel Akins, John Powell. John Powell made oath to James Starret, J. P., 18 May 1804.
Rec: 30 May 1804.

Pages 505-506:   Crosby Wilkes Miller for $100 sold William McFarlane 835 acres granted by Chas. Pinckney, 2 Mar. 1789, except small part of land which Miller sold to Anthony Griffen, where Griffen now lives, by resurvey made by Thomas Lofton, of 42 acres. Date: 10 May. 1804. Wit. J. Miller, J. Miller, Jr. John Miller made oath to A. Boyse, J. P., 2 April 1804. Rec: 2 Apr. 1804.

Pages 506-508:   28 May 1796, Howell (also Howlee) Dowdy, of Knox Co., Tenn. to George Willson of Pendleton Co., S. C. for ₤100 stg. for 100 acres on Dowdy's Creek of the Saluda River, bd. by Isaac Reeves, Ebenezer Bowline. Signed: Howell Dowdy. Wit: Sterling Hightower, Samuel Willson. Sterling Hightower made oath to George Foster, J. P., 28 May 1796. Rec: 13 Mar. 1804.

Pages 508-509:   By my note or obligation, I am bound unto James White for $200, payable by 24 March

(Pages 508-509 cont'd): 180_(?). I, Phillip Huff now secure to James White one horse, two featherbeds and covers, dishes, loom, plow, etc. Date: 24 Mar. 1804. Signed: Phillip(X) Huff. Wit: Moses Lister. Phillip Huff acknowledged he made above mortgage to Wm. Edmondson, J. Q., 24 Mar. 1804. Moses Lister made oath to Wm. Edmondson, 24 Mar. 1804. Rec: 3 Apr. 1804.

Pages 509-510: Watson Alison of Jackson Co., Ga. for Ł10 sold to William Stanton 150 acres, part of tract of 400 acres granted Alison by Wm. Moultrie, 4 Dec. 1786,......on SW side of Brushy Creek, bd. William McWilliams, Nimrod McWilliams. (No date). Signed: Watson (X) Allison. Wit: Frederick Thompson, Robert Allison, Josiah Johnston. Receipt dated 28 Jan. 1804. Josiah Johnston made oath to James Wilborn, J. P., 7 Mar.1804. Rec: 13 Mar. 1804.

Pages 511-512: Isaac Lynch for $1,500 sold to Henry Burch 600 acres on NE side of Keowee River, part of old fort tract surveyed by William Tate, bd. Burch and Abraham Hargis. Date: 18 Jul. 1800. Wit: Wm. McFarlane, Abraham Hargis, Sion Busby. William McFarlane made oath to David Murphree, J. P., 7 Nov. 1800. Rec: 4 Jun. 1804.

Pages 512-513: Commissioners to lay off and dispose of the Public lands adjoining the Village of Pendleton for $47 sold to David Sloan one lot of 1 acre, known as Lot #4, bd. on S. by Lot #5, by Lot #31 on E., on N. and W. by streets, lot which William Hany first settled. Date: 7 May 1803. Signed: Andw. Pickens, Robert Anderson, John Willson. Wit: J. B. Earle, D. C. McCaleb. David McCaleb made oath to M. Hammond, D. C., 5 Jun.1804. Rec: 5 Jun. 1804.

Pages 513-514: Pendleton Dist., William Reed, later of sd. County and State (lately?) for $100 sold to John Keath 100 acres, granted Colin Campbell on Woolonoy of Saluda River, bd. by line laid out to Robert Wilson, Keath, part conveyed by Reid to the Baptist Society, Samuel Watts, Mary Caswell. Date: 9 Mar. 1804. Wit: Cornelious Keath, Cornelious Keath,Jr. Cornelious Keith made oath to Colin Campbell, J. P., 9 Mar. 1804. Rec: 12 Mar. 1804.

Pages 514-515: Elizabeth Liddell and Andrew Liddell bound to Elijah Nicholson, and Elizabeth Liddell the Widow and Executrix of Moses Liddell, dec'd. convey 200 acres on Devil's Creek, part of 640 acres granted to James Martin, Esq., D. S. conveyed from Martin to Moses Liddell, dec'd. Date: ___ Mar. 1804. Signed: Elizabeth Liddell, Andrew Liddell. Wit: John Russell, Adam Davis. Adam Davis made oath to Nathan Lusk, J. P., 10 Mar. 1804. Rec: 13 Mar. 1804.

Pages 515-516: William Lesley of Abbeville Dist., for sum of $1,000 sold to John Cox of Pendleton Dist., two tracts of land of 340 acres,... 300 acres granted William Lesley, and 40 acres granted Samuel Wat, on Big Generostee Creek, bd. on W. by John Cox, on N. by John Hall, on E.by William Lesley, on S. by James Brazor. Date: 9 Dec. 1803. Wit: James Cox and Levi Cox. Levi Cox made oath to Wm. Lesley, J. P., 9 Dec. 1803. Rec: 4 Jun. 1804.

Pages 516-517: Ezekiel Buffington and Allis Harlin for Ł 15 sold to Stephen Whitmire 180 acres on N. fork of Cane Creek, of Keowee River. Date: 1 Jan. 1801. Signed: Ezekiel Buffington, Allis (X) Harlin. Wit: James Smith, Joshua Holden. Joshua Holden made oath to Henry Burch, J.P. ___ May 1801. Rec: 11 Jun. 1804.

Pages 517-518: Ezekiel Buffington and Allis Harlan for

(Pages 517-518 cont'd): Ł 15 stg. sold to Stephen Whitmire 247 ac. on N. fork of Cane Creek of the Keowee River. Date: 10 Jun. 1799. Signed: Ezekiel Buffington, Ellis (X) Harlen. Wit: Richard Cross, Joshua (X) Holding. Joshua Holden made oath to Henry Burch. J. P., 9 Mar. 1801. Rec: 4 Jun. 1804.

Pages 518-519: William Floyd for $700 sold to Champ Taylor 400 acres on Mile Creek, part of tract granted Duncan Camron, 1787, and part was granted Samuel Lofton, 1789, bd. by John Grisham, Daniel Alexander and Taylor. Date: 12 Mar. 1804. Wit: Ro. Stewart, Alex Floyd, John Grisham. Robert Stewart made oath to Thomas Hargis, J. P., 23 Apr. 1804. Rec: 2 Jun. 1804.

Pages 519-520: Andrew Boddan of Richland Dist., S. C. for $178 sold to Daniel Winchester of Pendleton Dist., 356 acres, on Big and Little Eastertoe (sic) Creek of the Keowee River, known by the name of Langstons Cove. Date: 15 Oct. 1802. Wit: John Stephens, James Wood. James Wood made oath to John Cochran, J. P., 14 Mar. 1804. Rec: 14 Mar. 1804.

Pages 520-521: 20 (?) Jan. 1804, Joshua Reeder to Gilbert Dunlap for $190(?) for 200 acres on both sides of 5 Mile Spring of the Keowee River bd. on NE(?) by John Toliver(?), granted by Wm. Moultrie, 2 Oct. 1786 to Gilbert Dunlap, now in Dunlap's possession. Wit: William McDow, Isaac Reeder. William McDow made oath to Samuel H. Dickson, J. P., 14 March 1804. Rec: 14 Mar. 1804.

Pages 521-522: Champ Taylor for $220(?) sold to Robert Stewart 180 acres, part of tract granted Duncan Camron, 1787, and part of the tract granted Saml Lofton, 1789, bd. by Daniel Alexander. Date: 12 Mar. 1804. Signed: Champ (X) Taylor. Wit: John Grisham, Alexander Floyd, and William Floyd. John Grisham made oath to Thos. Hargis, J. P.. 3 Apr. 1804. Rec: 2 May 1804.

Pages 522-523: Hardy Owens for $150 sold to John White 150 acres on 18 Mile Creek of the Keowee River part of 2 tracts, one granted John Young by Wm. Moultrie, the other granted Hardy Owens, bd. by William Steele, Hardy Owens, where White now lives. Date: 22 Sep. 1801. Wit: Archebald Farley, James Wood. Archebald Farley made oath to Peter Keys, J. P., 13 Oct.1801. Rec: 25 Feb. 1804.

Pages 523-524: William Murphree sold for $300 to William Thompson 160 acres on both sides of Town Creek of 12 Mile River, bd. by Pervis, Adam Gillecrist, line run by Joseph Whitner for Wm. Murphree, 5 Dec. 1791, Luke Barnard and Reuben Reed. Date: 1 Nov. 1803. Wit: Elijah Murphree, Alexander Burns. Elijah Murphree made oath to David Murphree, J. P., 1 Dec: 1803. Rec: 5 Jan. 1804.

Pages 524-525: James Hicks for $200 sold to Jesse Edwards 114 acres on Deep Creek, where Hicks now lives, granted William Nicholson, bd. on S by Geo. Bennison, NE by James Hamilton. Date: 20 Feb. 1804. Signed: James (X) Hix, Nancy (X)Hix. John Hix and William Edwards, Wit. John Hix made oath to John McMillin, J. P., 23 May 1804. Rec: 24 May 1804.

Pages 525-526: Thomas Garner, James Garner, John Garner & William Garner sold to Thomas Williams 133 acres on Rocky River, granted James Barr, part of real estate of James Garner, dec'd., where Thomas Garner now lives which was an inheritance of Thomas, James, William and John Garner on the death of their father, James Garner. Date: 9 Jan. 1804. Wit: Jonathan Ruth, George Taylor, Annanias Arvin. Jane (X) Garner and Elizabeth

(Pages 525-526 cont'd): (X) Garner, both wives of James and Thomas Garner, released dower to E. Browne, QU, 9 Jan. 1804. Jonathan Ruth made oath to E. Browne, 9 Jan. 1804. Rec: 12 Mar. 1804.

Pages 526-527: Isaac Alewaters for $200 sold Solomon Banks 70 acres on Wolf Creek, part of tract that Mark Ward formerly owned, bd. by Mark Ward and Earle, and John Langley, and John Galaspy. Date: 27 Feb. 1804. Wit: Alexander McElrath, John Childres. John Childres made oath to George Foster, J. P., 7 Mar. 1804. Rec: 12 Mar. 1804.

Pages 527-528: David Barton for $100 sold to Mashack Hanby 100 acres on Cane Creek, part of a tract surveyed for James Jarvis. Date: 8 Dec. 1803. Wit: William (X) Fortin, Peter Looney. William Fortin made oath to Wm. Cleveland, J. P., 24 Jan. 1804. Rec: 12 Mar. 1804.

Pages 528-529: 7 Jan. 1794, John Young to Charles Morgan for Ł 20 for 68 acres on Middle fork of 12 Mile River, generally known as Anderson's Mill Creek, part of tract granted Nathaniel Perry, 4 Sep. 1786, bd. S. by Willson, W. by William Young. Wit: Samuel Jackson, William Borin. Wm. Borin made oath to Baley Anderson, J. P., 15 May 1795. Rec: 12 Mar. 1804.

END OF BOOK G

PENDLETON DIST. CONVEYENCE BK. H 1804-1807

Page 1: Elijah Nicholson for $200 sold to Captain James Turner 201 acres on Devil's Fork of Great Generostee Creek of the Savannah River, conveyed to Nicholson by Elizabeth Liddell. Date: 1 Mar. 1804. Wit: Elam Sharpe, M. Hammond. Elam Sharpe made oath to J. B. Earle, 20 Jun. 1804. Rec: 20 Jun. 1804.

Pages 1-2: 6 Jan. 1804, Phillip Sutton to James McAdams for $500 for 100 acres granted on 1 Aug. 1785 by Wm. Moultrie to Craven Moffit on Crooked Creek of the Saluda River. Signed: Phillip (X) Sutton. Wit: Bailey Turner, John Sitton. John Sitton made oath to Wm. Edmondson, JQ, 18 Feb. 1804. Rec: 12 Mar. 1804.

Page 2: 5 Oct. 1803, Edward Bird, Attorney for Mark Bird, of Rutherford Co., N. C. to Joseph Hall of Pendleton Dist. for $150 for 145 acres on Beaver Creek, bd. SE by land laid out to James Martin, NW by John Jackson. Wit: John Bruce, Josiah Alexander. John Bruce made oath to E. Browne, Q. U., 24 Feb. 1804. Rec: 12 Mar. 1804.

Pages 2-3: Mathew Hooper of Pendleton Dist. for $500 sold to Jacob Shelor of Mecklenburg Co., Va., tract on Middle fork of Choestoe Crk. of Toogalo River, including old mill seat, on line of a tract granted to Thomas Lofton, part of tract granted John Skelton. Date: 29 Sep. 1803. Signed: Mathew B. Hooper. Wit: Richard Hooper, Nathaniel Perry, Kenneth McKenzie. Richard Hooper made oath to David Humphreys, J. P., 29 Sep. 1803. Rec: 12 Mar. 1804.

Pages 3-4: Nathaniel Perry of Pendleton Dist., for Ł 100 sold to Jacob Shelor of Mecklenburg Co., Va., 200 acres on Choestoe Creek of

(Pages 3-4 cont'd): Toogalo River, granted Thomas Lofton, Jul. 2, 1787. Date: 29 Sep. 1803. Wit: Richard Hooper, Matthew Hooper, Kenneth McKinzie. Matthew B. Hooper made oath to David Humphreys, J. P., 29 Sep. 1803.
Rec: 12 Mar. 1804.

Page 4: Martin Hewlett of Pendleton Dist. for $600 sold to John Hooper of Franklin Co., Ga., 160 acres on fork of Choestoe Creek, part of tract granted Robert Miscampbell, bd. by Nicholas Darnall, Martin Hewlett, Benjamin Perry. Date: 12 Oct. 1800. Wit: Matthew Hooper, Edward Hooper, Obadiah Hooper. Matthew Hooper made oath to David Humphreys, JP, Sep. ___ .
Rec: 12 Mar. 1804.

Pages 4-5: Commissioners for laying off and disposing of Public Lands adjoining Pendleton Courthouse for $149 sold to James Dorin the following lots of land: Lot #12 of 1 acre, Lot #14 of 3 acres, Lot #16 of 1 acre, Lot #9 of 7 acres and Lot #17 of 25 acres, agreeable to plat made by Robt. McCann, Esq. Date: 14 Oct. 1800. Signed: Andw. Pickens, John Wilson, Robert Anderson. Wit: John E. Calhoun, Thos. Hunter. Thomas Hunter made oath to J. B. Earle, Clk., 25 Jun. 1804.
Rec: 25 Jun. 1804.

Pages 5-6: John Eubanks, Sr., for $150 sold to James Parsons 40½ acres, part of tract granted Eubanks. Date: 9 Nov. 1803. Signed: John (X) Eubanks. Wit: Edmond Parsons, William Parsons. William Parsons made oath to John Willson, J. Q., 3 May 1804.
Rec: 5 May 1804.

Page 6: 12 Dec. 1801, George Rusel of Pendleton Dist., for $600 sold to Daniel Davis, of Stokes Co., N. C., 200 acres, part of 897 acres granted Rusel, 1 Oct. 1787 by Thos. Pinckney, on Camp Creek of the Keowee River, bd. by Samuel Crain, James Smith. Wit: Phillip Heath, Isaac Miers(?). Isaac Miers made oath to Colin Campbell, J.P., 15 Oct. 1803.
Rec: 14 Mar. 1804.

Pages 6-7: Peter Gray of Spartan (sic) Dist., for $100 sold to Benjamin Starret of Pendleton Co., 300 acres "which was the County right from the State" to Peter Gray for Services during the late war, on Connoross (96 Dist.) Date: 18 Oct. 1803. Wit: Benjamin Hawkins, William Montgomery.....Spartanburg Dist., Hannah Gray, wife of Peter Gray, released dower to Lewis Trezevant, Judge, 22 Oct. 1803. Pendleton Dist., William Montgomery made oath to Alexander Boyse, J. P., 13 Apr. 1804.
Rec: 12 Apr. 1804.

Pages 7-8: 4 Aug. 1797, James Hendrix of Franklin Co., Ga., to Stephen Whitmire of Pendleton Co. for Ł 100 stg. for 160 acres on N. fork of Keowee River, granted Robert Anderson, 5 Mar. 1787, recorded Bk. TTTT, p. 111 (or Bk. FFFF?), examined by Peter Freneau, Secretary. Wit: Benjamin Whorton, Mary Whorton. Benjamin Whorton made oath to Henry Burch, J. P. 16 Dec. 1799. Rec: 4 Jun. 1804.

Page 8: Orange Davis, yeoman, for $135 sold Samuel Melony, farmer, 135 acres, part of a tract granted Joseph Gouge on Wilson's Creek bd. Widow Parker, John Calhoun, Gouge, William Lesley, James Edings. Date: 7 Mar. 1804. Wit: Israel Pickens, Rot. Black. Robert Black made oath to Joseph Black, J. P., 7 Mar. 1804.
Rec: 13 Mar. 1804.

Pages 8-9: John Cochran for $600(?) sold William Bay? Winchester, (later called Willoughby Winchester), 157 acres on both sides of Little Eastertoe. Date: 5 Sep. 1803. Signed: John Cochran, Nancy Cochran. Wit:

(Pages 8-9 cont'd): Abraham Beach, James Stephens, Joel Terrell. James Stephens made oath to John Cochran, J. P., 28 Nov. 1803. Rec: 14 Mar. 1804.

Pages 9-10: 27 Jun. 1804, David McCaleb, Sheriff of Pendleton Dist. to Robert Dowdle, planter .....Robert Love, tanner, owned 2 tracts of land, one of 219 acres, the other of 363 acres. Giles Talbut(?) on 2 Monday of 1802 before Justices of the Court of Common Pleas at Pendle- Courthouse, obtained judgement against Robert Love for $80. On 7 Jan. 1803, Sheriff was ordered to sell goods, chattels, lands of Robert Love and levied $109.26. On Feb. 1803, at public auction the land was sold to Robert Dowdle, the highest bidder for $11, tracts of land, one granted by Chas. Pinckney for 219 acres to Robert Love, surveyed for James Moore, 24 Jul. 1792, on Great Rocky Creek of Rocky River, bd. on SE by land laid out to James Martin, on NE by John Moore; the other granted Robert Love by Edward Rutledge, 18 Oct. 1799, on Great Rocky Creek, of Rocky River, bd. on SW by Thomas Wadsworth, on SW and NW by Andrew Pickens, on NE and SE by Robert Love. Wit: Moses Liddell, A. Boyse. Moses Liddell made oath to M. Hammond, J. P., 27 Jun. 1804. (No recording date).

Page 11: Thomas Adams for $100 sold Rodger Murphy 50 acres on Little Beaverdam Creek of the Rocky River. Date: 3 Aug. 1803. Wit: Joseph (X) Ducksworth, Obadiah (X) Ducksworth. Joseph Ducksworth made oath to E. Browne, Q. U., 12 Mar. 1804. Rec: 12 Mar. 1804.

Pages 11-12: John Todd of Pendleton Dist., to William Tylor of Abbeville Dist., 100 acres on Rocky River of the Savannah River, bd. by James Askens, Thomas Waters, Adam Todd, part of 200 acres surveyed for Patrick Forbes by William Lesley, D. S., 1 Sep. 1786, granted by Thomas Pinckney, conveyed from Forbes to James Moore and from him to Todd...... Date: 14 Jan. 1804. Wit: John Alexander, Adam Todd. John Alexander made oath to E. Browne, Q. U., 18 Mar. 1804. Lucinda (X) Todd, wife of John Todd, released dower to Elijah Browne, 13 Mar. 1804. Rec: 13 Mar. 1804.

Page 12: 19 Jan. 1804, Edward Bird of Rutherford Co. N. C. to Jesse Davis of Pendleton Dist., for $120 for 367 acres, bd. by Jesse Davis. Wit: Van Davis, David Tate. Van Davis made oath to E. Browne, Q. U., 24 Feb. 1804. Rec: 13 Mar. 1804.

Pages 13-14: John Brice for $180 sold Jesse Davis 100 acres, part of 1,000 acres granted to John Jackson, being that part formerly occupied by Charles McClure, bd. by Jesse Davis, Wm. Hilhouse, Wm. Brice, Wm. Leonard. Date: 11 Feb. 1804. Wit: Van (X) Davis, John Armstrong. Ann Brice, wife of John Brice, released dower to E. Browne, Q. U. Signed: Anney (X) Brice, 24 Feb. 1804. Vann Davis made oath to E. Browne (no date shown). Rec: 13 Mar. 1804.

Pages 14-15: Obadiah Pinkston for $250 sold to Jehu Orr 125 acres surveyed 26 May 1784 for William Brook, on both sides of Hen Coop Creek, part of 250 acres granted Archibald Gillison, 5 Jun. 1786 by Wm. Moultrie, bd. by Archible Gillison, William Keaton. Date: 10 Mar. 1803. Wit: George Manning, Thos. Hanks. George Manning made oath to E. Browne, 19 March 1803. Ann (X) Pinkston, wife of Obadiah Pinkston, released dower to E. Browne, Q. U. 21 Apr. 1803. Rec: 29 Jun. 1804.

Pages 15-16: Andrew Bodden of the Town of Columbia, S.C. for $30 sold to Jacob Capehart of Pendleton Dist., 160 acres on Little River of the Keowee River, on Whetson's branch and on the path from Tomasa to River, surveyed for John Robins, 12 Jun. 1791, granted Andrew Bodden by Edward

(Pages 15-16 cont'd): Rutledge, 1 Apr. 1799. Date: 16 Mar.1804. Wit: Samuel Cherry, Moses Liddell. Samuel Cherry made oath to A. Boyse, J. P., 16 Mar. 1804. Rec: 16 Mar. 1804.

Page 16: Joseph Gouge of Abbeville Dist., farmer, for $400 sold to Orange Davis of Abbeville Dist., farmer, 235 acres, part of a tract granted Gouge, 27 Nov. 1792, bd. by John Callihan and Widow Parker, on Rocky River. Date: 7 Mar. 1804. Wit: Israel Perkins, Rob. Black. Robert Black made oath to Joseph Black, J. P., 7 Mar. 1804. Rec: 4 Jul. 1804.

Pages 16-17: Shadrack Chandler and his wife (not named) for $200 sold to Reuben Shinault 100 ac., part of tract granted Alerand Powers by Wm. Moultrie, 3 Apr. 1793, on branches of 23 and 26 Mile Creek, bd. Power's old line, John Morris, Charles Tavet's old line now belonging to Thomas Stribling,and Edw. T. McClure. Date: 15 Feb. 1804. Signed: Shadrack (X) Chandler. Wit: Caleb Baldwin, Henry Goodwin, Daniel Mason. Henry Goodwin made oath to M. Hammond, D. Clk., 4 Jul. 1804. Rec: 4 Jul. 1804.

Page 17: Benjamin Brimer for $50 sold to Joseph Brimer, part of tract granted Jacob Rice by Chas. Pinckney, 3 Ocr. 1791. Date: 7 Jul. 1802. Signed: Benjamin (X) Brimer. Wit: James Kennedy, Thomas (X) Commons. James Kennedy made oath to E. Browne, 28 Jan. 1804. Rec: 12 Mar. 1804.

Pages 17-18: Robert Anderson, planter, for $200 sold to Samuel Gibson, planter, 123 acres on N.W. fork of Great Rocky Creek of the Savannah River, in 96 Dist., granted Robert Anderson, Esq., 1 Jan. 1787 by Wil'm. Moultrie, recorded Bk. QQQQ, p. 513. "It will be observed that 274 ac. was originally granted Robert Anderson designated, part of which was taken from an older grant, the residue being released of 123 acres certified by David Greer, Esq., D.S.". Date: 19 Mar. 1804. Wit: John Reid, Robert Anderson, Jr. John Reid made oath to M. Hammond, D.C., 19 Jul. 1804. Rec: 19 Jul. 1804.

Pages 18-19: William Davidson, John Davidson and Andrew Thomas Davidson, heirs of James Davidson, dec'd. of Mecklenburg Co., N. C., for $10 sold to James Tuffnell of Pendleton Dist., 20 acres "not to exceed 30 ac. part of 835 acres" granted by Wm. Moultrie to sd. William, John and Andrew Thomas Davidson, children of James Davidson, dec'd, 4 Sep. 1786, being SE corner of tract which Tuffnell claims by deed made by Jacob Visage. Date: 28 Jun. 1804. Signed: Andrew T. Davidson, for self and Wm. Davidson and John Davidson. Wit: Samuel Cherry, Moses Liddell. Samuel Cherry made oath to J. B. Earle, 2 Jul. 1804. Rec: 2 Jul. 1804.

Pages 19-20: Samuel Henderson, Jr. of Laurens Dist.,SC, for $450 sold to Matthew Mulinginx of Pendleton Dist., one tract of 337 acres, one tract of 148 acres, part of 800 acres granted James Henderson, 10 Oct. 1785, on 18 Mile Creek. Date: 18 Jan. 1804. Signed: Samuel Henderson, Administrator. Wit: Frans. Dower, William Mullinnix. Plat shows the 148 acres on 18 Mile Creek, ...Francis Dower made oath to John Willson, JQ, 1 May 1804. Rec: 16 Jul. 1804.

Page 20: William Wakefield for $100 sold to John Verner 494 acres on Shoal Creek of Choestoe Creek, bd. by Enoch Berry, Thomas Shanklin, Mrs. Hall. Date: 24 Mar. 1804. Wit: Enoch Berry, Jane (X) Berry. Enoch Berry made oath to Jno. Barton, J. P., 20 Jul. 1804. Rec: 21 Jul. 1804.

Pages 20-21: Hannah West and Zachariah Morgan of Pendleton Dist., Administrators of Estate of Jacob West, dec'd., and also, Charles West & Polly West, heirs of the deceased, of N. C., for $45 sold Jonathan West, of Pendleton Dist., 33½ acres, part of 150 acres purchased by Jacob West of a 640 tract from John Robinson, on both sides of 23 Mile Creek of the Keowee River, this piece on NW side of the Creek. Date: 28 Jan. 1804. Signed: Hannah West, Zachariah Morgan, Charles West and Mary West. Wit: Wm. Sims, Wm. Pasmore, James (X) Grimes. James Grimes made oath to M. Hammond, 11 Jul. 1804. Rec: 11 Jul. 1804.

Page 21: Ellis Harlin for $300 paid by my slave, James, sell to sd. negro man James, his freedom and clear acquitance from my service forever and do warrant and defend his freedom from all persons. Date: 13 Feb. 1804. Signed: Ellis (X) Harlin. Wit: Caleb Starr, Berry Roe, Baalam Berryman, John Grisham. John Grisham made oath to Thomas Hargis, J. P., 12 Mar. 1804. Rec: 14 Mar. 1804.

Page 22: 2 Nov. 1793, John Bohannan of Abbeville Co. to David Alexander, Jr. of Pendleton Co., for Ł 20 stg. for 107 acres, being 1/4 of the plantation on Cherokee Creek of Hen Coop of the Savannah River,..... granted Bohannan, 7 Jul. 1788 by Thos. Pinckney. Wit: Stephen Willis, James Alexander. (Plat). Capt. Stephen Willis made oath to John McMillin, J. P., 13 Mar. 1804. Rec: 13 Mar. 1804.

Pages 22-23: Ellis Harlin and Ezekiel Buffington for Ł 30 stg. sold to Andrew Pickens 167 acres surveyed for Robert Craven, 6 Sep. 1790, granted to us, 12 Jun. 1792, on NW fork of Little River of Keowee River. Date: 24 May 1804. Signed: Ellis (X) Harlin, Ezekiel Buffington. Wit: David Files, James Smith. David Files made oath to James Starret, J.P., 9 Jan. 1804. Rec: 26 Jul. 1804.

Pages 23-24: James Hollagan for Ł 18 stg. sold to Thomas Word 66 Acres on Choestow Creek of Toogalow River, part of tract granted James Maxwell, 3 Nov. 1788 by Thos. Pinckney, bd. by Eli Davis. Date: 29 Mar. 1799. Signed: James (X) Holligan, Sarah (X) Holligan. Wit: W. H. Lacy, Samuel Burton, William Darnall. Samuel Burton made oath to John Barton, J. P., 2 Mar. 1801. Rec: 13 Mar. 1804.

Page 24: John Morrow of Abbeville Co., Attorney at Law, of John Millican, dec'd., for Ł 40 sold to Andrew Boddan 100 acres on N. side of 23 Mile Creek of Keowee River, granted John Millican, 26 Mar. 1785 by Wm. Moultrie. Date: 16 Oct. 1799. Wit: Robert Morrow, Wm. Morrow....96 Dist., Abbeville Co., Robert Morrow made oath to Wm. Linton, J.P., 24 October 1799. Rec: 13 Mar. 1804.

Pages 24-25: Andrew Boddan of Columbia, S. C. for $220 sold to John Gentry of Pendleton Dist. 100 acres on N. side of 23 Mile Creek of Keowee River, granted John Millican, 26 Mar. 1785 by Wm. Moultrie. Date: 26 Apr. 1802. Wit: Marlyn Alkin, Wm. Smith. (Dist. blank). Mar_tin_ Alkin made oath to D. R. Evans, J.P.Q.U., 26 Apr. 1802. Rec: 13 Mar. 1804.

Page 25: I, John Taylor, Justice of Quorum, certify that Margaret Millwee, wife of within named, released dower to John E. Calhoun. Date 8 Jul. 1804. Signed: Margaret Millwee (X). Rec: 28 Jul. 1804. (Note: no indication where this belongs...BW)

Pages 25-26: Jesse Bynam for $200 sold to James Bynam 58 acres on Rice's Creek. Date: 10 March 1804. Signed: Jesse (X) Bynam. Wit: Wm. O Bynam, Asa (X) O. Bynam. Asa Bynam made oath to John Willson, Q. U., 10 Mar. 1804. Elizabeth (X) Bynum released dower to John Willson, 10 March 1804. Rec: 12 Mar. 1804.

Page 26: Kenith Fendley for $400 sold to William Ramy 224 acres on Toogalow River and on both sides of Chauga Creek, granted John Perkins by Wm. Moultrie, no. 15, p. 125 (sic), conveyed from Perkins to Littleton Meeks. Date: 12 Apr. 1804. Wit: Joseph Taylor, Thomas (X) Ramy. Thomas Ramy made oath to John Barton, J. P., 12 Apr. 1804. Rec: 30 Jul. 1804.

Page 27: James Kell borrowed from William Richards $22 and gives bond for $44 on or before 1 Apr. 1804, mortgage one horse, bed and furniture. Date: 9 Feb. 1804. Wit: T. Farrar, David Files. David Files made oath to Nathan Lusk, J. P., 21 Feb. 1804. Rec: 13 Mar. 1804.

Pages 27-28: David Pruet for £ 60 sold to Drury Pruet 50 acres on Great Generostee Creek, part of tract granted Joseph Walker of 640 acres, recorded Vol. VIII, p. 475, bd. by Thomas Pruit. Date: __ Oct. 1800. Wit: Edw. T. McClure, Stephen (X) Sharton. Stephen Sharton made oath to P. Keys, J. P., 30 Oct. 1802. Rec: 31 Jul. 1804.

Pages 28-29: Daniel Davis and Elizabeth, his wife, for $600 sold to Moses Hendricks (also Hendrix) 200 acres, part of tract granted George Russell, 1 Oct. 1787 by Thos. Pinckney, conveyed from Russell to Davis, on Camp Creek of the Saluda River, on line between Samuel Crain and James Smith. Wit: Moses Hendricks, Sr., Isaac Miers. Isaac Miers made oath to Colin Campbell, J. P., 15 Oct. 1803. Rec: 12 Mar. 1804.

Page 29: Thomas Shockley for $80 sold to James Shockley 40 acres on S. side of Townhouse branch of Savannah River, part of larger tract granted "Thomas Shockley, Sr., to Thomas Shockley, Jr., to Thomas Shockley, Sr. by William Love by deed, 1788". Date: 11 Nov. 1803. Wit: Edward Cox, Jesse (X) Shockley. (No oath). Rec: 13 Mar. 1804.

Pages 29-30: Andrew Boddan for $100 sold Benjamin Starret 474 acres surveyed for Stephen Whitmire on 17 May 1797, bd. Cane Creek, land laid out to Buffington, granted Rolen Williams, 5 Feb. 1798, conveyed to Boddan in March 1798. Date: 14 Mar. 1804. Wit: Robert Anderson, Jesse (X) Coffee. Jesse Coffee made oath to John Barton, Esq. (No date). Rec: 14 Mar. 1804.

Page 30: Daniel Bryson for $50 sold to John Bryson, Sr., one negro boy about 16 years old, by name Tom, born of a wench, now the property of Mr. Daniel Hammick. Date: 4 Feb. 1804. Wit: William _____ (blank), Jean Bryson. (No oath). Rec: 13 Mar. 1804.

Pages 30-31: John Patterson for $100 sold to Robert Honey 100 acres, granted Hugh Brown, 3 Dec. 1798, part of a tract bd. by Thomas (blank), Bennoni Fowler, Kennedy and others. Date: 31 Mar. 1803. Signed: John (X) Patterson. Wit: Sol Humphreys, Edmond (X) Thomason. Solomon Humphreys made oath to David Humphreys, J. P., 31 May 1803. Rec: 12 Mar. 1804.

Page 31:	John McCoy for $306 sold to John Reeves -
273 acres, part of tract granted to Peter
Brimer 6 Feb. 1786. Date: 30 Dec. 1803.
Signed: John (X) McCoy. Wit: John Mauldin, William (X) Jackson, Mallachi Reeves. Plat shows land bd. Rocky River, N. by part of above tract, E. by Ansel Janott, SE by James Thompson, SW by Widow Norris. John Mauldin made oath to E. Browne, Q.U., 14 Jan. 1804.
Rec: 3 Feb. 1804.

Page 32:	Richard Willbanks for Ł 10 stg. sold Moses
Hendricks 50 acres, part of 897 acres -
granted George Rusel 1 Oct. 1787, on Camp
Creek, 97 acres sold to Willbanks. (No date). Wit: William Rackley, David Hendricks. William Rackley made oath to George Foster, J.P., 23 Jul. 1803.
Rec: 12 Mar. 1804.

Page 32:	George Carr and Judith, his wife, for $16½
sold to Cornelious Keith 50 acres on Woolanoia, part of tract granted Robert Anderson 7 Feb. 1791, now in Carr's possession, bd. by Keith, Thomas Leonard, Jacob Eddin. Date: 1 Oct. 1803. Signed: George (X) Carr, Judith (X) Carr. Wit: Thomas Stone, John Keith, John Keith made oath to Colin Campbell, 1 Oct. 1803.
Rec: 12 Mar. 1804.

Pages 33-34:	7 Nov. 1803, David McCaleb, Esq., Sheriff
of Pendleton Dist., to Captain Thomas Stribling......John Weekley was seized of 200
acres on 23 Mile Creek, bd. by Thomas Stribling, Vandover, lands claimed by Messrs. Frinea & Brimer. James Kennedy in Court of Common Pleas, at Charleston, obtained judgement against John Weekley for Ł 224, 1 April 1786. John Grimke, Clerk of Court of Charleston, directed all goods, chattels and lands of Weekley be sold at public auction 7 Nov. 1803.... Thomas Stribling being highest bidder for $50. Wit: Wm. Hunter, Wm. Hamilton. (Plat)......I hereby certify for John Weekley a tract of 200 ac. surveyed for Jacob J (sic) 22 Mar. 1785, in 96 Dist., on 23 Mile Creek. Date: 20 May 1785. Signed: Ephraim Mitchell, S.G.....Bernd. Glen, D.S., Charleston, 23 Aug. 1803, above is a true copy from State Record Vol. IX page 440, examined by Artimas B. Darby, D.S.G.....Pendleton Dist., Dr. William Hunter made oath to Obadiah Trimmier, Q.U., 7 May 1804.
Rec: 7 Apr. 1804.

Pages 34-35:	Reuben Brock of Pendleton Dist. for $365
sold to George Hackleman of Abbeville Dist.
247 acres on W. fork of Barker's Creek of
Little River and Savannah River, bd. by William Hunt, John Robinson, David Greer, Saml. Black, Reuben Brock, Wm. Armstrong, 100 acres was part of tract granted David Greer 14 Sep. 1794 by Wm. Moultrie, conveyed from him to Brock, 147 acres was granted William Wightman 5 Sep. 1785 by Wm. Moultrie. Date: 22 Feb. 1803.
Wit: John Robinson, Conrad Hackleman. Elizabeth (X) Brock released dower to E. Browne, Q.U., 1 Mar. 1803. Conrad Hackleman made oath to E. Browne, 1 Mar. 1803.
Rec: 27 Dec. 1804.

Page 35:	Thomas McTaggart and Mary, his wife, of
Morgan Dist., N. C. for $820 sold Joshua
Dyer of Pendleton Dist., 320 acres on both
sides of Little Eastertoe Creek, part of tract granted James Martin, 1784. Date: 5 Oct. 1803. Signed: Thomas McTaggart, Mary (X) McTaggart. Wit: James Connelly, Abner Dyer, William (X) Egan. Abner Dyer made oath to John Cochran, J.P., 19 Oct. 1803.
Rec: 14 Mar. 1804.

Page 36:	Pritchet Stone, carpenter, sold to William
Childers, planter, for Ł 20 stg. 247 acres
on W. side of Saluda River, surveyed by
Adam Crain and granted Stone, 3 Dec. 1792, bd. by James Mattison. Date: 5 Feb. 1793. Wit: Calvin Ward, Archable (X) Chilers. Archbald Childers

Page 36 cont'd: made oath to Aaron Broyles, J.P., 9 Nov. 1793. Rec: 12 Mar. 1804.

Pages 36-37: James Millwee for ₤5 sold to Jesse Step 176 acres on Toxaway Creek of Toogalowe River, granted by Charles Pinckney, 7 Nov. 1791. Date: 20 Dec. 1796. Wit: William Clark, Robert Glen, Darling Jones. William Clark made oath to David Humphreys, J.P., 15 Dec. 1803. Rec: 12 Mar. 1804.

Page 37: 15 Aug. 1804, Giddeon Hog sold to William McGuffin (no amount) 2 mares, cows, all pewter dishes and other items, share of crop of corn, cotton and tobacco, which he has 1/4 with William Hogg. Wit: John Miller, Crosby W. Miller. Crosby W. Miller made oath to M. Hammond, D. Clerk, 16 Aug. 1804. Rec: 21 Aug. 1804.

Page 37: James Simpson, planter, for love and affection to my grandchild, Eleanor Simpson, and for sum of $100 paid by Eleanor, one negro wench, named Kate, horses, cattle, household furniture which I now possess. Date: 12 Mar. 1804. Signed: James (X) Simpson. Wit: Geo. Bowie, Jas. Thomson. (No oath). Rec: 13 Mar. 1804.

Page 38: 31 Jan. 1795, Francis Borring to Joshua Dyer for 1 mare for 66 acres on 12 Mile River, bd. SE by Baylis Earle, NW by Amos Freeman. Signed: Francis Borin. Wit: Amos Freeman, Elisha Dyer. (blank-Elisha Dyer?) made oath to Bayley Anderson, J.P. (said he was witness with Amos Freeman. Rec: 14 Mar. 1804.

Page 38: Christon Atkins for myself and Legatees of John Atkins, dec'd. have sold to Jacob, formerly called Henry, the balance of his servitude for $300. Jacob is to pay $50 every year till whole is paid, unless Jacob should die. Date: 29 Jul. 1803. Signed: Christian (X) Atkins and Robert Atkins, William Arnold, Bartius Atkins, Sarah (X) Thomason, Ann (X) Hooker, Joseph Atkins, Martha Atkins. Wit: Robert Atkins, Robert Atkins (sic). Robert Atkins made oath to Samuel Houston, J.P., 10 Jan. 1804. Rec: 13 Mar. 1804.

Pages 38-39: David Smith for $325 sold to Jonathan Lindley 176 acres on 23 Mile Creek, bd. Rankin Mills, Esquire Willson. Date: 20 Mar.1804. Wit: Wm. Farris, Wm. McMahan, Wm. Coker. Rebecca (X) Smith, wife of David Smith, released dower to John Willson, J.Q., 24 Mar. 1804. William McMahan made oath to John Willson, 24 Mar. 1804. Rec: 24 Aug. 1804.

Page 39: James Linn, Sr. for $300 sold to Aron Smith 101 acres, part of 2 tracts, one granted James Linn 6 Oct. 1794, the other granted James Gillison 1 Aug. 1785, on 26 Mile Creek. Date: 20 Dec.1803. Wit: Jonathan Smith, Jonathan Montgomery. Jonathan Montgomery made oath to John George, J.P., 13 Mar. 1804. Rec: 13 Mar. 1804.

Pages 39-40: Samuel Burton for $400 sold to John Lawley 183 acres on N. side of Choestoe Creek of Toogalow River, part of tract granted to James Maxwell, 3 Nov. 1788 by Thos. Pinckney. Date: 4 Mar. 1801. Wit: Jacob Loudermilk, Thomas Word. Thomas Word made oath to John Barton, JP, 10 Mar. 1804. Rec: 13 Mar. 1804.

Pages 40-41: James Jett for $20 sold to John Field, Sr.

Pages 40-41 cont'd: 127 acres on 12 Mile River, granted James Jett, 2 Feb. 1801 by John Drayton. Date: 30 Mar. 1802. Wit: Abner Smith, John Morris. John Morris made oath to David Murphree, J.P., 3 Nov. 1803.
Rec: 12 Mar. 1804.

Page 41: Daniel Symmes for $100 sold to Thomas Hamilton 319 acres on 23 Creek, bd. Sw and NE by Merrick, NE and SE by Miller, NW and NE by William Forbes, NW by William Hamilton; also tract of 354 acres on branches of 18 and 23 Mile Creeks, bd. NW by John Hallum, NE by William Hamilton. Date: 5 Mar. 1804. Wit: Ambrose Dudley, Robert Clark. Robert Clark made oath to John Willson, Q.U., 29 __ 1804.
Rec: 31 Aug. 1804.

Pages 41-42: Brook Hall Davis for £60 stg. sold Samuel Burton 183 acres on N. side of Choestoe Creek of Toogalow River, part of a tract granted James Maxwell, 3 Nov. 1788 by Thos. Pinckney. Date: 13 Jan. 1799. Signed: Brook H. Davis, Sally Davis. Wit: William Darnall, Thomas Word. Thomas Word made oath to John Barton, J.P., 2 Mar. 1801.
Rec: 13 Mar. 1801.

Pages 42-43: Patrick Peace on 4 Jul. 1804 did cheat and defraud Elam Sharp out of $405 by pretending to purchase from Elam Sharp a mulatto boy, called Dick, age 14 years, and delivered him 405 forged and counterfiet dollar bills. Elam Sharp has appointed James Gillison, planter, attorney to recover from Patrick Peace the mulatto boy or lawful payment. Date: 1 Sep. 1804. Wit: M. Hammond, B. W. Finley. Barkley W. Finley made oath to Saml. H. Dickson, J.P., 1 Sep. 1804....Clerk's Office, John B. Earle, Clerk of General Session and Common Pleas, certify Samuel H. Dickson, Esq., is Acting Justice of Peace for Pendleton Dist. Date: 1 Sep. 1804.
Rec: 1 Sep. 1804.

Pages 43-44: William Hamby for $200 sold to Anthony Rick(?) 100 acres, part of all that tenth part of 1,000 acres on 18 and 23 Mile Crk. of Savannah River, (bd.) SW and SE by Ephraim Lindsey, NW by Thomas Gadson, SW by Charles Hughes and Thomas Pilgrim, granted William Burney 4 Jun. 1792, recorded Bk. T, no. 5, p. 39. Date: 1 Feb. 1804. Signed: William (X) Hamby. Wit: Wm. Allen, Wm. Walsh. William Allen made oath to John Willson, Q.U., 16 Jun. 1804. Selle (X) Hamby, wife of Wm. Hamby, released dower to John Willson, 5 Jul. 1804.
Rec: 28 Jul. 1804.

Page 44: 26 Mar. 1801, John and Lydia McMillian to Morgan Hood for $80 for 100 acres on the W. branch of Big Generostee Creek of the Savannah River, part of a tract granted John Williams 7 Jul. 1788 by Thos. Pinckney, bd. by Morgan Hood, John McMillian. Signed: John McMillian, Lydia McMillian. Wit: Laken Walker, Wm. Garner. Laken Walker made oath to P. Keys, J.P., 11 Oct. 1802.
Rec: 3 Sep. 1804.

Pages 44-45: John Pickens in his lifetime owned three negroes viz: a fellow named Peter, a wench named Luce and Prince, their child, which negroes were plundered and taken from John Pickens about 1 Feb. 1786. Since that time, John Pickens has deceased and appointed Sarah Pickens his wife Executrix and Joseph Pickens his son Executor of his last will and Testament. Joseph Pickens is since dead. I, Sarah Pickens, only survivor, Executrix of John Pickens, dec'd. have appointed John Pickens, my son, of the State of Tenesee (sic), my lawful attorney to seek and demand said negroes and child or children of negro woman and any sums of money or compensation for use of negroes. Date: 9 Sep. 1804. Wit: Samuel Taylor and M. Hammond. Samuel Taylor made oath to John Taylor, Q.U., 9 Sep.1804 ....Clerk's Office, John B. Earle, Clerk of Crt. of Common Pleas, certify John Taylor, Esq., as Acting Justice of Quorum. Date: 10 Sep. 1804.

Pages 44-45 cont'd: Rec: 10 Sep. 1804.

Pages 45-46:   George Salmon of Greenville Dist., S. C.,
                                   is bound to Charles Lay of Pendleton Dist.
                                   for Ł 65 stg. and mortgage 300 acres on 12
Mile River, sold by Salmon to Lewis Wimberly and by Wimberly to Charles
Lay, then obligation to be void. Date: 26 Oct. 1802. Signed: George Sal-
mon. Wit: Joab Lewis, Leroy Pullen, Benjamin Barton. Leroy Pullen made
oath to John Cochran, J.P., 9 Dec. 1802.
Rec: 12 Mar. 1804.

Page 46:   William Gray of Abbeville Dist. for $150
                                   sold to William Richards of Pendleton Dis-
                                   trict, 200 acres on Keowee River of Savan-
nah River, part of 993 acres granted John Reed 2 Sep. 1793, by Wm. Moultrie, recorded Bk. S, no. 5, p. 233, bd. by William Watson, land conveyed to Levi Robins, from him to James Gray, 10 Mar. 1800 and from James
Gray to William Gray, 15 Sep. 1801. Date: 13 Oct. 1800. Wit: David Mozly,
Lewis Jones. David Mozly made oath to Nathan Lusk, J.P., 21 Feb. 1804.
Rec: 13 Mar. 1804.

Pages 46-47:   John Hamilton of Union Co., S. C., for
                                   $217.50 sold to James Hamilton Bell of
                                   Pendleton Dist. 515 acres on 18 Mile (Crk)
of Savannah River, bd. by land granted John Hallum, Johnson, John Martin,
David Hamilton, granted John Hamilton by Thos. Pinckney, 7 Jan. 1788,
recorded Bk. NNNN (or VVVV), p. 285. Date: 2 Mar. 1804. Wit: Aaron Boggs,
William (X) Hendrix, John Hendricks. John Hendrix made oath to John
Willson, Q. U., 15 Mar. 1804.
Rec: 1 Sep. 1804.

Page 47:   John Ward for $300 sold to James Griffen
                                   300 acres on 23 Mile Creek, bd. NE and SE
                                   by land surveyed for Joseph Jenkins and
Andrew Roe. Date: 28 Oct. 1803. Wit: James Wood, Samuel Cherry. James
Wood made oath to M. Hammond, D. Clk., 11 Sep. 1804. Mary (X) Ward, wife
of John Ward, released dower to John Taylor, Q.U., 31 Dec. 1803.
Rec: 21 Apr. 1804.

Page 48:   Barak Norton for $100 sold to William Rich-
                                   ards 580 acres surveyed 27 Feb. 1800, on
                                   Occoney Creek and S. fork of Little River.
Date: 3 May 1800. Wit: David Files, Lewis Jones. David Files made oath
to Nathan Lusk, J.P., 1 Feb. 1804.
Rec: 13 Mar. 1804.

Page 48:   Turner Harwood for $200 sold to William
                                   Carle 112 acres on Wolf Creek part of 2
                                   surveys, on line laid out for William Mur-
phree, Joseph Duncan. Date: 4 Oct. 1800. Signed: Turner (X) Harwood. Wit:
William Brown, James Jett. William Brown made oath to David Murphree, JP
on 4 May 1801.
Rec: 3 Sep. 1804.

Page 49:   Thomas Farrar for $500 paid by Joseph Mit-
                                   chel and Obadiah Trimier, sold to Obadiah
                                   Trimier 515 acres on Little Beaverdam of
Tugaloo River, granted Farrar by Wm. Moultrie, 2 Dec. 1793. Date: 16 Nov.
1803. Wit: Charles Bond, B. Starrett. Benjamin Starrett made oath to Wm.
Cleveland, J.P., 13 Mar. 1804.
Rec: 17 Sep. 1804.

Pages 49-50:   Israel Pickens for $200 sold to Mary Pick-
                                   ens, Elizabeth Pickens, Matildy Pickens,
                                   Dilley Pickens and Rebecca Pickens one
mare, one colt, sheep. Date: 3 Sep. 1798. Wit: John Harkness, Jos. Erwin.
John Harkness made oath to E. Browne, J.P., 19 Sep. 1798.
Rec: 13 Sep. 1804.

Page 50:   Robert Baker, planter, for Ł 30 sold Henry
                           Garner, planter, 96 acres, part of 2 tracts
                           ...one granted by Moultrie, the other by
Pinckney, 5 Mar. 1787, on 18 Mile Creek, bd. by Ambrose Dudley, Gen'l.
Anderson, Thomas Hallum. Date: 19 Mar. 1804. Signed: Robert Baker, Sarah
(X) Baker. Wit: Ambrose Dudley, William Baker. Ambrose Dudley made oath
to John Willson, J.Q., 7 Sep. 1804.
Rec: 14 Sep. 1804.

Pages 50-51:   Nathaniel Dennis for $270 sold to Robert
                           Bell 100 acres on both sides of Ramsey's
                           Creek, fork of Chauga of Toogaloe River,
where Robert Bell now lives, bd. by line made by Bell and Joseph Louel-
len, in presents of Edward Robertson and Andrew Dennis, granted William
McCaleb by Thos. Pinckney, recorded Bk. WWWW, p. 142. Date: 20 Mar. 1804.
Wit: William Simpson, Wm. Findley. (No oath).
Rec: _____ 1804.

Pages 51-52:   James Legare, Esq., of St. John's Island,
                           Charleston Dist., S. C., for $50 sold to
                           James Gillison of Pendleton Dist., 200 ac.
in Pendleton Dist., formerly 96, on Lawrens Creek of Keowee River.......
granted Legare, 21 Jan. 1785. Date: 4 Dec. 1801. Wit: Stephen C. Wood,
Wm. Simmons. Proven in open Court, March Term, 1804. J. B. Earle.
Rec: 21 Sep. 1804.

Page 52:   James Gillison for $500 sold to Alexander
                           Ramsey 200 acres on Lawrens Creek of Keowee
                           granted James Legare, 21 Jan. 1785. Date:
19 May 1804. Signed: James (X) Gillison. Wit: J. B. Earle, B. Starrett.
Col. John B. Earle made oath to John Taylor, Q.U., 21 Sep. 1804.
Rec: 21 Sep. 1804.

Page 52:   James Jett for $50 sold to William Carle
                           100 acres on Wolf Creek of 12 Mile (River)
                           Date: 4 Feb. 1804. Wit: Abner Smith, Henry
Mills. Abner Smith made oath to David Murphree, J.P., 1 Sep. 1804.
Rec: 3 Sep. 1804.

Page 53:   22 Jan. 1803, Daniel McAllester for $300
                           sold to James Todd 325 acres on Broadway
                           Creek of Rocky River, part of 2 tracts
granted McAllester 5 Jan. 1786 by Wm. Moultrie; the other by Chas. Pinck-
ney, 5 Sep. 1791. Signed: Daniel McAlister. Wit: Ezekiel Mason, Daniel
Gray. Daniel Gray made oath to John George, J.P., 1 Feb. 1803. Agnes(X)
McAlester released dower to E. Browne, Q.U., 14 Mar. 1804.
Rec: 14 Mar. 1804.

Pages 53-54:   James Furguson for $290 sold to William
                           Dicky 80 acres. Date: 20 Feb. 1801. Wit:
                           Wm. Womack, John Gregory, Rebecca (X) Wom-
ack. John Gregory made oath to Josiah Foster, J.P., 7 Feb. 1804.
Rec: 22 Sep. 1804.

Page 54:   Jesse Miller for $100 sold to William Mill-
                           er one mare, one draught ox, shop tools and
                           plantation tools. Date: 28 Feb. 1804. Wit:
Daniel Bruce, George Miller. George Miller made oath to Phil. Meroney,
J.P., 25 Jul. 1804.
Rec: 8 Aug. 1804.

Page 55:   David Dunlap has borrowed of William Rich-
                           ards $248.97, and mortgages one negro wench
                           named Nancy, about 30 years of age, middle
sized, pitted with small pox, debt to be paid before 19 Feb. 1804. Date:
9 Feb. 1804. Wit: David Files, William H. Terrell. David Files made oath
to Nathan Lusk, J.P., 21 Feb. 1804.
Rec: 13 Mar. 1804.

Pages 55-56:   John Perkins and Fanny Perkins for $65 sold

Pages 55-56 cont'd: to John Gregory 10 acres on Connoross Crk. bd. by Gregory and Perkins. Date: 28 Nov. 1800. Signed: John (X) Perkins, Fanny (X) Perkins. Wit: William Womack, George Beaty, James (X) Beaty. James Beaty made oath to Joseph Reid, JP on 21 Feb. 1801.
Rec: 24 Sep. 1804.

Page 56: Solomon Perkins of Lewiston Co., Ky. for $12.50 sold to Hosea Tapley 80 acres on Connoross Creek, bd. by Miller, granted to Solomon Perkins, 7 Jun. 1790. Date: 12 Dec. 1803. Signed: Solomon (X) Perkins. Wit: Wm. Land, Dicy (X) Burchfield. William Land made oath to James Starrett, J.P., 24 Mar. 1804.
Rec: 27 Mar. 1804.

Pages 56-57: James Ferguson and Martha Ferguson for $100 sold to John Gregory 100 acres. Date: 11 Jun. 1799. Signed: James Ferguson, Martha (X) Ferguson. Wit: J. Foster, Wm. Womack, James (X) Baty. Martha Ferguson, wife of James Ferguson, released dower to Obadaiah Trimmier, Q.U. (No date) Josiah Foster made oath to Wm. Cleveland, J.P., 29 Jun. 1799.
Rec: 23 Sep. 1804.

Page 57: Jamea and Martha Ferguson for $150 sold to John Gregory 100 acres on Connoross, granted by John Drayton 4 Aug. 1800. Date: 27 Feb. 1803. Signed: James Ferguson, Martha (X) Ferguson. Wit: James Newman, David Handcock. Martha Ferguson released dower to Obadiah Trimmier, Q.U. (No date). David Handcock made oath to Josiah Foster, J.P., 15 Sep. 1804. Rec: 23 Sep. 1804.

Pages 57-58: Israel Pickens for $200 sold to John Pickens 200 acres on First Creek of Rocky River, bd. by Fenton Hall, Alexander Coven, John Pickens, Israel Pickens. Date: 17 Dec. 1803. Wit: William Pickens, Sarah (X) Pickens. Sally (X) Pickens, wife of Israel Pickens, released dower to (J.P. and date blank).
Rec: 13 Sep. 1804.

Pages 58-59: Israel Pickens for $200 sold to William Pickens a tract bd. by Fenton Hall, John Pickens, Israel Pickens. Date: 2 Mar. 1804. Wit: William Hall, Elizabeth (X) Baskin Pickens. Sarah Pickens, wife of Israel Pickens, released dower to (blank) 10 Sep. 1804. Elizabeth Baskin Pickens made oath to E. Browne, Q.U., 13 Sep. 1804.
Rec: 13 Sep. 1804.

Page 59: Daniel Sims for $300 sold to James Garvin 2 cotton machines, 22 head of cattle, 50 head of hogs, horses, feather beds and other utensels. Date: 10 Mar. 1804. Signed: Daniel Symmes. Wit: Ambrose Dudley, Robert Clark. Ambrose Dudley made oath to John Willson, Q.U., 7 Dec. 1804.
Rec: 8 Sep. 1804.

Pages 59-60: Israel Pickens for $200 sold to John Pickens, William Pickens and Israel Pickens,Jr. ...one waggon, geers, horse and mare. Date 3 Sep. 1798. Wit: John Harkness, Jos. Erwin. John Harkness made oath to E. Browne, J.P., 19 Sep. 1798.
Rec: 13 Sep. 1804.

Page 60: Isaac Lynch of Jackson Co., Ga. for $86 sold to Henry Burch of Pendleton Dist. 100 acres on NE side of Keowee River, part of a tract granted Lynch, bd. by John Grisham. Date: 28 Aug. 1804. Signed: Isaac (X) Lynch. Wit: James Kell, John Burch. James Kell made oath to Thomas Hargess, J.P., 28 Oct. 1804.
Rec: 3 Sep. 1804.

Pages 60-61: Thomas Edwards of Greenville Dist. for $100 sold to Richard Burdine, 100 acres purchased from Thomas Stone, part of tract granted John Logan, heir at law to Thomas Logan, dec'd. granted by Wm. Moultrie, 2 Oct. 1786, for 200 acres on N. side of Little George's Creek, bd. by Armstrong. Date: 4 Oct. 1803. Wit: Charles Armstrong, Reuben Marston, C. McVay....Greenville Dist., Mary Ann Edwards, wife of Thomas Edwards, released dower to D. Goodlett, J.P., 18 Oct. 1803. Reuben Marston and McVay made oath to Thos. Ferguson, J.P., 20 Oct. 1803.
Rec: 15 Mar. 1804.

Page 61: William Murphree, Jr. and John Lin, Jr., for divers good causes, appoint William Murphree, Sr., our attorney to ask, demand and sue to recover all debts, goods and chattels that we have right to obtain as lawful heirs of Robert Linn, dec'd. in every part of the United States. Date: 6 Mar. 1804. Wit: David Murphree, John Cochran. David Murphree made oath to John Cochran, J.P., 14 Mar. 1804.
Rec: 14 Mar. 1804.

Pages 61-62: James Shockley of Pendleton Dist., planter, for $200 sold to Levi Compton of Lawrence Dist., S. C., planter, 100 acres on W. side of Luvies(?) fork of Big Generostee Creek, part of tract conveyed to Shockley by George Brooks, to Brooks by James Martin by deed 2 Apr. 1796. Date: 27 Feb. 1804. Wit: Edward Cox, James Compton. James Compton made oath to James Tate, Q.U., 28 Feb. 1804.
Rec: 7 Oct. 1804.

Page 62: William Murphree for $120 sold to James Murphree 120 acres on 12 Mile River, part of tract granted William Murphree by Chas. Pinckney and divided by lines of Samuel Reed and David Murphree, on the bank of Town Creek. Date: 7 Jun. 1803. Wit: Reuben Reed, Jesse Murphree. Jesse Murphree made oath to David Murphree, J.P., 13 Mar. 1804.
Rec: 14 Mar. 1804.

Page 62: Before John Cochran, J.P., came Adam Thompson and made oath that Robert Lin, now deceased, was the lawful heir of John Lin, who fell in the late American War and that Sarah Lin, wife of William Murphree and John Lin, Jr. is the lawful representative, heirs of Robert Linn. Date: 6 Mar. 1804. Signed: Adam (X) Thompson.
Rec: 14 Mar. 1804.

Page 63: Benjamin Brimer for value received deliver to William Linard a negro woman named Beck, after Brimer's decease and Rebecca Brimer, his wife's decease. Date: 21 Sep. 1802. Wit: Joseph Dean, Samuel Dean...
....I, William Leonard sign over his right and claim to the within specified negro wench to Mr. Van Davis. Date: 13 Nov. 1803. Wit: James Kennedy, Thomas Dean. Joseph Dean made oath to Zh. Davis, J.P., 14 Mar. 1804.
Rec: 13 Mar. 1804.

Page 63: Jehu Lollar sold for $300 to James Allen, 242 acres on Shoal Creek of the Saluda,... granted Sutton Green 17 May 1787. Date: 8 Nov. 1798. Wit: Archer Harvey (Harry?), William Gorman, William Gorman made oath to Phil. Merony, J.P., 25 Sep. 1804.
Rec: 1 Oct. 1804.

Pages 63-64: William Harper for $200 sold to Robert Trotter 130 acres on Little Rocky Creek of the Savannah River, part of a grant to Borgues Snoddy, by Wm. Moultrie, 3 Oct. 1785. Date: 13 Jul. 1803. Wit: Daniel (X) Owens, Joel Braziel. Daniel Owens made oath to Aaron Broyles, JP, 31 Dec. 1800.
Rec: 13 Mar. 1804.

Page 64: John Chapman for $500 sold to William Pace

Page 64 cont'd: 140 acres granted by Wm. Moultrie 6 June 1786 on Golden's Creek of the 12 Mile River, bd. by Joseph Chapman. Date: 15 Mar. 1804. Wit: George (X) Jepson (also called Gibson in the oath), Thomas Byrd. Thomas Byrd made oath to John Willson, Q.U., 16 Mar. 1804. Christiana Chapman, wife of John Chapman, released dower to John Willson, 4 Aug. 1804. Signed: Christiany Champman.
Rec: 11 Sep. 1804.

Pages 64-65:   Ebenezer Bourland of Pendleton Co., S. C. and Edmond Johnson of Buncum Co., N. C. for $300 sold to John Bourland of Pendleton Co. 200 acres by Bourland and 170 acres by Johnson on S. side of the Saluda River, bd. by Asherst, Dody, Ebenezer Bourland, Alexander Starrett, and James Gates. Date: 28 Jul. 1797. Signed: Ebenezer Bourland, Edward Johnson. Wit: William (_blank), George Bradley, Benjamin Bourland. Benjamin Bourland made oath to Phil. Meroney, J.P., 28 Aug. 1804.
Rec: 1 Oct. 1804.

Page 65:   Frances Smith, widow, for love and goodwill to my loving neice, Nancy Hamilton, one negro boy named John, son of my negro woman Rody. Date: 27 Sep. 1804. Wit: Wm. Hunter, James Wood. Dr. William Hunter made oath to John Taylor, Q.U., 28 Sep. 1804.
Rec: 24 Sep. 1804.

Pages 65-66:   Frances Smith, widow, for love and affection to my nephew, Michael Edmondson, one negro boy named James, son of my negro woman Hester. Date: 27 Sep. 1804. Wit: Wm. Hunter, James Wood. Dr. William Hunter made oath to John Taylor, Q.U., 28 Sep. 1804.
Rec: 28 Sep. 1804.

Page 66:   Frances Smith, widow, for love and affection to my neice, Frances Wallace, one negro boy named Bosin(?), son of my negro woman Hester. Date: 27 Sep. 1804. Wit: Wm. Hunter, James Wood. Dr. William Hunter made oath to John Taylor, Q.U., 28 Sep. 1804.
Rec: 28 Sep. 1804.

Pages 66-67:   George Singleton Foster for $600 sold to John Crow Foster 140 acres on W. side of the Saluda River, part of 180 acres granted Charles Gates by Wm. Moultrie 5 Jun. 1786, conveyed from Gates to Foster 24 Jan. 1793, in Bk. B, p. 118. Date: 24 Mar. 1804. Wit: John Goode, James H. Foster. James H. Foster made oath to John Goode, J.P., 28 Mar. 1804. Rec: 5 Oct. 1804.

Page 67:   John Crow Foster for $600 sold to Howard Finley 140 acres on W. side of the Saluda River, part of 180 acres granted Charles Gates 5 Jun. 1786, conveyed to Geo. S. Foster. Date: 4 Apr. 1804. Wit: Gabriel Sisk, John Jefferies. John Jefferies made oath to J. B. Earle, Clk., 6 Oct. 1804.
Rec: 6 Oct. 1804.

Pages 67-68:   Charles Lay for $100 sold to Abram Beach a tract known as Clansy's Place on Little Eastatoa of the Keowee River. Date: 8 Dec. 1802. Signed: Charles (X) Lay, Ann (X) Lay. Wit: Leroy Patten, James Stephens. James Stephens made oath to John Cochran, J.P., 9 Dec. 1802.
Rec: 11 Oct. 1802.

Page 68:   James Zealy of Beauford Dist., S. C. for $200 sold to Adam Carruth of Greenville Dist., 200 acres in Pendleton Dist. on S. side of the Saluda River, surveyed for William Bruce 11 Jun. 1784, and granted Andrew Adams 1 Aug. 1784, conveyed 23 Dec. 1785. Date: 17 Nov. 1802. Wit: Geo. Maxwell, Jesse Howard. (Plat)....Greenville Dist., George Maxwell made oath to L. Tarrant, JP, 23 May 1804. Rec: 11 Oct. 1804.

Pages 68-69: 6 Oct. 1804, John Harris, Sheriff, late of Pendleton Co. to William Steele....whereas, William Hanie was seized of 200 acres, part of 398 acres granted Isaac Lych....William Steele and Co. obtained Judgement against William Haney for Ł 22...John B. Earle, Clk. of the Court of Pendleton Co. directed John Harris, Sheriff, that all goods, chattels and lands of William Haney be sold at public auction to the highest bidder... William Steele for Ł 27. Wit: B. Green, P. Norris. Benjamin Green made oath to Josiah Foster, J.P. (No date).
Rec: 17 Oct. 1804.

Pages 69-70: William Steele for Ł 50 stg. sold to James Armstrong 200 acres on 18 Mile Creek, adjoining one side of town lot in Pendleton Courthouse, part of 398 acres granted Isaac Lynch 2 Jul. 1787, referring to Sheriff's title made from John Harris, Esq. to Steele. Date: 17 Oct. 1804. Wit: M. Hammond, James Wood. Michael Hammond made oath to John Taylor, Q.U. 24 Oct. 1804.
Rec: 29 Oct. 1804.

Page 70: John McEntire for $100 sold to Edward Gregory 200 acres on both sides of Gregory's Creek of 12 Mile River. Date: 30 Apr. 1799. Signed: John (X) McEntire. Wit: James Jett, Reuben (X) Reed. Reuben Reed made oath to David Murphree, J.P. 10 Oct. 1804.
Rec: 11 Oct. 1804.

Page 71: David Silmon for $1,200 sold to Benjamin Silmon 200 acres on 12 Mile River, part of tract granted Baylis Earle, Sr., conveyed to Benjamin Silmon, Sr. and by him willed to David Silmon, son of Benjamin Silmon. Date: __ Oct. 1804. Wit: James Jett, Reuben Tarrant. Reuben Tarrant made oath to M. Hammond, D. Clk. 9 Oct. 1804.
Rec: 9 Oct. 1804.

Pages 71-72: William Turpin of Charleston, Merchant, for Ł 70 sold to Samuel Henry Dickson of Pendleton Dist., 240 acres, part of tract granted Lydia Mavrick by Gov. Guerard 15 Oct. 1804, on 23 Mile Creek, bounding Michael Dickson and part of sd. survey sold to Eliza Dickson, Lydia Mavrick, Wm. Hunter and Dickson. Date: 2 Mar. 1803. Wit: Andw. Pickens, Jr., Ezekiel Noble. Mary Turpin, wife of William Turpin, released dower to Paul Hamilton (Charleston?), 4 Mar. 1803. Andrew Pickens, Jr. made oath to John Willson, Q.U., 4 Jul. 1804.
Rec: 12 Nov. 1804.

Pages 72-73: Adam Caruth of Greenville Dist. for $200 sold to William Lafoon of Pendleton Dist., 200 acres on N. side of the Saluda River, about 2 miles below the fork, surveyed for William Bruce, 11 Jun. 1784, granted Andrew Adams 1 Aug. 1784, conveyed to James Zealy by Adams 23 Dec. 1785 and by Zealy to Caruth 17 Nov. 1802. Date: 19 Oct. 1804. Wit: Amb. Blackburn, James West....Greenville Dist., James West made oath to L. Tarrant, J.P., 20 Oct. 1804.
Rec: 20 Nov. 1804.

Page 73: Michael Kallison(?) for $70 sold to James Gillison 300 acres in 96 Dist., (formerly), now in Pendleton, on S. side of Richaland Creek of the Keowee River. Date: 25 Nov. 1804. Wit: James Files, Jeremiah Files. Proved in open court by James Files, J. B. Earle, CPD.
Rec: 10 Nov. 1804.

Pages 73-74: Samuel Homan has borrowed of Andrew Pickens, Esq., $252 and sell and release to Pickens my house and lot in Village of Pendleton... which I purchased of Samuel Waller. Date: 28 Aug. 1804. Wit: Alexander Shaw, J. B. Earle. Alexander Shaw made oath to M. Hammond, D. Clk. 28 Nov. 1804.
Rec: 29 Nov. 1804.

Page 74: 15 Apr. 1797, Absolom Faris(?) of Pendleton Dist., Washington Co., to George Hagood for ₤ 50 stg. for 175 acres on Doddy's Creek & Jones Creek of the Saluda River, granted Richard Hood. Wit: William Faris, John Longley(?). William Faris made oath to Wm. Reed, J.P., 29 Feb.1798. Rec: 16 Nov. 1804.

Pages 74-75: Reuben Reed for ₤ 50 sold to William Marchbanks 149 acres, including head of Marchbank's Branch. Date: 26 May 1804. Signed: Reuben (X) Reed. Wit: Jonathan Gregory, David Murphree. Jonathan Gregory made oath to (_____). Rec: 8 Dec. 1804.

Page 75: John H. Blackburn for $100 sold to William Addis (_____) land adjoining _____ and Mr. Jett, Mr. Kelison(?). Date: 30 Mar. 1804. Wit: James (X) Loggins, Jas. Wilborn. James Loggins made oath to Wm. Edmondson, J.P., 20 Apr. 1804. Rec: 29 Nov. 1804.

Pages 75-76: William Harrison for $70 sold to Thomas Harrison cattle, hogs, beds and furniture. Date: 7 Jul. 1804. (Cannot read witnesses, and there was not oath made).

Page 76: 16 Dec. 1803, Thomas Shockley, planter, for $300 sold to William Cook land (tract) on the bank of the Savannah River (cannot read) Wit: John (X) Sarter, James Shockley. James Shockley made oath to John George, J.P., 9 Oct. 1804. Rec: 9 Oct. 1804.

Pages 76-77: Jarred Nelson of Greenville (Dist.) for $450 sold to Sary Langford of Buncombe Co., N. C. 376 acres on Sugar Creek of the Keowee River, bd. by Eli Langford, Sr. and Eli Langford, Jr., William Tabor, part of tract granted Elia Langford, Sr. by Gov. Moultrie, 1786; also, part of tract granted Eli Langford, Sr. by 1793. Date: 21 Feb. 1804(?). Wit: Leander Langford, Robert (X) Langford. Robert Langford made oath to Wm. Edmondson, J.Q., 26 Mar. 1804. Rec: 10 Oct. 1804.

Pages 77-78: William Harrison for $500 sold to Thomas Harrison, Sr. 200 acres on Big Beaverdam of the Toogalow River, bd. by Harry Lowry, Pendleton Isbell, Jacob Holland, Bird Lanier, granted to Daniel Doily. Date: 5 Jul. 1804. Wit: Benjamin Harrison, J. W. D. Terrell. Benjamin Harrison made oath to Wm. Cleveland, J.P., 11 Aug. 1804. Rec: 3 Dec. 1804.

Page 78: William Hallum(?), dec'd., in his lifetime made his last will and testament 15 Sep. 1803, then being of sound mind and memory, did order a certain negro man slave named Peter, then the property of William Hallum (Cannot read.........) that we, being executors named desirous to comply (...........) sd. negro Peter from this day forward to act and do for himself without any hinderance (...........). Date: _ Nov. 1804. Signed: James Barr, husband of the Widow, Andrew Pickens, James Hallum. John Wilson, J.Q. Rec: 5 Dec. 1804. Mary (X) Barr, formerly wife of William Hallum, released dower to John Willson, 17 Nov. 1804.

Pages 78-79: Jacob Homes for $200 sold to Elizabeth Thrasher 320 acres granted James Swan on 8 Aug. 1795, bd. NW by John Wammack, NW by Desaussure and Reuben Nash. Date: 30 Mar. 1804. Signed: Jacob (X) Homes, Sary (X) Homes. Wit: Daniel Willis, John Thrasher. John Thrasher made oath to Obadiah Trimier, Q.U., 10 Dec. 1804. Rec: 20 Dec. 1804.

Page 79: Charles Rice for $400 sold to Joseph Whitner 100 acres on E. side of 18 Mile Creek part of 300 acres granted John Campbell and conveyed to Rice 5 Aug. 1794, recorded Pendleton Bk. B, p. 307, bd. by Charles (Lin?), George Capehart, Joseph Whitner. Date: 18 Dec. 1804.Wit: John Moorhead, James Wood. James Wood made oath to M. Hammond, D. Clk., 20 Dec. 1804.
Rec: 20 Dec. 1804.

Pages 79-80: 29 Dec. 1801, Robert Gray and Elizabeth his wife, to Eleanor Pickens for $100 for tract lying between her land and branch running to Beaver Creek of Great Rocky River, granted by Wm. Moultrie 5 Jun. in 1786(?) to John Dowdle, recorded Bk. LLLL, p. 405, certified by William Lesley, conveyed from Dowdle to John Caliham(?) 20 Jun. 1790, bd. John Dowdle, Eleanor Pickens. Signed: Robert Gray, Elizabeth Gray. Wit: Israel Pickens, John (X) Smith. Israel Pickens made oath to John George, J. P., 12 Aug. 1804.
Rec: 19 Dec. 1804.

Pages 80-81: 3 Aug. 1799. Robert Reid, taylor, to Eleanor Pickens, Sr., for Ł 50 stg. for 110 ac. on Beaver Creek of the Savannah River, part of tract granted John Dowdle, conveyed to Moses Estrage, bd. Wm. McClusky(?), Eliab Moore, where Eleanor Pickens now lives. Signed: Richard (X) Reid, Jean (X) Reid. Wit: James Drinnan, Moses Bean. Moses Bean made the oath to Patrick Norris, J.P., 12 Apr. 1800.
Rec: 9 Dec. 1804.

Page 81: John Eubanks has bargained 150 acres, part of 225 acres granted by Chas. Pinckney to Ferdnand Hopkins 2 Jan. 1792, bd. by John Eubanks, Sr., Henry Garner. Date: 9 Jan. 1803. Wit: John Stuart, Jonathan Reider(?). John Stuart made oath to Dd. Murphree, J.P., 13 Mar. 1803.
Rec: 12 Dec. 1804.

Pages 81-82: John Hunnycutt sold to John and James Dickson one bay mare, 4 cows and calves, one black cow bought from Alexander Boys, Esq., one red and white cow bought from Maxey Jolly. Date: 14 May 1804. Wit: Samuel H. Dickson, Robert Kelton. (No oath).
Rec: 26 Dec. 1804.

Page 82: William Lesley of Abbeville Dist. for $170 sold to William Wilson of Pendleton Dist., 200 acres on Wilson's Creek, bd. on N. by Joseph Trimble, on E. by Mark Bird, on S. by John Sailor, part of a tract granted Matthew Willson 5 Mar. 1792. Date: 2 Sep. 1801. Wit: John Sailor (X), Agnes (X) Sailors. John Sailors made oath to E. Browne, J.P., 27 Feb. 1802.
Rec: 10 Oct. 1804.

Pages 82-83: Matthew Mullinix for $75 sold to Michael Cannemore 60 acres, part of tract granted James Henderson by Wm. Moultrie, 10 Oct. 1786, on 18 Mile Creek, bd. by Henderson, George Cannemore. Date: 1 May 1804. Signed: Matthew (X) Mullinix. Wit: William Mullinix, George (X) Cannemore. George Cannemore made oath to John Willson, J.Q., 13 Sep.1804.
Rec: 9 Oct. 1804.

Page 83: James Jett for $7 sold to Sarah Sinkler 116 acres bd. by Murphree, John Fields, Sarah Sinkler. Date: 7 Mar. 1803. Wit: Nathaniel Newman, John Prince(?). Nathaniel Newman made oath to John Cochran, J.P., 16 Apr. 1803.
Rec: 2 Jan. 1805.

Pages 83-84: Robert Pickens for $600 sold to Stephen Booth a negro wench named Sall and her child, Allen. Date: 8 Jun. 1804. Wit:.....

(Pages 83-84 cont'd): Adam (?) Wimpee, Obid Wimpee. Edin Wimpee made oath to Alexander Boyse, J.P., 3 Nov. 1804. Rec: 6 Nov. 1804.

Page 84: John Eubanks for $150 sold to William Edwards 95 acres on Geldings Creek, bd. Bradey. Date: 8 Feb. 1804. Signed: John (X) Eubanks. Wit: Peter Edwards, Henry (X) Edwards. Peter Edwards made oath to John Willson, J.Q., 19 May 1804. Rec: 9 Oct. 1804.

Pages 84-85: Thomas Eubanks for $200 sold to William Edwards 103 acres granted John (___very dim) by Wm. Moultrie, 19 Feb. 1791. Date: 8 Feb. 1804. Wit: Peter Edwards, John (X) Eubanks. Peter Edwards made oath before John Willson, Q.U., 19 May 1804. Rec: 9 Oct. 1804.

Pages 85-86: 11 Feb. 1793, Joseph Brown to Ambrose Nichols for £ 30 for 200 acres in Washington Dist. on Rock Creek of the Savannah River, granted James Brown by Thos. Pinckney 1 Oct. 1787. Wit: Peter Acker, John Nichols, B. Starritt. John Nichols made oath to Jon. Montgomery, 9 Mar. 1802. Rec: 9 Oct. 1804.

Page 86: Abraham Larrow, planter, for love and good will to my daughter, Cesiah Larrow, one negro child named Harry. Date: 7 Sep. 1804. Wit: Stephen Anderson, John Larrow. Both made oath to John George, J. P., 8 Oct. 1804. Rec: 8 Oct. 1804.

Page 86: Personally came Thomas Buchannan and swore that on 6 Jul. last that he believes that in a quarrel with David Bearly (Bearty?), did bite off a piece of sd. Baty's right ear. Sworn 10 Oct. 1804 before Nathan Lusk, J.P., and recorded 10 Oct. 1804.

Pages 86-87: Abraham Larrow, planter, for love and affection for my son, Jacob Larrow, give him one negro woman named Ann now in my possession, provided above slave do live to have children, I give the first child she has to my son, Stephen Larrow, and the second to my son, William Larrow. Date: 7 Sep. 1804. Wit: Stephen Anderson, John Larrow. Both made oath before John George, J.P., 8 Oct. 1804. Rec: 8 Oct. 1804.

Page 87: James Brown of Washington Co., Tn. for $200 sold to Robert Hall of Pendleton Co., S.C. 428 acres on Golden's Creek of 12 Mile River, deducting 107 acres sold to Aron Boggs by Henry Burdine. Date: 29 Apr. 1797. Wit: Waddy Thompson, W. C. Hamilton. William Hamilton made oath to Samuel Houston, J.P., 9 Oct. 1804. Rec: 9 Oct. 1804.

Page 88: James Brown of Washington Co., Tn. for $500 sold to Robert Hall, 240 acres on 12 Mile River, reserving 8 acres sold to Aron Boggs and granted by Wm. Moultrie to Elijah Mayfield 5 Feb. 1787. Date: 9 Apr. 1797. Wit: Waddy Thompson, W. C. Hamilton. William Hamilton made oath to Samuel Houston 9 Oct. 1804. Rec: 9 Oct. 1804.

Pages 88-89: 2 Mar. 1796, Absolem Briant to William Bruer for £ 80 stg. for tract on Big Beaverdam of the Savannah River, bd. by Nathan Briant's old line. Signed: Absolem (X) Briant. Wit: Oliver Charles, Elizabeth (X) Charles, William (X) Moss. Oliver Charles made oath to Wm. Hall, J.P., 6 Aug. 1796. Rec: 9 Oct. 1804.

Page 89: Patterson Childers for $120 sold to Isaac

(Page 89 cont'd): January 100 acres on S. side of the Saluda River, bd. by John Thomas, John Southerland. Date: 30 Jun. 1804. Signed: Patterson (X) Childers. Wit: John Childers, Jacob Copelin. John Childers made oath to David Murphree, J.P., 30 June 1804. Rec: 29 Dec. 1804.

Pages 89-90: Michael Hutchens for 9 shillings stg. sold to William Sutherland 1 acre, part of 212 acres on Clevelands Creek, NE. of Tugaloo River, where Sutherland's grist mill now stands, granted Hutchens by Thos. Pinckney 9 Feb. 1797, bd. by Sutherland. Date: 27 Dec. 1802. Signed: Michael Hutchings. Wit: Nimrod Graham, Daniel Sutherland. Daniel Sutherland made oath to Colin Campbell, J.P. 20 Jul. 1804. Rec: 30 Jan. 1805.

Pages 90-91: Edward Graham for Ł 60 stg. sold to Wm. Sutherland 100 acres, part of 930 acres on Cleveland's Creek, NE of the Tugaloe River where Sutherland now lives, granted Edward Graham by Thos. Pinckney 12 Nov. 1792, bd. by Graham and Sutherland, John Robinson, Michael Hutchins, Robert Graham. Date: 27 Dec. 1802. Signed: Edward (X) Graham. Wit: Michael Hutchins, Daniel Sutherland. Daniel Sutherland made oath to Colin Campbell, J.P., 26 Jul. 1804. Rec: 30 Jan. 1805.

Page 91: John Williams of Franklin Co., Ga. for $300 sold to Phillip Smith of Pendleton Co. 177 acres on the S. side of Connoross, bd. by a tract of 772 acres granted William McKay, this land part of 3 tracts: 60 acres granted Geo. Weems(?) conveyed to Wm. McKay, from McKay to Williams, 45 acres granted Wm. Mackay and 70 acres granted John C. Kilpatrick, all conveyed to John Williams. Date: 26 Dec. 1799. Signed: John(X) Williams. Wit: John C. Kilpatrick, Wm. Smith. William Smith made oath to H. McCray, J.P., 31 Jan. 1805. Rec: 1 Feb. 1805.

Page 92: James McCarley for $300 sold to Jesse McGee 250 acres on Big Generostee of Savannah River, part of 3 tracts; one surveyed for Richard York 3 Feb. 1787 by John Kilpatrick and granted John Tallant 1787 by Chas. Pinckney, the other survey for Robert Boyd 23 Aug. 1785 by Thomas Finley and granted Robert Maxwell 3 Mar. 1788 by Thos. Pinckney, the 3rd part surveyed for Jonathan Gibbs by John McMahan, bd. by Gibbs. Date: 6 Apr. 1804. Wit: Jonathan Gibbs, Thomas (X) Commons, Elizabeth (X) McCarley released dower to James Tate, Q.U., 6 Apr. 1804. Jonathan Gibbs made oath to James Tate 6 Apr. 1804. Rec: 1 Feb. 1805.

Pages 92-93: Nathan Nall for $125 sold to John Murphey 150 acres on Cherokee Creek of Savannah River, bd. by Rodger Murphey, Sr., part of 371 acres granted Charles Clements 5 Nov. 1792, by Chas. Pinckney. Date: 27 Nov. 1802. Wit: Charles Clemons, Rodger Murphey. Mary (X) Nall, wife of Nathan Nall, released dower to James Willbourn, J.P., 11 Feb. 1803. Rodger Murphree made oath to James Wilbourn 11 Feb. 1803. Rec: 8 Oct. 1804.

Pages 93-94: Jesse Miller for $100 sold to Sally Miller and Emy Miller several head of cattle. Date 12 Apr. 1803. Wit: William (X) Tramble, Sampson (X) Tramble. William Tramble made oath to James Wardlaw, J.P., 6 Feb. 1805. Rec: 7 Feb. 1805.

Page 94: Jesse Miller for $100 sold to Sally Miller and Emy Miller feather beds and furniture, kitchen utinsels. Date: 12 Apr. 1803. Wit: William (X) Tramble, Sampson (X) Tramble. William Tramble made oath to James Wardlaw, J.P. 6 Feb. 1805. Rec: 7 Feb. 1805.

Pages 94-95: 5 Oct. 1799, Isham Blankingship to John Blankingship for $100 sue 1 March for 100 acres in Washington Dist. on Little Beaverdam of Rocky River, where George Slaton now lives. Signed: Isham (X) Blankingship. Wit: John Wallace, William Blankingship. John Wallace made oath to Michael Dickson, J.P., 11 Apr. 1803.
Rec: 9 Oct. 1804.

Pages 95-96: John Smith for $260 sold to William Tim (also spelled Timm) 135 acres on 26 Mile Creek of the Savannah River, bd. by McCoy, John Hunnicutt, Vinson Timms, Sr., John Smith, Lewis Jones, part of the tract granted Randolph Hunnicutt, who conveyed to Wm. Timms, by John Smith. Date: 7 Sep. 1804. Wit: Foster Golden, Jabes Timms. Foster Golden made oath to John Willson, J.Q., 8 Feb. 1805.
Rec: 9 Feb. 1805.

Page 96: Saml. Robinson for $85 sold to Azariah Anderson 95 acres, 1/2 tract granted Robinson on Seneca River of the Keowee River, bd by William Hamilton, Estate of Evan Thomas, dec'd., Samuel Robinson. Date: 1 Feb. 1804. Wit: Edwd. Adair, Robert Waugh. (Plat). Edwd. Adair made oath to John Adair, J.P., 15 Mar. 1804.
Rec: 9 Oct. 1804.

Page 96-97: William Hone for $350 sold to John Green 400 acres on Big Creek, granted William Stone by Chas. Pinckney 1 Oct. 1792. Date: 28 Dec. 1803. Signed: Willie Hone. Wit: William Anderson, Henry Green, Elizabeth (X) Honey released dower. Wit: Tobias Honey. (No date or J.P.) Henry Green made oath to Sam Houston, J.P., 2 Jan. 1804.
Rec: 12 Jan. 1805.

Pages 97-98: John Bird, planter, appoint my trusty and loving wife, Sarah Bird, my lawful attorney to recover a negro woman named Lett, together with all of Lett's children, also all sums of money, goods and wares from Daniel Vaughn, or other persons. Date: 15 Feb. 1805. Signed: John Byrd. Wit: Henry Garner, John Willson, J.Q. certified above Power of Attorney. J. B. Earle, Clk. of the Crt. of Gen. Sessions and Common Pleas certify John Willson is acting Justice of Quorom, 16 Feb. 1805.
Rec: 16 Feb. 1805.

Pages 98-99: 21 Mar. 1792, James Moore, planter, for Ł 10 stg. sold to James Park Adare and James Askens 200 acres granted James Moore 17 Jan. 1788 in 96 Dist. above the antient boundary line on Hencoop, waters of Savannah River. Wit: Alexander McAllister, Robert McWhorter, Alexander Moore. Alexander McAllister made oath to E. Browne, J.P. 30 May 1794.
Rec: 4 Feb. 1805.

Page 99: John Tapley for $40 sold to Henry McCray 32(?) acres on Big Beaverdam Creek bd. by McCambridge, Robert Smith and McCray. Date: 12 Oct. 1803. Wit: Ann Trimier, Nancy Harbin. Ann Trimmier made oath to Obadiah Trimmier, Q.U., 10 Nov. 1803.
Rec: 17 Dec. 1803.

Pages 99-100: Josiah Shipp, farmer, for $190 sold to Daniel Shipp 160 acres on 23 Mile Creek, granted Joseph Jenkins by Wm. Moultrie 4 Dec. 1786, where Josiah Shipp now lives. Date: 6 Oct. 1804. Signed: Josiah (X) Shipp. Wit: Simon Doyle, William Shipp. Simon Doyle made oath to James Starrett, J.P., 12 Oct. 1804.
Rec: 13 Oct. 1804.

Page 100: I am held and bound to James White for $167 to be paid on or before 9 Nov. 1805, now I, William Montgomery deliver to James White feather beds, furniture, kitchen utinsels, farm tools, wearing apparel,

(Page 100 cont'd): cattle, corn and fodder, sheep, waggon and complete geers, etc. Date: 9 Nov. 1804. Wit: Parthenia Edmondson who gave oath to Wm. Edmondson, Q.U., 9 Nov. 1804. Rec: 21 Jan. 1805.

Pages 100-101: William Guest of Pendleton Dist. for $250 sold to Thomas Harris of Abbeville Dist., 200 acres on Beaverdam Creek in fork of the Keowee and Toogalow Rivers, laid out for Lewis Desaussure, bd. on S. by Tucker Woodson. Date: 15 Sep. 1801. Wit: Asa Kemp, Henry Harris. Asa Kemp made oath to John Harris, J.P., 15 Sep. 1801. Ann Guest, wife of William Guest, released dower to Obadiah Trimmier, Q.U., 15 Sep. 1804. Rec: 8 Oct. 1804.

Pages 101-102: Adam Lackey for $200 sold to John Jones 72 acres on 26 Mile Creek of Savannah River, bd. on E. by Lewis Jones, N. by John Hunnicutt, on other sides by Robert Anderson and Mr. Reese, granted Sophia Case. Date: 7 Nov. 1803. Wit: Benjamin Gilbert, Jesse Jolly. Jesse Jolly made oath to Sam Houston, J.P., 5 Dec. 1803. Rec: 4 Oct. 1804.

Page 102: Thomas Putman for $280 sold to David Baty 150 acres on Lockuses fork of Big Generostee of the Savannah River, part of 360 ac. granted William Stephenson 14 Jan. 1791 and part of 505 acres granted to Thos. Osbin 17 Jan. 1788, bd. by Draton's old survey. Date: 11 Sep. 1802. Wit: David McCarley, Penuel Price. Mary Putman, wife of Thomas Putman, released dower to E. Browne, Q.U., 20 Jan. 1803. Penuel Price made oath to Nathan Lusk, J.P., 29 Nov. 1802. Rec: 10 Oct. 1804.

Pages 102-103: Abraham Elledge for $30 sold to Richard Harris 20 acres on 26 Mile Creek, part of 888 acres granted James Gillison by Thos. Pinckney 5 Dec. 1787, recorded Bk. VVVV, p. 207, bd. by Abram Elledge, William Butler, Mathew Dixon. Date: 26 Oct. 1800. Signed: Abraham (X) Elledge. Wit: Arthur Durley, Spencer (X) Haney. Spencer Haney made oath to John Taylor, Q.U., 22 Oct. 1804. Rec: 22 Oct. 1804.

Pages 103-104: 20 Sep. 1804, David Guest and Fanney, his wife, to Jacob Holland for $260 for 150 ac. on S. side of Big Beaverdam Creek, bd. by Jacob Holland, and Kilpatrick, part of 295 acres surveyed by Alexander Kilpatrick 26 Jul. 1785. Signed: David Guest (only). Wit: William Bates, Danl. Bates. Daniel Bates made oath to Obadiah Trimmier, Q.U, 5 Oct. 1804. Frances Guest, wife of David Guest, released dower to Obadiah Trimmier, 5 Oct. 1804. Rec: 8 Oct. 1804.

Page 104: John Chapman now of Pendleton Dist., planter, for $250 sold to William Brown 50 ac. part of tract granted Nathaniel Perry in 1786 by Wm. Moultrie, on Raven's Creek of 12 Mile River. Date: 8 October 1804. Wit: Jay Kirksey, Reuben Reed. Reuben (X) Reed made oath to John Cochran, J.P. (No date) Rec: 9 Oct. 1804.

Pages 104-105: 14 Jan. 1793, Eli Hunnicutt to Rolin Hunnicutt for ₤ 30 for 30 acres in Washington Dist. on 26 Mile Creek of the Savannah River, bd. by Lewis Jones, part of tract granted Eli Hunnicutt by Wm. Moultrie 4 Dec. 1786. Wit: John Hunnicutt, Jacob Capehart. John Hunnicutt made oath to John Wilson, J.P., 2 Feb. 1794. Rec: 25 Oct. 1804.

Page 105: William Wardlaw for $100 sold to Cannon Braziel 215 acres (no location given). (cont'd next page).

(Page 105 cont'd): Date: 5 Jan. 1794. Wit: George Dilworth, Elisha Rosson. Geo. Dilworth made oath to Aaron Broyles, 9 Oct. 1804.
Rec: 9 Oct. 1804.

Pages 105-106: Jonathan Clark for $1,000 sold to Thomas Coker 200 acres granted Boling Clark by Benj. Guerard, plantation where Jonathan Clark now lives, on E. side of 23 Mile Creek, bd. by Peter McLean. Date: 31 Aug. 1803. Wit: Jos. Clark, Wm. Coker, Lucinda (X) Rodgers. Wm. Coker made oath to John Wilson, J.Q., 2 Nov. 1803. Jenny Clark, wife of Jonathan Clark, released dower to John Wilson, 2 Nov. 1803.
Rec: 10 Jan. 1805.

Pages 106-107: James Neel for $160 sold to William Sims 150 acres as represented by plat (included) on Cuffey Creek of 23 Mile River of Keowee River, surveyed 13 Apr. 1802 by Samuel H. Dickson, D.S., bd. on E. by George Forbis, W. by Jonathan West. Date: 10 Apr. 1802. Wit: James Wood, A. Kilpatrick. Ann (X) Neel, wife of James Neel released dower to John Wilson, J.Q.
Rec: 8 Oct. 1804. (See p. 108).

Page 107: William Rose on 26 Sep. 1804, sold for $400 to James McAfee, 202 acres I now live on except one rod where my daughter, Patty is buried, part of a tract granted 7 Aug. 1799, on both sides of Fall Creek, bd. by Aaron Moore. Wit: Stephen Meritt, Joseph Boon. Joseph Boon made oath to Thomas Hargiss, J.P., 8 Oct. 1804.
Rec: 8 Oct. 1804.

Pages 107-108: James McKinney on 5 Oct. 1804, for $500... sold to Ratliff Boon 358 acres where Boon now lives, part of tract granted to Thomas Grant, 1 Aug. 1785, recorded Bk. EEEE (no page number), on both sides of Keowee River, below Toxaway Creek. Wit: James McAfee, Joseph Boon, Jeptha Norton. James McAfee made oath to Thomas Hargiss, J.P. 8 Oct. 1804.
Rec: 8 __ 1804.

Page 108: Joseph McClusky of Wilson Co., Tenn. for $10 sold to George Watts of Pendleton Dist. 381 acres on Little Generostee Creek of the Sacannah River, granted McClusky by Wm. Moultrie 6 Jul. 1784. Date: 7 Jan. 1804. Wit: George Weems, Edward (X) Landers. Edward Landers made oath he saw Capt. Joseph McClusky sign deed to Nathan Lusk, J.P., 29 Sep. 1804.
Rec: 8 Oct. 1804.

Page 108: James Wood made oath to M. Hammond, D.C., 7 Mar. 1804. (Refers to James Neel deed to Wm. Sims, page 106 above)

Pages 108-109: Lewis Davis for $300 sold to William Cox 100 acres on S. side of Little Creek of the Saluda River. Date: 5 Jan. 1802. Wit: Henry Gambrell, Patience Crenshaw. Henry Gambrel made oath to E. Browne, J.Q., 5 Jan. 1802. Peggy (X) Davis, wife of Lewis Davis, released dower to E. Browne, 5 Dec. 1802.
Rec: 8 Oct. 1802.

Page 109: Robert Trotter for $200 sold to Archibald Nichols 130 acres on N. fork of Little Creek of Rocky River, bd. by George Dilworth, Ambrose Nichols, Daniel Owens. Date: 19 Jul. 1804. Wit: Ambrose (X) Nichols, George Dilworth. George Dilworth made oath to James Wilborn, J.P., 6 Oct. 1804. Susanna (X) Trotter, wife of Robert Trotter, released dower to James Wilborn, 6 Oct. 1804.
Rec: 9 Oct. 1804.

Page 109: Abraham Elledge for $100 sold to Richard Harris 80 acres, on 26 Mile Creek, part of

(Page 109 cont'd): tract granted James Gillison by Thomas Pinckney 5 Dec. 1787, recorded Bk. VVVV, page 207, bd. by Abraham Elledge, Harris, Mathew Dixon, Wm. Hembrie, Calhoun, Crumbless and Welch. Date: 26 Oct. 1800. Signed: Abraham (X) Elledge. Wit: Arthur Durley, Spencer (X) Haney. Spencer Haney made oath to John Taylor, Q.U., 22 Oct. ___. Rec: 22 Oct. 1804.

Page 110: 24 Feb. 1804, Answell Griffen is bound to Joseph Chatham for $300 and made lawful deed to 234 acres on 12 Mile River. Wit: Green Collier, John Chapman. John Chapman made oath to John Taylor, Q.U., 8 Oct. 1804. Rec: 8 Oct. 1804.

Page 110: John Young for $500 sold to William Brown 100 acres on 12 Mile River, bd. by Brown and Morgan. Date: 19 Nov. 1803. Wit: Moses Hunt, Joseph Gibson. Moses Hunt made oath to John Cochran, J.P. 18 Feb. 1804. Rec: 9 Oct. 1804.

Pages 110-111: Charles Clements for $125 sold to Roger Murphey 250 acres on Cherokee Creek of the Savannah River, bd. by Peter Hall, James Todd, Samuel Smith, Curry, Vanderhorst and Nathan Nall, part of 871 ac. granted Clements 5 Nov. 1792, by Chas. Pinckney. Date: 20 Sep. 1802.Wit: John Murphey, Allis Day, Moses Rush. Agnes (X) Clements, wife of Charles Clements, released dower to James Welborn, J.P., 11 Feb. 1803. John Murphrey made oath to James Welborn 11 Feb. 1803. Rec: 8 Oct. 1803.

Page 111: John Miller for $300 sold to Hugh Miller tract on Barker's Creek of Little River, bd. on S. by Vanderhorst, W. by Barker's Creek, N. by Thomas Brown and John Robertson, granted to Miller by Chas. Pinckney, 5 Sep. 1791. Date: 30 Jun. 1804. Wit: Samuel Black, Oliver Woods. Samuel Black made oath to Aaron Broyles, J.P., 9 Oct. 1804. Rec: 9 Oct. 1804.

Page 112: John Miller for $300 sold to Henry Miller tract on Corner Creek and Barker's Creek, bd. S. by Vanderhorst, E. by Nathaniel Aldridge, N. by Alexander Snell, W. by Hugh Miller. Date: 13 Jun. 1804. Wit: Oliver Woods and Samuel Black. Samuel Black made oath to Aaron Broyles, J.P., 9 Oct. 1804. Rec: 9 Oct. 1804.

Pages 112-113: James Milwee for Ł 40 stg. sold to Thomas Garner 240 acres on S. side of Saluda River on Begg Creek, bd. by Thomas Garner's old line, Joel Halbert, part of tract of 300 acres granted Milwee (exclusive of Ambrose Nichols and Alexander's land, Joel Halbert's and Dolly Burdine's land) by Chas. Pinckney, 3 Sep. 1792, recorded Bk. F, no. 5, page 151. Date: 31 Aug. 1796. Wit: William Bell and Aaron Guyton. Margaret Milwee, wife of James Milwee, released dower and William Bell made oath to Wm. Hall, J.P., 23 Jan. 1798. Rec: 11 Oct. 1804.

Page 113: John Gillispie of Greenville Dist. for $750 sold to Ambrose Bradley 550(?) acres by 3 surveys on George's Creek of Saluda River, where Bradley now lives, bd. by Daniel McCollum, Wm. Jamison, Thomas Boyd, James Satterfield, Sr., Saml. Black, William Brown, and Henderson. Date: 10 Dec. 1801. Wit: Joab Mauldin, Elijah Hammond. Joab Mauldin made oath to Ro. Bowen, J.P., 17 Apr. 1802. Rec: 8 Oct. 1804.

Page 113: John Eubanks for $150 sold to William Edwards 95 acres on Bradley's line on Goldens Creek. Date: 28 Feb. 1804. Wit: Peter Edwards, Henry (X) Edwards. (No oath or recording date).

Page 114: Joseph Black for $867½ sold to Thomas Coker 265 acres, part of tracts granted Boling Clark by Benj. Guerard, where Joseph Clark now lives, on 23 Mile Creek. Date: 17 Dec. 1803. Wit: Wm. Coker, Josiah (X) Kees. Wm. Coker made oath to John Wilson, Q.U., 21 Apr. 1804. Mary (X) Clark, wife of Joseph Clark, released dower to John Wilson, 26 Apr. 1804. Rec: 10 Jan. 1805. (The deed was signed by Joseph Clark)

Pages 114-115: Susannah Tackett for $100 sold to David Barton 50 acres on Togaloo River, conveyed from Col. Benjamin Cleveland to William Tackett, dec'd., bd. by Looney. Date: 7 Sep. 1804. Signed: Susannah (X) Tackett. Wit: B. Starrett, Presley Barton. Benjamin Starrett made oath to Jno. Barton, J.P., 8 Sep. 1804. Rec: 10 Oct. 1804.

Page 115: James Millwee for ₤10 sold to John Millwee 100 acres on Wilson's Creek of Rocky River, granted James Millwee 5 Apr. 1789, recorded Bk. ZZZZ, p. 40. Date: 10 May 1804. Wit: James Warnock, Susannah Warnock. James Warnock made oath to Alexander Boyse, J.P., 11 Oct. 1804. Rec: 11 Oct. 1804.

Page 115: Robert Dowdle and James Dowdle for $400 sold to James Guy 200 acres on Neal's Crk. of Rocky River of Savannah River, bd. by Andrew McAllester, Glenn, Peter Greenlees, dec'd., Eliab Moore and Robert Dowdle; 176 acres is part of 320 acres granted Robert Dowdle 5 Jun. 1786 by Wm. Moultrie; 24 acres part of 771 acres granted James Dowdle on 14 Nov. 1793 by Arnoldus Vanderhorst. Date: 18 Oct. 1802. Wit: Adam Todd, Robt. Thompson. Adam Todd made oath to Sam. Houston, J.P. (No date). Rec: 9 Oct. 1804.

Pages 115-116: Ann Mathews, Joseph Mathews, Polly Mathews, Nancy Mathews and Jno. Mathews, heirs of Isaac Mathews, dec'd., of Abbeville Dist. for $231 sold to Thomas Haney of Pendleton Dist., 154 acres bd. on W. by Savannah River, S. by Joseph Calhoun, N. by Wm. Love, surveyed for Isaac Mathews for 200 acres, now deducting 46 acres, which is to be conveyed to Isaac Evans. Date: 19 Dec. 1801. Signed: Ann (X) Mathews, Joseph Mathews, Polly Mathews, Nancy Mathews, John Mathews. Wit: Hugh Simpson, Isaac Evans, Jos. Hutton. Isaac Evans made oath to James Tate, Q.U., 12 Oct.1803. Rec: 10 Oct. 1804.

Page 116: Andrew Pickens, Robert Anderson and John Wilson, Commissioners for laying off and disposing of the Public Lotts and lands adjoining Pendleton Courthouse, for ₤10 10 pence sold to Jane Marchbanks, Margaret Williams, John Young, Sarah Young, Ann Young, James Young, Nancy Young and Dicey Young, heirs of William Young, dec'd. of the State of Tennessee, one lot of land in the Town of Pendleton, no. 5, bd. on N. by no. 4, E. by no. 32, S. by street, W. by street, containing 1 acre. Date: 9 Oct. 1803. Wit: James Jett, Saml. Cherry. James Jett made oath to David Murphree, J.P., 10 Oct. 1804. Rec: 10 Oct. 1804.

Page 117: James Courtney for 50(?) sold to Belffe (called Belfield in oath) Wood 150 acres on Morrises branch of Little River of the Keowee River on Indian line, bd. by Courtney and Isaac Hill. Date: 3 Nov. 1804. Wit: Isaac Hill, Buckner Smith. Buckner Smith made oath to W. Nicholson, J.P., 23 Feb. 1805. Rec: 4 Mar. 1805.

Pages 117-118: John Hallum, planter, for $800 sold to Robert Baker, planter, 320 acres being 1/2 of tract granted William Marshall on 18 Mile Creek of Savannah River, bd. by Daniel Sims and Madrick, to include where Baker now lives. Date: 13 Oct. 1804. Signed: John Hallum, Mary (X) Hallum (called Ann in oath). Wit: John Hallum, Mary Hallum. James Hallum made

(Pages 117-118 cont'd): oath to James C. Griffen, J.P., 18 Feb.1805.
Rec: 18 Feb. 1805.

Pages 118-119: 10 Sep. 1793, Robert Anderson and Jane,his wife, to George Tubb for Ł 60 stg. for 284 acres in Washington Dist. on S. side of the Keowee River, bd. on NW by land surveyed for Major Warley, granted Robert Anderson 7 June. 1790 by Chas. Pinckney. Signed: Robert Anderson, Jane Anderson. Wit: William Tabour, Susana (X) Tabour. William Tabour made oath to Joseph Reed, J.P., 14 Jun. 1794.
Rec: 10 Mar. 1805.

Pages 119-120: 29 Aug. 1804, David McCaleb, Sheriff of Pendleton Dist. to Josiah Foster, Esq...... Joseph Hall on 2nd Monday of March 1802, in Court of Common Pleas obtained a judgement against Benjamin Starrett, Sr. for $66 plus $26 for cost and charges. On 14 Mar. 1802, Sheriff ordered all goods, chattels, and lands of Benj. Starrett, Sr. be sold at public auction, Josiah Foster being the highest bidder for $770 for 200 acres on Connoross Creek, granted John Davey by Benj. Guerard, bd. N. by Alexander Glen, E. by Robert Glen and Johh Bavick(?), S. by Joseph Griffen, W. by Capt. James Kennedy. Wit: J. B. Earle, J. Miller. John Miller made oath to M. Hammond, 17 Apr. 1805.
Rec: 17 Apr. 1805.

Pages 121-122: 14 Feb. 1804, David McCaleb, Sheriff, to Levi Graham.....David Sloan on 2nd Monday in March 1802 in Court of Common Please obtained judgement against John Rusk for $758.76 plus $17.36 charges. The Sheriff directed all goods, chattles and lands of John Rusk to be sold at public auction to highest bidder on 4 Sep. 1804, being Levi Graham for $125 for 157 acres, part of 207 acres, granted Alexander McDowall by Thos. Pinckney, bd. S. by Joshua and Richard Holden, N. by Samuel Harper and Joseph Wood. Wit: John R. Brown, William Anderson. John R. Brown made oath to M. Hammond, 14 Feb. 1804.
Rec: 14 Feb. 1805.

Page 122: 21 Aug. 1801, James Barnett to Abner Robinson for $50 for 30 acres on S. side of 12 Mile River, bd. by sd. Robertson, William Wight. Signed: James (X) Barnett. Wit: James Wardlaw, Nathl. Newman. James Wardlaw made oath to David Murphree, J.P., 30 Dec. 1801.
Rec: 14 Apr. 1805.

Pages 122-123: 16 Jan. 1804, John Barnett to Abner Robertson for $100 for 80 acres on N. fork of 12 Mile River, on both sides, bd. by James Wardlaw, Wight, Combs. Signed: John (X) Barnett, Nancy (X) Barnett. Wit: James Wardlaw, James Newman. Nancy (X) Barnett, wife of John Barnett, released dower to James Wardlaw, Q.U., 16 Jan. 1805. (No oath).
Rec: 19 Apr. 1804.

Pages 123-124: 25 Mar. 1797, John Morehead, to Abner Robertson (also Robinson) for Ł 35 for 179 ac. (later says 129 ac.) purchased from George Thompson on N. fork of 12 Mile River. Wit: Robert Stewart, James Jett. James Jett made oath to W. Reed, J.P., 22 Apr. 1797.
Rec: 19 Apr. 1805.

Page 124: William Lewis and Mary, his wife, for $30 sold to Richard Gray 77 acres, part of 385 acres granted William Lewis on 23 Mile Crk. to include improvement of Ambrose Barnett. Date: 23 Jul. 1804. Signed: William Lewis, Mary Lewis. Wit: Jesse H. Posey, Jesse Lewis. Jesse H. Posey made oath to James C. Griffen, J.P., 12 Feb. 1805.
Rec: 14 Feb. 1805.

Pages 124-125: John Miller for $200 sold to William Miller 200 acres on W. fork of Barker's Creek, granted by Chas. Pinckney 1796. Date: 28

(Pages 124-125 cont'd): Jun. 1804. Wit: Samuel Black and Oliver
Woods. Samuel Black made oath to Aaron
Broyles, J.P., 9 Oct. 1804.
Rec: 9 Oct. 1804.

Pages 125-126: John Brown of Pendleton Dist. for $300 sold
to Thomas Harris of Abbeville Dist., 339
acres on Little Beaverdam Creek in fork of
Keowee River and Toogalow River, laid out for John Brown, bd. NE by William Grant, SW by McCambridge. Date: 19 Oct. 1801. Wit: John Harris, Thomas Gorman, Andw. Harris. Thomas Gorman made oath to John Harris, J. P., 19 Oct. 1801.
Rec: 8 Oct. 1804.

Page 126: Thomas Coker for $2,500 sold to William
Coker 640 acres on 23 Mile Creek, granted
Boling Clark by Benj. Guerard, where Thomas Coker now lives, bd. by Cooper, Peter McMahan, former line of Coker and Joseph Clark. Date: 27 Nov. 1804. Wit: John Inlow, Lucy (X) Inlow. John Inlow made oath to Samuel H. Dickson, 10 Jan. 1805.
Rec: 10 Jan. 1805.

Pages 126-127: Trion Fuller for $640 sold to Jacob Laudermilk 100 acres on Choestoe Creek of Toogalow River, part of a tract granted James
McIlwee 2 May 1785 by Wm. Moultrie, bd. by Baker and Verner. Date: 26 Feb. 1804. Signed: Trion (X) Fuller. Wit: John Verner and John (X) Marsh. John Verner made oath to Josiah Foster, J.P., 9 Oct. 1804.
Rec: 9 Oct. 1804.

Page 127: James Brown for $180 sold to Samuel Earle
111 acres on Toogalow River. Date: 4 July
1804. Signed: James Brown, Elizabeth (X)
Brown. Wit: Nathl. Reed, Colin Campbell. Elizabeth (X) Brown, wife of James Brown, released dower to Henry M. Wood, J.Q., 23 Jul. 1804. Nathaniel Reed made oath to H. M. Wood, 29 Oct. 1804.
Rec: 13 Jan. 1805.

Pages 127-128: Ann Matthews, William Hamilton and Joseph
Hutton of Abbeville Dist. are bound unto
Thomas Haney of Pendleton Dist. for $1,500.
Date: 19 Dec. 1801. Obligation is that Ann Matthews, William Calhoun and Joseph Hutton give title to land executed by heirs of Isaac Matthews,deceased, namely: Ann Matthews, Joseph Polly Nancy and John Matthews (no punctuation). Signed: Ann (X) Matthews, Wm. Calhoun, Jos. Hutton. Wit: Isaac Evans, Hugh Simpson, Polly Matthews. Isaac Evans made oath to James Tate, Q.U., 12 Oct. 1803.
Rec: 10 Oct. 1804.

Page 128: James Jett for $1.00 sold to Zachariah Holcum 489 acres on fork of Cane Creek of the
Keowee River. Date: 26 Apr. 1804. Wit: Alexander White, Isaac Gray. Isaac Gray made oath to M. Hammond, D. Clk. 15 Feb. 1805. Rec: 15 Feb. 1805.

Pages 128-129: 18 Jun. 1803, Robert Norwood and William
Norwood of Abbeville Dist. to Jacob Earnest
of Pendleton Dist. for $200 for a tract on
23 Mile Creek of the Savannah River. Signed: Robert Norwood, William Norwood. Wit: James Wally, who made oath to Adam Cr. Jones, J.Q. of Abbeville Dist., 5 Oct. 1803. (Signature looks like James Watts).
Rec: 12 Feb. 1805.

Pages 129-130: Abiel Cobb for love and affection give to
my loving son, Lewis Cobb, all my stock,
goods and chattels. Date: 15 Dec. 1804.
Signed: Abiel (X) Cobb. Wit: A. Patterson, Mary (X) Patterson. Inventory, tract of land on E. side of 23 Mile Creek of the Keowee River of 191 ac. bought from Samuel Robinson, horses, cattle, waggon, plantation tools, household furniture. Archibald Patterson made oath to Jas. C. Griffen, JP

(Pages 129-130 cont'd): 15 Feb. 1803. Rec: 15 Jan. 1805.

Page 130: John Green for $80 sold to Isaac Horton 100 acres granted John Hamilton by James B. Richardson, Esq. bd. by Ellet, Wm. Honey. Date: 6 Jan. 1803. Wit: John Millwee, Henry Green. John Millwee made oath to Samuel Houston, 2 Jan. 1805. Rec: 12 Jan. 1805.

Pages 130-131: William McWhorter, planter, for love and affection to my son, Isaac McWhorter, horses, calf, 1 forty eight gallon still and vessels. Date: 17 Jan. 1805. Signed: William (X) McWhirter. Wit: Edley Linn, Thomas Drinnan. Rec: 17 Jan. 1805. (No oath).

Page 131: Thomas Garner for $162 sold to William Halbert 108 acres on Saluda River, part on a branch of Big Creek and part on a branch of Tonies Creek. Date: 14 Oct. 1803. Wit: William Hall, Thomas Smith, and Jamima (X) Hall. William Hall made oath to Aaron Broyles, J.P. (No date). Rec: 8 Feb. 1805.

Pages 131-132: William Cox of Pendleton Dist. for $350 sold to James Lawson of Franklin Co., Ga. a tract on both sides of Little Beaverdam Creek on the Togalow River, bd. by James Allen, Wm. Felton and Samuel Earle. Date: 8 Feb. 1804. Wit: Edwd. T. McClure, George Walker Read..... Mary Cox, wife of William Cox, released dower to Obadiah Trimmier, Q. U., 20 Feb. 1804. George Walker Reed made oath to Obadiah Trimmier, 4 Oct. 1804. Rec: 15 Feb. 1805.

Pages 132-133: 23 Feb. 1801, Ezekiel Buffington and Ellis Harlan to Daniel Treadaway for $171 for 150 acres on NE side of Little River of the Keowee River, granted Ezekiel Buffington and Ellis Harlan by Chas. Pinckney 1 Aug. 1790. Signed: Ezekiel Buffington and Ellis (X) Harlan. Wit: Thomas Lamar, Thomas (X) Ostin and Jesse Frost. Thomas Lamar made oath to Joseph Reed, J.P., 15 Jun. 1801. Rec: 7 Feb. 1805.

Page 133: Tobias Honey for $100 sold to John Green, 100 acres on Big Creek of the Saluda River, granted John Hamilton by James B. Richardson, Esq., bd. by Ellet, Mary Justist(?) and John Green. Date: 14 Nov. 1804. Signed: Tobias (X) Honey. Wit: Samuel Garner and Sampson (X) Nellson. Sampson Nellson made oath to Jas. Williams, J.P., 10 Jan. 1804. Rec: 12 Jan. 1805.

Pages 133-134: Zachariah Holcum for $320 sold to Isaac Gray 554 acres, part of 3 tracts: one conveyed by Benjamin Whorton to Holcum on N. branch of Cain Creek of Keowee River, one tract conveyed by Edward Hughy to Holcum of 15 acres, and one tract conveyed by James Jett of 489 acres. Date: 29 Oct. 1804. Signed: Zachariah (X) Holcum. Wit: B. Roe and John(X) Klien. Berry Roe made oath to James Starrett, J.P., 4 Jan. 1805. Rec: 15 Feb. 1805.

Pages 134: George Tucker for $800, with $200 due now, and $200 due the 1st of Jan. next, "the balance of $200 due 1st Jan. 1807", sold to Major John Taylor 2 negros, Tom and his wife, Suky. Date: 5 Feb. 1805. Wit: James Wood, John T. Ramsey. Capt. James Wood made oath to A. Boyse, J.P., 5 Feb. 1805. Rec: 15 Feb. 1805.

Pages 134-135: Robert Glenn for $500 sold to Abner Steele 390 acres on Middle fork of Keowee River, 200 acres originally granted John Harrison by Benj. Guerard, 190 acres granted Glenn by James B. Richardson. Date:

(Pages 134-135 cont'd): 25 Jan. 1805. Wit: John Taylor, Wm. Hunter. Mary (X) Glenn, wife of Robert Glenn, released dower to John Taylor, Q.U., 26 Feb. 1805. Dr. William Hunter made oath to M. Hammond, D.C., 25 May 1805.
Rec: 25 May 1805.

Pages 135-136: Ambrose Nichols for $164 sold to William Holbert 300 acres on Big Creek and Rock Crk. of the Saluda River. Date: 8 Oct. 1803.
Signed: Ambrose (X) Nichols. Wit: Enos Holbert, Wm. Arnold, Joseph Alkins. Enos Holbert made oath to James Wilbourn, J.P., 29 Jan. 1803.
Rec: 8 Feb. 1805.

Pages 136-137: John Wardlaw, son of Esquire(?) Wardlaw of Abbeville Dist., for $250 sold to Edward Vandiver of Pendleton Dist., 121 acres on Broadaway Creek of Rocky River, part of 311 acres granted John Wardlaw, 4 Jul. 1785 by Wm. Moultrie, recorded Bk. EEEE, p. 46, surveyed by David Green, D.S. Date: 3 Feb. 1801. Wit: James Caldwell, David Cochran, John Warnock. John Warnock made oath to E. Browne, J.Q., 1 Oct. 1801. Mary Ann (X) Wardlaw, wife of John Wardlaw, released dower to Andrew Hamilton, in Abbeville Dist., 3 Feb. 1801.
Rec: 23 Jan. 1805.

Page 137: John Green for $460 sold to Isaac Horton 400 acres on Big Creek, laid out for William Honey, Sr. by Chas. Pinckney 1 Oct. 1792.
Date: 8 Jan. 1805. Wit: John Millwee, Thos. W. Raulins. John Millwee made oath to Sam. Houston, J.P., 2 Jan. 1805.
Rec: 12 Jan. 1805.

Pages 137-138: Samuel Earle of Greenville Dist. for $700 sold to James Lawson of Franklin Co., Ga., a tract in Pendleton Dist. in fork of the Toogalow and Keowee Rivers, bd. corner at head of Main St. in the Town of Andersonville. Date: 15 Jul. 1803. Wit: Saml. Hawkins, Fanny (X) Hester. Harriot Earle, wife of Samuel Earle, released dower to Henry Machen Wood, J.Q. of Greenville Dist., 30 Jul. 1803. Samuel Earle acknowledged deed to Obadiah Trimmier, Q.U., 3 Sep. 1804.
Rec: 15 Jan. 1805. Plat certified was a tract of land sold from William Cox to James Lawson, resurvey bd. E. by James Al_en_, W. by Samuel Earle for 531 acres.
Rec: 15 Jan. 1805.

Page 139: James Wardlaw, J.Q. of Pendleton Dist., certify that Doratha Combs, wife of Bennet Combs, dec'd., relinquished dower to Nathaniel Merritt for 100 acres on 15 Mile Creek, bd. by John Gibson's old line. Date: 30 Mar. 1805. Signed: Do_litha_ (X) Combs.
Rec: 4 Jan. 1805.

Pages 139-140: 6 Sep. 1804, David McCaleb, Sheriff of Pendleton Dist. to Randson Thompson...whereas Jacob Brazelton on 2 Mar. 1804, in Court of Common Pleas entered judgement against Drury Thompson for $136.26, ..all goods, chattels and lands of Drury Thompson to be sold at public auction, highest bidder being Randson Thompson for $150, for 200 acres on Rocky River of Savannah River, part of tract granted William Thompson, bd. E. by James Gilliland, SE by John Stilts, S. by Robert Thompson, SW by John Hillhouse, W. by Adley Linn(?), N. by Thomas Drennan. Wit: M. Hammond & James Wood. Michael Hammond made oath to J. B. Earle, 12 Jan. 1805.
(No recording date).

Pages 140-141: 11 Feb. 1805, David McCaleb, Sheriff of Pendleton Dist. to Samuel C. Duff, Esq....... whereas Elias Earle on 2nd Mon. of October 1804, in Court of Common Pleas entered judgement against John McCrosky for $43, all goods, chattels and lands of McCrosky to be sold at public auction to highest bidder, being Samuel Carson Duff, Esq., for $130 for

(Pages 140-141 cont'd): 260 acres, part of 2 tracts, one originally granted William Gillispie, the other Enoch Williams, bd. on S. by John Bowen and Nathaniel Henderson, N. by John Boyd and William Gorman. Wit: A. Kilpatrick, John McCrosky. Alexander Kilpatrick made oath to M. Hammond, D. Clk, 11 Jun. 1805.
Rec: 11 Jun. 1805.

Pages 141-142: John Reeves for $400 sold to Benjamin Fuller for 101 acres on W. side of Rocky River, part of 640 acres granted Peter Bremar, Esq. by Wm. Moultrie, 6 Feb. 1736, recorded Bk. HH (sic), p. 292, bd. E. by Rocky River, S. by Estate of John Norris, dec'd., W. and N. by part of original survey conveyed by Bremar to David McCoy, then to John Reeves. Date: 19 Nov. 1804. Wit: John Mauldin, John Garner. Sarah (X) Reeves, wife of John Reeves, released dower to E. Browne, Q.U., 19 Nov. 1804. John Garner made oath to E. Browne, 19 Nov. 1804.
Rec: 25 Feb. 1805.

Pages 142-143: Thomas Garvin, Sr., planter, for $200 sold to Thomas Garvin, Jr., 100 acres on 15 Mile Creek of Savannah River, bd. SW and SE by Thomas Garvin, Sr., NE by Mr. Lizingby, part of a tract granted Thomas Shurley, 1785. Date: 21 Dec. 1804. Wit: Fredrick (X) Johnston, Martha(X) Garvin. Fredrick Johnston made oath to Saml. H. Dickson, J.P., 21 Dec. 1804. Rec: 4 Feb. 1805.

Page 143: John Perkins for $200 sold to David Herring 100 acres where Perkins now lives, purchased from William Sloan, granted by Charles Pinckney 2 Jan. 1792, except part sold to John Gregory, on E. side of Connoross of 10 acres, also part I purchased from William Perkins, where Josiah Foster now lives which was granted Capt. Charles Crowley, containing about 30 acres, on Gregory Spring. Date: 19 Mar. 1802. Signed: John (X) Perkins. Wit: John Young, Samuel Cannon. Both made oath to Josiah Foster, J.P. 27 Aug. 1804. (No recording date).

Page 144: 16 Sep. 1801, Ebenezer Fain of Buncumb Co., N. C. to Paterson Childers of Pendleton Dist., for $130 for 268 acres, part of 918 acres granted 12 Oct. 1787 by Thos. Pinckney, including Cornelus Ford(?) bd. James Fleming, Thomas, William Ford(?) and Henderson. Wit: John Childers, Alexander St. Clair. John Childers made oath to David Murphree, JP, 20 Jun. 1804.
Rec: 29 Dec. 1804.

Pages 144-145: Christopher Ramy for $130 sold to Samuel Burnett 100 acres, part of 640 acres granted Mary Preachard, bd. NW by Jean Deal, SW by John Woodall, E. by Mary Preachard, on 23 Mile Creek, conveyed by James Hobson to Ramy. Date: 1 Oct. 1804. Signed: Christopher (X) Ramy. Wit: R. D. Gray, Behethlem Posey. Richard Gray made oath to James C. Griffen, J.P., 12 Feb. 1805.
Rec: 12 Feb. 1805.

Page 145: James Barnett for $300 sold to Ambrose Barnett 226 acres conveyed by John Woodall, Thomas Hobson and Amos Nations to James Barnett, on 23 Mile Creek. Date: 3 Oct. 1804. Wit: R. D. Gray, Thos. Holland. Richard Gray made oath to James C. Griffen, 12 Feb. 1805.
Rec: 12 Feb. 1805.

Pages 145-146: Benjamin Land of Logan Dist., Ky. for divers good causes, appoint my friend, John Todd of Pendleton Dist., my attorney to sue and demand from persons indebted to me and in my name deliver 82 acres of land. Date: 21 Oct. 1804. Signed: Benjamin (X) Land. Wit: John Land, Elijah Land. John Land made oath to Samuel H. Dickson, J.P., 20 Jan. 1805. Rec: 29 Jan. 1805.

Pages 146-147: 4 Jan. 1805, John Smith, planter, to John Cannon Smith for ₤100 stg. for 254 acres, according to survey by Robt. McCann 10 Dec. 1792, granted by John Drayton, Governor, recorded Bk. WWW, (no page), on 23 Mile Creek of Savannah River, bd. E. by David Clark and Thomas Abit. Wit: Jabes Tims, Eleazer Smith. Jebes Tims made oath to John Willson, QU, 24 Jan. 1805. Rec: 25 Jan. 1805.

Page 147: Fredrick Moss for $725 sold to Thomas Harbin 225 acres on N. side of South Beaver Creek of Toogalow River, part of tract granted Samuel Watt by Chas. Pinckney 17 Jan. 1788, conveyed by Watt to John Gibson, from Gibson to Moss. Date: 19 Jan. 1805. Wit: Henry C. Barton, Caleb Barton. Caleb Barton made oath to Wm. Cleveland, J.P., 11 Mar. 1805. Rec: 14 Mar. 1805.

Pages 147-148: Samuel H. Dickson for $225 sold to Alexander White 282½ acres, surveyed 4 Feb. 1792, on Cain Creek of Keowee River of Savannah River. Date: 12 Nov. 1804. Wit: John R. Brown, Field Farrar. John R. Brown made oath to Hezekiah Davis, J.P., 13 Mar. 1805. Rec: 15 Mar. 1805.

Page 148: Orange Davis for $100 sold to Robert Todd 100 acres, part of 2 tracts granted William Lesley 1786 and 1791, bd. by Luck Hamilton, Wm. Lesley, Joseph Gouge, on Governor's Creek of Rocky River of Savannah River. Date: 18 Mar. 1805. Wit: Robert Harkness, Nathan McCallister. Nathan McCallister made oath to E. Browne, Q.U., 1 Apr. 1805. Rec: 11 Apr. 1805.

Pages 148-149: William Townsend for $1400 sold to John Stevenson 640 acres on Coxes Creek of Rocky Creek, part of 539 acres granted Mary Anderson 3 Oct. 1785, bd. by D. Gray, Pool, William Gogins and part bd. John Smith, of 494 acres. The other part on W. side being a tract of 110 ac. granted David Green 4 Jun. 1792, bd. by Gogin. Date: 8 Mar. 1804. Wit: William McElvany, Adam Todd. Margaret (X) Townsend, wife of William Townsend, released dower to E. Browne, QU, 13 Mar. 1804. William McElveny made oath to John George, J.P., 18 Jan. 1805. Rec: 13 Mar. 1805.

Pages 149-150: Garet Watts of Jackson Co., Ga. is bound to William Floyd of Pendleton Dist. for $300, and release to Floyd 110 acres, on E side of Keowee River, bd. Joseph White. Date: 6 Sep. 1801. Wit: George Tubb, William Tubb. George Tubb made oath to Thomas Hargiss, J.P., 19 Apr. 1804. Rec: 1 Jul. 1805.

Pages 150-151: Charles Rice is firmly bound to Arthur Grayham for $1400 on 10 Dec. 1804, and makes title to 362 acres on W. side of 18 Mile Creek where he lives, payment due by 25 Dec. 1808. Wit: Sam'l. Cherry and Moses Liddell. S. Cherry made oath 2 Apr. 1805....I assign within bond to Capt. Lewis Martin 1 Apr. 1805. Signed: Arthur Graham to J. B. Earle. Rec: 1 Apr. 1805.

Page 151: Richard Lancaster and Mary, his wife for $100 sold to Elisha Bennett 195 acres on Hencoop and Niel's Creek of Rocky River, a grant to Willm. Forbes, 5 Mar. 1787 by Thos. Pinckney, recorded Bk. BBBB, p. 434, conveyed from Forbes to John Buckhannon, from him to Lancaster, bd. by Adam Todd, Sam'l. McCoy, Sugar Mayfield, Dudley Pruit, dec'd. Date: 16 Feb. 1805. Signed: Richard Lancaster, Mary (X) Lancaster. Wit: Adam Todd and John Lard. Adam Todd made oath to John George, J.P., 1 Mar. 1805. Rec: 11 Mar. 1805.

Pages 151-152: John Patrick of Pendleton Dist. and County of Columbia of the State of S.C. for ₤50

(Pages 151-152 cont'd): stg. sold to Robert Lanier of Pendleton Dist., State of Ga. (sic) 50 ac., part of 450 acres granted Jacob Miligan on Big Beaverdam of the Toogaloo River, bd. by John Tapley. Date: 7 Sep. 1803. Wit: Jacob Holland, James Mitchell. Jacob Holland made oath to Wm. Cleveland, J.P., 9 Sep. 1803.
Rec: 13 Mar. 1805.

Page 152: I certy (sic) for Samuel Black that he has taken oath of office required by law to enable him to act as Justice of the Peace for Pendleton Dist., 1 Jan. 1805. E. Browne, Q.U.
Rec: 12 Jan. 1805.

Pages 152-153: James Stevenson, farmer, for $700 sold to Wiley Bishop 272 acres on Mountain Creek of Savannah River, one part granted Amos Roberts, 1784, by Benj. Garrett, Governor. Second part granted John Holcombe 20 Jan. 1788 by Chas. Pinckney. Last part formerly land of Richard York, bd. Jonathan Gibbs, William Anderson, John Ferguson, Thomas Skelton and Thomas Hays. Date: 25 Feb. 1804. Wit: Sam'l. Dean, Jas. Kennedy, Sandford Vandevere. Sanford Vandevere made oath to E. Browne, Q.U., 27 Feb. 1804. Elioner (X) Stevenson, wife of James Stevenson, released dower to E.Brown, 14 Mar. 1804.
Rec: 27 Feb. 1805.

Pages 153-154: William Townsend for $400 sold John Stevenson 342 acres on Coxes Creek of Rocky River bd. by Millwee, Samuel Lexon, granted Jesse Wood; also, 50 acres, part of 250 acres granted Elizabeth Riggs, bd. by Thomas Martin, William Townsend. Date: 21 Mar. 1804. Wit: John George & William Reed. Margaret (X) Townsend before me, then moving out of State, released dower to Jno. George, J.P., the reason it was not done before a Quorum was the want of time, as the land was sold the same day she started to leave the State, 21 Mar. 1804. William Reed made oath to Jno. George, 18 Jan. 1805.
Rec: 13 Mar. 1805.

Page 154: 5 Nov. 1804, Aquilla Greer and Hannah Greer convey to Jacob Holland for $16 for 4 ac. on Toogalo River, bd. by Jacob Holland and Eliab Moore. Date: 5 Nov. 1804. Signed: Aquilla Greer, Hannah (X) Greer. Wit: Wm. Bates, Wm. Jonston. Wm. Bates made oath to Wm. Cleveland, J.P., 3 Jun. 1805.
Rec: 3 Jun. 1805.

Page 155: John Calvert of the Town of Columbia, S.C. planter, for Ł 10-10 sh. sold to Andrew Boddan of the Town of Columbia, S.C., 200 acres in 96 Dist., Pendleton Co., on N. fork of Toxaway Creek, surveyed for James Madison, 2 Apr. 1793, granted John Calvert by Arnoldus Vanderhorst, 6 Jul. 1795. Date: 10 May 1796. Wit: James Douglass, Jas. Gillispie.....Richland Co., S. C., James Douglas made oath to Martyn Alken,JP, 31 May 1796.....This deed in the property of Capt. James Blair of Geo., which was sold to Thos. Crews and Capt. Blair is to pay for recording the same. A. Boddan ...
Rec: 3 Jun. 1805.

Page 155: James Wardlaw, one of the Justices of the Quorum, certify Dolitha (X) Combs, wife of Bennet Combs, dec'd., released dower to Joseph Chapman, to tract that Chapman now lives on that he bought from sd. Combs on 12 Mile River bd. by Wm. Brown. Date: 22 Feb. 1805.
Rec: 12 Mar. 1805.

Pages 155-156: James _____(blank) sold to Jacob Gillaspie a negro girl named Cann. Date: 11 Mar.1805. Signed: James Milwee. (see blank). Wit: James (X) Gillison.
Rec: 1 Apr. 1805.
(No oath).

Page 156: 14 Jan. 1805, James Brasher to Capt. James Turner for $119.89 for 210 acres granted 5 Jan. 1789 by Thos. Pinckney to John Simpson on Big Generostee Creek, from Simpson conveyed to Aaron James, then back to Brasher. Wit: Aaron James, Ishom Cox. John Cox made oath to Samuel Black, J. P., 8 Apr. 1805. Rec: 29 May 1805.

Pages 156-157: Charles Lay for $13 sold Abraham Beach 297 acres on Little Estatoa, surveyed by John Grisham 10 Mar. 1800, recorded 11 Feb. 1802 by William Lesley. Date: 9 Dec. 1802. Signed: Charles (X) Lay, Ann (X) Lay. Wit: Leroy Cullen, James Stevenson. James Stevenson made oath John Cochran, J.P., 9 Dec. 1802. Rec: 4 Mar. 1805.

Page 157: Joseph Brimer for $48.73 sold Van Davis 3 ewes, 1 yearling, lambs and a sorrel mare. Date: 9 Mar. 1805. Signed: Joseph (X) Brimer. Wit: Thomas Dean and James Stevenson. Joseph Brimer acknowledged the deed to Hez. Davis, J.P., 9 Mar. 1805. Rec: 10 Mar. 1805.

Pages 157-158: Anthony Griffen makes Deed of Trust to Arthur Dow for 69 acres on Conneross Creek, with grist mill, by bond of Security, the sd. Anthony (Griffen) to Gen. Andrew Pickings, which bond, if paid is null and void. Date: 28 Mar. 1804. Wit: Jno. Pounds. John Pounds made oath to M. Hammond, D. Clk., 13 Mar. 1805. Rec: 9 Mar. 1805.

Page 158: Ferdinand Hopkins for $118 sold Titus Atwater 237 acres, part of a larger tract... granted Hopkins 2 Jan. 1792, on Wolf Creek of 12 Mile River, bd. by Mr. Cannon and Charles Rice, being where Atwater now lives. Date: 22 ___ 1804. Wit: Jeremiah Ellis and Edward (X) Tatum. Edward Tatum made oath to James Wardlaw, 22 Jun. 1804. Rec: 1 Jun. 1805.

Pages 158-159: John Cannon for $85 sold to James McAdory 50 acres on Cane Creek of Keowee River,... part of a tract granted Humphrey Cobb by Chas. Pinckney, recorded Bk. F, no. 5, p. 178. Date: 5 Apr. 1805. Wit: Thos. Russell and Samuel Torbert. Thomas Russell made oath to Jno. Adair, J. P., 13 Apr. 1805. Rec: 24 Apr. 1805.

Page 159: John Clements for $1,000 sold William Harper 150 acres on S. side of the Saluda River, bd. by Henry Townley, Wm. Poor, James Riding(?) and Mr. Finley. Date: 15 Oct. 1803. Wit: John Halbert and Edwin Smith. John Halbert made oath to James Welborn, J.P., 4 Nov. 1804. Rec: 24 Apr. 1804. (1805?)

Pages 159-160: Samuel Gibson for $450 sold John McElroy 208 acres on Western branch of Rocky River, part of 2 tracts: one granted John Pickens 3 Jun. 1793 by Wm. Moultrie, recorded Bk. E, no. 5, p. 524, and one granted Robert Anderson, 1 Jan. 1787, recorded Bk. QQQQ, p. 513, bd. Thomas Drennan, Edley Linn, John Anderson, John McFall, Samuel and Joseph Drennan. Date: 25 Jul. 1804. Wit: Matthew Dickson and Samuel McElroy. Samuel McElroy made oath to John George, J.P., 18 Jan. 1804. Mary (X) Gibson, wife of Samuel Gibson, releaser dower to E. Browne, Q.U., 9 Oct. 1804. Rec: 6 Mar. 1805.

Pages 160-161: George Edmondson and Lettia (later Lettitia) Edmondson for $450 sold to Steele & Woods, Merchants, a mullato negro girl named Jane about 13 or 14 years of age. Date: 12 Feb. 1805. Wit: John Ramsey, Moses Liddell. John Ramsey made oath to M. Hammond, D. Clk.,*30 Mar. 1805.Rec.*

Page 161:   Jane (X) Selmon, wife of William Selmon, re-
            leased dower to John Garner for a tract on
            Brandy Creek, that Benjamin Selmon, dec'd.,
willed to William Selmon, dec'd., that Jane Selmon now lives on, she does
give up to Garner. Date: 22 Mar. 1805, James Wardlaw, J.Q.
Rec: 19 Apr. 1805.

Pages 161-162:   1 Apr. 1805, David McCaleb, Sheriff of Pen-
                 dleton Dist., to Joshua Barton........James
                 Jett was seized of a tract of land and John
Bourland on 2nd Monday, Mar. 1804 in the Court of Common Pleas obtained
judgement against James Jett and John Boyd for $150 plus $38 costs,tract
of 214 acres sold at public auction to Joshua Barton for $15 by his.....
friend, William Gray, being the highest bidder, land was part of 314 ac.
granted Jonathan Gregory by Arnoldus Vanderhorst, 4 Apr. 1792, bd. William Curley on branches of Town and Wolf Creeks of 12 Mile River. Wit: A.
Kilpatrick, Wm. Hamilton. Alexander Kilpatrick made oath to M. Hammond,
26 Jul. 1805.
Rec: 26 Jul. 1805.

Pages 162-163:   25 Dec. 1797, Elisha Bennet to Moses Holl-
                 and for $40 for 50 acres on branches of
                 Broadaway Creek of Rocky River, part of a
tract granted Thomas Burford, 4 Dec. 1786, by Wm. Moultrie. Wit: John
Allen, Alex. McLean, Edward Vandiver. Alexander McClean made oath to E.
Browne, J. P., 5 Apr. 1798.
Rec: 19 Apr. 1805.

Pages 163-164:   Samuel Rowen for $195 sold Samuel Earle 64½
                 acres on Beaverdam Creek, bd. by Earle and
                 granted Gen'l. William Henderson as his
Bounty, near a road leading to Alexander Barron. Date: 18 Feb. 1805. Wit:
Archd. Lawhon, Giddeon (X) Hester, Polly (X) Hester. Archibald Lawhon made
oath to H. McCroy, J.P., 23 Mar. 1805. Elizabeth (X) Rowen, wife of Sam-
uel Rowen, released dower to John Verner, J.Q., 23 Feb. 1805.
Rec: 1 Apr. 1805.

Pages 164-165:   Francis Moore for $200 sold John Moore, Sr.
                 100(?) ac. on fork of Bever(sic) Creek and
                 Rocky River, and on both sides of the old
trading path, part of 250 acres granted John Moore, 15 Mar. 1787, and at
his decease to fall to John Camble's son, John Moore Camble "unto John
Moore, Sr. and grandson, John Moor Camble". Date: 4 Dec. 1804. Wit: Josiah Alexander and John Campbell. Josiah Alexander made oath to E. Browne,
Q.U., 8 Mar. 1805.
Rec: 11 Mar. 1805.

Page 165:   13 Feb. 1796, William Young and Hugh Moore
            to Harry Terrell, all of Pendleton Dist.,
            for Ł 50 currency of Virginia, paid by Col.
Peter Perkins of Pittsylvania Co., Va., sold to Harry Terrell 250 acres
on both sides of Little Eastatoe of Keowee River, bd. on NW and NE by
John Young, Jr., granted William Young and Hugh Moore by Chas. Pinckney,
8 Apr. 1789. Signed: William Young and Hugh (X) Moore. William Young and
Hugh Moore acknowledge deed 13 Feb. 1796 to Wm. Reed, J.P. Wit: John D.
Terrell.
Rec: 19 Apr. 1805.

Pages 165-166:   Henry Townly for $380 sold Samuel Pepper
                 150 acres on SW side of the Saluda River,
                 bd. by William Poor and William Harper.
Date: 26 Jan. 1804. Wit: William Harper and Peter (X) Nees(?). William
Harper made oath to Aron Broyles, J.P. 9 Mar. 1805. _____ (cannot read)
Townley, wife of Hery Townley (Henry Townley) released dower....(no date
or signature).
Rec: 12 Mar. 1805.

Pages 166-167:   Thomas Boyd for $800 sold George Boyd 600
                 acres on Saluda and George's Creek, bd. by
                 Thomas M. Barrot and Thomas Boyd, Gillispie,

(Pages 166-167 cont'd):   part of 3 tracts.....(rest is too dim, but
                            appears to read...."Susan Boyd released
                            dower".)

Page 167:   (Dim..cannot read).........Date: 15 March
                            1805. Signed by William Montgomery. Thomas
                            Davis signed oath to Wm. Edmondson. Rec:
25 Jul. 1805.

Page 168:   William Smith and Rachel Smith of Pendleton
                            Dist. for $300 sold William Linn of Buncomb
                            (sic) Co., N.C., 126 acres on Big Generostee
of the Savannah River, bd. by William Herin, Elisha Herin and John Tuggle.
Date: 12 Dec. 1803. Signed: William Smith, Rachel (X) Smith. Wit: John
Linn, Edle Linn. John Linn made oath to H. Davis, J.P., 24 Dec. 1804.
Rec: 11 Mar. 1805.

Pages 168-169:   James Brouster for $300 sold Sturdy Garner
                            150 acres on Big Creek, part of 400 acres
                            granted Alex McDowel by Wm. Moultrie, 1785,
recorded Bk. 4 DDDD, p. 504. Date: 16 Jul. 1801. Wit: Samuel Pepper and
Samuel Brouster. Samuel Pepper made oath to Wm. Hall, J.P., 25 Dec. 1801.
Rec: 7 Jun. 1805.

Page 169:   Michael Byrd of Fairfield Co., S. C. for
                            $20 sold Moses Perkins of Pendleton Dist.,
                            171 acres, conveyed from John Burks 30 May
1793, in Washington Dist. on Connoross Creek, granted by Chas. Pinckney,
6 Aug. 1798. Date: 19 Jul. 1799. Signed: Michael (X) Byrd. Wit: Andrew
Boddan and Mark Mason. Andrew Boddan made oath to R. Witherspoon, J.Q.,
2 Nov. 1799.
Rec: __ Apr. 1805.

Pages 169-170:   Moses Perkins for $1,000 sold William Wat-
                            son 550 acres where Perkins now lives,part
                            granted George Brough, the other to Capt.
Urial Gudyn, another to Michael Byrd and another to Moses Perkins, on
Connoross Creek of Keowee River. Date: 24 Mar. 1805. Signed: Moses (X)
Perkins. Wit: John Watson, Jacob Watson. John Watson made oath to Thomas
Hargiss, J.P., 2 Mar. 1805.
Rec: 1 Apr. 1805.

Page 170:   John Abbett for $300 sold Josiah Foster 100
                            acres on E. side of Connoross of the Keowee
                            River, part of a tract granted James Brough
by Benj. Guerard, recorded Bk. BBBB, p. 22, bd. by Wadkins. Date: 19 Jan.
1805. Signed: John (X) Abbett. Wit: James Fuller and Isaac (X) Williams.
James Fuller made oath to James Barton, J.P., 12 Mar. 1805.
Rec: 1 Apr. 1805.

Pages 170-171:   Thomas Bailey for $100 sold Joseph Burk 41
                            acres on both sides of 12 Mile River. Date:
                            19 Dec. 1804. Signed: Thomas (X) Bailey.
Wit: Arch. W. Reynolds and Jordan (X) Bailey. Jordan Bailey made oath to
Phil. Meroney, J.P., 5 Jan. 1805.
Rec: 11 Mar. 1805.

Page 171:   Phillip Phagans is bound to Isaac Mitchell
                            for Ł 500 stg. Date: 4 Jul. 1790...he makes
                            title to Isaac Mitchell for 200 acres, bd.
by Steven Leverett, Willson creek and William Bladen, to be paid by 4 Jul.
1799, then obligation is null and void. Wit: George Tillman, Phillip Phagan, Jr. Phillip Phagan made oath his father signed the above deed, 14
Mar. 1805 to John McMillen, J.P.
Rec: 15 Mar. 1805.

Page 172:   James Barren for $150 sold John Grisham 50
                            acres on E. side of Keowee River, bd. John
                            Grisham, part of tract granted Samuel Lof-
ton, 1789. Date: 19 Jun. 1804. Wit: William McFarland, Timothy Stamps...

363

(Page 172 cont'd:) William McFarland made oath to Thomas Hargiss, J. P., 13 Nov. 1804. Rec: 11 Mar. 1805.

Pages 172-173: 21 Nov. 1801, Enoch Williams to John McCrosky for $450 for 100 acres on George's Crk., of the Saluda River. Signed: Enoch (X) Williams, Mary (X) Williams. Wit: William Groman, William Henderson and Wm. Jameson. Wm. Henderson made oath to Samuel C. Duff, J.P., 6 Mar. 1805. Rec: 12 Mar. 1805.

Page 173: Charles Williams for $50 sold William Norris 200 acres surveyed for George Askin, 20 Sep. 1784 on Little River of Keowee River. Date: 16 Oct. 1804. Signed: Charles (X) Williams. Wit: Jonathan Perry and Jeptha Norton. Jeptha Norton made oath to W. Nicholson, J.P., 5 Mar. 1805. Rec: 11 Mar. 1805.

Pages 173-174: Thomas Martin for $60 sold Daniel Williams 60 acres on Deep Creek of Seneca River, bd. Thomas Martin, John McCollum, Elijah Nicholson, part of tract granted Samuel McCollum, Jr., dec'd, on which John Martin now lives. Date: 19 Oct. 1804. Wit: Edw. T. McClure, John Martin. Edward T. McClure made oath to J. Stribling, Q.U., 22 Feb. 1804. Rec: 13 Mar. 1805.

Page 174: John Warnock for $230 sold John McWhorter 140 acres bd. by John Wornock, Edward Vandiver, Thomas Wade and James Erskin. Date: 14 Feb. 1804. Wit: John McWhorter, William Duff and Isaac McWhorter. Eleanor (X) Warnock released dower to E. Browne, Q.U., 7 Feb. 1804. John McWhorter made oath to E. Browne, 5 May 1804. Rec: 11 Mar. 1805.

Pages 174-175: 11 Mar. 1805, John Flanikan and Elizabeth, his wife, to Joseph Jolly for $600 for 145 acres on Town Creek of 26 Mile River, part of a tract granted Joseph Price. Wit: John Morehead, Jonathan Smith. John Morehead made oath to John Taylor, Q.U., 15 Mar. 1805. Elizabeth (X) Flenkin released dower to John Taylor, 16 Mar. 1805. Rec: 16 Mar. 1805.

Pages 175-176: William Pinkston for $50 sold Robert Orr 50 acres on Bear Creek, part of 269½ acres.. granted E. Browne. Date: 10 Aug. 1804. Wit: Robert McWhorter and John Morton. Robert McWhorter made oath to E. Browne, Q.U., 10 Aug. 1804. Levina (X) Pinkston released dower to E. Browne, 22 Aug. 1804. Rec: 11 Mar. 1804. (1805?)

Pages 176-177: Robert Anderson, Esq. for $38 sold George Weams 23 and 3/4 acres, part of 360 acres granted Robert Anderson, Robert Maxwell and James Floyd in Company on Big Generostee of Savannah River, surveyed by John McMahan, D.S. Date: 9 Aug. 1804. Wit: J. Miller and John Harris..... I do also relinquish and quit claim 33½ acres granted James Simpson to include above mentioned grant. John Harris, Esq. made oath to John Wilson, Q.U., 16 Aug. 1804. Rec: 11 Mar. 1805.

Page 177: Charles Clements, planter, for $34 sold to Nathan Nall 150 acres on Pee Creek of the Savannah River, it being part of grant to John Hallum 1 Feb. 1790 by Chas. Pinckney. Date: 14 Jan. 1805. Wit: Bennett ____ (?), Reuben Clements. Reuben Clements made oath to James C. Griffen, J. P., 11 Mar. 1805. Rec: 11 Mar. 1805.

Pages 177-178: Daniel Owen for $120 sold Joel Brazeal 120 acres on Rock Creek of Savannah River, bd. Ambrose Nichols(?), part of 402 ac. granted

(Pages 177-178 cont'd): Reuben Clements 1 Jan. 1793, surveyed by Robert McCann. Date: 2 Jan. 1803. Signed: Daniel (X) Owen. Wit: Hardy Clement, Kenon Brazeal, William Braze<u>l</u>..... Canon (sic) Brazeal made oath to John George, J.P., 12 Mar. 1805. Rec: 12 Mar. 1805.

Page 178: Thomas Garner for $30 sold William Harper 17 acres on Saludy River on Tory's Creek, bd. by Wilson's old line. Date: 9 Nov.1802. Wit: John Holbert and Henry Townley. John Holbert made oath to James Welbourn, J.P., 15 Nov. 1800. Rec: 11 Mar. 1805.

Pages 178-179: George Clark for $20 sold John Bryson 100 acres on Wilson's Creek of Savannah River, bd. by John Bryson, William Kee, Thomas Jones and Phebe Hardin, being S. end of 475 acres granted Samuel Green, conveyed to Daniel Bryson, recorded Bk. T, no. 5, p. 389. Date: 22 Nov. 1804. Wit: Daniel Bryson, William Bryson, Daniel Bryson, Jr. Maj. Daniel Bryson made oath to E. Browne, Q.U., 5 Jan. 1805. Rec: 11 Mar. 1805.

Page 179: Bennet Combs for $110 sold Nathaniel Merret 100 acres on W. side of 15 Mile branch of Savannah River, granted by Chas. Pinckney, 5 Mar. 1792, bd. by John Gibson. Date: 18 Dec. 1799. Signed: Banna<u>t</u> Come<u>bess</u> (Combs). Wit: Jeremiah (X) Chapman and John Eubanks. Jeremiah Chapman made oath to Basil Hallum, J.P., 1 Mar. 1800. Rec: 4 Mar. 1804.

Page 180: Willoughby Pugh for $700 sold John Verner 250 acres on Chestoe Creek of Tugalo River bd. by Willoughby Pugh, David Pugh and by land I sold to free negro Bob, also bd. by Vanderhorst, part of a tract granted Stephen Drayton, Esq., 15 Oct. 1784 by Benj. Guerard. Date: 25 Jan. 1804. Wit: Enoch Berry and David (X) Pugh. Enoch Berry made oath to Jno. Barton, J.P., 20 Jul. 1804. Rec: 6 May 1805.

Page 181: Alexander Brown of Mungumry co., Tenese(sic) for $500 sold Hamilton Brown of Chester Dist., S. C., 250 acres on Governor's Crk. of Rocky River, bd. on S. by Jas. Thomsen, W. by Wm. Lesley, S. by Luke Hamilton, E. by Harris Mauldin, dec'd., and Holloway. Date: 19 Jul. 1804. Wit: Edward Davis, James Thomson and Peggy Thomson. James Thomson made oath to E. Browne, Q.U., 4 <u>Jul. 1805</u>. Rec: 7 <u>May 1805</u>.

Pages 181-182: William Thompson for $500 sold Richard Thompson 200 acres on 12 Mile River, bd. by Richard Thompson, James Gibson, Bennet Combs. Date: 31 Oct. 1803. Signed: William (X) Thompson. Wit: Nat. Newman and Alex. Burns. Nathaniel Newman made oath to Davi<u>s</u> Murphree, J.P., 12 May 1804. Rec: 5 Aug. 1805.

Page 182: 23 Jan. 1801, William Eddins to Phillip D. Merony for $200 sold 150 acres on S. side of Hickory Nut Mountain and branch of Wolf Creek, 12 Mile River, part of 200 acres granted Samuel Earle, bd. Earle and part of 779 acres granted James Gillispie, 1791, by Chas. Pinckney and by deed conveyed to John Langley and by Langley to Eddins. Wit:David Cantrell and Richd. (X) Willbanks. <u>Joseph</u> Cantrell made oath to Phillip Merony, J.P., 6 Aug. 1804. Rec: 11 Mar. 1805.

Page 183: Josiah Houston of Pendleton Dist. and Thomas Houston of Buncum Co., N.C. for $450 sold James Taylor of Pendleton Dist., 214 acres on Rocky River of Savannah, bd. by John Henry, John Houston, John

(Page 183 cont'd): Still, William Drennen and John McWhorter.
Date: 3 Mar. 1804. Signed: Josiah Houston
and Thomas Houston. Wit: Adam Todd and Wm. Drinnan. William Drinnan made
oath to Samuel Taylor, J.P., 27 Mar. 1804. Ann Houston and Margaret (X)
Houston, wives of Josiah Houston and Thomas Houston, released dower to
E. Browne, Q.U., 13 Mar. 1804.
Rec: 11 Mar. 1805.

Pages 183-184: Hugh Porter, Executor, to Robert Porter for
$232 sold David Parker of Abbeville Co.,133
acres on Willson's Creek of Rocky River, bd
by Robert Parker's heirs, John Parker, James Parker and the Widow Adair.
Date: 4 Mar. 1805. Wit: Gab'l. Long, A. C. Hamilton and Joseph Spence.
Abbeville Co.....Gab'l. Long made oath to A. Hamilton, J.Q. 5 Mar. 1805.
Rec: 11 Mar. 1805.

Page 184: John Stephens for $100 sold Capt. William
Brown 50 acres "on Twelvewaters" bd. Brown
and Stephens. Date: 16 Mar. 1805. Wit:Moses
Hunt and Thomas (X) Stephens. Moses Hunt made oath to James Wardlaw, J.Q.
13 Mar. 1805.
Rec: 14 Mar. 1805.

Page 184: James Willbourn, J.Q., certifies Gean (X)
Clements, wife of John Clements, released
dower to William Harper for 150 acres sold
by her husband on S. side of Saluda near the mouth of Rones Creek. Date:
7 Nov. 1804.
Rec: 11 Mar. 1805.

Pages 184-185: Robert Rankin and Margaret Tuggle, Exors.
of Jesse Wood, dec'd., for $250 sold John
Tuggle 100 acres in Washington Dist. on the
Big Generostee, of Savannah River, bd. by John Tuggle. Date: 12 Jan. 180_.
Signed: Robert Rankin and Margaret (X) Tuggle. Wit: Peter Keys and Arthur
Durley. Peter Keys, J.P., certified deed, 14 Oct. 1801.
Rec: 11 Mar. 1805.

Page 185: 27 Jan. 1801, William Eddins to Phillip D.
Merony for $500 for 200 acres on SW side
of Hickory River, branch of Doddies Creek,
surveyed by William Barton(?) for Samuel Earle, who sold to Jane Cuningham by Cuningham to Eddins. Wit: William Jamison and Elizabeth Akins.
William Jamison made oath to Phil. Merony, J.P., 2 Oct. 1804.
Rec: 11 Mar. 1805.

Pages 185-186: John Greenwood for $300 sold Jacob Mauldin
(later Joab) 100 acres on George's Creek of
the Saluda River, bd. by Jas. Fleming,part
of 200 acres granted Gabriel Moffet 1 Aug. 1794. Date: 8 Dec. 1804. Wit:
James (X) Moore and Stephen (X) Huff. Stephen Huff made oath to William
Edmondson, Q.U., 19 Feb. 1805.
Rec: 12 Mar. 1805.

Pages 186-187: Charles Clements for $50 sold Edward Thomp-
son 250 acres between Little Rock Creek and
head of Broadaway of Rocky River, bd. Bal-
lard Day, Elijah Mathers(?), Kennon Brazeal, John Hugar(?), Keowee Road.
Date: 13 Jun. 1804. Wit: Ballard Day, James Hanney(?). Ballard Daye made
oath to John George, J.P., 12 Mar. 1805.
Rec: 12 Mar. 1805.

Page 187: Nathl. Reed, Sr., for love and affection he
bears son, Nathan'l. Reed, Jr., give him a
negro boy about 3 years old now in my cus-
tody, known as George. Date: 9 Mar. 1805. Wit: Jephs Moss, William (X)
Hood. Jeff Moss made oath to Colin Campbell, J.P., 9 Mar. 1805.
Rec: 11 Mar. 1805.

Page 188: Samuel Braden, carpenter, for $200 sold to

(Page 188 cont'd): William McCarley, planter, 350 acres, part of 712 acres granted John Scott, conveyed from Scott to Robert Forgeson 3 Feb. 1804, bd. by William Manson, Gilbert Mills and Benjamin Green. Date: __ Oct. 1804. Signed: Samuel Breden. Wit: George Weems, Thomas Weems. George Weems made oath to John Wilson, Q.U., 12 Oct. 1804.
Rec: 13 Mar. 1805.

Pages 188-189: William Wakefield for $250 sold William M. Cockerham 100 acres where William Wakefield now lives, on Choestoee Creek of Toogaloo River, part of tract granted William McCaleb by Thos. Pinckney 2 Jul.17__ and bd. by Mr. Jacob Loudermilk, Mr. Baker, Delaney's branch. Date: 29 Feb. 1804. Wit: John Carn and Mary (X) Fuller. John Cain made oath to David Humphreys, J.P. (No date).
Rec: 11 Mar. 1804.

Page 189: Robert Fergeson for $200 sold Samuel Braden 350 acres being SW and ___ on 714(?) acres granted Ferguson 3 Feb. ___, bd. by William Mason(?), Gilbert Mills and Benjamin Green(?). Date: 22 Aug. 1804. Wit: ___ Reed, Ezekiel Magill. John Reed made oath to James Tate, Q.U., 8 Oct. 1804. Rec: 13 Mar. 1805. (Dim; difficult to read).

Pages 189-190: William Linn of Buncombe Co., N. C. for $300 sold John Tuggle 126¼ acres on Big Generostee of the Savannah River, bd. by William Herrin and John Tuggle. Date: 24 Nov. 1804. Wit: John Linn, Edley Linn. John Linn made oath to Hh. Davis, J.P., 24 Dec. 1804.
Rec: 11 Mar. 1805.

Page 190: Timothy Stamps for $370 sold James Barron 100 acres on E. side of Keowee River, bd. by John Grisham(?), part of a tract granted Samuel Lofton, 1789. Date: 19 Jun. 1804. Wit: William McFarland and John Grisham. John Grisham made oath to Thomas Hargiss, J.P., 13 Dec. 1804. (No recording date).

Pages 190-191: Ebenezer Fain of French Broad Settlement, for $250 sold John Greenwood of Pendleton Dist., 100 acres on George's Creek, bd. by James Fleming. Date: 31 Oct. 1804. Wit: Hezekiah (X) Johnston and J. Mauldin. Joab Mauldin made oath to Wm. Edmondson, J.P., 16 Feb. 1806.
Rec: 12 Mar. 1805.

Page 191: William Honie for $150 sold Thomas Honie 100 acres on N. fork of Big Creek of the Saluda River, part of a tract granted James Hamilton by Wm. Moultrie, conveyed to William Honie. Date: 4 Dec. 1804. Signed: William (X) Honie. Wit: John Willson, Jr. and Hugh Wilson. John Wilson made oath to James Wilborn, J.P., 14 Nov. 1803.
Rec: 12 Mar. 1805.

Pages 191-192: William Silmon, now of Pendleton Dist., is bound to John Garner of Pendleton District, for $1,200 and makes title to a tract where Silmon now lives, on Brandy Creek of 12 Mile River and is his part agreeable to will of late Benjamin Silmon, dec'd. Date: 21 Jan. 1805. Signed: William (X) Silmon. Wit: George Combs and J. Meridith. James Meriday made oath to James Wardlaw, J.Q., 6 Mar. 1805.
Rec: 12 Mar. 1805.

Page 192: William Drennan for $300 sold Robert Richardson 218½ acres, bd. NE and N by Charles Wilson, E. by Martha Anderson, SE by Wm. Lesley, SW by John Taylor, W. by Rich'd. and James Gilliland(?). Date: 9 Mar. 1804. Signed: Wm. Drennan and Mary (X) Drennan. Wit: David Drennan and James Drennan. James Drennan made oath to Jno. George, J.P., 12 Mar. 1805.
Rec: 12 Mar. 1805.

Page 192: We, subscribing freeholders called upon to Examine and ascertain the property of Daniel Bryson ____ (cannot read this).... free a certain negro woman Sall(?) of yellow complection, do give our opinion that (she) is a proper subject for freedom being capable to support herself by actual labour, this opinion being formed by evidence of the appearance of the negro and from our own intuitive knowledge. Date: 30 Aug. 1805. Signed: Ch. Stark, John Milford, Robert Baird, Thomas Milford, Andrew McAlester, E. Browne, Q.U.
Rec: 19 Sep. 1805.

Pages 192-193: 17 Jan. 1805, Benjamin Silmon to Jeremiah Chapman for $1,000 for 150 acres on Brandy Creek, bd. by Drury Hutchins(?), Wimberly, James Barin, ____ (cannot read), mentions Benjamin Silmon and wife, Lydia. Signed: Benjamin Silmon, David Silmon and Lydia (X) Silmon. (Cannot read names of witnesses.) Lydia (X) Silmon released dower to James Wardlaw, QU on 17 Jan. 1803. Moses Hunt made oath he and William Brown witnessed the above deed to James Wardlaw, __ Jan. 1805.
Rec: 12 Mar. 1805.

Pages 193-194: 6 Apr. 1795, Reuben Clements for Ł 30 stg. sold Joel Brazeal 331 acres on Rocky Creek of Rocky River, granted Reuben Clements on 7 Jan. 1792, recorded Bk. F, no. 5, p. 430. Wit: Jas. Clements, Davis Collier and William Murphree. Reuben Clements acknowledge deed to John Willson, Q.U., 12 Mar. 1805.
Red: 12 Mar. 1805.

Pages 194-195: 27 Feb. 1805, John Swords and Eleanor, his wife, to Matthew Armstrong for $100 for 50 acres, bd. by Swords, Matthew Armstrong and Joseph Kemp, part of tract granted by Wm. Moultrie to William Shelby(X) on 23 Mile River. Wit: Thomas Garner, Nathaniel (X) Trother(?), John (X) Cress(?). Thomas Garner made oath to John Willson, Q.U., 2 Mar. 1805. Eleanor (X) Swords released dower to John Willson, 21 Mar. 1805.
Rec: 6 Apr. 1805.

Pages 195-196: Samuel Rowen for $80 sold Samuel Earle 85 (?) acres, part of 150 acres granted ____, bd. by Gen'l. William Anderson and William Liddell ____. Date: 18 Feb. 1805. Wit: Archd. Lawhon, Gideon (X) Hester, Polly (X) Hester. Archibald Laughlin made oath to H. McCray, J.P., 23 Mar. 1805. Elizabeth (X) Rowin, wife of Samuel Rowin, released dower to John Verner, J.Q., 23 Feb. 1805.
Rec: 1 Apr. 1805.

Pages 196-197: 9 Apr. 1805, George Tubb to Nathan Boon for $700 for 284 acres on S. side of the Keowee River, bd. on NW by Major Warley, the other sides by William Tabour, granted Robert Anderson 7 Jun. 1790 by Charles Pinckney, conveyed to George Tubb. Wit: Sam'l. Harbin, Nathaniel Harbin, Jesse Harbin. Nathaniel Harbin made oath to Henry Burch, J.P., 12 April 1805. Betta Tubb, wife of George Tubb, released dower to Henry Burch, QU on 15 Apr. 1805. Signed: Elizabeth Tubb.
Rec: 19 Apr. 1805.

Page 197: Samuel Orr of Carlagan in County of Monaghan, farmer; Robert Orr of Bellaheugh in the County of Armagh, weaver; Alexander Whiteraft(?) of Glasnknow(?) in County of Monagham, farmer, and Ann Whiteraft, otherwise Orr, his wife, all of the Kingdom of Ireland, appoint Thomas Orr of Bellaheagh in the County of Armagh, now age 21, our lawful attorney to demand and receive from the Administrators of Wm. Orr, formerly of Glenehiem(?) in the County of Monaghan and lately of South Carolina, in America, where he died, and which property, we the brothers and sisters are entitled. Given at Mariaghen in County of Monagahan in that part of the United Kingdom called Ireland. Date: 17 Apr. 1804. (Agness Orr signed with the above heirs.) Wit: David Hamilton, City of Charleston; Simon Maywood of Charleston, Merchant, who swore he was acquainted with the signa-

(Page 197 cont'd): ture of David Hamilton, 24 May 1804, to Jno. Mitchell, Q. U. Rec: 15 Jun. 1805.

Page 198: Thomas Honie for $200 sold William Elliott 100 acres on N. fork of Big Creek of the Saluda River, part of a tract granted James Hamilton by Wm. Moultrie 13 Mar. 1792. Date: 25 Feb. 1805. Signed: Thomas Honey. Wit: William Slaton, Aaron Wellborn. Elizabeth Honey, wife of Thomas Honey, released dower to James Wellborn, Q.U., 21 Feb. 1805. William Slaton made oath to James Wellborn, 21 Feb. 1805.
Rec: 6 Apr. 1805.

Pages 198-199: 3 Mar. 1804, Edward Wade of Elbert Co., Ga. to Moses Holland of Pendleton Dist. for Ł 20 for 79 acres on Neel's Creek, part of tract granted Samuel Dalrymple, 1787 by Chas. Pinckney. Wit: James Ridgeway, Abner Sutton, Thomas Burford. Thomas Burford made oath to Jno. George, J.P., 6 Mar. 1804. Mrs. Ann Wade released dower to R. B. Christian, J.P., 3 Mar. 1804.
Rec: 19 Apr. 1805.

Page 199: George Nelson for $50 sold William Owens 184 acres on Beaverdam Creek of Savannah bd. by William Owens and George Nelson on E. and SE. Date: 9 Apr. 1805. Wit: Barnebus (X) Fox (Far?), Owen Evans. Barnebus Far(?) made oath to Samuel Houston, J.P., 11 Apr. 1805.
Rec: 11 Apr. 1805.

Pages 199-200: John Jones for $20 sold John White 67 acres part of tract granted Eli Hunnicutt and Michael Dickson on Jones Creek, branch of Mile Creek of the Savannah River, bd. by Lewis Jones, John Jones. Date: 14 Jan. 1803. Wit: Jon Smith, Eli Hunnicutt. John Smith made oath Samuel H. Dickson, J.P., 12 Mar. 1805.
Rec: ___ Apr. 1805.

Pages 200-201: 4 Jan. 1805, David McCaleb, Sheriff of Pendleton Dist. to James McGuffin....Wm. Steel before Court of Common Pleas got judgement against Eli Hunnicutt for $29.66, all goods, chattels and lands included. On 2 Apr. 1804, land of 70 acres sold at public auction for $45 to James McGuffin by his friend, William McGuffin, being the highest bidder, on 26 Mile Creek, granted Eli Hunnicutt, bd. by John White, John E. Calhoun. Wit: A. Kilpatrick, Thomas W. Farrar. Thomas W. Farrar made oath to M. Hammond, D. Clk., 9 Oct. 1805.
Rec: 9 Oct. 1805.

Pages 201-202: 5 Mar. 1793, Thomas Farrar, Sheriff of Washington Dist. to Patrick Duncan of the City of Charleston....on suit of Adm. of David Baty(?), late resident of St. Thomas Parish of S. C., against Ephraim Mitchell. Thomas Farrar sold at public auction to the highest bidder for ready money at Pickensville for Ł 35 stg. to Patrick Duncan, 140 acres on both sides of George's Creek of the Saluda River, formerly in Old 96 District, now Washington, by survey to Ephraim Mitchell 10 Jul. 1784.(Plat). Wit: Jno. Hunter, B. Starrett. Benjamin Starret made oath to M. Hammond, D. Clk, 20 Aug. 1805.
Rec: 20 Aug. 1805.

Pages 202-203: John McCutchen for $650 sold Simon Doyle 500 acres, where McCutchen now lives on E. side of 23 Mile Creek of the Savannah, being 2 different tracts adjacent to each other, one granted Charles Saxon, the other to Wm. Turpin by Wm. Moultrie, bd. by Turpin. Date: 24 Nov.1803. (No witnesses or oath).

Page 203: 17 Jan. 1804, Benjamin Selmon and Lydia, his wife, to John Gibson for $900 for 150 acres on Brandy Creek on both sides, bd.by Thomas Stevens and Reuben Torrence, line made by will of Benjamin Selmon,

(Page 203 cont'd): Sr., now deceased. Signed: Benjamin Selmon, David Selmon and Lydia (X) Selmon. Wit: William Brown, Moses Hunt. Lydia Selmon released dower to James Wardlaw, J.Q., 17 Jan. 1805. William Brown made oath to James Wardlaw, 17 January 1805. Rec: 12 Mar. 1805.

Page 204: Thomas Black for $650 sold David Watkins 1/2 of 640 acres on N. side of 23 Mile Crk. bd. by Watkins, James Lyn, granted William Murphey 16 Jul. 1784. Date: 4 Dec. 1804. Wit: Andrew Warnock and Joseph Watkins. Eleanor Black, wife of Thomas Black, released dower to John Wilson, Q.U., 1 Apr. 1805. Joseph Watkins made oath to A. Boyse, J.P., 7 May 1805. Rec: 12 May 1805.

Pages 204-205: Robert Baker, gunsmith, for $700 sold John Prater, planter, 320 acres on 18 Mile Crk. of the Savannah River, part of tract surveyed by Thomas Garvin and granted William Mitchell. Date: 2 Apr. 1805. Wit: Wm. Baker, Wm. Prater, John (X) Baker, Sr. William Baker made oath to John Willson, Q.U., 2 Apr. 1805. Sarah (X) Baker, wife of Robert Baker, released dower to John Willson, Q.U., 2 Apr. 1805. Rec: 19 Apr. 1805.

Page 205: 30 Nov. 1801, Enock Williams to John McCrosky for $450 for 167 acres on George's Creek of the Saluda River. Signed: Enock Williams, Mary (X) Williams. Wit: Wm. Gorman, W. Henderson, Wm. Jameson. Wm. Henderson made oath to Samuel C. Duff, J.P., 6 Mar. 1805. Rec: 12 Mar. 1805.

Page 206: George Shotwell, of Abbeville Dist., for $50 sold Phillimon Bradford of Greenville Dist., tract in Pendleton Dist. on S. side of the Saluda River at the mouth of Woolanoy Creek, bd. by Henry Clark, granted Shotwell by John Drayton, 11 Jun. 1802. Date: 29 Jun. 1802. Wit: Henry Bradford, Reuben Talley. Henry Bradford made oath to Colin Campbell, J.P., 13 Feb. 1805. Rec: 12 Mar. 1805.

Page 206: 27 Oct. 1803, John Hunt to John Patterson for $300 for 30 acres on N. side of 12 Mile River on Mile Creek, where Patterson now lives. Wit: Isaac Hudson, John (X) Barnett. John Barnett made oath to James Wardlaw, J.Q., 26 Jan. 1805. Rec: 12 Mar. 1805.

Pages 206-207: Robert Baker, gunsmith, for $400 sold Thomas Johnston a tract where Ambrose Dudley(?) has lived for several years, part on 18 Mile Creek of the Savannah River (_____). Date: 1 Apr. ___. Wit: John Baker, Sr., Wm. ____ (?), Wm. ____ (?). John Baker made oath to John Willson, J.Q., 2 Apr. 1805. Plat shows 153 acres. Date: 18 Mar. 1805. Signed: D. Symmes. Rec: 29 Jul. 1805. Sarah (X) Baker, wife of Robert Baker, released dower to John Willson, J.Q., 2 Apr. 1805.

Pages 207-208: Vincent Tims, Sr. and William Timms, Sr., for $150 sold Thomas Johnston, storekeeper, 150 acres where Vincent Timms, Sr. now resides, including house, creek and cleared land. Date: 20 Feb. 1805. Signed: Vincent Timms, Sr. and Wm. Timms. Wit: Thomas Orr, John Hall and William Robinson. Thomas Orr made oath to M. Hammond, D. Clk. 21 Jan. 1806. (No recording date).

Page 208: William Reed for $200 sold John Leathers 136 acres on both sides of Weaver Creek of Woolenoy Creek of the Saluda River, bd. by Samuel Weaver and Hunter, granted Reed by Wm. Moultrie, _ Jul. 1793, recorded Bk. G., no. 5, p. 381. Date: 8 Apr. 1802. Signed: Wm. Reed, Violet Reed. Wit: Nathl. Reed, Abel(?) Anderson. Nathl. Reed made oath to Colin Campbell, J.P. 28 Aug. 1805. Rec: 3 Sep. 1805.

Pages 208-209: John Stewart for $50 sold John Rand(?) 190 acres on Crow Creek, granted Eli Langford 4 Feb. 1802 by John Drayton. Date: 8 Sep. 1803. (Cannot read witnesses). Rec: 4 Sep. 1805.

Pages 209: Thomas Orr to Andrew Warnock, Sr., John Dickson and Thomas Johnston _____..Estate of William Orr, late of Pendleton District, Merchant, dec'd., for $2,000(?). Date: 16 Jul. 1805. (appears to be a bond of secutiry). Wit: Andrew Oliver, John Hilton. John Hilton made oath to John Willson, Q.U., 2 Oct. 1809(?). Rec: 2 Oct. 1809. "Affec. recd. by John Lewis, C.C.".

Pages 209-210: John Moffet for $150 sold Samuel McColey 164 acres, less 1 acre, excepted for a burying place where the dead are now buryed, on Little Generostee Creek. Date: 16 May 1805. Wit: Wm. Simpson, Samuel Black. Ann Moffet, wife of John Moffet, released dower to Elijah Browne, Q.U., 16 May 1805. William Simpson made oath to E. Browne, 18 May 1805. Rec: 24 May 1805.

Page 210: Jeremiah Hubbard for $200 sold Nehemiah Hamm 147 acres where James Carson formerly lived, on W. side of 18 Mile Creek, surveyed for Peter Singlar and granted Thomas Farrar, who conveyed to Hubbard, 23 Mar. 1796. Date: 8 Jun. 1805. Wit: Richard Tomson, Joseph Whitner. Joseph Whitner made oath to M. Hammond, D. Clk., 10 Sep. 1805. Rec: 10 Sep. 1805. Dower, see Bk. K, p. 161.

Pages 210-211: William T. Rodgers for $87.77 sold Thomas Johnston one yellow sorrel filly, saddles, feather beds, furniture, cows and calves, etc. Date: 21 Feb. 1805. Teste: Thomas Coker.

Page 211: William Lesley of Abbeville Dist., for $200 sold Thomas Burford of Pendleton Dist.,part of a tract granted Margaret Lesley, on Broadaway Creek, bd. by Burford. Date: 23 Apr. 1805. (Plat). Wit: Adam Todd, Solomon Geer. Adam Todd made oath to Wm. Lesley, J.Q., 23 Apr.1805. Rec: 1 Aug. 1805. Margaret Browne, late Margaret Lesley, released dower to her interest in 640 acres on Broadaway Creek granted her 5 Jun. 1786. Date: 23 Apr. 1805. Elijah Browne, Q.U.

Pages 211-212: Samuel Earle of Greenville Dist., S.C. sold to James Lawson of Franklin Co., Ga. tract, part of which is in the Town which Gen'l. Robert Anderson, John Baylis Earle and Samuel Earle are appointed by Act of Assembly of S. C., Commissioners, accordingly, viz: 1st - that Commissioners or a Majority of them at any time they see proper, to lay off or divide the place into lots without varying the course of Main Street; 2nd - agreed all conditions and stricktions on establishment of a Town shall at all times be binding; 3rd - all springs found in the limits of the Town shall forever remain free for use of Earle and Lawson; 4th - Earle shall have full liberty to cultivate land this year and carry the crop off; 5th - agreed that neither party shall attempt to take advantage of this instrument by when difference of opinion shall arise a final descision will be left to a referee. Date: 16 Aug. 1803. Signed: Samuel Earle, Jas. Lawson. Wit: Samuel Hankins, Fanny (X) Hester. Fanny Hester made oath to J. B. Earle, 8 Aug. 1805. Rec: 8 Aug. 1805.

Page 212: Abraham Duff for $100 sold John Leatherdale 50 acres on Weaver's Creek. Date: 14 Jul. 1802. Signed: Abram Duff, Lanny(?)(X) Duff. (his mark). Wit: James Wardlaw, Dolly (X) Combs. James Wardlaw made oath to John Cochran, J.P., 30 Mar. 1805. (No recording date).

Pages 212-213: Nathaniel Perry for $250 sold William Goacher 87 acres, part of tract granted Moses Perkins, bd. by Coffee, Henson, on both sides of Conneross Creek. Date: 11 Oct. 1805. Wit: Sol J. Humphreys, Richard Hooper, John Y. Humphreys. Solomon Humphreys made oath to David Humphreys, J.P., 12 Oct. 1805. Rec: 18 Oct. 1805.

Page 213: Elisha Lake for $420 sold John Phillips 300 acres on Gregory's Creek of 12 Mile River. Date: 18 Feb. 1805. Wit: David Murphree, Alexander Burns. Alexander Burns made oath to David Murphree, J.P., 18 Feb. 1805. Rec: 18 Oct. 1805.

Pages 213-214: Charles Rice of Walton Co., Ga., lawful attorney for his father, Henry Rice of Tenesee(sic), for $234 sold Jesse Tatum of Pendleton Dist., 468 acres granted Henry Rice by Thos. Pinckney 5 Nov. 1787, on Wolf and Rice Creeks of 12 Mile River. Date: 15 Aug. 1804. Wit: T. W. Farrar, Wm. Hamilton. Thomas W. Farrar made oath to M. Hammond, D.C., 15 Aug. 1805. Rec: 15 Aug. 1805.

Page 214: Christopher Hargreaves for divers considerations, appoint my trusty friend, James Long, to be my lawful attorney to sell a tract of 99 acres on the Savannah River and deliver the sale money to apply to payment on my lawful debts and support of my family, and to collect debts due me. Date: 2 Apr. 1805. Wit: Wm. Bennett, Cynthia Jones. William Bennett made oath to John McMillin, J.P., 5 Oct. 1805. Rec: 7 Oct. 1805.

Page 215: Amos Roberts of Greenville Dist. for $130 sold Sturdy Garner of Pendleton Dist., a tract on Big Creek of the Saluda River... granted Roberts 2 Jul. 1792(?), recorded Bk. C, no. 5, p. 332. Date: ____ 1801. Signed: Amos (X) Roberts. Wit: William ____, ____(?). Thomas Thaxton made oath to Wm. Hall, J.P., 5 Jul. ___. Rec: 7 Jun. 1805.

Pages 215-216: William Steele for $150 sold Major Barkley W. Finley lot of 1 acre and 16 poles in the Village of Pendleton Courthouse, bd. on N. by lot #26, W. by lot #27, S. by street, according to plat made by Robt. McCann, Esq., in 1800. Date: 6 May 1805. Wit: Elam Sharp, John R. Brown. Elam Sharp made oath to M. Hammond, D.C., 22 Oct. 1807. Rec: 22 Oct. 1807. Dower, Bk. K, p. 135(?).

Page 216: Robert Portwood for $120 sold George Vandiver 100 acres on Conneross, bd. by Martin, Winn and Portwood. Date: ___ 1804. Wit: Thomas Edington, Peter Wagnon. Peter Wagnon made oath to John Taylor, QU, 9 Aug. 1805. Rec: 9 Aug. 1805.

Pages 216-217: John Butt to Trion Fuller for $373 for 138 acres granted Lewis D. Martin, also part of tract granted Butt, both on S. side of Conneross Creek, bd. by Butt, Elisha Miller. Date: 1 Oct. 1805. Wit: Thomas Delanry, John Nichols. Thomas Delany made oath to Josiah Foster, J.P., 8 Oct. 1805. Rec: 29 Oct. 1805.

Page 217: Jacob Skelton for $10 sold Ezekiel Green 130 acres where Skelton now lives on Hooker's(?) fork of Generostee of Savannah River. Date: 12 Mar. 1803. Wit: John Cox and Amos Barnett. Amos Barnett made oath to James Tate, Q.U., 28 Feb. 1804. Rec: 20 Nov. 1805.

Pages 217-218: 16 Mar. 1796, Rowland Burks to John Burks

(Pages 217-218 cont'd:) for ₤60 for 60 acres on Conneross Creek of the Keowee River, part of a tract granted Lewis D. Martin by Thos. Pinckney, 2 July 1787, bd. by John Burks, John Butt, Henry Mekee. Signed: Roland Burks, Rachel (X) Burks. Wit: Charles (X) Burks, Henry McKee. Henry McKee made oath to Joseph Reed, J.P., 24 Nov. 1800.
Rec: 18 Nov. 1805.

Pages 218-219: James Fuller for $20 sold John Towry tract on N. fork of Conneross Creek, part of the tract granted James Fuller by John Drayton 27 Sep. 1800, recorded Bk. WWW, p. 580, bd. by Wm. Towers and Abett.... John Towers made oath to Jno. Adair, J.P., 11 Nov. 1805.
Rec: 18 Nov. 1805.

Page 219: Joseph Thresher for $20(?) sold John Towery ___ acres on N. fork _____ part of tract granted Lewis D. Martin by Thos. Pinckney _____ 1787. Date: __ Mar. 1804(?). Wit: _____. John Towry signed oath _____ 1805. Rec: __ Nov. 1805.

Pages 219-220: John Abbet _____ to John Towry 100 (?) acres on N. fork of Conneross Creek of the Keowee River _____. Date: __ Mar. 1804. Signed: John (X) Abbett. Wit: _____. Aaron Hill made oath he and Richard Burks witnessed deed to Jno. Adair, J.P., 11 Nov. 1805.
Rec: 18 Nov. 1805.

Page 220: John Burks, Sr. for $18 sold Thomas Brown 50 acres, part of tract granted Andrew Boddan by Edward Rutledge. Date: 11 May 1803. Wit: B. Starrett, Alexander Glen. Mr. Benjamin Starrett made oath to Josiah Foster, J.P., 25 Apr. 1804.
Rec: 2 Dec. 1805.

Pages 220-221: Charles Varner and Mary Varner for $12 sold John Ledbetter 4 acres, part of tract granted John Varner, Jr. by Wm. Moultrie, 5 Jun. 1786, conveyed to John Varner, Sr., 4 Jan. 1793, recorded Pendleton Bk. D, p. 324, on the Savannah River, bd. by Joel Ledbetter, John Varner, Sr. and John Ledbetter. Date: 11 Mar. 1805. Signed: Mary (X) Verner, Charles Verner _____ Wit: _____. Henry Braselton signed oath.
Rec: _____

(Note: the next group of film was unreadable in part but have abstracted what was readable to the best of my ability).

Page 221: Robert Willson to Meshack Hall _____ for 100 acres on Little River _____

Page 222: 18 May 1797, William Beaty and Ellen, his wife, of Washington Dist., to William Stevenson of the same place, for $50 for 124 acres part of 378 acres granted Nathan Young by Wm. Moultrie 5 Apr. 1786. Signed: Wm. Beaty, Ellen (X) Beaty. Wit: Moses Purvines, Nathan Lusk. Moses Purvines made oath to Nathan Lusk, J.P., 23 Aug. 1798.
Rec: 12 Sep. 1805.

Pages 222-223: 7 May 1797, William Beaty and Ellen, his wife, to William Stevenson for 10 shillings _____ part of 378 acres granted Nathan Young by Wm. Moultrie 5 Jun. 1786. Signed: Wm. Beaty, Ellen (X) Beaty. Wit: _____. No oath.

Pages 223-225: 2 Sep. 1802(?) _____ judgement entered in Office of the Clerk of Court, Pendleton, on 2nd Monday of October 1804, direcred Sheriffs of State that all chattels, houses, lands, and Real Estate of William Montgomery be sold to highest bidder (suit for the sum of $314.38), which James Cahun(?) in Court of Common Pleas against

(Pages 223-225 cont'd): William Montgomery ......tract of 175 ac. sold to Thomas Davis(?) by his friend,... James Moore(?) as the last and highest bidder for $64. Signed: D. McCaleb, Sheriff. Wit: T. W. Farrar, A. Boyse. Thomas W. Farrar made oath to N. Hammond, D.C., 4 Sep. 1805.
Rec: 4 Sep. 1805.

Page 225: Lewis D. Martin for $500(?) sold Thomas Byrd 100 acres granted Ephraim Mitchell _____ Date: _____ Dec. 1805. Wit: _____
Rec: 16 Dec. 1805.

Pages 225-226: Joseph Land, Sr. and Sarah _____ sold to Hezekiah Davis _____ and by legal conveyance made by him to Jesse G_____ and from G____ to Joseph Land. Date: 8 Mar. 1802. Signed: Joseph (X) Land, Sarah (X) Land. Wit: Henry (X) Beshers, Joseph (X) Elledge. Joseph Elledge made oath to George Foster, J.P., 8 Mar. 1801(?).
Rec: 13 Nov. 1805.

Page 226: William Duncan for $100 sold Hugh Duncan, Jr. 400 acres (Plat), on Hencoop Creek of Rocky River, part of tract surveyed for William Bennum(?), conveyed from him to William Duncan 3 Nov. 1799(?),recorded Bk. B, no. 5, p. 80. Date: 11 Nov. 1805. Wit: Reuben Brock, Samuel Black. Samuel Black, J.P., certified as witness, 1 Nov. 1805.
Rec: 21 Jan. 1806.

Page 227: John McFall and Mary, his wife, for $500 sold Samuel Brown 280(?) acres on Bever(sic) Creek, granted Mary Smith by Wm. Moultrie, 178_, conveyed to William ____ and from him to McFall. Date: __ Dec. 1803. Signed: Jno. McFall. Wit: _____. Mary McFall signed dower. Date:_____

Pages 227-228: _____(first part unreadable).......... (sold to) sd. John Donaldson. Signed: John Land, Nightengale (X) Land. Wit: Richard Blackstock, John Todd. John Todd made oath to Samuel H. Dickson, J. P., 11 Mar. 1805.
Rec: 21 Oct. 1805.

Page 228: Major Lewis is firmly bound to Richard Gray for $640 and sells him 320 acres granted to Robert Scott 5 Jun. 1786, on 26 Mile Creek, including improvement of John McCutchen. Date: 10 Sep. 1805. Wit: John Gentry, Richard Riddels. John Gentry made oath to J. Stribling, Q.U., 30 Jan. 1806. Elizabeth (X) Lewis, wife of Major Lewis, released dower to John Taylor, Q.U., 23 Sep. 1805.
Rec: 30 Jan. 1806.

Pages 229-230: 27 Jan. 1797, Henry Lusk and Ellen, his wife, of Washington Dist., to William Stevenson for $3(?) for 28½ acres on Little Generostee, part of 200 acres granted Andrew Pickens by Wm. Moultrie, bd. William Beaty, Moses Parvines. Signed: Henry Loosk, Ellen (X) Lusk. Wit: Moses Parvines, Nathan Loosk. Moses Parvines made oath to Nathan Lusk,JP on 23 Aug. 1798.
Rec: 12 Sep. 1805.

Pages 230-231: Sheriff Brouster for $86 sold to David Drennan 100 acres where Drenan now lives. Date: 15 Mar. 1803. Wit: James Todd, John Watson. James Todd made oath to John George, J.P., 15 Mar. 1803.
Rec: 19 Nov. 1805.

Pages 231-232: Joseph Chapman and Mary Chapman for $250 sold John Byrd a tract at mouth of Goldens Creek. Date: 7 Feb. 1800. Signed: Joseph (X) Chapman. Wit: James Jett, Jesse Tatum. Mary (X) Chapman released

(Pages 231-232 cont'd):　　　　　　dower to John Willson, Q. U., 12 Mar. 1805.
　　　　　　　　　　　　　　　　　Jesse Tatum made oath to David Murphree,
J. P., 26 Feb. 1800. Rec: 17 Dec. 1805.

Page 232:　　　　　　　　　　　　John Armstrong for $550 sold William Car-
　　　　　　　　　　　　　　　　　ter 307 acres on S. fork of George's Crk.
　　　　　　　　　　　　　　　　　of the Saluda River, bd. by John Armstrong
and William McCamey. Date: 22 Mar. 1805. Wit: Jacob Hill, Jas. Linard.
Jacob Hill made oath to Samuel C. Duff, J.P., 30 Nov. 1805.
Rec: 2 Dec. 1805.

Pages 232-233:　　　　　　　　　　17 May 1805, James Taylor to Samuel Brown
　　　　　　　　　　　　　　　　　for $500(?) for 100 acres, bd. on NE by
　　　　　　　　　　　　　　　　　Andrew _____(rest unreadable).Date:
__May 180_.(Wit and oath unreadable).

Pages 233-234:　　　　　　　　　　(First part unreadable)......Power of At-
　　　　　　　　　　　　　　　　　torney, dated 15 Nov. 1805. Signed: Wilm.
　　　　　　　　　　　　　　　　　Davidson, Andrew T. Davidson. Wit: T. Mc-
Knitt, J.P., Dd. Cowan, J.P.....State of N. C., I, Isaac Alexander, Clk.
of the County Court of Mecklenburg, cettify Joseph McKnitt and David
Cowan, Esquires, who attested within Power of Attorney are Acting Jus-
tices (of this County?). Date: 16 Nov. 1805.
Rec: 22 Nov. 1805. (Index says Davidsons to John Davidson...BW)

Page 234:　　　　　　　　　　　　David Barton for $150 sold Peter Lewney &
　　　　　　　　　　　　　　　　　Hugh Lewney (later Looney) 344 acres on
　　　　　　　　　　　　　　　　　Cain and Beaverdam Creek of Tugaloe River,
granted Barton for 454 acres and formerly sold to Meshack Hamby, laid
out by John D. Terrell. Date: 21 Nov. 1805. Wit: Jno. D. Terrell and
Richard Shipp. Richard Shipp made oath to John Verner, J.P. (No date).
Rec: 15 Dec. 1805.

Pages 234-235:　　　　　　　　　　7 Jan. 1805, William Robinson to Sergant
　　　　　　　　　　　　　　　　　Griffen for $100 for 70 acres on N. fork
　　　　　　　　　　　　　　　　　of 12 Mile River, on both sides, bd. Griffen. Signed: William Robinson, Susannah Robinson. Wit: James Wardlaw and
Abner (X) Robinson. Susannah (X) Robinson released dower to James Wardlaw, Q.U., 23 Jan. 1805. Abner Robinson made oath to David Murphree, JP,
18 May 1805.
Rec: 22 Jan. 1806.

Pages 235-236:　　　　　　　　　　Ambrose Bradly for $2,000 sold Joseph Burk
　　　　　　　　　　　　　　　　　590 acres in 4 surveys on George's Creek,
　　　　　　　　　　　　　　　　　of Saluda River, bd. by Daniel McCollom &
Ambrose Bradly. Date: 11 Feb. 1806. Wit: Hezekiah Goodrich, Thos. Barrett.
Thomas Barrett made oath to Samuel C. Duff, J.P., 12 Feb. 1806.
Rec: 13 Feb. 1806.

Pages 236-237:　　　　　　　　　　Thomas Shockley for $2,000 sold James Shock-
　　　　　　　　　　　　　　　　　ley 150 acres on Savannah River, bd. Aquilla
　　　　　　　　　　　　　　　　　Shockley, Bond and Putman. Date: 10 Dec.
1804. Wit: William Sartor and Jesse (X) Shockley. William Sartor made
oath to James Tate, Q.U., 12 Feb. 1805.
Rec: 25 Sep. 1805.

Pages 237-238:　　　　　　　　　　William Lewis, Jr., planter, for $160 sold
　　　　　　　　　　　　　　　　　Benjamin Lewis, planter, 160 acres on 26
　　　　　　　　　　　　　　　　　Mile Creek, part of 320 acres purchased
from James Anderson, granted Jesse Webb by Wm. Moultrie 4 Dec. 1786.Date:
18 Feb. 1804. Wit: Major Lewis, Samuel Anderson. Capt. Major Lewis made
oath to James C. Griffen, 2 Nov. 1805.
Rec: 2 Nov. 1805.

Page 238:　　　　　　　　　　　　Lewis D. Martin of Pendleton Dist. for
　　　　　　　　　　　　　　　　　$2,000 sold William May of Anson Co., N.C.
　　　　　　　　　　　　　　　　　400 acres granted James Mitchell for 300
acres for his Bounty and 100 acres, part of 400 acres granted Ephraim
Mitchell for his Bounty. Date: 1 Oct. 1805. Wit: P. H. May, William Ham-

(Page 238 cont'd): ilton. William Hamilton made oath that he and Phillip May witnessed deed to M. Hammond, D. Clk. 1 Oct. 1805.
Rec: 1 Oct. 1805.

Pages 238-239: 3 Nov. 1804, Ranson Powell of Greenville Co., S. C. to Thomas Rowland of Rutherford Co., N. C. for $400 for 165 acres on Saluda River. Wit: John Robinson, Susanah Robinson. and John Robinson, Jr. John Robinson made oath to John ___, J.P., 12 Jan. 1805.
Rec: 10 Oct. 1805.

Pages 239-240: George Stamps for $50 sold Solomon Palmour 50 acres on Little River, part of tract granted Albert Robinson 1792, bd. by Stamps and Palmour. Date: 11 Jun. 1805. Wit: James Barron, Henry Burch. Henry Burch, Esq., made oath to Thomas Hargis, J.P., 1 Jan. 1805.
Rec: 2 Dec. 1805.

Page 240: Ezekial Buffington and Ellis Harlin for $400 sold Solomon Palmer 200 acres on Little River, part of a tract granted Field Pruett 1790, bd. by James Millwee. Date: 25 Mar. 1805. Signed: Ezekiel Buffington, Ellis (X) Harlin. Wit: Isaiah Beck, Jeffry Beck. Isaiah Beck made oath to Thomas Hargis, J.P., 11 Jun. 1805.
Rec: 2 Dec. 1805.

Pages 240-241: Wm. Steel and James Wood for $125 sold John Burns 200 acres including improvement where Francis Greenwood now lives near the road to Gen'l. Anderson's ferry, part of 1815 acres granted Francis Greenwood and conveyed to Gen'l. Robert Anderson 22 Feb. 1799. Date: 9 Jan. 1804. Wit: Wm. Hunter, Joseph B. Earle. Wm. Hunter made oath to James Starrett, J. P., 14 Mar. 1804.
Rec: 26 Sep. 1805.

Pages 241-242: John Harper for $160 sold Kenon Brazeale (later Cannon Brazeale) 272 acres on Rocky Creek of the Savannah River, part of 272 acres granted Benjamin Starrett by Chas. Pinckney 4 Jun. 1787, on NE fork of Little Rocky Creek. Date: 10 Nov. 1802. Wit: John Harper, Jr., George Dilworth. George Dilworth made oath to James Welborn, J.P., 11 Feb. 1803.
Rec: 29 Oct. 1805.

Page 242: Bartholay Laurence for $100 sold Joab Laurence one stud horse. Date: 12 Mar. 1805. Signed: Bartholomew Laurence. Wit: Robert Waugh, Edward Adair. (No oath).
Rec: 8 Apr. 1805.

Pages 242-243: Joseph Couch for Ł 40 sold Hezekiah Davis 120 acres on Big Generostee Creek, part of tract granted Henry Pearson, conveyed to Jesse Garland, then to William Gibson, then to Couch, bd. W. by Jesse Brown, S. by John Miller, NW by Joseph Lamb, E. by Jesse Garland, N. by James Long, including improvement made by Elisha Garland and William Gibson. Date: 5 Jan. 1799. Signed: Joseph (X) Couch. Wit: Jesse Brown, William McGregor, Solomon (X) Bennett. William McGregory made oath to John McMillen, J.P., 21 Oct. 1805.
Rec: 13 Oct. 1805.

Page 243: 13 Sep. 1790(?), Jesse Garland, planter, to Joseph Land _____, granted 18 May by Wm. Moultrie to Henry Pearson for 640(?)...... (cannot read rest).....Signed: Jesse (X) Garland. Wit: _____. Nathan McAllister signed oath.
Rec: __ Nov. 1805.

Page 244: William Crosby for $300 sold John Burns 104 Acres on Keowee River, granted by Thomas

(Page 244 cont'd): Pinckney 7 May 1787, recorded Bk. TTTT, p. 202. Date: 26 Sep. 1804. Wit: T. W. Farrar, A. Deal. Thomas W. Farrar made oath to M. Hammond, D.C., 21 Feb. 1806. Rec: 21 Feb. 1806.

Pages 244-245: Moses Harris for £ 54 stg. sold John Gibson 216 acres on S. side of Big Beaverdam Crk. part of 940 acres granted James Clark by Wm. Moultrie 6 Oct. 1794, bd. by Gibson, McKinsey. Date: 9 Apr. 1804. Wit: Frederick Moss, J. C. Kilpatrick. Frederick Moss made oath to William Cleveland, J.P., 19 Jul. 1805. Rec: 13 Aug. 1805.

Page 245: (First part unreadable).....for ___ hundred dollars sold William Stevenson 200 acres, laid off to William Young(?), 26 Jul. 1784, recorded Bk. FFFF, p. 176(?). Date: 6 Jan. 18___. Signed: Isom Young. Wit: William Young(?), Alexander Sherrard(?). Rachel Young signed release of dower 30 Jan. 1804. Oath to E. Browne, 30 Jan. 1804. Rec: 11 Sep. 1805.

Pages 245-246: John Phillips for $300 sold William Stuart 300 acres on Gregory's Creek of 12 Mile River. Date: 16 Jul. 1805. Wit: Elias Phillips and Nathl. Newman. Elias Phillips made oath to David Murphree, J.P., 16 Jul. 1805. Rec: 5 Aug. 1805.

Page 246: Eli Hunnicutt for £ 5 sold John Hunnicutt 150 acres on Jones Creek of 26 Mile Creek, part of 482 acres granted Eli Hunnicutt by Wm. Moultrie 4 Dec. 1786, recorded Bk. ___ (left out), p. 240. Date: 8 Nov. 1804. Wit: Jas. Millwee, Wm. Hunnicutt. James Millwee made oath to Samuel Houston, J.P., 18 Jun. 1805. Rec: 5 Aug. 1805.

Page 247: John Hamilton of Union Co., S. C. for $100 sold Peter Edwards of Pendleton Dist., 112 acres on Golden's Creek of Savannah River, granted Hamilton by Chas. Pinckney 1 Oct. 1798, recorded Bk. S, no. 5, p. 237. Date: 14 Mar. 1804. Wit: David Hamilton, Catherine (X) Edwards, and Margeret Hamilton. David Hamilton made oath to John Willson, Q.U., 8 Apr. 1805. Rec: 19 Sep. 1805.

Pages 247-248: William Wakefield of Smith Co., Tenesee (sic) for $120 sold Henry Braselton of Pendleton Dist., 50 acres, part of 194 acres granted George Verner by Arnoldus Vanderhorst 7 Nov. 1796, bd. by Ambrose Hugins, Thomas Finley. Date: 15 Nov. 1804. Wit: Samuel Anderson, Nicholas Edwards, Sr. Samuel Anderson made oath to John McMillin, J.P., 27 July 1805. Rec: 27 Sep. 1805.

Page 248: William Simms for $2,100 sold Taylor & Cherry, Merchants, 163 acres on 23 Mile Creek and Cuffe Creek, conveyed by James Neale to Sims on 10 Apr. 1802. Date: 3 Nov. 1804. Wit: Moses Liddell and M. Hammond. Moses Liddell made oath to A. Boyse, J.P., 16 Mar. 1805. Rec: 10 Sep. 1805.

Pages 248-249: 11 Jan. 1798(?) Nathaniel Reed to Robert Wilson for £ 33 for 100 acres surveyed for Reed 7 Aug. 1792 in 96 Dist., part of 223 acres granted by Wm. Moultrie, recorded Bk. T (or F), no. 5, p. 235. Signed: Nathaniel (X) Reed. Wit: Samuel Boydston, John (X) Head. John Head made oath to Joseph Reed, J.P., 16 Mar. 1798. Rec: 25 Nov. 1805.

Page 249: 20 May 1801, John Blyth of Greenville Co., S. C. to John Tarwater (of same?) for £ 50 stg. for 50 acres, part of grant to Joseph

(Page 249 cont'd): Copeland on S. side of Saluda, bd. by Blyth and Tarwater. Signed: John (X) Blyth. Wit: William Duncan, Wm. Blyth. William Blyth made oath to Absalon Blyth, JP, 25 Oct. ____.
Rec: 27 Oct. 1805.

Pages 249-250: James Hallum for $300 sold Henry Edwards 261 acres on 18 Mile Creek of Savannah River, bd. on S. by Widow Prater, W. by Widow Gibson, N. by James Passons, E. by tract granted Thomas Roberts 21 Jan. 1805. Date: 1 Apr. 1805. Signed: James Hallums, Nancy (X) Hallums. Wit: James Chapman, William (X) Edwards. William Edwards made oath to John Wilson, Q.U., 3 Aug. 1805.
Rec: 19 Sep. 1805.

Pages 250-251: By bond I am bound to Richard Tarrant for $567.62½ on or before Mar. 1806....I, Ambrose Bradley sold to Richard Tarrant, cows and calves, hogs, sheep, feather beds, furniture, household items and all my farming tools. Date: 15 Feb. 1806. Wit: James Wilson and John Tarrant. James Wilson made oath to Wm. Edmondson, Q.U., 18 Feb. 1806.
Rec: 19 Feb. 1806.

Page 251: William Thompson for $900 sold Elias Phillips 300 acres in N. fork of 12 Mile (River), bd. by Moses Murphree, Alexander Burns. Date: 21 Oct. 1803. Signed: William (X) Thompson. Wit: David Murphree and Jesse Murphree. Jesse Murphree made oath to David Murphree, J.P., 21 Oct. 1803. Rec: 8 Nov. 1805.

Pages 251-252: John James for $25 sold Thomas Dean 50 ac. on 26 Mile Creek, bd. by Caleb Edmondson, Beazley, Abraham Elledge and John James,... part of tract granted James Gillison by Thos. Pinckney 3 Dec. 1787, recorded Bk. RRRR, p. 207. Date: 28 Nov. 1803. Wit: James Kennedy and Samuel Dean. Samuel Dean made oath to Hez. Davis, J.P., 30 Apr. 1805.
Rec: 1 May 1805.

Page 252: Jacob Vance to Moses Hendricks for $60 for 60 acres on Camp Creek of Saluda River, bd. by Moses Hendricks, David Hendricks, Vance (Grant....Date:(?) 4 Aug. 1794. Date: 26 Oct. 1805. Signed: Jacob (X) Vance. Wit: William Rackley, Moses Hendricks. William Rackley made oath to Amos Ladd, J.P., 29 Oct. 1805.
Rec: 2 Nov. 1805.

Pages 252-253: William Hubbard for $26 sold John Byrd 26 acres, part of 2,225 acres granted Ferdinand Hopkins 2 Jan. 1792, on Golden's Creek. Date 6 Jul. 1805. Wit: Wm. Hallum, Ph. May. Phillip May made oath to John Wilson, Q.U., 3 Aug. 1805.
Rec: 17 Dec. 1805.

Pages 253-254: Alexander McDowell of the Town of Cambridge in Abbeville Co., Merchant, for Ł 40 10 sh. sold to Patrick McDowall, Merchant, of the same place, the following tracts: one of 202 acres surveyed 4 Dec. 1787 by James Millwee, D.S., granted 2 Jun. 1788, in 96 Dist. of Washington (Co.?) on 6(?) Mile Creek of Keowee River; one of 275 acres surveyed 7 Jun. 1788 in 96 Dist., now Washington Dist. on Little Beaverdam Creek, bd on SE by James Lincoln, Esq., SW by Moses Tomlan(?); one tract of 532 ac. surveyed 8 Nov. 1787, granted 2 Jun. 1788, in 96 Dist. on Crow Creek of Little Beaverdam and Rocky Creek, bd. SE by David Laurence Pearson, NW by John Beaver; one tract of 207 acres granted Jun. 1788 in 96 Dist. on the Keowee River, bd. on NW by Colonel Hopkins; one tract of 252 acres granted 2 Jun. 1788, on Mile Creek of Keowee; one tract of 210 acres granted 2 Jun. 1788 on Keowee River. Date: 14 Jun. 1796. Wit: T. Bostick, Thos. Anderson. Thomas Anderson, Q.U., certified deed 12 Sep. 1804.
Rec: 4 Mar. 1806.

Pages 254-255:   Farley Thompson, planter, for $450 sold to
                                  Charles Pitts 220 acres on W. side of Sene-
                                  ca River, granted Robert Tate in 1784, con-
veyed by him to Edwd. T. McClure, 1790, bd. NW by David Sloan, E. by the
Seneca River. Date: 17 Sep. 1805. Wit: James (X) Johnston, Saml. Tate and
Jeremiah Fowler. Samuel Tate made oath to James Tate, Q.U., 24 Sep. 1805.
Elizabeth Thompson, wife of Farley Thompson, released dower to James Tate
Q.U. 24 Sep. 1805.
Rec: 2 Dec. 1805.

Pages 255-256:   Presley Self for $200 sold David Sloan and
                                  Walter Adair 385 acres on both sides of a
                                  branch of Richland Creek of the Keowee Riv-
er, bd. NE by Jacob Chapman, granted Self by Chas. Pinckney. Date: 19 Jun.
1805. Signed: Presley (X) Self. Wit: James Fuller, Bartholomew (X) Daniel.
James Fuller made oath to James Adair, J.P., 19 Jun. 1805.
Rec: 3 Dec. 1805.

Page 256:   James Hallums, planter, for $200 sold Henry
                                  Edwards 129 acres on branches of 18 Mile
                                  Creek of the Savannah River, bd. by James
Passon, granted Thomas Roberts, 21 Jan. 1805. Date: 2 Jul. 1805. Wit:Sam-
uel Baker and Henry Gaines. Samuel Baker made oath to John Wilson, Q. U.,
3 Aug. 1804. Nancy (X) Hallums released dower to John Wilson, Q.U., 3 Aug.
1805.

Pages 256-257:   Henry D. Reece and Robert Anderson are both
                                  bound to Edwin Reese of Jackson Co., Ga.
                                  for $800 payable to Reese.....whereas dur-
ing the minority of Henry D. Reese, having chosen E. Reese as his guard-
ian, has sold at Public Sale one negro named Jack, bequeathed to Henry
D. Reese..(by his brother, E. G. Reese?...not sure of this wording...BW)
(Rest unreadable). Signed: H. Dobson Reese, Robert Anderson. (Cannot read
witnesses). Oath signed by Jane Anderson.
Rec: 7 Oct. 1805.

Pages 257-258:   William Matthews for $250 sold David Sell-
                                  ars, planter, _____ on 12 Mile Creek
                                  part of 3 tracts: one granted
by Chas. Pinckney, one granted Benjamin Starrett 6 Jan. 1794(?) and one
granted William Matthers, bd. by Kirksey ....(all very dim). Date: 9
Dec. 1797. Wit: Willoughy Pugh, David (X) Pugh, John Kirksey. Willoughby
Pugh made oath to John Varner, J.P., 27 Feb. ___.
Rec: 3 Jan. 1806.

Page 258:   Jesse Cain mortgaged for $200 to William
                                  Walson(?) tract where Cain now lives on the
                                  Keowee River, conveyed from William Floyd;
also one sorrell mare, 4 cows and calves, 4 sheep, household furniture,
___ acres cotton, 15 acres corn. Date: 2 Oct. 1805. Wit: James Williams,
John (X) Price. Rec: 10 Jan. 1806. (No oath).

Pages 258-259:   Andrew Oliver, planter, for $155 sold John
                                  Cross 168 acres; one tract of 120 acres
                                  granted Britian George 2 Jan. 1797, on 23
Mile Creek of Savannah River; the other of 48 acres, part of tract granted Hugh Warnock, adjoining above tract on SW, deed to Margaret Blair and
by her to William Blair, from him to John Wilkinson, from him to Britian
George and from him to Oliver. Date: 2 Feb. 1805. Wit: (very dim but appears to be...) Charles Willson, John Smith, Samuel Oliver. Samuel Oliver
made oath. Rebecca (X) Oliver, wife of Andrew Oliver, released dower to
John Wilson, Q.U., 2 Feb. 1805.
Rec: __ Jul. 1805.

Pages 259-260:   William May, Sr. of Anson Co., N. C. to Wil-
                                  liam May, Jr., carpenter, of Pendleton Dis-
                                  trict, for Ł 400 for tract on Connoross Crk
part of tract granted James Mitchel(?). Date: 25 Nov. 1805. Wit: Ph. May
and Daniel May. Phillip May made oath to M. Hammond, D.C., 28 Sep. 1805.
Rec: 28 Dec. 1805.

Page 260: John McCutchen for $650 sold Simon Doyle 500 acres where McCutchen now lives, part of 2 tracts: one granted Charles Saxon, the other to William Turpin(?) by Wm. Moultrie, on W. side of 23 Mile Creek, bd. by Turpin, Saxon. Date: 24 Nov. 1803. Wit: James Hembree, James Simmons. James Hembree made oath to M. Hammond, D.C., 28 Dec. 1805. Rec: 23 Apr. 1805.

Pages 260-261: Thomas Brown for $32 sold John Cobb 80 ac. bd. by John Cobb, Jesse Glen, part of tract granted Andrew Bodden by Edwd. Rutledge, 7 Oct. 1799. Date: 3 Oct. 1802. Wit: James Starrett, Moses Perkins. James Starrett, Esq. made oath to _____, 28 Oct. 1805. Rec: 28 Oct. 1805.

Pages 261-262: John Cobb for $400 sold Warren Fillpot 100 acres on Conneross Creek of Keowee River, part of tract granted George Brough 16 Jul. 1784 by Benj. Guerard, bd. Noland Burks and Richard Burks. Date: 25 Feb. 1801. Signed: John Cobb, Franky Cobb. Wit: Jas. Starrett, Mary (X) Starrett. James Starrett made oath to Joseph Reid, J.P., 24 Nov. 1800. Rec: 28 Oct. 1805.

Page 262: 17 Mar. 1796, Rowland Burks to John Cobb for £ 60 stg. for 100 acres on Conneross Creek of Keowee River, part of tract granted George Brough 16 Jul. 1784 by Benj. Guerard, bd. Rowland Burks and by Richard Burks. Signed: Rowland Burks and Rachel (X) Burks. Wit: John Burks and Henry McKie. Henry McKie made oath to Joseph Reid, J.P., 24 Nov. 1800. Rec: 28 Oct. 1805.

Pages 262-264: Theodore Gaillard of the City of Charleston, Attorney at Law, and wife, Cornelia Gaillard, for $300 sold to Israel Pickens 640 ac. in Old Dist. of 96, on First Creek of Rocky River, granted Cornelia Marshall for 640 acres (resurvey found to be 667 acres.). Date: 13 Feb. 1801. Wit: Lewis Tresevant, Catharine Tresevant.....Plat for 640 acres, Dd. Hopkins, D.S. recorded in Columbia __ Dec. 1799. Signed: J. G. Guignard, Surv. Genl. Also plat for 667 acres bd. S. by land laid out to Forga Cavin. At request of Gen. Andrew Pickens have resurveyed land, 24 Jan.1800. Samuel H. Dickson, D.S., Cornelia Gaillard released dower to Lewis Tresevant, 11 Mar. 1801....It is stipulated that within warranty shall not extend to claims of persons who at the time of execution have settled themselves on described tract, several persons, namely Fenton Hall, Israel Pickens, John Erwing, Alexr. Erwing and Maxwell Kennedy have encoached on said tract. Date: __ Mar. 1801. Signed: Theodore Gaillard. Hon. Lewis Tresevant made oath to E. Pickens, Q.U. 1 Dec. 1801. Rec: 1 Nov. 1805.

Page 264: 10 Feb. 1797, Robert Linn to Leeser Agustus (Augustus) for £ 20 stg. for 60 acres being lower end of tract that John Conn now lives on and bd. lower end of tract that Robert Linn lives on, line between William Wright and William Dun. Wit: John Evans, James Hues. John Evans made oath to Wm. Reed, J.P., 24 Mar. 1797. Rec: 28 Oct. 1805.

Pages 264-265: 30 Sep. 1803, Isaiah Lewis to Leason Augustus for tract on S. fork of 12 Mile River part of 2 surveys, one to David McAdoo, the other to Lewis Eaton, bd. James Martin, James Hughes above Old Mill, Lewis, John Boren. Wit: Joseph Duff, George (X) Glover. George Glover made oath to Henry Burch, J.P., 5 Jan. 1802. Rec: 28 Oct. 1805.

Page 265: York Co., S. C., 12 Dec. 1797, Nathaniel Henderson to Daniel Henderson for 233 ac. in Pendleton City on Mill Creek of George's Creek of Saluda River. Date: 12 Dec. 1797. Wit: Thomas Henderson, Samuel Henderson, Nathaniel H. Canseller. Pendleton Dist.: Thomas Henderson made

(Page 265 cont'd): oath to Samuel C. Duff, J.P., 10 Oct. 1805. Rec: 28 Oct. 1805.

Pages 265-266: William Mitchell of Henderson Co., Ky. for $500 sold William Nicholson of Pendleton Dist. 450 acres granted Burrell Bobo on 5 Feb. 1787, on old Indian path, line between Nicholson, Mitchell, George Shuler, Edward Hays, Smelcer, William Stuart. Signed: William (X) Mitchell. Wit: Andrew Roe, Jeremiah Slater. Catherine (X) Mitchell, wife of William Mitchell, released dower to Henry Burch, J.Q, 25 Sep. 1805. Andrew Roe made oath to Henry Burch, 25 Sep. 1805. Rec: 28 Oct. 1805.

Page 266: 11 Feb. 1805, Owen Evans to Mary Owens for $200 for 100 acres on Saluda River, being part of 2 tracts: one to John Hambelton for 80 acres, the other to Owen Evans for 81 acres, bd. by Owens, land laid out to John Dorrah, now belonging to James Welborn. Wit: John Evans and Elizabeth Evans. John Evans made oath to James Welborn, J.P., 28 Sept. 1805. Rec: 28 Oct. 1805.

Page 266: James Boren for $250 sold Leason Augusta 250 acres on branch of 12 Mile River, part on top of a mountain. Date: 12 Mar. 1804. Signed: James (X) Borne. Wit: James Wardlaw, Thomas Carpenter. James Wardlaw made oath to John Cochran, J.P., 30 Mar. 1804. Rec: 28 Oct. 1805.

Pages 266-267: Thomas Gasaway for $300 sold Joseph Smith 100 acres on Six Mile Creek, branch of the Keowee River, being NE part of 770 acres granted Henry Gasaway by John Drayton 6 Sep. 1802, bd. SE by Susannah Brown, NE by Moses Mays, NW by Robert Evans. (No date:) Wit: Benjamin Gasaway, Henry Gasaway. Benjamin Gasaway made oath to Colin Campbell, JP, 12 Mar. 1805. Rec: 29 Oct. 1805.

Page 267: Stephen Barton for $259 sold Thomas Milsap 172½ acres, being 1/2 tract granted John Tarwater by Wm. Moultrie 19 Nov. 1791, on Conneross Creek of Keowee River. Date: 10 Aug. 1803. Signed: Stephen (X) Barton. Wit: Josiah Foster, Daniel (X) Dulaney. Josiah Foster certified deed 11 Aug. 1803. No recording date.

Page 267: 20 Mar. 1805, William Fowler, Sr. to Shadrack Stevens for $150 for 138 acres on Beard's Creek of Rocky River, conveyed from John McCollough to Joel Calahan. Signed: William (X) Fowler, Lucy (X) Fowler. Wit: William McKay, Robert Fowler. Wm. McKay made oath to E. Brown Q.U., 10 Sep. 1805. Rec: 29 Oct. 1805.

Page 268: 16 Apr. 1805, Patrick Calhoun to David Stevenson for $30 for 121 acres bd. by Savannah River, John Moffett, David Stevenson, represented by plat dated 7 Nov. 1791. Wit: Alexander Sherrard, William Watson. Alexander Sherrard made oath to James Turner, J.P., 18 May 1803. Rec: 29 Oct. 1805.

Pages 268-269: 22 Feb. 1805, Enoch Fowler for $130 sold to William McKee 103 acres on Beard's Creek of Rocky River. Signed: Enoch Fowler, Sarah (X) Fowler. Wit: William McKay, James Moore. Wm. McKay made oath to E. Brown, Q.U., 10 Sep. 1805. Rec: 29 Oct. 1805.

Page 269: James Powell (called Sr. in oath) and Ales Powell, his wife, for love and affection they bear to beloved children, Sam Stevens

(Page 269 cont'd): and Polly Stevens, his wife, grant all household goods and property now in our possession, also all claims and demands we have against any person. Date: 19 Sep. 1805. Signed: James (X) Powell and Ales (X) Powell. Wit: David Murphree, Allen Powell. Allen Powell made oath to David Murphree, J. P., 26 Oct. 1805.
Rec: 30 Oct. 1805.

Pages 269-270: Timothy Toney for $400 sold Aaron Begerstaff 150 acres granted Zephaniah Roberts 17 Jul. 1784 by Wm. Moultrie. Date: 7 Nov. 1804. Wit: Josiah Carter, Wm. Edmondson. Sarah Toney, wife of Timothy Toney, released dower to Wm. Edmondson, J.Q., 7 Nov. 1804. Josiah Carter made oath to Wm. Edmondson, 7 Nov. 1804.
Rec: 29 Oct. 1805.

Page 270: James White, late of Pickensville, Pendleton Dist. for divers good causes appoint Moses Lister of Greenville Co., S. C. and James Lister of Ville (sic) of Pickensville, my lawful Attorney to ask and receive from my debtors in S. C. by bond, note or book account, all sums of money owed to me. Date: 25 Sep. 1805. Wit: Reuben Brock, Joshua Broyles. Both made oath to Aaron Broyles, J.P., 25 Sep. 1805.
Rec: 29 Oct. 1805.

Pages 270-271: Susannah Brown and Daniel Brown, Susannah (X) (her mark), Samuel Brown, Samuel Brown, Anna (X) Brown, Susannah Brown...(Note:.. this is as shown in record...BW) for $120 sold Joseph Smith 129 acres on 6 Mile Creek of Keowee River, granted John Waugh 7 Sep. 1795. Date: 14 Aug. 1805. Signed: Susannah (X) Brown, Samuel Brown, Daniel Brown, Anna (X) Brown. Wit: William Honey, James Fisher. William (X) Honey made oath to Thomas Hargiss, J.P., 21 Sep. 1805.
Rec: 29 Oct. 1805.

Page 271: 30 Sep. 1805, William Fortin of Pendleton Dist., to William Cawthon, Jr. of Franklin Co., Ga. for $100 for 100 acres on Cane Crk part of tract surveyed for James Garvis. Signed: William (X) Fortin. Wit: Jeremiah Cleveland, Tyra (X) Gentry. Jeremiah Cleveland made oath to Wm. Cleveland, J.P., 28 Oct. 1805.
Rec: 1 Nov. 1805.

Pages 271-272: William Crosby for $860 sold John Burns 150 acres on E. side of Keowee River, granted Crosby by Wm. Moultrie 14 Mar. 1785, recorded Bk. MMMM, p. 219. Date: 26 Sep. 1805. Wit: T. W. Farrar, A. Deal. Thomas W. Farrar made oath to M. Hammond, D.C, 22 Oct. 1806.
Rec: 22 Mar. 1806.

Page 272: 15 Dec. 1805, Moses B. Crafford is endebted to Walter Adair for $144.61 to be paid on or before 4 Feb. and made title to 180 ac. on Little River on E. side where Crafford now lives. Wit: Thos. Lamar and Jas. Mordah(?). Thomas Lamar made oath to John Adair, J.P., 27 Feb. 1806.
Rec: 1 Mar. 1806.

Pages 272-273: 30 Nov. 1805, Adam Sloan to Walter Adair for $70 for one sorrell horse on condition Adam Sloan repay Adair $35 on or before 25 Dec. 1806. Teste: Thomas Lamar.
Rec: 3 Dec. 1805.

Pages 273-274: Charles Gates, planter, for $1,000 dollars sold Allen Robinson tract of 2 surveys, one of 200 acres granted Charles Gates 21 Jan. 1780 on S. side of Saluda and 40 ac. taken out of 180 ac. tract, adjoining above 200 ac. Date: 23 Nov. 1805. Wit: Travis N. Hall, William Ellett. Anna (X) Gates, wife of Charles Gates, released dower to John McClure, JQ, 23 Nov. 1805. Travis N. Hall and William Ellett both made oath to John

(Pages 273-274 cont'd): McClure, 23 Nov. 1805. Rec: 14 Jan. 1806.

Page 274: Francis Beard for $100 sold John Hendrix a mare and colt, 3 cows and calves, all household furniture. Date: 4 Jan. 1806. Signed: Francis (X) Beard. Wit: John Hendricks, J. W. Nukles. John Hendrix made oath to John Willson, 4 Jan. 1806. Rec: 10 Jan. 1806.

Page 274: James Tuffnell has given to Clarymond Willson 2 cows and calves, bed and furniture, kitchen utinsels, one mare, saddle and bridle, 600 "slay nine head" of geese, etc., because she has always behaved herself well and has work (sic) faithfull for me. Date: 11 Mar. 1805. Wit: Jacob Capehart, Adam Rogers. Jacob Capehart made oath to Saml. Houston, J.P., 15 Aug. 1805. Rec: 4 Jan. 1806.

Page 275: Ludwick Earnest for $400 sold Col. John Brown 150 acres on 23 Mile Creek of Savannah River, bd. William Hamby, Charles Willson, granted Samuel Norwood 15 Oct. 1784 (no date). Signed: Leadwick Earnest. Wit: Thompson Sloan, Wm. Brown. William Brown made oath to Samuel C. Duff, J.P., 24 Dec. 1805. Rec: 25 Dec. 1805.

Page 275-276: Francis Genkins for $500 sold Thomas Harbin 175 acres on S. side of Beaver Creek of Toogalow River, bd. Genkins and Samuel Hawkins, granted Samuel Watt by Chas. Pinckney 7 Jan. 1786, conveyed by Watt to John Gibson, then by Gibson to Genkins. Date: 25 Feb. 1806. Signed: Frans. Jenkins. Wit: John Clayton, Thomas Harbin, Jr. John Clayton made oath to Wm. Cleveland, J.P., 22 Mar. 1806. Rec: 24 Mar. 1806.
See Bk. N, p. 256, W. C. Gibson to heirs of Thos. Harbin, dec'd.

Page 276: Abbeville Dist., James Curry appoints Henry Houston of St. (State) and County aforesaid, my lawful attorney to make good and sufficient titles to claim of half of tract of 200 acres on Cane Creek where John Adair, Esq. now lives, made over by Francis Miller to John Adair and James Curry as Tennants in Common. Date: 18 Nov. 1805. Wit: Francis Walker, William Willson. (No oath). Rec: 27 Nov. 1805.

Page 276: John Davidson of Mecklenburg Co., N. C. and Town of Charlotte, lawful attorney of William Davidson and Andrew Davidson, appoint Samuel Cherry of Pendleton Dist....my true and lawful attorney to sell and dispose of all our parts of 835 acres in Pendleton Dist. on 23 Mile Creek of the Savannah River, granted to the heirs of James Davidson, deceased......and to authorize our sd. attorney to pay and satisfy James Gillison(?) the sum of $55 which we allowed him for finding and showing sd. land. Date: 22 Nov. 1805. Wit: A. Lawhon, William Taylor. Archibald Lawhon made oath to M. Hammond, D.C., 12 Apr. 1806. No recording date.

Page 277: James Prichard for $50 sold Samuel Taylor 340 acres granted William Prichard, bd. by Dobson Reese, James Sims, James Griffen and Col. Earle. Date: 15 Feb. 1805. Wit: David Sloan, David Files. (No oath). Rec: 12 Apr. 1806.

Page 277: John Boyd, Sr. for natural affection for son, Ephraim Boyd, give him one negro man named Harry, colts, cattle, hogs, plantation tools and household furniture. Date: 12 Aug. 1805. Wit: James Jett and George Boyd. James Jett made oath to Samuel C. Duff, J.P., 12 Aug. 1805. Rec: 3 Jan. 1806.

Pages 277-278: Thomas Standridge for $250 sold James Cav-

(Pages 277-278 cont'd): ender 354 acres where Standridge now lives on NW branch of Choestoe Creek of Toogalow River, granted Joshua Lee by Thos. Pinckney, recorded Bk. NNNN, p. 68. Date: 20 Jan. 1798. Wit: Thos. Russell and Jean (X) Henery. Thomas Russell made oath to John Barton, J.P., 16 Aug. 1800. Rec: 17 Aug. 1805.

Page 278: Mark Castleberry for $40 sold Adam Davis 54 acres part of tract granted Robert Mayfield, which part of tract being land of John McMahan, 12 Oct. 1797. Date: 2 Dec. 1797. Wit: Jonathan Gibbs and John (X) Holcom. Jonathan Gibbs made oath to James Turner, J.P., 28 Dec. 1805. Rec: 7 Feb. 1806.

Page 279: Samuel and James Black for $500 sold Adam Davis 390 acres on Great Generostee of the Savannah River, surveyed by Edw. T. McClure D.S., part of tract granted Eleanor Black by Wm. Moultrie 17 Jun. 1785. Date: 21 ___ 1805. Wit: James Brice, Robert Davis, James Turner, J. P. Isabell Black and Agnes Black, wives of Samuel and James Black, released dower to E. Browne, Q.U., 21 Oct. 1805. Signed: Isbell (X) Black, Nancy Black. No oath. Rec: 7 Feb. 1806.

Pages 279-280: 6 Mar. 1806, Daniel Bates to Jacob Holland for $100 sold 30 acres on both sides of Big Beaverdam Creek bd. by Holland. Wit: Benjamin Holland and William Bates. Benjamin Holland made oath to William Cleveland, 8 Mar. 1806. Rec: 7 Feb. 1806.

Page 280: Henry D. Reese for $550 sold Ephraim Robinson a negro man named Moses. Date: 2 Jan. 1806. Signed: H. Dobson Reese. Wit: Samuel H. Dickson and John Dickson. Capt. John Dickson made oath to M. Hammond, D.C., 2 Feb. 1806. Rec: 2 Feb. 1806.

Pages 280-281: Reuben Reed for $200 sold Benjamin Bourland 70 acres on Wolf Creek of 12 Mile River, bd by line made by William Benson and William Marchbanks and Reuben Reed. Date: 29 Oct. 1804. Signed: Reuben (X) Reed. Wit: Abner Smith, Aron (X) Murphree. Aaron Murphree made oath to David Murphree, J.P., 22 Feb. 1806. Rec: 3 Mar. 1806.

Page 281: Daniel Southerland for $150 sold Samuel Earle 125 acres part of survey granted to Archelous(?) Reynolds 5 Dec. 1803. Date: 26 Aug. 1805. Wit: Burt (Bartemous in oath) Reynolds, A. Lawhon, Thos. Gibson. Archibald Lawhon made oath to M. Hammond, D.C., 23 Apr. 1806. Rec: 23 Feb. 1806.

Pages 281-282: James Broaster for $250 sold James Polick 227 acres, part of grant to James Doherty 3 Apr. 1786, recorded Bk. JJJJ, p. 200, by Wm. Moultrie, on 26 Mile Creek of Savannah River, bd. on ENE by William Laughlin, John Brouster, Jr., John Hunter, on W. by Jonathan Smith. Date 8 Feb. 1801. Wit: John Laughlin, Samuel Broaster. John Laughlin made oath to Samuel Houston, J.P., 1 Feb. 1806. Rec: 3 Feb. 1806.

Page 282: John Gibson for $729 sold Samuel Earle 243 acres where Gibson now lives, on S. fork of Beaverdam, bd. Armstead Barry. Date: 23 Sep. 1805. Wit: A. Lawhon, William Davis, Fredrick Moss. Fredrick Moss made oath to H. McCray, J.P., 23 Apr. 1805. Elizabeth (X) Gibson, wife of John Gibson, released dower to John Verner, Q.U., 23 Dec. 1805. Rec: 23 Feb. 1806.

Page 282:	George Hays of Jackson Co., Ga. for $300 sold James Carson of Pendleton Dist., 200 acres (except 28 acres which was cut off from original survey) granted George Kilson by Benj. Guerard on W. side of 18 Mile Creek of Keowee River. Date: 13 Feb. 1806. Wit: John Hays and John Burns. John Hays made oath to M. Hammond, D.C. Sarah (X) Hays released dower to John Taylor, Q.U., 13 Feb. 1806. Rec: 17 Feb. 1806.

Pages 283-284:	John Hamilton, Jr. and Martha Hamilton for $220 sold Zachariah Taliaferro 200 acres on 23 Mile Creek, part of tract granted Robert Pickens by Thos. Pinckney, bd. Robert Pickens, Zachariah Taliaferro, Samuel Barr, Francis Posey, devisees of James Foster, dec'd. Date: 7 Sep. 1805. Wit: Robert Macklin White, James White. Martha (X) Hamilton, wife of John Hamilton released dower to E. Browne, Q.U., 21 Oct. 1805. Robert Maclin White made oath to E. Browne, 22 Oct. 1805. Rec: 21 Mar. 1806.

Pages 284-285:	Daniel Shipp for $250 sold Ritter Smith 160 acres on 23 Mile Creek, granted Joseph Jenkins by Wm. Moultrie 4 Dec. 1786. Date: 11 Nov. 1805. Wit: James C. Griffen, David Wadkins. James C. Griffen, Esq. made oath to M. Hammond, D.C., 28 Apr. 1806. Rec: 28 Apr. 1806.

Page 285:	David Anderson of Laurens Dist., S. C. for $600 sold George Anderson of Pendleton Dist. 400 acres on Generostee Creek, bd. Joshua Saxon, J. Dalrymple. Date: 23 May 1804. Wit: ___ Adams, Wm. Grimes (?), Jno. Wait(?).......Laurens Dist., John Wait(?) made oath to Lewis Greaves (?), J.P., 24 May 1804. Rec: 15 Feb. 1806.

Pages 285-286:	Bennet Aden, planter, for $150 sold Joseph Land 100 acres on N. side of Keowee River, part of tract granted James Jordan by Wm. Moultrie. Date: 17 Aug. 1801. Signed: Bennet Aden, Martha Aden. Wit: John Reed, Hardy Owens. Hardy Owens made oath to Samuel H. Dickson, J.P., 9 Mar. 1802. Rec: 15 Feb. 1806.

Page 286:	12 Feb. 1806, Robert Rainwater binds his son, Hartgraves(?) Rainwater, age 9 years, to James Tuffnell, until he is 21 years of age ____ (cannot read this), in farming line and give the child ____ schooling, suit of clothes, a young horse and saddle and treat child as if he was his own. Signed: Robert (X) Rainwater, James Tuffnell. Wit: James C. Griffen, Edwd. Doyle. Robert Rainwater and James Tuffnell acknowledged deed to James Griffen, J.P., 12 Feb. 1806. Rec: 12 Feb. 1806.

Pages 282-287:	21 May 1804, William Gillaspie of Bunckim (sic) Co., N.C. to Robert Duff of Pendleton Dist., for $165 for 150 acres bd. by Col. Brown, Boyd and Samuel C. Duff. Wit: Samuel C. Duff, John McCrosky and James Duff. James Duff made oath to Samuel C. Duff, J.P., 10 Oct.1805. Rec: 10 May 1806.

Page 287:	Henry Sims, Sr. to William Richard for $500 _____ (cannot read) (Bond of Debt ?), for one negro woman named Milly about 20 years of age _____. Date: 3 Feb. ___. Wit: William McFarland, David Files. David Files made oath to M. Hammond, D.C., 12 Feb. 1806. Rec: 12 Feb. 1806.

Pages 287-288:	John McKinzie to Duncan McKinzie a horse & mare for $200. Date: 2 Feb. 1805. Wit: Archd. Lawhon who made oath to M. Hammond, DC on 8 May 1806. Rec: 8 May 1806.

Page 288:   William Beazley for $305 sold Rev. Andrew
                            Brown 100 acres granted John Rodgers by
                            Chas. Pinckney 21 Feb. 1792, recorded Bk.
D, no. 5, p. 484(?), on Cane Creek of Keowee River. Date: 18 Jan. 180_.
Signed: William (X) Beazley. Wit: Thomas Russel, William Russel. Thomas
Russel made oath to Jno. Adair, J.P., 22 Jan. 1806.
Rec: 19 Feb. 1806.

Pages 288-289:   William Lesley of Abbeville Dist. for $300
                            sold to John Sailors of Pendleton Dist.,
                            part of tract granted Matthew Wilson(?) on
5 May 1792 on W. side of Wilson's Creek, bd. on NW by William Wilson.
Date: 18 Dec. 1801. Wit: Robert C. Gordon and Andrew ____(?). (Plat).
Robert C. Gordon made oath to Samuel Watt, J.P., _____.
Rec: 1 Nov. 1805.

Page 289:   (Cannot read).....mentions Ephraim Boyd.
                            Signed: Solomon White. Wit: John Boyd, Sr.
                            and John Langston. John Boyd made oath to
Samuel C. Duff, 17 Aug. 1805.
Rec: 3 Jan. 1806.

Page 290:   4 Nov. 1805, David Guest to Daniel Bates
                            for £ 100 stg. for 180 acres on Togalow
                            River, excepting 1 acre to be laid off as
a grave yard, part of tract granted William Guest, 3 Mar. 1788, bd. by
Jacob Holland. Wit: Jacob Holland and William Bates. Jacob Holland made
oath to Wm. Cleveland, J.P., 18 Feb. 1806.
Rec: 10 Mar. 1806.

Page 290:   Richard Stevens of the City of Baltimore,
                            Mariner, appoint my friend, Lewis Daniel
                            Martin, of Pendleton Dist.,my lawful attor-
ney to sell or rent at his discretion 644 acres in Old 96 Dist. now Pendleton, on Conneross Creek of Keowee River, recorded Vol. XIX, p. 219.
Date: 19 Nov. 1803. Wit: Thos. Hunter, Joseph Taylor.
Rec: 10 Mar. 1806. (No oath).

Page 291:   Joshua Saxon for $8,000 sold James Burris
                            300 acres, bd. by Isaac Gatlin(?), John
                            Dernley, Saxon, part of tract granted Sax-
on by Wm. Moultrie, recorded Bk. LLL, p. 445; also 200 acres, part of
tract granted James M_____ by Thos. Pinckney, 7 Apr. 1788, conveyed to
Peter Keys, Esq., from Keys to Saxon, 25 Dec. 1799. Date: 21 Jan. 1801.
Wit: George Chandler, Zadick (X) Chambler, Langston Drew. Sally (X) Saxon, wife of Joshua Saxon, released dower to Joshua Saxon, J.Q., 17 Feb.
1801. Zaddock Shambler made oath to Peter Keys, J.P., 18 Nov. 1802.
Rec: 15 Feb. 1806.

Pages 291-292:   John Dickson for $550 sold James Rodgers
                            200 acres on Cuffy Creek on N. side of 23
                            Mile Creek of Savannah River, granted to
William Dunlap, 6 Feb. 1786, conveyed to Hugh Rodgers, Sr., late of Pen-
dleton Dist., dec'd., and was conveyed by Legatees of Hugh Rodgers to
Hugh Rodgers, Jr., and by him to John Dickson. Date: 24 Jan. 1806. Wit:
Nicholas Bishop, Joshua Camp, Jesse (X) Jones. Joshua Camp made oath to
M. Hammond, D.C., 27 Jan. 1806.
Rec: 27 Jan. 1806.

Page 292:   William Robinson in consideration of Rich-
                            ard Robinsin being my security for $110 to
                            Steele & Wood, sell to Richard Robinson one
waggon and geers, 4 horses, 3 featherbeds and furniture, cows and sows,
plantation tools, all corn and fodder I have at this time. Date: 6 Feb.
1806. Wit: Wm. Hamilton, Ephm. Robinson. William Hamilton made oath to M.
Hammond, D.C. 20 May 1806.
Rec: 20 May 1806.

Pages 293-294:   James Edmondson, Jr. by bond of obligation
                            dated: 17 Sep. 1805 to James White for.....

(Pages 293-294 cont'd): $1,098.16 and deliver the following property: horses, cows and calves, one 32 saw (sic) cotton gin, one 24 saw cotton gin, feather beds and furniture, carpenter tools, all corn on my tract where James Edmondson, Jr. now lives. Date: 17 Sep. 1805. Wit: James Willson, who made oath to Samuel C. Duff, J.P., 12 Mar. 1806.
Rec: 15 Mar. 1806.

Page 294: James Allison for $48 sold Isaac Cox 130 acres on Little Creek of Saluda River, bd. by Robert Kay, Thomas Mattison, Wm. Williamson, James Allison, Isaac Cox and Francis Clinkscales. Date: __ 1803. Wit: Wm. Clinkscales, Wm. (X) Cox. William Clinkscales made oath to George Grace, J.Q., 15 Mar. 1806. Sarah (X) Allison released dower to George Grace, 17 Mar. 1806. Signed: Sary (X) Allison.
Rec: 20 Mar. 1806.

Page 295: 5 Jan. 17__(?) ____ (cannot read)____ 900 (?) acres in Washington Dist. on Big Generostee. Signed: Henry Long. (Cannot read witnesses of oath. Index says Henry Long to Lesley Thomas...BW)

Pages 295-296: (Cannot read)_____ William Henry to Samuel Taylor _____...mentions Samuel Lovingood. Date: 30 Jan. 1806. Wit: Samuel Cherry, A. Lawhon. Archibald Lawhon made oath to M. Hammond, D.C., 26 May 1806. Rec: 26 May 1806.

Page 296: Bayly Anderson of Warren Co., Ky. for good causes and considerations, appoint James Jett of Pendleton Co., S. C. my lawful attorney to prosecute any suits in Law of Equity, and to recover sums of money or receive title for lands. Date: 3 Oct. 1797. Signed: Bayley Anderson......Warren Co., Ky. October Court, 1793, Bailey Anderson acknowledged power of Attorney to Will Chaplin, C.C., 3 Oct. 1797. James Garrard, Gov. of the Commonwealth of Ky. (certifies?) William Chapline is Clerk of Court of Warren Co., signed at Frankfort, 6 Dec. 1801. Harry Toulmin, Secretary.
Rec: 25 May 1806.

Pages 296-297: Malechi Ewell has purchased land whereon Thomas Garner now lives with two stills and stands for $300 part paid in hand, balance of $180 for which I give my notes, payable 31 Oct. 1807. Date: 6 Jul. 1805. Wit: P. H. May, Wm. Pace(?).
Rec: 10 Mar. 1806.

Page 297: ____ 1804, James Duff to Samuel C. Duff for £ 95 stg. for 320 acres on both sides of George's Creek of Saluda River. Signed: James Duff, Sr. Wit: Thomas Henderson, James Duff, Robert Duff. James Duff made oath to John McClure, J.Q, 25 Feb. 1806.
Rec: 10 Mar. 1806.

Page 298: William Burton of Edgefield Dist., S.C. for $30 sold to Joseph Smith of Pendleton Dist. 140 acres on 6 Mile Creek of Keowee River, bd. by Widow Brown. Date: 7 Jan. 1805. Wit: Henry Gasaway, Mary (X) Cary, and Elijah Hutchinson. Henry Gasaway made oath he saw Wm. Burton of Abbeville Dist. sign deed to Samuel H. Dickson, J.P., 12 Mar. 1805.
Rec: 6 Feb. 1806.

Page 298: Joel Moody for $50 sold Benjamin Bourland 150 acres on Wolf Creek of 12 Mile River, part of 1000 acres granted Reuben Reed on 2 Jul. ____ by Chas. Pinckney, bd. by William Lemons, John Tatom. Date: 6 Aug. 1804. Wit: Willm. Marchbanks, Joseph (X) Burk. William Marchbanks made oath to David Murphree, J.P., 18 Oct. 1804.
Rec: 3 Mar. 1806.

Pages 298-299: Henry Sims for $300 sold James C. Griffen planter, a negro woman named Rose about 28 years of age. Date: 23 Mar. 1804. Wit: John Robinson, William McGuffin. (No oath). Rec: 14 Mar. 1806.

Page 299: Joel Moody, Sr. for $20 sold Benjamin Bourland 15 acres on Wolf Creek of 12 Mile River, part of 28 acres bd. by Benton, William Marchbanks, and bank of Wolf Creek. Date: 15 Jan. 1802. Wit: Powel Regans and William Cannon, Jr. William Cannon made oath to David Murphree, J.P. 22 Feb. 1806. Rec: 3 Mar. 1806.

Page 299: 16 Dec. 1803, Rec'd of Joseph Taylor $300 in full for 1 negro girl named Lucy. Signed: Saml. Tate. Wit: David Sloan, Jr. Rec: 16 Dec. 1805.

Pages 299-300: Enoch Garner for $428 sold Joel Holbert 130 acres on Big Creek, part of 2 tracts: one granted John Nicholson, the other granted John Burdine. Date: 29 Sep. 1798. Wit: William Holbert, Edmond Lindsey, Jno. Holbert. John Holbert made oath to William Hall, J.P., 25 Jan. 1800. Winney (X) Garner, wife of Enoch Garner, released dower to John Willson, Q.U., 17 Apr. 1800. Rec: 4 Mar. 1806.

Pages 300-301: Benjamin Farmer for $300 sold Henry Cobb 100 acres on SW side of Saluda River, bd. Rachel Cobb. Date: 23 Sep. 1803. Signed: Benjamin (X) Farmer. Wit: John Holbert, Samuel Cobb. Samuel Cobb made oath to James Wilbourn, Q.U. 1 Mar. 1806. Rec: 4 Mar. 1806.

Pages 301-302: Thomas Garner for $100 sold Joel Holbert 19 acres on Big Creek of Saluda River, part of 2 surveys. Date: 7 Sep. 1797. (Plat). Wit: James (X) Eson, William Bell, Wm. Garner. James Eson made oath to Wm. Hall, J.P., 25 Jan. 1800. Rec: 4 Mar. 1806.

Page 302: William Bell for $30 sold Joel Holbert 15 acres on Big Creek of Saluda River, part of 125 Acres granted Bell 4 Feb. 1799, recorded Bk. T, no. 5, p. 41. Date: 27 Sep. 1790. Wit: James (X) Eson, Benjamin Clarity, Harper Garner. James Eason made oath to William Hall, JP, 25 Jan. 1800. Rec: 4 Mar. 1806.

Pages 302-303: John Harper for $100 sold John Holbert 61 acres on N. side of Big Creek of Saluda River. Wit: Edward Harper, Samuel Cobb. Edward Harper made oath to E. Browne, J.Q, 19 Jun. 1802. Rec: 4 Mar. 1806.

Page 303: I certify that James _____ (cannot read; mentions Mathew Dickson judged some of my family for cutting down ____ and request of me to have recorded.) I certify this to the Clerk of Pendleton Court, 3 May 1806. Signed: James Hembree. Rec: 1 Jun. 1806.

Page 303: Henry Gasaway for $100 sold John Tours (or Towers in oath) 100 acres on 6 Mile Creek of Keowee River, bd. by Widow Brown. Date: 2 Feb. 1805. Signed: Henry Gasaway, Rachel Gasaway. Wit: Joseph Smith, Judah (X) Hudson. Joseph Smith made oath to Henry Burch, J.Q., 19 Oct. 1805. Rec: 24 Mar. 1806.

page 304:   Hezekiah Posey for $75 sold Joseph Ducks-
                             worth 130 acres on Little Beaverdam Creek,
                             granted John Breavert, 4 Feb. 1792, record-
ed Bk. B, no. 5, p. 131. Date: 15 Mar. 1806. Wit: Wm. (X) Rodgers and
Barnabus (X) Fair, Sarah (X) Rodgers. (No oath).
Rec: 16 Apr. 1806.

Page 304:   Isaac West of Greenville Dist. for Ł 70 stg
                             sold to Richard Robinson of Pendleton Dist.
                             100 acres, part of survey granted to Andrew
Roe by Chas. Pinckney, on both sides of 23 Mile Creek on N. side of road
which leads from Pendleton Courthouse, by James Griffen to 23 Mile Creek
and by Topher Tanner. Date: 10 Aug. 1805. Wit: James C. Griffen, John Agnew. John Agnew made oath to James C. Griffen, J.P., 10 Aug. 1805.
Rec: 29 Mar. 1806.

Pages 304-305:   Benjamin Bourland for $350 sold Rusell Can-
                             non parts of tracts on Wolf Creek, of 12
                             Mile River, bd. by Willie Benson, William
Marchbanks, Reuben Reed and John Tatum. Date: 3 Aug. 1805. Wit: Wm. Cannon, James Cannon. Agnes (X) Bourland released dower to John McClure,JQ,
31 Aug. 1805. William Cannon made oath to John McClure, 31 Aug. 1803.
Rec: 25 Mar. 1806.

Pages 305-306:   Washington Dist., 2 Jan. 1797, Robert Max-
                             well, Sheriff of Washington Dist. to Am-
                             brose Hudgens, Sr. of Pendleton Co........
James Milwee was seized of 200 acres, bd. on SW by Charles Pitts, SE by
James Ross, NE and NW by Gen. Robert Anderson, granted by Benj. Guerard
in 1784....Robert King commenced suit against James Millwee for assault
and battery.....all goods, chattels, lands of Millwee be levied for Ł 4
16 sh., Robert Maxwell, Sheriff on 7 Mar. last sold to Ambrose Hudgens as
highest bidder for Ł 30. Wit: James Millwee, Margaret (X) Mann.   James
Millwee made oath to Samuel Houston, J.P., 20 Mar. 1806.
Rec: 22 Mar. 1806.

Pages 306-307:   Ambrose Hudgens for Ł 10 sold to Ambrose
                             Millwee 200 acres on Big Beaverdam Creek
                             of Savannah River, bd. SE by James Ross,
SW by Charles Pitts, NW by Gen. Robert Anderson, granted James Millwee
by Benj. Guerard 1785, and bought at public sale 2 Jan. 1797. Date: 2
Jan. 1797. Wit: Rt. Maxwell, Margaret (X) Mann, Henry (X) Green. Henry
Green made oath to Wm. Millwee, J.P., 11 Dec. 1797.
Rec: 25 Mar. 1806.

Page 307:   Henry Gasaway for $100 sold William Honea
                             100 acres on 6 Mile Creek of Keowee River,
                             bd. Honea, Hutson, Towers, Smith. (Cannot
read date). Signed: Henry Gasaway, Rachel (X) Gasaway. Wit: Charles Bradley, Abner Honea. Abner Honea made oath to James Wilbourn, J.P., 5 Mar.
1805.
Rec: 24 Mar. 1806.

Pages 307-308:   Andrew Roe for Ł 60 sold John Lindley 73
                             acres, part of 333 acres granted Roe by
                             Chas. Pinckney, on each side of 23 Mile Crk
the part conveyed on N. side of Creek. Date: 10 Aug. 1805. Wit: James C.
Griffen, John Agnew. John Agnew made oath to James C. Griffen, J.P., 10
Aug. 1805. Rec: 29 Mar. 1806.

Pages 308-309:   John Jones by bond of obligation 24 Jan.
                             1806 to Messrs. Steele & Wood, Merchants,
                             for $254, sold 72 acres on 26 Mile Creek,
bd. by Lewis Jones, John Hunnicutt, Gen. Anderson, Mr. Reese, granted to
Sophia Case. Date: 24 Jan. 1806. Signed: John (X) Jones. Wit: J. Miller,
Jesse (X) Jones. John Miller made oath to M. Hammond, D.C., 14 Jun. 1806.
Rec: 14 Jun. 1806.

Pages 309-310:   Randolph Hunnicutt by bond of security, 22
                             Feb. 1806, with William Hunnicutt as secur-

(Pages 309-310 cont'd): ity, to Messrs. Steele and Wood, Merchants, for $90.76 sold 200 acres on 26 Mile Creek of Savannah River, granted Thomas Entrican. Date: 22 Feb. 1806. Wit: J. Miller, Joseph B. Earle. John Miller made oath to M. Hammond, D.C., 14 Jun. 1806. Rec: 14 Jun. 1806.

Page 310: Luke Smith of Barron Co., Ky. for $400 sold Joel Swinney of Pendleton Dist., 200 acres on Little Beaverdam Creek of Toogalow River including part of the Harican(?) ground, NE of Dr. Fredrick Sunn, SE of Sylvanus(?), James Willson, originally granted John Martin 7 Aug. 1786 by Wm. Moultrie. Date: 3 Mar. 1806. Wit: William (X) Brian, John (X) Brian. John Brian made oath to J. Stribling, Q.U., 22 Mar. 1806. Rec: 7 Aug. 1806.

Pages 310-311: 2 Jan. 1806, Nathaniel Robinson for $200 sold John Duncan 200 acres granted James Scott by Wm. Moultrie 6 Jan. 1785, recorded Bk. BBBB, p. 276, on S. Broadaway of Savannah River. Wit: Anderson Duncan, Wm. Johnston. Elizabeth (X) Robinson, wife of Nathaniel Robinson, released dower to E. Browne, Q.U., 3 Jan. 1806. William Johnston made oath to E. Browne, 3 Jan. 1806. Rec: 25 Mar. 1806.

Pages 311-312: Henry Macwhorter for $600 sold Nathaniel Davis 575 acres on Deep Creek of Seneca River, bd. by John Hammon, part of a tract granted Edward McClure for 640 acres, 16 Jul. 1784 by Benj. Guerard. Date: 5 Dec. 1805. Wit: Ambrose (X) Barnett, Samson (X) Barnett, William (X) Gravet. Jane McWhorter, wife of Henry McWhorter, released dower to J. Stribling, Q.U., 4 Jan. 1806. Ambrose Barnett made oath to Jas. C. Griffen, J.P., 24 Mar. 1806. Rec: 24 Mar. 1806.

Page 312: James Slater for $100 sold William Brevart tract where Brevart now lives on both sides of Little River, N. fork of Keowee River, granted Thomas Fields, bd. Fields and Slater. Date: 9 Oct. 1805. Wit: Joshua Robins, John (X) Putteet. John Putteet made oath to W. Nicholson, J.P., 24 Feb. 1806. Rec: 26 Mar. 1806.

Pages 313-314: David Kelton for $350 sold John C. Dickson 180½ acres, part of 2 tracts: one of 102 acres, part of tract granted Thomas Lofton, by Wm. Moultrie, the other of 86½ acres, part of tract granted Henry Childs, on 5 Mile Creek of 18 Mile Creek of Keowee River, bd. Samuel Lofton, Sr. Date: ___ Jan. 1806. Wit: Edward Camp, Stephen Spruil. Esther Kelton, wife of David Kelton, released dower to John Willson, Q.U., 3 Mar. 1806. Edward Camp made oath to John Willson, 14 Apr. 1806. Rec: 20 Apr. 1806.

Page 314: John Gibson for $720 sold Armstead Barry 335 acres on S. Beaverdam Creek of Togalow River, bd. McKinzie, part of tract granted John Holcum by Chas. Pinckney, 7 Jan. 1788, conveyed to John Gibson, the other part granted Samuel Watt by Chas. Pinckney, 7 Jan. 1788 and conveyed to Gibson. Date: 10 May 1804. Wit: W. T. Barry, Fredrick Moss. Fredrick Moss made oath to William Cleveland, J.P., 12 May 1804. Elizabeth (X) Gibson, wife of John Gibson, released dower to John Verner, J.Q. 23 Dec. 1805. Rec: 31 Mar. 1806.

Pages 314-315: 7 May 1805, Sion (later appears to be Leon) Sanders to William Sanders for $360 for 177 acres on N. side of Little River, bd. Robert Craven, granted Thomas Wafer, 4 Feb. 1799, by Edwd. Rutledge. Signed: Leon (X) Sanders. Wit: George Tubb, Thos. Robertson. Thomas Robinson made oath to W. Nicholson, J.P., 29 Oct. 1805. Rec: 25 Mar. 1806.

Pages 315-316: 16 Oct. 1804, Henry M. Wood, Esq., late Sheriff of Washington Dist., to John Henry Stevelee, Merchant of Burk Co., N. C. .... Robert Looney was seized of 200 acres on Cane Creek of Toogalow River, bd. John Humphrey, granted 21 Jan. 1785 by Benj. Guerard.....John Henry Stevelee obtained judgement in Court of Common Pleas in Washington Dist. on 12 Apr. 1798 against Looney for $394.....all goods and chattels and lands of Looney sold at public auction to Stevelee for $58.59. Date: 16 Oct. 1804. Wit: W. Thompson, F. Stevelee. Fredrick Stevelee made oath to M. Hammond, D.C., 22 Mar. 1806.
Rec: 22 Mar. 1806.

Pages 316-317: Hezekiah Davis for $51 sold Jesse Davis 45 acres, part of a tract granted John Gabriel where John Heater now lives. Date: 16 Nov. 1805. Wit: Jesse Browne, George Stevenson. George Stevenson made oath to Jonathan Gibbs, J.P., 8 Mar. 1806.
Rec: 24 Mar. 1806.

Page 317: Henry Houston of Abbeville Dist., for $250 sold Walter Adair of Pendleton Dist., part of 244 acres granted Francis Miller, where John Adair, Sr. now lives, on both sides of Cane Creek of the Keowee River, bd. SW by Capt. David Sloan, NE by John Adair and James Curry and Richard Fowler. Date: 23 Nov. 1805. Wit: John Bell, Levi Robbins. Levi Robbins made oath to Jno. Adair, J.P., 10 Mar. 1806.
Rec: 8 Apr. 1806.

Pages 317-318: Richard and John Bullock for $100 sold to Ezekiel Potts 416 acres on fork of Chauga, known as Bone Camp Creek. Date: _ Apr. 1802. Signed: Richard Bullock, John (X) Bullock. Wit: John (X) Potts, Obadiah Fowler. John Potts made oath to Jas. Starrett, J.P., 22 Mar. 1806.
Rec: 24 Mar. 1806.

Page 318: 18 Apr. 1803, Jesse Nevil to George Potts for $200 for 100 acres bd. by land surveyed for William Sloan, 22 Oct. 1797, now deeded to George Potts by Ezekiel Potts, part of 300 acres granted Jesse Nevil, 19 Feb. 1791, bd. by Ezekiel Potts, Nevil and Sloan ...."In witness whereof the sd. Ezekiel Potts has set his name". Ezekiel Potts: signed. Wit: John Pound, Jesse Nevil. John Pound made oath to Jas. Starrett, J.P., 27 Jun. 1803. Rec: 24 Mar. 1806.

Pages 318-319: 18 Apr. 1803, Ezekiel Potts to George Potts for $200 for 50 acres, bd. Fields Prewitt, Anthony Griffen, on N. side of Cane Creek, part of tract surveyed for William Sloan, 22 Oct. 1791. (This deed was signed by Jesse Nevil.) Wit: John Pounds, Ezekiel Potts. Ezekiel Potts made oath to James Starrett, J.P., 27 Jun. 1803.
Rec: 24 Mar. 1806.

Pages 319-320: Samuel Taylor for $60 sold to James Dickson 100 acres on S. fork of Garvin's Crk. of 23 Mile River, bd. Major Michael Dickson, Samuel Taylor, Henry Dobson Reese, part of tract granted William Prichard in 1784 by Benj. Guerard. Date: 12 Apr. 1806. Wit: M. Hammond, J. Miller. John Miller made oath to M. Hammond, D.C., 20 Jun. 1806.
Rec: 20 Jun. 1806.

Page 320: Henry Dobson Reese for $300 sold to John and James Dickson 200 acres on Garvin's Creek of 23 Mile River on the Savannah River, bd. John Dickson, part of tract sold by James Martin to Thomas Reese. Date: 14 Apr. 1806. Wit: John Willson, Ephm. Robinson. John Willson, Esq. made oath to Saml. H. Dickson, J.P., 14 Apr. 1806. Rebecca Reese, wife of Henry Dobson Reese, released dower to John Willson, Q.U., 14 Apr.1806. Signed: Beckey E. Reese.
Rec: 21 Apr. 1806.

(Pages 320-321 cont'd): son 342 acres on Coxes Creek of Rocky River, bd. Millwee, Samuel Saxon, granted Jesse Wood; also 65 acres on Coxes Creek, part of 200 acres granted Elijah Williamson, bd. N. by Thos. Norwood, S. by Moses Anderson, W. by William Townsend, part of 200 acres granted Elizabeth Rigs, adj. Thomas Martin & William Townsend. Date: 22 Mar. 1806. Wit: John George, D. Hammond. Dudley Hammond made oath to (No J.P.) 22 Mar. 1806. Rec: 25 Mar. 1806.

Pages 321-322: William McClure for $300 sold John Hammond, now of this State and Dist., 112 acres on Deep Creek of Seneca River, part of tract granted Edward Tell McClure, conveyed from him to Josiah McClure(?) and from him to William McClure. Date: _ Aug. 1804. Wit: Henry McWhorter and Noah (X) Hammond. Noah Hammond made oath to J. Stribling, Q.U., 28 Oct. 1804. Mary McClure, wife of William McClure, released dower to Obadiah Trimmier, Q.U., 13 Oct. 1804. Rec: 25 Mar. 1806.

Page 322: 10 Sep. 1805. William Satter to Gideon Shockley for $100 for 100 acres on E. side of the Savannah River, bd. by Thomas Shockley, Sr. and Thomas Shockley, Jr., part of 2 tracts, granted Shelby Glenn and William Love. Signed: William Sarter. Wit: Peter Sarter, James Shockley. Peter Sarter made oath to James Tate, Q.U., 9 Sep. 1805. Delilah(X) Satter, wife of William Satter, released dower to James Tate, 7 Sep. 1805. Rec: 24 Mar. 1806.

Pages 322-323: I assign my right and title of within plat and grant to Mr. Alexander Barran for value received, 20 Jan. 1801. Signed: James Rutherford. Teste: Alexander Barran, Jr., who made oath to James Tate, Q.U., 9 Feb. 1805. Rec: 12 Jan. 1806.

Page 323: James Doran for $300 sold Samuel Torbet___ acres on Chauga Creek of Toogalow River, part of 2 tracts: one granted Mary Doran, the other to Jesse Willson. Date: 24 Feb. 1806. Wit: William Torbert and Andrew Brown and Jno. Barton. Wm. Torbert made oath to John Barton, J.P. (no date). Rec: 25 Mar. 1806.

Pages 323-324: 24 Mar. 1795, William Ross of Washington Dist. to Henry Ruckelsmer(?) for £ 27 stg. for 105 acres on George's Creek of Saluda River, where Rucklemen(?) now lives, bd. by Ross, William Jameson, Ruckelsmer(?), William Gillaspie and Robert Harper, part of 2 tract: one surveyed for Ross, the other for William Jameson. Wit: William Jameson, Sarah Jameson, Charles (X) Williams. William Jameson made oath to William Reed, J.P., 13 Jun. 1798. Rec: 24 Mar. 1806.

Pages 324-325: Edwin Smith for $250 sold Henry Gambrill 160 acres on Ready fork of Broadmouth Crk. of the Saluda River, bd. by Barney Lee,Jas. Bagwell, Fredrick Bagwell and Thomas Sadler. Date: 29 Oct. 1803. Wit: Benjamin Smith, John (X) Gambril. John Gambril made oath to James Wellborn, J.P., 19 Apr. 1804. Rec: 24 Mar. 1806.

Page 325: James Logan for $600 sold John Gambril 193 acres granted Samuel Tarbert on S. side of Craven's Creek of Saluda River. Date: 17 Mar. 1806. Signed: James Loggins. Wit: William Harper, Re. Verner (Rebecca in oath), Wm. Harper made oath to John Verner, J.Q., 17 Mar. 1806. Susannah (X) Loggins, wife of James Loggins, released dower to John Verner, 17 Mar. 1806. Rec: 24 Mar. 1806.

Page 326: William Murphree for $300 sold Aron Murph-

(Page 326 cont'd): ree 588 acres on Rock Bridge Branch of 12
Mile River. Date: 21 Jan. 1806. Wit: David
Murphree. Turner (X) Harwood. David Murphree made oath to John Cochran,
Q.U., 21 Jan. 1806.
Rec: 24 Mar. 1806.

Pages 326-327: Henry Rukelsmer, planter, for $100 paid by
Thomas Boyd, dec'd., sold to his heirs,...
John Boyd, William Boyd, Ephraim Boyd, Mary
Boyd and Jeremiah Boyd, 125 acres on George's Creek of Saluda River, same
tract Ruckelsmer (sic) formerly lived on, bd. by William Rose, William
Jameson, Ruckelsmer, Wm. Gillispie, Robert Harper, part of 2 tracts. Date:
22 Feb. 1806. Signed: Henry Pickelsmer. Wit: Stephen Meritt, Abraham
Picklesmer. Stephen Merritt made oath to Wm. Watson, J.P., 5 Mar. 1806.
Rec: 26 Mar. 1806.

Page 327: 1 Nov. 1802, John Roberts to David Andrews
for $400 for 172 acres including tract of
150 acres granted Hugh Simpson by Thomas
Pinckney, 4 Aug. 1788, also 22 acres granted Thomas Lesley, 15 Oct. 1784
by Benjamin Guerard, conveyed to Hugh Simpson. Signed: John (X) Roberts.
Wit: George Weems, Adam Davis. George Weems made oath to James Turner, JP,
11 Feb. 1806.
Rec: 24 Mar. 1806.

Page 327: John Brown sold John Millwee a negro girl
about 17 years old named Maria. Date: 10
Oct. 1805. Teste: Stephen Anderson who also made oath to Samuel Houston, 26 Mar. 1806. (No recording date).

Page 328: James Crafford for $500 sold John Eston...
(later Elston and also Easton) 325 acres
granted Crafford 4 Jan. 1796, bd. by land
granted Lewis Shelton and Aron Smith, the 325 acres to be divided by John
Eston and William Clark, on N. branch of Toogalow River. Date: 9 Sep. 1803.
Signed: James (X) Crafford. Wit: D. Jarritt, James Gibson. D. Jarritt
made oath to David Humphreys, J.P., 10 Apr. 1803.
Rec: 27 Mar. 1806.

Pages 328-329: James Crafford for $1,200 sold John Elston
100 acres on Toogalow River, part of tract
granted Aron Smith, a Lieutenant in the Army of the United States, in the Revolutionary War, 15 Oct. 1784, bd. by
river above Walton's ford, where James Crafford now lives. Date: 10 Sep.
1803. Wit: Deverus(?) Jarrett, James Gibson. Deverue Jarrett made oath to
David Humphrey, 10 Sep. 1803.
Rec: 27 Mar. 1806. Elizabeth Crawford, wife of James, released dower to
David Humphrey, 10 Sep. 1803.

Page 329: James Crafford for $500 sold William Clark
325 acres granted Crafford 4 Jan. 1791, bd.
Lewis Shelton and Smith(?), on Toogaloe River, lines to be divided by William Clark and John Elston. Date: 9 Sep.
1803. Signed: James Crawford. Wit: Deverue Jarrett made oath to David
Humphrey, J.P., 10 Sep. 1803.
Rec: 27 Mar. 1806.

Pages 329-330: James Crawford for $1,200 sold to William
Clark 100 acres, part of 200 acres granted
Aron Smith 15 Oct. 1784, on Toogalow River
and bd. by William Clark and James Crawford. Date: 10 Sep. 1803. Wit:
Deverue Jarrett, James Gibson. Deverue Jarrett made oath to David Humphrey, J.P., 10 Sep. 1803. Elizabeth Crawford released dower 10 Sep. 1803.

Pages 330-331: By Act of General Assembly, passed 20 Dec.
1800, entitled an act to run supplies and
make appropriation for the year of 1800....
whereas sundry borrowers of the paper medium loan have not the interest
due on same borrowed by them and sales have been made of the land mortgaged to secure the loan, and the Treasurers have bought in the sd. land

(Pages 330-331 cont'd): for defect of bidders and the same remain in the hands of the State unproductive.... whereas the sd. act it is enacted that the Treasurers shall be authorized to cause all lands brought in as aforesaid to be put up for sales in the District, where they lay, the Sheriff of the District on Public Sale day after giving lawful notice shall sell same to higest bidded (Note: this is very disjointed...BW)......Now, David McCaleb, Sheriff of Pendleton Dist., did expose at Public Sale all that tract in Pendleton District on Toogalow River of the Savannah River, 300 acres (bd.?) by Loderwick, James Crawford, surveyed for Hugh Milling and mortgaged by Milling, borrower of the paper medium loan on 1st Monday 1801 (no month given), did sell to William Clark for $33. Date: 9 Oct. 1804. Wit: William Hamilton, John Elston. John Elston made oath to David Humphrey, J.P., 15 Mar. 1806. Rec: 27 Mar. 1806.

Page 331: James Shirley for $600 sold John Turner 120 acres on 26 Mile Creek, bd. by Calhoun, Robert Dickeson, John Turner, part of 280 ac. granted Edward Kemp by Wm. Moultrie, 7 Aug. 1786, conveyed by Kemp to Jacob Capehart, then to James Shirley. Date: 7 Jan. 1806. Wit: Hezekiah Posey, Robt. (X) Dickeson. Hezekiah Posey made oath to Henry Burch, J. P., 25 Mar. 1806. Rec: 25 Mar. 1806.

Pages 331-332: Jonathan Lane of Oglethorpe Co., Ga. for $450 sold Aaron Guyton a negro man named Peter about 20 years of age of a yellow complexion. Date: 30 May 1801. Wit: Jas. Millwee, who made oath to Samuel Houston, J.P., 21 Dec. 1805. Rec: 25 Mar. 1806.

Page 332: Samuel Crafton of Edgefield Dist., S. C., is bound to Henry Bradford of Greenville Dist., for $800. Date: 28 Sep. 1804, and now make title to 240 acres, part of tract granted William Rigley, of 340 acres, 16 Sep. 1784, divided to Decree of Court at 96 (Dist.), Apr. 1796. Wit: James Jett, P. Bradford. Phil Bradford made oath to John Willson, QU on 24 Mar. 1806. Rec: 25 Mar. 1806.

Pages 332-334: John Miller by bond of obligation, dated 23 Jan. 1805, payable to Messrs. Steele & Wood Merchants, for $400 for security all my personal property, furniture, chest containing apparel, three trunks, carpet (and other itemized items). Date: 23 Jan. 1805. Wit: M. Hammond, J. Ramsey....I, John Miller, not being able to comply with the conditions of a bond for $300 to Wood & Steele, hereby acknowledge to have sold to Steele & Wood, all property specified. Date: 22 Mar. 1806. Wit: M. Hammond, Michael Hammond made oath to J. B. Earle, _ Mar. 1805. Rec: 23 Mar. 1805.

Page 334: Lewis D. Martin for $1,000 sold John Harris, Esq., 200 acres on Conneross Creek of Keowee River, part of tract granted Major Ephraim Mitchell on bounty 19 Jul. 1784 by Benj. Guerard. Date: 10 Mar. 1801. Wit: Joel Bond, John Adams. John Adams made oath to John Willson, Q. U., 26 Mar. 1806. Rec: 28 Mar. 1806.

Pages 334-335: 16 Mar. 1805, Abraham Nally, Jr. and Sarah, his wife, to John Childers for $244 for 83 acres on Craven's Creek of Saluda River, bd. by Andrew Cochran, James Loggins. Wit: William Addis, Major Loggins. William Addis made oath to Wm. Edmondson, J.P., 22 Mar. 1805. Sally (X) Nally, wife of Abraham Nally, released dower to Wm. Edmondson, 22 Mar. 1805. Rec: 24 Mar. 1806.

Pages 335-336: 3 Apr. 1805, John Childers and Nancy, his wife, to James Gambril for $240 for 83 ac. on fork of Craven's Creek and Saluda River, bd. by Andrew Cochran, James Loggins. Wit: John (X) Gambril, John (X)

(Pages 335-336 cont'd.): Gambrill, Jr. John Gambrill, Sr. made oath to Aron Broyles, J.P., 8 Mar. 1806. Mrs. Nancy (X) Childers, wife of John Childers, released dower to Benjamin Arnold, J.Q., 5 Mar. 1806. Rec: 24 Mar. 1806.

Page 336: Andrew Cochran of Jackson Co., Ga. for $160 sold James Gambril of Pendleton Dist., 56 acres on Saluda River, conveyed from James Loggins to Cochran, part of tract granted Samuel Talbert. Date: 17 Aug. 1805. Signed: Andrew Cochran, Lovinia (X) Cochran. Wit: Thomas Kelly and John Kelly. Thomas Kelly made oath to William Arnold, J.P., 24 Oct. 1805. Rec: 24 Mar. 1806.

Page 337: 1 Sep. 1797, William McKee, and Jane his wife, to Archibald McKee for Ł 40 stg. for 1/2 of 2 tracts: one for 400 acres, the other for 417 acres, on Willson's Creek, bd. by George Houston. Wit: James Bole, John McColough, William McKay. Jane (X) McKee released dower to E. Browne, Q.U., 22 Mar. 1806. William McKay made oath to E. Browne on 16 Sep. 1805. Rec: 24 Mar. 1806.

Pages 337-338: 5 Aug. 1805, Thomas Jones to Archibald McKee for $140 for 100 acres on Willson's Crk. Signed: Thomas (X) Jones, Sarah (X) Jones. Wit: William McKay, James Bole. Sarah Jones, wife of Thomas Jones, released dower to E. Browne, Q.U., 22 Mar. 1806. Wm. McKay made oath to E. Browne, 16 Sep. 1805. Rec: 24 Aug. 1806.

Pages 338-339: Alexander McCluskey and Jane, his wife, for Ł 50 stg. sold to William King 140 acres on Rocky River of the Savannah River, bd. by Joseph Culton, Drury Thompson. Date: 8 Oct. 1801(?). Signed: Alexr. McCluskey, Jean (X) McCluskey. Wit: Robert Thompson, William Anderson. Robert Thompson made oath to Joshua Saxon, J.Q., 13 Oct. ____. Rec: 28 Mar. 1806.

Page 339: William Pinkston for $200 sold to Stephen Holloway 120 acres on Bear Creek, bd. William Keaton and Robert Orr, William Pinkston. Date: 22 Sep. 1805. Wit: Jonathan Brown and Larkin (X) Holloway. Jonathan Brown made oath to E. Brown, Q.U., 7 Feb. 1806. Rec: 27 Mar. 1806.

Pages 339-340: Elisha Dyer, Sr. for $200 sold to William Hardage 100 acres on both sides of Big Estitoe (sic) Creek of Keowee River, part of 2 tracts granted Allenathan Thomas and James Jett, one on 6 Aug. 1784, the other 2 Sep. 1793, both by Wm. Moultrie, the one to Thomas for 335 acres, the one to Jett for 764 acres, and formerly deeded to my son, Elisha Dyer, bd. by Dyer and Edward Murdin, Thomas, Jett, Elisha Dyer, Jr., Manoah Dyer. Date: 1 Feb. 1806. Wit: Edward Murdin, Elisha Dyer, Cloee(X) Murdin. Edward Murdin made oath to John Cochran, J.Q., 8 Feb. 1806. Rec: 27 Mar. 1806.

Pages 340-341: Britton Willis for $500 sold Archibald Simpson 150 acres, part of tract granted Patrick Colhoun, Jr., 20 Jul. 1804, on Sadler's Crk and conveyed by Joseph Colhoun, heir at law of Patrick Colhoun, to Willis 31 Dec. 1794. Date: 26 Feb. 1806. Signed: Britton (X) Willis. Wit: John Simpson, Davis Simpson. Ann (X) Willis, wife of Britton Willis, released dower to James Tate, Q.U., 3 Mar. 1806. John Simpson made oath to James Tate, 5 Mar. 1806. Rec: 2 Apr. 1806.

Pages 341-342: 20 Dec. 1798, William Killen to Jacob Lewis for Ł 60 for 120 acres on 12 Mile River, bd by John Caruthers, E. by Joel _____, N. by

(Pages 341-342 cont'd): Lockspur Mountain, part of tract where Killen now lives, granted by Thos. Pinckney, 7 Apr. 1788. Wit: Leonard Reed and Isaiah Lewis. Isaiah Lewis made oath to Wm. Reed, J.P., 17 Feb. 1800.
Rec: 27 Mar. 1806.

Page 342: 26 Apr. 1799, Joab Lewis to Jacob Lewis for Ł 50 for 150 acres on S. fork of 12 Mile River. Wit: Catherine Lewis, Isaiah Lewis. Isaiah Lewis made oath to Wm. Reed, J.P., 27 Feb. 1800.
Rec: 27 Mar. 1806.

Pages 342-343: William Hays (or Kays) for $200 sold Benjamin Armstrong 320 acres surveyed for John Green 1 Jan. 1793, on 6 Mile Creek of Keowee River, part of 838 acres granted John Green by Wm. Moultrie. Date: 16 Sep. 1805. Wit: John Green(?), Saml. F. Green(?). Jno. Green made oath to Samuel H. Dickson, J.P., 7 Mar. 1806.
Rec: 28 Mar. 1806.

Page 343: James Doran _____(cannot read this)____ to Andrew Brown 191 acres on E. side of Chauga of Toogaloo River, bd. Samuel H. Dickson, _____ Walton (or Walters). Date: 24 Feb. 1806. Wit: William Tolbert and Samuel Torbert and John Barton. William Torbert made oath to John Barton.
Rec: 25 Mar. 1806.

Page 344: Hezekiah Posey for $111 sold to Aron Hardin 195 acres on 26 Mile Creek, bd. by John Miller, Hugh Mills, John Turner and Turpin, granted Jacob Capehart 6 Jan. 1794 for 262 acres. Date: 17 Nov. 1805. Wit: Joseph Jolly and Henry Jolly. Joseph Jolly made oath to M. Hammond, D.C. 25 Mar. 1806.
Rec: 28 Mar. 1806.

Page 344: Duncan McKinzie for $400 sold Henry C. Barton 230 acres on Big Beaverdam Creek of the Toogalow River, granted John Miller and James Millwee, 2 Jul. 1787 by Thos. Pinckney, bd. SW and NE by John Gibson, SE by Erwin(?) and Haney, SW by McKinzie and Benjamin Hickman. Date: 14 Jan. 1806. Wit: Caleb Barton, John McKinzie. John McKinzie made oath to H. McCray, J.P., 22 Mar. 1806.
Rec: 27 Mar. 1806.

Page 345: Moses Holland for $195 sold to John Taylor 120 acres on Neel's Creek of Rocky River, part of tract granted Thomas Burford 4 Dec. 1786 by Wm. Moultrie, another part granted Samuel Dalrymple 3 Jul. 1787 by Chas. Pinckney, surveyed by Adam Todd 29 Mar. 1805. (Plat shows land bd. S. by Thomas Burford, NE by John McFall, NW by Solomon Geer, E. by E. Vandiver.) Date: 4 Apr. 1805. Wit: John Gilliland, David Drennan. David Drennan made oath to James Willborn, J.Q., 4 Apr. 1805. Mary Holland, wife of Moses Holland, released dower to James Willborn, Q.U., 4 Apr. 1805.
Rec: 25 Mar. 1806.

Pages 345-346: James Kennedy of the City of Charleston, for $200 sold to James Pratt of Pendleton Dist., 640 acres in 96 Dist. on Conneross Creek, granted Kennedy 16 Jan. 1785. Date: 25 Feb. 1806. Wit: Francis Coran, Saml. H. Dickson. Mary Eliza Kennedy, wife of James Kennedy, released dower to Charles Few, Q.U., 5 Feb. 1806. Samuel H. Dickson, Esq., made oath to M. Hammond, D.C., 4 Aug. 1806.
Rec: 8 Jul. 1806.

Pages 346-347: Benjamin Ray Montgomery, Clergyman, by his note of 1 Jun. 1805, for $700 to be paid 1 Jun. 1806, sell to Andrew Pickens, Jr., 326 acres where Montgomery now lives on 23 Mile Creek, part of 2 tracts: one granted James Gillison 6 Nov. 1786, the other to Joseph Price 6 Nov. 1786, bd. on N. by Crosby W. Miller, NE and E. by Abner A. Steele and by

(Pages 346-347 cont'd): Thomas Hunter, S. by John Taylor, W. by
Isaac Lych, commonly called the Town Lands.
Date: 18 Apr. 1806. Wit: William Hunnicutt, James Wood. James Wood made
oath to M. Hammond, D.C., 7 Jul. 1806.
Rec: 7 Jul. 1806.

Pages 347-348: Archibald Pagan, John McDowall and John
Birney, assignees of the Estate of William
Stephens, Bankrupt, of the City of Charleston for $62.01 sold to James Pierson, Merchant, of the City, 2 tracts
containing 170 acres by the old survey, but by the new survey as follows:
one tract of 120 acres in 96 Dist., on Little Beaverdam Creek, part of a
tract granted John Huneycutt by Wm. Moultrie 6 Nov. 1787 as in titles
from Nathan Briant to James Eason; one lot of 65 acres in Washington District, on both sides of Little Beaverdam, granted George Slaton by Chas.
Pinckney, in title from Slaton to James Eason. Date: 12 Apr. 1805.
Signed: Archd. Pagan, John McDowall (only). Wit: Geo. Burger, James Mackie....Charleston, Geo. Burger made oath to Jno. Mitchell, Q.U., 23 May
1806. Rec: 6 Jun. 1806.

Page 348: Archibald Pagen, John McDowall and John Birney, assignees of the Estate of William
Stephens, Bankrupt, of Charleston, for $210
sold to James Pierson, Merchant, tract in 96 Dist. on 26 Mile Creek of
Keowee River, bd. SW and NW by Alexander Olayfer(?), SW by Peter McMahen,
SE by George Forbest. Date: 12 Apr. 1805. Signed: Archd. Pagan, John McDowall. Wit: Geo. Burger, James Mackie. ....Charleston, Geo. Burger made
oath to Jno. Mitchell, Q.U., 23 May 1806.
Rec: 6 Jun. 1806.

Page 348: Abbeville Dist., Joseph McMurtry of Abbeville Dist. for $500 sold John Faucheraud
(?) Grimke, Esq., 700 acres, part of 848
acres granted McMurtry 4 Aug. 1794, on Devil's fork of the Big Generostee
and bd. on W. by James Hamilton, being rest of the survey after deducting
part sold to Mr. Strange. Date: __ Mar. 1805. Wit: Wm. Hamilton and Jms.
Lesley.....Abbeville Dist., James Lesley made oath to Wm. Lesley, J. P.,
5 May 1806.
Rec: 9 Jun. 1806.

Pages 349-350: Robert Kyle for love and affection I bear
to my beloved nephew, James Henry Bankhead
Kyle, give him a black horse and waggon,
being property which Robert Kyle purchased at Sheriff's sale at Pendleton
on 7 Jul. 1806. Date: 4 Aug. 1806. Wit: Wm. Hamilton, Cecilia Hamilton.
William Hamilton made oath to M. Hammond, D.C., 6 Aug. 1806.
Rec: 6 Aug. 1806.

Page 350: Franklin Co., Ga., John Landers for $300
sold to William Massey of Spartanburg Dist.
S. C., 150 acres, 1/2 tract on Great Generostee Creek of the Savannah River (cannot read the boundaries...BW),
granted 15 Oct. 1784, recorded Bk. AAAA, p. 132(?). Date: 4 Sep. 1801.
Wit: Wm. Allen, Wm. Rackley....Pendleton Dist., William Rackley made oath
to James Kilgore, J.P., 6 Nov. 1802.
Rec: 26 May 1806.

Pages 350-351: 29 Jan. 1806, Andrew Barkley for $300 sold
to William Barkley 300 acres, bd. Keowee
River, part of 1,000 acres granted Benjamin Arnold 1 Sep. 1791. Wit: Samuel Barkley, Robt. (X) Smith. Samuel
Barkley made oath to Saml. Houston, J.P., 20 Jun. 1806.
Rec: 27 __ 1806.

Page 351: Benjamin Buchan for $50 sold to William
Beaty, Jr., 6½ acres on Little Generostee
Creek of the Savannah River, part of tract
granted William Buchanon 7 Sep. 1795, for 387 acres, recorded Bk. __, no.
5, p. 302 (sic) Wit: David Beaty, John Meloney, James Buchanon. Plat for
60½ acres, bd. N. by Wm. Buchan, E. by John Beaty, surveyed 17 Jan. 1800,

(Page 351 cont'd):   by Jno. McMahan, D.S. David Beaty made oath to Nathan Lusk, J.P., 13 Dec. 1800. Rec: 24 Mar. 1806.

Pages 351-352:   John Beaty for $100 sold William Beaty, Jr. 100 acres part of 296 acres granted 6 Apr. 1789, recorded Bk. ZZZZ, p. 230. Date: 13 Dec. 1800. Wit; Joseph McCarley, David Marley. Plat shows land bd. on E. by John Beaty, N. by William Buchanan, laid off 18 Jan. 1800 by Jno. McMahan, D.S., Joseph McCarley made oath to Nathan Lusk, J.P., 13 Dec.1800. Rec: 24 Mar. 1806.

Pages 352-353:   8 Jan. 1800, Ephraim Hearin for $115 sold William Phares 100 acres part of 779 acres granted James Gillaspy 22 Aug. 1791 by Chs. Pinckney, sold to Hearin, recorded Bk. D, p. 179, Pendleton records, bd. Samuel Duff, John Gillespie, James Gillispie, on Wolf Creek of Savannah River. Signed: Ephraim Herring. Wit: Absolom Faris, Wm. Edmondson. Absalom Faris made oath to Robert Bowen, J.P., 23 Apr. 1801. Rec: 28 Oct. 1805.

Pages 353-354:   David Henderson for $400 sold George Hagood 233 acres on Mile Creek of George's Creek of the Saluda River. Date: 10 Oct. 1805. Wit: William Jameson, Robert Duff, Gray (X) Jones. William Jameson made oath to Samuel C. Duff, J.P. Isbal (X) Henderson, wife of Daniel Henderson, released dower to John McClure, J.Q., 19 Oct. 1805. Rec: 28 Oct. 1805.

Pages 354-355:   John Dickson and James Dickson for $1,812 sold to Zachariah Taliaferro 3 tracts joining each other of 659 acres on 23 Mile Crk. and Garvin's Creek, bd. by James Symms, Major Michael Dickson, Samuel Taylor, Henry Dobson Reese, 359 acres was conveyed by John Dickson to Henry D. Reese 14 Apr. 1806, 100 acres sold to John Dickson and James Dickson by Samuel Taylor 12 Apr. 1806. Date: 16 Apr. 1806. Wit: Robert Kelton, Jno. Smith, Nicholas Bishop. Martha Dickson, wife of James Dickson, released dower to John Willson, Q.U., 10 Jun. 1806. Nicholas Bishop made oath to John Willson 4 Jul. 1806. Rec: 4 Jul. 1806.

Page 355:   George Goodwin sold to Crafford Goodwin(?) one negro woman named Sarah about 40(?) years old, one negro girl named Sal(?), about 7 years old, one negro boy named Cane(?) about 4 years old and her twin boys, about 18 months old named Tom and Landy. Date: 28 Jun. 1806. Wit: David Quorles(?), John (X) Putteet(?), W. Nicholson. W. Nicholson made oath. (No J.P.). 22 Jun. 1806. Rec: 30 Jun. 1806.

Pages 355-356:   Thomas Berit for $100 sold to my 2 sons, William Berit and Benjamin Berit 100 acres on George's Creek of Saluda River, bd. by Ambrose Bradley. Date: 14 Jan. 1806. Signed: Thomas Barrett, Mary Barrett. Wit: John Carson, Jesse Saterfield. John Carson made oath to Samuel C. Duff, J.P., 15 Jan. 1806. Rec: 11 Jul. 1806.

Page 356:   Hamilton Bell for $235.50 sold to John Prator Odell 550 acres on 18 Mile Creek of the Savannah River, bd. by John Hallums, Johnson, John Maritain(?) and David Hamilton, granted to John Hamilton by Thos. Pinckney, recorded Bk. VVVV, p. 285 (no date or witnesses, deed not finished...BW). Martha (X) Bell, wife of James Hamilton Bell, released dower to John Willson, Q.U., ___ Dec. 1801. (No oath).

Pages 356-357:   James Sims for $500 sold Zachariah Taliaferro, Esq., 230 acres on 23 Mile Creek, part of a tract granted William Prichard, on fork of Garvin's Creek. Date: 2 May 1806. Wit: Michael Dickson, Sam-

(Pages 356-357 cont'd): uel H. Dickson, Elizabeth ____ (Dickson in the oath). Samuel H. Dickson made oath to John Willson, Q.U., 4 Jul. 1806. Nancy (X) Sims, wife of James Sims, released dower to John Willson, 10 Jun. 1806.
Rec: 4 Jul. 1806.

Pages 357-358: William Steele for $225 sold William Thompson 925 acres on Conneross Creek, granted Charles Lay by Thos. Pinckney, 2 Jul. 1787, recorded Bk. FFFF, (no page no.). Date: 22 Sep. 1801. Wit: Thos. Hunter, Anty. Griffen (Anthony in oath). Thos. Hunter made oath to Saml. H. Dickson, J.P. (no date).
Rec: 4 Jul. 1806.

Page 358: Alexander Barren for $537.50 sold Samuel Hawkins tract on both sides of Hericane Creek, S. Beaverdam Creek of Toogalow River, bd. by Daniel Keith, Shields. Date: 13 Mar. 1805. Wit: W. T. Barry, Fras. Jenkins. William Barry made oath to H. McCray, J.P., 4 Jul. 1806.
Rec: 4 Jul. 1806.

Pages 358-359: Hezekiah Lincicum for $250 sold to John P. Odell 200 acres on 18 Mile Creek of Savannah River, granted David Hamilton by William Moultrie, 5 Jun. 1786, conveyed by David Hamilton to James Hamilton, 10 Nov. 1800 and by Hamilton to Lincicum, 12 Mar. 1804. Date: ____ 1805. Wit: James Odell, Mary (X) ____. James Odell made oath to John Wilson, Q.U., 23 Jan. 1805. Sarah (X) Lincicum released dower to John Willson, Q.U., 23 Jan. 1805.
Rec: 16 May 1806.

Pages 259-360: John Kees for love and good will, grant to my beloved son, Absalom Kees, a tract on the Toogalow River, on N. side of Mill Crk. including Mill and all acres(?) on S. side of Mill Creek. Date: 10 May 1806. Wit: William Brooks, Aaron (X) Anderson. Aron Anderson made oath to Wm. Cleveland, J.P., 20 Jun. 1806.
Rec: 21 Jun. 1806.

Page 360: John Kees for love and good will to my beloved son, Elijah Kees, a tract on the Toogalow River, bd. by Washington Kees, Elijah Kees and Phillip Hancock. Date: 10 May 1806. Wit: William Brooks, Aron (X) Anderson. Aron Anderson made oath to Wm. Cleveland, J.P., 20 Jun. 1806.
Rec: 21 ____.

Pages 360-361: John Kees for love and good will to my beloved son, Thomas Kees, give him five negros, names as follows: one fellow named June, one Will, one wench named Sarah, one girl named Lucy, one boy Curry (?), also, cattle, hogs, sheep, waggon and geers, household furniture; and unto son, Absalom Kees, horses; unto Martin Hardin, well beloved son-in-law of Franklin Co., Ga., one horse. Date: 19 Jun. 1806. Wit: Benjamin Magee, Aaron (X) Anderson. Aaron Anderson made oath to Wm. Cleveland, JP, 26 Jun. 1806.
Rec: 21 Jun. 1806.

Page 361: John Kees for love and good will give to my beloved son, Washington Kees, a tract on Toogalow River, where I now live, bd. on N by A. Kees, and Washington Kees, David Barton, Thomas Kees. Date: 10 May 1806. Wit: William Brook, Aron (X) Anderson. Aron Anderson made oath to Wm. Cleveland, J.P., 25 Jun. 1806.
Rec: 25 Jun. 1806.

Page 361: John Troutman of Abbeville Dist. for $434 sold to Dudley Hammond of Pendleton Dist. a negro fellow named Bill. Date: 5 Feb. 1806. S. J. Hammond (witness?). (No oath). Rec: 17 May 1806.

Page 362:	John Gentry for $500 sold to Matthew Clark 100 acres between 23 and 26 Mile Creeks, granted John Millican by Wm. Moultrie 1 Jan. 1787. Date: 11 Jan. 1806. Wit: Caleb Baldwin, William Morris. Caleb Baldwin made oath to J. Stribling, Q.U., 9 Jul. 1805. Ruth Gentry, wife of John Gentry, released dower to J. Stribling, 9 Jul. 1806. Rec: 17 Jul. 1806.

Pages 362-363:	Elizabeth Oliver, spinster, to John Cansler, Jr., planter, for $100 for 200 acres, granted Elizabeth Oliver by Wm. Moultrie 4 Sep. 1786, on 23 Mile Creek of Savannah River, being 1/2 of a tract, bd. John Willson. Date: 19 Aug. 1801. Wit: James Cansler, Ambrose Moffett(?) and John Willson. James Cansler made oath to John Willson, 19 Aug. ___. Rec: 4 Jul. 1806.

Page 363:	James Evett for $300 sold to William Kirby(?) 200 acres _____ on 12 Mile River _____ (rest unreadable). Date: 28 Apr. 1805. Signed: James (X) Evett, Susannah (X) Evett. Wit: Saml. Taylor and John Simpson. John Simpson made oath to M. Hammond, D.C., 28 Apr. 1806. Rec: 28 Apr. 1806.

Pages 363-364:	Saml. Taylor for $350 sold James Evett 290 acres on NE side of 18 Mile Creek of Seneca River, bd. NE by Tilly Merick, W by Simon Grist(?), S by David Kelton and Dr. Hunter, part of 2 tracts granted Samuel Lofton; one for 579 acres by Wm. Moultrie, 4 Feb. 1793, the other by Chas. Pinckney, 1 Aug. 179_. Date: 28 Apr. 1806. Wit: Josiah Wright and A. Lawhon. Leah Taylor, wife of Samuel Taylor, released dower to John Taylor, Q.U., 28 ___ 1806. Archibald Lawhon made oath to M. Hammond, D. C., 28 Apr. 1806. Rec: 28 Apr. 1806.

Pages 364-365:	John Dickson for $350 sold to Wm. McAdoo 188½ acres composed of 2 small tracts; one of 102 acres granted Thomas Lofton by Wm. Moultrie, the other of 86½ acres, part of tract granted Henry Childs on 5 Mile Branch of 18 Mile Creek, bd. NE by Saml. Lofton, Sr., both tracts occupied by John Dickson. Date: 12 Apr. 1806. Wit: Richd. Blackstock, James Dickson and Jesse Hillin. Jesse Hillin made oath to M. Hammond, DC on 10 May 1806. Rec: 10 May 1806.

Page 365:	Jacob Capehart for ₤5 stg. sold William Hunnicutt 163 acres on Whitstone Creek of Little Beaver of the Savannah River, granted Andrew Boddan by Edward Rutledge, 1 Apr. 1799. Date: 3 May 1805. Wit: Willis Dickinson, John Hunnicutt. John Hunnicutt made oath to M. Hammond, D.C., 21 Apr. 1806. Rec: 28 Apr. 1806.

Pages 365-366:	John Woodall for natural love and duty I have for my son, Thomas Holms Woodall give the following property: 244 acres where I now live, also, use of a negro woman named Jamimah, until Thomas becomes age 21, another child, Nancy, which said woman has and her issue during the nonage (sic) of Thomas to be his property forever, also, one negro boy named Jimmy, also all my household furniture, farming tools, mare & colt, etc., provided he, my son Thomas, shall live with his mother and let her have proper use of the property until he is 21, and his mother and guardian shall live my chaste widow after my decease, then Thomas shall make her, Judith Woodall, his mother, firm titles and deliver one horse and saddle to be valued at $50 and necessary furniture and $150. If Thomas should die before age 21, that property before mentioned shall be equally divided between his lawful heirs, excepting what is left to my wife, Judith, and Joseph Woodall to act as my sons guardian. Date: 25 Feb. 1806. Wit: Christian Tuck(?), Stephen B. Swinny. Stephen B. Swinny made oath to John Taylor, Q.U., 3 May 1806. Rec: 3 May. 1806.

Pages 366-367:   James Hamilton of Pendleton Dist., for $250 sold to Hezekiah Lincicum, late of State of Georgia,, 200 acres on 18 Mile Creek of the Savannah River, granted David Hamilton by Wm. Moultrie, 5 Jun. 1786, conveyed by David Hamilton to James Hamilton, 10 Nov. 1800. Wit: John Willson, Wm. F. Rogers. Susannah (X) Hamilton, wife of James Hamilton, released dower to John Willson, Q.U., 20 Mar. 1804. Wm. F. Rogers made oath to John Willson, 20 May 1804.
Rec: 16 May 1806.

Pages 367-368:   29 Mar. 1806, Andrew White by bond of obligation to William Richards, Merchant, for $355, gave indenture to Richards for these 2 tracts: one of 100 acres where White now lives, granted Samuel H. Dickson, conveyed to White, part of tract on Cain Creek of Keowee River, the other for 282 acres on Little Generostee of the Savannah River, granted Andrew White, Sr., conveyed to Andrew White, now in possession of William and Robert White. Wit: David Files, William Brown. William Brown made the oath to W. Nicholson, J.P., 28 Apr. 1806.
Rec: 5 May 1806.

Page 369:   James Bourland of Pendleton, Washington District, to John Kencellor(?)..(Canselor in the oath) for ___(blank)...for tract now in Kencellor's possession, on N. side of George's Creek of the Saluda River, bd. by John Armstrong, John Bowen, Bourland. Date: 6 Apr. 1804. Wit: Nathaniel Hendrickson, William Gorman. William Gorman made oath to John McClure, J.P., 20 May 1806.
Rec: 4 Jul. 1806.

Pages 369-370:   Benjamin Starrett has borrowed $50 and $30 from James Starrett and Capt. James Wood, also $450, making $935, and mortgages 300 acres where he now lives, horses, cattle, household furniture and profits arising by cultivation of the plantation. Date: 24 Mar. 1806. Wit: James Wood, Joseph B. Earle. Capt. James Wood made oath to James C. Griffen, JP, 7 Apr. 1806.
Rec: 4 Jun. 1806.

Page 370:   James Alexander for $100 sold to David Larance 100 acres on Cain Creek of Toogalow River, part of 2 tracts: one laid out for James Alexander, the other granted Jacob Boshman(?) by Chas. Pinckney in 1795, bd. by John Larance, James Alexander and Hillary Mills. Date: 14 Sep. 1805. Wit: Joseph Venable, John Haile. John Haile made oath to Wm. Cleveland, J.P., 20 Sep. 1805.
Rec: 22 May 1806.

Page 370:   James McGuffin sold to William McGuffin one mare, cow and calf, heifer, also land whereon I now live with all household furniture for value received. Date: 24 Feb. 1806. Wit: John Hunnicutt, Sarah Hunnicutt. John Hunnicutt made oath to M. Hammond, D.C., 2 Jun. 1806.
Rec: 2 Jun. 1806.

Page 371:   Martha Vann for $86 sold to ...(cannot read name)...(Note: James Linn in the index),bd. by Thomas Morton(?), 102 acres ____ (unreadable). Signed: Martha (X) Vann. Wit: (Appears to be Aaron Smith and John Turner.) Oath:(Cannot read).

Pages 371-372:   David McCaleb, Sheriff, to Thomas Garvin, planter....whereas Peter Freneau and Francis Bremar were seized of ....(unreadable) Justice of Court of Common Pleas obtained judgement against Freneau and Bremar......(cannot read)...directed Sheriff to sell all goods, chattels, lands for $71 which sd. Hezekiah Listenby received against them, sold to Thomas Garvin for $69 as the highest bidder for 587 acres, part of 640 acres granted Freneau and Bremar, on dividing ridge between 12 Mile and 18 Mile Creeks, bd. by land surveyed by John Cunningham, Gen. Robert An-

(Pages 371-372 cont'd): derson, Hezekiah Listenby. Wit: Rt. Brackinridge and Wm. Hamilton. William Hamilton
made oath (No J. P.) __ Sep. 1806. (No recording date).

Pages 372-373: Christopher Strong of Pendleton Dist., sold
for $1,800 to William Walker of Chester Dis-
trict, S. C., 713 acres where Strong now
lives on 18 Mile Creek, granted John Loyd, Esq. Date: __ Oct. __ (Note:
cannot read rest of this...BW)

Pages 373-374: ......(Cannot read)....date of deed 8 Aug.
1803. Signed: George Boyd. Wit: Henry(?)
Norton, John Boyd. (Oath shows deed to
Thomas Goss.) Henry Norton made oath to Wm. Edmondson, J.Q., 18 Jul.1806.
Rec: 18 Jul. 1806.

Pages 374-375: 2 Jun. 1806, David McCaleb, Sheriff, to John
Watson, blacksmith......James Millwee was
seized of a tract....Thomas Hunter and Bart-
lett Finley received judgement against Millwee for $41.33; at public
sale, land was sold to John Watson for $16.50 by his friend Sheriff Brus-
ter as the highest bidder for 150 acres on Willson's Creek of Rocky River
part of 1,000 acres, except part which was recovered of Millwee by Nathaniel McCallister, in a suit, said tract granted James Millwee and William Ebenezer Kennedy by Chas. Pinckney, ...(cannot read witnesses, but
appears Wm. Hamilton signed the oath.)

Page 375: .....(Cannot read). Signed: Randolph Hunni-
cutt. Wit: Meridith (X) Hunnicutt, William
Hunnicutt. Receipt was to John Hunnicutt,
Jr. William Hunnicutt made oath to M. Hammond, D.C., 1 Sep. 1806.
Rec: 1 Sep. 1806.

Pages 375-376: Samuel C. Duff and James Duff, Executors of
James Duff, Sr., dec'd., for $150 sold to
James Edmondson 213 acres on George's Crk.
Date: 14 Feb. 1806. Wit: J. Mauldin, John Edmondson. John Edmondson made
oath to Wm. Edmondson, J.Q., 2 Jun. 1806.
Rec: 15 Aug. 1806.

Page 376: Peter Akor to William Halbert for $100 for
30 acres on S. side of the Saluda River.
Date: 5 Apr. 1805. Signed: Peter Acher.Wit:
Thomas Bennett, Charles Bennett. Charles Bennett made oath to James Well-
born, L.W.(?), 12 Aug. 1806.
Rec: 11 Aug. 1806.

Pages 376-377: 3 May 1790, James Martin, planter, and his
wife, Ruth, to Alexander Keith for L60 for
250 acres on Willson's Creek of Rocky River-
er, granted James Martin 4 May 1787 by Thos. Pinckney. Signed: James Martin, Ruth (X) Martin. Wit: John Jackson, William Liddell. William Liddel
made oath to Samuel Black, J.P., 15 Mar. 1805.
Rec: 26 Aug. 1806.

Page 377: Edmond Manning for $40 sold to James Adams
20 acres on Goodland Creek of Connoross,
granted Benjamin Howard by Wm. Moultrie on
17 Jan. 1785, recorded Bk. HHHH, p. 168. Date: 13 Jan. 1806. Signed: Edmond (C) Maning. Wit: James Drennan, Isham Burks. Isham Burks made oath
to Wm. Towers, J.P., 9 Aug. 1806.
Rec: 4 Sep. 1806.

Page 378: Alexander Keith for $500 sold Samuel Rowan
a tract on Willson's Creek of Rocky River,
bd. by John Scott, Wm. Liddell, Wm. Lesley
and granted James Martin 4 Jun. 1787 by Thos. Pinckney. Date: 16 Mar.1805.
Wit: Jas. Thomson, William Tippen. Sarah (X) Keith, wife of Alexander
Keith, released dower to E. Browne, QU, 16 Mar. 1805. Capt. James Thomson
made oath to J. Stribling,QU, 2 Apr. 1805. Rec: 26 Aug. 1806.

Pages 378-379:   25 Sep. 1788, John McCarter, sadler, of Abbeville Co., to William McCarley of same county, planter, for £ 40 for 200 acres above the ancient boundary line on Big Creek of Big Generostee of Savannah River, bd. by Mills, granted Moses McCarter by Gov. Guerard, recorded Bk. CCCC, p. 477. Wit: Thos. Morrow, Joseph McCarley. Joseph McCarley made oath to Jonathan George, J.P., 7 Apr. 1806.
Rec: 7 Aug. 1806.

Page 379:   James Hamilton for $150 sold Thomas Eaves 100 acres on 26 Mile Creek, part of a grant to James Hamilton by John Drayton 8 July 1800, bd. by Jonathan Hemphill, and Hamilton. Date: 13 Aug. 1806. Wit: Thos. Stribling, Caleb Baldwin, both made oath to J. Stribling, 13 Aug. 1806. Rec: 15 Aug. 1806.

Pages 379-380:   14 Feb. 1787, Alexander Moore and Dorcus (or Darius), his wife, of York Co., Camden Dist., S. C. to Alexander Black of County aforesaid, for £ 100 stg. for 200 acres on Little Beaverdam of Savannah River. Wit: Robert Maclin, Charles Melure(?). .....York Co., Robert McClelan made oath to Alexander Moore, J.P., 31 Dec. 1793.
Rec: 16 Aug. 1806.

Pages 380-381:   Peter Freneau and Francis Bremar of Charleston for $45 sold to Robert McCann, Esq. of Pendleton Dist., a tract in 96 Dist. on 26 Mile Creek of Savannah River, surveyed for William Downs 14 Jan. 1805 and granted Francis Bremar and Peter Freneau on 3 Apr. 1806. Date: 17 Mar. 1806. Wit: James (X) Gillison, H. Pinckney. James Gillison made oath to John Willson, Q.U., 1 Sep. 1806.
Rec: 1 Sep. 1806.

Page 381:   20 Sep. 1803, Sarah Manner(?), single woman, has bound her son, Elijah, now 7 years old to William Armstrong, until he arrives at the age of 21, during which time he shall not contract matrimoney and shall when capable, obey instructions, he shall not waste or embezzel his master's property, etc......and then Armstrong shall give him 1 year and a half schooling......(rest unreadable)....a decent suit of clothing. Signed: William Armstrong, Sally(?) Maner. Wit: Aaron Broyles, Cain Broyles. Aaron Broyles made oath _____(unreadable), 22 Sep. 1806.
Rec: 23 Sep. 1806.

Page 381:   David Lewis for $22 sold to Joseph Pinson 15 acres, part of tract on Kellies Creek of the Keowee River, bd. by Samuel Brown, where Pinson now lives and Lewis. Date: 20 Aug. 1805. Wit: Tarleton Lewis, Micajah Alexander. Micajah Alexander made oath to Henry Burch, J.P., 21 Dec. 1805.
Rec: 8 Aug. 1806.

Page 382:   John Patterson, planter, for $60 sold to George Magee 104 acres on 12 Mile River of the Savannah River, bd. by Joseph Smith, part of tract granted John Patterson 7 Jul. 1801. Date: 16 Dec. 1801.Wit: Solomon (X) Magee, John Garner. Solomon Magee made oath to James Wardlaw, J.P., 25 ___ 1805. Nancy (X) Patterson, wife of John Patterson, released dower to James Wardlaw, Q.U., 25 May 1805.
Rec: 22 Sep. 1806.

Pages 382-383:   Isaac Hudson for $___ sold to John Patterson 265 acres on 12 Mile River, bd. Patrick Hay, part of tract granted Alexander McCannel. Date: 24 Nov. ___. Wit: Moses Hunt, _____. Moses Hunt made oath to David Murphree, J.P., 25 Sep. 1805.
Rec: 23 Aug. 1806.

Page 383:   John Barnett for $50 sold to Amos Barnett 30 acres on branch of Generostee Creek of

(Page 383 cont'd): Savannah River, bd. by Harper, Skelton, Thomas Portman(?), Lesley, Amos Barnett, part of 360 acres surveyed for William Stephens 4 Aug. 1786 by Thomas Finley, granted by Chas. Pinckney. Date: 6 Jun. 1801. Wit: Thomas Putman and Jacob Skelton. Jacob Skelton made oath to John Verner, J.P., 13 Feb. 1802. Rec: 4 Aug. 1806.

Page 384: Acquilla Niron has sold to Daniel Bryson a negro woman named Ame(?) about 18 or 19 yrs. of age, and her child, Fanny, about 2 yrs. old, for $450. Signed: Acquiller Nerron. Wit: Isaac Mitchell and William McKee. Rec: 2 Sep. 1806. (No oath).

Pages 384-385: Robert Harkness, Sr. for $1,500 sold Robert Harkness, Jr., the following: 3 negros - Ned, a boy about 17 years old, 2 Aprian(?) girls, one about 15 named Dinah, the other called Rachel, about 11 or 12 years old, cattle, sheep, horses, feather beds and furniture, all plantation tools, oats, cotton, and standing corn on Robert Harkness, Sr.'s plantation. Date: 16 Aug. 1806. Wit: William (X) Keeten, Alexander (X) Cater (oath says Caven). William Keaton made oath to E. Browne, Q. U., 28 Aug. 1806.
Rec: 1 Sep. 1806.

Page 385: Forester Upshaw for $300 sold Garret Fitzjarrel 200 acres on Coffee Creek of Toogalow River, part of 417 acres granted William McCaleb by Chas. Pinckney, bd. by John and William Doss, Smithen and Pugh. Date: 12 Sep. 1805. Wit: Enoch Berry, William Berry. Enoch Berry made oath to John Verner, J.Q., 12 Sep. 1805.
Rec: 18 Aug. 1806.

Pages 385-386: Henry Edwards, carpenter, for $300 sold to James Hallums 270 acres on 18 Mile Creek of Savannah River, bd. by James Passon, granted Thos. Roberts. Date: 10 Dec. 1805. Signed: Henry (X) Edwards. Wit: Saml. Baker, Martha (X) Baker. Samuel Baker made oath to John Willson, Q.U., 3 Jun. 1806. Mary Edwards, wife of Henry Edwards, released dower to John Willson, 3 May 1806.
Rec: 9 Jun. 1806.

Page 386: Samuel Taylor for $120 sold to Caleb Baldwin 100 acres on E. side of the Seneva River, bd. by McDaniel, Samuel Suthern. Date: 4 Feb. 1806. Wit: A. Lawhon, John Jones. Alexander Lawhon made oath to J. Stribling, Q.U., 26 Mar. 1806.
Rec: 17 Jul. 1806.

Pages 386-387: James Bourland to John Hamilton for $300 for 100 acres on Little George's Creek of Saluda River, bd. by Enoch Williams. Date: 5 Apr. 1804. Wit: Nathaniel Henderson, William Gorman. William Gorman made oath to ...(No J.P.), 20 May 1806.
Rec: 4 Jul. 1806.

Page 387: James Dickson for £35 sold Henry Jolly 65 acres on 26 Mile Creek, bd. by Lewis Jones. Date: 26 Dec. 1805. Wit: Richd. Robinson and John Hunnicutt. John Hunnicutt, Jr., made oath to Samuel Houston, JP, 25 Mar. 1806.
Rec: 29 Apr. 1806.

Pages 387-388: Joseph Waldrum of Pendleton Dist., sold to A. Harris of Abbeville Dist., 123 acres on Keowee River, the Village fork of Cain Crk. granted Charles Plunket 19 Feb. 1798. Date: 11 Apr. 1806. Wit: Jno. Pound and John McWhorter, Jr. John McWhorter made oath to Jas. Starrett, J. P. 16 Jul. 1806.
Rec: 18 Jul. 1806.

Page 388:	Isaac Hill for $300 sold to David Quarrels a tract granted Peter Fenn(?), bd. Isaac Hill and Amos(?) Hill, Thos. Field, William Stuart. Date: 13 Nov. 1804. Wit: James (X) Slatter, W. Nicholson. W. Nicholson, J. P., certified deed 23 Feb. 1805.
Rec: 6 Oct. 1806.

Pages 388-389:	William Murphree for $150 sold to Solomon Murphree 508 acres on 12 Mile River. Date: 11 May ___. Wit: David Murphree, Daniel(?) Murphree. David Murphree made oath to John Cochran, J.P., 4 Oct. 1806. Hannah Murphree released dower to John Cochran, 4 Oct. 1806.
Rec: 4 Oct. 1806.

Pages 389-390:	David Garvin for $205(?) sold Simon Grist 800 acres ___ (cannot read rest)......... Wit: William Evett, Ebr. (Ebenezer in oath) Jacob Walker. Jacob Walker made oath to John Willson, Q.U., 24 Sep. 1806.
Rec: 3 Oct. 1806.

Page 390:	John McCutchen is bound to Richard Gray for $20 for 100 acres, part of 177 acres surveyed for McCutchen 10 Jun. 1805, bd. Robert Scott, William Lewis, Martha Vann, Robert O. Buris(?). Date: 10 1805. Wit: Richard Riddel(?), John Gentry. Anne (X) McCutchen, wife of John McCutchen, released dower to John Taylor, Q.U., 23 Sep. 1805. John Gentry made oath to John McMillin, J.P., 30 Jul. 1806.
Rec: 1 Sep. 1806.

Page 390:	James Gibson for $180 sold to Moses Murphree 120 acres on fork of 12 Mile River, bd. by William Wiatt. Date: 16 Jul. 1803. Signed: James (X) Gibson. Wit: Archer Harris and David Adams. David Adams made oath to David Murphree, J.P., 6 Sep. 1804.
Rec: 6 Oct. 1806.

Page 391:	Samuel Hawkins for $1,000 sold John Crow Foster 250 acres, part of 300 acres granted 6 Aug. 1792 by Chas. Pinckney, bd. by Fredrick Moss. Date: 3 Jul. 1806. Wit: Samuel Earle, Fredrick Moss. Samuel Earle made oath to H. McCray, J.P., 2 Oct. 1806.
Rec: 2 Oct. 1806.

Page 391:	William Murphree for $500 sold David Murphree 200 acres on 12 Mile River, part of a tract known as Seconia, bd. by James Murphree, William Murphree. Date: 4 Oct. 1806. Wit: Jonathan Davis and William Brown. Jonathan Davis made oath to Jehu(?) Kirksey, J.P., 6 Oct. 1806.
Rec: 6 Oct. 1806.

Page 391:	Samuel Earle for $150 sold to Jesse H. Posey 2 lots joining each other of 1/2 acre each in the Town of Andersonville, known as Lot #38 and #39. Date: 9 Jul. 1806. Wit: Geo. D. Paine and James Barton. James Barton made oath to James Tate, Q.U., 21 Oct. 1806.
Rec: 14 Oct. 1806.

Page 392:	13 Jan. 1806, Capt. James Turner of Pendleton Dist., to Little Berry Roach of Greenville Co. for $119.18 for 40 acres, part of 210 acres granted in 1789 by Thos. Pinckney to John Simpson, on Big Generostee Creek, conveyed by Simpson to Aaron James, from James to James Brasher, from Brasher to Capt. Turner. Wit: Henry (X) Roach, Archd. Gilmer. Archd. Gilmer made oath to James Turner, J.P., 13 Jan. 1806.
Rec: 4 Aug. 1806.

Page 392:	James Millwee for $45 sold to John Millwee a negro wench named Winney about 50 or 60 years of age. Date: 14 Apr. 1806. Wit: David Shirrell(?), who made oath to Saml. Houston, J. P., 10 Sep. 1806.

(Page 392 cont'd):   Rec: 4 Oct. 1806.

Pages 392-393: 7 Jul. 1806, David McCaleb, Sheriff, to William Steele, Merchant,.....whereas Henry Kyle was possessed of lot of land and Mickey Denmon & Co. on 4th Mon. of March 1806, in the Court of Common Pleas, obtained judgement against Kyle for $761 and Sheriff ordered all goods, chattels, lands of Henry Kyle sold at public auction to highest bidder. On 7 Jul. 1806 for _____ 3 acres _____ in Village of Pendleton. _____(Unreadable). Wit: Daniel Symms, Wm. Hamilton. Wm. Hamilton made oath to M. Hammond, D.C., 22 Aug. 1806.
Rec: (Unreadable).

Page 393: _____(unreadable) to Jonathan(?) Thompson bd. by William Thompson _____ S. fork of Keowee River(?) _____. Date: 7 Apr. 1806. Signed: Rose(or Ross)(X) Reese. Wit: G. W. Terrell, Pamela Terrell. G. Washington Terrell made oath to David Murphree, J.P., 17 Apr 1806. Rec: 29 Sep. 1806.

Pages 393-394: Joel Smith of Granville Co., N. C. to James C. Griffen for $400 sold a negro woman Mary abour 23 years of age and her female child named Comfort. Date: 13 Jun. 1806. Wit: Jas. (X) Powers who made oath to M. Hammond, D.C., 25 Sep. 1806.
Rec: 25 Sep. 1806.

Page 394: Thomas Hargis for $395 sold Joseph Pinson 252 acres on branch of One Mile Creek, granted Alexr. McDowall, 1788, on Keowee Old Road. Date: 1 Mar. 1805. Wit; John Grisham, Martha Grisham. John Grisham made oath to Henry Burch, J.Q., 26 Aug. 1805.
Rec: 8 Aug. 1805.

Page 394: 17 Jul. 1804, John Tippen to my beloved son Sampson Tippen, a small tract whereon Sampson now lives, on branch of Big Generostee of Savannah River, part of survey made for Mathew Morgan 28 Oct. 1795 and conveyed to Francis Miller, from Miller to John Adam Miller, from Miller to James Hannah, from Hannah to Capt. John Tippen, 25 Feb. 1801, bd. by Capt. Wm. Tippen, John Adam Miller, and James Hannah. Wit: James Long, John L. Brooks, George Tippen. John L. Brooks made oath to Obadiah Trimmier, Q. U., 8 Oct. 1804.
Rec: 23 Aug. 1806.

Pages 394-395: 3 Mar. 1806, Ormand Morgan to Thomas Harrison for $80 for 250 acres where Morgan now lives, bd. by Rolston,and Peggy Echols; also, 100 acres where James Sullivan now lives, bd. by Rolson and Harrison; also 4 cows and 2 calves, horse, beds and household articles. Date: 25 Dec. ___. Wit: _____. John Cain signed oath.
Rec: _____

Page 395: 6 Sep. 1791, Moses Hopper to Amos Barnett for Ł 33 for ___ acres, on branch of Big Generostee Creek in 96 Dist., bd. by land surveyed for Martin, sold to William Shelton, bd. by John Barnett and Robert Skelton, granted William Stevens. Signed: Moses (X) Hopper. Wit: John Barnett, Rolly (X) Hopper....(very dim)....John Barnett made oath to John Willson, J.P., 17 Jul. 1793.
Rec: 4 Aug. 1806.

Pages 395-396: Daniel Brown of Kershaw Co., S. C. for Ł100 sold to Mathew Hooper of Pendleton Co., 200 acres where Hooper now lives on Choestoa Creek of Tugaloe River, granted John Skelton, a soldier, by Benj. Guerard on 21 Jan. 1785. Date: 8 Mar. 1799. Wit: John Fisher, John Brown........ Kershaw Dist., Mrs. Mary Brown, wife of Daniel Brown, released dower to Jas. Dubose, J.K.C., 8 Mar. 1799. John Fisher made oath to John Brown, JP on 8 Mar. 1799. Rec: 9 Jun. 1806.

Page 396: Aaron Terrell sold to Micajah Smithson for $20 for 6 acres, bd. by Smithson. Date: 30 Jul. 1805. Wit: Josiah Shipp, Asa Smithson. Asa Smithson made oath to John Verner, J.Q., 1 Aug. 1805. Rec: 6 Jun. 1806.

Pages 396-397: 30 Aug. 1795, John Smith of Charleston, baker, to John Moore of the same city, merchant, for ₤ 100 stg. for 1,000 acres in Washington Dist. (formerly 96 Dist.) on Generostee of Savannah River, bd. SE by Richard Morrow, S by Joshua Saxon. Signed: John Smith, Catherine (X) Smith. Wit: Peter Keys, George Moore. P. Keys made oath to Joshua Saxon, J.P., 14 Sep. 1796. Rec: 23 Sep. 1806.

Pages 397-398: Stephen Herring for $400 sold to Benjamin Crownover 200 acres on Big Generostee of the Savannah River. Date: 30 Feb. 1804. Signed: Stephen Herring, Rhoda (X) Herring. Wit: William (X) Crownover, Abraham Crownover. Abraham Crownover made oath to Hez.(?) Davis, J. P., 9 Nov. 1805. Rec: 23 Sep. 1806.

Page 398: Benjamin Covenhoven for $550 sold to Peter Keys 200 acres on Big Generostee of Savannah River. Date: 7 Apr. 1806. Wit: Alexander Moore, James Brown. Signed: Benjamin Covenhoven. Keziah (X) Houston, wife of Henry Houston, released dower to P. Keys for 200 acres on Big Generostee, sold and conveyed by her husband to Peter Keys, 22 Mar. 1804. Rec: 23 Sep. 1806.....Rachel (X) Covenhoven, wife of Benjamin Covenhoven, released dower to John Tippen, Q.U., 10 Jun. 1806. Alexander Moore made oath to John Tippen, 10 Jun. 1806. Rec: 23 Sep. 1806. (There is no explanation for the Houston dower release being included in this deed...BW)

Page 399: Samuel Cherry of Pendleton Dist., lawful attorney of William Davidson, Andrew Davidson and John Davidson, children of James Davidson, dec'd. of Maclenburg (sic) Co., N. C. for $75.50 sold Rhodam Doyle 101 acres, part of a tract adj. land formerly belonging to Robinson and Tuffnell. Date: 9 Apr. 1806. Wit: Wm. Hunter, Damuel (Samuel?) Taylor. Dr. William Hunter made oath to J. L. Lewis, Clerk & Q.U., 25 May 1808. Rec: ___ (cannot read).

Page 399: Samuel Moore appeared and made oath that he was present at Robert Stephenson's tavern on 25 Jan. last and saw William Forsyth and Robert Love quarrel and when the fight was over, the sd. Forsyth had lost a part of his ear and the sd. deponent heard Love say he (Love) bit off Forsyth's ear and swallowed (it). Sworn and subscribed to on the 22 Mar. 1806 to John George, J.P. Rec: 24 Mar. 1806.

Pages 399-400: 25 Oct. 1804, David Guest to Lee Allen for 190 acres on N side of Beaverdam Creek.... where Guest now lives, part of a grant to Col. Kilpatrick, bd. by Jacob Holland. Wit: William Ainsworth, Ann (X) Cox. Frances Guest, wife of David Guest, released dower to Obadiah Trimmier, Q.U., 10 Nov. 1804. William Ainsworth made oath to Samuel H. Dickson, J.P. 14 Oct. 1804. Rec: 14 Oct. 1804.

Page 400: John Morrow for $600 sold to James Morrow 227 acres on 26 Mile Creek of Savannah River, granted John Hunnicutt by Chas. Pinckney 7 Sep. 1789. Date: 1 Aug. 1805. Signed: John Morrow, Mary (X) Morrow. Wit: Thomas Walkee, Orwin (X) Moore. Orwin Moore made oath to Samuel Houston, J.P. 25 Mar. 1806. Rec: 14 Oct. 1806.

Page 401: Harold Felton for $215 sold Jesse H. Posey 290 acres, part of a tract granted Felton. Date: 25 Mar. 1804. Signed: Harold (X) Felton. Wit: Edwd. Tell McClure, B. Starrett. (Plat). B. Starrett made oath to John McMillen, J.P., __ Oct. 1806. Rec: 14 Oct. 1806.

Pages 401-402: Ebenezer Smith for $100 sold to Simon Grist (?), 92 acres on 5 Mile Branch of 18 Mile Creek of the Savannah River, part of tract granted to Samuel Lofton, Sr. Date: 1 Aug. 1806. Signed: Ebr. Smith and Margaret (X) Smith. Wit: James Watters and John Watters. James Watters made oath to M. Hammond, D.C., 13 Oct. 1806. Rec: 16 Oct. 1806.

Page 402: John McClain of Buncombe Co., N. C. for $300 sold to Abner McMillen of Pendleton Dist., 597 acres on Pea Creek of Rocky River, granted Wm. Neil by Gov. Moultrie, 6 Feb. 1786, bd. by George Miller, Wiley Bishop, Pouge, McClain. Date: ____ 1802. Signed: John McClain and Mary McClain. Wit: Wiley Bishop, who made oath to John George, J.P., 5 Mar. 1805. Rec: 13 Oct. 1806.

Pages 402-403: John McClain of Pendleton Co., farmer, for $159 sold to Wiley Bishop 100 acres on Broadaway Creek of Great Rocky River, part of 282½ acres granted Mathew Wilson. Date: 25 Nov. 1799. Wit: John Duncan and James Swofford. John Duncan made oath to Patrick Norris, J.P., 20 Dec. 1799. Rec: __ Oct. 1806.

Pages 403-404: 29 Oct. 1796, Thomas Norris to Joseph Dickson for £ 60 stg. for 200 acres, granted Thomas Norris 7 Jul. 1788, recorded Bk.BBBB and p. 54, bd. SE by Wm. ____ (?) and James Jordan, NW by Henry Barton. Wit: John Dixon and Thomas (X) Morris, Jr. John Dickson made oath to Joshua Saxon, J.P., 31 Oct. 1796. Rec: 14 Oct. 1806.

Page 404: Received of William Orr on 23 Aug. 1806 one horse which is to be my property if I discharge note of $50 payable in 6 months. Signed: Thos. Galloway. Wit: John Watson and William Anderson. John Watson made oath to John B. Earle, 22 Sep. 1806. Rec: 22 Sep. 1806.

Page 404: Hosea Tapley for $600 sold Samuel Martin 364 acres, part of tract granted Jeremiah Abel and part granted Lot Irby(?), another granted Thomas Commander Russel, on Conneross, bd. S by Richard Nall, W by Andrew Caddel, N by John Caddel, Twitty, Wm. Land. Date: 27 Jan. 1806. Wit: Robert Portwood, John (X) Lumpkin. Robert Portwood made oath to M. Hammond, D. C., 20 Sep. 1806. Rec: 20 Sep. 1806.

Pages 404-406: 1 Jul. 1805, David McCaleb, Sheriff, to.. William Richards, ...William Richards received Judgement on 2nd. Mond., Mar. 1805 in the Court of Common Pleas, against John Doss for $22.50...ordered all goods, chattels, lands of John Doss be sold at Public Auction to highest bidder, being William Richards for $65 by his friend, Maj. John Taylor.. for 200 acres, where John Doss now lives, part of a tract granted William McCaleb by Thos. Pinckney, 2 Jul. 1787 on Coffee Creek of Togalow River, being remainder of a tract sold by Doss to William Doss and Forester Upshaw. Wit: William Hamilton, Cecelia Hamilton. William Hamilton made oath to M. Hammond, D.C., 31 Mar. 1806. Rec: 31 Mar. 1806.

Page 406: John Morrow, planter, for $117 sold David Garvin 82 acres on W side of 18 Mile Creek of Savannah River, bd. W by Tilly Merrick,

(Page 406 cont'd): on S. by John McDowal, on E. by John Morrow and on N. by Maj. Strong. Date: 19 Dec. 1804. Wit: James Beard, James Garvin. James Beard made oath to Samuel H. Dickson, J.P., 21 Dec. 1804. Rec: 20 Sep. 1806.

Pages 406-407: Barak Norton for $124 sold to William Richards 298 acres, surveyed for James Jett on 21 Nov. 1799, conveyed to Norton. Date: 20 Aug. 1806. Wit: _____ Miller. Oath: (unreadable) A. Miller... signed. Mary Norton, wife of Barak Norton released dower to Henry Burch, J.Q. (Dates not readable).

Page 407: (Cannot read this deed).

Pages 407-408: __ Sep. 1801, James Gray to William Gray for __ for 200 acres, part of 443 acres granted John Read(?), 2 Sep. 1793 by Wm. Moultrie, recorded Bk. S.(?), no. 5, p. 233, bd. by William Watson. Wit: Mark (X) Wideman, who made oath to _____ Gilbert, J.P., __ Feb. 1802. Rec: 20 Sep. 1806.

Page 408: Hosea Tapley for $100 sold Samuel Martin 80 acres, part of 500 acres granted Solomon Perkins, bd. by Miller. Date: 27 Jan. 1806. Wit: Robert Portwood, John (X) Lumkin. Robert Portwood made oath to M. Hammond, D.C., 20 Sep. 1806. Rec: 20 Sep. 1806.

Pages 408-409: Nimrod Cally for $200 sold to William Turner 100 acres on Great Generostee Creek of the Savannah River, part of tract granted John Holcum 3 Sep. 1800. Date: 14 Dec. 1805. Wit: Michael (X) Hill, John Buckhannon(?). Sarah (X) Kelly, wife of Nimrod Kelly, released dower to E. Browne, Q.U., 20 Aug. 1806. John Buchannon made oath to E. Browne, 30 Aug. 1806. Rec: 15 Sep. 1806.

Pages 409-410: Pickensville.......an agreement between Elijah Browne of Pendleton Co. and Willey Browne of Greenville Co....Elijah Browne has exchanged a negro boy named Newry, about 9 years old, with Willey S. Browne, for a negro boy named _____, and his note for $40, and I..... Elijah Browne make sufficient bill of sale for boy Newry.....(cannot read this part)....if Capt. Benjamin Ruker(?), father-in-law of Elijah Browne at his departure from this life dispose of the property on loan to his daughter, Milly(?), wife of Elijah, so as to make it out of his power to make lawful right to said negro....then in that case he is to return the negro boy, Donas(?) and his note for $40. Date: 12 Apr. 1796. Signed by E. Browne, Willey S. Browne. Wit: Wm. Wood, William Poor, John McColough (very hard to read this.....)....John McColough made oath to John Scott, J.P., 24 Aug. 1806. Rec: 4 Oct. 1806.

Page 410: 24 Nov. 1801, Daniel Mazych, eldest, Capt., in the late 2nd. Reg. of foot (sic) of the State of S. C., on Continental Establishment commanded by Lieutenant Col. Commandant Francis Marion, to Jacob Holland of Pendleton Dist. for $130 for remaining part of 300 acres, the other part being held by Jacob Holland, on Beaverdam of Toogalow, granted Mazych. Wit: James (X) Gillison, Thomas W. Mazych. James Gillison made oath to Wm. Cleveland, J.P., 28 Oct. 1806. Rec: 28 Oct. 1806.

Pages 410-411: John Phillips for $400 sold to David Grimes 2 tracts of 572 acres on 12 Mile River, one on line between John Evans and Joseph Woodall, part of 427 acres. Date: 30 Jan. 1806. Wit: Wm. Farris, Gabriel Foster. Gabriel Foster made oath to John Willson, Q.U., 11 Feb. 1806. Rec: 14 Oct. 1806.

Page 411:   John Hampton Harrison of Greenville Dist., for $100 sold to Samuel Earle of Pendleton Dist., 217 acres granted by Paul Hamilton, 1 Jul.(?) 1804.........(difficult to read). Date: 3 Nov. 1806. Wit: Reuben Barrett, Robert Cooke, J.P., Shadrack Tramill.....Greenville Dist., Shadrack Tramill made oath to Elijah Green, J.P., 3 Nov. 1806. Rec: 8 Nov. 1806.

Pages 411-412:   Joseph Thompson for $300 sold Matthew Long 222 acres, part of a tract granted Matthew Thompson and part conveyed by Thomas Farrow to Mary Thompson, both deceased, on E. side of Big Rocky Creek of the Big Generostee Creek. Date: 7 Nov. 1806. Wit: William McGriger, Matiam (X) McGriger. William McGriger made oath to John Tippen, Q.U., 8 Nov. 1806. Rec: 10 Nov. 1806.

Page 412:   Matthew Thompson for $200 sold to Joseph Thompson 111 acres, all my part of land granted Mary Thompson, now dec'd., on E. side of Big Rocky fork of Big Generostee Creek. Date: 13 Feb. 1806. Wit: Anthony Griffen, Archer (X) Brooks. Anthony Griffen made oath to James Starrett, J.P., 13 Feb. 1806. Rec: 10 Nov. 1806.

Pages 412-413:   Major Lewis, house carpenter, for $160 sold to John Lewis, planter, 160 acres, 1/2 of a tract purchased from Robert Scott, granted him by Wm. Moultrie, 1 Jun. 1786, recorded Bk. NNNN, p. 124 and 141, on 26 Mile Creek of the Savannah River, bd. by Benjamin Lewis. Date: 22 Aug. 1806. Wit: William Lewis, Jr., Benj. Lewis. William Lewis made oath to M. Hammond, D.C., 11 Nov. 1806. Rec: 11 Nov. 1806.

Pages 413-414:   5 Nov. 1806, Lee Allen to Jacob Holland for $600 for 190 acres on Big Beaverdam, part of tract granted Alexander Kilpatrick where Lee Allen now lives. Wit: Daniel Willis, Squire Allen. Elizabeth Allen released dower to J. Stribling, Q.U., 13 Nov. 1806. Squire _Guest_ made oath to J. Stribling, 13 Nov. 1806. Rec: 15 Nov. 1806.

Page 414:   William Murphree for $100 sold Aron Murphree tract on 12 Mile River. Date: 15 Sep. 1806. Wit: David Murphree, Alen (X) Murphree. Allen Murphree made oath to David Murphree, J.P., 25 Oct. 1806. Rec: 27 Oct. 1806.

Pages 414-415:   David Murphree sold Aron Murphree for $500 for 200 acres on 12 Mile River on Seconia Tract, bd. by Wm. Murphree, James Murphree. Date: 4 Oct. 1806. Wit: William Murphree, Allen (X) Murphree. Allen Murphree made oath to J. Kirksey, J.P., 6 Oct. 1806. Rec: ___ (cannot read).

Pages 415-416:   Matthew Martin for $300 sold Obadiah Duckworth 130 acres on N. side of 26 Mile Crk. of Savannah River, part of 360 acres granted Joseph Martin by Benj. Guerard, 15 Oct. 1784, bd. by Obed Duckworth, Matthew Martin. Date: 3 Mar. 1806. Wit: D. Chamblin, John Caddell. John Caddell made oath to Robt. McCann, 14 Jan. 1807. Rec: 15 Jan. 1807.

Pages 416-417:   Samuel Robinson for $100 sold Joel Foster 171 acres, part of 198 acres granted Robinson 5 Feb. 1798, on NW side of Seneca Crk., bd. SW by John Knox, NW by Robert Waugh and Colonel Earle, SE and SW by Robert Armour. Date: 15 Nov. 1804. Wit: Robert Waugh, Edw. Adair. Robert Waugh made oath to Jno. Adair, J.P., 19 Apr. 1806. (Plat). Rec: 9 Jan. 1807.

Pages 417-418: 29 Oct. 1806, Benjamin Magee to William Cleveland, Esq., for Ł 30 for 50 acres on N. side of Toogaloo River, bd. by Magee, Thomas Kees. Wit: Robert Looney, Caleb Barton. Robert Looney made oath to H. McCray, J.P., 29 Oct. 1806.
Rec: 29 Oct. 1806.

Pages 418-419: James Cavender for $450 sold Thomas Stockstill 354 acres on NW branch of Choestoe Creek, of Toogaloo River, bd. on SW by Wm. McCaleb, NE by land granted to Joshua Lee by Thos. Pinckney, 2 Jul. 1787. Date: 29 Aug. 1805. Wit: John (X) March, Forister Upshaw. John Marsh made oath to John Verner, J.P., 27 Jan. 1805. Polly Cavender, wife of James Cavender, released dower to John Verner, 27 Jan. 1806.
Rec: 27 Oct. 1806.

Page 419: Richard Berry sold to Sarah Gandy a negro girl named Chainey for $15. Date: 26 June 1806. Teste: Thomas Mathews, who made oath to Wm. Towers, J. P., 19 Sep. 1806.
Rec: 15 Dec. 1806.

Pages 420-422: Andrew Pickens of Pendleton Dist., planter, for 5 shillings stg., sold to Ezekiel Pickens of St. Thomas Parish, S. C., 394½ ac. on E. side of Keowee River (lower half of Hopewell tract), part of 2 tracts: one of 326 acres and one of 67½ (ac.). Date: 17 Feb. 1805. Wit: B. R. Montgomery, Andrew Pickens, Jr. Andrew Pickens, Jr. made oath to M. Hammond, D.C. Plat shows land bd. by Andrew Pickens, Francis Pratt, Gen. Anderson, land laid out to Francis Greenwood, now Burn's land.....
"the above plat represents part of General Andrew Pickens land given to his son, Ezekiel Pickens, laid out 15 Jan. 1805".
Rec: 15 Dec. 1806.

Page 422: Jesse Cain is bound to Benjamin Smith for $800. Date: 7 Feb. 1806, and made deed for tract bought of Elisha Floyd. Wit: Robt. Kell, Nathan Boon. Nathan Boon made oath to Joseph Reid, J.P., 26 Nov. 1806. Rec: 29 Dec. 1806.

Pages 422-424: Jesse Tatum for $350 sold Jesse Binum 120 acres. Date: 1 Nov. 1802. Wit: John Edwards and Wm. Binum. Amara (X) Tatum, wife of Jesse Tatum, released dower to John Willson, Q.U., 3 Dec. 1804.
Rec: 2 Jan. 1807.

Pages 424-425: Hezekiah Davis for $400 sold William Tippen 210 acres, part of tract granted Henry Pearson by Wm. Moultrie, 18 May 1785, 110 acres was conveyed from Pearson to Jesse Garland, from Garland to William Gibson, from Gibson to Joseph Crouch and from Crouch to Hezekiah Davis, the balance of 90 acres was conveyed from Henry Pearson to Jesse Garland then to Joseph Land, who sold to Davis, bd. by Jesse Brown, John Miller, Edward McAllister, James Long and Jesse Garland. Date: 18 Oct. 1805. Wit: James Jones, James Long. James Long made oath to E. Browne, Q.U., 21 Oct. 1805. Sarah (X) Davis, wife of Hezekiah Davis, released dower to E. Browne, 21 Oct. 1805. Rec: 5 Jan. 1807.

Pages 425-426: Peter Freneau and Francis Bremar of Charleston, for $162.50 sold John Smith of Pendleton Dist., planter, 306 acres in 96 Dist. on S. side of Saluda on 23 Mile Creek, bd. NW by Andrew Warnock, surveyed for Robert Bradea(?), 9 Jan. 1805, granted Bremar & Freneau, 3 Apr. 1806. Date: 17 Mar. 1806. Wit: James (X) Gillison, H. Pinckney. James Gillison made oath to Wm. Cleveland, J.P., 26 Mar. 1806.
Rec: 4 Jan. 1807.

Pages 416-418: Washington Dist., 6 May 1794, Edward Cox of Lawrence Co., S. C. to Benjamin Dickson of Pendleton Co. for Ł 40 stg. for 72 acres,

(Pages 426-428 cont'd): part of 269 acres granted William Stone on 6 Apr. 1789, on 26 Mile Creek, bd. NE and SE by Benjamin Dickson, SW by Charles White. Wit: William Crosby, George Reeves. (No oath).
Rec: 27 Mar. 1806.

Pages 428-429: William Y. Glover of Pendleton Dist. for $150 sold to Reuben Tarrant of Greenville 250 acres granted Fredrick Glover 1 March 1790. Date: 6 May 1800. Wit: Isaac (X) Cox, Thomas Hall. Isaac Cox made oath to Wm. Hall, J.P., 6 May 1800.
Rec: 27 Mar. 1806.

Pages 429-430: John Woodall, Sr. for $100 sold John Woodall, Jr. 100 acres on branches of Big Generostee Creek, bd. by John Woodall, John Hogg, George Hogg. Date: 17 Apr. 1804. Wit: William Mullican, Edward T. McClure. Edward T. McClure made oath to John McMillion, J.P., 13 March 1806. Rec: 27 Mar. 1806.

Page 430: William Bennison of Abbeville Dist., for $150 sold to William Duncan of Pendleton Dist., 712 acres on Hen Coop of Rocky River of Savannah River, granted Bennison, 21 Jan. 1790, by Chas. Pinckney and recorded Bk. B, no. 5, p. 80. Date: 8 Jun. 1803. Wit: John Laughlin and Robert Duncan. Robert Duncan made oath to E. Browne, Q.U. 8 Oct. 1804.
Rec: 29 Oct. 1806.

Pages 430-431: Daniel Keith, Sr. of Pendleton Dist. for $800 sold to Alexander Colhoun of Newberry Dist., tract on Devil's fork of Generostee Creek where Keith now lives, bd. by Holden. Date: 11 Feb. 1804. Wit: Edward T. McClure, James Hamilton. Elizabeth (X) Keith, wife of Daniel, released dower to James Tate, Q.U., 26 Mar. 1804. Major James Hamilton made oath to James Tate, 22 Nov. 1804.
Rec: 29 Oct. 1806.

Pages 431-432: John Dickson of Pendleton Dist. for $600 sold to Alexander (Colhoun?) of sd. dist., 350 acres on Great Generostee Creek of the Savannah River. Date: 25 Oct. 1804. Wit: David Sloan, Jr., James McCollum. Sally Dickson, wife of John Dickson, released dower to J. Stribling, Q.U., 5 Nov. 1805. David Sloan, Jr., made oath to John McMillion, J. P., 26 Mar. 1806.
Rec: 29 Oct. 1806.

Pages 432-433: 24 Nov. 1801, Daniel Mazyck, eldest, Capt. in the 2nd Regt. (etc.) to Burrell Greene of Pendleton Dist., farmer, for $100 for 200 acres in 96 Dist. on S. branches of Conneross Creek of Keowee River, bd. by George Slaitor, granted Lt. Stephen Mazyck, 2 May 1785, on bounty of the State, who conveyed to Daniel Mazyck, 2 May 1785, recorded Bk. __, no. 6, p. 100 to 102 (Book P?), 3 Nov. 1795. Wit: James Gillison (X) and Thomas W. Mazyck. James Gillison made oath to W. Nicholson, J.P., 27 Oct. 1806. Rec: 28 Nov. 1806.

Pages 433-434: John Mills for $160 sold to T. Wall Funderburk 150 acres on 26 Mile Creek bd. Benjamin Harris, part of tract granted to Mills on 5 Jun. 1786 for 640 acres by Wm. Moultrie, recorded Bk. LLLL, p. 215. (No date). Wit: Joseph Green, William Black. Betsy Mills released dower to (No J.P.), 17 Nov. 1806. Signed: Elizabeth Mills. Joseph Green made oath to P. Norris, J.P., 2 Feb. 1807.
Rec: 2 Jan. 1807.

Page 434: Armistead Berry, Kesia Berry, William Barry, Polly Berry and Fredrick Moss, all of Pendleton Dist., are bound to Robert Walton and Swift Mullins, both of Franklin Co., Ga. for $8,000...Armstead

412

(Page 434 cont'd): Berry and Kesia Berry in 1802 were appointed as Administrators of the Estate of Andrew Berry, dec'd. and Robert Walton and Swift Mullins became bound with sd. Armstead and Kesia for $10,000 as security for their true administration of the Estate. Date: 13 Jan. 1807. Wit: Samuel Earle. (No oath).
Rec: 2 Feb. 1807.

Page 435: James Linsey for Ł 50 sold Alexander McCluskey 50 acres granted James Linsey on Big Generostee, bd. Jacob Chamberly, James Hillisy, Alexander Stephenson, William Leonard. Date: 8 Oct. 1796. Signed: James Lindsey. Wit: Colin Campbell, Wm. Moor Lindsey. Colin Campbell made oath to William Reed, J.P., 10 Oct. 1796.
Rec: 17 Jan. 1807.

Pages 435-436: William Leonard for Ł 100 sold to Alexander McClusky 160 acres, part of 200 acres where McCluskey now lives, granted by Wm. Moultrie, 1786, bd. by Alexander Stephenson, Thomas Skelton. Date: 28 October 1796. Wit: David Dickey, James Hillhouse. James Hillhouse made oath to Joshua Saxon, J.P., 5 Jan. 1797.
Rec: 17 Jan. 1807.

Pages 436-438: 8 Dec. 1804, David McCaleb, Sheriff, to Leonard Ellington.....Rebecca Jones, Administratrix, and Lewis Jones, Administrator, of the (Estate) of Willis Jones, dec'd., when William Steele on 2d. Mon. in Oct. in the Court of Common Pleas obtained judgement for $78.23, all goods, chattels, lands ordered sold at public auction to the highest bidder, being Leonard Ellington for $35, for 106 acres, part of 206 ac. granted Willis Jones by Wm. Moultrie on 23 Mile Creek. Wit: William Hamilton, Charles Bond. Charles Bond made oath to M. Hammond, D.C., 20 Feb. 1807. Rec: 26 Jan. 1807.

Page 438: Edly Lyn for $150 sold to John McCleroy 134 acres on W. side of Rocky River. Date: 29 Aug. 1805. Wit: James George, James Dickson. James Dickson made oath to John McMillion, J.P., 28 Oct. 1806.
Rec: 28 Oct. 1806.

Page 439: Bert Moore for $700 sold to Henry Garner 197 acres on N. fork of 12 Mile River. Date: 9 Mar. 1806. Signed: Bert (X) Moore. Wit: William Brown, James Dickson and Moses Hunt. Mary (X) Moore, wife of Bert Moore, released dower to John Cochran, Q.U., 12 Jan. 1807. Moses Hunt.... made oath to John Cochran, 22 Jan. 1807.
Rec: 24 Jan. 1807.

(Note: Written in the margin between deed above and deed below but with no indication to which it refers......"Handed to Wm. Choice, Esq., of Greenville."....BW)

Pages 439-440: Joseph Green for $200 sold Leonard Ellington 88 acres, part of 547 acres on E. side of 26 Mile Creek, bd. by Michael Dickson, granted Francis Ley by Thos. Pinckney, 4 Feb. 1788. Date: 4 Nov. 1805. Wit: John Clark, Hugh Mills. Annis (X) Green, wife of Joseph Green, released dower to John Taylor, Q.U. (no date). Hugh Mills made oath to Jno. McMillion, J.P., 6 Aug. 1806.
Rec: 26 Jan. 1807.

Pages 440-441: 10 May 1791, Eli Hunnicutt to William Jolley for Ł 60 for 150 acres on 26 Mile Crk. of the Savannah River, bd. by survey supposed to belong to Ewing Colhoun, Wm. Jolley, Randolph Hunnicutt, Robert Parker, part of a tract granted Eli Hunnicutt by Wm. Moultrie, 14 Dec. 1786. Wit: Jonathan Clark, H. Hunnicutt. Hartwell Hunnicutt made oath to M. Hammond, D.C., 21 Jan. 1807.
Rec: 21 Feb. 1807.

Page 441:   Solomon Stone sold to Fredrick Johnson one
                            negro boy named Wally. Date: 10 Jan. 1807.
                            Wit: Jno. Stuart, Thomas Garvin. John Stu-
art made oath to M. Hammond, D.C., 10 Jan. 1807.
Rec: 10 Jan. 1807.

Page 442:   John McEllroy for $450 sold to John Stephen-
                            son 208 acres, on W. branch of Rocky River,
                            part of tract granted John Pickens, 3 Jun.
1791 by Wm. Moultrie, recorded Bk. E., no. 5, p. 524; also, part of 274
acres granted Robert Anderson, 1 Jan. 1787 by Wm. Moultrie, recorded Bk.
QQQQ, p. 513, bd. by Thos. Drennan, Edly Lynn, Moses Land, John Anderson,
John McFall, Saml. and Joseph Drennan. Date: 25 Oct. 1806. Wit: Samuel
McEllroy, Thomas Drennan. Samuel McElroy made oath to Jno. George, J.P.,
27 Oct. 1806. Lattice McElroy, wife of John McElroy released dower to E.
Browne, Q.U., 28 Oct. 1806.
Rec: 28 Oct. 1806.

Page 443:   Edmond Mannen and Bedy, his wife, for $280
                            sold to John Lewis Glenn 100 acres, where
                            Mannen now lives, granted Benjamin Howard,
by Wm. Moultrie, 17 Jan. 1785, recorded Bk. KKKK, p. 161. Date: 2 March
1801. Signed: Edmond (X) Mannin (only). Wit: Jesse Glenn, James Glenn.
Jesse Glenn made oath to Henry Burch, J.P., 4 Sep. 1801.
Rec: 28 Feb. 1806.

Pages 443-444:   Mark Bird of the State of North Carolina by
                            my Attorney, Edward Bird, for $35 sold to
                            William Lesley of South Carolina, 200 ac.
now in possession of James Thompson on branch of Beaver Creek and on old
road called Leatherdale Road, bd. on E. by William Brown, part of 1,000
acres granted Mark Bird 7 Nov. 1791, bd. all other sides by this land.
Date: 1 Jul. 1806. Wit: P. Norris, W. Brown, Robert Dowdle, Sr. William
Brown made oath to Jno. George, J.P., 16 Aug. 1806.
Rec: 28 Oct. 1806.

Pages 444-445:   1 Oct. 1796, Reuben Pyles of Laurens Co.,
                            S. C., 96 Dist., to Levi Robbins for Ł 47
                            for 1,000 acres on Cane Creek, granted to
Pyles by Wm. Moultrie. Wit: John Vickrey, Albert Robins. Albert Robins
made oath to Joseph Reid, J.P., 18 Jun. 1798.
Rec: 19 Nov. 1806.

Pages 445-446:   Saml. Little of Franklin Co., Ga. for Ł 20
                            sold to Samuel Anderson of Pendleton Dist.,
                            40 acres, part of 204 acres granted David
Jordan, in Washington Dist. on 26 Mile Creek, bd. by Andrew Liddle. Date:
15 Apr. 1803. Wit: John McMillion, Andrew Liddle. (No oath).
Rec: 21 Nov. 1806.

Page 446:   William Gray for $275 sold to Levi Robbins
                            273 acres on Crooked Creek of Little River
                            of Keowee River, bd. by James Barton, Sr.,
granted William Gray by Chas. Pinckney, 3 Apr. 1797. Date: (blank). Wit:
Sampson Vickrey, Milley (X) Eaton. Sampson Vickrey made oath to Jno.
Adair, J.P., 19 Nov. 1806.
Rec: 19 Nov. 1806.

Pages 446-447:   Samuel Burks for $350 sold Forrister Upsher
                            180 acres on N. side of Chauga on Richaland
                            Creek, where Burks now lives. Date: 9 Nov.
1805. Wit: Jno. Barton, J.P., Charles Baker. Samuel Burks acknowledged
deed to John Barton, J.P. (no date).
Rec: 27 Oct. 1806.

Page 447:   Forrister Upshear of Pendleton Dist., for
                            $300 sold to William Faulkner of Georgia,
                            180 acres on N. side of Chauga, where Up-
shear now lives. Date: 8 Sep. 1806. Wit: Rhoda Barton, Anna Barton. For-
ister Upshear ack. deed to Jno. Barton, J.P. 8 Sep. 1806. Rec: 27 Oct. 1806.

Page 448: Phillip Meroney for $500 sold Reuben Copeland 200 acres on 12 Mile River of Saluda River. Date: 7 Feb. 1804. Signed: Phil. D. Maroney. Wit: David Murphree, Jesse Murphree. David Murphree made oath to Amos Ladd, J.P., 16 May 1805. Rec: 27 Oct. 1806.

Pages 448-449: Samuel McCully and Jenny McCully for $300 sold to Sugar Mayfield 327 acres on Rocky River of the Savannah River, part of tract granted Peter Graham, 5 Mar. 1792 by Chas. Pinckney, recorded Bk. D, no. 5, p. 452, conveyed from him to McCully; another part granted McCully, 20 Nov. 1802 by John Drayton, recorded Bk. XXX, no. 5 (sic), p. 164 for 107 acres; another part of 40 or 50 acres, part of tract granted Prichard Stone, 3 Sep. 1792, conveyed to Peter Graham, from him to McCully, bd. by Stephen Bennet, John (?) Duncan. Date: 26 Jan. 1805. Signed: Samuel McCully, Jain McCully. Wit: Abraham Mayfield, James McCoy. James McCoy made oath to Aaron Broyles, J.P., 2 Feb. 1805. Rec: 27 Oct. 1806.

Pages 449-450: (Very dim; cannot read the beginning but appears to be...) Jane Ann Butler, formerly Jane Ann Wise, for $115 sold to Thomas Harris 440 acres, laid out by John Martin, D.S., on Little Beaverdam Crk of the Toogaloo River, being bounty to Major Samuel Wise, Esq., bd. by Maj. Mools(?). Date: 21 Dec. 1802. Signed: Jane Ann Butler. Wit: Samuel Campbell, John Harris. Saml. Campbell made oath to John Harris, J. P., 21 Dec. 1802. Jane Ann Butler appeared to John Harris, J.P., and made the oath that at the time she had no lawful heirs or child, 21 Dec. 1802.

Pages 450-452: John Ewing Calhoun, dec'd., at time of his death, possessed the plantation described. On 8 Feb. 1799 he entered into a contract with William Floyd to sell the plantation for $600 and by bond from Alexander Floyd, Elisha Floyd and William Floyd and by will of John Ewing Calhoun, did execute on the date of 20 May 1802, appointed Henry William Desausure, Executor, and by codicil of 21 Oct. 1802, the testator appointed Ezekiel Pickens, Co-Executor......the sd. William Floyd did pay John Ewing Calhoun in his lifetime for tract as appears by receipt produced by William Floyd, he having sold the premises for valuable consideration to Mr. Joseph Read, and now demand from Henry William Desausure and Ezekiel Pickens to execute titles for 650 acres bd. W. on Keowee River, N. by Joseph Reed, Esq., E. by John Green, S. by Lamar, granted in 2 tracts: one to Joseph Spears for 150 acres, the other to John Ewing Calhoun for 500 acres. Date: 10 May 1805. Signed: Henry William Desaussure, E. Pickens, Exors. of J. E. Ewing(?) (Calhoun?). Wit: Eldred Simkins, R. Anderson, Jr. Robert Anderson, Jr. made oath to Samuel H. Dickson, J.P......We, the Executors certify tract, we have been informed and believe $1,600 instead of $600 was paid to the late J. E. Calhoun in his lifetime. Rec: 12 Nov. 1806.

Pages 452-453: William Murphree for $50 sold to Mary Murphree and Elijah Murphree, Administrators of Levi Murphree, dec'd., 100 acres. Date: 12 Jul. 1805. Wit: James Jett, Aaron (X) Murphree. Aaron Murphree made oath to David Murphree, J.P., 8 Oct. 1806. Rec: 9 Oct. 1806.

Pages 453-454: Ezekiel Pickens for 5 shillings sold Edward Landers 105 acres on Big Branch of Generostee, where Charleston Road crosses where Landers now lives, bd. by Jesse McGee, part of tract granted Thomas Lesley, laid off by Samuel Dickson, Esq. Date: 14 Nov. 1806. Wit: B. Greene and Michael Speed. Michael Speed made oath to M. Hammond, D.C., 26 Nov. 1806. (Plat). Rec: 26 Nov. 1806.

Pages 454-455: 25 Nov. 1789, Jehu Pope to John Cox for ₤20 stg. for 250 acres on 26 Mile Creek, part of tract granted Francis Guttery by Benjn.

(Pages 454-455 cont'd): Guerard on 15 Oct. 1784, recorded Bk. AAAA, p. 136, transferred from Guttery to Pope on 24 Oct. 1786. Wit: James Jones, William Stone. James Jones made oath to Jonathan Gibbs, J.P., 28 Oct. 1806, saying "the time being so long past, his memory has failed so that he cannot be positive, but knowing his own handwrite(sic) and remembering he was called on".
Rec: 28 Oct. 1806.

Pages 455-456: Thomas Lesley, farmer, for Ł 200 stg. sold Ezekiel Pickens, Attorney at Law, of St. Thomas Parish, S. C., 618 acres granted to Thomas Lesley on big branch of Great Generostee, surveyed by Samuel Dickson, Esq., bd. on N. by land laid out for Hugh Simpson, now owned by David Andrews, George Weems, NE. by Edward Landers and William Lesley, S. by William Lesley and Isaac Steele, in his lifetime, W. by land formerly owned by Isaac Steele and Michael Steele. Date: 25 Oct. 1805. Wit: Nathaniel Shotwell, Michael Speed. Mrs. Mary Lesley, wife of Thomas Lesley, released dower to Henry Burch, J.Q., 26 Oct. 1805. Nathaniel Shotwell made oath to M. Hammond, D.C., 4 Nov. 1806. Plat - resurvey for 640 ac. on 15 Sep. 1802, Samuel H. Dickson, D.S.
Rec: 1 Nov. 1806.

Page 457: Phillip D. Meroney for $200 sold to Reuben Copeland 150 acres on S. side of Hickory Mill Mountain on branch of Wolf Creek, bd. by Samuel Earle, part of 779 acres granted James Glasby. Date: 7 Feb.1804. Wit: David Murphree, Jesse Murphree. David Murphree made oath to Amos Ladd, J.P., 26 May 1805.
Rec: 27 Oct. 1805.

Pages 457-458: Job Smith for $100 sold to David Smith 144 acres on W. side of 23 Mile Creek. Wit: Benjn. Smith, Andrew Oliver, Wm. McMahan. Elizabeth (X) Smith, wife of Job Smith, released dower to John Willson, Q.U., 27 May 1806. Benjn. Smith made oath to John Willson, 27 May 1806.
Rec: 28 Oct. 1806.

Pages 458-460: David Smith of Laurence Dist., S. C. for $300 sold to John Cross of Pendleton Dist. 200 acres on 23 Mile Creek of Savannah River, part of 2 tracts: one granted Job Smith, Jr. by Wm. Moultrie, 1 May 1786 for 144 acres, bd. by Benjamin Smith, Wilson, Rankin's Mill, the other granted Job Smith, Sr. by Benj. Guerard, 14 Oct. 1784 for 200 ac., bd. by William Rankin's Mill pond, and Waggon Road. Date: 29 May 1806. Wit: Benjn. Smith, John Willson, Job Smith. Benjn. Smith made oath to John Willson, Q.U., 27 May 1806. Rebecca (X) Smith, wife of David Smith, released dower to John Willson, 27 May 1806.
Rec: 28 Oct. 1806.

Page 460: John Drennan for $150 sold to Edly Lynn 134 acres on W. side of Rocky River. Date: 23 Mar. 1804. Wit: James Drennan, Adam Todd. Adam Todd made oath to John George, J.P., 26 Sep. 1805.
Rec: 28 Oct. 1806.

Pages 460-462: James Gilliland for $460 sold to Samuel McElroy 224 acres on both sides of Rocky River, part of tract granted James Caldwell. Date: 4 Mar. 1805. Wit: John McElroy, Robert Stevenson. (Plat). John McElroy made oath to James Wellburn, Q.U., 4 Apr. 1805. Frances Gilliland the wife of James Gilliland, released dower to James Wellburn, 4 April 1805. Rec: 28 Oct. 1806.

Page 462: Essey Meeks and Fanny Meeks for $265 sold to James Starrett 200 acres on N. fork of Cain Creek, granted John Williams, as a bounty, 21 Jan. 1785 by Benj. Guerard, surveyed by Thomas Lewis, D.S. Date: ___ 1802. Signed: Nasse Meeks, Fanny Meeks. Wit: Littleton (X) Meeks, Isaac Crabtree. Isaac Crabtree made oath he saw Nese Meeks and his wife, Fanny, sign deed to John Verner, Q. U., 13 Oct. 1806. (cont'd):

(Page 462 cont'd):   Rec: 28 Oct. 1806.

Pages 462-463:   26 Oct. 1803, Edward Bird, Attorney for Mark
                          Bird of Rutherford Co., N. C., to Samuel Mc-
                          Cully of Pendleton Dist., for $200 for 464
acres on Neel's(?) Creek, bd. by William Smith. Wit: David Wade, Moses
Holland, Thomas Burford. David Wade made oath to Jno. George, J. P., 18
Oct. 1806.
Rec: 29 Oct. 1806.

Pages 463-464:   David Drennan and Mary Wheems Drennan for
                          $425 aols to Job Hammond 100 acres on Broad-
                          away of Rocky River of Savannah River, bd.
by Dudley Hammond, John George, John McCinstry, Martha Anderson. Date: 6
Jan. 1806. Signed: David Drennan, Mary (X) W. Drennan. Wit: S. J. Hammond
and D. Hammond. S. J. Hammond made oath to John George, J.P., 31 January
1807. Rec: 2 Feb. 1807.

Pages 464-465:   James Gilliland for $650 sold Jno. McFall
                          200 acres on W. side of Broadaway Creek of
                          Rocky River, part of 2 tracts: one granted
Thomas Burford by Wm. Moultrie 5 Jun. 1786, recorded Bk. NNNN, p. 207,the
other granted Thomas Burford by Benj. Guerard 21 Jan. 1785, recorded Bk.
DDDD, p. 44. Date: 8 Apr. 1805. Wit: Joseph Wornock, John Gilliland......
Frances Gilliland, wife of James Gilliland, released dower to E. Browne,
Q.U., 9 Apr. 1805. John Gilliland made oath to (cannot read)..........

Pages 465-466:   Samuel Robertson, of the City of Charleston
                          for $1,100 sold to John McFall of Pendle-
                          ton Dist., 640 acres near head of Wilson's
(?) Creek of Rocky River, granted John Kerr, surveyed by Patrick Colhoun,
Esq., also, 590 acres adjoining above tract, granted William Matthews(?),
except 50 acres I sold to William Lesley, Esq. Date: 28 Mar. 1805. Wit:
Geo. Robertson, Robert Dowdle. Mrs. Ann Robertson, wife of Samuel Rob-
ertson, released dower to Charles Few, J.P.Q.U., 28 Mar. 1805. Robert
Dowdle made oath to Jno. George, J.P., 25 Feb. 1806.
Rec: 2 Feb. 1807.

Pages 466-467:   William Townsend for $120 sold John McFall
                          97½ acres on Rocky River of Savannah River,
                          part of 539 acres granted Mary Anderson on
3 Oct. 1785, bd. by Samuel Duncan, Samuel Gipson, John Anderson, Coxe's
Creek, John Smith and William Townsend. Date: 10 Mar. 1804. Wit: Wm. Mc-
Elvaney, Joseph Black. Margaret (X) Townsend, wife of William Townsend,
released dower to E. Browne, Q.U., 13 Mar. 1804. Joseph Black made oath
to Jno. George, J.P., 21 Jan. 1807.
Rec: 2 Feb. 1807.

Pages 467-468:   Daniel Williams for $210 sold John Woodall
                          200 acres. Date: 25 Oct. 1806. Wit: Samuel
                          Power, Joseph Heaton. (No oath). Rec: 2 Feb.
                          1807.

Pages 468-469:   Robert Bowen for $100 sold to Richard Stea-
                          gall 600 acres , bd. W. by Col. John Brown.
                          Date: 8 Oct. 1805. Wit; John Brown, John
McClure, Hezekiah Goodrich. John McClure made oath to Wm. Edmondson, JQ,
8 Oct. 1805. (Mary (X) Bowen, wife of Robert Bowen, released dower to
Wm. Edmondson, 8 Oct. 1805.
Rec: 2 Feb. 1807.

Pages 469-470:   John Nickleson for $556 sold James Matkin
                          217 acres on Big Creek of Saluda River.
                          Date: 9 Mar. 1805. Signed: John Nicholson.
Wit: John Holbert, Geo. Dilworth. Jane Nicholson, wife of John Nicholson,
released dower to James Welbourn, Q.U., 9 Mar. 1805. Signed: Jean (X)
Nicholson. George Dilworth made oath to James Welbourn, 9 Mar. 1805.
Rec: 2 Feb. 1807.

Pages 470-471:   Shadrack Ingram for $250 sold James Hayes

(Pages 470-471 cont'd): 100 acres where Ingram now lives, on Great Generostee Creek, made over from Daniel Stringer to Ingram 9 Nov. 1799. Date: 19 Jan. 1802. Signed: Shadrack (X) Ingram. Wit: John Carrick who made oath to John Tippen, Q.U., 31 January 1807. Rec: 2 Feb. 1807.

Pages 471-472: Auldin Tucker for $250 sold John Sorrells, Sr., 93 acres being W. part of Robert Hall's land on First Creek of Rocky River (except 2 acres where Robert Hall's spring is), bd. by Bartley Tucker, Benjamin Farmer. Date: 24 Jan. 1804. Signed: Auldin (X) Tucker. Wit: Winston Hall and Robert Hall. Clary (X) Tucker, wife of Auldin Tucker, released dower to E. Browne, Q.U., 20 Jul. 1804. Robert Hall made oath to E. Browne, 22 Feb. 1804.
Rec: 3 Feb. 1807.

Page 472: 18 Jan. 1806, James Weems of Abbeville District, is bound to Isaac Goldin of Pendleton Dist., for $600, for security 407 ac. part of tract granted Harry Persons for 457 acres on 26 Mile River of the Savannah River. Wit: John Willson, Esq., who made oath to Rt. McCann, JP on 22 Jan. 1807.
Rec: 10 Feb. 1807.

Page 473: William Borland for $200 sold John Howard 100 acres on Crow Creek and Mile Creek. Date: 29 Oct. 1801. Signed: William Bourland. Wit: Robert Akins, Hugh Forgison. Robert Akins made oath to John McClure, J.Q., 21 Dec. 1805.
Rec: 17 Feb. 1807.

Pages 473-474: Charles Bradly for $200 sold John Howard 237 acres on Mile and Crow Creek of Keowee River, part of tract granted James Bradly in 1792, where Ridge road crosses that went from Patterson's to Joseph Woodall. Date: 10 Jun. 1803. Wit: Archibald Bourland, John McElroy. John McElroy made oath to John McClure, J.P., 4 Jan. 1806.
Rec: 17 Feb. 1807.

Page 474: John Howard for $425 sold Elisha Smith 337 acres on Crow and Mile Creek, part granted James Abit, bd. by William Bourland and Ross. Date: 5 Oct. 1805. Signed: John (X) Howard. Wit: James Young, Onely (X) Carney. James Young made oath to Henry Burch, J.Q., 10 Feb. 1807.
Rec: 17 Feb. 1807.

Page 475: Jesse Crane for $50 sold Elisha Smith 100 acres on Crow Creek of Keowee River. Date: 8 Dec. 1805. Signed: Jesse (X) Crane. Wit: James Young, Aaron (X) Crane. James Young made oath to Henry Burch, JQ, 10 Feb. 1807.
Rec: 17 Feb. 1807.

Pages 475-477: 7 Feb. 1806, David McCaleb, Sheriff, to John Hamilton....John Armstrong entered judgement in Court of Common Pleas for $50 against William Carter, all goods and chattels of Wm. Carter ordered to be sold at Public Auction to the highest bidder, being John Hamilton for $22, for 307 acres on George's Creek of the Saluda River, granted William Reed, bd. by John Armstrong, Wm. McCanrey(?). Wit: A. Lawhon, Jno. Hunter. Archibald Lawhon made oath to M. Hammond, D.C., 21 Feb. 1807.

Pages 477-478: Jonathan Kemp to Charles Bruce (no amount given) for 359½ acres in 96 Dist., on both sides of Grindal's Creek of Keowee River, bd. on E. by Alexander Kilpatrick, N. by Jno. Gradal, SW by Ezekiel Mason, E. by John Portman, granted Jonathan Kemp by Arnoldus Vanderhorst, recorded Bk. P, no. 5, p. 104, on 8 Jan. 1795. Date: 27 Sep. 1799. Wit: John Harris, Thomas Gorman. Elizabeth (X) Kemp, wife of Jonathan Kemp,

(Pages 477-478 cont'd): released dower to Joshua Saxon, J. Q., 13 May 1800. John Harris, Esq., made oath to Saml. H. Dickson, J. P., 9 Mar. 1802.
Rec: 21 Jan. 1807.

Pages 478-479: Jonathan Kemp for $1,098 sold Charles Bruce 158 acres on SW of Keowee River, granted to Alexander Kilpatrick in 1786 by Wm. Moultrie, recorded Bk. X, no. 3575(?), by James Mitchell, also recorded in Bk. MMMM, p. 209. Date: 8 Sep. 1799. Wit: John Harris, Thomas Gorman. Elizabeth Kemp released dower to Joshua Saxon, 13 May 1800. John Harris made oath to Saml. H. Dickson, 9 Mar. 1802. (No oath).

Pages 479-480: Jonathan Kemp, planter, for 4 shillings sold to Charles Bruce 109 acres in 96 Dist. surveyed for Kemp, 1795, on NE side of the Keowee River, including mouth of 18 Mile Creek, bd. N. by James Ditto, NE by Stephen Fuller, recorded Bk. O, no. (?), p. 3524(?). Date: 8 Sep.1799. Wit: John Harris, Thomas Gorman. Elizabeth Kemp released dower to Joshua Saxon, 13 May 1800. John Harris made oath to Saml. H. Dickson, 9 March 1802. (No recording date).

Page 481: John Bynum for $100 sold Benjamin Bynum 250 acres on Town Creek of 12 Mile River. Date: 6 Dec. 1804. Wit: James Jett, William (X) Bynum, Jr. William Bynum made oath to John Cochran, Q.U., 18 Feb. 1807.
Rec: 22 Feb. 1807.

Pages 481-482: John Midowal(?) for $300 sold Joseph Glenn, Jr., 130 acres part of 2 tracts, granted to John Hallum and Wm. Huggins, on NW side of 18 Mile Creek of the Savannah River, bd. E. and NE by Starrett Dobbins and John Morrow, NW by David Garvin and Tilly Merick, S. by Jonathan Reeder. Date: 23 Mar. 1805. Signed: John (X) Midowal, Margaret (X) Midowal. Wit: James Garvin, Starrett Dobbins. Starrett Dobbins made oath to Saml. H. Dickson, J.P., 25 May 1805.
Rec: 26 Sep. 1806.

Pages 482-483: William Fortain for $130 sold Ezekiel Pilgrim "all that tenth part" of 1,000 acres on 18 Mile and 23 Mile Creeks of Savannah River, bd. SW and SE by Ephraim Lindsey, NW by Thomas Gadson, SW by Charles Hughes, granted William Burney, 1792, recorded Bk. T, no. 5, p. 39. Date: 13 Nov. 1806. Signed: William (X) Fortain. Wit: John Hunnicutt, Peter Vandergrift, Amos Pilgram. Peter Vandergrift made oath to John Willson, Q.U., 13 Sep. 1806. Martha (X) Fortain, wife of William Fortain, released dower to John Willson, 15 Nov. 1806.
Rec: 26 Feb. 1807.

Pages 483-484: 10 Sep. 1794, Thomas Finley to Martha Henderson for £ 100 for 1,000 acres on both sides of Cain Creek of Toogaloe River, granted by Wm. Moultrie, 2 Sep. 1793. Wit: Jas. Brown, Elijah Mayfield. James Brown made oath to Aaron Broyles, Q.U., 28 Feb. 1807.
Rec: 2 Mar. 1807.

Pages 484-485: 14 Mar. 1793, John Hennington to William Henderson for £ 30 stg. for 131 acres granted 6 Jun. 1791 by Chas. Pinckney to Hennington, in Washington Dist. on N. side of Keowee River. Signed: John Hennington, Elizabeth Hennington. Wit: Ann Shepherd, John Moorhead. John Moorhead made oath to George Nash, J.P., 2 Mar. 1807.
Rec: 2 Mar. 1807.

Pages 485-486: Hezekiah Lizingby, planter, for $200 sold Thomas Garvin 125 acres on W. branches of 15 Mile Creek of the Savannah River, bd. E. by Fred Johnson, N. by Jonah Broughton, NW, SW and SE by Thomas Garvin, Jr., part of 2 tracts: one granted Thomas Sherley 1785, the other to Geo. Payne 1792. Date: 4 Feb. 1807. Signed: Hezekiah Lisenbe. Wit: David Gar-

(Pages 485-486 cont'd): vin, James Hall, Jehu Grayham. David Garvin made oath to Saml. H. Dickson, J.P., 10 Feb. 1807. Rec: 2 Mar. 1807.

Pages 486-487: William Robinson for $200 sold Richard Robinson 145-3/4 acres on 23 Mile Creek of the Seneca River, conveyed to Wm. Robinson by his father, John Robinson, by deed on 1 Apr. 1799, bd. by John West, Taylor & Cherry, Elisha Robinson. Date: 1 Feb. 1807. Wit: William Hamilton, Andrew Hamilton, Joseph Jolly. The within conveyed tract was sold by me as the Sheriff of Pendleton Dist. and bid off by Capt. Jas. Wood, but it was afterwards between the sd. Wood and Wm. Robinson that Robinson, giving Wood good security and that the land should again revert back to Wm. Robinson, 21 Feb. 1807. Signed: D. McCaleb. William Hamilton made oath to John Cochran, Q.U., 26 Mar. 1807.....Plat, at request of Major James Wood, I have surveyed the tract wherein Wm. Robinson now lives on 23 Mile Creek, 4 Sep. 1806. William Hamilton, D. S.

Pages 487-488: 21 Jun. 1797, Thomas Watson and Elizabeth, his wife, of Washington Dist., to William Laughton of same district, for Ł 50 stg., for 127 acres part of 640 acres granted James Daugherty by Wm. Moultrie, 19 Jan. 1785, recorded Bk. JJJJ, p. 200, on Town Creek of 26 Mile Creek bd. by William Milwee, Mr. Bruster, Mary Ridgdel, John Pollock. Signed: Thomas Watson, Elizabeth (X) Watson. Wit: Benjamin Land, James Anderson, Mary (X) Watson. James Anderson made oath to Wm. Mulwee, J.P., 11 Dec. 1797. Rec: 27 Oct. 1806.

Pages 488-489: 11 Jan. 1797, January (later spelled Ganeway) Johnston to David Hughs for Ł 100 stg. for 150½ acres where Hughs now lives, part of a tract granted Wm. Reed, bd. by William Jewel, William McAmey. Signed: January (X) Johnston. Wit: Charles (X) Hughes, Charles Armstrong. Charles Armstrong made oath to R. Bowen, J.P., 10 Dec. 1799. Rec: 2 Mar. 1807.

Page 489: John Brown for $400 sold Joab Mauldin 150 acres on George's Creek, bd. on E. by Wm. Edmondson, S. by John Armstrong, W. by Robert Norris and land late the property of Absolom Brown, S. by Francis Brown and Joab Mauldin. Date: 6 Nov. 1806. Wit: Joseph (X) Smith and James Rowland. James Rowland made oath to Wm. Edmondson, J.P., 24 Feb. 1806. Rec: 2 Mar. 1807.

Pages 489-490: George <u>Arcer</u> for $400 sold Absalom Brown 146 acres on S. branch of George's Creek of the Saluda River, bd. by Johnson. Date: 22 Jan. 1804. Signed: George <u>Archer</u>. Wit: John Brown, Jeremiah (X) Foster. John Brown made oath to Wm. Edmondson, J.P., 13 Aug. 1804. Rec: 22 Mar. 1807.

Pages 490-491: Absalom Brown for $150 sold Robert Norris 100 acres on S. branch of George's Creek, bd. by Brown, Joseph Smith, Francis Bremar, purchased by Brown from George Archer. Date: 23 Dec. 1805. Wit: Joab Mauldin, John Brown. Joab Mauldin made oath to Wm. Edmondson, J.Q., 24 Feb. 1807. Rec: 2 Mar. 1807.

Pages 491-492: Absalom Brown for $300 sold Joab Mauldin 150 acres where Brown now lives, on Georges Creek, bd. by Robert Norris, Joseph Smith, John Armstrong, Thos. Henderson, Frances Bremar, near the main road leading from Parris' ford to Pickensville. Date: 13 Sep. 1806. Wit: Robert Norris, Cornelius Green. Robert Norris made oath to Wm. Edmondson, Q.U., 24 Feb. 1807. Rec: 2 Mar. 1807.

Page 492: 12 Nov. 1804, David Hughs to Ledwick Earnest for Ł 100 stg. for 150½ acres where Hughs now lives, bd. by John Armstrong, Wm.

(Page 492 cont'd): Edmondson, Mr. Bremar, Absalom Brown. Wit: John Hamilton, William Hobbs. John Hamilton made oath to Wm. Edmondson, J.Q., 24 Nov. 1804.
Rec: 2 Mar. 1807.

Pages 492-493: Reuben Tarrant for $500 sold to John Mullinax 250 acres granted Fredrick Glover on 1 Mar. 1790. Date: 1 Dec. 1805. Wit: William Grimes, Joseph Mullinix. Joseph Mullinix made oath to John Willson, QU, 1 May 1806.
Rec: 7 Mar. 1807.

Page 493: Hugh Moore for $17 sold to John Mullinix (later called Joseph Mullinix) 40 acres on Cane Creek of Big Eastatoe Creek. Date: 15 May 1806. Signed: Hugh (X) Moore. Wit: James Jett, Richard Gibson. (Plat) Richard Gibson made oath to John Cochran, J.Q., 3 Mar. 1807. Sarah (X) Moore, wife of Hugh Moore, released dower to John Cochran, 2 Jan. 1807.
Rec: 27 Mar. 1807.

Page 494: 9 Sep. 1806, Benjamin Cleveland to Daniel Cleveland for $10 for 250 acres on Toogooloo River, part of 3 tracts where Benjamin now lives. Wit: John Cleveland, Nimrod Leathers. Nimrod Leathers made the oath to John Verner, J.Q., 15 Jan. 1807.
Rec: 30 Jan. 1807.

Pages 494-496: 7 Jul. 1806, David McCaleb, Sheriff, to Samuel Cherry.....John Cooke on 4th Monday of March 1806 in the Court of Common Pleas received judgement of $481.33 against Henry Kyle, ...all goods, chattels, lands of Kyle ordered sold at public auction to the highest bidder, being Samuel Cherry for $13 for lot of 1 acre known as Lot #12 in the Village of Pendleton. Wit: James Todd, Joseph Whitner. Joseph Whitner made oath to M. Hammond, D.C., 26 Dec. 1806.
Rec: 26 Dec. 1806.

Page 496: Andrew McCalister for $30 sold to William Beaty 15 acres on Little Generostee Creek, part of 37 acres granted Nathan Young by Wm. Moultrie, 15 Jun. 1786. Date: 22 Jan. 1807. Wit: Robert Loosk, Robert Love. Robert Loosk made oath to John Scott, J.P., 7 Mar. 1807.
Rec: 11 Mar. 1807.

Page 497: Andrew Pickens for $1,028.14 sold to William Beaty 163 acres surveyed for Robert Craven on 6 Sep. 1790 and granted to Ellis Harland and Ezekiel Buffington, 12 Jun. 1792, on NW fork of Little River of Keowee River. Date: 1 Jul. 1806. Wit: Nathan Lusk, Alexr. Keown. Alexander Keown made oath to W. Nicholson, J.P., 2 Mar. 1807. Plat surveyed 3 May 1806 by John Grisham, D.S., land bd. on N. by Wm. Nicholson, Esq., on E. by White, on S. by Nicholson.
Rec: 11 Mar. 1807.

Page 497: 27 Apr. 1805, Rowland Tankersly and Richard his son, sold to William Copeland a negro man named Tom now in the possession of Henry Paris and as soon as redeemed from sd. Parris servitude, for $450. Wit: Clara Tankersly.
Rec: 11 Mar. 1807. (No oath).

Pages 498-499: 5 May 1806, David McCaleb, Sheriff, to James Wood, Merchant.....James Gillison was possessed of a tract when Ezekiel Pickens, Executor of John E. Colhoun, dec'd., on 2nd Monday of March 1804 received judgement against James Gillison and James Dickson for $130 and all goods chattels and lands were ordered sold at public auction to the highest bidder being James Wood for $5 for 300 acres on S. branch of Richland Creek of the Keowee River, granted Capt. Michael Kaltison(?) by Benj. Guerard, 21 Jan. 1785. Wit: Joseph Whitner, William Steele, Jr. William Steele, Jr.

(Pages 498-499 cont'd): made oath to M. Hammond, D. C., 13 March 1807. Rec: 13 Mar. 1807.

Pages 499-501: 2 Jan. 1802, David McCaleb, Sheriff, to John Taylor....John Taylor, Esq. on 2nd Monday of October 1801 obtained judgement against Joseph Anglin for $48.43 and all goods, chattels and lands of sd. Anglin ordered sold at public auction to highest bidder, being John Taylor for $35 for 100 acres on 26 Mile Creek being the plantation where Joseph Anglin formerly lived, within 2 miles of Pickensville. Wit: William Hamilton, T. W. Farrar. Wm. Hamilton made oath to M. Hammond, D. C., 13 Mar. 1807. Rec: 13 Mar. 1807.

Pages 501-503: 6 Jan. 1806, David McCaleb, Sheriff, to Thomas Garvin, planter, ...whereas, Peter Freneau and Francis Bremar were..... seized of a tract when Hezekiah Listenby on 4th Monday of October 1805, received judgement in Court of Common Pleas for $17.10 against Freneau & Bremar, all goods, chattels, lands ordered sold at public auction to the highest bidder being Thomas Garvin for $69 by his friend, Jonathan Reeder, for 587 acres part of 640 acres granted Freneau & Bremar, on dividing ridge between 12 Mile and 18 Mile Creeks, bd. SE by Thomas Garvin,Sr. on W. by Robert Fullerton, S. by John Cunningham, N. by Gen. Robert Anderson, NE by Hezekiah Listenby. Wit: Robert Brackenridge, Wm. Hamilton. William Hamilton made oath to M. Hammond, D.C., 13 Mar. 1807. Rec: 13 Mar. 1807.

Page 503: Richard Wade, one of the Executors and Legatees of the Estate of David Wade, dec'd., for $52.64 sold to Thomas C. Wade and David Wade, his right to sd. Estate. Date: 7 Oct. 1805. Signed: Richard (X)Wade. Wit: Adam Todd, Hezekiah Rice. Hezekiah Rice made oath to Jno. George,JP, 23 Oct. 1806. Rec: 27 Oct. 1806.

Pages 503-504: 6 Mar. 1807, Benjamin Johnson to Peter Wagnon and Thomas Davis for $800 for 245 ac. on Toogooloo River, bd. by Hatten's ford, 19 acres granted John Fleek(?) and 35 acres that Greeor(?) bought from Capt. David Sloan and 14 acres (bought?) of Esquire Jacob Holland, bd. by Sloan and Greeor, Fleek's old line, made by Amose and his father, including where Johnson now lives. Wit: Robert Johnson, Mark Wagnon. Mark Wagnon made oath to M. Hammond, D.C., 13 Mar. 1807. Rec: 13 Mar. 1807.

Page 504: Adam Thompson in consideration of many good deeds and services done me by Elizabeth Widgion, give her a mare and colt, cow and calf, working tools and kitchen furniture, with crop now growing on my plantation. Date: 20 Aug. 1806. Wit: Prudence (X) Turner, Jean (X) Hollingsworth. Prudence Turner made oath to David Murphree, J.P., 20 Aug. 1806. Rec: 16 Mar. 1807.

Pages 504-505: William Rowen for $100 sold Samuel Earle 41 acres part of tract of 81 acres granted to Samuel Rowen by Edward Rutledge 4 Feb. 1799. Date: 18 Apr. 1806. Wit: John Pinkerton, James Corwine(?). Nancy Rowen, wife of William Rowen, released dower to J. Stribling, Q.U., 24 Apr.1806. James Carwine made oath to H. McCray, J.P., 24 Apr. 1806. Rec: 29 Oct. 1806.

Pages 505-506: James Lawson for $50 sold Samuel Earle lot of land in Town of Andersonville at Confluence of the Tugaloo and Keowee River known as Lot #30. Date: 12 Jul. 1806. Wit: James Barton, Geo. D. Paine. Ann Lawson, wife of James Lawson, released dower to Jesse Stribling, J.Q.,19 Jul. 1806. James Barton made oath to Jesse Stribling, J.P., 19 Jul. 1806. (No recording date).

Page 506: Samuel Taylor for $300 sold to William Mc-
Callister, planter, 200 acres granted James
Jordan, 1790, on Keowee River, bd. by John
Sportsman, Bennet Aden. Date: 20 Mar. 1807. Wit: Saml. Cherry, A. Lawhon.
(No oath).
Rec: 20 Mar. 1807.

Page 507: Barnet Putnam for Ł 40 sold Stephen Grifith
197 acres, part of 400 acres granted to Wm.
Love by Thos. Pinckney, 7 Jan. 1788, bd. by
Love and Green. Date: 29 Aug. 1803. Wit: Abraham Moore, James Moore. Abraham Moore made oath to Hezekiah Davis, J.P., 6 Oct. 1803.
Rec: 30 Oct. 1805.

Pages 507-508: John Morris for $200 sold Matthew Clark 73
acres part of 413 acres granted to Morris
on 21 Jul. 1795 by Wm. Moultrie on 26 Mile
Creek. Date: 17 Dec. 1806. Wit: William Brown, John Gentry. Susannah Morris, wife of John Morris, released dower to J. Stribling, Q.U., 17 Dec. 1806. Rec: 20 Mar. 1807.

Page 508: 12 Feb. 1801, Stephen Whitmire to Wm. Robins for $750 for 204½ acres, part of two
tracts: one bd. by Samuel Whitmire, also,
part of tract surveyed for Fields Prewet, bd. by Christopher Whitmire and
Stephen Whitmire, on N. fork of Cain Creek of the Keowee, granted to Ez.
Buffington, Ellis Warling (should by Harlan) and Field Prewet, recorded
Bk. FFFF, p. 111. Signed: Stephen Whitmire, Mary (X) Whitmire. Wit.: Peter Phrow, Francis (X) Bradley. Peter Phrow made oath to Henry Burch, JP
on 12 Feb. 1801. (No recording date).

Page 509: Rec'd. and settled with Capt. Lewis D. Martin the full amount due me rent of my house
which has been occupied by him in Village
of Pendleton, in full to 14 Mar. 1807. Signed: Edward Adair. Teste: Samuel Cherry, who made oath 20 Mar. 1807. (Cannot read J.P.).
Rec: __ Mar. 1807.

Page 509: (Note: much of this cannot be read...BW)
By John Willson, one of the Justices of the
Quoram, to any lawful constable, wherein
David _____ in Pendleton Courthouse there was a _____ reporting to
be a receipt for a large sum of money _____ was signed _____ seen by
complainant until _____ counterfiet and he has reason to believe Joab Lewis did sign this complaint's (sic) name _____ and bring him before me
or the next Justice _____ to be further dealt with _____. Date: 26 Mar.
1806. _____ (appears to be receipt of Joab Lewis in full for all
notes _____ dues and trespass _____ have given receipt.). __ Feb. ____.
Signed: David Hughs. Joseph (X) Woods made oath to receipt and that the
sd. Hughs was perfectly satisfied, 24 Oct. 1806, to John Cochran, Q. U.,
and Rec: 27 Oct. 1806.

Page 509-510: John Burks for $300 sold Phillip Smith 140
acres on N. fork of Coneross Creek of the
Keowee River, bd. by Towers, Abbett, Burk.
Date: 7 Dec. 1805. Wit: Josiah Foster, Christian Sloan. Josiah Foster
made oath to Wm. Towers, J.P., 13 Apr. 1807.
Rec: 13 Apr. 1807.

Pages 510-511: 12 Oct. 1806, John Adam Miller to Dudley
Hammond for $101 for 148 acres on Mountain
Creek of Big Generostee, granted William
Thackerby by Thos. Pinckney, recorded Bk. WWWW, p. 116, bd. by Vines,
Moore, Fowler. (Cannot read Witness). Jobe Hammond signed oath. Hester
(X) Miller released dower, __ Mar. 1807.

Page 511: (Note: much of this cannot read...BW)......
George _____, Executors of last will and
_____ of _____, waters of Keowee. Mentions Zachariah Hembree _____ bd. by Capt. John Dickson _____

(Page 511 cont'd): Signed: John Anderson, George Reed, John Harris(?), Rt. McCann. Wit: (cannot read). Michael Doyle made oath and said Simon Doyle was a witness, 20 Apr. 1807 to J. B. Earle.
Rec: 20 Apr. 1807.

Pages 512-513: 18 Oct. 1804, David McCaleb, Sheriff, to Dr. William Hunter......on 2nd Monday of March 1804, John Young entered judgement against Alexander Patterson for $32.....all goods, chattels, lands ordered to be sold at public auction to the highest bidder, being Dr. Hunter for $28 for 150 acres on E. side of Keowee River, of the Savannah River, granted John Young by John Drayton, Lt. Gov. of S. C., 14 Aug. 1800, bd. SW. by Robert Maxwell, NW. by Joshua Young, SE. by Charles Reese. Wit: John R. Brown, M. Hammond. Michael Hammond made oath to J. B. Earle, 17 Aug. 1807.
Rec: 17 Apr. 1807.

Pages 513-514: Articles of Agreement concluded 3 Apr.1807 between Edward Doyle, planter, and William Shaw, Attorney at Law, for $1,200, whereas Doyle sold to Shaw 350 acres on Mulwee Creek of 23 Mile Creek, purchased from William Mulwee, also tract adjoining, purchased from Spence Mitchell for 250 acres. Signed: Edward Doyle, W. Shaw. Wit: James Cooper, John B. Melonay. James Cooper made oath to James C. Griffen, 21 Apr. 1807.
Rec: 22 Apr. 1807.

Page 514: Thomas N. Gibson sold to his father, John Gibson, one cow and calf, one bed and furniture, other household items for value received, 28 Aug. 1806. Wit: Fras. Jenkins, Caleb Woodling. (No oath).
Rec: 30 Aug. 1806.

Page 514: Alexander Glenn and Mary Glenn for $200 sold to William Binam 128 acres part of a tract on both sides of Rice's Creek, granted David Hamilton by Wm. Moultrie, 4 Dec. 1786, recorded Bk. QQQQ, p.283, bd. by Binam, Wm. Killen, Isaac Miller. Date: 31 Jul. 1801. Wit: John Lewis Glenn. (only). Mary (X) Glenn, wife of Alexander Glenn, released dower to John Taylor, J.Q., 10 Aug. 1801. Jesse Glenn made oath to Henry Burch, J.P., 24 Sep. 1801.
Rec: 24 Mar. 1807.

Page 515: 9 Aug. 1799, Joel Breazeale to Elijah Breazeal for $60 for 200 acres on Rocky Creek of Rocky River, part of tract of 442 acres granted Reuben Clements, 7 Jan. 1793, recorded Bk. F, no. 5, p. 430, conveyed from Clements to Joel Breazeal. Signed: Joel (X) Breazeal. Wit: Ambrose (X) Nichols, Kinon (X) Breazeale. Kinon Breazeal made oath to Jno. George, J.P., 24 Mar. 1807.
Rec: 4 Mar. 1807.

Pages 515-516: Samuel Taylor, planter, for $300 sold Patrick White 273 acres granted Elinor Brook in July 1787, on N. fork of Cane Creek of the Keowee River. Date: 3 Apr. 1807. Wit: A. Lawhon, Jonathan Reeder. Archibald Lawhon made oath to M. Hammond, D.C., 4 Apr. 1807. (No recording date).

Page 516: Elisha Dyer, Sr. for $300 sold Joshua Dyer 300 acres on Big Eastatoo of Keowee River, surveyed by James Jett. Date: 15 Sep. 1806. Wit: Manoah Dyer, W. Hardag. William Hardag made oath to John Cochran, Q. U., 29 Dec. 1806.
Rec: 24 Mar. 1807.

Pages 516-517: Robert Boyd for $100 sold John Morris 93 ac on 12 Mile River. Date: 7 Jan. 1801. Wit: John Hunt, Adam Heath Thompson. John Hunt made oath to David Murphey, J.Q., 12 Oct. 1801. Rec: 23 Mar. 1807.

Page 517: Jesse Brown for $360 sold John Burris 166 acres part of tract granted John Lawderdale where Jesse Brown now lives, bd. by Joshua Prichard; also, tract adjoining above tract of 100 acres part of a grant to David Clark, conveyed to Benjamin Raney, from Raney to Timothy Reeves and from Reeves to Jesse Brown, bd. by James Long, Wm. Tippen, Matthew Long. Date: 11 Nov. 1806. Wit: Asa Castleberry, James Cooper. James Cooper made oath to Jno. George, J. P., 4 Mar. 1807. Rec: 24 Mar. 1807.

Page 518: David Lewis sold to Benjamin Lewis, horses, cattle, hogs, all working tools in possession of David Lewis, household furniture. Date: 2 Mar. 1807. Wit: John Grisham, Savage Littleton. Savage Littleton made oath to Henry Burch, J.P., 24 Mar. 1807. Rec: 24 Mar. 1807.

Page 518: Mathew Long for $200 sold to Peter Keys, Esq., 200 acres on Big Generostee of the Savannah River, being 2/3 of an undivided tract conveyed by Joseph Thompson to Mathew Long, bd. by Robert Hemphill, John Ross, George Hogg, John Woodall, Peter Keys, Drury Pruitt. Date: 7 Jan. 1807. Wit: William Gordon, Elisha Herring. Elisha Herring made oath to Jno. George, J.P., 25 Mar. 1807. Rec: 25 Mar. 1807.

Pages 518-519: William Cooker for $800 sold John Bates, blacksmith, late of the State of Georgia, 270 acres, part of 2 tracts granted Boling Clark, conveyed by Joseph Clark, son of Boling Clark, to Thomas Cooker and from him to his son, William Coker, one tract for 640 acres, deed dated 17 Dec. 1800, on bank of 23 Mile Creek. Date: 31 Oct. 1806. Signed: William Coker. Wit: Zachr. Taliaferro, Eliza Bates, Rebecca Oliver. Zachariah Taliaferro, Esq., made oath to (cannot read J. P. or recording date).

Page 519: John Bates for $800(?) sold to Warren Taliaferro, late of the State of Georgia, 270 acres part of 2 tracts granted Boling Clark and conveyed to Joseph Clark, son of Boling Clark, then to Thomas Coker by him to his son, William Coker. Date: _____. Wit: _____ Oath says Zachariah Taliaferro, Wm. Coker, Eliza Bates, 24 Mar. 1807 to Samuel H. Dickson. Frances (X) Bates, wife of John Bates, released dower to John Willson, Q.U., 3 Nov. 1806. Rec: 24 Mar. 1807.

Pages 519-520: William Boyce, Executor of last will and testament of Alexander Boyse, dec'd., for $300 sold to David Spearman, planter, 120 acres on Hurricane Creek, bd. by Shamlin. Date: 23 Mar., 1807. Wit: Amos Garison, John Booth. Amos Garitson made oath to James Welborn, J.P., 23 Mar. 1807. Signed: Amos Garrison. Rec: 23 Mar. 1807.

Page 520: Martha Henderson for $100 sold to William Nicholson 100 acres, part of tract granted Thomas Finley by Wm. Moultrie, 29 Aug. 1790 on Toxaway Creek. Date: 17 May 1807. Signed: Martha (X) Henderson. Wit: Demsy Pace, Abner Ratlick, Humphrey Lindsey. Humphrey Lindsey made oath to W. Nicholson, J.P., 7 Mar. 1807. Rec: 26 Mar. 1807.

Pages 520-521: David Lewis for $1,000 sold Benjamin Lewis 277 acres on Keowee River where David Lewis now lives, part of 2 tracts: one granted to John Thomas, 1785 of 140 acres, the other granted Lewis 1799. Date: 23 Mar. 1807. Wit: John Grisham, Savage Littleton. Savage Littleton made oath to (cannot read). Rec: 24 Mar. 1807.

Page 521: John Taylor for $25 sold Solomon Geer 50 ac.

(Page 521 cont'd): on Broadaway Creek of Rocky River, bd. by Geer, Edwin Vandiaver, Thos. Burford(?). Date: 28 Dec. 1806. Signed: John (X) Taylor. Wit: John McFall, Edward Thompson. Edward Thompson made oath to Jno. George, J.P., 26 Feb. 1807. Rec: 24 Mar. 1807.

Pages 521-522: Owin Shannon for $400 sold Jacob Jones 100 acres on both sides of Choestoe Creek, near the mouth of N. fork of Toogaloe River, bd. by Isaac Jones, John Shannon, part of tract laid out for John Shannon. Date: 6 Jan. 1800. Wit: Isaac Jones, John Barton, Jr. Isaac Jones made oath to Jno. Barton, J.P., 25 Jul. 1800. Rec: 23 Mar. 1807.

Page 522: John B. Earle for $250 sold Samuel Cherry 200 acres on branches of 18 and 23 Mile Creek of the Seneca River, part of tract granted Mathew Hunter, conveyed to Earle, bd. by Abner Stutes (or Steele) crossing road from Pendleton to Pickensville. Date: 15 Apr. 1807. Wit: Wm. Hamilton, James Cooper. James Cooper made oath to M. Hammond, 22 Apr. 1807. Rec: 22 Apr. 1807.

Pages 522-523: John Cary for $100 sold Josiah Houston 140 acres on Cuffy Creek of 23 Mile Creek. Date: 20 Dec. 1806. Wit: Josiah Camp, J. Miller. John Miller made oath to M. Hammond, D.C., 27 Apr. 1807. Rec: 27 Apr. 1807.

Page 523: Francis Bremar & Peter Freneau of Charleston, for $250 sold to John B. Earle, Esq., Clerk of Court of Pendleton Dist., 640 ac. on branches of 23 Mile Creek of the Savannah River, bd. on SE by Wadsworth, NE by Hunter. Date: 13 Mar. 1801. Signed: F. Bremar, Peter Freneau by Francis Bremar, his Attorney. Wit: Wm. Edmondson, Thomas Edmondson.... James Martin of Lincoln Co., N. C., for $200 paid by John B. Earle to Francis Bremar, do release, relinquish and quit claim to John B. Earle for described land. Date: 28 Jan. 1802. Wit: Wm. Cunningham, Moses Liddell. (No oath). Rec: 28 Apr. 1807.

Page 524: John Baylis Earle for $1500 sold Samuel Taylor 1,013 and 3/4 acres on 18 and 23 Mile Creeks, part of 2 tracts conveyed to Earle by different men, bd. by Samuel Cherry, Mr. Lee, Thomas Hunter, Richards, Major Dickson, Saml. H. Dickson; also, 19 acres bought of William Simms. Date: 15 Apr. 1807. Wit: James Cooper, Wm. Hamilton. James Cooper made oath to M. Hammond, D.C., 22 Apr. 1807. Rec: 22 Apr. 1807.

Pages 524-525: William McGuffin of Pendleton Dist., for $300 sold to Ezekiel Pickens of St. Thomas Parish, S. C., all tract where McGuffin now lives on 18 Mile Creek, granted McGuffin, 3 Dec. 1792 for 583 acres, by original grant, 40 acres have been taken off by prior granted belonging to Andrew Pickens, Jr. and Capt. Lewis D. Martin, bd. NE by Thomas Richard and Wm. Gaston, SE by Capt. Lewis D. Martin, SW by Francis Greenwood, NW by Ezekiel Pickens and Andrew Pickens, Jr. Date: 18 Sep. 1805. Wit: Andw. Pickens, Jr., Benjamin Green. Susannah (X) McGuffin released dower to (no J.P.) Andrew Pickens, Jr., Esq., made oath to M. Hammond, D. C. 14 Oct. 1806.

Page 525: William Herring for $70 sold to Peter Keys 50 acres on Big Generostee of Savannah River. Date: 20 Jan. 1807. Wit: Elisha Herring and John Tuggle. Elisha Herring made oath to Jno. George, J.P., 25 March 1807. Rec: 28 __ 1807.

Pages 525-526: Joseph Jolly for ₤150 sold Alexander Moorhead 100 acres on Town Creek, part of tract granted David Lewis Anderson, 5 Oct. 1884,

(Pages 525-526 cont'd): by Benj. Guerard, recorded Bk. ZZZ, p. 123. Date: 20 Mar. 1807. Wit: Jno. Moorhead and Whiteaher Smith. James Moorhead made oath to George Nash, J.P., 24 Mar. 1807. Rec: 24 Mar. 1807.

Page 526: Joshua Burres for $27 sold Lewis Shamley a tract on Generostee Creek. (No date). Wit: Elisha Herring, James Burris, Thomas Burris. Elisha Herring made oath to P. Keys, Q.U., 25 Mar. 1807. Rec: 25 Mar. 1807.

Page 526: William Brown of the District of Franklin, Georgia, for $10 sold to Henry Gambrill of Pendleton Dist., 25 acres on Ready fork of Broadmouth Creek of the Saludy River, bd. SE by Gambrill, Wm. Donelson, NW by Donelson, NE by Gambrill. Date: 25 Feb. 1807. Wit: Grief Hinton and Isaac Jordan. Isaac Jordan made oath to Aron Broyles, 25 Feb. 1807. Rec: 23 Mar. 1807.

Page 527: James Reden for $200 sold Henry Gambrell 200 acres, part of 2 tracts: one granted to James Reden, 14 May 1785, the other to William Poor, 1 Dec. 1788, conveyed to Garnbull(sic) on Toney's Creek of the Saluda River. Date: 15 Nov. 1806. Signed: James (X) Reden. Wit: Jael E. Grace, Isaac Jordan, William Barry. Isaac Jourdan made oath to Aron Broyles, Q. U., 25 Feb. 1807. Elizabeth (X) Reden, wife of James Reden, released dower to Aron Broyles, 25 Feb. 1807. Rec: 23 Mar. 1807.

Pages 527-528: John Thomas for $8 sold to Lewis Shamley 12 and 3/4 acres on Big Jenerostee Creek, part of a tract granted Elijah Herring by Wm. Moultrie, 25 Feb. 1804, recorded Bk. MMMM, p. 257. (No date). Wit: James Burris, Elisha Herrin. James Drimon. Elisha Herring made oath to P. Keys, J. P., 25 Mar. 1807. Rec: 25 Mar. 1807.

Page 528: Mark Ward for $250 sold to Peter Keys 150 acres, part of a tract granted Henry Pearson, bd. by Wm. Herring, land formerly held by Bradock McDonnel, James Long, Joseph Land, Joshua Burris, land that Wm. Dickey bought of Bradock McDonald, on Big Generostee Creek of Savannah River. Date: 7 Nov. 1806. Signed: Mark (X) Ward. Wit: Jesse Brown, Eli Hunnicutt, John Tuggle. John Tuggle made oath to Jno. George, J. P., 25 Mar. 1807. Rec: 25 Mar. 1807.

Page 528: Robert Anderson from principles of natural Justice, do of my own free will make the following statement: I hereby acknowledge my ever honoured wife of blessed memory was possessed in her own right of a negro woman by the name of Rose and one named Hannah, who has now 4 children, the oldest, Charlotte, my wife told me she intended to give to her daughter, Lydia Findley.....therefore, sd. negro girl I do hereby make over to my step daughter, Lydia Finley. Date: 23 Sep. 1806. Wit: Maria Anderson, Anne A. Maxwell. Anna Maxwell made oath to M. Hammond,DC, 4 Apr. 1807. Rec: 4 Apr. 1807.

Page 529: Ephraim Herring for $80 sold John Armstrong 100 acres on Beaver Creek, bd. by Hillhouse, Brice Stevenson, Hunter and Armstrong.Date: 6 Feb. 1807. Wit: William Hillhouse and James Hillhouse. Wm. Hillhouse made oath to John Stephenson, J.P., 12 Mar. 1807. Rec: 2 Apr. 1807.

Page 529: Thomas Farrar for $356 sold Jesse Putman 350 acres granted John Ellege(?) (this is difficult to read)...by Chas. Pinckney, on ____ Creek of Keowee River. Date: 6 Feb. 1806. Signed: Thomas Farrar and

(Page 529 cont'd):   Peggy Farrar. Wit: T. W. Farrar and Robt.
                                  Looney. Thomas W. Farrar made oath to Wm.
Cleveland, J. P., 6 Jan. 1806.
Rec: 4 Apr. 1807.

Page 530:   5 Apr. 1800, Edward Bird of Warren County,
                                  Georgia, to Ansel Jarret of Pendleton District, for $105 for 265 acres on Beaver
Creek bd. by Lesley and Bird's old line. Wit: James McCoy, John McCormack.
James McCoy made oath to Patr. Norris, J. P., 15 Mar. 1807.
Rec: 25 Mar. 1807.

Page 530:   James Fowler for $150 sold to Thomas Jones
                                  99 acres on branches of Verner's Creek, a
                                  part of 239 acres granted Christopher Hargraves, conveyed to James Fowler by James Jones, Attorney for Christopher
Hargraves, 31 Jan. 1806, bd. SW and S by James, W. by part of tract held
by James Johnson, E. by Capt. David Sloan's land, now claimed by Hardamon Bennett and NE by Cooper Bennett and Alexander Calhoun. Date: 12 Dec.
1806. Signed: James (X) Fowler. Wit: Jeremiah Fowler, Nehemiah Fowler.
Jeremiah Fowler made oath to John McMillen, J.P., 6 Jan. 1807.
Rec: 23 Mar. 1807.

Page 531:   George Capehart is bound to Joseph Whitner
                                  for $6,000(?), date 7 Apr. 1807 and makes
                                  good title to 2 adjoining pieces of land
near the Village of Pendleton, one of 131 acres, the other 14 (acres)
purchased from David McCaleb, Esq., the other part of 2 lots in Village
of Pendleton, Lot #8 and #15. Wit: P.(?) D. Murphy, J. B. Earle. John B.
Earle, made oath to M. Hammond, D.C., 24 Apr. 1807.
Rec: 28 Apr. 1807.

Pages 531-532:   Smith Heaton for $100 sold to John Hembree
                                  75 acres on 26 Mile Creek, part of 2 Surveys: one granted to John Harris, 19 Oct.
1791 by Chas. Pinckney, conveyed from Harris to Heaton, 23 Dec. 1799 and
the other granted to John Cannon, 1 Jan. 1787 by Wm. Moultrie, conveyed
to Heaton, 4 Feb. 1805, bd. by James Heaton, Hembree, Woodall and Cannon.
Date: 30 Mar. 1805. Wit: James Hembree and George Brown. James Hembree
made oath to P. Keys, Q.U., 7 Apr. 1807.
Rec: 15 Apr. 1807.

Page 532:   James Jones for $148.50 sold to James Fowler 99 acres on Verner's Creek, part of 239
                                  acres granted to Christopher Hargraves, bd.
S. by Capt. David Sloan's land, now claimed by Hardaman Bennett and Cooper Bennett, ENE by Alexander Calhoun (except small part laid off from the
Meeting house and grave yard). Date: 1 Jan. 1806. Wit: Pleasant Sullivant
and Thomas Jones. Thomas Jones made oath to John McMillen, J.P., 6 Jan.
1807. Rec: 23 Mar. 1807.

Pages 532-533:   Samuel Savage of Abbeville Dist. for $70
                                  sold to William Blair of Pendleton Dist.,
                                  102 acres on N. side of old Indian line and
on the dividing line between Abbeville and Pendleton Dist. Date: 17 Mar.
1807. Wit: Jos. Blair, Wm. McKea. William McKee made oath to Jos. Blair,
J.Q., 17 Mar. 1807. Milley Savage, wife of Samuel Savage, released dower
to Jos. Blair, J.Q. of Abbeville Dist., 17 Mar. 1807.
Rec: 23 Mar. 1807.

Page 533:   Washington Dist., Bennett Combs for $80 to
                                  John Morris 30 acres on S. side of 12 Mile
                                  River, bd. by Balay Anderson's old line.
Date: 23 Apr. 1800. Wit: Moses Murphree, James Wardlaw. James Wardlaw
made oath to David Murphree, 20 Mar. 1802.
Rec: 23 Mar. 1804.

Pages 533-534:   William Huggins, now of the State of Tenesee(sic), planter, for $400 sold Naaman
                                  Curtis 218 acres on 12 Mile River of Savan-

(Pages 533-534 cont'd):   nah River (except 8 or 10 acres running into John Todd's land). Date: 10 Jan. 1807. Wit: John Todd and Wm. Donaldson. William Donaldson made oath to Leonard Simpson, J.P., 24 Mar. 1807.
Rec: 24 Mar. 1807.

Page 534:   Elizabeth Griffen for $204 sold to Elijah Breazeal 68 acres on Big Rock Creek of the Savannah River, bd. by Hugar, Joel Breazeal, part of 140 acres granted Reuben Clements, 16 Jan. 1793. Date: 17 Feb. 1806. Signed: Elizabeth (X) Griffen. Wit: Joel (X) Breazeal, Hardy Clements, Kenon Breazeal. Kenon Breazeal made oath to Jno. George, J.P. on 24 Mar. 1807.
Rec: 24 Mar. 1807.

Pages 534-535:   John Cansler to Isham Fielding for $100 for 100 acres, part of a tract granted Elizabeth Oliver by Wm. Moultrie, 5 Sep. 1786, on 23 Mile Creek of the Savannah River, bd. by John Willson. Date: 2 Apr. 1806. Wit: John Willson, Andrew Blair. Andrew Blair made oath to John Willson, Q.U., 14 May 1806.
Rec: 11 Apr. 1807.

Pages 535-536:   Edwin L. Smith, physician, late of the City of Charleston ____ (cannot read this), 17 Apr. 1807 is bound to David McCaleb for $1,500 ____ on or before 1 Apr. 1809 ____ makes title to 1,211 acres where Smith now lives on N. side of the Seneca River. Wit: Richard B. North, Tucker North. Richard B. North made oath to M. Hammond. (No date). Rec: 20 Apr. 1802. Satisfaction recorded Bk. M., p. 135.

Page 536:   John Whitner and Elizabeth his wife, for $428 sold to Daniel Ledbetter, a tract on the W. side of 18 Mile Creek, granted in 1785 bd. by George Rease. Date: 10 Jan. 1807. Wit: J. B. Earle, Wm. Ledbetter. William Ledbetter made oath to John Tippen, 30 Jan. 1807. Elizabeth Whitner released dower to John Tippen, 23 Mar. 1807.
Rec: 23 Mar. 1807.

Pages 536-537:   David McCaleb for $3000 sold to Dr. Edwin B. Smith, late of the City of Charleston, 1,211 acres on N. side of Seneca River. Date: 17 Apr. 1807. It is understood that the ferry landing on the Tabor (?) place was previously conveyed to Col. John B. Earle. Wit: Richard B. North and Tucker North. Richard B. North made oath to M. Hammond. (No date). Mrs. Matilou(?) McCaleb, wife of David McCaleb, released dower to J. Stribling, Q. U., 18 Apr. 1807.
Rec: __ Apr. 1807.

Pages 537-538:   1 Sep. 1801, William Herring, planter, to Stephen Herring, planter, for Ł100 for 110 acres where Stephen Herring now lives, part of a tract granted to John Dalrymple on Generostee Creek of the Savannah River, bd. by William and Stephen Herring. Date: 1 Sep. 1801. Wit: Joel Wood and Isaac Herring. Joel Wood made oath to P. Keys, Q. U., 2 March 1807. Rec: 3 Apr. 1807.

Page 538:   Aron Bryant for $220 sold to Thomas Willson 97 acres on Saluda River, granted to Ann Bryant, wife of Aron Bryant, 4 Apr. 1791; also 50 acres, part of a tract granted to Robert Willson for 200 acres, 18 Nov. 1784, at the road laid out from Willson's ferry on the Saluda to Cambridge, bd. by Owen Evans, A. Bryant, John Willson, Jr. Date: 27 Nov. 1806. Signed: Aaron (X) Bryant. Wit: John Wilson, Jr., John Bryant. John Wilson, Jr. made oath to James Welboun, Q.U., 6 May 1807.
Rec: 15 May 1807.

Page 539:   Daniel Williams for $100 sold Roday Young 60 ac. on branches of Deep Creek of Senika River, bd. on S. by Jesse Chappel, John

(Page 539 cont'd): McCollum, Wm. McClusky, granted to Samuel McCollum, Jr., dec'd., where William McClusky now lives, conveyed by Thos. Martain to Daniel Williams. Date: ___ Sep. 1806. Wit: John Long, James Long and Edmond Strange. James Long made oath to John Tippen, Q. U., 27 Sep. 1806. Nancy (X) Williams released dower to John Tippen, 5 Oct. 1806. Rec: 23 Mar. 1807.

END OF BOOK H

(Index at back)

INDEX
by
Eileene Sandlin
Saginaw, Texas

_____, Alexr. 230
_____, Andrew 375,386
_____, Asa 165
_____, Benjamin 258
_____, Bennet 287
_____, Bennett 364
_____, Charles 259
_____, David 320,423
_____, Francis 277
_____, Henry 246
_____, Jacob 200,258
_____, Jacob J. 336
_____, James 200,211,226,
  229,246,248,277,288,
  360,388
_____, James McGuffin (?)
  213
_____, Jane 257
_____, Jessee 277
_____, Jesse G. 374
_____, John 220,229,246,
  280,347,376
_____, John, Sr. 280
_____, Joseph 231,254
_____, Margaret 277
_____, Mary 399
_____, Nathan 240
_____, Nathaniel 241
_____, Robert 232,239
_____, Stephen 244
_____, Thomas 233,244,253,
  335
_____, William 96,229,233,
  242,284,335,343,370,
  372,374
_oster, George 202

ABBET(ABBETT,ABBOTT,ABBUT,
  ABBUTT), _____ 373,423
  James 17,18,114,117,
  184,307,315,318
  John 363,373
  Margaret 114
  Thomas/Thos. 23,177,
  288
ABEL, Ezekiel 260
  Jeremiah 408
ABELS, Jeremiah 85
ABIL, Jeremiah 84
ABIT, James 419
  Thomas 359
ABLE, Abraham 217
  Elizabeth 244,315
  Ezekiel 235,315
  Jeremiah 37,244,315
ACKER(ACCOR), Peter 34,58,
  66,74,127,233,303,347
ACKER(ASHER), William 69
ADAIR, Edward/Edwd. 58,169,
  233,308,324,349,376,
  410,423
  Elizabeth 286
  James 379
  John/Jno. 44,58,62,68,
  82,85,93,104,187,196,232,
  259,260,261,305,308,
  323,325,349,361,373,
  382,383,386,391,410,
  414
  Walter 379,382,391
  Walter Scott 169
  "Widow" 366
ADAMS, _____ 385
  Andrew 31,343,344
  David 405
  Ezekiel 259
  Henry 159
  James 122,123,402
  Jodah 313

ADAMS, cont'd.:
  John 267,313,394
  John, Sr. 159
  Judith 313
  Nat 320
  Stephen 159
  Thomas/Thos. 5,130,179,
  260,332
  William 145
ADARE, James Park 349
ADDAMS, Andrew 232
ADDERHOLD(ADERHOLD,ADERHOLT)
  Conrad 48,106
  John Conrod(Conrad) 106,
  151,152,160
ADDINS, _____ 229
ADDIS, Richard 293
  William 345,394
ADEN(EDEN), Anne 199
  Bennet(t) 163,200,255,
  276,385,423
  John 130,194,199
  Martha/Marthy 255,385
ADIRS, George 252
ADKERSON, _____ 320
ADKINS, William 172
ADKISON, Amos 143
ADLY, John 44
AGNEW(EGNEW), James 20,29
  John 389
AIDEN, Bennett 104
AIKENS, Mr. _____ 50
  Mrs. _____ 51
AINSWORTH, William 407
AIRWICK, James 287
AKER, Joseph 229,230
  Peter 229,262,286
  Peter, Jr. 229
AKEY, Jonathan 241
AKINS, Ezekiel 327
  Elizabeth 366
  John 134
  Peter 286
  Robert 152,270,418
AKOR(ACHER), Peter 402
ALBERT, Thos. 238
ALBERTIA(?), Francis 90
ALDRIDGE(ALDERIDGE,ELDRIDGE)
  Benjamin 16,119,168,305
  Nathaniel 162,352
  Rebecca 16
ALDRUS, William 219
ALEXANDER, Aaron/Aron 114,
  145
  Aroph? 90
  Asaph 101,107,172,174,
  210,212
  Daniel 329
  David 84,88,180,181
  David, Jr. 334
  Elias 54
  Elinor 239
  Floid/Floyd (also see
  Elexander) 209
  Isaac 54,75,88,375
  James 146,180,268,284,
  285,322,334,401
  James, Jr. 101,172
  John/Jno. 21,138,239,
  260,285,332
  Joseph 56
  Josh. 222
  Josiah 330,362
  Margaret 54
  Martha 221
  Matthew/Mathew 16,27,
  31,88,127,129,157,190,
  205,221
  Micajah 403

ALEXANDER, cont'd.:
  Nat. 54
  Susannah 26
  Thomas 150
ALEWATERS, Alston 321
  Isaac (also Alewatters)
  152,169,179,311,321,
  330
ALFER, James 136
ALIN, Martyn 174
ALKINS(ALKEN,ALKIN),
  Jenny Marie(Maria) 174,
  175
  Joseph 357
  Marlyn 324,334
  Martyn/Martin 174,175,
  334,360
ALLARD, James 162
ALLEN, Elizabeth 410
  Gershim 302
  James/Jas. 160,239,
  269,288,322,342,356,
  357
  John 362
  Lee 106,407,410
  Mary 274
  Richd. 253
  Squire 106,184,186,
  193,410
  William 164,274,338,
  397
  Zachariah 219
ALLISON (ALLINSON), _____
  186
  David 175
  Elizabeth 189
  James 189,387
  James, Sr. 189
  John 9,118
  Rebeccah/Rebeca 306
  Robert 9,102,306,328
  Sarah/Sary 189,387
  Watson 10,13,122,164,
  244,328
  William/Wm. 10,13,164,
  222,244,306
ALLUM(HALLUM?), Basil 248
ALMAR, Ralph 40
ALSTON, L. A. 3
AMOSE, _____ 422
ANDERSON, _____ 317
  Aaron/Aron 399
  Abel 260,262,267,370
  Abraham 75
  Agnes 133,208
  Ails 74
  Archibald Cook John-
  ston 260
  Azariah 349
  Bailey/Baley/Bayley/
  Baily 6,7,11,12,13,17,
  30,42,43,44,47,50,54,
  58,63,65,68,71,74,75,
  84,88,89,93,104,105,
  107,117,119,123,125,
  140,149,157,165,217,
  237,324,330,337,387,
  428
  Col. 204,211
  David 91,128,130,140,
  203,292,385
  David Lewis 176,426
  Eliza Ann 177
  General 272,310,311,
  340,389,411
  Geo./George 6,79,130,
  136,190,256,385
  Jacob 75
  James 20,32,52,112,133,

ANDERSON, James cont'd:
137,145,171,175,208,
224,252,264,289,375,
420
  James, Jr. 294
  James, Sr. 294
  Jane 14,26,211,302,354,
379
  Jean 15,19
  John 74,80,81,82,92,
125,361,414,417,424
  John Calhoun 22
  Leonard 255
  Lydia 78,212,213
  Maria 427
  Martha 367,417
  Mary 105,106,125,149,
309,359,417
  Moses 125,392
  Robert 1,9,10,14,20,
22,25,26,29,34,35,45,
53,57,72,73,78,83,84,
85,88,90,92,101,107,
124,126,145,159,169,
172,176,192,202,203,
205,212,213,225,232,
234,238,241,247,253,
262,263,279,282,284,
294,309,311,313,319,
328,331,333,335,336,
350,353,354,361,364,
368,371,376,379,389,
401,414,422,427
  Robert, Jr. 104,192,
257,333,415
  Rosanah 267
  Sal. 264
  Samuel 249,375,377,414
  Sarah 44,58
  Stephen 104,347,393
  Thomas 54,87,132,177,
182,378
  Thompson 20
  Vinson 7
  Wiat 58
  William 7,33,37,142,
170,177,256,262,278,
349,354,360,368,395,
408
  William, Jr. 14
ANDREWS, David 393,416
ANGILLY(ALAGILLY), Alex-
  ander 253,262
ANGLIN, James 260
  Joseph 422
ANGLING, Joseph 170
ARCHER(ARCER), George 208,
420
ARMOUR, Robert 410
ARMSTRONG, _____ 290
  Ann 54
  Benjamin 95,308,396
  Charles 342,420
  James 229,249,284,344
  John 22,53,54,57,58,
72,79,208,227,293,332,
375,401,418,420,427
  Mathew/Matthew/Marthew
57,249,264,368
  Thomas 110,170,226
  William 57,79,336,403
ARNOLD(ARNALD), Benjamin
88,121,135,170,242,397
  John 124,170
  William 337,357,395
ARRATTS, William 273
ARTHUR, _____ 323
ARVIN, Annanias 329
ASBURN, Thomas 279
ASHER, _____ 269
  James 251
  William 152,269,286,
309
  Mrs. William 152

ASHERST, _____ 343
  William 69,191,192,286
ASHLOCK(ASHOLOK), James 291
ASHURST, Mary 152
  William 118,152,180
ASKENS, James 332,349
ASKEW, Samuel 260
ASKIN, George 364
ATCHINS, Mary 37
ATKINS, Bartius 337
  Christian/Christon
337
  Ezrel/Ezekiel 306
  Hugh 105,149
  Joseph 337
  Lewis 231
  Margarett 226
  Martha 337
  Robert 337
ATKINSON, Amos 205
ATTERSON, John 285
ATWATER, Isaac 300
  Titus 361
AUGUSTA, Leason 381
AUGUSTUS(AGUSTUS), Leeser/
  leason 380
AUSTIN, _____ 256
  Nathan 82,84
  Nathaniel 85

BAGWELL, Fredrick 392
  J. 229
  Jas. 392
BAILEY, H. (Henry) 27
  Jordan 363
  Robert 95
  Thomas 363
BAILY, Jas. 90
BAIRD, Robert 68,368
BAKER, _____ 355
  Mr. _____ 367
  Caleb 207
  Catherine 108
  Charles 414
  Elizabeth 192
  George A. 108
  Grace 48
  James 231
  Jesse 48,186
  John, Sr. 370
  Martha 404
  Robert 50,74,75,150,
340,353,370
  Samuel/Saml. 231,293,
379,404
  Sarah 75,340,370
  William 192,291,311,
340,370
BALDWIN, Caleb 315,333,400,
403,404
BALLARD, Nathaniel 17
  Stephen 156
  William 60,63
BALY, Margaret 123
BAMPFIELD, George 40
BANKS, Ransom 271
  Solomon 171,311,330
BANISTER, William/Wm. 76,
138,282
BANNISTER, William 217
BARBEE, Jacob 294
BARBOUR, Abose 313
  Ambrose 314
BARDON(RARDON), Patrick 217
BARIN, James 368
BARKLEY, Andrew 43,124,170,
292,397
  Samuel 42,43,44,124,292,
397
  William 397
BARLEY, Samuel 170
BARNARD, John 166
  Luke 314,324,329
BARNES, Dennis 62,202

BARNES, cont'd.:
  Moses 19,86
BARNETT(BARNET), _____ 326
  Ambrose 199,234,260,
354,358,390
  Amos 372,403,404,406
  Ezekiel 320
  James 144,157,217,279,
307,320,354,358
  John 2,6,19,279,307,
354,370,403,406
  Luke 86,198
  Nancy 354
  Samson 390
  Samuel 68
  William 12,252
BARR, James 329,345
  Mary 345
  Samuel 34,94,111,131,
174,179,244,248,264,
267,385
BARRAN, Alexander 392
  Alexander, Jr. 392
  Henry 291
BARREN, Abraham 176
  Alexander 399
  James 205,308,363
BARRETT, Mary 398
  Michael 174,175,213
  Reuben 410
  Thomas 375,398
BARRON, Abraham 124
  Alexander 95,362
  Charles 180
  James 77,367,376
  William 254
BARROT, Thomas M. 362
BARRY, Armstead 384,390
  William 412,427
  William T. 399
  W. T. 390
BARTLETT, _____ 251
BARTON, Anna 414
  Bailey 5
  Bavester/Baveaster
236,318
  Benjamin 7,54,109,110,
117,128,252,257,265,
339
  Benniston 262
  Caleb 147,359,396,411
  David 142,330,353,375,
399
  Henry 22,408
  Henry C. 147,359,396
  James 363,405,414,422
  Jno./John 7,29,31,73,
88,89,91,95,103,113,
134,138,141,145,148,
154,161,171,182,184,
195,198,220,225,234,
235,248,250,254,266,
269,270,278,283,284,
292,303,322,333,334,
335,337,338,353,365,
384,392,396,414,426
  John, Jr. 154,426
  Joseph 319
  Joshua 252,324,362
  Mary 236
  Presley 353
  Rhoda 414
  Saml. 141,220
  Stephen 163,316,381
  Thomas 51,192
  William 154,366
BARTY, John 311
BASKINS, _____? 229
BASKIN, Andrew 38
  Hugh 204
  William 68,69,201,229,
235,273,275,282,284
BASTROP, P. H. N. Tot 219
BATES, Daniel 350,384,386

BATES, cont'd.:
    Eliza 425
    Fleming 45
    F. M. 145
    F. N. 123
    Frances 425
    John 425
    William 162,319,350,
        360,386
BATEY, David 47
BATY, David 347,350,369
    Geo. 220
    James 220,341
    Margaret 123
BAUFMAN, Jacob 284
BAULHAM, Jacob 260
BAUGHMAN, Elizabeth 284
BAUTHMAN, ____ 284
BAVICK, John 354
BAXTER, Francis 227
BAY, Andrew 183,265
    Elihu Hall 265
BAYLEY, Patr(?) 179
    Peter 147,180
BEACH, A. 266
    Abraham/Abram 332,343,
        361
BEAN, Moses 346
BEARD, Francis 383
    James 409
    John 21,318
    Jonas 92
    Mary 59,320
    Robert 68
    William 59
BEARDEN, Edmond 85,86
    Winn 85
BEARLY(BEARTY?), David 347
BEATY, David 206,397,398
    Ellen 373
    Francis 206,230
    George 341
    James 164,238,341
    John 215,397,398
    Nathan 230
    Peter 196,199
    Robert 114,238,261
    Thomas 182
    William 215,373,374,
        421
    William, Jr. 397,398
BEAUDUET, Richard 153
BEAUHANNON, Thos. 265
BEAVART, Wilson 292
BEAVER, John 378
BEAVERT, John 19
BEAZLEY, ____ 378
    John 140,174,225,291
    William 30,103,105,106,
        174,386
BECK, Isaiah 376
    Jeffry 376
    William 96
BECKMAN, Saml. 260
BEDELLON, William 310
BECERSTAFF, Aaron 382
BELL, Hamilton 398
    James Hamilton 339,398
    John 391
    Kiziar 236
    Martha 398
    Robert 340
    Walter 177,191,236,260
    William 77,100,157,176,
        270,352,388
BENNETT(BENNET,BENITT),
    Charles 100,137,173,
        176,402
    Cooper 305,428
    Elijah 242
    Elisha 99,102,161,179,
        246,359,362
    Hardeman/Hardamon 311,
        428

BENNETT cont'd:
    Lewis 166
    Mason 48,67,71,75
    Michael 317
    Saml., Jr. 39
    Sarah 161
    Solomon 376
    Stephen 102,179,322,
        415
    Thomas 33,48,136,176,
        177,402
    William 18,27,39,88,
        129,191,242,305,372
BENNISON(BENISON,BENNESON),
    ? 120
    George 25,40,150,194,
        329
    William 25,40,194,412
BENNIT, William 288
BENNUM, William 374
BENSON, Caty 250,261
    Gabriel 303
    Joseph 116
    Thomas 213
    William 93,111,115,116,
        384
    Willie 389
    Willis 292
    Z. 116
BENTHAM, James 50,51
BENTON, ____ 388
BERIT, Benjamin 398
    William 398
BERKLEY, Andrew 256
BERRY(BARRY,BERY), Andrew
    413
    Armistead 412,413
    Enoch 91,97,153,333,
        365,404
    Jane 333
    Hudson 272
    Kesia 412,413
    Polly 412
    Richard 5,314,411
    William 404
    Wm. Linch 323
BERRYMAN, Baalam 334
BESHERS, Henry 374
BETTERTON, Joseph 207
BETTS, Thomas 52
BEVART(BEVERT,BREVERT),
    Cleamaindor 196
BIBB, Thos. 282
BIGGS, Robert 246
BINAM, William 424
BINUM, Jesse 411
    Wm. 411
BIRCH, Henry 114,240
BIRCHFIELD, John 278
BIRD, Edward 330,332,414,
        417,428
    John 151,349
    John, Sr. 179
    Mark 72,330,346,414,
        417
    Sarah 179,349
BIRDSONG, Jesse 105
    John 148
BIRNEY, John 397
BISHOP, Jonas (also Jones,
    and Janes) 160,237,260
    Isham/Isum 86
    Nicholas 5,118,306,386,
        398
    Wiley 139,360,408
BLACK, Agnes 384
    Alexander 238,403
    Elinor/Elenor/Eleanor
        96,370,384
    Isabell 384
    Jacob 10
    James 96,256,260,384
    John 10,13,86,109
    Joseph 99,201,281,309,

BLACK, Joseph cont'd.:
    331,333,353,417
    Nancy 384
    Peter 63
    Robert 203,286,331,333
    Samuel 96,239,260,336,
        352,355,360,361,371,
        374,384,402
    Thomas 4,63,184,199,
        256,296,315,327,370
    W. 281
    "Widow" 254
    William/Wm. 96,138,178,
        412
BLACKBOURN, Augusteen 143
BLACKBURN, ____ 295
    A. 3
    Ambrose 3,130,344
    Capt. 6
    John A. 267
    John H. 267,345
    Meridith 75,77
BLACKLEDGE, Ichabod/Icka-
        bod,Icabod 104
BLACKSTOCK, Richard 280,304,
        374,400
BLACKWELL, J. B. 249
    John Byas(s) 180,269
BLADDEN(BLADEN), William
        59,61,62,65,150,363
BLAG(BLAGG), Israel 255,
        256,260,265
    Nimrod Kelfin 298
BLAIR(BLARE), Andrew 429
    George 138,287
    James 50,51,70,71,99,
        104,126,133,140,144,
        148,184,270,287,303,
        360
    Jane 217
    John 190,267
    Jos. 428
    Hayes 226
    Margaret 202,261,306,
        379
    Thomas 97,104,194,208,
        217
    Wm. 184,205,251,288,
        306,379,428
BLAKE, ____? 28
    Robert 16,272
BLALOCK, Francis 152
BLANKENSHIP, Isum/Isham
        121,179
BLANKINGSHIP, Isham 349
    John 349
    William 349
BLANTON, John 70
BLASINGAME, Jas. 197
BLASSINGAME, John 58,59,
        121,152,197,250
BLASINGAME, Thomas 58,59,
        152,174,189
BLASSINGHAM, Thomas 76
BLEDSOE(BLEDSOW,BLEDSO),
    John 15,232,263,271,
        325
    William 325
BLERDIN, Jno. 263
BLISS, James 219
BLYTHE(BLITHE, BLYTH), Ab-
        solum 109,149,378
    James 30,327
    John 305,377,378
    William 61,378
BOAGES, Aaron 14
BOBO, ____ 218
    Burrell/Burrill 140,
        180,226,248,270,381
        (also Burrel)
    Chaney 180
    Elizabeth 140,180
BODDAN(BODDEN,BODDIN),
    Andrew 148,231,242,

BODDAN, Andrew cont'd.:
   252,256,260,261,263,
   265,324,329,332,334,
   335,360,363,373,380,
   400
BODENHAMMER, William 137
BODLEY, Thomas 219
BOG, Robert 235
BOGGS(BOGS), Aaron 9,28,
   48,68,218,270,291,339,
   347
   Elizabeth 28
   Ezekiel 317
   Jos. 175
   Rob. 260
BOGHMAN, Jacob 284
BOHANNAN, John 249,334
BOHANNON, Alexander 112
   Elexr. 311
BOID, John 18
BOIN, Daniel 310
BOISE, Alexander 211
BOKMAN, Jacob 261
BOLDING, James 310
BOLE, James 135,229,395
   J. P. 229
BOLES, _____ 222
   Jon 1
BOLING, William 313
BOLLAN, John 153
BOND, _____ 375
   Charles 7,29,127,224,
   276,297,300,304,339,
   413
   George 144
   Joel 394
   Micajah 289
BONNEAU, Francis 258
   Hannah 258,261
BOON, Daniel 281
   Joseph 351
   Nathan 240,368,411
   Ratliff 5,32,169,351
BOOTH, Eby Stephens 273
   John 118,194,244,295
   Stephen (also Boothe)
   99,198,236,290,346
BOREN(BORAN,BORING), Francis 71,337
BORNE(BOREN), James 381
BORNE(BORING), John 6,221,
   222,278,293,380
   J. M. 241
   William 6,130,187,221,
   222,241,243,260,330
BORLAND, Benjamin 180
BORRING, Francis 337
BOSTICK, T. 378
BOSHMAN, Jacob 290,401
BOUD, Robert 299
BOULAND, James 310
BOULGAR, Michael 174,175
BOULWAR, Mary 139
BOULWAR(E), Phillip 198
   Phillip P. 139,232,291
BOULYER, Michael 174
BOUN, James 132
   William 132
   William, Sr. 132
BOURDINE(BURDINE), John
   43
BOURLAND, Agnes 389
   Archibald 315,418
   Benjamin 270,313,343,
   384,387,388,389
   Benoyni/Benani 270
   Ebenezer 180,343
   Edward (also Borland)
   180
   Eli 118
   James 104,401,404
   John 33,105,153,162,
   270,313,343,362

BOURLAND, cont'd.:
   Martha 313
   William 69,105,164,270,
   302,313,314,418
BOUTHMAN, Jacob 238
BOUYER, Henry 288
   Joseph (also Bowyer)
   288
BOWE, R. 152
BOWEN(BOWAN), _____ 186
   Agnes 114
   Benjamin/Benjn. 33,66,
   74,168,242,274,319
   Charles 39,47,73,79,114
   Fredrick 164
   James 99
   John 35,39,211,358,401
   John, Jr. 322
   Mary 417
   R. 114,122,152,153,159,
   161,162,164,174,258,
   420
   Reese/Reece 299,321
   Robert 18,33,35,80,83,
   84,85,86,105,118,119,
   123,130,143,183,195,
   198,205,211,217,218,
   222,237,238,249,254,
   271,273,288,293,299,
   352,398,417
   Samuel 254,263
   William 115,141,167
BOWER, Henry 305,306
   Margery 306
BOWHANAN(BOWHANNON), John
   14,254
BOWIE, George 146,337
   John 11,38,127,146
   Major 167
BOWLAND, James 192
   John, Jr. 310
BOWLES, Phillip 241
BOWLIN, Joseph 14,176
   Valentine 176
BOWLINE, Ebenezer 327
BOWLING, William 270
BOWMAN, Hannah 166
   Jesse 166,177
BOWSMAN, Jacob 290
BOX, Ann 19
   Edward 64,138
   Joseph 1
   Robert 31,64,73,103,
   109
BOYD(BOID) _____ 73,214,385
   Archabald/Archable 190,
   208,300,301
   Caleb 206
   Elizabeth 145,300
   Ephraim 383,386,393
   George 218,236,256,260,
   362,383,402
   James P. 219,242,260
   Jeremiah 393
   John 66,93,94,118,128,
   153,197,205,256,260,
   358,362,393,402
   John, Jr. 205,207,218,
   236
   John, Sr. 207,236,383,
   386
   Mary 256,393
   Robert 208,209,215,236,
   300,311,325,348,424
   Susan 363
   Thomas 186,203,205,207,
   236,288,289,309,313,
   352,362,393
   William 199,235,260,
   393
BOYDSTON, Samuel 230,377
BOYSE(BOYCE/BOYS), A. .....
   267,299,320,326,327,

BOYSE(BOYCE), Cont'd.:
   A.....332,333,356,370,
   374,377
   Alexander 20,22,37,39,
   42,99,164,165,182,185,
   188,194,195,200,218,
   223,234,247,248,273,
   291,313,317,325,331,
   346,347,353,425
   Archibald 266
   James 64,92,110,120,
   148,166
   Jane/Jean 182,195
   Jenat 20
   Major 256
   Robert 199
   William 425
   William Alexander 39
   Wm. N. 326
BOYSES, Ezekiel 113
BOZBY, William 45
BOZEMAN, Lewis 86
BRACKENRIDGE(BRACKINRIDGE)
   Robert 187,402,422
BRADBERRY, James 184,186
BRADCUT, Richard 267
BRADCUT(T), Samuel 45,276,
   278,300
   Susanah 300
BRADEA, Robert 411
BRADEN(BREDEN), Samuel 366,
   367
BRADEY, _____ 347
BRADFORD, Henry 370,394
   Phil 305,394
   Phillimon 370
BRADLEY, _____ 107
BRADLEY(BRADLY), Ambrose
   118,198,254,352,375,
   378,398
   Andrew 290
   Charles 208,389,418
   Francis 217,423
   George 180,343
   James 418
   Lawrence/Laurence 68,
   198,237,254,260
BRADSHAW, Joel 97
BRADWELL, Nathaniel 202
BRAG(BRAGG), David 2,20,
   37,56,151
BRAILSFORD, Morton 319
BRANDLEY, Lawrence 254
BRANDON, George 289
BRANDON(BRANNON), Charles
   97,98,248,264
BRANNEN, Eugene 41
BRANYON, Henry 165
   John 165
   Thomas 165
BRASELTON, Henry 373,377
   John 67,277
BRASHER, Feeby 86
   James 361,405
   Phillip 174
   Robert Samuel (also
   Brashears) 86,216,230
   Samuel 86
BRATTON, Wm., Jr. 200
BRAZEAL(BRASEAL,BRAZEALE),
   Joel 305,364,368
   Kannon/Kenon/Cannon
   236,260,365,366,376
BRAZEL, William 365
   Willis 311
BRAZELTON, Jacob 59,357
BRAZIEL, Cannon 350
   Joel 342
BRAZOR, James 328
BREADON(BRAIDON,BRIDON),
   Saml. 316
BREAZEAL, Elijah 424,429
BREAZEALE, Joel 424,429

BREAZELE(BREAZEALE), contd
  Kenon/Kinon 244,424
BREEN, Francis 25,183
  Luke 25
BREMAR, ___ 98,421
  F. 183
  Francis 9,40,57,76,89,
    138,183,188,207,216,
    238,261,272,277,278,
    401,403,411,420,422,
    426
  Peter 76,145,159,183,
    225,358
BREMIS(?), James 107
BRENAN, Eugene 116
BREVERT(BREAVERT), John
  12,108,196,389
  W. 266
BREVART, William 390
BRIAN, John 390
  William 390
BRIANT, Absolum/Absolem/
  Absolom 33,121,347
  James 113
  John 3
  Nathan 3,33,347,397
  Nathaniel 121
BRICE, Ann/Anney 332
  James 7,95,384
  James, Jr. 81
  James, Sr. 81
  John 46,56,250,332
  William 250
BRIDEN, Samuel 101
BRIENT, Absolum 19
BRIMER(BRIMAR,BRIMOR),
  Mr. 76,336
  Benjamin 119,156,297,
    333,342
  Francis 196,238,282,
    308
  Joseph 37,119,227,333,
    361
  Peter 308,325,336
  Rebecca 342
BRINER, John 1
BRISON, Daniel 135,321
BRISTER, James 211
  Samuel 170
  William 170,184
BRISTOW, Charity 123
BROADLEY, Lawrence 68
BROASTER, James 384
BROCK(also see BROOKS),
  David 322
  Elizabeth 336
  Isaac 3,4
  James 142,322
  Loyed/Loid/Loyd 305-
    322
  Reuben 299,305,322,
    336,374,382
BROGDEN, ___ 279
BROOK(BROOKS), Archer 410
  Elenor/Elinor 314,424
  George 260,342
  John L. 406
  Margaret 22
  Mathew 230
  Sarah 22
  William 8,22,95,192,
    258,332,399
BROSE, William 31
BROTTON, Williby/Willoby
  154
BROUGH, Agnes 45
  George 73,363,380
  James 78,295,363
  Thomas 45
BROUGHTON, Jonah 419
BROUNETHEAU, Peter 148
BROUSTER, Elenor 172
  James/Jas. 128,134,150,
    363

BROUSTER, cont'd:
  John 163
  John, Jr. 128,384
  Margaret 145
  Samuel 363
BROWN(BROWNE), ___ 76
  Abner 60
  Absolom/Absalom 122,
    420,421
  Alexander 5,365
  Andrew 386,392,396
  Anna/Anne 87,222,244,
    382
  Benjamin 281,289,298,
    325
  Col. ___ 385
  Daniel 382,406
  David 26,32,65,115,143,
    168,170,192,193,205,
    226,274,319
  David, Jr. 32
  E. 72,75,76,77,78,80,
    81,82,84,85,86,87,88,
    90,94,95,96,97,99,100,
    101,103,104,107,108,
    112,113,114,115,116,
    117,120,121,126,127,
    130,131,132,133,134,
    135,136,138,139,140,
    143,150,153,156,158,
    159,160,161,162,163,
    172,174,178,180,181,
    182,204,206,225,251,
    258,268,271,272,273,
    274,278,280,286,287,
    290,292,294,298,300,
    301,304,308,309,316,
    322,330,332,333,336,
    339,340,341,346,349,
    350,351,357,358,359,
    360,362,364,365,366,
    368,377,381,384,385,
    388,390,395,402,404,
    409,411,412,414,417,
    418.
  Elijah 4,15,26-30,36,
    38,39,42,45,48-52,56,
    57,59-64,67,68,70,71,
   132,145,146,192,
    227,258,266,269,274,
    275,294,298,299,325,
    332,371,409
  Elisha 210,274
  Elizabeth 192,193,355
  Francis 420
  Griffen 276,287
  George 244,428
  Hamilton 365
  Hugh 3,4,9,87,200,222,
    259,272,335
  Isaac 299
  J. N. 25
  J. R. 186
  Jacob R. 227,273
  James 10,21,27,51,57,
    66,78,90,115,142,157,
    159,236,300,311,321,
    347,355,407,419
  Jamima/Jamina 29
  Jane 170,226
  Jean 170
  Jehu 222
  Jesse 60,63,67,77,85,
    98,119,135,140,150,170,
    215,267,296,322,376,
    391,411,425,427
  John 11,12,60,63,67,
    84,122,143,156,170,222,
    244,249,260,262,269,
    355,383,393,406,417,
    420
  John R. 354,359,372,
    424
  Jonathan 395

BROWN(BROWNE) cont'd:
  Joseph 10,66,76,130,
    143,162,168,170,173,
    207,215,222,226,238,
    259,292,310,347
  Joseph, Jr. 29,87,162
  Joseph, Sr. 29
  Larkin 226
  Margaret 149,371
  Mary 406
  Milley/Milly 51,409
  Richard 73
  Robert 25,95,133
  Roger 105
  Samuel 19,42,67,170,
    192,226,239,299,305,
    374,375,382,430
  Stewart 200
  Susanah/Susannah 289,
    327,381,382
  T. 236
  Thomas 78,218,299,305,
    352,373,380
  Violet 10
  "Widow" 387,388
  Willey S. 409
  Willey Spiers 4
  William 10,20,21,25,
    34,42,50,51,98,99,106,
    115,132,136,137,149,
    157,160,198,249,280,
    281,306,339,350,352,
    360,366,368,370,383,
    401,405,413,414,423,
    427
BROWSTER(BROUSTER,BRUSTER)
  Sheriff ___ 116,172,
    374,402
BROYLES(BROILS), Aaron/
  Aron 4,9,29,162,170,
    200,222,259,262,286,
    319,322,337,342,351,
    352,355,356,362,382,
    395,403,415,419,427
  Cain 403
  Elizabeth 170,235,289
  Joshua/Josh 20,170,235,
    260,288,289,382
  Phanny 286
BRUCE(BRUSE,BROOSE), ___
  255
  Charles 418,419
  Daniel 340
  James 217
  John 202,330
  W. W. 270
  William 48,187,202,232,
    320,343,344
  William M. 197
BRUER, William 347
BRUISTER, Margaret 116
BRUMMETT, William 10
BRUSTER, Mr. 420
  Hugh 233,260
  James 233
  John 210
  Samuel 210
BRYAN, Absolum 19
  Hardy 19
BRYANT, Absolom 189
  Ann 429
  Aron 429
  John 429
  Nathaniel 90
BRYMER, ___ 153
BRYSON(BRISON), Daniel 86,
  131,135,204,335,365,
  368,404
  Daniel, Jr. 365
  Jean 335
  Jenny 135
  John 130,165,174,204,
    365
  John, Sr. 335

BRYSON, cont'd:
  Saml. 131
  William 365
BUCHAN, Benjamin 397
  W. 397
BUCHANAN(BUCHANNON,BUCK-
  ANNON,BUCKMAN), Archibald
  49,207
  Benjamin 322
  Capt. 58
  Chas. 260
  Eben 5,9,68
  Ebnz. 260
  Jacob 146
  James 36,110,189,397
  John 13,14,68,82,95,
    151,161,180,206,230,
    232,237,249,259,260,
    261,290,322,359,409
  Joseph 322
  Patrick 8,43
  Robert 151,237
  Samuel 231,232
  Sarah 237
  Thomas 49,189,254,318,
    347
  William 68,102,125,232,
    260,309,322,397,398
  William, Jr. 68
BUCK, John 113
BUCKANN, William 232
BUFFINGTON, Abm. 91
  Ezekiel/Eziekeil 91,
    92,155,158,174,227,
    245,264,328,329,334,
    356,376,421,423
  Obern/Oburn 140,174,245
BUFORD, Thomas 102
BUGG, N. H. 70
BULLARD, Nathaniel 93,130
  Stephen 142
BULLER, William 42
BULLION, Mary 171
BULLOCK, John 391
  Richard 162,238,391
BUNNEY(BUNEY), William 316
BURBY, Robt. 104
BURCH, Henry/Hennery 1,89,
  114,117,185,194,197,
  201,204,205,206,208,
  209,210,214,217,218,
  219,220,221,222,224,
  226,240,246,247,248,
  250,259,270,275,281,
  284,286,287,289,292,
  296,298,302,319,328,
  329,331,341,368,376,
  380,381,388,394,403,
  406,409,414,416,418,
  423,424,425
  John 341
  Savannah 218
BURCHFIELD, Adam 246
  Dicy 341
  John 19
BURDINE(BOURDINE), Abra-
  ham 198
  Dolly 352
  Henry 157,159,270,291,
    347
  Jer./Jeremiah 20,43
  John 43,54,109,137,388
  Nancy 157,291
  Richard 208,342
  Samuel 109,198,271
BURFORD(BURFORT), John 87
  Mary 21,225
  Thomas 21,125,135,161,
    168,225,243,309,362,
    369,371,396,417,426
BURGER, Geo. 397
BURGESS, James 287
  John Carn Opea 287

BURGESS, cont'd:
  Rowland 64
BURK(S), Charles 373
  Isham 402
  John 207,363,372,373,
    380,423
  John, Sr. 373
  Joseph 363,375
  Nimrod 253
  Noland 380
  Rachel 373,380
  Randolph/Randlof 107
  Richard 73,373,380
  Roland/Rowland 60,73,
    107,372,373,380
  Samuel 414
BURNET(BURNETT), Samuel
  109,358
BURNEY, Adam 29,70
  Elizabeth 131,138,170
  Samuel 177
  W. W. 184
  William 33,131,138,141,
    170,177,211,338,419
  William W. 184
BURNS, Alexander 117,324,
  329,365,378
  John 83,376,382,385
  Joshua 133
  Peter 125
  Thomas 57
BURRELL(BURRILL), Harley
  135
  Hezekiah 135
  Peter 157
BURRIS(BURROUSE,BURROS),
  James 154,315,386,427
  Jean 10
  John 315,324,325,425
  Joshua 144,145,154,315,
    427
  Mrs. Kitty 10
  Robert O. 405
  Thomas 315,427
BURROWS, Edward 218
BURRY(BURRISS), Elisha 5
BURT, John 10
BURTON, Ann 269
  Elizabeth 275
  Hally 123
  John/Jno. 39,119,128,
    182,226,230,268,269
  Josiah 226
  Mary 226
  Samuel 85,179,217,275,
    334,337,338
  William 134,182,387
BUSBY, Sihon/Sinn/Sion 193,
  240,328
BUSH(BURK?), Daniel 115
BUSH, Samuel 143
  Wm. 171
BUSSON?, Andw. 94
BUTLER, James 301
  Jane Ann 415
  John 35
  Robert 35
  Thomas 302
  William 243,260,301,350
BUTT(S), John 72,103,124,
  320,372,373
BUZBIE, Jacob 291
BYNAM(BYNEHAM,BYNUM), Asa
  O. 335
  Benjamin 419
  Elizabeth 335
  Isaac 74,157
  James 335
  Jesse 235,264,335
  John 13,89,251,258,263,
    419
  William 268
  William, Jr. 419

BYNAM, Wm. O. 335
BYRD, John 169,349,374,378
  Michael 363
  Thomas 343,374

CABORNE, Geo. 196
CADDEL(CADDELL), Andrew
  408
  James 140
  John 408,410
CAHUN, James 373
CAIN, Jesse 379,411
  John 367,406
  Mary 201
  Michael 201
CALLAHAM(CALAHAM,CALLIHAM,
  CALLAHAN), Joel 59,84,94,
    257,381
  John 5,8,13,71,72,84,
    215,227,280,333,346
CALDWELL(CALWELL), David
  28,32,98,307,323
  Elizabeth 61,62
  James 15,274,282,317,
    323,357,416
  James, Jr. 323
  John 9,13,61,65,88,150,
    165,167,174,203,210
  John, Jr. 204
  John P. 98
  John Perkins 98
  Moses 88
  Nancy 203
  Robert 112
  Samuel 4,192
CALHOUN(CALHAON,COLHOUN),
    84,94,150,151,238,
    256,304,315,352
  Alexander 412,428
  Ewin 310
  Ewing 413
  Evin 272
  Howard 214
  James 71,72
  J. E. 261
  John 6,14,121,138,202,
    236,282,309,331
  John E. 77,121,164,214,
    241,247,267,283,312,
    331,334,369,421
  John Ewing 55,61,223,
    256,258,278,415
  John U. 263
  Joseph 112,123,140,353,
    395
  Patrick 116,251,284,
    316,381,395,417
  Patrick, Jr. 45,395
  William 355
  Wm., Jr. 292
CALLAWAY(CALLOWAY), ____
    259
  Francis 146,259
  Gaddeth/Gaddah/Gladdah
    284
  Thomas 325
CALOPSANE, ____? 140
CALVERT, John 148,360
CALVIN, Fergus 26
CAMP(CEMP), ____ 306
  Edward 84,150,151,193,
    249,390
  Elizabeth 84
  Holley 64
  Joshua 386,426
  L. 222
  Larkin 264
CAMPBELL(CAMBLE), Abraham
  62
  Collen/Collin/Colin
    104,149,187,266,286,
    301,305,306,311,313,
    326,328,331,335,336,

CAMPBELL, Colin cont'd:
    348,355,366,370,381,
    413
    Donald 78
    Jno./John 69,76,95,123,
    127,309,346,362
    John Moor(e) 362
    Samuel 415
CAMPONEL, Henry 152
CAMRON(CAMERON), ___ 198
    Duncan/Duncin/Dunkin
    12,17,18,37,56,58,114,
    115,163,194,209,222,
    224,253,284,329
    Mary 17,18
CANADY, ___ 15
CANNADY, W. E. 227
CANNIMORE(CANAMUR,CANNE-
MORE,CANNIMUR,CENNEMUR),
    George 254,256,260,
    262,346
    Michael 346
    Moses 283
    Noah 258
CANNON, ___ 309
    Mr. 361
    Abigale 129
    Elinor 129
    James 30,34,91,105,106,
    159,166,213,215,216,
    220,227,254,389
    James, Jr. 283
    James, Sr. 283
    John 129,158,215,228,
    234,261,283,361,428
    Kinson 5,220
    Mary 91
    Russell 292,389
    Samuel 358
    Sarah 30,34
    William 115,129,293,
    389
    William, Jr. 388
CANSELOR(CANSELLER,CANSLER,
KENSLER), Elizabeth 286
    James 146,286
    John 429
    John, Jr. 400
    Nathaniel H. 380
CANTREL(L), David 365
    John 276
    Joseph 365
    Levi 307
    Moses 139
    Stephen/Steven 208,209,
    250,299,306
CANTWELL, Stephen 125
CAPE, Brian 237
    Thomas 93
CAPEHART, ___ 320
    George 130,225,232,240,
    261,263,283,302,303,
    346,428
    Henry 130
    Jacob 5,94,115,151,165,
    177,178,183,196,197,
    199,224,238,240,249,
    259,261,264,273,283,
    304,320,326,332,350,
    383,394,396,400
    Margaret 151,326
    Paul 231
CARDEN, John 133
CARES, ___ 288
CAREWE(CAREW), John 174
CARLE, William 339,340
CARLTON, Henry 97
CARLETON, Joseph 206
    Joseph S. 97
CARLILE, James 210
    Samuel 220,257
CARMAN (see CAMRON)
CARN, John 367
CARNES, P. J. 47

CARNES, cont'd:
    Thomas Peter 47
CARNEY, Onely 418
CARNICK, Samuel 90
CARODINE, Hugh 264
    Jas. 263
CAROLAN, Phillip 237
CARPENTER, William 69,118.
    180,191,269,381
CARR, George 336
    Judith 336
CARRELL, Jno. 79,130
CARRICK, James 208,220,255
    John 212,237,320,418
CARRIDINE(CARIDINE), Thom-
    as 36,37,259
CARSON, James 371,385
    John 398
CART(CAST?), James 111
    John 94
CARTER, David 52,79,81,82,
    94,316
    Josiah 382
    Mehitable/Mahatabel 81
    Robert 37,69,217
    William 375,418
CARTON, David 275
CARRUTH(CARUTH), Adam 343,
    344
    Mary 309
CARUTHERS(CARRUTHERS),
    John 5,44,65,75,193,
    289,313,395
    Samuel 65
CARWINE, James 255,422
CARY(CAREY), ___ 306
    Graham 210
    John 301,426
    Mary 387
    Thomas 57,168,173,176,
    237
CASE, Sophia 177,350,389
    Thomas 16
    William 193
CASEY, ___ 269
    Abram 129
    Christopher 3,105,127,
    300,304
    Elizabeth 3
    Isaac 51
    Jesse 128
    Levi 307
    Moses 4
    Thomas 197
CASTLEBERRY(CASSELBURY),
    Adam 235
    Asa 425
    Edwin 292
    Mark 156,235,261,384
    Oden 292
    William 156,252
CASWELL, Mary 328
    "Widow" 165
CAUHARN(CAUHORN), Andrew
    268
    James 268
CAUDILL(CAUDELL), Thomas
    14,141
CAVIN, Alexander 120,178,
    278,404
    Fergus/Forga 139,181,
    189,380
    Hannah 181
CAVENDER, James 383,384,411
    Polly 411
CAVANDISH, William 134,292
    Wm. M. 59,137
CAVINDISH(see above)
CAWTHON, William, Jr. 382
CHADWICK, Thos. 129
CHALMERS, Elinor 191
CHAMBERLAIN, Jacob 87
CHAMBERLAND, Jacob 212

CHAMBERLY, Jacob 413
CHAMBERS, John 45
    Josiah 128
CHAMBLE, Benjamin 279,295
    Jacob 263,296
CHAMBLER, Zadick 386
CHAMBLES(CHAMBLESS), Jacob
    252
    Hugh 123,243
    Peter 139
CHAMBLIN, D. 410
CHAMLEE, Joel 36
    Jacob 36,292
    William 292
CHAMPMAN, Christiany 343
CHANDLER, Mrs. 333
    George 386
    James 151,170,223
    John 251,272
    Shadrack 240,264,295,
    333
    Tunstall 239
CHANEY, Isaac 253
CHAPLEY, Jane 183
CHAPLIN(E), William/Will
    387
CHAPMAN, Christiana 343
    Darkey 150
    Jacob 379
    James 5,169,292,378
    Jeremiah 365,368
    John 232,245,261,318,
    342,350,352
    Joseph 16,17,75,121,
    188,206,232,303,318,
    343,360,374
    Mary 206,374
    Thos. 93,114
    William 150,188
CHAPPEL, Jesse 429
CHAPPELL, Margaret 112
CHARLES, Oliver 121,179,
    347
CHARLESTON, Paul 344
CHASTAIN, Elijah 84
    John 84
    Stephen 279
CHATHAM, Joseph 352
CHERRY, ___ 317,420
    S. 261
    Samuel/Saml. 154,158,
    173,195,225,255,259,
    272,279,283,293,295,
    297,302,307,312,313,
    333,339,353,359,383,
    387,407,421,423,426
    Thomas 293
CHILDERS, Abraham 270
    Archbald 336
    John 348,358,394,395
    Joseph 115
    Nancy 394,395
    Paterson/Patterson 300,
    347,348,358
    William 257,336
CHILDRES(CHILDRESS,CHILD-
ERS), John 330
    Joseph 319
    Robert 211
CHILDS(CHILES), ___ 158
    Amilew 185
    Henry 6,26,27,69,156,
    390,400
    Moses 253,261
    Roland/Rowland 185
    Sarah 26,156
CHILERS, Archable 336
CHILOKE, Patterson 300
CHION, J. F. 252
    John F. 252
CHIRROUTH, Peter 231
CHIS(O)M, William/Wm. 197,
    209

CHOICE, Wm. 413
CHRISTIAN, R. B. 369
CILLA, Nimrod 318
CIMMON(CINAMORE,CINIMUR,
CINNEMUR),
   George 116
   John 164
   Noah 164
CLACK, Davis 322
CLARDY(CLARITY,CLARRIDY),
   Agnes 52,109,110
   Benjamin 52,64,109,110,
   233,241,242,259,261,
   262,388
   Elliott 218
   John 99,183,218,262
   Nancy 52
   Smith 110,233
CLARK(CLARKE), ___ 233
   Benjamin/Benjn. 13,15,
   31,72,103,119,149,171,
   206,273
   Bolen/Bolin/Boling/
   Bowlen/Bowling 15,155,
   172,177,219,282,288,
   295,318,351,353,355,
   425
   Boling, Jr. 155
   Charity 168
   David 15,16,117,134,
   137,145,148,153,165,
   168,169,184,197,267,
   268,281,288,295,359,
   425
   Davis 322
   George 365
   Gideon/Gedion 29,53,
   70,72
   Henry 1,118,119,149,
   252,281,370
   Henry, Jr. 119
   Isaac 119,128
   James 151,185,253,285,
   318,377
   Jenny 185,351
   John 153,318,413
   jon 149
   Jonathan 15,102,121,
   137,148,152,153,155,
   160,168,177,185,252,
   255,288,295,297,324,
   351,413
   Joseph 155,169,172,
   282,288,295,297,351,
   353,355,425
   Lurany 313
   Mary 172,282,288,353
   Matthew 400,423
   Mic(h)ach 295
   Micaiah 63,67,219,313
   Micajah 185,194
   Nathaniel 53,89,128
   Patience 171,206
   Robert 165,338,341
   Samuel 128
   Thomas 165,174
   William 13,292,337,
   393,394
   Wm. David 223
CLARKSON, John 276
   Matthew 175
CLAYTON(CLATON,CLEATON,
SLATON), Charles 244
   Isham 69,173,204
   James 267
   Jean 69
   John 220,244,383
   William 69,304,326
CLEARMAN, Jacob 111
CLEMENTS(CLEMEN,CLEMMENTS,
CLEMONS), Aaron 100
   Agnes 274,294,352
   Benjamin 236,244 251,
   288

CLEMENTS, cont'd:
   Charles 20,38,48,59,
   70,94,111,163,251,274,
   294,299,305,348,352,
   364,366
   Culliver/Culiver 12,20,
   262,264,270
   Gean 366
   Hardy 365,429
   Hugh 190
   James 65,121,135,163,
   236,261,270,274,368
   Jesse 12,20,59,65
   John 100,172,361,366
   Reuben/Reubin 111,121,
   135,163,270,364,365,
   368,424,429
   Thomas 243
CLEVELAND(CLEAVELAND,CLEA-
VELIN), Absolom (any var-
ious spellings) 70,89,99,
   133,182,280
   Anderson 166
   Benjamin 1,6,22,28,31,
   53,55,70,71,89,91,99,
   122,133,152,155,157,
   166,171,182,184,192,
   258,261,280,287,303,
   353,421
   Daniel 421
   David 308
   Jeremiah 258,382
   John 28,133,184,258,
   308,421
   Larkin 192,258,308
   Mary 258
   Mathew 159
   Mathias 92
   N. 251,308
   Neely 192
   Nell(Neil?) 258
   William 77,122,171,183,
   192,203,204,212,222,
   226,229,238,248,251,
   253,254,258,259,261,
   262,266,280,282,284,
   285,287,308,318,323,
   330,339,345,359,360,
   377,382,383,384,386,
   390,399,401,409,411,
   428
   Wm. (see above)

CLIFTON, Claiborn 230
CLINKSCALES, Francis 27,31,
   189,190,206,286,387
   William 189,387
CLOWNEY, Samuel 209
COB(COBB.COOB), ___ 326
   A. 276
   Abiel/Abial 4,93,98,
   113,130,355
   Ann 74
   Asa 100,136,176
   Franky 380
   Henry 17,56,88,388
   Humphrey/Humphree 215,
   216,272,283,361
   Jenny 272
   Jesse 56,100
   John 4,319,380
   Levise 272
   Lewis 44,52,82,93,98,
   112,113,152,178,194,197,
   200,209,320,355
   Rachel 388
   S. 261
   Sally 320
   Samuel 88,100,388
COBBIN, Hannah 56
COCHRAN(COCKRAN,COHRAN),
   Andrew 394,395
   David 274,357
   James 319,320

COCHRAN, cont'd:
   John 71,150,151,204,
   233,261,266.278,293,
   295,300,307,308,309,
   323,324,325,329,331,
   332,336,339,342,343,
   346,350,352,361,371,
   381,393,395,405,413,
   419,420,421,423,424
   Lovinia 395
   Nancy 331
   Richard 17
COCKERHAM, William H. 248
   William M. 367
   Wm. 263
CODDLE, Thomas 306
COFFEE, ___ 372
COFFEY, James 266,326
COFFEE, Jesse 50,77,122,
   133,142,151,161,226,
   335
COIL, Martha 294
COKER, ___ 289
   Thomas 9,137,172,252,
   261,282,318,351,353,
   355,371,425
   William/Wm. 252,261,
   337,351,353,355
COLCOCK, Charles J. 134
   Charles Jones 188
   Charles T. 56
COLCOM, John 325
COLE, Thomas 166
COLLER, William 138
COLLEY, Susannah 233
COLLIER, Davis 368
   Green 299,352
COLLINS, Mr. 114
   Hezekiah 97
   Rebekah 203
   Richard 203,324
   Thomas 285
COLTON, Joseph 224
COLWELL, Hennery 203
   Joseph 203
   Robert 296
COMBS, ___ 144,307,354
   Bennet/Bennett 16,54
   75,149,154,157,158,171,
   173,206,208,213,217,
   219,220,232,236,241,
   257,261,357,360,365,
   428
   (Also Comebess)
   Dolley/Dolly 206,303,
   304,324,371
   Dolitha 357,360-
   Doratha 54,357
   George 367
COMMING, John Boyd 116
COMMONS, Hermon 72
   Thomas 333,348
COMPTON, James 38,46,48,
   58,75,248,342
   Levi 342
CONAWAY, Caleb 16,32,57
   Mary 57
CONGER, Rachel 285
CONN, John 65,380
   Simeon 65
CONNELLY, James 336
CONNER, Christopher 123
   James 235,275
CONNOR, D. O. 201
CONWAY, Edwin 63
   Peter 63
COOK, Elisha 155
   Jehu 207
   John 310
   West 248
   William 178,345
COOKE, John 421
   Robert 410
COOKER, Thomas 255

COOKER(COKER), William 425
COOPER, ___ 355
  Enos 112
  James 153,251,317,424,
    425,426
  Jesse 112
  John 310
COPELAND, ___ 295
  Alr. 267
  Joseph 305,377,378
  Reuben 415,416
  Samuel 309
COPLAND, W. 222
COPELAND, William 164,238,
  261,267,290,421
COPELIN, Jacob 348
COPLING, Jean/Jain 282
CORAM, Robert 154
CORAN, Francis 396
CORBETT, Thomas 155
CORLEY, George 278
CORLS, James 181
  Matthew 181
CORNELIS, Benjamin 22
CORNELIUS, Auston/Austen/
  Austin 49,184
  Rowland 40
  Rowland, Jr. 40
  Rowland, Sr. 40
CORRES, John 49
CORRIS, John QV (also John
  Q. Norris?) 49
CORWINE, James 422
COSBY, John 133
  William 304
COUCH, John 4,85
  Joseph 376
COULTER, Wm. 138
COUN?, William 106
COURTNEY, James 201,353
COVEN, Alexander 341
COVENHOVEN, Benjamin 407
  Rachel 407
COWAN(COWEN), David 375
  John, Jr. 13,156
COX(COCKS,COXX), Ann 407
  Bevely/Beaverly/Bev-
    erly 101,172,244,261
  Edward 259,261,316,
    318,335,342,411
  George 244,261
  Henry 233,261
  Isaac 101,189,270,281,
    387,412
  Ishom 361
  James 101,107,163,306
  Joel 52
  John 87,101,172,178,
    261,304,316,318,328,
    361,372,415
  John, Jr. 101
  John, Sr. 244
  Levi 328
  Mary 6,101,356
  Phillip 225,291
  Polley/Polly 233,261
  Reuben 57,189,206
  Solomon 182
  Thomas 6,192
  William 115,129,134,
    189,197,210,270,281,
    319,320,351,356,357
COYLES, Martha 215
COZBY, James 302
CRABTREE, Isaac 416
  Samuel 34,166
CRAFFORD, James 393
  Moses B. 382
CRAFT, John 55
  Richard Wood 232
CRAFTON, Bennet 120,139,
  216
  Samuel 394

CRAGE, Andrew 65
CRAIG(CRAIGE), Benjamin 168
  John 32,187,194,276,
    292
  Robert 42
CRAIN(CRAINE,CRANE), Adam
  336
  Aaron 65,71,307,315,
    418
  Jesse 315,418
  John 311
  Philimon/Phillimon/
    Philemon 307,315
  Samuel 326,331,335
  William 111,209,214,
    215,286,307,315
  William C. 307,315
CRAKE, Henry 171
CRASLIN, Samuel 34
CRAUSBY, William 326
CRAVEN(CRAVENS,CRAVING,
  CRAVINS), Abigale 72,73
  Fergus 78
  Robert 32,72,89,173,
    185,193,208,214,284,
    286,308,334,390,421
CRAWFORD(CRAFFORD), David
  4,61
  Elizabeth 393
  Geo. 223
  James 161,393,394
  L. W. 21
CREDER, Christopher 190
CREEL, Thomas 56,60
CRENSHAW, Patience 116,351
CRESS, John 368
CRESWELL, ___ 288
  Mary 34,209
  Robert 209
CREWS, Thomas 148,360
CRIDINTON(CRIDIENTON,CRI-
  TINGTON), Jonathan 91,220
CROFT, Samuel 136
CROFTON, B. 232
  Samuel 94,234
CROMWELL, Oliver 252
CROSBY, William 100,120,
  144,376,382,412
CROSS, Dorrel 156
  John 379,416
  Richard 329
  William 115
CROUCH, Joseph 411
CROW, David 186
  Thomas 27,119,122,133,
    260
  William 184
CROWDER(CROUDER), James 2
  Martha 237,261
CROWLEY, Charles 192,358
CROWNOVER, Abraham 407
  Benjamin 407
  William 407
CROWTHER, James 18,47
CRUMBLESS(CRUMBLEY), ___
  352
  Hugh 213,226,287
CRUTCHFIELD, Susannah 90
CULLEN, Leroy 361
CULLON, Claiborn 230
CULTON(COULTON), Anne 46
  James 62
  Joseph 39,47,56,117,
    126,145,161,253,272,
    395
  Joseph, Sr. 38
  Norris J. 81
CUMMINGS(CUMMINS), Jas. 40
  Harman 134,153,279,280
  William 86
CUNNINGHAM(CUNINGHAM), ___
  39,187,274
  Andrew/Andw. 13,14,238

CUNNINGHAM, cont'd:
  Dd. 158
  Francis 124
  James 23,69,93,111,
    114,123,124,164,181,
    230,238,261
  Jane 366
  John 67,93,238,401,
    422
  William 26,223,250,
    251,426
CURETON, Thomas 289,299
CURL, William 314
CURLEY, William 362
CURRIER, Jno. 111
CURRY, ___ 324,352
  James 82,85,187,325,
    383,391
  John 44,58,68,82,93,
    96
  "Widow" 267
CURTIS, Christopher 248
  Naaman 428

D___, 229
DALRYMPLE(DALRIMPLE,DAL-
  RUMPLE), ___ 104
  J. 385
  James 309,324
  John 45,59,67,68,271,
    429
  Samuel 45,64,91,101,
    114,159,162,163,236,
    309,369,396
  Sarah 45,91,159,163,
    220
  "Widow" 129
DANALLY, John 35
DANIEL, Bartholomew 379
  Burton 325
  Richard 238
  Wm. 60
DARBY, Artemas B. 216,336
  Artemas Bernham(Burn-
    ham) 216
  B. 259
DARDEN, Charnel 285
DARNELL(DARNAL,DARNALL,
  DERNAL), ___ 287
  James 18
  Nancy 23
  Nicholas 2,18,125,128,
    168,331
  Thomas 23
  William 125,188,334,
    338
DARRAGH(DARRAH), John 43,
  44,162,292
DARRELL, E., Jr. 188
  Edward 11
DART, Isaac Motte 183
  John Sanford 3,55,94
DAUGHTY(DAUGHERTY,DAUGH-
  TRY), ___ 299
  Daniel (also Doty) 200
  James 56,129,158,420
DAVENPORT, Isaac 242,262
  James 122,133,226
DAVEY(DAVEYS), Daniel 78
  John 78,354
DAVID, ___ 308
DAVIDSON, Andrew 383,407
  Andrew T. 375
  Andrew Thomas 333
  James 333,383,407
  John 71,333,375,383,
    407
  William 333,375,383,
    407
DAVINEY, Hugh 203
DAVIS(DAVES), Abigaile 20
  Abijah 72,227
  Abner 114,318

DAVIS, cont'd:
  Adam 96,104,235,327,
    328,384,393
  Andrew 5
  Brook Hall 338
  Brooks 214
  Brooks H. 115,129
  Daniel 331,335
  Edward 120,132,139,
    365
  Eli 26,109,110,334
  Elizabeth 335
  H. 322,363
  Hezekiah/Hez./Hh. 72,
    227,297,298,301,305,
    319,322,325,359,361,
    367,374,376,378,391,
    407,411,423
  Hezekiah, Sr. 71
  Isaac 206
  James 84,141,190
  Jane 203
  Jesse 72,154,166,227,
    250,332,391
  Jfh(?) 315
  John 19,44,99,122,209,
    217,272,295,302,314
  John, Sr.? 225
  John Lewis 4,6,19,26,
    110,115,129,203
  Jonathan 59,235,273,
    405
  Joseph 274
  Keziah 206
  Lewis 190,203,239,281,
    351
  Nathaniel 130,132,152,
    199,234,260,326,390
  Orange 331,333,359
  Paul 239
  Peggy 351
  Richard 313
  Robert 228,384
  Sally 338
  Sarah 14,72,227,411
  Surry/Surkey 15,83,115
  Thomas 206,190,231,
    281,299,326,363,374,
    422
  Van/Vann 227,332,342,
    361
  Vincent 3,21
  William 14,116,157,
    228,270,272,291,302,
    308,384
  William Elson 18
  Zachariah/Zh. 27,342
DAWDY, Howell 302
DAY(DAYE), Allis 352
  Ballard 366
  Henson 251
DEALE,   138
DEAL(DEALE), A. 377
  Alexr. 29
  Clement 28,76,138
  Jane 146,152,183
  Jean 358
  Joseph (also Deen)
    280,319,324
  Samuel 45,113,134,153,
    236,280,342,360,378
  Thomas (also Deen) 30,
    342,361,378
DEARING(DEERING), John
    238,260,261,322
  John, Jr. 238
  Mary 322
DEASON, Benjamin 141
DEAVORS, George 111
de BLOCK, Francois/Francis 219,260
DEFLOOR, Andrew 96
DEGALY, Thomas 73

DEJERNIT(DEGARNET,DEGERNET), Elias 96
  Nancy 96
  Reuben 78,96
DELANEY(DELANY,DELINNY),
    367
  Daniel 91,153,193,220,
    235,261,285,317
DELANEY(DELANRY), Thomas
    372
DELIESSILINE, Francis C.
    227
DENHAM, Jas. 232
  Margarett 232
DENNIS, Andrew 340
  Nathaniel 74,76,340
  William 143,256
DENOM, Mickey 406
DENSON, James 260,261
DENTON, Benjamin 55
  Reuben 55,133,144,171
DERNALL(DARNELL), James
    115
  Joseph 201
DERNEY, Aaron 11
DERNLEY, John 386
DERSON, John 228
DESAUSSURE(DESAUSARE),___
    345
  Daniel 11,310
  Eliza 258
  H. W. 261
  Henry W. 97,310,311
  Henry William 2,9,50,
    51,64,96,247,258,415
  Lewis 350
  Mary 311
DETWORTH, George 5
DEURING, John 290
DEVANPORT, Charles 205
DEVANEY, Hugh 111
  Mary 111
DEVINEY, James 106
DICKASON, Anthony 256,272
  Matthew 255
  Robert 255
DICKENS, Ellander 235
DICKENSON, Robert 249
DICKERSON,   84
  mical 209
  Robert 94,151,209
DICKESON, Ellenor 16
  John 16
  Lyddia 16
  Michael 16
  Robert 16,238,312,394
DICKEY(DICKY,DICKIE), Ann
    145
  David 36,87,90,235,263,
    267,297,413
  John 174
  William 114,133,145,
    146,317,340,427
DICKINSON, Willis 400
DICKSON(DIXON),   121
  Benjamin 5,81,178,292,
    293,411,412
  David 60
  Eliza 344
  Elizabeth 310,399
  Hugh 177,186,209,269
  James 129,139,197,209,
    234,307,346,391,398,
    400,404,413,421
  John 177,182,200,221,
    346,371,384,386,390,
    391,398,400,412,423
  John, Jr. 223,269
  John, Sr. 106,167
  Joseph 408
  Martha 251,398
  Mathew/Matthew 108,207,
    251,361,388

DICKSON, cont'd:
  Matthew, Jr. 199,261
  Matthew, Sr. 251,261
  Mathew, Sr. 261
  Michael 131,164,167,
    178,192,197,202,209,
    210,227,230,240,243,
    247,251,255,265,278,
    306,310,312,344,349,
    369,391,398,413
  Mitchael 250
  Rebekah/Rebecca/Rebecah/Rebeckah 106,
    225,289,315
  Rob. 263
  Sally 412
  Samuel 178,213,254,
    304,310,312,315,318
  Samuel H./Saml. H. 6,
    19,36,42,102,106,167,
    209,214,225,279,280,
    285,289,297,304,306,
    312,313,314,315,329,
    338,344,346,351,355,
    358,359,369,374,380,
    384,385,387,391,396,
    398,399,401,407,409,
    415,416,419,420,425,
    426
  Samuel Henry 127,310
  Samuel J. 72
  Walter C. 251,292
  Walter Carson 108
  William 73,253
DILLARD, George 222
  Joseph 147
DILLON, Robert 201
DILSON, James 318
  James Harris 318
DILWORTH, G. 260
  George 95,133,191,270,
    274,293,351,376,417
DINIS, Samuel 323
DINKINS, Lewis 174
DINSON, James 259
DISON, John 233
DITTO, James 44,54,126,
    143,419
  Jane Star 307
DIVINE, Thomas 201
DIXON, John 408
  Mathew 350,352
DOBBING, James 224
DOBBIN(DOBBINS), James 42,
    46,126,255
  John 46
  Starrett 419
DOBBS, Hugh 64,158
  John 119,128
  Loddy 6,192
  Lodwick 171
  Sarah 192
DOBSON, Henry 20,21,27,
    35,244
DODD, Hugh 186,251
  Richard 222
DODDY, Howell 86,164
DODSON, Charles 77,117,214
  Delinham 214
  Henry 182,263
  Isaac 56
  Joshua 56,89
DODY,   343
DOGGETT, Thomas 164
DOHERTY, James 384
DOIL, James 130
DOILY, Daniel 345
DOLLAR(DALLAR,DILLARD),
  Ansel 105
  Reuben/Reubin 105
DOLLARS(also Dillard),
  George 222
DONALDSON, John 374

DONALDSON, cont'd:
    Thomas 160
    William 429
DONALSON, Thomas 160
DONELSON, Wm. 427
DONNALSON, John 250
DONOLSON, Wm. 310
DORAN(DORIN), James 5,25,
    261,295,331,392,396
    John 314
    Mary 392
DORRAH, John 381
DORSEY, William 44
DOSETT, Joseph 292
DOSEY(DASEY?), William
    209
DOSS, John 233,263,404,
    408
    Usley 189
    William 80,189,404,
    408
DOUBY, Artimas B. 319
DOUGHTY(DAUGHTY), Daniel
    201
    Joseph 45,46
DOUGLAS(DOUGLASS), James
    360
    James Alexander 7
    Joseph 141
DOUTHIT, Jas. 38
DOVER, John 270,314
DOW, Arthur 361
DOWDLE, James 8,225,353
    James Gwen 309
    John 8,163,227,346
    J. John 126
    Robert 4,8,16,28,66,
    68,100,164,168,332,
    353,417
    Robert, Sr. 414
    Samuel G. 309
DOWDY, Howell/Howlee 33,
    327
    Robert 219
DOWER, Francis 333
DOWNEN, Josiah 50
DOWNING, E. 52
DOWNS, James 155
    John 82
    Jonathan 8,92,211
    Joshua 30
    Joseph 166
    William 403
DOYLE, Arron 233
    Edward 5,134,385,424
DOYLE(also Doyal) James
    71,114,130,197,224
    Michael 424
    Rhodam 407
    Simon/Sim./Sin. 150,
    169,179,211,218,241,
    262,276,349,369,380,
    424
    William 211
D'OYLEY, Daniel 196,203
DRATON(DRAYTEN), ___ 289,
    350
DRAYTON, ___ 112,147
    H. 147
    Hannah 147
    Jacob 52,55,68,147,
    237,322
    John 275,304,327,338,
    341,359,370,371,373,
    381,403,415,424
    Sarah Motte 147
    Stephen 1,94,191,268,
    303,365
    Thomas 147
    William 52,55,87,147
DRENNAN(DRINNAN), David
    98,307,310,316,318,
    367,374,396,417

DRENNAN, James/Jas. 261,
    346,367,402,416
    John 75,130,134,253,
    324,325,416
    Joseph 323,361,414
    Mary 367
    Mary Wheems 417
    Samuel 361,414
    Thomas 253,317,323,356,
    357,361,414
    William 59,98,130,307,
    317,318,324,366,367
    William, Jr. 4,138
DREW, Langston 277,386
DRIMON, James 427
DRINNAN (see DRENNAN)
DROMGOOLE, Alexander 1,4,
    17,20,36,37,213,259
Dryden, Jonathan 25
DUBOSE, Jas. 406
DUCASS, John 221
DUCKWORTH(DUCKSWORTH),
    Benjamin 309,312,318
    Howard 309
    Joseph 332,389
    Obadiah 332,410
DUDLEY, Ambrose 74,150,338,
    340,341,370
DUFF, ___ 300
    Abraham/Abram 149,371
    James 27,97,109,114,
    123,143,171,181,271,385,
    387,402
    James, Jr. 159
    James, Sr. 387
    Joseph 214,215,380
    Lanny 371
    Robert 385,387,398
    Samuel 108,114,181,192,
    208,249,271,299,300,
    321,398
    Samuel/Saml. C. 181,
    271,357,364,370,375,
    381,383,385,386,387,
    398,402
    Samuel Carson 97,357
    William 364
DUKE(DUK,DUCK), Abraham
    152,160,300,324
DUKY, William 314
DULANEY, Daniel 214,220,
    381
DULLIS, Joseph 1
DUNCAN(DUNKIN), Anderson
    390
    Benjamin 226
    Charles 226
    Daniel 273,276,285
    David 273,276
    Hugh, Jr. 374
    John 105,273,390,408,
    415
    Joseph 63,101,115,117,
    169,179,181,261,339
    Nathaniel 122,273
    ooni(?) 226
    Patrick 213,261,369
    Rice 169,179,261
    Robert 97,102,109,141,
    251,412
    Samuel 417
    Thomas 213
    William 5,374,378,412
DUNKLIN, Joseph 11
DUNLAP, David 290,308,340
    Gilbert 329
    William 25,113,234,269,
    386
DUN(DUNN), Elizabeth 64
    Joseph 53,65,115,128,
    149
DUN. William 380
DUNNAGAN, Ezekiel 77,114

DUNSEETH, Jno. A. 125
DURHAM, Charles 169
    David 13,319
    Nathan 65,271
    William 267
DURLEY, Arthur 62,134,137,
    228,350,352,366
    John (also Durely) 45,
    201,207
    Rhatio 271
DURUMPLE, Samuel 30
DUTILLEY(DUTILLY), ___ 177
    James 98,265
DUTON, Jacob 232
DYCHE, ___ 143
DYAR(DYER), Abner 336
    Caleb 187
    Elijah 63
    Elisha 58,190,252,264,
    269,337
    Elisha, Jr. 395
    Elisha, Sr. 187,189,
    395,424
    Joshua 88,170,190,336,
    337,424
    Josiah 150,171
    Levina 269
    Manoah 395,424
    William 63

EAKER(EAKINS), Jane 233
    Peter 134
    Samuel 116,233
EARLE, ___ 58,300,330
    B. B. 125
    Balis/Baylis 6,13,17,
    129,157,174,233,261,
    301,303,337
    Baylis, Jr. 6
    Baylis, Sr. 116,344
    Col. 383,410
    Elias 93,103,111,173,
    202,357
    G. W./George Washing-
    ton 75,83,94,106,124,
    125,126,128,129,135,
    138,139,140,142,144,
    150,151,152,154,155,
    157,158,162,164,165,
    166,168,169,171,173,
    177,178,179,181,183,
    184,186,187,188,189,
    190,191,193,194,195,
    197,198,199,200,201,
    202,205,208,209,212,
    213,221,223,224,225,
    226,286,310
    Harriot 357
    J. B./ John Baylis
    35,57,59,61,62,64,67,
    69,72,73,74,75,76,77,
    78,79,80,82,83,84,85,
    87,88,89,91,93,94,96,
    98,99,101,102,103,104,
    106,107,109,111-115,
    120,122,124,128-131,
    133,136,139,141-146,
    148,153,158,159,163-
    165,167,168,174-178,
    186,187,192-195,197,
    203,204,206,207,214,
    215,216,220,221,223,
    225,227,229,232-235,
    237,239-242,244,248-
    253,255-257,259,261,
    272,274-281,283,285,
    286,287,294,297,298,
    302-309,312,317,322,
    323,324,328,330,331,
    333,338,340,343,344,
    349,354,357,359,371,
    394,408,424,426,428,
    429

EARLE, cont'd:
  J. P. 94
  Joseph B. 376,390,401
  Samuel 35,40,43,57,93,
    108,111,125,139,149,
    176,192,206,210,232,
    233,257,262,263,266,
    267,281,303,306,324,
    355,356,357,362,365,
    366,368,371,384,405,
    410,413,416,422
  Samuel, Jr. 95
  Sarah 259
  W. 41
EARLY, James 68,85
  Patrick 149
EARNEST, ___ 186
  Jacob 138,141,211,236,
    280,306,355
  Jacob, Jr. 124
  Jacob, Sr. 124,125
  Ludwick/Ledwick/Lead-
    wick 383,420
  Norman 125
  Thomas 126,183,198,218
EARP, Daniel 269
EASLEY, John 149,217
  Millington 58
  Pleasant 197
  Robert 58,59,65,121,
    152,174,250,261
  William 35
EASON, Abraham 3
  James 3,79,129,130,
    140,196,388,397
EAST, Joshua 166
  Josiah 59
EASTEST, Nathaniel 130
EASTRIDGE, Moses 8
EATEN(EASTEN), Lewis 300,
    301
EATON, John 53,65
  Joseph 164,238,261
  Lewis 221,222,293,321,
    380
  Milley 414
EAUST, Jacob 324
EAVES, Thomas 403
ECHOLS, Peggy 406
  Richard 168
ECKELS, Joshua 259
EDDIN(S), Alexander 15
  Benjamin 111
  Benjamin, Sr. 111
  Jacob 336
  James 49,83
  William 109,111,139,
    195,246,262,365,366
EDENS, Alexander 61
  Molley 61
  William 195
EDINGS, James 331
  William 299
EDINGTON, Thomas 372
EDNEY, Jacob 188
EDMONDSON, Benjamin 139,
    291
  Caleb 105,106,134,228,
    378
  George 139,291,304,312,
    314,361
  James 120,139,402
  James, Jr. 386,387
  John 138,139,291,402
  Lettia/Lettitia 361
  Mary 291
  Michael 343
  Nancy 120
  Parthenia 350
  Thomas 41,106,120,139,
    198,282,291,426
  Wm./William 13,40,41,
    47,48,52,53,54,57,58,

EDMONDSON, cont'd:
  William/Wm. 59,65,66,
    67,71,83,86,97,106,115,
    122,123,124,131,139,
    141,144,160,164,167,
    183,186,198,205,208,
    213,216,238,261,267,
    278,280,282,291,293,
    294,297,306,310,320,
    328,330,345,350,363,
    366,367,368,382,394,
    398,402,417,420,421,
    426
  Wm., Sr. 48
EDWARDS, ___ 162
  Catherine 377
  Edward 3,65,98,192
  Henry 347,352,378,379,
    404
  J. 2
  Jesse 329
  John 2,31,65,98,122,
    127,166,167,173,178,
    189,190,192,193,199,
    301,305,317,327,411
  Lewis 119,253,286
  Mary 404
  Mary Ann 143,342
  Nicholas, Sr. 377
  Peter 243,264,347,352,
    377
  Thomas 53,143,165,342
  William 39,143,329,347,
    352,378
EDWATERS, John 251
EGAN, William 336
ELDRIDGE, Nathaniel 119
ELENN, Barne 193
ELEY, A. 64
ELFE, Benj. 258
ELGIN, Robert 57
ELKINS, James 253
  Jno. 263
  Shadrack 204
ELLEDGE, Abraham/Abram 121,
    284,293,350,351,378
  Isaac 60
  Joseph 374
ELEGE, John 86,427
ELLET, ___ 356
  Thomas 196
ELLETT, William 382
ELLINGTON, Leonard 413
ELLIOT/ELLIOTT, Ann 183
  Barn'd 2
  Charles 291
  Jonah 250
  Josiah 207,215,279
  Robert 199
  Thomas 19
  William 191,369
ELLIS, Benj. 258
  Jeremiah 361
ELLITT, Charles 157
ELMORE, J. A. 285
  John 285
  John A. 291
ELROD, Abraham 143
  Isaac 198,295
  ELLROD, Jeremiah 179
ELROD, Samuel 145
ELSTON, John 308,394
ELTON, Anthony Wm. 166
  Elenor 166
ELWATERS, Isaac 300
ELWEL, Isaac 295
EMBERSON, Samuel 294
EMISON, Samuel 181,294
ENGLAND, Charles 140
ENTREKIN(ENTREKEN,ENTRICAN)
  John 59
  Mary 149
  Sarah 271

ENTREKIN, cont'd:
  Thomas 38,59,148,149,
    185,390
ERSKIN, James 364
ERWIN((ERWING,ERVIN)___
    396
  Alexander 6,21,26,31,
    165,181,298,380
  J. 197
  James 26,298
  John 38,165,298
  Joseph 40,165,166,184,
    191,203,288,315,339,
    341,380
  Susannah 21,31
  Unity 298
  William 96
ESON, James 388
ESTES, Moses 8
  Nathaniel 298
ESTHER, Frances 269
ESTON(ELSTON,EASTON),
  John 393
ESTR(E)AGE, Moses 8,346
EUBANKS, John 318,346,347,
    352,365
  John, Sr. 331,346
  Martin 160
  Thomas 347
EVANS(EVENS,EVINS), Agnes
    209
  D. 8,28
  D. R. 26
  David 8
  David Read 8,26
  Elizabeth 381
  Isaac 127,300,304,353,
    355
  Jean 137
  John 10,63,78,278,316,
    380,381,409
  Joseph 259
  Letitia 10
  Owen 43,172,176,209,
    369,381,429
  Robert 4,114,192,327
    381
  Samuel 305
  Walter 290
EVELIEGH, Nicholas 27
EVETT, James 304,400
  Susannah 400
  William 250,405
EVITTE, William 280
EWELL, Malechi 387
EWING, J. E. 415
  Joseph 61

FAFER, Francis 69
FAIN, Ebenezer 13,67,68,
    74,86,118,159,198,237,
    254,261,264,358,367
FAIR, Barnabas/Barnabus
    127,312,389
FAIRCHILD, Thos. 199
FALCONER(FALKNER), John 15
FARER, Leonard 149
FARIS(FARES,FARRIS,FARISS)
  Absolom 299,345,398
  John/Jno. 280,295
  Moses 305
  William 78,80,125,130,
    183,184,198,199,205,
    280,289,290,295,306,
    337,345,409
FARLEY, Archebald 329
FARMANDIS, Henry 27
FARMER, Benjamin 4,136,176,
    251,261,265,298,388,
    418
  Francis 289
  Frasiers 281
  John 298

FARMER, cont'd:
    John 298
    William 62,158,159,
      252
FARR(FAR), Barnabas/Bar-
    nebus 121,369
FARRAR, ___ 229
    Briton 251
    Cyprian 142,280
    Elizabeth 1,28
    Field 1,2,3,6,8,12,13,
      26,28,31,42,88,176,
      252,278,280,302,359
    John 251
    John Landers 88
    Matilda 60
    Peggy 298,428
    Richard/Richd. 30,58,
      307
    Seth 43,89
    T. 335
    T. W. 422
    Thomas 1,2,13,25,28,
      40,47,51,55,60,66,67,
      76,85,87,93,94,103,
      106,107,125,142,147,
      164,175,176,183,191,
      193,203,229,234,240,
      255,261,278,280,298,
      302,308,310,317,323,
      339,427
    Thomas W. 369,371,372,
      374,377,382,428
FARROW(FARO,FARRO), Brit-
    on 261
    John 251,261,317
    Sarah 251,317
    Rerin/Perron 251,261,
      274,317
    Thomas 105,410
FARY, William 242
FAULKNER, William 414
FAUST, Daniel 231,261
    Jacob 324
FAYSSOUX, Peter 44
FAZBY, James 302
FEEMSTER, Samuel 200
FELD, John 293
FELLOW(S), John 249
FELTON, Emeriah 5
    Harold 408
    William 307,356
FENDLEY, Kenith 335
FENN, Peter 218,405
FENNY, Patrick 186
FERBUSH, George 233
FERGUSON(FERGESON,FORGU-
    SON), James 314,322,341
    John 142,155,360
    Martha 314,341
    Robert 367
    Thos/Tom (also Forson)
      156,342
FERRELL, William 247
FERRIS, Jas. 57
FEW, Charles 252,396,417
FIELD(S), Jeremiah 229,
      265
    John 5,44,160,308,309,
      346
    John, Jr. 278,293
    Jno., Sr. 260,278,337
    Thomas 218,222,247,
      259,261,262,292,390,
      405
FIELDING, Isham 429
FIKE, Abel/Able 192,300,
      321
FILES, ___ 153
    Adam 13,17,95,100,120,
      134,139
    Adam T. (J.?) 17
    David 334,335,339,340,
      383,385,401

FILES, cont'd:
    James 159,298,344
    Jeremiah 100,134,313,
      344
    John 45,95,134
    John. Ja. Jos (sic) 7
    Mary/Marah 95
FILLPOT, Warren 380
FINDLEY, Goldin 253
    John 58
    Kenneth/Kinneth 95,226
    Lydia (also Finley) 427
    Thomas 136,239
    William 239,340
FINLEY, Mr. 361
    B. W. 301,312,326
    Barkley W. 338,372
    Bartlett 402
    Howard 343
    John 84
    Mathew 45
    Samuel 84
    Thomas (also Finely)
      169,261,279,235,325,
      348,377,404,419,425
    Wm. 261
FINN(FENN), Peter 218,222,
      248,261
FINNEY, Patrick 64
FINSON, Peter 3,6
FINTON, Sm. 196
FISHER, James 382
    John 406
FITZGER(R)ALD, Ambrose 3,
      31,73
    Sarah 73
FITZJARREL, Garret 404
FITZPATRICK, John Clarke
      31
FLAGG, Henry Collins 95
FLANAGAN(FELANIGAM,FILAN-
    AGAN), John 321
FLANIKAN, Elizabeth 364
    John 364
FLEEK(FLUK), John 88,422
FLEMING(FLEMAN,FLEMINS),
    ___ 174
    James 69,74,198,237,
      358,366,367
FLENKIN, Elizabeth 364
FLETCHER, William 210
FLEURY, John 301
FLEY, Saml. 261
FLOKER, John C. 92
FLOYD(FLOID), Alexander
      163,194,196,210,224,
      284,329,415
    Elijah 291
    Elisha 209,411,415
    James 364
    Nancy 284
    William 18,194,209,210,
      224,329,359,379,415
    William, Jr. 163
FOILS, Mary 28
FOLKNER, ___ 263
    David 242
FORBES(FORBIS,FORBUS,FOR-
    BEST), E. 261
    Elizabeth 297
    George 15,23,29,46,126,
      142,148,172,184,199,
      255,261,296,297,301,
      315,318,351,397
    Margaret 301,302
    Patrick 7,8,14,332
    U. 261
    William 14,126,281,300,
      301,302,338,359
FORBUSH, Patrick 161
FORD, Cornelius 198,358
    Jacob 247
    John 7,35,83,84,85,311
    Thomas 240

FORD, cont'd:
    Timothy/Timy 50,64,97
    William 358
FORGISON, Hugh 418
FORK, James 86
FORSYTH, William 407
FORTAIN(FORTIN), Martha
      419
    William 330,382,419
FORTUNE, William 259,264
FOSHER, Josiah 41
FOSTER, Ambrose 266,287
    Elizabeth 295
    Gabriel 194,409
    George 31,214,215,230,
      249,269,270,273,281,
      299,302,303,311,327,
      330,336,374
    George S. 171,343
    George Singleton 41,
      272
    Henry 124
    Isaac 36
    James 306,385
    James, Jr. 191
    James H. 343
    James J. 41
    Jeremiah 236,262,326,
      420
    Joel 186,410
    John Crow 306,343,405
    Josiah 41,268,283,285,
      291,292,296,317,322,
      340,341,344,354,355,
      358,363,372,373,381,
      423
    Samuel 128,202,210
    Tadira 275
    Thomas 9,10,36,164,
      198,231,295
FOUNTAIN, Paul 109
FOWLER, ___ 423
    Benoni/Benonia 76,220,
      238,261,310,335
    Enoch 381
    Esther 59
    James 428
    Jeremiah 238,250,261,
      379,428
    John 59,84
    Joshua 105,143
    Lucy 381
    Margaret 4
    Nehemiah 428
    Obadiah 391
    Richard 391
    Robert 381
    Sarah 381
    William 4,162,238,261,
      292
    William, Sr. 381
FOX(FAR?), Barnebus 369
    Titus 302
FR___ES, ___? 112
FRANKEY, ___ 247
FRANER, John 316
FREEMAN, Amos 132,271,337
    Robt. 40
FRENCH, Joseph 160
    Limon 159
    William 156
FRENEAU, ___ 265
    Peter 21,65,76,89,92,
      101,138,188,231,232,
      331,401,403,411,422,
      426
    Robert 45
FRINEA, Mr. 336
FROST, Jesse 325,356
FULCHER, Francis 62,97,169
FULLER, Benjamin 325,358
    James/Jas. 285,295,363,
      373,379
    Jeremiah 244

FULLER, cont'd:
  Mary 367
  Mordechai/Mordica 19,
    60,220
  Stephen 26,42,124,163,
    320,419
  Trion 311,355,372
FULLERTON, Robert 285,422
FULTON, Gasham/Gashem/
  Gashim/Gershim 18,30,
    100,316
FUNDERBURK, T. Wall 412
FURCE(FURSE), James 247,
  261
FURGUSON, James 340

GABIE(GABBY), Robert 52,82
GABRIEL, John 227,391
GADSEN(GADSON,GARSDEN),
  ___ 141,283
  Thomas 35,41,138,313,
    338,419
GAGE, John 175
GAILLARD, Cornelia 380
  Theodore 380
GAINES, Henry 379
GAIST, Moses 47
GALLEGLY(GALLIGLY), Joseph
  40,45,147
  Sarah 40
GALLERT(GALLIART), John M.
  136
GALLEYTON, Jacob 51
GALLOWAY, Thos. 408
GAMBLIN, William 314
GAMBREL(CAMBRELL,GAMBRIL,
GAMBRILL,GAMBRIEL),
  Henry 351,392,427
  James 394,395
  John 3,4,189,392,394
  John, Jr. 395
  John, Sr. 395
  William 166,263,314
GAMLETION, William 314
GANDY, Sarah 411
GANT(GANTT), Giles 162
  Thomas 123
  William 89
GARDNER, Jacob 89
  L. (S.?) 90
  S. M. 92,94,120
  Samuel/Saml. 80,104,
    107,112,131,212,356
  Samuel M. 119,120
GARISON, George 269
GARLAND, ___ 322
  Elisha 376
  Jesse 376,411
GARLANT, Elisha 267
GARNBULL, ___ 427
GARNER, Elizabeth 329,330
  Enoch 16,76,88,137,388
  Harper 78,191,388
  Henry 239,244,245,261,
    264,265,285,340,346,
    349,413
  James 45,59,161,221,
    222,251,279,329,330
  Jane 329
  John 285,329,358,362,
    367,403
  Lewis 78
  Thomas 35,43,54,75,78,
    137,329,330,352,356,
    365,368,387,388,401
  William/Wm. 329,338,
    388
  Winney 388
GARNIER,STURDY(STERDY) 17,
  32,35,124,137,363,372
GAROSON, James 192
GARRARD, James 387
GARRET(GARRETT), Benjamin
  86,87,360

GARRETT, cont'd:
  Dickerson/Dickeson 176,
    262
  Lidia 177
GARRISON(GARISON,GARITSON),
  Amos 425
  James 162
  Zebulon 197
GARROD, Ansel 159
GARVIN, Danl. 45
  David 405,408,419,420
  James 341,409,419
  John 79,113,155,171
  Martha 358
  Thomas 54,78,370,414,
    419,422
  Thomas, Jr. 358
  Thomas, Sr. 358,422
GARVIS, James 34,382
GARY(?), Timothy 133
GASAWAY(GASSAWAY), Benja-
  min 327,381
  Henry 75,154,326,327,
    381,387,388,389
  James 94,168
  Rachel 388,389
  Thomas 326,327,381
GASTON, Wm. 426
GATES, Anna 382
  Charles 29,41,70,72,
    103,124,202,320,343,
    382
  James 33,86,343
GAW, Thomas 80
GEER, Solomon 5,309,371,
  396,425,426
GELBLANKS, John 240
GENAWAY(GENEWAY), Joseph
  67,74
GENT, John 116,271
GENTRY, David 92
  John 334,374,400,405,
    423
  Major 92
  Ruth 400
  Tyra 382
GEONTOSE(?), Jesse 103
GEORGE, ___ 423
  Benjamin 239
  Britain/Britton 288,
    306,379
  J. 298
  John 99,110,115,205,
    239,262,309,310,311,
    316,318,323,324,337,
    340,345,346,347,359,
    360,365,366,367,369,
    374,392,407,408,413,
    414,416,417,422,424,
    425,426,427,429
  Jonathan 403
  Joseph 280
  Richard 115,239,262
  Robert 222
  Thomas 226
GERLD, James 159
GERVAIS(CERVICE), John Lew-
  is 40,49,58,151,176,
    312
GERVISON, Zebulon 152
GIBBIE, Robert 316
GIBBS, Jonathan 121,156,
  220,235,322,325,348,
  360,384,391,416
  Mary 325
  Shadrack 269
GIBSON, Ann 317,323
  Elizabeth 384,390
  George 343
  Humphrey 26,89,141
  Humphrey, Jr. 89
  Jacob 89
  James 171,318,365,393,
    405

GIBSON, cont'd:
  John 126,173,202,232,
    253,254,262,265,291,
    357,359,365,369,377,
    383,384,390,396,424
  Joseph 352
  Julius 4
  Mary 158,173,361
  Richard 421
  Samuel 145,325,333,
    361,417
  Thomas 138
  Thos. N. 292,424
  W. C. 383
  "Widow" 214,378
  William 306,376,411
GIGNARD (sic), Benjamin
  266
GILBERT, ___ 409
  Benjamin 350
GILCHRIST(GILLECRIST),
  Adam 65,98,323,329
GILDER(GILDED), Isaac 6,
  50
GILHAM(GILLHAM), Jacob
  5,9,46,101,170,248,
    311
  Jane 213,277,278,286
  John 273
  Sarah 213
  Thomas/Thos. 126,136,
    172,235
  William 213,223,251,
    254,263,273,277,278,
    285,286,301,303,312
GILL, Peter 135
GILLIAM, John 234
  Robert 79
GILLELAND(GILLILAND,GILL-
IAN,GILLIANG,GILLEYLEN,
GILLEYLIN), Frances 416,
  417
  Jacob 78,108,136,137,
    174
  James (also Gilliling)
    90,225,309,323,357,
    367,416,417
  John 41,54,90,396,417
  Robert 3,118
GILLISON, ___ 185
  Ann 32
  Archibald/Archible
    32,332
  Isc./Isaac 265
  Israel 263
  Jacob 116
  James 10,19,20,21,32,
    46,47,54,59,67,69,89,
    92,93,117,121,163,184,
    203,238,240,289,290,
    314,337,338,340,344,
    350,352,360,378,383,
    396,403,409,411,412,
    421
  Jane 10,19
  Jean 32
  John 32
  Jonathan 289
  Joseph 303
  Samuel 54,92
  William 216
GILLISPY(GILLISPIE,GALAS-
PIE,GALLESPIE,GILASPIE,
GILLASPIE,GOLASPY,GILLIS-
PEY,GILLASPEY), ___ 186,
  300,362
  Agnes 46
  Ann 46,101
  D. 308
  David 191
  Jacob 116,163,322,360
  James 74,93,104,108,
    115,128,139,152,153,
    192,208,209,214,215,

GILLESPIE (and variations cont'd:)...
  James (cont'd.) 288, 299,301,306,311,360, 365,398
  John 18,86,108,153,192, 214,271,288,300,321, 330,352,398
  Mary 74
  Nancy 108
  Samuel 208,209
  Susander (Golaspy) 249
  Thomas 152,153,211,288
  William 33,39,46,71, 100,101,170,181,249, 262,304,316,326,258, 385,392,393
  William, Jr. 73,153, 181,249
  William, Sr. 18,73,152, 153,181,249
GILMER, Archd. 405
GILMORE, Robert 320
GIPSON, James 157
  John 158,162
GIST, Jos. C. 175
GIVEN, James 199
GLASBY, James 416
GLASCOW, John 181,182
GLASS, John 248
GLEN(GLENN), ___ 32,298, 353
  Alexander 119,141,153, 354,373,424
  Bern./Bernd. 32,306, 336
  James 414
  Jean 10
  Jesse 380,414,424
  John 48,74,97,104,119, 158,220,253,259
  John Lewis 414
  Joseph, Jr. 419
  Mary 357,424
  Robert 27,57,94,96,176, 237,260,325,337,354, 356,357
  Samuel 155
  Shelby 392
  Spilsby 189,286
  Thomas 170
  William 213
GLOVER, Benj. 96
  Fredrick 64,96,186,251, 412,421
  George 380
  John 59
  Wiley 36,182
  William Y. 412
GOACHER, William 372
GODFREY, John 35
GODSON, Thomas 131
GOGGINS(GOGINS,GOGGINGS), William 42,178,359
GOLDEN(GOLDIN), Elizabeth 155
  Foster 349
  Isaac 418
  Richard 17,116,155
  Wm. 155
GOLDIN(GOLDING), ___ 225
  Anthony 28,29,146,168
  Michael 206
  Richard 62
  William 288
GOOD___TT, James 111
GOODE, Edward 3
  John 343
  Wm. 28
GOODLETT, D. 250,342
  David 173
  James 33,93
GOODRICH, Hezekiah 375,417

GOODWIN, ___ 225
  Charles 213
  Crafford 176,182,309, 398
  George 173,176,309,398
  Henry 333
  Jesse 13,301,306
  Jep 301
  John 173,182,280
  Josiah 44
  Mary 173,176
  Mecager 17
  Robert 17,32,306
GOODWINE, Uriah 73
GOODWYN, John 1
GORDAN(GORDON), James 112
  Robert C. 386
  Robert Campbell 96
  William 425
GORMAN, David 237
  Judith 103
  Thomas 23,103,121,144, 231,262,355,418,419
  William 342,358,370, 401,404
GOSS(also GAWZEY), Benjamin 289
  Thomas 66,90,106,160, 402
GOTCHER(GOCHER,GOLCHER, GOUCHER), Henry 28,31,32, 41,154,293
  Henry, Jr. 32
  Joshua 198,226,310
  Thomas 66
  William 319
COUDY, ___ 119
GOUGE, Joseph 331,333,359
GOWAN, Benjamin 231
GOWEN, Allen 7
  H. M. 174
  John 7,35,85,123,173, 198
GRACE, George 387
  Jael E. 427
GRADAL, Jno. 418
GRAHAM, Arthur 359
  David 273
  Edward 348
  James 298
  Levi 354
  Nancy 321,322
  Nimrod 348
  Peter 321,322,415
  Robert 348
GRANT, Thomas 35,42,178, 351
  William/Wm. 82,83,84, 217,315,355
GRASON, Jno./John 235,289
GRAVET, William 390
GRAY, D. 359
  Daniel 322,340
  Daniel J. 316
  David 316
  Elizabeth 227,346
  Hannah 331
  Huldah 229
  Isaac 355,356
  James 230,264,339,409
  Jesse/Jessey 58,127, 135,229,230,262,263
  Joseph 166
  Peter 303,331
  Richard 260,354,374, 405
  Richard D. 358
  Robert 185,227,346
  Thomas 4,51,76,119,128
  William 95,221,229,277, 314,339,362,409,414
GRAYHAM, ___ 139
  Arthur 359

GRAYHAM, cont'd:
  Jehu 420
  William 56,251
GRAYSON, John 170
GREAVES, Lewis 385
GREEN(GREENE), ___ 259,423
  Abednego/Ebednego 62, 191,234,326
  Aledness 262
  Ann ___ 242
  Annis 413
  B. 266,415
  B., Jr. 276
  Benjamin 256,278,344, 367,426
  Benjamin, Jr. 136,223
  Burrel/Burrell,Burrill
  Burwell 244,246,287, 315,319,412
  Caroline 233
  Col. 262
  Cornelius 232,265,236, 420
  Creasey 190
  David 299,357,359
  Elijah 410
  Ezekiel 372
  Garner/Gardner 62,134
  Hannah 324
  Henry 64,110,191,233, 242,262,349,356,389
  Isham 211
  James 224
  John 6,9,12,19,31,72, 90,104,127,130,133, 136,190,223,256,262, 309,326,349,356,357, 396,415
  Joseph 187,211,249, 412,413
  Lewis 9,122
  Mashack/Meshack 9,79, 136,190,313
  Neil 124
  Obediah 263
  Ralph 71
  Robert 103
  Samuel 41,103,365,396
  Sutton 53,93,103,115, 162,342
  Thomas 94,130
  William 120,121,132
GREENLEE(S), Peter 39,162, 172,176,353
GREENWOOD, Elizabeth 211
  Francis 84,192,211,213, 306,311,376,411,426
  John 366,367
GREEOR, ___ 422
GREER, Aquilla 202,360
  David 160,312,322,324, 333,336
  David 312,322,324,333, 336
  Equilar (also Green?) 88
  Hannah 360
  James 46
GREGORY, Edward 344
  John 114,192,285,314, 340,341,358
  Jonathan 104,171,345, 362
GRESHAM, ___ 119
GRIFFEN, Answell 352
  Anthony 90,101,102, 293,327,361,391,399, 410
  Britain 274,290
  Elinor 186
  Elizabeth 429
  Henry 299
  Horatio 167

GRIFFEN, cont'd:
    James 105,186,253,339,
       383,385,389
    James C. 106,281,354,
       355,358,364,375,388,
       389,390,401,406,424
    John 51,52,69,74,138,
       151,186,199,209,227,
       234,246,251,253,261,
       262,267,273,275,281,
       294,327
    Joseph 322,354
    Margaret 158
    Peter 290
    Richard 186,253
    Sarah/Sary 69,273
    Sargent/Sergant 198,
       375
    Spenser 288
    William 2,62,69,113,
       141,158,168,173,174,
       176,197,198,224,233,
       299,312
GRIFFIS, John 327
GRIFITH, Stephen 423
GRIGSBY, John B. 6,95,116
GRIMES, David 183,194,195,
       236,253,255,262,273,
       409
    James 334
    Nancy 273
    William 385,421
GRIMKIE, ___ 185
GRIMKE, John 336
GRIMKIE, John F. 178
GRIMKE, John F., Sr. 311
GRIMKIE, John Faucheraud
    (also Fishereaud) 72,
    201,397
    John T. 312,319
GRIMMET, Josiah 88
GRINDLE(GRINDEL), John
    54,98
GRINE, William Hives 231
GRISHAM, J. W. 285
    John 16,210,262,285,
       329,334,341,361,363,
       367,406,421,425
    John W. 244
    John, Jr. 274,284
    John, Sr. 16
    Joseph 5
    Martha 274,406
    Patsey 274
GRISSAM(GRISSAN,GRISSIM,
GRISSOM), Elizabeth 82
    J. W. 82
    John 52,53,66,79,81,
       82,94,169,194
    John, Jr. 168,194
    John, Sr. 168,194
    John W. 82,152
    Mary 152
    Susannah 152
GRIST, Simon 400,405,408
GRIZEL, George 140
GROMAN, William 364
GROOMS, Gilbert 133
GROSLIN, Samuel 8
GROUTER, Jesse 31,64
GROUTCHER, Jesse 64
GROWGAN, Elsa 248,249
GROWLY, John 58
GRURAND, Aquilla 85
GUARANTEE, Catherine 201
GUDYN, Urial 363
GUEREARD, ___ 286
    Benjamin 25,27,28,29,
       30,32,33,34,37,38,42,
       44,45,46,48,55,57,61,
       63,64,71,72,73,75,78,
       84,86,88,89,90,91,94,
       97,99,100,101,102,103,
       104,106,107,111,113,

GUERRARD, cont'd:
    Benjamin...114,117,119,
       120,122,125,126,127,
       128,129,133,134,136,
       141,142,144,145,149,
       151,152,154,155,157,
       158,161,162,164,165,
       167,168,170,171,172,
       176,181,182,187,189,
       194,195,198,199,200,
       201,202,206,222,223,
       225,227,228,232,237,
       238,253,254,267,268,
       270,278,280,282,285,
       287,289,291,292,295,
       303,304,305,306,308,
       312,324,351,353,354,
       355,363,365,380,385,
       389,390,391,393,394,
       406,410,415,416,417,
       421,427
    Governor 249,310,344,
       403
GUESS, Henry 262
    William 106
GUEST, Ann 350
    Benjamin 69,106
    David 69,289,350,386,
       407
    Fanney 350
    Frances 350,407
    Morgan 144
    Moses 69,144,253
    Saml. 144
    Simon 313,314
    Squire 410
    William 7,69,130,193,
       225,261,302,319,350,
       386
GUFFIN(GRIFFEN?), John 225
GUFFIN, William 302
GUILDER, Isaac 44
GUIGNARD, J. C. 243
    J. G. 380
    Jas. 262
    James L. (Guignand)256
    James Sanders 145,242,
       324
GUNN, Wm. 128,131
GUNTER(GUNTOR), Ann 212
    William 212
GURLEY, John 62
GURRIN, Ephraim 214
GUTHRIE(GUTRY,GUTHRY,GUT-
TERY), ___ 161,188
    Francis 26,79,81,94,
       223,277,415,416
    Henry 99
    Sarah 26
GUY, James 353
GUYTON, Aaron 134,149,172,
       352,394
GWIN, John 17

H_LL, William 233
HACKET(T), James 199,200,
       315
    Robert 221,272,276
HACKLEMAN, ___ 119
    Conrad 336
    George 336
HAGIS(HARGIS?), Abraham 214
HAGOOD, James 171,280,281
    George 300,345,398
HAIL, ___ 269
HAILE, J. 315
    John 323,401
    Saml. 317
HAIRE(HARE), Betty 195
    Caleb 245
    Elizabeth 195,196
    Matthew 158,195,196
HAIRSTON, John 38
HALBERT, Arthur 75,168

HALBERT, cont'd:
    Joel 11,21,71,352
    John 71,242,361
    W. W. 102
    William 4,12,14,25,27,
       29,30,31,32,33,34,35,
       36,42,43,44,46,48,51,
       56,58,59,63,65,66,71,
       73,75,76,84,88,100,101,
       102,136,230,251,291,
       356,402
HALCHELL, William 137
HALL, Mrs. 333
    Benj. 222
    Dorcys 298
    Fenton 26,165,278,341,
       380
    James 420
    Jamima(h) 168,356
    Jeremiah 96,181
    Jesse 285,305
    John 6,26,67,170,176,
       198,240,258,278,289,
       318,328,370
    John, Sr. 25,51
    Joseph 134,165,227,
       286,289,330,354
    Lent 15,160,258,269
    Leonard D. 213
    Meshack 373
    Nathan 64,115
    Nathaniel 15,116,298
    Nathl., Sr. 15
    Peter 87,103,352
    R. 115
    Robert 6,7,18,26,64,
       165,298,347,418
    Thomas 291,412
    Travis N. 382
    W. 170
    W. N. 88
    William 4,12,20,21,25,
       33,66,80,87,88,90,94,
       95,100,103,110,111,
       116,119,121,124,127,
       129,132,133,135,137,
       138,141,144,148,157,
       161,162,163,168,172,
       173,176,177,179,181,
       189,190,191,200,209,
       210,226,230,233,235,
       238,239,244,251,257,
       260,268,270,274,275,
       278,281,288,289,291,
       293,294,299,305,341,
       347,352,356,363,372,
       388,412
    Winston 258,269,418
    Zachariah 305
HALLUM(S), ___ 234
    Ann(e) 58,203,296
    Basil/Bazzel 125,239,
       245,292,293,365
    Elizabeth 9
    James 257,326,345,353,
       378,379,406
    John 22,23,32,33,35,
       43,50,57,58,83,84,85,
       125,138,144,202,203,
       206,207,208,211,212,
       216,230,239,262,264,
       265,282,293,296,305,
       316,338,339,353,364,
       398,419
    Martha 186
    Mary 74,296
    Mary (Ann) 353
    Nancy 326,378,379
    Paul 297
    Susanah 292,293
    Tho. 2,9,10,50,74,144,
       231,340
    William 5,6,17,33,50,
       62,74,243,257,262,...

HALLUMS, cont'd:
　　William cont'd: 285,
　　　293,316,345,378
HAM, Joshua 144,297,298
HAMBELTON(HAMILTON), John
　　170,381
HAMBRAY, Selah 244
　　William 244
HAMBY, Meshack 375
　　Selle 338
　　William 306,338,383
HAMILTON, ____ 208,256
　　A. C. 366
　　Alexander 127,169,254,
　　　255,262
　　Andrew 2,7,11,33,41,
　　　95,104,113,114,121,
　　　127,135,145,163,191,
　　　262,274,357,420
　　Archibald 45,184
　　Catherine 4
　　Cecilia 397,408
　　Charles 207
　　David 26,153,339,368,
　　　369,377,398,399,401,
　　　424
　　Horatio 18
　　James 4,32,42,45,48,
　　　50,55,59,61,80,97,127,
　　　136,140,145,169,176,
　　　184,262,275,299,304,
　　　321,329,367,369,397,
　　　399,401,403,412
　　James, Jr. 9
　　Jean 254,255
　　John 5,9,32,44,46,61,
　　　79,100,127,143,169,
　　　176,208,287,299,321,
　　　322,339,356,377,398,
　　　404,418,421
　　John, Jr. 385
　　John T. 162
　　Leon 87
　　Little James 260
　　Lock 359
　　Luke 280,365
　　M. 131
　　Margeret 377
　　Martha 385
　　Mary 176
　　Mathew 44
　　Nancy 343
　　Ninginbel(sic) 5
　　Ninian B. 18
　　Ninian Bell 5,18,44,
　　　65
　　Paul 306,310,313,344,
　　　410
　　Robert Sharp 122,222
　　Susannah 401
　　Thomas 32,146,160,161,
　　　235,240,259,262,264,
　　　312,338
　　W. C. 211,304,347
　　William 17,26,32,50,
　　　55,61,96,107,126,131,
　　　137,144,198,208,246,
　　　254,256,260,304,308,
　　　313,319,324,336,338,
　　　347,349,355,362,372,
　　　375,376,386,394,397,
　　　402,406,408,413,420,
　　　422,426
HAMM, Joshua 211
　　Nehemiah 371
HAMMACK, Daniel 171
HAMMANGER, James 145
HAMMATT, Robert 78
HAMMET, Robert 239,312
　　Thomas 240
HAMMICK, Daniel 335
HAMMON, David 256
　　John 390

HAMMOND(HAMMONDS), Dudley
　　274,392,399,417,423
　　Elijah 271,352
　　Job/Jobe 417,423
　　John 392
　　M. 301,312,321,327,328,
　　　330,332,333,334,337,
　　　338,339,346,351,354,
　　　355,357,358,361,362,
　　　369,370,371,372,376,
　　　377,379,380,382,383,
　　　384,385,386,387,389,
　　　390,391,394,396,397,
　　　400,401,402,406,408,
　　　409,410,411,413,414,
　　　415,416,418,421,422,
　　　426,427,428,429
　　Michael 284,285,294,
　　　295,303,304,312,344,
　　　357,394,424
　　N. 291,374
　　Noah 392
　　Robert 276
　　S. J. 399,417
　　William 13,271
HAMON, Robert 253,262
HAMPTON, Wade 107,108
HANBY, Mashack 330
　　Wm. 3
HANCOCK, Gilbert 223
　　Phillip 399
HAND, Joseph 7
HANDCOCK, David 341
HANDERSON, Nathaniel 358
HANDLEY, Joseph 88
　　Thomas 16
HANDLY, Peter 56
HANEY(HANIE,HAYNIE,HANY),
　　____ 396
　　Benjamin 165
　　Elizabeth 117
　　John 117,163
　　Richard 165,267
　　Spencer 350,352
　　Stephen 163
　　Thomas 353,355
　　William 328,344
HANKINS, Benjamin 213
　　John 232,233
　　Samuel 371
HANNA, Wm. 126
HANKS, Luke 59
　　Thos. 163,332
　　"Widow" 59
HANNAH, James 139,258,406
　　Margaret 258
HANNEY, James 366
HANNON, William 75
HARBIN, Ellis 218
　　Jesse 185,226,368
　　Nancy 349
　　Nathaniel 185,226,368
　　Samuel 185,226,240,262,
　　　302,368
　　Thomas 146,259,359,383
　　Thomas, Jr. 383
HARDAG(E), William 395,424
HARDEN, Comfort 51
　　Gabriel 51
　　Joseph 61
HARDIN, Aaron 130,396
　　Ann 220
　　Gabriel 54,281
　　Griffen 246
　　John 84,85,220,225,246
　　Martin 399
　　Phebe 365
HARE, Edward 266
　　Mathew 227
HARGES(HARGESS), Abraham
　　284
　　Thomas 239,284,321,341
HARGIS(HARGISS), Abraham
　　173,214,328

HARGIS, cont'd:
　　Thomas 209,225,313,
　　　314,325,329,334,351,
　　　359,363,364,367,376,
　　　382,406
HARGR(E)AVES, Christopher
　　191,305,372,428
HARKIN, ____ 260
HARKINS, ____ ____ 170
　　Hugh 119,235
　　Joseph 235
　　Ketron 235
　　Samuel 235
HARKNESS, James 181
　　John 120,139,150,181,
　　　339,341
　　Margaret 182
　　Robert 14,98,99,120,
　　　132,134,181,182,210,
　　　239,250,269,359
　　Robert, Jr. 14,404
　　Robert, Sr. 404
　　William 134
HARLEY, ____ 244
HARLIN(HARLEN,HARLAND,HAR-
　　LAN,HARLING), Ellis 79,
　　　222,245,246,329,334,
　　　356,376,421,423
　　(also see Ellis Warling on
　　　423)
HARLING, Allis 174
HARLSTON(HARLESTON), Isaac
　　155
　　William 155
HARMON, Christopher 160
HARNAGE, Isaac 145,146,159
HARPER, ____ 404
　　Banister 9,20,186
　　Edward 388
　　Elizabeth 185
　　Hance 184
　　John 20,35,177,288,
　　　376,388
　　John, Jr. 376
　　Rith 240
　　Robert 392,393
　　Robert Goodloe 70
　　Samuel 117,184,185,
　　　240,262,306,354
　　William 9,20,30,33,75,
　　　91,191,262,263,342,
　　　361,362,365,366,392
HARRIS, A. 404
　　Andrew/Andw. 228,255,
　　　355
　　Archer 405
　　Archibald 299
　　Auguston 268
　　Benjamin 33,51,77,124,
　　　125,231,262,278,412
　　Caleb 287
　　Cary 231
　　Charity 278
　　Chas. 236,237
　　Clabourn 271
　　David 271,311
　　Edward 299
　　Ephraim 108
　　Handy 106,228
　　Henry 350
　　J. 239
　　John 19,22,23,34,44,
　　　63,73,94,98,103,106,
　　　111,121,129,139,140,
　　　141,144,165,167,173,
　　　174,184,196,208,212,
　　　214,220,223,228,232,
　　　234,237,244,249,250,
　　　255,257,258,262,265,
　　　271,276,277,287,291,
　　　298,299,315,344,350,
　　　355,364,394,415,418,
　　　419,424,428

HARRIS, cont'd:
  Karenhappoch/Karenha-
  puck 32,231
  Mary 32,106,140,165,
  167,228,234
  Moses 253,262,377
  Reavriend 228
  Richard 350,351,352
  Sharpin 132
  Stephen 32,219,236,
  237,274
  Thomas 350,355,415
  Thomas, Sr. 34
  Turner 202
  W. V. 34
  William 114,192
  Zephaniah/Zephiniah
  173,224
HARRISON,   237
  Barzillai/Barzellai
  6,14,168
  Benjamin/Benj. 11,203,
  257,258,262,345
  Caty 257,266
  Elizabeth 162
  George 143,162
  Isham 198
  Jno./John 65,66,71,
  203,356
  John Hampton 410
  Nancy 287
  Richard 108
  Robert/Robt. 162,168,
  280,282,284,287
  Thomas 129,180,203,
  247,251,258,262,266,
  282,299,345,406
  Thomas, Sr. 266,280,345
  W. P. 284
  William 203,308,345
  William P. 284
  William T. 252
  Zephaniah 78,185
HARRY, Moses 290
HART, Jas. 80,82,104,155,
  164,194
  Jno. 262
  West 104
  William 259,262
HARTHORN(HAWTHORN), Ann
  96
HARTHORN(HATHORN), James
  96
HARTSELL, James 99
HARTSFIELD, Godfry 135
HARVEY(HARRY?), Archer 342
  T. 52
HARVICK(HARWICK), Jacob
  172,262
  Nicholas 172,262
HARWOOD, Turner 282,339,
  393
HASES(HASE), Edward 180,
  266
HASHEL, Robert 248
HASLEY, Talton 302
HATCHETT, William 43
HATHORN, John 173
HAWKINS, Benjamin 331
  Harmon 217
  Samuel/Saml. 357,383,
  399,405
HAWKS, Fras. 262
  John 266,288
  William 95,273
HAYAES, Moses 66
HAYINGS, Moses 66
HAYNES, Stephen 112
HAYNEY, Richard 322
  Sidney 322
HAYNIE, Charles 37,117,274
  Elizabeth 274
  John 39,117,163,271,274

HAYNIE, cont'd:
  Stephen 163
  William/Wm. 40,47,49,
  51
HAYES(HAYS,HAY), Edward
  224.270,381
  George 44,83,91,207,
  293,385
  Henry 83,131,144,297,
  298
  Henry, Jr. 201,202
  Henry, Sr. 202
  James 417
  John 20,80,83,84,91,
  144,156,175,201,202,
  385
  Margret 202
  Mary 201
  Patrick 403
  Peter 156
  Sarah 385
  Thomas 51,59,91,156,
  157,201,202,360
  William 163,276,396
HAYWARD, John 68
HEAD, George 205,320
  James 230,320
  John 216,230,319,320,
  377
  Peter 216
  Richard 205,211
HEANY, Thomas 321
HEAREL, Charles 301,302
HEARIN, Ephraim 398
HEART, John 245
HEATEN, John 301
HEATER, John 391
HEATH, Phillip 331
  William 139
HEATON, James 428
  Joseph 417
  Smith 428
HEMBREE, David 260
  James 42,48,161,244,
  380,388,428
  John 428
  William 262,284
  Zachariah 423
HEMBRIE, James 134
  Wm. 352
HEMBRY, David 301
HEMPHILL, Jonathan/Johna-
  than 275,296,305,403
  Robert 425
HENDERSON,   74,237,
  271,352
  Daniel 380,398
  David 208,214,398
  Isbal 398
  James 97,116,183,324,
  333,346
  Jane 152
  John 39,40,94,132,183,
  194,208,265
  Joseph 23
  Margaret 152
  Martha 151,152,208,419,
  425
  Matthew 183
  Nathaniel 106,151,152,
  380,404
  Robert 120,298
  Robert, Jr. 97
  Samuel 23,33,207,380
  Samuel, Jr. 333
  Thomas 73,94,380,387,
  420
  William 19,40,48,106,
  123,151,152,362,364,
  370,419
HENDREX, James 17,18
HENDRICK(HENDRICKS), David
  274,336,378

HENDRICKS, cont'd:
  John 32,339
  Moses 116,274,335,336,
  378
  Moses, Sr. 335
  R. 231
HENDRICKSON, Nathaniel 401
HENDRIX, Hannah 102
  James 74,89,90,92,101,
  102,209,331
  John 339,383
  Moses 187,188,283,324,
  335
  William 339
HENERY, Jean 384
HENEY, Richard 322
HENMAR, James 245
HENLY, Peter 30,43
HENNINGTON, Elizabeth 89,
  419
  John 89,419
HENRY, John 16,36,37,42,
  46,72,129,175,365
  Mary 156
  Richard 322
  Samuel 134,155,156,297
  Thomas 156
  William 297,387
HENSON,   372
  John 77
  Samuel 154,198
  William 198
HERD, Charles 300
HERNDON, Benjamin 306
HERONS, John 229
HERING(HERRIN,HERRING),
  David 358
  Elijah 5,154,215,216,
  235,237,283,285,427
  Elisha 216,311,315,
  363,425,426,427
  Ephraim 101,114,192,
  398,427
  Isaac 114,215,228,235,
  262,285,429
  Jacob 114,153
  Rhoda 407
  Stephen 218,317,407,
  429
  William 39,133,159,
  363,367,426,427,429
HERSTON(HAIRSTON), William
  21
HESTER, Fanny 357,371
  Gideon/Giddeon 306,362,
  368
  Polly 362,368
HEURY, John 301
HEWLET(HEWLETT), Martin
  125,149,168,287,331
HICKMAN, Benjamin 175,184,
  249,262,323,396
  William 323
HICKS, James 329
  Jonathan 36,71,182,188
  Jonathan, Jr. 165
  Jonathan, Sr. 273,274
HIGH, David 262
HIGHSAW, Henry 154
  James 5
HIGHSMITH, John 300
HIGHTOWER, Joseph 68,70
  Sterling 171,327
HILL, Aaron 144,373
  Amos 405
  Asa 292
  George 274
  Henry 110,197,220,284
  Isaac 259,262,292,296,
  353,405
  Jacob 375
  Jonas/Jones 110,160,
  197,208,217,276,280,
  296

HILL, cont'd:
    Joseph 45,85,163,192,
        323
    Joshua 13
    Michael 409
    Ward 13
    "Widow" 174
HILLEN(HILLIN,HILLION,HIL-
    LIAN), Jesse 5,215,216,
        247,254,262,400
    John 122,124,228
    Joseph 215
    Mary 216
HILLHOUSE, ____ 427
    James/Jas. 36,44,87,
        267,296,413,427
    John 134,157,163,357
    John, Sr. 279
    Samuel 305
    William 39,56,227,250,
        332,427
HILLIGAN, Wm. 285
HILLISY, James 413
HILTON, John 371
HIMLEY, John James 50,51
HINESLY(HINSLEY,HINDSLEY),
    Thomas 151,218
HININ, Stephen 113
HINSON, John 72,77
    Samuel 226
    William 161
HINTON, Grief 427
    Job 73
HIRT, William 286
HIX, James 329
    John 329
    Jonathan 191
    Nancy 329
    Prudence 179
    Robert 191,272,281
    Thomas 326
HOBBS, James 86
    William 10,78,198,280,
        421
HOBSON, ____ 178
    James 27,146,152,358
    James, Sr. 5
    Nicholas 70
    Thomas 43,98,146,320,
        358
HODGE(HODGES), Abel/Ebel
    278,288
    James 138,305
    John 138,182
    William 36,125
HOGGE(HOG,HOGE,HOGG),
    George 112,287,296,
        412,425
    Giddeon/Gideon 154,
        195,337
    Henry 298
    John 112,226,412
    Mary 296
    Thomas 136
    William 337
HOGWOOD, George 300
HOLBERT, Enos 357
    Joel 388
    John 365,388,417
    William 1,357,388
HOLCOM(HOLCOMB,HOLCOMBE),
    Joel 50,105
    John 102,121,156,235,
        261,318,325,360,384,
        390,409
    Phillip 1,2,156
    Rachel 156
    Tabitha 325
    Zachariah 2,156,157,
        175,287,290,355,356
HOLDEN, ____ 412
    Joshua 173,328,354
    Margaret 236
    Nemar (Holson?) 223

HOLDEN, cont'd:
    Richard 47,89,205,354
    Thomas 47,115,170,226,
        236,262,319,320
HOLDING, Joshua 329
HOLLAN, Dominic 19
    John 19,217
    Wilson 55
HOLLAND, Andrew 212
    Benjamin 384
    Danl. 225
    Domico 217
    Francis 19
    Jacob 129,153,210,212,
        247,253,262,263,289,
        298,319,345,350,360,
        384,386,407,409,410,
        422
    Jacob, Jr. 153
    James 212,253
    John 7,54,297
    Mary 102,319,396
    Moses 48,99,101,362,
        369,396,417
    Nancy 297
    Thomas 153,203,212,251,
        308,320,358
    Wm. 237
HOLLIGAN(HOLLAGAN), Sarah
    334
    James 334
HOLLEY, Richard 201
HOLLIMAN(HOLLYMAN), Edmund
    25
HOLLINGSWORTH, Elias 54,78,
    82,91,92,154,262
    Jean 422
    Jeremiah 270
    Joseph 189
    Thomas 92
HOLLOWAY(HOLOWAY,HOLAWAY)
    365
    Caleb 177
    Larkin 395
    Stephen 258,263,395
HOLLUM, William 144
HOLLY, Sion 151
HOLMAN, Jas. 229
HOLMES(HOLMS), James 6,7,
    65
    James, Sr. 78
    J. B. 11
    John 31
    John Bee 11,27
HOMAN, Samuel 344
    Richard 174,242,243
    Richard/Richd. H. 3,
        174,175
    Richard Hatfield 175
HOMES, Jacob 345
    Sary 345
HONEY(HONA,HONEA,HONIE),
    Abel 133,224
    Abner 124,137,214,225,
        257,262,389
    Abner, Sr. 225
    Betty 27,31
    Elizabeth (Betty) 27,
        349,369
    George 93
    Robert 224,335
    Sarah (Hone) 124
    Thomas (Hone) 124,138,
        176,191,257,304,367,
        369
    Tobias 349,356
    William 27,31,32,76,88,
        124,133,138,176,225,
        257,262,304,309,349,
        356,367,382,389
    William, Sr. 257,357
    Willie (Hone) 349
HOOD, Andrew 146,196
    James 227

HOOD, cont'd:
    John 123,271,299
    Morgan 123,135,171,
        279,289,338
    Richard 246,345
    Thomas 118,152,180,
        269,270,271,309
    Violet 271
HOOKER, Ann 337
HOOPER, Edward 331
    Enoch 35,38,39
    John 190,331
    Nathew/Matthew 317,
        330,331,406
    Matthew B. 190,330,
        331
    O. C., Jr. 103
    Obadiah 331
    Richard 66,144,248,
        330,331,372
HOPE, ____ 164
    John 172
HOPKINS, Col. 191
    D. 25,183
    David 4,7,16,29,38,
        42,59,65,156,171,189,
        191,205,217,274,280,
        300,380
    Ferdinand 268,296,346,
        361,378
    Mary 201
    Samuel 233
    Wm. 201,229
HOPPER, Moses 19,104,309,
    406
    Rolly 406
HOPSON, Anne 320
    Thomas 274,320
HORNADAY(HORNEDAY,HORNIDY)
    John 11,12,50
HORNE, Jas. 316
HORRY, Mary Margaret 227
    Peter 50,51,227
HORT, William 2,31,51,65,
    98,122,127,166,167,
    173,178,189,190,192,
    193,199,251,259,305,
    317,327
HORTON(HORTEN), Isaac 79,
    129,130,136,356,357
HOUGHTON, Tho. 60
HOUSE, Nimrod 252
HOUSTON, ____ 166
    Ann 366
    George 61,395
    Grizzel 191
    Henry 113,128,161,325,
        383,391,407
    James/Jas. 16,37,61,
        107,204,269,270,316,
        317,320,323
    John 365
    Jonah 61
    Joseph 292
    Josiah 42,139,365,366,
        426
    Keziah 407
    Margaret 366
    Samuel 16,62,134,153,
        187,191,225,307,310,
        325,337,347,349,350,
        353,356,357,369,377,
        383,384,389,393,394,
        397,404,405,407
    Thomas 42,61,145,365,
        366
HOW, William 250
HOWARD, Abraham 112,242
    Aquilla 68
    Benjamin 26,154,322,
        402,414
    Jesse 343
    John 155,418
    Lucy 154

HOWARD, cont'd:
  Martin 154
  Nathaniel 112
HOWELL, Isaac 93,108
  Jno. dela 127
  Robert 48
  Wm. 174
HUBBARD(HUBBART), Jeremiah 120,125,371
  Kerby 43
  William 293,296,318,378
HUDGENS(HUDGINS), Ambrose 138,233
  Ambrose, Sr. 110,389
  Wm. 126
HUDSON, Geo. 61
  Isaac 317,370,403
  John 187,238,318,326,327
  Judah 388
HUES, James 380
HUFF, Phillip 328
  Stephen 278,282,366
HUGAR,   429
  Daniel 167
  John 366
HUGER, General 298
  Isaac 323
  John 2,121
HUGGINS, Ambrose 262,377
  John 49,62,218,250,280,303
  John, Jr. 64
  John, Sr. 64
  Martha 57
  Mary 250,280
  Robert 26
  William 26,57,176,265,312,419,428
HUGHES(HUGHS), Andrew 320
  Charles 110,122,131,138,167,203,338,419,420
  David 174,230,282,420,423
  Henry 76
  John 176
HUGHEY(HUGHY), Edward 290,356
  James 287,291
HUKLEMAN, Conrad 112
  George 112
HULATE, Martin 43
HULL, Joseph 4
HUMPHREY(HUMPHREYS, HUM-PHRIES), Charlotte 241
  David 103,144,292,330,331,335,337,367,372,393,394
  George 67,124,191,234,236,241,262
  Isaac 224
  John 142,214,391
  John Y. 372
  Sol 335
  Solomon 335
  Solomon J. 372
  William 186,321
HUNLEY, Wm. 122
HUNNICUTT(HUNNEYCUTT,HUN-NYCUTT), Eli/Ely 47,164,178,256,262,272,310,312,350,369,377,413,427
  H. 47,148,256,262,272
  Hartwell 5,39,310,413
  Jas. 262
  John 3,6,19,33,47,84,130,140,145,146,148,153,177,197,223,297,346,349,350,377,389,397,400,401,402,407,419

HUNNICUTT, cont'd:
  John, Jr. 404
  Joseph 77,259,260
  Marady/Meridy 197
  Martha 178
  Meridith/Meridath 145,402
  Randol 149,150,310
  Randolph 168,242,310,349,389,402,413
  Robt. 177
  Rolin 148,350
  Sarah 401
  William 197,377,389,397,400,402
HUNT, Abraham 34
  Charles 173,184,214,256
  Charles, Jr. 173
  Elsi/Elsy 249
  Jesse 42,132
  John 204,219,234,241,289,317,370,424
  Moses 75,117,158,173,352,366,368,370,403,413
  Thomas 42
  Uriah 42,132
  Washington 173
  William 74,75,118,132,161,180,191,269,336
HUNTER,   370,426,427
  Alex 77,254
  Alexander 70,184
  Ann 283
  Dr. 313,314,400
  Hance 1
  Henry 306
  Jean 177
  John 40,52,57,64,72,110,113,121,147,149,166,177,223,224,225,227,228,232,243,249,250,253,261,304,309,312,322,369,384,418
  Margaret 177
  Mary 271
  Mathew 426
  Samuel, Jr. 304
  Sarah 64
  Thomas/Thos. 234,239,240,261,276,280,283,297,326,331,386,397,399,402,426
  William 120,138,154,224,227,232,234,239,240,241,249,250,255,261,262,264,271,272,276,283,297,305,312,326,336,343,344,357,376,407,424
HURTIN, Wm. 177
HUSE, Andrew 58,75,86
  Charles 44,58,122
  Henry 135
HUSTON(HUSTEN), Hennery 218
  Henry 67,68
  Kiza 218
HUTCHENS(HUTCHINGS), Michael 348
  Drury 368
HUTCHINSON, Elijah 387
HUTSON,   260,389
  John 20,156
HUTTON, Joseph 353,355
  William 178
HYDE, Joseph 198
HYNDMAN, Aug. H. 261
HYNES(HINES), Robert 196
HYRNE, Henry 70,71

INGLIS, George H. 237
INGRAM(INGRAN), Benjamin

INGRAM, Benjamin cont'd:
  36,85,92,141,255,256
  James 55,131,237,255,256,262
  Shadrack 216,310,417,418
INLOW, John 355
  Lucy 355
IOOR, Geo. 183
IRBY, Charles 93
  Henrietta 79
  Isham 93,151
  Lot 408
  William/Wm. 74,79
IRONS, Peter 229
IRWIN(ERWIN,Irvin,Irwine)
  Alexander 7,64
  John 62,64,188,189
  John, Jr. 62
  Joseph 45,55,166,232
  Milla 45
  Susannah 64
ISAAC, Eligah/Elijah 289
ISBEL(ISBELL), Godfrey 278,285,299
  Godpherry (Godfrey?) 238
  Hannah 285,299
  Pendleton 203,259,345
IVEY(IVIE), Jehu 101
  John 315
  Lott. 101,315,319
  Lott I. 315

JACK, James 15,94
  Sam'l. 68
  William H. 68
JACKS, John 8
JACKSON, Ann 72
  Anna 72
  Benjamin 173,197
  Ephraim 5
  Isabella 6,27
  John 39,47,71,72,126,140,224,227,330,332,402
  Nathaniel 3
  Ralph 4
  Samuel 5,18,63,160,221,241,330
  Sarah 258
  William 6,26,27,49,221,222,258,262,278,336
JAMES, Aaron/Aron 107,108,174,236,262,266,361,405
  David 316
  Griffith 153
  Isaac 210,246,264,271,276
  John 111,198,378
  Mary Ann 41
  Moses 292
  Stephen 246
  Wm. 41,262
JAMESON(JAMISON), James 172
  Joseph 172
  Margaret 198
  Sarah 392
  William 35,80,85,86,97,105,123,143,171,184,198,276,352,364,366,370,392,393,398
JANEWAY, Isaac 300
JANOTT, Ansel 336
JANUARY, Isaac 296,300,311,347,348
JARRET(JARROT), Ancil/Ansel 45,52,428
  James 159
  Deverus/Deverue 393
JARRITT, D. 393

JARVIS, James 330
JAY, Abigaile 20
    Aeson/Eason 20,36,87,
    296
JEFFERIES, John 343
JEFFRES, Thomas 146
JENDRIX(Hendrix?), James
    194
JENKINS(JINKENS), Daniel
    201
    Francis 210,291,323,
    383,399,424
    James 253
    John 179,241,262
    Joseph 1,18,51,54,78,
    143,192,339,349,385
    Pronus 323
    Simon 306
    Susanna 179
    Thomas 210,219,229,
    268
    William 210
JENNINGS, Isaac 237
JENSON, Reubin 262
JEPSON, George 343
JERVAIS, John L. 84
    John Lewis 51
JERVIS, J. 219
JETT, Mr. 345
    James 69,97,109,130,
    141,157,160,169,171,
    179,181,183,185,187,
    189,190,206,207,218,
    226,252,266,268,272,
    283,289,297,300,323,
    324,325,337,338,340,
    344,346,353,354,355,
    356,362,374,383,387,
    394,395,409,415,419,
    421,424
JEUETT, Ansel 325
JEULTON, Norris 81
JEWELL(JEWELE), ___ 186
    Elizabeth 208
    James 143
    William 54,79,122,208,
    420
JIMESON, W. 236
JOHN(JOHNS), ___ 323
    Arthur 317
    Ezekiel 64
    James 259
    Jacob 246,249,268
JOHNSON, ___ 339,398
    Benjamin 422
    Edmond 343
    Edward 180,343
    Elizabeth 11
    Fred 419
    Fredrick 414
    Hezekiah (also John-
    ston) 203
    James 72,305,428
    Jeptha 155
    John 11,22,62,63,137,
    185,230,295
    Jonathan 246,262
    Joseph 11,209
    Josiah 155,185
    Michael 39
    Noblet/Noblett 22,79,
    208
    Robert 422
    Rebin/Reuben 10,36,
    242
    Sarah 79
    Thomas 26
    William 5,35,36
    William, Jr. 36
JOHNSTON, ___ 104
    Edward 118,269
    Fredrick 5,154,358
    Hezekiah 203,277,367
    James 379

JOHNSTON, cont'd:
    January/Ganeway 420
    Jepthae 295
    John 9,50,100,258
    Joseph 240
    Josiah 295,328
    Noblet (also Johnson)
    79
    Rhuben/Reuben/Ruben
    (also Jonston) 30,33,
    176
    Sarah (also Johnson)
    79
    Thomas 247,370,371
    William 390
JOIE, Lott 319
JOLLEY(JOLLY), ___ 302
    Henry 396,404
    James 129,178,209
    Jesse 178,350
    John 220
    Joseph 84,115,172,176,
    193,249,255,263,310,
    364,396,420,426
    Maxey 346
    William 151,172,307,
    413
    Wilson 151,193
JONES, Adam Crain/Crane
    54,87,164,355
    Adam Crain, Jr. 20,49
    Andrew 11,41
    Ann 33,116
    Anna 292
    Betsy (Elizabeth) 1
    Cynthia 372
    Darling 337
    Elizabeth 11,164
    Francis 171
    Gray 398
    Isaac/Isaak 154,210,
    426
    Isai 20
    Henry 118
    Jacob 128,426
    James 11,12,13,29,74,
    90,101,119,128,172,243,
    244,262,268,269,272,
    281,311,411,416,428
    Jesse 386,389
    John 118,123,148,153,
    164,172,177,178,222,
    240,307,312,314,350,
    369,389,404
    Kile (also Jonas) 107
    Lewis 25,33,128,177,
    178,339,349,350,369,
    389,404,413
    Lewis, Jr. 279
    Lewis, Sr. 279
    Mary 304,305
    Moses 16,18,41,76,116,
    139,140,250,261,292
    Nancy 177,292
    Peter 19,164
    Phillip 13
    Rebecca 413
    Reece 85,302
    Samuel 54,73,127
    Sarah 395
    Thomas 1,2,4,5,86,135,
    365,395,428
    William 15,169,248,250
    Willis 279,413
JONSTON, Austin 100
    Reuben 30
    Wm. 360
JORDAN(JORDIN,JOURDAN),
    Adam 49
    David 43,84,85,161,188,
    210,285,414
    Isaac 427
    James 3,7,33,34,37,49,
    66,103,107,108,111,113,

JORDAN, cont'd:
    James cont'd: 126,141,
    151,152,163,184,200,
    276,303,310,317,323,
    385,408,423
    John 192
    Margaret 7
    Thomas 25,99,189
JULEEN, L. 214
JULIEN(JULLIN), John 273
    Peter 273
    William 272,273
JUNKINS, John 69
JUSTICE, John 311,315
JUSTIST, Mary 356

KALLISON(KALTISON), Mi-
    chael 344,421
KARR, George 159
KASEY, John 277
    Luvisy 277
KAY, Charles 310
    Robert 57,190,310,387
    Robert, Sr. 57
KAYS, Lettice 157,158
    Peter 98,99,137,157,
    158
KEATON(KEETON), William
    20,332,395,404
KEE, William 365
KEEL, Fredrick 148
KEELY, John 242
    Sebastion 319
KEES (see Keys)
    Absalom 399
    Elijah 399
    John 192,399
    Josiah 353
    Thomas 399,411
    Washington 399
KEITH(KEATH,KEETH), ___
    236
    Agnes/Agneth 254,263
    Alexander 68,254,402
    Cornelius/Cornelious
    5,149,328,336
    Cornelious, Jr. 328
    Daniel 34,220,254,323,
    399
    Daniel, Jr. 223
    Daniel, Sr. 223,412
    David 212
    Elizabeth 412
    George 286
    James 212
    John 48,149,209,328,
    336
    Matthew 311
    Sarah 402
    William 149
KELISON, Mr. 345
KELLISON, Robert 218
KELL, James 137,193,284,
    302,335,341
    Robert 302,411
KELLUM, John 90
KELLY, ___ 65,218,314
    Andrew 65,71,271
    Daniel 132,138,144
    Gesham 21
    James (Kellay) 141
    John 4,77,193,254,270,
    302,313,395
    John, Jr. 77
    Matw. 132
    Nancy 77
    Nimrod 266,409
    Sarah 409
    Thomas 89,155,395
KELSELL, John 64,97
KELTON, Daniel 49
    David 5,30,51,64,69,
    158,168,297,313,314,
    390,400

KELTON, cont'd:
  Esther 390
  Nichl. 262
  Robert 346,398
KEMP, Asa 256,258,261,265,
  275,350
  Demcy 237
  Edward 94,238,249,263,
  278,394
  Elizabeth 208,418,419
  Jonathan 95,131,207,
  208,237,262,418,419
  Jonathan K. 273
  Joseph 368
  Thomas 294
KENNEDY(KENADY,KENEDY),
  218,335
  Andrew 148
  C. 70
  Charles 99
  Ebenezer 140,141
  James 92,201,319,333,
  336,342,354,360,378,
  396
  Jesse 201
  Joseph 126,129,148,211
  Joshua 148
  Josiah 29,131
  Josiah N. 76,130,140,
  141,148
  Mary Eliza 396
  Maxfield 96
  Maxwell 380
  Sarah (Salley) 141
  Thomas 145,165,298
  William E. 131,140,148
  William Ebenezer 402
KENNON, Henry 25
KENSLER(KENCELLOR,CANSE-
  LOR), John 286,401
KEOWN, Alexander 421
KERLY, William 82
KERR, J. C. 223
  John 251,252,263,283,
  284,417
  Mary 8,34
KEY, Moses 88
  William 88
KEYS, Jno. 263
  Lettice 160,207
  P. 287,290,296,325,
  335,338,427,428,429
  Peter 147,160,161,164,
  177,180,196,199,201,
  207,218,236,255,264,
  265,267,289,295,298,
  329,366,386,407,425,
  426
  Thomas 282
KILBURN, Aaron 267
KILBURN(KILBOURN,KILBORN,
  KILBOURNE), Amos 129,162,
  257,263,306
  Elizabeth 306
  James 306
KILE, George 225
  James 94
  Thomas 107
KILGORE, James 167,187,
  266,397
  Kiziah 266
  Robert 91
KILLE, Jacob 137
KILLEN, Robert 144
  William 144,206,294,
  395,396,424
KILLIAM, William 245
KILLIGAN(HOLLIGAN?), Wil-
  liam 285
KILLISON(KILTISON), ___
  295
  Michael 99,183
KILLOUGH, David 66

KILPATRICK, ___ 282,350
  A. 351,369
  Alexander 8,10,46,49,
  95,101,131,204,225,233,
  253,277,278,289,297,
  306,312,315,350,358,
  362,410,418,419
  Andrew 96
  Col. 407
  J. A. 277
  J. C. 86,101,103,106,
  116,125,129,131,141,
  143,154,184,192,195,
  212,213,217,220,234,
  264,270,289,315,319,
  326,377
  James 46,195,233,266,
  275
  Joel 88
  John 95,325
  Jno./John C. 10,36,46,
  49,60,83,98,132,138,
  162,176,235,252,279,
  314,315,348
  John Clark 8,21,46,206
  Mary 101
  William 154,204
KILSON, George 2,42,91,125,
  385
KING, ___ 253
  Elizabeth 103
  Ezekiel 108
  Francis 54,92,103,131,
  237
  Henry 119,163
  James 309
  John 54,92,103,121
  Robert 103,145,160,389
  Sarah 131
  Solomon 7,54,98,120,
  244
  Solomon, Jr. 23,103,121
  T. Wm. 263
  Thomas 269
  William 101,119,144,145,
  157,163,190,265,266,395
  William ___ 246
  Wm. I. 265
  William J. 249,268
  William T. 250
KINLEY, Wm. 127
KINZA, Peter 157
KIRBY, David 164
  Jesse 110,124
  James 130
  William 130,400
KIRKS-KEEKS, ___ 217
KIRKSEY, ___ 379
  Christopher, Sr. 321
  Isaiah 327
  J. 410
  Jay 350
  Jehu 405
  John 379
  Josiah 327
  William 321
KIRKWOOD, Hugh 146
  Nathan 146
KIRSEY, Chrisr. 220
KITCHENS, Nathl. 262
  Mathew 241
KITLE, Jacob 43
KLIEN, John 356
KNAP, Timothy 147
KNOX, John 165,263,302,308,
  410
KYLE, Henry 224,261,406,
  421
  James Henry Bankhead
  397
  Robert 397

LABOON, Cate 294

LABOON, cont'd:
  Elizabeth 294
  Peter 244,262,265
LACY(LACY), Edward 55
  H. Wm. 263
  Martha 248
  W. H. 2,110,128,154,
  334
  William H. 248
  William Hughes 109,125,
  153,214
LACKEY, Adam 350
LADD, A. 309
  Amos 84,173,189,308,
  387,415,416
  Amos, Sr. 190
LAFFOON, Rutherford 271
  William 15,31,48,72,
  171,232,263,271,344
LAFOY, James 202
LAIN, Martin 118
LAKE, Elisha 372
LAMAN, Jennet 6
LAMAR, ___ 415
  Thomas 144,356,382
LAMB, Joseph 376
LAMBERT, James 308
LANCASTER, Mary 359
  Richard 14,15,359
  William 198
LANCE, Flora 320
  John 320
  Johnston 201
  Peter 320
  Samuel H. 269
LAND, Benjamin 40,215,216,
  358,420
  Doyle 211
  Elijah 358
  James 40
  John 27,156,295,358,
  374
  Joseph 15,130,133,156,
  298,307,310,376,385,
  411,427
  Joseph, Sr. 374
  Lewis 8
  Moses 414
  Nightengale 374
  Sarah 307,310,374
  William 105,341,408
LANDERS, Edward 351,415,
  416
  John 45,134,397
  Mary 134
LANDUS, J. L. 101
LANE, Jonathan 394
  Peter 319
LANGFORD, Eli/Ely 97,225,
  299,371
  Eli, Jr. 275,327,345
  Eli, Sr. 275,327,345
  Hetty 257
  Leander 345
  Matthew 275,327
  Robert 345
  Sarah 275
  Sary 345
  William 257
LANGLEY, John 11,17,93,139,
  214,299,301,321,330,
  365
  Noah 163
LANGSTON, Jesse 86
  John 386
LANIER, Bird 345
  Fredrick 196,203,308
  Robert 360
LANKSON, Joseph 210
LANTON, Jesse 56
LAPIER, Paul 227
LARD, John 359
  Henry 207,272

LARENCE, David 401
LARROW, Abraham 347
   Cesiah 347
   Jacob 347
   John 347
   Stephen 347
   William 347
LASLEY, William 227
LATHUM, Charles 219
LAUDERDALE(LAWDERDALE),
   James 76
   John 63,76,98,99,117,
     136,137,425
   Milberry 99,137
   Sarah 76
LAUDERMILK, Jacob 355
LAUGHLIN, Anthony 34
   Archibald(also Lawhon)
     368
   James 176
   John 34,104,163,187,
     271,384,412
   William 104,187,325,
     384
LAUGHTON, William 420
LAURENCE, Bartholomew/
   Bartholay 376
   Benjamin 204,263,323
   Jacob 323
   Joab/Job 72,133,291,
     376
   Rachel 323
LAWHON, A. 423
   Alexander 404
   Archibald 362,383,384,
     385,387,400,418,424
LAWLER, Jehu 161
LAWLEY, John 337
LAWRENCE, Benjamin 230
   Jacob 285
   Joab 29,63,133
   John 8,10,21,318
   Rachel 230
LAWSON, Ann 422
   James 356,357,371,422
LAX, William 80
LAXTON, Jesse 163
LAY, Anna 266,343,361
   Charles 18,30,47,71,
     213,229,266,303,308,
     309,339,343,361,399
   Thomas 254
LAYMAR, Thos. 301
LAYS, ___ 311
   William 78
LEATHERDALE, John 371
LEATHERS, John 370
   Nimrod 421
   Samuel 122,224
LEBOON, Mary 216
   Peter 230
LECY, Francis 249
LEDBETTER, ___ 223,236
   Daniel 39,63,88,179,
     201,265,429
   H. 311
   Joel/Jowl 87,88,179,
     191,272,281,311,373
   John 311,373
   Kitty(Katy) 179
   Martha 314
   Matthew 275
   Rebeckah 275
   Wiley 215
   William 429
LEE, ___ 225
   Mr. 426
   Andrew 14,181
   Barney 392
   Elizabeth 14
   Francis 193
   Joshua 94,153,154,191,
     268,291,311,384,411
   Major 313

LEE, cont'd:
   Thos. 14
   William 235
   William Powell 121,166,
     189,190
LEECH, Wm. 314
LEEPER, Joseph 270
LEGARE, James 340
LEGATE, Absalom 323
LEGRAND, Jesse 155
LEHRE(LEHERE), Thomas 245,
   263
LEMAN, Martha, Sr. 6
   Robert 6
LEMONS, William 387
LENDIES, Ephraim 313
LEONARD(LINARD,LINNEARD),
   John 169,254
   Larkin 254
   Mary 127,169,254
   Thomas 45,113,134,153,
     218,336
   William 104,332,342,
     413
LESLEY(LESLIE,LESLY), ___
   105,404,428
   Anne 16
   James 397
   Margaret 149,307,371
   Mary 108,416
   Thomas 77,108,129,149,
     174,266,287,393,415,
     416
   William 8,16,31,68,99,
     108,127,137,149,184,
     189,191,204,210,212,
     236,240,250,263,268,
     274,280,307,316,318,
     322,328,331,332,346,
     359,361,365,367,371,
     386,397,402,414,416,
     417
   William, Jr. 15,137
LEVERETE(LEVERETTE),
   Stephen/Steven 150,363
LEVY, Lyon 178
LEWIS, Benjamin 208,288,
   375,410,425
   Catherine 396
   Christopher 107,108
   David 201,218,302,309,
     403,425
   Earle 320
   Elizabeth 374
   George 339
   Isaiah 157,221,222,278,
     293,380,396
   J. L. 407
   Jacob 221,395,396
   Jesse 354
   Joab 221,396,423
   John 3,21,67,249,285,
     291,371,410,424
   John T. 5
   Major 126,129,247,281,
     285,291,297,374,375,
     410
   Mary 354
   Nenah 308
   Neriah 218
   Norsale 308
   Richard 5
   Samuel 173
   Tarleton 403
   Thomas 3,6,21,42,67,75,
     124,133,164,191,223,
     232,236,308,326,416
   Thomas Harrison 5
   V. 3
   Vincent 3,6
   Wm. 47,53,74,78,103,
     287,354,405
   William, Jr. 208,375,
     410

LEXON, Samuel 360
LEY, Francis 249,263,413
LIDDEL(LIDDELL,LIDDLE),
   Andrew 33,79,94,144,
     194,285,312,328,414
   Andrew, Jr. 307
   Andrew, Sr. 307
   Andrew Johnston, Jr.
     307
   Elizabeth 217,238,327,
     328,330
   George 95,126
   Jean 33
   Jesse 118
   Moses 6,18,30,31,34,
     39,66,77,97,100,104,
     108,132,164,212,217,
     223,238,249,264,294,
     295,304,307,312,313,
     314,317,321,327,328,
     332,333,359,361,377,
     426
   Moses, Sr. 194
   Stephen 118
   William 254,368,402
LIGHT, Abin 206
   Eben 115
   Elizabeth 294
   Jacob 206
   Jacob, Sr. 266
   Sanders 204
   Tire? 323
LIGON, Blackmon 53
LINARD, Jas. 375
   Thomas 187
   William 342
LINCH, Isaac 9
   Wm. 121
LINCICUM, Hezekiah 399,401
   Sarah 399
LINCOLN, James 378
LINDLEY(LINLEY), John 11,
   16,17,77,78,88,230,389
   Jonathan 264,337
   Sarah 11,17,77,78,263
   William 95,121,135,163
LINDSAY, Ephraim 126
   Esther 126
   Thomas, Sr. 326
LINDSEY, Caleb 302
   Edmond 133,388
   Elizabeth 152
   Ephraim 131,138,141,
     338,419
   Humphrey 425
   James 110,129,152,170,
     413
   James, Sr. 158
   John 132
   William 131
   Wm. Moor 413
LIN, Charles 346
   John 342
   John, Jr. 342
   Robert 342
   Sarah 342
LINN, Edley(Adley,Edle)
   126,356,357,361,363,
   367
   James 10,19,51,102,121,
     124,128,136,150,197,
     286,290,401
   James, Jr. 10,19
   James, Sr. 197,320,337
   John 126,298,363,367
   Robert 117,190,194,342,
     380
   Sarah 197,286
   William 126,363,367
LIN(N)EARD, Honour 104
   Thomas 266
   William 104
LINSE(LINCE), Henry 224,
   233,263

LINTON(LIUTON?), Sam 112
  Sm. 113
  Wm. 334
LINVILL, Wm. 205
LISTENBY, Hezekiah 401,
  402,422
LISTER, James 382
  Moses 328,382
LITHGOW, Robert 252
LITTLE(LITTEL,LITTELL),
  Capt. 58
  George 82
  Job 3
  Jonas 17,42,137
  Samuel 82,161,285,414
LITTLETON, Savage 425
LIVELY, John 202
LIVINGSTON, Thomas 207
LIZINGBY(LISENBE), Mr.358
  Hezekiah 419
LOCKERT(LOCHERT), Aaron
  69
LODERWICK, ____ 394
LOFTIN, Abigale 158
LOFTON, Agnes 234,283
  James 22
  Jean 285
  G. 94
  G. Jno. 263
  John 233,238
  John C. 279
  John G. 49,51,64,174,
  176,183,186,187,242,
  251,257,276,283,314
  John Guy 263
  Margaret 37,38
  Samuel 2,6,7,10,12,13,
  21,22,25,26,35,36,38,
  40,51,56,63,64,73,84,
  158,168,183,234,263,
  305,313,314,329,363,
  367,400
  Samuel, Jr. 25,30,35,
  36,37,43,51,56,73,
  176,186,187,194,210,
  251,257,279
  Samuel, Sr. 10,22,30,
  51,69,94,173,187,197,
  312,390,408
  Solomon, Sr. 186
  Thomas 6,10,17,30,37,
  38,49,51,60,64,69,96,
  131,162,171,173,183,
  186,187,189,193,197,
  205,226,233,238,240,
  241,276,285,293,305,
  312,327,330,331,390,
  400
  William 2,10,25,26,35,
  36,37,49,51,57,64,73,
  182,183,240
  William, Sr. 158
LOG(G)AN(LOGGINS), Alex-
  ander 58
  David 48,58
  Isaac 300
  James 23,122,268,293,
  345,392,394,395
  John 52,53,100,105,342
  Joseph 105,115,140,226
  Joseph, Jr. 226
  Joseph, Sr. 226
  Major 244
  Reuben/Reubin 163,224
  Susan(n)ah 268,392
  Thomas/Thos. 52,53,
  105,342
LOLLER(LOLLAR,LAWLER),
  John 162,180
  Jehu 342
LOLLOER, Thomas 324
LOMAX, James 28,29,70
  Jno. H. 221
LONG(also Lang), James...

LONG(also LANG), James Dav-
  is 15
LONG, Ann 293
  Benjamin 320
  Christopher 110,143
  Gab'l. 366
  Henry 174,204,266,387
  James 15,16,29,41,61,
  66,67,85,113,133,147,
  161,165,166,199,218,
  236,238,258,267,288,
  317,318,322,372,376,
  406,411,425,427
  James Davis (see above)
  John 430
  Margary/Margery 113
  Matthew 322,410,425
LONGFORD (see LANGFORD)
LONGLEY, John 345
LOONEY(LEWNEY), ____ 353
  David 196
  Hugh 375
  John 112,273
  Peter 330,375
  Robert 1,20,55,133,142,
  259,263,318,391,411,
  428
LOOPER, Joseph 302,309
  Samuel 286
LORD, Curtis 264
  Wm. 36
LOUDERMILK, Jacob 337,367
LOUELLEN, Joseph 340
LOUMBER, John 38
LOURANCE, William 248,249
LOURY, Edward 203
  Henry/Hennery 203,212
  Henry, Jr. 298
  Henry, Sr. 298
  Isaac 207
  John 212
LOVE, Elsa 249
  James 302
  John 149,292
  Joseph 300
  Robert 199,332,407,421
  Samuel 30,107,119,128,
  249,269,304
  Sarah 169,240,302
  Thomas 249
  William 12,29,66,112,
  126,127,128,189,286,
  300,304,335,353,392,
  423
LOVELADY, Jno./John 18,41,
  76
  Simon 162
LOVELL, Saml. 263
LOVINGOOD, Samuel 177,387
LOW(LOWE), Alice 18
  Craduk 117
  Joseph 300
  Margaret 135,144,275
  Stephen 164
  Thomas 30
  William 43,49,110,134,
  135,144,263,275
LOWRY(LOURY,LOWERY), George
  207
  Harry 345
  Henry/Hennery 212,323
  James 212
  John 2,3,56,104,273,
  275
  Sarah 273,275
LOYD, Charles 237
  John 2,175,319,402
  "Widow" 157
LUCKIE, James 142
  John 119,142
  Wm. L. 142
LUCKY, John 238
LUISTON, Jesse 109
LUKEY, Adam 177

LUMBAS, John 41
LUPER, Joseph 313
LUMPKIN, George 66
  John 408,409
LUNSFORD, Swanson 44
LUSK(LOOSK), Ellen 374
  Henry 173,223,374
  Janin 52
  Nathan 173,193,206,
  207,215,222,223,225,
  236,257,287,299,316,
  318,320,327,328,335,
  339,340,347,350,351,
  373,374,398,421
  Robert 69,215,421
LUSKEY, ____ 113
LYCH, Isaac 344,397
LYLE, John 242
LYN(LYNN), Edly 413,414,
  416
  James 370
LYNCH(LINCH,LYNTCH),
  Geter 186
  Isaac 1,2,14,37,60,
  151,169,173,185,190,
  226,233,273,285,323,
  328,341,344
  Jacob 178
  James 206
  John 239,265
LYTTLEYON, William Henry
  28

MC ADAM, ____ 267
MC ADAMS, James 13,256,
  262,330
  John 254
MCADOO (see MC ADOO)
MC ADOO(MC ADOW), Arthur
  187,213,251,254,293
  David(Daniel?) 18,221,
  380
  James 17,94
  Samuel 65
  William 251,400
MC ADORY, James 361
MC AFEE, James 221,281,351
  Robert 220,221
MC AL(L)ESTER(MC AL(L)IS-
  TER), Agnes(s) 205,340
  Alexander 168,205,294,
  349
  Andrew 168,294,353,
  368
  Daniel 36,110,205,340
  Edward 411
  James 205
  John 205,251
  Nathan 181,376
  Nathaniel 168,205
  William 36
MC AMEY, William 420
MC BEATH, John 103,204
MC BEE, Hugh 177
  Vardry 6
  William 42
MC BRIDE, ____ 280
  James 92,250
MC CALEB, Capt. 58
  D. 199,227,232,253,261,
  265,306,374,420
  D. C. 213,309,328
  David 63,74,85,125,136,
  151,164,186,199,200,
  213,225,229,232,234,
  239,240,252,253,263,
  265,272,275,283,303,
  312,319,323,324,328,
  332,336,354,357,362,
  369,394,401,402,406,
  408,413,418,421,422,
  424,428,429
  David C. 311

MC CALEB, cont'd:
    James 110,131,231,234,
        239,240,263
    Martha 225
    Matilda 240
    Matilou 429
    William 2,7,8,19,20,22,
        26,29,34,36,38,41,42,
        48,60,62,63,73,74,82,
        85,96,131,153,154,158,
        176,186,191,193,205,
        214,229,233,234,239,
        248,263,272,279,319,
        340,367,404,408,411
    William M. 60
    Wm. N. 50
    Wm. Neal/Neel 20,48
MC CALL, John 71,178
MC CALLISTER(MC CALASTER,
MC CALISTER), Andrew 421
    Francis 321
    John 5,229
    Nathan 359
    Nathaniel 402
    William 423
MC CAMBRIDGE, ___ 323,349
    John 175
MC CAMEY, William 375
MC CANE, Samuel 210
MC CANN, ___ 313
    Hannah 172,182
    Robert 25,32,39,75,
        118,172,175,177,181,
        182,183,184,185,186,
        188,190,191,194,195,
        196,198,200,205,206,
        208,211,218,222,223,
        224,225,230,232,234,
        236,241,256,260,263,
        268,269,274,280,282,
        283,288,290,295,297,
        303,305,309,312,318,
        331,359,365,372,403,
        410,418,424
MC CANNEL, Alexander 403
MC CANREY, Wm. 418
MC CANT(S) (MC CANCE),
    Thomas 15,235
MC CARLEY(MC CARELY),
    David 350
    Elizabeth 348
    James 144,154,157,325,
        348
    John 320,325
    Joseph 157,398,403
    Sarah 320
    William 403
MC CARTER, James 145
    John 403
    Moses 41,403
MC CARTY, Callagan/Calle-
    gan 17,18,27,34,223
MC CAY, Daniel 45
MC CEARLY, James 30
MC CHESNEY, Isabel/Isa-
    bellah 152
    Walter 152
MC CILLION, Aber 265
MC CINSTRY, John 417
MC CLAIN, Ann 309
    John 38,139,408
    Mary 408
    Wm. 310
MC CLANNAN, Hugh 280
MC CLANNIHAN, John 186
MC CLARDY, ___ 241
MC CLEAN, Alexander 309,
    362
MC CLEERY, John 270
MC CLELAN(MACLIN), Robert
    403
MC CLEROY, John 413
MC CLESK(E)Y, David 207

MC CLESKEY, Isabalah 196
    William 38,196,217,235
MC CLOSKY, Alexander 159
    Wm. 227
MC CLUCK, John 245
MC CLURE, Charles 61,225,
        332
    E. T. 138
    Edw. F. 57
    E. Tate 37
    Edward 57,184,194,390
    Edward T. 80,107,128,
        185,204,223,240,275,
        292,315,333,335,356,
        364,379,384,412
    Edward Tate 80,81,82,
        97,107,145,223,275
    Edward Tell 392,408
    James/Jas. 37,175,277,
        302
    John 39,218,382,383,
        387,389,398,401,417,
        418
    Josiah 37,145,184,204,
        292,392
    Margaret 145
    Mary 392
    "Widow" Mogot 292
    William 80,82,108,145,
        162,169,184,292,392
MC CLURY, John 313
MC CLUSKY, Alexander 96,
        296,395,413
MC CLUSKEY, Jane/Jean 395
    Joseph 351
    William/Wm. 346,430
MC COLEY, Samuel 371
MC COLLICTER, Mr. 32
MC COLISTER(MC COLLISTER,
MC ALISTER), Aeneas 314
    Alexander 274
    Danl. 263
    Edward 156
    Frs. 263
    Jesse 263
    John 181
    Math. 263
    Nathan 181
    Robt. 263
    Sarah 274
    Selah 263
    Wm. 274
MC COLLOCK, James 38
    John 31
    William 38,134
MC COLLOUGH(MC COLOUGH,MC
CULOUGH), ___ 94
    John 59,137,215,381,
        395,409
MC COLLUM, Daniel (also
MC COLLOM), 3,63,86,97,
        198,275,316,352,375
    James 221,412
    John 27,55,95,146,364,
        429,430
    Samuel 34
    Samuel, Jr. 364,430
    Sarah 25
MC CONNEL(MC CONNELL),
    Alexander 317
    James 173
    William 10
MC CORMACK, John 428
MC COURTY, William 225
MC COY, ___ 349
    Daniel 145,158,159,222,
        325
    David 358
    Henry 277
    James 415,428
    John 145,158,159,336
    Patrick 148,153,223
    Robert 31

MC COY, cont'd:
    Sam'l. 359
MC CRACKEN, J. 225
    James 87,135,258
    Wm. 126
MC CRAY, H. 315,348,368,
        384,396,399,405,411,
        422
    Henry 349
MC CREARY(MC CRARY,MC
CRERY), Alexander 145
    John 153
    Margaret 145
    Robert 153,281
MC CREE, John 161,198
MC CREIGHT, Jas. 264
    Robert 229
    Thomas 187
MC CRONE, William 308
MC CROSKY, John 123,171,
        198,357,364,370,385
    Margaret 171
MC CROWN, William 326
MC CROY, H. 362
MC CULLOUGH, John 17,94
    Mary 69
    William 69
MC CULLUM, Daniel 87
    James 253
    John 40
    Sarah 40
MC CULLY, Jenny/Jain 415
    Samuel 322,415,417
MC CUNE, Mary 121
    Samuel/Saml. 125,132
    Thos. 132
    William 121,132
MC CURDY, Elijah 7
    Wm. 120
MC CURON, Wm. 232
MC CUSHION, John 113
MC CUTCHIN(MC CUTCHEN),
    Ann 177
    Anne 405
    John 5,113,161,177,
        201,218,244,262,369,
        374,380,405
MC DANELL, William Hawkins
    291
MC DANIEL(S), ___ 133,404
    Archer 141
    Henry 89,200,298,302
    Henry, Jr. 298
    Henry, Sr. 188,223
    John 258,298
    Patty 298
    Thomas 302
MC DANNELLY, J. 291
    Martha 291
MC DOLE, ___ 282
    Jon 158
MC DONALD(MC DONALE,MC
DONNEL), Bradock 317,427
    James 291
    Stephen 317
MC DOW, Arthur 263,277,278
    William/Wm. 263,312,
        329
MC DOWELL(MC DOWAL(L),
    Alexander 36,87,116,
        135,172,225,354,363,
        378,406
    James/Jas. 234,291
    John 197,397,409
    Patrick 36,87,191,205,
        225,258,263,378
    Robert 202
MC EARLEY(MC CARLEY),John
    155
MC ELRATH, Alexander 330
MC ELROY(MC ELLROY), John
    3,80,105,118,123,155,
    185,361,414,416,418

MC ELROY, cont'd:
  Lattice 414
  Samuel 361,414,416
MC ELVAN(E),(MC ELVENY,MC
ELVINY), John 34,121,125
  Margaret 166
  Margaret, Jr. 166
  Margaret, Sr. 166
  William 98,166,359,
    417
MC ENTIRE, John 301,344
MC EVANNEY, John 132
MC EWEN, John 218
MC FALL, John 258,262,317,
  361,374,396,414,417,
  426
  Mary 374
MC FARLAND(MC FARLANE),
  William 284,302,327,
  328,363,364,367,385
MC FARRON(MC FARON), Isabel 83
  James 83
MC GEE, Jesse 348,415
  John 13
MC GEHEE, John 67,128,130,
  141
MC GILL, Samuel 223,321
MC GILLIARS, John 136
MC GLAULIN, Agnes 201
MC GREGGER(MC GREGOR),
  Thomas 296
  William 223,236,376
MC GREGORY, Robert 281
  Wm. 262,263,264
MC GREW, Peter 138
MC GRIGER, Matiam 410
  William 410
MC GUFFIN, ____ 76,84,193
  Hugh 311
  James 5,213,311,369,
    401
  Susannah 426
  William/Wm. 53,144,
    192,202,213,221,250,
    302,311,337,369,388,
    401,426
MC ILWEE, James 214,248,
  355
MC KAIN, William 122,172
MC KAY(MACKAY), William
  44,135,348,381,395
MC KEE, Archibald 395
MCKIE(MC KEE), Henry 373,
  380
  Jane 395
  William/Wm. 135,149,
    381,395,404,428
MC KEEN, James 311
MC KEESWICK, Felix 247
MC KEY (MACKIE), William
  111,112,131,297,298
MC KAM, Joseph 111
MC KAMEY(MC KAMY,MC KEMY),
  William 22,54,79
MC KINLEY, Elizabeth 178
  John W. 250
  Wm. 178
MC KINNEY, James 32,193,
  197,214,247,351
MC KINSEY(MC KENZIE, MC
KINZIE), ____ 377,390
  Duncan/Dunkan 50,95,
    253,323,385,396
  Farren/Ferrihan 50,95
  James 308
  John 63,99,108,183,204,
    255,263,272,277,385,
    396
  Kenneth 330,331
MC KNEEL, Jno. 86
MC KNITT, Joseph 375
  T. 375

MC KOURNEY, Jno. 236
MC LANE(MC LEAN), Alexander 99,101,102,135,161,
  243,246,362
  Peter 351
MC LEMORE, Jno. 220
MC MAHEN(MC MAHAN,MC MAHN,
MC MAHON), Adam 13
  J. 181
  James 197
  John 16,21,46,65,78,94,
    120,126,139,142,157,
    159,165,175,178,181,
    206,210,224,258,269,
    280,281,282,298,301,
    325,348,364,384,398
M(A)C MAHEN, Mary 6
  Peter 263,355,397
  Rowley 127
  William 6,138,281,282,
    337,416
MC MILLEN(MC MILLAN,MC
MILLIM), Abner 408
  Alexander 63,77,119,
    140
  Daniel 184
  John 326,329,334,363,
    372,376,377,405,408,
    428
  Rowley, Jr. 208
MC MILLIAN(MC MILLION),
  Abner 260
  Alexander 238,263,267,
    268,295
  Daniel 287
  John 276,272,276,281,
    314,316,321,338,412,
    413,414
  Lydia 338
MC MORRIES, Wm. 151
MC MULLEN, Alexander 142
MC MURRY, Jno. 169
MC MURTREY(MC MURTRY),
  Joseph 397
  Wm. 125
MC NEAL(MC NEEL), Neal
  237
  John 61,135,204
MC PHERSON, William 41,264
MC READY, John 173
MC REE, John 94
MC TAGGART, Mary 336
  Thomas 136,336
MC VAY(MC VEY), C. 342
  Fanny 288
  Hugh 16,288
  John 8,14,70,71,113,
    196
  Wm. 4,14,39,113
MC WHORTER (MC WHERTER,
MC WHIRTER), Henry 40,76,
  91,240,263,390,392
  Henry, Jr. 145
  Henry, Sr. 169
  Henry A. 240
  Isaac 356,364
  Jane 76,240,390
  John 145,188,225,304,
    305,307,318,364,366
  John, Jr. 404
  Robert 305,349,364
  William 356
MC WILLIAMS, Andrew 35
  Nimrod 328
  William 10,328

M____, James 386
MACADOW, Arthur 293
MACBRID, ____ 209
MAC CRARY, John 230
MACHEN, Henry 3
MACHCOLLINS, Robert 203
MACKELWEE, James 140

MACKEY(MACKIE,MC KEY),
  J. 286
  James 397
  Mary 83,195
  William 8,49,83,108,
    109,131,143,163,195,
    200
MACLED, David 293
MACLIN, Robert 403
  William 302
MAC MILLIM, John 210
MADGETT, Nicholas 252,265,
  289
MADISON, James 12,122,148,
  221,360
MADRICK, ____ 353
MAGEE, Benjamin 399,411
  George 403
  Solomon 403
MAGILL, Ezekiel 367
MAHAN(MAHEN,MAHAM,MAHON),
  A. W. 86
  Alexander 216,230,294
  Hezekiah 71
  Joseph 21
  Margaret 294
MAISTON, Reuben 269
MAJOR, Richard 294
MALLACK(MALLOCK), ____ 288
  Absolom 323
  Robert B. 323
  William 252,284
MALONEY, John 229
MANN, Margaret 389
MANNAN(MANNEN,MANNON),
  Bedy 414
  Edmond 154,414
  Edward 139
  Jno. 154
MANNER, Elijah 403
  Sally/Sarah 403
MANNING, Edmond 268,402
  Elizabeth 296
  Geo./George 219,268,
    332
  Walter 190
MAPLES, William 48,136
MARAH, Dominick 13
MARBROUGH, William 210
MARCH, John 411
MARCHBANKS, Elijah 50
  Jane 353
  Johnston 116,278
  William 17,50,107,110,
    116,179,183,237,252,
    276,324,345,384,387,
    388,389
MARION, Francis 409
MARITAIN, John 398
MARLEY, David 398
MARLOW, James 282
MARONEY, James 67,68
MARS, Samuel 272
MARSH, John 355
MARSHALL, Cornelia 380
  William 201,316,353
  William, Jr. 201
MARSLEY(or MASTERS?),
  Nolly 137
MARSTON, Reuben 342
MARTAIN, Thos. 430
MARTIALL, William 210
MARTIN, ____ 19,54,92,157,
  170,175,197,210,319,
  372,406
  A. C. 138
  Absalom 187,188
  Barkley 248,263
  Charity 222
  Charles 314
  Daniel Lewis 4
  Doctr. 146
  Frances 171

MARTIN, cont'd:
  George 222
  J. 128
  James 9,10,30,31,38,
    57,65,86,87,89,90,97,
    98,105,112,113,121,
    122,125,126,127,134,
    136,140,144,150,156,
    159,166,167,171,178,
    181,186,188,193,199,
    200,207,208,212,221,
    235,251,267,278,281,
    286,289,296,297,305,
    308,317,327,328,330,
    332,336,342,380,391,
    402,426
  John 1,2,10,41,63,65,
    97,100,120,122,123,
    127,134,147,172,173,
    175,191,201,207,232,
    233,234,235,248,249,
    263,267,280,314,325,
    339,364,390,415
  John C. 78
  Joseph 55,145,165,204,
    273,410
  Keath 233
  L. D. 260,262,263,265
  Lewis/Louis 55,359
  Louis D. 1,18,38,107,
    125,141,166,167,169,
    229,234,249,256,276,
    282,283,290,297,320,
    372,373,374,394,423,
    426 (also Lewis D.)

  Lewis Daniel 11,17,37,
    46,78,165,167,220,233,
    272,386
  Lilly 186
  Mart 275
  Mathias 100
  Matthew 104,410
  Merit 204
  Moses 3,140
  Norman 26,89,141
  Roger 45,52,117,161,
    221
  Ruth 45,277,402
  Samuel 35,89,90,135,
    188,265,283,299,408,
    409
  Sarah 1,18,38,125,165,
    167
  Tempy 222
  Thomas 59,65,212,277,
    309,312,360,364,392
  William 6,55,109,144,
    171,303
MASON, Daniel 243,333
  Ezekiel 340,418
  Hanah 216
  Mark 363
  William/Wm. 73,367
MASEY, Robert 301
MASSEY, William 397
MASTERS, Nolly 137
MASTON, John 4
MATHERS, Elijah 366
MATKIN, James 417
MATLOCK, A. B. 214
  Absolom 214
  Christian 313
  Littleberry 270,313
  William 284
MATTERS, William 379
MATTERSON, James 27
  Thomas 57
MATHEWS(MATTHEWS), Ann
    353,355
  George 66,144,252
  Isaac 353,355
  Isom 218
  John 353,355

MATTHEWS, cont'd:
  Joseph 353,355
  Nancy 353,355
  Polly 353,355
  Thomas 411
  William 91,268,269,379,
    417
MATTESON(MATTISON), Ben./
    Benjamin 239,263
  Frances 239
  James 16,31,190,221,
    239,263,286,299,336
  Nevil(1) 116,190
  Thomas 116,189,387
MATTOCK(S), William/Wm.
    229,284
MAULDIN, B. 316
  Bala(a)m 169,210
  Betsey 47,81
  Blake 15,19,45,47,50,
    53,54,78,81,82,128,
    129,132,143,144,186,
    194,199,210,234,269,
    297,303
  Capt. 49
  Elizabeth 81
  Harris 15,38,50,76,114,
    116,132,160,365
  J. 99,129,144,402
  Jacob (Joab) 366
  Jean 210
  Joab 45,50,52,69,77,
    78,96,121,129,132,139,
    143,150,151,158,161,
    165,196,230,238,239,
    262,263,271,310,352,
    367,420
  John 50,52,76,114,117,
    136,161,230,298,303,
    325,336,358
  John, Jr. 45
  John, Sr. 15,50,116,132
  Keziah 114
  Peggy 50
  Sarah 114
  Wesley 114,132
  "Widow" 137
  Wylie 230
MAV(E)RICK(MAVEK), Lydia
    306,310,344
  Samuel 225
MAXWELL, Anne A. 427
  Chas. 283
  Col. 216
  Edward 86
  Elisha 126,170
  George 74,343
  Hugh 40,41
  James 8,19,26,68,110,
    115,221,253,334,337,
    338
  John 40,41,100,189,301
  Joseph 255
  Mary 247,263
  R. 110
  Rob 263
  Rob Anderson 263
  Robert 9,35,40,41,43,
    52,60,83,84,85,90,99,
    100,144,166,211,229,
    235,247,309,325,348,
    364,389,424
  William 8
MAY, Daniel 379
  P. H. 375,387
  Phillip 326,378,379
  Phillip H. 376
  William 375,379
  William, Jr. 379
MAYES, John 75
MAYS, Moses 213,309,327,
    381
MAYFIELD, ___ 190

MAYFIELD, cont'd:
  Abraham 415
  Austin 251
  Elijah 150,151,159,
    208,263,300,301,347,
    419
  Elizabeth 151,159,208
  Isaac 159
  Isham/Isam 208
  Robert 384
  Stephen 208
  Sugar 359,415
  Thomas 251
MAYNARD, Richard 253
MAYSON, Robert 209
MAYWOOD, Simon 368
MAZYCK, D. 92,117,118
  Daniel 409,412
  Stephen 412
  Thomas W. 409,412
  (also spelled Mazych)
MEAD, Abrial 21
MEANS, Jane 143
  Robert 23
  Samuel 14,44,120,128
  William 14,143
MECLANE, Ellicksader 135
MECLURE, E. T. 238
MEDLIN, Lewis 184
  Richd. 184
MEDLING, William 41
MEDLOCK, Berry 270
  Littleberry 270
MEED, Abull(Abill) 21
MEEK, Adam 235
MEEKS, Asa 223
  Essey(Nasse/Nese) 416
  Fanny 416
  Littleton 225,335,416
  Isaac 48
MEGAHE, Jarel 277
MECREGORY, William 236
MEGROGOR, William 238
MEIRS, Isaac 299
MELICAN, Jawl 272
MELON(E)(MELONAY), John
    397
MELONEY (as above)
  John B. 424
MELONY, Samuel 331
MELURE, Charles 403
MERIAN, Samuel 51
MERIDITH(MERIDAY), James
    367
MERONY (MERONEY), Chil.
    300
  James 61
  Phil/Phillip 340,342,
    343,363,365,415
  Phillip D. 365,366,
    415,416
MERRELL, Charles 294
MER(R)ICK(MER(R)IK), ___
    338
  Augustus 3,132,225,
    300,301
  T. 64,228
  Tilly/Tilley/Telly
    3,6,7,17,64,99,132,
    225,251,300,313,314,
    400,408,419
MERRILL, John 319
  Stephen 207
MER(R)IT(T), ___ 243
  Ephraim 240
  James 222,244,260,261
  Nathaniel 357,365
  Obadiah/Obediah 244,
    295
  Stephen 240,241,264,
    351,393
MERRY, Benja. 96
METZKER, Geo. 70

MICHAM, Henry 229
MICHIE, Matt. 193
MIDDLETON, Hugh 67,68,70
   John 207
   Robert 67,68,70
MIDLINGO, William 116
MIDOWAL, John 419
   Margaret 419
MIERS, Isaac 331,335
MIFFLEN(MIFFLIN), Thomas 93,108
MILES, Aquilla 248
   Charles 126
   John 9
MILLEN, Wm. 300
MILLER, ___ 266,338,341
   A. 409
   Alexr. 60,123
   Catherine 106,228,277
   Crosby 4
   Crosby W. 14,19,49, 293,337,396
   Crosby Wilkes 19,22,37, 55,327
   Ebenezer 226
   Elisha 372
   Elizabeth 18,108
   Emy 348
   Francis (Millar) 17,18, 20,21,26,27,34,60,63, 85,126,140,223,322, 383,391,406
   George 151,340,408
   Henry 352
   Hester 423
   Howell 93,276,300
   Hugh 352
   Isaac 16,48,424
   J. 2,74,91,108,130, 254,364
   J., Jr. 327
   James 48,112
   James Robinson 48
   Jane 26,55,263
   Jean 21,63,85,126
   Jesse 80,143,278,300, 340,348
   John 1,4,14,16,18,19, 22,26,27,29,30,34,37, 38,40,41,45,47,48,49, 50,51,52,53,54,55,56, 71,76,78,86,95,139, 169,183,186,197,224, 229,263,301,303,312, 323,327,337,352,354, 376,389,390,391,394, 396,411,426
   John, Jr. 27,45,49,51, 55,57
   John A. 258,267
   John Adam 60,119,139, 140,406,423
   Katharine 134
   Mary 126,151
   Mary Ann 22
   Mirah 144
   R. 204
   Rachael 229
   Robert 119,134
   Sally 348
   W. 193
   William 276,300,340, 354
MILFORD(MILLFORD), Henry 150,181
   John 215,368
   Thomas 59,215,320,368
MILLICAN, John 334,400
   William, Jr. 213
   William, Sr. 213
MIL(L)IGAN, Henry 292
   Jacob 1,176,183,255, 277,360

MILLIN, Phillip 247
MILLING, David A. 13
   Hugh 13,394
MILLS, ___ 76,318
   Betsy (Elizabeth) 412
   Gilbert 41,367
   Henry 239,263,340
   Hillary/Hillery 323, 401
   Hugh 187,211,396,413
   James 239,263
   John 77,187,211,304, 412
   Martha 41
   Rankin 337
   Thomas 290
MILLWEE(MILWEE,MULLWEE, MULWEE), ___ 204,360,392
   Ambrose 389
   James/Jas. 32,33,36,45, 50,58,95,109,110,115, 116,126,128,129,135, 136,139,140,145,148, 150,155,156,162,168, 172,197,200,220,251, 256,263,272,278,279, 286,290,291,292,297, 337,352,353,360,376, 377,378,389,394,396, 402,405
   John 353,356,357,393, 405
   Margaret 155,200,334, 352
   Martha 134,149,187
   William/Wm. 16,85,89, 96,99,104,105,106,107, 114,115,116,120,126, 128,129,130,134,145, 148,149,150,151,161, 163,166,170,172,176, 178,180,185,187,210, 211,224,228,236,239, 307,389,420,424
MILNER, Daniel 316
MILLSAP(MILSAP), Kezia 258,294
   J. 99
   Thomas 114,115,132,137, 160,210,258,263,269, 294,316,317,381
MINTON, Richard 307
   Richard, Sr. 307
MISCAMPBELL(MISCAMPBLE,MS-CAMPRELL), Robert 2,18,19, 31,64,103,125,287,331
MISCANDERS, James 268
MITCHEL(L)(MICHFL), Arthur 179,276
   Catharine/Catherine 313,314,381
   Coren 270
   David W. 268
   Ephraim/Ephram 39,47, 59,65,132,216,237,240, 277,319,336,369,374, 375,394
   Isaac 167,280,363,404
   Isaac, Jr. 167
   James 39,243,375,379, 419
   Joab 109
   John 64,228,248,249, 255,264,369,397
   Joseph 339
   Mark 107
   Spence 211,218,424
   William/Wm. 77,122,127, 248,264,270,313,314, 370,381
MITTURE, James 255
MOFFETT(MOFFET,MOFFITT), ___ 254

MOFFETT, cont'd:
   Ambrose 400
   Ann 371
   Craven 13,255,263,330
   David 107
   Gabriel 2,13,29,41,44, 48,53,61,62,69,72,80, 86,366
   John 1,6,11,30,121, 128,132,371,381
   Nancy 255
MOLL, Peter 197
MOODY(MODY), Joel 74,117, 387
   Joel, Sr. 388
MOOLS, Maj. 415
MOON, James 100
MOOR, Bennit 214
   Eliab 247
   Elijah 295
   Hugh 214
   James 7
   John 119
MOORE, ___ 113,423
   Mr. 177
   Aaron 178,351
   Abraham 295,423
   Alexander 14,15,75, 290,349,403,407
   Berry 277
   Bert 413
   David 255
   Dorcus(or Darius) 403
   E. 81
   Eless? 71,72
   Eliab 46,56,66,67,146, 163,172,263,278,300, 346,353,360
   Elias 42
   Elijah 295
   Francis 123,362
   George 407
   Hugh 173,323,362,421
   Jacob 263
   James 8,14,15,22,36, 37,38,42,43,127,201, 239,310,332,349,366, 374,381,423
   Jean 127
   John 14,15,26,75,76, 110,123,127,161,178, 201,245,253,332,407
   Jonathan 124,231,259, 263
   John, Sr. 362
   Levi 192,193,263,264
   Lucy 184
   Mary 196,201,413
   Moris 81
   Orwin 407
   Rebecca 66,172,277
   Robert 74,127,230,263
   Samuel 262,407
   Sarah 421
   William 11,127,160, 289,290
MOOREHOUSE(MOREHOUSE), Abraham 175,218,219, 242
MOOREHEAD(MOORHEAD), ___ 144,241
   Alexander 5,416
   James 116,176,427
   John 89,217,220,346, 354,364,419,427
   John, Sr. 277
MOORS, Nichols 116
MONK, Jean 323
MONROE, Johnson 69
MONTGOMERY, ___ 233
   A. D. 317
   B. R. 411
   Benjamin Ray 396

MONTGOMERY, cont'd:
  H. 80
  Hugh 87,242,263
  James 10,88,135,136,
  311
  John 112,224,276,286,
  290,292,293
  Jonathan 10,19,51,134,
  193,197,213,217,218,
  337,347
  Sarah 88,136,217,311
  William 102,306,319,
  331,349,363,373,374
MORDAH, Jas. 382
MORE, John 212
  Joseph 178
  Levi/Levy 244,246
  Patrick 214
MOREHEAD, Sarah 217
MOREMAN, James 219
MORGAN, ___ 352
  Charles 271,317,330
  Edward 5,25
  Isaac 3
  Jeremiah 274
  John 178,193
  Leonard 123,171
  Mathew 60,140,150,406
  Orman/Ormand 146,147,
  318,406
  Polly 318
  Zachariah 167,334
MORRAH, Hugh 76,203
MORRILL(MORRIL,MORAL),
  William 136,292
MORRIS, Adam 55
  Drury 172
  E. 81
  George 284
  Hezekiah 281
  Jacob 252,284
  James 124
  John 42,161,178,188,
  240,316,333,338,423,
  424,428
  Mary 315
  Patrick 215
  Robert 76,92
  Samuel 224
  Susannah 423
  Thomas 47,81
  Thomas, Jr. 408
  William 400
MORRISON, Wm. 247
MORROW(MORRAH,MORROWSS),
  Elizabeth 320
  Hugh 84
  James 87,104,121,142,
  155,212,223,272,281,
  407
  John 2,51,148,153,334,
  407,408,409,419
  Leonard 97,132,155,170
  Margaret 51
  Mary 407
  Richard 51,67,68,77,
  91,129,170,407
  Robert 334
  Thomas 18,34,90,97,
  134,155,403
  Thomas, Jr. 155,320
  Thomas, Sr. 97,155,320
  Wm. 334
MORS, John 307,315,318
  Samuel 318
MORSE, John 307
  Samuel 272
MORTON, Joel, Jr. 268
  John 364
  Thomas 401
MOSS, ___ 153
  Fredrick 359,377,384,
  390,405,412
  James 60

MOSS, cont'd:
  Jeff/Jephs 73,85,281,
  366
  John 78
  Joseph 28
  Samuel 150
  Thomas 41,60,140,150,
  156,322
MOTHERS, Isaac 304
MOTTE, ___ 231
  Abraham 25
  Charles 231
  Jacob 231
MOULTRIE, Gov./William/Wm.
  25,26,27,28,30,31,32,
  33,35,36,37,38,39,40,
  42,43,45,47,48,49,50,
  51,52,54,55,57,58,59,
  61,62,63-66,69-80,82,
  84,86,87,89,92,94,95,
  96,98,99,100,103,104,
  105,106,107-110,112-
  118,121-126,128-135,
  137,138,140-144,146-
  154,156-159,161,163,
  165,166,168,170-181,
  183,184,187-193,195-
  197,200-202,204-210,
  214,215,217-220,222-
  225,227-231,233,234,
  236,238-240,244,245,
  248,249,251-256,258,
  266,267,270-277,279,
  281,282,284-286,288-
  290,292,296,298,299,
  301,303,304,307,309,
  310-318,320,322-330,
  332-336,339,340,342,
  343,345-347,350,353,
  355,357,358,361-363,
  367-369,373,374,377,
  380-382,384-386,390,
  394-397,399-402,408,
  409-411,413,414,416;
  417,419-421,423-425,
  427,429
MOZLEY, D. 221
MOZLY, David 339
MUDA, Joel 284
MULHERIN(MULHERING), Char-
  les 304
  John 91
MULICAN(MULLICAN), Benja-
  min 324
  William 152,163,184,
  226,242,264,412
  William, Jr. 151
MULLIGAN, Benjamin 324
MULLINIX(MULLINAS), John
  89,421
  Joseph 421
  Mathew 66,283,333,346
  William 333,346
MULLIN(MULLINS), ___ 298
  John 275
  Love(Lane?) 302
  Swift 412,413
MULRONEY, James 201
MUNRO, George 252,284
  John 117,118
MURDIN(MURDINE), Cloee 395
  Edward 189,395
MURDOCK, Rachel 55
  Wm. L. 249
MURLEW, John 282
MURPHY(MURPHEE,MURPHIES,
MURPHEY), D. 428
  David 251,424
  John 109,348,352
  Roger 241,260,332,352
  Rodger/Roger, Sr. 274,
  348
  William 63,89,266,370
MURRAY, Anna 161

MURRAY, cont'd:
  Benjamin 44
  John 161
  Johnston 125,161
  Margaret 37,42
  William 20,37,42,161
MURRY, Benjamin 82
  Johnston 135
  William, Jr. 125
MURPHREE(MURPHREY), Alex-
  ander 307
  Allen 410
  Aaron/Aron 104,294,
  384,392,393,410,415
  D. 305
  Daniel/Danl. 220,405
  David (also Muphie)
  (Murphee) 74,157,181,
  241,252,257,266,268,
  270,272,275,276,292,
  294,296,300,301,307,
  314,315,317,321,324,
  328,329,338,339,340,
  342,344,345,346,348,
  353,354,358,372,375,
  377,378,382,384,387,
  388,393,403,405,406,
  410,415,416,422,428
  Davis 365
  E. 266
  Elijah 116,292,324,
  329,415
  Hannah 321
  Izan 152
  James 117,342,405,410
  Jesse 149,171,268,314,
  342,378,415,416
  John 294,352
  Levi 7,128,164,165,188,
  415
  Mary 164,415
  Moses 104,117,128,152,
  160,181,378,405,428
  Rodger 348
  Solomon 181,405
  William/Wm. 101,104,
  109,117,181,206,208,
  251,264,282,294,300,
  301,314,321,324,329,
  339,342,368,392,405,
  410,415
  William, Jr. 342
  William, Sr. 272,342
MYRES(MEIRS,MYERS), David
  221
  Henry 16,204
  Samuel 95

NAIL, Gilbert 207
NALL(NALLE), Mary 301,348
  Nathan 65,103,171,274,
  348,352,364
  Nathaniel 301
  Richard 244,246,263,
  408
  William 211
NALLY, A. 262
  Aaron 231,280
  Abraham 124,125,231,
  261,280
  Abraham, Jr. 394
  Richard 230
  Sarah (sally) 394
NASH, Ann 219
  George 32,117,239,288,
  419,427
  James 32,288
  James, Jr. 219
  James, Sr. 219,268
  Larkin 32,268
  Reuben/Reubin 160,206,
  221,345
  Robert C. 271
  Valentine 32,219

NAST, John 16
NATE, Richard 246
NATION(NATIONS), Amos 178, 358
   Nathan 187
NAYLOR, George 175,176, 219,242
NEAL, Aaron 301
NEALE, James 377
NEALSON, George 4
NEEL, Aaron/Aron 233,263, 276
   Ann 351
   Archabauld 120
   James 230,233,263,351
   Samuel 4,20,109,151
   Thomas 233,263
NEES, Peter 362
NEIL(NEILL), Aaron 234
   Archib. 139
   James 296
   Samuel/Saml. 78,84,149
   William 38,139,148, 149,408
NEILSON, James S. 167
NELMS, William 141
NELSON(NELLSON), George 79,130,136,148,190,369
   Jared/Jarred 327,345
   John 72
   Lewis 75,100
   Martha 136
   Noah 154
   Sampson 356
   William 130
NERRON, Acquiller 404
NEVIL(NEVILE,NEVILLE),
   Jesse 141,275,293,316, 391
   John 95
   William 34,37,38,42, 43,44,46,51,56,59,60, 62,63,66,67,71,93,95, 136,192,203,254
   Yelverton 86
NEWHOUSE, Lewis 50,51
NEWMAN, Charles 189,190
   James 341,354
   John 30,107,119,189, 269
   Nathaniel 125,208,261, 299,346,354,365,377
   Natheal 299
NEWSOM, Benjamin 165
   Thomas J. 5
NEYLe, Gilbert/Guilbert 147,179,180
NIBBS, Wm. 225
NICHELSON, John 12
NICHOLS, Ambrose 347,351, 352,357,364,424
   Archibald 351
   John 295,347,372
   Julius 51,87
   Julius, Jr. 36,50,116
   Thos. 192
NICHOLSON(NICKELSON), ___ 270
   Benjamin 197,224
   Elijah 132,327,328, 330,364
   Isaac 69,104,293
   James 27,64,97,111,183
   Jane/Jean 417
   John 12,14,28,33,43,71, 77,86,92,126,206,213, 276,353,388,417
   W. 270,364,390,398,401, 405,412,425
   William 37,223,248,263, 264,266,296,329,381, 421,425
NIDLY, Bromfield 123

NINON, Baylis 234
NIRON, Acquilla 404
NIXON, Elizabeth 199
   Hugh Alexander 199
NOLAND(NOLEN,NOLING),David 192,286
   Shadrack/Shadrich 211, 284,286
NOLIND, Nancy 286
NOBLE, Alexander 251,284
   Ezekiel 312,313,344
NORRINGTON, David 83
NORRIS, ___ 81
   Andrew 222
   Andrew Middleton 114
   Jean 325
   John 159,358
   John Q. 49
   P. 274,288,322,344,412, 414
   Patrick 117,172,204, 219,221,222,258,278, 279,346,408,428
   Robert/Robt. 49,83,116, 132,210,269,420
   Thomas 408
   "Widow" 336
   William 364
NORTH, Richard B. 429
   Tucker 429
NORTON, Barak 339,409
   Edward 116
   Gideon 39,313
   Henry 35,39,43,66,205, 402
   James 124
   Jeptha 351,364
   Mary 409
   William 43,83,120,124, 247,270,314
NORWOOD, ___ 281
   Daniel 104,149
   John 26,42,96,104,110, 125,126,128,138,141,149, 164,171,209
   Jos. 263
   Robert 355
   Samuel 46,102,141,306, 315,383
   Thomas 392
   William 102,306,355
NOWLAND, Shirod 21
NUGENT, John 227
NUKLES, J. W. 383
NULL, John 312
   Phillip 312
NUNN, Francis 43,49,134, 135,144,275

OAKLEY(OKLEY), Leban 200, 201,207
OALDFIELD, William 12
OBRIEN, Denis 201
ODELL(ODLE), James 399
   John P. 265,399
   John Prater/Prator 246, 305,398
OGG, George 47
OLAYFER, Alexander 397
OLDHAM(ODAM), Abraham 87
   George 38,48,58,95,133, 135,144,275
   James 168
   John 56,243,264,300
   Richard 33,38,48,58,95, 121,135,163,211
   Taply (H) 39
OLIPHANT, ___ 207
OLIVANT, Dr. 127
OLIVER, Alexander 29,297
   Andrew 177,239,305,307, 371,379,416
   Benjamin 311,315,316

OLIVER, cont'd:
   Elijah 55
   Elizabeth 286,400,429
   John 50,248,297,311
   Joseph 165
   Rebecca 379,425
   Samuel 50,260,267,306, 315,379
ONEAL(O'NEAL), James 311, 313
ONEILLY, Jas. C. 253
ORR, Agness 368
   Alexander 37,264
   James John 72
   Jehu 219,268,332
   Robert 194,195,200, 274,364,368,395
   Samuel 368
   Thomas 368,370,371
   Timothy 274
   William 281,282,368, 371,408
OSBURN(OSBERN,OSBOURN, OSBOURNE), ___ 295
   Morgan 6,15,30,64,69, 186,251
   Thomas 13,350
   Thomas, Sr. 127
   William 13,30,64
OSIPHANT, Dr. 259
OSTIN, Thomas 356
OTTERY, Wm. 221
OTWELL, Deborah 218
   William 183,194,195, 218,264,289,290
   William, Jr. 183,184
OWENBY, Joel 202
OWEN(OWENS,OWIN,OWNE), ___ 211
   Clement 76,173,176
   Daniel 305,342,351, 364,365
   Elijah 4,12,14,16,48, 88,100,112
   Elizabeth 8
   Hardy 146,165,329,385
   John 29
   Mary 381
   Ralph 8,71,76,157
   Samuel 196
   William 102,110,167, 369
OWINGS, Archeble 212
OWL, William 237

PACE, Demsy 425
   William 326,342,387
PAGAN(PAGEN), Archibald 397
PAGE, Nathan 13
PALMER(PALMOUR), John 277
   Jonathan 217
   Jos. 200
   Solomon 107,217,264, 276,376
PAPON(PASSON?), Major 162
PARK(H)ADUR,(PARKADEN), James/Jas. 251,261,264
PARISH, Thomas 411,416
PARKER, ___ 75
   David 366
   James 42,298,366
   John 43,51,110,129, 305,316,366
   Matthew 288
   Robert 58,256,272,310, 366,413
   "Widow" 331,333
PARMORE(PARMER), William 167,266
PARNE, ___ 265
PARNEL, Edward 69
PARIS(PARRIS,PARRISSES), (next page)

PARIS (and variations)
  cont'd:
    George 123,171
    Henry 421
    Richd. 58,65,71
PARSONS, Edmund 173,218,
    254,326,331
  Henry 322
  James 326,331
  John 7,54,55,131
  Major 47,129,257,258,
    267,294,306
  Thomas 47
  William 28,173,218,
    224,326,331
PASHEL, Clayton 254
PASMORE(PASSMORE), William
    178,193,224,259,334
PASSON, Lewis 210
  James 378,379,404
  John 231,237,320
  Major 210
PATRICK, Hugh 212
  John 359
PATTEN, Leroy 343
PATERSON(PATTERSON), ____
    245,418
  Alexander 144,293,424
  Ann 244,245
  Archibald 355
  George 109
  Hugh 247
  James 109,120,131,143,
    199,251,308
  John 11,12,38,62,97,
    150,151,169,244,245,
    264,266,285,326,335,
    370,403
  John, Jr. 17
  John, Sr. 17
  Joseph 80
  Josiah 47,80,93,300,
    324
  Mary 355
  Nancy 403
  Thomas 120,243,264
  William 17,18,36,56,
    114,115
PAUL, William 29
PAYNE(PAINE)(PAYN?), Eb-
    enezer 261,264
  George 50,74,75,150,
    154,419
  Geo. D. 405,422
  Henry 50
  Isaac 231
  James 128
  Jane 257,264
  L. 297
  Ledford 47,105,106
  Mr. 299
  Mary 304
  Moses 43,111,178,197,
    231,259,295,304
  Seth 188
  Thomas 109,143,282
  William 146,147,153
PEACE, Patrick 338
PEACOCK, Robert 298
PEARCE, George 10,30,78,
    84,100,172,191
PEARCY, John 19
PEARMAN, Thomas 65
PEARSON, David Laurence
    378
  Harry 23
  Henry 133,168,376,411,
    427
  Mary 168
PEEK, John 244,264
PEEPLES, John 249
PEG,(PEGG), Saml. 320
  Wm. 222,320

PELLISON, William 216
PENDERGRASS, John 16,38,
    316
PENMAN(PERIMAN?), Edward
    245
PENNINGTON, W. 201
PENRY, Henry 245
PEPPER, John 38,48,58,100,
    176
  Samuel/Saml. 176,362,
    363
PEREMAN, Joel 236
PERENIEU, John 142
PERISEMON, ____ 86
PERKINS, Abraham 166,189,
    190,236
  Agnes 213
  Andrew 98
  Fanny 340,341
  Gabriel 252
  Israel 333
  John 45,46,134,325,335,
    340,341,358
  Moses 91,154,191,226,
    363,372,380
  N. 213
  Nicholas/Nicals 127,
    217,235,264
  Peter 58,141,166,189,
    190,213,236,362
  Robert 46
  Sabra 28
  Sarah 96
  Solomon 46,341,409
  Thos. 213
  William 358
  William Gabriel 269
PERRY, Benjamin 7,18,25,31,
    34,69,107,115,125,153,
    157,160,168,188,217,
    237,276,300,331
  Jonathan 364
  Nathan 25
  Nathaniel 2,7,18,25,31,
    34,43,49,66,69,73,85,
    88,91,95,96,109,110,
    125,129,144,146,147,
    153,154,157,160,168,
    169,188,190,203,214,
    217,265,285,287,291,
    318,330,350,372
  Susanna(h) 88,160
PERSON(PERSONS), Harry 165,
    317,418
PERVIS, ____ 329
PETERSON, John 289
PETTIGREW, James 14,59
PEWIT(PEWITT,PEUTT), Fields
    54,55,263
  Fiedl(Field?), Sr. 291
PEYNE, Lindsay 322
PHAGAN(PHAGANS,PHAGENS,
  PHEGANS), Phillip 21,61,
    86,150,167,363
  Phillip, Jr. 363
PHARES, William 398
PHEAGANS, Moses 292
PHILLIPS, Elias 315,377,
    378
  Jacob 36
  John 232,372,377,409
  Lemuel 199
  Robert 95
  Samuel 199
PHILPOTT, John 271
PHINNY(PHINNEY,PHINERY),
  Henry 245
  Patrick 187
PHROW, Peter 423
PICKLESMER, Abraham 393
  Henry 393
PICKENS, Andrew 1,2,21,22,
    28,35,41,46,53,62,72,

PICKENS, Andrew cont'd:
    73,77,83,84,85,90,91,
    94,131,138,152,166,
    168,169,185,221,232,
    234,241,272,283,301,
    309,312,313,320,328,
    331,332,334,345,353,
    361,374,411,421
  Andrew, Jr. 59,294,
    306,310,344,396,411,
    426
  Dilley 339
  E. 380
  Eleanor/Elenor/Elli-
    nor 215,255,346
  Eleanor, Sr. 346
  Elizabeth 339
  Elizabeth Baskins 341
  Elizabeth Sturd 19
  Ellender/Elander/El-
    linder 19,227,285
  Ezekiel 56,129,411,
    415,416,421,426
  Gabriel 110,143
  Israel 19,64,165,278,
    331,339,341,346,380
  Israel, Jr. 19,341
  John 19,59,62,68,125,
    206,211,250,338,341,
    361,414
  John, Sr. 66,146
  Joseph 66,172,250,263,
    274,338
  M. 165
  Margaret 59
  Mary 19,339
  Matilday 19
  Rebecca/Rebekah 41,339
  Robert 5,9,16,38,39,
    46,48,58,75,142,182,
    188,248,281,346,385
  Sally 341
  Sarah 125,146,338,341
  William 19,341
  William Gabriel 110
PIERCE, Elizabeth 72
  George 7
  Levi 15,72,90
PIERSON, James 397
  Joel 236
PILES, Reubin 47
PILGRAM(PILGRIM), Amos 419
  Michael 141,169,419
  Thomas 138,141,338
PINCKNEY, ____ 246,340
  Charles 21,31,32,33,
    35,36,37,39,42,44,51,
    60,62,64,65,69,71,72,
    73,75,78,79,82,85,86,
    87,88,89,93,96,00,101,
    102,104,105,108,109,
    111,120,121,122,123,
    124,126,128,130,131,
    133,135,136,137,138,
    139,140,141,143,145,
    146,148,150,151,152,
    153,154,156,158,159,
    160,162,163,164,165,
    167,169,172,173,174,
    178,181,182,184,185,
    189,192,193,194,196,
    200,202,203,204,205,
    206,207,208,209,210,
    211,214,215,216,217,
    219,220,222,224,226,
    229,233,235,238,240,
    242,244,257,259,266,
    268,270,271,272,273,
    274,275,279,281,284,
    285,286,289,291,293,
    295,296,297,299,301,
    303,305,306,308,311,
    313,315,319,320,324,

PINCKNEY, Charles cont'd:
  325,327,332,333,337,
  340,342,346,348,349,
  352,354,356,357,358,
  359,360,361,362,363,
  364,365,368,369,376,
  379,383,386,387,389,
  390,396,397,398,400,
  401,402,404,405,412,
  414,415,419,427,428
  Charles Cotesworth 35,
    36
  Genl. 139
  Gov. 227
  H. 403,411
  Mary 35,36
  Thomas/Thos. 25,27,29,
    30,31,32,34,37,45,46,
    47,48,49,50,51,57,59,
    61,62,64,65,66,67,68,
    69,74,75,76,79,85,86,
    95,97,106,107,109,110,
    111,114,115,116,117,
    119,121,123,126,127,
    129,131,132,143,146,
    148,149,150,153,154,
    159,160,162,163,165,
    168,169,180,183,190,
    194,195,198,202,207,
    209,210,213,214,216,
    221,224,227,228,230,
    233,235,237,248,254,
    269,272,275,278,279,
    285,287,291,294,296,
    300,304,311,321,322,
    325,326,331,332,334,
    335,337,338,339,340,
    347,348,350,352,354,
    358,359,361,367,372,
    373,376,377,378,384,
    385,386,393,396,398,
    399,402,405,408,411,
    413,423
PINEY, Thomas 140
PINKERTON, Matthew 291
  John 255,422
PINKSTON, Ann 332
  Levina 364
  Obadiah 332
  William 364,395
PINNELL, James 230
PINSON, Joseph 403,406
PIRONEAU, John 132
PITCHFORD, Daniel 280
  Eli 280
  Rebecah 280
PITMAN, Daniel 256
PITTMAN, John 233
  Noah 1
PITTS, Charles 379,389
  Mary 161
  William 59
PLUNKET, Charles 275,404
POGUE, Elizabeth 150
  James 150,187
POLLARD, Richard 43,120,
    314
POLLOCK(POLOCK,POLICK),
  Elizabeth 32,37,147,
    150
  James 147,150,187,384
  John 32,37,77,150,420
PONDER, Amos 119
  James 203
  John 142
POOL, ___ 359
  Walter 292
POOR(POORE), William 10,
    30,75,100,135,191,286,
    361,362,409,427
POPE, Jehu 26,76,79,81,
    84,94,149,150,192,193,
    415,416

PORTER, ___ 309
  Adam 70
  Andrew 29,70,177
  Hugh 366
  James 189
  John 138
  Robert 366
  Samuel/Saml. 100,101,
    119,120,128,132,172
PORTMAN, George 60
  John 43,49,60,82,93,
    98,107,109,111,141,
    146,153,161,188,207,
    208,210,264,273,276,
    282,418
  John, Jr. 126
  John, Sr. 98,112,126,
    200
  Thomas 404
PORTWOOD, Robert 255,262,
    372,408,409
POSEY, Behethlem 358
  Francis 385
  Hezekiah 196,197,389,
    394,396
  Jesse 313
  Jesse H. 313,314,354,
    405,408
POSTELL, John 2
POTTER, Henry 55
POTTS(POTS), Ezekiel 141,
    391
  George 86,287,391
  John 391
POUGE, ___ 408
POUND(POUNDS), John 293,
    361,391,404
POWEL(POWELL), Abraham 132,
    299
  Absalom 187
  Ales 381,382
  Allen 382
  James 104,243,261,381,
    382
  James, Sr. 282
  John 93,120,160,240,
    241,264,273,280,296,
    320,322
  Mark 12,13
  Mary 120
  Matilda 246
  Ranson 376
  Richard 131
  Robert 18,140,200,246,
    262,264
  William 282
POWERS, Alerand 333
  Alexander 93,240,264
  David 133
  Florence 240
  Jas. 406
  Samuel 417
PRATER, Archelaus 67,74
  Elianor 211
  John 46,182,195,210,
    370
  Phillip 39,195,200
  Thomas 313
  "Widow" 378
  William 370
PRATOR (see above)
PRATT, Francis 411
  James 192,396
  John 151,161
PREWIT(T),(PRUET(T),PRUIT,
  PRUITT), David 135,147,207,
    279,335
  Drury 335,425
  Dudley 359
  Field/Fields 92,101,
    102,131,141,185,226,
    237,245,246,264,291,
    376,391,423

PREWETT (and variations)
  cont'd:
  Field, Jr. 92,102,292
  Field, Sr. 79,92,102,
    158
  John 298
  Michael 207,279
  Patience 298
  Thomas 335
  W. Solomon 288
PRICE, Benja. 135
  Caleb 316
  Callum/Collum/Cullem/
    Cullum 66,220,254
  Elizabeth 32,34,321
  James 93
  John 379
  Joseph 37,106,117,185,
    271,321,364,396
  Kellum 34
  Lot 225
  Penuel 350
  Richard 93
  William 316
PRICHARD(PRITCHARD,PREACH-
  ARD), ___ 148
  Eleanor 177
  Elizabeth 182
  James 177,182,383
  Joshua 425
  Mary 27,146,152,358
  P. 199
  William 27,59,167,177,
    182,383,391,398
PRINCE, Edea 156
  Edward 67,68,70
  Isham 320
  Jas. 264
  John 346
  Joseph 242
  Josiah 156
  Levy 322
  Richard 155,156
  Robt. 29
  William 243,320
PRINE, Francis, Jr. 113
PUCKET(PUCKETT), James 6
  John 105
  Richd. 6
PUET, Fields 62
  Fields, Jr. 62
PUGH, ___ 404
  David 91,303,365,379
  Elizabeth 303
  J. H. Willoughby 62
  William 207
  Willoughby 91,97,268,
    303,365,379
PULLEN, Leroy 339
PURCELL, Henry 41
PURDY, Henry 312
PURSLEY, ___ 120
PURVIANES(PURVINES),Moses
    136,373,374
PURVIS, Col. 65
  Eliza Ann 89,117
  John 27
PUTMAN(PUTTMAN), ___ 375
  Barnard 12
  Barnet 269
  Daniel 127,149,257,
    264,265,279,287,300,
    304,316
  Ezekiel 235,309
  Jesse 427
  Mary 350
  Thomas 279,309,350,
    404
PUTNAM, Barnet 12,423
  Daniel 29,41
PUTTEET, John 390,398
PYLE(PYLES), Nicholas 129
  Reuben 54,143,414

PYLE(PYLES), cont'd:
    Samuel 129
    Wm. 77,78
    William, Jr. 11
QUARRELS, David 405
QUEAL(QUEL), John 178
QUILLEN, William 189,190
QUORLES, David 398

RACKLEY, William 336,378,
    397
RADEN, John 279
RAGLAND, Sarah 266
RAGSDALE, Asa 170
    Benjamin 126,141,170,
        302,320
    Jesse 170
    John 103,120,121,144,
        244,264
    Michael 306
    Peter 243,244,264,308
RAIN, Edwin 263
RAINES, Giles 70
RAINEY, Benjamin 267,268,
    322
    Capt. 153
RAINS, James (J) 30
RAINWATER, Hartgraves 385
    Robert 385
RALSTON(RAULSTON), Frances
    11
    John 11
    Lewis 11,73
    R. 11
RAME, Jacob 44,138,197
RAMEY, Christopher 152
RAMI, Jacob 76
RAMSEY, Alexander 1,9,12,
    16,73,90,212,255,264,
    322,340
    Christopher 98
    David 191,236,245,251,
        252,264,283,284
    E. 2
    Ephraim 2,247
    H. Jos. 264
    J. 394
    Jas. H. 247
    John 290,361
    John T. 356
    Joseph Hall 247
    Mary 73,247,302
RAMY, Christopher 358
    Thomas 335
    William 335
RAND, John 371
RANEY, Benjamin 425
RANFROW, Agnes 252
    William 252
RANKIN, ___ 161
    James 185
    John 21,158
    Leah 21
    Rachel 137
    Robert 21,30,37,105,
        106,111,137,185,366
    William/Wm. 146,241,
        281,282,416
RAPER(RAPIER), John 84
    Thomas 84,138,194,226
RATLICK, Abner 425
RAULINS, Thos. W. 357
RAVENELL, James 259
    Stephen 94,98,216,252,
        294
RAVENOR, David 288
RAVINEL, Danl. Jas. 196
READ (READE,REED,REEDE,
REID,REIDE),
    Abraham 51
    Archebald 126
    David 267

REED(and variations) cont'd:
    Elizabeth 39,237,264
    G. 237
    George 111,202,424
    George Miller 276
    George Walker 218,356
    Hamilton 152
    Harmon 89,302
    Isabella 192
    Jacob 4,126,156,162,
        200,224,297,319
    Jean 272,346
    Jehu 259,264,269
    John 115,196,252,269,
        297,298,303,333,339,
        367,385,409
    John L. 238
    Joseph 4,62,66,72,73,
        85,92,97,107,109,114,
        115,117,140,158,163,
        173,174,180,184,185,
        192,193,194,196,202,
        213,215,216,218,220,
        224,225,228,230,250,
        259,260,276,279,285,
        291,302,310,318,323,
        341,354,356,373,377,
        380,411,414,415
    Joseph, Sr. 218
    Joshua 146
    Leonard 396
    Mary 39
    Mathew 68
    Nathan 215,272
    Nathaniel 65,111,215,
        266,267,321,355,370,
        377
    Nathan'l. ,Jr. 366
    Nathl., Sr. 366
    Rebecca/Rebeckah/Re-
        beccah 216,282
    Reuben 128,171,329,344,
        345,350,384,387,389
    Richard 346
    Robert 346
    Sally 146
    Samuel 342
    Sarah 4,39,126
    Stephen 204
    Violet 370
    W. 93,160,163,171,182,
        188,190,192,202,204,
        206,207,213,221,222,
        272,288,316,318,320,
        354
    W. P. 117
    W. W. 88,89,93,101,103,
        104,108,109,110,111,
        115,121,122,123,127,
        128,132,144,149,151,
        152,157,169,185,209,
        William 3,4,9,13,22,
        39,79,114,115,130,159,
        160,162,164,171,173,
        174,177,187,188,189,
        198,208,214,215,216,
        221,225,234,236,237,
        244,247,262,264,266,
        267,269,276,283,301,
        316,328,345,360,362,
        370,380,392,396,413,
        418,420
REARDON, Patrick 127
REDEN(REDDAN,REDDEN),
    Elizabeth 427
    James 66,74,427
    Nancy 316
    Sidney 316
REEDER(READER,REIDER),
    Elizabeth 326
    Isaac 329
    Jonathan 183,305,312,
        346,419,422,424

REEDER, cont'd:
    Joshua 84,169,183,244,
        245,264,285,305,326,
        327,329
    Simon 183,245
REESE(REECE), ___ 144
    Mr. 189,350
    Anna 192
    Cabbin Jacob 185
    Charles 424
    Dobson 383
    E. 223,244,248
    E. G. 379
    Edmond 312
    Edward 248
    Edwin 182,186,223,264,
        379
    George 149,150,192,193,
        299,429
    H. Dobson 327,379
    Henry D. 379,384
    Henry Dobson 186,384,
        391,398
    Jacob 162,180,218
    Jane 131,182
    Leah 182
    Levi 247
    Peter 124,262,283
    Rebecca (Beckey E.)391
    Rose(or Ross) 262,296,
        406
    Susanna 196
    Thomas 186,264,391
    Thomas L. 41,93,150
    Thomas S. 131,152,174,
        175,241
    Thomas Sidney 164,174
    Wm. 159
REEVES(REAVES), Burgess 19
    Burril/Burrell 133,267
    George 165,412
    Isaac 327
    John 268,288,301,325,
        336,358
    John, Jr. 258
    John, Sr. 258
    Jordan 36,87,296
    Mallachi 336
    Sarah 325,358
    Simon 239
    Timothy 165,267,322,
        425
REGANS, Powel 388
REGGS, Wm. 264
REIGHLY, William 56
RENEY, Benjamin 267
    Thos. 2
RENFRO, Wm. 264
RENO, John 65,71,271
RESONER, William 309
REYNOLDS, Archelous 384
    Arch. W. 363
    Bartemous/Bartemius/
        burt 225,235,294,384
    Jeremiah 235
    Jno./John 173,225,231
    Milburton 225
RHEA, Matthew 195,196
RHODEN, ___ 291
RICE, Charles 9,69,84,119,
    153,193,197,225,226,
    312,346,359,361,372
    Duncan 261
    Edward 171
    Henry 226,372
    Hezekiah 38,133,135,
        144,260,264,422
    Isaac 207
    Jacob 333
    James 47,80,116,119,
        140,324
    Kezekiah 58
    Mary 213

RICE, cont'd:
    Otheneil 56
    Peter 247
RICHARD(RICHARDS), ___ 426
    Amos 259
    John 303
    Thomas 202,221,426
    W. 206
    William 41,92,125,145,
    159,196,199,221,286,
    290,299,327,335,339,
    340,385,401,408,409
    William P. 113
RICHARDSON, Amos 248,264,
    270
    James B. 356
    M. 261
    Mathias 64,110,259,
    262,263,275
    Matthew 243
    Richard 33,42,84,86,
    167
    Robert 367
    William 22,257,265
RICHEY(RICHY,RITCHEY),
    James 275
    John 163,275
    Robert 14
RICK, Anthony 338
RIDDLE(RIDDELS), Andrew
    42
    Randolph 217
    Richard 374,405
RIDEN, James 172
RIDGDEL, Mary 420
RIDGELL, John 115
RIDGEWAY, James 369
RIDGWAY, Carity 123
    Charles 194
    David 170
    Samuel 123,143,205
RIDING, James 75,361
RIGDALE, Mary 158
RIGGS(RIGS), ___ 326
    Elizabeth 360,392
    Robert 246
    Saml. 145
    Sarah 25,177
    William 20,145,177
RIGHLY(RIGLEY,RIEGHLEY),
    William 167,203,394
RIGHT, Adam 229
    James ___ 257
    John 239
RILEY, Patrick 118
RINGLAND, George 52,55
RISE, Chas. 264
RISENER(RISONER), Thomas
    288,312,318
RISENISON, Backster 290
RISLL, John 212
RIVES, William, Jr. 232
ROACH(ROCH), Anna 50
    Henry 405
    Jane 245
    L. Benj. 264
    Little B. 245
    Little Berry 62,405
    Rebeccah 299
    Stephen 50,120,299
    Thomas 59
    William/Wm. 8,50
ROANE, Archibald 302
ROARK, Christian 14
ROBB, John 151,161
ROBERTS(ROBERDS), ___ 143
    Alice 18
    Amos 86,87,90,360,372
    Brook 178
    Elias 48,58,59
    Isaac 137
    James 18,62
    Jane 115

ROBERTS, cont'd:
    John 18,55,159,220,248,
    249,264,279,287,393
    Joseph 165,238,249,265
    Joseph, Jr. 107
    Joseph, Sr. 107
    Margaret 14
    Mary 85,137
    Richard 18
    Richard B. 319
    Richard Brooke/Brooks
    26,173,319,322
    Stephen 218,233,263,
    276
    Thomas 14,18,48,248,
    249,296,326,378,379,
    404
    Wiley/Willey 317,323
    William 4,12,18,55,62,
    165
    Zachariah 95
    Zephaniah/Zaphaniah 58,
    115,216,237,277,288,
    382
ROBERTSON, ___ 198
    Abner 217,219,307,354
    Ann 417
    Edward 340
    Geo. 417
    James 28,45,104
    John 11,20,149,251,256,
    264,352
    Samuel 104,148,317,417
    Thomas 25,36,74,83,145,
    221,247,298
    William/Wm. 151,183,299
ROBINS(ROBBINS), Abner 318
    Albert 56,79,79,158,414
    John 332
    Joshua 296,309,390
    Levi 230,264,279,339,
    391,414
    William 165,423
ROBINSON, ___ 259,407
    Abner 354,375
    Albert 376
    Alexander 65,178,193
    Allen 382
    Amos Garrett 199
    Andrew 167
    Elisha 168,199,315,327,
    420
    Elizabeth 390
    Ephraim 177,259,384,386,
    391
    James 77
    Jean 164
    John 11,30,49,63,88,99,
    104,105,112,142,157,160,
    161,164,167,168,192,199,
    200,202,260,264,278,279,
    315,316,322,334,336,348,
    376,388,420
    John, Jr. 324,376
    John, Sr. 324
    Michael 83
    Nathaniel 33,150,390
    Peggy 324
    Richard 148,167,177,178,
    224,386,389,404,420
    Samuel 58,83,113,205,
    245,257,262,263,264,
    308,349,355,410
    Sarah (Robeson) 142
    Susannah 375,376
    Thomas 20,145,228,302
    Thomas Carter 315
    William 23,199,324,370,
    375,386,420
ROBITS, Joseph 318
ROBUCK(REOBUCK,ROEBUCK),
    George 12,149,324
    Nim. 253

ROE, Andrew 27,44,51,69,
    104,114,165,339,381,
    389
    Anselm 4,27,114,165,
    303,321
    Benjamin 51
    Berry 334,356
    Berryman 116,193
    Solomon 40,94,116,283
ROGERS(RODGERS), Adam 148,
    154,231,259,262,264,
    383
    Clayton 164
    H. 264
    Hugh 25,54,92,193,224,
    231,259,261,264,269,
    270
    Hugh, Jr. 231,259,386
    Hugh, Sr. 386
    James 5,148,231,269,
    270,386
    Jeany 270
    Jenny 270
    John 50,61,290,386
    John, Jr. 290
    John, Sr. 290
    Lucinda 351
    Margaret 259,269
    Nancy 270
    Sarah 231,389
    Samuel 1
    T. R. 68
    William 290,389
    Wm. F. 401
    William T. 371
ROLAND(ROLLAND,ROWLAND),
    Charles 154
    Peter 118
ROLSTON(ROLLSTON), ___
    282,406
    John 12,169
    Lewis 13,147,169,299
ROPE(ROSS?), William 18
ROSS(ROSE), ___ 144,207,
    241,275,418
    Andrew 22,116,274
    Barbarra 207,275
    Brown 87
    Daniel 213,259,264
    David 3,36,147,180,200,
    201
    Francis/Frank 121,131,
    132,236,289
    George 67,123,151
    Hugh 39,216,237,264,
    277
    Hudson/Hutson 217,241,
    300
    James 66,67,87,116,147,
    161,179,180,200,218,
    236,289,389
    John 147,161,207,236,
    264,275,278,425
    John, Sr. 67
    Patty 351
    Pricilla 132
    Rhoda/Rhody 132,236
    Samuel 121,132,236,264,
    289
    William 86,105,185,199,
    206,208,214,217,240,
    241,246,248,264,273,
    276,321,351,392,393
    Wm., Jr. 217
    William, Sr. 302
    William B. 147,180,289
    Wm. Brown 275
ROSSON, Elisha 351
ROSMOND(ROSAMOND,ROSEMOND),
    Capt. 52,64,110
    James 25,49
    James, Jr. 169

ROTTON(ROTTEN,ROTTIN),
  John 115,129,170,210,
    226,319,320
  Mary 115
ROW, Andrew 209
ROWAN(ROWEN), Elizabeth
    362,368
  Nancy 422
  Samuel 255,362,368,
    402,422
  William 422
ROWLAND,   186
  James 420
  Thomas 376
ROYSTON, R. C. 60
ROZELL, Solomon 297
ROZETT, Solomon 297
RU(C)KELSMER, Henry 392,
  393
RUCKLEMEN,   392
RUDDLE, Andrew 39,164
RUDIFILL, John 156
RUKER, Benjamin 409
  Milly 409
RUPEL(RUSSELL), William 96
RUSH, John 259,313
  Moses 352
RUSHTON, John L. (S.?) 196
RUSK, John 5,191,194,260,
    261,272,294,313,325,
    354
RUSSEL(RUSSELL,RUSEL,RUS-
ELL),   120
  Arnold 28
  George 208,209,297,
    301,326,331,335,336
  Harriet 204
  John 127,163,294,295,
    327,328
  Margaret 28
  Mary 41,204
  Mathew/Matthew 182,316
  Sara 209
  Thomas 291,361,384,386
  Thomas C. 120,139,204
  Thomas Commander 21,41,
    44,67,408
  William 386
RUSTIN, Thomas 107
RUSTON, John Baker 279,280
RUTH, Jonathan 222,325,329,
    330
  Mariam/Maryam 222
RUTHERFORD, James 392
RUTLAND, Lydia 174
RUTLEDGE, Edward 27,293,
    296,324,332,333,373,
    380,390,400,422
  Henry 27
  John 59,73,87,93,164,
    310,317
RYLIE, Patrick 3
RYNOLDS, Hugh 74

ST. CLAIR, Alexander 358
SADLER(SADDLER), Richard
    16,31,160,190,392
SAILOR(SAILORS), Agnes 346
  John 346,386
SALBERT, Samuel, Jr. 268
SALLOR(SALER), Phillip 168
SALMON,   308
  George 35,44,58,88,109,
    115,118,146,338
SALTER, Polley 286
  William 286
SANDERS, Isaac 293
  John 128
  Leon(Sion) 390
  Sarah (Sally) 293
  William 390
SANDERSON, General 256
SANDFORD, John 52

SARGENT, Daniel 169,222
SARTER, John 345
SARTOR, John P. 189
SARTER, Peter 392
  Sarah 189
  William 375,392
SATTER, Delilah 392
  William 392
SAT(T)ERFIELD, Jas. 230,
    264
  James, Sr. 352
  Jesse 398
  Rachel 143
  William 143,319
SAVAGE, Samuel 428
  Milley 428
SAXON, Mr. 32
  Charles 61,369,380
  Hugh 208
  Jacob 130
  James 140
  Jesse 30,275
  John 175,209
  Jonathan 215
  Joseph 130
  Joshua 32,67,68,76,77,
    87,90,91,97,106,107,
    112,113,114,119,121,
    130,131,133,134,135,
    137,139,140,142,143,
    145,147,156,157,158,
    159,161,163,164,166,
    177,179,187,199,207,
    216,218,220,223,226,
    227,230,235,237,238,
    254,274,277,279,296,
    317,385,386,395,407,
    408,413,419
  Judith 61
  Mary 30
  Nancy 187
  Sally 386
  Samuel 30,61,145,154,
    167,201,207,392
  Squire 201
SAXTON, Robert 284
SCELTON, Robert 316
SCHRIMSTER(SCHRIMSHERE),
  Robert 55,203
SCOOTS,   178
SCOTT, Francis 97
  Isabella 285,291
  James 9,14,127,137,147,
    157,260,265,390
  John 126,127,165,402,
    409,421
  Nancy 157,260
  Patrick 147
  Robert 147,285,291,374,
    405,410
  William 5,160,238
SCURLOCK, James 265
  Rebeca 265
SEABORN, James 122
SEARS, Thomas 234
SEAWRIGHT, William 18,27,
    34
SEEGO, Robert 204
SELF, Presley 379
SELFRI(D)GE, Robert 129,
    174
SELLARS, David 379
SELMSER(?), George 131
SELMON(SILMON), Benjamin
    6,362,369
  Benjamin, Sr. 369,370
  David 370
  Jane 362
  Lydia 369,370
  William 362
SEWRIGHT, Wm. 220
SESSON, James 217
SEXTON,   193,230

SHACKLEFORD(SHAKELFORT),
  W. M. 124
  William 165,232,253,
    259,261,264,274,276,
    296,297,312
SHADDIN(SHADON), David 105
SHAMBLER(CHAMBLER), Zad-
    dock/Zadick 386
SHAMBLY, Benjamin 57
SHAMLEY, Lewis 427
SHAMLIN,   425
SHANKLIN,   282
  Hannah 193,282,284
  Thomas 193,215,282,
    284,285,333
SHANNON, John 28,78,91,154,
    177,191,210,268,426
  Owin 426
SHARP(SHARPE), Elam 285,
    330,338,272
  Isham 66
  Robt. 133
SHARTON, Stephen 335
SHAW, Alexander 344
  Leonard 94
  Leonard D. 72,93,125
  Leonard D. Klyne 93
  William 53,173,424
SHELBY, Moses 20,21
  Sarah (Sally) 233,249,
    288,290
  William 233,249,257,
    265,276,288,290,296,
    301,368
SHELOR, Jacob 168,330
SHELTON(SCHELTON), Archi-
    bald 227
  John 19
  Lewis 19,393
  Robert 19
  Taliferro 144
  William 19,406
SHERARD(SHERRARD,SHARRAR,
  SHARRARD,SHERRAR),
    Abe 320
  Alex./Alexander 113,
    145,146,159,173,257,
    263,298,316,320,377,
    381
  John 113,114,145,159,
    173,196
  John, Jr. 146,196
  John, Sr. 146,196
  Miranda 287
SHERRIDAN, Alexander 113
SHERRILL(SHIRRELL), David
    405
  Lewis 16,129,162,211
SHEPPARD(SHEPHERD), Ann
    89,419
SHEW, Archibald 226
SHIELDS,   399
  George 254
  James 149,265,268,316
SHILLITO(SHILLETO), William
    31,186
SHILOR,   282
SHINAULT, Reuben 333
SHIPP(SHIPPE,SHIP),
    258
  Daniel 44,54,143,149,
    281,283,349,385
  Joseph 143,209
  Josiah 5,61,152,169,
    349,407
  Richard 5,213,258,266,
    280,375
  William 349
SHIPPEN, Edward 108
SHIRLEY(SHURLEY,SHERLEY),
  James 14,238,263,394
  John 168,194,274
  Joshua 168

SHIRLEY, cont'd:
  Mary (Margaret) 14,54
  Richard 54
  Lewis 246
  Thomas 14,54,154,358,
  419
  Wm. 264
SHOCKLEY, Aquilla/Aquilly
  269,375
  Gideon 392
  James 11,105,112,260,
  269,335,342,345,375,
  392
  Jesse 335,375
  Quil_ 286
  Thomas/Thos. 41,107,
  189,282,335,345,375
  Thomas, Jr. 12,189,269,
  286,335,392
  Thomas, Sr. 11,12,29,
  112,127,189,286,304,
  335
SHOTWELL, George 281,370
  Hannah 118,119,280,281
  John 111
  Moss 119
  Nathaniel 416
  Reuben 280,281
SHULER(SHOOLER,SHULOR,SU-
LER), George 16,38,46,140,
  180,224,247,248,266,
  268,270,381
  Mary 16,268
SHWANSEY (see SWANCY)
SIDDLE,___ 174
SILER(SILLER), Wimer 32,
  77
SILMON, Benjamin 344,367,
  368
  Benjamin, Sr. 344
  David 344,368
  Lydia 368
  William 367
SIMKINS, Arthur 182
  Eldred 415
SIMS(SIMMS,SYMMS,SYNNES),
  Avis 228,275
  Charles 29,173
  D. 370
  Daniel 1,79,214,228,
  275,338,341,353,406
  David 154
  Fanny 283
  Henry 49,53,67,134,
  149,186,283,385,388
  James 69,108,167,213,
  383,398,399
  Jane 283
  Nancy 399
  William 224,283,301,
  334,351,377,426
SIMMONS, James 179,380
  Thos. 36,233
  Wm. 340
SIMON, Thomas 237
SIMPSON, Archibald 395
  Baxter 290
  Davis 395
  Eleanor 337
  George 104
  Hugh 108,287,353,355,
  393,416
  James 16,40,120,337,
  364
  John 27,33,34,40,66,
  107,146,174,194,214,
  223,236,249,252,264,
  269,277,318,361,395,
  400,405
  Leonard 429
  Reuben 154
  William 146,340,371
SINGLAR, Peter 150,371
SINGLETON, George 343

SINGLETON, cont'd:
  John 246,264,276
  Lewis 246
  Robert 141
  Rutha 246
  William 275
SINKLER(SINCLER,SINKER),
  Margaret 259,260
  Peter 2,84,107,120,125,
  131,299
  Robert 278
  Sarah 63,221,346
SISELAND(?), William 16
SISK, Gabriel 343
SIS(S)ON, David 208
  James 298
  John 275,298
SITTON, John 28,254,330
SIZEMORE, James 9
SKELTON(SCELTON),___ 404
  Jacob 127,279,309,372,
  404
  John 37,69,330,406
  Lewis 289
  Patty 134
  Robert 127,268,406
  Thomas 87,156,360,413
  William 6,31,134,156,
  175,310,319
SLAITOR, George 412
  James George 212
  Jno. 212
  John, Sr. 212
  Levi 212
SLATER(SLATOR,SLATTER),
  James 247,261,302,309,
  390,405
  Jeremiah 381
SLATERN, James 246
SLATON, George 19,140,179,
  349,397
  James 302
  Sarah 304
  William 304,369
SLOAN, Adam 382
  Christian 423
  David 73,89,97,101,185,
  202,216,218,221,223,
  247,248,261,264,265,
  272,292,297,328,354,
  379,383,391,422,428
  David, Jr. 292,388,412
  James 258
  Richard 73
  Robert 66,74
  Thompson 383
  William/Will'm 28,78,
  83,86,90,91,101,140,
  141,216,243,248,273,
  291,323,358,391
SMART, Thomas 51
SMELCER,___ 381
SMELSER, George 266
SMITH,___ (also Smythe)
  81,135,161,389
  Aaron/Aron 19,102,286,
  290,337,393,401
  Abner 338,340,384
  Alexander 307
  Andrew 40
  Andrew, Jr. 45
  Andrew, Sr. 45
  Ann 316
  Anna 66,88
  Anne Louisa 35,36
  Bazzel 182
  Benjamin 46,160,169,
  183,202,392,411,416
  Buckner 273,353
  Catherine 407
  Charity 304
  Daniel 111,134,252
  Daniel Desausaure 11

SMITH, cont'd:
  David 25,77,86,146,
  153,160,240,241,264,
  270,281,313,337,416
  Ebenezer 295,408
  Edward 162
  Edward Darrell 11
  Edwin 30,33,36,100,
  127,162,361,392
  Edwin B. 429
  Edwin L. 429
  Elazon 177
  Eliazer/Eleazer 290,
  359
  Elisha 418
  Elizabeth 27,214,256,
  262,290,416
  Enoch/Enock 77,105,286
  Evin 92,96
  Ezekiel 8
  Frances 343
  George 11,91,137,158,
  159,213,214,224,237,
  304
  James 79,136,240,261,
  285,291,292,313,326,
  328,331,334,335
  Job 55,146,160,188,
  208,306,416
  Joel 406
  John 2,4,8,12,27,32,
  34,41,66,88,89,109,
  116,122,128,133,134,
  154,158,159,188,199,
  201,220,265,278,279,
  311,316,346,349,359,
  369,379,398,407,411,
  417
  John, Jr. 66
  John Cannon 359
  Jonathan 134,286,290,
  337,364,384
  Joseph 91,127,159,206,
  209,215,235,236,237,
  250,262,264,285,312,
  381,382,387,388,403,
  420
  Joshua 194,289,290
  Josiah 11,194
  Laban 288
  Lettice 299
  Luke 244,249,262,390
  Malinda 287
  Margaret 408
  Mary 36,110,137,145,
  258,278,316,374
  Matilda 287
  Michael 83,85,128,131,
  186,204,253,255,273
  Molly 95
  Nancy 287
  Nimrod 206,221,239,299
  Norris 81,145
  Phillip 348,423
  Rachel 91,137,157,158,
  159,363
  Rebecca/Rebecah 241,
  281,337,416
  Ritter 385
  Robert 27,106,117,118,
  193,202,214,233,256,
  264,265,302,307,324,
  349,397
  Ruth 169,250
  Samuel 87,252,352
  Solomon 249
  Thomas 76,162,281,356
  Thos. Rhett 73
  Whiteaher 427
  "Widow" 137,157,158,
  237
  William 4,36,42,120,
  127,135,139,157,158,

SMITH, cont'd:
    William cont'd: 246,
    287,314,334,348,363,
    417
    William G. 137
SMITHEN, ____ 404
SMITHSON, Albert 278
    Albert Francis 80,105
    Asa 407
    Bartley 199
    Basil/Basley 110
    Marsin/Marson 110,199
    Micajer/Micajah 190,
    199,407
    Sina 80
SNELL, Alexander 352
SNODDY, Borgues 342
    Fergus/Fargus 191,236,
    288
    Samuel 191
SNOWDEN, Charles 252,284
SORDS(SWORDS?), John 290
SORRELLS, John, Sr. 418
SOSSELAND, William 42
SOUTHERLAND, Daniel 384
  (also Sotherland)
    John 265,348
SOUTHERN, Samuel 200
SPEAK(E), H. 326
SPEAK, Hezekiah 128
    John 158,326
    Margaret 15
    Richard 37,80,81,82,
    104,107,216,247,264,
    316
SPEARMAN, David 425
SPEARSON, Robert 316
SPEED, Michael 133,415,
    416
    Robt. W. 29,85
SPEERS(SPEARS), David 66,
    272
    Jesse 41
    Joseph 415
SPENCE, Joseph 187,366
    Nancy 211
    Robert 211
SPENCER, Samuel 55
SPIEREN, Patrick 192
SPORTSMAN, John 423
SPRADLING, David 322
SPRIGG, Rezen/Rezin/Rizin
    258,285,290,322
SPRUIL, Stephen 390
SQUIB, Robt. 45
SQUIER, D. 39
STAGGS, William 281
STAMPS, George 158,376
    Timothy 117,363,367
STANDAGE, Thos. 122
STANDRIDGE, James 134
    Richard 293
    Thomas 383,384
STANLEY(STANDLEY), Ezekiel
    179,180,201
    John 12
    Joseph 4,12,100
    Mary 4
    Rhoda 180
    Thomas 4
STANTON, Christopher 90,
    143
    William 5,135,242,260,
    264,275,328
STANTON(STATON), Major 77
STARK, Ch. 368
STARKE, ____ 40
STARKS, Jeremiah 61
STARR, Caleb 155,287,334
STARRETT(STARRITT), Alex-
    ander 314,343
    B. 9,257,293,299,340,
    347,408

STARRETT, cont'd:
    Benjamin, Sr. 354
    Benjamin 3,7,9,10,15,21,
    25,35,84,131,183,207,
    295,305,325,326,331,335,
    339,353,369,373,376,
    379,401
    James 20,34,292,293,
    299,313,316,317,325,
    327,334,341,349,356,
    376,380,391,401,404,
    410,416
    Mary 314,380
    Moses 166
    William 122,127,166
STATON, George 3,79,80,130
    Major 77
STEAGALL, Richard 417
STEEL(STEELE), ____ 49,186
    Mr. 389,390,394
    Aaron/Arron 96,143,243,
    297,302,308
    Abner 356,426
    Abner A. 183,396
    Abner Alexander 138
    Charles 29,70
    Isaac 31,108,201,238,
    254,264,265,416
    James 108
    Martha 238,254
    Michael 266,287,318,
    416
    W. 77,85,121,134,138,
    149,158,196,282,320
    William/Wm. 22,47,53,54,
    78,94,96,108,109,130,
    136,142,151,155,161,
    165,166,179,193,196,
    197,204,212,213,227,
    229,241,263,265,269,
    283,303,306,307,311,
    313,319,325,329,344,
    369,372,376,399,406,
    413
    William, Jr. 421
STEELER, Wm. 54
STELL, John 290
STENSON, Elijah 58
    William 59
STEPHENS, A. Beach 266
    Henry 240
    Isaiah 5
    James 266,332,343
    John 329,366
    Meshack 171,185,219
    Milley 185
    Samuel 282,301
    Thomas 366
    William 140,397,404
STEPHENSON, Alexander 212,
    413
    Danl. 264
    David 34,235,260
    James 259,267
    John 414,427
    Robert 407
    William 350
STEP(STEPP,STAPP), Jesse
    337
    Joseph 70,99,104,134,
    184,287
    Joseph, Jr. 303
    Joseph, Sr. 303
STEVELEE(STEVELIE), Fred-
    rick 197,391
    John Henry 197,391
STEVENS, Charles 39,47,79,
    85,184,186,202
    Henry 28
    Jerv(a)is Henry 1,71
    Meshack 170
    Polly 382
    Richard 167,386

STEVENS, cont'd:
    Sam 381
    Samuel 301
    Shadrack 381
    William 406
STEVENSON, ____ 155
    Alexander 47,86,87,100,
    142,143
    Andrew 391,392
    Brice 427
    David 100,236,381
    Elijah 4,68,72,204
    Elioner 360
    George 191,391
    Isabel 81
    James 47,87,90,121,142,
    143,156,170,184,255,
    262,360,361
    Jenny 170
    John 132,359,360,391
    Margaret 168
    Robert 8,42,46,56,81,
    117,164,416
    Samuel 287
    Thomas 167,369
    "Widow" 168
    William 19,59,100,135,
    136,170,190,257,265,
    279,311,373,374,377
STEWART(STEUART), Charles
    70
    James 229,264,287
    John 33,44,245,275,
    309,371
    Margaret 229
    Mary A. 229
    Robert 329,354
    William 202,292
STILL, John 323,365,366
STILTS, John 357
STINSON, Elijah 9,82,205
STOCKSTILL, Thomas 411
STONE, B. 190
    Bannister 141
    David 302,323
    H. D. L. J. 217
    Mary 53
    Prichard/Pritchet 322,
    336,415
    Sary 53
    Solomon 414
    Thomas 52,53,65,105,
    336,342
    William/Wm. 264,293,
    349,412,416
STORY, Mary 299
STOVER, Nancy 327
    Obadiah 327
STOW, William 250,265
STRABEL, Joseph 16
STRABLER, ____ 121
STRANGE, Mr. 397
    Edmond 430
    Elizabeth 201,314
    Stephen 39,63,201,314
STRIBLING(STRIBBLING), ____
    292
    Elizabeth (Betsey) 204,
    315
    J. 250,364,374,390,392,
    400,403,404,410,412,
    420,422,423,429
    Jesse 250,276,422
    Nancy 163
    Thomas 103,163,204,216,
    250,263,310,315,317,
    319,323,333,336,403
STRINGER, Daniel 17,18,20,
    34,77,97,212,237,296,
    418
    George 135,181
    Mary 212
STROBEL, Joseph 303

STRONG, cont'd:
    Christopher 40,64,94,
      173,186,187,197,219,
      249,264,312,402
    Elizabeth 249
    Maj. 409
    Sarah 219
STROUD, James 161
STUART, Charles 94,163
    Daniel 152
    James 65,181
    John/Jon 153,268,272,
      320,346,414
    William 180,202,222,
      224,248,264,266,311,
      377,381,405
STURART, Joshua 326
STURGES, William 193
STUTES, Abner 426
SUGGS, Jesse 300
SULES, John 280
SULLIVAN, Andrew 128
    James 406
    William 240
SULLIVANT, ___ 143
    Pleasant 428
    Stephen 11
    Wm. 261
SUMMER, Elizabeth 180
SUMTER, Thomas 40,107
SUNN, Fredrick 249,390
    Dortos Fredrick 175
SUTHERLAND, ___ 257
    Daniel 348
    John 67,68,74,104,150,
      234,237,257
    William 190,348
SUTHERN, Samuel 404
SUTLIFFE, Ellis 267
    John 267
SUTTERFIELD, Robert 271
SUTTON, Abner 369
    James 291,311
    John 254,260,261,264
    Phillip 255,263,330
SWAN(SWANN), James 214,233,
      254,264,265,323,345
    Lewis 135
    Robert 110,167
SWANCY(SWANCEY), Elizabeth
      257
    John 257,286,290,294,
      296
SWAIN, Robert 160
SWEPSON, John 70
SWERLING, John 288
SWIFT, ___ 64
    Elizabeth 205
    Wm. 63,64,68,186,205,
      251
SWILLING, Joseph 77,91
SWILLIVANT(SWELLIVENT,
SWEVILLENT, SULLIVANT),___
      65,162
    Hewlit/Hewlet 53
    Millinder 53
    Moses 53
SWINNEY, Joel 390
SWINNY, Stephen B. 400
SWOFFORD, James 408
SWORDS(SUORDS,SEWARDS),
    Eleanor 66,368
    James 109,133
    John 11,17,37,66,125,
      257,265,288,368
    William 288,290
SYNARD, Jon. 264

TABOR(TABOUR), Susana 354
    William 97,225,228,275,
      327,345,354,368
TACKETT, Susannah 353
    William 353

TAGGART(MC TAGGART), Thomas
      M. 136
TALBERT, Samuel 222,244,293,
      395
    Samuel, Sr. 293
TALBOT(TALBUT), ___ 198
    Giles 332
    Samuel 164,238
TALIAFERRO(TALIFERRO),
    Richard 11
    Warren 425
    Zachariah 142,210,211,
      385,398,425
TALLANT, John 235,265,325,
      348
TALLEY(TALLY), Dyer 305
    John 195
    Reuben 370
TANKERSLY, Clara 421
    Richard 421
    Rowland 421
TANNER, Lophar 93
    Topher 113,389
TANZEY, Abraham 44
TAPLEY(TAPPLEY), H. 315
    Hosea 204,244,319,341,
      408,409
    John 204,214,255,272,
      275,323,349,360
TARBET(TARBERT), Samuel
      122,293,320
TARRANT, L. 41,77,343
    Larkin 262
    John 378
    Richard 378
    Reuben 344,412,421
TARVETOR, John 314
TARWATER, George 292
    John 317,377,378,381
TATE, Mr. 306
TATE(TEAT,TOTE), Andrew
      21,111,297
    David 332
    Edward 99
    James 39,80,81,83,128,
      185,207,211,269,311,
      316,318,320,325,342,
      348,353,355,367,372,
      379,392,395,405,412
    James, Jr. 57,74,80,81,
      82,97,107,119,207
    Peramon 236
    Robert 2,15,80,81,82,
      95,185,275,379
    Samuel 80,81,82,107,
      128,143,185,249,269,
      275,297,315,379,387,
      388
    Sun(?) 15
    Susan(Susn) 2,15
    Susannah 2
    William/Wm. 2,13,32,37,
      72,81,89,92,93,128,178,
      185,193,226,328
TATHAM(TATHUM), ___ 218
    Charles 219
TATUM(TATOM), Amara 411
    Edward 179,361
    Jesse 179,372,374,375,
      411
    John 300,324,387,389
    Nathaniel 324
    Wm. 292
TAVENER, James 120
TAVET, Charles 333
TAYLOR, ___ 317,420
    Champ 329
    Danuel(Samuel?) 407
    Elenor 158
    George 329
    J. 302
    James 365,375
    John, Jr. 277

TAYLOR, cont'd:
    John 133,158,162,177,
      187,200,232,249,253,
      255,256,261,262,265,
      272,273,275,283,284,
      285,286,292,293,294,
      295,302,303,304,305,
      306,307,308,311,314,
      315,317,319,321,327,
      334,338,339,340,343,
      344,350,352,356,357,
      364,367,372,374,385,
      396,397,400,405,408,
      413,422,424,425,426
    Joseph 5,212,213,234,
      276,302,314,335,386,
      388
    Leah 400
    Major 2,196
    Sam 48
    Samuel 2,6,7,8,22,28,
      34,38,42,45,72,73,83,
      133,158,177,186,195,
      200,227,247,261,265,
      272,283,284,285,286,
      295,309,313,314,317,
      323,338,366,383,391,
      398,400,404,423,424,
      426
    Samuel, Jr. 83
    Sarah 317
    William 155,317,383
TELFAIR, Edward 25,73,147
TELFORD(TELLFORD), Isabela
      281
    Robert 76,207,281
TELL, Charles 284
TENISON, John 299
TERRELL(TERRILL), Aaron 28,
      204,219,220,407
    Archabald 204
    Charles 294
    G. Washington 406
    George Washington 313
    Harry 121,122,204,362
    J. D. 229,266
    J. W. D. 345
    James 45
    Joel 185,204,219,266,
      307,332
    John 185,189,203,263
    John D. 229,280,362,
      375
    Martin 132
    Moses 27
    Pamela 406
    Saml. 219
    Samuel D./Saml. D. 220,
      229,263
    William H. 266,313,340
TERRET, Aaron 15
THACKER, Samuel 244
THACKERBY, William 423
THAKER, Ecor(Eaker) 159
    William 119
THARIN, Daniel 50,51
THAXTON, Thomas 100,372
THAYER, James 57
    Sarah 228
    William 57,113,228,229,
      265
THEUS, Simeon 178
THOMAS, ___ 219,358
    Aleenathan 395
    Alexr. 62
    Anderson 32,187,229
    Athanalius 189,190
    Athanatius(Athantious)
      "Qualhache" 187
    Drury 279
    Elizabeth 82
    Evan/Evin 30,82,98,113,
      130,194,209,326,349

THOMAS, cont'd:
    John 67,73,74,170,185,
    187,201,220,221,229,
    237,254,265,348,425,
    427
    Lesley 387
    Martha 279
    William 171,265,275
THOMASON(THOMSON,THOMSEN),
    Edmond 335
    James/Jas. 337,365,
    402
    Peggy 365
THOMPSON,   76
    Adam 342,422
    Adam H. 257
    Adam Heath 179,424
    Allis 95
    Andrew 140
    Archd. 47
    David 194
    Drury/Drewry 253,265,
    271,273,279,290,357,
    395
    Edward 366,426
    Eliza B. 207
    Elizabeth 379
    Farley 162,185,379
    Frederick 328
    George 75,123,124,144,
    157,164,171,190,206,
    208,266,275,354
    James 39,56,88,99,137,
    159,160,181,182,224,
    258,300,301,308,325,
    336,414
    James W. 125
    Jeremiah 179
    John 253,279
    Jonathan 296,406
    Joseph 163,410,425
    Mark 273,325
    Martha 279
    Mary 66,147,166,253,
    317,324,410
    Mathew/Matthew 87,410
    Peter 124,204,271
    Rachel 136
    Randsom 119,357
    Richard/Richd. 161,171,
    271,300,365
    Robert 47,163,237,353,
    357,395
    Samuel 171,191
    Sarah 337
    W. 57,67,120,247,265,
    310,391
    Waddy 47,76,139,152,
    175,223,347
    William/Wm. 21,38,42,
    46,52,62,68,72,75,99,
    117,123,133,134,171,
    190,221,230,232,235,
    253,257,260,265,266,
    276,279,285,296,301,
    317,323,324,329,357,
    365,378,399,406
THOPSON(sic), William 119
THORN(?), Jas. 26
THORNHILL, James 32,160
THORNTON,   81
    David 37,56
    J. 81
THRASHER, Elizabeth 345
    Isaac 199
    John 345
THRESHER, Elizabeth 319
    Joseph 373
THRISHER, Elizabeth 175
THROOP, William 27
THURSTON(HUISTON?), Buck-
    ner 219
THURSTON, William 180

THWEAT, Daniel 326
TILLMAN(TILLMON), George
    61,62,86,150,167,363
TILLEY(TILLY),   113
    Lazarus 67,68,137,207,
    298
    Jane 67,157,158
    "Widow" 161,177,201,
    218,236
TIMBERLAKE, Murwood 92
TIMMONS, John 250
TIMMS(TIMS), Jabes/Jebes
    349,359
    Vinson, Sr. 349,370
    William 265,349
    William, Sr. 370
TINKLER, Jno./John 13
TINNISON, John 209
TINSLEY,   138
    Adah 269
    Golden/Golding 29,76,
    186,227
    John 210,258,269
    Mary 227
TINSLEY(TINSALEY), Thomas
    210
TIPPEN(TIPPENS), George
    156,406
    John 41,57,84,113,150,
    156,175,223,258,262,
    267,279,305,322,406,
    407,410,418,429,430
    Sampson 406
    William 322,402,406,
    411,425
TITWORTH(TITSWORTH,TITTS-
WORTH), Isaac 2,18,20,56,
    173,185,226,273,285
TODD, Adam 161,243,246,317,
    332,353,359,366,371,
    396,416,422
    Archibald 66
    James 294,316,340,352,
    374,421
    Jenny 161
    John 8,161,280,332,358,
    374,429
    Lucinda 332
    Robert 359
    William 8,65,66
TOLBERT, William 396
TOLESSON, Erasmus 216
TOLICER, John 329
TOLINSON, Aaron/Aron 80
TOMLAN(TOMLIN), Genevary
    58
    Moses 50,51,378
TOMLINSON, Moses 88
TOMSON(also THOMPSON)
    Richard 371
TONEY,   174
    Little Berry 31
    Sarah 382
    Timothy 382
    Timothy, Jr. 58
TONN, Jacob 250
TOOD(TODD?), John 322
TOOMER, Joshua 252
TORBERT(TARBERT), Samuel
    13,23,164,361,392,396
    William 392,396
TORRENCE, Reuben 369
TORRENS, Robert 257
TOULMIN, Harry 387
TOURS, John 388
TO(U)TE(L)LOT(TOURTELOTT),
    Asa 99,228
    Avis 57,64,113,228
    Betsy 228,265
    Lydia 228,265
    Nancy 228,265
TOWERS,   389
    Wm. 373,402,411,423

TOWNES(TOWNS), Thomas 53,
    65,121,303
TOWNLEY, Mrs. 362
    Henry 191,361,362,365
TOWNSEND(TOUNSEND), Mar-
    garet 309,359,360,417
    William 324,359,360,
    392,417
TOWREY(TOWRY), Abraham 17
    Betsey 6
    Edward 6,7
TOWRY(TOWERY,TOWERS), John
    373
TRAMBLE, Sampson 348
    William 348
TRAMILL, Shadrack 410
TRAMMEL, Benjamin 80
    Isaac 80
TRAPIER, Paul 227
TRAPP, William 174
TRAVIS, Charles/Chs. 49,
    103,108,113,315
TREADWAY(TREDAWAY), Daniel
    325,356
    William 325
TREHERN, James 217
TRESCOTT, Edward 50,51
TRESEVANT(TREZEVANT),
    Catharine 380
    Lewis 140,167,331,380
TRIMBLE, James 93,108,127
    Joseph 127,346
TRIMMIER(TRIMIER,TRIMMER),
    Ann 349
    Obediah 218,227,276,
    277,282,284,286,297,
    306,308,314,315,317,
    319,320,323,336,339,
    341,345,349,350,356,
    357,391,406
TRIP(TRIPP), Ferrls 143
    John 143
    Michael 230
    William 319
TRIPPLETT, Daniel 208,209
TROTHER, Nathaniel 368
TROTTER, John 135,250
    Robert 342,351
    Susanna 351
TROUTMAN, John 399
TRUSSELL, Henry 190
TUBB,   225
    Betta (Elizabeth) 368
    George 163,166,196,354,
    359,368
    James 166
    John 97,105
    William 166,359
TUCK, Christian 400
TUCKER,   254
    Aulden/Auldin 65,181,
    205,251,418
    Bartley 21,31,78,96,
    181,298,418
    Charles 226,254,265
    Clary/Clery 181,205,
    418
    Elijah 56,115
    Fannie/Fanney 181,251
    George 6,7,15,26,31,
    56,114,131,301,312,
    326,356
    Hadbert 6
    Harbert 7,21,115,181,
    251,265,278,298
    Hart(?) 26
    Maldin (Aledon) 298
    Mary 254
    Robert 21,31,65,181,
    229
    Thomas T. 302
    William R. 229
TUFFNELL, ____ 407

TUFFNELL, cont'd:
    James 71,114,178,197,
        224,333,383,385
TUGGLE, John 157,158,363,
    366,367,426,427
    Margaret 366
TURIN, Pricilla 210
    Thomas 210
TURNBULL, John 7,31,44
    Joseph 44
TURNER, Alex. 318
    Ann 106
    Bailey 330
    Benjamin 106,150,179,
        286
    Eleazer/Eliazer 158,
        195,227
    Elias 179,193,224
    George 110
    Harris 174,175
    James 107,174,210,212,
        236,254,265,330,361,
        381,384,393,405
    John 33,105,106,150,
        151,179,193,238,249,
        394,396,401
    Matthias 218,224
    Nathan 220
    Pricilla 318
    Prudence 422
    Robert 318
    Sophia/Sophis 33
    Thomas 78,174,236,318
    William 107,318,409
TURPIN, ___ 49,110,241,
        265,396
    Hannah 47
    Mary 148,306,310,344
    William 41,52,53,54,
        64,78,82,92,99,110,
        116,147,148,166,209,
        225,247,249,306,310,
        344,369,380
    William, Jr. 148
TWITTY(TWENTY,TWILLY),___
        408
    Ann 80
    John 19,44,45,60,80,
        83,86,91,98,120,131,
        143,308
    Sarah 80
    William 10,44,80,91,
        143,293
TYLOR, William 332

UBANKS, John, Jr. 296
UMPHRIES(also see Humphries)
    George 232,265
    Isaac 214
    John 214
UNDERWOOD, J. 220
    Josiah (Isiah) 105,106,
        191
    Polly 106
UPSHAW, Forester/Forister
        404,408,411
UPSHEAR(UPSHER), Forrister 414
UPTON, John 254

VANCE, George 277
    Jacob 89,188,197,299,
        378
    John 274
VANDERGRIFFS, ___ 119
VANDERGRIFT, Chrt. 128
    Peter 419
VANDERHORST, ___ 265,303,
        352,365
    A., Jr. 167
    Arnoldus 112,148,158,
        163,167,170,184,186,

VANDERHORST, Arnoldus
    cont'd: 194,199,201,
        202,218,224,234,244,245,
        252,277,281,353,360,
        362,377,418
    John 86,94,119,159,167,
        252,266
VANDERPOOL, Samuel 109
VANDERPOOR, Samuel 109
VANDIVER(VANDEVERE,VANDIA-
    VER,VANDOVER), ___ 336
    E. 396
    Edward 135,161,274,287,
        357,362,364
    Edwin 426
    George 179,255,265,372
    George, Jr. 287
    George, Sr. 287
    Hollingsworth 257,304
    Holly 5
    James E. 274
    John 135
    Sandford/Sanford 360
VANN, Martha 218,224,401,
        405
    W. 198
    William/Wm. 61,130
VANUE, Jacob 128
VAUGHN(VEAUGN), Daniel 349
    James 40,88,100,189,
        270
    Joel 209,299
    William 40,41,100,101,
        189,270
VENABLE(VENEABLE), Joseph
        290,401
    Joseph E. 285
VERNER(VERNOR,VARNER),___
        355
    Charles 373
    David 190
    George 138,140,163,188,
        316,377
    John 150,151,154,155,
        157,162,169,170,174,
        179,184,185,188,189,
        191,194,201,208,218,
        222,232,235,236,237,
        238,240,243,252,253,
        269,272,275,277,279,
        281,300,303,305,309,
        310,311,322,325,333,
        355,362,365,368,375,
        379,384,390,392,404,
        407,411,416,421
    John, Jr. 59,138,140,
        163
    John, Sr. 136,138,163,
        190,373
    Mary 140,373
    Rebecca 392
    Relick 277
    Sarah 138,140,311
VICK, Nancy 184
    Thomas 131,170,184,207,
        273
VICKREY(VICKERY), Christopher 158,276
    John 158,279,414
    Sampson 414
VINES, ___ 423
    Isaiah 119
VISAGE, Elizabeth 71,114
    Jacob 11,71,114,197,224,
        333
    Thomas 197

WABBE, Alexander 283,284
WADDELL(WADDLE), John 301,
        312
    Robert 8,10,21
    William 206
WADE, ___ 174

WADE, cont'd:
    Ann 369
    Agnes 246
    Clement 246
    David 21,45,65,71,179,
        265,417,422
    David, Jr. 265
    Edward 45,102,162,168,
        179,369
    Edwin 101
    Mary 246
    Nancy 101,168
    Richard 422
    Thomas 135,179,251,364
    Thomas C. 265,422
    Thomas Clement 21,179,
        246
WADKINS, ___ 290,363
    David 385
WADSWORTH, ___ 49,104,110,
        120,129,265,426
    Mr. 312
    Jane 110
    Mss(?) 241
    Stephen 147
    Susannah 147
    Thomas 41,52,53,54,61,
        64,78,82,92,99,110,116,
        147,166,247,250,306,
        332
WAFER, Francis 69,286
    Thomas 171,201,205,
        246,390
WAFFORD, James 185,186
    Margaret 186
WAGGONER(WAGNER), Barbary
        111
    Christopher 57,93,111
WAGNON, John 135
    Mark 422
    Peter 184,287,372,422
WAIT, John 385
WAKEFIELD, Allen 91
    Henry 91
    John 246,276
    Mary 91
    William 40,91,163,277,
        303,333,367,377
WALBANKS, Henry 276
WALDRON, Joseph 275
WALDRUM, Joseph 404
WALKEE, Thomas 407
WALKER, ___ 134,186
    Eaton 303
    Ebenezer Jacob 405
    Elijah 154,296
    Francis 383
    James 58
    Jethro 166
    John 166
    Joseph 207,279,295,335
    Laken 338
    M. 41
    Robert 257
    Samuel 63,170,344
    Silv's. 1
    Vann 63,67,77
    William 5,402
    William J. 305
    Zachariah 77,170
WALL, Alexander 233
    Daniel 236
WALLACE, ___ 283
    Frances 343
    James 66,246
    John 55,349
    R. 184
    Richard 33
    Robert 110
    William 131,211,312,
        313
WALLER, Benj. 258
WALLIS, ___ 170

WALLIS, cont'd:
    Daniel 313
WALLS, George 287
WALLY, James 355
WALSH, Wm. 338
WALSON, William 379
WALTERS, ___ 396
    James 62
    Richard 204,322
    Richard, Jr. 26
    Thomas 26,28
WALTON, ___ 396
    Jesse 11,25
    Robert 412,413
    Walker 25
WAMMACK, John 345
WARD, Calvin 336
    David 62
    Fredrick 128
    Jesse 106,239
    John 22,54,69,143,281,
        283,339
    Mark 192,300,321,330,
        427
    Mary 339
    Samuel 101,108,192
WARDLAW(WORDLAW), ___ 177
    Esquire 357
    Hugh 70,96,139,146,
        192,203,274
    J. N. 274
    James 257,261,307,317,
        348,354,357,360,361,
        362,366,367,368,370,
        371,375,381,403,428
    John 274,357
    Mary 139
    Mary Anne 274,357
    Thomas 219
    William 139,152,163,
        350
WARDON, John 51
WARE(WERE), Edward 62,134,
    317
    Thomas 252,265
WARHURST, Tim 298
WARING, R. H. 256
    Robert H. 324
    Thomas 167
    Thomas, Sr. 252
WARLEY, Capt. 246
    Major 354,368
    Ann 206
    Calt. George 256
    Felix 163,206
    George 117,118,206,
        252,256,284
    Joseph 206
    Wm. 118
WARMACH, William 220
WARNER, George 67
WARNOCK(WARNAK), ___ 259,
    312
    Andrew 3,56,63,302,
        370,411
    Andrew, Sr. 371
    Eleanor/Ellenor 28,
        364
    Hugh 56,288,306,379
    James 353
    John 15,16,28,56,84,
        274,357,364
    Joseph 56,322
    Michael 56,63,255,261,
        302,314
    Samuel 56
    Susannah 353
WARREN, Rebecca 294,295
    William 59,73,214,277,
        294,295
WARTLAW, Hugh 42
    Jno. 135
WASHBURN, Samuel 106

WASHINGTON, William/Wm. 7,
    10,20,30
WATERS(WATTERS), Charles
    216,230,265
    David 29,70,256,320
    Fanny 216,320
    James 234,238,277,303,
        304,305,408
    John 271,408
    Mary 216
    Philmon 8
    Samuel 303
    Thomas 332
    Thomas W. 320
    Thomas Willoughby 320
WATKINS, David 63,260,
    261,288,296,370
    Ezekiel 260
    Joseph 370
    Tempy 296
WATSON(WHATSON), Elizabeth
    420
    Jacob 363
    James 29,291,303
    John 14,69,268,316,321,
        363,374,402,408
    Jonathan 150,153,156,
        301,325
    Mary 420
    Samuel 44
    Thomas 129,420
    William 321,339,363,
        381,393,409
WATTS(WAT,WATT), Edward
    269
    Garet 359
    George 120,351
    Gregory 192
    Isaac 322
    James 355
    John 146
    Samuel/Saml. 33,56,62,
        141,149,162,187,190,
        191,209,210,291,328,
        359,383,386,390
WAUGH, James Adair 82
    John 382
    Robert 58,62,187,194,
        233,290,308,349,376,
        410
    Sarah 58
WEAMS, George 364
WEAVER, Daniel 288
    David 267,288
    Nathaniel 267
    Peter 266,267
    Samuel 15,370
WEBB, Jesse 375
    Joel 141,151,152,184,
        200
    Joseph 151,208
WEED, Nathaniel 145
    Nathaniel, Sr. 145
WEEKLEY(WEEKLY), John 250,
    265,315,336
WEEMS, Bartholomew 22
    George 6,8,10,21,195,
        348,351,367,393,416
    James 418
    Samuel 210
    Thomas 367
WEIR, Elizabeth 293
WEITZEL, Eleanor 28
    John 28
WELCH, ___ 352
    David 122,263,294
    Jamima 99
    John 232
    Nicholas 134,228,277,
        290
    Robert 249
    William 48,67,99,134,
        162,267,279,294,295

WELCHEL(WELCHELL,WHELCHEL)
    Davis 19
    Francis 19,21,62,202
    Francis, Jr. 202
    William 21,202
WELIHISTINE, David 244
WELLBORN(WELBORN,WELBOURN)
    Aaron 369
    James 352,361,365,369,
        376,381,392,402,416,
        417,425,429
WELLS, Clement 29
    George 326
    Hiram 252
WEST, Charles 334
    Hannah 334
    Isaac 104,389
    Jacob 104,167,168,178,
        199,200,334
    James 344
    Jane 245
    Jean 318
    John 420
    Jonathan 178,193,224,
        334,351
    Mary 334
    Michael 178
    Polly 334
    Sarah 104
    Solomon 245,265,318
    Solomon Redmon 62
WHAREY, John 11
    Thomas 11
WHATSON, Jonathan 156
WHEELER, John 15,31,95,
    149,171
    Joseph 95
    Susannah 95
    William 21(Wheller)
WHERTER, ___ 325
WHILELL, Davis 272
WHISENHUNT, John 187
WHITCHEL, David 272
WHITE, Alexander 193,355,
    359
    Alexander, Sr. 193
    Andrew 401
    Andrew, Sr. 401
    Bartholomew 48,49,119,
        298
    Charles 48,49,178,293,
        412
    Hugh 54
    Jacob 73
    James 224,253,255,273,
        280,291,294,327,328,
        349,382,385,386
    Jno./John 262,312,329,
        369
    Joseph 106,359
    Mary 149
    Patrick 424
    Robert/Robt. 255,265,
        401
    Robert Macklin 385
    Sam 156
    Solomon 214,386
    Thomas 66
    William 4,33,66,149,
        168,190,199,248,401
WHITEFIELD, John 70
WHITEMAN, Wm. 239
WHITERAFT, Alexander 368
    Ann 368
WHITLEY, Moses 163,203
WHITLOW, Moses 163
WHITMIRE(WHITMER), Chris-
    topher 298,423
    George 153
    Henry 132,265,298
    Mary 423
    Michael 26,320
    Michael, Sr. 132

WHITMIRE, cont'd:
   Samuel 423
   Stephen 142,156,328,
   329,331,335,423
WHITNER, ___ 192,193
   Elizabeth 429
   J. 42,54,107
   John 429
   Joseph 15,19,29,42,57,
   76,77,93,94,103,111,
   138,150,187,193,197,
   223,229,265,272,282,
   313,324,329,346,371,
   421,428
WHITNEY, John 69
   Joseph 70
WHITTEN, Jonathan 306
WHITTENDEL, John T. 136
WHIT(T)WORTH, John 191,
   316
WHORTON, Benjamin 74,90,92,
   101,102,140,141,145,
   287,291,298,331,356
   Mary 102,287,293,331
WIATT, William 144,405
WICKLEY, John 249,265
WIDEMAN, Mark 409
WIDGION, Elizabeth 422
WIGGLESWORTH, Thos. 27
WIGHT, William 289,354
WIGHTMAN, Nichs. Jno. 3
   William 94,299,336
WILBORN(WILLBERN,WILLBORN,
WILLBOURN), Aaron 124,191
WILLBURN, James 44,73,124,
   133,137,191,310,328,
   345,348,351,357,366,
   367,388,389,396
   James M. 176
WILEMAN, Elias 289
WILKINSON, A. 198
   Michael 192
   John 288,306,379
WILKISON, Betsy 1
WILLBANKS(WILBANKS), Henry
   237,238,260,264,300
   John 300
   Richard 336,365
WILLET, Stephen 19
WILEY(WILLEY,WILIE,WILLIE,
WILLY,WILY,WYLWY,WYLLEY),
   Bettie 116
   Harris McKinley 103
   Jas. 148
   Jean 311
   John 46,101,114,145,
   311
   Samuel 46,101,159,311
WILLIA, M. 271
WILLIAM(WILLIAMS), ___ 143
   Alexander 236
   Ann 10
   B. 129
   Caleb 279
   Cassander 129
   Charles 28,208,257,263,
   364,392
   D. 264
   Daniel 129,287,314,364,
   417,429,430
   E. 144
   Edward 103,193,201,202
   Elizabeth 85
   Enoch 358,364,370,404
   Fredrick 296
   Griaff 109
   Isaac 131,143,239,243,
   247,264,265,297,298,
   363
   James 233,253,356,379
   John 75,195,210,221,
   223,338,348,416,417
   John, Jr. 52

WILLIAMS, cont'd:
   Joseph 75,109
   Margaret 353
   Martin 303
   Mary 364,370
   Nancy 430
   Nathaniel 85,217
   Nimrod 9,10
   Price 150
   Robert 230
   Rolen 335
   Sarah 297
   Thomas 287,329
   William 105,273,292
WILLIAMSON, ___ 254
   Andrew 207
   Elijah 166,392
   William 189,198,254,
   300,387
WILLIMAN(WILLIMON,WILLIAMS?)
   Christopher 70,111,212
WILLINGHAM, Jesse 119
WILLIS, Ann 395
   Brittan/Britten/Brit-
   ton 216,395
   Daniel 173,184,345,410
   Henry 34
   Stephen 34,59,99,117,
   162,163,180,181,271,
   274,308,334
   Susannah 112
WILLMEN, John 323
WILLOMON, ___ 245
WILLS, Ezekiel 315
WILMON, John 323
WILSON(WILLSON), ___ 155,
   174,330,394,411,416
   Ann 126
   Andrew 58,59,277,315
   Charles 22,25,28,36,
   108,110,141,167,169,
   196,260,307,310,323,
   367,379,383
   Charles Desley 318
   Charles Wesley 310,318
   Clarymond 383
   Edward 161
   Elizabeth 10,162,172
   George 115,162,327
   George G. 10
   Hugh 124,176,209,304,
   309,310,367
   Hugh, Jr. 172
   Isaac 100,191
   James 43,45,122,175,
   249,273,294,299,304,
   307,318,378,387,390
   James Harris 318
   James W. 10
   James Wharey 10
   Jane 10
   Jean 108
   Jesse 93,392
   John 1,4,20,25,26,27,
   28,29-39,41-46,48-51,
   55,56,58,60,61,63,64,
   66,67,73-75,77,79,84,
   90,91,94,97,99,104,106,
   110,116,118,120-123,
   125-127,129-131,137,
   138,141-144,146,148-
   150,152,153,156,160-
   162,164-170,173,176,
   177,182-186,188-190,
   194,197,199,200,203,
   205-207,209-213,218,
   219,222,232,234,236,
   239,241,244,247,248,
   252,254-256,260,267,
   268,270,272,273,277,
   278,281,283,286,288,
   290,293,295,299,301-
   310,315,318,320-322,

WILSON, John cont'd:
   324,326,327,328,331,
   335-341,343-345,347,
   349-351,353,359,364,
   367,368,370,375,378,
   388,398,400-409,416,
   418,421,423,425,429
   John, Jr. 162,176,209,
   292,309,367,429
   John, Sr. 176
   Keziah 43,49
   Margaret 286
   Mary Charlotte 147
   Mathew/Matthew 92,139,
   346,386,408
   Ralph 10,11,34,166
   Robert 43,157,159,172,
   267,279,328,373,377,
   429
   Samuel 45,327
   Sarah D. 10
   Stephen, Jr. 11
   Thomas 43,76,209,429
   Toney 59
   William 44,75,77,100,
   143,168,304,315,316,
   346,383,386
WIMBERLY, ___ 368
   Isaac 157
   Lewis 44,58,157,160,
   308,309,339
   Noah 160
   Polly 308,309
WIMPEE(WIMPEY,WIMPY), Adam
   347
   Adin/Eden 200
   David 182,188,194,200
   Levi 182,188,194
   Obid 347
WIMPLE, David 200
WINCHESTER, Daniel 329
   William Bay 331
   Willoughby 331
WINDER, Chris. 174
WINN(WIN), ___ 372
   John 26,216,265
   John/Jon., Jr. 2,8,26
   M. 8
   Minor 27,42,44,91,120,
   143,285
WINTER, Fredrick 28
WIOMER, Alexander 34
WISAGE, Jacob 167,168
WISE, Jane Ann 415
   Samuel 415
WITHERSPOON, R. 242,363
WITT, ___ 307
WOLDROP, Thomas 105
WOLLENS, Absolum 18
   Bartholeme 18
WOLLUM, William 131
WOMACK(WOMOCK), Jacob 84
   Rebecca 340
   W. 191
   William 202,220,314,
   340,341
WONDER, Christopher 217
WOOD(WOODS), ___ 285
   Mr. 389,390,394
   Alis 253
   Belffe 353
   Belfield 289,308,309,
   353
   Frame 11
   H. ___ 229
   H. M. 146,229
   Henry M. 355,391
   Henry Machen 146,357
   Henry William 229
   James 83,105,129,139,
   151,161,165,183,193,
   196,197,221,223,227,
   234,238,253,276,278,

WOOD(WOODS), James cont'd:
  294,296,297,303,306,
  307,311,312,325,329,
  339,343,344,346,351,
  356,357,376,397,401,
  420,421
  Jesse 11,21,34,137,
    158,360,366,392
  Joel 429
  John 1,9,12,16
  Joseph 354,423
  L. 3
  Loraina 246
  M. H. 265
  Margaret 137
  Margarite 158
  Oliver 5,352,355
  Robert 307
  Stephen C. 340
  Thomas 10,246,265,334,
    338
  William 5,246,409
WOODALL,   428
  John 32,98,113,146,152,
    287,296,321,358,400,
    425
  John, Jr. 112,296,314,
    412
  John, Sr. 112,412
  Joseph 11,12,130,150,
    166,226,279,295,400,
    409,418
  Judith 400
  Thomas Holms 400
WOODARD, Thomas 112
WOODHALL, Joseph 82
WOODLAW,   133
WOODLING, Caleb 424
WOODSIDE, Jane 63
WOODSIDES, John 20,63,64,
    301,312
WOODSON, Tucker 9,258,350
WOODWARD, Wm. 82
WOOLBANKS, Henry 300
  Phebe 300
  Richard 195,326
WOOLBRIDGE, Gibson 112
WORD, Thomas 337
WORNOCK, Andrew 99,117,
    153,202,282
  Hugh 99,102,117,168,
    259
  Jane/Jean 99,102
  John 100,101,110,135,
    178,300,364
  Joseph 99,102,117,163,
    417
  Mary 202
WORTMAN, John 313
WRIGHT, Adam 92,99,122
  Danl. 236
  James Walker 71
  Josiah 400
  William 96,380
WRIGHTMAN, Wm. 111
WYATT, Elijah 221,286
  Peyton 112
  Theopolis 41

YAGER(YEAGER), George 301
  John 109,111,159,214,
    215,301,311
  Samuel 111,139,159
YANCY, Cyrus 290
  James 61
  James Lewis 222
YEARWOOD, Robert 220
YORK, Richard 132,142,235,
    325,348,360
YOUNG,   17,241
  Agnes 120
  Alex. 120,188,222,316
  Andrew 222,322

YOUNG, cont'd:
  Ann 353
  Dicey 353
  Enoch 321
  Henry 231,282
  Isom 377
  James 52,64,65,68,82,
    92,110,120,166,222,248,
    263,299,321,353,418
  Jane 206,215
  Jean 152
  John 16,28,30,68,109,
    146,157,160,197,213,
    230,233,246,248,250,
    260,298,299,318,321,
    329,330,352,353,358,
    424
  John, Jr. 362
  Joshua 8,10,50,255,265,
    424
  Mary 68
  Matthew/Mathew 196,230,
    299
  Nancy 353
  Nathan 70,113,206,215,
    373,421
  P. 261
  Polly 241
  R. 261
  Rachel 230,377
  Rebecca 241
  Robert 33,75,90
  Roday 429
  Sam'l. 80
  Sarah 353
  W. 147
  William 8,28,34,35,41,
    68,87,125,132,152,157,
    198,220,233,252,253,
    261,270,299,307,330,
    353,362,377
YOWELL, Joel 133,144
  James 122,133

ZEALY, James 343,344

INDEX TO BLACKS

ANDERSON,   oll 294
  Alice 294
  Charlotte 427
  Hannah 427
  Henry 294
  Rose 427
  Sam 294
ARMSTRONG, Nancy 308
ATKINS, Henry 337
  Jacob 337
BANISTER, Cheaney 9
  Daniel 9
BARR, Joe 179
BERRY, Chainey 411
BETTS, Billey 52
BIRD, Lett 349
BOOTH, Cato 118
  Cloe 118
BOWEN, Cate 211
BOWMAN, Rigne 166
BOYD, Harry 383
BRIMER, Beck 342
BROWN, Jacob 67
  Maria 393
  "Negro boy Donas?" 409
  Newry 409
BROYLES, Joe 222
  Lucy 222
  Peter 222
BRYSON, Jack 131
  Sall 368
  Tom 335
CAPEHART, Abrom 303
CLARKE, Sambo 155

COKER, Jacob 252
  Jeany 252
  Sary 252
COLLINS, Winnie Rebeka 203
CORNELIUS, Tap 40
CRAIG, Tom 194
CRUTCHFIELD, Nan/Nancy 90
DAVIS, Jack 129
EDMONDSON, Jane 361
  Jeff 139
  Nancy 139
  Punch 139
  Samuel 139
  Terris 139
  Toney 139
FARROW, Abraham 317
FIELD, Ceasor 278
FINDLEY, Agga 226
GEORGE, Jean 239
GILLASPIE, Cann 360
GILLISON, Boowain 46
  Joe 46
GILLISPIE, Jack 153
GOODWIN, Cane 398
  Landy 398
  Sal 398
  Sarah 398
  Tom 398
GREENLEES, Charlotte 39
HALLUM, Peter 345
HAMILTON, Charlot 287
  Gin 113
  Jaible 299
  Let 113
HAMMICK, Tom 335
HAMON, Sam 253
HARKNESS, Dinah 404
  Ned 404
  Rachel 404
HARLIN, James 334
HARRISON, Cooper 266
  David 280
  Hannah 257,266
  Jenny 280
  Jude 280
  Lucy 280
  Sollomon 280
HILL, Hester 110
HOOPER, Sarah 317
HUNTER, Isobel 224
JOHNSTON, Winnie 203
KEES, Curry 399
  June 399
  Lucy 399
  Sarah 399
  Will 399
KEYS, Esther 207
  Nancy 207
KING, James 54
  Luce 54
LANE, Peter 394
LARROW, Ann 347
  Harry 347
LESLEY, Ciel 77
  Sambo 77
LIDDLE, Charlott 217
  Sarah 217
MC CALEB, Minerva 60
  Rose 60
  Samson 193
MC CANN, Byna 118
MC WHORTER, Lib 240
  Rachel 240
  Sharlot 240
MARTIN, Hannah 297
MAULDIN, Alyce 78
  Tom 78,96
MILLWEE, Mary 115
  Winney 405
NASH, Harry 288
  Rose 288
NEVILL, Phillis 93
NIRON, Ame 404

NIRON, cont'd:
   Fanny 404
PARKADUR, Abraham 251
   Charlot 251
   Hannah 251
PAYNE, John 106
PICKENS, Allen 346
   Luce 338
   Peter 338
   Sall 346
PUGH, Bob 365
REED, George 366
REEDER, Leah 305
   Lusa 305
REESE, Jack 379
   Moses 384
RICHARDS, Nancy 340
RICHARDSON, Bob 257
ROBINSON, Jefey (or Jesse) 105
RUSK, Daniel 294
SHARP, Dick 338
SIMPSON, Kate 337
SIMS, Milly 385
   Rose 388
SLOAN, Isaac (also see Williams) 90
   Joe 101
   Sambo 101
SMITH, Bosin 343
   Comfort 406
   Hester 343
   Jacob 88
   James 343
   John 343
   Mary 406
   Rody 343
STEELE, Hannah 161
   Isaac 161
   Molly 161
   Tour 183
STEVENSON, Nancy 68
STONE, Wally 414
STRONG, hennery 219
   Milley 219
   tom 219
   Tomm 219
TANKERSLY, Tom 421
TATE, Jacob 97
   Lucy 388
TAYLOR, Betty 265
   Bob 265
   Caesar 265
   Ceasor 265
   Cela 265
   Dine 286
   Frank 286
   Jim 286
   Nero 286
   Ransome 286
   Tom 187
TERREL, hennery 219
   Milley 219
   tom 219
   Tom 219
THOMPSON, Jack 223
   Marie 76
TROUTMAN, Bill 399
TUCKER, Jim 115
   Suky 356
   Tom 356
WAKEFIELD, Bob 91
WARE, Patty 252,289
WILSON, Joseph 273
   Ned 273,283
WOODALL, Jamimah 400
   Jimmy 400
   Nancy 400
YOUNG, Tom 248

NO GIVEN NAMES SHOWN:

HAMMICK, "mother of Tom" 335
HARRISON, "negro man" 257
MARTIN, "negro man" 105
PICKENS, "child" 338
WILLIAMS (also under Sloan)
   Isaac 90

www.ingramcontent.com/pod-product-compliance
Lightning Source LLC
Chambersburg PA
CBHW020633300426
44112CB00007B/103